UNDER THE GENERAL EDITORSHIP OF

GORDON N. RAY

THE UNIVERSITY OF ILLINOIS

HOUGHTON MIFFLIN COMPANY, BOSTON

The Riverside Press Cambridge

MASTERS OF

AMERICAN LITERATURE

VOLUME TWO

Whitman, Dickinson, Twain, Adams, James,
Crane, O'Neill, Frost, Eliot, Faulkner

EDITORS

Leon Edel, New York University
Thomas H. Johnson, The Lawrenceville School
Sherman Paul, The University of Illinois
Claude Simpson, The Ohio State University

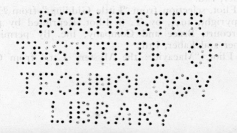

The Riverside Press
CAMBRIDGE, MASSACHUSETTS
PRINTED IN THE U.S.A.

Henry Adams, *Mont-Saint-Michel and Chartres*. Reprinted by
permission of Houghton Mifflin Company.

Henry Adams, *The Education of Henry Adams*. Reprinted by
permission of Houghton Mifflin Company.

Emily Dickinson, Numbers 1295 and 1409 from *The Life and Letters of Emily Dickinson*, by Martha Dickinson Bianchi. Reprinted by permission of Houghton Mifflin Company.

Emily Dickinson, Number 298 from *Emily Dickinson Face to
Face*, by Martha Dickinson Bianchi. Reprinted by permission
of Houghton Mifflin Company.

Emily Dickinson, Numbers 306, 341, 391, 754, 974 from *Poems by
Emily Dickinson*, edited by Martha Dickinson Bianchi and Al-
fred Leete Hampson. Copyright 1929 by Martha Dickinson
Bianchi. Selections reprinted by permission of Little, Brown &
Company.

Emily Dickinson, other poems reprinted by permission of the publishers from *The Poems of Emily Dickinson*, Thomas H. Johnson, editor. Cambridge, Mass.: Harvard University Press. Copyright, 1955, by The President and Fellows of Harvard College.

T. S. Eliot, "The Love Song of J. Alfred Prufrock," "Landscapes,"
"Sweeney Among the Nightingales," "The Waste Land" (and
Notes), "The Hollow Men," Section vi from "Ash-Wednes-
day," "Journey of the Magi," and "Preludes," from *Collected
Poems 1909-1935*, by T. S. Eliot. Copyright, 1936, by Harcourt,
Brace and Company, Inc. By permission also of Faber and
Faber, Ltd.

T. S. Eliot, selection from "Little Gidding," from *Four Quartets*.
Copyright, 1943, by T. S. Eliot. Reprinted by permission of
Harcourt, Brace and Company, Inc. By permission also of
Faber and Faber, Ltd.

T. S. Eliot, "Macavity: the Mystery Cat," from *Old Possum's*

PREFATORY NOTE

THIS BOOK OFFERS EXTENSIVE SELECTIONS FROM THE WRITINGS OF
eighteen master authors of our native tradition. Like Houghton Mifflin's
companion *Masters of British Literature*, it reflects in its plan three convictions which are coming to be increasingly accepted by American
teachers of literature: that the student is better introduced to their subject through close familiarity with a few writers than through superficial acquaintance with many, that he will profit more from regarding
the works he reads to be studied and enjoyed on their own terms than
he will from viewing them as illustrations of the course of literary or
cultural history, and that at the same time he must have a competent
knowledge of the historical setting from which these authors and their
works emerged if he is to see them as they really are.

In choosing authors up to the present century, the editors were of one
mind, even though Edward Taylor here appears for the first time in an
anthology of major American writers. Our own age offered more difficult problems of choice, but Frost and Eliot, O'Neill and Faulkner were
at length selected as its greatest and most representative figures. It should
be mentioned, however, that the claims of Hemingway had to be dismissed without a hearing, since copyright restrictions precluded the possibility of representing him adequately.

The task of making selections from the novelists was simplified by
the assumption that teachers would choose to supplement this book by
a choice from among the classic American novels available in several
well-edited and inexpensive paperback series. So Hawthorne and Melville are represented by the shorter narratives which best complement
The Scarlet Letter and *Moby-Dick*. Similarly several of the selections
from Mark Twain are relevant to *Huckleberry Finn*. The excerpts
from his *Autobiography* concern Twain's boyhood memories of Hannibal. The chapters from *Life on the Mississippi* include the celebrated
"raftsmen" passage which Twain removed from his novel along with the
account of the Watkins-Darnell feud, an analogue to the Shepherdson-
Grangerford episode in *Huckleberry Finn*. Such stories as *Daisy Miller*,
in which the "international theme" is explored, and "The Pupil," with
its delicate probing of human relationships, prepare the student for *The
Portrait of a Lady* and James's other longer fictions. With Faulkner
"Red Leaves" leads to "The Bear" and "That Evening Sun" to *The
Sound and the Fury*, while "My Grandmother Millard" gives the stu-
dent a sense of the Civil War South and prepares him for the legendary
Snopeses.

Our remaining writers of fiction concerned themselves primarily with
the short story. The tales by Poe illustrate his main themes and interests
in familiar and unfamiliar works. Crane's major shorter narratives are

here as well as an early Bowery piece and a Civil War tale. Again it is possible to supplement with a paperback *Red Badge of Courage.*

Except for T. S. Eliot, in choosing from whose verse we have been restricted, like other editors, to a thousand lines, the poets are represented with unusual fullness. The several phases of Edward Taylor's work are exampled. All of Poe's best poems are here. The best and most significant poems of Whitman are given in the order of their first appearance in the successive editions of *Leaves of Grass.* Thus the student is enabled to comprehend Whitman's development as well as his variety. Not only do we provide the best of Emily Dickinson but also far more of her poems than are available in trustworthy texts in any other volume. The many moods and poetic forms that have marked Frost's long career are generously sampled, and his notable essay on the art of poetry, "The Figure a Poem Makes," is included.

Desire Under the Elms was chosen from the works of O'Neill, our one dramatist, because it embodies better than any other piece the theme of conflict within the family basic to *Mourning Becomes Electra* and to his posthumous plays.

The remaining writers of prose have been presented not only through familiar, indeed inevitable, selections but also through some fresh and unhackneyed passages. Over against Franklin, the type of the wisely worldly man and a famous American worthy, is placed Edwards, a deeply understanding philosopher. With Adams the stress is on his ability to think historically and his grace in reviving past relationships. Emerson and Thoreau are too varied to be adequately displayed in terms of a single theme. Hence the development of their thought has been emphasized.

Particular care has been taken to provide the text most appropriate to each author. In the cases of Edward Taylor and Emily Dickinson, whose work was published posthumously, we have used the definitive texts established from the manuscripts by Mr. Johnson. Mark Twain is printed from first-edition texts throughout, since later editions incorporate many minor unauthorized changes. Elsewhere the usual practice has been to follow the last text which the author can be presumed to have seen.

The editors have written illuminating essays introducing the work of each author. Headnotes and discreet annotation have been provided where necessary. (Contrary to recent editorial fashion, Mr. Edel has elected to leave *The Waste Land* unannotated, a decision which Eliot would presumably approve.) Each volume concludes with a highly selective bibliography. It may also be noted that certain selections from Eliot and Faulkner parallel these authors' recorded readings from their own works, a hint which students and perhaps some instructors may wish to follow up.

It should be added that Hawthorne, James, O'Neill, Eliot, and Faulkner were edited by Mr. Edel; Edwards, Taylor, Franklin, Emily Dickinson, and Adams by Mr. Johnson; Emerson, Thoreau, Melville, and Whitman by Mr. Paul; and Poe, Crane, Twain, and Frost by Mr. Simpson.

GORDON N. RAY

CONTENTS

WALT WHITMAN   1

CONTENTS

MARK TWAIN 173

CONTENTS

HENRY ADAMS

HENRY JAMES

STEPHEN CRANE

CONTENTS

CONTENTS

MASTERS OF

AMERICAN LITERATURE

VOLUME TWO

WALT WHITMAN

1819–1892

No OTHER POET HAS BEEN SO GREAT A CENTER OF CONTROVERSY IN
America as Whitman has. From the very beginning he was troublesome
to the genteel critics who were offended by his "egotism," the unortho-
doxies of his form, and his open treatment of sex. E. P. Whipple said that
Whitman "had every leaf but the fig leaf," and E. C. Stedman spoke of
his "repulsive exhibitionism" and his trespassing on "the consummate
processes of nature." At the same time, Whitman had his champions:
William O'Connor, who in *The Good Gray Poet, A Vindication* (1866)
introduced Whitman-the-Messiah, and John Burroughs and Dr. Maurice
Bucke, who, with Whitman's help, wrote his first biographies. Moreover,
to later critics who were reassessing American literature before and after
World War I, Whitman, because of his frankness, realism, and the democratic mission he had proposed for the writer, became a culture-hero
and the starting point of the modern American literary tradition. Van
Wyck Brooks, for example, wrote in *America's Coming-of-Age* (1915)
that Whitman was the poet who gave the "nation a certain focal centre
in the consciousness of its own character." And in *The Golden Day*
(1926), Lewis Mumford wrote that "one might remove Longfellow without changing a single possibility of American life; had Whitman died in
the cradle, however, the possibilities of American life would have been
definitely impoverished. He created a new pattern of experience and
character. The work he conceived still remains to be done: the America
he evoked does not as yet exist." More recently, because of extensive
scholarship, especially that of Emory Holloway, C. J. Furness, and F. O.
Matthiessen in America, and Jean Catel and Frederick Schyberg in
Europe, the contours of Whitman's life and art have been better understood; and in Gay Wilson Allen's definitive critical biography, *The
Solitary Singer* (1955), the poet has finally been domesticated and normal-
ized. And yet, as a culture-hero, Whitman still raises voices: in the inter-

est of poetic freedom and renewal in our time, William Carlos Williams
has put Whitman against T. S. Eliot and claimed that "free verse was
his great idea"; and others, reacting against Whitman's democratic program, like Richard Chase in *Walt Whitman Reconsidered* (1955), have
stripped Whitman of his "poses" and reduced him to a comic poet and
elegist.

When one considers that Whitman had to print and sell his own poems
and often review them, that he lost a governmental clerkship because of
his poetry, and that though unpopular and little read, *Leaves of Grass*
grew in edition after edition, one can grant Whitman the pride with
which he spoke of his "unkillable work!" But apart from the assertiveness
and the freedom of the form, was there so much that was new to the
reader in 1855 who had read Emerson or even periodicals like the *Democratic Review?* Wasn't the shock mainly one of recognition, that here at
last was the actual fulfillment of what Emerson had called for, the native,
original literature that critics and journalists had heralded for a generation? Whitman had found a form in which to realize the professed ideas
of his age, but perhaps the fact that he had assumed the role of prophet
of democracy and had begun to "tally" American experience in his own
personality was an affront; an affront, because in his bold lines and in his
identification with the common man the aspirations of democracy were
put on record, gathered into a personality which was to be its witness and
justification—and model.

Like Emerson, who, he said, had brought his simmering genius to a
boil, Whitman subscribed to the faith in the divinity and infinitude of
man. He proclaimed the individual—"One's-self I sing, a simple separate
person"—and most important to him was "the great pride of man in himself." He too struck up for a new world, and envisaged the American,
born anew, with no shackles, working out his destiny by facing the universe freshly. And he too knew something of that "history" which "is
folded, folded inward and inward again, in the single word I." In fact, his
poems were about the self (or the soul) and its relations to matter. Somehow the self of Emerson's essays came alive in Whitman's poems and began to speak "without check." This was the crudeness of which even
Emerson and Thoreau spoke. And to many, undoubtedly, the lack of reticence was too much, not only on grounds of taste, but, one suspects, because the lack of reticence—the very daring of his frankness—implied as
well a lack of qualification in the expression of one's democratic sentiments.

For Whitman carried the democratization of life to its deepest citadel
—the personality. This was his achievement. Much of his program was
announced in the inscription he added to *Leaves of Grass* in 1867, the
opening poem of all subsequent editions:

> One's-self I sing, a simple separate person,
> Yet utter the word Democratic, the word En-Masse.

Of physiology from top to toe I sing,
Not physiognomy alone nor brain alone is worthy for
  the Muse, I say the Form complete is worthier far,
The Female equally with the Male I sing.

Of Life immense in passion, pulse, and power,
Cheerful, for freest action form'd under the laws divine,
The Modern Man I sing.

Where Emerson or Thoreau had celebrated the self it was indeed the "soul." More ascetic than Whitman, still somewhat Puritan, their self was bodiless; its passion, pulse, and power were spiritual, and its senses were rightly called "lofty senses" by the younger William Ellery Channing. Until Whitman, no one in America had celebrated the body—"Come, said my Soul,/ Such verses for my body let us write, (for we are one)." No one had spoken so joyously of merely physical experience, and no one had spoken so freely and naturally of sex. Others, Henry Adams later remarked, had used sex for sentiment, but only Whitman had "insisted on the power of sex. . . ." In fact, in his open letter to Emerson in 1856, Whitman said that the "main matter . . . so far quite unexpressed in poems" was the body and sex, that the test of the poet of America would be his celebration of "the eternal decency of the amativeness of Nature, the motherhood of all" rather than the silence that acknowledged "the fashionable delusion of the inherent nastiness of sex. . . ." For this power suffused the universe: "Urge and urge and urge,/ Always the procreant urge of the world." And this power, manifest in man, solved the seeming paradox of the separate person and the en-masse of democracy; properly expressed, this power was the fusing spiritual principle. In his own self-realization through Nature, which had given him his profound assurance and which he believed to be essential to the liberation of the democratic personality, Whitman had learned that "all men ever born are . . . my brothers, and the women my sisters and lovers." It was this experience that made him the "caresser of life," who claimed that "what is common-est, cheapest, nearest, easiest, is Me" and who announced defiantly, "By God! I will accept nothing which all cannot have their counterpart of on the same terms."

That Whitman rather than Emerson or Thoreau was able to enact the social ideal—the running together of souls—implicit in Transcendentalism was due to many things. No doubt the "long foreground" of which Emerson spoke in his letter of praise on receiving the first edition of *Leaves of Grass* had much to do with it. For Whitman was not of New England; the soil from which his poems grew, and which he felt made him the representative American bard, was that of New York. Whitman was born in West Hills, Long Island, of humble but well-descended farming folk, and was soon to move to Brooklyn; his education and experience were hardly those of his Concord contemporaries. He had neither the support of a cohesive family nor the security of an established life. His father, whom he hated, was a carpenter dogged and hardened by failure; his mother, whom he loved, was (like Dreiser's mother) the emotional stay of a wayward, impoverished family. If the one imbued his son with a Jeffersonian free-thinking rationalism and the other with the inward spirit of Quakerism, the actual life they provided for his youth was that of a slum. He was more familiar with the "roughs," with Fulton Street and the ferry slips of a village quickly becoming a city, than with academies—and no Harvard awaited him. After six years in the public schools he became a printer's apprentice, and like Franklin before him and Twain after him, had his education in the print shop. A journeyman printer, and by sixteen, a migrant schoolteacher, he spent most of his life before the "*Leaves of Grass* bee" came to him in virulent political journalism.

Printing and politics were one, and from his first political activity in behalf of Van Buren in 1840 until his disenchantment with political parties around 1848, Whitman was the editor of Democratic newspapers. His most important post was on the Brooklyn *Daily Eagle*. During these years he was also contributing to various magazines and newspapers the stock-in-trade writing of the times: conventional, sentimental, didactic stories, essays, and sketches, some imitative of Hawthorne and Poe, and most, heavily dependent on the conventions of the graveyard school. He even wrote on commission a temperance novel, *Franklin Evans, or the Inebriate*. With this experience in popular literature, Whitman's achievement in *Leaves of Grass* seems all the more remarkable (in fact, like Emily Dickinson, he was able to transform the sentimental theme of death into something genuinely sublime). But if the printing office had its liabilities, it also had its assets: it placed Whitman in the arena of his times. Here he learned the politics of America first hand, received and reviewed the books that were shaping the times, and was given his passport to the theatre and opera, the latter being, he said, one of the sources of inspiration for his poems.

Throughout this period, and later in 1851–1854 when he withdrew from what might have been a successful career in journalism to take up carpentering, Whitman assimilated the materials of his poems. He was not unlearned, as his own epithet "barbaric" has led many to believe; he was a serious reader in libraries, and in his informal way had come upon significant ideas. He knew the painters William S. Mount and Walter Libby, he listened to the discussions in Henry K. Brown's studio, and he even gave a lecture before the Brooklyn Art Union. A devoted reader of the British reviews, he was familiar with the romantic theories of art and genius, and through his connection with the *Democratic Review*, the literary organ of "Young America," he found these theories dressed out in an acceptable nationalism. Though gathered from popular lectures and books, his knowledge of astronomy was accurate; it was the fundamental science of his poems, providing him with the notion of cosmic evolution. From Dr. Henry Abbott and his Egyptian Museum he quickened his sense of the long reaches of human history and the flow of human time.

And in Epictetus—a life-long favorite—and Lucretius, he found many of the ideas that characterized his poems: manly love, the injunction to enjoy, the atomic flux, the fearlessness of death, the importance of "amativeness" (the phrenological word for heterosexual love).

More was needed than this education, however, to transform a journalist-carpenter into a poet. For Whitman was anything but the confident poet who first addressed the readers of *Leaves of Grass*. Behind the public pose of bard, which he honestly tried to live up to, was an introspective and a troubled man. No hearty "rough" at all, but a lonely and secretive man, who confessed his longing for love in many of his poems and hoped to find communion with other people through them, he tried throughout his life to reconcile the duality within himself. This tension impelled his poems; in fact, his passivity and his feminine traits of tenderness and receptivity had much to do with their strength. His best poems were often the expression and resolution of his personal conflicts, and even his public program for America was the projection of or compensation for his inner needs. Frequently the editions of *Leaves of Grass* marked the stages of his self-distrust and his assurance; and that the first edition was confident—that it appeared at all—was due to the fact that Whitman had found at last the springs of courage. These springs, as Haniel Long pointed out in *Walt Whitman and the Springs of Courage* (1938), were released when Whitman discovered the depths and resources of his own self; when he found in phrenology (a pseudo-science, then popular, in which one's character was read from the "bumps" of one's head) the certification of his own powers. Emerson had also helped him recognize and had taught him to respect these deeper powers within the self. And one might add that when Whitman needed assurance most, at the time when his small first edition appeared, it was Emerson's letter of recognition almost alone that encouraged him to continue his work.

His work, of course, was *Leaves of Grass*, the book of poems that grew with him during the remainder of his life. In some nine editions, he added to, revised, and rearranged his poems, trying to give them the organic form of a human life from birth to death. From the start he had determined to write a "this side book," for the literature of the past was "feudal," unsuited in its sentiments and its forms to democratic America. The form of his poems, accordingly, was programmatically different: new ideas require new forms of expression. But the expression was also organic in the sense that it grew out of the poet, that it expressed him, the American nativity of which he was so proud, the very people, landscape, speech he had taken into himself. "Who are you indeed who would talk or sing to America?" he asked. "Have you studied out the land, its idioms and men?" This he had tried to do, in his public role of bard, and by becoming or dramatizing himself as a stock personality who would represent the kind of character needed in the new world.

The poems, moreover, were as democratic in form as in idea. They were "natural" rather than conventional or artificial; they took their shape from the poet's experience, and formally were as free and all-absorbing as he was. And if they were, as Whitman said, an attempt "to cast into literature . . . his own grit and arrogance," they were also intended to "bestow . . . no less than the entrance to all the gifts of the universe." Their aim was to stir one's sense of life, to awaken the senses and the consciousness, to prepare one for the glory of simply being and experiencing. They indicated the stance and provided the road that, beginning in any well-founded self, opens into the universe. They were not substitutes for experience, they were appeals to experience: "Not I, not any one else can travel that road for you,/ You must travel it for yourself." Spurning the "second or third hand," spurning the past and even the poet, they were to enable man "to listen to all sides and filter them from your self"; through the poems one was to learn that the road is "within reach,/ Perhaps you have been on it since you were born and did not know." Not only in the sense that his poems were "clues and indirections," were symbolically suggestive, did they require the reader to complete them; they required him to go beyond the poems to the "origin of all poems," to the experience itself of man in nature.

To say that the poems were open and natural does not mean that they were formless, but simply that they had a different form. Just as the poem grew out of the poet and was his expression, so the poem took its shape from the unfolding of an inner idea, was formed not from the outside, but from within—literally formed and informed by what the poet was trying to express. The clue to such a form, again, is the poet's experience: the images and language he has taken into himself in his occupations, his actual contact with the world, and the rhythms he has known and that have naturally become the cadences of his being. One immediately notices in Whitman's poems a declamatory style, a resourceful use of the human voice, and the oceanic largeness of his rhythms. For the most important influences in the shaping of his poems, as F. O. Matthiessen pointed out, were the native tradition of oratory, the opera, and the sea. Many of his poems, especially the public ones, were simply the versified orations of the leader who had "the divine power to speak words." Others were called carols and songs, and some employed the aria and recitative of the opera and the leitmotif and modulated volumes of music. Some had the resurgent melody of the sea. And though he seldom controlled and fused these resources, when he did, as in "Out of the Cradle Endlessly Rocking," he produced his most successful poems.

The best poems, moreover, came from the deepest soil of the poet. The public ones have the weakness of oratory; they proclaimed the program of the prophet of democracy, they did not intimately express him. This, of course, does not discredit Whitman's faith, but turns one instead to the lonely poet who wanted his poems to substantiate him. "This is no book," he said, "Who touches this, touches a man." Toward the end of his life, he confessed: "I also sent out *Leaves of Grass* to arouse and set flowing in men's and women's hearts, young and old, (my present and future readers,) endless streams of living, pulsating love and friendship, directly from them to myself, now and ever. To this terrible, irrepressible yearning, (surely more or less down underneath in most human souls,) —this never-satisfied appetite for sympathy, and this boundless offering of sympathy—this universal democratic comradeship—this old, eternal, yet ever-new interchange of adhesiveness [the phrenological word for manly love], so fitly emblematic of America—I have given in that book, undisguisedly, declaredly, the openest expression. . . ." It is here, in the "underneath in most human souls" that the public and private poet join. For the common center of both was the need to find in sympathy the answer to the question that disturbed him from his youth: "Wherefore is there no response?"

⚭

From LEAVES OF GRASS

First Edition, 1855

Except for its handsome reception by Emerson, this remarkable book did not readily find appreciation. Even its preface, with its summary pronouncements of the fervid literary nationalism and organic theory of the period, did not alert readers to the fact that, though self-proclaimed, Whitman was indeed the poet Emerson had called for. And even the green cover with its design of leaves and flowers and sprouting roots did not prepare the reader for the poems that had grown out of the poet.

Of the twelve untitled poems in this edition, the first (later called "A Poem of Walt Whitman, An American," "Walt Whitman," and finally "Song of Myself") was the longest and most important. For it was the poet's celebration of the self—the constant hero of his poems—the exuberant expression of his discovery of the "Me myself" (§4). Not egoistic, as many readers assumed, Whitman's celebration of "myself" was representative; the self he glorified was the "real" or "spiritual" self, the divinity common to all men, and hence the ground of human equality and the bond of democracy. The poem, accordingly, tells us how Whitman found, and everyone might find, the confidence, the centrality of being, which made him a truly democratic person.

Covering a day from morning to evening, the poem also covered a life; its contents were the substance of Whitman's thirty-six years, as in the act of "observing a spear of summer grass" the self poured forth the images it had long contained. By leaving the house (the conventions of society), by returning to nature, and by confronting its mysteries in a blade of grass, Whitman invited his soul "to speak at every hazard." His experience, however, was not only one of release, but one of cosmic self-realization (§5), and it taught him what the rest of the poem expressed, that "a kelson of the creation is love."

If this dramatization of the self put his readers off, so did the form of the poem: not only the defiantly free verse, but the symphonic and stream-of-consciousness techniques that Whitman here pioneered. Images proposed the themes, and by the "logic" of association the poem circled about them—if one takes the trouble to translate images into ideas the poem will be found to have a meaningful structure. The fundamental symbols, however, were apparent: the self and the grass, man and nature. And they helped the poet unfold the essential drama of the poem, the coming into *identity* (the way the self takes on form through birth and subsequently through its relations to things) and the passing into *diffusion* (the return of the self at death to the immortal, everflowing flux or "float" of "atoms" which is nature). Thus, at the end of the poem, in that confident expectation of the deathlessness of death, the self and the grass become one as the poet bequeathes "myself to the dirt to grow from the grass I love."

Of the remaining poems, "There Was a Child Went Forth," "The Sleepers," and "I Sing the Body Electric" were perhaps the most significant. The first reveals the process of identification and is richly autobiographical; here are some of the deepest sources of experience from which the poet drew. The second is a dream poem in which the poet takes his characteristic flight in—or out of—time and space, and in the freedom of his "vision" (his dream, his release into the unconscious) merges with the sleepers—humanity equalized by sleep, by night and death, the symbols here of the "float" from which all will be delivered into new life. The last poem of the group, later included in *Children of Adam*, is a rhapsodic praise of the body in all its "performances," but especially of healthy procreation, which brings forth the body necessary to the identification of the soul.

PREFACE

America does not repel the past or what it has produced under its forms or amid other politics or the idea of castes or the old religions . . . accepts the lesson with calmness . . . is not so impatient as has been supposed that the slough still sticks to opinions and manners and literature while the life which served its requirements has passed into the new life of the new forms . . . perceives that the corpse is slowly borne from the eating and sleeping rooms of the house . . . perceives that it waits a little while in the door . . . that it was fittest for its days . . . that its action has descended to the stalwart and wellshaped heir who approaches . . . and that he shall be fittest for his days.

The Americans of all nations at any time upon the earth have probably the fullest poetical nature. The United States themselves are essentially the greatest poem. In the history of the earth hitherto the largest and most stirring appear tame and orderly to their ampler largeness and stir. Here at last is something in the doings of man that corresponds with the broadcast doings of the day and night. Here is not merely a nation but a teeming nation of nations. Here is action untied from strings necessarily blind to particulars and details magnificently moving in vast masses. Here is the hospitality which forever indicates heroes. . . . Here are the roughs and beards and space and ruggedness and nonchalance that the soul loves. Here the performance disdaining the trivial unapproached in the tremendous audacity of its crowds and groupings and the push of its perspective spreads with crampless and flowing breadth and showers its prolific and splendid extravagance. One sees it must indeed own the riches of the summer and winter, and need never be bankrupt while corn grows from the ground or the orchards drop apples or the bays contain fish or men beget children upon women.

Other states indicate themselves in their deputies . . . but the genius of the United States is not best or most in its executives or legislatures, nor in its ambassadors or authors or colleges or churches or parlors, nor even in its newspapers or inventors . . . but always most in the common people. Their manners speech dress friendships—the freshness and candor of their physiognomy—the picturesque looseness of their carriage . . . their deathless attachment to freedom—their aversion to anything indecorous or soft or mean—the practical acknowledgment of the citizens of one state by the citizens of all other states—the fierceness of their roused resentment—their curiosity and welcome of novelty—their self-esteem and wonderful sympathy—their susceptibility to a slight—the air they have of persons who never knew how it felt to stand in the presence of superiors—the fluency of their speech—their delight in music, the sure symptom of manly tenderness and native elegance of soul . . . their good temper and openhandedness—the terrible significance of their elections—the President's taking off his hat to them not they to him—these too are unrhymed poetry. It awaits the gigantic and generous treatment worthy of it.

The largeness of nature or the nation were monstrous without a corresponding largeness and generosity of the spirit of the citizen. Not nature nor swarming states nor streets and steamships nor prosperous business nor farms nor capital nor learning may suffice for the ideal of man . . . nor suffice the poet. No reminiscences may suffice either. A live nation can always cut a deep mark and can have the best authority the cheapest . . . namely from its own soul. This is the sum of the profitable uses of individuals or states and of present action and grandeur and of the subjects of poets.—As if it were necessary to trot back generation after generation to the eastern records! As if the beauty and sacredness of the demonstrable must fall behind that of the mythical! As if men do not make their mark out of any times! As if the opening of the western continent by discovery and what has transpired since in North and South America were less than the small theatre of the antique or the aimless sleepwalking of the middle ages! The pride of the United States leaves the wealth and finesse of the cities and all returns of commerce and agriculture and all the magnitude of geography or shows of exterior victory

to enjoy the breed of fullsized men or one fullsized man unconquerable
and simple.

The American poets are to enclose old and new for America is the race
of races. Of them a bard is to be commensurate with a people. To him the
other continents arrive as contributions . . . he gives them reception for
their sake and his own sake. His spirit responds to his country's spirit . . .
he incarnates its geography and natural life and rivers and lakes. Mississippi with annual freshets and changing chutes, Missouri and Columbia
and Ohio and Saint Lawrence with the falls and beautiful masculine Hudson, do not embochure where they spend themselves more than they embochure into him. The blue breadth over the inland sea of Virginia and
Maryland and the sea off Massachusetts and Maine and over Manhattan
bay and over Champlain and Erie and over Ontario and Huron and Michigan and Superior, and over the Texan and Mexican and Floridian and
Cuban seas and over the seas off California and Oregon, is not tallied by
the blue breadth of the waters below more than the breadth of above
and below is tallied by him. When the long Atlantic coast stretches longer
and the Pacific coast stretches longer he easily stretches with them north
or south. He spans between them also from east to west and reflects what
is between them. On him rise solid growths that offset the growths of
pine and cedar and hemlock and liveoak and locust and chestnut and cypress and hickory and limetree and cottonwood and tuliptree and cactus
and wildvine and tamarind and persimmon . . . and tangles as tangled as
any canebrake or swamp . . . and forests coated with transparent ice and
icicles hanging from the boughs and crackling in the wind . . . and sides
and peaks of mountains . . . and pasturage sweet and free as savannah
or upland or prairie . . . with flights and songs and screams that answer
those of the wildpigeon and highhold and orchard-oriole and coot and
surf-duck and redshouldered-hawk and fish-hawk and white-ibis and
indian-hen and cat-owl and water-pheasant and qua-bird and pied-shel-
drake and blackbird and mockingbird and buzzard and condor and night-
heron and eagle. To him the hereditary countenance descends both mother's and father's. To him enter the essences of the real things and past and
present events—of the enormous diversity of temperature and agriculture
and mines—the tribes of red aborigines—the weather-beaten vessels entering new ports or making landings on rocky coasts—the first settlements
north or south—the rapid stature and muscle—the haughty defiance of '76,
and the war and peace and formation of the constitution . . . the union
always surrounded by blatherers and always calm and impregnable—the
perpetual coming of immigrants—the wharfhem'd cities and superior marine—the unsurveyed interior—the loghouses and clearings and wild animals and hunters and trappers . . . the free commerce—the fisheries and
whaling and gold-digging—the endless gestation of new states—the con-
vening of Congress every December, the members duly coming up from
all climates and the uttermost parts . . . the noble character of the young
mechanics and of all free American workmen and workwomen . . . the

general ardor and friendliness and enterprise—the perfect equality of the female with the male . . . the large amativeness—the fluid movement of the population—the factories and mercantile life and laborsaving machinery—the Yankee swap—the New-York firemen and the target excursion—the southern plantation life—the character of the northeast and of the northwest and southwest—slavery and the tremulous spreading of hands to protect it, and the stern opposition to it which shall never cease till it ceases or the speaking of tongues and the moving of lips cease. For such the expression of the American poet is to be transcendant and new. It is to be indirect and not direct or descriptive or epic. Its quality goes through these to much more. Let the age and wars of other nations be chanted and their eras and characters be illustrated and that finish the verse. Not so the great psalm of the republic. Here the theme is creative and has vista. Here comes one among the wellbeloved stonecutters and plans with decision and science and sees the solid and beautiful forms of the future where there are now no solid forms.

Of all nations the United States with veins full of poetical stuff most need poets and will doubtless have the greatest and use them the greatest. Their Presidents shall not be their common referee so much as their poets shall. Of all mankind the great poet is the equable man. Not in him but off from him things are grotesque or eccentric or fail of their sanity. Nothing out of its place is good and nothing in its place is bad. He bestows on every object or quality its fit proportions neither more nor less. He is the arbiter of the diverse and he is the key. He is the equalizer of his age and land . . . he supplies what wants supplying and checks what wants checking. If peace is the routine out of him speaks the spirit of peace, large, rich, thrifty, building vast and populous cities, encouraging agriculture and the arts and commerce—lighting the study of man, the soul, immortality—federal, state or municipal government, marriage, health, freetrade, intertravel by land and sea . . . nothing too close, nothing too far off . . . the stars not too far off. In war he is the most deadly force of the war. Who recruits him recruits horse and foot . . . he fetches parks of artillery the best that engineer ever knew. If the time becomes slothful and heavy he knows how to arouse it . . . he can make every word he speaks draw blood. Whatever stagnates in the flat of custom or obedience or legislation he never stagnates. Obedience does not master him, he masters it. High up out of reach he stands turning a concentrated light . . . he turns the pivot with his finger . . . he baffles the swiftest runners as he stands and easily overtakes and envelops them. The time straying toward infidelity and confections and persiflage he withholds by his steady faith . . . he spreads out his dishes . . . he offers the sweet firmfibred meat that grows men and women. His brain is the ultimate brain. He is no arguer . . . he is judgment. He judges not as the judge judges but as the sun falling around a helpless thing. As he sees the farthest he has the most faith. His thoughts are the hymns of the praise of things. In the talk on the soul and eternity and God off of his equal plane he is silent. He sees eternity less like a play with a prologue and denouement . . . he sees eternity in men and women . . . he does not see men and women as dreams or dots. Faith is the antiseptic of the soul . . . it pervades the common people and preserves them . . . they never give up believing and expecting and trusting. There is that indescribable freshness and unconsciousness about an illiterate person that humbles and mocks the power of the noblest expressive genius. The poet sees for a certainty how one not a great artist may be just as sacred as the greatest artist. . . . The power to destroy or remould is freely used by him but never the power of attack. What is past is past. If he does not expose superior models and prove himself by every step he takes he is not what is wanted. The presence of the greatest poet conquers . . . not parleying or struggling or any prepared attempts. Now he has passed that way see after him! there is not left any vestige of despair or misanthropy or cunning or exclusiveness or the ignominy of a nativity or color or delusion of hell or the necessity of hell . . . and no man thenceforward shall be degraded for ignorance or weakness or sin.

The greatest poet hardly knows pettiness or triviality. If he breathes into any thing that was before thought small it dilates with the grandeur and life of the universe. He is a seer . . . he is individual . . . he is complete in himself . . . the others are as good as he, only he sees it and they do not. He is not one of the chorus . . . he does not stop for any regulations . . . he is the president of regulation. What the eyesight does to the rest he does to the rest. Who knows the curious mystery of the eyesight? The other senses corroborate themselves, but this is removed from any proof but its own and foreruns the identities of the spiritual world. A single glance of it mocks all the investigations of man and all the instruments and books of the earth and all the reasoning. What is marvelous? what is unlikely? what is impossible or baseless or vague? after you have once just opened the space of a peachpit and given audience to far and near and to the sunset and had all things enter with electric swiftness softly and duly without confusion or jostling or jam.

The land and sea, the animals, fishes and birds, the sky of heaven and the orbs, the forests mountains and rivers, are not small themes . . . but folks expect of the poet to indicate more than the beauty and dignity which always attach to dumb real objects . . . they expect him to indicate the path between reality and their souls. Men and women perceive the beauty well enough . . . probably as well as he. The passionate tenacity of hunters, woodmen, early risers, cultivators of gardens and orchards and fields, the love of healthy women for the manly form, seafaring persons, drivers of horses, the passion for light and the open air, all is an old varied sign of the unfailing perception of beauty and of a residence of the poetic in outdoor people. They can never be assisted by poets to perceive . . . some may but they never can. The poetic quality is not marshalled in rhyme or uniformity or abstract addresses to things nor in melancholy complaints or good precepts, but is the life of these and much else and is in the soul. The profit of rhyme is that it drops seeds of a sweeter and more luxuriant rhyme, and of uniformity that it conveys itself into its own roots in the ground out of sight. The rhyme and uniformity of perfect poems show the free growth of metrical laws and bud from them as unerringly and loosely as lilacs or roses on a bush, and take shapes as compact as the shapes of chestnuts and oranges and melons and pears, and shed the perfume impalpable to form. The fluency and ornaments of the finest poems or music or crations or recitations are not independent but dependent. All beauty comes from beautiful blood and a beautiful brain. If the greatnesses are in conjunction in a man or woman it is enough . . . the fact will prevail through the universe . . . but the gaggery and gilt of a million years will not prevail. Who troubles himself about his ornaments or fluency is lost. This is what you shall do: Love the earth and sun and the animals, despise riches, give alms to every one that asks, stand up for the stupid and crazy, devote your income and labor to others, hate tyrants, argue not concerning God, have patience and indulgence toward the people, take off your hat to nothing known or unknown or to any man or number of men, go freely with powerful uneducated persons and with the young and with the mothers of families, read these leaves in the open air every season of every year of your life, re-examine all you have been told at school or church or in any book, dismiss whatever insults your own soul, and your very flesh shall be a great poem and have the richest fluency not only in its words but in the silent lines of its lips and face and between the lashes of your eyes and in every motion and joint of your body. . . . The poet shall not spend his time in unneeded work. He shall know that the ground is always ready plowed and manured . . . others may not know it but he shall. He shall go directly to the creation. His trust shall master the trust of everything he touches . . . and shall master all attachment.

The known universe has one complete lover and that is the greatest poet. He consumes an eternal passion and is indifferent which chance happens and which possible contingency of fortune or misfortune and persuades daily and hourly his delicious pay. What balks or breaks others is fuel for his burning progress to contact and amorous joy. Other proportions of the reception of pleasure dwindle to nothing to his proportions. All expected from heaven or from the highest he is rapport with in the sight of the daybreak or a scene of the winter-woods or the presence of children playing or with his arm round the neck of a man or woman. His love above all love has leisure and expanse . . . he leaves room ahead of himself. He is no irresolute or suspicious lover . . . he is sure . . . he scorns intervals. His experience and the showers and thrills are not for nothing. Nothing can jar him . . . suffering and darkness cannot—death and fear cannot. To him complaint and jealousy and envy are corpses buried and rotten in the earth . . . he saw them buried. The sea is not surer of the shore or the shore of the sea than he is of the fruition of his love and of all perfection and beauty.

The fruition of beauty is no chance of hit or miss . . . it is inevitable as life . . . it is exact and plumb as gravitation. From the eyesight proceeds another eyesight and from the hearing proceeds another hearing and from the voice proceeds another voice eternally curious of the harmony of things with man. To these respond perfections not only in the committees that were supposed to stand for the rest but in the rest themselves just the same. These understand the law of perfection in masses and floods . . . that its finish is to each for itself and onward from itself . . . that it is profuse and impartial . . . that there is not a minute of the light or dark nor an acre of the earth or sea without it—nor any direction of the sky nor any trade or employment nor any turn of events. This is the reason that about the proper expression of beauty there is precision and balance . . . one part does not need to be thrust above another. The best singer is not the one who has the most lithe and powerful organ . . . the pleasure of poems is not in them that take the handsomest measure and similes and sound.

Without effort and without exposing in the least how it is done the greatest poet brings the spirit of any or all events and passions and scenes and persons some more and some less to bear on your individual character as you hear or read. To do this well is to compete with the laws that pursue and follow time. What is the purpose must surely be there and the clue of it must be there . . . and the faintest indication is the indication of the best and then becomes the clearest indication. Past and present and future are not disjoined but joined. The greatest poet forms the consistence of what is to be from what has been and is. He drags the dead out of their coffins and stands them again on their feet . . . he says to the past, Rise and walk before me that I may realize you. He learns the lesson . . . he places himself where the future becomes present. The greatest poet does not only dazzle his rays over character and scenes and passions . . . he finally ascends and finishes all . . . he exhibits the pinnacles that no man can tell what they are for or what is beyond . . . he glows a moment on the extremest verge. He is most wonderful in his last half-hidden smile or frown . . . by that flash of the moment of parting the one that sees it shall be encouraged or terrified afterwards for many years. The greatest poet does not moralize or make applications of morals . . . he knows the soul. The soul has that measureless pride which consists in never acknowledging any lessons but its own. But it has sympathy as measureless as its pride and the one balances the other and neither can stretch too far while it stretches in company with the other. The inmost secrets of art sleep with the twain. The greatest poet has lain close betwixt both and they are vital in his style and thoughts.

The art of art, the glory of expression and the sunshine of the light of letters is simplicity. Nothing is better than simplicity . . . nothing can make up for excess or for the lack of definiteness. To carry on the heave of impulse and pierce intellectual depths and give all subjects their articulations are powers neither common nor very uncommon. But to speak in literature with the perfect rectitude and insouciance of the movements of animals and the unimpeachableness of the sentiment of trees in the woods and grass by the roadside is the flawless triumph of art. If you have looked on him who has achieved it you have looked on one of the masters of the artists of all nations and times. You shall not contemplate the flight of the graygull over the bay or the mettlesome action of the blood horse or the tall leaning of sunflowers on their stalk or the appearance of the sun journeying through heaven or the appearance of the moon afterward with any more satisfaction than you shall contemplate him. The greatest poet has less a marked style and is more the channel of thoughts and things without increase or diminution, and is the free channel of himself. He swears to his art, I will not be meddlesome, I will not have in my writing any elegance or effect or originality to hang in the way between me and the rest like curtains. I will have nothing hang in the way, not the richest curtains. What I tell I tell for precisely what it is. Let who may exalt or startle or fascinate or sooth I will have purposes as health or heat or snow has and be as regardless of observation. What I experience or portray shall go from my composition without a shred of my composition. You shall stand by my side and look in the mirror with me.

The old red blood and stainless gentility of great poets will be proved by their unconstraint. A heroic person walks at his ease through and out of that custom or precedent or authority that suits him not. Of the traits of the brotherhood of writers savans musicians inventors and artists nothting is finer than silent defiance advancing from new free forms. In the need of poems philosophy politics mechanism science behaviour, the craft of art, an appropriate native grand-opera, shipcraft, or any craft, he is greatest forever and forever who contributes the greatest original practical example. The cleanest expression is that which finds no sphere worthy of itself and makes one.

The messages of great poets to each man and woman are, Come to us on equal terms, Only then can you understand us, We are no better than you, What we enclose you enclose, What we enjoy you may enjoy. Did you suppose there could be only one Supreme? We affirm there can be unnumbered Supremes, and that one does not countervail another any more than one eyesight countervails another . . . and that men can be good or grand only of the consciousness of their supremacy within them. What do you think is the grandeur of storms and dismemberments and the deadliest battles and wrecks of the wildest fury of the elements and the power of the sea and the motion of nature and of the throes of human desires and dignity and hate and love? It is that something in the soul which says, Rage on, Whirl on, I tread master here and everywhere, Master of the spasms of the sky and of the shatter of the sea, Master of nature and passion and death, And of all terror and all pain.

The American bards shall be marked for generosity and affection and for encouraging competitors. . . . They shall be kosmos . . . without monopoly or secrecy . . . glad to pass any thing to any one . . . hungry for equals night and day. They shall not be careful of riches and privilege . . . they shall be riches and privilege . . . they shall perceive who the most affluent man is. The most affluent man is he that confronts all the shows he sees by equivalents out of the stronger wealth of himself. The American bard shall delineate no class of persons nor one or two out of the strata of interests nor love most nor truth most nor the soul most nor the body most . . . and not be for the eastern states more than the western or the northern states more than the southern.

Exact science and its practical movements are no checks on the greatest poet but always his encouragement and support. The outset and remembrance are there . . . there are the arms that lifted him first and brace him best . . . there he returns after all his goings and comings. The sailor and traveler . . . the atomist chemist astronomer geologist phrenologist spiritualist mathematician historian and lexicographer are not poets, but they are the lawgivers of poets and their construction underlies the structure of every perfect poem. No matter what rises or is uttered they sent the seed of the conception of it . . . of them and by them stand the visible proofs of souls . . . always of their fatherstuff must be begotten the sinewy races of bards. If there shall be love and content between the father and the son and if the greatness of the son is the exuding of the greatness of the father there shall be love between the poet and the man of demonstrable science. In the beauty of poems are the tuft and final applause of science.

Great is the faith of the flush of knowledge and of the investigation of the depths of qualities and things. Cleaving and circling here swells the soul of the poet yet is president of itself always. The depths are fathomless and therefore calm. The innocence and nakedness are resumed . . . they are neither modest not immodest. The whole theory of the special and supernatural and all that was twined with it or reduced out of it departs as a dream. What has ever happened . . . what happens and whatever may or shall happen, the vital laws enclose all . . . they are sufficient for any case and for all cases . . . none to be hurried or retarded . . . any miracle of affairs or persons inadmissible in the vast clear scheme where every motion and every spear of grass and the frames and spirits of men and women and all that concerns them are unspeakably perfect miracles all referring to all and each distinct and in its place. It is also not consistent with the reality of the soul to admit that there is anything in the known universe more divine than men and women.

Men and women and the earth and all upon it are simply to be taken as they are, and the investigation of their past and present and future shall be unintermitted and shall be done with perfect candor. Upon this basis philosophy speculates ever looking toward the poet, ever regarding the eternal tendencies of all toward happiness never inconsistent with what is clear to the senses and to the soul. For the eternal tendencies of all toward happiness make the only point of sane philosophy. Whatever comprehends less than that . . . whatever is less than the laws of light and of astronomical motion . . . or less than the laws that follow the thief the liar the glutton and the drunkard through this life and doubtless afterward . . . or less than vast stretches of time or the slow formation of density or the patient upheaving of strata—is of no account. Whatever would put God in a poem or system of philosophy as contending against some being or influence, is also of no account. Sanity and ensemble characterise the great master . . . spoilt in one principle all is spoilt. The great master has nothing to do with miracles. He sees health for himself in being one of the mass . . . he sees the hiatus in singular eminence. To the perfect shape comes common ground. To be under the general law is great for that is to correspond with it. The master knows that he is unspeakably great and that all are unspeakably great . . . that nothing for instance is greater than to conceive children and bring them up well . . . that to be is just as great as to perceive or tell.

In the make of the great masters the idea of political liberty is indispensable. Liberty takes the adherence of heroes wherever men and women exist . . . but never takes any adherence or welcome from the rest more than from poets. They are the voice and exposition of liberty. They out of ages are worthy the grand idea . . . to them it is confided and they must sustain it. Nothing has precedence of it and nothing can warp or degrade it. The attitude of great poets is to cheer up slaves and horrify despots. The turn of their necks, the sound of their feet, the motions of their wrists, are full of hazard to the one and hope to the other. Come nigh them awhile and though they neither speak or advise you shall learn the faithful American lesson. Liberty is poorly served by men whose good intent is quelled from one failure or two failures or any number of failures, or from the casual indifference or ingratitude of the people, or from the sharp show of the tushes of power, or the bringing to bear soldiers and cannon or any penal statutes. Liberty relies upon itself, invites no one, promises nothing, sits in calmness and light, is positive and composed, and knows no discouragement. The battle rages with many a loud alarm and frequent advance and retreat . . . the enemy triumphs . . . the prison, the handcuffs, the iron necklace and anklet, the scaffold, garrote and leadballs do their work . . . the cause is asleep . . . the strong throats are choked with their own blood . . . the young men drop their eyelashes toward the ground when they pass each other . . . and is liberty gone out of that place? No never. When liberty goes it is not the first to go nor the second nor third to go . . . it waits for all the rest to go . . . it is the last. . . . When the memories of the old martyrs are faded utterly away . . . when the large names of patriots are laughed at in the public halls from the lips of the orators . . . when the boys are no more christened after the same but christened after tyrants and traitors instead . . . when the laws of the free are grudgingly permitted and laws for informers and bloodmoney are sweet to the taste of the people . . . when I and you walk abroad upon the earth stung with compassion at the sight of numberless brothers answering our equal friendship and calling no man master—and when we are elated with noble joy at the sight of slaves . . . when the soul retires in the cool communion of the night and surveys its experience and has much extasy over the word and deed that put back a helpless innocent person into the gripe of the gripers or into any cruel inferiority . . . when those in all parts of these states who could easier realize the true American character but do not yet—when the swarms of cringers, suckers, doughfaces, lice of politics, planners of sly involutions for their own preferment to city offices or state legislatures or the judiciary or congress or the presidency, obtain a response of love and natural deference from the people whether they get the offices or no . . . when it is better to be a bound booby and rogue in office at a high salary than the poorest free mechanic or farmer with his hat unmoved from his head and firm eyes and a candid and generous heart . . . and when servility by town or state or the federal government or any oppression on a large scale or small scale can be tried on without its own punishment following duly after in exact proportion against the smallest chance of escape . . . or rather when all life and all the souls of men and women are discharged from any part of the earth— then only shall the instinct of liberty be discharged from that part of the earth.

As the attributes of the poets of the kosmos concentre in the real body and soul and in the pleasure of things they possess the superiority of genuineness over all fiction and romance. As they emit themselves facts are showered over with light . . . the daylight is lit with more volatile light . . . also the deep between the setting and rising sun goes deeper many fold. Each precise object or condition or combination or process exhibits a beauty . . . the multiplication table its—old age its—the carpenter's trade its—the grand-opera its . . . the hugehulled cleanshaped New-York clipper at sea under steam or full sail gleams with unmatched beauty . . . the American circles and large harmonies of government gleam with theirs . . . and the commonest definite intentions and actions with theirs. The poets of the kosmos advance through all interpositions and coverings and turmoils and stratagems to first principles. They are of use . . . they dissolve poverty from its need and riches from its conceit. You large proprietor they say shall not realize or perceive more than any one else. The owner of the library is not he who holds a legal title to it having bought and paid for it. Any one and every one is owner of the library who can read the same through all the varieties of tongues and subjects and styles, and in whom they enter with ease and take residence and force toward paternity and maternity, and make supple and powerful and rich and large. . . . These American states strong and healthy and accomplished shall receive no pleasure from violations of natural models and must not permit them. In paintings or mouldings or carvings in mineral or wood, or in the illustrations of books or newspapers, or in any comic or tragic prints, or in the patterns of woven stuffs or anything to beautify

rooms or furniture or costumes, or to put upon cornices or monuments
or on the prows or sterns of ships, or to put anywhere before the human
eye indoors or out, that which distorts honest shapes or which creates unearthly beings or places or contingencies is a nuisance and revolt. Of the
human form especially it is so great it must never be made ridiculous. Of
ornaments to a work nothing outre can be allowed . . . but those ornaments can be allowed that conform to the perfect facts of the open air
and that flow out of the nature of the work and come irrepressibly from
it and are necessary to the completion of the work. Most works are most
beautiful without ornament. . . . Exaggerations will be revenged in human physiology. Clean and vigorous children are jetted and conceived
only in those communities where the models of natural forms are public
every day. . . . Great genius and the people of these states must never
be demeaned to romances. As soon as histories are properly told there is
no more need of romances.

The great poets are also to be known by the absence in them of tricks
and by the justification of perfect personal candor. Then folks echo a
new cheap joy and a divine voice leaping from their brains: How beautiful is candor! All faults may be forgiven of him who has perfect candor.
Henceforth let no man of us lie, for we have seen that openness wins the
inner and outer world and that there is no single exception, and that never
since our earth gathered itself in a mass have deceit or subterfuge or pre-
varication attracted its smallest particle or the faintest tinge of a shade—
and that through the enveloping wealth and rank of a state or the whole
republic of states a sneak or sly person shall be discovered and despised
. . . and that the soul has never been once fooled and never can be
fooled . . . and thrift without the loving nod of the soul is only a fœtid
puff . . . and there never grew up in any of the continents of the globe
nor upon any planet or satellite or star, nor upon the asteroids, nor in any
part of ethereal space, nor in the midst of density, nor under the fluid wet
of the sea, nor in that condition which precedes the birth of babes, nor at
any time during the changes of life, nor in that condition that follows
what we term death, nor in any stretch of abeyance or action afterward
of vitality, nor in any process of formation or reformation anywhere, a
being whose instinct hated the truth.

Extreme caution or prudence, the soundest organic health, large hope
and comparison and fondness for women and children, large alimentive-
ness and destructiveness and causality, with a perfect sense of the oneness
of nature and the propriety of the same spirit applied to human affairs
. . . these are called up of the float of the brain of the world to be parts
of the greatest poet from his birth out of his mother's womb and from
her birth out of her mother's. Caution seldom goes far enough. It has
been thought that the prudent citizen was the citizen who applied himself
to solid gains and did well for himself and his family and completed a
lawful life without debt or crime. The greatest poet sees and admits
these economies as he sees the economies of food and sleep, but has higher

notions of prudence than to think he gives much when he gives a few slight attentions at the latch of the gate. The premises of the prudence of life are not the hospitality of it or the ripeness and harvest of it. Beyond the independence of a little sum laid aside for burial-money, and of a few clapboards around and shingles overhead on a lot of American soil owned, and the easy dollars that supply the year's plain clothing and meals, the melancholy prudence of the abandonment of such a great being as a man is to the toss and pallor of years of moneymaking with all their scorching days and icy nights and all their stifling deceits and underhanded dodgings, or infinitessimals of parlors, or shameless stuffing while others starve . . . and all the loss of the bloom and odor of the earth and of the flowers and atmosphere and of the sea and of the true taste of the women and men you pass or have to do with in youth or middle age, and the issuing sickness and desperate revolt at the close of a life without elevation or naivete, and the ghastly chatter of a death without serenity or majesty, is the great fraud upon modern civilization and forethought, blotching the surface and system which civilization undeniably drafts, and moistening with tears the immense features it spreads and spreads with such velocity before the reached kisses of the soul. . . . Still the right explanation remains to be made about prudence. The prudence of the mere wealth and respectability of the most esteemed life appears too faint for the eye to observe at all when little and large alike drop quietly aside at the thought of the prudence suitable for immortality. What is wisdom that fills the thinness of a year or seventy or eighty years to wisdom spaced out by ages and coming back at a certain time with strong reinforcements and rich presents and the clear faces of wedding-guests as far as you can look in every direction running gaily toward you? Only the soul is of itself . . . all else has reference to what ensues. All that a person does or thinks is of consequence. Not a move can a man or woman make that affects him or her in a day or a month or any part of the direct lifetime or the hour of death but the same affects him or her onward afterward through the indirect lifetime. The indirect is always as great and real as the direct. The spirit receives from the body just as much as it gives to the body. Not one name or word or deed . . . not of venereal sores or discolorations . . . not the privacy of the onanist . . . not of the putrid veins of gluttons or rum-drinkers . . . not peculation or cunning or betrayal or murder . . . no serpentine poison of those that seduce women . . . not the foolish yielding of women . . . not prostitution . . . not of any depravity of young men . . . not of the attainment of gain by discreditable means . . . not any nastiness of appetite . . . not any harshness of officers to men or judges to prisoners or fathers to sons or sons to fathers or of husbands to wives or bosses to their boys . . . not of greedy looks or malignant wishes . . . nor any of the wiles practised by people upon themselves . . . ever is or ever can be stamped on the programme but it is duly realized and returned, and that returned in further performances . . . and they returned again. Nor can the push of charity or personal force ever be any thing else than the profoundest reason, whether it bring arguments to hand or no. No specification is necessary . . . to add or subtract or divide is in vain. Little or big, learned or unlearned, white or black, legal or illegal, sick or well, from the first inspiration down the windpipe to the last expiration out of it, all that a male or female does that is vigorous and benevolent and clean is so much sure profit to him or her in the unshakable order of the universe and through the whole scope of it forever. If the savage or felon is wise it is well . . . if the greatest poet or savan is wise it is simply the same . . . if the President or chief justice is wise it is the same . . . if the young mechanic or farmer is wise it is no more or less . . . if the prostitute is wise it is no more nor less. The interest will come round . . . all will come round. All the best actions of war and peace . . . all help given to relatives and strangers and the poor and old and sorrowful and young children and widows and the sick, and to all shunned persons . . . all furtherance of fugitives and of the escape of slaves . . . all the self-denial that stood steady and aloof on wrecks and saw others take the seats of the boats . . . all offering of substance or life for the good old cause, or for a friend's sake or opinion's sake . . . all pains of enthusiasts scoffed at by their neighbors . . . all the vast sweet love and precious suffering of mothers . . . all honest men baffled in strifes recorded or unrecorded . . . all the grandeur and good of the few ancient nations whose fragments of annals we inherit . . . and all the good of the hundreds of far mightier and more ancient nations unknown to us by name or date or location . . . all that was ever manfully begun, whether it succeeded or not . . . all that has at any time been well suggested out of the divine heart of man or by the divinity of his mouth or by the shaping of his great hands . . . and all that is well thought or done this day on any part of the surface of the globe . . . or on any of the wandering stars or fixed stars by those there as we are here . . . or that is henceforth to be well thought or done by you whoever you are, or by any one—these singly and wholly inured at their time and inure now and will inure always to the identities from which they sprung or shall spring. . . . Did you guess any of them lived only its moment? The world does not so exist . . . no parts palpable or impalpable so exist . . . no result exists now without being from its long antecedent result, and that from its antecedent, and so backward without the farthest mentionable spot coming a bit nearer to the beginning than any other spot. . . . Whatever satisfies the soul is truth. The prudence of the greatest poet answers at last the craving and glut of the soul, is not contemptuous of less ways of prudence if they conform to its ways, puts off nothing, permits no let-up for its own case or any case, has no particular sabbath or judgment-day, divides not the living from the dead or the righteous from the unrighteous, is satisfied with the present, matches every thought or act by its correlative, knows no possible forgiveness or deputed atonement . . . knows that the young man who composedly periled his life and lost it has done exceeding well for himself, while the man who has not periled his life and retains it to old age in riches and ease has perhaps achieved nothing for himself worth mentioning . . . and that only that person has no great prudence to learn who has learnt to prefer real longlived things, and favors body and soul the same, and perceives the indirect assuredly following the direct, and what evil or good he does leaping onward and waiting to meet him again —and who in his spirit in any emergency whatever neither hurries or avoids death.

The direct trial of him who would be the greatest poet is today. If he does not flood himself with the immediate age as with vast oceanic tides . . . and if he does not attract his own land body and soul to himself and hang on its neck with incomparable love and plunge his semitic muscle into its merits and demerits . . . and if he be not himself the age transfigured . . . and if to him is not opened the eternity which gives similitude to all periods and locations and processes and animate and inanimate forms, and which is the bond of time, and rises up from its inconceivable vagueness and infiniteness in the swimming shape of today, and is held by the ductile anchors of life, and makes the present spot the passage from what was to what shall be, and commits itself to the representation of this wave of an hour and this one of the sixty beautiful children of the wave—let him merge in the general run and wait his development. . . . Still the final test of poems or any character or work remains. The prescient poet projects himself centuries ahead and judges performer or performance after the changes of time. Does it live through them? Does it still hold on untired? Will the same style and the direction of genius to similar points be satisfactory now? Has no new discovery in science or arrival at superior planes of thought and judgment and behaviour fixed him or his so that either can be looked down upon? Have the marches of tens and hundreds and thousands of years made willing detours to the right hand and the left hand for his sake? Is he beloved long and long after he is buried? Does the young man think often of him? and the young woman think often of him? and do the middle-aged and the old think of him?

A great poem is for ages and ages in common and for all degrees and complexions and all departments and sects and for a woman as much as a man and a man as much as a woman. A great poem is no finish to a man or woman but rather a beginning. Has any one fancied he could sit at last under some due authority and rest satisfied with explanations and realize and be content and full? To no such terminus does the greatest poet bring . . . he brings neither cessation or sheltered fatness and ease. The touch of him tells in action. Whom he takes he takes with firm sure grasp into live regions previously unattained . . . thenceforward is no rest . . . they see the space and ineffable sheen that turn the old spots and lights into dead vacuums. The companion of him beholds the birth and progress of stars and learns one of the meanings. Now there shall be a man cohered out of tumult and chaos . . . the elder encourages the younger and shows him how . . . they too shall launch off fearlessly together till the new world fits an orbit for itself and looks unabashed on the lesser orbits of the stars and sweeps through the ceaseless rings and shall never be quiet again.

There will soon be no more priests. Their work is done. They may wait awhile . . . perhaps a generation or two . . . dropping off by degrees. A superior breed shall take their place . . . the gangs of kosmos and prophets en masse shall take their place. A new order shall arise and they shall be the priests of man, and every man shall be his own priest. The churches built under their umbrage shall be the churches of men and women. Through the divinity of themselves shall the kosmos and the new breed of poets be interpreters of men and women and of all events and things. They shall find their inspiration in real objects today, symptoms of the past and future . . . They shall not deign to defend immortality or God or the perfection of things or liberty or the exquisite beauty and reality of the soul. They shall arise in America and be responded to from the remainder of the earth.

The English language befriends the grand American expression . . . it is brawny enough and limber and full enough. On the tough stock of a race who through all change of circumstances was never without the idea of political liberty, which is the animus of all liberty, it has attracted the terms of daintier and gayer and subtler and more elegant tongues. It is the powerful language of resistance . . . it is the dialect of common sense. It is the speech of the proud and melancholy races and of all who aspire. It is the chosen tongue to express growth faith self-esteem freedom justice equality friendliness amplitude prudence decision and courage. It is the medium that shall well nigh express the inexpressible.

No great literature nor any like style of behaviour or oratory or social intercourse or household arrangements or public institutions or the treatment by bosses of employed people, nor executive detail or detail of the army or navy, nor spirit of legislation or courts or police or tuition or architecture or songs or amusements or the costumes of young men, can long elude the jealous and passionate instinct of American standards. Whether or no the sign appears from the mouths of the people, it throbs a live interrogation in every freeman's and freewoman's heart after that which passes by or this built to remain. Is it uniform with my country? Are its disposals without ignominious distinctions? Is it for the evergrowing communes of brothers and lovers, large, well-united, proud beyond the old models, generous beyond all models? Is it something grown fresh out of the fields or drawn from the sea for use to me today here? I know that what answers for me an American must answer for any individual or nation that serves for a part of my materials. Does this answer? or is it without reference to universal needs? or sprung of the needs of the less developed society of special ranks? or old needs of pleasure overlaid by modern science and forms? Does this acknowledge liberty with audible and absolute acknowledgment, and set slavery at naught for life and death? Will it help breed one goodshaped and wellhung man, and a woman to be his perfect and independent mate? Does it improve manners? Is it for the nursing of the young of the republic? Does it solve readily with the sweet milk of the nipples of the breasts of the mother of many children? Has it too the old ever-fresh forbearance and impartiality? Does it look with the same love on the last born and those hardening toward stature, and on the errant, and on those who disdain all strength of assault outside of their own?

The poems distilled from other poems will probably pass away. The coward will surely pass away. The expectation of the vital and great can only be satisfied by the demeanor of the vital and great. The swarms of the polished deprecating and reflectors and the polite float off and leave no remembrance. America prepares with composure and goodwill for the visitors that have sent word. It is not intellect that is to be their warrant and welcome. The talented, the artist, the ingenious, the editor, the statesman, the erudite . . . they are not unappreciated . . . they fall in their place and do their work. The soul of the nation also does its work. No disguise can pass on it . . . no disguise can conceal from it. It rejects none, it permits all. Only toward as good as itself and toward the like of itself will it advance half-way. An individual is as superb as a nation when he has the qualities which make a superb nation. The soul of the largest and wealthiest and proudest nation may well go half-way to meet that of its poets. The signs are effectual. There is no fear of mistake. If the one is true the other is true. The proof of a poet is that his country absorbs him as affectionately as he has absorbed it.

Song of Myself

1

I celebrate myself, and sing myself,
And what I assume you shall assume,
For every atom belonging to me as good belongs to you.

I loafe and invite my soul,
I lean and loafe at my ease observing a spear of summer grass.   5

My tongue, every atom of my blood, form'd from this soil, this air,
Born here of parents born here from parents the same, and their parents the same,
I, now thirty-seven years old in perfect health begin,
Hoping to cease not till death.

Creeds and schools in abeyance,   10
Retiring back a while sufficed at what they are, but never forgotten,
I harbor for good or bad, I permit to speak at every hazard,
Nature without check with original energy.

2

Houses and rooms are full of perfumes, the shelves are crowded with
   perfumes,
I breathe the fragrance myself and know it and like it,   15
The distillation would intoxicate me also, but I shall not let it.

The atmosphere is not a perfume, it has no taste of the distillation, it is
   odorless,
It is for my mouth forever, I am in love with it,
I will go to the bank by the wood and become undisguised and naked,
I am mad for it to be in contact with me.   20

The smoke of my own breath,
Echoes, ripples, buzz'd whispers, love-root, silk-thread, crotch and
   vine,
My respiration and inspiration, the beating of my heart, the passing of
   blood and air through my lungs,
The sniff of green leaves and dry leaves, and of the shore and dark-
   color'd sea-rocks, and of hay in the barn,
The sound of the belch'd words of my voice loos'd to the eddies of
   the wind,   25
A few light kisses, a few embraces, a reaching around of arms,
The play of shine and shade on the trees as the supple boughs wag,
The delight alone or in the rush of the streets, or along the fields and
   hill-sides,
The feeling of health, the full-noon trill, the song of me rising from
   bed and meeting the sun.

Have you reckon'd a thousand acres much? have you reckon'd the
   earth much?   30
Have you practis'd so long to learn to read?
Have you felt so proud to get at the meaning of poems?

Stop this day and night with me and you shall possess the origin of all
   poems,
You shall possess the good of the earth and sun, (there are millions of
   suns left,)
You shall no longer take things at second or third hand, nor look
   through the eyes of the dead, nor feed on the spectres in
   books,   35
You shall not look through my eyes either, nor take things from me,
You shall listen to all sides and filter them from your self.

3

I have heard what the talkers were talking, the talk of the beginning
   and the end,
But I do not talk of the beginning or the end.

There was never any more inception than there is now, 　　40
Nor any more youth or age than there is now,
And will never be any more perfection than there is now,
Nor any more heaven or hell than there is now.

Urge and urge and urge,
Always the procreant urge of the world. 　　45
Out of the dimness opposite equals advance, always substance and in-
　　crease, always sex,
Always a knit of identity, always distinction, always a breed of life.

To elaborate is no avail, learn'd and unlearn'd feel that it is so.

Sure as the most certain sure, plumb in the uprights, well entretied,
　　braced in the beams,
Stout as a horse, affectionate, haughty, electrical, 　　50
I and this mystery here we stand.

Clear and sweet is my soul, and clear and sweet is all that is not my
　　soul.

Lack one lacks both, and the unseen is proved by the seen,
Till that becomes unseen and receives proof in its turn.

Showing the best and dividing it from the worst age vexes age, 　　55
Knowing the perfect fitness and equanimity of things, while they
　　discuss I am silent, and go bathe and admire myself.

Welcome is every organ and attribute of me, and of any man hearty
　　and clean,
Not an inch nor a particle of an inch is vile, and none shall be less
　　familiar than the rest.

I am satisfied—I see, dance, laugh, sing;
As the hugging and loving bed-fellow sleeps at my side through the
　　night, and withdraws at the peep of the day with stealthy tread,
Leaving the baskets cover'd with white towels swelling the house with
　　their plenty, 　　61
Shall I postpone my acceptation and realization and scream at my eyes,
That they turn from gazing after and down the road,
And forthwith cipher and show me to a cent,
Exactly the value of one and exactly the value of two, and which is
　　ahead? 　　65

4

Trippers and askers surround me,
People I meet, the effect upon me of my early life or the ward and
　　city I live in, or the nation,

The latest dates, discoveries, inventions, societies, authors old and new,
My dinner, dress, associates, looks, compliments, dues,
The real or fancied indifference of some man or woman I love, 70
The sickness of one of my folks or of myself, or ill-doing or loss or
    lack of money, or depressions or exaltations,
Battles, the horrors of fratricidal war, the fever of doubtful news, the
    fitful events;
These come to me days and nights and go from me again,
But they are not the Me myself.

Apart from the pulling and hauling stands what I am, 75
Stands amused, complacent, compassionating, idle, unitary,
Looks down, is erect, or bends an arm on an impalpable certain rest,
Looking with side-curved head curious what will come next,
Both in and out of the game and watching and wondering at it.

Backward I see in my own days where I sweated through fog with
    linguists and contenders, 80
I have no mockings or arguments, I witness and wait.

5

I believe in you my soul, the other I am must not abase itself to you,
And you must not be abased to the other.

Loafe with me on the grass, loose the stop from your throat,
Not words, not music or rhyme I want, not custom or lecture, not
    even the best, 85
Only the lull I like, the hum of your valvèd voice.

I mind how once we lay such a transparent summer morning,
How you settled your head athwart my hips and gently turn'd over
    upon me,
And parted the shirt from my bosom-bone, and plunged your tongue
    to my bare-stript heart,
And reach'd till you felt my beard, and reach'd till you held my
    feet. 90

Swiftly arose and spread around me the peace and knowledge that pass
    all the argument of the earth,
And I know that the hand of God is the promise of my own,
And I know that the spirit of God is the brother of my own,
And that all the men ever born are also my brothers, and the women
    my sisters and lovers,
And that a kelson of the creation is love, 95
And limitless are leaves stiff or drooping in the fields,
And brown ants in the little wells beneath them,
And mossy scabs of the worm fence, heap'd stones, elder, mullein and
    poke-weed.

6

A child said *What is the grass?* fetching it to me with full hands,
How could I answer the child? I do not know what it is any more
  than he.   100

I guess it must be the flag of my disposition, out of hopeful green stuff
  woven.

Or I guess it is the handkerchief of the Lord,
A scented gift and remembrancer designedly dropt,
Bearing the owner's name someway in the corners, that we may see
  and remark, and say *Whose?*

Or I guess the grass is itself a child, the produced babe of the
  vegetation.   105

Or I guess it is a uniform hieroglyphic,
And it means, Sprouting alike in broad zones and narrow zones,
Growing among black folks as among white,
Kanuck, Tuckahoe, Congressmen, Cuff, I give them the same, I receive
  them the same.

And now it seems to me the beautiful uncut hair of graves.   110

Tenderly will I use you curling grass,
It may be you transpire from the breasts of young men,
It may be if I had known them I would have loved them,
It may be you are from old people, or from offspring taken soon out
  of their mothers' laps,
And here you are the mothers' laps.   115

This grass is very dark to be from the white heads of old mothers,
Darker than the colorless beards of old men,
Dark to come from under the faint red roofs of mouths.
O I perceive after all so many uttering tongues,
And I perceive they do not come from the roofs of mouths for
  nothing.   120

I wish I could translate the hints about the dead young men and
  women,
And the hints about old men and mothers, and the offspring taken
  soon out of their laps.

What do you think has become of the young and old men?
And what do you think has become of the women and children?

They are alive and well somewhere,   125
The smallest sprout shows there is really no death,

And if ever there was it led forward life, and does not wait at the end
    to arrest it,
And ceas'd the moment life appear'd.

All goes onward and outward, nothing collapses,
And to die is different from what any one supposed, and luckier.   130

7

Has any one supposed it lucky to be born?
I hasten to inform him or her it is just as lucky to die, and I know it.

I pass death with the dying and birth with the new-wash'd babe, and
    am not contain'd between my hat and boots,
And peruse manifold objects, no two alike and every one good,
The earth good and the stars good, and their adjuncts all good.   135

I am not an earth nor an adjunct of an earth,
I am the mate and companion of people, all just as immortal and
    fathomless as myself,
(They do not know how immortal, but I know.)

Every kind for itself and its own, for me mine male and female,
For me those that have been boys and that love women,   140
For me the man that is proud and feels how it stings to be slighted,
For me the sweet-heart and the old maid, for me mothers and the
    mothers of mothers,
For me lips that have smiled, eyes that have shed tears,
For me children and the begetters of children.

Undrape! you are not guilty to me, nor stale nor discarded,   145
I see through the broadcloth and gingham whether or no,
And am around, tenacious, acquisitive, tireless, and cannot be shaken
    away.

8

The little one sleeps in its cradle,
I lift the gauze and look a long time, and silently brush away flies with
    my hand.

The youngster and the red-faced girl turn aside up the bushy hill,   150
I peeringly view them from the top.

The suicide sprawls on the bloody floor of the bedroom,
I witness the corpse with its dabbled hair, I note where the pistol has
    fallen.

The blab of the pave, tires of carts, sluff of boot-soles, talk of the
promenaders,
The heavy omnibus, the driver with his interrogating thumb, the clank
of the shod horses on the granite floor,   155
The snow-sleighs, clinking, shouted jokes, pelts of snow-balls,
The hurrahs for popular favorites, the fury of rous'd mobs,
The flap of the curtain'd litter, a sick man inside borne to the hospital,
The meeting of enemies, the sudden oath, the blows and fall,
The excited crowd, the policeman with his star quickly working his
passage to the centre of the crowd,   160
The impassive stones that receive and return so many echoes,
What groans of over-fed or half-starv'd who fall sunstruck or in fits,
What exclamations of women taken suddenly who hurry home and
give birth to babes,
What living and buried speech is always vibrating here, what howls
restrain'd by decorum,
Arrests of criminals, slights, adulterous offers made, acceptances, rejec-
tions with convex lips,   165
I mind them or the show or resonance of them—I come and I depart.

9

The big doors of the country barn stand open and ready,
The dried grass of the harvest-time loads the slow-drawn wagon,
The clear light plays on the brown gray and green intertinged,
The armfuls are pack'd to the sagging mow.   170

I am there, I help, I came stretch'd atop of the load,
I felt its soft jolts, one leg reclined on the other,
I jump from the cross-beams and seize the clover and timothy,
And roll head over heels and tangle my hair full of wisps.

10

Alone far in the wilds and mountains I hunt,   175
Wandering amazed at my own lightness and glee,
In the late afternoon choosing a safe spot to pass the night,
Kindling a fire and broiling the fresh-kill'd game,
Falling asleep on the gather'd leaves with my dog and gun by my side.

The Yankee clipper is under her sky-sails, she cuts the sparkle and
scud,   180
My eyes settle the land, I bend at her prow or shout joyously from the
deck.

The boatmen and clam-diggers arose early and stopt for me,
I tuck'd my trowser-ends in my boots and went and had a good time;
You should have been with us that day round the chowder-kettle.

I saw the marriage of the trapper in the open air in the far west, the
    bride was a red girl,   185
Her father and his friends sat near cross-legged and dumbly smoking,
    they had moccasins to their feet and large thick blankets hanging
    from their shoulders,
On a bank lounged the trapper, he was drest mostly in skins, his lux-
    uriant beard and curls protected his neck, he held his bride by the
    hand,
She had long eyelashes, her head was bare, her coarse straight locks
    descended upon her voluptuous limbs, and reach'd to her feet.

The runaway slave came to my house and stopt outside,
I heard his motions crackling the twigs of the woodpile,   190
Through the swung half-door of the kitchen I saw him limpsy and
    weak,
And went where he sat on a log and led him in and assured him,
And brought water and fill'd a tub for his sweated body and bruis'd
    feet,
And gave him a room that enter'd from my own, and gave him some
    coarse clean clothes,
And remember perfectly well his revolving eyes and his awkwardness,
And remember putting plasters on the galls of his neck and ankles;   196
He staid with me a week before he was recuperated and pass'd north,
I had him sit next me at table, my fire-lock lean'd in the corner.

11

Twenty-eight young men bathe by the shore,
Twenty-eight young men and all so friendly;   200
Twenty-eight years of womanly life and all so lonesome.

She owns the fine house by the rise of the bank,
She hides handsome and richly drest aft the blinds of the window.

Which of the young men does she like the best?
Ah the homeliest of them is beautiful to her.   205

Where are you off to lady? for I see you,
You splash in the water there, yet stay stock still in your room.

Dancing and laughing along the beach came the twenty-ninth bather,
The rest did not see her, but she saw them and loved them.

The beards of the young men glisten'd with wet, it ran from their long
    hair,   210
Little streams pass'd all over their bodies.

An unseen hand also pass'd over their bodies,
It descended trembling from their temples and ribs.

The young men float on their backs, their white bellies bulge to the
    sun, they do not ask who seizes fast to them,
They do not know who puffs and declines with pendant and bending
    arch,   215
They do not think whom they souse with spray.

12

The butcher-boy puts off his killing-clothes, or sharpens his knife at
    the stall in the market,
I loiter enjoying his repartee and his shuffle and break-down.

Blacksmiths with grimed and hairy chests environ the anvil,
Each has his main-sledge, they are all out, there is a great heat in the
    fire.

From the cinder-strew'd threshold I follow their movements,   221
The lithe sheer of their waists plays even with their massive arms,
Overhand the hammers swing, overhand so slow, overhand so sure,
They do not hasten, each man hits in his place.

13

The negro holds firmly the reins of his four horses, the block swags
    underneath on its tide-over chain,   225
The negro that drives the long dray of the stone-yard, steady and tall
    he stands pois'd on one leg on the string-piece,
His blue shirt exposes his ample neck and breast and loosens over his
    hip-band,
His glance is calm and commanding, he tosses the slouch of his hat
    away from his forehead,
The sun falls on his crispy hair and mustache, falls on the black of his
    polish'd and perfect limbs.

I behold the picturesque giant and love him, and I do not stop there,
I go with the team also.   231

In me the caresser of life wherever moving, backward as well as fore-
    ward sluing,
To niches aside and junior bending, not a person or object missing,
Absorbing all to myself and for this song.

Oxen that rattle the yoke and chain or halt in the leafy shade, what is
    that you express in your eyes?   235
It seems to me more than all the print I have read in my life.

My tread scares the wood-drake and wood-duck on my distant and
    day-long ramble,
They rise together, they slowly circle around.

I believe in those wing'd purposes,
And acknowledge red, yellow, white, playing within me,   240
And consider green and violet and the tufted crown intentional,
And do not call the tortoise unworthy because she is not something
    else,
And the jay in the woods never studied the gamut, yet trills pretty
    well to me,
And the look of the bay mare shames silliness out of me.

14

The wild gander leads his flock through the cool night,   245
Ya-honk he says, and sounds it down to me like an invitation,
The pert may suppose it meaningless, but I listening close,
Find its purpose and place up there toward the wintry sky.

The sharp-hoof'd moose of the north, the cat on the house-sill, the
    chickadee, the prairie-dog,
The litter of the grunting sow as they tug at her teats,   250
The brood of the turkey-hen and she with her half-spread wings,
I see in them and myself the same old law.

The press of my foot to the earth springs a hundred affections,
They scorn the best I can do to relate them.

I am enamour'd of growing out-doors,   255
Of men that live among cattle or taste of the ocean or woods,
Of the builders and steerers of ships and the wielders of axes and
    mauls, and the drivers of horses,
I can eat and sleep with them week in and week out.

What is commonest, cheapest, nearest, easiest, is Me,
Me going in for my chances, spending for vast returns,   260
Adorning myself to bestow myself on the first that will take me,
Not asking the sky to come down to my good will,
Scattering it freely forever.

15

The pure contralto sings in the organ loft,
The carpenter dresses his plank, the tongue of his foreplane whistles
    its wild ascending lisp,   265
The married and unmarried children ride home to their Thanksgiving
    dinner,
The pilot seizes the king-pin, he heaves down with a strong arm,
The mate stands braced in the whale-boat, lance and harpoon are
    ready,
The duck-shooter walks by silent and cautious stretches,
The deacons are ordain'd with cross'd hands at the altar,   270
The spinning-girl retreats and advances to the hum of the big wheel,

The farmer stops by the bars as he walks on a First-day loafe and
    looks at the oats and rye,
The lunatic is carried at last to the asylum a confirm'd case,
(He will never sleep any more as he did in the cot in his mother's
    bedroom;)
The jour printer with gray head and gaunt jaws works at his case, 275
He turns his quid of tobacco while his eyes blurr with the manuscript;
The malform'd limbs are tied to the surgeon's table,
What is removed drops horribly in a pail;
The quadroon girl is sold at the auction-stand, the drunkard nods by
    the bar-room stove,
The machinist rolls up his sleeves, the policeman travels his beat, the
    gate-keeper marks who pass, 280
The young fellow drives the express-wagon, (I love him, though I do
    not know him;)
The half-breed straps on his light boots to compete in the race,
The western turkey-shooting draws old and young, some lean on their
    rifles, some sit on logs,
Out from the crowd steps the marksman, takes his position, levels his
    piece;
The groups of newly-come immigrants cover the wharf or levee, 285
As the woolly-pates hoe in the sugar-field, the overseer views them
    from his saddle,
The bugle calls in the ball-room, the gentlemen run for their partners,
    the dancers bow to each other,
The youth lies awake in the cedar-roof'd garret and harks to the
    musical rain,
The Wolverine sets traps on the creek that helps fill the Huron,
The squaw wrapt in her yellow-hemm'd cloth is offering moccasins
    and bead-bags for sale, 290
The connoisseur peers along the exhibition-gallery with half-shut eyes
    bent sideways,
As the deck-hands make fast the steamboat the plank is thrown for
    the shore-going passengers,
The young sister holds out the skein while the elder sister winds it off
    in a ball, and stops now and then for the knots,
The one-year wife is recovering and happy having a week ago borne
    her first child,
The clean-hair'd Yankee girl works with her sewing-machine or in the
    factory or mill, 295
The paving-man leans on his two-handed rammer, the reporter's lead
    flies swiftly over the note-book, the sign-painter is lettering with
    blue and gold,
The canal boy trots on the tow-path, the book-keeper counts at his
    desk, the shoemaker waxes his thread,
The conductor beats time for the band and all the performers follow
    him,
The child is baptized, the convert is making his first professions,

The regatta is spread on the bay, the race is begun, (how the white
    sails sparkle!) 300
The drover watching his drove sings out to them that would stray,
The pedler sweats with his pack on his back, (the purchaser higgling
    about the odd cent;)
The bride unrumples her white dress, the minute-hand of the clock
    moves slowly,
The opium-eater reclines with rigid head and just-open'd lips,
The prostitute draggles her shawl, her bonnet bobs on her tipsy and
    pimpled neck, 305
The crowd laugh at her blackguard oaths, the men jeer and wink to
    each other,
(Miserable! I do not laugh at your oaths nor jeer you;)
The President holding a cabinet council is surrounded by the great
    Secretaries,
On the piazza walk three matrons stately and friendly with twined
    arms,
The crew of the fish-smack pack repeated layers of halibut in the hold,
The Missourian crosses the plains toting his wares and his cattle, 311
As the fare-collector goes through the train he gives notice by the jin-
    gling of loose change,
The floor-men are laying the floor, the tinners are tinning the roof,
    the masons are calling for mortar,
In single file each shouldering his hod pass onward the laborers;
Seasons pursuing each other the indescribable crowd is gather'd, it is
    the fourth of Seventh-month, (what salutes of cannon and small
    arms!) 315
Seasons pursuing each other the plougher ploughs, the mower mows,
    and the winter grain falls in the ground; 316
Off on the lakes the pike-fisher watches and waits by the hole in the
    frozen surface,
The stumps stand thick round the clearing, the squatter strikes deep
    with his axe,
Flatboatmen make fast towards dusk near the cotton-wood or pecan-
    trees,
Coon-seekers go through the regions of the Red river or through those
    drain'd by the Tennessee, or through those of the Arkansas, 320
Torches shine in the dark that hangs on the Chattahooche or Al-
    tamahaw,
Patriarchs sit at supper with sons and grandsons and great-grandsons
    around them,
In walls of adobe, in canvas tents, rest hunters and trappers after their
    day's sport,
The city sleeps and the country sleeps,
The living sleep for their time, the dead sleep for their time, 325
The old husband sleeps by his wife and the young husband sleeps by
    his wife;
And these tend inward to me, and I tend outward to them,

And such as it is to be of these more or less I am,
And of these one and all I weave the song of myself.

16

I am of old and young, of the foolish as much as the wise, 330
Regardless of others, ever regardful of others,
Maternal as well as paternal, a child as well as a man,
Stuff'd with the stuff that is coarse and stuff'd with the stuff that is fine,
One of the Nation of many nations, the smallest the same and the largest the same,
A Southerner soon as a Northerner, a planter nonchalant and hospitable down by the Oconee I live, 335
A Yankee bound my own way ready for trade, my joints the limberest joints on earth and the sternest joints on earth,
A Kentuckian walking the vale of the Elkhorn in my deer-skin leggings, a Louisianian or Georgian,
A boatman over lakes or bays or along coasts, a Hoosier, Badger, Buckeye;
At home on Kanadian snow-shoes or up in the bush, or with fishermen off Newfoundland,
At home in the fleet of ice-boats, sailing with the rest and tacking, 340
At home on the hills of Vermont or in the woods of Maine, or the Texan ranch,
Comrade of Californians, comrade of free North-Westerners, (loving their big proportions,)
Comrade of raftsmen and coalmen, comrade of all who shake hands and welcome to drink and meat,
A learner with the simplest, a teacher of the thoughtfullest,
A novice beginning yet experient of myriads of seasons, 345
Of every hue and caste am I, of every rank and religion,
A farmer, mechanic, artist, gentleman, sailor, quaker,
Prisoner, fancy-man, rowdy, lawyer, physician, priest.

I resist any thing better than my own diversity,
Breathe the air but leave plenty after me, 350
And am not stuck up, and am in my place.

(The moth and the fish-eggs are in their place,
The bright suns I see and the dark suns I cannot see are in their place,
The palpable is in its place and the impalpable is in its place.)

17

These are really the thoughts of all men in all ages and lands, they are not original with me, 355
If they are not yours as much as mine they are nothing, or next to nothing,

If they are not the riddle and the untying of the riddle they are
    nothing,
If they are not just as close as they are distant they are nothing.

This is the grass that grows wherever the land is and the water is,
This is the common air that bathes the globe. 360

18

With music strong I come, with my cornets and my drums,
I play not marches for accepted victors only, I play marches for con-
    quer'd and slain persons.

Have you heard that it was good to gain the day?
I also say it is good to fall, battles are lost in the same spirit in which
    they are won.

I beat and pound for the dead, 365
I blow through my embouchures my loudest and gayest for them.

Vivas to those who have fail'd!
And to those whose war-vessels sank in the sea!
And to those themselves who sank in the sea!
And to all generals that lost engagements, and all overcome heroes!
And the numberless unknown heroes equal to the great heroes known!

19

This is the meal equally set, this the meat for natural hunger, 372
It is for the wicked just the same as the righteous, I make appointments
    with all,
I will not have a single person slighted or left away,
The kept-woman, sponger, thief, are hereby invited, 375
The heavy-lipp'd slave is invited, the venerealee is invited;
There shall be no difference between them and the rest.

This is the press of a bashful hand, this the float and odor of hair,
This is the touch of my lips to yours, this the murmur of yearning,
This the far-off depth and height reflecting my own face, 380
This the thoughtful merge of myself, and the outlet again.

Do you guess I have some intricate purpose?
Well I have, for the Fourth-month showers have, and the mica on the
    side of a rock has.

Do you take it I would astonish?
Does the daylight astonish? does the early redstart twittering through
    the woods? 385
Do I astonish more than they?

This hour I tell things in confidence,
I might not tell everybody, but I will tell you.

20

Who goes there? hankering, gross, mystical, nude;
How is it I extract strength from the beef I eat? 390

What is a man anyhow? what am I? what are you?

All I mark as my own you shall offset it with your own,
Else it were time lost listening to me.

I do not snivel that snivel the world over,
That months are vacuums and the ground but wallow and filth. 395

Whimpering and truckling fold with powders for invalids, conformity
    goes to the fourth remov'd,
I wear my hat as I please indoors or out.

Why should I pray? why should I venerate and be ceremonious?

Having pried through the strata, analyzed to a hair, counsel'd with
    doctors and calculated close,
I find no sweeter fat than sticks to my own bones. 400

In all people I see myself, none more and not one a barley-corn less,
And the good or bad I say of myself I say of them.

I know I am solid and sound,
To me the converging objects of the universe perpetually flow,
All are written to me, and I must get what the writing means. 405

I know I am deathless,
I know this orbit of mine cannot be swept by a carpenter's compass,
I know I shall not pass like a child's carlacue cut with a burnt stick at
    night.

I know I am august,
I do not trouble my spirit to vindicate itself or be understood, 410
I see that the elementary laws never apologize,
(I reckon I behave no prouder than the level I plant my house by,
    after all.)

I exist as I am, that is enough,
If no other in the world be aware I sit content,
And if each and all be aware I sit content. 415

One world is aware and by the far largest to me, and that is myself,
And whether I come to my own to-day or in ten thousand or ten
 million years,
I can cheerfully take it now, or with equal cheerfulness I can wait.

My foothold is tenon'd and mortis'd in granite,
I laugh at what you call dissolution, 420
And I know the amplitude of time.

21

I am the poet of the Body and I am the poet of the Soul,
The pleasures of heaven are with me and the pains of hell are with me,
The first I graft and increase upon myself, the latter I translate into a
 new tongue.

I am the poet of the woman the same as the man, 425
And I say it is as great to be a woman as to be a man,
And I say there is nothing greater than the mother of men.

I chant the chant of dilation or pride,
We have had ducking and deprecating about enough,
I show that size is only development. 430

Have you outstript the rest? are you the President?
It is a trifle, they will more than arrive there every one, and still pass
 on.

I am he that walks with the tender and growing night,
I call to the earth and sea half-held by the night.

Press close bare-bosom'd night—press close magnetic nourishing night!
Night of south winds—night of the large few stars! 436
Still nodding night—mad naked summer night.

Smile O voluptuous cool-breath'd earth!
Earth of the slumbering and liquid trees!
Earth of departed sunset—earth of the mountains misty-topt! 440
Earth of the vitreous pour of the full moon just tinged with blue!
Earth of shine and dark mottling the tide of the river!
Earth of the limpid gray of clouds brighter and clearer for my sake!
Far-swooping elbow'd earth—rich apple-blossom'd earth!
Smile, for your lover comes. 445

Prodigal, you have given me love—therefore I to you give love!
O unspeakable passionate love.

22

You sea! I resign myself to you also—I guess what you mean,
I behold from the beach your crooked inviting fingers,

I believe you refuse to go back without feeling of me,   450
We must have a turn together, I undress, hurry me out of sight of the
    land,
Cushion me soft, rock me in billowy drowse,
Dash me with amorous wet, I can repay you.

Sea of stretch'd ground-swells,
Sea breathing broad and convulsive breaths,   455
Sea of the brine of life and of unshovell'd yet always-ready graves,
Howler and scooper of storms, capricious and dainty sea,
I am integral with you, I too am of one phase and of all phases.

Partaker of influx and efflux, I, extoller of hate and conciliation,
Extoller of amies and those that sleep in each other's arms.   460

I am he attesting sympathy,
(Shall I make my list of things in the house and skip the house that
    supports them?)

I am not the poet of goodness only, I do not decline to be the poet
    of wickedness also.

What blurt is this about virtue and about vice?
Evil propels me and reform of evil propels me, I stand indifferent,   465
My gait is no fault-finder's or rejecter's gait,
I moisten the roots of all that has grown.

Did you fear some scrofula out of the unflagging pregnancy?
Did you guess the celestial laws are yet to be work'd over and rec-
    tified?

I find one side a balance and the antipodal side a balance,   470
Soft doctrine as steady help as stable doctrine,
Thoughts and deeds of the present our rouse and early start.

This minute that comes to me over the past decillions,
There is no better than it and now.

What behaved well in the past or behaves well to-day is not such a
    wonder,   475
The wonder is always and always how there can be a mean man or an
    infidel.

23

Endless unfolding of words of ages!
And mine a word of the modern, the word En-Masse.

A word of the faith that never balks,
Here or henceforward it is all the same to me, I accept Time abso-
    lutely.   480

It alone is without flaw, it alone rounds and completes all,
That mystic baffling wonder alone completes all.

I accept Reality and dare not question it,
Materialism first and last imbuing.

Hurrah for positive science! long live exact demonstration!   485
Fetch stonecrop mixt with cedar and branches of lilac,
This is the lexicographer, this the chemist, this made a grammar of
   the old cartouches,
These mariners put the ship through dangerous unknown seas,
This is the geologist, this works with the scalpel, and this is a mathe-
   matician.

Gentlemen, to you the first honors always!   490
Your facts are useful, and yet they are not my dwelling,
I but enter by them to an area of my dwelling.

Less the reminders of properties told my words,
And more the reminders they of life untold, and of freedom and extri-
   cation,
And make short account of neuters and geldings, and favor men and
   women fully equipt,   495
And beat the gong of revolt, and stop with fugitives and them that
   plot and conspire.

24

Walt Whitman, a kosmos, of Manhattan the son,
Turbulent, fleshy, sensual, eating, drinking and breeding,
No sentimentalist, no stander above men and women or apart from
   them,
No more modest than immodest.   500

Unscrew the locks from the doors!
Unscrew the doors themselves from their jambs!

Whoever degrades another degrades me,
And whatever is done or said returns at last to me.

Through me the afflatus surging and surging, through me the current
   and index.   505

I speak the pass-word primeval, I give the sign of democracy,
By God! I will accept nothing which all cannot have their counterpart of on the same terms.

Through me many long dumb voices,
Voices of the interminable generations of prisoners and slaves,

Voices of the diseas'd and despairing and of thieves and dwarfs,   510
Voices of cycles of preparation and accretion,
And of the threads that connect the stars, and of wombs and of the
    father-stuff,
And of the rights of them the others are down upon,
Of the deform'd, trivial, flat, foolish, despised,
Fog in the air, beetles rolling balls of dung.   515

Through me forbidden voices,
Voices of sexes and lusts, voices veil'd and I remove the veil,
Voices indecent by me clarified and transfigur'd.

I do not press my fingers across my mouth,
I keep as delicate around the bowels as around the head and heart,   520
Copulation is no more rank to me than death is.

I believe in the flesh and the appetites,
Seeing, hearing, feeling, are miracles, and each part and tag of me is a
    miracle.

Divine am I inside and out, and I make holy whatever I touch or am
    touch'd from,
The scent of these arm-pits aroma finer than prayer,   525
This head more than churches, bibles, and all the creeds.

If I worship one thing more than another it shall be the spread of my
    own body, or any part of it,
Translucent mould of me it shall be you!
Shaded ledges and rests it shall be you!
Firm masculine colter it shall be you!   530
Whatever goes to the tilth of me it shall be you!
You my rich blood! your milky stream pale strippings of my life!
Breast that presses against other breasts it shall be you!
My brain it shall be your occult convolutions!
Root of wash'd sweet-flag! timorous pond-snipe! nest of guarded
    duplicate eggs! it shall be you!   535
Mix'd tussled hay of head, beard, brawn, it shall be you!
Trickling sap of maple, fibre of manly wheat, it shall be you!
Sun so generous it shall be you!
Vapors lighting and shading my face it shall be you!
You sweaty brooks and dews it shall be you!   540
Winds whose soft-tickling genitals rub against me it shall be you!
Broad muscular fields, branches of live oak, loving lounger in my
    winding paths, it shall be you!
Hands I have taken, face I have kiss'd, mortal I have ever touch'd, it
    shall be you.

I dote on myself, there is that lot of me and all so luscious,
Each moment and whatever happens thrills me with joy, 545
I cannot tell how my ankles bend, nor whence the cause of my faintest
    wish,
Nor the cause of the friendship I emit, nor the cause of the friendship
    I take again.

That I walk up my stoop, I pause to consider if it really be,
A morning-glory at my window satisfies me more than the meta-
    physics of books.

To behold the day-break! 550
The little light fades the immense and diaphanous shadows,
The air tastes good to my palate.

Hefts of the moving world at innocent gambols silently rising, freshly
    exuding,
Scooting obliquely high and low.

Something I cannot see puts upward libidinous prongs, 555
Seas of bright juice suffuse heaven.

The earth by the sky staid with, the daily close of their junction,
The heav'd challenge from the east that moment over my head,
The mocking taunt, See then whether you shall be master!

25

Dazzling and tremendous how quick the sun-rise would kill me, 560
If I could not now and always send sun-rise out of me.

We also ascend dazzling and tremendous as the sun,
We found our own O my soul in the calm and cool of the daybreak.

My voice goes after what my eyes cannot reach,
With the twirl of my tongue I encompass worlds and volumes of
    worlds. 565
Speech is the twin of my vision, it is unequal to measure itself,
It provokes me forever, it says sarcastically,
Walt you contain enough, why don't you let it out then?

Come now I will not be tantalized, you conceive too much of articula-
    tion,
Do you not know O speech how the buds beneath you are folded? 570
Waiting in gloom, protected by frost,
The dirt receding before my prophetical screams,
I underlying causes to balance them at last,
My knowledge my live parts, it keeping tally with the meaning of all
    things,

Happiness, (which whoever hears me let him or her set out in search
    of this day.) 575

My final merit I refuse you, I refuse putting from me what I really am,
Encompass worlds, but never try to encompass me,
I crowd your sleekest and best by simply looking toward you.

Writing and talk do not prove me,
I carry the plenum of proof and every thing else in my face, 580
With the hush of my lips I wholly confound the skeptic.

26

Now I will do nothing but listen,
To accrue what I hear into this song, to let sounds contribute toward it.

I hear bravuras of birds, bustle of growing wheat, gossip of flames,
    clack of sticks cooking my meals,
I hear the sound I love, the sound of the human voice, 585
I hear all sounds running together, combined, fused or following,
Sounds of the city and sounds out of the city, sounds of the day and
    night,
Talkative young ones to those that like them, the loud laugh of work-
    people at their meals,
The angry base of disjointed friendship, the faint tones of the sick,
The judge with hands tight to the desk, his pallid lips pronouncing a
    death-sentence, 590
The heave'e'yo of stevedores unlading ships by the wharves, the re-
    frain of the anchor-lifters,
The ring of alarm-bells, the cry of fire, the whirr of swift-streaking
    engines and hose-carts with premonitory tinkles and color'd lights,
The steam-whistle, the solid roll of the train of approaching cars,
The slow march play'd at the head of the association marching two
    and two,
(They go to guard some corpse, the flag-tops are draped with black
    muslin.) 595

I hear the violoncello, ('tis the young man's heart's complaint,)
I hear the key'd cornet, it glides quickly in through my ears,
It shakes mad-sweet pangs through my belly and breast.

I hear the chorus, it is a grand opera,
Ah this indeed is music—this suits me. 600

A tenor large and fresh as the creation fills me,
The orbic flex of his mouth is pouring and filling me full.

I hear the train'd soprano (what work with hers is this?)
The orchestra whirls me wider than Uranus flies,

It wrenches such ardors from me I did not know I possess'd them, 605
It sails me, I dab with bare feet, they are lick'd by the indolent waves,
I am cut by bitter and angry hail, I lose my breath,
Steep'd amid honey'd morphine, my windpipe throttled in fakes of
    death,
At length let up again to feel the puzzle of puzzles,
And that we call Being. 610

27

To be in any form, what is that?
(Round and round we go, all of us, and ever come back thither,)
If nothing lay more develop'd the quahaug in its callous shell were
    enough.

Mine is no callous shell,
I have instant conductors all over me whether I pass or stop, 615
They seize every object and lead it harmlessly through me.

I merely stir, press, feel with my fingers, and am happy,
To touch my person to some one else's is about as much as I can
    stand.

28

Is this then a touch? quivering me to a new identity,
Flames and ether making a rush for my veins, 620
Treacherous tip of me reaching and crowding to help them,
My flesh and blood playing out lightning to strike what is hardly dif-
    ferent from myself,
On all sides prurient provokers stiffening my limbs,
Straining the udder of my heart for its withheld drip,
Behaving licentious toward me, taking no denial, 625
Depriving me of my best as for a purpose,
Unbuttoning my clothes, holding me by the bare waist,
Deluding my confusion with the calm of the sunlight and pasture-
    fields,
Immodestly sliding the fellow-senses away,
They bribed to swap off with touch and go and graze at the edges of
    me,
No consideration, no regard for my draining strength or my anger, 630
Fetching the rest of the herd around to enjoy them a while,
Then all uniting to stand on a headland and worry me.

The sentries desert every other part of me,
They have left me helpless to a red marauder, 635
They all come to the headland to witness and assist against me.

I am given up by traitors,
I talk wildly, I have lost my wits, I and nobody else am the greatest
    traitor,
I went myself first to the headland, my own hands carried me there.

You villain touch! what are you doing? my breath is tight in its throat,
Unclench your floodgates, you are too much for me.   641

29

Blind loving wrestling touch, sheath'd hooded sharp-tooth'd touch!
Did it make you ache so, leaving me?

Parting track'd by arriving, perpetual payment of perpetual loan,
Rich showering rain, and recompense richer afterward.   645

Sprouts take and accumulate, stand by the curb prolific and vital,
Landscapes projected masculine, full-sized and golden.

30

All truths wait in all things,
They neither hasten their own delivery nor resist it,
They do not need the obstetric forceps of the surgeon,   650
The insignificant is as big to me as any,
(What is less or more than a touch?)

Logic and sermons never convince,
The damp of the night drives deeper into my soul.

(Only what proves itself to every man and woman is so,   655
Only what nobody denies is so.)

A minute and a drop of me settle my brain,
I believe the soggy clods shall become lovers and lamps,
And a compend of compends is the meat of a man or woman,
And a summit and flower there is the feeling they have for each
    other,   660
And they are to branch boundlessly out of that lesson until it becomes
    omnific,
And until one and all shall delight us, and we them.

31

I believe a leaf of grass is no less than the journey-work of the stars,
And the pismire is equally perfect, and a grain of sand, and the egg of
    the wren,
And the tree-toad is a chef-d'œuvre for the highest,   665
And the running blackberry would adorn the parlors of heaven,
And the narrowest hinge in my hand puts to scorn all machinery,
And the cow crunching with depress'd head surpasses any statue,
And a mouse is miracle enough to stagger sextillions of infidels.

I find I incorporate gneiss, coal, long-threaded moss, fruits, grains,
    esculent roots,   670

And am stucco'd with quadrupeds and birds all over,
And have distanced what is behind me for good reasons,
But call any thing back again when I desire it.

In vain the speeding or shyness,
In vain the plutonic rocks send their old heat against my approach   675
In vain the mastodon retreats beneath its own powder'd bones,
In vain objects stand leagues off and assume manifold shapes,
In vain the ocean settling in hollows and the great monsters lying low,
In vain the buzzard houses herself with the sky,
In vain the snake slides through the creepers and logs,   680
In vain the elk takes to the inner passes of the woods,
In vain the razor-bill'd auk sails far north to Labrador,
I follow quickly, I ascend to the nest in the fissure of the cliff.

32

I think I could turn and live with animals, they're so placed and self-
contain'd,
I stand and look at them long and long.   685

They do not sweat and whine about their condition,
They do not lie awake in the dark and weep for their sins,
They do not make me sick discussing their duty to God,
Not one is dissatisfied, not one is demented with the mania of owning
things,
Not one kneels to another, nor to his kind that lived thousands of
years ago,   690
Not one is respectable or unhappy over the whole earth.

So they show their relations to me and I accept them,
They bring me tokens of myself, they evince them plainly in their
possession.

I wonder where they get those tokens,
Did I pass that way huge times ago and negligently drop them?   695

Myself moving forward then and now and forever,
Gathering and showing more always and with velocity,
Infinite and omnigenous, and the like of these among them,
Not too exclusive toward the reachers of my remembrancers,
Picking out here one that I love, and now go with him on brotherlv
terms.   700

A gigantic beauty of a stallion, fresh and responsive to my caresses,
Head high in the forehead, wide between the ears,
Limbs glossy and supple, tail dusting the ground,
Eyes full of sparkling wickedness, ears finely cut, flexibly moving.

His nostrils dilate as my heels embrace him, 705
His well-built limbs tremble with pleasure as we race around and
return.
I but use you a minute, then I resign you, stallion,
Why do I need your paces when I myself out-gallop them?
Even as I stand or sit passing faster than you.

33

Space and Time! now I see it is true, what I guess'd at, 710
What I guess'd when I loaf'd on the grass,
What I guess'd while I lay alone in my bed,
And again as I walk'd the beach under the paling stars of the morning.

My ties and ballasts leave me, my elbows rest in sea-gaps,
I skirt sierras, my palms cover continents, 715
I am afoot with my vision.

By the city's quadrangular houses—in log huts, camping with lumber-
men,
Along the ruts of the turnpike, along the dry gulch and rivulet bed,
Weeding my onion-patch or hoeing rows of carrots and parsnips,
crossing savannas, trailing in forests,
Prospecting, gold-digging, girdling the trees of a new purchase, 720
Scorch'd ankle-deep by the hot sand, hauling my boat down the shal-
low river,
Where the panther walks to and fro on a limb overhead, where the
buck turns furiously at the hunter,
Where the rattlesnake suns his flabby length on a rock, where the
otter is feeding on fish,
Where the alligator in his tough pimples sleeps by the bayou,
Where the black bear is searching for roots or honey, where the
beaver pats the mud with his paddle-shaped tail; 725
Over the growing sugar, over the yellow-flower'd cotton plant, over
the rice in its low moist field,
Over the sharp-peak'd farm house, with its scallop'd scum and slender
shoots from the gutters,
Over the western persimmon, over the long-leav'd corn, over the deli-
cate blue-flower flax,
Over the white and brown buckwheat, a hummer and buzzer there
with the rest,
Over the dusky green of the rye as it ripples and shades in the breeze;
Scaling mountains, pulling myself cautiously up, holding on by low
scragged limbs, 731
Walking the path worn in the grass and beat through the leaves of the
brush,
Where the quail is whistling betwixt the woods and the wheat-lot,
Where the bat flies in the Seventh-month eve, where the great gold-
bug drops through the dark,

Where the brook puts out of the roots of the old tree and flows to the
    meadow,   735
Where cattle stand and shake away flies with the tremulous shudder-
    ing of their hides,
Where the cheese-cloth hangs in the kitchen, where andirons straddle
    the hearth-slab, where cobwebs fall in festoons from the rafters;
Where trip-hammers crash, where the press is whirling its cylinders,
Wherever the human heart beats with terrible throes under its ribs,
Where the pear-shaped balloon is floating aloft, (floating in it myself
    and looking composedly down,)   740
Where the life-car is drawn on the slip-noose, where the heat hatches
    pale-green eggs in the dented sand,
Where the she-whale swims with her calf and never forsakes it,
Where the steam-ship trails hind-ways its long pennant of smoke,
Where the fin of the shark cuts like a black chip out of the water,
Where the half-burn'd brig is riding on unknown currents,   745
Where shells grow to her slimy deck, where the dead are corrupting
    below;
Where the dense-starr'd flag is borne at the head of the regiments,
Approaching Manhattan up by the long-stretching island,
Under Niagara, the cataract falling like a veil over my countenance,
Upon a door-step, upon the horse-block of hard wood outside,   750
Upon the race-course, or enjoying picnics or jigs or a good game of
    baseball,
At he-festivals, with blackguard gibes, ironical license, bull-dances,
    drinking, laughter,
At the cider-mill tasting the sweets of the brown mash, sucking the
    juice through a straw,
At apple-peelings wanting kisses for all the red fruit I find,
At musters, beach-parties, friendly bees, huskings, house-raisings;   755
Where the mocking-bird sounds his delicious gurgles, cackles,
    screams, weeps,
Where the hay-rick stands in the barn-yard, where the dry-stalks are
    scatter'd, where the brood-cow waits in the hovel,
Where the bull advances to do his masculine work, where the stud to
    the mare, where the cock is treading the hen,
Where the heifers browse, where geese nip their food with short
    jerks,
Where sun-down shadows lengthen over the limitless and lonesome
    prairie,   760
Where herds of buffalo make a crawling spread of the square miles
    far and near,
Where the humming-bird shimmers, where the neck of the long-lived
    swan is curving and winding,
Where the laughing-gull scoots by the shore, where she laughs her
    near-human laugh,
Where bee-hives range on a gray bench in the garden half hid by the
    high weeds,

Where band-neck'd partridges roost in a ring on the ground with
their heads out,   765
Where burial coaches enter the arch'd gates of a cemetery,
Where winter wolves bark amid wastes of snow and icicled trees,
Where the yellow-crown'd heron comes to the edge of the marsh at
night and feeds upon small crabs,
Where the splash of swimmers and divers cools the warm noon,
Where the katy-did works her chromatic reed on the walnut-tree
over the well,   770
Through patches of citrons and cucumbers with silver-wired leaves,
Through the salt-lick or orange glade, or under conical firs,
Through the gymnasium, through the curtain'd saloon, through the
office or public hall;
Pleas'd with the native and pleas'd with the foreign, pleas'd with the
new and old,
Pleas'd with the homely woman as well as the handsome,   775
Pleas'd with the quakeress as she puts off her bonnet and talks melo-
diously,
Pleas'd with the tune of the choir of the whitewash'd church,
Pleas'd with the earnest words of the sweating Methodist preacher,
impress'd seriously at the camp-meeting;
Looking in at the shop-windows of Broadway the whole forenoon,
flatting the flesh of my nose on the thick plate glass,
Wandering the same afternoon with my face turn'd up to the clouds,
or down a lane or along the beach,   780
My right and left arms round the sides of two friends, and I in the
middle;
Coming home with the silent and dark-cheek'd bush-boy, (behind me
he rides at the drape of the day,)
Far from the settlements studying the print of animals' feet, or the
moccasin print,
By the cot in the hospital reaching lemonade to a feverish patient,
Nigh the coffin'd corpse when all is still, examining with a candle;   785
Voyaging to every port to dicker and adventure,
Hurrying with the modern crowd as eager and fickle as any,
Hot toward one I hate, ready in my madness to knife him,
Solitary at midnight in my back yard, my thoughts gone from me a
long while,
Walking the old hills of Judæa with the beautiful gentle God by my
side,   790
Speeding through space, speeding through heaven and the stars,
Speeding amid the seven satellites and the broad ring, and the diam-
eter of eighty thousand miles,
Speeding with tail'd meteors, throwing fire-balls like the rest,
Carrying the crescent child that carries its own full mother in its belly,
Storming, enjoying, planning, loving, cautioning,   795
Backing and filling, appearing and disappearing,
I tread day and night such roads.

I visit the orchards of spheres and look at the product,
And look at quintillions ripen'd and look at quintillions green.

I fly those flights of a fluid and swallowing soul, 800
My course runs below the soundings of plummets.

I help myself to material and immaterial,
No guard can shut me off, no law prevent me.

I anchor my ship for a little while only,
My messengers continually cruise away or bring their returns to me.

I go hunting polar furs and the seal, leaping chasms with a pike-
pointed staff, clinging to topples of brittle and blue. 806

I ascend to the foretruck,
I take my place late at night in the crow's-nest,
We sail the arctic sea, it is plenty light enough,
Through the clear atmosphere I stretch around on the wonderful
beauty, 810
The enormous masses of ice pass me and I pass them, the scenery is
plain in all directions,
The white-topt mountains show in the distance, I fling out my fancies
toward them,
We are approaching some great battle-field in which we are soon to be
engaged,
We pass the colossal outposts of the encampment, we pass with still
feet and caution,
Or we are entering by the suburbs some vast and ruin'd city, 815
The blocks and fallen architecture more than all the living cities of the
globe.

I am a free companion, I bivouac by invading watchfires,
I turn the bridegroom out of bed and stay with the bride myself,
I tighten her all night to my thighs and lips.

My voice is the wife's voice, the screech by the rail of the stairs, 820
They fetch my man's body up dripping and drown'd.

I understand the large hearts of heroes,
The courage of present times and all times,
How the skipper saw the crowded and rudderless wreck of the steam-
ship, and Death chasing it up and down the storm,
How he knuckled tight and gave not back an inch, and was faithful
of days and faithful of nights, 825
And chalk'd in large letters on a board, *Be of good cheer, we will not
desert you;*

How he follow'd with them and tack'd with them three days and
    would not give it up,
How he saved the drifting company at last,
How the lank loose-gown'd women look'd when boated from the side
    of their prepared graves,
How the silent old-faced infants and the lifted sick, and the sharp-
    lipp'd unshaven men;   830
All this I swallow, it tastes good, I like it well, it becomes mine,
I am the man, I suffer'd, I was there.

The disdain and calmness of martyrs,
The mother of old, condemn'd for a witch, burnt with dry wood, her
    children gazing on,
The hounded slave that flags in the race, leans by the fence, blowing,
    cover'd with sweat.   835
The twinges that sting like needles his legs and neck, the murderous
    buckshot and the bullets,
All these I feel or am.

I am the hounded slave, I wince at the bite of the dogs,
Hell and despair are upon me, crack and again crack the marksmen,
I clutch the rails of the fence, my gore drips, thinn'd with the ooze of
    my skin,   840
I fall on the weeds and stones,
The riders spur their unwilling horses, haul close,
Taunt my dizzy ears and beat me violently over the head with whip-
    stocks.

Agonies are one of my changes of garments,
I do not ask the wounded person how he feels, I myself become the
    wounded person,   845
My hurts turn livid upon me as I lean on a cane and observe.

I am the mash'd fireman with breast-bone broken,
Tumbling walls buried me in their debris,
Heat and smoke I inspired, I heard the yelling shouts of my comrades,
I heard the distant click of their picks and shovels,   850
They have clear'd the beams away, they tenderly lift me forth.

I lie in the night air in my red shirt, the pervading hush is for my sake,
Painless after all I lie exhausted but not so unhappy,
White and beautiful are the faces around me, the heads are bared of
    their fire-caps,
The kneeling crowd fades with the light of the torches.   855

Distant and dead resuscitate,
They show as the dial or move as the hands of me, I am the clock
    myself.

I am an old artillerist, I tell of my fort's bombardment,
I am there again.

Again the long roll of the drummers,   860
Again the attacking cannon, mortars,
Again to my listening ears the cannon responsive.

I take part, I see and hear the whole,
The cries, curses, roar, the plaudits for well-aim'd shots,
The ambulanza slowly passing trailing its red drip,   865
Workmen searching after damages, making indispensable repairs,
The fall of grenades through the rent roof, the fan-shaped explosion,
The whizz of limbs, heads, stone, wood, iron, high in the air.

Again gurgles the mouth of my dying general, he furiously waves with
    his hand,   869
He gasps through the clot *Mind not me—mind—the entrenchments.*

34

Now I tell what I knew in Texas in my early youth,
(I tell not the fall of Alamo,
Not one escaped to tell the fall of Alamo,
The hundred and fifty are dumb yet at Alamo,)
'Tis the tale of the murder in cold blood of four hundred and twelve
    young men.   875

Retreating they had form'd in a hollow square with their baggage for
    breastworks,
Nine hundred lives out of the surrounding enemy's, nine times their
    number, was the price they took in advance,
Their colonel was wounded and their ammunition gone,
They treated for an honorable capitulation, receiv'd writing and seal,
    gave up their arms and march'd back prisoners of war.

They were the glory of the race of rangers,   880
Matchless with horse, rifle, song, supper, courtship,
Large, turbulent, generous, handsome, proud, and affectionate,
Bearded, sunburnt, drest in the free costume of hunters,
Not a single one over thirty years of age.

The second First-day morning they were brought out in squads and
    massacred, it was beautiful early summer,   885
The work commenced about five o'clock and was over by eight.

None obey'd the command to kneel,
Some made a mad and helpless rush, some stood stark and straight,
A few fell at once, shot in the temple or heart, the living and dead lay
    together,

The maim'd and mangled dug in the dirt, the new-comers saw them there,   890
Some half-kill'd attempted to crawl away,
These were despatch'd with bayonets or batter'd with the blunts of muskets,
A youth not seventeen years old seiz'd his assassin till two more came to release him.
The three were all torn and cover'd with the boy's blood.

At eleven o'clock began the burning of the bodies;   895
That is the tale of the murder of the four hundred and twelve young men.

35

Would you hear of an old-time sea-fight?
Would you learn who won by the light of the moon and stars?
List to the yarn, as my grandmother's father the sailor told it to me.

Our foe was no skulk in his ship I tell you, (said he,)   900
His was the surly English pluck, and there is no tougher or truer, and never was, and never will be;
Along the lower'd eve he came horribly raking us.

We closed with him, the yards entangled, the cannon touch'd,
My captain lash'd fast with his own hands.

We had receiv'd some eighteen pound shots under the water,   905
On our lower-gun-deck two large pieces had burst at the first fire, killing all around and blowing up overhead.

Fighting at sun-down, fighting at dark,
Ten o'clock at night, the full moon well up, our leaks on the gain, and five feet of water reported,
The master-at-arms loosing the prisoners confined in the after-hold to give them a chance for themselves.

The transit to and from the magazine is now stopt by the sentinels,
They see so many strange faces they do not know whom to trust. 911

Our frigate takes fire,
The other asks if we demand quarter?
If our colors are struck and the fighting done?

Now I laugh content, for I hear the voice of my little captain,   915
We have not struck, he composedly cries, *we have just begun our part of the fighting.*

Only three guns are in use,
One is directed by the captain himself against the enemy's main-mast,
Two well serv'd with grape and canister silence his musketry and clear
his decks.

The tops alone second the fire of this battery, especially the main-
top,   920
They told out bravely during the whole of the action.

Not a moment's cease,
The leaks gain fast on the pumps, the fire eats toward the powder-
magazine.

One of the pumps has been shot away, it is generally thought we are
sinking.

Serene stands the little captain,   925
He is not hurried, his voice is neither high nor low,
His eyes give more light to us than our battle-lanterns.

Toward twelve there in the beams of the moon they surrender to us.

36

Stretch'd and still lies the midnight,
Two great hulls motionless on the breast of the darkness,   930
Our vessel riddled and slowly sinking, preparations to pass to the one
we have conquer'd,
The captain on the quarter-deck coldly giving his orders through a
countenance white as a sheet,
Near by the corpse of the child that serv'd in the cabin,
The dead face of an old salt with long white hair and carefully curl'd
whiskers,
The flames spite of all that can be done flickering aloft and below,   935
The husky voices of the two or three officers yet fit for duty,
Formless stacks of bodies and bodies by themselves, dabs of flesh upon
the masts and spars,
Cut of cordage, dangle of rigging, slight shock of the soothe of waves,
Black and impassive guns, litter of powder-parcels, strong scent,
A few large stars overhead, silent and mournful shining,   940
Delicate sniffs of sea-breeze, smells of sedgy grass and fields by the
shore, death-messages given in charge to survivors,
The hiss of the surgeon's knife, the gnawing teeth of his saw,
Wheeze, cluck, swash of falling blood, short wild screams, and long,
dull, tapering groan,
These so, these irretrievable.

37

You laggards there on guard! look to your arms!   945
In at the conquer'd doors they crowd! I am possess'd!
Embody all presences outlaw'd or suffering,
See myself in prison shaped like another man,
And feel the dull unintermitted pain.

For me the keepers of convicts shoulder their carbines and keep watch,
It is I let out in the morning and barr'd at night.   951

Not a mutineer walks handcuff'd to jail but I am handcuff'd to him
          and walk by his side,
(I am less the jolly one there, and more the silent one with sweat on
          my twitching lips.)

Not a youngster is taken for larceny but I go up too, and am tried and
          sentenced.   954

Not a cholera patient lies at the last gasp but I also lie at the last gasp,
My face is ash-color'd, my sinews gnarl, away from me people retreat.

Askers embody themselves in me and I am embodied in them,
I project my hat, sit shame-faced, and beg.

38

Enough! enough! enough!
Somehow I have been stunn'd. Stand back!   960
Give me a little time beyond my cuff'd head, slumbers, dreams, gaping,
I discover myself on the verge of a usual mistake.

That I could forget the mockers and insults!
That I could forget the trickling tears and the blows of the bludgeons
          and hammers!
That I could look with a separate look on my own crucifixion and
          bloody crowning.   965

I remember now,
I resume the overstaid fraction,
The grave of rock multiplies what has been confided to it, or to any
          graves,
Corpses rise, gashes heal, fastenings roll from me.

I troop forth replenish'd with supreme power, one of an average un-
          ending procession,   970
Inland and sea-coast we go, and pass all boundary lines,
Our swift ordinances on their way over the whole earth,
The blossoms we wear in our hats the growth of thousands of years.

Eleves, I salute you! come forward!
Continue your annotations, continue your questionings.   975

39

The friendly and flowing savage, who is he?
Is he waiting for civilization, or past it and mastering it?

Is he some Southwesterner rais'd out-doors? is he Kanadian?
Is he from the Mississippi country? Iowa, Oregon, California?
The mountains? prairie-life? bush-life? or sailor from the sea?   980

Wherever he goes men and women accept and desire him,
They desire he should like them, touch them, speak to them, stay with
    them.

Behavior lawless as snow-flakes, words simple as grass, uncomb'd head,
    laughter, and naiveté,
Slow-stepping feet, common features, common modes and emanations,
They descend in new forms from the tips of his fingers,   985
They are wafted with the odor of his body or breath, they fly out of
    the glance of his eyes.

40

Flaunt of the sunshine I need not your bask—lie over!
You light surfaces only, I force surfaces and depths also.

Earth! you seem to look for something at my hands,
Say, old top-knot, what do you want?   990

Man or woman, I might tell how I like you, but cannot,
And might tell what it is in me and what it is in you, but cannot,
And might tell that pining I have, that pulse of my nights and days.

Behold, I do not give lectures or a little charity,
When I give I give myself.   995

You there, impotent, loose in the knees,
Open your scarf'd chops till I blow grit within you,
Spread your palms and lift the flaps of your pockets,
I am not to be denied, I compel, I have stores plenty and to spare,
And any thing I have I bestow.   1000

I do not ask who you are, that is not important to me,
You can do nothing and be nothing but what I will infold you.

To cotton-field drudge or cleaner of privies I lean,
On his right cheek I put the family kiss,
And in my soul I swear I never will deny him.   1005

On women fit for conception I start bigger and nimbler babes,
(This day I am jetting the stuff of far more arrogant republics.)

To any one dying, thither I speed and twist the knob of the door,
Turn the bed-clothes toward the foot of the bed,
Let the physician and the priest go home.   1010

I seize the descending man and raise him with resistless will,
O despairer, here is my neck,
By God, you shall not go down! hang your whole weight upon me.

I dilate you with tremendous breath, I buoy you up,
Every room of the house do I fill with an arm'd force,   1015
Lovers of me, bafflers of graves.

Sleep—I and they keep guard all night,
Not doubt, not decease shall dare to lay finger upon you,
I have embraced you, and henceforth possess you to myself,
And when you rise in the morning you will find what I tell you is so.

                              41

I am he bringing help for the sick as they pant on their backs,   1021
And for strong upright men I bring yet more needed help.

I heard what was said of the universe,
Heard it and heard it of several thousand years;
It is middling well as far as it goes—but is that all?   1025

Magnifying and applying come I,
Outbidding at the start the old cautious hucksters,
Taking myself the exact dimensions of Jehovah,
Lithographing Kronos, Zeus his son, and Hercules his grandson,
Buying drafts of Osiris, Isis, Belus, Brahma, Buddha,   1030
In my portfolio placing Manito loose, Allah on a leaf, the crucifix en-
      graved,
With Odin and the hideous-faced Mexitli and every idol and image,
Taking them all for what they are worth and not a cent more,
Admitting they were alive and did the work of their days,
(They bore mites as for unfledg'd birds who have now to rise and fly
      and sing for themselves,)   1035
Accepting the rough deific sketches to fill out better in myself, be-
      stowing them freely on each man and woman I see,
Discovering as much or more in a framer framing a house,
Putting higher claims for him there with his roll'd-up sleeves driving
      the mallet and chisel,
Not objecting to special revelations, considering a curl of smoke or a
      hair on the back of my hand just as curious as any revelation,

Lads ahold of fire-engines and hook-and-ladder ropes no less to me
than the gods of the antique wars, 1040
Minding their voices peal through the crash of destruction,
Their brawny limbs passing safe over charr'd laths, their white fore-
heads whole and unhurt out of the flames;
By the mechanic's wife with her babe at her nipple interceding for
every person born,
Three scythes at harvest whizzing in a row from three lusty angels
with shirts bagg'd out at their waists,
The snag-tooth'd hostler with red hair redeeming sins past and to
come, 1045
Selling all he possesses, traveling on foot to fee lawyers for his brother
and sit by him while he is tried for forgery;
What was strewn in the amplest strewing the square rod about me,
and not filling the square rod then,
The bull and the bug never worshipp'd half enough,
Dung and dirt more admirable than was dream'd,
The supernatural of no account, myself waiting my time to be one of
the supremes, 1050
The day getting ready for me when I shall do as much good as the
best, and be as prodigious;
By my life-lumps! becoming already a creator,
Putting myself here and now to the ambush'd womb of the shadows.

42

A call in the midst of the crowd,
My own voice, orotund sweeping and final. 1055

Come my children,
Come my boys and girls, my women, household and intimates,
Now the performer launches his nerve, he has pass'd his prelude on the
reeds within.

Easily written loose-finger'd chords—I feel the thrum of your climax
and close.

My head slues round on my neck,
Music rolls, but not from the organ, 1060
Folks are around me, but they are no household of mine.

Ever the hard unsunk ground,
Ever the eaters and drinkers, ever the upward and downward sun, ever
the air and the ceaseless tides,
Ever myself and my neighbors, refreshing, wicked, real,
Ever the old inexplicable query, ever that thorn'd thumb, that breath
of itches and thirsts,
Ever the vexer's *hoot! hoot!* till we find where the sly one hides and
bring him forth,

Ever love, ever the sobbing liquid of life,
Ever the bandage under the chin, ever the trestles of death.

Here and there with dimes on the eyes walking,   1070
To feed the greed of the belly the brains liberally spooning,
Tickets buying, taking, selling, but in to the feast never once going,
Many sweating, ploughing, thrashing, and then the chaff for payment
    receiving,
A few idly owning, and they the wheat continually claiming.

This is the city and I am one of the citizens,   1075
Whatever interests the rest interests me, politics, wars, markets, news-
    papers, schools,
The mayor and councils, banks, tariffs, steamships, factories, stocks,
    stores, real estate and personal estate.

The little plentiful manikins skipping around in collars and tail'd coats,
I am aware who they are, (they are positively not worms or fleas,)
I acknowledge the duplicates of myself, the weakest and shallowest is
    deathless with me,   1080
What I do and say the same waits for them,
Every thought that flounders in me the same flounders in them.

I know perfectly well my own egotism,
Know my omnivorous lines and must not write any less,
And would fetch you whoever you are flush with myself.   1085

Not words of routine this song of mine,
But abruptly to question, to leap beyond yet nearer bring;
This printed and bound book—but the printer and the printing-office
    boy?
The well-taken photographs—but your wife or friend close and solid in
    your arms?
The black ship mail'd with iron, her mighty guns in her turrets—but
    the pluck of the captain and engineers?   1090
In the houses the dishes and fare and furniture—but the host and
    hostess, and the look out of their eyes?
The sky up there—yet here or next door, or across the way?
The saints and sages in history—but you yourself?
Sermons, creeds, theology—but the fathomless human brain,
And what is reason? and what is love? and what is life?   1095

43

I do not despise you priests, all time, the world over,
My faith is the greatest of faiths and the least of faiths,
Enclosing worship ancient and modern and all between ancient and
    modern,
Believing I shall come again upon the earth after five thousand years,

Waiting responses from oracles, honoring the gods, saluting the sun,
Making a fetich of the first rock or stump, powowing with sticks in
    the circle of obis,   1101
Helping the llama or brahmin as he trims the lamps of the idols,
Dancing yet through the streets in a phallic procession, rapt and aus-
    tere in the woods a gymnosophist,
Drinking mead from the skull-cup, to Shastas and Vedas admirant,
    minding the Koran,
Walking the teokallis, spotted with gore from the stone and knife,
    beating the serpent-skin drum,   1105
Accepting the Gospels, accepting him that was crucified, knowing as-
    suredly that he is divine,
To the mass kneeling or the puritan's prayer rising, or sitting patiently
    in a pew,
Ranting and frothing in my insane crisis, or waving dead-like till my
    spirit arouses me,
Looking forth on pavement and land, or outside of pavement and land,
Belonging to the winders of the circuit of circuits.   1110

One of that centripetal and centrifugal gang I turn and talk like a man
    leaving charges before a journey.

Down-hearted doubters dull and excluded,
Frivolous, sullen, moping, angry, affected, disheartwhich'd, atheistical,
I know every one of you, I know the sea of torment, doubt, despair
    and unbelief.

How the flukes splash!   1115
How they contort rapid as lightning, with spasms and spouts of blood!

Be at peace bloody flukes of doubters and sullen mopers,
I take my place among you as much as among any,
The past is the push of you, me, all, precisely the same,
And what is yet untried and afterward is for you, me, all, precisely the
    same.   1120

I do not know what is untried and afterward,
But I know it will in its turn prove sufficient, and cannot fail.

Each who passes is consider'd, each who stops is consider'd, not a
    single one can it fail.

It cannot fail the young man who died and was buried,
Nor the young woman who died and was put by his side,   1125
Nor the little child that peep'd in at the door, and then drew back
    and was never seen again,
Nor the old man who has lived without purpose, and feels it with
    bitterness worse than gall,

Nor him in the poor house tubercled by rum and the bad disorder,
Nor the numberless slaughter'd and wreck'd, nor the brutish koboo
    call'd the ordure of humanity,   1129
Nor the sacs merely floating with open mouths for food to slip in,
Nor any thing in the earth, or down in the oldest graves of the earth,
Nor any thing in the myriads of spheres, nor the myriads of myriads
    that inhabit them,
Nor the present, nor the least wisp that is known.

44

It is time to explain myself—let us stand up.

What is known I strip away,   1135
I launch all men and women forward with me into the Unknown.

The clock indicates the moment—but what does eternity indicate?

We have thus far exhausted trillions of winters and summers,
There are trillions ahead, and trillions ahead of them.

Births have brought us richness and variety,   1140
And other births will bring us richness and variety.

I do not call one greater and one smaller,
That which fills its period and place is equal to any.

Were mankind murderous or jealous upon you, my brother, my sister?
I am sorry for you, they are not murderous or jealous upon me,   1145
All has been gentle with me, I keep no account with lamentation,
(What have I to do with lamentation?)

I am an acme of things accomplish'd, and I an encloser of things to be.

My feet strike an apex of the apices of the stairs,
On every step bunches of ages, and larger bunches between the steps,
All below duly travel'd, and still I mount and mount.   1151

Rise after rise bow the phantoms behind me,
Afar down I see the huge first Nothing, I know I was even there,
I waited unseen and always, and slept through the lethargic mist,
And took my time, and took no hurt from the fetid carbon.   1155

Long I was hugg'd close—long and long.

Immense have been the preparations for me,
Faithful and friendly the arms that have help'd me.

Cycles ferried my cradle, rowing and rowing like cheerful boatmen,
For room to me stars kept aside in their own rings, 1160
They sent influences to look after what was to hold me.

Before I was born out of my mother generations guided me,
My embryo has never been torpid, nothing could overlay it.

For it the nebula cohered to an orb,
The long slow strata piled to rest it on, 1165
Vast vegetables gave it sustenance,
Monstrous sauroids transported it in their mouths and deposited it with
care.

All forces have been steadily employ'd to complete and delight me,
Now on this spot I stand with my robust soul.

45

O span of youth! ever-push'd elasticity! 1170
O manhood, balanced, florid and full.

My lovers suffocate me,
Crowding my lips, thick in the pores of my skin,
Jostling me through streets and public halls, coming naked to me at
night,
Crying by day *Ahoy!* from the rocks of the river, swinging and chirp-
ing over my head, 1175
Calling my name from flower-beds, vines, tangled underbrush,
Lighting on every moment of my life,
Bussing my body with soft balsamic busses,
Noiselessly passing handfuls out of their hearts and giving them to be
mine. 1179

Old age superbly rising! O welcome, ineffable grace of dying days!

Every condition promulges not only itself, it promulges what grows
after and out of itself,
And the dark hush promulges as much as any.

I open my scuttle at night and see the far-sprinkled systems,
And all I see multiplied as high as I can cipher edge but the rim of the
farther systems.

Wider and wider they spread, expanding, always expanding, 1185
Outward and outward and forever outward.

My sun has his sun and round him obediently wheels,
He joins with his partners a group of superior circuit,
And greater sets follow, making specks of the greatest inside them.

There is no stoppage and never can be stoppage,   1190
If I, you, and the worlds, and all beneath or upon their surfaces, were
  this moment reduced back to a pallid float, it would not avail in
  the long run,
We should surely bring up again where we now stand,
And surely go as much farther, and then farther and farther.

A few quadrillions of eras, a few octillions of cubic leagues, do not
  hazard the span or make it impatient,
They are but parts, any thing is but a part.   1195

See ever so far, there is limitless space outside of that,
Count ever so much, there is limitless time around that.

My rendezvous is appointed, it is certain,
The Lord will be there and wait till I come on perfect terms,
The great Camerado, the lover true for whom I pine will be there.   1200

46

I know I have the best of time and space, and was never measured and
  never will be measured.

I tramp a perpetual journey, (come listen all!)
My signs are a rain-proof coat, good shoes, and a staff cut from the
  woods,
No friend of mine takes his ease in my chair,
I have no chair, no church, no philosophy,   1205
I lead no man to a dinner-table, library, exchange,
But each man and each woman of you I lead upon a knoll,
My left hand hooking you round the waist,
My right hand pointing to landscapes of continents and the public
  road.

Not I, not any one else can travel that road for you,   1210
You must travel it for yourself.

It is not far, it is within reach,
Perhaps you have been on it since you were born and did not know,
Perhaps it is everywhere on water and on land.

Shoulder your duds dear son, and I will mine, and let us hasten forth,
Wonderful cities and free nations we shall fetch as we go.   1216

If you tire, give me both burdens, and rest the chuff of your hand on
  my hip,
And in due time you shall repay the same service to me,
For after we start we never lie by again.

This day before dawn I ascended a hill and look'd at the crowded
    heaven,   1220
And I said to my spirit *When we become the enfolders of those orbs,*
    and the pleasure and knowledge of every thing in them, shall we
    be fill'd and satisfied then?
And my spirit said *No, we but level that lift to pass and continue*
    beyond.

You are also asking me questions and I hear you,
I answer that I cannot answer, you must find out for yourself.

Sit a while dear son,
Here are biscuits to eat and here is milk to drink,   1225
But as soon as you sleep and renew yourself in sweet clothes, I kiss you
    with a good-by kiss and open the gate for your egress hence.

Long enough have you dream'd contemptible dreams,
Now I wash the gum from your eyes,
You must habit yourself to the dazzle of the light and of every mo-
    ment of your life.   1230

Long have you timidly waded holding a plank by the shore,
Now I will you to be a bold swimmer,
To jump off in the midst of the sea, rise again, nod to me, shout, and
    laughingly dash with your hair.

47

I am the teacher of athletes,
He that by me spreads a wider breast than my own proves the width
    of my own,   1235
He most honors my style who learns under it to destroy the teacher.

The boy I love, the same becomes a man not through derived power,
    but in his own right,
Wicked rather than virtuous out of conformity or fear,
Fond of his sweetheart, relishing well his steak,
Unrequited love or a slight cutting him worse than sharp steel cuts,
First-rate to ride, to fight, to hit the bull's eye, to sail a skiff, to sing a
    song or play on the banjo,   1241
Preferring scars and the beard and faces pitted with small-pox over all
    latherers,
And those well-tann'd to those that keep out of the sun.

I teach straying from me, yet who can stray from me?
I follow you whoever you are from the present hour,
My words itch at your ears till you understand them.   1245

I do not say these things for a dollar or to fill up the time while I wait
   for a boat,
(It is you talking just as much as myself, I act as the tongue of you,
Tied in your mouth, in mine it begins to be loosen'd.)

I swear I will never again mention love or death inside a house,   1250
And I swear I will never translate myself at all, only to him or her
   who privately stays with me in the open air.

If you would understand me go to the heights or water-shore,
The nearest gnat is an explanation, and a drop or motion of waves a
   key,
The maul, the oar, the hand-saw, second my words.

No shutter'd room or school can commune with me,   1255
But roughs and little children better than they.

The young mechanic is closest to me, he knows me well,
The woodman that takes his axe and jug with him shall take me with
   him all day,
The farm-boy ploughing in the field feels good at the sound of my
   voice,
In vessels that sail my words sail, I go with fishermen and seamen
   and love them.   1260

The soldier camp'd or upon the march is mine,
On the night ere the pending battle may seek me, and I do not fail
   them,
On that solemn night (it may be their last) those that know me seek
   me.

My face rubs to the hunter's face when he lies down alone in his
   blanket,
The driver thinking of me does not mind the jolt of his wagon,   1265
The young mother and old mother comprehend me,
The girl and the wife rest the needle a moment and forget where they
   are,
They and all would resume what I have told them.

48

I have said that the soul is not more than the body,
And I have said that the body is not more than the soul,   1270
And nothing, not God, is greater to one than one's self is,
And whoever walks a furlong without sympathy walks to his own
   funeral drest in his shroud,
And I or you pocketless of a dime may purchase the pick of the earth,
And to glance with an eye or show a bean in its pod confounds the
   learning of all times,

And there is no trade or employment but the young man following it
    may become a hero,   1275
And there is no object, so soft but it makes a hub for the wheel'd
    universe,
And I say to any man or woman, Let your soul stand cool and com-
    posed before a million universes.

And I say to mankind, Be not curious about God,
For I who am curious about each am not curious about God,
(No array of terms can say how much I am at peace about God and
    about death.)   1280

I hear and behold God in every object, yet understand God not in the
    least,
Nor do I understand who there can be more wonderful than myself.

Why should I wish to see God better than this day?
I see something of God each hour of the twenty-four, and each mo-
    ment then,
In the faces of men and women I see God, and in my own face in the
    glass,   1285
I find letters from God dropt in the street, and every one is sign'd by
    God's name,
And I leave them where they are, for I know that wheresoe'er I go,
Others will punctually come for ever and ever.

49

And as to you Death, and you bitter hug of mortality, it is idle to try
    to alarm me.

To his work without flinching the accoucheur comes,   1290
I see the elder-hand pressing receiving supporting,
I recline by the sills of the exquisite flexible doors,
And mark the outlet, and mark the relief and escape.

And as to you Corpse I think you are good manure, but that does not
    offend me,
I smell the white roses sweet-scented and growing,   1295
I reach to the leafy lips, I reach to the polish'd breasts of melons.

And as to you Life I reckon you are the leavings of many deaths,
(No doubt I have died myself ten thousand times before.)

I hear you whispering there O stars of heaven,
O suns—O grass of graves—O perpetual transfers and promotions,
If you do not say any thing how can I say any thing?   1301

Of the turbid pool that lies in the autumn forest,
Of the moon that descends the steeps of the soughing twilight,
Toss, sparkles of day and dusk—toss on the black stems that decay in
   the muck,
Toss to the moaning gibberish of the dry limbs.   1305

I ascend from the moon, I ascend from the night,
I perceive that the ghastly glimmer is noonday sunbeams reflected,
And debouch to the steady and central from the offspring great or
   small.

50

There is that in me—I do not know what it is—but I know it is in me.

Wrench'd and sweaty—calm and cool then my body becomes,   1310
I sleep—I sleep long.

I do not know it—it is without name—it is a word unsaid,
It is not in any dictionary, utterance, symbol.

Something it swings on more than the earth I swing on,
To it the creation is the friend whose embracing awakes me.   1315

Perhaps I might tell more. Outlines! I plead for my brothers and
   sisters.

Do you see O my brothers and sisters?
It is not chaos or death—it is form, union, plan—it is eternal life—it is
   Happiness.

51

The past and present wilt—I have fill'd them, emptied them,
And proceed to fill my next fold of the future.   1320

Listener up there! what have you to confide to me?
Look in my face while I snuff the sidle of evening,
(Talk honestly, no one else hears you, and I stay only a minute
   longer.)

Do I contradict myself?
Very well then I contradict myself,   1325
(I am large, I contain multitudes.)

I concentrate toward them that are nigh, I wait on the door-slab.

Who has done his day's work? who will soonest be through with his
   supper?
Who wishes to walk with me?

Will you speak before I am gone? will you prove already too late?

52

The spotted hawk swoops by and accuses me, he complains of my gab
    and my loitering.   1331

I too am not a bit tamed, I too am untranslatable,
I sound my barbaric yawp over the roofs of the world.

The last scud of day holds back for me,
It flings my likeness after the rest and true as any on the shadow'd
    wilds,   1335
It coaxes me to the vapor and the dusk.

I depart as air, I shake my white locks at the runaway sun,
I effuse my flesh in eddies, and drift it in lacy jags.

I bequeath myself to the dirt to grow from the grass I love,
If you want me again look for me under your boot-soles.   1340

You will hardly know who I am or what I mean,
But I shall be good health to you nevertheless,
And filter and fibre your blood.

Failing to fetch me at first keep encouraged,
Missing me one place search another,   1345
I stop somewhere waiting for you.

There Was a Child Went Forth

There was a child went forth every day,
And the first object he look'd upon, that object he became,
And that object became part of him for the day or a certain part of
    the day,
Or for many years or stretching cycles of years.

The early lilacs became part of this child,   5
And grass and white and red morning-glories, and white and red
    clover, and the song of the phœbe-bird,
And the Third-month lambs and the sow's pink-faint litter, and the
    mare's foal and the cow's calf,
And the noisy brood of the barnyard or by the mire of the pond-side,
And the fish suspending themselves so curiously below there, and the
    beautiful curious liquid,
And the water-plants with their graceful flat heads, all became part of
    him.   10

The field-sprouts of Fourth-month and Fifth-month became part of
    him,

Winter-grain sprouts and those of the light-yellow corn, and the es-
culent roots of the garden,
And the apple-trees cover'd with blossoms and the fruit afterward,
and wood-berries, and the commonest weeds by the road,
And the old drunkard staggering home from the outhouse of the tav-
ern whence he had lately risen,
And the schoolmistress that pass'd on her way to the school,   15
And the friendly boys that pass'd, and the quarrelsome boys,
And the tidy and fresh-cheek'd girls, and the barefoot negro boy and
girl,
And all the changes of city and country wherever he went.

His own parents, he that had father'd him and she that had conceiv'd
him in her womb and birth'd him,
They gave this child more of themselves than that,   20
They gave him afterward every day, they became part of him.

The mother at home quietly placing the dishes on the supper-table,
The mother with mild words, clean her cap and gown, a wholesome
odor falling off her person and clothes as she walks by,
The father, strong, self-sufficient, manly, mean, anger'd, unjust,
The blow, the quick loud word, the tight bargain, the crafty lure,   25
The family usages, the language, the company, the furniture, the
yearning and swelling heart,
Affection that will not be gainsay'd, the sense of what is real, the
thought if after all it should prove unreal,
The doubts of day-time and the doubts of night-time, the curious
whether and how,
Whether that which appears so is so, or is it all flashes and specks?
Men and women crowding fast in the streets, if they are not flashes
and specks what are they?   30
The streets themselves and the façades of houses, and goods in the
windows,
Vehicles, teams, the heavy-plank'd wharves, the huge crossing at the
ferries,
The village on the highland seen from afar at sunset, the river be-
tween,
Shadows, aureola and mist, the light falling on roofs and gables of
white or brown two miles off,
The schooner near by sleepily dropping down the tide, the little boat
slack-tow'd astern,   35
The hurrying tumbling waves, quick-broken crests, slapping,
The strata of color'd clouds, the long bar of maroon-tint away solitary
by itself, the spread of purity it lies motionless in,
The horizon's edge, the flying sea-crow, the fragrance of salt marsh
and shore mud,
These became part of that child who went forth every day, and who
now goes, and will always go forth every day.

THE SLEEPERS

I

I wander all night in my vision,
Stepping with light feet, swiftly and noiselessly stepping and stopping,
Bending with open eyes over the shut eyes of sleepers,
Wandering and confused, lost to myself, ill-assorted, contradictory,
Pausing, gazing, bending, and stopping.   5

How solemn they look there, stretch'd and still,
How quiet they breathe, the little children in their cradles.

The wretched features of ennuyés, the white features of corpses, the
   livid faces of drunkards, the sick-gray faces of onanists,
The gash'd bodies on battle-fields, the insane in their strong-door'd
   rooms, the sacred idiots, the new-born emerging from gates, and
   the dying emerging from gates,
The night pervades them and infolds them.   10

The married couple sleep calmly in their bed, he with his palm on the
   hip of the wife, and she with her palm on the hip of the husband,
The sisters sleep lovingly side by side in their bed,
The men sleep lovingly side by side in theirs,
And the mother sleeps with her little child carefully wrapt.

The blind sleep, and the deaf and dumb sleep,   15
The prisoner sleeps well in the prison, the runaway son sleeps,
The murder that is to be hung next day, how does he sleep?
And the murder'd person, how does he sleep?

The female that loves unrequited sleeps,
And the male that loves unrequited sleeps,   20
The head of the money-maker that plotted all day sleeps,
And the enraged and treacherous dispositions, all, all sleep.

I stand in the dark with drooping eyes by the worst-suffering and the
   most restless,
I pass my hands soothingly to and fro a few inches from them,
The restless sink in their beds, they fitfully sleep.   25

Now I pierce the darkness, new beings appear,
The earth recedes from me into the night,
I saw that it was beautiful, and I see that what is not the earth is
   beautiful.

I go from bedside to bedside, I sleep close with the other sleepers each
   in turn,

I dream in my dream all the dreams of the other dreamers, 30
And I become the other dreamers.

I am a dance—play up there! the fit is whirling me fast!

I am the ever-laughing—it is new moon and twilight,
I see the hiding of douceurs, I see nimble ghosts whichever way I look,
Cache and cache again deep in the ground and sea, and where it is
  neither ground nor sea. 35

Well do they do their jobs those journeymen divine,
Only from me can they hide nothing, and would not if they could,
I reckon I am their boss and they make me a pet besides,
And surround me and lead me and run ahead when I walk,
To lift their cunning covers to signify me with stretch'd arms, and
  resume the way; 40
Onward we move, a gay gang of blackguards! with mirth-shouting
  music and wild-flapping pennants of joy!

I am the actor, the actress, the voter, the politician,
The emigrant and the exile, the criminal that stood in the box,
He who has been famous and he who shall be famous after to-day,
The stammerer, the well-formed person, the wasted or feeble person.

I am she who adorn'd herself and folded her hair expectantly, 46
My truant lover has come, and it is dark.

Double yourself and receive me darkness,
Receive me and my lover too, he will not let me go without him.

I roll myself upon you as upon a bed, I resign myself to the dusk. 50

He whom I call answers me and takes the place of my lover,
He rises with me silently from the bed.

Darkness, you are gentler than my lover, his flesh was sweaty and
  panting,
I feel the hot moisture yet that he left me.

My hands are spread forth, I pass them in all directions, 55
I would sound up the shadowy shore to which you are journeying.

Be careful darkness! already what was it touch'd me?
I thought my lover had gone, else darkness and he are one,
I hear the heart-beat, I follow, I fade away.

2

I descend my western course, my sinews are flaccid, 60
Perfume and youth course through me and I am their wake.

It is my face yellow and wrinkled instead of the old woman's,
I sit low in a straw-bottom chair and carefully darn my grandson's
   stockings.

It is I too, the sleepless widow looking out on the winter midnight,
I see the sparkles of starshine on the icy and pallid earth.   65

A shroud I see and I am the shroud, I wrap a body and lie in the
   coffin,
It is dark here under ground, it is not evil or pain here, it is blank
   here, for reasons.

(It seems to me that everything in the light and air ought to be happy,
Whoever is not in his coffin and the dark grave let him know he has
   enough.)

3

I see a beautiful gigantic swimmer swimming naked throught the eddies of the sea,   70
His brown hair lies close and even to his head, he strikes out with
   courageous arms, he urges himself with his legs,
I see his white body, I see his undaunted eyes,
I hate the swift-running eddies that would dash him head-foremost on
   the rocks.

What are you doing unruffianly red-trickled waves?
Will you kill the courageous giant? will you kill him in the prime of
   his middle age?   75

Steady and long he struggles,
He is baffled, bang'd, bruis'd, he holds out while his strength holds out,
The slapping eddies are spotted with his blood, they bear him away,
   they roll him, swing him, turn him,
His beautiful body is borne in the circling eddies, it is continually
   bruis'd on rocks,
Swiftly and out of sight is borne the brave corpse.   80

4

I turn but do not extricate myself,
Confused, a past-reading, another, but with darkness yet.

The beach is cut by the razory ice-wind, the wreck-guns sound,
The tempest lulls, the moon comes floundering through the drifts.

I look where the ship helplessly heads end on, I hear the burst as she
   strikes, I hear the howls of dismay, they grow fainter and fainter.

I cannot aid with my wringing fingers,   86
I can but rush to the surf and let it drench me and freeze upon me.

I search with the crowd, not one of the company is wash'd to us alive,
In the morning I help pick up the dead and lay them in rows in a
barn.

5

Now of the older war-days, the defeat at Brooklyn,   90
Washington stands inside the lines, he stands on the intrench'd hills
amid a crowd of officers,
His face is cold and damp, he cannot repress the weeping drops,
He lifts the glass perpetually to his eyes, the color is blanch'd from his
cheeks,
He sees the slaughter of the southern braves confided to him by their
parents.

The same at last and at last when peace is declared,   95
He stands in the room of the old tavern, the well-belov'd soldiers all
pass through,
The officers speechless and slow draw near in their turns,
The chief encircles their necks with his arm and kisses them on the
cheek,
He kisses lightly the wet cheeks one after another, he shakes hands and
bids good-by to the army.

6

Now what my mother told me one day as we sat at dinner together,
Of when she was a nearly grown girl living home with her parents
on the old homestead.   101

A red squaw came one breakfast-time to the old homestead,
On her back she carried a bundle of rushes for rush-bottoming chairs,
Her hair, straight, shiny, coarse, black, profuse, half-envelop'd her
face,
Her step was free and elastic, and her voice sounded exquisitely as she
spoke.   105

My mother look'd in delight and amazement at the stranger,
She look'd at the freshness of her tall-borne face and full and pliant
limbs,
The more she look'd upon her she loved her,
Never before had she seen such wonderful beauty and purity,
She made her sit on a bench by the jamb of the fireplace, she cook'd
food for her,   110
She had no work to give her, but she gave her remembrance and
fondness.

The red squaw staid all the forenoon, and toward the middle of the
afternoon she went away,
O my mother was loth to have her go away,

All the week she thought of her, she watch'd for her many a month
She remember'd her many a winter and many a summer, 115
But the red squaw never came nor was heard of there again.

7

A show of the summer softness—a contact of something unseen—an
    amour of the light and air,
I am jealous and overwhelm'd with friendliness,
And will go gallivant with the light and air myself.

O love and summer, you are in the dreams and in me, 120
Autumn and winter are in the dreams, the farmer goes with his thrift,
The droves and crops increase, the barns are well-fill'd.

Elements merge in the night, ships make tacks in the dreams,
The sailor sails, the exile returns home,
The fugitive returns unharm'd, the immigrant is back beyond months
    and years, 125
The poor Irishman lives in the simple house of his childhood with the
    well-known neighbors and faces,
They warmly welcome him, he is barefoot again, he forgets he is well
    off,
The Dutchman voyages home, and the Scotchman and Welshman
    voyage home, and the native of the Mediterranean voyages home,
To every port of England, France, Spain, enter well-fill'd ships,
The Swiss foots it toward his hills, the Prussian goes his way, the
    Hungarian his way, and the Pole his way, 130
The Swede returns, and the Dane and Norwegian return.

The homeward bound and the outward bound,
The beautiful lost swimmer, the ennuyé, the onanist, the female that
    loves unrequited, the money-maker,
The actor and actress, those through with their parts and those wait-
    ing to commence,
The affectionate boy, the husband and wife, the voter, the nominee
    that is chosen and the nominee that has fail'd, 135
The great already known and the great any time after to-day,
The stammerer, the sick, the perfect-form'd, the homely,
The criminal that stood in the box, the judge that sat and sentenced
    him, the fluent lawyers, the jury, the audience,
The laugher and weeper, the dancer, the midnight widow, the red
    squaw,
The consumptive, the erysipalite, the idiot, he that is wrong'd, 140
The antipodes, and every one between this and them in the dark,
I swear they are averaged now—one is no better than the other,
The night and sleep have liken'd them and restored them.

I swear they are all beautiful,
Every one that sleeps is beautiful, every thing in the dim light is beau-
tiful, 145
The wildest and bloodiest is over, and all is peace.

Peace is always beautiful,
The myth of heaven indicates peace and night.

The myth of heaven indicates the soul,
The soul is always beautiful, it appears more or it appears less, it
comes or it lags behind, 150
It comes from its embower'd garden and looks pleasantly on itself and
encloses the world,
Perfect and clean the genitals previously jetting, and perfect and clean
the womb cohering,
The head well-grown proportion'd and plumb, and the bowels and
joints proportion'd and plumb.

The soul is always beautiful,
The universe is duly in order, every thing is in its place, 155
What has arrived is in its place and what waits shall be in its place,
The twisted skull waits, the watery or rotten blood waits,
The child of the glutton or venerealee waits long, and the child of the
drunkard waits long, and the drunkard himself waits long,
The sleepers that lived and died wait, the far advanced are to go on
in their turns, and the far behind are to come on in their turns,
The diverse shall be no less diverse, but they shall flow and unite—
they unite now. 160

8

The sleepers are very beautiful as they lie unclothed,
They flow hand in hand over the whole earth from east to west as
they lie unclothed,
The Asiatic and African are hand in hand, the European and American are hand to hand,
Learn'd and unlearn'd are hand in hand, and male and female are hand
in hand,
The bare arm of the girl crosses the bare breast of her lover, they
press close without lust, his lips press her neck, 165
The father holds his grown or ungrown son in his arms with measureless love, and the son holds the father in his arms with measureless love,
The white hair of the mother shines on the white wrist of the
daughter,
The breath of the boy goes with the breath of the man, friend is
inarm'd by friend,
The scholar kisses the teacher and the teacher kisses the scholar, the
wrong'd is made right,

The call of the slave is one with the master's call, and the master sa-
 lutes the slave, 170
The felon steps forth from the prison, the insane becomes sane, the
 suffering of sick persons is reliev'd,
The sweatings and fevers stop, the throat that was unsound is sound,
 the lungs of the consumptive are resumed, the poor distress'd
 head is free,
The joints of the rheumatic move as smoothly as ever, and smoother
 than ever,
Stiflings and passages open, the paralyzed become supple,
The swell'd and convuls'd and congested awake to themselves in
 condition, 175
They pass the invigoration of the night and the chemistry of the night,
 and awake.

I too pass from the night,
I stay a while away O night, but I return to you again and love you.

Why should I be afraid to trust myself to you?
I am not afraid, I have been well brought forward by you, 180
I love the rich running day, but I do not desert her in whom I lay so
 long,
I know not how I came of you and I know not where I go with you,
 but I know I came well and shall go well.

I will stop only a time with the night, and rise betimes,
I will duly pass the day O my mother, and duly return to you.

I Sing the Body Electric

1

I sing the body electric,
The armies of those I love engirth me and I engirth them,
They will not let me off till I go with them, respond to them,
And discorrupt them, and charge them full with the charge of the
 soul.

Was it doubted that those who corrupt their own bodies conceal
 themselves? 5
And if those who defile the living are as bad as they who defile the
 dead?
And if the body does not do fully as much as the soul?
And if the body were not the soul, what is the soul?

2

The love of the body of man or woman balks account, the body itself
 balks account,
That of the male is perfect, and that of the female is perfect. 10

The expression of the face balks account,
But the expression of a well-made man appears not only in his face,
It is in his limbs and joints also, it is curiously in the joints of his hips and wrists,
It is in his walk, the carriage of his neck, the flex of his waist and knees, dress does not hide him,
The strong sweet quality he has strikes through the cotton and broadcloth, 15
To see him pass conveys as much as the best poem, perhaps more,
You linger to see his back, and the back of his neck and shoulder-side.

The sprawl and fulness of babes, the bosoms and heads of women, the folds of their dress, their style as we pass in the street, the contour of their shape downwards,
The swimmer naked in the swimming-bath, seen as he swims through the transparent green-shine, or lies with his face up and rolls silently to and fro in the heave of the water,
The bending forward and backward of rowers in row-boats, the horseman in his saddle, 20
Girls, mothers, house-keepers, in all their performances,
The group of laborers seated at noon-time with their open dinner kettles, and their wives waiting,
The female soothing a child, the farmer's daughter in the garden or cow-yard,
The young fellow hoeing corn, the sleigh-driver driving his six horses through the crowd,
The wrestle of wrestlers, two apprentice-boys, quite grown, lusty, good-natured, native-born, out on the vacant lot at sundown after work, 25
The coats and caps thrown down, the embrace of love and resistance,
The upper-hold and under-hold, the hair rumpled over and blinding the eyes;
The march of firemen in their own costumes, the play of masculine muscle through clean-setting trowsers and waist-straps,
The slow return from the fire, the pause when the bell strikes suddenly again, and the listening on the alert,
The natural, perfect, varied attitudes, the bent head, the curv'd neck and the counting; 30
Such-like I love—I loosen myself, pass freely, am at the mother's breast with the little child,
Swim with the swimmers, wrestle with wrestlers, march in line with the firemen, and pause, listen, count.

3

I knew a man, a common farmer, the father of five sons,
And in them the fathers of sons, and in them the fathers of sons.

This man was of wonderful vigor, calmness, beauty of person,   35
The shape of his head, the pale yellow and white of his hair and
    beard, the immeasurable meaning of his black eye, the richness
    and breadth of his manners,
These I used to go and visit him to see, he was wise also,
He was six feet tall, he was over eighty years old, his sons were mas-
    sive, clean, bearded, tan-faced, handsome,
They and his daughters loved him, all who saw him loved him,
They did not love him by allowance, they loved him with personal
    love,   40
He drank water only, the blood show'd like scarlet through the clear-
    brown skin of his face,
He was a frequent gunner and fisher, he sail'd his boat himself, he had
    a fine one presented to him by a ship-joiner, he had fowling-pieces
    presented to him by men that loved him,
When he went with his five sons and many grand-sons to hunt or fish,
    you would pick him out as the most beautiful and vigorous of the
    gang,
You would wish long and long to be with him, you would wish to sit
    by him in the boat that you and he might touch each other.

4

I have perceiv'd that to be with those I like is enough,   45
To stop in company with the rest at evening is enough,
To be surrounded by beautiful, curious, breathing, laughing flesh is
    enough,
To pass among them or touch any one, or rest my arm ever so lightly
    round his or her neck for a moment, what is this then?
I do not ask any more delight, I swim in it as in a sea.
There is something in staying close to men and women and looking on
    them, and in the contact and odor of them, that pleases the soul
    well,   50
All things please the soul, but these please the soul well.

5

This is the female form,
A divine nimbus exhales from it from head to foot,
It attracts with fierce undeniable attraction,
I am drawn by its breath as if I were no more than a helpless vapor, all
    falls aside but myself and it,   55
Books, art, religion, time, the visible and solid earth, and what was ex-
    pected of heaven or fear'd of hell, are now consumed,
Mad filaments, ungovernable shoots play out of it, the response like-
    wise ungovernable,
Hair, bosom, hips, bend of legs, negligent falling hands all diffused,
    mine too diffused,
Ebb stung by the flow and flow stung by the ebb, love-flesh swelling
    and deliciously aching,

Limitless limpid jets of love hot and enormous, quivering jelly of love,
    white-blow and delirious juice,   60
Bridegroom night of love working surely and softly into the prostrate
    dawn,
Undulating into the willing and yielding day,
Lost in the cleave of the clasping and sweet-flesh'd day.

This is the nucleus—after the child is born of woman, man is born of
    woman,
This the bath of birth, this the merge of small and large, and the out-
    let again.   65

Be not ashamed women, your privileges encloses the rest, and is the
    exit of the rest,
You are the gates of the body, and you are the gates of the soul.

The female contains all qualities and tempers them,
She is in her place and moves with perfect balance,
She is all things duly veil'd, she is both passive and active,   70
She is to conceive daughters as well as sons, and sons as well as
    daughters.

As I see my soul reflected in Nature,
As I see through a mist, One with inexpressible completeness, sanity,
    beauty,
See the bent head and arms folded over the breast, the Female I see.

6

The male is not less the soul nor more, he too is in his place,   75
He too is all qualities, he is action and power,
The flush of the known universe is in him,
Scorn becomes him well, and appetite and defiance become him well,
The wildest largest passions, bliss that is utmost, sorrow that is utmost
    become him well, pride is for him,
The full-spread pride of man is calming and excellent to the soul,   80
Knowledge becomes him, he likes it always, he brings every thing to
    the test of himself,
Whatever the survey, whatever the sea and the sail he strikes sound-
    ings at last only here,
(Where else does he strike soundings except here?)

The man's body is sacred and the woman's body is sacred,
No matter who it is, it is sacred—is it the meanest one in the laborers'
    gang?   85
Is it one of the dull-faced immigrants just landed on the wharf?
Each belongs here or anywhere just as much as the well-off, just as
    much as you,
Each has his or her place in the procession.

(All is a procession,
The universe is a procession with measured and perfect motion.)   90

Do you know so much yourself that you call the meanest ignorant?
Do you suppose you have a right to a good sight, and he or she has no
    right to a sight?
Do you think matter has cohered together from its diffuse float, and
    the soil is on the surface, and water runs and vegetation sprouts,
For you only, and not for him and her?

7

A man's body at auction,   95
(For before the war I often go to the slave-mart and watch the sale,)
I help the auctioneer, the sloven does not half know his business.

Gentlemen look on this wonder,
Whatever the bids of the bidders they cannot be high enough for it,
For it the globe lay preparing quintillions of years without one animal
    or plant,   100
For it the revolving cycles truly and steadily roll'd.

In this head the all-baffling brain,
In it and below it the makings of heroes.

Examine these limbs, red, black, or white, they are cunning in tendon
    and nerve,
They shall be stript that you may see them.   105

Exquisite senses, life-lit eyes, pluck, volition,
Flakes of breast-muscle, pliant backbone and neck, flesh not flabby,
    good-sized arms and legs,
And wonders within there yet.

Within there runs blood,
The same old blood! the same red-running blood!   110
There swells and jets a heart, there all passions, desires, reachings,
    aspirations,
(Do you think they are not there because they are not express'd in
    parlors and lecture-rooms?)

This is not only one man, this the father of those who shall be fathers
    in their turns,
In him the start of populous states and rich republics,
Of him countless immortal lives with countless embodiments and en-
    joyments.   115

How do you know who shall come from the offspring of his offspring
 through the centuries?
(Who might you find you have come from yourself, if you could
 trace back through the centuries?)

8

A woman's body at auction,
She too is not only herself, she is the teeming mother of mothers,
She is the bearer of them that shall grow and be mates to the mothers.

Have you ever loved the body of a woman?   121
Have you ever loved the body of a man?

Do you not see that these are exactly the same to all in all nations and
 times all over the earth?

If anything is sacred the human body is sacred,
And the glory and sweet of a man is the token of manhood untainted,
And in man or woman a clean, strong, firm-fibred body, is more beau-
 tiful than the most beautiful face.   126

Have you seen the fool that corrupted his own live body? or the fool
 that corrupted her own live body?
For they do not conceal themselves, and cannot conceal themselves.

9

O my body! I dare not desert the likes of you in other men and
 women, nor the likes of the parts of you,
I believe the likes of you are to stand or fall with the likes of the soul,
 (and that they are the soul,)   130
I believe the likes of you shall stand or fall with my poems, and that
 they are my poems,
Man's, woman's, child's, youth's, wife's, husband's, mother's, father's,
 young man's, young woman's poems,
Head, neck, hair, ears, drop and tympan of the ears,
Eyes, eye-fringes, iris of the eye, eyebrows, and the waking or sleep-
 ing of the lids,
Mouth, tongue, lips, teeth, roof of the mouth, jaws, and the jaw-
 hinges,   135
Nose, nostrils of the nose, and the partition,
Cheeks, temples, forehead, chin, throat, back of the neck, neck-slue,
Strong shoulders, manly beard, scapula, hind-shoulders, and the ample
 side-round of the chest,
Upper-arm, armpit, elbow-socket, lower-arm, arm-sinews, arm-bones,
Wrist and wrist-joints, hand, palm, knuckles, thumb, forefinger,
 finger-joints, finger-nails,   140
Broad breast-front, curling hair of the breast, breast-bone, breast-side,
Ribs, belly, backbone, joints of the backbone,

Hips, hip-sockets, hip-strength, inward and outward round, man-balls, man-root,
Strong set of thighs, well carrying the trunk above,
Leg-fibres, knee, knee-pan, upper-leg, under-leg,   145
Ankles, instep, foot-ball, toes, toe-joints, the heel;
All attitudes, all the shapeliness, all the belongings of my or your body
    or of any one's body, male or female,
The lung-sponges, the stomach-sac, the bowels sweet and clean,
The brain in its folds inside the skull-frame,
Sympathies, heart-valves, palate-valves, sexuality, maternity,   150
Womanhood and all that is a woman, and the man that comes from
    woman,
The womb, the teats, nipples, breast-milk, tears, laughter, weeping,
    love-looks, love-perturbations and risings,
The voice, articulation, language, whispering, shouting aloud,
Food, drink, pulse, digestion, sweat, sleep, walking, swimming,
Poise on the hips, leaping, reclining, embracing, arm-curving and
    tightening,   155
The continual changes of the flex of the mouth, and around the eyes,
The skin, the sunburnt shade, freckles, hair,
The curious sympathy one feels when feeling with the hand the naked
    meat of the body,
The circling rivers the breath, and breathing it in and out,
The beauty of the waist, and thence of the hips, and thence downward
    toward the knees,   160
The thin red jellies within you or within me, the bones and the mar-
    row in the bones,
The exquisite realization of health;
O I say these are not the parts and poems of the body only, but of the
    soul,
O I say now these are the soul!

From LEAVES OF GRASS

Second Edition, 1856

The second edition of *Leaves of Grass* was Whitman's response to
Emerson's reception of the first edition. It contained twenty new
poems of which the best, and one of his supreme achievements, was
the "Sun-Down Poem," later called "Crossing Brooklyn Ferry." This
poem celebrates the continuity of experience—"The similitudes of the
past and those of the future"—the common deliverance into life (the
passage), the common experience of places and things, the common
facts of human nature. What makes it so remarkable and exciting,
however, is the subtle way in which the poet, by means of these

similitudes, evokes his own presence: "What I promis'd without mentioning it, have you not accepted?" As in "Full of Life Now"—

When you read these I that was visible am become invisible,
Now it is you, compact, visible, realizing my poems, seeking me,
Fancying how happy you were if I could be with you and become your comrade;
Be it as if I were with you. (Be not too certain but I am now with you.)

—so here, and not in statement but in deed, Whitman creates the very bond of love that brings him to life for the reader.

More programmatic, "Song of the Open Road" is one of the best translations into Whitman's symbols of the transcendental values of Emerson and Thoreau. For here he calls for self-reliance ("Allons! from all formules!"), for an openness to experience, for the liberation that comes when one knows "the universe itself as a road, as many roads, as roads for traveling souls." Extolling the liberation of the "open air," the poem describes a world in flux, mankind in procession, life as the journey of the self. The appeal of this adventure on life for Whitman, however, was that it permitted him to satisfy his "old delicious burdens"; for the first time he introduced the word "adhesiveness." On the open road, he wrote, the love of comrades (which is the emotional center of the poem) is "apropos." Here he could "scatter myself among men and women as I go."

Finally, among the poems of sex that Whitman now added to this edition, "Spontaneous Me" (originally more suggestively called "Bunch Poem") is the most interesting. Later placed among the *Children of Adam* poems, it was not so much a poem of procreation, as a catalog of erotic images, a recognition of the "sexual fibre" of all things, which, in himself, the poet has not found satisfactorily expressed, but for which his poem ("this bunch") is a substitute.

Crossing Brooklyn Ferry

1

Flood-tide below me! I see you face to face!
Clouds of the west—sun there half an hour high—I see you also face to face.

Crowds of men and women attired in the usual costumes, how curious you are to me!
On the ferry-boats the hundreds and hundreds that cross, returning home, are more curious to me than you suppose,
And you that shall cross from shore to shore years hence are more to me, and more in my meditations, than you might suppose.   5

2

The impalpable sustenance of me from all things at all hours of the day,

The simple, compact, well-join'd scheme, myself disintegrated, every
    one disintegrated yet part of the scheme,
The similitudes of the past and those of the future,
The glories strung like beads on my smallest sights and hearings, on
    the walk in the street and the passage over the river,
The current rushing so swiftly and swimming with me far away,   10
The others that are to follow me, the ties between me and them,
The certainty of others, the life, love, sight, hearing of others.

Others will enter the gates of the ferry and cross from shore to shore,
Others will watch the run of the flood-tide,
Others will see the shipping of Manhattan north and west, and the
    heights of Brooklyn to the south and east,   15
Others will see the islands large and small;
Fifty years hence, others will see them as they cross, the sun half an
    hour high,
A hundred years hence, or ever so many hundred years hence, others
    will see them,
Will enjoy the sunset, the pouring-in of the flood-tide, the falling-back
    to the sea of the ebb-tide.

3

It avails not, time nor place—distance avails not,   20
I am with you, you men and women of a generation, or ever so many
    generations hence,
Just as you feel when you look on the river and sky, so I felt,
Just as any of you is one of a living crowd, I was one of a crowd,
Just as you are refresh'd by the gladness of the river and the bright
    flow, I was refresh'd,
Just as you stand and lean on the rail, yet hurry with the swift current,
    I stood yet was hurried,   25
Just as you look on the numberless masts of ships and the thick-
    stemm'd pipes of steamboats, I look'd.

I too many and many a time cross'd the river of old,
Watched the Twelfth-month sea-gulls, saw them high in the air float-
    ing with motionless wings, oscillating their bodies,
Saw how the glistening yellow lit up parts of their bodies and left the
    rest in strong shadow,
Saw the slow-wheeling circles and the gradual edging toward the
    south,   30
Saw the reflection of the summer sky in the water,
Had my eyes dazzled by the shimmering track of beams,
Look'd at the fine centrifugal spokes of light round the shape of my
    head in the sunlit water,
Look'd on the haze on the hills southward and south-westward,
Look'd on the vapor as it flew in fleeces tinged with violet,   35
Look'd toward the lower bay to notice the vessels arriving,

Saw their approach, saw aboard those that were near me,
Saw the white sails of schooners and sloops, saw the ships at anchor,
The sailors at work in the rigging or out astride the spars,
The round masts, the swinging motion of the hulls, the slender-serpen-
    tine pennants,   40
The large and small steamers in motion, the pilots in their pilot-houses,
The white wake left by the passage, the quick tremulous whirl of the
    wheels,
The flags of all nations, the falling of them at sunset,
The scallop-edged waves in the twilight, the ladled cups, the frolic-
    some crests and glistening,
The stretch afar growing dimmer and dimmer, the gray walls of the
    granite storehouses by the docks,   45
On the river the shadowy group, the big steam-tug closely flank'd on
    each side by the barges, the hay-boat, the belated lighter,
On the neighboring shore the fires from the foundry chimneys burn-
    ing high and glaringly into the night,
Casting their flicker of black contrasted with wild red and yellow
    light over the tops of houses and down into the clefts of streets.

4

These and all else were to me the same as they are to you,
I loved well those cities, loved well the stately and rapid river,   50
The men and women I saw were all near to me,
Others the same—others who look back on me because I look'd for-
    ward to them,
(The time will come, though I stop here to-day and to-night.)

5

What is it then between us?
What is the count of the scores or hundreds of years between us?   55

Whatever it is, it avails not—distance avails not, and place avails not,
I too lived, Brooklyn of ample hills was mine,
I too walk'd the streets of Manhattan island, and bathed in the waters
    around it,
I too felt the curious abrupt questionings stir within me,
In the day among crowds of people sometimes they came upon me,
In my walks home late at night or as I lay in my bed they came upon
    me,   61
I too had been struck from the float forever held in solution,
I too had receiv'd identity by my body,
That I was I knew was of my body, and what I should be I knew I
    should be of my body.

6

It is not upon you alone the dark patches fall,   65
The dark threw its patches down upon me also,

The best I had done seem'd to me blank and suspicious,
My great thoughts as I supposed them, were they not in reality
    meagre?
Nor is it you alone who know what it is to be evil,
I am he who knew what it was to be evil, 70
I too knitted the old knot of contrariety,
Blabb'd, blush'd, resented, lied, stole, grudg'd,
Had guile, anger, lust, hot wishes I dared not speak,
Was wayward, vain, greedy, shallow, sly, cowardly, malignant,
The wolf, the snake, the hog, not wanting in me, 75
The cheating look, the frivolous word, the adulterous wish, not want-
    ing,
Refusals, hates, postponements, meanness, laziness, none of these want-
    ing,
Was one with the rest, the days and haps of the rest,
Was call'd my nighest name by clear loud voices of young men as
    they saw me approaching or passing,
Felt their arms on my neck as I stood, or the negligent leaning of their
    flesh against me as I sat, 80
Saw many I loved in the street or ferry-boat or public assembly, yet
    never told them a word,
Lived the same life with the rest, the same old laughing, gnawing,
    sleeping,
Play'd the part that still looks back on the actor or actress,
The same old role, the role that is what we make it, as great as we like,
Or as small as we like, or both great and small. 85

7

Closer yet I approach you,
What thought you have of me now, I had as much of you—I laid in
    my stores in advance,
I consider'd long and seriously of you before you were born.
Who was to know what should come home to me?
Who knows but I am enjoying this? 90
Who knows, for all the distance, but I am as good as looking at you
    now, for all you cannot see me?

8

Ah, what can ever be more stately and admirable to me than mast-
    hemm'd Manhattan?
River and sunset and scallop-edg'd waves of flood-tide?
The sea-gulls oscillating their bodies, the hay-boat in the twilight, and
    the belated lighter?

What gods can exceed these that clasp me by the hand, and with
    voices I love call me promptly and loudly by my nighest name
    as I approach? 95

What is more subtle than this which ties me to the woman or man
  that looks in my face?
Which fuses me into you now, and pours my meaning into you?

We understand then do we not?
What I promis'd without mentioning it, have you not accepted?
What the study could not teach—what the preaching could not accom-
  plish is accomplish'd, is it not?   100

9

Flow on, river! flow with the flood-tide, and ebb with the ebb-tide!
Frolic on, crested and scallop-edg'd waves!
Gorgeous clouds of the sunset! drench with your splendor me, or the
  men and women generations after me!
Cross from shore to shore, countless crowds of passengers!
Stand up, tall masts of Mannahatta! stand up, beautiful hills of
  Brooklyn!   105
Throb, baffled and curious brain! throw out questions and answers!
Suspend here and everywhere, eternal float of solution!
Gaze, loving and thirsting eyes, in the house or street or public assem-
  bly!
Sound out, voices of young men! loudly and musically call me by my
  nighest name!
Live, old life! play the part that looks back on the actor or actress!
Play the old role, the role that is great or small according as one makes
  it!   111
Consider, you who peruse me, whether I may not in unknown ways
  be looking upon you;
Be firm, rail over the river, to support those who lean idly, yet haste
  with the hasting current;
Fly on, sea-birds! fly sideways, or wheel in large circles high in the air;
Receive the summer sky, you water, and faithfully hold it till all
  downcast eyes have time to take it from you!   115
Diverge, fine spokes of light, from the shape of my head, or any one's
  head, in the sunlit water!
Come on, ships from the lower bay! pass up or down, white-sail'd
  schooners, sloops, lighters!
Flaunt away, flags of all nations! be duly lower'd at sunset!
Burn high your fires, foundry chimneys! cast black shadows at night-
  fall! cast red and yellow light over the tops of the houses!
Appearances, now or henceforth, indicate what you are,   120
You necessary film, continue to envelop the soul,
About my body for me, and your body for you, be hung our divinest
  aromas,
Thrive, cities—bring your freight, bring your shows, ample and suffi-
  cient rivers,
Expand, being than which none else is perhaps more spiritual,
Keep your places, objects than which none else is more lasting.   125

You have waited, you always wait, you dumb, beautiful ministers,
We receive you with free sense at last, and are insatiate henceforward,
Not you any more shall be able to foil us, or withhold yourselves
from us,
We use you, and do not cast you aside—we plant you permanently
within us,
We fathom you not—we love you—there is perfection in you also,   130
You furnish your parts toward eternity,
Great or small, you furnish your parts toward the soul.

Song of the Open Road

1

Afoot and light-hearted I take to the open road,
Healthy, free, the world before me,
The long brown path before me leading wherever I choose.

Henceforth I ask not good-fortune, I myself am good-fortune,
Henceforth I whimper no more, postpone no more, need nothing,   5
Done with indoor complaints, libraries, querulous criticisms,
Strong and content I travel the open road.

The earth, that is sufficient,
I do not want the constellations any nearer,
I know they are very well where they are,
I know they suffice for those who belong to them.   10

(Still here I carry my old delicious burdens,
I carry them, men and women, I carry them with me wherever I go,
I swear it is impossible for me to get rid of them,
I am fill'd with them; and I will fill them in return.)   15

2

You road I enter upon and look around, I believe you are not all that
is here,
I believe that much unseen is also here.

Here the profound lesson of reception, nor preference nor denial,
The black with his woolly head, the felon, the diseas'd, the illiterate
person, are not denied;
The birth, the hasting after the physician, the beggar's tramp, the
drunkard's stagger, the laughing party of mechanics,   20
The escaped youth, the rich person's carriage, the fop, the eloping
couple,
The early market-man, the hearse, the moving of furniture into the
town, the return back from the town,
They pass, I also pass, any thing passes, none can be interdicted,
None but are accepted, none but shall be dear to me.

3

You air that serves me with breath to speak!   25
You objects that call from diffusion my meanings and give them shape!
You light that wraps me and all things in delicate equable showers!
You paths worn in the irregular hollows by the roadsides!
I believe you are latent with unseen existences, you are so dear to me.

You flagg'd walks of the cities! you strong curbs at the edges!   30
You ferries! you planks and posts of wharves! you timber-lined sides!
    you distant ships!
You rows of houses! you window-pierc'd façades! you roofs!
You porches and entrances! you copings and iron guards!
You windows whose transparent shells might expose so much!
You doors and ascending steps! you arches!   35
You gray stones of interminable pavements! you trodden crossings!
From all that has touch'd you I believe you have imparted to your-
    selves, and now would impart the same secretly to me,
From the living and the dead you have peopled your impassive sur-
    faces, and the spirits thereof would be evident and amicable with
    me.

4

The earth expanding right hand and left hand,
The picture alive, every part in its best light,   40
The music falling in where it is wanted, and stopping where it is not
    wanted,
The cheerful voice of the public road, the gay fresh sentiment of the
    road.

O highway I travel, do you say to me *Do not leave me?*
Do you say *Venture not—if you leave me you are lost?*
Do you say *I am already prepared, I am well-beaten and undenied,
    adhere to me?*   45
O public road, I say back I am not afraid to leave you, yet I love you,
You express me better than I can express myself,
You shall be more to me than my poem.

I think heroic deeds were all conceiv'd in the open air, and all free
    poems also,
I think I could stop here myself and do miracles,   50
I think whatever I shall meet on the road I shall like, and whoever be-
    holds me shall like me,
I think whoever I see must be happy.

5

From this hour I ordain myself loos'd of limits and imaginary lines,
Going where I list, my own master total and absolute,
Listening to others, considering well what they say,   55

Pausing, searching, receiving, contemplating,
Gently, but with undeniable will, divesting myself of the holds that
would hold me.

I inhale great draughts of space,
The east and the west are mine, and the north and the south are mine.

I am larger, better than I thought,   60
I did not know I held so much goodness.

All seems beautiful to me,
I can repeat over to men and women, You have done such good to me
    I would do the same to you,
I will recruit for myself and you as I go,
I will scatter myself among men and women as I go,   65
I will toss a new gladness and roughness among them,
Whoever denies me it shall not trouble me,
Whoever accepts me he or she shall be blessed and shall bless me.

6

Now if a thousand perfect men were to appear it would not amaze me,
Now if a thousand beautiful forms of women appear'd it would not
    astonish me.   70
Now I see the secret of the making of the best persons,
It is to grow in the open air and to eat and sleep with the earth.

Here a great personal deed has room,
(Such a deed seizes upon the hearts of the whole race of men,
Its effusion of strength and will overwhelms law and mocks all au-
    thority and all argument against it.)   75

Here is the test of wisdom,
Wisdom is not finally tested in schools,
Wisdom cannot be pass'd from one having it to another not having it,
Wisdom is of the soul, is not susceptible of proof, is its own proof,
Applies to all stages and objects and qualities and is content,   80
Is the certainty of the reality and immortality of things, and the excel-
    lence of things;
Something there is in the float of the sight of things that provokes it
    out of the soul.

Now I re-examine philosophies and religions,
They may prove well in lecture-rooms, yet not prove at all under the
    spacious clouds and along the landscape and flowing currents.

Here is realization,   85
Here is a man tallied—he realizes here what he has in him,
The past, the future, majesty, love—if they are vacant of you, you are
    vacant of them.

Only the kernel of every object nourishes;
Where is he who tears off the husks for you and me?
Where is he that undoes stratagems and envelopes for you and me?   90

Here is adhesiveness, it is not previously fashion'd, it is apropos;
Do you know what it is as you pass to be loved by strangers?
Do you know the talk of those turning eye-balls?

7

Here is the efflux of the soul,
The efflux of the soul comes from within through embower'd gates,
    ever provoking questions,   95
These yearnings why are they? these thoughts in the darkness why are
    they?
Why are there men and women that while they are nigh me the sun-
    light expands my blood?
Why when they leave me do my pennants of joy sink flat and lank?
Why are there trees I never walk under but large and melodious
    thoughts descend upon me?
(I think they hang there winter and summer on those trees and al-
    ways drop fruit as I pass;)   100
What is it I interchange so suddenly with strangers?
What with some driver as I ride on the seat by his side?
What with some fisherman drawing his seine by the shore as I walk by
    and pause?
What gives me to be free to a woman's and man's good-will? what
    gives them to be free to mine?

8

The efflux of the soul is happiness, here is happiness,   105
I think it pervades the open air, waiting at all times,
Now it flows unto us, we are rightly charged.

Here rises the fluid and attaching character,
The fluid and attaching character is the freshness and sweetness of man
    and woman,
(The herbs of the morning sprout no fresher and sweeter every day
    out of the roots of themselves, than it sprouts fresh and sweet
    continually out of itself.)   110

Toward the fluid and attaching character exudes the sweat of the love
    of young and old,
From it falls distill'd the charm that mocks beauty and attainments,
Toward it heaves the shuddering longing ache of contact.

9

Allons! whoever you are come travel with me!
Traveling with me you find what never tires.   115

The earth never tires,
The earth is rude, silent, incomprehensible at first, Nature is rude and
    incomprehensible at first,
Be not discouraged, keep on, there are divine things well envelop'd,
I swear to you there are divine things more beautiful than words can
    tell.

Allons! we must not stop here, 120
However sweet these laid-up stores, however convenient this dwelling
    we cannot remain here,
However shelter'd this port and however calm these waters we must
    not anchor here,
However welcome the hospitality that surrounds us we are permitted
    to receive it but a little while.

10

Allons! the inducements shall be greater,
We will sail pathless and wild seas, 125
We will go where winds blow, waves dash, and the Yankee clipper
    speeds by under full sail.

Allons! with power, liberty, the earth, the elements,
Health, defiance, gayety, self-esteem, curiosity;
Allons! from all formules!
From your formules, O bat-eyes and materialistic priests. 130

The stale cadaver blocks up the passage—the burial waits no longer.

Allons! yet take warning!
He traveling with me needs the best blood, thews, endurance,
None may come to the trial till he or she bring courage and health,
Come not here if you have already spent the best of yourself, 135
Only those may come who come in sweet and determin'd bodies,
No diseas'd person, no rum-drinker or venereal taint is permitted here.

(I and mine do not convince by arguments, similes, rhymes,
We convince by our presence.)

11

Listen! I will be honest with you, 140
I do not offer the old smooth prizes, but offer rough new prizes,
These are the days that must happen to you:
You shall not heap up what is call'd riches,
You shall scatter with lavish hand all that you earn or achieve,
You but arrive at the city to which you were destin'd, you hardly
    settle yourself to satisfaction before you are call'd by an irresisti-
    ble call to depart, 145

You shall be treated to the ironical smiles and mockings of those who
   remain behind you,
What beckonings of love you receive you shall only answer with passionate kisses of parting,
You shall not allow the hold of those who spread their reach'd hands
   toward you.

12

Allons! after the great Companions, and to belong to them!
They too are on the road—they are the swift and majestic men—they
   are the greatest women,   150
Enjoyers of calms of seas and storms of seas,
Sailors of many a ship, walkers of many a mile of land,
Habituès of many distant countries, habituès of far-distant dwellings,
Trusters of men and women, observers of cities, solitary toilers,
Pausers and contemplators of tufts, blossoms, shells of the shore,   155
Dancers at wedding-dances, kissers of brides, tender helpers of chil-
   dren, bearers of children,
Soldiers of revolts, standers by gaping graves, lowerers-down of
   coffins,
Journeyers over consecutive seasons, over the years, the curious years
   each emerging from that which preceded it,
Journeyers as with companions, namely their own diverse phases,
Forth-steppers from the latent unrealized baby-days,   160
Journeyers gayly with their own youth, journeyers with their bearded
   and well-grain'd manhood,
Journeyers with their womanhood, ample, unsurpass'd, content,
Journeyers with their own sublime old age of manhood or woman-
   hood,
Old age, calm, expanded, broad with the haughty breadth of the uni-
   verse,   164
Old age, flowing free with the delicious near-by freedom of death.

13

Allons! to that which is endless as it was beginningless,
To undergo much, tramps of days, rests of nights,
To merge all in the travel they tend to, and the days and nights they
   tend to,
Again to merge them in the start of superior journeys,
To see nothing anywhere but what you may reach it and pass it,   170
To conceive no time, however distant, but what you may reach it and
   pass it,
To look up or down no road but it stretches and waits for you, how-
   ever long but it stretches and waits for you,
To see no being, not God's or any, but you also go thither,
To see no possession but you may possess it, enjoying all without labor
   or purchase, abstracting the feast yet not abstracting one particle
   of it,

To take the best of the farmer's farm and the rich man's elegant villa,
and the chaste blessings of the well-married couple, and the fruits
of orchards and flowers of gardens, 175
To take to your use out of the compact cities as you pass through,
To carry buildings and streets with you afterward wherever you go,
To gather the minds of men out of their brains as you encounter them,
to gather the love out of their hearts,
To take your lovers on the road with you, for all that you leave them
behind you,
To know the universe itself as a road, as many roads, as roads for
traveling souls. 180

All parts away for the progress of souls,
All religion, all solid things, arts, governments—all that was or is apparent upon this globe or any globe, falls into niches and corners
before the procession of souls along the grand roads of the
universe.

Of the progress of the souls of men and women along the grand roads
of the universe, all other progress is the needed emblem and sustenance.

Forever alive, forever forward,
Stately, solemn, sad, withdrawn, baffled, mad, turbulent, feeble, dis-
satisfied, 185
Desperate, proud, fond, sick, accepted by men, rejected by men,
They go! they go! I know that they go, but I know not where they
go,
But I know that they go toward the best—toward something great.

Whoever you are, come forth! or man or woman come forth!
You must not stay sleeping and dallying there in the house, though
you built it, or though it has been built for you. 190

Out of the dark confinement! out from behind the screen!
It is useless to protest, I know all and expose it.

Behold through you as bad as the rest,
Through the laughter, dancing, dining, supping, of people,
Inside of dresses and ornaments, inside of those wash'd and trimm'd
faces, 195
Behold a secret silent loathing and despair.

No husband, no wife, no friend, trusted to hear the confession,
Another self, a duplicate of every one, skulking and hiding it goes,
Formless and wordless through the streets of the cities, polite and
bland in the parlors,
In the cars of railroads, in steamboats, in the public assembly, 200

Home to the houses of men and women, at the table, in the bedroom, everywhere,
Smartly attired, countenance smiling, form upright, death under the breast-bones, hell under the skull-bones,
Under the broadcloth and gloves, under the ribbons and artificial flowers,
Keeping fair with the customs, speaking not a syllable of itself,
Speaking of any thing but never of itself.   205

14

Allons! through struggles and wars!
The goal that was named cannot be countermanded.

Have the past struggles succeeded?
What has succeeded? yourself? your nation? Nature?
Now understand me well—it is provided in the essence of things that from any fruition of success, no matter what, shall come forth something to make a greater struggle necessary.   210
My call is the call of battle, I nourish active rebellion,
He going with me must go well arm'd,
He going with me goes often with spare diet, poverty, angry enemies, desertions.

15

Allons! the road is before us!
It is safe—I have tried it—my own feet have tried it well—be not detain'd!   215
Let the paper remain on the desk unwritten, and the book on the shelf unopen'd!
Let the tools remain in the workshop! let the money remain unearn'd!
Let the school stand! mind not the cry of the teacher!
Let the preacher preach in his pulpit! let the lawyer plead in the court, and the judge expound the law.

Camerado, I give you my hand!   220
I give you my love more precious than money,
I give you myself before preaching or law;
Will you give me yourself? will you come travel with me?
Shall we stick by each other as long as we live?

SPONTANEOUS ME

Spontaneous me, Nature,
The loving day, the mounting sun, the friend I am happy with,
The arm of my friend hanging idly over my shoulder,
The hillside whiten'd with blossoms of the mountain ash,
The same late in autumn, the hues of red, yellow, drab, purple, and light and dark green,   5

The rich coverlet of the grass, animals and birds, the private un-
trimm'd bank, the primitive apples, the pebble-stones,
Beautiful dripping fragments, the negligent list of one after another as
I happen to call them to me or think of them,
The real poems, (what we call poems being merely pictures,)
The poems of the privacy of the night, and of men like me,
This poem drooping shy and unseen that I always carry, and that all
men carry, 10
(Know once for all, avow'd on purpose, wherever are men like me, are
our lusty lurking masculine poems,)
Love-thoughts, love-juice, love-odor, love-yielding, love-climbers, and
the climbing sap,
Arms and hands of love, lips of love, phallic thumb of love, breasts of
love, bellies press'd and glued together with love,
Earth of chaste love, life that is only life after love,
The body of my love, the body of the woman I love, the body of the
man, the body of the earth, 15
Soft forenoon airs that blow from the south-west,
The hairy wild-bee that murmurs and hankers up and down, that
gripes the full-grown lady-flower, curves upon her with amorous
firm legs, takes his will of her, and holds himself tremulous and
tight till he is satisfied;
The wet of woods through the early hours,
Two sleepers at night lying close together as they sleep, one
with an arm slanting down across and below the waist of the
other,
The smell of apples, aromas from crush'd sage-plant, mint, birch-
bark, 20
The boy's longings, the glow and pressure as he confides to me what
he was dreaming,
The dead leaf whirling its spiral whirl and falling still and content to
the ground,
The no-form'd stings that sights, people, objects, sting me with,
The hubb'd sting of myself, stinging me as much as it ever can any
one,
The sensitive, orbic, underlapp'd brothers, that only privileged feelers
may be intimate where they are, 25
The curious roamer the hand roaming all over the body, the bashful
withdrawing of flesh where the fingers soothingly pause and edge
themselves,
The limpid liquid within the young man,
The vex'd corrosion so pensive and so painful,
The torment, the irritable tide that will not be at rest,
The like of the same I feel, the like of the same in others, 30
The young man that flushes and flushes, and the young woman that
flushes and flushes,
The young man that wakes deep at night, the hot hand seeking to re-
press what would master him,

The mystic amorous night, the strange half-welcome pangs, visions, sweats,

The pulse pounding through palms and trembling encircling fingers, the young man all color'd, red, ashamed, angry;

The souse upon me of my lover the sea, as I lie willing and naked,   35

The merriment of the twin babes that crawl over the grass in the sun, the mother never turning her vigilant eyes from them,

The walnut-trunk, the walnut-husks, and the ripening or ripen'd long-round walnuts,

The continence of vegetables, birds, animals,

The consequent meanness of me should I skulk or find myself indecent, while birds and animals never once skulk or find themselves indecent,

The great chastity of paternity to match the great chastity of maternity,   40

The oath of procreation I have sworn, my Adamic and fresh daughters,

The greed that eats me day and night with hungry gnaw, till I saturate what shall produce boys to fill my place when I am through,

The wholesome relief, repose, content,

And this bunch pluck'd at random from myself,

It has done its work—I toss it carelessly to fall where it may.   45

⚜

From LEAVES OF GRASS

Third Edition, 1860

In the third edition the abounding confidence and nationalism of the earlier editions gave way to dejection. The poet of unity confessed his own personal conflict and division, and signified his intention of completing his work by ending this, the largest outpouring of his poems, with "So Long!" How defeated he was can be seen in "As I Ebb'd with the Ocean of Life," where he speaks of being "baffled, balk'd, bent to the very earth,/Oppress'd with myself that I have dared to open my mouth." Lacking biographical information—and Whitman was most secretive about the crises of his life—one can only guess from the confessional nature of many of the poems, and from "Out of the Cradle Endlessly Rocking," the major poem of this edition, that he was troubled by the despair of his unsatisfied longing for love. This longing for comradeship, for manly love, was confessed in the *Calamus* poems, the theme and tone of which were originally set by "I Saw in Louisiana a Live-Oak Growing." These poems were preceded by *Children of Adam*, a group of poems in which, without convincing personal accent, the poet proposed healthy procreation as part of his program for America; but unlike the *Calamus* poems, which they

served to offset, they did not, as he said of these "frailest leaves of me,"
"expose me more than all my other poems." Though Whitman was to
sublimate his longing in a public vision of democratic brotherhood
(see "For You, O Democracy") and, during the Civil War, in his work
as a "wound dresser," more privately he found his welcome response
in the "delicious word death." In death he hoped that he would at last
meet the "Great Comrade." Thus this edition fully announces the
theme of love and introduces its companion theme of death.

OUT OF THE CRADLE ENDLESSLY ROCKING

Out of the cradle endlessly rocking,
Out of the mocking-bird's throat, the musical shuttle,
Out of the Ninth-month midnight,
Over the sterile sands and the fields beyond, where the child leaving
    his bed wander'd alone, bareheaded, barefoot,
Down from the shower'd halo,   5
Up from the mystic play of shadows twining and twisting as if they
    were alive,
Out from the patches of briers and blackberries,
From the memories of the bird that chanted to me,
From your memories sad brother, from the fitful risings and fallings I
    heard,
From under that yellow half-moon late-risen and swollen as if with
    tears,   10
From those beginning notes of yearning and love there in the mist,
From the thousand responses of my heart never to cease,
From the myriad thence-arous'd words,
From the word stronger and more delicious than any,
From such as now they start the scene revisiting,   15
As a flock, twittering, rising, or overhead passing,
Borne hither, ere all eludes me, hurriedly,
A man, yet by these tears a little boy again,
Throwing myself on the sand, confronting the waves,
I, chanter of pains and joys, uniter of here and hereafter,   20
Taking all hints to use them, but swiftly leaping beyond them,
A reminiscence sing.

Once Paumanok,
When the lilac-scent was in the air and Fifth-month grass was grow-
    ing,
Up this seashore in some briers,   25
Two feather'd guests from Alabama, two together,
And their nest, and four light-green eggs spotted with brown,
And every day the he-bird to and fro near at hand,
And every day the she-bird crouch'd on her nest, silent, with bright
    eyes,

And every day I, a curious boy, never too close, never disturbing
    them,   30
Cautiously peering, absorbing, translating.

Shine! shine! shine!
Pour down your warmth, great sun!
While we bask, we two together.

Two together!   35
Winds blow south, or winds blow north,
Day come white, or night come black,
Home, or rivers and mountains from home,
Singing all time, minding no time,
While we two keep together.   40

Till of a sudden,
May-be kill'd, unknown to her mate,
One forenoon the she-bird crouch'd not on the nest,
Nor return'd that afternoon, nor the next,
Nor ever appear'd again.   45

And thenceforward all summer in the sound of the sea,
And at night under the full of the moon in calmer weather,
Over the hoarse surging of the sea,
Or flitting from brier to brier by day,
I saw, I heard at intervals the remaining one, the he-bird,   50
The solitary guest from Alabama.

Blow! blow! blow!
Blow up sea-winds along Paumanok's shore;
I wait and I wait till you blow my mate to me.

Yes, when the stars glisten'd,   55
All night long on the prong of a moss-scallop'd stake,
Down almost amid the slapping waves,
Sat the lone singer wonderful causing tears.

He call'd on his mate,
He pour'd forth the meanings which I of all men know.   60

Yes my brother I know,
The rest might not, but I have treasur'd every note,
For more than once dimly down to the beach gliding,
Silent, avoiding the moonbeams, blending myself with the shadows,
Recalling now the obscure shapes, the echoes, the sounds and sights
    after their sorts,   65
The white arms out in the breakers tirelessly tossing,

I, with bare feet, a child, the wind wafting my hair,
Listen'd long and long.

Listen'd to keep, to sing, now translating the notes,
Following you my brother. 70

Soothe! soothe! soothe!
Close on its wave soothes the wave behind,
And again another behind embracing and lapping, every one close,
But my love soothes not me, not me.

Low hangs the moon, it rose late, 75
It is lagging—O I think it is heavy with love, with love.

O madly the sea pushes upon the land,
With love, with love.

O night! do I not see my love fluttering out among the breakers?
What is that little black thing I see there in the white? 80

Loud! loud! loud!
Loud I call to you, my love!
High and clear I shoot my voice over the waves,
Surely you must know who is here, is here,
You must know whom I am, my love. 85

Low-hanging moon!
What is that dusky spot in your brown yellow?
O it is the shape, the shape of my mate!
O moon do not keep her from me any longer.

Land! land! O land! 90
Whichever way I turn, O I think you could give me my mate back
    again if you only would,
For I am almost sure I see her dimly whichever way I look.

O rising stars!
Perhaps the one I want so much will rise, will rise with some of you.

O throat! O trembling throat! 95
Sound clearer through the atmosphere!
Pierce the woods, the earth,
Somewhere listening to catch you must be the one I want.

Shake out carols!
Solitary here, the night's carols! 100
Carols of lonesome love! death's carols!

Carols under that lagging, yellow, waning moon!
O under that moon where she droops almost down into the sea!
O reckless despairing carols.

But soft! sink low!   105
Soft! let me just murmur,
And do you wait a moment you husky-nois'd sea,
For somewhere I believe I heard my mate responding to me,
So faint, I must be still, be still to listen,
But not altogether still, for then she might not come immediately to
*   me.*   110

Hither my love!
Here I am! here!
With this just-sustain'd note I announce myself to you,
This gentle call is for you my love, for you.

Do not be decoy'd elsewhere,   115
That is the whistle of the wind, it is not my voice,
That is the fluttering, the fluttering of the spray,
Those are the shadows of leaves.

O darkness! O in vain!
O I am very sick and sorrowful.   120

O brown halo in the sky near the moon, drooping upon the sea!
O troubled reflection in the sea!
O throat! O throbbing heart!
And I singing uselessly, uselessly all the night.

O past! O happy life! O songs of joy!   125
In the air, in the woods, over fields,
Loved! loved! loved! loved! loved!
But my mate no more, no more with me!
We two together no more.

The aria sinking,   130
All else continuing, the stars shining,
The winds blowing, the notes of the bird continuous echoing,
With angry moans the fierce old mother incessantly moaning,
On the sands of Paumanok's shore gray and rustling,
The yellow half-moon enlarged, sagging down, drooping, the face of
    the sea almost touching,   135
The boy ecstatic, with his bare feet the waves, with his hair the atmos-
    phere dallying,
The love in the heart long pent, now loose, now at last tumultuously
    bursting,
The aria's meaning, the ears, the soul, swiftly depositing,

The strange tears down the cheeks coursing,
The colloquy there, the trio, each uttering, 140
The undertone, the savage old mother incessantly crying,
To the boy's soul's questions sullenly timing, some drown'd secret
     hissing,
To the outsetting bard.

Demon or bird! (said the boy's soul,)
Is it indeed toward your mate you sing? or is it really to me? 145
For I, that was a child, my tongue's use sleeping, now I have heard
     you,
Now in a moment I know what I am for, I awake,
And already a thousand singers, a thousand songs, clearer, louder and
     more sorrowful than yours,
A thousand warbling echoes have started to life within me, never to
     die.

O you singer solitary, singing by yourself, projecting me, 150
O solitary me listening, never more shall I cease perpetuating you,
Never more shall I escape, never more the reverberations,
Never more the cries of unsatisfied love be absent from me,
Never again leave me to be the peaceful child I was before what there
     in the night,
By the sea under the yellow and sagging moon, 155
The messenger there arous'd, the fire, the sweet hell within,
The unknown want, the destiny of me.

O give me the clew! (it lurks in the night here somewhere,)
O if I am to have so much, let me have more!

A word then, (for I will conquer it,) 160
The word final, superior to all,
Subtle, sent up—what is it?—I listen;
Are you whispering it, and have been all the time, you sea waves?
Is that it from your liquid rims and wet sands?

Whereto answering, the sea, 165
Delaying not, hurrying not,
Whisper'd me through the night, and very plainly before daybreak,
Lisp'd to me the low and delicious word death,
And again death, death, death, death,
Hissing melodious, neither like the bird nor like my arous'd child's
     heart, 170
But edging near as privately for me rustling at my feet,
Creeping thence steadily up to my ears and laving me softly all over,
Death, death, death, death, death.

Which I do not forget,
But fuse the song of my dusky demon and brother, 175

That he sang to me in the moonlight on Paumanok's gray beach,
With the thousand responsive songs at random,
My own songs awaked from that hour,
And with them the key, the word up from the waves,
The word of the sweetest song and all songs,   180
That strong and delicious word which, creeping to my feet,
(Or like some old crone rocking the cradle, swathed in sweet gar-
    ments, bending aside,)
The sea whisper'd me.

As I Ebb'd with the Ocean of Life

1

As I ebb'd with the ocean of life,
As I wended the shores I know,
As I walk'd where the ripples continually wash you Paumanok,
Where they rustle up hoarse and sibilant,
Where the fierce old mother endlessly cries for her castaways,   5
I musing late in the autumn day, gazing off southward,
Held by this electric self out of the pride of which I utter poems,
Was seiz'd by the spirit that trails in the lines underfoot,
The rim, the sediment that stands for all the water and all the land of
    the globe.

Fascinated, my eyes reverting from the south, dropt, to follow those
    slender windrows,   10
Chaff, straw, splinters of wood, weeds, and the sea-gluten,
Scum, scales from shining rocks, leaves of salt-lettuce, left by the tide,
Miles walking, the sound of breaking waves the other side of me,
Paumonok there and then as I thought the old thought of likenesses,
These you presented to me you fish-shaped island,   15
As I wended the shores I know,
As I walk'd with that electric self seeking types.

2

As I wend to the shores I know not,
As I list to the dirge, the voices of men and women wreck'd,
As I inhale the impalpable breezes that set in upon me,
As the ocean so mysterious rolls toward me closer and closer,   20
I too but signify at the utmost a little wash'd-up drift,
A few sands and dead leaves to gather,
Gather, and merge myself as part of the sands and drift.

O baffled, balk'd, bent to the very earth,   25
Oppress'd with myself that I have dared to open my mouth,
Aware now that amid all that blab whose echoes recoil upon me I have
    not once had the least idea who or what I am,

But that before all my arrogant poems the real Me stands yet un-
touch'd, untold, altogether unreach'd,
Withdrawn far, mocking me with mock-congratulatory signs and
bows,
With peals of distant ironical laughter at every word I have written,
Pointing in silence to these songs, and then to the sand beneath. 31

I perceive I have not really understood any thing, not a single object,
and that no man ever can,
Nature here in sight of the sea taking advantage of me to dart upon
me and sting me,
Because I have dared to open my mouth to sing at all.

3

You oceans both, I close with you,   35
We murmur alike reproachfully rolling sands and drift, knowing not
why,
These little shreds indeed standing for you and me and all.

You friable shore with trails of debris,
You fish-shaped island, I take what is underfoot,
What is yours is mine my father.   40

I too Paumanok,
I too have bubbled up, floated the measureless float, and been wash'd
on your shores,
I too am but a trail of drift and debris,
I too leave little wrecks upon you, you fish-shaped island.

I throw myself upon your breast my father,   45
I cling to you so that you cannot unloose me,
I hold you so firm till you answer me something.

Kiss me my father,
Touch me with your lips as I touch those I love,
Breathe to me while I hold you close the secret of the murmuring I
envy.   50

4

Ebb, ocean of life, (the flow will return,)
Cease not your moaning you fierce old mother,
Endlessly cry for your castaways, but fear not, deny not me,
Rustle not up so hoarse and angry against my feet as I touch you or
gather from you.

I mean tenderly by you and all,   55
I gather for myself and for this phantom looking down where we
lead, and following me and mine.

Me and mine, loose windrows, little corpses,
Froth, snowy white, and bubbles,
(See, from my dead lips the ooze exuding at last,
See, the prismatic colors glistening and rolling,)   60
Tufts of straw, sands, fragments,
Buoy'd hither from many moods, one contradicting another,
From the storm, the long calm, the darkness, the swell,
Musing, pondering, a breath, a briny tear, a dab of liquid or soil,   64
Up just as much out of fathomless workings fermented and thrown,
A limp blossom or two, torn just as much over waves floating, drifted
    at random,
Just as much for us that sobbing dirge of Nature,
Just as much whence we come that blare of the cloud-trumpets,
We, capricious, brought hither we know not whence, spread out be-
    fore you,
You up there walking or sitting,   70
Whoever you are, we too lie in drifts at your feet.

From CALAMUS

In Paths Untrodden

In paths untrodden,
In the growth by margins of pond-waters,
Escaped from the life that exhibits itself,
From all the standards hitherto publish'd, from the pleasures, profits,
    conformities,
Which too long I was offering to feed my soul,   5
Clear to me now standards not yet publish'd, clear to me that my soul,
That the soul of the man I speak for rejoices in comrades,
Here by myself away from the clank of the world,
Tallying and talk'd to here by tongues aromatic,
No longer abash'd, (for in this secluded spot I can respond as I would
    not dare elsewhere,)   10
Strong upon me the life that does not exhibit itself, yet contains all
    the rest,
Resolv'd to sing no songs to-day but those of manly attachment,
Projecting them along that substantial life,
Bequeathing hence types of athletic love,
Afternoon this delicious Ninth-month in my forty-first year,   15
I proceed for all who are or have been young men,
To tell the secret of my nights and days,
To celebrate the need of comrades.

SCENTED HERBAGE OF MY BREAST

Scented herbage of my breast,
Leaves from you I gleam, I write, to be perused best afterwards,
Tomb-leaves, body-leaves growing up above me above death,
Perennial roots, tall leaves, O the winter shall not freeze you delicate
    leaves,
Every year shall you bloom again, out from where you retired you
    shall emerge again;   5
O I do not know whether many passing by will discover you or inhale
    your faint odor, but I believe a few will;
O slender leaves! O blossoms of my blood! I permit you to tell in your
    own way of the heart that is under you,
O I do not know what you mean there underneath yourselves, you are
    not happiness,
You are often more bitter than I can bear, you burn and sting me,
Yet you are beautiful to me you faint-tinged roots, you make me think
    of death,   10
Death is beautiful from you, (what indeed is finally beautiful except
    death and love?)
O I think it is not for life I am chanting here my chant of lovers, I
    think it must be for death,
For how calm, how solemn it grows to ascend to the atmosphere of
    lovers,
Death or life I am then indifferent, my soul declines to prefer,
(I am not sure but the high soul of lovers welcomes death most,)   15
Indeed O death, I think now these leaves mean precisely the same as
    you mean,
Grow up taller sweet leaves that I may see! grow up out of my breast!
Spring away from the conceal'd heart there!
Do not fold yourself so in your pink-tinged roots timid leaves!
Do not remain down there so ashamed, herbage of my breast!   20
Come I am determin'd to unbare this broad breast of mine, I have long
    enough stifled and choked;
Emblematic and capricious blades I leave you, now you serve me
    not,
I will say what I have to say by itself,
I will sound myself and comrades only, I will never again utter a call
    only their call,
I will raise with it immortal reverberations through the States,   25
I will give an example to lovers to take permanent shape and will
    through the States,
Through me shall the words be said to make death exhilarating,
Give me your tone therefore O death, that I may accord with it,
Give me yourself, for I see that you belong to me now above all, and
    are folded inseparably together, you love and death are,
Nor will I allow you to balk me any more with what I was calling life,
For now it is convey'd to me that you are the purports essential,   31

That you hide in these shifting forms of life, for reasons, and that they
 are mainly for you,
That you beyond them come forth to remain, the real reality,
That behind the mask of materials you patiently wait, no matter how
 long,
That you will one day perhaps take control of all,   35
That you will perhaps dissipate this entire show of appearance,
That may-be you are what it is all for, but it does not last so very
 long,
But you will last very long.

For You O Democracy

Come, I will make the continent indissoluble,
I will make the most splendid race the sun ever shone upon,
I will make divine magnetic lands,
 With the love of comrades,
 With the life-long love of comrades.   5

I will plant companionship thick as trees along all the rivers of
 America, and along the shores of the great lakes, and all over the
 prairies,
I will make inseparable cities with their arms about each other's necks,
 By the love of comrades,
 By the manly love of comrades,

For you these from me, O Democracy, to serve you ma femme!   10
For you, for you I am trilling these songs.

When I Heard at the Close of the Day

When I heard at the close of the day how my name had been receiv'd
 with plaudits in the capitol, still it was not a happy night for me
 that follow'd,
And else when I carous'd, or when my plans were accomplish'd, still
 I was not happy,
But the day when I rose at dawn from the bed of perfect health, re-
 fresh'd, singing, inhaling the ripe breath of autumn,
When I saw the full moon in the west grow pale and disappear in the
 morning light,
When I wander'd alone over the beach, and undressing bathed, laughing with the cool waters, and saw the sun rise,   5
And when I thought how my dear friend my lover was on his way
 coming, O then I was happy,
O then each breath tasted sweeter, and all that day my food nourish'd
 me more, and the beautiful day pass'd well,
And the next came with equal joy, and with the next at evening came
 my friend,

And that night while all was still I heard the waters roll slowly continually up the shores,
I heard the hissing rustle of the liquid and sands as directed to me whispering to congratulate me,   10
For the one I love most lay sleeping by me under the same cover in the cool night,
In the stillness in the autumn moonbeams his face was inclined toward me,
And his arm lay lightly around my breast—and that night I was happy.

I Saw in Louisiana a Live-Oak Growing

I saw in Louisiana a live-oak growing,
All alone stood it and the moss hung down from the branches,
Without any companion it grew there uttering joyous leaves of dark green,
And its look, rude, unbending, lusty, made me think of myself,
But I wonder'd how it could utter joyous leaves standing alone there without its friend near, for I knew I could not,   5
And I broke off a twig with a certain number of leaves upon it, and twined around it a little moss,
And brought it away, and I have placed it in sight in my room,
It is not needed to remind me as of my own dear friends,
(For I believe lately I think of little else than of them,)
Yet it remains to me a curious token, it makes me think of manly love;   10
For all that, and though the live-oak glistens there in Louisiana solitary in a wide flat space,
Uttering joyous leaves all its life without a friend a lover near,
I know very well I could not.

Here the Frailest Leaves of Me

Here the frailest leaves of me and yet my strongest lasting,
Here I shade and hide my thoughts, I myself do not expose them,
And yet they expose me more than all my other poems.

So Long

To conclude, I announce what comes after me.

I remember I said before my leaves sprang at all,
I would raise my voice jocund and strong with reference to consummations.

When America does what was promis'd,   4
When through these States walk a hundred millions of superb persons,
When the rest part away for superb persons and contribute to them,
When breeds of the most perfect mothers denote America,
Then to me and mine our due fruition.

I have press'd through in my own right,
I have sung the body and the soul, war and peace have I sung, and the
    songs of life and death,   10
And the songs of birth, and shown that there are many births.

I have offer'd my style to every one, I have journey'd with confident
    step;
While my pleasure is yet at the full I whisper *So long!*
And take the young woman's hand and the young man's hand for the
    last time.

I announce natural persons to arise,   15
I announce justice triumphant,
I announce uncompromising liberty and equality,
I announce the justification of candor and the justification of pride.

I announce that the identity of these States is a single identity only,
I announce the Union more and more compact, indissoluble,   20
I announce splendors and majesties to make all the previous politics of
    the earth insignificant.

I announce adhesiveness, I say it shall be limitless, unloosen'd,
I say you shall yet find the friend you were looking for.

I announce a man or woman coming, perhaps you are the one, (*So
    long!*)
I announce the great individual, fluid as Nature, chaste, affectionate,
    compassionate, fully arm'd.   25

I announce a life that shall be copious, vehement, spiritual, bold,
I announce an end that shall lightly and joyfully meet its translation.

I announce myriads of youths, beautiful, gigantic, sweet-blooded,
I announce a race of splendid and savage old men.

O thicker and faster—(*So long!*)   30
O crowding too close upon me,
I foresee too much, it means more than I thought,
It appears to me I am dying.

Hasten throat and sound your last,
Salute me—salute the days once more. Peal the old cry once more.   35

Screaming electric, the atmosphere using,
At random glancing, each as I notice absorbing,
Swiftly on, but a little while alighting,
Curious envelop'd messages delivering,
Sparkles hot, seed ethereal down in the dirt dropping,   40
Myself unknowing, my commission obeying, to question it never dar-
    ing,
To ages and ages yet the growth of the seed leaving,
To troops out of the war arising, they the task I have set promulging,
To women certain whispers of myself bequeathing, their affection me
    more clearly explaining,
To young men my problems offering—no dallier I—I the muscle of
    their brains crying,   45
So I pass, a little time vocal, visible, contrary,
Afterward a melodious echo, passionately bent for, (death making me
    really undying,)
The best of me then when no longer visible, for toward that I have
    been incessantly preparing.

What is there more, that I lag and pause and crouch extended with
    unshut mouth?
Is there a single final farewell?   50

My songs cease, I abandon them,
From behind the screen where I hid I advance personally solely to
    you.

Camerado, this is no book,
Who touches this touches a man,
(Is it night? are we here together alone?)   55
It is I you hold and who holds you,
I spring from the pages into your arms—decease calls me forth.

O how your fingers drowse me,
Your breath falls around me like dew, your pulse lulls the tympans of
    my ears,
I feel immerged from head to foot,   60
Delicious, enough.

Enough O deed impromptu and secret,
Enough O gliding present—enough O summ'd-up past.

Dear friend whoever you are take this kiss,
I give it especially to you, do not forget me,   65
I feel like one who has done work for the day to retire awhile,
I receive now again of my many translations, from my avataras as-
    cending, while others doubtless await me,

An unknown sphere more real than I dream'd, more direct, darts
    awakening rays about me, *So long!*
Remember my words, I may again return,
I love you, I depart from materials,   70
I am as one disembodied, triumphant, dead.

From LEAVES OF GRASS

Drum-Taps and *Sequel*, 1865–1866

For the poet as well as for the nation he had hoped to tally in his
poems, the Civil War was a momentous crisis. It expressed his own
disunity, but it also provided the purgative experience by which the
poet re-integrated himself. Called to the battlefield at Fredericksburg
in search of his wounded brother George, Whitman learned first-
hand the horror of death and the glory of sacrifice. And remaining
to serve the wounded, Whitman found the vocation for his sympathy. His whole life was changed: he stayed on in Washington not
only to visit the soldiers in the hospitals but perhaps because it kept
him at the throbbing center of the nation. For the next eleven years
in fact, until his paralytic stroke in 1873, Washington was his city,
replacing the Brooklyn and Manhattan of his earlier years; and his
residence there undoubtedly strengthened his sense of being the
poet of the nation.

In *Drum-Taps*, Whitman covered the emotions of war, from the
righteous shock and patriotic upsurge in the city and the weariness
and slaughter of the battlefield to the reconciliation that came of
costly death and sacrificial love. The most important poem, however,
his great elegy on the death of Lincoln—on the death and resurrection of the nation—was printed in *Sequel*. "When Lilacs Last in the
Dooryard Bloom'd" recalls "Out of the Cradle Endlessly Rocking,"
not only in the themes of love and death, but in its management of
symbols and its symphonic and operatic techniques. Unlike the earlier
poem, however, we are able to see something of the genesis of the
lilac poem in the records Whitman left in *Specimen Days* and "Death
of Abraham Lincoln." For convenience, these materials precede the
poem.

CAVALRY CROSSING A FORD

A line in long array where they wind betwixt green islands,
They take a serpentine course, their arms flash in the sun—hark to the
    musical clank,
Behold the silvery river, in it the splashing horses loitering stop to
    drink,

Behold the brown-faced men, each group, each person a picture, the
    negligent rest on the saddles,
Some emerge on the opposite bank, others are just entering the ford—
    while,   5
Scarlet and blue and snowy white,
The guidon flags flutter gayly in the wind.

A SIGHT IN CAMP IN THE DAYBREAK GRAY AND DIM

A sight in camp in the daybreak gray and dim,
As from my tent I emerge so early sleepless,
As slow I walk in the cool fresh air the path near by the hospital tent,
Three forms I see on stretchers lying, brought out there untended
    lying,
Over each the blanket spread, ample brownish woolen blanket,   5
Gray and heavy blanket, folding, covering all.

Curious I halt and silent stand,
Then with light fingers I from the face of the nearest the first just lift
    the blanket;
Who are you elderly man so gaunt and grim, with well-gray'd hair,
    and flesh all sunken about the eyes?
Who are you my dear comrade?   10

Then to the second I step—and who are you my child and darling?
Who are you sweet boy with cheeks yet blooming?

Then to the third—a face nor child nor old, very calm, as of beautiful
    yellow-white ivory;
Young man I think I know you—I think this face is the face of the
    Christ himself,
Dead and divine and brother of all, and here again he lies.   15

AS TOILSOME I WANDER'D VIRGINIA'S WOODS

As toilsome I wander'd Virginia's woods,
To the music of rustling leaves kick'd by my feet, (for 'twas autumn,)
I mark'd at the foot of a tree the grave of a soldier;
Mortally wounded he and buried on the retreat, (easily all could I
    understand,)
The halt of a mid-day hour, when up! no time to lose—yet this sign
    left,   5
On a tablet scrawl'd and nail'd on the tree by the grave,
Bold, cautious, true, and my loving comrade.

Long, long I muse, then on my way go wandering,
Many a changeful season to follow, and many a scene of life,

Yet at times through changeful season and scene, abrupt, alone, or in
  the crowded street,   10
Comes before me the unknown soldier's grave, comes the inscription
  rude in Virginia's woods,
Bold, cautious, true, and my loving comrade.

The Wound-Dresser

1

An old man bending I come among new faces,
Years looking backward resuming in answer to children,
Come tell us old man, as from young men and maidens that love me,
(Arous'd and angry, I'd thought to beat the alarum, and urge relentless
  war,   4
But soon my fingers fail'd me, my face droop'd and I resign'd myself,
To sit by the wounded and soothe them, or silently watch the dead;)
Years hence of these scenes, of these furious passions, these chances,
Of unsurpass'd heroes, (was one side so brave? the other was equally
  brave;)
Now be witness again, paint the mightiest armies of earth,
Of those armies so rapid so wondrous what saw you to tell us?   10
What stays with you latest and deepest? of curious panics,
Of hard-fought engagements or sieges tremendous what deepest re-
  mains?

2

O maidens and young men I love and that love me,
What you ask of my days those the strangest and sudden your talk-
  ing recalls,   14
Soldier alert I arrive after a long march cover'd with sweat and dust,
In the nick of time I come, plunge in the fight, loudly shout in the
  rush of successful charge,
Enter the captur'd works—yet lo, like a swift-running river they fade,
Pass and are gone they fade—I dwell not on soldiers' perils or soldiers'
  joys,
(Both I remember well—many of the hardships, few the joys, yet I was
  content.)

But in silence, in dreams' projections,   20
While the world of gain and appearance and mirth goes on,
So soon what is over forgotten, and waves wash the imprints off the
  sand,
With hinged knees returning I enter the doors, (while for you up
  there,
Whoever you are, follow without noise and be of strong heart.)

Bearing the bandages, water and sponge,   25
Straight and swift to my wounded I go,

Where they lie on the ground after the battle brought in,
Where their priceless blood reddens the grass the ground,
Or to the rows of the hospital tent, or under the roof'd hospital,
To the long rows of cots up and down each side I return,   30
To each and all one after another I draw near, not one do I miss,
An attendant follows holding a tray, he carries a refuse pail,
Soon to be fill'd with clotted rags and blood, emptied, and fill'd again.

I onward go, I stop,
With hinged knees and steady hand to dress wounds,   35
I am firm with each, the pangs are sharp yet unavoidable,
One turns to me his appealing eyes—poor boy! I never knew you,
Yet I think I could not refuse this moment to die for you, if that
    would save you.

3

On, on I go, (open doors of time! open hospital doors!)
The crush'd head I dress, (poor crazed hand tear not the bandage
    away,)   40
The neck of the cavalry-man with the bullet through and through I
    examine,
Hard the breathing rattles, quite glazed already the eye, yet life strug-
    gles hard,
(Come sweet death! be persuaded O beautiful death!
In mercy come quickly.)

From the stump of the arm, the amputated hand,   45
I undo the clotted lint, remove the slough, wash off the matter and
    blood,
Back on his pillow the soldier bends with curv'd neck and side-falling
    head,
His eyes are closed, his face is pale, he dares not look on the bloody
    stump,
And has not yet look'd on it.

I dress a wound in the side, deep, deep,   50
But a day or two more, for see the frame all wasted and sinking,
And the yellow-blue countenance see.

I dress the perforated shoulder, the foot with the bullet-wound,
Cleanse the one with a gnawing and putrid gangrene, so sickening, so
    offensive,
While the attendant stands behind aside me holding the tray and pail.

I am faithful, I do not give out,   56
The fractur'd thigh, the knee, the wound in the abdomen,
These and more I dress with impassive hand, (yet deep in my breast a
    fire, a burning flame.)

4

Thus in silence in dreams' projections,
Returning, resuming, I thread my way through the hospitals,   60
The hurt and wounded I pacify with soothing hand,
I sit by the restless all the dark night, some are so young,
Some suffer so much, I recall the experience sweet and sad,
(Many a soldier's loving arms about this neck have cross'd and rested,
Many a soldier's kiss dwells on these bearded lips.)   65

PENSIVE ON HER DEAD GAZING

Pensive on her dead gazing I heard the Mother of All,
Desperate on the torn bodies, on the forms covering the battle-fields
    gazing,
(As the last gun ceased, but the scent of the powder-smoke linger'd,)
As she call'd to her earth with mournful voice while she stalk'd,
Absorb them well O my earth, she cried, I charge you lose not my
    sons, lose not an atom,   5
And you streams absorb them well, taking their dear blood,
And you local spots, and you airs that swim above lightly impalpable,
And all you essences of soil and growth, and you my rivers' depths,
And you mountain sides, and the woods where my dear children's
    blood trickling redden'd,
And you trees down in your roots to bequeath to all future trees,   10
My dead absorb or South or North—my young men's bodies absorb,
    and their precious precious blood,
Which holding in trust for me faithfully back again give me many a
    year hence,
In unseen essence and odor of surface and grass, centuries hence,
In blowing airs from the fields back again give me my darlings, give
    my immortal heroes,
Exhale me them centuries hence, breathe me their breath, let not an
    atom be lost,   15
O years and graves! O air and soil! O my dead, an aroma sweet!
Exhale them perennial sweet death, years, centuries hence.

From SPECIMEN DAYS

August 12th [1863]. I see the President almost every day, as I happen
to live where he passes to or from his lodging out of town. . . . I see very
plainly ABRAHAM LINCOLN'S dark brown face, with the deep-cut
lines, the eyes, always to me with a deep latent sadness in the expression.
We have got so that we exchange bows, and very cordial ones. . . .
None of the artists or pictures has caught the deep, though subtle and indirect expression of this man's face. There is something else there. . . .

March 4 [1865] [Lincoln's second inaugural]

. . . [Lincoln] look'd very much worn and tired; the lines, indeed, of vast responsibilities, intricate questions, and demands of life and death, cut deeper than ever upon his dark brown face; yet all the old goodness, tenderness, sadness, and canny shrewdness, underneath the furrows. (I never see that man without feeling that he is one to become personally attach'd to, for his combination of purest, heartiest tenderness, and native western form of manliness.). . . .

The Weather—Does It Sympathize with These Times?

Whether the rains, the heat and cold, and what underlies them all, are affected with what affects man in masses, and follow his play of passionate action, strain'd stronger than usual, and on a larger scale than usual—whether this, or no, it is certain that there is now, and has been for twenty months or more, on this American continent north, many a remarkable, many an unprecedented expression of the subtle world of air above us and around us. There, since this war, and the wide and deep national agitation, strange analogies, different combinations, a different sunlight, or absence of it; different products even out of the ground. After every great battle, a great storm. Even civic events the same. On Saturday last, a forenoon like whirling demons, dark, with slanting rain, full of rage; and then the afternoon, so calm, so bathed, with flooding splendor for heaven's most excellent sun, with atmosphere of sweetness; so clear, it show'd the stars, long, long before they were due. As the President came out on the capitol portico, a curious little white cloud, the only one in that part of the sky, appear'd like a hovering bird, right over him.

Indeed, the heavens, the elements, all the meteorological influences, have run riot for weeks past. Such caprices, abruptest alternations of frowns and beauty, I never knew. It is a common remark that (as last summer was different in its spells of intense heat from any preceding it,) the winter just completed has been without parallel. It has remain'd so down to the hour I am writing. Much of the daytime of the past month was sulky, with leaden heaviness, fog, interstices of bitter cold, and some insane storms. But there have been samples of another description. Nor earth nor sky ever knew spectacles of superber beauty than some of the nights lately here. The western star, Venus, in the earlier hours of evening, has never been so large, so clear; it seems as if it told something, as if it held rapport indulgent with humanity, with us Americans. Five or six nights since, it hung close by the moon, then a little past its first quarter. The star was wonderful, the moon like a young mother. The sky, dark blue, the transparent night, the planets, the moderate west wind, the elastic temperature, the miracle of that great star, and the young and swelling moon swimming in the west, suffused the soul. Then I heard, slow and clear, the deliberate notes of a bugle come up out of the silence, sounding so good through the night's mystery, no hurry, but firm and faithful, floating along, rising, falling leisurely, with here and there a long-drawn note; the bugle, well play'd, sounding tattoo, in one of the army hospitals near here, where the wounded (some of them personally so dear to me,) are lying in their cots, and many a sick boy come down to the war from Illinois, Michigan, Wisconsin, Iowa, and the rest.

Death of President Lincoln

April 16, '65.—I find in my notes of the time, this passage on the death of Abraham Lincoln: He leaves for America's history and biography, so far, not only its most dramatic reminiscence—he leaves, in my opinion, the greatest, best, most characteristic, artistic, moral personality. Not but that he had faults, and show'd them in the Presidency; but honesty, goodness, shrewdness, conscience, and (a new virtue, unknown to other lands, and hardly yet really known here, but the foundation and tie of all, as the future will grandly develop,) UNIONISM, in its truest and amplest sense, form'd the hardpan of his character. These he seal'd with his life. The tragic splendor of his death, purging, illuminating all, throws round his form, his head, an aureole that will remain and will grow brighter through time, while history lives, and love of country lasts. By many has this Union been help'd; but if one name, one man, must be pick'd out, he most of all, is the conservator of it, to the future. He was assassinated—but the Union is not assassinated—*ça ira!* One falls, and another falls. The soldier drops, sinks like a wave—but the ranks of the ocean eternally press on. Death does its work, obliterates a hundred, a thousand—President, general, captain, private, but the Nation is immortal.

From "Death of Abraham Lincoln"

The day, April 14, 1865, seems to have been a pleasant one throughout the whole land—the moral atmosphere pleasant too—the long storm, so dark, so fratricidal, full of blood and doubt and gloom, over and ended at last by the sun-rise of such an absolute National victory, and utter break-down of Secessionism—we almost doubted our own senses! Lee had capitulated beneath the apple-tree of Appomattox. The other armies, the flanges of the revolt, swiftly follow'd. And could it really be, then? Out of all the affairs of this world of woe and failure and disorder, was there really come the confirm'd, unerring sign of plan, like a shaft of pure light—of rightful rule—of God? So the day, as I say, was propitious. Early herbage, early flowers, were out. (I remember where I was stopping at the time, the season being advanced, there were many lilacs in full bloom. By one of those caprices that enter and give tinge to events without being at all a part of them, I find myself always reminded of the great tragedy of that day by the sight and odor of these blossoms. It never fails.)

When Lilacs Last in the Dooryard Bloom'd

Whitman was in Brooklyn when he heard the news of Lincoln's death. It is significant, as Professor Allen points out, that Whitman heard the news on the Saturday preceding Easter Sunday, and that when he returned to Washington on the following Monday the President's casket was banked with lilacs. Whitman, however, had used lilacs before, and perhaps they had associations for him, not only with the spring, but with his homecoming.

1

When lilacs last in the dooryard bloom'd,
And the great star early droop'd in the western sky in the night,
I mourn'd, and yet shall mourn with ever-returning spring.

Ever-returning spring, trinity sure to me you bring,
Lilac blooming perennial and drooping star in the west,   5
And thought of him I love.

2

O powerful western fallen star!
O shades of night—O moody, tearful night!
O great star disappear'd—O the black murk that hides the star!
O cruel hands that hold me powerless—O helpless soul of me!   10
O harsh surrounding cloud that will not free my soul.

3

In the dooryard fronting an old farm-house near the white-wash'd
  palings,
Stands the lilac-bush tall-growing with heart-shaped leaves of rich
  green,
With many a pointed blossom rising delicate, with the perfume strong
  I love,
With every leaf a miracle—and from this bush in the dooryard,   15
With delicate-color'd blossoms and heart-shaped leaves of rich green,
A sprig with its flower I break.

4

In the swamp in secluded recesses,
A shy and hidden bird is warbling a song.

Solitary the thrush,
The hermit withdrawn to himself, avoiding the settlements,   20
Sings by himself a song.

Song of the bleeding throat,
Death's outlet song of life, (for well dear brother I know,
If thou wast not granted to sing thou would'st surely die.)   25

5

ℓ Over the breast of the spring, the land, amid cities,
  Amid lanes and through old woods, where lately the violets peep'd
    from the ground, spotting the gray debris,
  Amid the grass in the fields each side of the lanes, passing the endless
    grass,
  Passing the yellow-spear'd wheat, every grain from its shroud in the
    dark-brown fields uprisen,
  Passing the apple-tree blows of white and pink in the orchards,   30
  Carrying a corpse to where it shall rest in the grave,
  Night and day journeys a coffin.

6

Coffin that passes through lanes and streets,
Through day and night with the great cloud darkening the land,
With the pomp of the inloop'd flags with the cities draped in black,
With the show of the states themselves as of crape-veil'd women
  standing,   36
With processions long and winding and the flambeaus of the night,
With the countless torches lit, with the silent sea of faces and the un-
  bared heads,
With the waiting depot, the arriving coffin, and the sombre faces,
With dirges through the night, with the thousand voices rising strong
  and solemn,   40
With all the mournful voices of the dirges pour'd around the coffin,
The dim-lit churches and the shuddering organs—where amid these
  you journey,
With the tolling bells' perpetual clang,
Here, coffin that slowly passes,
I give you my sprig of lilac.   45

7

(Nor for you, for one alone,
Blossoms and branches green to coffins all I bring,
For fresh as the morning, thus would I chant a song for you O sane
  and sacred death.

All over bouquets of roses,
O death, I cover you over with roses and early lilies,   50
But mostly and now the lilac that blooms the first,
Copious I break, I break the sprigs from the bushes,
With loaded arms I come, pouring for you,
For you and the coffins all of you O death.)

8

O western orb sailing the heaven,   55
Now I know what you must have meant as a month since I walk'd,
As I walk'd in silence the transparent shadowy night,

As I saw you had something to tell as you bent to me night after night,
As you droop'd from the sky low down as if to my side, (while the
other stars all look'd on,)
As we wander'd together the solemn night, (for something I know not
what kept me from sleep,)   60
As the night advanced, and I saw on the rim of the west how full you
were of woe,
As I stood on the rising ground in the breeze in the cool transparent
night,
As I watch'd where you pass'd and was lost in the netherward black
of the night,
As my soul in its trouble dissatisfied sank, as where you sad orb,
Concluded, dropt in the night, and was gone.   65

9

Sing on there in the swamp,
O singer bashful and tender, I hear your notes, I hear your call,
I hear, I come presently, I understand you,
But a moment I linger, for the lustrous star has detain'd me,
The star my departing comrade holds and detains me.   70

10

O how shall I warble myself for the dead one there I loved?
And how shall I deck my song for the large sweet soul that has gone?
And what shall my perfume be for the grave of him I love?

Sea-winds blown from east and west,
Blown from the Eastern sea and blown from the Western sea, till there
on the prairies meeting,   75
These and with these and the breath of my chant,
I'll perfume the grave of him I love.

11

O what shall I hang on the chamber walls?
And what shall the pictures be that I hang on the walls,
To adorn the burial-house of him I love?   80

Pictures of growing spring and farms and homes,
With the Fourth-month eve at sundown, and the gray smoke lucid and
bright,
With floods of the yellow gold of the gorgeous, indolent, sinking sun,
burning, expanding the air,
With the fresh sweet herbage under foot, and the pale green leaves of
the trees prolific,
In the distance the flowing glaze, the breast of the river, with a wind-
dapple here and there,   85
With ranging hills on the banks, with many a line against the sky, and
shadows,

And the city at hand with dwellings so dense, and stacks of chimneys,
And all the scenes of life and the workshops, and the workmen home-
    ward returning.

12

Lo, body and soul—this land,
My own Manhattan with spires, and the sparkling and hurrying tides,
    and the ships,   90
The varied and ample land, the South and the North in the light,
    Ohio's shores and flashing Missouri,
And ever the far-spreading prairies cover'd with grass and corn.

Lo, the most excellent sun so calm and haughty,
The violet and purple morn with just-felt breezes,
The gentle soft-born measureless light,   95
The miracle spreading bathing all, the fulfill'd noon,
The coming eve delicious, the welcome night and the stars,
Over my cities shining all, enveloping man and land.

13

Sing on, sing on you gray-brown bird,
Sing from the swamps, the recesses, pour your chant from the bushes,
Limitless out of the dusk, out of the cedars and pines.   101

Sing on dearest brother, warble your reedy song,
Loud human song, with voice of uttermost woe.

O liquid and free and tender!
O wild and loose to my soul—O wondrous singer!   105
You only I hear—yet the star holds me, (but will soon depart,)
Yet the lilac with mastering odor holds me.

14

Now while I sat in the day and look'd forth,
In the close of the day with its light and the fields of spring, and the
    farmers preparing their crops,
In the large unconscious scenery of my land with its lakes and forests,
In the heavenly aerial beauty, (after the perturb'd winds and the
    storms,)   111
Under the arching heavens of the afternoon swift passing, and the
    voices of children and women,
The many-moving sea-tides, and I saw the ships how they sail'd,
And the summer approaching with richness, and the fields all busy
    with labor,
And the infinite separate houses, how they all went on, each with its
    meals and minutia of daily usages,   115
And the streets how their throbbings throbb'd, and the cities pent—
    lo, then and there,

Falling upon them all and among them all, enveloping me with the
rest,
Appear'd the cloud, appear'd the long black trail,
And I knew death, its thought, and the sacred knowledge of death.

Then with the knowledge of death as walking one side of me,   120
And the thought of death close-walking the other side of me,
And I in the middle as with companions, and as holding the hands of
companions,
I fled forth to the hiding receiving night that talks not,
Down to the shores of the water, the path by the swamp in the dim-
ness,
To the solemn shadowy cedars and ghostly pines so still.   125

And the singer so shy to the rest receiv'd me,
The gray-brown bird I know receiv'd us comrades three,
And he sang the carol of death, and a verse for him I love.

From deep secluded recesses,
From the fragrant cedars and the ghostly pines so still,   130
Came the carol of the bird.

And the charm of the carol rapt me,
As I held as if by their hands my comrades in the night,
And the voice of my spirit tallied the song of the bird.

Come lovely and soothing death,   135
Undulate round the world, serenely arriving, arriving,
In the day, in the night, to all, to each,
Sooner or later delicate death.

Prais'd be the fathomless universe,
For life and joy, and for objects and knowledge curious,   140
And for love, sweet love—but praise! praise! praise!
For the sure-enwinding arms of cool-enfolding death.

Dark mother always gliding near with soft feet,
Have none chanted for thee a chant of fullest welcome?
Then I chant it for thee, I glorify thee above all,   145
I bring thee a song that when thou must indeed come, come unfalter-
ingly.

Approach strong deliveress,
When it is so, when thou hast taken them, I joyously sing the dead,
Lost in the loving floating ocean of thee,
Laved in the flood of thy bliss O death.   150

From me to thee glad serenades,
Dances for thee I propose saluting thee, adornments and feastings for
thee,

*And the sights of the open landscape and the high-spread sky are fit-
   ting,*
And life and the fields, and the huge and thoughtful night.

The night in silence under many a star,   155
The ocean shore and the husky whispering wave whose voice I know,
And the soul turning to thee O vast and well-veil'd death,
And the body gratefully nestling close to thee.

Over the tree-tops I float thee a song,
*Over the rising and sinking waves, over the myriad fields and the
   prairies wide,*   160
Over the dense-pack'd cities all and the teeming wharves and ways,
I float this carol with joy, with joy to thee O death.

15

To the tally of my soul,
Loud and strong kept up the gray-brown bird,
With pure deliberate notes spreading filling the night.   165

Loud in the pines and cedars dim,
Clear in the freshness moist and swamp-perfume,
And I with my comrades there in the night.

While my sight that was bound in my eyes unclosed,
As to long panoramas of visions.   170

And I saw askant the armies,
I saw as in noiseless dreams hundreds of battle-flags,
Borne through the smoke of the battles and pierc'd with missiles I saw
   them,
And carried hither and yon through the smoke, and torn and bloody,
And at last but a few shreds left on the staffs, (and all in silence,)   175
And the staffs all splinter'd and broken.

I saw battle-corpses, myriads of them,
And the white skeletons of young men, I saw them,
I saw the debris and debris of all the slain soldiers of the war,
But I saw they were not as was thought,   180
They themselves were fully at rest, they suffer'd not,
The living remain'd and suffer'd, the mother suffer'd,
And the wife and the child and the musing comrades suffer'd,
And the armies that remain'd suffer'd.

16

Passing the visions, passing the night,   185
Passing, unloosing the hold of my comrades' hands,
Passing the song of the hermit bird and the tallying song of my soul,

Victorious song, death's outlet song, yet varying ever-altering song,
As low and wailing, yet clear the notes, rising and falling, flooding the
 night,
Sadly sinking and fainting, as warning and warning, and yet again
 bursting with joy,   190
Covering the earth and filling the spread of the heaven,
As that powerful psalm in the night I heard from recesses,
Passing, I leave the lilac with heart-shaped leaves,
I leave thee there in the door-yard, blooming, returning with spring.

I cease from my song for thee,   195
From my gaze on thee in the west, fronting the west, communing
 with thee,
O comrade lustrous with silver face in the night.

Yet each to keep and all, retrievements out of the night,
The song, the wondrous chant of the gray-brown bird,
And the tallying chant, the echo arous'd in my soul,   200
With the lustrous and drooping star with the countenance full of woe,
With the holders holding my hand hearing the call of the bird,
Comrades mine and I in the midst, and their memory ever to keep,
 for the dead I loved so well,
For the sweetest, wisest soul of all my days and lands—and this for his
 dear sake,
Lilac and star and bird twined with the chant of my soul, 205
There in the fragrant pines and the cedars dusk and dim.

CHANTING THE SQUARE DEIFIC

1

Chanting the square deific, out of the One advancing, out of the sides,
Out of the old and new, out of the square entirely divine,
Solid, four-sided, (all the sides needed,) from this side Jehovah am I,
Old Brahm I, and I Saturnius am;
Not Time affects me—I am Time, old, modern as any,   5
Unpersuadable, relentless, executing righteous judgments,
As the Earth, the Father, the brown old Kronos, with laws,
Aged beyond computation, yet ever new, ever with those mighty laws
 rolling,
Relentless I forgive no man—whoever sins dies—I will have that man's
 life;
Therefore let none expect mercy—have the seasons, gravitation, the
 appointed days, mercy? no more have I,   10
But as the seasons and gravitation, and as all the appointed days that
 forgive not,
I dispense from this side judgments inexorable without the least re-
 morse.

2

Consolator most mild, the promis'd one advancing,
With gentle hand extended, the mightier God am I,
Foretold by prophets and poets in their most rapt prophecies and
poems,   15
From this side, lo! the Lord Christ gazes—lo! Hermes—I—lo! mine is
Hercules' face,
All sorrow, labor, suffering, I, tallying it, absorb in myself,
Many times have I been rejected, taunted, put in prison, and crucified,
and many times shall be again,
All the world have I given up for my dear brothers' and sisters' sake,
for the soul's sake,
Wending my way through the homes of men, rich or poor, with the
kiss of affection,   20
For I am affection, I am the cheer-bringing God, with hope and all en-
closing charity,
With indulgent words as to children, with fresh and sane words, mine
only,
Young and strong I pass knowing well I am destin'd myself to an early
death;
But my charity has no death—my wisdom dies not, neither early nor
late,
And my sweet love bequeath'd here and elsewhere never dies.   5

3

Aloof, dissatisfied, plotting revolt,
Comrade of criminals, brother of slaves,
Crafty, despised, a drudge, ignorant,
With sudra face and worn brow, black, but in the depths of my heart,
proud as any,   29
Lifted now and always against whoever scorning assumes to rule me,
Morose, full of guile, full of reminiscences, brooding, with many wiles,
(Though it was thought I was baffled and dispel'd, and my wiles done,
but that will never be,)
Defiant, I, Satan, still live, still utter words, in new lands duly appear-
ing, (and old ones also,)
Permanent here from my side, warlike, equal with any, real as any,
Nor time nor change shall ever change me or my words.   35

4

Santa Spirita, breather, life,
Beyond the light, lighter than light,
Beyond the flames of hell, joyous, leaping easily above hell,
Beyond Paradise, perfumed solely with mine own perfume,
Including all life on earth, touching, including God, including Saviour
and Satan,   40
Ethereal, pervading all, (for without me what were all? what were
God?)

Essence of forms, life of the real identities, permanent, positive,
(namely the unseen,)
Life of the great round world, the sun and stars, and of man, I, the
general soul,
Here the square finishing, the solid, I, the most solid,
Breathe my breath also through these songs.   45

When I Heard the Learn'd Astronomer

When I heard the learn'd astronomer,
When the proofs, the figures, were ranged in columns before me,
When I was shown the charts and diagrams, to add, divide, and meas-
ure them,
When I sitting heard the astronomer where he lectured with much ap-
plause in the lecture-room,
How soon unaccountable I became tired and sick,   5
Till rising and gliding out I wander'd off by myself,
In the mystical moist night-air, and from time to time,
Look'd up in perfect silence at the stars.

From LEAVES OF GRASS

Fifth Edition, 1871–1872

This edition, with its "Passage to India" supplement and the group
of poems called "Whispers of Heavenly Death," turned *Leaves of
Grass* in a new direction. For, though "Passage to India" commemo-
rated the physical unification of the world, it also opened up a "Passage to more than India"—a passage to the secret of nature, which
Whitman now announced he was ready to make on the unknown seas
of "Time and Space and Death." The sounds he heard in "Proud
Music of the Storm" told him of "The journey done, the journeyman
come home,/And man and art with Nature fused again," and taught
him that now his work was to write "Poems bridging the way from
Life to Death."

Passage to India

1

Singing my days,
Singing the great achievements of the present,
Singing the strong light works of engineers,
Our modern wonders, (the antique ponderous Seven outvied,)
In the Old World the east the Suez canal,   5
The New by its mighty railroad spann'd,

The seas inlaid with eloquent gentle wires;
Yet first to sound, and ever sound, the cry with thee O soul,
The Past! the Past! the Past!

The Past—the dark unfathom'd retrospect!   10
The teeming gulf—the sleepers and the shadows!
The past—the infinite greatness of the past!
For what is the present after all but a growth out of the past?
(As a projectile form'd, impell'd, passing a certain line, still keeps on,
So the present, utterly form'd, impell'd by the past.)   15

2

Passage O soul to India!
Eclaircise the myths Asiatic, the primitive fables.

Not you alone proud truths of the world,
Nor you alone ye facts of modern science,
But myths and fables of eld, Asia's, Africa's fables,   20
The far-darting beams of the spirit, the unloos'd dreams,
The deep diving bibles and legends,
The daring plots of the poets, the elder religions;
O you temples fairer than lilies pour'd over by the rising sun!
O you fables spurning the known, eluding the hold of the known,
     mounting to heaven!   25
You lofty and dazzling towers, pinnacled, red as roses, burnish'd with
     gold!
Towers of fables immortal fashion'd from mortal dreams!
You too I welcome and fully the same as the rest!
You too with joy I sing.

Passage to India!   30
Lo, soul, seest thou not God's purpose from the first?
The earth to be spann'd, connected by network,
The races, neighbors, to marry and be given in marriage,
The oceans to be cross'd, the distant brought near,
The lands to be welded together.   35

A worship new I sing,
You captains, voyagers, explorers, yours,
You engineers, you architects, machinists, yours,
You, not for trade or transportation only,
But in God's name, and for thy sake O soul.   40

3

Passage to India!
Lo soul for thee of tableaus twain,
I see in one the Suez canal initiated, open'd,

I see the procession of steamships, the Empress Eugenie's leading the
  van,
I mark from on deck the strange landscape, the pure sky, the level
  sand in the distance,   45
I pass swiftly the picturesque groups, the workmen gather'd,
The gigantic dredging machines.

In one again, different, (yet thine, all thine, O soul, the same,)
I see over my own continent the Pacific railroad surmounting every
  barrier,
I see continual trains of cars winding along the Platte carrying freight
  and passengers,   50
I hear the locomotives rushing and roaring, and the shrill steam-
  whistle,
I hear the echoes reverberate through the grandest scenery in the
  world,
I cross the Laramie plains, I note the rocks in grotesque shapes, the
  buttes,
I see the plentiful larkspur and wild onions, the barren, colorless, sage-
  deserts
I see in glimpses afar or towering immediately above me the great
  mountains, I see the Wind river and the Wahsatch mountains,   55
I see the Monument mountain and the Eagle's Nest, I pass the Prom-
  ontory, I ascend the Nevadas,
I scan the noble Elk mountain and wind around its base,
I see the Humboldt range, I thread the valley and cross the river,
I see the clear waters of lake Tahoe, I see forests of majestic pines,
Or crossing the great desert, the alkaline plains, I behold enchanting
  mirages of waters and meadows,   60
Marking through these and after all, in duplicate slender lines,
Bridging the three or four thousand miles of land travel,
Tying the Eastern to the Western sea,
The road between Europe and Asia.

(Ah Genoese thy dream! thy dream!   65
Centuries after thou art laid in thy grave,
The shore thou foundest verifies thy dream.)

4

Passage to India!
Struggles of many a captain, tales of many a sailor dead,
Over my mood stealing and spreading they come,   70
Like clouds and cloudlets in the unreach'd sky.

Along all history, down the slopes,
As a rivulet running, sinking now, and now again to the surface rising,
A ceaseless thought, a varied train—lo, soul, to thee, thy sight, they rise,
The plans, the voyages again, the expeditions;   75

Again Vasco de Gama sails forth,
Again the knowledge gain'd, the mariner's compass,
Lands found and nations born, thou born America,
For purpose vast, man's long probation fill'd,
Thou rondure of the world at last accomplish'd.   80

5

O vast Rondure, swimming in space,
Cover'd all over with visible power and beauty,
Alternate light and day and the teeming spiritual darkness,
Unspeakable high processions of sun and moon and countless stars
      above,
Below, the manifold grass and waters, animals, mountains, trees,   85
With inscrutable purpose, some hidden prophetic intention,
Now first it seems my thought begins to span thee.

Down from the gardens of Asia descending radiating,
Adam and Eve appear, then their myriad progeny after them,
Wandering, yearning, curious, with restless explorations,   90
With questionings, baffled, formless, feverish, with never-happy hearts,
With that sad incessant refrain, *Wherefore unsatisfied soul?* and
      Whither O mocking life?

Ah who shall soothe these feverish children?
Who justify these restless explorations?
Who speak the secret of impassive earth?   95
Who bind it to us? what is this separate Nature so unnatural?
What is this earth to our affections? (unloving earth, without a throb
      to answer ours,
Cold earth, the place of graves.)

Yet soul be sure the first intent remains, and shall be carried out,
Perhaps even now the time has arrived.   100

After the seas are all cross'd, (as they seem already cross'd,)
After the great captains and engineers have accomplish'd their work,
After the noble inventors, after the scientists, the chemist, the geol-
      ogist, ethnologist,
Finally shall come the poet worthy of that name,
The true son of God shall come singing his songs.   105

Then not your deeds only O voyagers, O scientists and inventors, shall
      be justified,
All these hearts as of fretted children shall be sooth'd,
All affection shall be fully responded to, the secret shall be told,
All these separations and gaps shall be taken up and hook'd and link'd
      together,

The whole earth, this cold, impassive, voiceless earth, shall be completely justified, 110
Trinitas divine shall be gloriously accomplish'd and compacted by the true son of God, the poet,
(He shall indeed pass the straits and conquer the mountains,
He shall double the cape of Good Hope to some purpose,)
Nature and Man shall be disjoin'd and diffused no more,
The true son of God shall absolutely fuse them. 115

6

Year at whose wide-flung door I sing!
Year of the purpose accomplish'd!
Year of the marriage of continents, climates and oceans!
(No mere doge of Venice now wedding the Adriatic,)
I see O year in you the vast terraqueous globe given and given all,
Europe to Asia, Africa join'd, and they to the New World, 121
The lands, geographies, dancing before you, holding a festival garland,
As brides and bridegrooms hand in hand.

Passage to India!
Cooling airs from Caucasus, far, soothing cradle of man, 125
The river Euphrates flowing, the past lit up again.

Lo soul, the retrospect brought forward,
The old, most populous, wealthiest of earth's lands,
The streams of the Indus and the Ganges and their many affluents,
(I my shores of America walking to-day behold, resuming all,) 130
The tale of Alexander on his warlike marches suddenly dying,
On one side China and on the other Persia and Arabia,
To the south the great seas and the bay of Bengal,
The flowing literatures, tremendous epics, religions, castes,
Old occult Brahma interminably far back, the tender and junior Buddha, 135
Central and southern empires and all their belongings, possessors,
The wars of Tamerlane, the reign of Aurungzebe,
The traders, rulers, explorers, Moslems, Venetians, Byzantium, the Arabs, Portuguese,
The first travelers famous yet, Marco Polo, Patouta, the Moor,
Doubts to be solv'd, the map incognita, blanks to be fill'd, 140
The foot of man unstay'd, the hands never at rest,
Thyself O soul that will not brook a challenge.

The mediæval navigators rise before me,
The world of 1492, with its awaken'd enterprise,
Something swelling in humanity now like the sap of the earth in spring, 145
The sunset splendor of chivalry declining.

And who art thou sad shade?
Gigantic, visionary, thyself a visionary,
With majestic limbs and pious beaming eyes,
Spreading around with every look of thine a golden world, 150
Enhuing it with gorgeous hues.

As the chief histrion,
Down to the footlights walks in some great scena,
Dominating the rest I see the Admiral himself,
(History's type of courage, action, faith,) 155
Behold him sail from Palos leading his little fleet,
His voyage behold, his return, his great fame,
His misfortunes, calumniators, behold him a prisoner, chain'd,
Behold his dejection, poverty, death.

(Curious in time I stand, noting the efforts of heroes, 160
Is the deferment long? bitter the slander, poverty, death?
Lies the seed unreck'd for centuries in the ground? lo, to God's due
    occasion,
Uprising in the night, it sprouts, blooms,
And fills the earth with use and beauty.)

                              7

Passage indeed O soul to primal thought, 165
Not lands and seas alone, thy own clear freshness,
The young maturity of brood and bloom,
To realms of budding bibles.

O soul, repressless, I with thee and thou with me,
Thy circumnavigation of the world begin, 170
Of man, the voyage of his mind's return,
To reason's early paradise,
Back, back to wisdom's birth, to innocent intuitions,
Again with fair creation.

                              8

O we can wait no longer, 175
We too take ship O soul,
Joyous we too launch out on trackless seas,
Fearless for unknown shores on waves of ecstasy to sail,
Amid the wafting winds, (thou pressing me to thee, I thee to me, O
    soul,)
Caroling free, singing our song of God, 180
Chanting our chant of pleasant exploration.

With laugh and many a kiss,
(Let others deprecate, let others weep for sin, remorse, humiliation,)
O soul thou pleasest me, I thee.

Ah more than any priest O soul we too believe in God,   185
But with the mystery of God we dare not dally.

O soul thou pleasest me, I thee,
Sailing these seas or on the hills, or waking in the night,
Thoughts, silent thoughts, of Time and Space and Death, like waters
    flowing,
Bear me indeed as through the regions infinite,   190
Whose air I breathe, whose ripples hear, lave me all over,
Bathe me O God in thee, mounting to thee,
I and my soul to range in range of thee.

O Thou transcendent,
Nameless, the fibre and the breath,   195
Light of the light, shedding forth universes, thou centre of them,
Thou mightier centre of the true, the good, the loving,
Thou moral, spiritual fountain—affection's source—thou reservoir,
(O pensive soul of me—O thirst unsatisfied—waitest not there?
Waitest not haply for us somewhere there the Comrade perfect?)
Thou pulse—thou motive of the stars, suns, systems,   201
That, circling, move in order, safe, harmonious,
Athwart the shapeless vastnesses of space,
How should I think, how breathe a single breath, how speak, if out
    of myself,
I could not launch, to those, superior universes?   205

Swiftly I shrivel at the thought of God,
At Nature and its wonders, Time and Space and Death,
But that I, turning, call to thee O soul, thou actual Me,
And lo, thou gently masterest the orbs,
Thou matest Time, smilest content at Death,   210
And fillest, swellest full the vastnesses of Space.

Greater than stars or suns,
Bounding O soul thou journeyest forth;
What love than thine and ours could wider amplify?
What aspirations, wishes, outvie thine and ours O soul?   215
What dreams of the ideal? what plans of purity, perfection, strength,
What cheerful willingness for others' sake to give up all?
For others' sake to suffer all?

Reckoning ahead O soul, when thou, the time achiev'd,
The seas all cross'd, weather'd the capes, the voyage done,   220
Surrounded, copest, frontest God, yieldest, the aim attain'd,
As fill'd with friendship, love complete, the Elder Brother found,
The Younger melts in fondness in his arms.

9

Passage to more than India!
Are thy wings plumed indeed for such far flights?   225
O soul, voyagest thou indeed on voyages like those?
Disportest thou on waters such as those?
Soundest below the Sanscrit and the Vedas?
Then have thy bent unleash'd.

Passage to you, your shores, ye aged fierce enigmas!   230
Passage to you, to mastership of you, ye strangling problems!
You, strew'd with the wrecks of skeletons, that, living, never reach'd
      you.

Passage to more than India!
O secret of the earth and sky!
Of you O waters of the sea! O winding creeks and rivers!   235
Of you O woods and fields! of you strong mountains of my land!
Of you O prairies! of you gray rocks!
O morning red! O clouds! O rain and snows!
O day and night, passage to you!

O sun and moon and all you stars! Sirius and Jupiter!   240
Passage to you!

Passage, immediate passage! the blood burns in my veins!
Away O soul! hoist instantly the anchor!
Cut the hawsers—haul out—shake out every sail!
Have we not stood here like trees in the ground long enough?   245
Have we not grovel'd here long enough, eating and drinking like mere
      brutes?
Have we not darken'd and dazed ourselves with books long enough?

Sail forth—steer for the deep waters only,
Reckless O soul, exploring, I with thee, and thou with me,
For we are bound where mariner has not yet dared to go,   250
And we will risk the ship, ourselves and all.

O my brave soul!
O farther farther sail!
O daring joy, but safe! are they not all the seas of God?
O farther, farther, farther sail!   255

PROUD MUSIC OF THE STORM

I

Proud music of the storm,
Blast that careers so free, whistling across the prairies,
Strong hum of forest tree-tops—wind of the mountains,

Personified dim shapes—you hidden orchestras,
You serenades of phantoms with instruments alert,   5
Bending with Nature's rhythmus all the tongues of nations;
You chords left as by vast composers—you choruses,
You formless, free, religious dances—you from the Orient,
You undertone of rivers, roar of pouring cataracts,
You sounds from distant guns with galloping cavalry,   10
Echoes of camps with all the different bugle-calls,
Trooping tumultuous, filling the midnight late, bending me powerless,
Entering my lonesome slumber-chamber, why have you seiz'd me?

2

Come forward O my soul, and let the rest retire,
Listen, lose not, it is toward thee they tend,   15
Parting the midnight, entering my slumber-chamber,
For thee they sing and dance O soul.

A festival song,
The duet of the bridegroom and the bride, a marriage-march,
With lips of love, and hearts of lovers fill'd to the brim with love,   20
The red-flush'd cheeks and perfumes, the cortege swarming full of
     friendly faces young and old,
To flutes' clear notes and sounding harps' cantabile.

Now loud approaching drums,
Victoria! see'st thou in powder-smoke the banners torn but flying? the
     rout of the baffled?
Hearest those shouts of a conquering army?   25

(Ah soul, the sobs of women, the wounded groaning in agony,
The hiss and crackle of flames, the blacken'd ruins, the embers of
     cities,
The dirge and desolation of mankind.)

Now airs antique and mediæval fill me,
I see and hear old harpers with their harps at Welsh festivals,   30
I hear the minnesingers singing their lays of love,
I hear the minstrels, gleemen, troubadours, of the middle ages.

Now the great organ sounds,
Tremulous, while underneath, (as the hid footholds of the earth,
On which arising rest, and leaping forth depend,   35
All shapes of beauty, grace and strength, all hues we know,
Green blades of grass and warbling birds, children that gambol and
     play, the clouds of heaven above,)
The strong base stands, and its pulsations intermits not,
Bathing, supporting, merging all the rest, maternity of all the rest,
And with it every instrument in multitudes,   40

The players playing, all the world's musicians,
The solemn hymns and masses rousing adoration,
All passionate heart-chants, sorrowful appeals,
The measureless sweet vocalists of ages,
And for their solvent setting earth's own diapason,   45
Of winds and woods and mighty ocean waves,
A new composite orchestra, binder of years and climes, ten-fold re-
    newer,
As of the far-back days the poets tell, the Paradiso,
The straying thence, the separation long, but now the wandering done,
The journey done, the journeyman come home,   50
And man and art with Nature fused again.

Tutti! for earth and heaven;
(The Almighty leader now for once has signal'd with his wand.)

The manly strophe of the husbands of the world,
And all the wives responding.   55

The tongues of violins,
(I think O tongues ye tell this heart, that cannot tell itself,
This brooding yearning heart, that cannot tell itself.)

3

Ah from a little child,
Thou knowest soul how to me all sounds became music,   60
My mother's voice in lullaby or hymn,
(The voice, O tender voices, memory's loving voices,
Last miracle of all, O dearest mother's, sister's, voices;)
The rain, the growing corn, the breeze among the long-leav'd corn,
The measur'd sea-surf beating on the sand,   65
The twittering bird, the hawk's sharp scream,
The wild-fowl's notes at night as flying low migrating north or south,
The psalm in the country church or mid the clustering trees, the open
    air camp-meeting,
The fiddler in the tavern, the glee, the long-strung sailor-song,
The lowing cattle, bleating sheep, the crowing cock at dawn.   70

All songs of current lands come sounding round me,
The German airs of friendship, wine and love,
Irish ballads, merry jigs and dances, English warbles,
Chansons of France, Scotch tunes, and o'er the rest,
Italia's peerless compositions.   75

Across the stage with pallor on her face, yet lurid passion,
Stalks Norma brandishing the dagger in her hand.

I see poor crazed Lucia's eyes' unnatural gleam,
Her hair down her back falls loose and dishevel'd.

I see where Ernani walking the bridal garden,   80
Amid the scent of night-roses, radiant, holding his bride by the hand,
Hears the infernal call, the death-pledge of the horn.

To crossing swords and gray hairs bared to heaven,
The clear electric base and baritone of the world,
The trombone duo, Libertad forever!   85

From Spanish chestnut trees' dense shade,
By old and heavy convent walls a wailing song,
Song of lost love, the torch of youth and life quench'd in despair,
Song of the dying swan, Fernando's heart is breaking.

Awaking from her woes at last retriev'd Amina sings,   90
Copious as stars and glad as morning light the torrents of her joy.

(The teeming lady comes,
The lustrous orb, Venus contralto, the blooming mother,
Sister of loftiest gods, Alboni's self I hear.)

4

I hear those odes, symphonies, operas,   95
I hear in the *William Tell* the music of an arous'd and angry people,
I hear Meyerbeer's *Huguenots*, the *Prophet*, or *Robert*,
Gounod's *Faust*, or Mozart's *Don Juan*.

I hear the dance-music of all nations,
The waltz, some delicious measure, lapsing, bathing me in bliss,   100
The bolero to tinkling guitars and clattering castanets.

I see religious dances old and new,
I hear the sound of the Hebrew lyre,
I see the crusaders marching bearing the cross on high, to the martial
    clang of cymbals,
I hear dervishes monotonously chanting, interspers'd with frantic
    shouts, as they spin around turning always towards Mecca,   105
I see the rapt religious dances of the Persians and the Arabs,
Again, at Eleusis, home of Ceres, I see the modern Greeks dancing,
I hear them clapping their hands as they bend their bodies,
I hear the metrical shuffling of their feet.

I see again the wild old Corybantian dance, the performers wounding
    each other,   110
I see the Roman youth to the shrill sound of flageolets throwing and
    catching their weapons,
As they fall on their knees and rise again.

I hear from the Mussulman mosque the muezzin calling,
I see the worshippers within, nor form nor sermon, argument nor
    word,
But silent, strange, devout, rais'd, glowing heads, ecstatic faces.   115

I hear the Egyptian harp of many strings,
The primitive chants of the Nile boatmen,
The sacred imperial hymns of China,
To the delicate sounds of the king, (the stricken wood and stone,)
Or to Hindu flutes and the fretting twang of the vina,   120
A band of bayaderes.

5

Now Asia, Africa leave me, Europe seizing inflates me,
To organs huge and bands I hear as from vast concourses of voices,
Luther's strong hymn *Eine feste Burg ist unser Gott*,
Rossini's *Stabat Mater dolorosa*,   125
Or floating in some high cathedral dim with gorgeous color'd win-
    dows,
The passionate *Agnus Dei* or *Gloria in Excelsis*.

Composers! mighty maestros!
And you, sweet singers of old lands, soprani, tenori, bassi!
To you a new bard caroling in the West,   130
Obeisant sends his love.

(Such led to thee O soul,
All senses, shows and objects, lead to thee,
But now it seems to me sound leads o'er all the rest.)

I hear the annual singing of the children in St. Paul's cathedral,   135
Or, under the high roof of some colossal hall, the symphonies, ora-
    torios of Beethoven, Handel, or Haydn,
The *Creation* in billows of godhood laves me.

Give me to hold all sounds, (I madly struggling cry,)
Fill me with all the voices of the universe,
Endow me with their throbbings, Nature's also,   140
The tempests, waters, winds, operas and chants, marches and dances,
Utter, pour in, for I would take them all!

6

Then I woke softly,
And pausing, questioning awhile the music of my dream,
And questioning all those reminiscences, the tempest in its fury,   145
And all the songs of sopranos and tenors,
And those rapt oriental dances of religious fervor,
And the sweet varied instruments, and the diapason of organs,

And all the artless plaints of love and grief and death,
I said to my silent curious soul out of the bed of the slumber-chamber,
Come, for I have found the clew I sought so long,   151
Let us go forth refresh'd amid the day,
Cheerfully tallying life, walking the world, the real,
Nourish'd henceforth by our celestial dream.

And I said, moreover,   155
Haply what thou hast heard O soul was not the sound of winds,
Nor dream of raging storm, nor sea-hawk's flapping wings nor harsh
     scream,
Nor vocalism of sun-bright Italy,
Nor German organ majestic, nor vast concourse of voices, nor layers
     of harmonies,   160
Nor strophes of husbands and wives, nor sound of marching soldiers,
Nor flutes, nor harps, nor the bugle-calls of camps,
But to a new rhythmus fitted for thee,
Poems bridging the way from Life to Death, vaguely wafted in night
     air, uncaught, unwritten,
Which let us go forth in the bold day and write.   165

WHISPERS OF HEAVENLY DEATH

Whispers of heavenly death murmur'd I hear,
Labial gossip of night, sibilant chorals,
Footsteps gently ascending, mystical breezes wafted soft and low,
Ripples of unseen rivers, tides of a current flowing, forever flowing,
(Or is it the plashing of tears? the measureless waters of human
     tears?)   5

I see, just see skyward, great cloud-masses,
Mournfully slowly they roll, silently swelling and mixing,
With at times a half-dimm'd sadden'd far-off star,
Appearing and disappearing.

(Some parturition rather, some solemn immortal birth;   10
On the frontiers to eyes impenetrable,
Some soul is passing over.)

ON THE BEACH AT NIGHT

On the beach at night,
Stands a child with her father,
Watching the east, the autumn sky.

Up through the darkness,
While ravening clouds, the burial clouds, in black masses spreading,   5
Lower sullen and fast athwart and down the sky,

Amid a transparent clear belt of ether yet left in the east,
Ascends large and calm the lord-star Jupiter,
And nigh at hand, only a very little above,
Swim the delicate sisters the Pleiades.   10

From the beach the child holding the hand of her father,
Those burial clouds that lower victorious soon to devour all,
Watching, silently weeps.

Weep not, child,
Weep not, my darling,   15
With these kisses let me remove your tears,
The ravening clouds shall not long be victorious,
They shall not long possess the sky, they devour the stars only in ap-
    parition,
Jupiter shall emerge, be patient, watch again another night, the Plei-
    ades shall emerge,
They are immortal, all those stars both silvery and golden shall shine
    out again,   20
The great stars and the little ones shall shine out again, they endure,
The vast immortal suns and the long-enduring pensive moons shall
    again shine.

Then dearest child mournest thou only for Jupiter?
Considerest thou alone the burial of the stars?

Something there is,   25
(With my lips soothing thee, adding I whisper,
I give thee the first suggestion, the problem and indirection,)
Something there is more immortal even than the stars,
(Many the burials, many the days and nights, passing away,)
Something that shall endure longer even than lustrous Jupiter,   30
Longer than sun or any revolving satellite,
Or the radiant sisters the Pleiades.

A Noiseless Patient Spider

A noiseless patient spider,
I mark'd where on a little promontory it stood isolated,
Mark'd how to explore the vacant vast surrounding,
It launch'd forth filament, filament, filament, out of itself,
Ever unreeling them, ever tirelessly speeding them.   5

And you O my soul where you stand,
Surrounded, detached, in measureless oceans of space,
Ceaselessly musing, venturing, throwing, seeking the spheres to con-
    nect them,
Till the bridge you will need be form'd, till the ductile anchor hold,
Till the gossamer thread you fling catch somewhere, O my soul.   10

From LEAVES OF GRASS

Sixth Edition, 1876

Though Whitman had always sung the songs of the "unseen Soul," it was appropriate that he proposed in his later years to balance "The songs of the Body and Existence" with another volume of poems on "Death, Immortality, and a free entrance into the Spiritual world." For in 1873, the remarkable physical strength of the poet was shattered by paralysis—and perhaps doubly so, by the death of his mother. Now in Camden, New Jersey, his residence for the remainder of his life, Whitman was uprooted and lonely, broken in health and removed from his friends. Indeed, as he wrote in "Prayer of Columbus," he was "A batter'd, wreck'd old man." His faith, however, expressed in the "death-chant" of the redwood tree, was still in the future, in the America for which he now felt his poems had been only a preparation.

PRAYER OF COLUMBUS

A batter'd, wreck'd old man,
Thrown on this savage shore, far, far from home,
Pent by the sea and dark rebellious brows, twelve dreary months,
Sore, stiff with many toils, sicken'd and nigh to death,
I take my way along the island's edge,   5
Venting a heavy heart.

I am too full of woe!
Haply I may not live another day;
I cannot rest O God, I cannot eat or drink or sleep,
Till I put forth myself, my prayer, once more to Thee,   10
Breathe, bathe myself once more in Thee, commune with Thee,
Report myself once more to Thee.

Thou knowest my years entire, my life,
My long and crowded life of active work, not adoration merely;
Thou knowest the prayers and vigils of my youth,   15
Thou knowest my manhood's solemn and visionary meditations,
Thou knowest how before I commenced I devoted all to come to
    Thee,
Thou knowest I have in age ratified all those vows and strictly kept
    them,
Thou knowest I have not once lost nor faith nor ecstasy in Thee,
In shackles, prison'd, in disgrace, repining not,   20
Accepting all from Thee, as duly come from Thee.

All my emprises have been fill'd with Thee,
My speculations, plans, begun and carried on in thought of Thee,
Sailing the deep or journeying the land for Thee;
Intentions, purports, aspirations mine, leaving results to Thee.   25

O I am sure they really came from Thee,
The urge, the ardor, the unconquerable will,
The potent, felt, interior command, stronger than words,
A message from the Heavens whispering to me even in sleep,
These sped me on.   30

By me and these the work so far accomplish'd,
By me earth's elder cloy'd and stifled lands uncloy'd, unloos'd,
By me the hemispheres rounded and tied, the unknown to the known.

The end I know not, it is all in Thee,
O small or great I know not—haply what broad fields, what lands,   35
Haply the brutish measureless human undergrowth I know,
Transplanted there may rise to stature, knowledge worthy Thee,
Haply the swords I know may there indeed be turn'd to reaping-tools,
Haply the lifeless cross I know, Europe's dead cross, may bud and
          blossom there.

One effort more, my altar this bleak sand;   40
That Thou O God my life hast lighted,
With ray of light, steady, ineffable, vouchsafed of Thee,
Light rare untellable, lighting the very light,
Beyond all signs, descriptions, languages;
For that O God, be it my latest word, here on my knees,   45
Old, poor, and paralyzed, I thank Thee.

My terminus near,
The clouds already closing in upon me,
The voyage balk'd, the course disputed, lost,
I yield my ships to Thee.   50

My hands, my limbs grow nerveless,
My brain feels rack'd, bewilder'd,
Let the old timbers part, I will not part,
I will cling fast to Thee, O God, though the waves buffet me,
Thee, Thee at least I know.   55

Is it the prophet's thought I speak, or am I raving?
What do I know of life? what of myself?
I know not even my own work past or present,
Dim ever-shifting guesses of it spread before me,
Of newer better worlds, their mighty parturition,   60
Mocking, perplexing me.

And these things I see suddenly, what mean they?
As if some miracle, some hand divine unseal'd my eyes,
Shadowy vast shapes smile through the air and sky,
And on the distant waves sail countless ships,   65
And anthems in new tongues I hear saluting me.

Song of the Redwood-Tree

1

A California song,
A prophecy and indirection, a thought impalpable to breathe as air,
A chorus of dryads, fading, departing, or hamadryads departing,
A murmuring, fateful, giant voice, out of the earth and sky,
Voice of a mighty dying tree in the redwood forest dense.   5

Farewell my brethren,
Farewell O earth and sky, farewell ye neighboring waters,
My time has ended, my term has come.

Along the northern coast,
Just back from the rock-bound shore and the caves,   10
In the saline air from the sea in the Mendocino country,
With the surge for base and accompaniment low and hoarse,
With crackling blows of axes sounding musically driven by strong
    arms,
Riven deep by the sharp tongues of the axes, there in the redwood
    forest dense,
I heard the mighty tree its death-chant chanting.   15

The choppers heard not, the camp shanties echoed not,
The quick-ear'd teamsters and chain and jack-screw men heard not,
As the wood-spirits came from their haunts of a thousand years to join
    the refrain,
But in my soul I plainly heard.

Murmuring out of its myriad leaves,   20
Down from its lofty top rising two hundred feet high,
Out of its stalwart trunk and limbs, out of its foot-thick bark,
That chant of the seasons and time, chant not of the past only but the
    future.

You untold life of me,
And all you venerable and innocent joys,   25
Perennial hardy life of me with joys 'mid rain and many a summer
    sun,
And the white snows and night and the wild winds;
O the great patient rugged joys, my soul's strong joys unreck'd by
    man,

*(For know I bear the soul befitting me, I too have consciousness, iden-
tity,*
And all the rocks and mountains have, and all the earth,) 30
Joys of the life befitting me and brothers mine,
Our time, our term has come.

Nor yield we mournfully majestic brothers,
We who have grandly fill'd our time;
With Nature's calm content, with tacit huge delight, 35
We welcome what we wrought for through the past,
And leave the field for them.

For them predicted long,
For a superber race, they too to grandly fill their time,
For them we abdicate, in them ourselves ye forest kings! 40
In them these skies and airs, these mountain peaks, Shasta, Nevadas,
*These huge precipitous cliffs, this amplitude, these valleys, far Yo-
semite,*
To be in them absorb'd, assimilated.

Then to a loftier strain,
Still prouder, more ecstatic rose the chant, 45
As if the heirs, the deities of the West,
Joining with master-tongue bore part.

Not wan from Asia's fetiches,
Nor red from Europe's old dynastic slaughter-house,
*(Area of murder-plots of thrones, with scent left yet of wars and scaf-
folds everywhere,)* 50
*But come from Nature's long and harmless throes, peacefully builded
thence,*
These virgin lands, lands of the Western shore,
To the new culminating man, to you, the empire new,
You promis'd long, we pledge, we dedicate.

You occult deep volitions, 55
*You average spiritual manhood, purpose of all, pois'd on yourself,
giving not taking law,*
*You womanhood divine, mistress and source of all, whence life and
love and aught that comes from life and love,*
*You unseen moral essence of all the vast materials of America, (age
upon age working in death the same as life,)*
*You that, sometimes known, oftener unknown, really shape and
mould the New World, adjusting it to Time and Space,*
*You hidden national will lying in your abysms, conceal'd but ever
alert,* 60
*You past and present purposes tenaciously pursued, may-be uncon-
scious of yourselves,*

Unswerv'd by all the passing errors, perturbations of the surface;
You vital, universal, deathless germs, beneath all creeds, arts, statutes,
literatures,
Here build your homes for good, establish here, these areas entire,
lands of the Western shore,
We pledge, we dedicate to you. 65

For man of you, your characteristic race,
Here may be hardy, sweet, gigantic grow, here tower proportionate
to Nature,
Here climb the vast pure spaces unconfined, uncheck'd by wall or
roof,
Here laugh with storm or sun, here joy, here patiently inure,
Here heed himself, unfold himself, (not others' formulas heed,) here
fill his time, 70
To duty fall, to aid, unreck'd at last,
To disappear, to serve.

Thus on the northern coast,
In the echo of teamsters' calls and the clinking chains, and the music
of choppers' axes,
The falling trunk and limbs, the crash, the muffled shriek, the groan,
Such words combined from the redwood-tree, as of voices ecstatic,
ancient and rustling, 76
The century-lasting, unseen dryads, singing, withdrawing,
All their recesses of forests and mountains leaving,
From the Cascade range to the Wahsatch, or Idaho far, or Utah,
To the deities of the modern henceforth yielding, 80
The chorus and indications, the vistas of coming humanity, the settle-
ments, features all,
In the Mendocino woods I caught.

2

The flashing and golden pageant of California,
The sudden and gorgeous drama, the sunny and ample lands,
The long and varied stretch from Puget sound to Colorado south, 85
Lands bathed in sweeter, rarer, healthier air, valleys and mountain
cliffs,
The fields of Nature long prepared and fallow, the silent, cyclic chem-
istry,
The slow and steady ages plodding, the unoccupied surface ripening,
the rich ores forming beneath;
At last the New arriving, assuming, taking possession,
A swarming and busy race settling and organizing everywhere, 90
Ships coming in from the whole round world, and going out to the
whole world,
To India and China and Australia and the thousand island paradises of
the Pacific,

Populous cities, the latest inventions, the steamers on the rivers, the
   railroads, with many a thrifty farm, with machinery,
And wool and wheat and the grape, and diggings of yellow gold.

3

But more in you than these, lands of the Western shore,   95
(These but the means, the implements, the standing-ground,)
I see in you, certain to come, the promise of thousands of years, till
   now deferr'd,
Promis'd to be fulfill'd, our common kind, the race.

The new society at last, proportionate, to Nature,
In man of you, more than your mountain peaks or stalwart trees imperial,   100
In woman more, far more, than all your gold or vines, or even vital
   air.

Fresh come, to a new world indeed, yet long prepared,
I see the genius of the modern, child of the real and ideal,
Clearing the ground for broad humanity, the true America, heir of the
   past so grand,
To build a grander future.   105

To a Locomotive in Winter

Thee for my recitative,
Thee in the driving storm even as now, the snow, the winter-day de-
   clining,
Thee in thy panoply, thy measur'd dual throbbing and thy beat con-
   vulsive,
The black cylindric body, golden brass and silvery steel,
Thy ponderous side-bars, parallel and connecting rods, gyrating, shut-
   tling at thy sides,   5
Thy metrical, now swelling pant and roar, now tapering in the dis-
   tance,
Thy great protruding head-light fix'd in front,
Thy long, pale, floating vapor-pennants, tinged with delicate purple,
The dense and murky clouds out-belching from thy smoke-stack,
Thy knitted frame, thy springs and valves, the tremulous twinkle of
   thy wheels,   10
Thy train of cars behind, obedient, merrily following,
Through gale or calm, now swift, now slack, yet steadily careering;
Type of the modern—emblem of motion and power—pulse of the con-
   tinent,
For once come serve the Muse and merge in verse, even as here I see
   thee,
With storm and buffeting gusts of wind and falling snow,   15

By day thy warning ringing bell to sound its notes,
My night thy silent signal lamps to swing.

Fierce-throated beauty!
Roll through my chant with all thy lawless music, thy swinging lamps
 at night,
Thy madly-whistled laughter, echoing, rumbling like an earthquake,
 rousing all,   20
Law of thyself complete, thine own track firmly holding,
(No sweetness debonair of tearful harp or glib piano thine,)
Thy trills of shrieks by rocks and hills return'd,
Launch'd o'er the prairies wide, across the lakes,
To the free skies unpent and glad and strong.   25

From LEAVES OF GRASS

Seventh Edition, 1881–1882

Two other editions were to follow, but in this edition Whitman
finally completed the revision and rearrangement of his poems.

THE DALLIANCE OF THE EAGLES

Skirting the river road, (my forenoon walk, my rest,)
Skyward in air a sudden muffled sound, the dalliance of the eagles,
The rushing amorous contact high in space together,
The clinching interlocking claws, a living, fierce, gyrating wheel,
Four beating wings, two beaks, a swirling mass tight grappling, 5
In tumbling turning clustering loops, straight downward falling,
Till o'er the river pois'd, the twain yet one, a moment's lull,
A motionless still balance in the air, then parting, talons loosing,
Upward again on slow-firm pinions slanting, their separate diverse
 flight,
She hers, he his, pursuing.   10

EMILY DICKINSON

1830–1886

THERE ARE STRIKING PARALLELS IN THE LIVES OF WALT WHITMAN AND Emily Dickinson. They never knew each other but they were contemporaries, writing the most original English poetry of their day. Both at first were ridiculed for "posing," in their lives as in their poetry, and late nineteenth- and early twentieth-century histories of literature either ignored them or treated them with supercilious disdain. Now, a century after they began to write, both have won first rank and are acclaimed world poets. Their differences are equally arresting. Whitman identified himself with history, in particular with the history of a new, expanding nation. His boldness is felt in the long, free stroke of his verse, wherein the form itself sweeps the reader along in the cumulative power of his chant. Dickinson lived intensively, and outside both history and time. Her poems are brief, taut, and metaphysical in the sense that they are always concerned with the mystery behind the commonplace. When her verses focus upon events, they do so to universalize routine experience, and the setting is bounded by her small village. Here she sees and describes a storm, a pebble, a neighbor's death, a harvest of grain, or the gossip of local women.

Emily Dickinson was born, December 10, 1830, in Amherst, Massachusetts, in the substantial brick homestead built by her grandfather Samuel Fowler Dickinson, a lawyer, and one of the founders of Amherst College. Her father Edward Dickinson, eldest of nine children, upon graduation from Yale College married Emily Norcross of nearby Monson, and settled in Amherst in his father's profession. For thirty-five years he served as Treasurer of Amherst College, and throughout his life was actively concerned with the political welfare of his state. The parents and the three Dickinson children were a singularly close knit unit. Emily's older brother Austin, upon his marriage in 1856 to Emily's friend Susan Gilbert, settled in a house built for them next door by his father, took up the practice of law, and succeeded the elder Dickinson as college treasurer. Emily attended Mount Holyoke Female Seminary in nearby South Hadley for one year (1847–1848), but did not thereafter return because the ties at home seemed more important to her than the benefits of a good institution. Her younger sister Lavinia, after a year away in a boarding school, likewise returned to live, unmarried, under the parental roof. After their father's death in 1874, the domestic routine of the sisters was circumscribed by the needs of their mother, bedridden most of the eight years that she survived her husband. Emily's own health declined after her mother's death in 1882, and she died four years later, May 15, 1886. During the last twenty years of her life, though she welcomed the friends and relatives of her selection, she spent her time solely within the limits of her home and gardens, accessible always to children, especially to the niece and two nephews next door, and their friends. But she herself never voluntarily visited away after the early months of 1855, when she and Lavinia joined their father for a few weeks in Washington, where he was serving a term in Congress. They also on their return stopped to visit Eliza Coleman, a school friend, in Philadelphia, where Emily almost certainly met the Reverend Charles Wadsworth, pastor of the church attended by the Colemans. Her sojourns in Cambridge during the summer months of 1864 and 1865 were enforced by an eye affliction requiring the care of a Boston specialist. The nature of the trouble is unknown, but her sight was never impaired.

Though in her physical activity Emily Dickinson lived austerely, in her intellectual travels she found amplitude by way of her voluminous correspondence and her poetry. Even her earliest letters, written when she was a child, fascinate by that candor, originality, and ebullience which in later years give individuality to her poetry, and magnetically drew or repelled those in her presence. The intensity of her nature she herself faced as a handicap, and her withdrawal from physical associations was in part a clear recognition of its acuteness.

It is reasonable to assume that Emily Dickinson began writing poetry with serious purpose in her early twenties, encouraged by Benjamin Franklin Newton, a law student in her father's office. He set up practice at Worcester in 1850, later married, and died of consumption in 1853. Emily was corresponding with him in the months after he left Amherst, and cherished his memory throughout her life as one who had first given assurance to her hopes. If early poems survive, they are not now identifiable. Some may have been incorporated into the manuscript "volumes" or small packets which she began to assemble in 1858: a few folded sheets of stationery loosely threaded at the spine. Some half dozen packets were so gathered in 1858 and 1859, a total of about one hundred fifty poems. In the six years following she assembled the bulk of the remaining fifty packets, and it was in those years that she wrote most of her poetry.

April 15, 1862 is significant in the life of Emily Dickinson, for on that day she wrote the essayist and critic Thomas Wentworth Higginson to ask his judgment about four poems which she enclosed (see nos. 216, 318, 319, 320).[1] Her letter was written in response to an article Higginson had contributed to the current issue of the *Atlantic Monthly* in which he had offered practical advice to beginning authors. Her enclosures display in fact a technical virtuosity which leads one to believe that she now felt assurance in her destiny as a poet. The metrical innovations, hovering rhymes, startling juxtaposition of ideas and phrases; above all, her indulgence in what he later termed her "fracture of grammar," clearly bewildered him. He replied nevertheless, asking to see more, and thus began a correspondence that continued throughout her life. But his first letters made clear to her that she could not expect him (and by implication the public) to regard her "beautiful thoughts and words" as poetry. Thus she learned at the start that she could never achieve recognition in her lifetime. Unlike Whitman, who circumvented the hostility of publishers by becoming his own printer, Dickinson reacted by resisting all publication. Except for "Success" (no. 67), the half-dozen poems issued in her lifetime were published surreptitiously by well-wishing friends who felt no compunction about making alterations which were intended to "correct" rhyme or idiom. It was therefore only by a complex process that Helen Hunt Jackson, famous in her day as poet and story writer, succeeded in gaining Dickinson's consent even to the anonymous publication of "Success" in the anthology *A Masque of Poets* (1878). Among qualified judges, Mrs. Jackson alone recognized the stature of Emily Dickinson.

Few poets repay close study of verse techniques more fully than Dickinson. Her "flood subjects" were her responses to love, to nature, to death; and the moods she evoked from them are as various as the days we undergo or the weather we endure. She continually reaches out to capture the fleeting or vivify a moment of almost insupportable tension, whether her emotion derives from the delight of observation ("A Route of Evanescence," no. 1463); from inner stress ("After great pain," no. 341); or from contemplation of the unknowable ("The Soul's Superior instants," no. 306).

On occasion the wit is directed as social commentary: in such a *jeu d'esprit* as "The Show is not the Show" (no. 1206); or in "I like to see it lap the miles" (no. 585), a poem similar in theme to Whitman's "To a Locomotive in Winter," but written with a totally different intent, one which is realized by the structure of the poem itself. Whitman feels the power, the throb and convulsive beat of the engine, and sees belching smoke. Dickinson creates a toy, an iron horse. The form derives in part from the grammatical ingenuity. There is but one subject and one predi-

---

[1] These four poems are analyzed in T. H. Johnson, *Emily Dickinson: An Interpretive Biography*, 1955, pp. 105–110, where the student will also find a discussion of the hymn meters which Dickinson used.

cate: the opening phrase "I like," after which the poet watches from a distance, while the cars are pulled along in a series of object complements: *lap, lick; stop, step; peer, pare; crawl, chase; neigh, stop.* And the circuit of this amusing contraption is completed. Is the idea of progress in this bustling age of steam delicately caricatured? There must have been many solemn words spoken about it around the Dickinson dining table in the early eighteen fifties, for Edward Dickinson was a director of the newly completed Amherst and Belchertown Railroad.[2]

In her poems of contemplation the word-strategy at times is masterful. Let one example suffice. The poem beginning "Of Bronze—and Blaze" (no. 290) opens as a paean on the aurora borealis, but moves into a contemplation of God's matchless plan wherein the human ego, infected by the taint of pride, seeks to emulate the splendors which it sees displayed. Then, in the third and final view, comes the acceptance of man's insignificance. The trifold order of the thought is matched by three metric patterns: common meter, sevens and sixes, and one eight-six syllable pair of lines that halves the common meter. There are three types of rhymes: vowel, identical, and exact—the exact at the end, rhyming in triplicate.

So adequately does the north blaze, the poet states, so sovereignly unconcerned, so preconcertedly distant from human alarms, that the writer's "simple spirit" is infected with "taints" of "Majesty." Here "simple" suggests both humility and naiveté, but naiveness to the point of being foolish; so that when she takes vaster attitudes, she becomes a poseur, and struts upon her "stem." She says: "I am an object to be admired like a flower." But the word *stem*, like *simple*, is controlled by its context to imply, as we shortly see, that she is in fact earthbound and transient, the creature of an hour. She disdains *oxygen*, the life-filling sustenance of being as we know being, for sheer arrogance. Then comes the only stanza-break in the poem, and she continues: "My Splendors, are Menagerie,"—that is, they are entertainment merely. But the "Competeless Show," the spectacle she witnesses, will entertain the centuries forever, or as she phrases it, even "When I, am long ago/An Island in dishonored Grass." The picture of elapsed time is sketched as the slightly raised mound of the grave, an island, now so long forgotten that its inhabitant is unremembered: "Whom none but Beetles, know." Does not the word *beetles* in the last line create with shattering effect the contrast she intends? The imagery draws the whole together, and by a verbal artifice it antiphonally echoes the first line. It sets man's transitoriness against the Creator's perturbless bronze and blaze.

There is a further prospect from which Dickinson's way of writing poetry can be viewed. Like many poets, Shelley set himself, during a given period of composition, the task of writing a certain number of lines which he thereafter polished. One surmises that this method of com-

---

[2] This analysis and the one that follows gladly acknowledge a debt to conversations with Professor Charles R. Anderson, whose forthcoming *Stairway to Surprise* is an important study of Dickinson's word strategy.

posing leads poets to think in terms of panorama, of wishing to convey readers over expanse. They conceive spacially. Keats worked likewise, as did Byron. All three could think in terms of story, on some occasions in terms of a narrative of involved complexity, and though they attempted no innovations of rhyme or metrics, they could handle with virtuoso ease the most intricate prosodic measures. On a few occasions Dickinson tried to write narratively, in such poems as "Wolfe demanded during dying," and "Tell, as a marksman, were forgotten." But the fact that she wrote so few witnesses to her sense of inadequacy in visualizing situations, for the few that she wrote communicate at a pedestrian level. She is much more akin to such seventeenth-century metaphysical writers as Donne, Vaughan, Marvell (in poetry), and Browne (in prose) in her ability to make the word itself become flesh. She loved words ardently, and her selection of them was ritualistic. "A Word made Flesh is seldom/ And tremblingly partook," she begins one poem, and many of her verses deal with the subject of language. At the same time, she knew how to see things "New Englandly," and like all writers of first rank, knew how to use the idioms of speech common to her countrymen, her locale, as in "A Field of Stubble" (no. 1409). Yet her two great masters always remained Shakespeare and the King James Bible. In fact, it is the idiom of the Bible that formed the texture of her imagery and appears in almost every poem that she wrote. In a sense one might say that the Bible was the catalyst by which in her verse the great traditions of English thought and expression were made to vitalize the universals in all villages. Though borne by the main stream, she yet clung to metaphysical modes of expression.

Because she sought primarily to call forth a moment of intensity, her poems are brief. All are composed in meters familiar to her from the hymns of her childhood. Yet her metric combinations of them, her shifts from iambs to trochees, trochees to dactyls, are maneuvered dexterously. This experimentation she carried over into her rhyme patterns, where identical, vowel, and suspended rhymes are used with uncanny effectiveness, as the analysis of the poem "Of Bronze—and Blaze" sets forth. Such possibilities of prosodic variety, now accepted as legitimate tools for the artisan of verse, were her innovations, and they gave a new dimension to English poetry.

Though outwardly uneventful, Emily Dickinson's inner life was extraordinarily alive. The intensity of her love poems, on occasion as erotic as anything written by Whitman (see no. 249, for instance), suggests a personal disturbance of some magnitude. It is true that most of them were written when the Reverend Charles Wadsworth, with whom she was in correspondence, removed from Philadelphia to San Francisco in 1862, and she then adopted her "white election," never again dressing in any other color. But it is improbable that Wadsworth shared the emotion, and it is quite possible that he was not aware of its nature. These events coincide with the period of greatest poetic creativeness, and with the initiation of the correspondence with Higginson, whom she later termed her "safest friend" and the person who once "saved my life." In later years she and Judge Otis Lord of Salem, an old friend of her father's and a widower, clearly were in love, but the circumstance was one of which she became aware in the final decade of her life, and if marriage was broached, as it seems to have been, the idea of interrupting the pattern of her living was clearly out of the question.

When Emily Dickinson discovered, by Higginson's verdict in 1862, that she could not expect to win public audiences as a poet, she chose to gain private ones by incorporating or enclosing verses in her letters. Indeed, after 1870 letters were her chief agency for maintaining fellowship, and she lavished attention upon them, as the springs of her poetic creativeness slacked, preparing them frequently from a first draft which she then revised. But the total of her poems she thus communicated or divulged proved in the end to be but a fraction of the whole number. Everyone knew of course that Emily "wrote poetry," but Lavinia's surprise was genuine when she discovered after her sister's death nearly 1700 neatly transcribed poems locked in a box in a bureau drawer. The long and complicated publishing history then commenced.

Lavinia prevailed on the reluctant Colonel Higginson to act as editor of a slender first volume. With the assistance of Mabel Loomis Todd, the young wife of a new member of the Amherst College faculty, he brought out *Poems by Emily Dickinson* in 1890. The editors approached their task with misgivings, rightly fearing that the "public ear" was not yet attuned to the words and thoughts which might or might not be judged as poetry. To cushion the shock, they undertook a job of "creative editing," whereby words were altered to effect rhyme, achieve "smoothness," and otherwise meet standards then practiced. Their procedure should not, in the light of history, be harshly judged, for Higginson expertly assessed the taste of his era. Reviews conceded that the poems were "remarkable" or "fascinating," but lacking technical skill they would give delight "mingled with regret." Their reception in England was less gracious. Such "scornful disregard" for poetic techniques branded them as "drivel" and "utter nonsense." Yet copies of the volume sold rapidly, and the demand for new editions encouraged the editors to prepare *Poems*, Second Series, issued a year later. Though such "experimental vagaries" were still deemed "exasperating," a gradual tempering is evident in the tone of the reviews. The effect of the poems now is becoming "cumulative." Only one voice in the first year had been raised in estimation that is neither querulous nor hedged. William Dean Howells called them "a distinctive addition to the literature of the world." Mrs. Todd's *Poems*, Third Series (1896), together with the verses included in the *Letters* (1894), which she edited as a labor of love, brought the total published canon to some five hundred fifty items, and no further were issued in the nineteenth century.

But already their effect had been made. Howells had read some to Stephen Crane, whose first volume of poems, *The Black Riders* (1895), shows the effect of their sound patterns. There is similar suggestion in the earliest publication of Edwin Arlington Robinson, *The Torrent and the Night Before* (1896). By 1912 a revolution had taken place. In that year Harriet Monroe founded *Poetry: A Magazine of Verse*, which immediately became an important journal for many modes and theories, and over the years has extended the vital influence of the craft of the poet. Mitchell Kennerley issued *The Lyric Year*, an anthology of one selection each from one hundred new poets. And Amy Lowell introduced Imagiste forms in *A Dome of Many-Coloured Glass*. Though the word *imagism* was new and used by Europeans to bespeak their interest in their own varieties of free expression, they willingly acknowledged their debt to Whitman and Dickinson. Soon to follow were the earliest collections of Vachel Lindsay, Carl Sandburg, Gertrude Stein, Ezra Pound, and other experimenters whose eclectic standards aroused such feeling that poetry, now a subject for editorial controversy throughout the country, became news.

Thus when Emily Dickinson's niece, Martha Dickinson Bianchi, issued a new collection in 1914, *The Single Hound*, the way had been prepared for Emily Dickinson clear, without editorial construction; and eight years later one of the younger poets and critics could observe: "Her first admirers feel somewhat ashamed of the patronizing or apologetic tone they once adopted towards her writing, and speak in bolder phrases." [3] Mrs. Bianchi published two additional collections (*Further Poems*, 1929; *Unpublished Poems*, 1935); and virtually the entire canon was completed in 1945, when Millicent Todd Bingham issued *Bolts of Melody*. By midcentury collections of Dickinson poetry were standard items for a beginner's library, translations were appearing in many languages, and no anthology was complete without selections from her verses.

It was in 1862 that the poet had said: "This is my letter to the World/ That never Wrote to Me." Some eighty years later she had received her reply.

49	67
I never lost as much but twice,	Success is counted sweetest
And that was in the sod.	By those who ne'er succeed.
Twice have I stood a beggar	To comprehend a nectar
Before the door of God!	Requires sorest need.
Angels—twice descending 5	
Reimbursed my store—	Not one of all the purple Host 5
Burglar! Banker— Father!	Who took the Flag today
I am poor once more!	Can tell the definition
1858	*1890* So clear of Victory

---

[3] Robert Hillyer, in *The Freeman*, VI (Oct. 18, 1922), 129.

As he defeated—dying—
On whose forbidden ear 10
The distant strains of triumph
Burst agonized and clear!
1859 *1878*

76

Exultation is the going
Of an inland soul to sea,
Past the houses—past the head-
lands—
Into deep Eternity—

Bred as we, among the mountains,
Can the sailor understand 6
The divine intoxication
Of the first league out from land?
1859 *1890*

89

Some things that fly there be—
Birds—Hours—the Bumblebee—
Of these no Elegy.

Some things that stay there be—
Grief—Hills—Eternity— 5
Nor this behooveth me.

There are that resting, rise.
Can I expound the skies?
How still the Riddle lies!
1859 *1890*

105

To hang our head—ostensibly—
And subsequent, to find
That such was not the posture
Of our immortal mind—

Affords the sly presumption 5
That in so dense a fuzz—
You—too—take Cobweb attitudes
Upon a plane of Gauze!
1859 *1896*

128

Bring me the sunset in a cup,
Reckon the morning's flagon's up

And say how many Dew,
Tell me how far the morning
leaps—
Tell me what time the weaver
sleeps 5
Who spun the breadths of blue!

Write me how many notes there
be
In the new Robin's extasy
Among astonished boughs—
How many trips the Tortoise
makes— 10
How many cups the Bee partakes,
The Debauchee of Dews!

Also, who laid the Rainbow's piers,
Also, who leads the docile spheres
By withes of supple blue? 15
Whose fingers string the stalac-
tite—
Who counts the wampum of the
night
To see that none is due?

Who built this little Alban House
And shut the windows down so
close 20
My spirit cannot see?
Who'll let me out some gala day
With implements to fly away,
Passing Pomposity?
1859 *1891*

130

These are the days when Birds
come back—
A very few—a Bird or two—
To take a backward look.

These are the days when skies
resume
The old—old sophistries of June—
A blue and gold mistake. 6

Oh fraud that cannot cheat the
Bee—
Almost thy plausibility
Induces my belief.

Till ranks of seeds their witness
   bear—   10
And softly thro' the altered air
Hurries a timid leaf.

Oh Sacrament of summer days,
Oh Last Communion in the Haze—
Permit a child to join.   15

Thy sacred emblems to partake—
Thy consecrated bread to take
And thine immortal wine!
1859   *1890*

160

Just lost, when I was saved!
Just felt the world go by!
Just girt me for the onset with
   Eternity,
When breath blew back,
And on the other side   5
I heard recede the disappointed
   tide!

Therefore, as One returned, I feel,
Odd secrets of the line to tell!
Some Sailor, skirting foreign
   shores—
Some pale Reporter, from the aw-
   ful doors   10
Before the Seal!

Next time, to stay!
Next time, the things to see
By Ear unheard,
Unscrutinized by Eye—   15

Next time, to tarry,
While the Ages steal—
Slow tramp the Centuries,
And the Cycles wheel!
1860   *1891*

174

At last, to be identified!
At last, the lamps upon thy side
The rest of Life to *see!*

Past Midnight! Past the Morning
   Star!
Past Sunrise!   5
Ah, What leagues there *were*
Between our feet, and Day!
1860   *1890*

187

How many times these low feet
   staggered—
Only the soldered mouth can tell—
Try—can you stir the awful rivet—
Try—can you lift the hasps of
   steel!

Stroke the cool forehead—hot so
   often—   5
Lift—if you care—the listless hair—
Handle the adamantine fingers
Never   a   thimble—more—shall
   wear—

Buzz the dull flies—on the chamber
   window—
Brave—shines the sun through the
   freckled pane—   10
Fearless—the cobweb swings from
   the ceiling—
Indolent   Housewife—in   Daisies—
   lain!
1860   *1890*

189

It's such a little thing to weep—
So short a thing to sigh—
And yet—by Trades—the size of
   these
We men and women die!
1860   *1896*

214

I taste a liquor never brewed—
From Tankards scooped in Pearl—
Not all the Frankfort Berries
Yield such an Alcohol!

Inebriate of Air—am I—   5
And Debauchee of Dew—

Reeling—thro endless summer
days—
From inns of Molten Blue—

When "Landlords" turn the
drunken Bee
Out of the Foxglove's door— 10
When Butterflies—renounces their
"drams"—
I shall but drink the more!

Till Seraphs swing their snowy
Hats—
And Saints—to windows run—
To see the little Tippler 15
From Manzanilla come!
1860 *1861*

216

Safe in their Alabaster Chambers—
Untouched by Morning
And untouched by Noon—
Sleep the meek members of the
Resurrection—
Rafter of satin, 5
And Roof of stone.

Light laughs the breeze
In her Castle above them—
Babbles the Bee in a stolid Ear,
Pipe the Sweet Birds in ignorant
cadence— 10
Ah, what sagacity perished here!
version of 1859 *1862*

Safe in their Alabaster Chambers—
Untouched by Morning—
And untouched by Noon—
Lie the meek members of the
Resurrection—
Rafter of Satin—and Roof of
Stone! 5

Grand go the Years—in the Cres-
cent—above them—
Worlds scoop their Arcs—
And Firmaments—row—

Diadems—drop—and Doges—surrender—
Soundless as dots—on a Disc of
Snow— 10
version of 1861 *1890*

228

Blazing in Gold and quenching in
Purple
Leaping like Leopards to the Sky
Then at the feet of the old Hori-
zon
Laying her spotted Face to die
Stooping as low as the Otter's
Window 5
Touching the Roof and tinting the
Barn
Kissing her Bonnet to the Meadow
And the Juggler of Day is gone
1861 *1864*

239

"Heaven"—is what I cannot reach!
The Apple on the Tree—
Provided it do hopeless—hang—
That—"Heaven" is—to Me!

The Color, on the Cruising
Cloud— 5
The interdicted Land—
Behind the Hill—the House be-
hind—
There—Paradise—is found!

Her teazing Purples—Afternoons—
The credulous—decoy— 10
Enamored—of the Conjuror—
That spurned us—Yesterday!
1861 *1896*

241

I like a look of Agony,
Because I know it's true—
Men do not sham Convulsion,
Nor simulate, a Throe—

The Eyes glaze once—and that is
    Death—   5
Impossible to feign
The Beads upon the Forehead
By homely Anguish strung.
1861   *1890*

245

I held a Jewel in my fingers—
And went to sleep—
The day was warm, and winds
    were prosy—
I said, " 'Twill keep"—

I woke—and chid my honest
    fingers,   5
The Gem was gone—
And now, an Amethyst remem-
    brance
Is all I own—
1861   *1891*

249

Wild Nights—Wild Nights!
Were I with thee
Wild Nights should be
Our luxury!

Futile—the Winds—   5
To a Heart in port—
Done with the Compass—
Done with the Chart!

Rowing in Eden—
Ah, the Sea!   10
Might I but moor—Tonight—
In Thee!
1861   *1891*

258

There's a certain Slant of light,
Winter Afternoons—
That oppresses, like the Heft
Of Cathedral Tunes—

Heavenly Hurt, it gives us—   5
We can find no scar,

But internal difference,
Where the Meanings, are—

None may teach it—Any—
'Tis the Seal Despair—   10
An imperial affliction
Sent us of the Air—

When it comes, the Landscape
    listens—
Shadows—hold their breath—
When it goes, 'tis like the Distance
On the look of Death—   16
1861   *1890*

272

I breathed enough to take the
    Trick—
And now, removed from Air—
I simulate the Breath, so well—
That One, to be quite sure—

The Lungs are stirless—must de-
    scend   5
Among the Cunning Cells—
And touch the Pantomine—Him-
    self,
How numb, the Bellows feels!
1861   *1896*

280

I felt a Funeral, in my Brain,
And Mourners to and fro
Kept   treading—treading—till   it
    seemed
That Sense was breaking through—

And when they all were seated, 5
A Service, like a Drum—
Kept   beating—beating—till   I
    thought
My Mind was going numb—

And then I heard them lift a Box
And creak across my Soul   10
With those same Boots of Lead,
    again,
Then Space—began to toll,

As all the Heavens were a Bell,
And Being, but an Ear,
And I, and Silence, some strange
    Race   15
Wrecked, solitary, here—

And then a Plank in Reason,
    broke,
And I dropped down, and down—
And hit a World, at every plunge,
And finished knowing—then— 20
1861   *1896*

287

A Clock stopped—
Not the Mantel's—
Geneva's farthest skill
Can't put the puppet bowing—
That just now dangled still— 5

An awe came on the Trinket!
The Figures hunched, with pain—
Then quivered out of Decimals—
Into Degreeless Noon—

It will not stir for Doctor's— 10
This Pendulum of snow—
The Shopman importunes it—
While cool—concernless No—

Nods from the Gilded pointers—
Nods from the Seconds slim— 15
Decades of Arrogance between
The Dial life—
And Him—
1861   *1896*

288

I'm Nobody! Who are you?
Are you—Nobody—too?
Then there's a pair of us!
Dont tell! they'd banish us—you
    know!

How dreary—to be—Somebody! 5
How public—like a Frog—

To tell your name—the livelong
    June—
To an admiring Bog!
1861   *1891*

290

Of Bronze—and Blaze—
The North—Tonight—
So adequate—it forms—
So preconcerted with itself—
So distant—to alarms— 5
An Unconcern so sovreign
To Universe, or me—
Infects my simple spirit
With Taints of Majesty—
Till I take vaster attitudes— 10
And strut upon my stem—
Disdaining Men, and Oxygen,
For Arrogance of them—

My Splendors, are Menagerie—
But their Completeless Show 15
Will entertain the Centuries
When I, am long ago,
An Island in dishonored Grass—
Whom none but Beetles, know.
1861   *1896*

298

Alone, I cannot be—
The Hosts—do visit me—
Recordless Company—
Who baffle Key—

They have no Robes, nor Names—
No Almanacs—nor Climes— 6
But general Homes
Like Gnomes—

Their Coming, may be known
By Couriers within— 10
Their going—is not—
For they're never gone—
1861   *1932*

303

The Soul selects her own Society—
Then—shuts the Door—

To her divine Majority—
Present no more—

Unmoved—she notes the Char-
    iots—pausing—   5
At her low Gate—
Unmoved—an Emperor be kneel-
    ing
Upon her Mat—

I've known her—from an ample
    nation—
Choose One—   10
Then—close the Valves of her at-
    tention—
Like Stone—
1862   *1890*

306

The Soul's Superior instants
Occur to Her—alone—
When friend—and Earth's occasion
Have infinite withdrawn—

Or She—Herself—ascended   5
To too remote a Hight
For lower Recognition
Than Her Omnipotent—

This Mortal Abolition
Is seldom—but as fair   10
As Apparition—subject
To Autocratic Air—

Eternity's disclosure
To favorites—a few—
Of the Colossal substance   15
Of Immortality
1862   *1914*

311

It sifts from Leaden Sieves—
It powders all the Wood.
It fills with Alabaster Wool
The Wrinkles of the Road—

It makes an Even Face   5
Of Mountain, and of Plain—

Unbroken Forehead from the East
Unto the East again—
It reaches to the Fence—
It wraps it Rail by Rail   10
Till it is lost in Fleeces—
It deals Celestial Vail

To Stump, and Stack—and Stem—
A Summer's empty Room—
Acres of Joints, where Harvests
    were,   15
Recordless, but for them—

It Ruffles Wrists of Posts
As Ankles of a Queen—
Then stills it's Artisans—like
    Ghosts—
Denying they have been—   20
1862   *1891*

318

I'll tell you how the Sun rose—
A Ribbon at a time—
The Steeples swam in Amethyst—
The news, like Squirrels, ran—
The Hills untied their Bonnets—
The Bobolinks—begun—   6
Then I said softly to myself—
"That must have been the Sun"!
But how he set—I know not—
There seemed a purple stile   10
That little Yellow boys and girls
Were climbing all the while—
Till when they reached the other
    side,
A Dominie in Gray—
Put gently up the evening Bars—
And led the flock away—   16
1862   *1890*

319

The nearest Dream recedes—un-
    realized—
The Heaven we chase,
Like the June Bee—before the
    School Boy,
Invites the Race—

Stoops—to an easy Clover— 5
Dips—evades—teazes—deploys—
Then—to the Royal Clouds
Lifts his light Pinnace—
Heedless of the Boy—
Staring—bewildered—at the mock-
    ing sky— 10

Homesick for steadfast Honey—
Ah, the Bee flies not
That brews that rare variety!
1862   *1891*

320

We play at Paste—
Till qualified, for Pearl—
Then, drop the Paste—
And deem ourself a fool—

The Shapes—though—were sim-
    ilar— 5
And our new Hands
Learned *Gem*-Tactics—
Practicing *Sands*—
1862   *1891*

321

Of all the Sounds despatched
    abroad,
There's not a Charge to me
Like that old measure in the
    Boughs—
That phraseless Melody—
The Wind does—working like a
    Hand, 5
Whose fingers Comb the Sky—
Then quiver down—with tufts of
    Tune—
Permitted Gods, and me—

Inheritance, it is, to us—
Beyond the Art to Earn— 10
Beyond the trait to take away
By Robber, since the Gain
Is gotten not of fingers—
And inner than the Bone—
Hid golden, for the whole of
    Days, 15

And even in the Urn,
I cannot vouch the merry Dust
Do not arise and play
In some old fashion of it's own,
Some quainter Holiday, 20
When Winds go round and round
    in Bands—
And thrum upon the door,
And Birds take places, overhead,
To bear them Orchestra.

I crave Him grace of Summer
    Boughs, 25
If such an Outcast be—
Who never heard that fleshless
    Chant—
Rise—solemn—on the Tree,
As if some Caravan of Sound
Off Deserts, in the Sky, 30
Had parted Rank,
Then knit, and swept—
In Seamless Company—
1862   *1890*

341

After great pain, a formal feeling
    comes—
The Nerves sit ceremonious, like
    Tombs—
The stiff Heart questions was it
    He, that bore,
And Yesterday, or Centuries be-
    fore?

The Feet, mechanical, go round—
A Wooden way 6
Of Ground, or Air, or Ought—
Regardless grown,
A Quartz contentment, like a
    stone—

This is the Hour of Lead— 10
Remembered, if outlived,
As Freezing persons, recollect the
    Snow—
First—Chill—then Stupor—then the
    letting go—
1862   *1929*

369

She lay as if at play
Her life had leaped away—
Intending to return—
But not so soon—

Her merry Arms, half dropt— 5
As if for lull of sport—
An instant had forgot
The Trick to start—

Her dancing Eyes—ajar—
As if their Owner were 10
Still sparkling through
For fun—at you—

Her Morning at the door—
Devising, I am sure—
To force her sleep— 15
So light—so deep—
1862   *1935*

389

There's been a Death, in the Op-
    posite House,
As lately as Today—
I know it, by the numb look
Such Houses have—alway—

The Neighbors rustle in and out—
The Doctor—drives away— 6
A Window opens like a Pod—
Abrupt—mechanically—

Somebody flings a Mattrass out—
The Children hurry by— 10
They wonder if it died—on that—
I used to—when a Boy—

The Minister—goes stiffly in—
As if the House were His—
And He owned all the Mourners—
    now— 15
And little Boys—besides—

And then the Milliner—and the
    Man
Of the Appalling Trade—

To take the measure of the
    House—

There'll be that Dark Parade— 20

Of Tassels—and of Coaches—
    soon—
It's easy as a Sign—
The Intuition of the News—
In just a Country Town—
1862   *1896*

391

A Visitor in Marl—
Who influences Flowers—
Till they are orderly as Busts—
And Elegant—as Glass—

Who visits in the Night— 5
And just before the Sun—
Concludes his glistening inter-
    view—
Caresses—and is gone—

But whom his fingers touched—
And where his feet have run— 10
And whatsoever Mouth he kissed—
Is as it had not been—
1862   *1935*

441

This is my letter to the World
That never wrote to Me—
The simple News that Nature
    told—
With tender Majesty

Her Message is committed 5
To Hands I cannot see—
For love of Her—Sweet—country-
    men—
Judge tenderly—of Me
1862   *1890*

449

I died for Beauty—but was scarce
Adjusted in the Tomb

When One who died for Truth,
   was lain
In an adjoining Room—

He questioned softly "Why I
   failed"?   5
"For Beauty", I replied—
"And I—for Truth—Themselves
   are One—
We Bretheren, are", He said—

And so, as Kinsmen, met a Night—
We talked between the Rooms—
Until the Moss had reached our
   lips—   11
And covered up—our names—
1862   *1890*

465

I heard a Fly buzz—when I died—
The Stillness in the Room
Was like the Stillness in the Air—
Between the Heaves of Storm—

The Eyes around—had wrung
   them dry—   5
And Breaths were gathering firm
For that last Onset—when the King
Be witnessed—in the Room—

I willed my Keepsakes—Signed
   away
What portion of me be   10
Assignable—and then it was
There interposed a Fly—

With Blue—uncertain stumbling
   Buzz—
Between the light—and me—
And then the Windows failed—and
   then   15
I could not see to see—
1862   *1896*

478

I had no time to Hate—
Because
The Grave would hinder Me—

And Life was not so
Ample I   5
Could finish—Enmity—

Nor had I time to Love—
But since
Some Industry must be—
The little Toil of Love—   10
I thought
Be large enough for Me—
1862   *1890*

502

At least—to pray—is left—is left—
Oh Jesus—in the Air—
I know not which thy chamber is—
I'm knocking—everywhere—

Thou settest Earthquake in the
   South—   5
And Maelstrom, in the Sea—
Say, Jesus Christ of Nazareth—
Hast thou no Arm for Me?
1862   *1891*

585

I like to see it lap the Miles—
And lick the Valleys up—
And stop to feed itself at Tanks—
And then—prodigious step

Around a Pile of Mountains—   5
And supercilious peer
In Shanties—by the sides of
   Roads—
And then a Quarry pare

To fit it's sides
And crawl between   10
Complaining all the while
In horrid—hooting stanza—
Then chase itself down Hill—

And neigh like Boanerges—
Then—prompter than a Star   15
Stop—docile and omnipotent
At it's own stable door—
1862   *1891*

621

I asked no other thing—
No other—was denied—
I offered Being—for it—
The Mighty Merchant sneered—

Brazil? He twirled a Button—   5
Without a glance my way—
"But—Madam—is there nothing
          else—
That We can show—Today?"
1862   *1890*

632

The Brain—is wider than the Sky—
For—put them side by side—
The one the other will contain
With ease—and You—beside—

The Brain is deeper than the sea—
For—hold them—Blue to Blue—   6
The one the other will absorb—
As Sponges—Buckets—do—

The Brain is just the weight of
          God—
For—Heft   them—Pound   for
          Pound—   10
And they will differ—if they do—
As Syllable from Sound—
1862   *1896*

640

I cannot live with You—
It would be Life—
And Life is over there—
Behind the Shelf

The Sexton keeps the Key to—   5
Putting up
Our Life—His Porcelain—
Like a Cup—

Discarded of the Housewife—
Quaint—or Broke—   10
A newer Sevres pleases—
Old Ones crack—

I could not die—with You—
For One must wait
To shut the Other's Gaze down—
You—could not—   16

And I—Could I stand by
And see You—freeze—
Without my Right of Frost—
Death's privilege?   20

Nor could I rise—with You—
Because Your Face
Would put out Jesus'—
That New Grace

Glow plain—and foreign   25
On my homesick Eye—
Except that You than He
Shone closer by—

They'd judge Us—How—
For You—served Heaven—You
          know,   30
Or sought to—
I could not—

Because You saturated Sight—
And I had no more Eyes
For sordid excellence   35
As Paradise

And were You lost, I would be—
Though My Name
Rang loudest
On the Heavenly fame—   40

And were You—saved—
And I—condemned to be
Where You were not—
That self—were Hell to Me—

So We must meet apart—   45
You there—I—here—
With just the Door ajar
That Oceans are—and Prayer—
And that White Sustenance—
Despair—   50
1862   *1890*

712

Because I could not stop for
    Death—
He kindly stopped for me—
The Carriage held but just Our-
    selves—
And Immortality.

We slowly drove—He knew no
    haste   5
And I had put away
My labor and my leisure too,
For His Civility—

We passed the School, where Chil-
    dren strove
At Recess—in the Ring—   10
We passed the Fields of Gazing
    Grain—
We passed the Setting Sun—

Or rather—He passed Us—
The Dews drew quivering and
    chill—
For only Gossamer, my Gown—
My Tippet—only Tulle—   16

We paused before a House that
    seemed
A Swelling of the Ground—
The Roof was scarcely visible—
The Cornice—in the Ground— 20

Since then—'tis Centuries—and yet
Feels shorter than the Day
I first surmised the Horses Heads
Were toward Eternity—
1863   *1890*

744

Remorse—is Memory—awake—
Her Parties all astir—
A Presence of Departed Acts—
At window—and at Door—

It's Past—set down before the Soul
And lighted with a Match—   6

Perusal—to facilitate—
And help Belief to stretch—

Remorse is cureless—the Disease
Not even God—can heal—   10
For 'tis His institution—and
The Adequate of Hell—
1863   *1891*

746

Never for Society
He shall seek in vain—
Who His own acquaintance
Cultivate—Of Men
Wiser Men may weary—   5
But the Man within

Never knew Satiety—
Better entertain
Than could Border Ballad—
Or Biscayan Hymn—   10
Neither introduction
Need You—unto Him—
1863   *1894*

754

My life had stood—a Loaded
    Gun—
In Corners—till a Day
The Owner passed—identified—
And carried Me away—

And now We roam in Sovrign
    Woods—   5
And now We hunt the Doe—
And every time I speak for Him—
The Mountains straight reply—

And do I smile, such cordial light
Upon the Valley glow—   10
It is as a Vesuvian face
Had let it's pleasure through—

And when at Night—Our good
    Day done—
I guard My Master's Head—
'Tis better than the Eider-Duck's
Deep Pillow—to have shared— 16

To foe of His—I'm deadly foe—
None stir the second time—
On whom I lay a Yellow Eye—
Or an emphatic Thumb—   20

Though I than He—may longer
    live
He longer must—than I—
For I have but the power to kill,
Without—the power to die—
1863   *1929*

764

Presentiment—is that long Shadow
    —on the Lawn—
Indicative that Suns go down—

The Notice to the startled Grass
That Darkness—is about to pass—
1863   *1890*

784

Bereaved of all, I went abroad—
No less bereaved was I
Upon a New Peninsula—
The Grave preceded me—

Obtained my Lodgings, ere my-
    self—   5
And when I sought my Bed—
The Grave it was reposed upon
The Pillow for my Head—

I waked, to find it first awake—
I rose—It followed me—   10
I tried to drop it in the Crowd—
To lose it in the Sea—

In Cups of artificial Drowse
To steep it's shape away—
The Grave—was finished—but the
    Spade   15
Remained in Memory—
1863   *1896*

792

Through the strait pass of suffer-
    ing—
The Martyrs—even—trod.
Their feet—upon Temptation—
Their faces—upon God—

A stately—shriven—Company—   5
Convulsion—playing round—
Harmless—as streaks of Meteor—
Upon a Planet's Bond—

Their faith—the everlasting troth—
Their Expectation—fair—   10
The Needle—to the North De-
    gree—
Wades—so—thro' polar Air!
1863   *1891*

824

The Wind begun to knead the
    Grass—
As Women do a Dough—
He flung a Hand full at the Plain—
A Hand full at the Sky—
The Leaves unhooked themselves
    from Trees—   5
And started all abroad—
The Dust did scoop itself like
    Hands—
And throw away the Road—
The Wagons quickened on the
    Street—
The Thunders gossiped low—   10
The Lightning showed a Yellow
    Head—
And then a lived Toe—
The Birds put up the Bars to
    Nests—
The Cattle flung to Barns—
Then came one drop of Giant
    Rain—   15
And then, as if the Hands
That held the Dams—had parted
    hold—
The Waters Wrecked the Sky—

But overlooked my Father's
   House—
Just Quartering a Tree— 20
1864 *1891*

829

Ample make this Bed—
Make this Bed with Awe—
In it wait till Judgment break
Excellent and Fair.

Be it's Mattress straight— 5
Be it's Pillow round—
Let no Sunrise' yellow noise
Interrupt this Ground—
1864 *1891*

917

Love—is anterior to Life—
Posterior—to Death—
Initial of Creation, and
The Exponent of Earth—
1864 *1896*

974

The Soul's distinct connection
With immortality
Is best disclosed by Danger
Or quick Calamity—

As Lightning on a Landscape 5
Exhibits Sheets of Place—
Not yet suspected—but for Flash—
And Click—and Suddenness.
1864 *1929*

986

A narrow Fellow in the Grass
Occasionally rides—
You may have met Him—did you
   not
His notice sudden is—

The Grass divides as with a
   Comb— 5
A spotted shaft is seen—

And then it closes at your feet
And opens further on—

He likes a Boggy Acre
A Floor too cool for Corn— 10
Yet when a Boy, and Barefoot—
I more than once at Noon
Have passed, I thought, a Whip
   lash
Unbraiding in the Sun
When stooping to secure it 15
It wrinkled, and was gone—

Several of Nature's People
I know, and they know me—
I feel for them a transport
Of cordiality— 20

But never met this Fellow
Attended, or alone
Without a tighter breathing
And Zero at the Bone—
1865 *1866*

1052

I never saw a Moor—
I never saw the Sea—
Yet know I how the Heather looks
And what a Billow be.

I never spoke with God 5
Nor visited in Heaven—
Yet certain am I of the spot
As if the Checks were given—
1865 *1890*

1055

The Soul should always stand ajar
That if the Heaven inquire
He will not be obliged to wait
Or shy of troubling Her

Depart, before the Host have slid
The Bolt unto the Door— 6
To search for the accomplished
   Guest,
Her Visitor, no more—
1865 *1896*

1067

Except the smaller size
No lives are round—
These—hurry to a sphere
And show and end—
The larger—slower grow   5
And later hang—
The Summers of Hesperides
Are long.
1866   *1891*

1068

Further in Summer than the Birds
Pathetic from the Grass
A minor Nation celebrates
It's unobtrusive Mass.

No Ordinance be seen   5
So gradual the Grace
A pensive Custom it becomes
Enlarging Loneliness.

Antiquest felt at Noon
When August burning low   10
Arise this spectral Canticle
Repose to typify

Remit as yet no Grace
No Furrow on the Glow
Yet a Druidic Difference   15
Enhances Nature now
1866   *1891*

1073

Experiment to me
Is every one I meet
If it contain a Kernel?
The Figure of a Nut

Presents upon a Tree   5
Equally plausibly
But Meat within, is requisite
To Squirrels and to Me
1866   *1891*

1078

The Bustle in a House
The Morning after Death

Is solemnest of industries
Enacted upon Earth—

The Sweeping up the Heart   5
And putting Love away
We shall not want to use again
Until Eternity.
1866   *1890*

1084

At Half past Three, a single Bird
Unto a silent Sky
Propounded but a single term
Of cautious melody.

At Half past Four, Experiment   5
Had subjugated test
And lo, Her silver Principle
Supplanted all the rest.

At Half past Seven, Element
Nor Implement, be seen—   10
And Place was where the Presence
          was
Circumference between.
1866   *1891*

1182

Remembrance has a Rear and
          Front—
'Tis something like a House—
It has a Garret also
For Refuse and the Mouse.

Besides the deepest Cellar   5
That ever Mason laid—
Look to it by it's Fathoms
Ourselves be not pursued—
1871   *1896*

1206

The Show is not the Show
But they that go—
Menagerie to me
My Neighbor be—
Fair Play—   5
Both went to see—
1872   *1891*

1263

There is no Frigate like a Book
To take us Lands away
Nor any Coursers like a Page
Of prancing Poetry—
This Travel may the poorest take
Without offence of Toll—   6
How frugal is the Chariot
That bears the Human soul.
1873   *1894*

1269

I worked for chaff and earning
    Wheat
Was haughty and betrayed.
What right had Fields to arbitrate
In matters ratified?

I tasted Wheat and hated Chaff   5
And thanked the ample friend—
Wisdom is more becoming viewed
At distance than at hand.
1873   *1896*

1274

The Bone that has no Marrow,
What Ultimate for that?
It is not fit for Table
For Beggar or for Cat.

A Bone has obligations—   5
A Being has the same—
A Marrowless Assembly
Is culpabler than shame.

But how shall finished Creatures
A function fresh obtain?   10
Old Nicodemus' Phantom
Confronting us again!
1873   *1896*

1295

Two Lengths has every Day—
It's absolute extent
And Area superior
By Hope or Horror lent—

Eternity will be   5
Velocity or Pause
At Fundamental Signals
From Fundamental Laws.

To die is not to go—
On Doom's consummate Chart   10
No Territory new is staked—
Remain thou as thou art.
1874   *1914*

1298

The Mushroom is the Elf of
    Plants—
At Evening, it is not—
At Morning, in a Truffled Hut
It stop upon a Spot

As if it tarried always   5
And yet it's whole Career
Is shorter than a Snake's Delay
And fleeter than a Tare—

'Tis Vegetation's Juggler—
The Germ of Alibi—   10
Doth like a Bubble antedate
And like a Bubble, hie—

I feel as if the Grass was pleased
To have it intermit—
This surreptitious scion   15
Of Summer's circumspect.

Had Nature any supple Face
Or could she one contemn—
Had Nature an Apostate—
That Mushroom—it is Him!   20
1874   *1891*

1304

Not with a Club, the Heart is
    broken
Nor with a Stone—
A Whip so small you could not
    see it
I've known

To lash the Magic Creature   5
Till it fell,
Yet that Whip's Name
Too noble then to tell.

Magnanimous as Bird
By Boy descried—   10
Singing unto the Stone
Of which it died—

Shame need not crouch
In such an Earth as Our's—
Shame—stand erect—   15
The Universe is your's.
1874   *1896*

1332

Pink—small—and punctual—
Aromatic—low—
Covert—in April—
Candid—in May—
Dear to the Moss—   5
Known to the Knoll—
Next to the Robin
In every human Soul—
Bold little Beauty
Bedecked with thee   10
Nature forswears
Antiquity—
1875   *1890*

1333

A little Madness in the Spring
Is wholesome even for the King,
But God be with the Clown—
Who ponders this tremendous
    scene—
This whole Experiment of Green—
As if it were his own!   6
1875   *1914*

1393

Lay this Laurel on the One
Too intrinsic for Renown—
Laurel—vail your deathless tree—
Him you chasten, that is He!
1877   *1891*

1407

A Field of Stubble, lying sere
Beneath the second Sun—
It's Toils to Brindled People
    thrust—
It's Triumphs—to the Bin—
Accosted by a timid Bird   5
Irresolute of Alms—
Is often seen—but seldom felt,
On our New England Farms—
1877   *1932*

1409

Could mortal lip divine
The undeveloped Freight
Of a delivered syllable
'Twould crumble with the weight.
1877   *1896*

1430

Who never wanted—maddest Joy
Remains to him unknown—
The Banquet of Abstemiousness
Defaces that of Wine—

Within it's reach, though yet un-
    grasped   5
Desire's perfect Goal—
No nearer—lest the Actual—
Should disenthrall thy soul—
1877   *1896*

1433

How brittle are the Piers
On which our Faith doth tread—
No Bridge below doth totter so—
Yet none hath such a Crowd.

It is as old as God—   5
Indeed—'twas built by him—
He sent his Son to test the Plank,
And he pronounced it firm.
1878   *1894*

1437

A Dew suffced itself—
And satisfied a Leaf

And felt "how vast a destiny"—
"How trivial is Life!"

The Sun went out to work—   5
The Day went out to play—
But not again that Dew be seen
By Physiognomy.

Whether by Day abducted
Or emptied by the Sun   10
Into the Sea in passing
Eternally unknown.

Attested to this Day
That awful Tragedy
By Transport's instability   15
And Doom's celerity.
1878   *1896*

1463

A Route of Evanescence
With a revolving Wheel—
A Resonance of Emerald—
A Rush of Cochineal—
And every Blossom on the Bush   5
Adjusts it's tumbled Head—
The mail from Tunis, probably,
An easy Morning's Ride—
1879   *1891*

1483

The Robin is a Gabriel
In humble circumstances—
His Dress denotes him socially,
Of Transport's Working Classes—
He has the punctuality   5
Of the New England Farmer—
The same oblique integrity,
A Vista vastly warmer—

A small but sturdy Residence,
A self denying Household,   10
The Guests of Perspicacity
Are all that cross his Threshold—
As covert as a Fugitive,
Cajoling Consternation

By Ditties to the Enemy   15
And Sylvan Punctuation—
1880   *1894*

1510

How happy is the little Stone
That rambles in the Road alone,
And does'nt care about Careers
And Exigencies never fears—
Whose Coat of elemental Brown
A passing Universe put on,   6
And independent as the Sun
Associates or glows alone,
Fulfilling absolute Decree
In casual simplicity—   10
1882   *1891*

1585

The Bird her punctual music
     brings
And lays it in its place—
It's place is in the Human Heart
And in the Heavenly Grace—
What respite from her thrilling toil
Did Beauty ever take—   6
But Work might be electric Rest
To those that Magic make—
1883   *1955*

1624

Apparently with no surprise
To any happy Flower
The Frost beheads it at it's play—
In accidental power—
The blonde Assassin passes on—   5
The Sun proceeds unmoved
To measure off another Day
For an Approving God.
1884   *1890*

1732

My life closed twice before its
     close;
It yet remains to see
If Immortality unveil
A third event to me,

So huge, so hopeless to conceive   5
As these that twice befel.
Parting is all we know of heaven,
And all we need of hell.
?   *1896*

1755

To make a prairie it takes a clover
       and one bee,
One clover, and a bee,
And revery.
The revery alone will do,
If bees are few.   5
?   *1894*

1760

Elysium is as far as to
The very nearest Room
If in that Room a Friend await
Felicity or Doom—

What fortitude the Soul contains,
That it can so endure   6
The accent of a coming Foot—
The opening of a Door—
1882   *1890*

MARK TWAIN
(Samuel Langhorne Clemens)

1835–1910

*U*NLIKE WHITMAN AND MELVILLE, WHOSE REPUTATIONS ARE A RESULT of twentieth-century revaluation, Mark Twain enjoyed great popular success and critical esteem in his own day and continues to be regarded as one of our foremost contributions to world literature. But this is not to say that we see him exactly as did his contemporaries. To them he was a literary "funny man," a kind of public comedian who could be expected to interpret the day's news wryly or to provide the humorous climax at a testimonial dinner. That he was, even more than Emerson or Lowell, a public figure may have been due rather to his newsworthiness than to the numerous lecture tours which made his *nom de plume* a byword throughout the English-speaking world. He was in fact an entertainer who might have disappeared into historical limbo along with Artemus Ward or Josh Billings. Indeed, he felt himself so "typed" that when he wished his book on Joan of Arc to be seriously received he issued it anonymously.

But there was another side to Twain. As a student of human nature he saw man's foibles and inconsistencies and moral puniness, first as a frontier phenomenon and later as a universal expression of the human condition. The scourge of folly is satire, which he applied liberally wherever he encountered pretension or inhumanity or hypocrisy. It was an ingredient in almost everything he wrote, from his youthful sketch "The Dandy Frightening the Squatter" to *The Mysterious Stranger.* But the predominant tone was humorous, and even satire might partake of amusement if the target were distant enough, as in the Arthurian England of *A Connecticut Yankee.* Often Twain provided an emotional catharsis through pathos, so that *The Prince and the Pauper* and even

Huckleberry Finn could be read appreciatively by Victorian sentimentalists. Beneath the surface of amusement and pathos, however, there lies a deeper layer of meaning, a knowing judgment of an imperfect world. The books for boys are not boys' books; they speak to a more mature audience not only with their nostalgia but also with a moralist's serious concern for the values by which men live. It is this double vision that accounts for the twentieth-century recognition of Twain as a complex figure. For us he is more than the literary comedian, the international public man, the critic of individual and social morality. He is also an artist, consciously concerned with giving form to his ideas, unconsciously embodying the myths and traditions of his culture.

The single most important fact in Sam Clemens' inheritance was Hannibal. He was four years old when his family moved to the river town from nearby Florida, Missouri, where he had been born in 1835. Hannibal was his home until he was eighteen, and those impressionable years loaded his imagination with the adventures of boyhood, the friends and cronies, the town characters, the fires and mobs and murders, and above all the spell of the Mississippi River, a magical highway which brought the outer world to the doorstep of Hannibal. In his boyhood years Missouri was a frontier state, full of brave prospects but raw realities as civilization fitfully took hold. Existence was not bleak and joyless, as Van Wyck Brooks maintained in *The Ordeal of Mark Twain;* the correction administered by Bernard DeVoto in *Mark Twain's America* and the body of solid fact assembled by Dixon Wecter in *Sam Clemens of Hannibal* point to an exciting and entertaining pattern of life. The world of Hannibal became the imaginative center for Twain, who returned to it again and again: it is St. Petersburg in *Tom Sawyer* and *Huckleberry Finn,* Dawson's Landing in *Pudd'nhead Wilson,* Eseldorf in *The Mysterious Stranger.* He could picture the riverside village warmly in his idyls of boyhood or serve an indictment against its leading citizens in "The Man that Corrupted Hadleyburg"; his autobiographical reminiscences of the seasons, the food, the river and shore (see p. 301 below) are almost sentimental. Instinctively he strikes a balance in *Huckleberry Finn,* where the proprieties of Judge Thatcher and the "sivilizing" influences of the Widow Douglas are offset by the delirium tremens and homicidal tendencies of Pap Finn. The art of Mark Twain surely transmuted the stuff of experience, but the Hannibal years saturated him with knowledge which he could later transform into understanding.

Young Clemens got little formal schooling; when he was twelve his father died and soon afterward he became an apprentice in the printing trade. At eighteen he was a journeyman printer and for three years drifted about the country holding jobs in St. Louis, New York, Philadelphia, Keokuk and Cincinnati. He was absorbing all sorts of popular journalism, notably the examples of tall-tale humor which newspapers freely appropriated from their "exchanges." In such stories as "Simon Suggs Attends a Camp-Meeting" (traces of which appear in the revival episode in *Huck Finn*), the Sut Lovingood tales, T. B. Thorpe's "The Big Bear of Arkansas," and the legendary exploits fathered on David Crockett, he found a well-developed yarnspinning technique in which the colloquial language of earthy frontier types was both a source of humor and a means of character revelation. As a compositor, Sam Clemens must have set up many a piece of frontier humor; he could scarcely have escaped reading many more or hearing local variations spun by the whittlers and loafers of Hannibal. From these influences, at any rate, we may explain his mastery of the tones of speech, his sensitive use of colloquial vocabulary. Hemingway has said that all modern American literature comes from one book—*Huckleberry Finn;* but behind that novel lay half a century of sub-literary stories and sketches that made Mark Twain possible.

In April 1857 young Clemens left Cincinnati for New Orleans and the Amazon River, but his far-fetched dream of exploration was suddenly abandoned when he persuaded Horace Bixby to accept him as an apprentice pilot. *Life on the Mississippi* is a somewhat imaginative ordering of the rich experience that followed. Having gone through the exacting job of learning the river, he became a well-paid glamorous figure in the heyday of the Mississippi steamboat. The onset of the Civil War put an end to this prestigious career, and after a brief period in what must have been the most loosely organized military unit of modern times (affectionately described in "The Private History of a Campaign that Failed"), he set out for Nevada with his brother Orion, who had been appointed secretary to the territorial governor.

The years 1861–66 were a final apprenticeship. He tried his hand at mining, but soon exhausted his savings without making a strike; he became a professional journalist, first with the Virginia City *Territorial Enterprise* and later with papers in San Francisco, developing a lucid style for factual reporting and a distinctive flair for recording the oral anecdote; he tried his hand at travel dispatches from Hawaii in which the blend of fact, anecdote and rambling fancy became the model for his later volumes of autobiographical prose; and he took up lecturing, which he enjoyed and despised by turns, regardless of his evident success. Late in 1865 "Jim Smiley and His Jumping Frog" appeared in a New York newspaper; it was widely reprinted and marked the beginning of something more than local fame. By the time he came to New York in the spring of 1867 he was known as "The Wild Humorist of the Pacific Slope" and "The Moralist of the Main." His local grounding in the traditions and folkways of the Mississippi Valley and the Far West was firm; all his important work henceforth would build imaginatively upon these foundations.

In 1870 he married Olivia Langdon and two years later settled in Hartford, Connecticut, where he made his home until the end of the century. But he was a frequent visitor to Europe and made several long sojourns in Germany, Italy and England. Besides his writing he devoted untold time and enthusiasm to the promotion of inventions, the most disastrous of which was the Paige typesetting machine which eventually bankrupted his publishing firm and finally himself. Saddled with mountainous debts, he made a round-the-world lecture tour in 1895–96 and by 1900 succeeded in satisfying his creditors in full. The Hartford home was now so full of tragic family memories that he moved to New York City. His last years were clouded by his wife's death in 1904 and the loss of his daughter Jean in 1909; he himself died at Stormfield, Connecticut, the following year, survived only by his daughter Clara.

The Celebrated Jumping Frog of Calaveras County, and Other Sketches (1867) was his first book, but it was *The Innocents Abroad* (1869) that established him before a national public. Based on letters describing a Mediterranean cruise of the *Quaker City* in 1867, it is Twain's intensely individual view of southern Europe, Egypt and the Holy Land, mingling awe with disdain, enthusiasm with impatience; he is the self-confident American passing judgment on an old civilization, a Protestant confronting the Catholicism of France and Italy, a self-proclaimed amateur inspecting the treasures of museums and art galleries. What distinguishes it from the conventional travel book is not only its personal point of view but also its humorous anecdotes and the constant play of wit and irony over its pages. Mark Twain saw the human comedy with a mixture of cynicism and kindliness, and this spirit characterizes his other accounts of travel—*A Tramp Abroad* (1880) and *Following the Equator* (1897). Akin to this genre are *Roughing It* (1872), an account of his Western adventures, and the last two-thirds of *Life on the Mississippi* (1883), describing his return to the river after twenty-one years' absence. In all these books he let imagination play over facts ("I could remember anything, whether it had happened or not"), and his loose chronological structures were always subject to interruption when a good yarn occurred to him. Some of his best short stories and sketches are, in fact, imbedded in these narratives; sometimes, as in "Buck Fanshaw's Funeral," they are an integral part of the context, but pieces like "Baker's Blue-Jay Yarn" are introduced upon very slight pretext. For Twain was an episodic writer, an extemporizer always ready to exploit the inspiration of the moment, generally careless of form. Such artlessness lent charm and freshness to chronicle but it could imperil a novel.

At their worst, Twain's novels fell apart. *The Gilded Age* (1873) was a collaboration, and it is no wonder that he and Warner were unsuccessful in combining plots of satire and sentiment. *Pudd'nhead Wilson* (1894), as Twain describes it, started as farce and ended as tragedy; with two irreconcilable stories on his hands he performed what he called "a kind of literary Caesarian operation" and published "Those Extraordinary Twins" as a separate piece. His trouble had been that he started with some people, a setting, and an incident or two, but with no central problem to motivate a plot; he improvised, letting the tale grow as it would. This was indeed the way he approached all his novels, and such unity as they possess was accidental and instinctive, not the result of careful planning. In *The Prince and the Pauper* (1881) the plot line was dictated by Prince Edward and Tom Canty's exchange of roles; in *A Connecticut Yankee* (1889) it derived from the juxtaposition of nine-teenth-century technology and the world of Arthurian romance. But these novels, like *Tom Sawyer* (1876) and *The Adventures of Huckle-berry Finn* (1885), are composed of a string of episodes which depend on the central characters to hold the picaresque structure together. Even the best of these, *Huckleberry Finn*, does not begin to find its direction until Huck has discovered Nigger Jim on Jackson Island and the fate of the runaway slave becomes the central problem. And Twain seriously compromises the unity of tone and character in the closing chapters with an elaborate burlesque of romantic fiction which would have been more appropriate to *Tom Sawyer, Detective*. The world of the river was real and Huck had come to grips with fundamental problems of right and wrong; with a humanitarian instinct far in advance of his powers of analysis he divined the essential pathos in the fourflushing antics of the spurious king and duke, as he sensed the inherent dignity of illiterate Jim. The unfolding of Huck's ethical awareness is at the heart of the novel, and is one important reason for its greatness. The reappearance of Tom Sawyer leads to anticlimax, for Huck and the reader have moved far beyond the buffooneries that could be tolerated at the beginning of the novel.

If Twain lacked the ability to confront the exacting demands of novelistic form, he was saved by the vitality and energy he put into character creation. Perhaps his soundest strategies were subconscious rather than contrived; there is no denying his serious concern for hu-manity and its problems, even when the vehicle is primarily comic. The Yankee amuses and delights us, but we are sobered by the crushing weight on the human spirit he finds in superstition and squalor, in the oppressions of state and church. Often Twain looks at society through the eyes and heart of the dispossessed: both the prince and the pauper make us aware of social evils in Tudor England; Pudd'nhead Wilson is written off by his neighbors as a fool, but his uncommon sense leads to an act of justice which the established institutions could not bring about. Huck Finn, too, is an outsider who must mediate between the powerful claims of conventionality and the frail strength of his conscience; we cannot blame him for confusing the two and censuring himself ("All right, then, I'll *go* to hell"), but we recognize that he has stumbled onto the transcendence of right over law which Emerson and Thoreau preached.

In another mood Twain translated his personal crises and frustrations into cosmic terms and denied the ability of the human race to shape its destiny. A bleak determinism motivates his tract *What Is Man?* and a number of other late pieces reflect an almost unrelieved cynicism. This attitude underlies "The Man that Corrupted Hadleyburg" and the post-humous *Mysterious Stranger* (1916). In the former he develops the thesis that every man has his price, while in the latter he moves to a complete denial of reality as the only explanation of man's pretensions and cruelties. DeVoto's penetrating chapter "The Symbols of Despair" in his *Mark Twain at Work* studies these pieces along with a mass of unfinished manuscripts in relation to the financial ruin that followed the failure of his typesetting machine in 1894 and the family tragedies that deepened his gloom. DeVoto thus gives us a far more circumstantial basis for Twain's pessimism than Brooks' Freudian theorizing. But if Twain as essayist and thinker jibed bitterly at the human race, the imaginative side of the artist was never able to lose sympathy with individuals. The weakness of Richards is relentlessly exposed in "Hadleyburg" but he is not held up to scorn. And the simple village folk of Eseldorf, especially the young, are treated with Twain's customary warmth; Satan, the mysterious stranger, is in most respects simply a worker of evil magic like his earthly counterpart in "Hadleyburg." Ultimately it is Twain's doctrine, not his people, that must seem contrived. Had he possessed the cool detachment of Crane he might have found a suitable vehicle for his ideas.

Temperamentally Sam Clemens was mercurial. The American dream of vast financial success was his, and he pursued it feverishly with all the optimism of his Colonel Sellers. He could as easily be depressed by ill luck or suspicion. He could be reduced to tears by acts of kindness or moved to wrath by the hint of a slur against him. In his calmer moods he saw beneath and behind the comforts of religious orthodoxy, as had his free-thinking father before him. During the last twenty years of his life the gaiety that had accompanied the sting of his satire was vanishing; for like Henry Adams he saw little sign of progress in the human race, and his spiritual doubts were reinforced by personal calamity and the slowing down of the human machine.

For all his uniqueness Mark Twain is an embodiment of his age. In him we see the continental heartland challenging an earlier domination by the Eastern seaboard. In him we find the laughter of the frontier—a laughter not of innocence only; an earthiness which bespeaks a knowledge of uncouth realities; and an anti-genteel attitude which mingles the grotesque with the humorous. In the last decades of the nineteenth century the vernacular was becoming ever more conspicuous in literature and Twain's work played a major part in its gradual acceptance. He was seriously concerned with America as a land of promise, but he also wrestled with the doubts that plagued Victorians on both sides of the ocean. Like Chaucer he lacks that high seriousness which Matthew Arnold demanded for greatness; but the comic vision of Chaucer, Cervantes, and Twain is a fortunate legacy for the world, and in this sense Twain has earned for himself a place in good company.

The texts here reprinted are based on first publications in book form. Because the "house style" of his several publishers differed, and because canons of usage altered through the years, Twain's books reflect great inconsistency in punctuation, compounding, and spelling. The present texts preserve first edition readings except for obvious inaccuracies; minor modifications in punctuation are made only in the interest of clarity and internal consistency within the piece. It should be noted that when the original illustrated subscription editions were superseded they were reset with wholesale punctuation changes and with occasional textual alterations which Twain, so far as we know, had no hand in.

THE CELEBRATED JUMPING FROG OF CALAVERAS COUNTY

During bad weather when a group of miners were gathered around the stove in a hotel at Angel's Camp, Mark Twain heard Ben Coon relate in his monotonous flat drawl the story of Jim Smiley and his jumping frog. He made a note of it at the time and later wrote the story for inclusion in a book of Artemus Ward's. It reached the publisher too late and fell into the hands of the New York *Saturday Press*, where it appeared November 18, 1865. It was copied far and wide and introduced Twain's name to the national public. In 1867 it became the title story in Twain's first book, *The Celebrated Jumping Frog of Calaveras County, and Other Sketches*, from which the present text is derived. "The Jumping Frog" in *Sketches New and Old* (1875) includes a slightly different version of the tale along with a French translation and Twain's word-by-word re-translation into English (a stock device which he repeatedly employed in the mistaken belief that it was exceedingly funny).

The yarn was not original with Ben Coon; in fact, versions of it had appeared in print at least three times before 1860, including Henry P. Leland's "Frogs Shot without Powder" in the New York *Spirit of the Times*, May 26, 1855. It had probably circulated orally for some time and may be ultimately of Negro origin. At any rate, as DeVoto observed, "It was American folklore here wrought into literature."

In compliance with the request of a friend of mine, who wrote me from the East, I called on good-natured, garrulous old Simon Wheeler, and inquired after my friend's friend, *Leonidas W*. Smiley, as requested to do, and I hereunto append the result. I have a lurking suspicion that *Leonidas W*. Smiley is a myth; that my friend never knew such a personage; and that he only conjectured that, if I asked old Wheeler about him, it would remind him of his infamous *Jim* Smiley, and he would go to work and bore me nearly to death with some infernal reminiscence of him as long and tedious as it should be useless to me. If that was the design, it certainly succeeded.

I found Simon Wheeler dozing comfortably by the bar-room stove of the old, dilapidated tavern in the ancient mining camp of Angel's, and I noticed that he was fat and bald-headed, and had an expression of winning gentleness and simplicity upon his tranquil countenance. He roused up and gave me good-day. I told him a friend of mine had commissioned me to make some inquiries about a cherished companion of his boyhood named *Leonidas W. Smiley—Rev. Leonidas W.* Smiley—a young minister of the Gospel, who he had heard was at one time a resident of Angel's Camp. I added that, if Mr. Wheeler could tell me any thing about this Rev. Leonidas W. Smiley, I would feel under many obligations to him.

Simon Wheeler backed me into a corner and blockaded me there with his chair, and then sat me down and reeled off the monotonous narrative which follows this paragraph. He never smiled, he never frowned, he never changed his voice from the gentle-flowing key to which he tuned the initial sentence, he never betrayed the slightest suspicion of enthusiasm; but all through the interminable narrative there ran a vein of impressive earnestness and sincerity, which showed me plainly that, so far from his imagining that there was any thing ridiculous or funny about his story, he regarded it as a really important matter, and admired its two heroes as men of transcendent genius in *finesse*. To me, the spectacle of a man drifting serenely along through such a queer yarn without ever smiling, was exquisitely absurd. As I said before, I asked him to tell me what he knew of Rev. Leonidas W. Smiley, and he replied as follows. I let him go on in his own way, and never interrupted him once:

There was a feller here once by the name of *Jim* Smiley, in the winter of '49—or may be it was the spring of '50—I don't recollect exactly, somehow, though what makes me think it was one or the other is because I remember the big flume wasn't finished when he first came to the camp; but any way, he was the curiousest man about always betting on any thing that turned up you ever see, if he could get any body to bet on the other side; and if he couldn't, he'd change sides. Any way that suited the other man would suit him—any way just so's he got a bet, *he* was satisfied. But still he was lucky, uncommon lucky; he most always come out winner. He was always ready and laying for a chance; there couldn't be no solit'ry thing mentioned but that feller'd offer to bet on it, and take any side you please, as I was just telling you. If there was a horse-race, you'd find him flush, or you'd find him busted at the end of it; if there was a dog-fight, he'd bet on it; if there was a cat-fight, he'd bet on it; if there was a chicken-fight, he'd bet on it; why, if there was two birds setting on a fence, he would bet you which one would fly first; or if there was a camp-meeting, he would be there reg'lar, to bet on Parson Walker, which he judged to be the best exhorter about here, and so he was, too, and a good man. If he even seen a straddle-bug start to go anywheres, he would bet you how long it would take him to get wherever he was going to, and if you took him up, he would follow that straddle-bug to Mexico but what he would find out where he was bound for and how long he was on the road. Lots of the boys here has seen that Smiley, and can tell you about him. Why, it never made no difference to *him*—he would bet on *any* thing—the dangdest feller. Parson Walker's wife laid very sick once, for a good while, and it seemed as if they warn't going to save her; but one morning he come in, and Smiley asked how she was, and he said she was considerable better—thank the Lord for his inf'nit mercy—and coming on so smart that, with the blessing of Prov'dence, she'd get well yet; and Smiley, before he thought, says, "Well, I'll risk two-and-a-half that she don't, any way."

Thish-yer Smiley had a mare—the boys called her the fifteen-minute nag, but that was only in fun, you know, because, of course, she was faster than that—and he used to win money on that horse, for all she was so slow and always had the asthma, or the distemper, or the consumption, or something of that kind. They used to give her two or three hundred yards start, and then pass her under way; but always at the fag-end of the race she'd get excited and desperate-like, and come cavorting and straddling up, and scattering her legs around limber, sometimes in the air, and sometimes out to one side amongst the fences, and kicking up m-o-r-e dust, and raising m-o-r-e racket with her coughing and sneezing and blowing her nose—and always fetch up at the stand just about a neck ahead, as near as you could cipher it down.

And he had a little small bull pup, that to look at him you'd think he wa'n't worth a cent, but to set around and look ornery, and lay for a chance to steal something. But as soon as money was up on him, he was a different dog; his under-jaw'd begin to stick out like the fo'castle of a steamboat, and his teeth would uncover, and shine savage like the furnaces. And a dog might tackle him, and bully-rag him, and bite him, and throw him over his shoulder two or three times, and Andrew Jackson—which was the name of the pup—Andrew Jackson would never let on but what *he* was satisfied, and hadn't expected nothing else—and the bets being doubled and doubled on the other side all the time, till the money was all up; and then all of a sudden he would grab that other dog jest by the j'int of his hind leg and freeze to it—not chaw, you understand, but only jest grip and hang on till they throwed up the sponge, if it was a year. Smiley always come out winner on that pup, till he harnessed a dog once that didn't have no hind legs, because they'd been sawed off by a circular saw, and when the thing had gone along far enough, and the money was all up, and he come to make a snatch for his pet holt, he saw in a minute how he'd been imposed on, and how the other dog had him in the door, so to speak, and he 'peared surprised, and then he looked sorter discouraged-like, and didn't try no more to win the fight, and so he got shucked out bad. He give Smiley a look, as much as to say his heart was broke, and it was *his* fault, for putting up a dog that hadn't no hind legs for him to take holt of, which was his main dependence in a fight, and then he limped off a piece and laid down and died. It was a

good pup, was that Andrew Jackson, and would have made a name for
hisself if he'd lived, for the stuff was in him, and he had genius—I know
it, because he hadn't had no opportunities to speak of, and it don't stand
to reason that a dog could make such a fight as he could under them circumstances, if he hadn't no talent. It always makes me feel sorry when I
think of that last fight of his'n, and the way it turned out.

Well, thish-yer Smiley had rat-tarriers, and chicken cocks, and tom-
cats, and all them kind of things, till you couldn't rest, and you couldn't
fetch nothing for him to bet on but he'd match you. He ketched a frog
one day, and took him home, and said he calk'lated to edercate him; and
so he never done nothing for three months but set in his back yard and
learn that frog to jump. And you bet he *did* learn him, too. He'd give
him a little punch behind, and the next minute you'd see that frog whirling in the air like a doughnut—see him turn one summerset, or may be a
couple, if he got a good start, and come down flat-footed and all right,
like a cat. He got him up so in the matter of catching flies, and kept him
in practice so constant, that he'd nail a fly every time as far as he could
see him. Smiley said all a frog wanted was education, and he could do
most anything—and I believe him. Why, I've seen him set Dan'l Webster down here on this floor—Dan'l Webster was the name of the frog—
and sing out, "Flies, Dan'l, flies!" and quicker'n you could wink, he'd
spring straight up, and snake a fly off'n the counter there, and flop down
on the floor again as solid as a gob of mud, and fall to scratching the side
of his head with his hind foot as indifferent as if he hadn't no idea he'd
been doin' any more'n any frog might do. You never see a frog so modest
and straightfor'ard as he was, for all he was so gifted. And when it come
to fair and square jumping on a dead level, he could get over more ground
at one straddle than any animal of his breed you ever see. Jumping on a
dead level was his strong suit, you understand; and when it come to that,
Smiley would ante up money on him as long as he had a red. Smiley
was monstrous proud of his frog, and well he might be, for fellers that
had traveled and been everywheres, all said he laid over any frog that
ever *they* see.

Well Smiley kept the beast in a little lattice box, and he used to fetch
him down town sometimes and lay for a bet. One day a feller—a stranger
in the camp, he was—come across him with his box, and says:

"What might it be that you've got in the box?"

And Smiley says, sorter indifferent like, "It might be a parrot, or it
might be a canary, may be, but it an't—it's only just a frog."

And the feller took it, and looked at it careful, and turned it round this
way and that, and says, "H'm—so 'tis. Well, what's *he* good for?"

"Well," Smiley says, easy and careless, "he's good enough for *one*
thing, I should judge—he can outjump ary frog in Calaveras county."

The feller took the box again, and took another long, particular look,
and give it back to Smiley, and says, very deliberate, "Well, I don't see
no p'ints about that frog that's any better'n any other frog."

"May be you don't," Smiley says. "May be you understand frogs, and may be you don't understand 'em; may be you've had experience, and may be you an't only a amature, as it were. Anyways, I've got *my* opinion, and I'll risk forty dollars that he can outjump any frog in Calaveras county."

And the feller studied a minute, and then says, kinder sad like, "Well, I'm only a stranger here, and I an't got no frog, but if I had a frog, I'd bet you."

And then Smiley says, "That's all right—that's all right—if you'll hold my box a minute, I'll go and get you a frog." And so the feller took the box, and put up his forty dollars along with Smiley's, and set down to wait.

So he set there a good while thinking and thinking to hisself, and then he got the frog out and prized his mouth open and took a teaspoon and filled him full of quail shot—filled him pretty near up to his chin—and set him on the floor. Smiley he went to the swamp and slopped around in the mud for a long time, and finally he ketched a frog, and fetched him in, and give him to this feller, and says:

"Now, if you're ready, set him alongside of Dan'l, with his fore-paws just even with Dan'l, and I'll give the word." Then he says, "One—two—three—jump!" and him and the feller touched up the frogs from behind, and the new frog hopped off, but Dan'l give a heave, and hysted up his shoulders—so—like a Frenchman, but it wan't no use—he couldn't budge; he was planted as solid as an anvil, and he couldn't no more stir than if he was anchored out. Smiley was a good deal surprised, and he was disgusted too, but he didn't have no idea what the matter was, of course.

The feller took the money and started away; and when he was going out at the door, he sorter jerked his thumb over his shoulders—this way—at Dan'l, and says again, very deliberate, "Well, *I* don't see no p'ints about that frog that's any better'n any other frog."

Smiley he stood scratching his head and looking down at Dan'l a long time, and at last he says, "I do wonder what in the nation that frog throw'd off for—I wonder if there an't something the matter with him—he 'pears to look mighty baggy, somehow." And he ketched Dan'l by the nap of the neck, and lifted him up and says, "Why, blame my cats, if he don't weigh five pound!" and turned him upside down, and he belched out a double handful of shot. And then he see how it was, and he was the maddest man—he set the frog down and took out after that feller, but he never ketched him. And—

[Here Simon Wheeler heard his name called from the front yard, and got up to see what was wanted.] And turning to me as he moved away, he said: "Just set where you are, stranger, and rest easy—I an't going to be gone a second."

But, by your leave, I did not think that a continuation of the history of the enterprising vagabond *Jim* Smiley would be likely to afford me much information concerning the *Rev. Leonidas W.* Smiley, and so I started away.

At the door I met the sociable Wheeler returning, and he buttonholed me and recommenced:

"Well, thish-yer Smiley had a yaller one-eyed cow that didn't have no tail, only jest a short stump like a bannanner, and—"

"Oh! hang Smiley and his afflicted cow!" I muttered, good-naturedly, and bidding the old gentleman good-day, I departed.

1865   *1867*

From THE INNOCENTS ABROAD

In June 1867 the *Quaker City* embarked on a five-month Mediterranean tour with some seventy-five passengers, the first "cruise" in modern times. Mark Twain was aboard as correspondent for the *Alta California*, which had underwritten his $1250 passage and was paying him $20 for each letter. He sent back fifty-three dispatches to the *Alta* and wrote a few others for New York papers. The ship called at all the principal ports of southern Europe, Asia Minor and North Africa and passengers took overland trips to interior cities of France, Italy, the Holy Land and Egypt according to a prearranged program. Twain's letters gave a running account of his adventures, usually in company with his roommate Dan Slote and Dr. A. Reeves Jackson, a physician from Stroudsburg, Pennsylvania. He recorded all the sights, often with considerable guide-book background, always with the flavor of personal reaction. He was instructive, but he was also humorous and he could be critical; therein lay the freshness of his approach. Soon after his return he was approached by the American Publishing Company of Hartford to turn his letters into a book, and thus began a profitable but often stormy relationship with a firm that sold its books by subscription only. *The Innocents Abroad, or the New Pilgrim's Progress* appeared in 1869 and enjoyed immediate success.

The selections here reprinted show how Twain adapted the conventions of travel literature to his own purposes. He was always interested in concrete information and his travel books are filled with accurate descriptions and masses of fact. But he was a story-teller too, and he often abandoned the scene of the moment to recall a character or an episode from some other locale. Thus we get his reminiscence of the patient Nevada judge in Chapter XXVII. Above all, the play of humor dictated an atmosphere of levity in which Twain was free to spoof pretension or enjoy a merry anecdote.

Chapter XI on Marseilles is a good example of his range of interests, not the least of which is his absorption in the mystery and romance of Château d'If. He was storing up details which he would later use in the closing chapters of *Huckleberry Finn;* there he would satirize the cloak-and-sword romance, but here he is the humanitarian moved by the pathos of prisoners' lonely and hopeless wearing out of time.

Chapter XV begins as a conventional account of the famous Paris cemetery of Père Lachaise but quickly moves to the story of Abélard and Héloïse, which Twain tells in a style which is a mixture of burlesque and seriousness. The reason for introducing it is the underlying moral indignation he feels toward Abélard, but he is also bent on destroying the romantic aura investing the common reputation of the two "ideal lovers."

The excerpt from Chapter XXVII enters a minority report on Michaelangelo and reflects a justified irritation at the set spiels of guides. Mark and his friends called all their guides "Ferguson," and the book contains several other episodes at their expense.

Chapter XI

We are getting foreignized rapidly, and with facility. We are getting reconciled to halls and bed-chambers with unhomelike stone floors, and no carpets—floors that ring to the tread of one's heels with a sharpness that is death to sentimental musing. We are getting used to tidy, noiseless waiters, who glide hither and thither, and hover about your back and your elbows like butterflies, quick to comprehend orders, quick to fill them; thankful for a gratuity without regard to the amount; and always polite—never otherwise than polite. That is the strangest curiosity yet— a really polite hotel waiter who isn't an idiot. We are getting used to driving right into the central court of the hotel, in the midst of a fragrant circle of vines and flowers, and in the midst, also, of parties of gentlemen sitting quietly reading the paper and smoking. We are getting used to ice frozen by artificial process in ordinary bottles—the only kind of ice they have here. We are getting used to all these things; but we are *not* getting used to carrying our own soap. We are sufficiently civilized to carry our own combs and tooth-brushes; but this thing of having to ring for soap every time we wash is new to us, and not pleasant at all. We think of it just after we get our heads and faces thoroughly wet, or just when we think we have been in the bath-tub long enough, and then, of course, an annoying delay follows. These Marseillaise make Marseillaise hymns, and Marseilles vests, and Marseilles soap for all the world; but they never sing their hymns, or wear their vests, or wash with their soap themselves.

We have learned to go through the lingering routine of the table d'hôte with patience, with serenity, with satisfaction. We take soup; then wait a few minutes for the fish; a few minutes more and the plates are changed, and the roast beef comes; another change and we take peas; change again and take lentils; change and take snail patties (I prefer grasshoppers); change and take roast chicken and salad; then strawberry pie and ice cream; then green figs, pears, oranges, green almonds, &c.; finally coffee. Wine with every course, of course, being in France. With such a cargo on board, digestion is a slow process, and we must sit long in the cool chambers and smoke—and read French newspapers, which have a strange fashion of telling a perfectly straight story till you get to the "nub" of it, and then a word drops in that no man can translate, and that story is ruined. An embankment fell on some Frenchmen yesterday, and the papers are full of it to-day—but whether those sufferers were killed, or crippled, or bruised, or only scared, is more than I can possibly make out, and yet I would just give any thing to know.

We were troubled a little at dinner to-day, by the conduct of an American, who talked very loudly and coarsely, and laughed boisterously where all others were so quiet and well-behaved. He ordered wine with a royal flourish, and said: "I never dine without wine, sir" (which was a pitiful falsehood), and looked around upon the company to bask in the admiration he expected to find in their faces. All these airs in a land where they would as soon expect to leave the soup out of the bill of fare as the wine!—in a land where wine is nearly as common among all ranks as water! This fellow said: "I am a free-born sovereign, sir, an American, sir, and I want every body to know it!" He did not mention that he was a lineal descendant of Balaam's ass; but every body knew that without his telling it.

We have driven in the Prado—that superb avenue bordered with patrician mansions and noble shade-trees—and have visited the Chateau Borély [1] and its curious museum. They showed us a miniature cemetery there—a copy of the first graveyard that was ever in Marseilles, no doubt. The delicate little skeletons were lying in broken vaults, and had their household gods and kitchen utensils with them. The original of this cemetery was dug up in the principal street of the city a few years ago. It had remained there, only twelve feet under ground, for a matter of twenty-five hundred years, or thereabouts. Romulus was here before he built Rome, and thought something of founding a city on this spot, but gave up the idea. He may have been personally acquainted with some of these Phœnicians whose skeletons we have been examining.

In the great Zoölogical Gardens, we found specimens of all the animals the world produces, I think, including a dromedary, a monkey ornamented with tufts of brilliant blue and carmine hair—a very gorgeous monkey he was—a hippopotamus from the Nile, and a sort of tall, long-legged bird with a beak like a powder-horn, and close-fitting wings like the tails of a dress coat. This fellow stood up with his eyes shut and his shoulders stooped forward a little, and looked as if he had his hands under his coat tails. Such tranquil stupidity, such supernatural gravity, such self-righteousness, and such ineffable self-complacency as were in

[1] The Château Borély (Twain wrote it "Boarely") is notable for its museum of antiquities in which the Phoenician origins of Marseilles are established.

the countenance and attitude of that gray-bodied, dark-winged, bald-headed, and preposterously uncomely bird! He was so ungainly, so pimply about the head, so scaly about the legs; yet so serene, so unspeakably satisfied! He was the most comical-looking creature that can be imagined. It was good to hear Dan and the doctor laugh—such natural and such enjoyable laughter had not been heard among our excursionists since our ship sailed away from America. This bird was a god-send to us, and I should be an ingrate if I forgot to make honorable mention of him in these pages. Ours was a pleasure excursion; therefore we stayed with that bird an hour, and made the most of him. We stirred him up occasionally, but he only unclosed an eye and slowly closed it again, abating no jot of his stately piety of demeanor or his tremendous seriousness. He only seemed to say, "Defile not Heaven's anointed with unsanctified hands." We did not know his name, and so we called him "The Pilgrim." Dan said:

"All he wants now is a Plymouth Collection." [2]

The boon companion of the colossal elephant was a common cat! This cat had a fashion of climbing up the elephant's hind legs, and roosting on his back. She would sit up there, with her paws curved under her breast, and sleep in the sun half the afternoon. It used to annoy the elephant at first, and he would reach up and take her down, but she would go aft and climb up again. She persisted until she finally conquered the elephant's prejudices, and now they are inseparable friends. The cat plays about her comrade's forefeet or his trunk often, until dogs approach, and then she goes aloft out of danger. The elephant has annihilated several dogs lately, that pressed his companion too closely.

We hired a sail-boat and a guide and made an excursion to one of the small islands in the harbor to visit the Castle d'If. This ancient fortress has a melancholy history. It has been used as a prison for political offenders for two or three hundred years, and its dungeon walls are scarred with the rudely carved names of many and many a captive who fretted his life away here, and left no record of himself but these sad epitaphs wrought with his own hands. How thick the names were! And their long-departed owners seemed to throng the gloomy cells and corridors with their phantom shapes. We loitered through dungeon after dungeon, away down into the living rock below the level of the sea, it seemed. Names every where!—some plebeian, some noble, some even princely. Plebeian, prince, and noble, had one solicitude in common—they would not be forgotten! They could suffer solitude, inactivity, and the horrors of a silence that no sound ever disturbed; but they could not bear the thought of being utterly forgotten by the world. Hence the carved names. In one cell, where a little light penetrated, a man had lived twenty-seven years without seeing the face of a human being—lived in filth and wretchedness,

[2] The *Quaker City* "pilgrims" were provided with copies of Henry Ward Beecher's *Plymouth Collection of Hymns and Tunes* (1855).

with no companionship but his own thoughts, and they were sorrowful enough, and hopeless enough, no doubt. Whatever his jailers considered that he needed was conveyed to his cell by night, through a wicket. This man carved the walls of his prison-house from floor to roof with all manner of figures of men and animals, grouped in intricate designs. He had toiled there year after year, at his self-appointed task, while infants grew to boyhood—to vigorous youth—idled through school and college—acquired a profession—claimed man's mature estate—married and looked back to infancy as to a thing of some vague, ancient time, almost. But who shall tell how many ages it seemed to this prisoner? With the one, time flew sometimes; with the other, never—it crawled always. To the one, nights spent in dancing had seemed made of minutes instead of hours; to the other, those self-same nights had been like all other nights of dungeon life, and seemed made of slow, dragging weeks, instead of hours and minutes.

One prisoner of fifteen years had scratched verses upon his walls, and brief prose sentences—brief, but full of pathos. These spoke not of himself and his hard estate; but only of the shrine where his spirit fled the prison to worship—of home and the idols that were templed there. He never lived to see them.

The walls of these dungeons are as thick as some bed-chambers at home are wide—fifteen feet. We saw the damp, dismal cells in which two of Dumas' heroes passed their confinement—heroes of *Monte Cristo*. It was here that the brave Abbé wrote a book with his own blood; with a pen made of a piece of iron hoop, and by the light of a lamp made out of shreds of cloth soaked in grease obtained from his food; and then dug through the thick wall with some trifling instrument which he wrought himself out of a stray piece of iron or table cutlery, and freed Dantès from his chains. It was a pity that so many weeks of dreary labor should have come to naught at last.

They showed us the noisome cell where the celebrated "Iron Mask"— that ill-starred brother of a hard-hearted king of France—was confined for a season, before he was sent to hide the strange mystery of his life from the curious in the dungeons of St. Marguerite.[3] The place had a far greater interest for us than it could have had if we had known beyond all question who the Iron Mask was, and what his history had been, and why this most unusual punishment had been meted out to him. Mystery! That was the charm. That speechless tongue, those prisoned features, that heart so freighted with unspoken troubles, and that breast so oppressed with its piteous secret, had been here. These dank walls had known the man whose dolorous story is a sealed book forever! There was fascination in the spot.

[3] The Man in the Iron Mask, whose identity has never been definitively established, figured in *Le Vicomte de Brage-* *lonne* (1848–50), one of Dumas' continuations of his popular novel, *The Three Musketeers*.

Chapter XV

One of our pleasantest visits was to Père la Chaise, the national bury-ing-ground of France, the honored resting-place of some of her greatest and best children, the last home of scores of illustrious men and women who were born to no titles, but achieved fame by their own energy and their own genius. It is a solemn city of winding streets, and of minia-ture marble temples and mansions of the dead gleaming white from out a wilderness of foliage and fresh flowers. Not every city is so well peo-pled as this, or has so ample an area within its walls. Few palaces exist in any city that are so exquisite in design, so rich in art, so costly in mate-rial, so graceful, so beautiful.

We had stood in the ancient church of St. Denis, where the marble effi-gies of thirty generations of kings and queens lay stretched at length upon the tombs, and the sensations invoked were startling and novel; the curi-ous armor, the obsolete costumes, the placid faces, the hands placed palm to palm in eloquent supplication—it was a vision of gray antiquity. It seemed curious enough to be standing face to face, as it were, with old Dagobert I, and Clovis and Charlemagne, those vague, colossal heroes, those shadows, those myths of a thousand years ago! I touched their dust-covered faces with my finger, but Dagobert was deader than the sixteen centuries that have passed over him, Clovis slept well after his labor for Christ, and old Charlemagne went on dreaming of his paladins, of bloody Roncesvalles, and gave no heed to me.

The great names of Père la Chaise impress one, too, but differently. There the suggestion brought constantly to his mind is, that this place is sacred to a nobler royalty—the royalty of heart and brain. Every faculty of mind, every noble trait of human nature, every high occupation which men engage in seems represented by a famous name. The effect is a curi-ous medley. Davoust and Massena, who wrought in many a battle-tragedy, are here, and so also is Rachel, of equal renown in mimic trag-edy on the stage. The Abbé Sicard sleeps here—the first great teacher of the deaf and dumb—a man whose heart went out to every unfortunate, and whose life was given to kindly offices in their service; and not far off, in repose and peace at last, lies Marshal Ney, whose stormy spirit knew no music like the bugle call to arms. The man who originated pub-lic gas-lighting, and that other benefactor who introduced the cultiva-tion of the potato and thus blessed millions of his starving countrymen, lie with the Prince of Masserano, and with exiled queens and princes of Further India. Gay-Lussac the chemist, Laplace the astronomer, Larrey the surgeon, de Sèze the advocate, are here, and with them are Talma, Bellini, Rubini; de Balzac, Beaumarchais, Béranger; Molière and Lafon-taine, and scores of other men whose names and whose worthy labors are as familiar in the remote by-places of civilization as are the historic deeds of the kings and princes that sleep in the marble vaults of St. Denis.

But among the thousands and thousands of tombs in Père la Chaise, there is one that no man, no woman, no youth of either sex, ever passes by without stopping to examine. Every visitor has a sort of indistinct idea of the history of its dead, and comprehends that homage is due there, but not one in twenty thousand clearly remembers the story of that tomb and its romantic occupants. This is the grave of Abelard and Heloise—a grave which has been more revered, more widely known, more written and sung about and wept over, for seven hundred years, than any other in Christendom, save only that of the Saviour. All visitors linger pensively about it; all young people capture and carry away keepsakes and mementoes of it; all Parisian youths and maidens who are disappointed in love come there to bail out when they are full of tears; yea, many stricken lovers make pilgrimages to this shrine from distant provinces to weep and wail and "grit" their teeth over their heavy sorrows, and to purchase the sympathies of the chastened spirits of that tomb with offerings of immortelles and budding flowers.

Go when you will, you find somebody snuffling over that tomb. Go when you will, you find it furnished with those bouquets and immortelles. Go when you will, you find a gravel-train from Marseilles arriving to supply the deficiencies caused by memento-cabbaging vandals whose affections have miscarried.

Yet who really knows the story of Abelard and Heloise? Precious few people. The names are perfectly familiar to every body, and that is about all. With infinite pains I have acquired a knowledge of that history, and I propose to narrate it here, partly for the honest information of the public and partly to show that public that they have been wasting a good deal of marketable sentiment very unnecessarily.

STORY OF ABELARD AND HELOISE.

Heloise was born seven hundred and sixty-six years ago. She may have had parents. There is no telling. She lived with her uncle Fulbert, a canon of the cathedral of Paris. I do not know what a canon of a cathedral is, but that is what he was. He was nothing more than a sort of a mountain howitzer, likely, because they had no heavy artillery in those days. Suffice it, then, that Heloise lived with her uncle the howitzer, and was happy. She spent the most of her childhood in the convent of Argenteuil—never heard of Argenteuil before, but suppose there was really such a place. She then returned to her uncle, the old gun, or son of a gun, as the case may be, and he taught her to write and speak Latin, which was the language of literature and polite society at that period.

Just at this time, Pierre Abelard, who had already made himself widely famous as a rhetorician, came to found a school of rhetoric in Paris. The originality of his principles, his eloquence, and his great physical strength and beauty created a profound sensation. He saw Heloise, and was captivated by her blooming youth, her beauty and her charming disposition. He wrote to her; she answered. He wrote again, she answered again. He was now in love. He longed to know her—to speak to her face to face.

His school was near Fulbert's house. He asked Fulbert to allow him to call. The good old swivel saw here a rare opportunity: his niece, whom he so much loved, would absorb knowledge from this man, and it would not cost him a cent. Such was Fulbert—penurious.

Fulbert's first name is not mentioned by any author, which is unfortunate. However, George W. Fulbert will answer for him as well as any other. We will let him go at that. He asked Abelard to teach her.

Abelard was glad enough of the opportunity. He came often and stayed long. A letter of his shows in its very first sentence that he came under that friendly roof, like a cold-hearted villain as he was, with the deliberate intention of debauching a confiding, innocent girl. This is the letter:

> "I cannot cease to be astonished at the simplicity of Fulbert; I was as much surprised as if he had placed a lamb in the power of a hungry wolf. Heloise and I, under pretext of study, gave ourselves up wholly to love, and the solitude that love seeks our studies procured for us. Books were open before us, but we spoke oftener of love than philosophy, and kisses came more readily from our lips than words."

And so, exulting over an honorable confidence which to his degraded instinct was a ludicrous "simplicity," this unmanly Abelard seduced the niece of the man whose guest he was. Paris found it out. Fulbert was told of it—told often—but refused to believe it. He could not comprehend how a man could be so depraved as to use the sacred protection and security of hospitality as a means for the commission of such a crime as that. But when he heard the rowdies in the streets singing the love-songs of Abelard to Heloise, the case was too plain—love-songs come not properly within the teachings of rhetoric and philosophy.

He drove Abelard from his house. Abelard returned secretly and carried Heloise away to Palais, in Brittany, his native country. Here, shortly afterward, she bore a son, who, from his rare beauty, was surnamed Astrolabe—William G. The girl's flight enraged Fulbert, and he longed for vengeance, but feared to strike lest retaliation visit Heloise—for he still loved her tenderly. At length Abelard offered to marry Heloise—but on a shameful condition: that the marriage should be kept secret from the world, to the end that (while her good name remained a wreck, as before) his priestly reputation might be kept untarnished. It was like that miscreant. Fulbert saw his opportunity and consented. He would see the parties married, and then violate the confidence of the man who had taught him that trick; he would divulge the secret and so remove somewhat of the obloquy that attached to his niece's fame. But the niece suspected his scheme. She refused the marriage, at first; she said Fulbert would betray the secret to save her, and besides, she did not wish to drag down a lover who was so gifted, so honored by the world, and who had such a splendid career before him. It was noble, self-sacrificing love, and characteristic of the pure-souled Heloise, but it was not good sense.

But she was overruled, and the private marriage took place. Now for Fulbert! The heart so wounded should be healed at last; the proud spirit so tortured should find rest again; the humbled head should be lifted up once more. He proclaimed the marriage in the high places of the city, and rejoiced that dishonor had departed from his house. But lo! Abelard denied the marriage! Heloise denied it! The people, knowing the former circumstances, might have believed Fulbert, had only Abelard denied it, but when the person chiefly interested—the girl herself—denied it, they laughed despairing Fulbert to scorn.

The poor canon of the cathedral of Paris was spiked again. The last hope of repairing the wrong that had been done his house was gone. What next? Human nature suggested revenge. He compassed it. The historian says:

"Ruffians, hired by Fulbert, fell upon Abelard by night, and inflicted upon him a terrible and nameless mutilation."

I am seeking the last resting-place of those "ruffians." When I find it I shall shed some tears on it, and stack up some bouquets and immortelles, and cart away from it some gravel whereby to remember that howsoever blotted by crime their lives may have been, these ruffians did one just deed, at any rate, albeit it was not warranted by the strict letter of the law.

Heloise entered a convent and gave good-bye to the world and its pleasures for all time. For twelve years she never heard of Abelard—never even heard his name mentioned. She had become prioress of Argenteuil, and led a life of complete seclusion. She happened one day to see a letter written by him, in which he narrated his own history. She cried over it, and wrote him. He answered, addressing her as his "sister in Christ." They continued to correspond, she in the unweighed language of unwavering affection, he in the chilly phraseology of the polished rhetorician. She poured out her heart in passionate, disjointed sentences; he replied with finished essays, divided deliberately into heads and subheads, premises and argument. She showered upon him the tenderest epithets that love could devise, he addressed her from the North Pole of his frozen heart as the "Spouse of Christ!" The abandoned villain!

On account of her too easy government of her nuns, some disreputable irregularities were discovered among them, and the Abbot of St. Denis broke up her establishment. Abelard was the official head of the monastery of St. Gildas de Ruys, at that time, and when he heard of her homeless condition a sentiment of pity was aroused in his breast (it is a wonder the unfamiliar emotion did not blow his head off), and he placed her and her troop in the little oratory of the Paraclete, a religious establishment which he had founded. She had many privations and sufferings to undergo at first, but her worth and her gentle disposition won influential friends for her, and she built up a wealthy and flourishing nunnery. She became a great favorite with the heads of the church, and also the people, though she seldom appeared in public. She rapidly advanced in esteem, in good report and in usefulness, and Abelard as rapidly lost ground. The Pope so honored her that he made her the head of her order. Abelard, a man of splendid talents, and ranking as the first debater of his time, became timid, irresolute, and distrustful of his powers. He only needed a great misfortune to topple him from the high position he held in the world of intellectual excellence, and it came. Urged by kings and princes to meet the subtle St. Bernard in debate and crush him, he stood up in the presence of a royal and illustrious assemblage, and when his antagonist had finished he looked about him, and stammered a commencement; but his courage failed him, the cunning of his tongue was gone: with his speech unspoken, he trembled and sat down, a disgraced and vanquished champion.

He died a nobody, and was buried at Cluny, A.D. 1144. They removed his body to the Paraclete afterward, and when Heloise died, twenty years later, they buried her with him, in accordance with her last wish. He died at the ripe age of 64, and she at 63. After the bodies had remained entombed three hundred years, they were removed once more. They were removed again in 1800, and finally, seventeen years afterward, they were taken up and transferred to Père la Chaise, where they will remain in peace and quiet until it comes time for them to get up and move again.

History is silent concerning the last acts of the mountain howitzer. Let the world say what it will about him, *I*, at least, shall always respect the memory and sorrow for the abused trust, and the broken heart, and the troubled spirit of the old smooth-bore. Rest and repose be his!

Such is the story of Abelard and Heloise. Such is the history that Lamartine has shed such cataracts of tears over. But that man never could come within the influence of a subject in the least pathetic without overflowing his banks. He ought to be dammed—or leveed, I should more properly say. Such is the history—not as it is usually told, but as it is when stripped of the nauseous sentimentality that would enshrine for our loving worship a dastardly seducer like Pierre Abelard. I have not a word to say against the misused, faithful girl, and would not withhold from her grave a single one of those simple tributes which blighted youths and maidens offer to her memory, but I am sorry enough that I have not time and opportunity to write four or five volumes of my opinion of her friend the founder of the Parachute, or the Paraclete, or whatever it was.

The tons of sentiment I have wasted on that unprincipled humbug, in my ignorance! I shall throttle down my emotions hereafter, about this sort of people, until I have read them up and know whether they are entitled to any tearful attentions or not. I wish I had my immortelles back, now, and that bunch of radishes. . . .

Chapter XXVII

So far, good. If any man has a right to feel proud of himself, and satisfied, surely it is I. For I have written about the Coliseum and the gladiators, the martyrs and the lions, and yet have never once used the phrase "butchered to make a Roman holiday." I am the only free white man of mature age who has accomplished this since Byron originated the expression.

Butchered to make a Roman holiday sounds well for the first seventeen or eighteen hundred thousand times one sees it in print, but after that it begins to grow tiresome. I find it in all the books concerning Rome—and here latterly it reminds me of Judge Oliver. Oliver was a young lawyer, fresh from the schools, who had gone out to the deserts of Nevada to begin life. He found that country, and our ways of life there, in those early days, different from life in New England or Paris. But he put on a woollen shirt and strapped a navy revolver to his person, took to the bacon and beans of the country, and determined to do in Nevada as Nevada did. Oliver accepted the situation so completely that, although he must have sorrowed over many of his trials, he never complained—that is, he never complained but once. He, two others, and myself, started to the new silver mines in the Humboldt mountains—he to be Probate Judge of Humboldt county, and we to mine. The distance was two hundred miles. It was dead of winter. We bought a two-horse wagon and put eighteen hundred pounds of bacon, flour, beans, blasting-powder, picks and shovels in it; we bought two sorry-looking Mexican "plugs," with the hair turned the wrong way and more corners on their bodies than there are on the mosque of Omar; we hitched up and started. It was a dreadful trip. But Oliver did not complain. The horses dragged the wagon two miles from town and then gave out. Then we three pushed the wagon seven miles, and Oliver moved ahead and pulled the horses after him by the bits. We complained, but Oliver did not. The ground was frozen, and it froze our backs while we slept; the wind swept across our faces and froze our noses. Oliver did not complain. Five days of pushing the wagon by day and freezing by night brought us to the bad part of the journey—the Forty Mile Desert, or the Great American Desert, if you please. Still, this mildest-mannered man that ever was had not complained. We started across at eight in the morning, pushing through sand that had no bottom; toiling all day long by the wrecks of a thousand wagons, the skeletons of ten thousand oxen; by wagon-tires enough to hoop the Washington Monument to the top, and ox-chains enough to girdle Long Island; by human graves; with our throats parched always, with thirst; lips bleeding from the alkali dust; hungry, perspiring, and very, very weary—so weary that when we dropped in the sand every fifty yards to rest the horses, we could hardly keep from going to sleep— no complaints from Oliver: none the next morning at three o'clock, when we got across, tired to death. Awakened two or three nights afterward at midnight, in a narrow cañon, by the snow falling on our faces, and appalled at the imminent danger of being "snowed in," we harnessed up and pushed on till eight in the morning, passed the "Divide" and knew we were saved. No complaints. Fifteen days of hardship and fatigue brought us to the end of the two hundred miles, and the Judge had not complained. We wondered if any thing *could* exasperate him. We built a Humboldt house. It is done in this way. You dig a square in the steep base of the mountain, and set up two uprights and top them with two joists. Then you stretch a great sheet of "cotton domestic" from the point where the joists join the hill-side down over the joists to the ground; this makes the roof and the front of the mansion; the sides and back are the dirt walls your digging has left. A chimney is easily made by turning up one corner of the roof. Oliver was sitting alone in this dismal den, one night, by a sage-brush fire, writing poetry; he was very fond of digging poetry out of himself—or blasting it out when it came hard. He heard an animal's footsteps close to the roof; a stone or two and some dirt came through and fell by him. He grew uneasy and said "Hi!—clear out from there, can't you!"—from time to time. But by and by he fell asleep where he sat, and pretty soon a mule fell down the chimney! The fire flew in every direction, and Oliver went over backwards. About ten nights after that, he recovered confidence enough to go to writing poetry again. Again he dozed off to sleep, and again a mule fell down the chimney. This time, about half of that side of the house came in with the mule. Struggling to get up, the mule kicked the candle out and smashed most of the kitchen furniture, and raised considerable dust. These violent awakenings must have been annoying to Oliver, but he never complained. He moved to a mansion on the opposite side of the cañon, because he had noticed the mules did not go there. One night about eight o'clock he was endeavoring to finish his poem, when a stone rolled in—then a hoof appeared below the canvas—then part of a cow—the after part. He leaned back in dread, and shouted "Hooy! hooy! get out of this!" and the cow struggled manfully—lost ground steadily—dirt and dust streamed down, and before Oliver could get well away, the entire cow crashed through on to the table and made a shapeless wreck of every thing!

Then, for the first time in his life, I think, Oliver complained. He said, *"This thing is growing monotonous!"*

Then he resigned his judgeship and left Humboldt county. "Butchered to make a Roman holiday" has grown monotonous to me.

In this connection I wish to say one word about Michael Angelo Buonarotti. I used to worship the mighty genius of Michael Angelo—that man who was great in poetry, painting, sculpture, architecture—great in every thing he undertook. But I do not want Michael Angelo for breakfast —for luncheon—for dinner—for tea—for supper—for between meals. I like a change, occasionally. In Genoa, he designed every thing; in Milan he or his pupils designed every thing; he designed the Lake of Como; in

Padua, Verona, Venice, Bologna, who did we ever hear of, from guides, but Michael Angelo? In Florence, he painted every thing, designed every thing, nearly, and what he did not design he used to sit on a favorite stone and look at, and they showed us the stone. In Pisa he designed every thing but the old shot-tower, and they would have attributed that to him if it had not been so awfully out of the perpendicular. He designed the piers of Leghorn and the custom house regulations of Civita Vecchia. But, here—here it is frightful. He designed St. Peter's; he designed the Pope; he designed the Pantheon, the uniform of the Pope's soldiers, the Tiber, the Vatican, the Coliseum, the Capitol, the Tarpeian Rock, the Barberini Palace, St. John Lateran, the Campagna, the Appian Way, the Seven Hills, the Baths of Caracalla, the Claudian Aqueduct, the Cloaca Maxima—the eternal bore designed the Eternal City, and unless all men and books do lie, he painted every thing in it! Dan said the other day to the guide, "Enough, enough, enough! Say no more! Lump the whole thing! say that the Creator made Italy from designs by Michael Angelo!"

I never felt so fervently thankful, so soothed, so tranquil, so filled with a blessed peace, as I did yesterday when I learned that Michael Angelo was dead.

But we have taken it out of this guide. He has marched us through miles of pictures and sculpture in the vast corridors of the Vatican; and through miles of pictures and sculpture in twenty other palaces; he has shown us the great picture in the Sistine Chapel, and frescoes enough to fresco the heavens—pretty much all done by Michael Angelo. So with him we have played that game which has vanquished so many guides for us—imbecility and idiotic questions. These creatures never suspect—they have no idea of a sarcasm.

He shows us a figure and says: "Statoo brunzo." (Bronze statue.)

We look at it indifferently and the doctor asks: "By Michael Angelo?"

"No—not know who."

Then he shows us the ancient Roman Forum. The doctor asks: "Michael Angelo?"

A stare from the guide. "No—thousan' year before he is born."

Then an Egyptian obelisk. Again: "Michael Angelo?"

"Oh, *mon dieu*, genteelmen! Zis is *two* thousan' year before he is born!"

He grows so tired of that unceasing question sometimes, that he dreads to show us any thing at all. The wretch has tried all the ways he can think of to make us comprehend that Michael Angelo is only responsible for the creation of a *part* of the world, but somehow he has not succeeded yet. Relief for overtasked eyes and brain from study and sightseeing is necessary, or we shall become idiotic sure enough. Therefore this guide must continue to suffer. If he does not enjoy it, so much the worse for him. We do.

In this place I may as well jot down a chapter concerning those necessary nuisances, European guides. Many a man has wished in his heart he could do without his guide; but knowing he could not, has wished he could get some amusement out of him as a remuneration for the affliction of his society. We accomplished this latter matter, and if our experience can be made useful to others they are welcome to it.

Guides know about enough English to tangle every thing up so that a man can make neither head or tail of it. They know their story by heart —the history of every statue, painting, cathedral or other wonder they show you. They know it and tell it as a parrot would—and if you interrupt, and throw them off the track, they have to go back and begin over again. All their lives long, they are employed in showing strange things to foreigners and listening to their bursts of admiration. It is human nature to take delight in exciting admiration. It is what prompts children to say "smart" things, and do absurd ones, and in other ways "show off" when company is present. It is what makes gossips turn out in rain and storm to go and be the first to tell a startling bit of news. Think, then, what a passion it becomes with a guide, whose privilege it is, every day, to show to strangers wonders that throw them into perfect ecstasies of admiration! He gets so that he could not by any possibility live in a soberer atmosphere. After we discovered this, we *never* went into ecstasies any more—we never admired any thing—we never showed any but impassible faces and stupid indifference in the presence of the sublimest wonders a guide had to display. We had found their weak point. We have made good use of it ever since. We have made some of those people savage, at times, but we have never lost our own serenity.

The doctor asks the questions, generally, because he can keep his countenance, and look more like an inspired idiot, and throw more imbecility into the tone of his voice than any man that lives. It comes natural to him.

The guides in Genoa are delighted to secure an American party, because Americans so much wonder, and deal so much in sentiment and emotion before any relic of Columbus. Our guide there fidgeted about as if he had swallowed a spring mattress. He was full of animation—full of impatience. He said:

"Come wis me, genteelmen!—come! I show you ze letter writing by Christopher Colombo!—write it himself!—write it wis his own hand!—come!"

He took us to the municipal palace. After much impressive fumbling of keys and opening of locks, the stained and aged document was spread before us. The guide's eyes sparkled. He danced about us and tapped the parchment with his finger:

"What I tell you, genteelmen! Is it not so? See! hand-writing Christopher Colombo!—write it himself!"

We looked indifferent—unconcerned. The doctor examined the document very deliberately, during a painful pause.—Then he said, without any show of interest.

"Ah—Ferguson—what—what did you say was the name of the party who wrote this?"

"Christopher Colombo! ze great Christopher Colombo!"

Another deliberate examination.

"Ah—did he write it himself, or—or how?"

"He write it himself!—Christopher Colombo! he's own hand-writing, write by himself!"

Then the doctor laid the document down and said:

"Why, I have seen boys in America only fourteen years old that could write better than that."

"But zis is ze great Christo——"

"I don't care who it is! It's the worst writing I ever saw. Now you mustn't think you can impose on us because we are strangers. We are not fools, by a good deal. If you have got any specimens of penmanship of real merit, trot them out!—and if you haven't, drive on!"

We drove on. The guide was considerably shaken up, but he made one more venture. He had something which he thought would overcome us. He said:

"Ah, genteelmen, you come wis me! I show you beautiful, O, magnificent bust Christopher Colombo!—splendid, grand, magnificent!"

He brought us before the beautiful bust—for it *was* beautiful—and sprang back and struck an attitude:

"Ah, look, genteelmen!—beautiful, grand,—bust Christopher Colombo!—beautiful bust, beautiful pedestal!"

The doctor put up his eye-glass—procured for such occasions:

"Ah—what did you say this gentleman's name was?"

"Christopher Colombo!—ze great Christopher Colombo!"

"Christopher Colombo!—the great Christopher Colombo. Well, what did *he* do?"

"Discover America!—discover America, Oh, ze devil!"

"Discover America. No—that statement will hardly wash. We are just from America ourselves. We heard nothing about it. Christopher Colombo—pleasant name—is—is he dead?"

"Oh, corpo di Baccho!—three hundred year!"

"What did he die of?"

"I do not know!—I cannot tell."

"Small-pox, think?"

"I do not know, genteelmen!—I do not know *what* he die of!"

"Measles, likely?"

"May be—may be—I do *not* know—I think he die of somethings."

"Parents living?"

"Im-posseeble!"

"Ah—which is the bust and which is the pedestal?"

"Santa Maria!—zis ze bust! zis ze pedestal!"

"Ah, I see, I see—happy combination—very happy combination, indeed. Is—is this the first time this gentleman was ever on a bust?"

That joke was lost on the foreigner—guides can not master the subtleties of the American joke.

We have made it interesting for this Roman guide. Yesterday we spent three or four hours in the Vatican again, that wonderful world of curiosities. We came very near expressing interest, sometimes—even admiration—it was very hard to keep from it. We succeeded though. Nobody else ever did, in the Vatican museums. The guide was bewildered—non-plussed. He walked his legs off, nearly, hunting up extraordinary things, and exhausted all his ingenuity on us, but it was a failure; we never showed any interest in any thing. He had reserved what he considered to be his greatest wonder till the last—a royal Egyptian mummy, the best preserved in the world, perhaps. He took us there. He felt so sure, this time, that some of his old enthusiasm came back to him:

"See, genteelmen!—Mummy! Mummy!"

The eye-glass came up as calmly, as deliberately as ever.

"Ah,—Ferguson—what did I understand you to say the gentleman's name was?"

"Name?—he got no name!—Mummy!—'Gyptian mummy!"

"Yes, yes. Born here?"

"No! *'Gyptian* mummy!"

"Ah, just so. Frenchman, I presume?"

"No!—*not* Frenchman, not Roman!—born in Egypt!"

"Born in Egypt. Never heard of Egypta before. Foreign locality, likely. Mummy—mummy. How calm he is—how self-possessed. Is, ah—is he dead?"

"Oh, *sacré bleu*, been dead three thousan' year!"

The doctor turned on him savagely:

"Here, now, what do you mean by such conduct as this! Playing us for Chinamen because we are strangers and trying to learn! Trying to impose your vile second-hand carcasses on *us!*—thunder and lightning, I've a notion to—to—if you've got a nice *fresh* corpse, fetch him out!—or by George we'll brain you!"

We make it exceedingly interesting for this Frenchman. However, he has paid us back, partly, without knowing it. He came to the hotel this morning to ask if we were up, and he endeavored as well as he could to describe us, so that the landlord would know which persons he meant. He finished with the casual remark that we were lunatics. The observation was so innocent and so honest that it amounted to a very good thing for a guide to say.

There is one remark (already mentioned) which never yet has failed to disgust these guides. We use it always, when we can think of nothing else to say. After they have exhausted their enthusiasm pointing out to us and praising the beauties of some ancient bronze image or broken-legged statue, we look at it stupidly and in silence for five, ten, fifteen minutes—as long as we can hold out, in fact—and then ask:

"Is—is he dead?"

That conquers the serenest of them. It is not what they are looking for—especially a new guide. Our Roman Ferguson is the most patient, unsuspecting, long-suffering subject we have had yet. We shall be sorry to part with him. We have enjoyed his society very much. We trust he has enjoyed ours, but we are harassed with doubts. . . .

1867　　　　　　　　　　　　　　　　　　　　　　*1869*

From ROUGHING IT

After *The Innocents Abroad* Mark Twain's next successful work was *Roughing It* (1872), an autobiographical chronicle of his Western years enlivened with anecdotes, tall tales, and a play of wit tender and caustic by turns. The first quarter of the book concerns Sam Clemens' stagecoach trip from Missouri to Nevada with his brother Orion; the last quarter tells of his sojourn in the Sandwich Islands, as the Hawaiian Islands were then called. The forty central chapters introduce us to an untamed frontier region during the Civil War years, but the war is a distant echo; Nevada was enjoying a silver mining boom, and even Twain got caught up by it. In *Roughing It* he succeeds in capturing the atmosphere of "flush times" with its quick fortunes, its tragedies, its physical ugliness and its violence. And everywhere he has caught the ring of colloquial speech, the vernacular he often raised to the pitch of unexpected eloquence.

The two passages here reprinted are both in the tradition of vernacular humor that Twain knew from his early newspaper reading and had himself experimented with on the *Enterprise*. "Buck Fanshaw's Funeral" rather overplays the differences between the worlds of minister and fireman, but the very exaggeration of misunderstanding typifies the genre. "Dick Baker and His Cat" is a tall tale, told with a straight face and with a fine regard for circumstantial detail that almost forces the listener to believe that all elements of the story are equally true.

Chapter XLVII

[BUCK FANSHAW'S FUNERAL]

Somebody has said that in order to know a community, one must observe the style of its funerals and know what manner of men they bury with most ceremony. I cannot say which class we buried with most eclat in our "flush times," the distinguished public benefactor or the distinguished rough—possibly the two chief grades or grand divisions of society honored their illustrious dead about equally; and hence, no doubt the philosopher I have quoted from would have needed to see two representative funerals in Virginia [1] before forming his estimate of the people.

There was a grand time over Buck Fanshaw when he died. He was a representative citizen. He had "killed his man"—not in his own quarrel, it is true, but in defence of a stranger unfairly beset by numbers. He had kept a sumptuous saloon. He had been the proprietor of a dashing help-meet whom he could have discarded without the formality of a divorce. He had held a high position in the fire department and been a very War-wick [2] in politics. When he died there was great lamentation throughout the town, but especially in the vast bottom-stratum of society.

On the inquest it was shown that Buck Fanshaw, in the delirium of a wasting typhoid fever, had taken arsenic, shot himself through the body, cut his throat, and jumped out of a four-story window and broken his neck—and after due deliberation, the jury, sad and tearful, but with in-telligence unblinded by its sorrow, brought in a verdict of death "by the visitation of God." What could the world do without juries?

Prodigious preparations were made for the funeral. All the vehicles in town were hired, all the saloons put in mourning, all the municipal and fire-company flags hung at half-mast, and all the firemen ordered to muster in uniform and bring their machines duly draped in black. Now—let us remark in parenthesis—as all the peoples of the earth had representative adventurers in the Silverland, and as each adventurer had brought the slang of his nation or his locality with him, the combination made the slang of Nevada the richest and the most infinitely varied and copious that had ever existed anywhere in the world, perhaps, except in the mines of California in the "early days." Slang was the language of Nevada. It was hard to preach a sermon without it, and be understood. Such phrases as "You bet!" "Oh, no, I reckon not!" "No Irish need ap-ply," and a hundred others, became so common as to fall from the lips of a speaker unconsciously—and very often when they did not touch the subject under discussion and consequently failed to mean anything.

After Buck Fanshaw's inquest, a meeting of the short-haired brother-hood was held, for nothing can be done on the Pacific coast without a public meeting and an expression of sentiment. Regretful resolutions were passed and various committees appointed; among others, a commit-tee of one was deputed to call on the minister, a fragile, gentle, spirituel new fledgling from an Eastern theological seminary, and as yet unac-quainted with the ways of the mines. The committeeman, "Scotty" Briggs, made his visit; and in after days it was worth something to hear the minister tell about it. Scotty was a stalwart rough, whose customary suit, when on weighty official business, like committee work, was a fire helmet, flaming red flannel shirt, patent leather belt with spanner and revolver attached, coat hung over arm, and pants stuffed into boot tops. He formed something of a contrast to the pale theological student. It is

---

[1] Virginia City, Nevada.

[2] In allusion to Richard Neville (1428–71), called Warwick the King-maker be-cause during the Wars of the Roses he schemed to depose Henry VI in favor of Edward IV and later restored Henry.

fair to say of Scotty, however, in passing, that he had a warm heart, and a strong love for his friends, and never entered into a quarrel when he could reasonably keep out of it. Indeed, it was commonly said that whenever one of Scotty's fights was investigated, it always turned out that it had originally been no affair of his, but that out of native goodheartedness he had dropped in of his own accord to help the man who was getting the worst of it. He and Buck Fanshaw were bosom friends, for years, and had often taken adventurous "pot-luck" together. On one occasion, they had thrown off their coats and taken the weaker side in a fight among strangers, and after gaining a hard-earned victory, turned and found that the men they were helping had deserted early, and not only that, but had stolen their coats and made off with them! But to return to Scotty's visit to the minister. He was on a sorrowful mission, now, and his face was the picture of woe. Being admitted to the presence he sat down before the clergyman, placed his fire-hat on an unfinished manuscript sermon under the minister's nose, took from it a red silk handkerchief, wiped his brow and heaved a sigh of dismal impressiveness, explanatory of his business. He choked, and even shed tears; but with an effort he mastered his voice and said in lugubrious tones:

"Are you the duck that runs the gospel-mill next door?"

"Am I the—pardon me, I believe I do not understand?"

With another sigh and a half-sob, Scotty rejoined:

"Why you see we are in a bit of trouble, and the boys thought maybe you would give us a lift, if we'd tackle you—that is, if I've got the rights of it and you are the head clerk of the doxology-works next door."

"I am the shepherd in charge of the flock whose fold is next door."

"The which?"

"The spiritual adviser of the little company of believers whose sanctuary adjoins these premises."

Scotty scratched his head, reflected a moment, and then said:

"You ruther hold over me, pard. I reckon I can't call that hand. Ante and pass the buck."

"How? I beg pardon. What did I understand you to say?"

"Well, you've ruther got the bulge on me. Or maybe we've both got the bulge, somehow. You don't smoke me and I don't smoke you. You see, one of the boys has passed in his checks and we want to give him a good send-off, and so the thing I'm on now is to roust out somebody to jerk a little chin-music for us and waltz him through handsome."

"My friend, I seem to grow more and more bewildered. Your observations are wholly incomprehensible to me. Cannot you simplify them in some way? At first I thought perhaps I understood you, but I grope now. Would it not expedite matters if you restricted yourself to categorical statements of fact unencumbered with obstructing accumulations of metaphor and allegory?"

Another pause, and more reflection. Then, said Scotty:

"I'll have to pass, I judge."

"How?"

"You've raised me out, pard."

"I still fail to catch your meaning."

"Why, that last lead of yourn is too many for me—that's the idea. I can't neither trump nor follow suit."

The clergyman sank back in his chair perplexed. Scotty leaned his head on his hand and gave himself up to thought. Presently his face came up, sorrowful but confident.

"I've got it now, so's you can savvy," he said. "What we want is a gospel-sharp. See?"

"A what?"

"Gospel-sharp. Parson."

"Oh! Why did you not say so before? I am a clergyman—a parson."

"Now you talk! You see my blind and straddle it like a man. Put it there!"—extending a brawny paw, which closed over the minister's small hand and gave it a shake indicative of fraternal sympathy and fervent gratification.

"Now we're all right, pard. Let's start fresh. Don't you mind my snuffling a little—becuz we're in a power of trouble. You see, one of the boys has gone up the flume—"

"Gone where?"

"Up the flume—throwed up the sponge, you understand."

"Thrown up the sponge?"

"Yes—kicked the bucket—"

"Ah—has departed to that mysterious country from whose bourne no traveler returns."

"Return! I reckon not. Why pard, he's *dead!*"

"Yes, I understand."

"Oh, you do? Well I thought maybe you might be getting tangled some more. Yes, you see he's dead again—"

"*Again?* Why, has he ever been dead before?"

"Dead before? No! Do you reckon a man has got as many lives as a cat? But you bet you he's awful dead now, poor old boy, and I wish I'd never seen this day. I don't want no better friend than Buck Fanshaw. I knowed him by the back; and when I know a man and like him, I freeze to him—you hear *me*. Take him all round, pard, there never was a bullier man in the mines. No man ever knowed Buck Fanshaw to go back on a friend. But it's all up, you know, it's all up. It ain't no use. They've scooped him."

"Scooped him?"

"Yes—death has. Well, well, well, we've got to give him up. Yes indeed. It's a kind of a hard world, after all, *ain't* it? But pard, he was a rustler! You ought to seen him get started once. He was a bully boy with a glass eye! Just spit in his face and give him room according to his strength, and it was just beautiful to see him peel and go in. He was the worst son of a thief that ever drawed breath. Pard, he was *on* it! He was on it bigger than an Injun!"

"On it? On what?"

"On the shoot. On the shoulder. On the fight, you understand. *He* didn't give a continental for *any*body. *Beg* your pardon, friend, for coming so near saying a cuss-word—but you see I'm on an awful strain, in this palaver, on account of having to cramp down and draw everything so mild. But we've got to give him up. There ain't any getting around that, I don't reckon. Now if we can get you to help plant him—"

"Preach the funeral discourse? Assist at the obsequies?"

"Obs'quies is good. Yes. That's it—that's our little game. We are going to get the thing up regardless, you know. He was always nifty himself, and so you bet you his funeral ain't going to be no slouch—solid silver door-plate on his coffin, six plumes on the hearse, and a nigger on the box in a biled shirt and a plug hat—how's that for high? And we'll take care of *you*, pard. We'll fix you all right. There'll be a kerridge for you; and whatever you want, you just 'scape out and we'll 'tend to it. We've got a shebang fixed up for you to stand behind, in No. 1's house, and don't you be afraid. Just go in and toot your horn, if you don't sell a clam. Put Buck through as bully as you can, pard, for anybody that knowed him will tell you that he was one of the whitest men that was ever in the mines. You can't draw it too strong. He never could stand it to see things going wrong. He's done more to make this town quiet and peaceable than any man in it. I've seen him lick four Greasers in eleven minutes, myself. If a thing wanted regulating, *he* warn't a man to go browsing around after somebody to do it, but he would prance in and regulate it himself. He warn't a Catholic. Scasely. He was down on 'em. His word was, 'No Irish need apply!' But it didn't make no difference about that when it came down to what a man's rights was—and so, when some roughs jumped the Catholic bone-yard and started in to stake out town-lots in it he *went* for 'em! And he *cleaned* 'em, too! I was there, pard, and I seen it myself."

"That was very well indeed—at least the impulse was—whether the act was strictly defensible or not. Had deceased any religious convictions? That is to say, did he feel a dependence upon, or acknowledge allegiance to a higher power?"

More reflection.

"I reckon you've stumped me again, pard. Could you say it over once more, and say it slow?"

"Well, to simplify it somewhat, was he, or rather had he ever been connected with any organization sequestered from secular concerns and devoted to self-sacrifice in the interests of morality?"

"All down but nine—set 'em up on the other alley, pard."

"What did I understand you to say?"

"Why, you're most too many for me, you know. When you get in with your left I hunt grass every time. Every time you draw, you fill; but I don't seem to have any luck. Let's have a new deal."

"How? Begin again?"

"That's it."

"Very well. Was he a good man, and—"

"There—I see that; don't put up another chip till I look at my hand. A good man, says you? Pard, it ain't no name for it. He was the best man that ever—pard, you would have doted on that man. He could lam any galoot of his inches in America. It was him that put down the riot last election before it got a start; and everybody said he was the only man that could have done it. He waltzed in with a spanner in one hand and a trumpet in the other, and sent fourteen men home on a shutter in less than three minutes. He had that riot all broke up and prevented nice before anybody ever got a chance to strike a blow. He was always for peace, and he would *have* peace—he could not stand disturbances. Pard, he was a great loss to this town. It would please the boys if you could chip in something like that and do him justice. Here once when the Micks got to throwing stones through the Methodis' Sunday school windows, Buck Fanshaw, all of his own notion, shut up his saloon and took a couple of six-shooters and mounted guard over the Sunday school. Says he, 'No Irish need apply!' And they didn't. He was the bulliest man in the mountains, pard! He could run faster, jump higher, hit harder, and hold more tangle-foot whisky without spilling it than any man in seventeen counties. Put that in, pard—it'll please the boys more than anything you could say. And you can say, pard, that he never shook his mother."

"Never shook his mother?"

"That's it—any of the boys will tell you so."

"Well, but why *should* he shake her?"

"That's what *I* say—but some people does."

"Not people of any repute?"

"Well, some that averages pretty so-so."

"In my opinion the man that would offer personal violence to his own mother, ought to—"

"Cheese it, pard; you've banked your ball clean outside the string. What I was a drivin' at, was, that he never *throwed off* on his mother— don't you see? No indeedy. He give her a house to live in, and town lots, and plenty of money; and he looked after her and took care of her all the time; and when she was down with the small-pox I'm d——d if he didn't set up nights and nuss her himself! *Beg* your pardon for saying it, but it hopped out too quick for yours truly. You've treated me like a gentleman, pard, and I ain't the man to hurt your feelings intentional. I think you're white. I think you're a square man, pard. I like you, and I'll lick any man that don't. I'll lick him till he can't tell himself from a last year's corpse! Put it *there!*" [Another fraternal handshake—and exit.]

The obsequies were all that "the boys" could desire. Such a marvel of funeral pomp had never been seen in Virginia. The plumed hearse, the dirge-breathing brass bands, the closed marts of business, the flags drooping at half mast, the long, plodding procession of uniformed secret societies, military battalions and fire companies, draped engines, carriages of officials, and citizens in vehicles and on foot, attracted multitudes of spectators to the sidewalks, roofs and windows; and for years afterward, the degree of grandeur attained by any civic display in Virginia was determined by comparison with Buck Fanshaw's funeral.

Scotty Briggs, as a pall-bearer and a mourner, occupied a prominent place at the funeral, and when the sermon was finished and the last sentence of the prayer for the dead man's soul ascended, he responded, in a low voice, but with feeling:

"AMEN. No Irish need apply."

As the bulk of the response was without apparent relevancy, it was probably nothing more than a humble tribute to the memory of the friend that was gone; for, as Scotty had once said, it was "his word."

Scotty Briggs, in after days, achieved the distinction of becoming the only convert to religion that was ever gathered from the Virginia roughs; and it transpired that the man who had it in him to espouse the quarrel of the weak out of inborn nobility of spirit was no mean timber whereof to construct a Christian. The making him one did not warp his generosity or diminish his courage; on the contrary it gave intelligent direction to the one and a broader field to the other. If his Sunday-school class progressed faster than the other classes, was it matter for wonder? I think not. He talked to his pioneer small-fry in a language they understood! It was my large privilege, a month before he died, to hear him tell the beautiful story of Joseph and his brethren to his class "without looking at the book." I leave it to the reader to fancy what it was like, as it fell, riddled with slang, from the lips of that grave, earnest teacher, and was listened to by his little learners with a consuming interest that showed that they were as unconscious as he was that any violence was being done to the sacred proprieties!

Chapter LXI

DICK BAKER AND HIS CAT

One of my comrades there—another of those victims of eighteen years of unrequited toil and blighted hopes—was one of the gentlest spirits that ever bore its patient cross in a weary exile: grave and simple Dick Baker, pocket-miner of Dead-Horse Gulch.—He was forty-six, gray as a rat, earnest, thoughtful, slenderly educated, slouchily dressed and clay-soiled, but his heart was finer metal than any gold his shovel ever brought to light—than any, indeed, that ever was mined or minted.

Whenever he was out of luck and a little down-hearted, he would fall to mourning over the loss of a wonderful cat he used to own (for where women and children are not, men of kindly impulses take up with pets, for they must love something). And he always spoke of the strange sagacity of that cat with the air of a man who believed in his secret heart that there was something human about it—may be even supernatural.

I heard him talking about this animal once. He said:

"Gentlemen, I used to have a cat here, by the name of Tom Quartz, which you'd a took an interest in I reckon—most any body would. I had him here eight year—and he was the remarkablest cat *I* ever see. He was a large gray one of the Tom specie, an' he had more hard, natchral sense than any man in this camp—'n' a *power* of dignity—he wouldn't let the Gov'ner of Californy be familiar with him. He never ketched a rat in his life—'peared to be above it. He never cared for nothing but mining. He knowed more about mining, that cat did, than any man *I* ever, ever see. You couldn't tell *him* noth'n' 'bout placer diggin's— 'n' as for pocket mining, why he was just born for it. He would dig out after me an' Jim when we went over the hills prospect'n', and he would trot along behind us for as much as five mile, if we went so fur. An' he had the best judgment about mining ground—why you never see anything like it. When we went to work, he'd scatter a glance around, 'n' if he didn't think much of the indications, he would give a look as much as to say, 'Well, I'll have to get you to excuse *me*,' 'n' without another word he'd hyste his nose into the air 'n' shove for home. But if the ground suited him, he would lay low 'n' keep dark till the first pan was washed, 'n' then he would sidle up 'n' take a look, an' if there was about six or seven grains of gold *he* was satisfied—he didn't want no better prospect 'n that—'n' then he would lay down on our coats and snore like a steamboat till we'd struck the pocket, an' then get up 'n' superintend. He was nearly lightnin' on superintending.

"Well, by an' by, up comes this yer quartz excitement. Every body was into it—every body was pick'n' 'n' blast'n' instead of shovelin' dirt on the hill side—every body was put'n' down a shaft instead of scrapin' the surface. Noth'n' would do Jim, but *we* must tackle the ledges, too, 'n' so we did. We commenced put'n' down a shaft, 'n' Tom Quartz he begin to wonder what in the Dickens it was all about. *He* hadn't ever seen any mining like that before, 'n' he was all upset, as you may say— he couldn't come to a right understanding of it no way—it was too many for *him*. He was down on it, too, you bet you—he was down on it pow- erful—'n' always appeared to consider it the cussedest foolishness out. But that cat, you know, was *always* agin new fangled arrangements—some- how he never could abide 'em. *You* know how it is with old habits. But by an' by Tom Quartz begin to git sort of reconciled a little, though he never *could* altogether understand that eternal sinkin' of a shaft an' never pannin' out any thing. At last he got to comin' down in the shaft, hisself, to try to cipher it out. An' when he'd git the blues, 'n' feel kind o' scruffy, 'n' aggravated 'n' disgusted—knowin' as he did, that the bills was runnin' up all the time an' we warn't makin' a cent—he would curl up on a gunny sack in the corner an' go to sleep. Well, one day when the shaft was down about eight foot, the rock got so hard that we had to put in a blast—the first blast'n' we'd ever done since Tom Quartz was born. An' then we lit the fuse 'n' clumb out 'n' got off 'bout fifty yards—'n' forgot 'n' left Tom Quartz sound asleep on the gunny sack. In 'bout a minute we seen a puff of smoke bust up out of the hole, 'n' then everything let go with an awful crash, 'n' about four million ton of rocks 'n' dirt 'n' smoke 'n' splinters shot up 'bout a mile an' a half into the air, an' by George, right in the dead centre of it was old Tom Quartz a goin' end over end, an' a snortin' an' a sneez'n', an' a clawin' an' a reachin' for things like all possessed. But it warn't no use, you know, it warn't no use. An' that was the last we see of *him* for about two minutes 'n' a half, an' then all of a sudden it begin to rain rocks and rubbage, an' directly he come down ker-whop about ten foot off f'm where we stood. Well, I reckon he was p'raps the orneriest lookin' beast you ever see. One ear was sot back on his neck, 'n' his tail was stove up, 'n' his eye-winkers was swinged off, 'n' he was all blacked up with powder an' smoke, an' all sloppy with mud 'n' slush f'm one end to the other. Well sir, it warn't no use to try to apologize—we couldn't say a word. He took a sort of a disgusted look at hisself, 'n' then he looked at us—an' it was just exactly the same as if he had said—'Gents, may be *you* think it's smart to take advantage of a cat that ain't had no experience of quartz minin', but *I* think *different*'—an' then he turned on his heel 'n' marched off home without ever saying another word.

"That was jest his style. An' may be you won't believe it, but after that you never see a cat so prejudiced agin quartz mining as what he was. An' by an' by when he *did* get to goin' down in the shaft agin, you'd a been astonished at his sagacity. The minute we'd tetch off a blast 'n' the fuse'd begin to sizzle, he'd give a look as much as to say: 'Well, I'll have to git you to excuse *me*,' an' it was surpris'n' the way he'd shin out of that hole 'n' go f'r a tree. Sagacity? It ain't no name for it. 'Twas *inspiration!*"

I said, "Well, Mr. Baker, his prejudice against quartz-mining *was* remarkable, considering how he came by it. Couldn't you ever cure him of it?"

"*Cure him!* No! When Tom Quartz was sot once, he was *always* sot—and you might a blowed him up as much as three million times 'n' you'd never a broken him of his cussed prejudice agin quartz mining."

The affection and the pride that lit up Baker's face when he delivered this tribute to the firmness of his humble friend of other days, will always be a vivid memory with me. . . .

1872

From THE GILDED AGE

The partnership of Mark Twain and his Hartford neighbor Charles Dudley Warner produced a book of uneven interest, but it was important as Twain's first experience with the novel form. *The Gilded Age* (1873) was originally drafted in sections, Warner having most to do with a romantic plot which never became quite integrated into the story that Twain had begun. In the first eleven chapters Twain drew upon the early history of the Clemens family, the legendary Tennessee lands which were supposed to make them rich one day, the migration to Missouri where poverty continued to dog his father, the frontier atmosphere which had formed his own childhood, rich with memories. His mother's cousin James Lampton became the memorable figure of Colonel Beriah Sellers, whom Twain built into an archetypal financial visionary, always on the verge of making millions, ebullient with enthusiastic talk of surefire schemes, yet seldom solvent.

The Gilded Age devoted many chapters to speculation, centering chiefly around the exploitation of railroad lands. Despite its wealth of topical detail, the novel failed—as Henry Adams' *Democracy* failed—to take full account of economic drives unleashed in the expansionist decades after the Civil War. Both books symbolized the corruption of government in dishonest politicians and venal judges, but these are only the small fry—the great moneyed interests of Wall Street, the large-scale manipulators, went virtually unnoticed. And the thesis that the "Robber Barons" were themselves in the grip of irresistible forces remained for a later generation to explore. But Adams' title was ironic and only reinforced the Twain-Warner view that the promise of a Golden Day was unfulfilled.

The chapters of *The Gilded Age* here reprinted give a vivid portrait of Colonel Sellers. The Hawkins family has become so straitened that Clay, an adopted son, and Washington have left home to seek work. Washington is on his way to Hawkeye where the Colonel has represented the prospects as brilliant.

Chapter VII

[Col. Sellers at Home]

Bearing Washington Hawkins and his fortunes, the stage-coach tore out of Swansea at a fearful gait, with horn tooting gaily and half the town admiring from doors and windows. But it did not tear any more after it got to the outskirts; it dragged along stupidly enough, then—till it came in sight of the next hamlet; and then the bugle tooted gaily again, and again the vehicle went tearing by the houses. This sort of conduct marked every entry to a station and every exit from it; and so in those days children grew up with the idea that stage-coaches always tore and always tooted; but they also grew up with the idea that pirates went into action in their Sunday clothes, carrying the black flag in one hand and pistolling people with the other, merely because they were so represented in the pictures—but these illusions vanished when later years brought their disenchanting wisdom. They learned then that the stage-coach is but a poor, plodding, vulgar thing in the solitudes of the high-

way; and that the pirate is only a seedy, unfantastic "rough," when he is
out of the pictures.

Toward evening, the stage-coach came thundering into Hawkeye with
a perfectly triumphant ostentation—which was natural and proper, for
Hawkeye was a pretty large town for interior Missouri. Washington,
very stiff and tired and hungry, climbed out, and wondered how he was
to proceed now. But his difficulty was quickly solved. Col. Sellers came
down the street on a run and arrived panting for breath. He said:

"Lord bless you—I'm glad to see you, Washington—perfectly delighted
to see you, my boy! I got your message. Been on the look-out for you.
Heard the stage horn, but had a party I couldn't shake off—man that's
got an enormous thing on hand—wants me to put some capital into it—
and I tell you, my boy, I could do worse, I could do a deal worse. No,
now, let that luggage alone; I'll fix that. Here, Jerry, got anything to do?
All right—shoulder this plunder and follow me. Come along, Washington. Lord, I'm glad to see you! Wife and the children are just perishing
to look at you. Bless you, they won't know you, you've grown so. Folks
all well, I suppose? That's good—glad to hear that. We're always going
to run down and see them, but I'm into so many operations, and they're
not things a man feels like trusting to other people, and so somehow we
keep putting it off. Fortunes in them! Good gracious, it's the country to
pile up wealth in! Here we are—here's where the Sellers dynasty hangs
out. Dump it on the door-step, Jerry—the blackest niggro in the State,
Washington, but got a good heart—mighty likely boy, is Jerry. And now
I suppose you've got to have ten cents, Jerry. That's all right—when a
man works for me—when a man—in the other pocket, I reckon—when a
man—why, where the mischief *is* that portmonnaie!—when a—well now
that's odd—Oh, now I remember, must have left it at the bank; and
b'George I've left my check-book, too—Polly says I ought to have a
nurse—well, no matter. Let me have a dime, Washington, if you've got—
ah, thanks. Now clear out, Jerry, your complexion has brought on the
twilight half an hour ahead of time. Pretty fair joke—pretty fair. Here
he is, Polly! Washington's come, children!—come now, don't eat him
up—finish him in the house. Welcome, my boy, to a mansion that is
proud to shelter the son of the best man that walks on the ground. Si
Hawkins has been a good friend to me, and I believe I can say that
whenever I've had a chance to put him into a good thing I've done it,
and done it pretty cheerfully, too. I put him into that sugar speculation—what a grand thing that was, if we hadn't held on too long!"

True enough; but holding on too long had utterly ruined both of
them; and the saddest part of it was, that they never had had so much
money to lose before, for Sellers' sale of their mule crop that year in
New Orleans had been a great financial success. If he had kept out of
sugar and gone back home content to stick to mules it would have been
a happy wisdom. As it was, he managed to kill two birds with one
stone—that is to say, he killed the sugar speculation by holding for high

rates till he had to sell at the bottom figure, and that calamity killed the mule that laid the golden egg—which is but a figurative expression and will be so understood. Sellers had returned home cheerful but empty-handed, and the mule business lapsed into other hands. The sale of the Hawkins property by the Sheriff had followed, and the Hawkins hearts been torn to see Uncle Dan'l and his wife pass from the auction-block into the hands of a negro trader and depart for the remote South to be seen no more by the family. It had seemed like seeing their own flesh and blood sold into banishment.

Washington was greatly pleased with the Sellers mansion. It was a two-story-and-a-half brick, and much more stylish than any of its neighbors. He was borne to the family sitting room in triumph by the swarm of little Sellerses, the parents following with their arms about each other's waists.

The whole family were poorly and cheaply dressed; and the clothing, although neat and clean, showed many evidences of having seen long service. The Colonel's "stovepipe" hat was napless and shiny with much polishing, but nevertheless it had an almost convincing expression about it of having been just purchased new. The rest of his clothing was napless and shiny, too, but it had the air of being entirely satisfied with itself and blandly sorry for other people's clothes. It was growing rather dark in the house, and the evening air was chilly, too. Sellers said:

"Lay off your overcoat, Washington, and draw up to the stove and make yourself at home—just consider yourself under your own shingles, my boy—I'll have a fire going, in a jiffy. Light the lamp, Polly, dear, and let's have things cheerful—just as glad to see you, Washington, as if you'd been lost a century and we'd found you again!"

By this time the Colonel was conveying a lighted match into a poor little stove. Then he propped the stove-door to its place by leaning the poker against it, for the hinges had retired from business. This door framed a small square of isinglass, which now warmed up with a faint glow. Mrs. Sellers lit a cheap, showy lamp, which dissipated a good deal of the gloom, and then everybody gathered into the light and took the stove into close companionship.

The children climbed all over Sellers, fondled him, petted him, and were lavishly petted in return. Out from this tugging, laughing, chattering disguise of legs and arms and little faces, the Colonel's voice worked its way and his tireless tongue ran blithely on without interruption; and the purring little wife, diligent with her knitting, sat near at hand and looked happy and proud and grateful; and she listened as one who listens to oracles and gospels and whose grateful soul is being refreshed with the bread of life. By and by the children quieted down to listen; clustered about their father, and resting their elbows on his legs, they hung upon his words as if he were uttering the music of the spheres.

A dreary old hair-cloth sofa against the wall; a few damaged chairs; the small table the lamp stood on; the crippled stove—these things constituted the furniture of the room. There was no carpet on the floor; on the wall were occasional square-shaped interruptions of the general tint of the plaster which betrayed that there used to be pictures in the house—but there were none now. There were no mantel ornaments, unless one might bring himself to regard as an ornament a clock which never came within fifteen strokes of striking the right time, and whose hands always hitched together at twenty-two minutes past anything and traveled in company the rest of the way home.

"Remarkable clock!" said Sellers, and got up and wound it. "I've been offered—well, I wouldn't expect you to believe what I've been offered for that clock. Old Gov. Hager never sees me but he says, 'Come, now, Colonel, name your price—I *must* have that clock!' But my goodness I'd as soon think of selling my wife. As I was saying to—silence in the court, now, she's begun to strike! You can't talk against her—you have to just be patient and hold up till she's said her say. Ah—well, as I was saying, when—she's beginning again! Nineteen, twenty, twenty-one, twenty-two, twen——ah, that's all. Yes, as I was saying to old Judge—go it, old girl, don't mind me. Now how is that? Isn't that a good, spirited tone? She can wake the dead! Sleep? Why you might as well try to sleep in a thunder-factory. Now just listen at that. She'll strike a hundred and fifty, now, without stopping,—you'll see. There ain't another clock like that in Christendom."

Washington hoped that this might be true, for the din was distracting—though the family, one and all, seemed filled with joy; and the more the clock "buckled down to her work" as the Colonel expressed it, and the more insupportable the clatter became, the more enchanted they all appeared to be. When there was silence, Mrs. Sellers lifted upon Washington a face that beamed with a childlike pride, and said:

"It belonged to his grandmother."

The look and the tone were a plain call for admiring surprise, and therefore Washington said—(it was the only thing that offered itself at the moment):

"Indeed!"

"Yes, it did, didn't it, father!" exclaimed one of the twins. "She was my great-grandmother—and George's too; wasn't she, father! *You* never saw her, but Sis has seen her, when Sis was a baby—didn't you, Sis! Sis has seen her most a hundred times. She was awful deaf—she's dead, now. Ain't she, father!"

All the children chimed in, now, with one general Babel of information about deceased—nobody offering to read the riot act or seeming to discountenance the insurrection or disapprove of it in any way—but the head twin drowned all the turmoil and held his own against the field:

"It's our clock, now—and it's got wheels inside of it, and a thing that flutters every time she strikes—don't it, father! Great-grandmother died before hardly any of us was born—she was an Old-School Baptist and had warts all over her—you ask father if she didn't. She had an uncle once that was bald-headed and used to have fits; he wasn't *our* uncle. I don't know what he was to us—some kin or another I reckon—father's seen him a thousand times—hain't you, father! We used to have a calf that et apples and just chawed up dishrags like nothing, and if you stay here you'll see lots of funerals—won't he, Sis! Did you ever see a house afire? *I* have! Once me and Jim Terry——"

But Sellers began to speak now, and the storm ceased. He began to tell about an enormous speculation he was thinking of embarking some capital in—a speculation which some London bankers had been over to consult with him about—and soon he was building glittering pyramids of coin, and Washington was presently growing opulent under the magic of his eloquence. But at the same time Washington was not able to ignore the cold entirely. He was nearly as close to the stove as he could get, and yet he could not persuade himself that he felt the slightest heat, notwithstanding the isinglass door was still gently and serenely glowing. He tried to get a trifle closer to the stove, and the consequence was, he tripped the supporting poker and the stove-door tumbled to the floor. And then there was a revelation—there was nothing in the stove but a lighted tallow-candle!

The poor youth blushed and felt as if he must die with shame. But the Colonel was only disconcerted for a moment—he straightway found his voice again:

"A little idea of my own, Washington—one of the greatest things in the world! You must write and tell your father about it—don't forget that, now. I have been reading up some European scientific reports—friend of mine, Count Fugier, sent them to me—sends me all sorts of things from Paris—he thinks the world of me, Fugier does. Well, I saw that the Academy of France had been testing the properties of heat, and they came to the conclusion that it was a non-conductor or something like that, and of course its influence must necessarily be deadly in nervous organizations with excitable temperaments, especially where there is any tendency toward rheumatic affections. Bless you I saw in a moment what was the matter with us, and says I, out goes your fires!—no more slow torture and certain death for me, sir. What you want is the *appearance* of heat, not the heat itself—that's the idea. Well how to do it was the next thing. I just put my head to work, pegged away a couple of days, and here you are! Rheumatism? Why a man can't any more start a case of rheumatism in this house than he can shake an opinion out of a mummy! Stove with a candle in it and a transparent door—that's it—it has been the salvation of this family. Don't you fail to write your father about it, Washington. And tell him the idea is mine—I'm no more conceited than most people, I reckon, but you know it is human nature for a man to want credit for a thing like that."

Washington said with his blue lips that he would, but he said in his secret heart that he would promote no such iniquity. He tried to believe in the healthfulness of the invention, and succeeded tolerably well; but after all he could not feel that good health in a frozen body was any real improvement on the rheumatism.

Chapter VIII

[COL. SELLERS' SPECULATION SCHEMES]

The supper at Col. Sellers' was not sumptuous, in the beginning, but it improved on acquaintance. That is to say, that what Washington regarded at first sight as mere lowly potatoes, presently became awe-inspiring agricultural productions that had been reared in some ducal garden beyond the sea, under the sacred eye of the duke himself, who had sent them to Sellers; the bread was from corn which could be grown in only one favored locality in the earth and only a favored few could get it; the Rio coffee, which at first seemed execrable to the taste, took to itself an improved flavor when Washington was told to drink it slowly and not hurry what should be a lingering luxury in order to be fully appreciated—it was from the private stores of a Brazilian nobleman with an unrememberable name. The Colonel's tongue was a magician's wand that turned dried apples into figs and water into wine as easily as it could change a hovel into a palace and present poverty into imminent future riches.

Washington slept in a cold bed in a carpetless room and woke up in a palace in the morning; at least the palace lingered during the moment that he was rubbing his eyes and getting his bearings—and then it disappeared and he recognized that the Colonel's inspiring talk had been influencing his dreams. Fatigue had made him sleep late; when he entered the sitting room he noticed that the old hair-cloth sofa was absent; when he sat down to breakfast the Colonel tossed six or seven dollars in bills on the table, counted them over, said he was a little short and must call upon his banker; then returned the bills to his wallet with the indifferent air of a man who is used to money. The breakfast was not an improvement upon the supper, but the Colonel talked it up and transformed it into an oriental feast. By and by, he said:

"I intend to look out for you, Washington, my boy. I hunted up a place for you yesterday, but I am not referring to that, now—that is a mere livelihood—mere bread and butter; but when I say I mean to look out for you I mean something very different. I mean to put things in your way that will make a mere livelihood a trifling thing. I'll put you in a way to make more money than you'll ever know what to do with. You'll be right here where I can put my hand on you when anything turns up. I've got some prodigious operations on foot; but I'm keeping quiet; mum's the word; your old hand don't go around pow-wowing and letting everybody see his k'yards and find out his little game. But all in good time, Washington, all in good time. You'll see. Now, there's an operation in corn that looks well. Some New York men are trying to get me to go into it—buy up all the growing crops and just boss the market when they mature—ah, I tell you it's a great thing. And it only costs a trifle; two millions or two and a half will do it. I haven't exactly promised yet—there's no hurry—the more indifferent I seem, you know, the more anxious those fellows will get. And then there is the hog speculation—that's bigger still. We've got quiet men at work," [he was very impressive here] "mousing around, to get propositions out of all the farmers in the whole West and Northwest for the hog crop, and other agents quietly getting propositions and terms out of all the manufactories—and don't you see, if we can get all the hogs and all the slaughter houses into our hands on the dead quiet—whew! it would take three ships to carry the money. I've looked into the thing—calculated all the chances for and all the chances against, and though I shake my head and hesitate and keep on thinking, apparently, I've got my mind made up that if the thing can be done on a capital of six millions, that's the horse to put up money on! Why, Washington—but what's the use of talking about it—any man can see that there's whole Atlantic oceans of cash in it, gulfs and bays thrown in. But there's a bigger thing than that, yet—a bigger——"

"Why, Colonel, you can't want anything bigger!" said Washington, his eyes blazing. "Oh, I wish I could go into either of those speculations—I only wish I had money—I wish I wasn't cramped and kept down and fettered with poverty, and such prodigious chances lying right here in sight! Oh, it is a fearful thing to be poor. But don't throw away those things—they are so splendid and I can see how sure they are. Don't throw them away for something still better and maybe fail in it! I wouldn't, Colonel. I would stick to these. I wish father were here and were his old self again—Oh, he never in his life had such chances as these are. Colonel, you *can't* improve on these—no man can improve on them!"

A sweet, compassionate smile played about the Colonel's features, and he leaned over the table with the air of a man who is "going to show you" and do it without the least trouble:

"Why, Washington, my boy, these things are nothing. They *look* large—of course they look large to a novice, but to a man who has been all his life accustomed to large operations—shaw! They're well enough to while away an idle hour with, or furnish a bit of employment that will give a trifle of idle capital a chance to earn its bread while it is waiting for something to *do*, but—now just listen a moment—just let me give you an idea of what we old veterans of commerce call 'business.' Here's the Rothschilds' proposition—this is between you and me, you understand——"

Washington nodded three or four times impatiently, and his glowing eyes said, "Yes, yes—hurry—I understand——"

"——for I wouldn't have it get out for a fortune. They want me to go in with them on the sly—agent was here two weeks ago about it—go

ι the sly" [voice down to an impressive whisper, now] "and buy up
a hundred and thirteen wildcat banks in Ohio, Indiana, Kentucky, Illinois and Missouri—notes of these banks are at all sorts of discount now—average discount of the hundred and thirteen is forty-four per cent—buy them all up, you see, and then all of a sudden let the cat out of the bag! Whiz! the stock of every one of those wildcats would spin up to a tremendous premium before you could turn a handspring—profit on the speculation not a dollar less than forty millions!" [An eloquent pause, while the marvelous vision settled into W.'s focus.] "Where's your hogs now! Why, my dear innocent boy, we would just sit down on the front door-steps and peddle banks like lucifer matches!"

Washington finally got his breath and said:

"Oh, it is perfectly wonderful! Why couldn't these things have happened in father's day? And I—it's of no use—they simply lie before my face and mock me. There is nothing for me but to stand helpless and see other people reap the astonishing harvest."

"Never mind, Washington, don't you worry. I'll fix you. There's plenty of chances. How much money have you got?"

In the presence of so many millions, Washington could not keep from blushing when he had to confess that he had but eighteen dollars in the world.

"Well, all right—don't despair. Other people have been obliged to begin with less. I have a small idea that may develop into something for us both, all in good time. Keep your money close and add to it. I'll make it breed. I've been experimenting (to pass away the time) on a little preparation for curing sore eyes—a kind of decoction nine-tenths water and the other tenth drugs that don't cost more than a dollar a barrel; I'm still experimenting; there's one ingredient wanted yet to perfect the thing, and somehow I can't just manage to hit upon the thing that's necessary, and I don't dare talk with a chemist, of course. But I'm progressing, and before many weeks I wager the country will ring with the fame of Eschol [1] Sellers' Infallible Imperial Oriental Optic Liniment and Salvation for Sore Eyes—the Medical Wonder of the Age! Small bottles fifty cents, large ones a dollar. Average cost, five and seven cents for the two sizes. The first year sell, say, ten thousand bottles in Missouri, seven thousand in Iowa, three thousand in Arkansas, four thousand in Kentucky, six thousand in Illinois, and say twenty-five thousand in the rest of the country. Total, fifty-five thousand bottles; profit clear of all expenses, twenty thousand dollars at the very lowest calculation. All the capital needed is to manufacture the first two thousand bottles—say a hundred and fifty dollars—then the money would begin to flow in. The second year, sales would reach 200,000 bottles—clear profit, say, $75,000—and in the meantime the great factory would be building in St. Louis, to cost, say,

---

[1] When an Eschol Sellers appeared and threatened suit, the name was changed to "Beriah." It was further altered to "Mulberry" when the novel was dramatized in 1874. Under the latter name Colonel Sellers figured in *The American Claimant*.

$100,000. The third year we could easily sell 1,000,000 bottles in the United States and——"

"O, splendid!" said Washington. "Let's commence right away—let's——"

"——1,000,000 bottles in the United States—profit at least $350,000—and *then* it would begin to be time to turn our attention toward the *real* idea of the business."

"The *real* idea of it! ain't $350,000 a year a pretty real——"

"Stuff! Why, what an infant you are, Washington—what a guileless, short-sighted, easily-contented innocent you are, my poor little country-bred know-nothing! Would I go to all that trouble and bother for the poor crumbs a body might pick up in *this* country? Now do I look like a man who—does my history suggest that I am a man who deals in trifles, contents himself with the narrow horizon that hems in the common herd, sees no further than the end of his nose? Now, *you* know that that is not me—couldn't *be* me. *You* ought to know that if I throw my time and abilities into a patent medicine, it's a patent medicine whose field of operations is the solid earth! its clients the swarming nations that inhabit it! Why what is the republic of America for an eye-water country? Lord bless you, it is nothing but a barren highway that you've got to cross to get *to* the true eye-water market! Why, Washington, in the Oriental countries people swarm like the sands of the desert; every square mile of ground upholds its thousands upon thousands of struggling human creatures—and every separate and individual devil of them's got the ophthalmia! It's as natural to them as noses are—and sin. It's born with them, it stays with them, it's all that some of them have left when they die. Three years of introductory trade in the Orient and what will be the result? Why, our headquarters would be in Constantinople and our hindquarters in Further India! Factories and warehouses in Cairo, Ispahan, Bagdad, Damascus, Jerusalem, Yedo, Peking, Bangkok, Delhi, Bombay and Calcutta! Annual income—well, God only knows how many millions and millions apiece!"

Washington was so dazed, so bewildered—his heart and his eyes had wandered so far away among the strange lands beyond the seas, and such avalanches of coin and currency had fluttered and jingled confusedly down before him, that he was now as one who has been whirling round and round for a time, and, stopping all at once, finds his surroundings still whirling and all objects a dancing chaos. However, little by little the Sellers family cooled down and crystallized into shape, and the poor room lost its glitter and resumed its poverty. Then the youth found his voice and begged Sellers to drop everything and hurry up the eye-water; and he got his eighteen dollars and tried to force it upon the Colonel—pleaded with him to take it—implored him to do it. But the Colonel would not; said he would not need the capital (in his native magnificent way he called that eighteen dollars Capital) till the eye-water was an accomplished fact. He made Washington easy in his mind, though, by promising that he would call for it just as soon as the invention was finished, and he added the glad tidings that nobody but just they two should be admitted to a share in the speculation.

When Washington left the breakfast table he could have worshiped that man. Washington was one of that kind of people whose hopes are in the very clouds one day and in the gutter the next. He walked on air, now. The Colonel was ready to take him around and introduce him to the employment he had found for him, but Washington begged for a few moments in which to write home; with his kind of people, to ride to-day's new interest to death and put off yesterday's till another time, is nature itself. He ran up stairs and wrote glowingly, enthusiastically, to his mother about the hogs and the corn, the banks and the eye-water—and added a few inconsequential millions to each project. And he said that people little dreamed what a man Col. Sellers was, and that the world would open its eyes when it found out. And he closed his letter thus:

"So make yourself perfectly easy, mother—in a little while you shall have everything you want, and more. I am not likely to stint *you* in anything, I fancy. This money will not be for me, alone, but for all of us. I want all to share alike; and there is going to be far more for each than one person can spend. Break it to father cautiously—you understand the need of that—break it to him cautiously, for he has had such cruel hard fortune, and is so stricken by it that great good news might prostrate him more surely than even bad, for he is used to the bad but is grown sadly unaccustomed to the other. Tell Laura—tell all the children. And write to Clay about it if he is not with you yet. You may tell Clay that whatever I get he can freely share in—freely. He knows that that is true—there will be no need that I should swear to that to make him believe it. Good-bye—and mind what I say: Rest perfectly easy, one and all of you, for our troubles are nearly at an end."

Poor lad, he could not know that his mother would cry some loving, compassionate tears over his letter and put off the family with a synopsis of its contents which conveyed a deal of love to them but not much idea of his prospects or projects. And he never dreamed that such a joyful letter could sadden her and fill her night with sighs, and troubled thoughts, and bodings of the future, instead of filling it with peace and blessing it with restful sleep.

When the letter was done, Washington and the Colonel sallied forth, and as they walked along Washington learned what he was to be. He was to be a clerk in a real estate office. Instantly the fickle youth's dreams forsook the magic eye-water and flew back to the Tennessee Land. And the gorgeous possibilities of that great domain straightway began to occupy his imagination to such a degree that he could scarcely manage to keep even enough of his attention upon the Colonel's talk to retain the general run of what he was saying. He was glad it was a real estate office —he was a made man now, sure.

The Colonel said that General Boswell was a rich man and had a good and growing business; and that Washington's work would be light and he would get forty dollars a month and be boarded and lodged in the General's family—which was as good as ten dollars more; and even better, for he could not live as well even at the "City Hotel" as he would there, and yet the hotel charged fifteen dollars a month where a man had a good room.

General Boswell was in his office; a comfortable looking place, with plenty of outline maps hanging about the walls and in the windows, and a spectacled man was marking out another one on a long table. The office was in the principal street. The General received Washington with a kindly but reserved politeness. Washington rather liked his looks. He was about fifty years old, dignified, well preserved and well dressed. After the Colonel took his leave, the General talked a while with Washington—his talk consisting chiefly of instructions about the clerical duties of the place. He seemed satisfied as to Washington's ability to take care of the books, he was evidently a pretty fair theoretical bookkeeper, and experience would soon harden theory into practice. By and by dinnertime came, and the two walked to the General's house; and now Washington noticed an instinct in himself that moved him to keep not in the General's rear, exactly, but yet not at his side—somehow the old gentleman's dignity and reserve did not inspire familiarity.

Chapter XI [2]

[A DINNER WITH COL. SELLERS]

Two months had gone by and the Hawkins family were domiciled in Hawkeye. Washington was at work in the real estate office again, and was alternately in paradise or the other place just as it happened that Louise was gracious to him or seemingly indifferent—because indifference or preoccupation could mean nothing else than that she was thinking of some other young person. Col. Sellers had asked him several times to dine with him, when he first returned to Hawkeye, but Washington, for no particular reason, had not accepted. No particular reason except one which he preferred to keep to himself—viz., that he could not bear to be away from Louise. It occurred to him, now, that the Colonel had not invited him lately—could he be offended? He resolved to go that very day, and give the Colonel a pleasant surprise. It was a good idea; especially as Louise had absented herself from breakfast that morning, and torn his heart; he would tear hers, now, and let her see how it felt.

The Sellers family were just starting to dinner when Washington burst

[2] In the omitted chapters Washington has been dazzled by General Boswell's daughter Louise, who behaves somewhat coquettishly toward him. He returns home to help nurse his father, whose dying words are an injunction to hold onto the Tennessee lands. With his return to Hawkeye the narrative resumes.

upon them with his surprise. For an instant the Colonel looked non-plussed, and just a bit uncomfortable; and Mrs. Sellers looked actually distressed; but the next moment the head of the house was himself again, and exclaimed:

"All right, my boy, all right—always glad to see you—always glad to hear your voice and take you by the hand. Don't wait for special invitations—that's all nonsense among friends. Just come whenever you can, and come as often as you can—the oftener the better. You can't please us any better than that, Washington; the little woman will tell you so herself. We don't pretend to style. Plain folks, you know—plain folks. Just a plain family dinner, but such as it is, our friends are *always* welcome, I reckon you know that yourself, Washington. Run along, children, run along; Lafayette,[3] stand off the cat's tail, child, can't you see what you're doing? Come, come, come, Roderick Dhu, it isn't nice for little boys to hang onto young gentlemen's coat tails—but never mind him, Washington, he's full of spirits and don't mean any harm. Children will be children, you know. Take the chair next to Mrs. Sellers, Washington—tut, tut, Marie Antoinette, let your brother have the fork if he wants it, you are bigger than he is."

Washington contemplated the banquet, and wondered if he were in his right mind. Was this the plain family dinner? And was it all present? It was soon apparent that this was indeed the dinner: it was all on the table: it consisted of abundance of clear, fresh water, and a basin of raw turnips—nothing more.

Washington stole a glance at Mrs. Sellers' face, and would have given the world, the next moment, if he could have spared her that. The poor woman's face was crimson, and the tears stood in her eyes. Washington did not know what to do. He wished he had never come there and spied out this cruel poverty and brought pain to that poor little lady's heart and shame to her cheek; but he was there, and there was no escape. Col. Sellers hitched back his coat sleeves airily from his wrists as who should say "*Now* for solid enjoyment!" seized a fork, flourished it and began to harpoon turnips and deposit them in the plates before him:

"Let me help you, Washington—Lafayette, pass this plate to Washington—ah, well, well, my boy, things are looking pretty bright, now, *I* tell you. Speculation—my! the whole atmosphere's full of money. I wouldn't take three fortunes for one little operation I've got on hand now—have anything from the casters? No? Well, you're right, you're right. Some people like mustard with turnips, but—now there was Baron Poniatowski—Lord, but that man did know how to live!—true Russian

---

[3] In those old days the average man called his children after his most revered literary and historical idols; consequently there was hardly a family, at least in the West, but had a Washington in it—and also a Lafayette, a Franklin, and six or eight sounding names from Byron, Scott, and the Bible, if the offspring held out. To visit such a family was to find one's self confronted by a congress made up of representatives of the imperial myths and the majestic dead of all the ages. There was something thrilling about it, to a stranger, not to say awe-inspiring. (Twain's note.)

you know, Russian to the back bone; I say to my wife, give me a Russian every time, for a table comrade. The Baron used to say, 'Take mustard, Sellers, try the mustard,—a man *can't* know what turnips are in perfection without mustard,' but I always said, 'No, Baron, I'm a plain man, and I want my food plain—none of your embellishments for Eschol Sellers—no made dishes for me! And it's the best way—high living kills more than it cures in this world, you can rest assured of that. Yes indeed, Washington, I've got one little operation on hand that—take some more water—help yourself, won't you? help yourself, there's plenty of it. You'll find it pretty good, I guess. How does that fruit strike you?"

Washington said he did not know that he had ever tasted better. He did not add that he detested turnips even when they were cooked—loathed them in their natural state. No, he kept this to himself, and praised the turnips to the peril of his soul.

"I thought you'd like them. Examine them—examine them—they'll bear it. See how perfectly firm and juicy they are—they can't start any like them in this part of the country, I can tell you. These are from New Jersey—I imported them myself. They cost like sin, too; but Lord bless me, I go in for having the best of a thing, even if it does cost a little more—it's the best economy, in the long run. These are the Early Malcolm—it's a turnip that can't be produced except in just one orchard, and the supply never is up to the demand. Take some more water, Washington—you can't drink too much water with fruit—all the doctors say that. The plague can't come where this article is, my boy!"

"Plague? What plague?"

"What plague, indeed? Why the Asiatic plague that nearly depopulated London a couple of centuries ago."

"But how does that concern us? There is no plague here, I reckon."

"Sh! I've let it out! Well, never mind—just keep it to yourself. Perhaps I oughtn't said anything, but it's *bound* to come out sooner or later, so what is the odds? Old McDowells wouldn't like me to—to—bother it all, I'll just tell the whole thing and let it go. You see, I've been down to St. Louis, and I happened to run across old Dr. McDowells—thinks the world of me, does the doctor. He's a man that keeps himself to himself, and well he may, for he knows that he's got a reputation that covers the whole earth—he won't condescend to open himself out to many people, but Lord bless you, he and I are just like brothers; he won't let me go to a hotel when I'm in the city—says I'm the only man that's company to him, and I don't know but there's some truth in it, too, because although I never like to glorify myself and make a great to-do over what I am or what I can do or what I know, I don't mind saying here among friends that I *am* better read up in most sciences, maybe, than the general run of professional men in these days. Well, the other day he let me into a little secret, strictly on the quiet, about this matter of the plague.

"You see it's booming right along in our direction—follows the Gulf Stream, you know, just as all those epidemics do,—and within three months it will be just waltzing through this land like a whirlwind! And whoever it touches can make his will and contract for the funeral. Well, you can't *cure* it, you know, but you can prevent it. How? Turnips! that's it! Turnips and water! Nothing like it in the world, old McDowells says, just fill yourself up two or three times a day, and you can snap your fingers at the plague. Sh!—keep mum, but just you confine yourself to that diet and you're all right. I wouldn't have old McDowells know that I told about it for anything—he never would speak to me again. Take some more water, Washington—the more water you drink, the better. Here, let me give you some more of the turnips. No, no, no, now, I insist. There, now. Absorb those. They're mighty sustaining—brim full of nutriment—all the medical books say so. Just eat from four to seven good-sized turnips at a meal, and drink from a pint and a half to a quart of water, and then just sit around a couple of hours and let them ferment. You'll feel like a fighting cock next day."

Fifteen or twenty minutes later the Colonel's tongue was still chattering away—he had piled up several future fortunes out of several incipient "operations" which he had blundered into within the past week, and was now soaring along through some brilliant expectations born of late promising experiments upon the lacking ingredient of the eye-water. And at such a time Washington ought to have been a rapt and enthusiastic listener, but he was not, for two matters disturbed his mind and distracted his attention. One was, that he discovered, to his confusion and shame, that in allowing himself to be helped a second time to the turnips, he had robbed those hungry children. He had not needed the dreadful "fruit," and had not wanted it; and when he saw the pathetic sorrow in their faces when they asked for more and there was no more to give them, he hated himself for his stupidity and pitied the famishing young things with all his heart. The other matter that disturbed him was the dire inflation that had begun in his stomach. It grew and grew, it became more and more insupportable. Evidently the turnips were "fermenting." He forced himself to sit still as long as he could, but his anguish conquered him at last.

He rose in the midst of the Colonel's talk and excused himself on the plea of a previous engagement. The Colonel followed him to the door, promising over and over again that he would use his influence to get some of the Early Malcolms for him, and insisting that he should not be such a stranger but come and take pot-luck with him every chance he got. Washington was glad enough to get away and feel free again. He immediately bent his steps toward home.

In bed he passed an hour that threatened to turn his hair gray, and then a blessed calm settled down upon him that filled his heart with gratitude. Weak and languid, he made shift to turn himself about and seek rest and sleep; and as his soul hovered upon the brink of unconsciousness, he heaved a long, deep sigh, and said to himself that in his heart he had cursed the Colonel's preventive of rheumatism, before, and now *let* the plague come if it must—he was done with preventives; if ever any man beguiled him with turnips and water again, let him die the death. . . .

1873

From A TRAMP ABROAD

The following tall tale is a part of Chapters II and III of *A Tramp Abroad* (1880). The immediate locale is Heidelberg, and Twain has been describing a walk into a forest about a mile from his hotel. He is enjoying the afternoon solitude when he hears the croak of a raven and discovers that the bird is eyeing him. It is joined by two others who look him over critically, and the ensuing croaks are, he is sure, insults in raven language. At this point he makes the skillful transition into the recollection of Jim Baker and his blue-jay story.

The figure of Jim Baker is faithfully drawn from Twain's memory of Jim Gillis, a pocket-miner at whose cabin on Jackass Hill both Mark Twain and Bret Harte had stayed. Gillis was wise in the ways of animals and birds; he was also a capital storyteller, and Twain was indebted to him not only for the blue-jay anecdote but also for his yarn about Dick Baker's cat, Tom Quartz. In both the chief interest is in the careful circumstantial detail which makes narrator and scene come alive. The manner of telling the oral anecdote had evolved into an art through the generation of newspaper humorists that prepared the ground for Twain. His essay "How to Tell a Story" shows his devotion to this tradition in which the teller is grave, never hinting that he intends to amuse. In contrast to the humorous story is the comic, which exists for its point and requires little art in the telling. Occasionally Twain combines the two, but, as in the blue-jay yarn, success does not depend on the surprise of the closing lines.

Baker's Blue-Jay Yarn

Animals talk to each other, of course. There can be no question about that; but I suppose there are very few people who can understand them. I never knew but one man who could. I knew he could, however, because he told me so himself. He was a middle-aged, simple-hearted miner who had lived in a lonely corner of California, among the woods and mountains, a good many years, and had studied the ways of his only neighbors, the beasts and the birds, until he believed he could accurately translate any remark which they made. This was Jim Baker. According to Jim Baker, some animals have only a limited education, and use only very simple words, and scarcely ever a comparison or a flowery figure; whereas, certain other animals have a large vocabulary, a fine command of language and a ready and fluent delivery; consequently these latter talk a great deal; they like it; they are conscious of their talent, and they enjoy "showing off." Baker said, that after long and careful observation, he had come to the conclusion that the blue-jays were the best talkers he had found among birds and beasts. Said he:

"There's more *to* a blue-jay than any other creature. He has got more moods, and more different kinds of feelings than other creatures; and mind you, whatever a blue-jay feels, he can put into language. And no mere commonplace language, either, but rattling, out-and-out book-talk —and bristling with metaphor, too—just bristling! And as for command of language—why *you* never see a blue-jay get stuck for a word. No man ever did. They just boil out of him! And another thing: I've noticed a good deal, and there's no bird, or cow, or anything that uses as good grammar as a blue-jay. You may say a cat uses good grammar. Well, a cat does—but you let a cat get excited once; you let a cat get to pulling fur with another cat on a shed, nights, and you'll hear grammar that will give you the lockjaw. Ignorant people think it's the *noise* which fighting cats make that is so aggravating, but it ain't so; it's the sickening grammar they use. Now I've never heard a jay use bad grammar but very seldom; and when they do, they are as ashamed as a human; they shut right down and leave.

"You may call a jay a bird. Well, so he is, in a measure—because he's got feathers on him, and don't belong to no church, perhaps; but otherwise he is just as much a human as you be. And I'll tell you for why. A jay's gifts, and instincts, and feelings, and interests, cover the whole ground. A jay hasn't got any more principle than a Congressman. A jay will lie, a jay will steal, a jay will deceive, a jay will betray; and four times out of five, a jay will go back on his solemnest promise. The sacredness of an obligation is a thing which you can't cram into no blue-jay's head. Now on top of all this, there's another thing: a jay can out-swear any gentleman in the mines. You think a cat can swear. Well, a cat can; but you give a blue-jay a subject that calls for his reserve-powers, and where is your cat? Don't talk to *me*—I know too much about this thing. And there's yet another thing: in the one little particular of scolding—just good, clean, out-and-out scolding—a blue-jay can lay over anything, human or divine. Yes, sir, a jay is everything that a man is. A jay can cry, a jay can laugh, a jay can feel shame, a jay can reason and plan and discuss, a jay likes gossip and scandal, a jay has got a sense of humor, a jay knows when he is an ass just as well as you do—maybe better. If a jay ain't human, he better take in his sign, that's all. Now I'm going to tell you a perfectly true fact about some blue-jays.

"When I first begun to understand jay language correctly, there was a little incident happened here. Seven years ago, the last man in this region but me moved away. There stands his house,—been empty ever since; a log house, with a plank roof—just one big room, and no more; no ceiling —nothing between the rafters and the floor. Well, one Sunday morning I was sitting out here in front of my cabin, with my cat, taking the sun, and looking at the blue hills, and listening to the leaves rustling so lonely in the trees, and thinking of the home away yonder in the States, that I hadn't heard from in thirteen years, when a blue-jay lit on that house, with an acorn in his mouth, and says, 'Hello, I reckon I've struck something.' When he spoke, the acorn dropped out of his mouth and rolled down the roof, of course, but he didn't care; his mind was all on the thing he had struck. It was a knot-hole in the roof. He cocked his head to one side, shut one eye and put the other one to the hole, like a 'possum looking down a jug; then he glanced up with his bright eyes, gave a wink or two with his wings—which signifies gratification, you understand,—and says, 'It looks like a hole, it's located like a hole,—blamed if I don't believe it *is* a hole!'

"Then he cocked his head down and took another look; he glances up perfectly joyful, this time; winks his wings and his tail both, and says, 'O, no, this ain't no fat thing, I reckon! If I ain't in luck!—why it's a perfectly elegant hole!' So he flew down and got that acorn, and fetched it up and dropped it in, and was just tilting his head back, with the heavenliest smile on his face, when all of a sudden he was paralyzed into a listening attitude and that smile faded gradually out of his countenance like breath off'n a razor, and the queerest look of surprise took its place. Then he says, 'Why, I didn't hear it fall!' He cocked his eye at the hole again, and took a long look; raised up and shook his head; stepped around to the other side of the hole and took another look from that side; shook his head again. He studied a while, then he just went into the *de*tails— walked round and round the hole and spied into it from every point of the compass. No use. Now he took a thinking attitude on the comb of the roof and scratched the back of his head with his right foot a minute, and finally says, 'Well, it's too many for *me*, that's certain; must be a mighty long hole; however, I ain't got no time to fool around here, I got to 'tend to business; I reckon it's all right—chance it, anyway.'

"So he flew off and fetched another acorn and dropped it in, and tried to flirt his eye to the hole quick enough to see what become of it, but he was too late. He held his eye there as much as a minute; then he raised up and sighed, and says, 'Confound it, I don't seem to understand this thing, no way; however, I'll tackle her again.' He fetched another acorn, and done his level best to see what become of it, but he couldn't. He says, 'Well, *I* never struck no such a hole as this before; I'm of the opinion it's a totally new kind of a hole.' Then he begun to get mad. He held in for a spell, walking up and down the comb of the roof and shaking his head and muttering to himself; but his feelings got the upper hand of him, presently, and he broke loose and cussed himself black in the face. I never see a bird take on so about a little thing. When he got through he walks to the hole and looks in again for half a minute; then he says, 'Well, you're a long hole, and a deep hole, and a mighty singular hole altogether—but I've started in to fill you, and I'm d—d if I *don't* fill you, if it takes a hundred years!'

"And with that, away he went. You never see a bird work so since you was born. He laid into his work like a nigger, and the way he hove acorns into that hole for about two hours and a half was one of the most exciting and astonishing spectacles I ever struck. He never stopped to take a look any more—he just hove 'em in and went for more. Well, at last he could hardly flop his wings, he was so tuckered out. He comes a-drooping down, once more, sweating like an ice-pitcher, drops his acorn in and says, '*Now* I guess I've got the bulge on you by this time!' So he bent down for a look. If you'll believe me, when his head come up again he was just pale with rage. He says, 'I've shoveled acorns enough in there to keep the family thirty years, and if I can see a sign of one of 'em I wish I may land in a museum with a belly full of sawdust in two minutes!'

"He just had strength enough to crawl up on to the comb and lean his back agin the chimbly, and then he collected his impressions and begun to free his mind. I see in a second that what I had mistook for profanity in the mines was only just the rudiments, as you may say.

"Another jay was going by, and heard him doing his devotions, and stops to inquire what was up. The sufferer told him the whole circumstance, and says, 'Now yonder's the hole, and if you don't believe me, go and look for yourself.' So this fellow went and looked, and comes back and says, 'How many did you say you put in there?' 'Not any less than two tons,' says the sufferer. The other jay went and looked again. He couldn't seem to make it out, so he raised a yell, and three more jays come. They all examined the hole, they all made the sufferer tell it over again, then they all discussed it, and got off as many leather-headed opinions about it as an average crowd of humans could have done.

"They called in more jays; then more and more, till pretty soon this whole region 'peared to have a blue flush about it. There must have been five thousand of them; and such another jawing and disputing and ripping and cussing, you never heard. Every jay in the whole lot put his eye to the hole and delivered a more chuckle-headed opinion about the mystery than the jay that went there before him. They examined the house all over, too. The door was standing half open, and at last one old jay happened to go and light on it and look in. Of course that knocked the mystery galley-west in a second. There lay the acorns, scattered all over the floor. He flopped his wings and raised a whoop. 'Come here!' he says, 'Come here, everybody; hang'd if this fool hasn't been trying to fill up a house with acorns!' They all came a-swooping down like a blue cloud, and as each fellow lit on the door and took a glance, the whole absurdity of the contract that that first jay had tackled hit him home and he fell over backwards suffocating with laughter, and the next jay took his place and done the same.

"Well, sir, they roosted around here on the house-top and the trees for an hour, and guffawed over that thing like human beings. It ain't any use to tell me a blue-jay hasn't got a sense of humor, because I know better. And memory, too. They brought jays here from all over the United States to look down that hole, every summer for three years. Other birds too. And they could all see the point, except an owl that come from

Nova Scotia to visit the Yo Semite, and he took this thing in on his way back. He said he couldn't see anything funny in it. But then he was a good deal disappointed about Yo Semite, too."

1880

From LIFE ON THE MISSISSIPPI

At the urging of W. D. Howells, Twain wrote a series of papers called "Old Times on the Mississippi" which ran in the *Atlantic Monthly* from January through July, 1875. The series was too short for a book, and Twain proposed that Howells join him in revisiting the river to gather additional material. The plan fell through and it was not until 1882 that Twain made the journey with his publisher Osgood and a secretary. In the following year *Life on the Mississippi* was published. Its principal importance lies in the first twenty chapters, which are reminiscences of the great steamboating days before the Civil War, particularized and made personal through the focus on young Sam Clemens' apprenticeship as a pilot. This part of the book has a simple dramatic unity: it is the Alger story of poor boy making good despite obstacles. Beyond that, Twain has captured even more imperishably than in *Roughing It* the spirit of a locale in its brief period of special distinction. The river itself becomes a formidable protagonist in some of Twain's most evocative writing; but the foreground is dominated by men and their wonderful world of talk as they appear to the mind of a youth. These chapters, rapidly and lovingly set down, remain among the very best of all Twain's work.

The last forty chapters of *Life on the Mississippi* have their interest, but it is of a different sort. The famous middle-aged author, unsuccessful in his attempt to travel the river incognito, gives us a celebrity's view of once-familiar scenes now, alas, transformed by time and by the narrator's own change of perspective. As travel literature it is less buoyant than *The Innocents Abroad;* Twain's keen eye for detail is still apparent, but the magic has departed from the scene and often from his own prose. Nonetheless, the trip itself was of first importance in reawakening Twain's interest in the manuscript of *Huckleberry Finn* which he had abandoned when his "inspiration tank" ran dry some years before. A single sentence records the memory of two Englishmen "in cheap royal finery" acting out the sword fight from *Richard III*, and we may be witnessing the birth of the king and the duke; longer passages, here reprinted, contain the germinal ideas for the Grangerford-Shepherdson feud and Huck's engaging description of the Grangerford home. The stimulation of finishing *Life on the Mississippi* led him to take up the older manuscript with renewed zest. The result was to be the high point of his career.

Chapter III

FRESCOS FROM THE PAST

. . . The river's earliest commerce was in great barges—keelboats, broadhorns. They floated and sailed from the upper rivers to New Orleans, changed cargoes there, and were tediously warped and poled back by hand. A voyage down and back sometimes occupied nine months. In time this commerce increased until it gave employment to hordes of rough and hardy men; rude, uneducated, brave, suffering terrific hardships with sailor-like stoicism; heavy drinkers, coarse frolickers in moral sties like the Natchez-under-the-hill of that day, heavy fighters, reckless fellows, every one, elephantinely jolly, foul-witted, profane; prodigal of their money, bankrupt at the end of the trip, fond of barbaric finery, prodigious braggarts; yet, in the main, honest, trustworthy, faithful to promises and duty, and often picturesquely magnanimous.

By and by the steamboat intruded. Then, for fifteen or twenty years, these men continued to run their keelboats down-stream, and the steamers did all of the up-stream business, the keelboatmen selling their boats in New Orleans, and returning home as deck passengers in the steamers.

But after a while the steamboats so increased in number and in speed that they were able to absorb the entire commerce; and then keelboating died a permanent death. The keelboatman became a deck hand, or a mate, or a pilot on the steamer; and when steamer-berths were not open to him, he took a berth on a Pittsburgh coal-flat, or on a pine-raft constructed in the forests up toward the sources of the Mississippi.

In the heyday of the steamboating prosperity, the river from end to end was flaked with coal-fleets and timber rafts, all managed by hand, and employing hosts of the rough characters whom I have been trying to describe. I remember the annual processions of mighty rafts that used to glide by Hannibal when I was a boy—an acre or so of white, sweet-smelling boards in each raft, a crew of two dozen men or more, three or four wigwams scattered about the raft's vast level space for storm-quarters—and I remember the rude ways and the tremendous talk of their big crews, the ex-keelboatmen and their admiringly patterning successors; for we used to swim out a quarter or third of a mile and get on these rafts and have a ride.

By way of illustrating keelboat talk and manners, and that now-departed and hardly-remembered raft-life, I will throw in, in this place, a chapter from a book which I have been working at, by fits and starts, during the past five or six years, and may possibly finish in the course of five or six more. The book is a story which details some passages in the life of an ignorant village boy, Huck Finn, son of the town drunkard of my time out West, there. He has run away from his persecuting father, and from a persecuting good widow who wishes to make a nice, truth-telling, respectable boy of him; and with him a slave of the widow's has also escaped. They have found a fragment of a lumber raft (it is high water and dead summer time), and are floating down the river by night, and hiding in the willows by day—bound for Cairo, whence the negro will seek freedom in the heart of the free States. But in a fog, they pass Cairo without knowing it. By and by they begin to suspect the truth, and Huck Finn is persuaded to end the dismal suspense by swimming down to a huge raft which they have seen in the distance ahead of them, creeping aboard under cover of the darkness, and gathering the needed information by eavesdropping:

But you know a young person can't wait very well when he is impatient to find a thing out. We talked it over, and by and by Jim said it was such a black night, now, that it wouldn't be no risk to swim down to the big raft and crawl aboard and listen—they would talk about Cairo, because they would be calculating to go ashore there for a spree, maybe, or anyway they would send boats ashore to buy whisky or fresh meat or something. Jim had a wonderful level head, for a nigger: he could most always start a good plan when you wanted one.

I stood up and shook my rags off and jumped into the river, and struck out for the raft's light. By and by, when I got down nearly to her, I eased up and went slow and cautious. But everything was all right—nobody at the sweeps. So I swum down along the raft till I was most abreast the camp fire in the middle, then I crawled aboard and inched along and got in amongst some bundles of shingles on the weather side of the fire. There was thirteen men there—they was the watch on deck of course. And a mighty rough-looking lot, too. They had a jug, and tin cups, and they kept the jug moving. One man was singing—roaring, you may say; and it wasn't a nice song—for a parlor, anyway. He roared through his nose, and strung out the last word of every line very long. When he was done they all fetched a kind of Injun war-whoop, and then another was sung. It begun:

> "There was a woman in our towdn,
>   In our towdn did dwed'l [dwell],
> She loved her husband dear-i-lee,
>   But another man twyste as wed'l.
>
> "Singing too, riloo, riloo, riloo,
>   Ri-too, riloo, rilay - - - e,
> She loved her husband dear-i-lee,
>   But another man twyste as wed'l." [1]

And so on—fourteen verses. It was kind of poor, and when he was going to start on the next verse one of them said it was the tune the old cow

[1] An American ballad probably of British origin (called "The Old Woman of Slapsadam," "The Wily Auld Carle," or "Eggs and Marrowbone") in which a woman who tries to blind and drown her husband is herself drowned. For a version still current in Mississippi Valley tradition, see *Ballads and Songs Collected by the Missouri Folk-Lore Society*, ed. H. M. Belden (1940), pp. 238–39.

died on; and another one said, "Oh, give us a rest." And another one told him to take a walk. They made fun of him till he got mad and jumped up and begun to cuss the crowd, and said he could lam any thief in the lot.

They was all about to make a break for him, but the biggest man there jumped up and says:

"Set whar you are, gentlemen. Leave him to me; he's my meat."

Then he jumped up in the air three times and cracked his heels together every time. He flung off a buckskin coat that was all hung with fringes, and says, "You lay thar tell the chawin-up's done"; and flung his hat down, which was all over ribbons, and says, "You lay thar tell his sufferins is over."

Then he jumped up in the air and cracked his heels together again and shouted out:

"Whoo-oop! I'm the old original iron-jawed, brass-mounted, copper-bellied corpse-maker from the wilds of Arkansaw!—Look at me! I'm the man they call Sudden Death and General Desolation! Sired by a hurricane, dam'd by an earthquake, half-brother to the cholera, nearly related to the small-pox on the mother's side! Look at me! I take nineteen alligators and a bar'l of whisky for breakfast when I'm in robust health, and a bushel of rattlesnakes and a dead body when I'm ailing! I split the everlasting rocks with my glance, and I squench the thunder when I speak! Whoo-oop! Stand back and give me room according to my strength! Blood's my natural drink, and the wails of the dying is music to my ear! Cast your eye on me, gentlemen!—and lay low and hold your breath, for I'm 'bout to turn myself loose!"

All the time he was getting this off, he was shaking his head and looking fierce, and kind of swelling around in a little circle, tucking up his wrist-bands, and now and then straightening up and beating his breast with his fist, saying, "Look at me, gentlemen!" When he got through, he jumped up and cracked his heels together three times, and let off a roaring "Whoo-oop! I'm the bloodiest son of a wildcat that lives!"

Then the man that had started the row tilted his old slouch hat down over his right eye; then he bent stooping forward, with his back sagged and his south end sticking out far, and his fists a-shoving out and drawing in in front of him, and so went around in a little circle about three times, swelling himself up and breathing hard. Then he straightened, and jumped up and cracked his heels together three times before he lit again (that made them cheer), and he began to shout like this:

"Whoo-oop! bow your neck and spread, for the kingdom of sorrow's a-coming! Hold me down to the earth, for I feel my powers a-working! whoo-oop! I'm a child of sin, *don't* let me get a start! Smoked glass, here, for all! Don't attempt to look at me with the naked eye, gentlemen! When I'm playful I use the meridians of longitude and parallels of latitude for a seine, and drag the Atlantic Ocean for whales! I scratch my head with the lightning and purr myself to sleep with the thunder! When

I'm cold, I bile the Gulf of Mexico and bathe in it; when I'm hot I fan myself with an equinoctial storm; when I'm thirsty I reach up and suck a cloud dry like a sponge; when I range the earth hungry, famine follows in my tracks! Whoo-oop! Bow your neck and spread! I put my hand on the sun's face and make it night in the earth; I bite a piece out of the moon and hurry the seasons; I shake myself and crumble the mountains! Contemplate me through leather—*don't* use the naked eye! I'm the man with a petrified heart and biler-iron bowels! The massacre of isolated communities is the pastime of my idle moments, the destruction of nationalities the serious business of my life! The boundless vastness of the great American desert is my enclosed property, and I bury my dead on my own premises!" He jumped up and cracked his heels together three times before he lit (they cheered him again), and as he come down he shouted out: "Whoo-oop! bow your neck and spread, for the Pet Child of Calamity's a-coming!"

Then the other one went to swelling around and blowing again—the first one—the one they called Bob; next, the Child of Calamity chipped in again, bigger than ever; then they both got at it at the same time, swelling round and round each other and punching their fists most into each other's faces, and whooping and jawing like Injuns; then Bob called the Child names, and the Child called him names back again; next, Bob called him a heap rougher names and the Child come back at him with the very worst kind of language; next, Bob knocked the Child's hat off, and the Child picked it up and kicked Bob's ribbony hat about six foot; Bob went and got it and said never mind, this warn't going to be the last of this thing, because he was a man that never forgot and never forgive, and so the Child better look out, for there was a time a-coming, just as sure as he was a living man, that he would have to answer to him with the best blood in his body. The Child said no man was willinger than he was for that time to come, and he would give Bob fair warning, *now*, never to cross his path again, for he could never rest till he had waded in his blood, for such was his nature, though he was sparing him now on account of his family, if he had one.

Both of them was edging away in different directions, growling and shaking their heads and going on about what they was going to do; but a little black-whiskered chap skipped up and says:

"Come back here, you couple of chicken-livered cowards, and I'll thrash the two of ye!"

And he done it, too. He snatched them, he jerked them this way and that, he booted them around, he knocked them sprawling faster than they could get up. Why, it warn't two minutes till they begged like dogs— and how the other lot did yell and laugh and clap their hands all the way through, and shout, "Sail in, Corpse-Maker!" "Hi! at him again, Child of Calamity!" "Bully for you, little Davy!" Well, it was a perfect pow-wow for a while. Bob and the Child had red noses and black eyes when they got through. Little Davy made them own up that they was sneaks and

cowards and not fit to eat with a dog or drink with a nigger; then Bob
and the Child shook hands with each other, very solemn, and said they
had always respected each other and was willing to let bygones be bygones. So then they washed their faces in the river; and just then there
was a loud order to stand by for a crossing, and some of them went forward to man the sweeps there, and the rest went aft to handle the after-
sweeps.

I laid still and waited for fifteen minutes, and had a smoke out of a
pipe that one of them left in reach; then the crossing was finished, and
they stumped back and had a drink around and went to talking and singing again. Next they got out an old fiddle, and one played, and another
patted juba,[2] and the rest turned themselves loose on a regular old-
fashioned keel-boat break-down. They couldn't keep that up very long
without getting winded, so by and by they settled around the jug again.

They sung "Jolly, Jolly Raftsman's the Life for Me," with a rousing
chorus, and then they got to talking about differences betwixt hogs, and
their different kind of habits; and next about women and their different
ways; and next about the best ways to put out houses that was afire; and
next about what ought to be done with the Injuns; and next about what a
king had to do, and how much he got; and next about how to make cats
fight; and next about what to do when a man has fits; and next about differences betwixt clear-water rivers and muddy-water ones. The man
they called Ed said the muddy Mississippi water was wholesomer to
drink than the clear water of the Ohio; he said if you let a pint of this
yaller Mississippi water settle, you would have about a half to three-
quarters of an inch of mud in the bottom, according to the stage of the
river, and then it warn't no better than Ohio water—what you wanted to
do was to keep it stirred up—and when the river was low, keep mud on
hand to put in and thicken the water up the way it ought to be.

The Child of Calamity said that was so; he said there was nutritious-
ness in the mud, and a man that drunk Mississippi water could grow corn
in his stomach if he wanted to. He says:

"You look at the graveyards; that tells the tale. Trees won't grow
worth shucks in a Cincinnati graveyard, but in a Sent Louis graveyard
they grow upwards of eight hundred foot high. It's all on account of the
water the people drunk before they laid up. A Cincinnati corpse don't
richen a soil any."

And they talked about how Ohio water didn't like to mix with Mississippi water. Ed said if you take the Mississippi on a rise when the
Ohio is low, you'll find a wide band of clear water all the way down the
east side of the Mississippi for a hundred mile or more, and the minute
you get out a quarter of a mile from shore and pass the line, it is all thick
and yaller the rest of the way across. Then they talked about how to
keep tobacco from getting mouldy, and from that they went into ghosts
and told about a lot that other folks had seen; but Ed says:

---

2 A lively Negro dance accompanied by patting thighs and knees and clapping.

"Why don't you tell something that you've seen yourselves? Now let me have a say. Five years ago I was on a raft as big as this, and right along here it was a bright moonshiny night, and I was on watch and boss of the stabboard oar forrard, and one of my pards was a man named Dick Allbright, and he come along to where I was sitting, forrard—gaping and stretching, he was—and stooped down on the edge of the raft and washed his face in the river, and come and set down by me and got out his pipe, and had just got it filled, when he looks up and says:

" 'Why looky-here,' he says, 'ain't that Buck Miller's place, over yander in the bend?'

" 'Yes,' says I, 'it is—why?' He laid his pipe down and leant his head on his hand, and says:

" 'I thought we'd be furder down.' I says:

" 'I thought it too, when I went off watch'—we was standing six hours on and six off—'but the boys told me,' I says, 'that the raft didn't seem to hardly move, for the last hour,' says I, 'though she's a-slipping along all right, now,' says I. He give a kind of a groan, and says:

" 'I've seed a raft act so before, along here,' he says, ' 'pears to me the current has most quit above the head of this bend durin' the last two years,' he says.

"Well, he raised up two or three times, and looked away off and around on the water. That started me at it, too. A body is always doing what he sees somebody else doing, though there mayn't be no sense in it. Pretty soon I see a black something floating on the water away off to stabboard and quartering behind us. I see he was looking at it, too. I says:

" 'What's that?' He says, sort of pettish:

" ' 'Tain't nothing but an old empty bar'l.'

" 'An empty bar'l!' says I, 'why,' says I, 'a spy-glass is a fool to *your* eyes. How can you tell it's an empty bar'l?' He says:

" 'I don't know; I reckon it ain't a bar'l, but I thought it might be,' says he.

" 'Yes,' I says, 'so it might be, and it might be anything else, too; a body can't tell nothing about it, such a distance as that,' I says.

"We hadn't nothing else to do, so we kept on watching it. By and by I says:

" 'Why, looky-here, Dick Allbright, that thing's a-gaining on us, I believe.'

"He never said nothing. The thing gained and gained, and I judged it must be a dog that was about tired out. Well, we swung down into the crossing, and the thing floated across the bright streak of the moonshine, and by George, it *was* a bar'l. Says I:

" 'Dick Allbright, what made you think that thing was a bar'l, when it was a half a mile off?' says I. Says he:

" 'I don't know.' Says I:

" 'You tell me, Dick Allbright.' He says:

" 'Well, I knowed it was a bar'l; I've seen it before; lots has seen it; they says it's a ha'nted bar'l.'

"I called the rest of the watch, and they come and stood there, and I told them what Dick said. It floated right along abreast, now, and didn't gain any more. It was about twenty foot off. Some was for having it aboard, but the rest didn't want to. Dick Allbright said rafts that had fooled with it had got bad luck by it. The captain of the watch said he didn't believe in it. He said he reckoned the bar'l gained on us because it was in a little better current than what we was. He said it would leave by and by.

"So then we went to talking about other things, and we had a song, and then a breakdown; and after that the captain of the watch called for another song; but it was clouding up, now, and the bar'l stuck right thar in the same place, and the song didn't seem to have much warm-up to it, somehow, and so they didn't finish it, and there warn't any cheers, but it sort of dropped flat, and nobody said anything for a minute. Then everybody tried to talk at once, and one chap got off a joke, but it warn't no use, they didn't laugh, and even the chap that made the joke didn't laugh at it, which ain't usual. We all just settled down glum, and watched the bar'l, and was oneasy and oncomfortable. Well, sir, it shut down black and still, and then the wind began to moan around, and next the lightning began to play and the thunder to grumble. And pretty soon there was a regular storm, and in the middle of it a man that was running aft stumbled and fell and sprained his ankle so that he had to lay up. This made the boys shake their heads. And every time the lightning come, there was that bar'l with the blue lights winking around it. We was always on the look-out for it. But by and by, towards dawn, she was gone. When the day come we couldn't see her anywhere, and we warn't sorry, neither.

"But next night about half-past nine, when there was songs and high jinks going on, here she comes again, and took her old roost on the stabboard side. There warn't no more high jinks. Everybody got solemn; nobody talked; you couldn't get anybody to do anything but set around moody and look at the bar'l. It begun to cloud up again. When the watch changed, the off watch stayed up, 'stead of turning in. The storm ripped and roared around all night, and in the middle of it another man tripped and sprained his ankle, and had to knock off. The bar'l left towards day, and nobody see it go.

"Everybody was sober and down in the mouth all day. I don't mean the kind of sober that comes of leaving liquor alone—not that. They was quiet, but they all drunk more than usual—not together, but each man sidled off and took it private, by himself.

"After dark the off watch didn't turn in; nobody sung, nobody talked; the boys didn't scatter around, neither; they sort of huddled together, forrard; and for two hours they set there, perfectly still, looking steady in the one direction, and heaving a sigh once in a while. And then, here comes the bar'l again. She took up her old place. She stayed there all night; nobody turned in. The storm come on again, after midnight. It got awful dark; the rain poured down; hail, too; the thunder boomed and roared and bellowed; the wind blowed a hurricane; and the lightning spread over everything in big sheets of glare, and showed the whole raft as plain as day; and the river lashed up white as milk as far as you could see for miles, and there was that bar'l jiggering along, same as ever. The captain ordered the watch to man the after sweeps for a crossing, and no-body would go—no more sprained ankles for them, they said. They wouldn't even *walk* aft. Well, then, just then the sky split wide open, with a crash, and the lightning killed two men of the after watch, and crippled two more. Crippled them how, say you? Why, *sprained their ankles!*

"The bar'l left in the dark betwixt lightnings, towards dawn. Well, not a body eat a bite at breakfast that morning. After that the men loafed around, in two and threes, and talked low together. But none of them herded with Dick Allbright. They all give him the cold shake. If he come around where any of the men was, they split up and sidled away. They wouldn't man the sweeps with him. The captain had all the skiffs hauled up on the raft, alongside of his wigwam, and wouldn't let the dead men be took ashore to be planted; he didn't believe a man that got ashore would come back; and he was right.

"After night come, you could see pretty plain that there was going to be trouble if that bar'l come again; there was such a muttering going on. A good many wanted to kill Dick Allbright, because he'd seen the bar'l on other trips, and that had an ugly look. Some wanted to put him ashore. Some said, 'Let's all go ashore in a pile, if the bar'l comes again.'

"This kind of whispers was still going on, the men being bunched to-gether forrard watching for the bar'l, when, lo and behold you, here she comes again. Down she comes, slow and steady, and settles into her old tracks. You could a heard a pin drop. Then up comes the captain, and says:

"'Boys, don't be a pack of children and fools; I don't want this bar'l to be dogging us all the way to Orleans, and *you* don't; well, then, how's the best way to stop it? Burn it up—that's the way. I'm going to fetch it aboard,' he says. And before anybody could say a word, in he went.

"He swum to it, and as he come pushing it to the raft, the men spread to one side. But the old man got it aboard and busted in the head, and there was a baby in it! Yes sir, a stark naked baby. It was Dick All-bright's baby; he owned up and said so.

"'Yes,' he says, a-leaning over it, 'yes, it is my own lamented darling, my poor lost Charles William Allbright deceased,' says he—for he could curl his tongue around the bulliest words in the language when he was a mind to, and lay them before you without a jint started, anywheres. Yes, he said, he used to live up at the head of this bend, and one night he choked his child, which was crying, not intending to kill it—which was prob'ly a lie—and then he was scared, and buried it in a bar'l, before his wife got home, and off he went, and struck the northern trail and went to rafting; and this was the third year that the bar'l had chased him. He said the bad luck always begun light, and lasted till four men was killed, and then the bar'l didn't come any more after that. He said if the men would stand it one more night—and was a-going on like that—but the men had got enough. They started to get out a boat to take him ashore and lynch him, but he grabbed the little child all of a sudden and jumped overboard with it hugged up to his breast and shedding tears, and we never see him again in this life, poor old suffering soul, nor Charles William neither."

"*Who* was shedding tears?" says Bob; "was it Allbright or the baby?"

"Why, Allbright, of course; didn't I tell you the baby was dead? Been dead three years—how could it cry?"

"Well, never mind how it could cry—how could it *keep* all that time?" says Davy. "You answer me that."

"I don't know how it done it," says Ed. "It done it, though—that's all I know about it."

"Say—what did they do with the bar'l?" says the Child of Calamity.

"Why, they hove it overboard, and it sunk like a chunk of lead."

"Edward, did the child look like it was choked?" says one.

"Did it have its hair parted?" says another.

"What was the brand on that bar'l, Eddy?" says a fellow they called Bill.

"Have you got the papers for them statistics, Edmund?" says Jimmy.

"Say, Edwin, was you one of the men that was killed by the lightning?" says Davy.

"Him? Oh, no, he was both of 'em," says Bob. Then they all haw-hawed.

"Say, Edward, don't you reckon you'd better take a pill? You look bad—don't you feel pale?" says the Child of Calamity.

"O, come, now, Eddy," says Jimmy, "show up; you must a kept part of that bar'l to prove the thing by. Show us the bunghole—*do*—and we'll all believe you."

"Say, boys," says Bill, "less divide it up. Thar's thirteen of us. I can swaller a thirteenth of the yarn, if you can worry down the rest."

Ed got up mad and said they could all go to some place which he ripped out pretty savage, and then walked off aft, cussing to himself, and they yelling and jeering at him, and roaring and laughing so you could hear them a mile.

"Boys, we'll split a watermelon on that," says the Child of Calamity; and he come rummaging around in the dark amongst the shingle bundles where I was, and put his hand on me. I was warm and soft and naked; so he says "Ouch!" and jumped back.

"Fetch a lantern or a chunk of fire here, boys—there's a snake here as big as a cow!"

So they run there with a lantern and crowded up and looked in on me.

"Come out of that, you beggar!" says one.

"Who are you?" says another.

"What are you after here? Speak up prompt, or overboard you go."

"Snake him out, boys. Snatch him out by the heels."

I began to beg, and crept out amongst them trembling. They looked me over, wondering, and the Child of Calamity says:

"A cussed thief! Lend a hand and less heave him overboard!"

"No," says Big Bob, "less get out the paint-pot and paint him a sky blue all over from head to heel, and *then* heave him over!"

"Good! that's it. Go for the paint, Jimmy."

When the paint come, and Bob took the brush and was just going to begin, the others laughing and rubbing their hands, I begun to cry, and that sort of worked on Davy, and he says:

" 'Vast there! He's nothing but a cub. I'll paint the man that tetches him!"

So I looked around on them, and some of them grumbled and growled, and Bob put down the paint, and the others didn't take it up.

"Come here to the fire, and less see what you're up to here," says Davy. "Now set down there and give an account of yourself. How long have you been aboard here?"

"Not over a quarter of a minute, sir," says I.

"How did you get dry so quick?"

"I don't know, sir. I'm always that way, mostly."

"Oh, you are, are you? What's your name?"

I warn't going to tell my name. I didn't know what to say, so I just says:

"Charles William Allbright, sir."

Then they roared—the whole crowd; and I was mighty glad I said that, because maybe laughing would get them in a better humor.

When they got done laughing, Davy says:

"It won't hardly do, Charles William. You couldn't have growed this much in five year, and you was a baby when you come out of the bar'l, you know, and dead at that. Come, now, tell a straight story, and no-body'll hurt you, if you ain't up to anything wrong. What *is* your name?"

"Aleck Hopkins, sir. Aleck James Hopkins."

"Well, Aleck, where did you come from, here?"

"From a trading scow. She lays up the bend yonder. I was born on her. Pap has traded up and down here all his life; and he told me to swim off here, because when you went by he said he would like to get some of you to speak to a Mr. Jonas Turner, in Cairo, and tell him—"

"Oh, come!"

"Yes, sir, it's as true as the world; Pap he says—"

"Oh, your grandmother!"

They all laughed, and I tried again to talk, but they broke in on me and stopped me.

"Now, looky-here," says Davy; "you're scared, and so you talk wild. Honest, now, do you live in a scow, or is it a lie?"

"Yes, sir, in a trading scow. She lays up at the head of the bend. But I warn't born in her. It's our first trip."

"Now you're talking! What did you come aboard here for? To steal?"

"No, sir, I didn't. It was only to get a ride on the raft. All boys does that."

"Well, I know that. But what did you hide for?"

"Sometimes they drive the boys off."

"So they do. They might steal. Looky-here; if we let you off this time, will you keep out of these kind of scrapes hereafter?"

" 'Deed I will, boss. You try me."

"All right, then. You ain't but little ways from shore. Overboard with you, and don't you make a fool of yourself another time this way. Blast it, boy, some raftsmen would rawhide you till you were black and blue!"

I didn't wait to kiss good-bye, but went overboard and broke for shore. When Jim come along by and by, the big raft was away out of sight around the point. I swum out and got aboard, and was mighty glad to see home again.

The boy did not get the information he was after, but his adventure has furnished the glimpse of the departed raftsman and keelboatman which I desire to offer in this place.

I now come to a phase of the Mississippi River life of the flush times of steamboating, which seems to me to warrant full examination—the marvelous science of piloting, as displayed there. I believe there has been nothing like it elsewhere in the world.

Chapter IV

THE BOYS' AMBITION

When I was a boy, there was but one permanent ambition among my comrades in our village [3] on the west bank of the Mississippi River. That was, to be a steamboatman. We had transient ambitions of other sorts, but they were only transient. When a circus came and went, it left us all burning to become clowns; the first negro minstrel show that came to our section left us all suffering to try that kind of life; now and then we had a hope that if we lived and were good, God would permit us to be pirates. These ambitions faded out, each in its turn; but the ambition to be a steamboatman always remained.

Once a day a cheap, gaudy packet arrived upward from St. Louis, and another downward from Keokuk. Before these events, the day was glorious with expectancy; after them, the day was a dead and empty thing.

[3] Hannibal, Missouri. (Twain's note.)

Not only the boys, but the whole village, felt this. After all these years I can picture that old time to myself now, just as it was then: the white town drowsing in the sunshine of a summer's morning; the streets empty, or pretty nearly so; one or two clerks sitting in front of the Water Street stores, with their splint-bottomed chairs tilted back against the wall, chins on breasts, hats slouched over their faces, asleep—with shingle-shavings enough around to show what broke them down; a sow and a litter of pigs loafing along the sidewalk, doing a good business in water-melon rinds and seeds; two or three lonely little freight piles scattered about the "levee"; a pile of "skids" on the slope of the stone-paved wharf, and the fragrant town drunkard asleep in the shadow of them; two or three wood flats at the head of the wharf, but nobody to listen to the peaceful lapping of the wavelets against them; the great Missis-sippi, the majestic, the magnificent Mississippi, rolling its mile-wide tide along, shining in the sun; the dense forest away on the other side; the "point" above the town, and the "point" below, bounding the river-glimpse and turning it into a sort of sea, and withal a very still and bril-liant and lonely one. Presently a film of dark smoke appears above one of those remote "points"; instantly a negro drayman, famous for his quick eye and prodigious voice, lifts up the cry, "S-t-e-a-m-boat a-comin'!" and the scene changes! The town drunkard stirs, the clerks wake up, a furious clatter of drays follows, every house and store pours out a human contribution, and all in a twinkling the dead town is alive and moving. Drays, carts, men, boys, all go hurrying from many quar-ters to a common center, the wharf. Assembled there, the people fasten their eyes upon the coming boat as upon a wonder they are seeing for the first time. And the boat *is* rather a handsome sight, too. She is long and sharp and trim and pretty; she has two tall, fancy-topped chimneys, with a gilded device of some kind swung between them; a fanciful pilot-house, all glass and "gingerbread," perched on top of the "texas" deck be-hind them; the paddle-boxes are gorgeous with a picture or with gilded rays above the boat's name; the boiler deck, the hurricane deck, and the texas deck are fenced and ornamented with clean white railings; there is a flag gallantly flying from the jack-staff; the furnace doors are open and the fires glaring bravely; the upper decks are black with passengers; the captain stands by the big bell, calm, imposing, the envy of all; great vol-umes of the blackest smoke are rolling and tumbling out of the chim-neys—a husbanded grandeur created with a bit of pitch pine just before arriving at a town; the crew are grouped on the forecastle; the broad stage is run far out over the port bow, and an envied deck-hand stands picturesquely on the end of it with a coil of rope in his hand; the pent steam is screaming through the gauge-cocks; the captain lifts his hand, a bell rings, the wheels stop; then they turn back, churning the water to foam, and the steamer is at rest. Then such a scramble as there is to get aboard, and to get ashore, and to take in freight and to discharge freight, all at one and the same time; and such a yelling and cursing as the mates facilitate it all with! Ten minutes later the steamer is under way again, with no flag on the jack-staff and no black smoke issuing from the chimneys. After ten more minutes the town is dead again, and the town drunkard asleep by the skids once more.

My father was a justice of the peace, and I supposed he possessed the power of life and death over all men and could hang anybody that offended him. This was distinction enough for me as a general thing; but the desire to be a steamboatman kept intruding, nevertheless. I first wanted to be a cabin-boy, so that I could come out with a white apron on and shake a table-cloth over the side, where all my old comrades could see me; later I thought I would rather be the deck-hand who stood on the end of the stage-plank with the coil of rope in his hand, because he was particularly conspicuous. But these were only day-dreams—they were too heavenly to be contemplated as real possibilities. By and by one of our boys went away. He was not heard of for a long time. At last he turned up as apprentice engineer or "striker" on a steamboat. This thing shook the bottom out of all my Sunday-school teachings. That boy had been notoriously worldly, and I just the reverse; yet he was exalted to this eminence, and I left in obscurity and misery. There was nothing generous about this fellow in his greatness. He would always manage to have a rusty bolt to scrub while his boat tarried at our town, and he would sit on the inside guard and scrub it, where we could all see him and envy him and loathe him. And whenever his boat was laid up he would come home and swell around the town in his blackest and greasiest clothes, so that nobody could help remembering that he was a steamboatman; and he used all sorts of steamboat technicalities in his talk, as if he were so used to them that he forgot common people could not understand them. He would speak of the "labboard" side of a horse in an easy, natural way that would make one wish he was dead. And he was always talking about "St. Looy" like an old citizen; he would refer casually to occasions when he was "coming down Fourth Street," or when he was "passing by the Planter's House," or when there was a fire and he took a turn on the brakes of "the old Big Missouri"; and then he would go on and lie about how many towns the size of ours were burned down there that day. Two or three of the boys had long been persons of consideration among us because they had been to St. Louis once and had a vague general knowledge of its wonders, but the day of their glory was over now. They lapsed into a humble silence, and learned to disappear when the ruthless "cub"-engineer approached. This fellow had money, too, and hair oil. Also an ignorant silver watch and a showy brass watch chain. He wore a leather belt and used no suspenders. If ever a youth was cordially admired and hated by his comrades, this one was. No girl could withstand his charms. He "cut out" every boy in the village. When his boat blew up at last, it diffused a tranquil contentment among us such as we had not known for months. But when he came home the next week, alive, renowned, and appeared in church all battered up and bandaged, a shining hero, stared at and wondered over by everybody, it seemed to us that the partiality of Providence for an undeserving reptile had reached a point where it was open to criticism.

This creature's career could produce but one result, and it speedily followed. Boy after boy managed to get on the river. The minister's son became an engineer. The doctor's and the post-master's sons became "mud clerks"; the wholesale liquor dealer's son became a bar-keeper on a boat; four sons of the chief merchant, and two sons of the county judge, became pilots. Pilot was the grandest position of all. The pilot, even in those days of trivial wages, had a princely salary—from a hundred and fifty to two hundred and fifty dollars a month, and no board to pay. Two months of his wages would pay a preacher's salary for a year. Now some of us were left disconsolate. We could not get on the river—at least our parents would not let us.

So by and by I ran away. I said I never would come home again till I was a pilot and could come in glory. But somehow I could not manage it. I went meekly aboard a few of the boats that lay packed together like sardines at the long St. Louis wharf, and very humbly inquired for the pilots, but got only a cold shoulder and short words from mates and clerks. I had to make the best of this sort of treatment for the time being, but I had comforting day-dreams of a future when I should be a great and honored pilot, with plenty of money, and could kill some of these mates and clerks and pay for them.

Chapter V

I WANT TO BE A CUB-PILOT

Months afterward the hope within me struggled to a reluctant death, and I found myself without an ambition. But I was ashamed to go home. I was in Cincinnati, and I set to work to map out a new career. I had been reading about the recent exploration of the river Amazon by an expedition sent out by our government.[4] It was said that the expedition, owing to difficulties, had not thoroughly explored a part of the country lying about the head-waters, some four thousand miles from the mouth of the river. It was only about fifteen hundred miles from Cincinnati to New Orleans, where I could doubtless get a ship. I had thirty dollars left; I would go and complete the exploration of the Amazon. This was all the thought I gave to the subject. I never was great in matters of detail. I packed my valise, and took passage on an ancient tub called the *Paul Jones*, for New Orleans. For the sum of sixteen dollars I had the scarred and tarnished splendors of "her" main saloon principally to myself, for she was not a creature to attract the eye of wiser travelers.

When we presently got under way and went poking down the broad

---

[4] The book, a copy of which he had given his mother, was William L. Herndon and Lardner Gibbon's *Exploration of the Valley of the Amazon* (1853–54).

Ohio, I became a new being, and the subject of my own admiration. I was a traveler! A word never had tasted so good in my mouth before. I had an exultant sense of being bound for mysterious lands and distant climes which I never have felt in so uplifting a degree since. I was in such a glorified condition that all ignoble feelings departed out of me, and I was able to look down and pity the untraveled with a compassion that had hardly a trace of contempt in it. Still, when we stopped at villages and wood-yards, I could not help lolling carelessly upon the railings of the boiler deck to enjoy the envy of the country boys on the bank. If they did not seem to discover me, I presently sneezed to attract their attention, or moved to a position where they could not help seeing me. And as soon as I knew they saw me I gaped and stretched, and gave other signs of being mightily bored with traveling.

I kept my hat off all the time, and stayed where the wind and the sun could strike me, because I wanted to get the bronzed and weather-beaten look of an old traveler. Before the second day was half gone, I experienced a joy which filled me with the purest gratitude; for I saw that the skin had begun to blister and peel off my face and neck. I wished that the boys and girls at home could see me now.

We reached Louisville in time—at least the neighborhood of it. We stuck hard and fast on the rocks in the middle of the river, and lay there four days. I was now beginning to feel a strong sense of being a part of the boat's family, a sort of infant son to the captain and younger brother to the officers. There is no estimating the pride I took in this grandeur, or the affection that began to swell and grow in me for those people. I could not know how the lordly steamboatman scorns that sort of presumption in a mere landsman. I particularly longed to acquire the least trifle of notice from the big stormy mate, and I was on the alert for an opportunity to do him a service to that end. It came at last. The riotous powwow of setting a spar was going on down on the forecastle, and I went down there and stood around in the way—or mostly skipping out of it—till the mate suddenly roared a general order for somebody to bring him a capstan bar. I sprang to his side and said: "Tell me where it is—I'll fetch it!"

If a rag-picker had offered to do a diplomatic service for the Emperor of Russia, the monarch could not have been more astounded than the mate was. He even stopped swearing. He stood and stared down at me. It took him ten seconds to scrape his disjointed remains together again. Then he said impressively: "Well, if this don't beat hell!" and turned to his work with the air of a man who had been confronted with a problem too abstruse for solution.

I crept away, and courted solitude for the rest of the day. I did not go to dinner; I stayed away from supper until everybody else had finished. I did not feel so much like a member of the boat's family now as before. However, my spirits returned, in instalments, as we pursued our way down the river. I was sorry I hated the mate so, because it was not in (young) human nature not to admire him. He was huge and muscular, his face was bearded and whiskered all over; he had a red woman and a blue woman tattooed on his right arm—one on each side of a blue anchor with a red rope to it; and in the matter of profanity he was sublime. When he was getting out cargo at a landing, I was always where I could see and hear. He felt all the majesty of his great position, and made the world feel it, too. When he gave even the simplest order, he discharged it like a blast of lightning, and sent a long, reverberating peal of profanity thundering after it. I could not help contrasting the way in which the average landsman would give an order with the mate's way of doing it. If the landsman should wish the gang-plank moved a foot farther forward, he would probably say: "James, or William, one of you push that plank forward, please"; but put the mate in his place, and he would roar out: "Here, now, start that gang-plank for'ard! Lively, now! *What*'re you about! Snatch it! *snatch* it! There! there! Aft again! aft again! Don't you hear me? Dash it to dash! are you going to *sleep* over it! 'V*ast* heaving. 'Vast heaving, I tell you! Going to heave it clear astern? WHERE're you going with that barrel! *for'ard* with it 'fore I make you swallow it, you dash-dash-dash-*dashed* split between a tired mud-turtle and a crippled hearse-horse!"

I wished I could talk like that.

When the soreness of my adventure with the mate had somewhat worn off, I began timidly to make up to the humblest official connected with the boat—the night watchman. He snubbed my advances at first, but I presently ventured to offer him a new chalk pipe, and that softened him. So he allowed me to sit with him by the big bell on the hurricane deck, and in time he melted into conversation. He could not well have helped it, I hung with such homage on his words and so plainly showed that I felt honored by his notice. He told me the names of dim capes and shadowy islands as we glided by them in the solemnity of the night, under the winking stars, and by and by got to talking about himself. He seemed over-sentimental for a man whose salary was six dollars a week—or rather he might have seemed so to an older person than I. But I drank in his words hungrily, and with a faith that might have moved mountains if it had been applied judiciously. What was it to me that he was soiled and seedy and fragrant with gin? What was it to me that his grammar was bad, his construction worse, and his profanity so void of art that it was an element of weakness rather than strength in his conversation? He was a wronged man, a man who had seen trouble, and that was enough for me. As he mellowed into his plaintive history his tears dripped upon the lantern in his lap, and I cried, too, from sympathy. He said he was the son of an English nobleman—either an earl or an alderman, he could not remember which, but believed was both; his father, the nobleman, loved him, but his mother hated him from the cradle; and so while he was still a little boy he was sent to "one of them old, ancient colleges"—he couldn't remember which; and by and by his father died and his mother seized the property and "shook" him, as he phrased it. After his mother shook him, members of the nobility with whom he was acquainted used their influence to get him the position of "loblolly-boy in a ship";[5] and from that point my watchman threw off all trammels of date and locality and branched out into a narrative that bristled all along with incredible adventures; a narrative that was so reeking with bloodshed and so crammed with hair-breadth escapes and the most engaging and unconscious personal villainies, that I sat speechless, enjoying, shuddering, wondering, worshipping.

It was a sore blight to find out afterwards that he was a low, vulgar, ignorant, sentimental, half-witted humbug, an untraveled native of the wilds of Illinois, who had absorbed wildcat literature and appropriated its marvels, until in time he had woven odds and ends of the mess into this yarn, and then gone on telling it to fledglings like me, until he had come to believe it himself.

Chapter VI

A CUB-PILOT'S EXPERIENCE

What with lying on the rocks four days at Louisville, and some other delays, the poor old *Paul Jones* fooled away about two weeks in making the voyage from Cincinnati to New Orleans. This gave me a chance to get acquainted with one of the pilots, and he taught me how to steer the boat, and thus made the fascination of river life more potent than ever for me.

It also gave me a chance to get acquainted with a youth who had taken deck passage—more's the pity; for he easily borrowed six dollars of me on a promise to return to the boat and pay it back to me the day after we should arrive. But he probably died or forgot, for he never came. It was doubtless the former, since he had said his parents were wealthy, and he only traveled deck passage because it was cooler.[6]

I soon discovered two things. One was that a vessel would not be likely to sail for the mouth of the Amazon under ten or twelve years; and the other was that the nine or ten dollars still left in my pocket would not suffice for so impossible an exploration as I had planned, even if I could afford to wait for a ship. Therefore it followed that I must contrive a new career. The *Paul Jones* was now bound for St. Louis. I planned a siege against my pilot, and at the end of three hard days he surrendered. He agreed to teach me the Mississippi River from New Orleans to St. Louis for five hundred dollars, payable out of the first wages I should receive after graduating. I entered upon the small enterprise of "learning" twelve or thirteen hundred miles of the great Mississippi River with the easy confidence of my time of life. If I had really known

---

[5] Surgeon's assistant; the term also signified messboy.

[6] "Deck" passage—*i.e.*, steerage passage. (Twain's note.)

what I was about to require of my faculties, I should not have had the courage to begin. I supposed that all a pilot had to do was to keep his boat in the river, and I did not consider that that could be much of a trick, since it was so wide.

The boat backed out from New Orleans at four in the afternoon, and it was "our watch" until eight. Mr. Bixby, my chief, "straightened her up," plowed her along past the sterns of the other boats that lay at the Levee, and then said, "Here, take her; shave those steamships as close as you'd peel an apple." I took the wheel, and my heart-beat fluttered up into the hundreds; for it seemed to me that we were about to scrape the side off every ship in the line, we were so close. I held my breath and began to claw the boat away from the danger; and I had my own opinion of the pilot who had known no better than to get us into such peril, but I was too wise to express it. In half a minute I had a wide margin of safety intervening between the *Paul Jones* and the ships; and within ten seconds more I was set aside in disgrace, and Mr. Bixby was going into danger again and flaying me alive with abuse of my cowardice. I was stung, but I was obliged to admire the easy confidence with which my chief loafed from side to side of his wheel, and trimmed the ships so closely that disaster seemed ceaselessly imminent. When he had cooled a little he told me that the easy water was close ashore and the current outside, and therefore we must hug the bank, up-stream, to get the benefit of the former, and stay well out, down-stream, to take advantage of the latter. In my own mind I resolved to be a down-stream pilot and leave the up-streaming to people dead to prudence.

Now and then Mr. Bixby called my attention to certain things. Said he, "This is Six-Mile Point." I assented. It was pleasant enough information, but I could not see the bearing of it. I was not conscious that it was a matter of any interest to me. Another time he said, "This is Nine-Mile Point." Later he said, "This is Twelve-Mile Point." They were all about level with the water's edge; they all looked about alike to me; they were monotonously unpicturesque. I hoped Mr. Bixby would change the subject. But no; he would crowd up around a point, hugging the shore with affection, and then say: "The slack water ends here, abreast this bunch of China-trees; now we cross over." So he crossed over. He gave me the wheel once or twice, but I had no luck. I either came near chipping off the edge of a sugar plantation, or I yawed too far from shore, and so dropped back into disgrace again and got abused.

The watch was ended at last, and we took supper and went to bed. At midnight the glare of a lantern shone in my eyes, and the night watchman said:

"Come! turn out!"

And then he left. I could not understand this extraordinary procedure; so I presently gave up trying to, and dozed off to sleep. Pretty soon the watchman was back again, and this time he was gruff. I was annoyed. I said:

"What do you want to come bothering around here in the middle of the night for? Now as like as not I'll not get to sleep again to-night."

The watchman said:

"Well, if this an't good, I'm blest."

The "off-watch" was just turning in, and I heard some brutal laughter from them, and such remarks as "Hello, watchman! an't the new cub turned out yet? He's delicate, likely. Give him some sugar in a rag and send for the chambermaid to sing 'Rock-a-by Baby' to him."

About this time Mr. Bixby appeared on the scene. Something like a minute later I was climbing the pilot-house steps with some of my clothes on and the rest in my arms. Mr. Bixby was close behind, commenting. Here was something fresh—this thing of getting up in the middle of the night to go to work. It was a detail in piloting that had never occurred to me at all. I knew that boats ran all night, but somehow I had never happened to reflect that somebody had to get up out of a warm bed to run them. I began to fear that piloting was not quite so romantic as I had imagined it was; there was something very real and work-like about this new phase of it.

It was a rather dingy night, although a fair number of stars were out. The big mate was at the wheel, and he had the old tub pointed at a star and was holding her straight up the middle of the river. The shores on either hand were not much more than half a mile apart, but they seemed wonderfully far away and ever so vague and indistinct. The mate said:

"We've got to land at Jones's plantation, sir."

The vengeful spirit in me exulted. I said to myself, "I wish you joy of your job, Mr. Bixby; you'll have a good time finding Mr. Jones's plantation such a night as this; and I hope you never *will* find it as long as you live."

Mr. Bixby said to the mate:

"Upper end of the plantation, or the lower?"

"Upper."

"I can't do it. The stumps there are out of water at this stage. It's no great distance to the lower, and you'll have to get along with that."

"All right, sir. If Jones don't like it he'll have to lump it, I reckon."

And then the mate left. My exultation began to cool and my wonder to come up. Here was a man who not only proposed to find this plantation on such a night, but to find either end of it you preferred. I dreadfully wanted to ask a question, but I was carrying about as many short answers as my cargo-room would admit of, so I held my peace. All I desired to ask Mr. Bixby was the simple question whether he was ass enough to really imagine he was going to find that plantation on a night when all plantations were exactly alike and all the same color. But I held in. I used to have fine inspirations of prudence in those days.

Mr. Bixby made for the shore and soon was scraping it, just the same as if it had been daylight. And not only that, but singing:

"Father in heaven, the day is declining," etc.

It seemed to me that I had put my life in the keeping of a peculiarly reckless outcast. Presently he turned on me and said:

"What's the name of the first point above New Orleans?"

I was gratified to be able to answer promptly, and I did. I said I didn't know.

"Don't *know?*"

This manner jolted me. I was down at the foot again, in a moment. But I had to say just what I had said before.

"Well, you're a smart one," said Mr. Bixby. "What's the name of the *next* point?"

Once more I didn't know.

"Well, this beats anything. Tell me the name of *any* point or place I told you."

I studied a while and decided that I couldn't.

"Look here! What do you start out from, above Twelve-Mile Point, to cross over?"

"I—I—don't know."

"You—you—don't know?" mimicking my drawling manner of speech. "What *do* you know?"

"I—I—nothing, for certain."

"By the great Cæsar's ghost, I believe you! You're the stupidest dunderhead I ever saw or ever heard of, so help me Moses! The idea of *you* being a pilot—*you!* Why, you don't know enough to pilot a cow down a lane."

Oh, but his wrath was up! He was a nervous man, and he shuffled from one side of his wheel to the other as if the floor was hot. He would boil a while to himself, and then overflow and scald me again.

"Look here! What do you suppose I told you the names of those points for?"

I tremblingly considered a moment, and then the devil of temptation provoked me to say:

"Well—to—to—be entertaining, I thought."

This was a red rag to the bull. He raged and stormed so (he was crossing the river at the time) that I judge it made him blind, because he ran over the steering-oar of a trading-scow. Of course the traders sent up a volley of red-hot profanity. Never was a man so grateful as Mr. Bixby was: because he was brim full, and here were subjects who would *talk back*. He threw open a window, thrust his head out, and such an irruption followed as I never had heard before. The fainter and farther away the scowmen's curses drifted, the higher Mr. Bixby lifted his voice and the weightier his adjectives grew. When he closed the window he was empty. You could have drawn a seine through his system and not caught curses enough to disturb your mother with. Presently he said to me in the gentlest way:

"My boy, you must get a little memorandum-book, and every time I tell you a thing, put it down right away. There's only one way to be a pilot, and that is to get this entire river by heart. You have to know it just like A B C."

That was a dismal revelation to me; for my memory was never loaded with anything but blank cartridges. However, I did not feel discouraged long. I judged that it was best to make some allowances, for doubtless Mr. Bixby was "stretching." Presently he pulled a rope and struck a few strokes on the big bell. The stars were all gone now, and the night was as black as ink. I could hear the wheels churn along the bank, but I was not entirely certain that I could see the shore. The voice of the invisible watchman called up from the hurricane deck:

"What's this, sir?"

"Jones's plantation."

I said to myself, "I wish I might venture to offer a small bet that it isn't." But I did not chirp. I only waited to see. Mr. Bixby handled the engine bells, and in due time the boat's nose came to the land, a torch glowed from the forecastle, a man skipped ashore, a darky's voice on the bank said, "Gimme de k'yarpet-bag, Mars' Jones," and the next moment we were standing up the river again, all serene. I reflected deeply a while, and then said—but not aloud—"Well, the finding of that plantation was the luckiest accident that ever happened; but it couldn't happen again in a hundred years." And I fully believed it *was* an accident, too.

By the time we had gone seven or eight hundred miles up the river, I had learned to be a tolerably plucky up-stream steersman, in daylight, and before we reached St. Louis I had made a trifle of progress in night-work, but only a trifle. I had a note-book that fairly bristled with the names of towns, "points," bars, islands, bends, reaches, etc.; but the information was to be found only in the note-book—none of it was in my head. It made my heart ache to think I had only got half of the river set down; for as our watch was four hours off and four hours on, day and night, there was a long four-hour gap in my book for every time I had slept since the voyage began.

My chief was presently hired to go on a big New Orleans boat, and I packed my satchel and went with him. She was a grand affair. When I stood in her pilot-house I was so far above the water that I seemed perched on a mountain; and her decks stretched so far away, fore and aft, below me, that I wondered how I could ever have considered the little *Paul Jones* a large craft. There were other differences, too. The *Paul Jones's* pilot-house was a cheap, dingy, battered rattle-trap, cramped for room: but here was a sumptuous glass temple; room enough to have a dance in; showy red and gold window-curtains; an imposing sofa; leather cushions and a back to the high bench where visiting pilots sit, to spin yarns and "look at the river"; bright, fanciful "cuspadores" instead of a broad wooden box filled with sawdust; nice new oilcloth on the floor; a hospitable big stove for winter; a wheel as high as my head, costly with inlaid work; a wire tiller-rope; bright brass knobs for the bells; and a tidy, white-aproned, black "texas-tender," to bring up tarts and ices and coffee during mid-watch, day and night. Now this was "something like"; and so I began to take heart once more to believe that piloting was a romantic sort of occupation after all. The moment we were under way I began to prowl about the great steamer and fill myself with joy. She was as clean and as dainty as a drawing-room; when I looked down her long, gilded saloon, it was like gazing through a splendid tunnel; she had an oil-picture, by some gifted sign-painter, on every state-room door; she glittered with no end of prism-fringed chandeliers; the clerk's office was elegant, the bar was marvelous, and the bar-keeper had been barbered and upholstered at incredible cost. The boiler deck (*i. e.*, the second story of the boat, so to speak) was as spacious as a church, it seemed to me; so with the forecastle; and there was no pitiful handful of deck-hands, firemen, and roustabouts down there, but a whole battalion of men. The fires were fiercely glaring from a long row of furnaces, and over them were eight huge boilers! This was unutterable pomp. The mighty engines—but enough of this. I had never felt so fine before. And when I found that the regiment of natty servants respectfully "sir'd" me, my satisfaction was complete.

Chapter VIII

Perplexing Lessons

At the end of what seemed a tedious while, I had managed to pack my head full of islands, towns, bars, "points," and bends; and a curiously inanimate mass of lumber it was, too. However, inasmuch as I could shut my eyes and reel off a good long string of these names without leaving out more than ten miles of river in every fifty, I began to feel that I could take a boat down to New Orleans if I could make her skip those little gaps. But of course my complacency could hardly get start enough to lift my nose a trifle into the air, before Mr. Bixby would think of something to fetch it down again. One day he turned on me suddenly with this settler:

"What is the shape of Walnut Bend?"

He might as well have asked me my grandmother's opinion of protoplasm. I reflected respectfully, and then said I didn't know it had any particular shape. My gunpowdery chief went off with a bang, of course, and then went on loading and firing until he was out of adjectives.

I had learned long ago that he only carried just so many rounds of ammunition, and was sure to subside into a very placable and even remorseful old smooth-bore as soon as they were all gone. That word "old" is merely affectionate; he was not more than thirty-four. I waited. By and by he said:

"My boy, you've got to know the *shape* of the river perfectly. It is all there is left to steer by on a very dark night. Everything else is blotted out and gone. But mind you, it hasn't the same shape in the night that it has in the day-time."

"How on earth am I ever going to learn it, then?"

"How do you follow a hall at home in the dark? Because you know the shape of it. You can't see it."

"Do you mean to say that I've got to know all the million trifling variations of shape in the banks of this interminable river as well as I know the shape of the front hall at home?"

"On my honor, you've got to know them *better* than any man ever did know the shapes of the halls in his own house."

"I wish I was dead!"

"Now I don't want to discourage you, but—"

"Well, pile it on me; I might as well have it now as another time."

"You see, this has got to be learned; there isn't any getting around it. A clear starlight night throws such heavy shadows that if you didn't know the shape of a shore perfectly you would claw away from every bunch of timber, because you would take the black shadow of it for a solid cape; and you see you would be getting scared to death every fifteen minutes by the watch. You would be fifty yards from shore all the time when you ought to be within fifty feet of it. You can't see a snag in one of those shadows, but you know exactly where it is, and the shape of the river tells you when you are coming to it. Then there's your pitch-dark night; the river is a very different shape on a pitch-dark night from what it is on a starlight night. All shores seem to be straight lines, then, and mighty dim ones, too; and you'd *run* them for straight lines only you know better. You boldly drive your boat right into what seems to be a solid, straight wall (you knowing very well that in reality there is a curve there), and that wall falls back and makes way for you. Then there's your gray mist. You take a night when there's one of these grisly, drizzly, gray mists, and then there isn't *any* particular shape to a shore. A gray mist would tangle the head of the oldest man that ever lived. Well, then, different kinds of *moonlight* change the shape of the river in different ways. You see—"

"Oh, don't say any more, please! Have I got to learn the shape of the river according to all these five hundred thousand different ways? If I tried to carry all that cargo in my head it would make me stoop-shouldered."

"*No!* you only learn *the* shape of the river; and you learn it with such absolute certainty that you can always steer by the shape that's *in your head*, and never mind the one that's before your eyes."

"Very well, I'll try it; but after I have learned it can I depend on it? Will it keep the same form and not go fooling around?"

Before Mr. Bixby could answer, Mr. W—— came in to take the watch, and he said:

"Bixby, you'll have to look out for President's Island and all that country clear away up above the Old Hen and Chickens. The banks are caving and the shape of the shores changing like everything. Why, you wouldn't know the point above 40. You can go up inside the old syca-more snag, now." [7]

So that question was answered. Here were leagues of shore changing shape. My spirits were down in the mud again. Two things seemed pretty apparent to me. One was, that in order to be a pilot a man had got to learn more than any one man ought to be allowed to know; and the other was, that he must learn it all over again in a different way every twenty-four hours.

That night we had the watch until twelve. Now it was an ancient river custom for the two pilots to chat a bit when the watch changed. While the relieving pilot put on his gloves and lit his cigar, his partner, the re-tiring pilot, would say something like this:

"I judge the upper bar is making down a little at Hale's Point; had quarter twain with the lower lead and mark twain [8] with the other."

"Yes, I thought it was making down a little, last trip. Meet any boats?"

"Met one abreast the head of 21, but she was away over hugging the bar, and I couldn't make her out entirely. I took her for the *Sunny South* —hadn't any skylights forward of the chimneys."

And so on. And as the relieving pilot took the wheel his partner [9] would mention that we were in such-and-such a bend, and say we were abreast of such-and-such a man's wood-yard or plantation. This was cour-tesy; I supposed it was *necessity*. But Mr. W—— came on watch full twelve minutes late on this particular night—a tremendous breach of eti-quette; in fact, it is the unpardonable sin among pilots. So Mr. Bixby gave him no greeting whatever, but simply surrendered the wheel and marched out of the pilot-house without a word. I was appalled; it was a villainous night for blackness, we were in a particularly wide and blind part of the river, where there was no shape or substance to anything, and it seemed incredible that Mr. Bixby should have left that poor fellow to kill the boat trying to find out where he was. But I resolved that I would stand by him anyway. He should find that he was not wholly friendless. So I stood around, and waited to be asked where we were. But Mr. W—— plunged on serenely through the solid firmament of black cats that stood for an atmosphere, and never opened his mouth. "Here is a proud devil," thought I; "here is a limb of Satan that would rather send us all to de-struction than put himself under obligations to me, because I am not yet one of the salt of the earth and privileged to snub captains and lord it over everything dead and alive in a steamboat." I presently climbed up on the bench; I did not think it was safe to go to sleep while this lunatic was on watch.

However, I must have gone to sleep in the course of time, because the

[7] It may not be necessary, but still it can do no harm to explain that "inside" means between the snag and the shore. (Twain's note.) A snag is a dangerous submerged tree trunk.

[8] Two fathoms. Quarter twain is 2¼ fathoms, 13½ feet. Mark three is three fathoms. (Twain's note.)

[9] "Partner" is technical for "the other pilot." (Twain's note.)

next thing I was aware of was the fact that day was breaking, Mr. W——
gone, and Mr. Bixby at the wheel again. So it was four o'clock and all
well—but me; I felt like a skinful of dry bones and all of them trying to
ache at once.

Mr. Bixby asked me what I had stayed up there for. I confessed that
it was to do Mr. W—— a benevolence—tell him where he was. It took
five minutes for the entire preposterousness of the thing to filter into Mr.
Bixby's system, and then I judge it filled him nearly up to the chin; because he paid me a compliment—and not much of a one either. He said:

"Well, taking you by and large, you do seem to be more different
kinds of an ass than any creature I ever saw before. What did you suppose he wanted to know for?"

I said I thought it might be a convenience to him.

"Convenience! D——nation! Didn't I tell you that a man's got to know
the river in the night the same as he'd know his own front hall?"

"Well, I can follow the front hall in the dark if I know it *is* the front
hall; but suppose you set me down in the middle of it in the dark and not
tell me which hall it is; how am *I* to know?"

"Well, you've *got* to, on the river!"

"All right. Then I'm glad I never said anything to Mr. W——."

"I should say so. Why, he'd have slammed you through the window
and utterly ruined a hundred dollars' worth of window-sash and stuff."

I was glad this damage had been saved, for it would have made me unpopular with the owners. They always hated anybody who had the name
of being careless, and injuring things.

I went to work now to learn the shape of the river; and of all the eluding and ungraspable objects that ever I tried to get mind or hands on,
that was the chief. I would fasten my eyes upon a sharp, wooded point
that projected far into the river some miles ahead of me, and go to laboriously photographing its shape upon my brain; and just as I was beginning to succeed to my satisfaction, we would draw up toward it and the
exasperating thing would begin to melt away and fold back into the bank!
If there had been a conspicuous dead tree standing upon the very point
of the cape, I would find that tree inconspicuously merged into the general forest, and occupying the middle of a straight shore, when I got
abreast of it! No prominent hill would stick to its shape long enough for
me to make up my mind what its form really was, but it was as dissolving
and changeful as if it had been a mountain of butter in the hottest corner
of the tropics. Nothing ever had the same shape when I was coming
down-stream that it had borne when I went up. I mentioned these little
difficulties to Mr. Bixby. He said:

"That's the very main virtue of the thing. If the shapes didn't change
every three seconds they wouldn't be of any use. Take this place where
we are now, for instance. As long as that hill over yonder is only one
hill, I can boom right along the way I'm going; but the moment it splits
at the top and forms a V, I know I've got to scratch to starboard in a

hurry, or I'll bang this boat's brains out against a rock; and then the moment one of the prongs of the V swings behind the other, I've got to
waltz to larboard again, or I'll have a misunderstanding with a snag that
would snatch the keelson out of this steamboat as neatly as if it were a
sliver in your hand. If that hill didn't change its shape on bad nights
there would be an awful steamboat grave-yard around here inside of a
year."

It was plain that I had got to learn the shape of the river in all the different ways that could be thought of—upside down, wrong end first, inside out, fore-and-aft, and "thort-ships"—and then know what to do on
gray nights when it hadn't any shape at all. So I set about it. In the course
of time I began to get the best of this knotty lesson, and my self-complacency moved to the front once more. Mr. Bixby was all fixed, and ready
to start it to the rear again. He opened on me after this fashion:

"How much water did we have in the middle crossing at Hole-in-the-
Wall, trip before last?"

I considered this an outrage. I said:

"Every trip, down and up, the leadsmen are singing through that tangled place for three-quarters of an hour on a stretch. How do you reckon
I can remember such a mess as that?"

"My boy, you've got to remember it. You've got to remember the exact spot and the exact marks the boat lay in when we had the shoalest
water, in every one of the five hundred shoal places between St. Louis
and New Orleans; and you mustn't get the shoal soundings and marks of
one trip mixed up with the shoal soundings and marks of another, either,
for they're not often twice alike. You must keep them separate."

When I came to myself again, I said:

"When I get so that I can do that, I'll be able to raise the dead, and
then I won't have to pilot a steamboat to make a living. I want to retire
from this business. I want a slush-bucket and a brush; I'm only fit for a
roustabout. I haven't got brains enough to be a pilot; and if I had I
wouldn't have strength enough to carry them around, unless I went on
crutches."

"Now drop that! When I say I'll learn [10] a man the river, I mean it.
And you can depend on it, I'll learn him or kill him."

Chapter XXVI

[FEUDING FAMILIES]

. . . We struck down through the chute of Island No. 8, and I went
below and fell into conversation with a passenger, a handsome man, with
easy carriage and an intelligent face. We were approaching Island No.
10, a place so celebrated during the war. This gentleman's home was on
the main shore in its neighborhood. I had some talk with him about the

[10] "Teach" is not in the river vocabulary. (Twain's note.)

war times; but presently the discourse fell upon "feuds," for in no part of the South has the vendetta flourished more briskly, or held out longer between warring families, than in this particular region. This gentleman said:

"There's been more than one feud around here, in old times, but I reckon the worst one was between the Darnells and the Watsons. Nobody don't know now what the first quarrel was about, it's so long ago; the Darnells and the Watsons don't know, if there's any of them living, which I don't think there is. Some says it was about a horse or a cow—anyway, it was a little matter; the money in it wasn't of no consequence —none in the world—both families was rich. The thing could have been fixed up, easy enough; but no, that wouldn't do. Rough words had been passed; and so, nothing but blood could fix it up after that. That horse or cow, whichever it was, cost sixty years of killing and crippling! Every year or so somebody was shot, on one side or the other; and as fast as one generation was laid out, their sons took up the feud and kept it a-going. And it's just as I say; they went on shooting each other, year in and year out—making a kind of a religion of it, you see—till they'd done forgot, long ago, what it was all about. Wherever a Darnell caught a Watson, or a Watson caught a Darnell, one of 'em was going to get hurt—only question was, which of them got the drop on the other. They'd shoot one another down, right in the presence of the family. They didn't *hunt* for each other, but when they happened to meet, they pulled and begun. Men would shoot boys, boys would shoot men. A man shot a boy twelve years old—happened on him in the woods, and didn't give him no chance. If he *had* 'a' given him a chance, the boy'd 'a' shot *him*. Both families belonged to the same church (everybody around here is religious); through all this fifty or sixty years' fuss, both tribes was there every Sunday, to worship. They lived each side of the line, and the church was at a landing called Compromise. Half the church and half the aisle was in Kentucky, the other half in Tennessee. Sundays you'd see the families drive up, all in their Sunday clothes—men, women, and children—and file up the aisle, and set down, quiet and orderly, one lot on the Tennessee side of the church and the other on the Kentucky side; and the men and boys would lean their guns up against the wall, handy, and then all hands would join in with the prayer and praise; though they say the man next the aisle didn't kneel down, along with the rest of the family; kind of stood guard. I don't know; never was at that church in my life; but I remember that that's what used to be said.

"Twenty or twenty-five years ago, one of the feud families caught a young man of nineteen out and killed him. Don't remember whether it was the Darnells and Watsons, or one of the other feuds; but anyway, this young man rode up—steamboat laying there at the time—and the first thing he saw was a whole gang of the enemy. He jumped down behind a wood-pile, but they rode around and begun on him, he firing back, and they galloping and cavorting and yelling and banging away with all their might. Think he wounded a couple of them; but they closed in on him and chased him into the river; and as he swum along down stream, they followed along the bank and kept on shooting at him; and when he struck shore he was dead. Windy Marshall told me about it. He saw it. He was captain of the boat.

"Years ago, the Darnells was so thinned out that the old man and his two sons concluded they'd leave the country. They started to take steamboat just above No. 10; but the Watsons got wind of it; and they arrived just as the two young Darnells was walking up the companion-way with their wives on their arms. The fight begun then, and they never got no further—both of them killed. After that, old Darnell got into trouble with the man that run the ferry, and the ferry-man got the worst of it—and died. But his friends shot old Darnell through and through—filled him full of bullets, and ended him." . . .

Chapter XXXVIII

THE HOUSE BEAUTIFUL

We took passage in a Cincinnati boat for New Orleans; or on a Cincinnati boat—either is correct; the former is the Eastern form of putting it, the latter the Western.

Mr. Dickens declined to agree that the Mississippi steamboats were "magnificent," or that they were "floating palaces"—terms which had always been applied to them; terms which did not over-express the admiration with which the people viewed them.[11]

Mr. Dickens's position was unassailable, possibly; the people's position was certainly unassailable. If Mr. Dickens was comparing these boats with the crown jewels; or with the Taj, or with the Matterhorn; or with some other priceless or wonderful thing which he had seen, they were not magnificent—he was right. The people compared them with what *they* had seen; and, thus measured, thus judged, the boats were magnificent—the term was the correct one, it was not at all too strong. The people were as right as was Mr. Dickens. The steamboats were finer than anything on shore. Compared with superior dwelling-houses and first-class hotels in the Valley, they were indubitably magnificent, they were "palaces." To a few people living in New Orleans and St. Louis they were not magnificent, perhaps; not palaces; but to the great majority of those populations, and to the entire populations spread over both banks between Baton Rouge and St. Louis, they were palaces; they tallied with the citizen's dream of what magnificence was, and satisfied it.

Every town and village along that vast stretch of double river-frontage had a best dwelling, finest dwelling, mansion—the home of its

---

[11] Chapters XI and XII of Charles Dickens' *American Notes* (1842) contain vivid but often unflattering impressions of steamboat travel on the Ohio and Mississippi, emphasizing the crudity of men and boats alike.

wealthiest and most conspicuous citizen. It is easy to describe it: large grassy yard, with paling fence painted white—in fair repair; brick walk from gate to door; big, square, two-story "frame" house, painted white and porticoed like a Grecian temple—with this difference, that the imposing fluted columns and Corinthian capitals were a pathetic sham, being made of white pine, and painted; iron knocker; brass door knob—discolored, for lack of polishing. Within, an uncarpeted hall, of planed boards; opening out of it, a parlor, fifteen feet by fifteen—in some instances five or ten feet larger; ingrain carpet; mahogany center-table; lamp on it, with green-paper shade—standing on a gridiron, so to speak, made of high-colored yarns, by the young ladies of the house, and called a lamp-mat; several books, piled and disposed, with cast-iron exactness, according to an inherited and unchangeable plan; among them, Tupper, much penciled; [12] also, *Friendship's Offering*, and *Affection's Wreath*, with their sappy inanities illustrated in die-away mezzotints; [13] also, Ossian; [14] *Alonzo and Melissa*; [15] maybe *Ivanhoe*; also "Album," full of original "poetry" of the Thou-hast-wounded-the-spirit-that-loved-thee breed; two or three goody-goody works—*Shepherd of Salisbury Plain*,[16] etc.; current number of the chaste and innocuous *Godey's Lady's Book*,[17] with painted fashion-plate of wax-figure women with mouths all alike—lips and eyelids the same size—each five-foot woman with a two-inch wedge sticking from under her dress and letting-on to be half of her foot. Polished air-tight stove (new and deadly invention), with pipe passing through a board which closes up the discarded good old fireplace. On each end of the wooden mantel, over the fireplace, a large basket of peaches and other fruits, natural size, all done in plaster, rudely, or in wax, and painted to resemble the originals—which they don't. Over middle of mantel, engraving—"Washington Crossing the Delaware"; on the wall by the door, copy of it done in thunder-and-lightning crewels by one of the young ladies—work of art which would have made Washington hesitate about crossing, if he could have foreseen what advantage was going to be taken of it. Piano—kettle in disguise—with music, bound and unbound, piled on it, and on a stand near by: "Battle of Prague"; "Bird Waltz"; "Arkansas Traveler"; "Rosin the Bow"; "Marseilles Hymn"; "On a Lone Barren Isle" (St. Helena); "The Last Link Is Broken"; "She

[12] Martin Tupper's *Proverbial Philosophy* (1838–42) was an extremely popular collection of poetical maxims.

[13] Gift-book "annuals" popular in the generation before the Civil War. Designed more for display than for intellectual stimulation, they usually contained sentimental verse and genteel essays and fiction. No *Affection's Wreath* exists, but several issues of *Affection's Gift* have survived.

[14] The poems of Ossian, introduced to the public by a Scotsman James Macpherson (1736–96) and very largely his own

work, were long admired for their romantic spirit.

[15] *The Asylum, or, Alonzo and Melissa* (1811), a popular Gothic novel by Isaac Mitchell.

[16] The best known of Hannah More's *Cheap Repository Tracts* (1795–98).

[17] A leading magazine of fashion (1830–98) which published generally undistinguished prose and poetry, though such authors as Emerson, Poe and Hawthorne contributed occasionally to its pages.

Wore a Wreath of Roses the Night When Last We Met"; "Go, Forget
Me, Why Should Sorrow o'er That Brow a Shadow Fling"; "Hours
There Were to Memory Dearer"; "Long, Long Ago"; "Days of Absence"; "A Life on the Ocean Wave, a Home on the Rolling Deep";
"Bird at Sea"; and spread open on the rack, where the plaintive singer
has left it, "*Ro*-holl on, silver *moo*-hoon, guide the *trav*-el-err on his
way," etc. Tilted pensively against the piano, a guitar—guitar capable of
playing the Spanish fandango by itself, if you give it a start. Frantic
work of art on the wall—pious motto, done on the premises, sometimes in
colored yarns, sometimes in faded grasses: progenitor of the "God Bless
Our Home" of modern commerce. Framed in black mouldings on the
wall, other works of art, conceived and committed on the premises, by
the young ladies; being grim black-and-white crayons; landscapes,
mostly: lake, solitary sail-boat, petrified clouds, pre-geological trees on
shore, anthracite precipice; name of criminal conspicuous in the corner.
Lithograph, "Napoleon Crossing the Alps." Lithograph, "The Grave at
St. Helena." Steel-plates, Trumbull's "Battle of Bunker Hill," and the
"Sally from Gibraltar." Copper-plates, "Moses Smiting the Rock," and
"Return of the Prodigal Son." In big gilt frame, slander of the family in
oil: papa holding a book ("Constitution of the United States"); guitar
leaning against mamma, blue ribbons fluttering from its neck; the young
ladies, as children, in slippers and scalloped pantalettes, one embracing
toy horse, the other beguiling kitten with ball of yarn, and both simper-
ing up at mamma, who simpers back. These persons all fresh, raw, and
red—apparently skinned. Opposite, in gilt frame, grandpa and grandma,
at thirty and twenty-two, stiff, old-fashioned, high-collared, puff-sleeved,
glaring pallidly out from a background of solid Egyptian night. Under a
glass French clock dome, large bouquet of stiff flowers done in corpsy
white wax. Pyramidal what-not in the corner, the shelves occupied
chiefly with bric-a-brac of the period, disposed with an eye to best effect: shell, with the Lord's Prayer carved on it; another shell—of the
long-oval sort, narrow, straight orifice, three inches long, running from
end to end—portrait of Washington carved on it; not well done; the shell
had Washington's mouth, originally—artist should have built to that.
These two are memorials of the long-ago bridal trip to New Orleans and
the French Market. Other bric-a-brac: Californian "specimens"—quartz,
with gold wart adhering; old Guinea-gold locket, with circlet of ancestral hair in it; Indian arrow-heads, of flint; pair of bead moccasins, from
uncle who crossed the Plains; three "alum" baskets of various colors—
being skeleton-frame of wire, clothed-on with cubes of crystallized alum
in the rock-candy style—works of art which were achieved by the young
ladies; their doubles and duplicates to be found upon all what-nots in the
land; convention of desiccated bugs and butterflies pinned to a card;
painted toy-dog, seated upon bellows attachment—drops its under jaw
and squeaks when pressed upon; sugar-candy rabbit—limbs and features
merged together, not strongly defined; pewter presidential-campaign

MARK TWAIN*

medal; miniature card-board wood-sawyer, to be attached to the stove-pipe and operated by the heat; small Napoleon, done in wax; spread-open daguerreotypes of dim children, parents, cousins, aunts, and friends, in all attitudes but customary ones; no templed portico at back, and manu-factured landscape stretching away in the distance—that came in later, with the photograph; all these vague figures lavishly chained and ringed —metal indicated and secured from doubt by stripes and splashes of vivid gold bronze; all of them too much combed, too much fixed up; and all of them uncomfortable in inflexible Sunday-clothes of a pattern which the spectator cannot realize could ever have been in fashion; husband and wife generally grouped together—husband sitting, wife standing, with hand on his shoulder—and both preserving, all these fading years, some traceable effect of the daguerreotypist's brisk "Now smile, if you please!" Bracketed over what-not—place of special sacredness—an outrage in water-color, done by the young niece that came on a visit long ago, and died. Pity, too; for she might have repented of this in time. Horse-hair chairs, horse-hair sofa which keeps sliding from under you. Window shades, of oil stuff, with milk-maids and ruined castles stenciled on them in fierce colors. Lambrequins dependent from gaudy boxings of beaten tin, gilded. Bedrooms with rag carpets; bedsteads of the "corded" sort, with a sag in the middle, the cords needing tightening; snuffy feather-bed—not aired often enough; cane-seat chairs, splint-bottomed rocker; looking-glass on wall, school-slate size, veneered frame; inherited bureau; wash-bowl and pitcher, possibly—but not certainly; brass candlestick, tal-low candle, snuffers. Nothing else in the room. Not a bathroom in the house; and no visitor likely to come along who has ever seen one.

That was the residence of the principal citizen, all the way from the suburbs of New Orleans to the edge of St. Louis. When he stepped aboard a big fine steamboat, he entered a new and marvelous world: chimney-tops cut to counterfeit a spraying crown of plumes—and maybe painted red; pilot-house, hurricane deck, boiler-deck guards, all gar-nished with white wooden filigree-work of fanciful patterns; gilt acorns topping the derricks; gilt deer-horns over the big bell; gaudy symbolical picture on the paddle-box, possibly; big roomy boiler-deck, painted blue, and furnished with Windsor arm-chairs; inside, a far receding snow-white "cabin"; porcelain knob and oil-picture on every state-rooom door; curving patterns of filigree-work touched up with gilding, stretching overhead all down the converging vista; big chandeliers every little way, each an April shower of glittering glass-drops; lovely rainbow-light fall-ing everywhere from the colored glazing of the skylights; the whole a long-drawn, resplendent tunnel, a bewildering and soul-satisfying spec-tacle! in the ladies' cabin a pink and white Wilton carpet, as soft as mush, and glorified with a ravishing pattern of gigantic flowers. Then the Bridal Chamber—the animal that invented that idea was still alive and unhanged, at that day—Bridal Chamber whose pretentious flummery was necessarily overawing to the now tottering intellect of that hosannahing citizen. Every state-room had its couple of cozy clean bunks, and perhaps a looking-glass and a snug closet; and sometimes there was even a wash-bowl and pitcher, and part of a towel which could be told from mosquito netting by an expert—though generally these things were absent, and the shirt-sleeved passengers cleansed themselves at a long row of stationary bowls in the barber shop, where were also public towels, public combs, and public soap.

Take the steamboat which I have just described, and you have her in her highest and finest, and most pleasing, and comfortable, and satisfactory estate. Now cake her over with a layer of ancient and obdurate dirt, and you have the Cincinnati steamer awhile ago referred to. Not all over—only inside; for she was ably officered in all departments except the steward's.

But wash that boat and repaint her, and she would be about the counterpart of the most complimented boat of the old flush times: for the steamboat architecture of the West has undergone no change; neither has steamboat furniture and ornamentation undergone any.

1883

THE MAN THAT CORRUPTED
HADLEYBURG

This short story was published in *Harper's Magazine*, December 1899, and the next year was reprinted in *The Man that Corrupted Hadleyburg and Other Essays and Stories*. Theoretically, Twain's target here is the vanity of the human race, whose pretensions to virtue cannot stand serious onslaught. The only exceptions are Jack Halliday, a grownup Huck whose indifference to convention gives him a penetrating but charitable insight into his neighbors' flaws, and the stranger, who pretends to no virtue. The simple prose of the tale is splendidly controlled, and there is more irony than satire here; evidences of the younger Twain are clear in part III, for he always enjoyed courtroom scenes and other public gatherings into which he could introduce shifts of sympathy, clever reasoning, surprise witnesses. Satan as tempter is symbolized in the stranger, and his success is only for a moment in doubt. The moral cowardice of the townspeople is devastatingly laid bare, but if we accept the story as real we may feel that the Richardses and their kind are too weak to make for tragedy. As parable the story partakes of the indictment in *What Is Man?* although the determinism ("we couldn't help it") is of minor concern here.

I

It was many years ago. Hadleyburg was the most honest and upright town in all the region round about. It had kept that reputation unsmirched during three generations, and was prouder of it than of any other of its possessions. It was so proud of it, and so anxious to insure its perpetuation, that it began to teach the principles of honest dealing to its babies in the cradle, and made the like teachings the staple of their culture thenceforward through all the years devoted to their education. Also, throughout the formative years temptations were kept out of the way of the young people, so that their honesty could have every chance to harden and solidify, and become a part of their very bone. The neighboring towns were jealous of this honorable supremacy, and affected to sneer at Hadleyburg's pride in it and call it vanity; but all the same they were obliged to acknowledge that Hadleyburg was in reality an incorruptible town; and if pressed they would also acknowledge that the mere fact that a young man hailed from Hadleyburg was all the recommendation he needed when he went forth from his natal town to seek for responsible employment.

But at last, in the drift of time, Hadleyburg had the ill luck to offend a passing stranger—possibly without knowing it, certainly without caring, for Hadleyburg was sufficient unto itself, and cared not a rap for strangers or their opinions. Still, it would have been well to make an exception in this one's case, for he was a bitter man and revengeful. All through his wanderings during a whole year he kept his injury in mind, and gave all his leisure moments to trying to invent a compensating satisfaction for it. He contrived many plans, and all of them were good, but none of them was quite sweeping enough; the poorest of them would hurt a great many individuals, but what he wanted was a plan which would comprehend the entire town, and not let so much as one person escape unhurt. At last he had a fortunate idea, and when it fell into his brain it lit up his whole head with an evil joy. He began to form a plan at once, saying to himself, "That is the thing to do—I will corrupt the town."

Six months later he went to Hadleyburg, and arrived in a buggy at the house of the old cashier of the bank about ten at night. He got a sack out of the buggy, shouldered it, and staggered with it through the cottage yard, and knocked at the door. A woman's voice said "Come in," and he entered, and set his sack behind the stove in the parlor, saying politely to the old lady who sat reading the *Missionary Herald* by the lamp:

"Pray keep your seat, madam, I will not disturb you. There—now it is pretty well concealed; one would hardly know it was there. Can I see your husband a moment, madam?"

No, he was gone to Brixton, and might not return before morning.

"Very well, madam, it is no matter. I merely wanted to leave that sack in his care, to be delivered to the rightful owner when he shall be found. I am a stranger; he does not know me; I am merely passing through the town to-night to discharge a matter which has been long in my mind. My errand is now completed, and I go pleased and a little proud, and you will never see me again. There is a paper attached to the sack which will explain everything. Good-night, madam."

The old lady was afraid of the mysterious big stranger, and was glad to see him go. But her curiosity was roused, and she went straight to the sack and brought away the paper. It began as follows:

"To be Published; *or, the right man sought out by private inquiry—either will answer. This sack contains gold coin weighing a hundred and sixty pounds four ounces—*"

"Mercy on us, and the door not locked!"

Mrs. Richards flew to it all in a tremble and locked it, then pulled down the window-shades and stood frightened, worried, and wondering if there was anything else she could do toward making herself and the money more safe. She listened awhile for burglars, then surrendered to curiosity and went back to the lamp and finished reading the paper:

"*I am a foreigner, and am presently going back to my own country, to remain there permanently. I am grateful to America for what I have received at her hands during my long stay under her flag; and to one of her citizens—a citizen of Hadleyburg—I am especially grateful for a great kindness done me a year or two ago. Two great kindnesses, in fact. I will explain. I was a gambler. I say I* was. *I was a ruined gambler. I arrived in this village at night, hungry and without a penny. I asked for help—in the dark; I was ashamed to beg in the light. I begged of the right man. He gave me twenty dollars—that is to say, he gave me life, as I considered it. He also gave me fortune; for out of that money I have made myself rich at the gaming-table. And finally, a remark which he made to me has remained with me to this day, and has at last conquered me; and in conquering has saved the remnant of my morals: I shall gamble no more. Now I have no idea who that man was, but I want him found, and I want him to have this money, to give away, throw away, or keep, as he pleases. It is merely my way of testifying my gratitude to him. If I could stay, I would find him myself; but no matter, he will be found. This is an honest town, an incorruptible town, and I know I can trust it without fear. This man can be identified by the remark which he made to me; I feel persuaded that he will remember it.*

"*And now my plan is this: If you prefer to conduct the inquiry privately, do so. Tell the contents of this present writing to any one who is likely to be the right man. If he shall answer, 'I am the man; the remark I made was so-and-so,' apply the test—to wit: open the sack, and in it you will find a sealed envelope containing that remark. If the remark mentioned by the candidate tallies with it, give him the money, and ask no further questions, for he is certainly the right man.*

"*But if you shall prefer a public inquiry, then publish this present writing in the local paper—with these instructions added, to wit: Thirty days from now, let the candidate appear at the town-hall at eight in the evening (Friday), and hand his remark, in a sealed envelope, to the Rev. Mr.*

*Burgess (if he will be kind enough to act); and let Mr. Burgess there and
then destroy the seals of the sack, open it, and see if the remark is correct;
if correct, let the money be delivered, with my sincere gratitude, to my
benefactor thus identified."*

Mrs. Richards sat down, gently quivering with excitement, and was
soon lost in thinkings—after this pattern: "What a strange thing it is! . . .
And what a fortune for that kind man who set his bread afloat upon the
waters! . . . If it had only been my husband that did it!—for we are so
poor, so old and poor! . . ." Then, with a sigh—"But it was not my Edward; no, it was not he that gave a stranger twenty dollars. It is a pity
too; I see it now. . . ." Then, with a shudder—"But it is *gambler's* money!
the wages of sin; we couldn't take it; we couldn't touch it. I don't like
to be near it; it seems a defilement." She moved to a farther chair. . . .
"I wish Edward would come, and take it to the bank; a burglar might
come at any moment; it is dreadful to be here all alone with it."

At eleven Mr. Richards arrived, and while his wife was saying, "I am
so glad you've come!" he was saying, "I'm so tired—tired clear out; it is
dreadful to be poor, and have to make these dismal journeys at my time
of life. Always at the grind, grind, grind, on a salary—another man's slave,
and he sitting at home in his slippers, rich and comfortable."

"I am so sorry for you, Edward, you know that; but be comforted; we
have our livelihood; we have our good name—"

"Yes, Mary, and that is everything. Don't mind my talk—it's just a moment's irritation and doesn't mean anything. Kiss me—there, it's all gone
now, and I am not complaining any more. What have you been getting?
What's in the sack?"

Then his wife told him the great secret. It dazed him for a moment;
then he said:

"It weighs a hundred and sixty pounds? Why, Mary, it's for-ty thousand dollars—think of it—a whole fortune! Not ten men in this village are
worth that much. Give me the paper."

He skimmed through it and said:

"Isn't it an adventure! Why, it's a romance; it's like the impossible
things one reads about in books, and never sees in life." He was well
stirred up now; cheerful, even gleeful. He tapped his old wife on the
cheek, and said, humorously, "Why, we're rich, Mary, rich; all we've got
to do is to bury the money and burn the papers. If the gambler ever
comes to inquire, we'll merely look coldly upon him and say: 'What is
this nonsense you are talking? We have never heard of you and your
sack of gold before'; and then he would look foolish, and—"

"And in the mean time, while you are running on with your jokes, the
money is still here, and it is fast getting along toward burglar-time."

"True. Very well, what shall we do—make the inquiry private? No,
not that; it would spoil the romance. The public method is better. Think
what a noise it will make! And it will make all the other towns jealous;

for no stranger would trust such a thing to any town but Hadleyburg, and they know it. It's a great card for us. I must get to the printing-office now, or I shall be too late."

"But stop—stop—don't leave me here alone with it, Edward!"

But he was gone. For only a little while, however. Not far from his own house he met the editor-proprietor of the paper, and gave him the document, and said, "Here is a good thing for you, Cox—put it in."

"It may be too late, Mr. Richards, but I'll see."

At home again he and his wife sat down to talk the charming mystery over; they were in no condition for sleep. The first question was, Who could the citizen have been who gave the stranger the twenty dollars? It seemed a simple one; both answered it in the same breath—

"Barclay Goodson."

"Yes," said Richards, "he could have done it, and it would have been like him, but there's not another in the town."

"Everybody will grant that, Edward—grant it privately, anyway. For six months, now, the village has been its own proper self once more—honest, narrow, self-righteous, and stingy."

"It is what he always called it, to the day of his death—said it right out publicly, too."

"Yes, and he was hated for it."

"Oh, of course; but he didn't care. I reckon he was the best-hated man among us, except the Reverend Burgess."

"Well, Burgess deserves it—he will never get another congregation here. Mean as the town is, it knows how to estimate *him*. Edward, doesn't it seem odd that the stranger should appoint Burgess to deliver the money?"

"Well, yes—it does. That is—that is—"

"Why so much that-*is*-ing? Would *you* select him?"

"Mary, maybe the stranger knows him better than this village does."

"Much *that* would help Burgess!"

The husband seemed perplexed for an answer; the wife kept a steady eye upon him, and waited. Finally Richards said, with the hesitancy of one who is making a statement which is likely to encounter doubt,

"Mary, Burgess is not a bad man."

His wife was certainly surprised.

"Nonsense!" she exclaimed.

"He is not a bad man. I know. The whole of his unpopularity had its foundation in that one thing—the thing that made so much noise."

"That 'one thing,' indeed! As if that 'one thing' wasn't enough, all by itself."

"Plenty. Plenty. Only he wasn't guilty of it."

"How you talk! Not guilty of it! Everybody knows he *was* guilty."

"Mary, I give you my word—he was innocent."

"I can't believe it, and I don't. How do you know?"

"It is a confession. I am ashamed, but I will make it. I was the only man who knew he was innocent. I could have saved him, and—and—well, you know how the town was wrought up—I hadn't the pluck to do it. It would have turned everybody against me. I felt mean, ever so mean; but I didn't dare; I hadn't the manliness to face that."

Mary looked troubled, and for a while was silent. Then she said, stammeringly:

"I—I don't think it would have done for you to—to— One mustn't—er—public opinion—one has to be so careful—so—" It was a difficult road, and she got mired; but after a little she got started again. "It was a great pity, but— Why, we couldn't afford it, Edward—we couldn't indeed. Oh, I wouldn't have had you do it for anything!"

"It would have lost us the good-will of so many people, Mary; and then —and then—"

"What troubles me now is, what *he* thinks of us, Edward."

"He? *He* doesn't suspect that I could have saved him."

"Oh," exclaimed the wife, in a tone of relief, "I am glad of that. As long as he doesn't know that you could have saved him, he—he—well, that makes it a great deal better. Why, I might have known he didn't know, because he is always trying to be friendly with us, as little encouragement as we give him. More than once people have twitted me with it. There's the Wilsons, and the Wilcoxes, and the Harknesses, they take a mean pleasure in saying, '*Your friend* Burgess,' because they know it pesters me. I wish he wouldn't persist in liking us so; I can't think why he keeps it up."

"I can explain it. It's another confession. When the thing was new and hot, and the town made a plan to ride him on a rail, my conscience hurt me so that I couldn't stand it, and I went privately and gave him notice, and he got out of the town and staid out till it was safe to come back."

"Edward! If the town had found it out—".

"*Don't!* It scares me yet, to think of it. I repented of it the minute it was done; and I was even afraid to tell you, lest your face might betray it to somebody. I didn't sleep any that night, for worrying. But after a few days I saw that no one was going to suspect me, and after that I got to feeling glad I did it. And I feel glad yet, Mary—glad through and through."

"So do I, now, for it would have been a dreadful way to treat him. Yes, I'm glad; for really you did owe him that, you know. But, Edward, suppose it should come out yet, some day!"

"It won't."

"Why?"

"Because everybody thinks it was Goodson."

"Of course they would!"

"Certainly. And of course *he* didn't care. They persuaded poor old Sawlsberry to go and charge it on him, and he went blustering over there and did it. Goodson looked him over, like as if he was hunting for a place on him that he could despise the most, then he says, 'So you are the Committee of Inquiry, are you?' Sawlsberry said that was about what he was. 'Hm. Do they require particulars, or do you reckon a kind of a *general* answer will do?' 'If they require particulars, I will come back, Mr. Goodson; I will take the general answer first.' 'Very well, then, tell them to go to hell—I reckon that's general enough. And I'll give you some advice, Sawlsberry; when you come back for the particulars, fetch a basket to carry the relics of yourself home in.' "

"Just like Goodson; it's got all the marks. He had only one vanity; he thought he could give advice better than any other person."

"It settled the business, and saved us, Mary. The subject was dropped."

"Bless you, I'm not doubting *that*."

Then they took up the gold-sack mystery again, with strong interest. Soon the conversation began to suffer breaks—interruptions caused by absorbed thinkings. The breaks grew more and more frequent. At last Richards lost himself wholly in thought. He sat long, gazing vacantly at the floor, and by-and-by he began to punctuate his thoughts with little nervous movements of his hands that seemed to indicate vexation. Meantime his wife too had relapsed into a thoughtful silence, and her movements were beginning to show a troubled discomfort. Finally Richards got up and strode aimlessly about the room, ploughing his hands through his hair, much as a somnambulist might do who was having a bad dream. Then he seemed to arrive at a definite purpose; and without a word he put on his hat and passed quickly out of the house. His wife sat brooding, with a drawn face, and did not seem to be aware that she was alone. Now and then she murmured, "Lead us not into t . . . but—but—we are so poor, so poor! . . . Lead us not into . . . Ah, who would be hurt by it?—and no one would ever know. . . . Lead us . . . ." The voice died out in mumblings. After a little she glanced up and muttered in a half-frightened, half-glad way—

"He is gone! But, oh dear, he may be too late—too late. . . . Maybe not—maybe there is still time." She rose and stood thinking, nervously clasping and unclasping her hands. A slight shudder shook her frame, and she said, out of a dry throat, "God forgive me—it's awful to think such things—but . . . Lord, how we are made—how strangely we are made!"

She turned the light low, and slipped stealthily over and kneeled down by the sack and felt of its ridgy sides with her hands, and fondled them lovingly; and there was a gloating light in her poor old eyes. She fell into fits of absence; and came half out of them at times to mutter, "If we had only waited!—oh, if we had only waited a little, and not been in such a hurry!"

Meantime Cox had gone home from his office and told his wife all about the strange thing that had happened, and they had talked it over eagerly, and guessed that the late Goodson was the only man in the town who could have helped a suffering stranger with so noble a sum as twenty dollars. Then there was a pause, and the two became thoughtful and silent. And by-and-by nervous and fidgety. At last the wife said, as if to herself,

"Nobody knows this secret but the Richardses . . . and us . . . nobody."

The husband came out of his thinkings with a slight start, and gazed wistfully at his wife, whose face was become very pale; then he hesitatingly rose, and glanced furtively at his hat, then at his wife—a sort of mute inquiry. Mrs. Cox swallowed once or twice, with her hand at her throat, then in place of speech she nodded her head. In a moment she was alone, and mumbling to herself.

And now Richards and Cox were hurrying through the deserted streets, from opposite directions. They met, panting, at the foot of the printing-office stairs; by the night-light there they read each other's face. Cox whispered,

"Nobody knows about this but us?"

The whispered answer was,

"Not a soul—on honor, not a soul!"

"If it isn't too late to—"

The men were starting up-stairs; at this moment they were overtaken by a boy, and Cox asked,

"Is that you, Johnny?"

"Yes, sir."

"You needn't ship the early mail—nor *any* mail; wait till I tell you."

"It's already gone, sir."

"*Gone?*" It had the sound of an unspeakable disappointment in it.

"Yes, sir. Time-table for Brixton and all the towns beyond changed to-day, sir—had to get the papers in twenty minutes earlier than common. I had to rush; if I had been two minutes later—"

The men turned and walked slowly away, not waiting to hear the rest. Neither of them spoke during ten minutes; then Cox said, in a vexed tone,

"What possessed you to be in such a hurry, *I* can't make out."

The answer was humble enough:

"I see it now, but somehow I never thought, you know, until it was too late. But the next time—"

"Next time be hanged! It won't come in a thousand years."

Then the friends separated without a good-night, and dragged themselves home with the gait of mortally stricken men. At their homes their wives sprang up with an eager "Well?"—then saw the answer with their eyes and sank down sorrowing, without waiting for it to come in words. In both houses a discussion followed of a heated sort—a new thing; there had been discussions before, but not heated ones, not ungentle ones. The discussions to-night were a sort of seeming plagiarisms of each other. Mrs. Richards said,

"If you had only waited, Edward—if you had only stopped to think; but no, you must run straight to the printing-office and spread it all over the world."

"It *said* publish it."

"That is nothing; it also said do it privately, if you liked. There, now—is that true, or not?"

"Why, yes—yes, it is true; but when I thought what a stir it would make, and what a compliment it was to Hadleyburg that a stranger should trust it so—"

"Oh, certainly, I know all that; but if you had only stopped to think, you would have seen that you *couldn't* find the right man, because he is in his grave, and hasn't left chick nor child nor relation behind him; and as long as the money went to somebody that awfully needed it, and nobody would be hurt by it, and—and—"

She broke down, crying. Her husband tried to think of some comforting thing to say, and presently came out with this:

"But after all, Mary, it must be for the best—it *must* be; we know that. And we must remember that it was so ordered—"

"Ordered! Oh, everything's *ordered*, when a person has to find some way out when he has been stupid. Just the same, it was *ordered* that the money should come to us in this special way, and it was you that must take it on yourself to go meddling with the designs of Providence—and who gave you the right? It was wicked, that is what it was—just blasphemous presumption, and no more becoming to a meek and humble professor of—"

"But, Mary, you know how we have been trained all our lives long, like the whole village, till it is absolutely second nature to us to stop not a single moment to think when there's an honest thing to be done—"

"Oh, I know it, I know it—it's been one everlasting training and training and training in honesty—honesty shielded, from the very cradle, against every possible temptation, and so it's *artificial* honesty, and weak as water when temptation comes, as we have seen this night. God knows I never had shade nor shadow of a doubt of my petrified and indestructible honesty until now—and now, under the very first big and real temptation, I—Edward, it is my belief that this town's honesty is as rotten as mine is; as rotten as yours is. It is a mean town, a hard, stingy town, and hasn't a virtue in the world but this honesty it is so celebrated for and so conceited about; and so help me, I do believe that if ever the day comes that its honesty falls under great temptation, its grand reputation will go to ruin like a house of cards. There, now, I've made confession, and I feel better; I am a humbug, and I've been one all my life, without knowing it. Let no man call me honest again—I will not have it."

"I— Well, Mary, I feel a good deal as you do; I certainly do. It seems strange, too, so strange. I never could have believed it—never."

A long silence followed; both were sunk in thought. At last the wife looked up and said,

"I know what you are thinking, Edward."

Richards had the embarrassed look of a person who is caught.

"I am ashamed to confess it, Mary, but—"

"It's no matter, Edward, I was thinking the same question myself."

"I hope so. State it."

"You were thinking, if a body could only guess out *what the remark was* that Goodson made to the stranger.*"

"It's perfectly true. I feel guilty and ashamed. And you?"

"I'm past it. Let us make a pallet here; we've got to stand watch till the bank vault opens in the morning and admits the sack. . . . Oh, dear, oh, dear—if we hadn't made the mistake!"

The pallet was made, and Mary said:

"The open sesame—what could it have been? I do wonder what that remark could have been? But come; we will get to bed now."

"And sleep?"

"No; think."

"Yes, think."

By this time the Coxes too had completed their spat and their reconciliation, and were turning in—to think, to think, and toss, and fret, and worry over what the remark could possibly have been which Goodson made to the stranded derelict: that golden remark; that remark worth forty thousand dollars, cash.

The reason that the village telegraph-office was open later than usual that night was this: The foreman of Cox's paper was the local representative of the Associated Press. One might say its honorary representative, for it wasn't four times a year that he could furnish thirty words that would be accepted. But this time it was different. His despatch stating what he had caught got an instant answer:

"Send the whole thing—all the details—twelve hundred words."

A colossal order! The foreman filled the bill; and he was the proudest man in the State. By breakfast-time the next morning the name of Hadleyburg the Incorruptible was on every lip in America, from Montreal to the Gulf, from the glaciers of Alaska to the orange-groves of Florida; and millions and millions of people were discussing the stranger and his money-sack, and wondering if the right man would be found, and hoping some more news about the matter would come soon—right away.

II

Hadleyburg village woke up world-celebrated—astonished—happy—vain. Vain beyond imagination. Its nineteen principal citizens and their wives went about shaking hands with each other, and beaming, and smiling, and congratulating, and saying *this* thing adds a new word to the dictionary—*Hadleyburg*, synonym for *incorruptible*—destined to live in dictionaries forever! And the minor and unimportant citizens and their wives went around acting in much the same way. Everybody ran to the bank to see the gold-sack; and before noon grieved and envious crowds began to flock in from Brixton and all neighboring towns; and that afternoon and next day reporters began to arrive from everywhere to verify the sack and its history and write the whole thing up anew, and make dashing free-hand pictures of the sack and of Richards's house, and the bank, and the Presbyterian church, and the Baptist church, and the public square, and the town-hall where the test would be applied and the money delivered; and damnable portraits of the Richardses, and Pinkerton the banker, and Cox, and the foreman, and Reverend Burgess, and the postmaster—and even of Jack Halliday, who was the loafing, good-natured, no-account, irreverent fisherman, hunter, boys' friend, stray-dogs' friend, typical "Sam Lawson" [1] of the town. The little mean, smirking, oily Pinkerton showed the sack to all comers, and rubbed his sleek palms together pleasantly, and enlarged upon the town's fine old reputation for honesty and upon this wonderful endorsement of it, and hoped and believed that the example would now spread far and wide over the American world, and be epoch-making in the matter of moral regeneration. And so on, and so on.

By the end of a week things had quieted down again; the wild intoxication of pride and joy had sobered to a soft, sweet, silent delight—a sort of deep, nameless, unutterable content. All faces bore a look of peaceful, holy happiness.

Then a change came. It was a gradual change: so gradual that its beginnings were hardly noticed; maybe were not noticed at all, except by Jack Halliday, who always noticed everything; and always made fun of it, too, no matter what it was. He began to throw out chaffing remarks about people not looking quite so happy as they did a day or two ago; and next he claimed that the new aspect was deepening to positive sadness; next, that it was taking on a sick look; and finally he said that everybody was become so moody, thoughtful, and absent-minded that he could rob the meanest man in town of a cent out of the bottom of his breeches pocket and not disturb his revery.

At this stage—or at about this stage—a saying like this was dropped at bedtime—with a sigh, usually—by the head of each of the nineteen principal households:

"Ah, what *could* have been the remark that Goodson made!"

And straightway—with a shudder—came this, from the man's wife:

"Oh, *don't!* What horrible thing are you mulling in your mind? Put it away from you, for God's sake!"

But that question was wrung from those men again the next night—and got the same retort. But weaker.

And the third night the men uttered the question yet again—with anguish, and absently. This time—and the following night—the wives fidgeted feebly, and tried to say something. But didn't.

And the night after that they found their tongues and responded—longingly,

"Oh, if we *could* only guess!"

Halliday's comments grew daily more and more sparklingly disagree-

---

[1] A simple but shrewd Yankee yarn-spinner in *Sam Lawson's Oldtown Fire-* *side Stories* (1872), by Harriet Beecher Stowe.

able and disparaging. He went diligently about, laughing at the town, individually and in mass. But his laugh was the only one left in the village: it fell upon a hollow and mournful vacancy and emptiness. Not even a smile was findable anywhere. Halliday carried a cigar-box around on a tripod, playing that it was a camera, and halted all passers and aimed the thing and said, "Ready!—now look pleasant, please," but not even this capital joke could surprise the dreary faces into any softening.

So three weeks passed—one week was left. It was Saturday evening—after supper. Instead of the aforetime Saturday-evening flutter and bustle and shopping and larking, the streets were empty and desolate. Richards and his old wife sat apart in their little parlor—miserable and thinking. This was become their evening habit now: the life-long habit which had preceded it, of reading, knitting, and contented chat, or receiving or paying neighborly calls, was dead and gone and forgotten, ages ago—two or three weeks ago; nobody talked now, nobody read, nobody visited—the whole village sat at home, sighing, worrying, silent. Trying to guess out that remark.

The postman left a letter. Richards glanced listlessly at the superscription and the post-mark—unfamiliar, both—and tossed the letter on the table and resumed his might-have-beens and his hopeless dull miseries where he had left them off. Two or three hours later his wife got wearily up and was going away to bed without a good-night—custom now—but she stopped near the letter and eyed it awhile with a dead interest, then broke it open, and began to skim it over. Richards, sitting there with his chair tilted back against the wall and his chin between his knees, heard something fall. It was his wife. He sprang to her side, but she cried out:

"Leave me alone, I am too happy. Read the letter—read it!"

He did. He devoured it, his brain reeling. The letter was from a distant State, and it said:

"I am a stranger to you, but no matter: I have something to tell. I have just arrived home from Mexico, and learned about that episode. Of course you do not know who made that remark, but I know, and I am the only person living who does know. It was GOODSON. I knew him well, many years ago. I passed through your village that very night, and was his guest till the midnight train came along. I overheard him make that remark to the stranger in the dark—it was in Hale Alley. He and I talked of it the rest of the way home, and while smoking in his house. He mentioned many of your villagers in the course of his talk—most of them in a very uncomplimentary way, but two or three favorably: among these latter yourself. I say 'favorably'—nothing stronger. I remember his saying he did not actually LIKE any person in the town—not one; but that you—I THINK he said you—am almost sure—had done him a very great service once, possibly without knowing the full value of it, and he wished he had a fortune, he would leave it to you when he died, and a curse apiece for the rest of the citizens. Now, then, if it was you that did him that service,

*you are his legitimate heir, and entitled to the sack of gold. I know that I
can trust to your honor and honesty, for in a citizen of Hadleyburg these
virtues are an unfailing inheritance, and so I am going to reveal to you
the remark, well satisfied that if you are not the right man you will seek
and find the right one and see that poor Goodson's debt of gratitude for
the service referred to is paid. This is the remark:* 'YOU ARE FAR FROM BE-
ING A BAD MAN: GO, AND REFORM.'

"HOWARD L. STEPHENSON."

"Oh, Edward, the money is ours, and I am so grateful, *oh*, so grateful
—kiss me, dear, it's forever since we kissed—and we needed it so—the
money—and now you are free of Pinkerton and his bank, and nobody's
slave any more; it seems to me I could fly for joy."

It was a happy half-hour that the couple spent there on the settee caressing each other; it was the old days come again—days that had begun
with their courtship and lasted without a break till the stranger brought
the deadly money. By-and-by the wife said:

"Oh, Edward, how lucky it was you did him that grand service, poor
Goodson! I never liked him, but I love him now. And it was fine and
beautiful of you never to mention it or brag about it." Then, with a
touch of reproach, "But you ought to have told *me*, Edward, you ought
to have told your wife, you know."

"Well, I—er—well, Mary, you see—"

"Now stop hemming and hawing, and tell me about it, Edward. I always loved you, and now I'm proud of you. Everybody believes there
was only one good generous soul in this village, and now it turns out that
you— Edward, why don't you tell me?"

"Well—er—er— Why, Mary, I can't!"

"You *can't*? *Why* can't you?"

"You see, he—well, he—he made me promise I wouldn't."

The wife looked him over, and said, very slowly,

"Made—you—promise? Edward, what do you tell me that for?"

"Mary, do you think I would lie?"

She was troubled and silent for a moment, then she laid her hand
within his and said:

"No . . . no. We have wandered far enough from our bearings—God
spare us that! In all your life you have never uttered a lie. But now—now
that the foundations of things seem to be crumbling from under us, we—
we—" She lost her voice for a moment, then said, brokenly, "Lead us not
into temptation. . . . I think you made the promise, Edward. Let it rest
so. Let us keep away from that ground. Now—that is all gone by; let us
be happy again; it is no time for clouds."

Edward found it something of an effort to comply, for his mind kept
wandering—trying to remember what the service was that he had done
Goodson.

The couple lay awake the most of the night, Mary happy and busy, Edward busy, but not so happy. Mary was planning what she would do with the money. Edward was trying to recall that service. At first his conscience was sore on account of the lie he had told Mary—if it was a lie. After much reflection—suppose it *was* a lie? What then? Was it such a great matter? Aren't we always *acting* lies? Then why not *tell* them? Look at Mary—look what she had done. While he was hurrying off on his honest errand, what was she doing? Lamenting because the papers hadn't been destroyed and the money kept! Is theft better than lying?

That point lost its sting—the lie dropped into the background and left comfort behind it. The next point came to the front: *had* he rendered that service? Well, here was Goodson's own evidence as reported in Stephenson's letter; there could be no better evidence than that—it was even *proof* that he had rendered it. Of course. So that point was settled. . . . No, not quite. He recalled with a wince that this unknown Mr. Stephenson was just a trifle unsure as to whether the performer of it was Richards or some other—and, oh dear, he had put Richards on his honor! He must himself decide whither that money must go—and Mr. Stephenson was not doubting that if he was the wrong man he would go honorably and find the right one. Oh, it was odious to put a man in such a situation—ah, why couldn't Stephenson have left out that doubt! What did he want to intrude that for?

Further reflection. How did it happen that *Richards's* name remained in Stephenson's mind as indicating the right man, and not some other man's name? That looked good. Yes, that looked very good. In fact, it went on looking better and better, straight along—until by-and-by it grew into positive *proof*. And then Richards put the matter at once out of his mind, for he had a private instinct that a proof once established is better left so.

He was feeling reasonably comfortable now, but there was still one other detail that kept pushing itself on his notice: of course he had done that service—that was settled; but what *was* that service? He must recall it—he would not go to sleep till he had recalled it; it would make his peace of mind perfect. And so he thought and thought. He thought of a dozen things—possible services, even probable services—but none of them seemed adequate, none of them seemed large enough, none of them seemed worth the money—worth the fortune Goodson had wished he could leave in his will. And besides, he couldn't remember having done them, anyway. Now, then—now, then—what *kind* of a service would it be that would make a man so inordinately grateful? Ah—the saving of his soul! That must be it. Yes, he could remember, now, how he once set himself the task of converting Goodson, and labored at it as much as—he was going to say three months; but upon closer examination it shrunk to a month, then to a week, then to a day, then to nothing. Yes, he remembered now, and with unwelcome vividness, that Goodson had told him to go to thunder and mind his own business—*he* wasn't hankering to follow Hadleyburg to heaven!

So that solution was a failure—he hadn't saved Goodson's soul. Richards was discouraged. Then after a little came another idea: had he saved Goodson's property? No, that wouldn't do—he hadn't any. His life? That is it! Of course. Why, he might have thought of it before. This time he was on the right track, sure. His imagination-mill was hard at work in a minute, now.

Thereafter during a stretch of two exhausting hours he was busy saving Goodson's life. He saved it in all kinds of difficult and perilous ways. In every case he got it saved satisfactorily up to a certain point; then, just as he was beginning to get well persuaded that it had really happened, a troublesome detail would turn up which made the whole thing impossible. As in the matter of drowning, for instance. In that case he had swum out and tugged Goodson ashore in an unconscious state with a great crowd looking on and applauding, but when he had got it all thought out and was just beginning to remember all about it a whole swarm of disqualifying details arrived on the ground: the town would have known of the circumstance, Mary would have known of it, it would glare like a limelight in his own memory instead of being an inconspicuous service which he had possibly rendered "without knowing its full value." And at this point he remembered that he couldn't swim, anyway.

Ah—*there* was a point which he had been overlooking from the start: it had to be a service which he had rendered "possibly without knowing the full value of it." Why, really, that ought to be an easy hunt—much easier than those others. And sure enough, by-and-by he found it. Goodson, years and years ago, came near marrying a very sweet and pretty girl, named Nancy Hewitt, but in some way or other the match had been broken off; the girl died, Goodson remained a bachelor, and by-and-by became a soured one and a frank despiser of the human species. Soon after the girl's death the village found out, or thought it had found out, that she carried a spoonful of negro blood in her veins. Richards worked at these details a good while, and in the end he thought he remembered things concerning them which must have gotten mislaid in his memory through long neglect. He seemed to dimly remember that it was *he* that found out about the negro blood; that it was he that told the village; that the village told Goodson where they got it; that he thus saved Goodson from marrying the tainted girl; that he had done him this great service "without knowing the full value of it," in fact without knowing that he *was* doing it; but that Goodson knew the value of it, and what a narrow escape he had had, and so went to his grave grateful to his benefactor and wishing he had a fortune to leave him. It was all clear and simple now, and the more he went over it the more luminous and certain it grew; and at last, when he nestled to sleep satisfied and happy, he remembered the whole thing just as if it had been yesterday. In fact, he dimly remembered Goodson's *telling* him his gratitude once. Meantime Mary had spent six thousand dollars on a new house for herself and a pair of slippers for her pastor, and then had fallen peacefully to rest.

That same Saturday evening the postman had delivered a letter to each of the other principal citizens—nineteen letters in all. No two of the envelopes were alike, and no two of the superscriptions were in the same hand, but the letters inside were just like each other in every detail but one. They were exact copies of the letter received by Richards—handwriting and all—and were all signed by Stephenson, but in place of Richards's name each receiver's own name appeared.

All night long eighteen principal citizens did what their caste-brother Richards was doing at the same time—they put in their energies trying to remember what notable service it was that they had unconsciously done Barclay Goodson. In no case was it a holiday job; still they succeeded.

And while they were at this work, which was difficult, their wives put in the night spending the money, which was easy. During that one night the nineteen wives spent an average of seven thousand dollars each out of the forty thousand in the sack—a hundred and thirty-three thousand altogether.

Next day there was a surprise for Jack Halliday. He noticed that the faces of the nineteen chief citizens and their wives bore that expression of peaceful and holy happiness again. He could not understand it, neither was he able to invent any remarks about it that could damage it or disturb it. And so it was his turn to be dissatisfied with life. His private guesses at the reasons for the happiness failed in all instances, upon examination. When he met Mrs. Wilcox and noticed the placid ecstasy in her face, he said to himself, "Her cat has had kittens"—and went and asked the cook; it was not so; the cook had detected the happiness, but did not know the cause. When Halliday found the duplicate ecstasy in the face of "Shadbelly" Billson (village nickname), he was sure some neighbor of Billson's had broken his leg, but inquiry showed that this had not happened. The subdued ecstasy in Gregory Yates's face could mean but one thing—he was a mother-in-law short; it was another mistake. "And Pinkerton—Pinkerton—he has collected ten cents that he thought he was going to lose." And so on, and so on. In some cases the guesses had to remain in doubt, in the others they proved distinct errors. In the end Halliday said to himself, "Anyway it foots up that there's nineteen Hadleyburg families temporarily in heaven: I don't know how it happened; I only know Providence is off duty to-day."

An architect and builder from the next State had lately ventured to set up a small business in this unpromising village, and his sign had now been hanging out a week. Not a customer yet; he was a discouraged man, and sorry he had come. But his weather changed suddenly now. First one and then another chief citizen's wife said to him privately:

"Come to my house Monday week—but say nothing about it for the present. We think of building."

He got eleven invitations that day. That night he wrote his daughter and broke off her match with her student. He said she could marry a mile higher than that.

Pinkerton the banker and two or three other well-to-do men planned country-seats—but waited. That kind don't count their chickens until they are hatched.

The Wilsons devised a grand new thing—a fancy-dress ball. They made no actual promises, but told all their acquaintanceship in confidence that they were thinking the matter over and thought they should give it —"and if we do, you will be invited, of course." People were surprised, and said, one to another, "Why, they are crazy, those poor Wilsons, they can't afford it." Several among the nineteen said privately to their husbands, "It is a good idea, we will keep still till their cheap thing is over, then *we* will give one that will make it sick."

The days drifted along, and the bill of future squanderings rose higher and higher, wilder and wilder, more and more foolish and reckless. It began to look as if every member of the nineteen would not only spend his whole forty thousand dollars before receiving-day, but be actually in debt by the time he got the money. In some cases light-headed people did not stop with planning to spend, they really spent—on credit. They bought land, mortgages, farms, speculative stocks, fine clothes, horses, and various other things, paid down the bonus, and made themselves liable for the rest—at ten days. Presently the sober second thought came, and Halliday noticed that a ghastly anxiety was beginning to show up in a good many faces. Again he was puzzled, and didn't know what to make of it. "The Wilcox kittens aren't dead, for they weren't born; nobody's broken a leg; there's no shrinkage in mother-in-laws; *nothing* has happened—it is an insolvable mystery."

There was another puzzled man, too—the Rev. Mr. Burgess. For days, wherever he went, people seemed to follow him or to be watching out for him; and if he ever found himself in a retired spot, a member of the nineteen would be sure to appear, thrust an envelope privately into his hand, whisper "To be opened at the town-hall Friday evening," then vanish away like a guilty thing. He was expecting that there might be one claimant for the sack—doubtful, however, Goodson being dead—but it never occurred to him that all this crowd might be claimants. When the great Friday came at last, he found that he had nineteen envelopes.

III

The town-hall had never looked finer. The platform at the end of it was backed by a showy draping of flags; at intervals along the walls were festoons of flags; the gallery fronts were clothed in flags; the supporting columns were swathed in flags; all this was to impress the stranger, for he would be there in considerable force, and in a large degree he would be connected with the press. The house was full. The 412 fixed seats were occupied; also the 68 extra chairs which had been packed into the aisles; the steps of the platform were occupied; some distinguished strangers were given seats on the platform; at the horseshoe of tables which fenced the front and sides of the platform sat a strong force of special correspondents who had come from everywhere. It was the best-dressed house the town had ever produced. There were some tolerably expensive toilets there, and in several cases the ladies who wore them had the look of being unfamiliar with that kind of clothes. At least the town thought they had that look, but the notion could have arisen from the town's knowledge of the fact that these ladies had never inhabited such clothes before.

The gold-sack stood on a little table at the front of the platform where all the house could see it. The bulk of the house gazed at it with a burning interest, a mouth-watering interest, a wistful and pathetic interest; a minority of nineteen couples gazed at it tenderly, lovingly, proprietarily, and the male half of this minority kept saying over to themselves the moving little impromptu speeches of thankfulness for the audience's applause and congratulations which they were presently going to get up and deliver. Every now and then one of these got a piece of paper out of his vest pocket and privately glanced at it to refresh his memory.

Of course there was a buzz of conversation going on—there always is; but at last when the Rev. Mr. Burgess rose and laid his hand on the sack he could hear his microbes gnaw, the place was so still. He related the curious history of the sack, then went on to speak in warm terms of Hadleyburg's old and well-earned reputation for spotless honesty, and of the town's just pride in this reputation. He said that this reputation was a treasure of priceless value; that under Providence its value had now become inestimably enhanced, for the recent episode had spread this fame far and wide, and thus had focussed the eyes of the American world upon this village, and made its name for all time, as he hoped and believed, a synonym for commercial incorruptibility. [*Applause.*] "And who is to be the guardian of this noble treasure—the community as a whole? No! The responsibility is individual, not communal. From this day forth each and every one of you is in his own person its special guardian, and individually responsible that no harm shall come to it. Do you—does each of you —accept this great trust? [*Tumultuous assent.*] Then all is well. Transmit it to your children and to your children's children. To-day your purity is beyond reproach—see to it that it shall remain so. To-day there is not a person in your community who could be beguiled to touch a penny not his own—see to it that you abide in this grace. ["*We will! we will!*"] This is not the place to make comparisons between ourselves and other communities—some of them ungracious toward us; they have their ways, we have ours; let us be content. [*Applause.*] I am done. Under my hand, my friends, rests a stranger's eloquent recognition of what we are: through him the world will always henceforth know what we are. We do not know who he is, but in your name I utter your gratitude, and ask you to raise your voices in endorsement."

The house rose in a body and made the walls quake with the thunders of its thankfulness for the space of a long minute. Then it sat down, and Mr. Burgess took an envelope out of his pocket. The house held its breath while he slit the envelope open and took from it a slip of paper. He read its contents—slowly and impressively—the audience listening with tranced attention to this magic document, each of whose words stood for an ingot of gold:

" *The remark which I made to the distressed stranger was this: "You are very far from being a bad man; go, and reform." ' "* Then he continued: "We shall know in a moment now whether the remark here quoted corresponds with the one concealed in the sack; and if that shall prove to be so—and it undoubtedly will—this sack of gold belongs to a fellow-citizen who will henceforth stand before the nation as the symbol of the special virtue which has made our town famous throughout the land— Mr. Billson!"

The house had gotten itself all ready to burst into the proper tornado of applause; but instead of doing it, it seemed stricken with a paralysis; there was a deep hush for a moment or two, then a wave of whispered murmurs swept the place—of about this tenor: "*Billson!* oh, come, this is *too* thin! Twenty dollars to a stranger—or *anybody—Billson!* Tell it to the marines!" And now at this point the house caught its breath all of a sudden in a new access of astonishment, for it discovered that whereas in one part of the hall Deacon Billson was standing up with his head meekly bowed, in another part of it Lawyer Wilson was doing the same. There was a wondering silence now for a while. Everybody was puzzled, and nineteen couples were surprised and indignant.

Billson and Wilson turned and stared at each other. Billson asked, biringly,

"Why do *you* rise, Mr. Wilson?"

"Because I have a right to. Perhaps you will be good enough to explain to the house why *you* rise?"

"With great pleasure. Because I wrote that paper."

"It is an impudent falsity! I wrote it myself."

It was Burgess's turn to be paralyzed. He stood looking vacantly at first one of the men and then the other, and did not seem to know what to do. The house was stupefied. Lawyer Wilson spoke up, now, and said,

"I ask the Chair to read the name signed to that paper."

That brought the Chair to itself, and it read out the name,

" 'John Wharton *Billson.*' "

"There!" shouted Billson, "what have you got to say for yourself, now? And what kind of apology are you going to make to me and to this insulted house for the imposture which you have attempted to play here?"

"No apologies are due, sir; and as for the rest of it, I publicly charge you with pilfering my note from Mr. Burgess and substituting a copy of it signed with your own name. There is no other way by which you could have gotten hold of the test-remark; I alone, of living men, possessed the secret of its wording."

There was likely to be a scandalous state of things if this went on; everybody noticed with distress that the short-hand scribes were scribbling like mad; many people were crying "Chair, Chair! Order! order!" Burgess rapped with his gavel, and said:

"Let us not forget the proprieties due. There has evidently been a mistake somewhere, but surely that is all. If Mr. Wilson gave me an envelope —and I remember now that he did—I still have it."

He took one out of his pocket, opened it, glanced at it, looked surprised and worried, and stood silent a few moments. Then he waved his hand in a wandering and mechanical way, and made an effort or two to say something, then gave it up, despondently. Several voices cried out:

"Read it! read it! What is it?"

So he began in a dazed and sleep-walker fashion:

"*The remark which I made to the unhappy stranger was this: "You are far from being a bad man. [The house gazed at him, marvelling.] Go, and reform."*' [*Murmurs:* "Amazing! what can this mean?"] This one," said the Chair, "is signed Thurlow G. Wilson."

"There!" cried Wilson, "I reckon that settles it! I knew perfectly well my note was purloined."

"Purloined!" retorted Billson. "I'll let you know that neither you nor any man of your kidney must venture to—"

The Chair. "Order, gentlemen, order! Take your seats, both of you, please."

They obeyed, shaking their heads and grumbling angrily. The house was profoundly puzzled; it did not know what to do with this curious emergency. Presently Thompson got up. Thompson was the hatter. He would have liked to be a Nineteener; but such was not for him; his stock of hats was not considerable enough for the position. He said:

"Mr. Chairman, if I may be permitted to make a suggestion, can both of these gentlemen be right? I put it to you, sir, can both have happened to say the very same words to the stranger? It seems to me—"

The tanner got up and interrupted him. The tanner was a disgruntled man; he believed himself entitled to be a Nineteener, but he couldn't get recognition. It made him a little unpleasant in his ways and speech. Said he:

"Sho, *that's* not the point! *That* could happen—twice in a hundred years—but not the other thing. *Neither* of them gave the twenty dollars!" [*A ripple of applause.*]

Billson. "*I* did!"

Wilson. "*I* did!"

Then each accused the other of pilfering.

The Chair. "Order! Sit down, if you please—both of you. Neither of the notes has been out of my possession at any moment."

A Voice. "Good—that settles that!"

The Tanner. "Mr. Chairman, one thing is now plain: one of these men has been eavesdropping under the other one's bed, and filching family secrets. If it is not unparliamentary to suggest it, I will remark that both are equal to it. [*The Chair.* "Order! order!"] I withdraw the remark, sir, and will confine myself to suggesting that *if* one of them has overheard the other reveal the test-remark to his wife, we shall catch him now."

A Voice. "How?"

The Tanner. "Easily. The two have not quoted the remark in exactly the same words. You would have noticed that, if there hadn't been a considerable stretch of time and an exciting quarrel inserted between the two readings."

A Voice. "Name the difference."

The Tanner. "The word *very* is in Billson's note, and not in the other."

Many Voices. "That's so—he's right!"

The Tanner. "And so, if the Chair will examine the test-remark in the sack, we shall know which of these two frauds—[*The Chair.* "Order!"]—which of these two adventurers—[*The Chair.* "Order! order!"]—which of these two gentlemen—[*laughter and applause*]—is entitled to wear the belt as being the first dishonest blatherskite ever bred in this town—which he has dishonored, and which will be a sultry place for him from now out!" [*Vigorous applause.*]

Many Voices. "Open it!—open the sack!"

Mr. Burgess made a slit in the sack, slid his hand in and brought out an envelope. In it were a couple of folded notes. He said:

"One of these is marked, 'Not to be examined until all written communications which have been addressed to the Chair—if any—shall have been read.' The other is marked '*The Test.*' Allow me. It is worded—to wit:

" 'I do not require that the first half of the remark which was made to me by my benefactor shall be quoted with exactness, for it was not striking, and could be forgotten; but its closing fifteen words are quite striking, and I think easily rememberable; unless *these* shall be accurately reproduced, let the applicant be regarded as an impostor. My benefactor began by saying he seldom gave advice to any one, but that it always bore the hall-mark of high value when he did give it. Then he said this—and it has never faded from my memory: "*You are far from being a bad man—*" ' "

Fifty Voices. "That settles it—the money's Wilson's! Wilson! Wilson! Speech! Speech!"

People jumped up and crowded around Wilson, wringing his hand and congratulating fervently—meantime the Chair was hammering with the gavel and shouting:

"Order, gentlemen! Order! Order! Let me finish reading, please." When quiet was restored, the reading was resumed—as follows:

" ' "*Go, and reform—or, mark my words—some day, for your sins, you will die and go to hell or Hadleyburg—*TRY AND MAKE IT THE FORMER." ' "

A ghastly silence followed. First an angry cloud began to settle darkly upon the faces of the citizenship; after a pause the cloud began to rise, and a tickled expression tried to take its place; tried so hard that it was only kept under with great and painful difficulty; the reporters, the Brixtonites, and other strangers bent their heads down and shielded their faces with their hands, and managed to hold in by main strength and heroic courtesy. At this most inopportune time burst upon the stillness the roar of a solitary voice—Jack Halliday's:

"*That's* got the hall-mark on it!"

Then the house let go, strangers and all. Even Mr. Burgess's gravity broke down presently, then the audience considered itself officially absolved from all restraint, and it made the most of its privilege. It was a good long laugh, and a tempestuously whole-hearted one, but it ceased at last—long enough for Mr. Burgess to try to resume, and for the people to get their eyes partially wiped; then it broke out again; and afterward yet again; then at last Burgess was able to get out these serious words:

"It is useless to try to disguise the fact—we find ourselves in the presence of a matter of grave import. It involves the honor of your town, it strikes at the town's good name. The difference of a single word between the test-remarks offered by Mr. Wilson and Mr. Billson was itself a serious thing, since it indicated that one or the other of these gentlemen had committed a theft—"

The two men were sitting limp, nerveless, crushed; but at these words both were electrified into movement, and started to get up—

"Sit down!" said the Chair, sharply, and they obeyed. "That, as I have said, was a serious thing. And it was—but for only one of them. But the matter has become graver; for the honor of *both* is now in formidable peril. Shall I go even further, and say in inextricable peril? *Both* left out the crucial fifteen words." He paused. During several moments he allowed the pervading stillness to gather and deepen its impressive effects, then added: "There would seem to be but one way whereby this could happen. I ask these gentlemen—Was there *collusion?—agreement?*"

A low murmur sifted through the house; its import was, "He's got them both."

Billson was not used to emergencies; he sat in a helpless collapse. But Wilson was a lawyer. He struggled to his feet, pale and worried, and said:

"I ask the indulgence of the house while I explain this most painful matter. I am sorry to say what I am about to say, since it must inflict irreparable injury upon Mr. Billson, whom I have always esteemed and respected until now, and in whose invulnerability to temptation I entirely believed—as did you all. But for the preservation of my own honor I must speak—and with frankness. I confess with shame—and I now beseech your pardon for it—that I said to the ruined stranger all of the words contained in the test-remark, including the disparaging fifteen. [*Sensation.*] When the late publication was made I recalled them, and I resolved to claim the sack of coin, for by every right I was entitled to it. Now I will ask you to consider this point, and weigh it well: that stranger's gratitude to me that night knew no bounds; he said himself that he could find no words for it that were adequate, and that if he should ever be able he would repay me a thousandfold. Now, then, I ask you this: could I expect—could I believe

—could I even remotely imagine—that, feeling as he did, he would do so ungrateful a thing as to add those quite unnecessary fifteen words to his test?—set a trap for me?—expose me as a slanderer of my own town before my own people assembled in a public hall? It was preposterous; it was impossible. His test would contain only the kindly opening clause of my remark. Of that I had no shadow of doubt. You would have thought as I did. You would not have expected a base betrayal from one whom you had befriended and against whom you had committed no offence. And so, with perfect confidence, perfect trust, I wrote on a piece of paper the opening words—ending with 'Go, and reform,'—and signed it. When I was about to put it in an envelope I was called into my back office, and without thinking I left the paper lying open on my desk." He stopped, turned his head slowly toward Billson, waited a moment, then added: "I ask you to note this: when I returned, a little later, Mr. Billson was retiring by my street door." [*Sensation.*]

In a moment Billson was on his feet and shouting:

"It's a lie! It's an infamous lie!"

The Chair. "Be seated, sir! Mr. Wilson has the floor."

Billson's friends pulled him into his seat and quieted him, and Wilson went on:

"Those are the simple facts. My note was now lying in a different place on the table from where I had left it. I noticed that, but attached no importance to it, thinking a draught had blown it there. That Mr. Billson would read a private paper was a thing which could not occur to me; he was an honorable man, and he would be above that. If you will allow me to say it, I think his extra word *'very'* stands explained; it is attributable to a defect of memory. I was the only man in the world who could furnish here any detail of the test-remark—by *honorable* means. I have finished."

There is nothing in the world like a persuasive speech to fuddle the mental apparatus and upset the convictions and debauch the emotions of an audience not practised in the tricks and delusions of oratory. Wilson sat down victorious. The house submerged him in tides of approving applause; friends swarmed to him and shook him by the hand and congratulated him, and Billson was shouted down and not allowed to say a word. The Chair hammered and hammered with its gavel, and kept shouting,

"But let us proceed, gentlemen, let us proceed!"

At last there was a measurable degree of quiet, and the hatter said,

"But what is there to proceed with, sir, but to deliver the money?"

Voices. "That's it! That's it! Come forward, Wilson!"

The Hatter. "I move three cheers for Mr. Wilson, Symbol of the special virtue which—"

The cheers burst forth before he could finish; and in the midst of them—and in the midst of the clamor of the gavel also—some enthusiasts mounted Wilson on a big friend's shoulder and were going to fetch him in triumph to the platform. The Chair's voice now rose above the noise—

"Order! To your places! You forget that there is still a document to be read." When quiet had been restored he took up the document, and was going to read it, but laid it down again, saying, "I forgot; this is not to be read until all written communications received by me have first been read." He took an envelope out of his pocket, removed its enclosure, glanced at it—seemed astonished—held it out and gazed at it—stared at it.

Twenty or thirty voices cried out:

"What is it? Read it! read it!"

And he did—slowly, and wondering:

" 'The remark which I made to the stranger—[*Voices.* "Hello! how's this?"]—was this: "You are far from being a bad man. [*Voices.* "Great Scott!"] Go, and reform." ' [*Voice.* "Oh, saw my leg off!"] Signed by Mr. Pinkerton the banker."

The pandemonium of delight which turned itself loose now was of a sort to make the judicious weep. Those whose withers were unwrung laughed till the tears ran down; the reporters, in throes of laughter, set down disordered pot-hooks which would never in the world be decipherable; and a sleeping dog jumped up, scared out of its wits, and barked itself crazy at the turmoil. All manner of cries were scattered through the din: "We're getting rich—*two* Symbols of Incorruptibility!—without counting Billson!" "*Three!*—count Shadbelly in—we can't have too many!" "All right—Billson's elected!" "Alas, poor Wilson—victim of *two* thieves!"

A Powerful Voice. "Silence! The Chair's fished up something more out of its pocket."

Voices. "Hurrah! Is it something fresh? Read it! read! read!"

The Chair [*reading*]. " 'The remark which I made,' etc. ' "You are far from being a bad man. Go," ' etc. Signed, 'Gregory Yates.' "

Tornado of Voices. "Four Symbols!" " 'Rah for Yates!" "Fish again!"

The house was in a roaring humor now, and ready to get all the fun out of the occasion that might be in it. Several Nineteeners, looking pale and distressed, got up and began to work their way toward the aisles, but a score of shouts went up:

"The doors, the doors—close the doors; no Incorruptible shall leave this place! Sit down, everybody!"

The mandate was obeyed.

"Fish again! Read! read!"

The Chair fished again, and once more the familiar words began to fall from its lips—" 'You are far from being a bad man—' "

"Name! name! What's his name?"

" 'L. Ingoldsby Sargent.' "

"Five elected! Pile up the Symbols! Go on, go on!"

" 'You are far from being a bad—' "

"Name! name!"

" 'Nicholas Whitworth.' "

"Hooray! hooray! it's a symbolical day!"

Somebody wailed in, and began to sing this rhyme (leaving out "it's") to the lovely "Mikado" tune of "When a man's afraid of a beautiful maid"; [2] the audience joined in, with joy; then, just in time, somebody contributed another line—

"And don't you this forget—"

The house roared it out. A third line was at once furnished—

"Corruptibles far from Hadleyburg are—"

The house roared that one too. As the last note died, Jack Halliday's voice rose high and clear, freighted with a final line—

"But the Symbols are here, you bet!"

That was sung, with booming enthusiasm. Then the happy house started in at the beginning and sang the four lines through twice, with immense swing and dash, and finished up with a crashing three-times-three and a tiger for "Hadleyburg the Incorruptible and all Symbols of it which we shall find worthy to receive the hall-mark to-night."

Then the shoutings at the Chair began again, all over the place:

"Go on! go on! Read! read some more! Read all you've got!"

"That's it—go on! We are winning eternal celebrity!"

A dozen men got up now and began to protest. They said that this farce was the work of some abandoned joker, and was an insult to the whole community. Without a doubt these signatures were all forgeries—

"Sit down! sit down! Shut up! You are confessing. We'll find *your* names in the lot."

"Mr. Chairman, how many of those envelopes have you got?"

The Chair counted.

"Together with those that have been already examined, there are nineteen."

A storm of derisive applause broke out.

"Perhaps they all contain the secret. I move that you open them all and read every signature that is attached to a note of that sort—and read also the first eight words of the note."

"Second the motion!"

It was put and carried—uproariously. Then poor old Richards got up, and his wife rose and stood at his side. Her head was bent down, so that none might see that she was crying. Her husband gave her his arm, and so supporting her, he began to speak in a quavering voice:

"My friends, you have known us two—Mary and me—all our lives, and I think you have liked us and respected us—"

The Chair interrupted him:

---

[2] Gilbert and Sullivan's *The Mikado* was produced in London in 1885 and its popularity quickly spread to America. Twain has paraphrased a song in Act II: "When a man's afraid,/A beautiful maid/ Is a cheering sight to see . . ."

"Allow me. It is quite true—that which you are saying, Mr. Richards; this town *does* know you two; it *does* like you; it *does* respect you; more—it honors you and *loves* you—"

Halliday's voice rang out:

"That's the hall-marked truth, too! If the Chair is right, let the house speak up and say it. Rise! Now, then—hip! hip! hip!—all together!"

The house rose in mass, faced toward the old couple eagerly, filled the air with a snow-storm of waving handkerchiefs, and delivered the cheers with all its affectionate heart.

The Chair then continued:

"What I was going to say is this: We know your good heart, Mr. Richards, but this is not a time for the exercise of charity toward offenders. [*Shouts of "Right! right!"*] I see your generous purpose in your face, but I cannot allow you to plead for these men—"

"But I was going to—"

"Please take your seat, Mr. Richards. We must examine the rest of these notes—simple fairness to the men who have already been exposed requires this. As soon as that has been done—I give you my word for this—you shall be heard."

Many Voices. "Right!—the Chair is right—no interruption can be permitted at this stage! Go on!—the names! the names!—according to the terms of the motion!"

The old couple sat reluctantly down, and the husband whispered to the wife, "It is pitifully hard to have to wait; the shame will be greater than ever when they find we were only going to plead for *ourselves.*"

Straightway the jollity broke loose again with the reading of the names.

" 'You are far from being a bad man—' Signature, 'Robert J. Titmarsh.'

" 'You are far from being a bad man—' Signature, 'Eliphalet Weeks.'

" 'You are far from being a bad man—' Signature, 'Oscar B. Wilder.' "

At this point the house lit upon the idea of taking the eight words out of the Chairman's hands. He was not unthankful for that. Thenceforward he held up each note in its turn, and waited. The house droned out the eight words in a massed and measured and musical deep volume of sound (with a daringly close resemblance to a well-known church chant)—" 'You are f-a-r from being a b-a-a-a-d man.' " Then the Chair said, "Signature, 'Archibald Wilcox.' " And so on, and so on, name after name, and everybody had an increasingly and gloriously good time except the wretched Nineteen. Now and then, when a particularly shining name was called, the house made the Chair wait while it chanted the whole of the test-remark from the beginning to the closing words, "And go to hell or Hadleyburg—try and make it the for-or-m-e-r!" and in these special cases they added a grand and agonized and imposing "A-a-a-*men!*"

The list dwindled, dwindled, dwindled, poor old Richards keeping tally of the count, wincing when a name resembling his own was pro-

nounced, and waiting in miserable suspense for the time to come when
it would be his humiliating privilege to rise with Mary and finish his
plea, which he was intending to word thus: ". . . for until now we have
never done any wrong thing, but have gone our humble way unre-
proached. We are very poor, we are old, and have no chick nor child to
help us; we were sorely tempted, and we fell. It was my purpose when
I got up before to make confession and beg that my name might not be
read out in this public place, for it seemed to us that we could not bear
it; but I was prevented. It was just; it was our place to suffer with the
rest. It has been hard for us. It is the first time we have ever heard our
name fall from any one's lips—sullied. Be merciful—for the sake of the
better days; make our shame as light to bear as in your charity you can."
At this point in his revery Mary nudged him, perceiving that his mind
was absent. The house was chanting, "You are f-a-r," etc.

"Be ready," Mary whispered. "Your name comes now; he has read
eighteen."

The chant ended.

"Next! next! next!" came volleying from all over the house.

Burgess put his hand into his pocket. The old couple, trembling, began
to rise. Burgess fumbled a moment, then said,

"I find I have read them all."

Faint with joy and surprise, the couple sank into their seats, and Mary
whispered,

"Oh, bless God, we are saved!—he has lost ours—I wouldn't give this
for a hundred of those sacks!"

The house burst out with its "Mikado" travesty, and sang it three
times with ever-increasing enthusiasm, rising to its feet when it reached
for the third time the closing line—

"But the Symbols are here, you bet!"

and finishing up with cheers and a tiger for "Hadleyburg purity and our
eighteen immortal representatives of it."

Then Wingate, the saddler, got up and proposed cheers "for the cleanest man in town, the one solitary important citizen in it who didn't try to
steal that money—Edward Richards."

They were given with great and moving heartiness; then somebody
proposed that Richards be elected sole Guardian and Symbol of the now
Sacred Hadleyburg Tradition, with power and right to stand up and look
the whole sarcastic world in the face.

Passed, by acclamation; then they sang the "Mikado" again, and ended
it with,

"And there's *one* Symbol left, you bet!"

There was a pause; then—

A Voice. "Now, then, who's to get the sack?"

The Tanner [*with bitter sarcasm*]. "That's easy. The money has to be divided among the eighteen Incorruptibles. They gave the suffering stranger twenty dollars apiece—and that remark—each in his turn—it took twenty-two minutes for the procession to move past. Staked the stranger —total contribution, $360. All they want is just the loan back—and interest—forty thousand dollars altogether."

Many Voices [*derisively*]. "That's it! Divvy! divvy! Be kind to the poor—don't keep them waiting!"

The Chair. "Order! I now offer the stranger's remaining document. It says: 'If no claimant shall appear [*grand chorus of groans*], I desire that you open the sack and count out the money to the principal citizens of your town, they to take it in trust [*Cries of "Oh! Oh! Oh!"*], and use it in such ways as to them shall seem best for the propagation and preservation of your community's noble reputation for incorruptible honesty [*more cries*]—a reputation to which their names and their efforts will add a new and far-reaching lustre.' [*Enthusiastic outburst of sarcastic applause.*] That seems to be all. No—here is a postscript:

"'P. S.—CITIZENS OF HADLEYBURG: There *is* no test-remark—nobody made one. [*Great sensation.*] There wasn't any pauper stranger, nor any twenty-dollar contribution, nor any accompanying benediction and compliment—these are all inventions. [*General buzz and hum of astonishment and delight.*] Allow me to tell my story—it will take but a word or two. I passed through your town at a certain time, and received a deep offence which I had not earned. Any other man would have been content to kill one or two of you and call it square, but to me that would have been a trivial revenge, and inadequate; for the dead do not *suffer*. Besides, I could not kill you all—and, anyway, made as I am, even that would not have satisfied me. I wanted to damage every man in the place, and every woman—and not in their bodies or in their estate, but in their vanity—the place where feeble and foolish people are most vulnerable. So I disguised myself and came back and studied you. You were easy game. You had an old and lofty reputation for honesty, and naturally you were proud of it—it was your treasure of treasures, the very apple of your eye. As soon as I found out that you carefully and vigilantly kept yourselves and your children *out of temptation*, I knew how to proceed. Why, you simple creatures, the weakest of all weak things is a virtue which has not been tested in the fire. I laid a plan, and gathered a list of names. My project was to corrupt Hadleyburg the Incorruptible. My idea was to make liars and thieves of nearly half a hundred smirchless men and women who had never in their lives uttered a lie or stolen a penny. I was afraid of Goodson. He was neither born nor reared in Hadleyburg. I was afraid that if I started to operate my scheme by getting my letter laid before you, you would say to yourselves, "Goodson is the only man among us who would give away twenty dollars to a poor devil"—and then you might not bite at my bait. But Heaven took Goodson; then I knew I was safe, and I set my trap and baited it. It may be that I shall not catch all the men to whom I mailed the pretended test secret, but I shall catch the most of them, if I know Hadleyburg nature. [*Voices.* "Right—he got every last one of them."] I believe they will even steal ostensible *gamble*-money, rather than miss, poor, tempted, and mistrained fellows. I am hoping to eternally and everlastingly squelch your vanity and give Hadleyburg a new renown—one that will *stick*—and spread far. If I have succeeded, open the sack and summon the Committee on Propagation and Preservation of the Hadleyburg Reputation.' "

A Cyclone of Voices. "Open it! Open it! The Eighteen to the front! Committee on Propagation of the Tradition! Forward—the Incorruptibles!"

The Chair ripped the sack wide, and gathered up a handful of bright, broad, yellow coins, shook them together, then examined them—

"Friends, they are only gilded disks of lead!"

There was a crashing outbreak of delight over this news, and when the noise had subsided, the tanner called out:

"By right of apparent seniority in this business, Mr. Wilson is Chairman of the Committee on Propagation of the Tradition. I suggest that he step forward on behalf of his pals, and receive in trust the money."

A Hundred Voices. "Wilson! Wilson! Wilson! Speech! Speech!"

Wilson [*in a voice trembling with anger*]. "You will allow me to say, and without apologies for my language, *damn* the money!"

A Voice. "Oh, and him a Baptist!"

A Voice. "Seventeen Symbols left! Step up, gentlemen, and assume your trust!"

There was a pause—no response.

The Saddler. "Mr. Chairman, we've got *one* clean man left, anyway, out of the late aristocracy; and he needs money, and deserves it. I move that you appoint Jack Halliday to get up there and auction off that sack of gilt twenty-dollar pieces, and give the result to the right man—the man whom Hadleyburg delights to honor—Edward Richards."

This was received with great enthusiasm, the dog taking a hand again; the saddler started the bids at a dollar, the Brixton folk and Barnum's representative fought hard for it, the people cheered every jump that the bids made, the excitement climbed moment by moment higher and higher, the bidders got on their mettle and grew steadily more and more daring, more and more determined, the jumps went from a dollar up to five, then to ten, then to twenty, then fifty, then to a hundred, then—

At the beginning of the auction Richards whispered in distress to his wife: "Oh, Mary, can we allow it? It—it—you see, it is an honor-reward, a testimonial to purity of character, and—and—can we allow it? Hadn't I better get up and—Oh, Mary, what ought we to do?—what do you think we—" [*Halliday's voice.* "Fifteen I'm bid!—fifteen for the sack!—twenty!—ah, thanks!—thirty—thanks again! Thirty, thirty, thirty!—do I hear forty?—forty it is! Keep the ball rolling, gentlemen, keep it rolling!—fifty!—thanks, noble Roman!—going at fifty, fifty, fifty!—seventy!—ninety!—splendid!—a hundred!—pile it up, pile it up!—hundred and twenty—forty!*

*—just in time!—hundred and fifty!—*TWO *hundred!—superb! Do I hear two h— thanks!—two hundred and fifty!—*"]

"It is another temptation, Edward—I'm all in a tremble—but, oh, we've escaped *one* temptation, and that ought to warn us, to— [*"Six did I hear?—thanks!—six fifty, six f—* SEVEN *hundred!"*] And yet, Edward, when you think—nobody susp— [*"Eight hundred dollars!—hurrah!—make it nine!—Mr. Parsons, did I hear you say—thanks!—nine!—this noble sack of virgin lead going at only nine hundred dollars, gilding and all—come! do I hear—a thousand!—gratefully yours!—did some one say eleven?—a sack which is going to be the most celebrated in the whole Uni—"*] Oh, Edward" (beginning to sob), "we are *so* poor!—but—but—do as you think best—do as you think best."

Edward fell—that is, he sat still; sat with a conscience which was not satisfied, but which was overpowered by circumstances.

Meantime a stranger, who looked like an amateur detective gotten up as an impossible English earl, had been watching the evening's proceedings with manifest interest, and with a contented expression in his face; and he had been privately commenting to himself. He was now soliloquizing somewhat like this: "None of the Eighteen are bidding; that is not satisfactory; I must change that—the dramatic unities require it; they must buy the sack they tried to steal; they must pay a heavy price, too—some of them are rich. And another thing, when I make a mistake in Hadleyburg nature the man that puts that error upon me is entitled to a high honorarium, and some one must pay it. This poor old Richards has brought my judgment to shame; he is an honest man;—I don't understand it, but I acknowledge it. Yes, he saw my deuces-*and* with a straight flush, and by rights the pot is his. And it shall be a jack-pot, too, if I can manage it. He disappointed me, but let that pass."

He was watching the bidding. At a thousand, the market broke; the prices tumbled swiftly. He waited—and still watched. One competitor dropped out; then another, and another. He put in a bid or two, now. When the bids had sunk to ten dollars, he added a five; some one raised him a three; he waited a moment, then flung in a fifty-dollar jump, and the sack was his—at $1282. The house broke out in cheers—then stopped; for he was on his feet, and had lifted his hand. He began to speak.

"I desire to say a word, and ask a favor. I am a speculator in rarities, and I have dealings with persons interested in numismatics all over the world. I can make a profit on this purchase, just as it stands; but there is a way, if I can get your approval, whereby I can make every one of these leaden twenty-dollar pieces worth its face in gold, and perhaps more. Grant me that approval, and I will give part of my gains to your Mr. Richards, whose invulnerable probity you have so justly and so cordially recognized to-night; his share shall be ten thousand dollars, and I will hand him the money to-morrow. [*Great applause from the house.* But the "invulnerable probity" made the Richardses blush prettily; however, it went for modesty, and did no harm.] If you will pass my proposition by a good majority—I would like a two-thirds vote—I will regard that as the town's consent, and that is all I ask. Rarities are always helped by any device which will rouse curiosity and compel remark. Now if I may have your permission to stamp upon the faces of each of these ostensible coins the names of the eighteen gentlemen who—"

Nine-tenths of the audience were on their feet in a moment—dog and all—and the proposition was carried with a whirlwind of approving applause and laughter.

They sat down, and all the Symbols except "Dr." Clay Harkness got up, violently protesting against the proposed outrage, and threatening to—

"I beg you not to threaten me," said the stranger, calmly. "I know my legal rights, and am not accustomed to being frightened at bluster." [*Applause.*] He sat down. "Dr." Harkness saw an opportunity here. He was one of the two very rich men of the place, and Pinkerton was the other. Harkness was proprietor of a mint; that is to say, a popular patent medicine. He was running for the Legislature on one ticket, and Pinkerton on the other. It was a close race and a hot one, and getting hotter every day. Both had strong appetites for money; each had bought a great tract of land, with a purpose; there was going to be a new railway, and each wanted to be in the Legislature and help locate the route to his own advantage; a single vote might make the decision, and with it two or three fortunes. The stake was large, and Harkness was a daring speculator. He was sitting close to the stranger. He leaned over while one or another of the other Symbols was entertaining the house with protests and appeals, and asked, in a whisper,

"What is your price for the sack?"

"Forty thousand dollars."

"I'll give you twenty."

"No."

"Twenty-five."

"No."

"Say thirty."

"The price is forty thousand dollars; not a penny less."

"All right, I'll give it. I will come to the hotel at ten in the morning. I don't want it known; will see you privately."

"Very good." Then the stranger got up and said to the house:

"I find it late. The speeches of these gentlemen are not without merit, not without interest, not without grace; yet if I may be excused I will take my leave. I thank you for the great favor which you have shown me in granting my petition. I ask the Chair to keep the sack for me until to-morrow, and to hand these three five-hundred-dollar notes to Mr. Richards." They were passed up to the Chair. "At nine I will call for the sack, and at eleven will deliver the rest of the ten thousand to Mr. Richards in person, at his home. Good-night."

Then he slipped out, and left the audience making a vast noise, which was composed of a mixture of cheers, the "Mikado" song, dog-disapproval, and the chant, "You are f-a-r from being a b-a-a-d man—a-a-a-a-men!"

IV

At home the Richardses had to endure congratulations and compliments until midnight. Then they were left to themselves. They looked a little sad, and they sat silent and thinking. Finally Mary sighed and said,

"Do you think we are to blame, Edward—*much* to blame?" and her eyes wandered to the accusing triplet of big bank-notes lying on the table, where the congratulators had been gloating over them and reverently fingering them. Edward did not answer at once; then he brought out a sigh and said, hesitatingly:

"We—we couldn't help it, Mary. It—well, it was ordered. *All* things are."

Mary glanced up and looked at him steadily, but he didn't return the look. Presently she said:

"I thought congratulations and praises always tasted good. But—it seems to me, now— Edward?"

"Well?"

"Are you going to stay in the bank?"

"N-no."

"Resign?"

"In the morning—by note."

"It does seem best."

Richards bowed his head in his hands and muttered:

"Before, I was not afraid to let oceans of people's money pour through my hands, but— Mary, I am so tired, so tired—"

"We will go to bed."

At nine in the morning the stranger called for the sack and took it to the hotel in a cab. At ten Harkness had a talk with him privately. The stranger asked for and got five checks on a metropolitan bank—drawn to "Bearer,"—four for $1500 each, and one for $34,000. He put one of the former in his pocket-book, and the remainder, representing $38,500, he put in an envelope, and with these he added a note, which he wrote after Harkness was gone. At eleven he called at the Richards house and knocked. Mrs. Richards peeped through the shutters, then went and received the envelope, and the stranger disappeared without a word. She came back flushed and a little unsteady on her legs, and gasped out:

"I am sure I recognized him! Last night it seemed to me that maybe I had seen him somewhere before."

"He is the man that brought the sack here?"

"I am almost sure of it."

"Then he is the ostensible Stephenson too, and sold every important citizen in this town with his bogus secret. Now if he has sent checks instead of money, we are sold too, after we thought we had escaped. I was beginning to feel fairly comfortable once more, after my night's rest, but the look of that envelope makes me sick. It isn't fat enough; $8500 in even the largest bank-notes makes more bulk than that."

"Edward, why do you object to checks?"

"Checks signed by Stephenson! I am resigned to take the $8500 if it could come in bank-notes—for it does seem that it was so ordered, Mary—but I have never had much courage, and I have not the pluck to try to market a check signed with that disastrous name. It would be a trap. That man tried to catch me; we escaped somehow or other; and now he is trying a new way. If it is checks—"

"Oh, Edward, it is *too* bad!" and she held up the checks and began to cry.

"Put them in the fire! quick! we mustn't be tempted. It is a trick to make the world laugh at *us*, along with the rest, and— Give them to *me*, since you can't do it!" He snatched them and tried to hold his grip till he could get to the stove; but he was human, he was a cashier, and he stopped a moment to make sure of the signature. Then he came near to fainting.

"Fan me, Mary, fan me! They are the same as gold!"

"Oh, how lovely, Edward! Why?"

"Signed by Harkness. What can the mystery of that be, Mary?"

"Edward, do you think—"

"Look here—look at this! Fifteen—fifteen—fifteen—thirty-four. Thirty-eight thousand five hundred! Mary, the sack isn't worth twelve dollars, and Harkness—apparently—has paid about par for it."

"And does it all come to us, do you think—instead of the ten thousand?"

"Why, it looks like it. And the checks are made to 'Bearer,' too."

"Is that good, Edward? What is it for?"

"A hint to collect them at some distant bank, I reckon. Perhaps Harkness doesn't want the matter known. What is that—a note?"

"Yes. It was with the checks."

It was in the "Stephenson" handwriting, but there was no signature. It said:

"I am a disappointed man. Your honesty is beyond the reach of temptation. I had a different idea about it, but I wronged you in that, and I beg pardon, and do it sincerely. I honor you—and that is sincere, too. This town is not worthy to kiss the hem of your garment. Dear sir, I made a square bet with myself that there were nineteen debauchable men in your self-righteous community. I have lost. Take the whole pot, you are entitled to it."

Richards drew a deep sigh, and said:

"It seems written with fire—it burns so. Mary—I am miserable again."

"I, too. Ah, dear, I wish—"

"To think, Mary—he *believes* in me."

"Oh, don't, Edward—I can't bear it."

"If those beautiful words were deserved, Mary—and God knows I believed I deserved them once—I think I could give the forty thousand dollars for them. And I would put that paper away, as representing more than gold and jewels, and keep it always. But now— We could not live in the shadow of its accusing presence, Mary."

He put it in the fire.

A messenger arrived and delivered an envelope. Richards took from it a note and read it; it was from Burgess.

"You saved me, in a difficult time. I saved you last night. It was at cost of a lie, but I made the sacrifice freely, and out of a grateful heart. None in this village knows so well as I know how brave and good and noble you are. At bottom you cannot respect me, knowing as you do of that matter of which I am accused, and by the general voice condemned; but I beg that you will at least believe that I am a grateful man; it will help me to bear my burden.

[Signed]   "BURGESS."

"Saved, once more. And on such terms!" He put the note in the fire. "I—I wish I were dead, Mary, I wish I were out of it all."

"Oh, these are bitter, bitter days, Edward. The stabs, through their very generosity, are so deep—and they come so fast!"

Three days before the election each of two thousand voters suddenly found himself in possession of a prized memento—one of the renowned bogus double-eagles. Around one of its faces was stamped these words: "THE REMARK I MADE TO THE POOR STRANGER WAS—" Around the other face was stamped these: "GO, AND REFORM. [SIGNED] PINKERTON." Thus the entire remaining refuse of the renowned joke was emptied upon a single head, and with calamitous effect. It revived the recent vast laugh and concentrated it upon Pinkerton; and Harkness's election was a walk-over.

Within twenty-four hours after the Richardses had received their checks their consciences were quieting down, discouraged; the old couple were learning to reconcile themselves to the sin which they had committed. But they were to learn, now, that a sin takes on new and real terrors when there seems a chance that it is going to be found out. This gives it a fresh and most substantial and important aspect. At church the morning sermon was of the usual pattern; it was the same old things said in the same old way; they had heard them a thousand times and found them innocuous, next to meaningless, and easy to sleep under; but now it was different: the sermon seemed to bristle with accusations; it seemed aimed straight and specially at people who were concealing deadly sins. After church they got away from the mob of congratulators as soon as they could, and hurried homeward, chilled to the bone at they did not know what—vague, shadowy, indefinite fears. And by chance they caught a glimpse of Mr. Burgess as he turned a corner. He paid no attention to their nod of recognition! He hadn't seen it; but they did not know that. What could his conduct mean? It might mean—it might mean—oh, a dozen dreadful things. Was it possible that he knew that Richards could have cleared him of guilt in that bygone time, and had been silently waiting for a chance to even up accounts? At home, in their distress they got to imagining that their servant might have been in the next room listening when Richards revealed the secret to his wife that he knew of Burgess's innocence; next, Richards began to imagine that he had heard the swish of a gown in there at that time; next, he was sure he *had* heard it. They would call Sarah in, on a pretext, and watch her face: if she had been betraying them to Mr. Burgess, it would show in her manner. They asked her some questions—questions which were so random and incoherent and seemingly purposeless that the girl felt sure that the old people's minds had been affected by their sudden good fortune; the sharp and watchful gaze which they bent upon her frightened her, and that completed the business. She blushed, she became nervous and confused, and to the old people these were plain signs of guilt—guilt of some fearful sort or other—without doubt she was a spy and a traitor. When they were alone again they began to piece many unrelated things together and get horrible results out of the combination. When things had got about to the worst, Richards was delivered of a sudden gasp, and his wife asked,

"Oh, what is it?—what is it?"

"The note—Burgess's note! Its language was sarcastic, I see it now." He quoted: "'At bottom you cannot respect me, *knowing*, as you do, of *that matter* of which I am accused'—oh, it is perfectly plain, now, God help me! He knows that I know! You see the ingenuity of the phrasing. It was a trap—and like a fool, I walked into it. And Mary—?"

"Oh, it is dreadful—I know what you are going to say—he didn't return your transcript of the pretended test-remark."

"No—kept it to destroy us with. Mary, he has exposed us to some already. I know it—I know it well. I saw it in a dozen faces after church. Ah, he wouldn't answer our nod of recognition—*he* knew what he had been doing!"

In the night the doctor was called. The news went around in the morning that the old couple were rather seriously ill—prostrated by the exhausting excitement growing out of their great windfall, the congratulations, and the late hours, the doctor said. The town was sincerely distressed; for these old people were about all it had left to be proud of, now.

Two days later the news was worse. The old couple were delirious, and were doing strange things. By witness of the nurses, Richards had exhibited checks—for $8500? No—for an amazing sum—$38,500! What could be the explanation of this gigantic piece of luck?

The following day the nurses had more news—and wonderful. They had concluded to hide the checks, lest harm come to them; but when they searched they were gone from under the patient's pillow—vanished away. The patient said:

"Let the pillow alone; what do you want?"

"We thought it best that the checks—"

"You will never see them again—they are destroyed. They came from Satan. I saw the hell-brand on them, and I knew they were sent to betray me to sin." Then he fell to gabbling strange and dreadful things which were not clearly understandable, and which the doctor admonished them to keep to themselves.

Richards was right; the checks were never seen again.

A nurse must have talked in her sleep, for within two days the forbidden gabblings were the property of the town; and they were of a surprising sort. They seemed to indicate that Richards had been a claimant for the sack himself, and that Burgess had concealed that fact and then maliciously betrayed it.

Burgess was taxed with this and stoutly denied it. And he said it was not fair to attach weight to the chatter of a sick old man who was out of his mind. Still, suspicion was in the air, and there was much talk.

After a day or two it was reported that Mrs. Richards's delirious deliveries were getting to be duplicates of her husband's. Suspicion flamed up into conviction, now, and the town's pride in the purity of its one undiscredited important citizen began to dim down and flicker toward extinction.

Six days passed, then came more news. The old couple were dying. Richards's mind cleared in his latest hour, and he sent for Burgess. Burgess said:

"Let the room be cleared. I think he wishes to say something in privacy."

"No!" said Richards; "I want witnesses. I want you all to hear my confession, so that I may die a man, and not a dog. I was clean—artificially—like the rest; and like the rest I fell when temptation came. I signed a lie, and claimed the miserable sack. Mr. Burgess remembered that I had done him a service, and in gratitude (and ignorance) he suppressed my claim and saved me. You know the thing that was charged against Burgess years ago. My testimony, and mine alone, could have cleared him, and I was a coward, and left him to suffer disgrace—"

"No—no—Mr. Richards, you—"

"My servant betrayed my secret to him—"

"No one has betrayed anything to me—"

"—and then he did a natural and justifiable thing, he repented of the saving kindness which he had done me, and he *exposed* me—as I deserved—"

"Never!—I make oath—"

"Out of my heart I forgive him."

Burgess's impassioned protestations fell upon deaf ears; the dying man passed away without knowing that once more he had done poor Burgess a wrong. The old wife died that night.

The last of the sacred Nineteen had fallen a prey to the fiendish sack; the town was stripped of the last rag of its ancient glory. Its mourning was not showy, but it was deep.

By act of the Legislature—upon prayer and petition—Hadleyburg was allowed to change its name to (never mind what—I will not give it away), and leave one word out of the motto that for many generations had graced the town's official seal.

It is an honest town once more, and the man will have to rise early that catches it napping again.

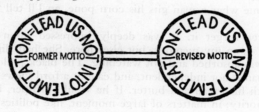

1899

From EUROPE AND ELSEWHERE

"Corn-Pone Opinions" was written in 1900 and "The War Prayer" was dictated in 1904–05; both were included in a posthumous miscellany volume, *Europe and Elsewhere* (1923). Neither piece credits the human race with effective powers of reasoning; in this respect man can scarcely be held responsible for his beliefs and actions: the voice of reason in "The War Prayer" must be dismissed as mad. This harsh view of humanity is reminiscent of Swift in the last book of *Gulliver's Travels*. For Twain, it was, as DeVoto has suggested, one stage in the working out of his own personal dilemmas. If each essay is an extreme statement of a position, it is nonetheless true that a frightening degree of truth is contained in these pages.

CORN-PONE OPINIONS

Fifty years ago, when I was a boy of fifteen and helping to inhabit a Missourian village on the banks of the Mississippi, I had a friend whose society was very dear to me because I was forbidden by my mother to partake of it. He was a gay and impudent and satirical and delightful young black man—a slave—who daily preached sermons from the top of his master's woodpile, with me for sole audience. He imitated the pulpit style of the several clergymen of the village, and did it well, and with fine passion and energy. To me he was a wonder. I believed he was the greatest orator in the United States and would some day be heard from. But it did not happen; in the distribution of rewards he was overlooked. It is the way, in this world.

He interrupted his preaching, now and then, to saw a stick of wood; but the sawing was a pretense—he did it with his mouth; exactly imitating the sound the bucksaw makes in shrieking its way through the wood. But it served its purpose; it kept his master from coming out to see how the work was getting along. I listened to the sermons from the open window of a lumber room at the back of the house. One of his texts was this:

"You tell me whar a man gits his corn pone, en I'll tell you what his 'pinions is."

I can never forget it. It was deeply impressed upon me. By my mother. Not upon my memory, but elsewhere. She had slipped in upon me while I was absorbed and not watching. The black philosopher's idea was that a man is not independent, and cannot afford views which might interfere with his bread and butter. If he would prosper, he must train with the majority; in matters of large moment, like politics and religion, he must think and feel with the bulk of his neighbors, or suffer damage in his social standing and in his business prosperities. He must restrict himself to corn-pone opinions—at least on the surface. He must get his opinions from other people; he must reason out none for himself; he must have no first-hand views.

I think Jerry was right, in the main, but I think he did not go far enough.

1. It was his idea that a man conforms to the majority view of his locality by calculation and intention.

This happens, but I think it is not the rule.

2. It was his idea that there is such a thing as a first-hand opinion, an original opinion, an opinion which is coldly reasoned out in a man's head, by a searching analysis of the facts involved, with the heart unconsulted, and the jury room closed against outside influences. It may be that such an opinion has been born somewhere, at some time or other, but I suppose it got away before they could catch it and stuff it and put it in the museum.

I am persuaded that a coldly-thought-out and independent verdict upon a fashion in clothes, or manners, or literature, or politics, or religion, or any other matter that is projected into the field of our notice and interest, is a most rare thing—if it has indeed ever existed.

A new thing in costume appears—the flaring hoopskirt, for example— and the passers-by are shocked, and the irreverent laugh. Six months later everybody is reconciled; the fashion has established itself; it is admired, now, and no one laughs. Public opinion resented it before, public opinion accepts it now, and is happy in it. Why? Was the resentment reasoned out? Was the acceptance reasoned out? No. The instinct that moves to conformity did the work. It is our nature to conform; it is a force which not many can successfully resist. What is its seat? The inborn requirement of self-approval. We all have to bow to that; there are no exceptions. Even the woman who refuses from first to last to wear the hoopskirt comes under that law and is its slave; she could not wear the skirt and have her own approval; and that she *must* have, she cannot help herself. But as a rule our self-approval has its source in but one place and not elsewhere—the approval of other people. A person of vast consequences can introduce any kind of novelty in dress and the general world will presently adopt it—moved to do it, in the first place, by the natural instinct to passively yield to that vague something recognized as authority, and in the second place by the human instinct to train with the multitude and have its approval. An empress introduced the hoopskirt, and we know the result. A nobody introduced the bloomer, and we know the result. If Eve should come again, in her ripe renown, and reintroduce her quaint styles—well, we know what would happen. And we should be cruelly embarrassed, along at first.

The hoopskirt runs its course and disappears. Nobody reasons about it. One woman abandons the fashion; her neighbor notices this and follows her lead; this influences the next woman; and so on and so on, and presently the skirt has vanished out of the world, no one knows how nor why; nor cares, for that matter. It will come again, by and by; and in due course will go again.

Twenty-five years ago, in England, six or eight wine glasses stood grouped by each person's plate at a dinner party, and they were used, not left idle and empty; to-day there are but three or four in the group, and the average guest sparingly uses about two of them. We have not adopted this new fashion yet, but we shall do it presently. We shall not think it out; we shall merely conform, and let it go at that. We get our notions and habits and opinions from outside influences; we do not have to study them out.

Our table manners, and company manners, and street manners change from time to time, but the changes are not reasoned out; we merely notice and conform. We are creatures of outside influences; as a rule we do not think, we only imitate. We cannot invent standards that will stick; what we mistake for standards are only fashions, and perishable. We may continue to admire them, but we drop the use of them. We notice this in literature. Shakespeare is a standard, and fifty years ago we used to write tragedies which we couldn't tell from—from somebody else's; but we don't do it any more, now. Our prose standard, three quarters of a century ago, was ornate and diffuse; some authority or other changed it in the direction of compactness and simplicity, and conformity followed, without argument. The historical novel starts up suddenly, and sweeps the land. Everybody writes one, and the nation is glad. We had historical novels before; but nobody read them, and the rest of us conformed—

without reasoning it out. We are conforming in the other way, now, because it is another case of everybody.

The outside influences are always pouring in upon us, and we are always obeying their orders and accepting their verdicts. The Smiths like the new play; the Joneses go to see it, and they copy the Smith verdict. Morals, religions, politics, get their following from surrounding influences and atmospheres, almost entirely; not from study, not from thinking. A man must and will have his own approval first of all, in each and every moment and circumstance of his life—even if he must repent of a self-approved act the moment after its commission, in order to get his self-approval *again:* but, speaking in general terms, a man's self-approval in the large concerns of life has its source in the approval of the peoples about him, and not in a searching personal examination of the matter. Mohammedans are Mohammedans because they are born and reared among that sect, not because they have thought it out and can furnish sound reasons for being Mohammedans; we know why Catholics are Catholics; why Presbyterians are Presbyterians; why Baptists are Baptists; why Mormons are Mormons; why thieves are thieves; why monarchists are monarchists; why Republicans are Republicans and Democrats, Democrats. We know it is a matter of association and sympathy, not reasoning and examination; that hardly a man in the world has an opinion upon morals, politics, or religion which he got otherwise than through his associations and sympathies. Broadly speaking, there are none but corn-pone opinions. And broadly speaking, corn pone stands for self-approval. Self-approval is acquired mainly from the approval of other people. The result is conformity. Sometimes conformity has a sordid business interest—the bread-and-butter interest—but not in most cases, I think. I think that in the majority of cases it is unconscious and not calculated; that it is born of the human being's natural yearning to stand well with his fellows and have their inspiring approval and praise—a yearning which is commonly so strong and so insistent that it cannot be effectually resisted, and must have its way.

A political emergency brings out the corn-pone opinion in fine force in its two chief varieties—the pocketbook variety, which has its origin in self-interest, and the bigger variety, the sentimental variety—the one which can't bear to be outside the pale; can't bear to be in disfavor; can't endure the averted face and the cold shoulder; wants to stand well with his friends, wants to be smiled upon, wants to be welcome, wants to hear the precious words, *"He's* on the right track!" Uttered, perhaps by an ass, but still an ass of high degree, an ass whose approval is gold and diamonds to a smaller ass, and confers glory and honor and happiness, and membership in the herd. For these gauds many a man will dump his life-long principles into the street, and his conscience along with them. We have seen it happen. In some millions of instances.

Men think they think upon great political questions, and they do; but they think with their party, not independently; they read its literature, but not that of the other side; they arrive at convictions, but they are drawn from a partial view of the matter in hand and are of no particular value. They swarm with their party, they feel with their party, they are happy in their party's approval; and where the party leads they will follow, whether for right and honor, or through blood and dirt and a mush of mutilated morals.

In our late canvass half of the nation passionately believed that in silver lay salvation, the other half as passionately believed that that way lay destruction. Do you believe that a tenth part of the people, on either side, had any rational excuse for having an opinion about the matter at all? I studied that mighty question to the bottom—came out empty. Half of our people passionately believe in high tariff, the other half believe otherwise. Does this mean study and examination, or only feeling? The latter, I think. I have deeply studied that question, too—and didn't arrive. We all do no end of feeling, and we mistake it for thinking. And out of it we get an aggregation which we consider a boon. Its name is Public Opinion. It is held in reverence. It settles everything. Some think it the Voice of God.

THE WAR PRAYER

It was a time of great and exalting excitement. The country was up in arms, the war was on, in every breast burned the holy fire of patriotism; the drums were beating, the bands playing, the toy pistols popping, the bunched firecrackers hissing and spluttering; on every hand and far down the receding and fading spread of roofs and balconies a fluttering wilderness of flags flashed in the sun; daily the young volunteers marched down the wide avenue gay and fine in their new uniforms, the proud fathers and mothers and sisters and sweethearts cheering them with voices choked with happy emotion as they swung by; nightly the packed mass meetings listened, panting, to patriot oratory which stirred the deepest deeps of their hearts, and which they interrupted at briefest intervals with cyclones of applause, the tears running down their cheeks the while; in the churches the pastors preached devotion to flag and country, and invoked the God of Battles, beseeching His aid in our good cause in outpouring of fervid eloquence which moved every listener. It was indeed a glad and gracious time, and the half dozen rash spirits that ventured to disapprove of the war and cast a doubt upon its righteousness straightway got such a stern and angry warning that for their personal safety's sake they quickly shrank out of sight and offended no more in that way.

Sunday morning came—next day the battalions would leave for the front; the church was filled; the volunteers were there, their young faces alight with martial dreams—visions of the stern advance, the gathering momentum, the rushing charge, the flashing sabers, the flight of the foe, the tumult, the enveloping smoke, the fierce pursuit, the surrender!— then home from the war, bronzed heroes, welcomed, adored, submerged in golden seas of glory! With the volunteers sat their dear ones, proud, happy, and envied by the neighbors and friends who had no sons and brothers to send forth to the field of honor, there to win for the flag, or, failing, die the noblest of noble deaths. The service proceeded, a war chapter from the Old Testament was read; the first prayer was said; it was followed by an organ burst that shook the building, and with one impulse the house rose, with glowing eyes and beating hearts, and poured out that tremendous invocation—

"God the all-terrible! Thou who ordainest,
Thunder thy clarion and lightning thy sword!"

Then came the "long" prayer. None could remember the like of it for passionate pleading and moving and beautiful language. The burden of its supplication was that an ever-merciful and benignant Father of us all would watch over our noble young soldiers, and aid, comfort, and encourage them in their patriotic work; bless them, shield them in the day of battle and the hour of peril, bear them in His mighty hand, make them strong and confident, invincible in the bloody onset; help them to crush the foe, grant to them and to their flag and country imperishable honor and glory—

An aged stranger entered and moved with slow and noiseless step up the main aisle, his eyes fixed upon the minister, his long body clothed in a robe that reached to his feet, his head bare, his white hair descending in a frothy cataract to his shoulders, his seamy face unnaturally pale, pale even to ghastliness. With all eyes following him and wondering, he made his silent way; without pausing, he ascended to the preacher's side and stood there, waiting. With shut lids the preacher, unconscious of his presence, continued his moving prayer, and at last finished it with the words, uttered in fervent appeal, "Bless our arms, grant us the victory, O Lord our God, Father and Protector of our land and flag!"

The stranger touched his arm, motioned him to step aside—which the startled minister did—and took his place. During some moments he surveyed the spellbound audience with solemn eyes, in which burned an uncanny light; then in a deep voice he said:

"I come from the Throne—bearing a message from Almighty God!" The words smote the house with a shock; if the stranger perceived it he gave no attention. "He has heard the prayer of His servant your shepherd, and will grant it if such shall be your desire after I, His messenger, shall have explained to you its import—that is to say, its full import. For it is like unto many of the prayers of men, in that it asks for more than he who utters it is aware of—except he pause and think.

"God's servant and yours has prayed his prayer. Has he paused and taken thought? Is it one prayer? No, it is two—one uttered, the other not. Both have reached the ear of Him Who heareth all supplications, the spoken and the unspoken. Ponder this—keep it in mind. If you would beseech a blessing upon yourself, beware! lest without intent you invoke a curse upon a neighbor at the same time. If you pray for the blessing of rain upon your crop which needs it, by that act you are possibly praying for a curse upon some neighbor's crop which may not need rain and can be injured by it.

"You have heard your servant's prayer—the uttered part of it. I am commissioned of God to put into words the other part of it—that part which the pastor—and also you in your hearts—fervently prayed silently. And ignorantly and unthinkingly? God grant that it was so! You heard these words: 'Grant us the victory, O Lord our God!' That is sufficient. The *whole* of the uttered prayer is compact into those pregnant words. Elaborations were not necessary. When you have prayed for victory you have prayed for many unmentioned results which follow victory—*must* follow it, cannot help but follow it. Upon the listening spirit of God the Father fell also the unspoken part of the prayer. He commandeth me to put it into words. Listen!

"O Lord our Father, our young patriots, idols of our hearts, go forth to battle—be Thou near them! With them—in spirit—we also go forth from the sweet peace of our beloved firesides to smite the foe. O Lord our God, help us to tear their soldiers to bloody shreds with our shells; help us to cover their smiling fields with the pale forms of their patriot dead; help us to drown the thunder of the guns with the shrieks of their wounded, writhing in pain; help us to lay waste their humble homes with a hurricane of fire; help us to wring the hearts of their unoffending widows with unavailing grief; help us to turn them out roofless with their little children to wander unfriended the wastes of their desolated land in rags and hunger and thirst, sports of the sun flames of summer and the icy winds of winter, broken in spirit, worn with travail, imploring Thee for the refuge of the grave and denied it—for our sakes who adore Thee, Lord, blast their hopes, blight their lives, protract their bitter pilgrimage, make heavy their steps, water their way with their tears, stain the white snow with the blood of their wounded feet! We ask it, in the spirit of love, of Him Who is the Source of Love, and Who is the ever-faithful refuge and friend of all that are sore beset and seek His aid with humble and contrite hearts. Amen."

(*After a pause.*) "Ye have prayed it; if ye still desire it, speak! The messenger of the Most High waits."

It was believed afterward that the man was a lunatic, because there was no sense in what he said.

1923

FROM MARK TWAIN'S AUTOBIOGRAPHY

It has been remarked that Twain's most successful autobiography is to be found in his fiction, especially those novels that re-create the Hannibal scene. It is equally true that his formal attempt at a memoir is a disappointment: most of it was dictated during the last decade of his life, with no attempt to record the "facts" in sequence. Instead, Twain took up any topic that happened to interest him at the moment, sure that this was the ideal way to combine the vividness of the present with warm recollections of the past. What resulted is a chaotic combination of diary and scrap book, undeniably interesting despite its gaps, its formlessness, and the capriciousness of his memory. Albert B. Paine used about half the manuscript in his edition of *Mark Twain's Autobiography* (1924) and Bernard DeVoto published further significant sections as *Mark Twain in Eruption* (1940).

The two passages here printed from the earlier work are not dictations but were written in longhand about 1897–98. They are rich with evocations of mid-century Missouri, which by extension is the universal world of boyhood, a physical paradise of sights and sounds and tastes. This is the world that Twain in a sense never outgrew, and from its memories came the characters, the locale, and the folkways he most imaginatively, yet most authentically, captured in his fiction.

I

My parents removed to Missouri in the early 'thirties; I do not remember just when, for I was not born then and cared nothing for such things. It was a long journey in those days, and must have been a rough and tiresome one. The home was made in the wee village of Florida, in Monroe County, and I was born there in 1835. The village contained a hundred people and I increased the population by 1 per cent. It is more than many of the best men in history could have done for a town. It may not be modest in me to refer to this, but it is true. There is no record of a person doing as much—not even Shakespeare. But I did it for Florida, and it shows that I could have done it for any place—even London, I suppose.

Recently some one in Missouri has sent me a picture of the house I was born in. Heretofore I have always stated that it was a palace, but I shall be more guarded now.

I used to remember my brother Henry walking into a fire outdoors when he was a week old. It was remarkable in me to remember a thing like that, and it was still more remarkable that I should cling to the delusion, for thirty years, that I *did* remember it—for of course it never happened; he would not have been able to walk at that age. If I had stopped to reflect, I should not have burdened my memory with that impossible rubbish so long. It is believed by many people that an impression deposited in a child's memory within the first two years of its life cannot remain there five years, but that is an error. The incident of Benvenuto Cellini and the salamander must be accepted as authentic and trustworthy; and then that remarkable and indisputable instance in the experience of Helen Keller— However, I will speak of that at another time.[1] For many years I believed that I remembered helping my grandfather drink his whisky toddy when I was six weeks old, but I do not tell about that any more, now; I am grown old and my memory is not as active as it used to be. When I was younger I could remember anything, whether it had happened or not; but my faculties are decaying now, and soon I shall be so I cannot remember any but the things that never happened. It is sad to go to pieces like this, but we all have to do it.

My uncle, John A. Quarles, was a farmer, and his place was in the country four miles from Florida. He had eight children and fifteen or twenty negroes, and was also fortunate in other ways, particularly in his character. I have not come across a better man than he was. I was his guest for two or three months every year, from the fourth year after we removed to Hannibal till I was eleven or twelve years old. I have never consciously used him or his wife in a book, but his farm has come very handy to me in literature once or twice. In *Huck Finn* and in *Tom Sawyer, Detective* I moved it down to Arkansas. It was all of six hundred miles, but it was no trouble; it was not a very large farm—five hundred acres, perhaps—but I could have done it if it had been twice as large. And as for the morality of it, I cared nothing for that; I would move a state if the exigencies of literature required it.

It was a heavenly place for a boy, that farm of my Uncle John's. The house was a double log one, with a spacious floor (roofed in) connecting it with the kitchen. In the summer the table was set in the middle of that shady and breezy floor, and the sumptuous meals—well, it makes me cry to think of them. Fried chicken, roast pig; wild and tame turkeys, ducks, and geese; venison just killed; squirrels, rabbits, pheasants, partridges, prairie-chickens; biscuits, hot batter cakes, hot buckwheat cakes, hot "wheat bread," hot rolls, hot corn pone; fresh corn boiled on the ear, succotash, butter-beans, string-beans, tomatoes, peas, Irish potatoes, sweet potatoes; buttermilk, sweet milk, "clabber"; watermelons, muskmelons, cantaloupes—all fresh from the garden; apple pie, peach pie, pumpkin pie, apple dumplings, peach cobbler—I can't remember the rest. The way that the things were cooked was perhaps the main splendor—particularly a certain few of the dishes. For instance, the corn bread, the hot biscuits and wheat bread, and the fried chicken. These things have never been properly cooked in the North—in fact, no one there is able to learn the art, so far as my experience goes. The North thinks it knows how to make corn bread, but this is mere superstition. Perhaps no bread in the world is quite so good as Southern corn bread, and perhaps no bread in the world is quite so bad as the Northern imitation of it. The North seldom tries to fry chicken, and this is well; the art cannot be learned

---

[1] Cellini remembered seeing a salamander in the fire when he was a boy of five, his father having boxed his ears to make the experience unforgettable. Helen Keller retained an acute visual memory of fields, flowers, and domestic details she had known before losing her sight and hearing at the age of twenty months.

north of the line of Mason and Dixon, nor anywhere in Europe. This is not hearsay; it is experience that is speaking. In Europe it is imagined that the custom of serving various kinds of bread blazing hot is "American," but that is too broad a spread; it is custom in the South, but is much less than that in the North. In the North and in Europe hot bread is considered unhealthy. This is probably another fussy superstition, like the European superstition that ice-water is unhealthy. Europe does not need ice-water and does not drink it; and yet, notwithstanding this, its word for it is better than ours, because it describes it, whereas ours doesn't. Europe calls it "iced" water. Our word describes water made from melted ice—a drink which has a characterless taste and which we have but little acquaintance with.

It seems a pity that the world should throw away so many good things merely because they are unwholesome. I doubt if God has given us any refreshment which, taken in moderation, is unwholesome, except microbes. Yet there are people who strictly deprive themselves of each and every eatable, drinkable, and smokable which has in any way acquired a shady reputation. They pay this price for health. And health is all they get for it. How strange it is! It is like paying out your whole fortune for a cow that has gone dry.

The farmhouse stood in the middle of a very large yard, and the yard was fenced on three sides with rails and on the rear side with high palings; against these stood the smoke-house; beyond the palings was the orchard; beyond the orchard were the negro quarters and the tobacco fields. The front yard was entered over a stile made of sawed-off logs of graduated heights; I do not remember any gate. In a corner of the front yard were a dozen lofty hickory trees and a dozen black walnuts, and in the nutting season riches were to be gathered there.

Down a piece, abreast the house, stood a little log cabin against the rail fence; and there the woody hill fell sharply away, past the barns, the corn-crib, the stables, and the tobacco-curing house, to a limpid brook which sang along over its gravelly bed and curved and frisked in and out and here and there and yonder in the deep shade of overhanging foliage and vines—a divine place for wading, and it had swimming pools, too, which were forbidden to us and therefore much frequented by us. For we were little Christian children and had early been taught the value of forbidden fruit.

In the little log cabin lived a bedridden white-headed slave woman whom we visited daily and looked upon with awe, for we believed she was upward of a thousand years old and had talked with Moses. The younger negroes credited these statistics and had furnished them to us in good faith. We accommodated all the details which came to us about her; and so we believed that she had lost her health in the long desert trip coming out of Egypt, and had never been able to get it back again. She had a round bald place on the crown of her head, and we used to creep around and gaze at it in reverent silence, and reflect that it was caused by fright through seeing Pharaoh drowned. We called her "Aunt" Hannah, Southern fashion. She was superstitious, like the other negroes; also, like them, she was deeply religious. Like them, she had great faith in prayer and employed it in all ordinary exigencies, but not in cases where a dead certainty of result was urgent. Whenever witches were around she tied up the remnant of her wool in little tufts, with white thread, and this promptly made the witches impotent.

All the negroes were friends of ours, and with those of our own age we were in effect comrades. I say in effect, using the phrase as a modification. We were comrades, and yet not comrades; color and condition interposed a subtle line which both parties were conscious of and which rendered complete fusion impossible. We had a faithful and affectionate good friend, ally, and adviser in "Uncle Dan'l," a middle-aged slave whose head was the best one in the negro quarter, whose sympathies were wide and warm, and whose heart was honest and simple and knew no guile. He has served me well these many, many years. I have not seen him for more than half a century, and yet spiritually I have had his welcome company a good part of that time, and have staged him in books under his own name and as "Jim," and carted him all around—to Hannibal, down the Mississippi on a raft, and even across the Desert of Sahara in a balloon—and he has endured it all with the patience and friendliness and loyalty which were his birthright.[2] It was on the farm that I got my strong liking for his race and my appreciation of certain of its fine qualities. This feeling and this estimate have stood the test of sixty years and more, and have suffered no impairment. The black face is as welcome to me now as it was then.

In my schoolboy days I had no aversion to slavery. I was not aware that there was anything wrong about it. No one arraigned it in my hearing; the local papers said nothing against it; the local pulpit taught us that God approved it, that it was a holy thing, and that the doubter need only look in the Bible if he wished to settle his mind—and then the texts were read aloud to us to make the matter sure; if the slaves themselves had an aversion to slavery, they were wise and said nothing. In Hannibal we seldom saw a slave misused; on the farm, never.

There was, however, one small incident of my boyhood days which touched this matter, and it must have meant a good deal to me or it would not have stayed in my memory, clear and sharp, vivid and shadowless, all these slow-drifting years. We had a little slave boy whom we had hired from some one, there in Hannibal. He was from the eastern shore of Maryland, and had been brought away from his family and his friends, halfway across the American continent, and sold. He was a cheery spirit, innocent and gentle, and the noisiest creature that ever was, perhaps. All day long he was singing, whistling, yelling, whooping, laughing—it was maddening, devastating, unendurable. At last, one day, I lost

[2] He appeared under his own name in *The Gilded Age* and as Jim in *Huckleberry Finn, Tom Sawyer Abroad*, and *Tom Sawyer, Detective*.

all my temper, and went raging to my mother and said Sandy had been singing for an hour without a single break, and I couldn't stand it, and *wouldn't* she please shut him up. The tears came into her eyes and her lip trembled, and she said something like this:

"Poor thing, when he sings it shows that he is not remembering, and that comforts me; but when he is still I am afraid he is thinking, and I cannot bear it. He will never see his mother again; if he can sing, I must not hinder it, but be thankful for it. If you were older, you would understand me; then that friendless child's noise would make you glad."

It was a simple speech and made up of small words, but it went home, and Sandy's noise was not a trouble to me any more. She never used large words, but she had a natural gift for making small ones do effective work. She lived to reach the neighborhood of ninety years and was capable with her tongue to the last—especially when a meanness or an injustice roused her spirit. She has come handy to me several times in my books, where she figures as Tom Sawyer's Aunt Polly. I fitted her out with a dialect and tried to think up other improvements for her, but did not find any. I used Sandy once, also; it was in *Tom Sawyer*. I tried to get him to whitewash the fence, but it did not work. I do not remember what name I called him by in the book.

I can see the farm yet, with perfect clearness. I can see all its belongings, all its details; the family room of the house, with a "trundle" bed in one corner and a spinning-wheel in another—a wheel whose rising and falling wail, heard from a distance, was the mournfulest of all sounds to me, and made me homesick and low spirited, and filled my atmosphere with the wandering spirits of the dead; the vast fireplace, piled high, on winter nights, with flaming hickory logs from whose ends a sugary sap bubbled out, but did not go to waste, for we scraped it off and ate it; the lazy cat spread out on the rough hearthstones; the drowsy dogs braced against the jambs and blinking; my aunt in one chimney corner, knitting; my uncle in the other, smoking his corn-cob pipe; the slick and carpetless oak floor faintly mirroring the dancing flame tongues and freckled with black indentations where fire coals had popped out and died a leisurely death; half a dozen children romping in the background twilight; "split"-bottomed chairs here and there, some with rockers; a cradle—out of service, but waiting, with confidence; in the early cold mornings a snuggle of children, in shirts and chemises, occupying the hearthstone and procrastinating—they could not bear to leave that comfortable place and go out on the wind-swept floor space between the house and kitchen where the general tin basin stood, and wash.

Along outside of the front fence ran the country road, dusty in the summertime, and a good place for snakes—they liked to lie in it and sun themselves; when they were rattlesnakes or puff adders, we killed them; when they were black snakes, or racers, or belonged to the fabled "hoop" breed, we fled, without shame; when they were "house snakes," or "garters," we carried them home and put them in Aunt Patsy's work basket for a surprise; for she was prejudiced against snakes, and always when she took the basket in her lap and they began to climb out of it it disordered her mind. She never could seem to get used to them; her opportunities went for nothing. And she was always cold toward bats, too, and could not bear them; and yet I think a bat is as friendly a bird as there is. My mother was Aunt Patsy's sister and had the same wild superstitions. A bat is beautifully soft and silky; I do not know any creature that is pleasanter to the touch or is more grateful for caressings, if offered in the right spirit. I know all about these coleoptera, because our great cave, three miles below Hannibal, was multitudinously stocked with them, and often I brought them home to amuse my mother with. It was easy to manage if it was a school day, because then I had ostensibly been to school and hadn't any bats. She was not a suspicious person, but full of trust and confidence; and when I said, "There's something in my coat pocket for you," she would put her hand in. But she always took it out again, herself; I didn't have to tell her. It was remarkable, the way she couldn't learn to like private bats. The more experience she had, the more she could not change her views.

I think she was never in the cave in her life; but everybody else went there. Many excursion parties came from considerable distances up and down the river to visit the cave. It was miles in extent and was a tangled wilderness of narrow and lofty clefts and passages. It was an easy place to get lost in; anybody could do it—including the bats. I got lost in it myself, along with a lady, and our last candle burned down to almost nothing before we glimpsed the search party's lights winding about in the distance.

"Injun Joe," the half-breed, got lost in there once, and would have starved to death if the bats had run short. But there was no chance of that; there were myriads of them. He told me all his story. In the book called *Tom Sawyer* I starved him entirely to death in the cave, but that was in the interest of art; it never happened: "General" Gaines, who was our first town drunkard before Jimmy Finn got the place, was lost in there for the space of a week, and finally pushed his handkerchief out of a hole in a hilltop near Saverton, several miles down the river from the cave's mouth, and somebody saw it and dug him out. There is nothing the matter with his statistics except the handkerchief. I knew him for years and he hadn't any. But it could have been his nose. That would attract attention.

The cave was an uncanny place, for it contained a corpse—the corpse of a young girl of fourteen. It was in a glass cylinder inclosed in a copper one which was suspended from a rail which bridged a narrow passage. The body was preserved in alcohol, and it was said that loafers and rowdies used to drag it up by the hair and look at the dead face. The girl was the daughter of a St. Louis surgeon of extraordinary ability and wide celebrity. He was an eccentric man and did many strange things. He put the poor thing in that forlorn place himself.

II

Beyond the road where the snakes sunned themselves was a dense young thicket, and through it a dim-lighted path led a quarter of a mile; then out of the dimness one emerged abruptly upon a level great prairie which was covered with wild strawberry plants, vividly starred with prairie pinks, and walled in on all sides by forests. The strawberries were fragrant and fine, and in the season we were generally there in the crisp freshness of the early morning, while the dew beads still sparkled upon the grass and the woods were ringing with the first songs of the birds.

Down the forest slopes to the left were the swings. They were made of bark stripped from hickory saplings. When they became dry they were dangerous. They usually broke when a child was forty feet in the air, and this was why so many bones had to be mended every year. I had no ill luck myself, but none of my cousins escaped. There were eight of them, and at one time and another they broke fourteen arms among them. But it cost next to nothing, for the doctor worked by the year—twenty-five dollars for the whole family. I remember two of the Florida doctors, Chowning and Meredith. They not only tended an entire family for twenty-five dollars a year, but furnished the medicines themselves. Good measure, too. Only the largest persons could hold a whole dose. Castor oil was the principal beverage. The dose was half a dipperful, with half a dipperful of New Orleans molasses added to help it down and make it taste good, which it never did. The next standby was calomel; the next, rhubarb; and the next, jalap. Then they bled the patient, and put mustard plasters on him. It was a dreadful system, and yet the death rate was not heavy. The calomel was nearly sure to salivate the patient and cost him some of his teeth. There were no dentists. When teeth became touched with decay or were otherwise ailing, the doctor knew of but one thing to do—he fetched his tongs and dragged them out. If the jaw remained, it was not his fault. Doctors were not called in cases of ordinary illness; the family grandmother attended to those. Every old woman was a doctor, and gathered her own medicines in the woods, and knew how to compound doses that would stir the vitals of a cast-iron dog. And then there was the "Indian doctor"; a grave savage, remnant of his tribe, deeply read in the mysteries of nature and the secret properties of herbs; and most backwoodsmen had high faith in his powers and could tell of wonderful cures achieved by him. In Mauritius, away off yonder in the solitudes of the Indian Ocean, there is a person who answers to our Indian doctor of the old times. He is a negro, and has had no teaching as a doctor, yet there is one disease which he is master of and can cure and the doctors can't. They send for him when they have a case. It is a child's disease of a strange and deadly sort, and the negro cures it with a herb medicine which he makes, himself, from a prescription which has come down to him from his father and grandfather. He will not let anyone see it. He keeps the secret of its components to himself, and it is feared that he will die without divulging it; then there will be consternation in Mauritius. I was told these things by the people there, in 1896.

We had the "faith doctor," too, in those early days—a woman. Her specialty was toothache. She was a farmer's old wife and lived five miles from Hannibal. She would lay her hand on the patient's jaw and say, "Believe!" and the cure was prompt. Mrs. Utterback. I remember her very well. Twice I rode out there behind my mother, horseback, and saw the cure performed. My mother was the patient.

Dr. Meredith removed to Hannibal, by and by, and was our family physician there, and saved my life several times. Still, he was a good man and meant well. Let it go.

I was always told that I was a sickly and precarious and tiresome and uncertain child, and lived mainly on allopathic medicines during the first seven years of my life. I asked my mother about this, in her old age—she was in her eighty-eighth year—and said:

"I suppose that during all that time you were uneasy about me?"

"Yes, the whole time."

"Afraid I wouldn't live?"

After a reflective pause—ostensibly to think out the facts—"No—afraid you would."

The country schoolhouse was three miles from my uncle's farm. It stood in a clearing in the woods and would hold about twenty-five boys and girls. We attended the school with more or less regularity once or twice a week, in summer, walking to it in the cool of the morning by the forest paths, and back in the gloaming at the end of the day. All the pupils brought their dinners in baskets—corn dodger, buttermilk, and other good things—and sat in the shade of the trees at noon and ate them. It is the part of my education which I look back upon with the most satisfaction. My first visit to the school was when I was seven. A strapping girl of fifteen, in the customary sunbonnet and calico dress, asked me if I "used tobacco"—meaning did I chew it. I said no. It roused her scorn. She reported me to all the crowd, and said:

"Here is a boy seven years old who can't chew tobacco."

By the looks and comments which this produced I realized that I was a degraded object, and was cruelly ashamed of myself. I determined to reform. But I only made myself sick; I was not able to learn to chew tobacco. I learned to smoke fairly well, but that did not conciliate anybody and I remained a poor thing, and characterless. I longed to be respected, but I never was able to rise. Children have but little charity for one another's defects.

As I have said, I spent some part of every year at the farm until I was twelve or thirteen years old. The life which I led there with my cousins was full of charm, and so is the memory of it yet. I can call back the solemn twilight and mystery of the deep woods, the earthy smells, the faint odors of the wild flowers, the sheen of rain-washed foliage, the rattling clatter of drops when the wind shook the trees, the far-off hammering of woodpeckers and the muffled drumming of wood pheasants in the remoteness of the forest, the snapshot glimpses of disturbed wild creatures scurrying through the grass—I can call it all back and make it as real as it ever was, and as blessed. I can call back the prairie, and its loneliness and peace, and a vast hawk hanging motionless in the sky, with his wings spread wide and the blue of the vault showing through the fringe of their end feathers. I can see the woods in their autumn dress, the oaks purple, the hickories washed with gold, the maples and the sumachs luminous with crimson fires, and I can hear the rustle made by the fallen leaves as we plowed through them. I can see the blue clusters of wild grapes hanging among the foliage of the saplings, and I remember the taste of them and the smell. I know how the wild blackberries looked, and how they tasted, and the same with the pawpaws, the hazelnuts, and the persimmons; and I can feel the thumping rain, upon my head, of hickory nuts and walnuts when we were out in the frosty dawn to scramble for them with the pigs, and the gusts of wind loosed them and sent them down. I know the stain of blackberries, and how pretty it is, and I know the stain of walnut hulls, and how little it minds soap and water, also what grudged experience it had of either of them. I know the taste of maple sap, and when to gather it, and how to arrange the troughs and the delivery tubes, and how to boil down the juice, and how to hook the sugar after it is made, also how much better hooked sugar tastes than any that is honestly come by, let bigots say what they will. I know how a prize watermelon looks when it is sunning its fat rotundity among pumpkin vines and "simblins"; [3] I know how to tell when it is ripe without "plugging" it; I know how inviting it looks when it is cooling itself in a tub of water under the bed, waiting; I know how it looks when it lies on the table in the sheltered great floor space between house and kitchen, and the children gathered for the sacrifice and their mouths watering; I know the crackling sound it makes when the carving knife enters its end, and I can see the split fly along in front of the blade as the knife cleaves its way to the other end; I can see its halves fall apart and display the rich red meat and the black seeds, and the heart standing up, a luxury fit for the elect; I know how a boy looks behind a yard-long slice of that melon, and I know how he feels; for I have been there. I know the taste of the watermelon which has been honestly come by, and I know the taste of the watermelon which has been acquired by art. Both taste good, but the experienced know which tastes best. I know the look of green apples and peaches and pears on the trees, and I know how entertaining they are when they are inside of a person. I know how ripe ones look when they are piled in pyramids under the trees, and how pretty they are and how vivid their colors. I know how a frozen apple looks, in a barrel down cellar in the wintertime, and how hard it is to bite, and how the frost

[3] Cymlings, scalloped summer squash.

makes the teeth ache, and yet how good it is, notwithstanding. I know the disposition of elderly people to select the specked apples for the children, and I once knew ways to beat the game. I know the look of an apple that is roasting and sizzling on a hearth on a winter's evening, and I know the comfort that comes of eating it hot, along with some sugar and a drench of cream. I know the delicate art and mystery of so cracking hickory nuts and walnuts on a flatiron with a hammer that the kernels will be delivered whole, and I know how the nuts, taken in conjunction with winter apples, cider, and doughnuts, make old people's old tales and old jokes sound fresh and crisp and enchanting, and juggle an evening away before you know what went with the time. I know the look of Uncle Dan'l's kitchen as it was on the privileged nights, when I was a child, and I can see the white and black children grouped on the hearth, with the firelight playing on their faces and the shadows flickering upon the walls, clear back toward the cavernous gloom of the rear, and I can hear Uncle Dan'l telling the immortal tales which Uncle Remus Harris was to gather into his book and charm the world with, by and by; and I can feel again the creepy joy which quivered through me when the time for the ghost story was reached—and the sense of regret, too, which came over me, for it was always the last story of the evening and there was nothing between it and the unwelcome bed.

I can remember the bare wooden stairway in my uncle's house, and the turn to the left above the landing, and the rafters and the slanting roof over my bed, and the squares of moonlight on the floor, and the white cold world of snow outside, seen through the curtainless window. I can remember the howling of the wind and the quaking of the house on stormy nights, and how snug and cozy one felt, under the blankets, listening; and how the powdery snow used to sift in, around the sashes, and lie in little ridges on the floor and make the place look chilly in the morning and curb the wild desire to get up—in case there was any. I can remember how very dark that room was, in the dark of the moon, and how packed it was with ghostly stillness when one woke up by accident away in the night, and forgotten sins came flocking out of the secret chambers of the memory and wanted a hearing; and how ill chosen the time seemed for this kind of business; and how dismal was the hoo-hooing of the owl and the wailing of the wolf, sent mourning by on the night wind.

I remember the raging of the rain on that roof, summer nights, and how pleasant it was to lie and listen to it, and enjoy the white splendor of the lightning and the majestic booming and crashing of the thunder. It was a very satisfactory room, and there was a lightning rod which was reachable from the window, an adorable and skittish thing to climb up and down, summer nights, when there were duties on hand of a sort to make privacy desirable.

I remember the 'coon and 'possum hunts, nights, with the negroes, and the long marches through the black gloom of the woods, and the excitement which fired everybody when the distant bay of an experienced dog announced that the game was treed; then the wild scramblings and stumblings through briers and bushes and over roots to get to the spot; then the lighting of a fire and the felling of the tree, the joyful frenzy of the dogs and the negroes, and the weird picture it all made in the red glare—I remember it all well, and the delight that everyone got out of it, except the 'coon.

I remember the pigeon seasons, when the birds would come in millions and cover the trees and by their weight break down the branches. They were clubbed to death with sticks; guns were not necessary and were not used. I remember the squirrel hunts, and prairie-chicken hunts, and wild-turkey hunts, and all that; and how we turned out, mornings, while it was still dark, to go on these expeditions, and how chilly and dismal it was, and how often I regretted that I was well enough to go. A toot on a tin horn brought twice as many dogs as were needed, and in their happiness they raced and scampered about, and knocked small people down, and made no end of unnecessary noise. At the word, they vanished away toward the woods, and we drifted silently after them in the melancholy gloom. But presently the gray dawn stole over the world, the birds piped up, then the sun rose and poured light and comfort all around, everything was fresh and dewy and fragrant, and life was a boon again. After three hours of tramping we arrived back wholesomely tired, overladen with game, very hungry, and just in time for breakfast.

1924

HENRY ADAMS

1838–1918

WHEN *THE EDUCATION OF HENRY ADAMS* WAS PUBLISHED IN 1918, SOON after Adams had died in his eighty-first year, there was a public eager to acclaim it. Purportedly an autobiography, it immediately took its place as one of the notable documents of its century, and it is not likely to be forgotten in times to come. But the public which applauded this testament to stoicism, hope, and doubt was not the remnant of Adams's generation, or even of that succeeding his. It was the generation, on both sides of the Atlantic, which had participated in the First World War.

As spiritual revelation it was Adams's last book, written shortly before it was privately printed in 1907. In retrospect one sees why Adams withheld publication, and why the older generation, even in the next decade, was irritated by it. Its color, wit, and charm were captivating, but the author's obsession with his "failure" in life, his aloofness, his cynicism repelled readers who believed that the United States had entered its period of manifest destiny. The fact that in the preface he coupled his name with that of St. Augustine as a writer of confessions was deemed especially inappropriate. Perversely, it seemed, he stressed the wastefulness of his life. He viewed as outmoded a childhood upbringing that should have been the envy of most children; he bewailed the emptiness of his college years; he insisted that he had learned nothing while serving during the Civil War as secretary to his father, one of America's great envoys to England; he felt that his days as newspaper reporter in Washington were barren; and thenceforth after chapter twenty, titled "Failure," the mood is one of unrelieved gloom.

But younger generations, stimulated by his anger at indifference, venality, and self-interest in public servants, see a different accomplishment. Like Augustine, Adams is not confessing his own failure merely, but mankind's. He speaks as a representative of his time, and the more fortunate his place and his gifts, the more serious the failure. Twentieth-century man, Adams foresaw, has been able to unleash enormous forces. In the light of past experience, from which few have learned to profit, he raises the question whether time may not be running out: whether men in this century of accelerating scientific knowledge understand how close they stand to the brink of annihilation. Adams speaks as a historian, not a scientist; and though he chose the medium of history to express his ideas, like Cervantes or Fielding, or Hawthorne or Melville, he is essentially a moralist.

Henry Brooks Adams was born, February 16, 1838, in his father's house on Mount Vernon Street in Boston, the fourth of the seven children of Charles Francis Adams and Abigail Brooks Adams. Nearby, while the children were growing up, lived their grandfather, the former president John Quincy Adams, now serving as a member of Congress. It was grand-father Adams whom Henry recalled among his earliest memories, when all members of the family moved to the Old House in Quincy to spend long summers. The family was closely knit, and the interdependence of the keen-minded children is evident from the letters they exchanged over the years. All had ability, and following the Adams tradition, the boys were expected to put it to use for public good. Since their other grand-father, Peter Chardon Brooks, was a very wealthy man, they were enabled to shape their careers without undue consideration of financial needs. They were nurtured in an atmosphere of politics, both in theory and practice, for presidents had been traditional in the family since the time of great-grandfather John Adams. Early friendships and associations were colored by the support their father gave to the Free Soil, or anti-slavery, wing of the Whig party in New England, which slated him in 1848 for vice president on the national ticket. Though the party lost the election, Charles Francis Adams still had a political future. He was chosen a Republican member of Congress in 1859, and served there until 1861, when Lincoln sent him as Minister to England.

Meanwhile Henry had attended Harvard College, from which he was graduated in 1858. His own account of student-teacher relationship at that time, which he describes as oppressively formal and unstimulating (with the notable exceptions of Louis Agassiz and James Russell Lowell), is confirmed by the recollections of other undergraduates. But he was active in student affairs and made lasting friendships, in particular with H. H. Richardson, who later shaped the taste in architecture, and with Alexander Agassiz, the distinguished geologist son of Adams's teacher. In September of 1858 he embarked for Europe, in the company of a few other classmates, having as his purpose the study of law in Berlin; but he found that his knowledge of both German and Latin was too elementary to serve his aim, and soon abandoned his plans. He now wandered about, and while residing in Dresden came to the conclusion that he wanted to write. The decision made, he set out for Italy, recording his impressions as he traveled. These through his brother Charles he placed with the Boston *Courier*, for which he now became a paid correspondent. With a newspaperman's desire to be in the midst of exciting events, he went to Palermo in May 1860, immediately after Garibaldi descended on Sicily with his one thousand volunteers. There, along with other correspondents, he met the liberator, and the impression of personal force, by which Garibaldi held his motley brigands together, never left him. But events at home were coming to a crisis. Aware that his father was under an increasing burden of affairs, he volunteered for any service he could render. The offer was accepted, and by autumn he had joined his family in Washington and taken on the duties of secretary to his father.

In his free evenings Henry Adams now found outlet to express ideas about events as he experienced them. He contributed anonymous letters to the Boston *Advertiser*, detailing week-to-week occurrences on Capitol Hill in this tense moment of national history. Lincoln, assuming office at this time, brought with him as secretary young John Hay, and thus began a lifelong friendship, of great importance to both Hay and Adams. The elder Adams's diplomatic appointment followed immediately, and the father was firm in his opinion that Henry's duty lay in going to England as his aide, not gaining a commission in the army as his son Charles did and as Henry wished to do. Henry Adams remained abroad for seven years, and the account of that sojourn furnishes some of the most enthralling chapters of the *Education*.

Throughout his life Adams enjoyed society, and sought out gatherings of his own choosing. Among his English friends Charles Milnes Gaskell most fully responded to Adams's views and shared his ironies; the two remained lifelong correspondents. But Adams's frequent claim that he merely liked to be diverted or amused can deceive no one who ponders his accomplishment as a writer. Even while he kept abreast of routine tasks, he made opportunity in after hours to record his impressions of people and events. Henry J. Raymond, whom Adams had known as a Washington correspondent, was now editor of the New York *Times*, and during the latter months of 1861 Adams sent Raymond commentaries on the British domestic and political scene which Raymond was glad to use. But Adams's reporting abruptly ended when the Boston *Courier*, in December, placed on the front page an account of a visit Adams had made in Manchester to study the cotton shortage. The author was identified, and the London *Times* took notice in a way intended to embarrass the American minister.

The burden of increasing work, as the war years lengthened, gave little opportunity for penning much besides official dispatches, but after 1865 the situation altered, though the writing was channeled into a different course. Adams immersed himself in research, and his first historical essay appeared in the *North American Review* for January 1867, "Captain John Smith," a notable examination of the Pocahontas episode. It was followed shortly by "British Finance in 1816." The success of these articles gave Adams enough repute so that, after the family's return to the United States in 1868, he could pick up again as an independent journalist. He gravitated, as he always felt impelled, to Washington, and now contributed to such reviews as the *Edinburgh* and the *Westminster*, as well as to the *North American*. Filled with the young reformer's zeal, he set out to expose corrupt practices as they affected government administration, business, and finance. The investigations resulted in his first published book, a collection of articles written by his brother Charles and himself on railroads and the land grab: *Chapters of Erie and Other Essays* (1871).

Meantime the young president of Harvard, Charles Eliot, casting about for new blood, for men who could enrich the classroom with vigorous ideas, persuaded Adams in 1870 to join the history department under Whitman Gurney, its head and the editor of the *North American Review*. Because Gurney was taking on new administrative duties, he wished to relinquish his editor's chair, which he turned over to Adams. During the summer of 1871, to break the routine of preparing lectures in medieval history and soliciting manuscripts for the *Review*, Adams journeyed to the Far West, to explore canyons and mountains. His chance meeting at this time with the brilliant young geologist Clarence King was to develop into one of the most meaningful associations of his life.

The significant event for Adams lay just ahead. On June 27, 1872, he married Marian Hooper of Boston. Witty and vivacious, she shared her husband's tastes, interests, and friendships, and thus began a singularly happy union. An inner harmony now reflects itself in the quality of his teaching and writing. Adams's most lasting contribution as teacher was his introduction of the seminar method at the graduate level. With his advanced classes he himself worked up studies in the area under research. When his first graduate students, Henry Cabot Lodge, Ernest Young, and J. Laurence Laughlin, received their degrees in June 1876, Adams published their theses as *Essays in Anglo-Saxon Law*, a volume which included his own study of early English courts of law. But his interest increasingly was in writing history rather than teaching it. By chance he had been put in a position to edit two important manuscript collections: documents relating to New England Federalism during 1800–1815 (illustrating a controversial episode in his grandfather's political career), and the writings of Jefferson's secretary of the treasury, Albert Gallatin. He resigned from the *Review* late in 1876, from his teaching post as of the following June, and in the autumn of 1877 Henry and Marian Adams were settled in Washington.

The *Documents* were published before the year ended, and both the *Life* and the *Writings* (3 volumes) of Gallatin followed in 1879. Adams was now working prodigiously. The man Gallatin, he had come to feel, needed a biographer, who should be himself. Even as he worked at the task he was assembling material for a life of Aaron Burr, whose "veneered profligacy," as Adams later termed it in his *History*, made Burr the polar opposite of Gallatin. While engaged in these historical under-takings, he began and completed *Democracy: An American Novel*, and delivered it to the publisher Henry Holt, who, sworn to secrecy, pub-lished it anonymously in 1880. Though actually only on the threshold of his most productive years, Adams was by no means "driven" by this burst of energy; he and Mrs. Adams found ample leisure to enjoy the so-ciety of their friends. John Hay had been brought to Washington as as-sistant secretary of state in 1878, and the Hays and Adamses were insep-arable. Clarence King, now living nearby, completed the group that came to call themselves "the Five of Hearts." Richardson, Agassiz, and many other friends were free to come and go, but only the most intimate knew the identity of the author of the novel which set tongues wagging in an effort to recognize persons and situations transparently drawn from current politics. In the next three years Adams would write yet another biography (*John Randolph*, 1882), and another novel (*Esther*, 1884). Be-cause there is a tie that links the biographies and the novels, they will be discussed together. While he was writing them, he was planning his most ambitious work, his *History*.

The *History of the United States of America during the Administra-tions of Thomas Jefferson and James Madison* will continue to rank among the major creative accomplishments of nineteenth-century writ-ers. Its breadth of concept and imaginative sweep are matched by its liter-ary quality and balanced perspectives. Adams had wished to settle in Washington not only because the associations there, as well as the envi-rons themselves, would be enjoyable. He needed to be near the sources of the documents he would use. The idea appealed likewise to Mrs. Ad-ams, and they soon established themselves in a house on Lafayette Square. But the roots of the problem, in an age of international turmoil, were in Europe, so both immediately laid plans for an extended sojourn abroad, which they undertook during 1879–1880, where Adams culled the necessary source material from archives in the foreign offices of Paris, Madrid, and London, and arranged to have it transcribed. On their re-turn he was granted a desk in the State Department building, and began the work of collating the transcripts now arriving by ship with those documents he was uncovering in the files at hand. Every summer when the Adamses went to Beverley Farms, Massachusetts, specially con-structed boxes transferred the large accumulation. The labors, engaging Adams for eleven years, ended in 1888, when the last of the nine volumes was drafted.

Adams chose to write about the sixteen years from the inauguration of Jefferson in 1801 until the retirement of Madison in 1817 because he felt them to be a unit, and the period of time in which the American charac-ter was formed. As Adams saw it, the accession of Jefferson ended the revolutionary era in American history; Jefferson not only had shaped the character of the nation in which Adams lived, but had molded the destiny of generations yet unborn. The narrative itself is introduced by a prologue of six chapters, the last of them titled "American Ideals"; it concludes with an epilogue of four chapters, the last titled "American Character." The recital between intends to show the extent to which the ideals of 1800 had become the distinctive reality for later generations. Though the emphasis throughout is on politics, no facet is neglected in the portrayal of events and persons. Adams examined not only the pertinent state papers of four nations, but also the available private papers (and his resources were uniquely extensive), together with pamphlets, newspapers, military and naval memoirs, statistical reports and charts, fiction, poetry, and the many accounts written by foreign and domestic travelers. The compelling figure, even in the last five volumes, is Jefferson, whom Adams sees as the shaper of the new society. He identifies Jefferson's contradictions—doubt and hope—with his own. Jefferson the statesman had learned by experience that he must accept the tragic necessities of all civilizations: war, tyrannies, and the bitternesses thus engendered, aroused by seizure—and likewise by relinquishment—of lands and cargoes.

Once Adams had set to work, he labored steadily to the end. His task was not stopped even in midstream by Marian Adams's suicide in December 1885. Her profound depression was a disorder which had been recurrent, and today could have been meliorated or perhaps cured. The loss to Adams created a permanent trauma. Though it did not change his character, it deepened his perversities: his aloofness, his self-pity. But it also, paradoxically, gave him strength. He had completed the first two volumes of the *History* in 1884 (through Jefferson's first administration), and printed six copies, partly for safety, partly for convenience. Such continued to be his procedure, the last volume issued privately in 1889, the year after the writing was finished. Publication of the first two volumes, in the same year, was followed in 1890 by the next four volumes, and in 1891 the entire work was before the public. Though it was immediately hailed for its scholarship, its bulk limited the number of readers, most of whom of course assumed it to be a picture of the era which the title named. The fact is that Adams attempted no less a feat than to present his ideas about the lines of force by which a nation was shaped and being impelled. His concern with "force" continued to be his abiding interest, almost an obsession.

As a work of art the *History* combines the wit, irony, and inclusiveness characteristic of Adams at his best. The portraits have a bias inevitable when strong minds reach conclusions. Perhaps the brief summary of John Quincy Adams will exemplify the nature of the style:

> Anxious by temperament, with little confidence in his own good fortune,—fighting his battles with energy, but rather that of despair than hope,—the younger Adams never allowed himself to enjoy the full relish of a triumph before it staled, while he never failed to taste with its fullest flavor, as though it were a precious wine, every drop in the bitter cup of his defeats.

The two biographies were completed while the *History* was in progress and are treatments in small, applied to individuals, of the general theme. In *Gallatin* it is the problem of a man of great talent who, working to produce a new society free from the ills of the past, finds himself caught up in the turbulence he deplores. In *Randolph* the issues are the same, but the subject is a man whose arrogance and intemperance led him to a gross misuse of his gifts. Both studies, the first warmly sympathetic, the second unsparing, tell much about Adams. Gallatin was a Swiss aristocrat who devoted his great abilities to the service of democracy. Randolph, with like talent, wealth, and background, also served his country, but dissipated his energies by malicious attacks on friend and foe. The studies complement each other, and as reflections on human capacity for success and failure they should be read together.

The vitality of Adams's creativeness when he deals directly with figures in history does not carry over into his fictional characters. In *Democracy* an intelligent, attractive woman refuses to marry a senator with a political future when she becomes convinced that he lacks integrity; the setting is Washington during the corrupt Grant administration, but the satire recalls Adams's disillusionment fifteen years earlier, when he first closely observed political maneuvering. *Esther*, written in 1883 and published in 1884 under the pseudonym Frances Snow Compton, presents a similar dilemma: a sensitive woman rejects a clergyman when she comes to feel that he lacks integrity in facing questions posed by science. But there is another problem in *Esther*, quite apart from the issues with which it deals. Elizabeth Stevenson in her biography of Adams makes a strong case for her belief that the characters are often, in part at least, the people whom Adams knew most intimately; there is much in Esther herself that is Marian Adams. He carefully guarded the authorship and virtually suppressed publication by refusing to allow it to be advertised. Yet over the years he valued it with an intimacy so personal as to make clear its special place in that part of him which after 1885 was irrecoverable. As a novel it was indeed a failure. But as a document written by one who felt compulsion to reveal even as he hides, it has unique importance.

Needing to relax and steady his nerves, in the summer of 1886 Adams set off with his artist friend John La Farge for Japan, Samoa, and the South Seas. In the autumn he returned to the new house which Richardson had designed, completed just after Marian's death, at 1603 H Street, next to that built for the Hays. (The structures, an architectural unit, were built together.) In Japan, Adams had discussed with La Farge the monument he wished to place over his wife's grave in Rock Creek cemetery. His friend Augustus St. Gaudens undertook the commission, and the hooded figure placed there in 1890, a masterpiece of American sculpture, is clearly influenced by Adams's trip to Japan and his feeling about the Great Buddha at Kamakura, for it also reflects a limitless repose in a world of tension and anxiety.

Travel for Adams was both a diversion and a way of sharpening his perceptions. With the *History* completed in 1890, Adams wished to divest himself of the past. For the next decade he moved restlessly, for varying periods of time, to the South Seas, the Orient, Europe, the Caribbean. The year 1895 was to prove immensely significant. His former pupil and good friend Henry Cabot Lodge had recently begun a term in the Senate that was destined to be renewed many times. With Cabot and Anna Lodge and their two boys, Adams embarked for France, and in Normandy made a new discovery of himself by way of a study of the great cathedrals. Their fascination was a totally unexpected emotion. He literally imbued himself with churches, for he wished to get the feel not only of monuments in stone and glass, but of the poetry and songs and philosophy of the twelfth and thirteenth centuries. After he had attended the Paris Exposition of 1900, and seen the huge dynamo whose mysterious and amoral force seemed to typify the twentieth century, he felt impelled to draw a comparison between it and the equally mysterious but moral force exerted by the Virgin in the thirteenth century. The seeds thus sown yielded in the next seven years his two best-known books, the companion pieces *Mont-Saint-Michel and Chartres* (1904), "a study in thirteenth-century unity," as he termed it, and *The Education of Henry Adams* (1907), "a study of twentieth-century multiplicity," both privately printed. (*Chartres* he revised and published in 1913; the *Education*, though distributed among friends, was not released to the public until after his death.)

These books are written by a different Adams. The *Chartres*, from beginning to end, glows with the feeling for color and form that he had absorbed from his travels in the Orient with La Farge. The work is of course the sound historical study which one would expect. But it is much more. As Ralph Adams Cram states in his 1913 preface: "it is no phantasm of the past that shines dimly before us in these magical pages; it is the very time itself in which we are merged; . . . we dispute with Abélard . . . we take our parts in the Court of Love, or sing the sublime and sounding praises of God with the Canons of Saint Victor. . . ." Adams, now past sixty, had discovered feeling itself. The Force is that which touches the heart because it measures life and thought outside and above the tensions and anxieties.

The *Education*, good as it is, suffers by comparison, for the skepticism, almost cynicism, of the later chapters, becomes oppressive. In them Adams sets forth his dynamic theory of history: that human thought is subject to physical laws, passing through phases determined by attraction, acceleration, and dissipation. Such is also the substance of *A Letter to American Teachers of History*, which he distributed to fellow historians in 1910. He raises the question whether men can expect much longer to control their affairs, and the issues are perhaps less easily dismissed today than they were fifty years ago. But the *Education* has this power: that in it Adams universalizes the problems of young men about to embark upon careers, by selecting from his own life, under review, the elements that symbolize what he believes all must face into. If he concludes that stoicism alone can carry him through, he leaves readers free to reach their own assumptions.

By now Adams was past seventy, and few of his friends remained on the scene. Richardson had died the year after Marian Adams, King in 1901, Hay four years after King, and most recently Agassiz and La Farge. He himself suffered a stroke in April 1912, but rapidly improved and was able to enjoy the society of the nieces who now meant the most to him, and who accompanied him to Paris in the following year. He lived into the period of the First World War and past his eightieth birthday. It was after his death, March 27, 1918, that general recognition was granted his accomplishments, not only as a historian, but as a fascinating guide into the region of ideas, and a distinguished man of letters.

HISTORY OF THE UNITED STATES

Book I—Chapter 6

AMERICAN IDEALS

Nearly every foreign traveller who visited the United States during these early years, carried away an impression sober if not sad. A thousand miles of desolate and dreary forest, broken here and there by settlements; along the sea-coast a few flourishing towns devoted to commerce; no arts, a provincial literature, a cancerous disease of negro slavery, and differences of political theory fortified within geographical lines,—what could be hoped for such a country except to repeat the story of violence and brutality which the world already knew by heart, until repetition for thousands of years had wearied and sickened mankind? Ages must probably pass before the interior could be thoroughly settled; even Jefferson, usually a sanguine man, talked of a thousand years with acquiescence, and in his first Inaugural Address, at a time when the Mississippi River formed the Western boundary, spoke of the country as having "room enough for our descendants to the hundredth and thousandth generation." No prudent person dared to act on the certainty that when settled, one government could comprehend the whole; and when the day of separation should arrive, and America should have her Prussia, Austria, and Italy, as she already had her England, France, and Spain, what else could follow but a return to the old conditions of local jealousies, wars, and corruption which had made a slaughter-house of Europe?

The mass of Americans were sanguine and self-confident, partly by temperament, but partly also by reason of ignorance; for they knew little of the difficulties which surrounded a complex society. The Duc de Liancourt,[1] like many critics, was struck by this trait. Among other in-

---

[1] François de La Rochefoucauld-Liancourt (1747–1827), philanthropist and politician, wrote *Voyage dans les États-Unis d'Amérique* (1798), translated in 1800.

stances, he met with one in the person of a Pennsylvania miller, Thomas Lea, "a sound American patriot, persuading himself that nothing good is done, and that no one has any brains, except in America; that the wit, the imagination, the genius of Europe are already in decrepitude;" and the duke added: "This error is to be found in almost all Americans,—legislators, administrators, as well as millers, and is less innocent there." In the year 1796 the House of Representatives debated whether to insert in the Reply to the President's Speech a passing remark that the nation was "the freest and most enlightened in the world,"—a nation as yet in swaddling-clothes, which had neither literature, arts, sciences, nor history; nor even enough nationality to be sure that it was a nation. The movement was peculiarly ill-chosen for such a claim, because Europe was on the verge of an outburst of genius. Goethe and Schiller, Mozart and Haydn, Kant and Fichte, Cavendish and Herschel were making way for Walter Scott, Wordsworth, and Shelley, Heine and Balzac, Beethoven and Hegel, Oersted and Cuvier, great physicists, biologists, geologists, chemists, mathematicians, metaphysicians, and historians by the score. Turner was painting his earliest landscapes, and Watt completing his latest steam-engine; Napoleon was taking command of the French armies, and Nelson of the English fleets; investigators, reformers, scholars, and philosophers swarmed, and the influence of enlightenment, even amid universal war, was working with an energy such as the world had never before conceived. The idea that Europe was in her decrepitude proved only ignorance and want of enlightenment, if not of freedom, on the part of Americans, who could only excuse their error by pleading that notwithstanding these objections, in matters which for the moment most concerned themselves Europe was a full century behind America. If they were right in thinking that the next necessity of human progress was to lift the average man upon an intellectual and social level with the most favored, they stood at least three generations nearer than Europe to their common goal. The destinies of the United States were certainly staked, without reserve or escape, on the soundness of this doubtful and even improbable principle, ignoring or overthrowing the institutions of church, aristocracy, family, army, and political intervention, which long experience had shown to be needed for the safety of society. Europe might be right in thinking that without such safeguards society must come to an end; but even Europeans must concede that there was a chance, if no greater than one in a thousand, that America might, at least for a time, succeed. If this stake of temporal and eternal welfare stood on the winning card; if man actually should become more virtuous and enlightened, by mere process of growth, without church or paternal authority, if the average human being could accustom himself to reason with the logical processes of Descartes and Newton!—what then?

Then, no one could deny that the United States would win a stake such as defied mathematics. With all the advantages of science and capital, Europe must be slower than America to reach the common goal.

American society might be both sober and sad, but except for negro slavery it was sound and healthy in every part. Stripped for the hardest work, every muscle firm and elastic, every ounce of brain ready for use, and not a trace of superfluous flesh on his nervous and supple body, the American stood in the world a new order of man. From Maine to Florida, society was in this respect the same, and was so organized as to use its human forces with more economy than could be approached by any society of the world elsewhere. Not only were artificial barriers carefully removed, but every influence that could appeal to ordinary ambition was applied. No brain or appetite active enough to be conscious of stimulants could fail to answer the intense incentive. Few human beings, however sluggish, could long resist the temptation to acquire power; and the elements of power were to be had in America almost for the asking. Reversing the old-world system, the American stimulant increased in energy as it reached the lowest and most ignorant class, dragging and whirling them upward as in the blast of a furnace. The penniless and homeless Scotch or Irish immigrant was caught and consumed by it; for every stroke of the axe and the hoe made him a capitalist, and made gentlemen of his children. Wealth was the strongest agent for moving the mass of mankind; but political power was hardly less tempting to the more intelligent and better-educated swarms of American-born citizens, and the instinct of activity, once created, seemed heritable and permanent in the race.

Compared with this lithe young figure, Europe was actually in decrepitude. Mere class distinctions, the *patois* or dialect of the peasantry, the fixity of residence, the local costumes and habits marking a history that lost itself in the renewal of identical generations, raised from birth barriers which paralyzed half the population. Upon this mass of inert matter rested the Church and the State, holding down activity of thought. Endless wars withdrew many hundred thousand men from production, and changed them into agents of waste; huge debts, the evidence of past wars and bad government, created interests to support the system and fix its burdens on the laboring class; courts, with habits of extravagance that shamed common-sense, helped to consume private economics. All this might have been borne; but behind this stood aristocracies, sucking their nourishment from industry, producing nothing themselves, employing little or no active capital or intelligent labor, but pressing on the energies and ambition of society with the weight of an incubus. Picturesque and entertaining as these social anomalies were, they were better fitted for the theatre or for a museum of historical costumes than for an active workshop preparing to compete with such machinery as America would soon command. From an economical point of view, they were as incongruous as would have been the appearance of a mediæval knight in helmet and armor, with battle-axe and shield, to run the machinery of Arkwright's [2] cotton-mill; but besides their bad economy they also tended to

---

[2] Sir Richard Arkwright (1732–1792) invented the cotton-spinning frame.

prevent the rest of society from gaining a knowledge of its own capacities. In Europe, the conservative habit of mind was fortified behind power. During nearly a century Voltaire himself—the friend of kings, the wit and poet, historian and philosopher of his age—had carried on, in daily terror, in exile and excommunication, a protest against an intellectual despotism contemptible even to its own supporters. Hardly was Voltaire dead, when Priestley,[3] as great a man if not so great a wit, trying to do for England what Voltaire tried to do for France, was mobbed by the people of Birmingham and driven to America. Where Voltaire and Priestley failed, common men could not struggle; the weight of society stifled their thought. In America the balance between conservative and liberal forces was close; but in Europe conservatism held the physical power of government. In Boston a young Buckminster[4] might be checked for a time by his father's prayers or commands in entering the path that led toward freer thought; but youth beckoned him on, and every reward that society could offer was dangled before his eyes. In London or Paris, Rome, Madrid, or Vienna, he must have sacrificed the worldly prospects of his life.

Granting that the American people were about to risk their future on a new experiment, they naturally wished to throw aside all burdens of which they could rid themselves. Believing that in the long run interest, not violence, would rule the world, and that the United States must depend for safety and success on the interests they could create, they were tempted to look upon war and preparations for war as the worst of blunders; for they were sure that every dollar capitalized in industry was a means of overthrowing their enemies more effective than a thousand dollars spent on frigates or standing armies. The success of the American system was, from this point of view, a question of economy. If they could relieve themselves from debts, taxes, armies, and government interference with industry, they must succeed in outstripping Europe in economy of production; and Americans were even then partly aware that if their machine were not so weakened by these economics as to break down in the working, it must of necessity break down every rival. If their theory was sound, when the day of competition should arrive, Europe might choose between American and Chinese institutions, but there would be no middle path; she might become a confederated democracy, or a wreck.

Whether these ideas were sound or weak, they seemed self-evident to those Northern democrats who, like Albert Gallatin,[5] were comparatively free from slave-owning theories, and understood the practical

---

[3] Joseph Priestley (1733–1804), English chemist and discoverer of oxygen, removed to America in 1794, after his house and property were destroyed by a mob which attacked him for his support of the French Revolution.

[4] Joseph Stevens Buckminster (1784–

1812) was a Unitarian clergyman; his library became the foundation of the Boston Athenaeum.

[5] Albert Gallatin (1761–1849), Jefferson's secretary of the treasury, is the subject of one of Adams's best biographies.

forces of society. If Gallatin wished to reduce the interference of government to a minimum, and cut down expenditures to nothing, he aimed not so much at saving money as at using it with the most certain effect. The revolution of 1800 [6] was in his eyes chiefly political, because it was social; but as a revolution of society, he and his friends hoped to make it the most radical that had occurred since the downfall of the Roman empire. Their ideas were not yet cleared by experience, and were confused by many contradictory prejudices, but wanted neither breadth nor shrewdness.

Many apparent inconsistencies grew from this undeveloped form of American thought, and gave rise to great confusion in the different estimates of American character that were made both at home and abroad.

That Americans should not be liked was natural; but that they should not be understood was more significant by far. After the downfall of the French republic they had no right to expect a kind word from Europe, and during the next twenty years they rarely received one. The liberal movement of Europe was cowed, and no one dared express democratic sympathies until the Napoleonic tempest had passed. With this attitude Americans had no right to find fault, for Europe cared less to injure them than to protect herself. Nevertheless, observant readers could not but feel surprised that none of the numerous Europeans who then wrote or spoke about America seemed to study the subject seriously. The ordinary traveller was apt to be little more reflective than a bee or an ant, but some of these critics possessed powers far from ordinary; yet Talleyrand [7] alone showed that had he but seen America a few years later than he did, he might have suggested some sufficient reason for apparent contradictions that perplexed him in the national character. The other travellers—great and small, from the Duc de Liancourt to Basil Hall,[8] a long and suggestive list—were equally perplexed. They agreed in observing the contradictions, but all, including Talleyrand, saw only sordid motives. Talleyrand expressed extreme astonishment at the apathy of Americans in the face of religious sectarians; but he explained it by assuming that the American ardor of the moment was absorbed in money-making. The explanation was evidently insufficient, for the Americans were capable of feeling and showing excitement, even to their great pecuniary injury, as they frequently proved; but in the foreigner's range of observation, love of money was the most conspicuous and most common trait of American character. "There is, perhaps, no civilized country in the world," wrote Félix de Beaujour,[9] soon after 1800, "where there is less generosity in the souls, and in the heads fewer of those illusions

---

[6] That is, the election of Jefferson, a Democratic-Republican, brought an end to Federalist control.

[7] Charles Maurice de Talleyrand-Périgord (1754–1838), distinguished French statesman, visited the United States in 1794–1795.

[8] Basil Hall (1788–1844), British naval officer, wrote *Travels in North America* (1829).

[9] French diplomatist (1765–1836), who wrote *A Survey of the United States to the Beginning of the Nineteenth Century* (1814).

which make the charm or the consolation of life. Man here weighs every-thing, calculates everything, and sacrifices everything to his interest." An Englishman named Fearon,[10] in 1818, expressed the same idea with more distinctness: "In going to America, I would say generally, the emigrant must expect to find, not an economical or cleanly people; not a social or generous people; not a people of enlarged ideas; not a people of liberal opinions, or toward whom you can express your thoughts free as air; not a people friendly to the advocates of liberty in Europe; not a people who understand liberty from investigation and principle; not a people who comprehend the meaning of the words 'honor' and 'generosity.'" Such quotations might be multiplied almost without limit. Rapacity was the accepted explanation of American peculiarities; yet every traveller was troubled by inconsistencies that required explanations of a different kind. "It is not in order to hoard that the Americans are rapacious," observed Liancourt as early as 1796. The extravagance, or what economical Euro-peans thought extravagance, with which American women were allowed and encouraged to spend money, was as notorious in 1790 as a century later; the recklessness with which Americans often risked their money, and the liberality with which they used it, were marked even then, in comparison with the ordinary European habit. Europeans saw such con-tradictions, but made no attempt to reconcile them. No foreigner of that day—neither poet, painter, nor philosopher—could detect in American life anything higher than vulgarity; for it was something beyond the range of their experience, which education and culture had not framed a formula to express. Moore [11] came to Washington, and found there no loftier inspiration than any Federalist rhymester of Dennie's [12] school.

"Take Christians, Mohawks, democrats and all,
From the rude wigwam to the Congress hall,—
From man the savage, whether slaved or free,
To man the civilized, less tame than he:
'T is one dull chaos, one unfertile strife
Betwixt half-polished and half-barbarous life;
Where every ill the ancient world can brew
Is mixed with every grossness of the new;
Where all corrupts, though little can entice,
And nothing's known of luxury but vice."

Moore's two small volumes of Epistles, printed in 1807, contained much more so-called poetry of the same tone,—poetry more polished and less respectable than that of Barlow and Dwight; [13] while, as though to prove that the Old World knew what grossness was, he embalmed in his lines

[10] James Fearon, author of *Sketches of America* (1818).

[11] Thomas Moore (1779–1852), the Irish poet, traveled in America in 1803–1804. The quotation following is from *Epistles, Odes, and Other Poems* (1807).

[12] Joseph Dennie (1768–1812), widely read journalist, essayist, and poet, was a staunch Federalist.

[13] Joel Barlow (1715–1812) and Timothy Dwight (1752–1817) were two of the best known Connecticut Wits.

the slanders which the Scotch libeller Callender [14] invented against Jefferson:—

"The weary statesman for repose hath fled
From halls of council to his negro's shed;
Where, blest, he woos some black Aspasia's grace,
And dreams of freedom in his slave's embrace."

To leave no doubt of his meaning, he explained in a footnote that his allusion was to the President of the United States; and yet even Moore, trifler and butterfly as he was, must have seen, if he would, that between the morals of politics and society in America and those then prevailing in Europe, there was no room for comparison,—there was room only for contrast.

Moore was but an echo of fashionable England in his day. He seldom affected moral sublimity; and had he in his wanderings met a race of embodied angels, he would have sung of them or to them in the slightly erotic notes which were so well received in the society he loved to frequent and flatter. His remarks upon American character betrayed more temper than truth; but even in this respect he expressed only the common feeling of Europeans, which was echoed by the Federalist society of the United States. Englishmen especially indulged in unbounded invective against the sordid character of American society, and in shaping their national policy on this contempt they carried their theory into practice with so much energy as to produce its own refutation. To their astonishment and anger, a day came when the Americans, in defiance of self-interest and in contradiction of all the qualities ascribed to them, insisted on declaring war; and readers of this narrative will be surprised at the cry of incredulity, not unmixed with terror, with which Englishmen started to their feet when they woke from their delusion on seeing what they had been taught to call the meteor flag of England, which had burned terrific at Copenhagen and Trafalgar, suddenly waver and fall on the bloody deck of the "Guerriere." [15] Fearon and Beaujour, with a score of other contemporary critics, could see neither generosity, economy, honor, nor ideas of any kind in the American breast; yet the obstinate repetition of these denials itself betrayed a lurking fear of the social forces whose strength they were candid enough to record. What was it that, as they complained, turned the European peasant into a new man within half an hour after landing at New York? Englishmen were never at a loss to understand the poetry of more prosaic emotions. Neither they nor any of their kindred failed in later times to feel the "large excitement" of the country boy, whose "spirit leaped within him to be gone before him," when the lights of London first flared in the distance; yet

[14] James Thomson Callender (1758–1803) did not receive from the President a coveted appointment as postmaster of Richmond.

[15] The American frigate *Constitution* (Old Ironsides) brought the surrender of the British *Guerrière* in the War of 1812.

none seemed ever to feel the larger excitement of the American immigrant. Among the Englishmen who criticized the United States was one
greater than Moore,—one who thought himself at home only in the stern
beauty of a moral presence. Of all poets, living or dead, Wordsworth felt
most keenly what he called the still, sad music of humanity; yet the highest conception he could create of America was not more poetical than
that of any Cumberland beggar he might have met in his morning walk:—

> "Long-wished-for sight, the Western World appeared;
> And when the ship was moored, I leaped ashore
> Indignantly,—resolved to be a man,
> Who, having o'er the past no power, would live
> No longer in subjection to the past,
> With abject mind—from a tyrannic lord
> Inviting penance, fruitlessly endured.
> So, like a fugitive whose feet have cleared
> Some boundary which his followers may not cross
> In prosecution of their deadly chase,
> Respiring, I looked round. How bright the sun,
> The breeze how soft! Can anything produced
> In the Old World compare, thought I, for power
> And majesty, with this tremendous stream
> Sprung from the desert? And behold a city
> Fresh, youthful, and aspiring! . . .
>   Sooth to say,
> On nearer view, a motley spectacle
> Appeared, of high pretensions—unreproved
> But by the obstreperous voice of higher still;
> Big passions strutting on a petty stage,
> Which a detached spectator may regard
> Not unamused. But ridicule demands
> Quick change of objects; and to laugh alone,
> . . . in the very centre of the crowd
> To keep the secret of a poignant scorn,
>   . . . is least fit
> For the gross spirit of mankind." [16]

Thus Wordsworth, although then at his prime, indulging in what
sounded like a boast that he alone had felt the sense sublime of something
interfused, whose dwelling is the light of setting suns, and the round
ocean, and the living air, and the blue sky, and in the mind of man,—even
he, whose moods the heavy and the weary weight of all this unintelligible world was lightened by his deepest sympathies with nature and the
soul, could do no better, when he stood in the face of American democracy, than "keep the secret of a poignant scorn."

Possibly the view of Wordsworth and Moore, of Weld, Dennie, and

[16] *The Excursion,* Book III: "Despondency," ll. 870–911.

Dickens [17] was right. The American democrat possessed little art of expression, and did not watch his own emotions with a view of uttering them either in prose or verse; he never told more of himself than the world might have assumed without listening to him. Only with diffidence could history attribute to such a class of men a wider range of thought or feeling than they themselves cared to proclaim. Yet the difficulty of denying or even ignoring the wider range was still greater, for no one questioned the force or the scope of an emotion which caused the poorest peasant in Europe to see what was invisible to poet and philosopher,—the dim outline of a mountain-summit across the ocean, rising high above the mist and mud of American democracy. As though to call attention to some such difficulty, European and American critics, while affirming that Americans were a race without illusions or enlarged ideas, declared in the same breath that Jefferson was a visionary whose theories would cause the heavens to fall upon them. Year after year, with endless iteration, in every accent of contempt, rage, and despair, they repeated this charge against Jefferson. Every foreigner and Federalist agreed that he was a man of illusions, dangerous to society and unbounded in power of evil; but if this view of his character was right, the same visionary qualities seemed also to be a national trait, for every one admitted that Jefferson's opinions, in one form or another, were shared by a majority of the American people.

Illustrations might be carried much further, and might be drawn from every social class and from every period in national history. Of all presidents, Abraham Lincoln has been considered the most typical representative of American society, chiefly because his mind, with all its practical qualities, also inclined, in certain directions, to idealism. Lincoln was born in 1809, the moment when American character stood in lowest esteem. Ralph Waldo Emerson, a more distinct idealist, was born in 1803. William Ellery Channing, another idealist, was born in 1780. Men like John Fitch, Oliver Evans, Robert Fulton, Joel Barlow, John Stevens, and Eli Whitney [18] were all classed among visionaries. The whole society of Quakers belonged in the same category. The records of the popular religious sects abounded in examples of idealism and illusion to such an extent that the masses seemed hardly to find comfort or hope in any authority, however old or well established. In religion as in politics, Americans seemed to require a system which gave play to their imagination and their hopes.

---

[17] Isaac Weld wrote his *Travels . . .*, in 1799. Dickens's visit to America in 1842, during which he was lionized, was followed by *American Notes for General Circulation* (1842), and *Martin Chuzzlewit* (1843–1844), portions of which unfavorably recall his impressions of the country.

[18] Channing the elder (d. 1842), Unitarian minister, was a spokesman for transcendentalism. Fitch (1743–1798) and Fulton (1765–1815) invented steamboats; Evans (1755–1819) and Stevens (1749–1838) made practical contributions to steam engines and railroads. Barlow supported principles of democracy in his *Advice to the Privileged Orders* (1792), while residing in France.

Some misunderstanding must always take place when the observer is at cross-purposes with the society he describes. Wordsworth might have convinced himself by a moment's thought that no country could act on the imagination as America acted upon the instincts of the ignorant and poor, without some quality that deserved better treatment than poignant scorn; but perhaps this was only one among innumerable cases in which the unconscious poet breathed an atmosphere which the self-conscious poet could not penetrate. With equal reason he might have taken the opposite view,—that the hard, practical, money-getting American democrat, who had neither generosity nor honor nor imagination, and who inhabited cold shades where fancy sickened and where genius died, was in truth living in a world of dream, and acting a drama more instinct with poetry than all the avatars of the East, walking in gardens of emeralds and rubies, in ambition already ruling the world and guiding Nature with a kinder and wiser hand than had ever yet been felt in human history. From this point his critics never approached him,—they stopped at a stone's throw; and at the moment when they declared that the man's mind had no illusions, they added that he was a knave or a lunatic. Even on his practical and sordid side, the American might easily have been represented as a victim to illusion. If the Englishman had lived as the American speculator did,—in the future,—the hyperbole of enthusiasm would have seemed less monstrous. "Look at my wealth!" cried the American to his foreign visitor. "See these solid mountains of salt and iron, of lead, copper, silver, and gold! See these magnificent cities scattered broadcast to the Pacific! See my cornfields rustling and waving in the summer breeze from ocean to ocean, so far that the sun itself is not high enough to mark where the distant mountains bound my golden seas! Look at this continent of mine, fairest of created worlds, as she lies turning up to the sun's never-failing caress her broad and exuberant breasts, overflowing with milk for her hundred million children! See how she glows with youth, health, and love!" Perhaps it was not altogether unnatural that the foreigner, on being asked to see what needed centuries to produce, should have looked about him with bewilderment and indignation. "Gold! cities! cornfields! continents! Nothing of the sort! I see nothing but tremendous wastes, where sickly men and women are dying of home-sickness or are scalped by savages! mountain-ranges a thousand miles long, with no means of getting to them, and nothing in them when you get there! swamps and forests choked with their own rotten ruins! nor hope of better for a thousand years! Your story is a fraud, and you are a liar and swindler!"

Met in this spirit, the American, half perplexed and half defiant, retaliated by calling his antagonist a fool, and by mimicking his heavy tricks of manner. For himself he cared little, but his dream was his whole existence. The men who denounced him admitted that they left him in his forest-swamp quaking with fever, but clinging in the delirium of death to the illusions of his dazzled brain. No class of men could be required to support their convictions with a steadier faith, or pay more devotedly with their persons for the mistakes of their judgment. Whether imagination or greed led them to describe more than actually existed, they still saw no more than any inventor or discoverer must have seen in order to give him the energy of success. They said to the rich as to the poor, "Come and share our limitless riches! Come and help us bring to light these unimaginable stores of wealth and power!" The poor came, and from them were seldom heard complaints of deception or delusion. Within a moment, by the mere contact of a moral atmosphere, they saw the gold and jewels, the summer cornfields and the glowing continent. The rich for a long time stood aloof,—they were timid and narrow-minded; but this was not all,—between them and the American democrat was a gulf.

The charge that Americans were too fond of money to win the confidence of Europeans was a curious inconsistency; yet this was a common belief. If the American deluded himself and led others to their death by baseless speculations; if he buried those he loved in a gloomy forest where they quaked and died while he persisted in seeing there a splendid, healthy, and well-built city,—no one could deny that he sacrificed wife and child to his greed for gain, that the dollar was his god, and a sordid avarice his demon. Yet had this been the whole truth, no European capitalist would have hesitated to make money out of his grave; for, avarice against avarice, no more sordid or meaner type existed in America than could be shown on every 'Change in Europe. With much more reason Americans might have suspected that in America Englishmen found everywhere a silent influence, which they found nowhere in Europe, and which had nothing to do with avarice or with the dollar, but, on the contrary, seemed likely at any moment to sacrifice the dollar in a cause and for an object so illusory that most Englishmen could not endure to hear it discussed. European travellers who passed through America noticed that everywhere, in the White House at Washington and in log-cabins beyond the Alleghanies, except for a few Federalists, every American, from Jefferson and Gallatin down to the poorest squatter, seemed to nourish an idea that he was doing what he could to overthrow the tyranny which the past had fastened on the human mind. Nothing was easier than to laugh at the ludicrous expressions of this simple-minded conviction, or to cry out against its coarseness, or grow angry with its prejudices; to see its nobler side, to feel the beatings of a heart underneath the sordid surface of a gross humanity, was not so easy. Europeans seemed seldom or never conscious that the sentiment could possess a noble side, but found only matter for complaint in the remark that every American democrat believed himself to be working for the overthrow of tyranny, aristocracy, hereditary privilege, and priesthood, wherever they existed. Even where the American did not openly proclaim this conviction in words, he carried so dense an atmosphere of the sentiment with him in his daily life as to give respectable Europeans an uneasy sense of remoteness.

Of all historical problems, the nature of a national character is the most difficult and the most important. Readers will be troubled, at almost every chapter of the coming narrative, by the want of some formula to explain what share the popular imagination bore in the system pursued by government. The acts of the American people during the administrations of Jefferson and Madison were judged at the time by no other test. According as bystanders believed American character to be hard, sordid, and free from illusion, they were severe and even harsh in judgment. This rule guided the governments of England and France. Federalists in the United States, knowing more of the circumstances, often attributed to the democratic instinct a visionary quality which they regarded as sentimentality, and charged with many bad consequences. If their view was correct, history could occupy itself to no better purpose than in ascertaining the nature and force of the quality which was charged with results so serious; but nothing was more elusive than the spirit of American democracy. Jefferson, the literary representative of the class, spoke chiefly for Virginians, and dreaded so greatly his own reputation as a visionary that he seldom or never uttered his whole thought. Gallatin and Madison were still more cautious. The press in no country could give shape to a mental condition so shadowy. The people themselves, although millions in number, could not have expressed their finer instincts had they tried, and might not have recognized them if expressed by others.

In the early days of colonization, every new settlement represented an idea and proclaimed a mission. Virginia was founded by a great, liberal movement aiming at the spread of English liberty and empire. The Pilgrims of Plymouth, the Puritans of Boston, the Quakers of Pennsylvania, all avowed a moral purpose, and began by making institutions that consciously reflected a moral idea. No such character belonged to the colonization of 1800. From Lake Erie to Florida, in long, unbroken line, pioneers were at work, cutting into the forests with the energy of so many beavers, and with no more express moral purpose than the beavers they drove away. The civilization they carried with them was rarely illumined by an idea; they sought room for no new truth, and aimed neither at creating, like the Puritans, a government of saints, nor, like the Quakers, one of love and peace; they left such experiments behind them, and wrestled only with the hardest problems of frontier life. No wonder that foreign observers, and even the educated, well-to-do Americans of the seacoast, could seldom see anything to admire in the ignorance and brutality of frontiersmen, and should declare that virtue and wisdom no longer guided the United States! What they saw was not encouraging. To a new society, ignorant and semi-barbarous, a mass of demagogues insisted on applying every stimulant that could inflame its worst appetites, while at the same instant taking away every influence that had hitherto helped to restrain its passions. Greed for wealth, lust for power, yearning for the blank void of savage freedom such as Indians and wolves delighted in,— these were the fires that flamed under the caldron of American society, in which, as conservatives believed, the old, well-proven, conservative crust of religion, government, family, and even common respect for age, education, and experience was rapidly melting away, and was indeed already broken into fragments, swept about by the seething mass of scum ever rising in greater quantities to the surface.

Against this Federalist and conservative view of democratic tendencies, democrats protested in a thousand forms, but never in any mode of expression which satisfied them all, or explained their whole character. Probably Jefferson came nearest to the mark, for he represented the hopes of science as well as the prejudices of Virginia; but Jefferson's writings may be searched from beginning to end without revealing the whole measure of the man, far less of the movement. Here and there in his letters a suggestion was thrown out, as though by chance, revealing larger hopes,—as in 1815, at a moment of despondency, he wrote: "I fear from the experience of the last twenty-five years that morals do not of necessity advance hand in hand with the sciences." In 1800, in the flush of triumph, he believed that his task in the world was to establish a democratic republic, with the sciences for an intellectual field, and physical and moral advancement keeping pace with their advance. Without an excessive introduction of more recent ideas, he might be imagined to define democratic progress, in the somewhat affected precision of his French philosophy: "Progress is either physical or intellectual. If we can bring it about that men are on the average an inch taller in the next generation than in this; if they are an inch larger around the chest; if their brain is an ounce or two heavier, and their life a year or two longer,— that is progress. If fifty years hence the average man shall invariably argue from two ascertained premises where he now jumps to a conclusion from a single supposed revelation,—that is progress! I expect it to be made here, under our democratic stimulants, on a great scale, until every man is potentially an athlete in body and an Aristotle in mind." To this doctrine the New Englander [19] replied, "What will you do for moral progress?" Every possible answer to this question opened a chasm. No doubt Jefferson held the faith that men would improve morally with their physical and intellectual growth; but he had no idea of any moral improvement other than that which came by nature. He could not tolerate a priesthood, a state church, or revealed religion. Conservatives, who could tolerate no society without such pillars of order, were, from their point of view, right in answering, "Give us rather the worst despotism of Europe,—there our souls at least may have a chance of salvation!" To their minds vice and virtue were not relative, but fixed terms. The Church was a divine institution. How could a ship hope to reach port when the crew

[19] John Adams (1735–1826) was Jefferson's political foe during his years of public service, but they corresponded genially in later years.

threw overboard sails, spars, and compass, unshipped their rudder, and all the long day thought only of eating and drinking. Nay, even should the new experiment succeed in a worldly sense, what was a man profited if he gained the whole world, and lost his own soul? The Lord God was a jealous God, and visited the sins of the parents upon the children; but what worse sin could be conceived than for a whole nation to join their chief in chanting the strange hymn with which Jefferson, a new false prophet, was deceiving and betraying his people: "It does me no injury for my neighbor to say there are twenty Gods or no God!" [20]

On this ground conservatism took its stand, as it had hitherto done with success in every similar emergency in the world's history, and fixing its eyes on moral standards of its own, refused to deal with the subject as further open to argument. The two parties stood facing opposite ways, and could see no common ground of contact.

Yet even then one part of the American social system was proving itself to be rich in results. The average American was more intelligent than the average European, and was becoming every year still more active-minded as the new movement of society caught him up and swept him through a life of more varied experiences. On all sides the national mind responded to its stimulants. Deficient as the American was in the machinery of higher instruction; remote, poor; unable by any exertion to acquire the training, the capital, or even the elementary textbooks he needed for a fair development of his natural powers,—his native energy and ambition already responded to the spur applied to them. Some of his triumphs were famous throughout the world; for Benjamin Franklin had raised high the reputation of American printers, and the actual President of the United States, who signed with Franklin the treaty of peace with Great Britain, was the son of a small farmer, and had himself kept a school in his youth. In both these cases social recognition followed success; but the later triumphs of the American mind were becoming more and more popular. John Fitch was not only one of the poorest, but one of the least-educated Yankees who ever made a name; he could never spell with tolerable correctness, and his life ended as it began,—in the lowest social obscurity. Eli Whitney was better educated than Fitch, but had neither wealth, social influence, nor patron to back his ingenuity. In the year 1800 Eli Terry, another Connecticut Yankee of the same class, took into his employ two young men to help him make wooden clocks, and this was the capital on which the greatest clock-manufactory in the world began its operations. In 1797 Asa Whittemore, a Massachusetts Yankee, invented a machine to make cards for carding wool, which "operated as if it had a soul, and became the foundation for a hundred subsequent patents. In 1790 Jacob Perkins, of Newburyport, invented a machine capable of cutting and turning out two hundred thousand nails a day; and then invented a process for transferring engraving from a very small steel cylinder to copper, which revolutionized cotton-printing. The

[20] From *Notes on the State of Virginia* (1784–85), Query XVII.

British traveller Weld, passing through Wilmington, stopped, as Liancourt had done before him, to see the great flour-mills on the Brandywine. "The improvements," he said, "which have been made in the machinery of the flour-mills in America are very great. The chief of these consist in a new application of the screw, and the introduction of what are called elevators, the idea of which was evidently borrowed from the chain-pump." This was the invention of Oliver Evans, a native of Delaware, whose parents were in very humble life, but who was himself, in spite of every disadvantage, an inventive genius of the first order. Robert Fulton, who in 1800 was in Paris with Joel Barlow, sprang from the same source in Pennsylvania. John Stevens, a native of New York, belonged to a more favored class, but followed the same impulses. All these men were the outcome of typical American society, and all their inventions transmuted the democratic instinct into a practical and tangible shape. Who would undertake to say that there was a limit to the fecundity of this teeming source? Who that saw only the narrow, practical, money-getting nature of these devices could venture to assert that as they wrought their end and raised the standard of millions, they would not also raise the creative power of those millions to a higher plane? If the priests and barons who set their names to Magna Charta had been told that in a few centuries every swine-herd and cobbler's apprentice would write and read with an ease such as few kings could then command, and reason with better logic than any university could then practise, the priest and baron would have been more incredulous than any man who was told in 1800 that within another five centuries the ploughboy would go a-field whistling a sonata of Beethoven, and figure out in quaternions the relation of his furrows. The American democrat knew so little of art that among his popular illusions he could not then nourish artistic ambition; but leaders like Jefferson, Gallatin, and Barlow might without extravagance count upon a coming time when diffused ease and education should bring the masses into familiar contact with higher forms of human achievement, and their vast creative power, turned toward a nobler culture, might rise to the level of that democratic genius which found expression in the Parthenon; might revel in the delights of a new Buonarotti [21] and a richer Titian; might create for five hundred million people the America of thought and art which alone could satisfy their omnivorous ambition.

Whether the illusions, so often affirmed and so often denied to the American people, took such forms or not, there were in effect the problems that lay before American society: Could it transmute its social power into the higher forms of thought? Could it provide for the moral and intellectual needs of mankind? Could it take permanent political shape? Could it give new life to religion and art? Could it create and maintain in the mass of mankind those habits of mind which had hitherto belonged to men of science alone? Could it physically develop the convolutions of the human brain? Could it produce, or was it compatible

[21] Michelangelo.

with, the differentiation of a higher variety of the human race? Nothing less than this was necessary for its complete success.

1884

Book IX—Chapter 106

AMERICAN CHARACTER

Until 1815 nothing in the future of the American Union was regarded as settled. As late as January, 1815, division into several nationalities was still thought to be possible. Such a destiny, repeating the usual experience of history, was not necessarily more unfortunate than the career of a single nationality wholly American; for if the effects of divided nationality were certain to be unhappy, those of a single society with equal certainty defied experience or sound speculation. One uniform and harmonious system appealed to the imagination as a triumph of human progress, offering prospects of peace and ease, contentment and philanthropy, such as the world had not seen; but it invited dangers, formidable because unusual or altogether unknown. The corruption of such a system might prove to be proportionate with its dimensions, and uniformity might lead to evils as serious as were commonly ascribed to diversity.

The laws of human progress were matter not for dogmatic faith, but for study; and although society instinctively regarded small States, with their clashing interests and incessant wars, as the chief obstacle to improvement, such progress as the world knew had been coupled with those drawbacks. The few examples offered by history of great political societies, relieved from external competition or rivalry, were not commonly thought encouraging. War had been the severest test of political and social character, laying bare whatever was feeble, and calling out whatever was strong; and the effect of removing such a test was an untried problem.

In 1815 for the first time Americans ceased to doubt the path they were about to follow. Not only was the unity of their nation established, but its probable divergence from older societies was also well defined. Already in 1817 the difference between Europe and America was decided. In politics the distinction was more evident than in social, religious, literary, or scientific directions; and the result was singular. For a time the aggressions of England and France forced the United States into a path that seemed to lead toward European methods of government; but the popular resistance, or inertia, was so great that the most popular party leaders failed to overcome it, and no sooner did foreign dangers disappear than the system began to revert to American practices; the national government tried to lay aside its assumed powers. When Madison vetoed the bill for internal improvements he could have had no other motive than that of restoring to the government, as far as possible, its original American character.

The result was not easy to understand in theory or to make efficient in practice; but while the drift of public opinion, and still more of practical necessity, drew the government slowly toward the European standard of true political sovereignty, nothing showed that the compromise, which must probably serve the public purpose, was to be European in form or feeling. As far as politics supplied a test, the national character had already diverged from any foreign type. Opinions might differ whether the political movement was progressive or retrograde, but in any case the American, in his political character, was a new variety of man.

The social movement was also decided. The war gave a severe shock to the Anglican sympathies of society, and peace seemed to widen the breach between European and American tastes. Interest in Europe languished after Napoleon's overthrow.[22] France ceased to affect American opinion. England became an object of less alarm. Peace produced in the United States a social and economical revolution which greatly curtailed the influence of New England, and with it the social authority of Great Britain. The invention of the steamboat counterbalanced ocean commerce. The South and West gave to society a character more aggressively American than had been known before. That Europe, within certain limits, might tend toward American ideas was possible, but that America should under any circumstances follow the experiences of European development might thenceforward be reckoned as improbable. American character was formed, if not fixed.

The scientific interest of American history centred in national character, and in the workings of a society destined to become vast, in which individuals were important chiefly as types. Although this kind of interest was different from that of European history, it was at least as important to the world. Should history ever become a true science, it must expect to establish its laws, not from the complicated story of rival European nationalities, but from the economical evolution of a great democracy. North America was the most favorable field on the globe for the spread of a society so large, uniform, and isolated as to answer the purposes of science. There a single homogeneous society could easily attain proportions of three or four hundred million persons, under conditions of undisturbed growth.

In Europe or Asia, except perhaps in China, undisturbed social evolution had been unknown. Without disturbance, evolution seemed to cease. Wherever disturbance occurred, permanence was impossible. Every people in turn adapted itself to the law of necessity. Such a system as that of the United States could hardly have existed for half a century in Europe except under the protection of another power. In the fierce struggle characteristic of European society, systems were permanent in nothing except in the general law, that, whatever other character they might possess, they must always be chiefly military.

The want of permanence was not the only or the most confusing ob-

---

[22] At the Battle of Waterloo, June 18, 1815.

stacle to the treatment of European history as a science. The intensity of the struggle gave prominence to the individual, until the hero seemed all, society nothing; and what was worse for science, the men were far more interesting than the societies. In the dramatic view of history, the hero deserved more to be studied than the community to which he belonged; in truth, he was the society, which existed only to produce him and to perish with him. Against such a view historians were among the last to protest, and protested but faintly when they did so at all. They felt as strongly as their audiences that the highest achievements were alone worth remembering either in history or in art, and that a reiteration of commonplaces was commonplace. With all the advantages of European movement and color, few historians succeeded in enlivening or dignifying the lack of motive, intelligence, and morality, the helplessness characteristic of many long periods in the face of crushing problems, and the futility of human efforts to escape from difficulties religious, political, and social. In a period extending over four or five thousand years, more or less capable of historical treatment, historians were content to illustrate here and there the most dramatic moments of the most striking communities. The hero was their favorite. War was the chief field of heroic action, and even the history of England was chiefly the story of war.

The history of the United States promised to be free from such disturbances. War counted for little, the hero for less; on the people alone the eye could permanently rest. The steady growth of a vast population without the social distinctions that confused other histories,—without kings, nobles, or armies; without church, traditions, and prejudices,— seemed a subject for the man of science rather than for dramatists or poets. To scientific treatment only one great obstacle existed. Americans, like Europeans, were not disposed to make of their history a mechanical evolution. They felt that they even more than other nations needed the heroic element, because they breathed an atmosphere of peace and industry where heroism could seldom be displayed; and in unconscious protest against their own social conditions they adorned with imaginary qualities scores of supposed leaders, whose only merit was their faculty of reflecting a popular trait. Instinctively they clung to ancient history as though conscious that of all misfortunes that could befall the national character, the greatest would be the loss of the established ideals which alone ennobled human weakness. Without heroes, the national character of the United States had few charms of imagination even to Americans.

Historians and readers maintained Old-World standards. No historian cared to hasten the coming of an epoch when man should study his own history in the same spirit and by the same methods with which he studied the formation of a crystal. Yet history had its scientific as well as its human side, and in American history the scientific interest was greater than the human. Elsewhere the student could study under better conditions the evolution of the individual, but nowhere could he study so well the evolution of a race. The interest of such a subject exceeded that of any other branch of science, for it brought mankind within sight of its own end.

Travellers in Switzerland who stepped across the Rhine where it flowed from its glacier could follow its course among mediæval towns and feudal ruins, until it became a highway for modern industry, and at last arrived at a permanent equilibrium in the ocean. American history followed the same course. With prehistoric glaciers and mediæval feudalism the story had little to do; but from the moment it came within sight of the ocean it acquired interest almost painful. A child could find his way in a river-valley, and a hoy could float on the waters of Holland; but science alone could sound the depths of the ocean, measure its currents, foretell its storms, or fix its relations to the system of Nature. In a democratic ocean science could see something ultimate. Man could go no further. The atom might move, but the general equilibrium could not change.

Whether the scientific or the heroic view were taken, in either case the starting-point was the same, and the chief object of interest was to define national character. Whether the figures of history were treated as heroes or as types, they must be taken to represent the people. American types were especially worth study if they were to represent the greatest democratic evolution the world could know. Readers might judge for themselves what share the individual possessed in creating or shaping the nation; but whether it was small or great, the nation could be understood only by studying the individual. For that reason, in the story of Jefferson and Madison individuals retained their old interest as types of character, if not as sources of power.

In the American character antipathy to war ranked first among political traits. The majority of Americans regarded war in a peculiar light, the consequence of comparative security. No European nation could have conducted a war, as the people of America conducted the War of 1812. The possibility of doing so without destruction explained the existence of the national trait, and assured its continuance. In politics, the divergence of America from Europe perpetuated itself in the popular instinct for peaceable methods. The Union took shape originally on the general lines that divided the civil from the military elements of the British constitution. The party of Jefferson and Gallatin was founded on dislike of every function of government necessary in a military system. Although Jefferson carried his pacific theories to an extreme, and brought about a military reaction, the reactionary movement was neither universal, violent, nor lasting; and society showed no sign of changing its convictions. With greater strength the country might acquire greater familiarity with warlike methods, but in the same degree was less likely to suffer any general change of habits. Nothing but prolonged intestine contests could convert the population of an entire continent into a race of warriors.

A people whose chief trait was antipathy to war, and to any system organized with military energy, could scarcely develop great results in national administration; yet the Americans prided themselves chiefly on their political capacity. Even the war did not undeceive them, although the incapacity brought into evidence by the war was undisputed, and was most remarkable among the communities which believed themselves to be most gifted with political sagacity. Virginia and Massachusetts by turns admitted failure in dealing with issues so simple that the newest societies, like Tennessee and Ohio, understood them by instinct. That incapacity in national politics should appear as a leading trait in American character was unexpected by Americans, but might naturally result from their conditions. The better test of American character was not political but social, and was to be found not in the government but in the people.

The sixteen years of Jefferson's and Madison's rule furnished international tests of popular intelligence upon which Americans could depend. The ocean was the only open field for competition among nations. Americans enjoyed there no natural or artificial advantages over Englishmen, Frenchmen, or Spaniards; indeed, all these countries possessed navies, resources, and experience greater than were to be found in the United States. Yet the Americans developed, in the course of twenty years, a surprising degree of skill in naval affairs. The evidence of their success was to be found nowhere so complete as in the avowals of Englishmen who knew best the history of naval progress. The American invention of the fast-sailing schooner or clipper was the more remarkable because, of all American inventions, this alone sprang from direct competition with Europe. During ten centuries of struggle the nations of Europe had labored to obtain superiority over each other in ship-construction, yet Americans instantly made improvements which gave them superiority, and which Europeans were unable immediately to imitate even after seeing them. Not only were American vessels better in model, faster in sailing, easier and quicker in handling, and more economical in working than the European, but they were also better equipped. The English complained as a grievance that the Americans adopted new and unwarranted devices in naval warfare; that their vessels were heavier and better constructed, and their missiles of unusual shape and improper use. The Americans resorted to expedients that had not been tried before, and excited a mixture of irritation and respect in the English service, until Yankee smartness became a national misdemeanor.

The English admitted themselves to be slow to change their habits, but the French were both quick and scientific; yet Americans did on the ocean what the French, under stronger inducements, failed to do. The French privateer preyed upon British commerce for twenty years without seriously injuring it; but no sooner did the American privateer sail from French ports, than the rates of insurance doubled in London, and an outcry for protection arose among English shippers which the Admiralty could not calm. The British newspapers were filled with assertions that the American cruiser was the superior of any vessel of its class, and threatened to overthrow England's supremacy on the ocean.

Another test of relative intelligence was furnished by the battles at sea. Instantly after the loss of the "Guerriere" the English discovered and complained that American gunnery was superior to their own. They explained their inferiority by the length of time that had elapsed since their navy had found on the ocean an enemy to fight. Every vestige of hostile fleets had been swept away, until, after the battle of Trafalgar, British frigates ceased practice with their guns.[23] Doubtless the British navy had become somewhat careless in the absence of a dangerous enemy, but Englishmen were themselves aware that some other cause must have affected their losses. Nothing showed that Nelson's line-of-battle ships, frigates, or sloops were as a rule better fought than the "Macedonian" and "Java," the "Avon" and "Reindeer."[24] Sir Howard Douglas, the chief authority on the subject, attempted in vain to explain British reverses by the deterioration of British gunnery. His analysis showed only that American gunnery was extraordinarily good. Of all vessels, the sloop-of-war,—on account of its smallness, its quick motion, and its more accurate armament of thirty-two-pound carronades,—offered the best test of relative gunnery, and Sir Howard Douglas in commenting upon the destruction of the "Peacock" and "Avon" could only say,—

"In these two actions it is clear that the fire of the British vessels was thrown too high, and that the ordnance of their opponents were expressly and carefully aimed at and took effect chiefly in the hull."[25]

The battle of the "Hornet" and "Penguin" as well as those of the "Reindeer" and "Avon," showed that the excellence of American gunnery continued till the close of the war. Whether at point-blank range or at long-distance practice, the Americans used guns as they had never been used at sea before.

None of the reports of former British victories showed that the British fire had been more destructive at any previous time than in 1812, and no report of any commander since the British navy existed showed so much damage inflicted on an opponent in so short a time as was proved to have been inflicted on themselves by the reports of British commanders in the American war. The strongest proof of American superiority was given by the best British officers, like Broke, who strained every nerve to maintain an equality with American gunnery. So instantaneous and energetic was the effort that, according to the British historian of the war, "a British forty-six-gun frigate of 1813 was half as effective again as a British forty-six-gun frigate of 1812;" and, as he justly said, "the slaughtered crews and the shattered hulks" of the captured British ships proved that

[23] Nelson's victory occurred on October 21, 1805.

[24] These were British frigates defeated by American, in the War of 1812.

[25] From *Treatise on Naval Gunnery* (1820), a standard textbook.

no want of their old fighting qualities accounted for their repeated and almost habitual mortifications.[26] Unwilling as the English were to admit the superior skill of Americans on the ocean, they did not hesitate to admit it, in certain respects, on land. The American rifle in American hands was affirmed to have no equal in the world. This admission could scarcely be withheld after the lists of killed and wounded which followed almost every battle; but the admission served to check a wider inquiry. In truth, the rifle played but a small part in the war. Winchester's men at the river Raisin may have owed their over-confidence, as the British Forty-first owed its losses, to that weapon, and at New Orleans five or six hundred of Coffee's men, who were out of range, were armed with the rifle; but the surprising losses of the British were commonly due to artillery and musketry fire. At New Orleans the artillery was chiefly engaged. The artillery battle of January 1, according to British accounts, amply proved the superiority of American gunnery on that occasion, which was probably the fairest test during the war. The battle of January 8 was also chiefly an artillery battle; the main British column never arrived within fair musket range; Pakenham was killed by a grapeshot, and the main column of his troops halted more than one hundred yards from the parapet.[27]

The best test of British and American military qualities, both for men and weapons, was Scott's battle of Chippawa.[28] Nothing intervened to throw a doubt over the fairness of the trial. Two parallel lines of regular soldiers, practically equal in numbers, armed with similar weapons, moved in close order toward each other, across a wide open plain, without cover or advantage of position, stopping at intervals to load and fire, until one line broke and retired. At the same time two three-gun batteries, the British being the heavier, maintained a steady fire from positions opposite each other. According to the reports, the two infantry lines in the centre never came nearer than eighty yards. Major-General Riall reported that then, owing to severe losses, his troops broke and could not be rallied. Comparison of the official reports showed that the British lost in killed and wounded four hundred and sixty-nine men; the Americans, two hundred and ninety-six. Some doubts always affect the returns of wounded, because the severity of the wound cannot be known; but dead men tell their own tale. Riall reported one hundred and forty-eight killed; Scott reported sixty-one. The severity of the losses showed that the battle was sharply contested, and proved the personal bravery of both armies. Marksmanship decided the result, and the returns proved that the American fire was superior to that of the British in the proportion of more than fifty per cent if estimated by the entire loss, and of two hundred and forty-two to one hundred if estimated by the deaths alone. The conclusion seemed incredible, but it was supported by the results

[26] Adams here quotes from William James, *Naval Occurrences* (1817).

[27] Winchester was defeated in Michigan, Jan. 22, 1813. Col. John Coffee commanded troops at the Battle of New Orleans, Jan. 8, 1815, in which the British commander Pakenham was killed.

[28] Near Fort Erie, Gen. Winfield Scott defeated the British under Riall, July 5, 1814.

of the naval battles. The Americans showed superiority amounting in some cases to twice the efficiency of their enemies in the use of weapons. The best French critic of the naval war, Jurien de la Gravière, said: "An enormous superiority in the rapidity of precision of their fire can alone explain the difference in the losses sustained by the combatants." So far from denying this conclusion the British press constantly alleged it, and the British officers complained of it. The discovery caused great surprise, and in both British services much attention was at once directed to improvement in artillery and musketry. Nothing could exceed the frankness with which Englishmen avowed their inferiority. According to Sir Francis Head, "gunnery was in naval warfare in the extraordinary state of ignorance we have just described, when our lean children, the American people, taught us, rod in hand, our first lesson in the art." The English textbook on Naval Gunnery, written by Major-General Sir Howard Douglas immediately after the peace, devoted more attention to the short American war than to all the battles of Napoleon, and began by admitting that Great Britain had "entered with too great confidence on war with a marine much more expert than that of any of our European enemies." The admission appeared "objectionable" even to the author; but he did not add, what was equally true, that it applied as well to the land as to the sea service.

No one questioned the bravery of the British forces, or the ease with which they often routed larger bodies of militia; but the losses they inflicted were rarely as great as those they suffered. Even at Bladensburg, where they met little resistance, their loss was several times greater than that of the Americans. At Plattsburg, where the intelligence and quickness of Macdonough and his men alone won the victory, his ships were in effect stationary batteries, and enjoyed the same superiority in gunnery. "The 'Saratoga,' " said his official report, "had fifty-five round-shot in her hull; the 'Confiance,' one hundred and five. The enemy's shot passed principally just over our heads, as there were not twenty whole hammocks in the nettings at the close of the action."

The greater skill of the Americans was not due to special training, for the British service was better trained in gunnery, as in everything else, than the motley armies and fleets that fought at New Orleans and on the Lakes. Critics constantly said that every American had learned from his childhood the use of the rifle, but he certainly had not learned to use the cannon in shooting birds or hunting deer, and he knew less than the Englishman about the handling of artillery and muskets. As if to add unnecessary evidence, the battle of Chrystler's Farm proved only too well that this American efficiency was not confined to citizens of the United States.[29]

Another significant result of the war was the sudden development of scientific engineering in the United States. This branch of the military service owed its efficiency and almost its existence to the military school at West Point, established in 1802. The school was at first much neglected by the government. The number of graduates before the year 1812 was very small; but at the outbreak of the war the corps of engineers was already efficient. Its chief was Colonel Joseph Gardner Swift, of Massachusetts, the first graduate of the academy: Colonel Swift planned the defences of New York harbor. The lieutenant-colonel in 1812 was Walker Keith Armistead, of Virginia,—the third graduate, who planned the defences of Norfolk. Major William McRee, of North Carolina, became chief engineer to General Brown, and constructed the fortifications at Fort Erie, which cost the British General Gordon Drummond the loss of half his army, besides the mortification of defeat. Captain Eleazer Derby Wood, of New York, constructed Fort Meigs, which enabled Harrison to defeat the attack of Proctor in May, 1813. Captain Joseph Gilbert Totten, of New York, was chief engineer to General Izard at Plattsburg, where he directed the fortifications that stopped the advance of Prevost's great army. None of the works constructed by a graduate of West Point was captured by the enemy; and had an engineer been employed at Washington by Armstrong and Winder, the city would have been easily saved.[30]

Perhaps without exaggeration the West Point Academy might be said to have decided, next to the navy, the result of the war. The works at New Orleans were simple in character, and as far as they were due to engineering skill were directed by Major Latour, a Frenchman; but the war was already ended when the battle of New Orleans was fought. During the critical campaign of 1814, the West Point engineers doubled the capacity of the little American army for resistance, and introduced a new and scientific character into American life.

In the application of science the steamboat was the most striking success; but Fulton's invention, however useful, was neither the most original nor the most ingenious of American efforts, nor did it offer the best example of popular characteristics. Perhaps Fulton's torpedo and Stevens's screw-propeller showed more originality than was proved by the "Clermont." The fast-sailing schooner with its pivot-gun—an invention that grew out of the common stock of nautical intelligence—best illustrated the character of the people.

That the individual should rise to a higher order either of intelligence or morality than had existed in former ages was not to be expected, for the United States offered less field for the development of individuality than had been offered by older and smaller societies. The chief function of the American Union was to raise the average standard of popular intelligence and well-being, and at the close of the War of 1812 the superior average intelligence of Americans was so far admitted that Yankee acuteness, or smartness, became a national reproach; but much doubt remained

[30] John Armstrong (1758–1843) was Madison's secretary of war.

whether the intelligence belonged to a high order, or proved a high morality. From the earliest ages, shrewdness was associated with unscrupulousness; and Americans were freely charged with wanting honesty. The charge could neither be proved nor disproved. American morality was such as suited a people so endowed, and was high when compared with the morality of many older societies; but, like American intelligence, it discouraged excess. Probably the political morality shown by the government and by public men during the first sixteen years of the century offered a fair gauge of social morality. Like the character of the popular inventions, the character of the morals corresponded to the wants of a growing democratic society; but time alone could decide whether it would result in a high or a low national ideal.

Finer analysis showed other signs of divergence from ordinary standards. If Englishmen took pride in one trait more than in another, it was in the steady uniformity of their progress. The innovating and revolutionary quality of the French mind irritated them. America showed an un-English rapidity in movement. In politics, the American people between 1787 and 1817 accepted greater changes than had been known in England since 1688. In religion, the Unitarian movement of Boston and Harvard College would never have been possible in England, where the defection of Oxford or Cambridge, and the best educated society in the United Kingdom, would have shaken Church and State to their foundations. In literature the American school was chiefly remarkable for the rapidity with which it matured. The first book of Irving was a successful burlesque of his own ancestral history; the first poem of Bryant sang of the earth only as a universal tomb; the first preaching of Channing assumed to overthrow the Trinity; and the first paintings of Allston aspired to recover the ideal perfection of Raphael and Titian. In all these directions the American mind showed tendencies that surprised Englishmen more than they struck Americans. Allston defended himself from the criticism of friends who made complaint of his return to America.[31] He found there, as he maintained, not only a growing taste for art, but "a quicker appreciation" of artistic effort than in any European land. If the highest intelligence of American society were to move with such rapidity, the time could not be far distant when it would pass into regions which England never liked to contemplate.

Another intellectual trait, as has been already noticed, was the disposition to relax severity. Between the theology of Jonathan Edwards and that of William Ellery Channing was an enormous gap, not only in doctrines but also in methods. Whatever might be thought of the conclusions reached by Edwards and Hopkins,[32] the force of their reasoning commanded respect. Not often had a more strenuous effort than theirs

---

[31] Washington Allston (1779-1843) was the leading American painter of his day. After study abroad, he returned home in 1809.

[32] Samuel Hopkins (1721-1803) was a pupil and follower of Edwards.

been made to ascertain God's will, and to follow it without regard to weaknesses of the flesh. The idea that the nature of God's attributes was to be preached only as subordinate to the improvement of man, agreed little with the spirit of their religion. The Unitarian and Universalist movements marked the beginning of an epoch when ethical and humanitarian ideas took the place of metaphysics, and even New England turned from contemplating the omnipotence of the Deity in order to praise the perfections of his creatures.

The spread of great popular sects like the Universalists and Campbellites, founded on assumptions such as no orthodox theology could tolerate, showed a growing tendency to relaxation of thought in that direction. The struggle for existence was already mitigated, and the first effect of the change was seen in the increasing cheerfulness of religion. Only when men found their actual world almost a heaven, could they lose overpowering anxiety about the world to come. Life had taken a softer aspect, and as a consequence God was no longer terrible. Even the wicked became less mischievous in an atmosphere where virtue was easier than vice. Punishments seemed mild in a society where every offender could cast off his past, and create a new career. For the first time in history, great bodies of men turned away from their old religion, giving no better reason than that it required them to believe in a cruel Deity, and rejected necessary conclusions of theology because they were inconsistent with human self-esteem.

The same optimism marked the political movement. Society was weary of strife, and settled gladly into a political system which left every disputed point undetermined. The public seemed obstinate only in believing that all was for the best, as far as the United States were concerned, in the affairs of mankind. The contrast was great between this temper of mind and that in which the Constitution had been framed; but it was no greater than the contrast in the religious opinions of the two periods, while the same reaction against severity marked the new literature. The rapid accumulation of wealth and increase in physical comfort told the same story from the standpoint of economy. On every side society showed that ease was for a time to take the place of severity, and enjoyment was to have its full share in the future national existence.

The traits of intelligence, rapidity, and mildness seemed fixed in the national character as early as 1817, and were likely to become more marked as time should pass. A vast amount of conservatism still lingered among the people; but the future spirit of society could hardly fail to be intelligent, rapid in movement, and mild in method. Only in the distant future could serious change occur, and even then no return to European characteristics seemed likely. The American continent was happier in its conditions and easier in its resources than the regions of Europe and Asia, where Nature revelled in diversity and conflict. If at any time American character should change, it might as probably become sluggish as revert to the violence and extravagances of Old-World development. The inertia of several hundred million people, all formed in a similar social mould, was as likely to stifle energy as to stimulate evolution.

With the establishment of these conclusions, a new episode in American history began in 1815. New subjects demanded new treatment, no longer dramatic but steadily tending to becoming scientific. The traits of American character were fixed; the rate of physical and economical growth was established; and history, certain that at a given distance of time the Union would contain so many millions of people, with wealth valued at so many millions of dollars, became thenceforward chiefly concerned to know what kind of people these millions were to be. They were intelligent, but what paths would their intelligence select? They were quick, but what solution of insoluble problems would quickness hurry? They were scientific, and what control would their science exercise over their destiny? They were mild, but what corruptions would their relaxations bring? They were peaceful, but by what machinery were their corruptions to be purged? What interests were to vivify a society so vast and uniform? What ideals were to ennoble it? What object, besides physical content, must a democratic continent aspire to attain? For the treatment of such questions history required another century of experience.

MONT-SAINT-MICHEL AND CHARTRES

To give a clear idea in brief space of the philosophical position of the schoolmen discussed in this chapter is made difficult because the subtleties in their arguments were never-ending, and often their definitions shade, or merge, or alter in such a way as to make classifications into "schools" of thought virtually impossible. But for readers of Adams's presentation of Abélard, perhaps the following analysis will not be an oversimplification.

The scholastic philosophers were concerned with the problem of the nature of true reality, and approached it through a study of Greek thought: is the general idea (the genus) or the particular object (the species) the more truly real? The two main tendencies of thought came to be known as Nominalism and Realism. Abélard's teacher Roscellinus (d. *c.* 1125) was a Nominalist, that is, he asserted that genera and species are only the names of things, mere words; and he denied any reality to the *parts* of a whole, since in essence, he said, the whole is indivisible: there is no redness, there is only a red fox or red barn. This doctrine, which makes universality merely subjective, if carried far enough, leads to pure materialism, to the doctrine that phenomena make up the sum of existence, fortuitously arranged, and constitute the universe. When applied to the theological mysteries of the Trinity, it forced Roscellinus to argue either that the Persons are one (in which case the Father and the Holy Ghost are incarnate with the Son), or that there are three Gods.

This most heretical position was countered by the Realists with a point of view which became established as the orthodox philosophical creed. Realists, like William of Champeaux (also a pupil of Roscellinus), maintained that only universals (genera) are substantially real. Yet even this position must be held within limits, for in its most uncompromising form it reduces individuals to accidents of one identical substance, and leads directly to the pantheism of Benedict Spinoza (1632–1677), who held that God is the one substance, of which man and nature are but manifestations.

Abélard took the mean position, customarily designated Conceptualism, which holds that universals have a real existence (Realism), but only in the mind (Nominalism); that is, the mind can conceive and distinguish a "chair" from other objects, but "chair" at the same time is purely abstract or conceptual. Roscellinus came to see the subversiveness of his logic and modified it. William later modified his own position when he saw the implications of it.

The difficulty, as Adams points out, was that Abélard tried to storm the "mysteries" of the Trinity and the Incarnation by the force of dialectics. For this unorthodoxy, Bernard of Clairvaux (1091–1152), the recognized guardian of sound doctrine, called him to account. It remained for the next century, in the persons of Albertus Magnus (1193–1280) and his still greater pupil Thomas Aquinas (1227–1274) to detach the mysteries from the sphere of rational theology.

XIV. Abélard

> Super cuncta, subter cuncta,
> Extra cuncta, intra cuncta,
> Intra cuncta nec inclusus,
> Extra cuncta nec exclusus,
> Super cuncta nec elatus,
> Subter cuncta nec substratus,
> Super totus, praesidendo,
> Subter totus, sustinendo,
> Extra totus, complectendo,
> Intra totus est, implendo.

According to Hildebert, Bishop of Le Mans and Archbishop of Tours, these verses describe God. Hildebert was the first poet of his time; no small merit, since he was contemporary with the "Chanson de Roland" and the first crusade; he was also a strong man, since he was able, as Bishop of Le Mans, to gain great credit by maintaining himself against William the Norman and Fulk of Anjou; and finally he was a prelate of high authority. He lived between 1055 and 1133. Supposing his verses to have been written in middle life, toward the year 1100, they may be taken to represent the accepted doctrine of the Church at the time of the first crusade. They were little more than a versified form of the Latin of Saint Gregory the Great who wrote five hundred years before: "Ipse manet intra omnia, ipse extra omnia, ipse supra omnia, ipse infra omnia; et superior est per potentiam et inferior per sustentationem; exterior per magnitudinem et interior per subtilitatem; sursum regens, deorsum continens, extra circumdans, interius penetrans; nec alia parte superior, alia inferior, aut alia ex parte exterior atque ex alia manet interior, sed unus idemque totus ubique." According to Saint Gregory, in the sixth century, God was "one and the same and wholly everywhere"; "immanent within everything, without everything, above everything, below everything, *sursum regens, deorsum continens"*; while according to Archbishop Hildebert in the eleventh century: "God is over all things, under all things; outside all, inside all; within but not enclosed; without but not excluded; above but not raised up; below but not depressed; wholly above, presiding; wholly beneath, sustaining; wholly without, embracing; wholly within, filling." Finally, according to Benedict Spinoza, another five hundred years later still: "God is a being, absolutely infinite; that is to say, a substance made up of an infinity of attributes, each one of which expresses an eternal and infinite essence."

Spinoza was the great pantheist, whose name is still a terror to the orthodox, and whose philosophy is—very properly—a horror to the Church; and yet Spinoza never wrote a line that, to the unguided student, sounds more Spinozist than the words of Saint Gregory and Archbishop Hildebert. If God is everywhere; wholly; presiding, sustaining, embracing and filling, "sursum regens, deorsum continens," He is the only possible energy, and leaves no place for human will to act. A force which is "one and the same and wholly everywhere" is more Spinozist than Spinoza, and is likely to be mistaken for frank pantheism by the large majority of religious minds who must try to understand it without a theological course in a Jesuit college. In the year 1100 Jesuit colleges did not exist, and even the great Dominican and Franciscan schools were far from sight in the future; but the School of Notre Dame at Paris existed, and taught the existence of God much as Archbishop Hildebert described it. The most successful lecturer was William of Champeaux, and to any one who ever heard of William at all, the name instantly calls up the figure of Abélard, in flesh and blood, as he sang to Héloïse the songs which he says resounded through Europe. The twelfth century, with all its sparkle, would be dull without Abélard and Héloïse.

With infinite regret, Héloïse must be left out of the story, because she was not a philosopher or a poet or an artist, but only a Frenchwoman to the last millimetre of her shadow. Even though one may suspect that her famous letters to Abélard are, for the most part, by no means above scepticism, she was, by French standards, worth at least a dozen Abélards, if only because she called Saint Bernard a false apostle. Unfortunately, French standards, by which she must be judged in our ignorance, take for granted that she philosophized only for the sake of Abélard, while

Abélard taught philosophy to her not so much because he believed in philosophy or in her as because he believed in himself. To this day, Abélard remains a problem as perplexing as he must have been to Héloïse, and almost as fascinating. As the west portal of Chartres is the door through which one must of necessity enter the Gothic architecture of the thirteenth century, so Abélard is the portal of approach to the Gothic thought and philosophy within. Neither art nor thought has a modern equivalent; only Héloïse, like Isolde, unites the ages.

The first crusade seems, in perspective, to have filled the whole field of vision in France at the time; but, in fact, France seethed with other emotions, and while the crusaders set out to scale heaven by force at Jerusalem, the monks, who remained at home, undertook to scale heaven by prayer and by absorption of body and soul in God; the Cistercian Order was founded in 1098, and was joined in 1112 by young Bernard, born in 1090 at Fontaines-lès-Dijon, drawing with him or after him so many thousands of young men into the self-immolation of the monastery as carried dismay into the hearts of half the women of France. At the same time—that is, about 1098 or 1100—Abélard came up to Paris from Brittany, with as much faith in logic as Bernard had in prayer or Godfrey of Bouillon in arms, and led an equal or even a greater number of combatants to the conquest of heaven by force of pure reason. None showed doubt. Hundreds of thousands of young men wandered from their provinces, mostly to Palestine, largely to cloisters, but also in great numbers to Paris and the schools, while few ever returned.

Abélard had the advantage of being well-born; not so highly descended as Albertus Magnus and Thomas Aquinas who were to complete his work in the thirteenth century, but, like Bernard, a gentleman born and bred. He was the eldest son of Bérenger, Sieur du Pallet, a château in Brittany, south of the Loire, on the edge of Poitou. His name was Pierre du Pallet, although, for some unknown reason, he called himself Pierre Abailard, or Abeillard, or Esbaillart, or Beylard; for the spelling was never fixed. He was born in 1079, and when, in 1096, the young men of his rank were rushing off to the first crusade, Pierre, a boy of seventeen, threw himself with equal zeal into the study of science, and, giving up his inheritance or birthright, at last came to Paris to seize a position in the schools. The year is supposed to have been 1100.

The Paris of Abélard's time was astonishingly old; so old that hardly a stone of it can be now pointed out. Even the oldest of the buildings still standing in that quarter—Saint-Julien-le-Pauvre, Saint-Séverin, and the tower of the Lycée Henri IV—are more modern; only the old Roman Thermae, now part of the Musée de Cluny, within the walls, and the Abbey Tower of Saint-Germain-des-Prés, outside, in the fields, were standing in the year 1100. Politically, Paris was a small provincial town before the reign of Louis-le-Gros (1108–37), who cleared its gates of its nearest enemies; but as a school, Paris was even then easily first. Students crowded into it by thousands, till the town is said to have contained more students than citizens. Modern Paris seems to have begun as a university town before it had a university. Students flocked to it from great distances, encouraged and supported by charity, and stimulated by privileges, until they took entire possession of what is still called the Latin Quarter from the barbarous Latin they chattered; and a town more riotous, drunken, and vicious than it became, in the course of time, hardly existed even in the Middle Ages. In 1100, when enthusiasm was fresh and faith in science was strong, the great mass of students came there to study, and, having no regular university organization or buildings, they thronged the cloister of Notre Dame—not our Notre Dame, which dates only from 1163, but the old Romanesque cathedral which stood on the same spot—and there they listened, and retained what they could remember, for they were not encouraged to take notes even if they were rich enough to buy notebooks, while manuscripts were far beyond their means. One valuable right the students seem to have had—that of asking questions and even of disputing with the lecturer provided they followed the correct form of dialectics. The lecturer himself was licenced by the Bishop.

Five thousand students are supposed to have swarmed about the cloister of Notre Dame, across the Petit Pont, and up the hill of Sainte-Geneviève; three thousand are said to have paid fees to Abélard in the days of his great vogue and they seem to have attached themselves to their favourite master as a champion to be upheld against the world. Jealousies ran high, and neither scholars nor masters shunned dispute. Indeed, the only science they taught or knew was the art of dispute—dialectics. Rhetoric, grammar, and dialectics were the regular branches of science, and bold students, who were not afraid of dabbling in forbidden fields, extended their studies to mathematics—"exercitium nefarium," according to Abélard, which he professed to know nothing about but which he studied nevertheless. Abélard, whether pupil or master, never held his tongue if he could help it, for his fortune depended on using it well; but he never used it so well in dialectics or theology as he did, toward the end of his life, in writing a bit of autobiography, so admirably told, so vivid, so vibrating with the curious intensity of his generation, that it needed only to have been written in "Romieu" to be the chief monument of early French prose, as the western portal of Chartres is the chief monument of early French sculpture, and of about the same date. Unfortunately Abélard was a noble scholar, who necessarily wrote and talked Latin, even with Héloïse, and, although the Latin was mediaeval, it is not much the better on that account, because, in spite of its quaintness, the naïvetés of a young language—the egotism, jealousies, suspicions, boastings, and lamentations of a childlike time—take a false air of outworn Rome and Byzantium, although, underneath, the spirit lives:

> I arrived at last in Paris where for a long time dialectics had specially flourished under William of Champeaux, rightly reckoned the first of my masters in that branch of study. I stayed some time in his

school, but, though well received at first, I soon got to be an annoyance to him because I persisted in refuting certain ideas of his, and because, not being afraid to enter into argument against him, I sometimes got the better. This boldness, too, roused the wrath of those fellow-students who were classed higher, because I was the youngest and the last comer. This was the beginning of my series of misfortunes which still last; my renown every day increasing, envy was kindled against me in every direction.

This picture of the boy of twenty, harassing the professor, day after day, in his own lecture-room before hundreds of older students, paints Abélard to the life; but one may safely add a few touches that heighten the effect; as that William of Champeaux himself was barely thirty, and that Abélard throughout his career, made use of every social and personal advantage to gain a point, with little scruple either in manner or in sophistry. One may easily imagine the scene. Teachers are always much the same. Pupils and students differ only in degrees of docility. In 1100, both classes began by accepting the foundations of society, as they have to do still; only they then accepted laws of the Church and Aristotle, while now they accept laws of the legislature and of energy. In 1100, the students took for granted that, with the help of Aristotle and syllogisms, they could build out the Church intellectually, as the architects, with the help of the pointed arch, were soon to enlarge it architecturally. They never doubted the certainty of their method. To them words had fixed values, like numbers, and syllogisms were hewn stones that needed only to be set in place, in order to reach any height or support any weight. Every sentence was made to take the form of a syllogism. One must have been educated in a Jesuit or Dominican school in order to frame these syllogisms correctly, but merely by way of illustration one may timidly suggest how the phrases sounded in their simplest form. For example, Plato or other equally good authority defined substance as that which stands underneath phenomena; the most universal of universals, the ultimate, the highest in order of generalization. The ultimate essence or substance is indivisible; God is substance; God is indivisible. The divine substance is incapable of alteration or accident; all other substance is liable to alteration or accident; therefore, the divine substance differs from all other substance. A substance is a universal; as for example, Humanity, or the Human, is a universal and indivisible; the Man Socrates, for instance, is not a universal, but an individual; therefore, the substance Humanity, being indivisible, must exist entire and undivided in Socrates.

The form of logic most fascinating to youthful minds, as well as to some minds that are only too acute, is the *reductio ad absurdum;* the forcing an opponent into an absurd alternative or admission; and the syllogism lent itself happily to this use. Socrates abused the weapon and Abélard was the first French master of the art; but neither State nor Church likes to be reduced to an absurdity, and, on the whole, both Socrates and Abélard fared ill in the result. Even now, one had best be civil toward the idols of the forum. Abélard would find most of his old problems sensitive to his touch today. Time has settled few or none of the essential points of dispute. Science hesitates, more visibly than the Church ever did, to decide once for all whether unity or diversity is ultimate law; whether order or chaos is the governing rule of the universe, if universe there is; whether anything, except phenomena, exists. Even in matters more vital to society, one dares not speak too loud. Why, and for what, and to whom, is man a responsible agent? Every jury and judge, every lawyer and doctor, every legislator and clergyman has his own views, and the law constantly varies. Every nation may have a different system. One court may hang and another may acquit for the same crime, on the same day; and science only repeats what the Church said to Abélard, that where we know so little, we had better hold our tongues.

According to the latest authorities, the doctrine of universals which convulsed the schools of the twelfth century has never received an adequate answer. What is a species? what is a genus or a family or an order? More or less convenient terms of classification, about which the twelfth century cared very little, while it cared deeply about the essence of classes! Science has become too complex to affirm the existence of universal truths, but it strives for nothing else, and disputes the problem, within its own limits, almost as earnestly as in the twelfth century, when the whole field of human and superhuman activity was shut between these barriers of substance, universals, and particulars. Little has changed except the vocabulary and the method. The schools knew that their society hung for life on the demonstration that God, the ultimate universal, was a reality, out of which all other universal truths or realities sprang. Truth was a real thing, outside of human experience. The schools of Paris talked and thought of nothing else. John of Salisbury, who attended Abélard's lectures about 1136, and became Bishop of Chartres in 1176, seems to have been more surprised than we need be at the intensity of the emotion. "One never gets away from this question," he said. "From whatever point a discussion starts, it is always led back and attached to that. It is the madness of Rufus about Naevia; 'He thinks of nothing else; talks of nothing else, and if Naevia did not exist, Rufus would be dumb.'"

Abélard began it. After his first visit to Paris in 1100, he seems to have passed several years elsewhere, while Guillaume de Champeaux in 1108, retired from the school in the cloister of Notre Dame, and, taking orders, established a class in a chapel near by, afterwards famous as the Abbaye-de-Saint-Victor. The Jardin des Plantes and the Gare d'Orléans now cover the ground where the Abbey stood, on the banks of the Seine outside the Latin Quarter, and not a trace is left of its site; but there William continued his course in dialectics, until suddenly Abélard reappeared among his scholars, and resumed his old attacks. This time Abélard could hardly call himself a student. He was thirty years old, and long since had been himself a teacher; he had attended William's course on dialectics nearly ten years before, and was past master in the art; he had nothing to learn from William in theology, for neither William nor he was yet a theologist by profession. If Abélard went back to school, it was certainly not to learn; but indeed, he himself made little or no pretence of it, and told with childlike candour not only why he went, but also how brilliantly he succeeded in his object:

I returned to study rhetoric in his school. Among other controversial battles, I succeeded, by the most irrefutable argument, in making him change, or rather ruin his doctrine of universals. His doctrine consisted in affirming the perfect identity of the essence in every individual of the same species, so that according to him there was no difference in the essence but only in the infinite variety of accidents. He then came to amend his doctrine so as to affirm, not the identity any longer, but the absence of distinction—the want of difference—in the essence. And as this question of universals had always been one of the most important questions of dialectics—so important that Porphyry, touching on it in his Preliminaries, did not dare to take the responsibility of cutting the knot, but said, "It is a very grave point,"—Champeaux, who was obliged to modify his idea and then renounce it, saw his course fall into such discredit that they hardly let him make his dialectical lectures, as though dialectics consisted entirely in the question of universals.

Why was this point so "very grave"? Not because it was mere dialectics! The only part of the story that seems grave today is the part that Abélard left out; the part which Saint Bernard, thirty years later put in, on behalf of William. We should be more credulous than twelfth-century monks, if we believed, on Abélard's word in 1135, that in 1110 he had driven out of the schools the most accomplished dialectician of the age by an objection so familiar that no other dialectician was ever silenced by it—whatever may have been the case with theologians—and so obvious that it could not have troubled a scholar of fifteen. William stated a settled doctrine as old as Plato; Abélard interposed an objection as old as Aristotle. Probably Plato and Aristotle had received the question and answer from philosophers ten thousand years older than themselves. Certainly the whole of philosophy has always been involved in the dispute.

The subject is as amusing as a comedy; so amusing that ten minutes may be well given to playing the scene between William and Abélard, not as it happened, but in a form nearer our ignorance, with liberty to invent arguments for William, and analogies—which are figures intended to serve as fatal weapons if they succeed, and as innocent toys if they fail—such as he never imagined; while Abélard can respond with his true rejoinder, fatal in a different sense. For the chief analogy, the notes of music would serve, or the colours of the solar spectrum, or an energy, such as gravity;—but the best is geometrical, because Euclid was as scholastic as William of Champeaux himself, and his axioms are even more familiar to the schoolboy of the twentieth, than to the schoolman of the twelfth century.

In these scholastic tournaments the two champions started from opposite points:—one, from the ultimate substance, God—the universal, the ideal, the type;—the other from the individual, Socrates, the concrete, the observed fact of experience, the object of sensual perception. The first champion—William in this instance—assumed that the universal was a real thing; and for that reason he was called a realist. His opponent—Abélard—held that the universal was only nominally real; and on that account he was called a nominalist. Truth, virtue, humanity, exist as units and realities, said William. Truth, replied Abélard, is only the sum of all possible facts that are true, as humanity is the sum of all actual human beings. The ideal bed is a form, made by God, said Plato. The ideal bed is a name, imagined by ourselves, said Aristotle. "I start from the universe," said William. "I start from the atom," said Abélard; and, once having started, they necessarily came into collision at some point between the two.

William of Champeaux, lecturing on dialectics or logic, comes to the question of universals, which he says, are substances. Starting from the highest substance, God, all being descends through created substances by stages, until it reaches the substance animality, from which it descends to the substance humanity: and humanity being, like other essences or substances, indivisible, passes wholly into each individual, becoming Socrates, Plato, and Aristotle, much as the divine substance exists wholly and undivided in each member of the Trinity.

Here Abélard interrupts. The divine substance, he says, operates by laws of its own, and cannot be used for comparison. In treating of human substance, one is bound by human limitations. If the whole of humanity is in Socrates, it is wholly absorbed by Socrates, and cannot be at the same time in Plato, or elsewhere. Following his favourite *reductio ad absurdum*, Abélard turns the idea round, and infers from it that, since Socrates carries all humanity in him, he carries Plato, too; and both must be in the same place, though Socrates is at Athens and Plato in Rome.

The objection is familiar to William, who replies by another commonplace:

"Mr. Abélard, might I, without offence, ask you a simple matter? Can you give me Euclid's definition of a point?"

"If I remember right it is, 'illud cujus nulla pars est'; that which has no parts."

"Has it existence?"

"Only in our minds."

"Not, then, in God?"

"All necessary truths exist first in God. If the point is a necessary truth, it exists first there."

"Then might I ask you for Euclid's definition of the line?"

"The line is that which has only extension; 'Linea vocatur illa quae solam longitudinem habet.' "

"Can you conceive an infinite straight line?"

"Only as a line which has no end, like the point extended."

"Supposing we imagine a straight line, like opposite rays of the sun, proceeding in opposite directions to infinity—is it real?"

"It has no reality except in the mind that conceives it."

"Supposing we divide that line which has no reality into two parts at its origin in the sun or star, shall we get two infinities?—or shall we say, two halves of the infinite?"

"We conceive of each as partaking the quality of infinity."

"Now, let us cut out the diameter of the sun; or rather—since this is what our successors in the school will do—let us take a line of our earth's longitude which is equally unreal, and measure a degree of this thing which does not exist, and then divide it into equal parts which we will use as a measure or metre. This metre, which is still nothing, as I understand you, is infinitely divisible into points? and the point itself is infinitely small? Therefore we have the finite partaking the nature of the infinite?"

"Undoubtedly!"

"One step more, Mr. Abélard, if I do not weary you! Let me take three of these metres which do not exist, and place them so that the ends of one shall touch the ends of the others. May I ask what is that figure?"

"I presume you mean it to be a triangle."

"Precisely! and what sort of a triangle?"

"An equilateral triangle, the sides of which measure one metre each."

"Now let me take three more of these metres which do not exist, and construct another triangle which does not exist;—are these two triangles or one triangle?"

"They are most certainly one—a single concept of the only possible equilateral triangle measuring one metre on each face."

"You told us a moment ago that a universal could not exist wholly and exclusively in two individuals at once. Does not the universal by definition—*the* equilateral triangle measuring one metre on each face—does it not exist wholly, in its integrity of essence, in each of the two triangles we have conceived?"

"It does—as a conception."

"I thank you! Now, although I fear wearying you, perhaps you will consent to let me add matter to mind. I have here on my desk an object not uncommon in nature, which I will ask you to describe."

"It appears to be a crystal."

"May I ask its shape?"

"I should call it a regular octahedron."

"That is, two pyramids, set base to base? making eight plane surfaces, each a perfect equilateral triangle?"

"Concedo triangula (I grant the triangles)."

"Do you know, perchance, what is this material which seems to give substantial existence to these eight triangles?"

"I do not."

"Nor I! nor does it matter, unless you conceive it to be the work of man?"

"I do not claim it as man's work."

"Whose, then?"

"We believe all actual creation of matter, united with form, to be the work of God."

"Surely not the substance of God himself? Perhaps you mean that this form—this octahedron—is a divine concept."

"I understand such to be the doctrine of the Church."

"Then it seems that God uses this concept habitually to create this very common crystal. One question more, and only one, if you will permit me to come to the point. Does the matter—the material—of which this crystal is made affect in any way the form—the nature, the soul—of the universal equilateral triangle as you see it bounding these eight plane surfaces?"

"That I do not know, and do not think essential to decide. As far as these triangles are individual, they are made so by the will of God, and not by the substance you call triangle. The universal—the abstract right angle, or any other abstract form—is only an idea, a concept, to which reality, individuality, or what we might call energy is wanting. The only true energy, except man's free will, is God."

"Very good, Mr. Abélard! we can now reach our issue. You affirm that, just as the line does not exist in space, although the eye sees little else in space, so the triangle does not exist in this crystal, although the crystal shows eight of them, each perfect. You are aware that on this line which does not exist, and its combination in this triangle which does not exist, rests the whole fabric of mathematics with all its necessary truths. In other words, you know that in this line, though it does not exist, is bound up the truth of the only branch of human knowledge which claims absolute certainty for human processes. You admit that this line and triangle, which are mere figments of our human imagination, not only exist independent of us in the crystal, but are, as we suppose, habitually and invariably used by God Himself to give form to the matter contained within the planes of the crystal. Yet to this line and triangle you deny reality. To mathematical truth, you deny compulsive force. You hold that an equilateral triangle may, to you and all other human individuals, be a right-angled triangle if you choose to imagine it so. Allow me to say, without assuming any claim to superior knowledge, that to me your logic results in a different conclusion. If you are compelled, at one point or another of the chain of being, to deny existence to a substance, surely it should be to the last and feeblest. I see nothing to hinder you from denying your own existence, which is, in fact, impossible to demonstrate. Certainly you are free, in logic, to argue that Socrates and Plato are mere names—that men and matter are phantoms and dreams. No one ever has proved or ever can prove the contrary. Infallibly, a great philosophical school will some day be founded on that assumption. I venture even to recommend it to your acute and sceptical mind; but I cannot conceive how, by any process of reasoning, sensual or supersensual, you can reach the conclusion that the single form of truth which instantly and inexorably compels our submission to its laws—is nothing."

Thus far, all was familiar ground; certainly at least as familiar as the Pons Asinorum [1]; and neither of the two champions had need to feel ruffled in temper by the discussion. The real struggle began only at this point; for until this point was reached, both positions were about equally tenable. Abélard had hitherto rested quietly on the defensive, but William's last thrust obliged him to strike in his turn, and he drew himself up for what, five hundred years later, was called the "Coup de Jarnac": [2]

"I do not deny," he begins; "on the contrary, I affirm that the universal, whether we call it humanity, or equilateral triangle, has a sort of reality as a concept; that it is something; even a substance, if you insist upon it. Undoubtedly the sum of all individual men results in the concept of humanity. What I deny is that the concept results in the individual. You have correctly stated the essence of the point and the line as sources of our concept of the infinite; what I deny is that they are divisions of the infinite. Universals cannot be divided; what is capable of division cannot be a universal. I admit the force of your analogy in the case of the crystal; but I am obliged to point out to you that, if you insist on this analogy, you will bring yourself and me into flagrant contradiction with the fixed foundations of the Church. If the energy of the triangle gives form to the crystal, and the energy of the line gives reality to the triangle, and the energy of the infinite gives substance to the line, all energy at last becomes identical with the ultimate substance, God Himself. Socrates becomes God in small; Judas is identical with both; humanity is of the divine essence, and exists, wholly and undivided, in each of us. The equilateral triangle we call humanity exists, therefore, entire, identical, in you and me, as a subdivision of the infinite line, space, energy, or substance, which is God. I need not remind you that this is pantheism, and that if God is the only energy, human free will merges in God's free will; the Church ceases to have a reason for existence; man cannot be held responsible for his own acts, either to the Church or to the State; and finally, though very unwillingly, I must, in regard for my own safety, bring the subject to the attention of the Archbishop, which, as you know better than I, will lead to your seclusion, or worse."

[1] "Bridge of (for) asses." The fifth proposition of the first book of Euclid is traditionally so called, for it is the first one involving any mathematical puzzle.

[2] A proverbial phrase, meaning an unexpected blow. Gui Chabot, comte de Jarnac (d. *c.* 1575), by a lucky backstroke, won a famous duel.

Whether Abélard used these precise words is nothing to the point. The words he left on record were equivalent to these. As translated by M. de Rémusat from a manuscript entitled: "Glossulae magistri Petri Baelardi super Porphyrium," the phrase runs: "A grave heresy is at the end of this doctrine; for, according to it, the divine substance which is recognized as admitting of no form, is necessarily identical with every substance in particular and with all substance in general." Even had he not stated the heresy so bluntly, his objection necessarily pushed William in face of it. Realism, when pressed, always led to pantheism. William of Champeaux and Bishop or Archbishop Hildebert were personal friends, and Hildebert's divine substance left no more room for human free will than Abélard saw in the geometric analogy imagined for William. Throughout the history of the Church for fifteen hundred years, whenever this theological point has been pressed against churchmen it has reduced them to evasion or to apology. Admittedly, the weak point of realism was its fatally pantheistic term.

Of course, William consulted his friends in the Church, probably Archbishop Hildebert among the rest, before deciding whether to maintain or to abandon his ground, and the result showed that he was guided by their advice. Realism was the Roman arch—the only possible foundation for any Church; because it assumed unity, and any other scheme was compelled to prove it, for a starting-point. Let us see, for a moment, what became of the dialogue, when pushed into theology, in order to reach some of the reasons which reduced William to tacit abandonment of a doctrine he could never have surrendered unless under compulsion. That he was angry is sure, for Abélard, by thus thrusting theology into dialectics, had struck him a foul blow; and William knew Abélard well: "Ah!" he would have rejoined; "you are quick, M. du Pallet, to turn what I offered as an analogy, into an argument of heresy against my person. You are at liberty to take that course if you choose, though I give you fair warning that it will lead you far. But now I must ask you still another question. This concept that you talk about—this image in the mind of man, of God, of matter; for I know not where to seek it—whether is it a reality or not?"

"I hold it as, in a manner, real."

"I want a categorical answer: Yes or No!"

"Distinguo! (I must qualify.)"

"I will have no qualifications. A substance either is, or not. Choose!"

To this challenge Abélard had the choice of answering Yes, or of answering No, or of refusing to answer at all. He seems to have done the last; but we suppose him to have accepted the wager of battle, and to answer:

"Yes, then!"

"Good!" William rejoins; "now let us see how your pantheism differs from mine. My triangle exists as a reality, or what science will call an energy, outside my mind, in God, and is impressed on my mind as it is on a mirror, like the triangle on the crystal, its energy giving form. Your triangle you say is also an energy, but an essence of my mind itself; you thrust it into the mind as an integral part of the mirror; identically the same concept, energy, or necessary truth which is inherent in God. Whatever subterfuge you may resort to, sooner or later you have got to agree that your mind is identical with God's nature as far as that concept is concerned. Your pantheism goes further than mine. As a doctrine of the Real Presence peculiar to yourself, I can commend it to the Archbishop together with your delation of me."

Supposing that Abélard took the opposite course, and answered: "No! my concept is a mere sign."

"A sign of what, in God's name!"

"A sound! a word! a symbol! an echo only of my ignorance."

"Nothing, then! So truth and virtue and charity do not exist at all. You suppose yourself to exist, but you have no means of knowing God; therefore, to you God does not exist except as an echo of your ignorance; and, what concerns you most, the Church does not exist except as your concept of certain individuals, whom you cannot regard as a unity, and who suppose themselves to believe in a Trinity which exists only as a sound, or a symbol. I will not repeat your words, M. du Pallet, outside this cloister, because the consequences to you would certainly be fatal; but it is only too clear that you are a materialist, and as such your fate must be decided by a Church Council, unless you prefer the stake by judgment of a secular court."

In truth, pure nominalism—if, indeed, any one ever maintained it—afforded no cover whatever. Nor did Abélard's concept help the matter, although for want of a better refuge, the Church was often driven into it. Conceptualism was a device, like the false wooden roof, to cover and conceal an inherent weakness of construction. Unity either is, or is not. If soldiers, no matter in what number, can never make an army, and worshippers, though in millions, do not make a Church, and all humanity united would not necessarily constitute a State, equally little can their concepts, individual or united, constitute the one or the other. Army, Church, and State, each is an organic whole, complex beyond all possible addition of units, and not a concept at all, but rather an animal that thinks, creates, devours, and destroys. The attempt to bridge the chasm between multiplicity and unity is the oldest problem of philosophy, religion, and science, but the flimsiest bridge of all is the human concept, unless somewhere, within or beyond it, an energy not individual is hidden; and in that case the old question instantly reappears: What is that energy?

Abélard would have done well to leave William alone, but Abélard was an adventurer, and William was a churchman. To win a victory over a churchman is not very difficult for an adventurer, and is always a tempting amusement, because the ambition of churchmen to shine in worldly contests is disciplined and checked by the broader interests of the Church: but the victory is usually sterile, and rarely harms the churchman. The Church cares for its own. Probably the bishops advised William not to insist on his doctrine, although every bishop may have held the same view. William allowed himself to be silenced without a judgment, and in that respect stands almost if not quite alone among schoolmen. The students divined that he had sold himself to the Church, and consequently deserted him. Very soon he received his reward in the shape of the highest dignity open to private ambition—a bishopric. As Bishop of Chalons-sur-Marne he made for himself a great reputation, which does not concern us, although it deeply concerned the unfortunate Abélard, for it happened, either by chance or design, that within a year or two after William established himself at Chalons, young Bernard of Citeaux chose a neighbouring diocese in which to establish a branch of the Cistercian Order, and Bishop William took so keen an interest in the success of Bernard as almost to claim equal credit for it. Clairvaux was, in a manner, William's creation, although not in his diocese, and yet, if there was a priest in all France who fervently despised the schools, it was young Bernard. William of Champeaux, the chief of schoolmen, could never have gained Bernard's affections. Bishop William of Chalons must have drifted far from dialectics into mysticism in order to win the support of Clairvaux, and train up a new army of allies who were to mark Abélard for an easy prey.

Meanwhile Abélard pursued his course of triumph in the schools, and in due time turned from dialectics to theology, as every ambitious teacher could hardly fail to do. His affair with Héloïse and their marriage seem to have occupied his time in 1117 or 1118, for they both retired into religious orders in 1119, and he resumed his lectures in 1120. With his passion for rule, he was fatally certain to attempt ruling the Church as he ruled the schools; and, as it was always enough for him that any point should be tender in order that he should press upon it, he instantly and instinctively seized on the most sensitive nerve of the Church system to wrench it into his service. He became a sort of apostle of the Holy Ghost.

That the Trinity is a mystery was a law of theology so absolute as in a degree to hide the law of philosophy that the Trinity was meant as a solution of a greater mystery still. In truth, as a matter of philosophy, the Trinity was intended to explain the eternal and primary problem of the process by which unity could produce diversity. Starting from unity alone, philosophers found themselves unable to stir hand or foot until they could account for duality. To the common, ignorant peasant, no such trouble occurred, for he knew the Trinity in its simpler form as the first condition of life, like time and space and force. No human being was so stupid as not to understand that the father, mother, and child made a trinity, returning into each other, and although every father, every mother, and every child, from the dawn of man's intelligence, had asked why, and had never received an answer more intelligible to them than to philosophers, they never showed difficulty in accepting that trinity as a fact. They might even, in their beneficent blindness, ask the Church why that trinity, which had satisfied the Egyptians for five or ten thousand years, was not good enough for churchmen. They themselves were doing their utmost, though unconsciously, to identify the Holy Ghost with the Mother, while philosophy insisted on excluding the human symbol precisely because it was human and led back to an infinite series. Philosophy required three units to start from; it posed the equilateral triangle, not the straight line, as the foundation of its *deometry*. The first straight line, infinite in extension, must be assumed, and its reflection engendered the second, but whence came the third? Under protest, philosophy was compelled to accept the symbol of Father and Son as a matter of faith, but, if the relation of Father and Son were accepted for the two units which reflected each other, what relation expressed the Holy Ghost? In philosophy, the product of two units was not a third unit, but diversity, multiplicity, infinity. The subject was, for that reason, better handled by the Arabs, whose reasoning worked back on the Christian theologians and made the point more delicate still. Common people, like women and children and ourselves, could never understand the Trinity; naturally, intelligent people understood it still less, but for them it did not matter; they did not need to understand it provided their neighbours would leave it alone.

The mass of mankind wanted something nearer to them than either the Father or the Son; they wanted the Mother, and the Church tried, in what seems to women and children and ourselves rather a feeble way, to give the Holy Ghost, as far as possible, the Mother's attributes—Love, Charity, Grace; but in spite of conscientious effort and unswerving faith, the Holy Ghost remained to the mass of Frenchmen somewhat apart, feared rather than loved. The sin against the Holy Ghost was a haunting spectre, for no one knew what else it was.

Naturally the Church, and especially its official theologians, took an instinctive attitude of defence whenever a question on this subject was asked, and were thrown into a flutter of irritation whenever an answer was suggested. No man likes to have his intelligence or good faith questioned, especially if he has doubts about it himself. The distinguishing essence of the Holy Ghost, as a theological substance, was its mystery. That this mystery should be touched at all was annoying to every one who knew the dangers that lurked behind the veil, but that it should be freely handled before audiences of laymen by persons of doubtful character was impossible. Such licence must end in discrediting the whole Trinity under pretence of making it intelligible.

Precisely this licence was what Abélard took, and on it he chose to insist. He said nothing heretical; he treated the Holy Ghost with almost exaggerated respect, as though other churchmen did not quite appreciate its merits; but he would not let it alone, and the Church dreaded every moment lest, with his enormous influence in the schools, he should raise a new storm by his notorious indiscretion. Yet so long as he merely lectured, he was not molested; only when he began to publish his theology did the Church interfere. Then a council held at Soissons in 1121 abruptly condemned his book in block, without reading it, without specifying its errors, and without hearing his defence; obliged him to throw the manuscript into the fire with his own hands, and finally shut him up in a monastery.

He had invited the jurisdiction by taking orders, but even the Church was shocked by the summary nature of the judgment, which seems to have been quite irregular. In fact, the Church has never known what it was that the council condemned. The latest great work on the Trinity, by the Jesuit Father de Régnon, suggests that Abélard's fault was in applying to the Trinity his theory of concepts. "Yes!" he says; "the mystery is explained; the key of conceptualism has opened the tabernacle, and Saint Bernard was right in saying that, thanks to Abélard, every one can penetrate it and contemplate it at his ease; 'even the graceless, even the uncircumcised.' Yes! the Trinity is explained, but after the manner of the Sabellians.[3] For to identify the Persons in the terms of human concepts is, in the same stroke, to destroy their 'subsistances propres.' "

Although the Saviour seems to have felt no compunctions about identifying the persons of the Trinity in the terms of human concepts, it is clear that tourists and heretics had best leave the Church to deal with its "subsistances propres," and with its own members, in its own way. In sum, the Church preferred to stand firm on the Roman arch, and the architects seem now inclined to think it was right; that scholastic science and the pointed arch proved to be failures. In the twelfth century the world may have been rough, but it was not stupid. The Council of Soissons was held while the architects and sculptors were building the west porch of Chartres and the Aquilon at Mont-Saint-Michel. Averroës was born at Cordova in 1126; Omar Khayyám died at Naishapur in 1123.[4] Poetry and metaphysics owned the world, and their quarrel with theology was a private, family dispute. Very soon the tide turned decisively in Abélard's favour. Suger, a political prelate, became minister of the King, and in March, 1122, Abbot of Saint-Denis. In both capacities he took the part of Abélard, released him from restraint, and even restored to him liberty of instruction, at least beyond the jurisdiction of the Bishop of Paris. Abélard then took a line of conduct singularly parallel with that of Bernard. Quitting civilized life he turned wholly to religion. "When the agreement," he said, "had been executed by both parties to it, in presence of the King and his ministers, I next retired within the territory of Troyes, upon a desert spot which I knew, and on a piece of

---

[3] Sabellius, a third-century philosopher, differed from orthodox Trinitarians by denying the real personality of the Son, and recognizing the Trinity not as real and eternal, but as temporal and modalistic, that is, as different manifestations of one and the same person, not as three separate persons.

[4] Averroës was a distinguished Spanish-Arabian philosopher, physician and commentator on Aristotle. Omar Khayyám was a Persian poet and astronomer.

ground given me by certain persons, I built, with the consent of the bishop of the diocese, a sort of oratory of reeds and thatch, which I placed under the invocation of the Holy Trinity. . . . Founded at first in the name of the Holy Trinity, then placed under its invocation, it was called 'Paraclete' in memory of my having come there as a fugitive and in my despair having found some repose in the consolations of divine grace. This denomination was received by many with great astonishment, and some attacked it with violence under pretext that it was not permitted to consecrate a church specially to the Holy Ghost any more than to God the Father, but that, according to ancient usage, it must be dedicated either to the Son alone or to the Trinity."

The spot is still called Paraclete, near Nogent-sur-Seine, in the parish of Quincey about halfway between Fontainebleau and Troyes. The name Paraclete as applied to the Holy Ghost meant the Consoler, the Comforter, the Spirit of Love and Grace; as applied to the oratory by Abélard it meant a renewal of his challenge to theologists, a separation of the Persons in the Trinity, a vulgarization of the mystery; and, as his story frankly says, it was so received by many. The spot was not so remote but that his scholars could follow him, and he invited them to do so. They came in great numbers, and he lectured to them. "In body I was hidden in this spot; but my renown overran the whole world and filled it with my word." Undoubtedly Abélard taught theology, and, in defiance of the council that had condemned him, attempted to define the persons of the Trinity. For this purpose he had fallen on a spot only fifty or sixty miles from Clairvaux where Bernard was inspiring a contrary spirit of religion; he placed himself on the direct line between Clairvaux and its source at Citeaux near Dijon; indeed, if he had sought for a spot as central as possible to the active movement of the Church and the time, he could have hit on none more convenient and conspicuous unless it were the city of Troyes itself, the capital of Champagne, some thirty miles away. The proof that he meant to be aggressive is furnished by his own account of the consequences. Two rivals, he says, one of whom seems to have been Bernard of Clairvaux, took the field against him, "and succeeded in exciting the hostility of certain ecclesiastical and secular authorities, by charging monstrous things, not only against my faith, but also against my manner of life, to such a point as to detach from me some of my principal friends; even those who preserved some affection for me dared no longer display it, for fear. God is my witness that I never heard of the union of an ecclesiastical assembly without thinking that its object was my condemnation." The Church had good reason, for Abélard's conduct defied discipline; but far from showing harshness, the Church this time showed a true spirit of conciliation most creditable to Bernard. Deeply as the Cistercians disliked and distrusted Abélard, they did not violently suppress him, but tacitly consented to let the authorities buy his silence with Church patronage.

The transaction passed through Suger's hands, and offered an ordinary example of political customs as old as history. An abbey in Brittany became vacant; at a hint from the Duke Conan, which may well be supposed to have been suggested from Paris, the monks chose Abélard as their new abbot, and sent some of their number to Suger to request permission for Abélard, who was a monk of Saint-Denis, to become Abbot of Saint-Gildas-de-Rhuys, near Vannes, in Brittany. Suger probably intimated to Abélard, with a certain degree of authority, that he had better accept. Abélard, "struck with terror, and as it were under the menace of a thunderbolt," accepted. Of course the dignity was in effect banishment and worse, and was so understood on all sides. The Abbaye-de-Saint-Gildas-de-Rhuys, though less isolated than Mont-Saint-Michel, was not an agreeable winter residence. Though situated in Abélard's native province of Brittany, only sixty or eighty miles from his birthplace, it was for him a prison with the ocean around it and a singularly wild people to deal with; but he could have endured his lot with contentment, had not discipline or fear or pledge compelled him to hold his tongue. From 1125, when he was sent to Brittany until 1135 when he reappeared in Paris, he never opened his mouth to lecture. "Never, as God is my witness—never would I have acquiesced in such an offer, had it not been to escape, no matter how, from the vexations with which I was incessantly overwhelmed."

A greater career in the Church was thus opened for him against his will, and if he did not die an archbishop it was not wholly the fault of the Church. Already he was a great prelate, the equal in rank of the Abbé Suger, himself, of Saint-Denis; of Peter the Venerable of Cluny; of Bernard of Clairvaux. He was in a manner a peer of the realm. Almost immediately he felt the advantages of the change. Barely two years passed when, in 1127, the Abbé Suger, in reforming his subordinate Abbey of Argenteuil, was obliged to disturb Héloïse, then a sister in that congregation. Abélard was warned of the necessity that his wife should be protected, and with the assistance of every one concerned, he was allowed to establish his wife at the Paraclete as head of a religious sisterhood. "I returned there; I invited Héloïse to come there with the nuns of her community; and when they arrived, I made them the entire donation of the oratory and its dependencies. . . . The bishops cherished her as their daughter; the abbots as their sister; the laymen as their mother." This was merely the beginning of her favour and of his. For ten years they were both of them petted children of the Church.

The formal establishment of Héloïse at the Paraclete took place in 1129. In February, 1130, on the death of the Pope at Rome, a schism broke out, and the cardinals elected two popes, one of whom took the name of Innocent II, and appealed for support to France. Suger saw a great political opportunity and used it. The heads of the French Church agreed in supporting Innocent, and the King summoned a Church council at Étampes to declare its adhesion. The council met in the late summer; Bernard of Clairvaux took the lead; Peter the Venerable, Suger of

Saint-Denis, and the Abbot of Saint-Gildas-de-Rhuys supported him; Innocent himself took refuge at Cluny in October, and on January 20, 1131, he stopped at the Benedictine Abbey of Morigny. The Chronicle of the monastery, recording the abbots present on this occasion—the Abbot of Morigny itself, of Feversham; of Saint-Lucien of Beauvais, and so forth—added especially: "Bernard of Clairvaux, who was then the most famous pulpit orator in France; and Peter Abélard, Abbot of Saint-Gildas, also a monk and the most eminent master of the schools to which the scholars of almost all the Latin races flowed."

Innocent needed popular support; Bernard and Abélard were the two leaders of popular opinion in France. To attach them, Innocent could refuse nothing. Probably Abélard remained with Innocent, but in any case Innocent gave him, at Auxerre, in the following November, a diploma, granting to Héloïse, prioress of the Oratory of the Holy Trinity, all rights of property over whatever she might possess, against all assailants; which proves Abélard's favour. At this time he seems to have taken great interest in the new sisterhood. "I made them more frequent visits," he said, "in order to work for their benefit." He worked so earnestly for their benefit that he scandalized the neighbourhood and had to argue at unnecessary length his innocence of evil. He went so far as to express a wish to take refuge among them and to abandon his abbey in Brittany. He professed to stand in terror of his monks; he excommunicated them; they paid no attention to him; he appealed to the Pope, his friend, and Innocent sent a special legate to enforce their submission "in presence of the Count and the Bishops."

> Even since that, they would not keep quiet. And quite recently, since the expulsion of those of whom I have spoken, when I returned to the abbey, abandoning myself to the rest of the brothers who inspired me with less distrust, I found them even worse than the others. It was no longer a question of poison; it was the dagger that they now sharpened against my breast. I had great difficulty in escaping from them under the guidance of one of the neighbouring lords. Similar perils menace me still and every day I see the sword raised over my head. Even at table I can hardly breathe. . . . This is the torture that I endure every moment of the day; I, a poor monk, raised to the prelacy, becoming more miserable in becoming more great, that by my example the ambitious may learn to curb their greed.

With this, the "Story of Calamity" ends. The allusions to Innocent II seem to prove that it was written not earlier than 1132; the confession of constant and abject personal fear suggests that it was written under the shock caused by the atrocious murder of the Prior of Saint-Victor by the nephews of the Archdeacon of Paris, who had also been subjected to reforms. This murder was committed a few miles outside of the walls of Paris, on August 20, 1133. The "Story of Calamity" is evidently a long plea for release from the restraints imposed on its author by his position in the prelacy and the tacit, or possibly the express, contract he had made, or to which he had submitted, in 1125. This plea was obviously written in order to serve one of two purposes: either to be placed before the authorities whose consent alone could relieve Abélard from his restraints; or to justify him in throwing off the load of the Church, and resuming the profession of schoolman. Supposing the second explanation, the date of the paper would be more or less closely fixed by John of Salisbury, who coming to Paris as a student, in 1136, found Abélard lecturing on the Mont-Sainte-Geneviève; that is to say, not under the licence of the Bishop of Paris or his Chancellor, but independently, in a private school of his own, outside the walls. "I attached myself to the Palatine Peripatician who then presided on the hill of Sainte-Geneviève, the doctor illustrious, admired by all. There, at his feet, I received the first elements of the dialectic art, and according to the measure of my poor understanding I received with all the avidity of my soul everything that came from his mouth."

This explanation is hardly reasonable, for no prelate who was not also a temporal lord would have dared throw off his official duties without permission from his superiors. In Abélard's case the only superior to whom he could apply, as Abbot of Saint-Gildas in Brittany, was probably the Pope himself. In the year 1135 the moment was exceedingly favourable for asking privileges. Innocent, driven from Rome a second time, had summoned a council at Pisa for May 30 to help him. Louis-le-Gros and his minister Suger gave at first no support to this council, and were overruled by Bernard of Clairvaux who in a manner drove them into giving the French clergy permission to attend. The principal archbishops, a number of bishops, and sixteen abbots went to Pisa in May, 1135, and some one of them certainly asked Innocent for favours on behalf of Abélard, which the Pope granted.

The proof is a papal bull, dated in 1136, in favour of Héloïse, giving her the rank and title of Abbess, accompanied by another giving to the Oratory of the Holy Trinity the rank and name of Monastery of the Paraclete, a novelty in Church tradition so extraordinary or so shocking that it still astounds churchmen. With this excessive mark of favour Innocent could have felt little difficulty in giving Abélard the permission to absent himself from his abbey, and with this permission in his hands Abélard might have lectured on dialectics to John of Salisbury in the summer or autumn of 1136. He did not, as far as known, resume lectures on theology.

Such success might have turned heads much better balanced than that of Abélard. With the support of the Pope and at least one of the most prominent cardinals, and with relations at court with the ministers of Louis-le-Gros, Abélard seemed to himself as strong as Bernard of Clairvaux, and a more popular champion of reform. The year 1137, which has marked a date for so many great points in our travels, marked also the moment of Abélard's greatest vogue. The victory of Aristotle and the pointed arch seemed assured when Suger effected the marriage of the young Prince Louis to the heiress Eleanor of Guienne. The exact moment was stamped on the façade of his exquisite creation, the Abbey Church of Saint-Denis, finished in 1140 and still in part erect. From Saint-Denis to Saint-Sulpice was but a step. Louis-le-Grand seems to stand close in succession to Louis-le-Gros.

Fortunately for tourists, the world, restless though it might be, could not hurry, and Abélard was to know of the pointed arch very little except its restlessness. Just at the apex of his triumph, August 1, 1137, Louis-le-Gros died. Six months afterwards the anti-pope also died, the schism ended, and Innocent II needed Abélard's help no more. Bernard of Clairvaux became Pope and King at once. Both Innocent and Louis-le-Jeune were in a manner his personal creations. The King's brother Henry, next in succession, actually became a monk at Clairvaux not long afterwards. Even the architecture told the same story, for at Saint-Denis, though the arch might simulate a point, the old Romanesque lines still assert as firmly as ever their spiritual control. The flèche that gave the façade a new spirit was not added until 1215, which marks Abélard's error in terms of time.

Once arrived at power, Bernard made short work of all that tried to resist him. During 1139 he seems to have been too busy or too ill to take up the affair of Abélard, but in March, 1140, the attack was opened in a formal letter from William of Saint-Thierry, who was Bernard's closest friend, bringing charges against Abélard before Bernard and the Bishop of Chartres. The charges were simple enough:

> Pierre Abélard seized the moment, when all the masters of ecclesiastical doctrine have disappeared from the scene of the world, to conquer a place apart, for himself, in the schools, and to create there an exclusive domination. He treats Holy Scripture as though it were dialectics. It is a matter with him of personal invention and annual novelties. He is the censor and not the disciple of the faith; the corrector and not the imitator of the authorized masters.

In substance, this is all. The need of action was even simpler. Abélard's novelties were becoming a danger; they affected not only the schools, but also even the Curia at Rome. Bernard must act because there was no one else to act: "This man fears you; he dreads you! if you shut your eyes, whom will he fear? . . . The evil has become too public to allow a correction limited to amicable discipline and secret warning." In fact, Abélard's works were flying about Europe in every direction, and every year produced a novelty. One can still read them in M. Cousin's collected edition; among others, a volume on ethics: "Ethica, seu Scito teipsum"; on theology in general, an epitome; a "Dialogus inter Philosophum, Judaeum et Christianum"; and, what was perhaps the most alarming of all, an abstract of quotations from standard authorities, on the principle of the parallel column, showing the fatal contradictions of the authorized masters, and entitled "Sic et Non"! Not one of these works but dealt with sacred matters in a spirit implying that the Essence of God was better understood by Pierre du Pallet than by the whole array of bishops and prelates in Europe! Had Bernard been fortunate enough to light upon the "Story of Calamity," which must also have been in existence, he would have found there Abélard's own childlike avowal that he taught theology because his scholars "said that they did not want mere words; that one can believe only what one understands; and that it is ridiculous to preach to others what one understands no better than they do." Bernard himself never charged Abélard with any presumption equal to this. Bernard said only that "he sees nothing as an enigma, nothing as in a mirror, but looks on everything face to face." If this had been all, even Bernard could scarcely have complained. For several thousand years mankind has stared Infinity in the face without pretending to be the wiser; the pretension of Abélard was that, by his dialectic method, he could explain the Infinite, while all other theologists talked mere words; and by way of proving that he had got to the bottom of the matter, he laid down the ultimate law of the universe as his starting-point: "All that God does," he said, "He wills necessarily and does it necessarily; for His goodness is such that it pushes Him necessarily to do all the good He can, and the best He can, and the quickest He can. . . . Therefore it is of necessity that God willed and made the world." Pure logic admitted no contingency; it was bound to be necessitarian or ceased to be logical; but the result, as Bernard understood it, was that Abélard's world, being the best and only possible, need trouble itself no more about God, or Church, or man.

Strange as the paradox seems, Saint Bernard and Lord Bacon, though looking at the world from opposite standpoints, agreed in this: that the scholastic method was false and mischievous, and that the longer it was followed, the greater was its mischief. Bernard thought that because dialectics led wrong, therefore faith led right. He saw no alternative, and perhaps in fact there was none. If he had lived a century later, he would have said to Thomas Aquinas what he said to a schoolman of his own day: "if you had once tasted true food"—if you knew what true religion is—"how quick you would leave those Jew makers of books (literatoribus judaeis) to gnaw their crusts by themselves!" Locke or Hume might perhaps still have resented a little the "literator judaeus," but Faraday or Clerk-Maxwell [5] would have expressed the same opinion with only the change of a word: "If the twelfth century had once tasted true science, how quick they would have dropped Avicenna and Averroës!" Science admits that Bernard's disbelief in scholasticism was well founded, whatever it may think of his reasons. The only point that remains is personal: Which is the more sympathetic, Bernard or Abélard?

The Church feels no doubt, but is a bad witness. Bernard is not a char-

---

[5] John Locke (1632–1704) was the founder of the English and French "sensational" philosophy and psychology; and the skeptical application of his principles by the Scottish philosopher David Hume (1711–1776) led Kant to develop the "critical" philosophy. James Clerk-Maxwell (1831–1879) was a celebrated theoretical physicist. Michael Faraday (1791–1867), physicist and chemist, discovered magneto-electric induction, and magnetization of light.

acter to be taken or rejected in a lump. He was many-sided, and even toward Abélard he showed more than one surface. He wanted no unnecessary scandals in the Church; he had too many that were not of his seeking. He seems to have gone through the forms of friendly negotiation with Abélard although he could have required nothing less than Abélard's submission and return to Brittany, and silence; terms which Abélard thought worse than death. On Abélard's refusal, Bernard began his attack. We know, from the "Story of Calamity," what Bernard's party could not have certainly known then—the abject terror into which the very thought of a council had for twenty years thrown Abélard whenever he was threatened with it; and in 1140 he saw it to be inevitable. He preferred to face it with dignity, and requested to be heard at a council to meet at Sens in June. One cannot admit that he felt the shadow of a hope to escape. At the utmost he could have dreamed of nothing more than a hearing. Bernard's friends, who had a lively fear of his dialectics, took care to shut the door on even this hope. The council was carefully packed and overawed. The King was present; archbishops, bishops, abbots, and other prelates by the score; Bernard acted in person as the prosecuting attorney; the public outside were stimulated to threaten violence. Abélard had less chance of a judicial hearing than he had had at Soissons twenty years before. He acted with a proper sense of their dignity and his own by simply appearing and entering an appeal to Rome. The council paid no attention to the appeal, but passed to an immediate condemnation. His friends said that it was done after dinner; that when the volume of Abélard's "Theology" was produced and the clerk began to read it aloud, after the first few sentences the bishops ceased attention, talked, joked, laughed, stamped their feet, got angry, and at last went to sleep. They were waked only to growl "Damnamus—namus," and so made an end. The story may be true, for all prelates, even in the twelfth century, were not Bernards of Clairvaux or Peters of Cluny; all drank wine, and all were probably sleepy after dinner; while Abélard's writings are, for the most part, exceedingly hard reading. The clergy knew quite well what they were doing; the judgment was certain long in advance, and the council was called only to register it. Political trials were usually mere forms.

The appeal to Rome seems to have been taken seriously by Bernard, which is surprising unless the character of Innocent II inspired his friends with doubts unknown to us. Innocent owed everything to Bernard, while Abélard owed everything to Innocent. The Pope was not in a position to alienate the French Church or the French King. To any one who knows only what is now to be known, Bernard seems to have been sure of the Curia, yet he wrote in a tone of excitement as though he feared Abélard's influence there even more than at home. He became abusive; Abélard was a crawling viper (coluber tortuosus) who had come out of his hole (egressus est de caverna sua), and after the manner of a hydra (in similitudinem hydrae), after having one head cut off at Soissons, had thrown out seven more. He was a monk without rule; a prelate without responsibility; an abbot without discipline; "disputing with boys; conversing with women." The charges in themselves seem to be literally true, and would not in some later centuries have been thought very serious; neither faith nor morals were impugned. On the other hand, Abélard never affected or aspired to be a saint, while Bernard always affected to judge the acts and motives of his fellow-creatures from a standpoint of more than worldly charity. Bernard had no right to Abélard's vices; he claimed to be judged by a higher standard; but his temper was none of the best, and his pride was something of the worst; which gave to Peter the Venerable occasion for turning on him sharply with a rebuke that cut to the bone: "You perform all the difficult religious duties," wrote Peter to the saint who wrought miracles; "you fast; you watch; you suffer; but you will not endure the easy ones—you do not love (non vis levia ferre, ut diligas)."

This was the end of Abélard. Of course the Pope confirmed the judgment, and even hurried to do so in order that he might not be obliged to give Abélard a hearing. The judgment was not severe, as judgments went; indeed, it amounted to little more than an order to keep silence, and, as it happened, was never carried into effect. Abélard, at best a nervous invalid, started for Rome, but stopped at Cluny, perhaps the most agreeable stopping-place in Europe. Personally he seems to have been a favourite of Abbot Peter the Venerable, whose love for Bernard was not much stronger than Abélard's or Suger's. Bernard was an excessively sharp critic, and spared worldliness, or what he thought lack of spirituality, in no prelate whatever; Clairvaux existed for nothing else, politically, than as a rebuke to them all, and Bernard's enmity was their bond of union. Under the protection of Peter the Venerable, the most amiable figure of the twelfth century, and in the most agreeable residence in Europe, Abélard remained unmolested at Cluny, occupied, as is believed, in writing or revising his treatises, in defiance of the council. He died there two years later, April 21, 1142, in full communion, still nominal Abbot of Saint-Gildas, and so distinguished a prelate that Peter the Venerable thought himself obliged to write a charming letter to Héloïse at the Paraclete not far away, condoling with her on the loss of a husband who was the Socrates, the Aristotle, the Plato, of France and the West; who, if among logicians he had rivals, had no master; who was the prince of study, learned, eloquent, subtle, penetrating; who overcame everything by the force of reason, and was never so great as when he passed to true philosophy, that of Christ.

All this was in Latin verses, and seems sufficiently strong, considering that Abélard's philosophy had been so recently and so emphatically condemned by the entire Church, including Peter the Venerable himself. The twelfth century had this singular charm of liberty in practice, just as its architecture knew no mathematical formula of precision; but Peter's letter to Héloïse went further still, and rang with absolute passion:

Thus, dear and venerable sister in God, he to whom you are united, after your tie in the flesh, by the better and stronger bond of the divine love; he, with whom, and under whom, you have served the Lord, the Lord now takes, in your place, like another you, and warms in His bosom; and, for the day of His coming, when shall sound the voice of the archangel and the trumpet of God descending from heaven, He keeps him to restore him to you by His grace.

THE EDUCATION OF HENRY ADAMS

These two chapters are a unit, and perhaps as good as any in the *Education* to document Adams's thesis that in human dealings even the most intelligent, upright, and experienced men of action, such as his father in this instance, can act on judgments quite erroneously formed.

Chapter X

POLITICAL MORALITY (1862)

On Moran's promotion to be Secretary,[1] Mr. Seward inquired whether Minister Adams would like the place of Assistant Secretary for his son. It was the first—and last—office ever offered him, if indeed he could claim what was offered in fact to his father. To them both, the change seemed useless. Any young man could make some sort of Assistant Secretary; only one, just at that moment, could make an Assistant Son. More than half his duties were domestic; they sometimes required long absences; they always required independence of the Government service. His position was abnormal. The British Government by courtesy allowed the son to go to Court as Attaché, though he was never attached, and after five or six years' toleration, the decision was declared irregular. In the Legation, as private secretary, he was liable to do Secretary's work. In society, when official, he was attached to the Minister; when unofficial, he was a young man without any position at all. As the years went on, he began to find advantages in having no position at all except that of young man. Gradually he aspired to become a gentleman; just a member of society like the rest. The position was irregular; at that time many positions were irregular; yet it lent itself to a sort of irregular education that seemed to be the only sort of education the young man was ever to get.

Such as it was, few young men had more. The spring and summer of 1863 saw a great change in Secretary Seward's management of foreign affairs.[2] Under the stimulus of danger, he too got education. He felt, at

---

[1] Benjamin Moran, secretary of legation.

[2] William Henry Seward (1801–1872) was Lincoln's secretary of state (1861–1869), and was so continued in the cabinet of Andrew Johnson.

last, that his official representatives abroad needed support. Officially he could give them nothing but despatches, which were of no great value to any one; and at best the mere weight of an office had little to do with the public. Governments were made to deal with Governments, not with private individuals or with the opinions of foreign society. In order to affect European opinion, the weight of American opinion had to be brought to bear personally, and had to be backed by the weight of American interests. Mr. Seward set vigorously to work and sent over every important American on whom he could lay his hands. All came to the Legation more or less intimately, and Henry Adams had a chance to see them all, bankers or bishops, who did their work quietly and well, though, to the outsider, the work seemed wasted and the "influential classes" more indurated with prejudice than ever. The waste was only apparent; the work all told in the end, and meanwhile it helped education.

Two or three of these gentlemen were sent over to aid the Minister and to coöperate with him. The most interesting of these was Thurlow Weed,[3] who came to do what the private secretary himself had attempted two years before, with boyish ignorance of his own powers. Mr. Weed took charge of the press, and began, to the amused astonishment of the secretaries, by making what the Legation had learned to accept as the invariable mistake of every amateur diplomat; he wrote letters to the London Times. Mistake or not, Mr. Weed soon got into his hands the threads of management, and did quietly and smoothly all that was to be done. With his work the private secretary had no connection; it was he that interested. Thurlow Weed was a complete American education in himself. His mind was naturally strong and beautifully balanced; his temper never seemed ruffled; his manners were carefully perfect in the style of benevolent simplicity, the tradition of Benjamin Franklin. He was the model of political management and patient address; but the trait that excited enthusiasm in a private secretary was his faculty of irresistibly conquering confidence. Of all flowers in the garden of education, confidence was becoming the rarest; but before Mr. Weed went away, young Adams followed him about not only obediently—for obedience had long since become a blind instinct—but rather with sympathy and affection, much like a little dog.

The sympathy was not due only to Mr. Weed's skill of management, although Adams never met another such master, or any one who approached him; nor was the confidence due to any display of professions, either moral or social, by Mr. Weed. The trait that astounded and confounded cynicism was his apparent unselfishness. Never, in any man who wielded such power, did Adams meet anything like it. The effect of power and publicity on all men is the aggravation of self, a sort of tumor that ends by killing the victim's sympathies; a diseased appetite, like a

[3] Thurlow Weed (1797-1882), noted journalist and politician, a close friend of Seward, was sent by Lincoln on a mission to Europe in 1861-1862.

passion for drink or perverted tastes; one can scarcely use expressions too strong to describe the violence of egotism it stimulates; and Thurlow Weed was one of the exceptions; a rare immune. He thought apparently not of himself, but of the person he was talking with. He held himself naturally in the background. He was not jealous. He grasped power, but not office. He distributed offices by handfuls without caring to take them. He had the instinct of empire: he gave, but he did not receive. This rare superiority to the politicians he controlled, a trait that private secretaries never met in the politicians themselves, excited Adams's wonder and curiosity, but when he tried to get behind it, and to educate himself from the stores of Mr. Weed's experience, he found the study still more fascinating. Management was an instinct with Mr. Weed; an object to be pursued for its own sake, as one plays cards; but he appeared to play with men as though they were only cards; he seemed incapable of feeling himself one of them. He took them and played them for their face-value; but once, when he had told, with his usual humor, some stories of his political experience which were strong even for the Albany lobby, the private secretary made bold to ask him outright: "Then, Mr. Weed, do you think that no politician can be trusted?" Mr. Weed hesitated for a moment; then said in his mild manner: "I never advise a young man to begin by thinking so."

This lesson, at the time, translated itself to Adams in a moral sense, as though Mr. Weed had said: "Youth needs illusions!" As he grew older he rather thought that Mr. Weed looked on it as a question of how the game should be played. Young men most needed experience. They could not play well if they trusted to a general rule. Every card had a relative value. Principles had better be left aside; values were enough. Adams knew that he could never learn to play politics in so masterly a fashion as this: his education and his nervous system equally forbade it, although he admired all the more the impersonal faculty of the political master who could thus efface himself and his temper in the game. He noticed that most of the greatest politicians in history had seemed to regard men as counters. The lesson was the more interesting because another famous New Yorker came over at the same time who liked to discuss the same problem. Secretary Seward sent William M. Evarts [4] to London as law counsel, and Henry began an acquaintance with Mr. Evarts that soon became intimate. Evarts was as individual as Weed was impersonal; like most men, he cared little for the game, or how it was played, and much for the stakes, but he played it in a large and liberal way, like Daniel Webster, "a great advocate employed in politics." Evarts was also an economist of morals, but with him the question was rather how much morality one could afford. "The world can absorb only doses of truth," he said; "too much would kill it." One sought education in order to adjust the dose.

[4] William Maxwell Evarts (1818–1901), New York lawyer and politician, later became secretary of state under Hayes (1877–1881), and senator (1885–1891).

The teachings of Weed and Evarts were practical, and the private secretary's life turned on their value. England's power of absorbing truth was small. Englishmen, such as Palmerston, Russell, Bethell, and the society represented by the *Times* and *Morning Post*, as well as the Tories represented by Disraeli, Lord Robert Cecil, and the *Standard*, offered a study in education that sickened a young student with anxiety.[5] He had begun—contrary to Mr. Weed's advice—by taking their bad faith for granted. Was he wrong? To settle this point became the main object of the diplomatic education so laboriously pursued, at a cost already stupendous, and promising to become ruinous. Life changed front, according as one thought one's self dealing with honest men or with rogues.

Thus far, the private secretary felt officially sure of dishonesty. The reasons that satisfied him had not altogether satisfied his father, and of course his father's doubts gravely shook his own convictions, but, in practice, if only for safety, the Legation put little or no confidence in Ministers, and there the private secretary's diplomatic education began. The recognition of belligerency, the management of the Declaration of Paris, the Trent Affair,[6] all strengthened the belief that Lord Russell had started in May, 1861, with the assumption that the Confederacy was established; every step he had taken proved his persistence in the same idea; he never would consent to put obstacles in the way of recognition; and he was waiting only for the proper moment to interpose. All these points seemed so fixed—so self-evident—that no one in the Legation would have doubted or even discussed them except that Lord Russell obstinately denied the whole charge, and persisted in assuring Minister Adams of his honest and impartial neutrality.

With the insolence of youth and zeal, Henry Adams jumped at once to the conclusion that Earl Russell—like other statesmen—lied; and, although the Minister thought differently, he had to act as though Russell were false. Month by month the demonstration followed its mathematical stages; one of the most perfect educational courses in politics and diplomacy that a young man ever had a chance to pursue. The most costly tutors in the world were provided for him at public expense—Lord Palmerston, Lord Russell, Lord Westbury, Lord Selborne, Mr.

[5] Henry John Temple, viscount Palmerston (1784–1865) was prime minister (1859–1865) during the period Adams served as United States minister. Lord John Russell (later Earl Russell) (1792–1878) was foreign secretary (1859–1865). He later became prime minister, and first lord of the treasury. Richard Bethell, baron Westbury (1800–1873), was lord chancellor (1861–1865). Benjamin Disraeli (1804–1881), created earl of Beaconsfield in 1876, had been chancellor of the exchequer and leader in the House in 1852, 1858–1859, but he held no office during

Minister Adams's service abroad. He later twice became prime minister. Lord Robert Cecil, marquis of Salisbury (1830–1903), supported Disraeli's reform bill in 1859. He later held high office, four times as prime minister.

[6] The *Trent*, a British steamer, was intercepted by an American ship, Nov. 8, 1861, commanded by Capt. Charles Wilkes, who removed from the *Trent* the Confederate commissioners, Mason and Slidell, thus creating the "Trent Affair." Later the United States government disavowed the act, preventing serious complications.

Gladstone, Lord Granville, and their associates, paid by the British Government; William H. Seward, Charles Francis Adams, William Maxwell Evarts, Thurlow Weed, and other considerable professors employed by the American Government; [7] but there was only one student to profit by this immense staff of teachers. The private secretary alone sought education.

To the end of his life he labored over the lessons then taught. Never was demonstration more tangled. Hegel's metaphysical doctrine of the identity of opposites was simpler and easier to understand. Yet the stages of demonstration were clear. They began in June, 1862, after the escape of one rebel cruiser, by the remonstrances of the Minister against the escape of "No. 290," which was imminent. Lord Russell declined to act on the evidence. New evidence was sent in every few days, and with it, on July 24, was included Collier's legal opinion: "It appears difficult to make out a stronger case of infringement of the Foreign Enlistment Act, which, if not enforced on this occasion, is little better than a dead letter." Such language implied almost a charge of collusion with the rebel agents— an intent to aid the Confederacy. In spite of the warning, Earl Russell let the ship, four days afterwards, escape.[8]

Young Adams had nothing to do with law; that was business of his betters. His opinion of law hung on his opinion of lawyers. In spite of Thurlow Weed's advice, could one afford to trust human nature in politics? History said not. Sir Robert Collier seemed to hold that Law agreed with History. For education the point was vital. If one could not trust a dozen of the most respected private characters in the world, composing the Queen's Ministry, one could trust no mortal man.

Lord Russell felt the force of this inference, and undertook to disprove it. His effort lasted till his death. At first he excused himself by throwing the blame on the law officers. This was a politician's practice, and the lawyers overruled it. Then he pleaded guilty to criminal negligence, and said in his "Recollections":—"I assent entirely to the opinion of the Lord Chief Justice of England that the Alabama ought to have been detained during the four days I was waiting for the opinion of the law officers. But I think that the fault was not that of the commissioners of customs, it was my fault as Secretary of State for Foreign Affairs." This concession brought all parties on common ground. Of course it was his fault!

---

[7] Roundell Palmer, earl of Selborne (1812–1895), was solicitor-general in 1861–1863, and attorney-general, 1863–1866; he later became lord chancellor. William Ewart Gladstone (1809–1898), chancellor of the exchequer (1859–1866) later became prime minister. George Granville Leveson-Gower, earl Granville (1815–1891), was president of the council under Palmerston, and later secretary for foreign affairs.

[8] Robert Porrett Collier, baron Monks-well (1817–1886) was at this time counsel to the admiralty and judge advocate to the fleet. The *Alabama*, a sloop built for the Confederate states at Birkenhead, England, was commanded by Capt. Raphael Semmes of the Confederate navy, but with a crew and equipment entirely British. She cruised during 1862–1864, destroying American shipping, until she was sunk. In 1872 an international arbitration commission awarded the United States fifteen million dollars in claims.

The true issue lay not in the question of his fault, but of his intent. To a young man, getting an education in politics, there could be no sense in history unless a constant course of faults implied a constant motive.

For his father the question was not so abstruse; it was a practical matter of business to be handled as Weed or Evarts handled their bargains and jobs. Minister Adams held the convenient belief that, in the main, Russell was true, and the theory answered his purposes so well that he died still holding it. His son was seeking education, and wanted to know whether he could, in politics, risk trusting any one. Unfortunately no one could then decide; no one knew the facts. Minister Adams died without knowing them. Henry Adams was an older man than his father in 1862, before he learned a part of them. The most curious fact, even then, was that Russell believed in his own good faith and that Argyll [9] believed in it also.

Argyll betrayed a taste for throwing the blame on Bethell, Lord Westbury, then Lord Chancellor, but this escape helped Adams not at all. On the contrary, it complicated the case of Russell. In England, one half of society enjoyed throwing stones at Lord Palmerston, while the other half delighted in flinging mud at Earl Russell, but every one of every party united in pelting Westbury with every missile at hand. The private secretary had no doubts about him, for he never professed to be moral. He was the head and heart of the whole rebel contention, and his opinions on neutrality were as clear as they were on morality. The private secretary had nothing to do with him, and regretted it, for Lord Westbury's wit and wisdom were great; but as far as his authority went, he affirmed the law that in politics no man should be trusted.

Russell alone insisted on his honesty of intention and persuaded both the Duke and the Minister to believe him. Every one in the Legation accepted his assurances as the only assertions they could venture to trust. They knew he expected the rebels to win in the end, but they believed he would not actively interpose to decide it. On that—on nothing else—they rested their frail hopes of remaining a day longer in England. Minister Adams remained six years longer in England; then returned to America to lead a busy life till he died in 1886 still holding the same faith in Earl Russell, who had died in 1878. In 1889, Spencer Walpole published the official life of Earl Russell, and told a part of the story which had never been known to the Minister and which astounded his son, who burned with curiosity to know what his father would have said of it.

The story was this: The Alabama escaped, by Russell's confessed negligence, on July 28, 1862. In America the Union armies had suffered great disasters before Richmond and at the second Bull Run, August 29–30, followed by Lee's invasion of Maryland, September 7, the news of which, arriving in England on September 14, roused the natural idea that the crisis was at hand. The next news was expected by the Confederates to

<hr />

[9] George Douglas Campbell, duke of Argyll (1823–1900), was lord privy seal, 1859–1866.

announce the fall of Washington or Baltimore. Palmerston instantly, September 14, wrote to Russell: "If this should happen, would it not be time for us to consider whether in such a state of things England and France might not address the contending parties and recommend an arrangement on the basis of separation?"

This letter, quite in the line of Palmerston's supposed opinions, would have surprised no one, if it had been communicated to the Legation; and indeed, if Lee had captured Washington, no one could have blamed Palmerston for offering intervention. Not Palmerston's letter but Russell's reply, merited the painful attention of a young man seeking a moral standard for judging politicians:—

GOTHA, September, 17, 1862.

MY DEAR PALMERSTON:—
    Whether the Federal army is destroyed or not, it is clear that it is driven back to Washington and has made no progress in subduing the insurgent States. Such being the case, I agree with you that the time is come for offering mediation to the United States Government with a view to the recognition of the independence of the Confederates. I agree further that in case of failure, we ought ourselves to recognize the Southern States as an independent State. For the purpose of taking so important a step, I think we must have a meeting of the Cabinet. The 23d or 30th would suit me for the meeting.
    We ought then, if we agree on such a step, to propose it first to France, and then on the part of England and France, to Russia and other powers, as a measure decided upon by us.
    We ought to make ourselves safe in Canada, not by sending more troops there, but by concentrating those we have in a few defensible posts before the winter sets in. . . .

Here, then, appeared in its fullest force, the practical difficulty in education which a mere student could never overcome; a difficulty not in theory, or knowledge, or even want of experience, but in the sheer chaos of human nature. Lord Russell's course had been consistent from the first, and had all the look of rigid determination to recognize the Southern Confederacy "with a view" to breaking up the Union. His letter of September 17 hung directly on his encouragement of the Alabama and his protection of the rebel navy; while the whole of his plan had its root in the Proclamation of Belligerency, May 13, 1861. The policy had every look of persistent forethought, but it took for granted the deliberate dishonesty of three famous men: Palmerston, Russell, and Gladstone. This dishonesty, as concerned Russell, was denied by Russell himself, and disbelieved by Argyll, Forster,[10] and most of America's friends in England, as well as by Minister Adams. What the Minister would have thought had he seen this letter of September 17, his son would have greatly liked to know, but he would have liked still more to know what the Minister would have thought of Palmerston's answer, dated September 23:—

[10] William Edward Forster (1818–1886), a Liberal member of Parliament (1861–1885), was under-secretary of state for the colonies, 1865–1866.

. . . It is evident that a great conflict is taking place to the north-west of Washington, and its issue must have a great effect on the state of affairs. If the Federals sustain a great defeat, they may be at once ready for mediation, and the iron should be struck while it is hot. If, on the other hand, they should have the best of it, we may wait a while and see what may follow. . .

The rôles were reversed. Russell wrote what was expected from Palmerston, or even more violently; while Palmerston wrote what was expected from Russell, or even more temperately. The private secretary's view had been altogether wrong, which would not have much surprised even him, but he would have been greatly astonished to learn that the most confidential associates of these men knew little more about their intentions than was known in the Legation. The most trusted member of the Cabinet was Lord Granville, and to him Russell next wrote. Granville replied at once decidedly opposing recognition of the Confederacy, and Russell sent the reply to Palmerston, who returned it October 2, with the mere suggestion of waiting for further news from America. At the same time Granville wrote to another member of the Cabinet, Lord Stanley of Alderley, a letter published forty years afterwards in Granville's "Life" (I, 442)—to the private secretary altogether the most curious and instructive relic of the whole lesson in politics:—

. . . I have written to Johnny my reasons for thinking it decidedly premature. I, however, suspect you will settle to do so. Pam., Johnny, and Gladstone would be in favor of it, and probably Newcastle. I do not know about the others. It appears to me a great mistake. . . .

Out of a Cabinet of a dozen members, Granville, the best informed of them all, could pick only three who would favor recognition. Even a private secretary thought he knew as much as this, or more. Ignorance was not confined to the young and insignificant, nor were they the only victims of blindness. Granville's letter made only one point clear. He knew of no fixed policy or conspiracy. If any existed, it was confined to Palmerston, Russell, Gladstone, and perhaps Newcastle. In truth, the Legation knew, then, all that was to be known, and the true fault of education was to suspect too much.

By that time, October 3, news of Antietam and of Lee's retreat into Virginia had reached London. The Emancipation Proclamation arrived. Had the private secretary known all that Granville or Palmerston knew, he would surely have thought the danger past, at least for a time, and any man of common sense would have told him to stop worrying over phantoms. This healthy lesson would have been worth much for practical education, but it was quite upset by the sudden rush of a new actor upon the stage with a rhapsody that made Russell seem sane, and all education superfluous.

This new actor, as every one knows, was William Ewart Gladstone, then Chancellor of the Exchequer. If, in the domain of the world's politics, one point was fixed, one value ascertained, one element serious, it was the British Exchequer; and if one man lived who could be certainly counted as sane by overwhelming interest, it was the man who had in charge the finances of England. If education had the smallest value, it should have shown its force in Gladstone, who was educated beyond all record of English training. From him, if from no one else, the poor student could safely learn.

Here is what he learned! Palmerston notified Gladstone, September 24, of the proposed intervention: "If I am not mistaken, you would be inclined to approve such a course." Gladstone replied the next day: "He was glad to learn what the Prime Minister had told him; and for two reasons especially he desired that the proceedings should be prompt: the first was the rapid progress of the Southern arms and the extension of the area of Southern feeling; the second was the risk of violent impatience in the cotton-towns of Lancashire such as would prejudice the dignity and disinterestedness of the proffered mediation."

Had the puzzled student seen this letter, he must have concluded from it that the best educated statesman England ever produced did not know what he was talking about, an assumption which all the world would think quite inadmissible from a private secretary—but this was a trifle. Gladstone having thus arranged, with Palmerston and Russell, for intervention in the American war, reflected on the subject for a fortnight from September 25 to October 7, when he was to speak on the occasion of a great dinner at Newcastle. He decided to announce the Government's policy with all the force his personal and official authority could give it. This decision was no sudden impulse; it was the result of deep reflection pursued to the last moment. On the morning of October 7, he entered in his diary: "Reflected further on what I should say about Lancashire and America, for both these subjects are critical." That evening at dinner, as the mature fruit of his long study, he deliberately pronounced the famous phrase:—

... We know quite well that the people of the Northern States have not yet drunk of the cup—they are still trying to hold it far from their lips—which all the rest of the world see they nevertheless must drink of. We may have our own opinions about slavery; we may be for or against the South; but there is no doubt that Jefferson Davis and other leaders of the South have made an army; they are making, it appears, a navy; and they have made, what is more than either, they have made a nation. ...

Looking back, forty years afterwards, on this episode, one asked one's self painfully what sort of a lesson a young man should have drawn, for the purposes of his education, from this world-famous teaching of a very great master. In the heat of passion at the moment, one drew some harsh moral conclusions: Were they incorrect? Posed bluntly as rules of conduct, they led to the worst possible practices. As morals, one could detect no shade of difference between Gladstone and Napoleon except to the advantage of Napoleon. The private secretary saw none; he accepted the teacher in that sense; he took his lesson of political morality as learned, his notice to quit as duly served, and supposed his education to be finished.

Every one thought so, and the whole City was in a turmoil. Any intelligent education ought to end when it is complete. One would then feel fewer hesitations and would handle a surer world. The old-fashioned logical drama required unity and sense: the actual drama is a pointless puzzle, without even an intrigue. When the curtain fell on Gladstone's speech, any student had the right to suppose the drama ended; none could have affirmed that it was about to begin; that one's painful lesson was thrown away.

Even after forty years, most people would refuse to believe it; they would still insist that Gladstone, Russell, and Palmerston were true villains of melodrama. The evidence against Gladstone in special seemed overwhelming. The word "must" can never be used by a responsible Minister of one Government towards another, as Gladstone used it. No one knew so well as he that he and his own officials and friends at Liverpool were alone "making" a rebel navy, and that Jefferson Davis had next to nothing to do with it. As Chancellor of the Exchequer he was the Minister most interested in knowing that Palmerston, Russell, and himself were banded together by mutual pledge to make the Confederacy a nation the next week, and that the Southern leaders had as yet no hope of "making a nation" but in them. Such thoughts occurred to every one at the moment and time only added to their force. Never in the history of political turpitude had any brigand of modern civilization offered a worse example. The proof of it was that it outraged even Palmerston, who immediately put up Sir George Cornewall Lewis [11] to repudiate the Chancellor of the Exchequer, against whom he turned his press at the same time. Palmerston had no notion of letting his hand be forced by Gladstone.

Russell did nothing of the kind; if he agreed with Palmerston, he followed Gladstone. Although he had just created a new evangel of nonintervention for Italy, and preached it like an apostle, he preached the gospel of intervention in America as though he were a mouthpiece of the Congress of Vienna. On October 13, he issued his call for the Cabinet to meet, on October 23, for discussion of the "duty of Europe to ask both parties, in the most friendly and conciliatory terms, to agree to a suspension of arms." Meanwhile Minister Adams, deeply perturbed and profoundly anxious, would betray no sign of alarm, and purposely delayed to ask explanation. The howl of anger against Gladstone became louder every day, for every one knew that the Cabinet was called for October 23, and then could not fail to decide its policy about the United States. Lord Lyons [12] put off his departure for America till October 25 expressly

---

[11] Sir George Cornewall Lewis (1806–1863) was secretary of state for war, 1861–1863.

[12] Richard Bickerton Pemell Lyons, earl Lyons (1817–1887) was minister to the United States, 1858–1865.

to share in the conclusions to be discussed on October 23. When Minister Adams at last requested an interview, Russell named October 23 as the day. To the last moment every act of Russell showed that, in his mind, the intervention was still in doubt.

When Minister Adams, at the interview, suggested that an explanation was due him, he watched Russell with natural interest, and reported thus:—

. . . His lordship took my allusion at once, though not without a slight indication of embarrassment. He said that Mr. Gladstone had been evidently much misunderstood. I must have seen in the newspapers the letters which contained his later explanations. That he had certain opinions in regard to the nature of the struggle in America, as on all public questions, just as other Englishmen had, was natural enough. And it was the fashion here for public men to express such as they held in their public addresses. Of course it was not for him to disavow anything on the part of Mr. Gladstone; but he had no idea that in saying what he had, there was a serious intention to justify any of the inferences that had been drawn from it of a disposition in the Government now to adopt a new policy. . . .

A student trying to learn the processes of politics in a free government could not but ponder long on the moral to be drawn from this "explanation" of Mr. Gladstone by Earl Russell. The point set for study as the first condition of political life, was whether any politician could be believed or trusted. The question which a private secretary asked himself, in copying this despatch of October 24, 1862, was whether his father believed, or should believe, one word of Lord Russell's "embarrassment." The "truth" was not known for thirty years, but when published, seemed to be the reverse of Earl Russell's statement. Mr. Gladstone's speech had been drawn out by Russell's own policy of intervention and had no sense except to declare the "disposition in the Government now to adopt" that new policy. Earl Russell never disavowed Gladstone, although Lord Palmerston and Sir George Cornewall Lewis instantly did so. As far as the curious student could penetrate the mystery, Gladstone exactly expressed Earl Russell's intent.

As political education, this lesson was to be crucial; it would decide the law of life. All these gentlemen were superlatively honorable; if one could not believe them, Truth in politics might be ignored as a delusion. Therefore the student felt compelled to reach some sort of idea that should serve to bring the case within a general law. Minister Adams felt the same compulsion. He bluntly told Russell that while he was "willing to acquit" Gladstone of "any deliberate intention to bring on the worst effects," he was bound to say that Gladstone was doing it quite as certainly as if he had one; and to this charge, which struck more sharply at Russell's secret policy than at Gladstone's public defence of it, Russell replied as well as he could:—

. . . His lordship intimated as guardedly as possible that Lord Palmerston and other members of the Government regretted the speech, and Mr. Gladstone himself was not disinclined to correct, as far as he could, the misinterpretation which had been made of it. It was still their intention to adhere to the rule of perfect neutrality in the struggle, and to let it come to its natural end without the smallest interference, direct or otherwise. But he could not say what circumstances might happen from month to month in the future. I observed that the policy he mentioned was satisfactory to us, and asked if I was to understand him as saying that no change of it was now proposed. To which he gave his assent. . . .

Minister Adams never knew more. He retained his belief that Russell could be trusted, but that Palmerston could not. This was the diplomatic tradition, especially held by the Russian diplomats. Possibly it was sound, but it helped in no way the education of a private secretary. The cat's-paw theory offered no safer clue, than the frank, old-fashioned, honest theory of villainy. Neither the one nor the other was reasonable.

No one ever told the Minister that Earl Russell, only a few hours before, had asked the Cabinet to intervene, and that the Cabinet had refused. The Minister was led to believe that the Cabinet meeting was not held, and that its decision was informal. Russell's biographer said that, "with this memorandum [of Russell's, dated October 13] the cabinet assembled from all parts of the country on October 23; but . . . members of the Cabinet doubted the policy of moving, or moving at that time." The Duke of Newcastle and Sir George Grey joined Granville in opposition. As far as known, Russell and Gladstone stood alone. "Considerations such as these prevented the matter being pursued any further."

Still no one has distinctly said that this decision was formal; perhaps the unanimity of opposition made the formal Cabinet unnecessary; but it is certain that, within an hour or two before or after this decision, "his lordship said [to the United States Minister] that the policy of the Government was to adhere to a strict neutrality and to leave this struggle to settle itself." When Mr. Adams, not satisfied even with this positive assurance, pressed for a categorical answer: "I asked him if I was to understand that policy as not now to be changed; he said: Yes!"

John Morley's comment on this matter, in the "Life of Gladstone," forty years afterwards, would have interested the Minister, as well as his private secretary: "If this relation be accurate," said Morley of a relation officially published at the time, and never questioned, "then the Foreign Secretary did not construe strict neutrality as excluding what diplomatists call good offices." For a vital lesson in politics, Earl Russell's construction of neutrality mattered little to the student, who asked only Russell's intent, and cared only to know whether his construction had any other object than to deceive the Minister.

In the grave one can afford to be lavish of charity, and possibly Earl Russell may have been honestly glad to reassure his personal friend Mr. Adams; but to one who is still in the world even if not of it, doubts are as plenty as days. Earl Russell totally deceived the private secretary, whatever he may have done to the Minister. The policy of abstention was not settled on October 23. Only the next day, October 24, Gladstone circulated a rejoinder to G. C. Lewis, insisting on the duty of England, France, and Russia to intervene by representing, "with moral authority and force, the opinion of the civilized world upon the conditions of the case." Nothing had been decided. By some means, scarcely accidental, the French Emperor was led to think that his influence might turn the scale, and only ten days after Russell's categorical "Yes!" Napoleon officially invited him to say "No!" He was more than ready to do so. Another Cabinet meeting was called for November 11, and this time Gladstone himself reports the debate:—

> Nov. 11. We have had our Cabinet to-day and meet again to-morrow. I am afraid we shall do little or nothing in the business of America. But I will send you definite intelligence. Both Lords Palmerston and Russell are *right*.
> Nov. 12. The United States affair has ended and not well. Lord Russell rather turned tail. He gave way without resolutely fighting out his battle. However, though we decline for the moment, the answer is put upon grounds and in terms which leave the matter very open for the future.
> Nov. 13. I think the French will make our answer about America public; at least it is very possible. But I hope they may not take it as a positive refusal, or at any rate that they may themselves act in the matter. It will be clear that we concur with them, that the war should cease. Palmerston gave to Russell's proposal a feeble and half-hearted support.

Forty years afterwards, when every one except himself, who looked on at this scene, was dead, the private secretary of 1862 read these lines with stupor, and hurried to discuss them with John Hay, who was more astounded than himself. All the world had been at cross-purposes, had misunderstood themselves and the situation, had followed wrong paths, drawn wrong conclusions, had known none of the facts. One would have done better to draw no conclusions at all. One's diplomatic education was a long mistake.

These were the terms of this singular problem as they presented themselves to the student of diplomacy in 1862: Palmerston, on September 14, under the impression that the President was about to be driven from Washington and the Army of the Potomac dispersed, suggested to Russell that in such a case, intervention might be feasible. Russell instantly answered that, in any case, he wanted to intervene and should call a Cabinet for the purpose. Palmerston hesitated; Russell insisted; Granville protested. Meanwhile the rebel army was defeated at Antietam, September 17, and driven out of Maryland. Then Gladstone, October 7, tried to force Palmerston's hand by treating the intervention as a *fait accompli*. Russell assented, but Palmerston put up Sir George Cornewall Lewis to contradict Gladstone and treated him sharply in the press, at the very moment when Russell was calling a Cabinet to make Gladstone's words good. On October 23, Russell assured Adams that no change in policy was now proposed. On the same day he had proposed it, and was voted down. Instantly Napoleon III appeared as the ally of Russell and Gladstone with a proposition which had no sense except as a bribe to Palmerston to replace America, from pole to pole, in her old dependence on Europe, and to replace England in her old sovereignty of the seas, if Palmerston would support France in Mexico. The young student of diplomacy, knowing Palmerston, must have taken for granted that Palmerston inspired this motion and would support it; knowing Russell and his Whig antecedents, he would conceive that Russell must oppose it; knowing Gladstone and his lofty principles, he would not doubt that Gladstone violently denounced the scheme. If education was worth a straw, this was the only arrangement of persons that a trained student would imagine possible, and it was the arrangement actually assumed by nine men out of ten, as history. In truth, each valuation was false. Palmerston never showed favor to the scheme and gave it only "a feeble and half-hearted support." Russell gave way without resolutely fighting out "*his*battle." The only resolute, vehement, conscientious champion of Russell, Napoleon, and Jefferson Davis was Gladstone.

Other people could afford to laugh at a young man's blunders, but to him the best part of life was thrown away if he learned such a lesson wrong. Henry James had not yet taught the world to read a volume for the pleasure of seeing the lights of his burning-glass turned on alternate sides of the same figure. Psychological study was still simple, and at worst—or at best—English character was never subtle. Surely no one would believe that complexity was the trait that confused the student of Palmerston, Russell, and Gladstone. Under a very strong light human nature will always appear complex and full of contradictions, but the British statesman would appear, on the whole, among the least complex of men.

Complex these gentlemen were not. Disraeli alone might, by contrast, be called complex, but Palmerston, Russell, and Gladstone deceived only by their simplicity. Russell was the most interesting to a young man because his conduct seemed most statesmanlike. Every act of Russell, from April, 1861, to November, 1862, showed the clearest determination to break up the Union. The only point in Russell's character about which the student thought no doubt to be possible was its want of good faith. It was thoroughly dishonest, but strong. Habitually Russell said one thing and did another. He seemed unconscious of his own contradictions even when his opponents pointed them out, as they were much in the habit of doing, in the strongest language. As the student watched him deal with the Civil War in America, Russell alone showed persistence, even obstinacy, in a definite determination, which he supported, as was necessary, by the usual definite falsehoods. The young man did not complain of the falsehoods; on the contrary, he was vain of his own insight in detecting them; but he was wholly upset by the idea that Russell should think himself true.

Young Adams thought Earl Russell a statesman of the old school, clear about his objects and unscrupulous in his methods—dishonest but strong. Russell ardently asserted that he had no objects, and that though he might be weak he was above all else honest. Minister Adams leaned to Russell personally and thought him true, but officially, in practice, treated him as false. *Punch*, before 1862, commonly drew Russell as a schoolboy telling lies, and afterwards as prematurely senile, at seventy. Education stopped there. No one, either in or out of England, ever offered a rational explanation of Earl Russell.

Palmerston was simple—so simple as to mislead the student altogether—but scarcely more consistent. The world thought him positive, decided, reckless; the record proved him to be cautious, careful, vacillating. Minister Adams took him for pugnacious and quarrelsome; the "Lives" of Russell, Gladstone, and Granville show him to have been good-tempered, conciliatory, avoiding quarrels. He surprised the Minister by refusing to pursue his attack on General Butler. He tried to check Russell. He scolded Gladstone. He discouraged Napoleon. Except Disraeli none of the English statesmen were so cautious as he in talking of America. Palmerston told no falsehoods; made no professions; concealed no opinions; was detected in no double-dealing. The most mortifying failure in Henry Adams's long education was that, after forty years of confirmed dislike, distrust, and detraction of Lord Palmerston, he was obliged at last to admit himself in error, and to consent in spirit—for by that time he was nearly as dead as any of them—to beg his pardon.

Gladstone was quite another story, but with him a student's difficulties were less because they were shared by all the world including Gladstone himself. He was the sum of contradictions. The highest education could reach, in this analysis, only a reduction to the absurd, but no absurdity that a young man could reach in 1862 would have approached the level that Mr. Gladstone admitted, avowed, proclaimed, in his confessions of 1896, which brought all reason and all hope of education to a still-stand:—

> I have yet to record an undoubted error, the most singular and palpable, I may add the least excusable of them all, especially since it was committed so late as in the year 1862 when I had outlived half a century. . . . I declared in the heat of the American struggle that Jefferson Davis had made a nation. . . . Strange to say, this declaration, most unwarrantable to be made by a Minister of the Crown with no authority other than his own, was not due to any feeling of partisanship for the South or hostility to the North. . . . I really, though most strangely, believed that it was an act of friendliness to all America to recognize that the struggle was virtually at an end. . . . That my opinion was founded upon a false estimate of the facts was the very least part of my fault. I did not perceive the gross impropriety of such an utterance from a Cabinet Minister of a power allied in blood and language, and bound to loyal neutrality; the case being further exaggerated by the fact that we were already, so to speak, under indictment before the world for not (as was alleged) having strictly enforced the laws of neutrality in the matter of the cruisers. My offense

was indeed only a mistake, but one of incredible grossness, and with such consequences of offence and alarm attached to it, that my failing to perceive them justly exposed me to very severe blame. It illustrates vividly that incapacity which my mind so long retained, and perhaps still exhibits, an incapacity of viewing subjects all round. . . .

Long and patiently—more than patiently—sympathetically, did the private secretary, forty years afterwards in the twilight of a life of study, read and re-read and reflect upon this confession. Then, it seemed, he had seen nothing correctly at the time. His whole theory of conspiracy—of policy—of logic and connection in the affairs of man, resolved itself into "incredible grossness." He felt no rancor, for he had won the game; he forgave, since he must admit, the "incapacity of viewing subjects all round" which had so nearly cost him life and fortune; he was willing even to believe. He noted, without irritation, that Mr. Gladstone, in his confession, had not alluded to the understanding between Russell, Palmerston, and himself; had even wholly left out his most "incredible" act, his ardent support of Napoleon's policy, a policy which even Palmerston and Russell had supported feebly, with only half a heart. All this was indifferent. Granting, in spite of evidence, that Gladstone had no set plan of breaking up the Union; that he was party to no conspiracy; that he saw none of the results of his acts which were clear to every one else; granting in short what the English themselves seemed at last to conclude—that Gladstone was not quite sane; that Russell was verging on senility; and that Palmerston had lost his nerve—what sort of education should have been the result of it? How should it have affected one's future opinions and acts?

Politics cannot stop to study psychology. Its methods are rough; its judgments rougher still. All this knowledge would not have affected either the Minister or his son in 1862. The sum of the individuals would still have seemed, to the young man, one individual—a single will or intention—bent on breaking up the Union "as a diminution of a dangerous power." The Minister would still have found his interest in thinking Russell friendly and Palmerston hostile. The individual would still have been identical with the mass. The problem would have been the same; the answer equally obscure. Every student would, like the private secretary, answer for himself alone.

Chapter XI

THE BATTLE OF THE RAMS (1863)

Minister Adams troubled himself little about what he did not see of an enemy. His son, a nervous animal, made life a terror by seeing too much. Minister Adams played his hand as it came, and seldom credited his opponents with greater intelligence than his own. Earl Russell suited him; perhaps a certain personal sympathy united them; and indeed Henry

Adams never saw Russell without being amused by his droll likeness to John Quincy Adams. Apart from this shadowy personal relation, no doubt the Minister was diplomatically right; he had nothing to lose and everything to gain by making a friend of the Foreign Secretary, and whether Russell were true or false mattered less, because, in either case, the American Legation could act only as though he were false. Had the Minister known Russell's determined effort to betray and ruin him in October, 1862, he could have scarcely used stronger expressions than he did in 1863. Russell must have been greatly annoyed by Sir Robert Collier's hint of collusion with the rebel agents in the Alabama Case, but he hardened himself to hear the same innuendo repeated in nearly every note from the Legation. As time went on, Russell was compelled, though slowly, to treat the American Minister as serious. He admitted nothing so unwillingly, for the nullity or fatuity of the Washington Government was his *idée fixe;* but after the failure of his last effort for joint intervention on November 12, 1862, only one week elapsed before he received a note from Minister Adams repeating his charges about the Alabama, and asking in very plain language for redress. Perhaps Russell's mind was naturally slow to understand the force of sudden attack, or perhaps age had affected it; this was one of the points that greatly interested a student, but young men have a passion for regarding their elders as senile, which was only in part warranted in this instance by observing that Russell's generation were mostly senile from youth. They had never got beyond 1815. Both Palmerston and Russell were in this case. Their senility was congenital, like Gladstone's Oxford training and High Church illusions, which caused wild eccentricities in his judgment. Russell could not conceive that he had misunderstood and mismanaged Minister Adams from the start, and when, after November 12, he found himself on the defensive, with Mr. Adams taking daily a stronger tone, he showed mere confusion and helplessness.

Thus, whatever the theory, the action of diplomacy had to be the same. Minister Adams was obliged to imply collusion between Russell and the rebels. He could not even stop at criminal negligence. If, by an access of courtesy, the Minister were civil enough to admit that the escape of the Alabama had been due to criminal negligence, he could make no such concession in regard to the ironclad rams which the Lairds were building; for no one could be so simple as to believe that two armored ships-of-war could be built publicly, under the eyes of the Government, and go to sea like the Alabama, without active and incessant collusion. The longer Earl Russell kept on his mask of assumed ignorance, the more violently in the end, the Minister would have to tear it off. Whatever Mr. Adams might personally think of Earl Russell, he must take the greatest possible diplomatic liberties with him if this crisis were allowed to arrive.

As the spring of 1863 drew on, the vast field cleared itself for action. A campaign more beautiful—better suited for training the mind of a youth eager for training—has not often unrolled itself for study, from the beginning, before a young man perched in so commanding a position. Very slowly, indeed, after two years of solitude, one began to feel the first faint flush of new and imperial life. One was twenty-five years old, and quite ready to assert it; some of one's friends were wearing stars on their collars; some had won stars of a more enduring kind. At moments one's breath came quick. One began to dream the sensation of wielding unmeasured power. The sense came, like vertigo, for an instant, and passed, leaving the brain a little dazed, doubtful, shy. With an intensity more painful than that of any Shakespearean drama, men's eyes were fastened on the armies in the field. Little by little, at first only as a shadowy chance of what might be, if things could be rightly done, one began to feel that, somewhere behind the chaos in Washington power was taking shape; that it was massed and guided as it had not been before. Men seemed to have learned their business—at a cost that ruined—and perhaps too late. A private secretary knew better than most people how much of the new power was to be swung in London, and almost exactly when; but the diplomatic campaign had to wait for the military campaign to lead. The student could only study.

Life never could know more than a single such climax. In that form, education reached its limits. As the first great blows began to fall, one curled up in bed in the silence of night, to listen with incredulous hope. As the huge masses struck, one after another, with the precision of machinery, the opposing mass, the world shivered. Such development of power was unknown. The magnificent resistance and the return shocks heightened the suspense. During the July days Londoners were stupid with unbelief. They were learning from the Yankees how to fight.

An American saw in a flash what all this meant to England, for one's mind was working with the acceleration of the machine at home; but Englishmen were not quick to see their blunders. One had ample time to watch the process, and had even a little time to gloat over the repayment of old scores. News of Vicksburg and Gettysburg reached London one Sunday afternoon, and it happened that Henry Adams was asked for that evening to some small reception at the house of Monckton Milnes.[13] He went early in order to exchange a word or two of congratulation before the rooms should fill, and on arriving he found only the ladies in the drawing-room; the gentlemen were still sitting over their wine. Presently they came in, and, as luck would have it, Delane of the *Times* came first. When Milnes caught sight of his young American friend, with a whoop of triumph he rushed to throw both arms about his neck and kiss him on both cheeks. Men of later birth who knew too little to realize the passions of 1863—backed by those of 1813—and reënforced by those of 1763—might conceive that such publicity embarrassed a private secretary who came from Boston and called himself shy; but that

---

[13] Richard Monckton Milnes, lord Houghton (1809–1885), was a statesman and poet of whom Henry Adams was especially fond.

evening, for the first time in his life, he happened not to be thinking of himself. He was thinking of Delane,[14] whose eye caught his, at the moment of Milnes's embrace. Delane probably regarded it as a piece of Milnes's foolery; he had never heard of young Adams, and never dreamed of his resentment at being ridiculed in the *Times*; he had no suspicion of the thought floating in the mind of the American Minister's son, for the British mind is the slowest of all minds, as the files of the *Times* proved, and the capture of Vicksburg had not yet penetrated Delane's thick cortex of fixed ideas. Even if he had read Adams's thought he would have felt for it only the usual amused British contempt for all that he had not been taught at school. It needed a whole generation for the *Times* to reach Milnes's standpoint.

Had the Minister's son carried out the thought, he would surely have sought an introduction to Delane on the spot, and assured him that he regarded his own personal score as cleared off—sufficiently settled, then and there—because his father had assumed the debt, and was going to deal with Mr. Delane himself. "You come next!" would have been the friendly warning. For nearly a year the private secretary had watched the board arranging itself for the collision between the Legation and Delane who stood behind the Palmerston Ministry. Mr. Adams had been steadily strengthened and reënforced from Washington in view of the final struggle. The situation had changed since the Trent Affair. The work was efficiently done; the organization was fairly complete. No doubt, the Legation itself was still as weakly manned and had as poor an outfit as the Legations of Guatemala or Portugal. Congress was always jealous of its diplomatic service, and the Chairman of the Committee of Foreign Relations was not likely to press assistance on the Minister to England. For the Legation not an additional clerk was offered or asked. The Secretary, the Assistant Secretary, and the private secretary did all the work that the Minister did not do. A clerk at five dollars a week would have done the work as well or better, but the Minister could trust no clerk; without express authority he could admit no one into the Legation; he strained a point already by admitting his son. Congress and its committees were the proper judges of what was best for the public service, and if the arrangement seemed good to them, it was satisfactory to a private secretary who profited by it more than they did. A great staff would have suppressed him. The whole Legation was a sort of improvised, volunteer service, and he was a volunteer with the rest. He was rather better off than the rest, because he was invisible and unknown. Better or worse, he did his work with the others, and if the secretaries made any remarks about Congress, they made no complaints, and knew that none would have received a moment's attention.

If they were not satisfied with Congress, they were satisfied with Secretary Seward. Without appropriations for the regular service, he

14 John Thaddeus Delane (1817–1879) was the influential editor of the London *Times* (1841–1877).

had done great things for its support. If the Minister had no secretaries, he had a staff of active consuls; he had a well-organized press; efficient legal support; and a swarm of social allies permeating all classes. All he needed was a victory in the field, and Secretary Stanton undertook that part of diplomacy. Vicksburg and Gettysburg cleared the board, and, at the end of July, 1863, Minister Adams was ready to deal with Earl Russell or Lord Palmerston or Mr. Gladstone or Mr. Delane, or any one else who stood in his way; and by the necessity of the case, was obliged to deal with all of them shortly.

Even before the military climax at Vicksburg and Gettysburg, the Minister had been compelled to begin his attack; but this was history, and had nothing to do with education. The private secretary copied the notes into his private books, and that was all the share he had in the matter, except to talk in private.

No more volunteer services were needed; the volunteers were in a manner sent to the rear; the movement was too serious for skirmishing. All that a secretary could hope to gain from the affair was experience and knowledge of politics. He had a chance to measure the motive forces of men; their qualities of character; their foresight; their tenacity of purpose.

In the Legation no great confidence was felt in stopping the rams. Whatever the reason, Russell seemed immovable. Had his efforts for intervention in September, 1862, been known to the Legation in September, 1863, the Minister must surely have admitted that Russell had, from the first, meant to force his plan of intervention on his colleagues. Every separate step since April, 1861, led to this final coercion. Although Russell's hostile activity of 1862 was still secret—and remained secret for some five-and-twenty years—his *animus* seemed to be made clear by his steady refusal to stop the rebel armaments. Little by little, Minister Adams lost hope. With loss of hope came the raising of tone, until at last, after stripping Russell of every rag of defence and excuse, he closed by leaving him loaded with connivance in the rebel armaments, and ended by the famous sentence: "It would be superfluous in me to point out to your lordship that this is war!"

What the Minister meant by this remark was his own affair; what the private secretary understood by it, was a part of his education. Had his father ordered him to draft an explanatory paragraph to expand the idea as he grasped it, he would have continued thus:—

"It would be superfluous: 1st. Because Earl Russell not only knows it already, but has meant it from the start. 2d. Because it is the only logical and necessary consequence of his unvarying action. 3d. Because Mr. Adams is not pointing out to *him* that 'this is war,' but is pointing it out to the world, to complete the record."

This would have been the matter-of-fact sense in which the private secretary copied into his books the matter-of-fact statement with which, without passion or excitement, the Minister announced that a state of war existed. To his copying eye, as clerk, the words, though on the extreme verge of diplomatic propriety, merely stated a fact, without novelty, fancy, or rhetoric. The fact had to be stated in order to make clear the issue. The war was Russell's war—Adams only accepted it.

Russell's reply to this note of September 5 reached the Legation on September 8, announcing at last to the anxious secretaries that "instructions have been issued which will prevent the departure of the two ironclad vessels from Liverpool." The members of the modest Legation in Portland Place accepted it as Grant had accepted the capitulation of Vicksburg. The private secretary conceived that, as Secretary Stanton had struck and crushed by superior weight the rebel left on the Mississippi, so Secretary Seward had struck and crushed the rebel right in England, and he never felt a doubt as to the nature of the battle. Though Minister Adams should stay in office till he were ninety, he would never fight another campaign of life and death like this; and though the private secretary should covet and attain every office in the gift of President or people, he would never again find education to compare with the life-and-death alternative of this two-year-and-a-half struggle in London, as it had racked and thumb-screwed him in its shifting phases; but its practical value as education turned on his correctness of judgment in measuring the men and their forces. He felt respect for Russell as for Palmerston because they represented traditional England and an English policy, respectable enough in itself, but which, for four generations, every Adams had fought and exploited as the chief source of his political fortunes. As he understood it, Russell had followed this policy steadily, ably, even vigorously, and had brought it to the moment of execution. Then he had met wills stronger than his own, and, after persevering to the last possible instant, had been beaten. Lord North and George Canning had a like experience.

This was only the idea of a boy, but, as far as he ever knew, it was also the idea of his Government. For once, the volunteer secretary was satisfied with his Government. Commonly the self-respect of a secretary, private or public, depends on, and is proportional to, the severity of his criticism, but in this case the English campaign seemed to him as creditable to the State Department as the Vicksburg campaign to the War Department, and more decisive. It was well planned, well prepared, and well executed. He could never discover a mistake in it. Possibly he was biassed by personal interest, but his chief reason for trusting his own judgment was that he thought himself to be one of only half a dozen persons who knew something about it. When others criticised Mr. Seward, he was rather indifferent to their opinions because he thought they hardly knew what they were talking about, and could not be taught without living over again the London life of 1862. To him Secretary Seward seemed immensely strong and steady in leadership; but this was no discredit to Russell or Palmerston or Gladstone. They, too, had shown power, patience and steadiness of purpose. They had persisted for two years and a half in their plan for breaking up the Union, and had yielded at last only in the jaws of war. After a long and desperate struggle, the American Minister had trumped their best card and won the game.

Again and again, in after life, he went back over the ground to see whether he could detect error on either side. He found none. At every stage the steps were both probable and proved. All the more he was disconcerted that Russell should indignantly and with growing energy, to his dying day, deny and resent the axiom of Adams's whole contention, that from the first he meant to break up the Union. Russell affirmed that he meant nothing of the sort; that he had meant nothing at all; that he meant to do right; that he did not know what he meant. Driven from one defence after another, he pleaded at last, like Gladstone, that he had no defence. Concealing all he could conceal—burying in profound secrecy his attempt to break up the Union in the autumn of 1862—he affirmed the louder his scrupulous good faith. What was worse for the private secretary, to the total derision and despair of the lifelong effort for education, as the final result of combined practice, experience, and theory—he proved it.

Henry Adams had, as he thought, suffered too much from Russell to admit any plea in his favor; but he came to doubt whether this admission really favored him. Not until long after Earl Russell's death was the question reopened. Russell had quitted office in 1866; he died in 1878; the biography was published in 1889. During the Alabama controversy and the Geneva Conference in 1872, his course as Foreign Secretary had been sharply criticised, and he had been compelled to see England pay more than £3,000,000 penalty for his errors. On the other hand, he brought forward—or his biographer for him—evidence tending to prove that he was not consciously dishonest, and that he had, in spite of appearances, acted without collusion, agreement, plan, or policy, as far as concerned the rebels. He had stood alone, as was his nature. Like Gladstone, he had thought himself right.

In the end, Russell entangled himself in a hopeless ball of admissions, denials, contradictions, and resentments which led even his old colleagues to drop his defence, as they dropped Gladstone's; but this was not enough for the student of diplomacy who had made a certain theory his law of life, and wanted to hold Russell up against himself; to show that he had foresight and persistence of which he was unaware. The effort became hopeless when the biography in 1889 published papers which upset all that Henry Adams had taken for diplomatic education; yet he sat down once more, when past sixty years old, to see whether he could unravel the skein.

Of the obstinate effort to bring about an armed intervention, on the lines marked out by Russell's letter to Palmerston from Gotha, 17 September, 1862, nothing could be said beyond Gladstone's plea in excuse for his speech in pursuance of the same effort, that it was "the most singular and palpable error," "the least excusable," "a mistake of incredible grossness," which passed defence; but while Gladstone threw himself on the mercy of the public for his speech, he attempted no excuse for Lord Russell who led him into the "incredible grossness" of announcing the Foreign Secretary's intent. Gladstone's offence, "singular and palpable," was not the speech alone, but its cause—the policy that inspired the speech. "I weakly supposed . . . I really, though most strangely, believed that it was an act of friendliness." Whatever absurdity Gladstone supposed, Russell supposed nothing of the sort. Neither he nor Palmerston "most strangely believed" in any proposition so obviously and palpably absurd, nor did Napoleon delude himself with philanthropy. Gladstone, even in his confession, mixed up policy, speech, motives, and persons, as though he were trying to confuse chiefly himself.

There Gladstone's activity seems to have stopped. He did not reappear in the matter of the rams. The rebel influence shrank in 1863, as far as is known, to Lord Russell alone, who wrote on September 1 that he could not interfere in any way with those vessels, and thereby brought on himself Mr. Adams's declaration of war on September 5. A student held that, in this refusal, he was merely following his policy of September, 1862, and of every step he had taken since 1861.

The student was wrong. Russell proved that he had been feeble, timid, mistaken, senile, but not dishonest. The evidence is convincing. The Lairds had built these ships in reliance on the known opinion of the lawofficers that the statute did not apply, and a jury would not convict. Minister Adams replied that, in this case, the statute should be amended, or the ships stopped by exercise of the political power. Bethell rejoined that this would be a violation of neutrality; one must preserve the *status quo*. Tacitly Russell connived with Laird, and, had he meant to interfere, he was bound to warn Laird that the defect of the statute would no longer protect him, but he allowed the builders to go on till the ships were ready for sea. Then, on September 3, two days before Mr. Adams's "superfluous" letter, he wrote to Lord Palmerston begging for help; "The conduct of the gentlemen who have contracted for the two ironclads at Birkenhead is so very suspicious,"—he began, and this he actually wrote in good faith and deep confidence to Lord Palmerston, his chief, calling "the conduct" of the rebel agents "suspicious" when no one else in Europe or America felt any suspicion about it, because the whole question turned not on the rams, but on the technical scope of the Foreign Enlistment Act—"that I have thought it necessary to direct that they should be detained," not, of course, under the statute, but on the ground urged by the American Minister, of international obligation above the statute. "The Solicitor General has been consulted and concurs in the measure as one of policy though not of strict law. We shall thus test the law, and, if we have to pay damages, we have satisfied the opinion which prevails here as well as in America that that kind of neutral hostility should not be allowed to go on without some attempt to stop it."

For naïveté that would be unusual in an unpaid attaché of Legation, this sudden leap from his own to his opponent's ground, after two years and a half of dogged resistance, might have roused Palmerston to inhuman scorn, but instead of derision, well earned by Russell's old attacks on himself, Palmerston met the appeal with wonderful loyalty. "On consulting the law officers he found that there was no lawful ground for meddling with the ironclads," or, in unprofessional language, that he could trust neither his law officers nor a Liverpool jury; and therefore he suggested buying the ships for the British Navy. As proof of "criminal negligence" in the past, this suggestion seemed decisive, but Russell, by this time, was floundering in other troubles of negligence, for he had neglected to notify the American Minister. He should have done so at once, on September 3. Instead he waited till September 4, and then merely said that the matter was under "serious and anxious consideration." This note did not reach the Legation till three o'clock on the afternoon of September 5—after the "superfluous" declaration of war had been sent. Thus, Lord Russell had sacrificed the Lairds: had cost his Ministry the price of two ironclads, besides the Alabama Claims—say, in round numbers, twenty million dollars—and had put himself in the position of appearing to yield only to a threat of war. Finally he wrote to the Admiralty a letter which, from the American point of view, would have sounded youthful from an Eton schoolboy:—

September 14, 1863.

My Dear Duke:—

It is of the utmost importance and urgency that the ironclads building at Birkenhead should not go to America to break the blockade. They belong to Monsieur Bravay of Paris. If you will offer to buy them on the part of the Admiralty you will get money's worth if he accepts your offer; and if he does not, it will be presumptive proof that they are already bought by the Confederates. I should state that we have suggested to the Turkish Government to buy them; but you can easily settle that matter with the Turks. . . .

The hilarity of the secretaries in Portland Place would have been loud had they seen this letter and realized the muddle of difficulties into which Earl Russell had at last thrown himself under the impulse of the American Minister; but, nevertheless, these letters upset from top to bottom the results of the private secretary's diplomatic education forty years after he had supposed it complete. They made a picture different from anything he had conceived and rendered worthless his whole painful diplomatic experience.

To reconstruct, when past sixty, an education useful for any practical purpose, is no practical problem, and Adams saw no use in attacking it as only theoretical. He no longer cared whether he understood human nature or not; he understood quite as much of it as he wanted; but he found in the "Life of Gladstone" (II, 464) a remark several times repeated that gave him matter for curious thought. "I *always* hold," said

Mr. Gladstone, "that politicians are the men whom, as a rule, it is most difficult to comprehend"; and he added, by way of strengthening it: "For my own part, I never have thus understood, or thought I understood, *above one or two.*"

Earl Russell was certainly not one of the two.

Henry Adams thought he also had understood one or two; but the American type was more familiar. Perhaps this was the sufficient result of his diplomatic education; it seemed to be the whole.

HENRY JAMES

1843–1916

THE CAREER OF HENRY JAMES, WHICH EXTENDED FROM THE LAST DAYS of the Civil War to the middle of the First World War, was one of the longest and most prolific in American letters. During his five decades of writing, James reared a vast literary edifice—novels, tales, plays, criticism, books of travel, fugitive essays—and created certain novels which are regarded as supreme examples of that form. He was not only a practitioner of the novel: he was one of its great modern explicators, and much of the terminology used in discussion of the art of fiction stems from his various writings. His vision was that of the role of the American, the New Man, in his relations with the Old World, a vision even more significant in our century than in the last. His major fictional theme, treated both as comedy and as tragedy, was the New Man's loss of innocence upon exposure to the wider world. His major search was for new techniques with which to render his material and the truths of human consciousness. He was the first of the modern psychological analysts in the novel.

In the annals of American literature he stands as the prototype of the dedicated artist—one who from the first determined upon literature as a career and achieved it by a high and intense professionalism, an almost legendary fertility; he was, indeed, so productive that at one time during his life he glutted his own market. If Melville surpassed James in the poetry of his passion and the range of his vision, James possessed on his side a craftsmanship unsurpassed by his contemporaries and most of his successors. This does not mean that he wrote the "perfect" novel, or that rougher works have not achieved greater power. Some critics, indeed, have seen James's work, especially the later novels, as over-weighted with design and over-elaborate in style; they have argued, with some justification, that in certain of his fictions, James places the reader too close to the blue-prints and the architectural drawings and not close enough to life and experience. A kind of stubborn intellectual structure tends to impose itself upon the groundwork of James's original impulse. He conceives a story and promptly brings to bear on it a quantity of theory and artifice that at times—as his notebooks show—smother his original intention. But he created many kinds of fiction; and if some of his works possess a cathedral-like intricacy (and therefore a cathedral grandeur) others seem spider-spun. And there are still others which are lucid and lyrical and retain their freshness and spontaneity to this day. Henry James wrote for so many years and went through so many phases that he possessed not one "manner" or "style" but several. The world has been discovering that it is difficult, for this reason, to generalize about Henry James's work.

The influence of his work has been pervasive. Even when he is not read, he seems to furnish abundant quotation; few discussions of the craft of fiction are held without invoking his name, whether to quote his phrase about the quantity of "felt life" needed to produce a work of art, or his metaphor of "the house of fiction" and its many windows upon the world; or his continual experiments with "point of view" and his demand that there be, in a novel, some radiant intelligence capable of illuminating the drama for the reader. All of James's innovations were directed to one end: to remove the presence of the narrator, to permit the reader closer access to the unfolding story—to make the reader, indeed, a participant in the story. In his later work he sought to take his readers into the inner life of his characters, and in his attempts to capture "the very atmosphere of the mind" he foreshadowed the introspections of Marcel Proust, and the angle-of-vision and stream-of-consciousness of James Joyce.

Henry James was born in New York, just off Washington Square, which was to give its name to one of his most celebrated short novels. Like Melville, also a New Yorker, he did not belong to Concord and Boston, where American literature had taken deepest root, but was associated with the less parochial squares and avenues of Manhattan, a city that looked seaward to the Old World. His grandfather, an Irish immigrant, had made his fortune in Albany. His father was a religious visionary who had embraced the exaltations of Swedenborg and of Blake. His elder brother, William James, grew up to be the founder of psychological research in the United States and America's philosopher of pragmatism. Henry's father, living on a comfortable income, was a restless wanderer. He crossed and re-crossed the Atlantic with his family, gave his sons governesses and tutors instead of sending them to school, and provided them with a continuing view of people and places on either side of the ocean. From the first, the future novelist was exposed to the old culture of Europe and the nascent culture of America.

Henry was a shy boy, a second son who assumed the role of quiet observer beside his active elder brother. He was a "devourer of libraries"; he read largely fiction, and from the first was content to be simply "literary." He spent his young manhood at Newport, in Rhode Island, when the family was not abroad, and here in late adolescence began to write tales and book reviews which he had little difficulty in getting published. An injury to his back, while helping to put out a fire just after the outbreak of the Civil War, for a while caused him to lead a sedentary life and kept him from participating in the conflict. For a few months he entertained the illusion that he should have a professional career; he registered in the Harvard Law School, but instead of reading law, read French novelists and critics. His first story appeared anonymously in February 1864 in a New York magazine, the *Continental Monthly*. His second tale, dealing with life behind the lines of the Civil War, appeared in the *Atlantic Monthly* in 1865 when he was twenty-two. He reviewed books regularly for the *North American Review* and the *Nation*, and when William Dean Howells became an editor of the *Atlantic*, James found in him a literary friend and mentor who published him readily.

By the time Henry had brought out half a dozen short stories in his early twenties critics spoke of him as one of the most skilful writers of fiction in America. From the first, however, they deplored his tendency to be reflective and the failure of his heroes to lead a life of action. The stories of these early years deal entirely with the American scene, and show the leisurely existence of the well-to-do on the eastern seaboard. They reveal a close study of James's French models, Balzac, Merimée, George Sand. They also show how attentively he had read George Eliot and Hawthorne.

In 1869–70 he made his first adult journey abroad. He met writers and painters in England, journeyed in Italy, and glimpsed for the first time the theme that was to be central to most of his writing—that of the American in Europe. While he was in England his beloved cousin, Minny Temple, to whom he had formed a deep but reticent attachment, died. This shock, and the high emotion of his "passionate pilgrimage," provided much of the experience which was to be reflected in *The Portrait of a Lady* and *The Wings of the Dove*. And the year of wandering in England, France, and Italy set the stage for a lifetime of continental travel.

But first James tried to live and work in the United States. On his return he wrote "A Passionate Pilgrim," the only early tale he was willing later to acknowledge, and an awkward short novel, *Watch and Ward*. A second journey to Italy, followed by an attempt to be an art and drama critic in New York, confirmed him in his determination to reside abroad. He had discovered that he had a ready American market for travel articles; on the practical side, he also could live more cheaply in Europe; and in Europe he was finding material best suited for his fiction. Thus began his long expatriation. It was heralded by the publication of his first full-length novel, *Roderick Hudson*, the story of an American sculptor's struggle and decline in Rome; his first book of travel, *Transatlantic Sketches;* and his first collection of stories, *A Passionate Pilgrim and Other Tales.*

His creative life can be divided into three distinct periods. The first, from 1865 to 1882, was the period symbolized by "Daisy Miller"— marked by his discovery of the "international theme" and his full exploitation of it. During his lifetime his fame rested largely upon his handling of this theme: the meeting of America and Europe, the study of the moral and psychological problems of his fellow-countrymen and country-women in relation to the morals and customs of Europe. Like Hawthorne's Young Goodman Brown the Americans have to learn that the world is not as innocent as it appears, that it contains a fund of evil which they tend to overlook in their dreams of brave new worlds and a Garden of Eden existence. "Daisy Miller" dramatizes this on a tragicomical level—the tale of a young girl from Schenectady who goes to Rome and never realizes for one moment that European standards and European manners can be different from what she has known in her home town; that what she deems a mild flirtation is viewed by the Europeans, and above all by the Europeanized Americans, with deadly seriousness. The fresh Daisy withers in this environment; she dies in Rome after a "rumpus" that goes on, as James remarked, quite over her head.

In *Roderick Hudson* James had portrayed the American artist in Rome; in *The American* he had shown how a forthright American business man, possessing great charm of character, fared among the French nobility; but now he recognized that his public liked best of all stories about young American girls moving against European settings. With professional promptness the novelist produced a series of pictures of innocent little school teachers yearning for Europe; of "self-made" American girls creating calculated careers for themselves abroad; of Anglo-American marriages; of young heiresses involved in European entanglements. When Londoners laughed too heartily at Daisy and her compatriots, James chastened them by reversing his "international" picture and showing (in such tales as "An International Episode") how Englishmen in America could be the subject of laughter also. But he was playing upon national sensitivities; the Americans and the English enjoyed laughing at each other; they did not care to laugh at themselves.

As demands for his work increased, James met them with great rapidity and unflagging inventiveness. Thus in little over a year he produced three short novels, *Confidence*, *Washington Square*, and *The Europeans*, and kept three magazines supplied with his fiction. The proceeds were devoted to a year of leisurely production during which he planned and wrote *The Portrait of a Lady*, a calculated performance, intended to be his best novel to date. This is what it turned out to be. He was not quite forty when it was published, in 1881, and had his career ended then he would still rank as a major American novelist. As it was, another thirty years of creation lay before him. His "lady"—one of those splendid young

American girls James could evoke with great warmth and human sympathy—arrives in Europe full of great hopes and a will to live her life freely. How she is "ground in the very mill of the conventional," in spite of her dreams of freedom and nobleness, because of her innocence and unawareness of evil, is the drama of the work, and it is a psychological drama of great power.

With this novel James dropped the "international" theme. The second period of his writings extended from 1882 to 1895. During this time he wrote *The Bostonians, The Princess Casamassima,* and *The Tragic Muse.* The Boston novel was about reformers and suffragettes; the *Princess* dealt with revolutionaries in London; *The Tragic Muse* tried to capture the problems confronted by a young politician-painter and an actress seeking to make their careers in the world of art. Although during this phase James was trying to write deterministic novels, after the manner of the French naturalists, he created in reality subtle studies of individuals caught up in inter-personal relationships, undone by conflict between their temperament and their environment. In 1890, finding that these novels had been poorly received, he renounced long fiction and turned to the stage. His plays were also failures. And while they were failing he wrote autobiographical stories of misunderstood and unappreciated authors, as well as a series of ghostly tales. With the collapse of his play *Guy Domville* in 1895—it was booed by an ill-tempered London audience—he abandoned the stage and returned to the novel.

Now began the third and final phase of his creativity. First, between 1895 and 1900, he set down a series of short novels and tales dealing with childhood and adolescence, but in reality with his old theme of innocence in a corrupting world. The most famous of this group is the ghost story "The Turn of the Screw." Others were *What Maisie Knew, The Other House,* "In the Cage," and *The Awkward Age.* In 1898 the novelist moved from London to Lamb House, in Rye, Sussex, where he spent his final years, an honored but little-read novelist, creating to the end with undiminished power. Drawing upon the technical devices mastered in his writing for the stage and his recent fictional experiments, he now wrote in fast succession, in the first four years of the new century, *The Ambassadors, The Wings of the Dove,* and *The Golden Bowl.* In these massive works, regarded by most critics as the summit of his art, he used certain of his tested story-telling methods, but more boldly and experimentally than ever: the consistent "point of view," the omission of climactic scenes, the employment of large symbolic effects. James had begun as a Balzacian novelist who described minutely his crowded stage and his characters; he ended by leaving his stage almost bare, and allowing the characters to describe themselves. His style had become crowded and allusive, a tapestry heavy with metaphor and rich in verbal refinement. The novels of the second period had been largely set in England. Now he returned to his old ground. *The Ambassadors* is a comedy of American-European international manners, of a middle-aged American who goes to Paris to bring back a young man who has lingered there too long, and is himself captivated by life abroad. It is a study in the growth of awareness, and it balances the relaxed moral standards of the Continent against the more rigid code of New England. *The Wings of the Dove* is the sombre drama of an American heiress, doomed to die young, who is the victim of a mendacious plot in which a young man trifles with her affections in order to inherit her money. The theme of *The Ambassadors* is built around the idea of "live all you can"; *The Wings of the Dove* suggests that there can be no "life" without love. These themes coalesced in the creation of James's powerful short story, "The Beast in the Jungle," which he wrote at this time. In this tale, whose thirty pages encompass the entire life of an individual, James set down the dark drama of a man whose sole adventure has been his own egotism. Too late he discovers that he has not known what it is to love; and with this awareness comes insight into the emptiness of his life. *The Golden Bowl*, James's last major novel, considered by many to be his best, is a study of adultery within a family setting; in this work the American heiress not only achieves understanding of her predicament, but learns how to cope with her husband's infidelity and to win him back. In the process she attains her own maturity.

Upon the completion of these three major works, Henry James revisited the United States. He had been away for twenty years—all of his middle-age. He was enthusiastically received, lectured widely and wrote a series of American impressions titled *The American Scene*, an appraisal of the old and the new in his homeland in which he expressed misgivings over the material side of American life. On his return to England he assembled and revised his novels and tales for a "Definitive Edition." It was called the *New York Edition* and it contained only the cosmopolitan and European novels, and only about half of his hundred tales. Those writings which he had deemed hack-work, written only for money, were excluded. Some of the early novels were extensively rewritten and to the edition James affixed a series of prefaces defining his theories of fiction. Just before his seventieth year James wrote his autobiographies, *A Small Boy and Others* and *Notes of a Son and Brother*. He became a British subject during the First World War, received the Order of Merit from George V and died in 1916 leaving the beginning of a third autobiographical work, *The Middle Years*, and two unfinished novels, *The Ivory Tower* and *The Sense of the Past*.

Both as a writer of light comedies in prose, and as a man whose tragic vision prevails in his larger novels, Henry James has had a marked and continuing influence. He was a Balzacian in his concept of realism and in his belief that the novelist is, in effect, a historian of the intimate life of his time; but unlike Balzac's, his realism was psychological, and focused on human beings rather than on their environment. His insight into human behaviour anticipated the psychological insights of the Freudian era.

To list Henry James's large contributions to the art of the novel, so various and intricate, is to give but a partial view of his half century of writing. Somewhere James speaks of the "addicted artist." These words perfectly describe him. He was "addicted" to literature and to style; he believed that art alone gives form and perpetuity to a life otherwise evanescent. In his work the New World interrogates its brief past, weighs its future, appraises its ties with the Old World. That appraisal is still going on: it is one of the large facts of our century. James's writings, as a consequence, take their place not only in the world of literary art, but as concrete elements in America's culture and its civilization.

From HAWTHORNE

BROOK FARM AND CONCORD

Henry James's study of Hawthorne (1879) is a notable example in American letters of the tribute of one American master of the novel form to another. It was commissioned for the "English Men of Letters Series" and was written by James in a very few weeks in 1878. Although depreciated by certain Hawthorne enthusiasts as "condescending," and fiercely attacked because of James's observations on what was lacking in the American scene for the novelist of manners, it has come to be recognized as a masterpiece of interpretive writing. James relied for his facts largely on the biographical study by Hawthorne's son-in-law, G. P. Lathrop, but his analysis and interpretation of these facts, and the manner in which he placed Hawthorne's work in its proper setting, made his little book an admirable introduction for the English—for whom it was primarily intended—into the American literary scene of the time.

The chapter on Hawthorne's experiences at Brook Farm, his marriage and removal to the Old Manse at Concord, is here given. It is characteristic of the felicitous style of the entire book. In it, James drew upon his own memories when, as a boy, he often saw in his father's study, various of the Transcendentalist members associated with the Brook Farm experiment in communal living. Readers of the chapter will notice with what care James briefly gives the background of each fact; and how, with his swift economy of words, he offers us vignettes of Emerson, of Thoreau, of Ellery Channing, and of Margaret Fuller.

James's attachment to Hawthorne was profound. Certain of his stories show clearly the Hawthorne influence and his incomplete novel, *The Sense of the Past,* as well as *The Golden Bowl,* hark back in a certain measure to his reading of his American predecessor. James felt that Hawthorne had been the only practitioner of the novel on the American scene who had struck an individual note and cultivated a style, and he freely absorbed from him certain of his moods and atmospheres. While he had little sympathy for Hawthorne's allegorical excursions, James was deeply interested in his use of symbols and in his faculty for rendering realistic detail imaginatively. Other writings of James on Hawthorne include a shorter essay on him, a review of his French and Italian notebooks, and a centenary letter read at the commemoration observances in Salem in 1904.

The history of the little industrial and intellectual association which formed itself at this time in one of the suburbs of Boston has not, to my knowledge, been written; though it is assuredly a curious and interesting chapter in the domestic annals of New England. It would, of course, be easy to overrate the importance of this ingenious attempt of a few speculative persons to improve the outlook of mankind. The experiment came and went very rapidly and quietly, leaving very few traces behind it. It became simply a charming personal reminiscence for the small number of amiable enthusiasts who had had a hand in it. There were degrees of enthusiasm, and I suppose there were degrees of amiability; but a certain generous brightness of hope and freshness of conviction pervaded the whole undertaking, and rendered it, morally speaking, important to an extent of which any heed that the world in general ever gave to it is an insufficient measure. Of course it would be a great mistake to represent the episode of Brook Farm as directly related to the manners and morals of the New England world in general—and in especial to those of the prosperous, opulent, comfortable part of it. The thing was the experiment of a coterie—it was unusual, unfashionable, unsuccessful. It was, as would then have been said, an amusement of the Transcendentalists—a harmless effusion of Radicalism. The Transcendentalists were not, after all, very numerous, and the Radicals were by no means of the vivid tinge of those of our own day. I have said that the Brook Farm community left no traces behind it that the world in general can appreciate; I should rather say that the only trace is a short novel, of which the principal merits reside in its qualities of difference from the affair itself. *The Blithedale Romance* is the main result of Brook Farm; but *The Blithedale Romance* was, very properly, never recognised by the Brook Farmers as an accurate portrait of their little colony.

Nevertheless, in a society as to which the more frequent complaint is that it is monotonous, that it lacks variety of incident and of type, the episode, our own business with which is simply that it was the cause of Hawthorne's writing an admirable tale, might be welcomed as a picturesque variation. At the same time, if we do not exaggerate its proportions, it may seem to contain a fund of illustration as to that phase of human life with which our author's own history mingled itself. The most graceful account of the origin of Brook Farm is probably to be found in these words of one of the biographers of Margaret Fuller: "In Boston and its vicinity, several friends, for whose character Margaret felt the highest honour, were earnestly considering the possibility of making such industrial, social, and educational arrangements as would simplify economies, combine leisure for study with healthful and honest toil, avert unjust collisions of caste, equalise refinements, awaken generous affections, diffuse courtesy, and sweeten and sanctify life as a whole." The reader will perceive that this was a liberal scheme, and that if the experiment failed, the greater was the pity. The writer goes on to say that a gentleman, who afterwards distinguished himself in literature (he had begun by being a clergyman), "convinced by his experience in a faithful ministry that the need was urgent for a thorough application of the professed principles of Fraternity to actual relations, was about staking his all of fortune, reputation, and influence in an attempt to organise a joint-stock company at Brook Farm." As Margaret Fuller passes for having suggested to Hawthorne the figure of Zenobia in *The Blithedale Romance*, and as she is probably, with one exception, the person connected with the affair who, after Hawthorne, offered most of what is called a personality to the world, I may venture to quote a few more passages from her Memoirs—a curious, in some points of view almost a grotesque, and yet, on the whole, as I have said, an extremely interesting book. It was a strange history and a strange destiny, that of this brilliant, restless, and unhappy woman—this ardent New Englander, this impassioned Yankee, who occupied so large a place in the thoughts, the lives, the affections, of an intelligent and appreciative society, and yet left behind her nothing but the memory of a memory. Her function, her reputation, were singular, and not altogether reassuring: she was a talker; she was *the* talker; she was the genius of talk. She had a magnificent, though by no means an unmitigated, egotism; and in some of her utterances it is difficult to say whether pride or humility prevails—as, for instance, when she writes that she feels "that there is plenty of room in the Universe for my faults, and as if I could not spend time in thinking of them when so many things interest me more." She has left the same sort of reputation as a great actress. Some of her writing has extreme beauty, almost all of it has a real interest; but her value, her activity, her sway (I am not sure that one can say her charm), were personal and practical. She went to Europe, expanded to new desires and interests, and, very poor herself, married an impoverished Italian nobleman. Then, with her husband and child, she embarked to return to her own country, and was lost at sea in a terrible storm, within sight of its coasts. Her tragical death combined with many of the elements of her life to convert her memory into a sort of legend, so that the people who had known her well grew at last to be envied by later comers. Hawthorne does not appear to have been intimate with her; on the contrary, I find such an entry as this in the American Note-Books in 1841: "I was invited to dine at Mr. Bancroft's yesterday, with Miss Margaret Fuller; but Providence had given me some business to do; for which I was very thankful!" It is true that, later, the lady is the subject of one or two allusions of a gentler cast. One of them, indeed, is so pretty as to be worth quoting:—

"After leaving the book at Mr. Emerson's, I returned through the woods, and, entering Sleepy Hollow, I perceived a lady reclining near the path which bends along its verge. It was Margaret herself. She had been there the whole afternoon, meditating or reading, for she had a book in her hand, with some strange title which I did not understand and have forgotten. She said that nobody had broken her solitude, and was just giving utterance to a theory that no inhabitant of Concord ever visited Sleepy Hollow, when we saw a group of people entering the sacred precincts. Most of them followed a path which led them away from us; but an old man passed near us, and smiled to see Margaret reclining on the ground and me standing by her side. He made some remark upon the beauty of the afternoon, and withdrew himself into the shadow of the wood. Then we talked about autumn, and about the pleasures of being lost in the woods, and about the crows, whose voices Margaret had heard; and about the experiences of early childhood, whose influence remains upon the character after the recollection of them has passed away; and about the sight of mountains from a distance, and the view from their summits; and about other matters of high and low philosophy."

It is safe to assume that Hawthorne could not, on the whole, have had a high relish for the very positive personality of this accomplished and argumentative woman, in whose intellect high noon seemed ever to reign, as twilight did in his own. He must have been struck with the glare of her understanding, and, mentally speaking, have scowled and blinked a good deal in conversation with her. But it is tolerably manifest, nevertheless, that she was, in his imagination, the starting-point of the figure of Zenobia; and Zenobia is, to my sense, his only very definite attempt at the representation of a character. The portrait is full of alteration and embellishment; but it has a greater reality, a greater abundance of detail, than any of his other figures, and the reality was a memory of the lady whom he had encountered in the Roxbury pastoral or among the woodwalks of Concord, with strange books in her hand and eloquent discourse on her lips. *The Blithedale Romance* was written just after her unhappy death, when the reverberation of her talk would lose much of its harshness. In fact, however, very much the same qualities that made Hawthorne a Democrat in politics—his contemplative turn and absence of a keen perception of abuses, his taste for old ideals, and loitering paces, and muffled tones—would operate to keep him out of active sympathy with a woman of the so-called progressive type. We may be sure that in women his taste was conservative.

It seems odd, as his biographer says, "that the least gregarious of men should have been drawn into a socialistic community;" but although it is apparent that Hawthorne went to Brook Farm without any great Transcendental fervour, yet he had various good reasons for casting his lot in this would-be happy family. He was as yet unable to marry, but he naturally wished to do so as speedily as possible, and there was a prospect that Brook Farm would prove an economical residence. And then it is only fair to believe that Hawthorne was interested in the experiment; and that, though he was not a Transcendentalist, an Abolitionist, or a Fourierite, as his companions were in some degree or other likely to be, he was willing, as a generous and unoccupied young man, to lend a hand in any reasonable scheme for helping people to live together on better terms than the common. The Brook Farm scheme was, as such things go, a reasonable one; it was devised and carried out by shrewd and sober-minded New Englanders, who were careful to place economy first and idealism afterwards, and who were not afflicted with a Gallic passion for completeness of theory. There were no formulas, doctrines, dogmas; there was no interference whatever with private life or individual habits, and not the faintest adumbration of a rearrangement of that difficult business known as the relations of the sexes. The relations of the sexes were neither more nor less than what they usually are in American life, excellent; and in such particulars the scheme was thoroughly conservative and irreproachable. Its main characteristic was that each individual concerned in it should do a part of the work necessary for keeping the whole machine going. He could choose his work, and he could live as he liked; it was hoped, but it was by no means demanded, that he would make himself agreeable, like a gentleman invited to a dinner-party. Allowing, however, for everything that was a concession to worldly traditions and to the laxity of man's nature, there must have been in the enterprise a good deal of a certain freshness and purity of spirit, of a certain noble credulity and faith in the perfectibility of man, which it would have been easier to find in Boston in the year 1840, than in London five-and-thirty years later. If that was the era of Transcendentalism, Transcendentalism could only have sprouted in the soil peculiar to the general locality of which I speak —the soil of the old New England morality, gently raked and refreshed by an imported culture. The Transcendentalists read a great deal of French and German, made themselves intimate with George Sand and Goethe, and many other writers; but the strong and deep New England conscience accompanied them on all their intellectual excursions, and there never was a so-called "movement" that embodied itself, on the whole, in fewer eccentricities of conduct, or that borrowed a smaller license in private deportment. Henry Thoreau, a delightful writer, went to live in the woods; but Henry Thoreau was essentially a sylvan personage, and would not have been, however the fashion of his time might have turned, a man about town. The brothers and sisters at Brook Farm ploughed the fields and milked the cows; but I think that an observer from another clime and society would have been much more struck with their spirit of conformity than with their *déréglements*. Their ardour was a moral ardour, and the lightest breath of scandal never rested upon them, or upon any phase of Transcendentalism.

A biographer of Hawthorne might well regret that his hero had not been more mixed up with the reforming and free-thinking class, so that he might find a pretext for writing a chapter upon the state of Boston society forty years ago. A needful warrant for such regret should be, properly, that the biographer's own personal reminiscences should stretch back to that period and to the persons who animated it. This would be a guarantee of fulness of knowledge and, presumably, of kindness of tone. It is difficult to see, indeed, how the generation of which Hawthorne has given us, in *Blithedale*, a few portraits, should not, at this time of day, be spoken of very tenderly and sympathetically. If irony enter into the allusion, it should be of the lightest and gentlest. Certainly, for a brief and imperfect chronicler of these things, a writer just touching them as he passes, and who has not the advantage of having been a contemporary, there is only one possible tone. The compiler of these pages, though his recollections date only from a later period, has a memory of a certain number of persons who had been intimately connected, as Hawthorne was not, with the agitations of that interesting time. Something of its interest adhered to them still—something of its aroma clung to their garments; there was something about them which seemed to say that when they were young and enthusiastic, they had been initiated into moral mysteries, they had played at a wonderful game. Their usual mark (it is true I can think of exceptions) was that they seemed excellently good. They appeared unstained by the world, unfamiliar with worldly desires and standards, and with those various forms of human depravity which flourish in some high phases of civilisation; inclined to simple and democratic ways, destitute of pretensions and affectations, of jealousies, of cynicisms, of snobbishness. This little epoch of fermentation has three or four drawbacks for the critics—drawbacks, however, that may be overlooked by a person for whom it has an interest of association. It bore, intellectually, the stamp of provincialism; it was a beginning without a fruition, a dawn without a noon; and it produced, with a single exception, no great talents. It produced a great deal of writing, but (always putting Hawthorne aside, as a contemporary but not a sharer) only one writer in whom the world at large has interested itself. The situation was summed up and transfigured in the admirable and exquisite Emerson. He expressed all that it contained, and a good deal more, doubtless, besides; he was the man of genius of the moment; he was the Transcendentalist *par excellence*. Emerson expressed, before all things, as was extremely natural at the hour and in the place, the value and importance of the individual, the duty of making the most of one's self, of living by one's own personal light, and carrying out one's own disposition. He reflected with beautiful irony upon the exquisite impudence of those institutions which claim to have appropriated the truth and to dole it out, in proportionate morsels, in exchange for a subscription. He talked about the beauty and dignity of life, and about every one who is born into the world being born to the whole, having an interest and a stake in the whole. He said "all that is clearly due to-day is not to lie," and a great many other things which it would be still easier to present in a ridiculous light. He insisted upon sincerity and independence and spontaneity, upon acting in harmony with one's nature, and not conforming and compromising for the sake of being more comfortable. He urged that a man should await his call, his finding the thing to do which he should really believe in doing, and not be urged by the world's opinion to do simply the world's work. "If no call should come for years, for centuries, then I know that the want of the Universe is the attestation of faith by my abstinence. . . . If I cannot work, at least I need not lie." The doctrine of the supremacy of the individual to himself, of his originality, and, as regards his own character, *unique* quality, must have had a great charm for people living in a society in which introspection—thanks to the want of other entertainment—played almost the part of a social resource.

In the United States, in those days, there were no great things to look out at (save forests and rivers); life was not in the least spectacular; society was not brilliant; the country was given up to a great material prosperity, a homely *bourgeois* activity, a diffusion of primary education and the common luxuries. There was, therefore, among the cultivated classes, much relish for the utterances of a writer who would help one to take a picturesque view of one's internal responsibilities, and to find in the landscape of the soul all sorts of fine sunrise and moonlight effects. "Meantime, while the doors of the temple stand open, night and day, before every man, and the oracles of this truth cease never, it is guarded by one stern condition; this, namely—it is an intuition. It cannot be received at second hand. Truly speaking, it is not instruction but provocation that I can receive from another soul." To make one's self so much more interesting would help to make life interesting, and life was probably, to many of this aspiring congregation, a dream of freedom and fortitude. There were faulty parts in the Emersonian philosophy; but the general tone was magnificent; and I can easily believe that, coming when it did and where it did, it should have been drunk in by a great many fine moral appetites with a sense of intoxication. One envies, even, I will not say the illusions, of that keenly sentient period, but the convictions and interests—the moral passion. One certainly envies the privilege of having heard the finest of Emerson's orations poured forth in their early newness. They were the most poetical, the most beautiful productions of the American mind, and they were thoroughly local and national. They had a music and a magic, and when one remembers the remarkable charm of the speaker, the beautiful modulation of his utterance, one regrets in especial that one might not have been present on a certain occasion which made a sensation, an era—the delivery of an address to the Divinity School of Harvard University, on a summer evening in 1838. In the light, fresh American air, unthickened and undarkened by customs and institutions established, these things, as the phrase is, told.

Hawthorne appears, like his own Miles Coverdale, to have arrived at

Brook Farm in the midst of one of those April snowstorms which, during the New England spring, occasionally diversify the inaction of the vernal process. Miles Coverdale, in *The Blithedale Romance,* is evidently as much Hawthorne as he is any one else in particular. He is, indeed, not very markedly any one, unless it be the spectator, the observer; his chief identity lies in his success in looking at things objectively, and spinning uncommunicated fancies about them. This, indeed, was the part that Hawthorne played socially in the little community at West Roxbury. His biographer describes him as sitting "silently, hour after hour, in the broad, old-fashioned hall of the house, where he could listen almost unseen to the chat and merriment of the young people, himself almost always holding a book before him, but seldom turning the leaves." He put his hand to the plough, and supported himself and the community, as they were all supposed to do, by his labour; but he contributed little to the hum of voices. Some of his companions, either then or afterwards, took, I believe, rather a gruesome view of his want of articulate enthusiasm, and accused him of coming to the place as a sort of intellectual vampire, for purely psychological purposes. He sat in a corner, they declared, and watched the inmates when they were off their guard, analysing their characters, and dissecting the amiable ardour, the magnanimous illusions, which he was too cold-blooded to share. In so far as this account of Hawthorne's attitude was a complaint, it was a singularly childish one. If he was at Brook Farm without being of it, this is a very fortunate circumstance from the point of view of posterity, who would have preserved but a slender memory of the affair if our author's fine novel had not kept the topic open. The complaint is, indeed, almost so ungrateful a one as to make us regret that the author's fellow-communists came off so easily. They certainly would not have done so if the author of *Blithedale* had been more of a satirist. Certainly, if Hawthorne was an observer, he was a very harmless one; and when one thinks of the queer specimens of the reforming genus with which he must have been surrounded, one almost wishes that, for our entertainment, he had given his old companions something to complain of in earnest. There is no satire whatever in the *Romance;* the quality is almost conspicuous by its absence. Of portraits there are only two; there is no sketching of odd figures—no reproduction of strange types of radicalism; the human background is left vague. Hawthorne was not a satirist, and if at Brook Farm he was, according to his habit, a good deal of a mild sceptic, his scepticism was exercised much more in the interest of fancy than in that of reality.

There must have been something pleasantly bucolic and pastoral in the habits of the place during the fine New England summer; but we have no retrospective envy of the denizens of Brook Farm in that other season which, as Hawthorne somewhere says, leaves in those regions "so large a blank—so melancholy a death-spot—in lives so brief that they ought to be all summer-time." "Of a summer night, when the moon was full," says

Mr. Lathrop,[1] "they lit no lamps, but sat grouped in the light and shadow, while sundry of the younger men sang old ballads, or joined Tom Moore's songs to operatic airs. On other nights there would be an original essay or poem read aloud, or else a play of Shakespeare, with the parts distributed to different members; and these amusements failing, some interesting discussion was likely to take their place. Occasionally, in the dramatic season, large delegations from the farm would drive into Boston, in carriages and wagons, to the opera or the play. Sometimes, too, the young women sang as they washed the dishes in the Hive; and the youthful yeomen of the society came in and helped them with their work. The men wore blouses of a checked or plaided stuff, belted at the waist, with a broad collar folding down about the throat, and rough straw hats; the women, usually, simple calico gowns and hats." All this sounds delightfully Arcadian and innocent, and it is certain that there was something peculiar to the clime and race in some of the features of such a life; in the free, frank, and stainless companionship of young men and maidens, in the mixture of manual labour and intellectual flights— dish-washing and aesthetics, wood-chopping and philosophy. Wordsworth's "plain living and high thinking" were made actual. Some passages in Margaret Fuller's journals throw plenty of light on this. (It must be premised that she was at Brook Farm as an occasional visitor; not as a labourer in the Hive.)

"All Saturday I was off in the woods. In the evening we had a general conversation, opened by me, upon Education, in its largest sense, and on what we can do for ourselves and others. I took my usual ground:—The aim is perfection; patience the road. Our lives should be considered as a tendency, an approximation only. . . . Mr. R. spoke admirably on the nature of loyalty. The people showed a good deal of the *sans-culotte* tendency in their manners, throwing themselves on the floor, yawning, and going out when they had heard enough. Yet, as the majority differ with me, to begin with—that being the reason this subject was chosen—they showed, on the whole, more interest and deference than I had expected. As I am accustomed to deference, however, and need it for the boldness and animation which my part requires, I did not speak with as much force as usual. . . . Sunday.—A glorious day; the woods full of perfume; I was out all the morning. In the afternoon Mrs. R. and I had a talk. I said my position would be too uncertain here, as I could not work.—— said 'they would all like to work for a person of genius.' . . . 'Yes,' I told her; 'but where would be my repose when they were always to be judging whether I was worth it or not? . . . Each day you must prove yourself anew.' . . . We talked of the principles of the community. I said I had not a right to come, because all the confidence I had in it was as an *experiment* worth trying, and that it was part of the great wave of inspired thought. . . . We had valuable discussion on these points. All Monday morning in the woods again. Afternoon, out with the drawing party; I felt the evils

[1] George Parsons Lathrop (1851– 1898), associate editor of the *Atlantic Monthly* 1875–77, married Hawthorne's daughter, Rose, and wrote the first biography of the novelist, *A Study of Hawthorne*, 1876.

of the want of conventional refinement, in the impudence with which one of the girls treated me. She has since thought of it with regret, I notice; and by every day's observation of me will see that she ought not to have done it. In the evening a husking in the barn . . . a most picturesque scene. . . . I stayed and helped about half an hour, and then took a long walk beneath the stars. Wednesday. . . . In the evening a conversation on Impulse. . . . I defended nature, as I always do;—the spirit ascending through, not superseding, nature. But in the scale of Sense, Intellect, Spirit, I advocated the claims of Intellect, because those present were rather disposed to postpone them. On the nature of Beauty we had good talk.——seemed in a much more reverent humour than the other night, and enjoyed the large plans of the universe which were unrolled. . . . Saturday.—Well, good-bye, Brook Farm. I know more about this place than I did when I came; but the only way to be qualified for a judge of such an experiment would be to become an active, though unimpassioned, associate in trying it. . . . The girl who was so rude to me stood waiting, with a timid air, to bid me good-bye."

The young girl in question cannot have been Hawthorne's charming Priscilla; nor yet another young lady, of a most humble spirit, who communicated to Margaret's biographers her recollections of this remarkable woman's visits to Brook Farm; concluding with the assurance that "after a while she seemed to lose sight of my more prominent and disagreeable peculiarities, and treated me with affectionate regard."

Hawthorne's farewell to the place appears to have been accompanied with some reflections of a cast similar to those indicated by Miss Fuller; in so far, at least, as we may attribute to Hawthorne himself some of the observations that he fathers upon Miles Coverdale. His biographer justly quotes two or three sentences from *The Blithedale Romance*, as striking the note of the author's feeling about the place. "No sagacious man," says Coverdale, "will long retain his sagacity if he live exclusively among reformers and progressive people, without periodically returning to the settled system of things, to correct himself by a new observation from that old standpoint." And he remarks elsewhere, that "it struck me as rather odd that one of the first questions raised, after our separation from the greedy, struggling, self-seeking world, should relate to the possibility of getting the advantage over the outside barbarians in their own field of labour. But to tell the truth, I very soon became sensible that, as regarded society at large, we stood in a position of new hostility rather than new brotherhood." He was doubtless oppressed by the "sultry heat of society," as he calls it in one of the jottings in the Note-Books. "What would a man do if he were compelled to live always in the sultry heat of society, and could never bathe himself in cool solitude?" His biographer relates that one of the other Brook Farmers, wandering afield one summer's day, discovered Hawthorne stretched at his length upon a grassy hill-side, with his hat pulled over his face, and every appearance, in his attitude, of the desire to escape detection. On his asking him whether he had any particular reason for this shyness of posture—"Too much of a party up there!" Hawthorne contented himself with replying, with a nod in the direction of the Hive. He had, nevertheless, for a time looked forward to remaining indefinitely in the community; he meant to marry as soon as possible, and bring his wife there to live. Some sixty pages of the second volume of the American Note-Books are occupied with extracts from his letters to his future wife and from his journal (which appears, however, at this time to have been only intermittent), consisting almost exclusively of descriptions of the simple scenery of the neighbourhood, and of the state of the woods, and fields, and weather. Hawthorne's fondness for all the common things of nature was deep and constant, and there is always something charming in his verbal touch, as we may call it, when he talks to himself about them. "Oh," he breaks out, of an October afternoon, "the beauty of grassy slopes, and the hollow ways of paths winding between hills, and the intervals between the road and wood-lots, where Summer lingers and sits down, strewing dandelions of gold and blue asters as her parting gifts and memorials!" He was but a single summer at Brook Farm; the rest of his residence had the winter-quality.

But if he returned to solitude, it was henceforth to be, as the French say, a *solitude à deux.* He was married in July, 1842, and betook himself immediately to the ancient village of Concord, near Boston, where he occupied the so-called Manse which has given the title to one of his collections of tales, and upon which this work, in turn, has conferred a permanent distinction. I use the epithets "ancient" and "near" in the foregoing sentence, according to the American measurement of time and distance. Concord is some twenty miles from Boston; and even to-day, upwards of forty years after the date of Hawthorne's removal thither, it is a very fresh and well-preserved looking town. It had already a local history when, a hundred years ago, the larger current of human affairs flowed for a moment around it. Concord has the honour of being the first spot in which blood was shed in the war of the Revolution; here occurred the first exchange of musket-shots between the King's troops and the American insurgents. Here—as Emerson says in the little hymn which he contributed, in 1836, to the dedication of a small monument commemorating this circumstance—

"Here once the embattled farmers stood,
And fired the shot heard round the world."

The battle was a small one, and the farmers were not destined, individually, to emerge from obscurity; but the memory of these things has kept the reputation of Concord green, and it has been watered, moreover, so to speak, by the life-long presence there of one of the most honoured of American men of letters—the poet from whom I just quoted two lines. Concord is, indeed, in itself decidedly verdant, and is an excellent specimen of a New England village of the riper sort. At the time of Hawthorne's first going there, it must have been an even better specimen than to-day—more homogeneous, more indigenous, more absolutely democratic. Forty years ago the tide of foreign immigration had scarcely begun to break upon the rural strongholds of the New England race; it had at most begun to splash them with the salt Hibernian spray. It is very possible, however, that at this period there was not an Irishman in Concord; the place would have been a village community operating in excellent conditions. Such a village community was not the least honourable item in the sum of New England civilisation. Its spreading elms and plain white houses, its generous summers and ponderous winters, its immediate background of promiscuous field and forest, would have been part of the composition. For the rest, there were the selectmen and the town-meetings, the town-schools and the self-governing spirit, the rigid morality, the friendly and familiar manners, the perfect competence of the little society to manage its affairs itself. In the delightful introduction to the *Mosses,* Hawthorne has given an account of his dwelling, of his simple occupations and recreations, and of some of the characteristics of the place. The Manse is a large, square wooden house, to the surface of which—even in the dry New England air, so unfriendly to mosses, and lichens, and weather-stains, and the other elements of a picturesque complexion—a hundred and fifty years of exposure have imparted a kind of tone, standing just above the slow-flowing Concord river, and approached by a short avenue of over-arching trees. It had been the dwelling-place of generations of Presbyterian ministers, ancestors of the celebrated Emerson, who had himself spent his early manhood, and written some of his most beautiful essays there. "He used," as Hawthorne says, "to watch the Assyrian dawn, and Paphian sunset and moonrise, from the summit of our eastern hill." From its clerical occupants the place had inherited a mild mustiness of theological association —a vague reverberation of old Calvinistic sermons, which served to deepen its extramundane and somnolent quality. The three years that Hawthorne passed here were, I should suppose, among the happiest of his life. The future was, indeed, not in any special manner assured; but the present was sufficiently genial. In the American Note-Books there is a charming passage (too long to quote) descriptive of the entertainment the new couple found in renovating and re-furnishing the old parsonage, which, at the time of their going into it, was given up to ghosts and cobwebs. Of the little drawing-room, which had been most completely reclaimed, he writes that "the shade of our departed host will never haunt it; for its aspect has been as completely changed as the scenery of a theatre. Probably the ghost gave one peep into it, uttered a groan, and vanished forever." This departed host was a certain Doctor Ripley, a venerable scholar, who left behind him a reputation of learning and sanctity which was reproduced in one of the ladies of his family, long the most distinguished woman in the little Concord circle. Doctor Ripley's predecessor had been, I believe, the last of the line of the Emerson ministers— an old gentleman who, in the earlier years of his pastorate, stood at the window of his study (the same in which Hawthorne handled a more irresponsible quill), watching, with his hands under his long coattails, the progress of Concord fight. It is not by any means related, however, I should add, that he waited for the conclusion to make up his mind which was the righteous cause.

Hawthorne had a little society (as much, we may infer, as he desired), and it was excellent in quality. But the pages in the Note-Books which relate to his life at the Manse, and the introduction to the *Mosses,* make more of his relations with vegetable nature, and of his customary contemplation of the incidents of wood-path and way-side, than of the human elements of the scene; though these also are gracefully touched upon. These pages treat largely of the pleasures of a kitchen-garden, of the beauty of summer-squashes, and of the mysteries of apple-raising. With the wholesome aroma of apples (as is, indeed, almost necessarily the case in any realistic record of New England rural life) they are especially pervaded; and with many other homely and domestic emanations; all of which derive a sweetness from the medium of our author's colloquial style. Hawthorne was silent with his lips; but he talked with his pen. The tone of his writing is often that of charming talk—ingenious, fanciful, slow-flowing, with all the lightness of gossip, and none of its vulgarity. In the preface to the tales written at the Manse he talks of many things, and just touches upon some of the members of his circle—especially upon that odd genius, his fellow-villager, Henry Thoreau. I said, a little way back, that the New England Transcendental movement had suffered, in the estimation of the world at large, from not having (putting Emerson aside) produced any superior talents. But any reference to it would be ungenerous which should omit to pay a tribute, in passing, to the author of *Walden.* Whatever question there may be of his talent, there can be none, I think, of his genius. It was a slim and crooked one, but it was eminently personal. He was imperfect, unfinished, inartistic; he was worse than provincial—he was parochial; it is only at his best that he is readable. But at his best he has an extreme natural charm, and he must always be mentioned after those Americans—Emerson, Hawthorne, Longfellow, Lowell, Motley—who have written originally. He was Emerson's independent moral man made flesh—living for the ages, and not for Saturday and Sunday; for the Universe, and not for Concord. In fact, however, Thoreau lived for Concord very effectually; and by his remarkable genius for the observation of the phenomena of woods and streams, of plants and trees, and beasts and fishes, and for flinging a kind of spiritual interest over these things, he did more than he perhaps intended towards consolidating the fame of his accidental human sojourn. He was as shy and ungregarious as Hawthorne; but he and the latter appear to have been sociably disposed towards each other, and there are some charming touches in the preface to the *Mosses* in regard to the hours they spent in boating together on the large, quiet Concord river. Thoreau was a great voyager, in a canoe which he had constructed himself, and which he eventually made over to Hawthorne, and as expert in the use of the paddle as the Red men who had once haunted the same silent stream. The most frequent of Hawthorne's companions on these excursions appears, however, to have been a local celebrity—as well as Thoreau a high Transcendentalist—Mr. Ellery Channing, whom I may mention, since he is mentioned very explicitly in the preface to the *Mosses,* and also because no account of the little Concord world would be complete which should omit him. He was the son of the distinguished Unitarian moralist, and, I believe, the intimate friend of Thoreau, whom he resembled in having produced literary compositions more esteemed by the few than by the many. He and Hawthorne were both fishermen, and the two used to set themselves afloat in the summer afternoons. "Strange and happy times were those," exclaims the more distinguished of the two writers, "when we cast aside all irksome forms and strait-laced habitudes, and delivered ourselves up to the free air, to live like the Indians or any less conventional race, during one bright semicircle of the sun. Rowing our boat against the current, between wide meadows, we turned aside into the Assabeth. A more lovely stream than this, for a mile above its junction with the Concord, has never flowed on earth —nowhere, indeed, except to lave the interior regions of a poet's imagination. . . . It comes flowing softly through the midmost privacy and deepest heart of a wood which whispers it to be quiet; while the stream whispers back again from its sedgy borders, as if river and wood were hushing one another to sleep. Yes; the river sleeps along its course and dreams of the sky and the clustering foliage. . . ." While Hawthorne was looking at these beautiful things, or, for that matter, was writing them, he was well out of the way of a certain class of visitants whom he alludes to in one of the closing passages of this long Introduction. "Never was a poor little country village infested with such a variety of queer, strangely-dressed, oddly-behaved mortals, most of whom took upon themselves to be important agents of the world's destiny, yet were simply bores of a very intense character." "These hobgoblins of flesh and blood," he says, in a preceding paragraph, "were attracted thither by the wide-spreading influence of a great original thinker who had his earthly abode at the opposite extremity of our village. . . . People that had lighted on a new thought, or a thought they fancied new, came to Emerson, as the finder of a glittering gem hastens to a lapidary, to ascertain its quality and value;" and Hawthorne enumerates some of the categories of pilgrims to the shrine of the mystic counsellor, who as a general thing was probably far from abounding in their own sense (when this sense was perverted), but gave them a due measure of plain practical advice. The whole passage is interesting, and it suggests that little Concord had not been ill-treated by the fates—with "a great original thinker" at one end of the village, an exquisite teller of tales at the other, and the rows of New England elms between. It contains, moreover, an admirable sentence about Hawthorne's pilgrim-haunted neighbour, with whom, "being happy," as he says, and feeling, therefore, "as if there were no question to be put," he was not in metaphysical communion. "It was good, nevertheless, to meet him in the wood-paths, or sometimes in our avenue, with that pure intellectual gleam diffused about his presence, like the garment of a shining one; and he so quiet, so simple, so without pretension, encountering each man alive as if expecting to receive more than he could impart!" One may without indiscretion risk the surmise that Hawthorne's perception of the "shining" element in his distinguished friend was more intense than his friend's appreciation of whatever luminous property might reside within the somewhat dusky envelope of our hero's identity as a collector of "mosses." Emerson, as a sort of spiritual sun-worshipper, could have attached but a moderate value to Hawthorne's catlike faculty of seeing in the dark.

"As to the daily course of our life," the latter writes, in the spring of 1843, "I have written with pretty commendable diligence, averaging from two to four hours a day; and the result is seen in various magazines. I might have written more if it had seemed worth while, but I was content to earn only so much gold as might suffice for our immediate wants, having prospect of official station and emolument which would do away with the necessity of writing for bread. These prospects have not yet had their fulfilment; and we are well content to wait, for an office would inevitably remove us from our present happy home—at least from an outward home; for there is an inner one that will accompany us wherever we go. Meantime, the magazine people do not pay their debts; so that we taste some of the inconveniences of poverty. It is an annoyance, not a trouble." And he goes on to give some account of his usual habits. (The passage is from his Journal, and the account is given to himself, as it were, with that odd, unfamiliar explicitness which marks the tone of this record throughout.) "Every day I trudge through snow and slush to the village, look into the post-office, and spend an hour at the reading-room; and then return home, generally without having spoken a word to any human being. . . . In the way of exercise I saw and split wood, and physically I was never in a better condition than now." He adds a mention of an absence he had lately made. "I went alone to Salem, where I resumed all my bachelor habits for nearly a fortnight, leading the same life in which ten years of my youth flitted away like a dream. But how much changed was I! At last I had got hold of a reality which never could be taken from me. It was good thus to get apart from my happiness for the sake of contemplating it."

These compositions, which were so unpunctually paid for, appeared in the *Democratic Review,* a periodical published at Washington, and having, as our author's biographer says, "considerable pretensions to a national character." It is to be regretted that the practice of keeping its creditors waiting should, on the part of the magazine in question, have been thought compatible with these pretensions. The foregoing lines are a description of a very monotonous but a very contented life, and Mr. Lathrop justly remarks upon the dissonance of tone of the tales Hawthorne produced under these happy circumstances. It is, indeed, not a little of an anomaly. The episode of the Manse was one of the most agreeable he had known, and yet the best of the *Mosses* (though not the greater number of them) are singularly dismal compositions. They are redolent of M. Montégut's [2] pessimism. "The reality of sin, the pervasiveness of evil," says Mr. Lathrop, "had been but slightly insisted upon in the earlier tales: in this series the idea bursts up like a long-buried fire, with earth-shaking strength, and the pits of hell seem yawning beneath us." This is very true (allowing for Mr. Lathrop's rather too emphatic way of putting it); but the anomaly is, I think, on the whole, only superficial. Our writer's imagination, as has been abundantly conceded, was a gloomy one; the old Puritan sense of sin, of penalties to be paid, of the darkness and wickedness of life, had, as I have already suggested, passed into it. It had not passed into the parts of Hawthorne's nature corresponding to those occupied by the same horrible vision of things in his ancestors; but it had still been determined to claim this later comer as its own, and since his heart and his happiness were to escape, it insisted on setting its mark upon his genius—upon his most beautiful organ, his admirable fancy. It may be said that when his fancy was strongest and keenest, when it was most itself, then the dark Puritan tinge showed in it most richly; and there cannot be a better proof that he was not the man of a sombre *parti-pris* whom M. Montégut describes, than the fact that these duskiest flowers of his invention sprang straight from the soil of his happiest days. This surely indicates that there was but little direct connection between the products of his fancy and the state of his affections. When he was lightest at heart, he was most creative; and when he was most creative, the moral picturesqueness of the old secret of mankind in general and of the Puritans in particular, most appealed to him—the secret that we are really not by any means so good as a well-regulated society requires us to appear. It is not too much to say, even, that the very condition of production of some of these unamiable tales would be that they should be superficial, and, as it were, insincere. The magnificent little romance of *Young Goodman Brown*, for instance, evidently means nothing as regards Hawthorne's own state of mind, his conviction of human depravity and his consequent melancholy; for the simple reason that, if it meant anything, it would mean too much. Mr. Lathrop speaks of it as a "terrible and lurid parable;" but this, it seems to me, is just what it is not. It is not a parable, but a picture, which is a very different thing. What does M. Montégut make, one would ask, from the point of view of Hawthorne's pessimism, of the singularly objective and unpreoccupied tone of the Introduction to the *Old Manse*, in which the author speaks from himself, and in which the cry of metaphysical despair is not even faintly sounded?

[2] Émile Montégut (1826–1895), a French critic, whose essays on American literature, particularly on Hawthorne and Emerson, attracted wide attention. His first essay on the novelist appeared as early as 1860, when Hawthorne was still alive. In 1864 he wrote also an obituary study of him.

We have seen that when he went into the village he often came home without having spoken a word to a human being. There is a touching entry made a little later, bearing upon his mild taciturnity. "A cloudy veil stretches across the abyss of my nature. I have, however, no love of secrecy and darkness. I am glad to think that God sees through my heart, and if any angel has power to penetrate into it, he is welcome to know everything that is there. Yes, and so may any mortal who is capable of full sympathy, and therefore worthy to come into my depths. But he must find his own way there; I can neither guide nor enlighten him." It must be acknowledged, however, that if he was not able to open the gate of conversation, it was sometimes because he was disposed to slide the bolt himself. "I had a purpose," he writes, shortly before the entry last quoted, "if circumstances would permit, of passing the whole term of my wife's absence without speaking a word to any human being." He beguiled these incommunicative periods by studying German, in Tieck [3] and Bürger,[4] without apparently making much progress; also in reading French, in Voltaire and Rabelais. "Just now," he writes, one October noon, "I heard a sharp tapping at the window of my study, and, looking up from my book (a volume of Rabelais), behold, the head of a little bird, who seemed to demand admittance." It was a quiet life, of course, in which these diminutive incidents seemed noteworthy; and what is noteworthy here to the observer of Hawthorne's contemplative simplicity, is the fact that, though he finds a good deal to say about the little bird (he devotes several lines more to it), he makes no remark upon Rabelais. He had other visitors than little birds, however, and their demands were also not Rabelaisian. Thoreau comes to see him, and they talk "upon the spiritual advantages of change of place, and upon the *Dial*, and upon Mr. Alcott, and other kindred or concatenated subjects." Mr. Alcott was an arch-transcendentalist, living in Concord, and the *Dial* was a periodical to which the illuminated spirits of Boston and its neighbourhood used to contribute. Another visitor comes and talks "of Margaret Fuller, who, he says, has risen perceptibly into a higher state since their last meeting." There is probably a great deal of Concord five-and-thirty years ago in that little sentence!

※

DAISY MILLER

Henry James's *Daisy Miller*, the tale which made him famous in the late 1870's, continues to be read today even though its theme is now regarded as rather "old-fashioned." A younger generation, in an

---

[3] Ludwig Tieck (1773–1853), German romantic poet, dramatist and novelist whose works of fantasy and satire were widely read.

[4] Gottfried August Bürger (1747–1794), revived the German ballad. His most famous work in this form was *Lenore*, 1773.

era when co-education and easy "dating" has altered the Victorian relationships between the sexes, tends to regard the story of Daisy's flirtations as a silly tempest in a diminutive tea-pot. Indeed flirtation, so integral a part of society and manners in the Jamesian era, seems to be on the way out in our time. But in the 1870's, when young American travelers for the first time appeared upon the horizon of Europe, the differences between American informality and European customs of courtship and wooing, were considerable; and the inability of Americans and Europeans to understand each other's habits and manners was beginning to be remarked. Daisy's "crime," in the eyes of the Europeanized Americans who have lost touch with their native land, is that she goes walking unescorted in the moonlight with a genteel but not very interesting Italian and thereby ruins her social reputation. Her mother, impassive and permissive, seems oblivious of her daughter's problem; and the daughter's morality, in essence, is that of a strange, hard innocence, a naive belief that what is the custom in Schenectady, New York, is necessarily the custom among the Romans as well.

In these circumstances Daisy generates a social storm which, as James sought to show, is completely over her head. To the end, she does not really understand what has happened. When the novelist first published the tale in the *Cornhill Magazine* in 1878 he subtitled it "A Study" and doubtless was adapting to his needs the French phrase *étude de moeurs*—study of manners. Later he removed the sub-title. Yet the story remains essentially a study, a picture, a dramatization, of a social situation which could not occur today yet which has in it certain fundamental human values distinctly relevant to our time. Dramatized for us is the conflict between European sophistication and American innocence. Daisy remains an innocent to the end because she is unable to reach awareness of the difference between her own world and that into which she has voyaged. All she is able to experience is Winterbourne's frostiness and the fact that she somehow has suffered social rejection, and for actions which seem to her harmless enough. This is a pathetic tale and James's handling of it has a freshness and lightness that remain to this day.

The story, when James first offered it to an American journal, was rejected as an "outrage" on American girlhood; but its appearance in England and its rapid publication in American journals who "pirated" it in Boston and New York, testified promptly to its popularity. It went through many editions and launched James on a series of tales about American girls abroad. He played out this theme in all its variations of comedy and pathos, and it culminated in a major novel, *The Portrait of a Lady*.

I

At the little town of Vevey, in Switzerland, there is a particularly comfortable hotel; there are indeed many hotels, since the entertainment

of tourists is the business of the place, which, as many travellers will remember, is seated upon the edge of a remarkably blue lake—a lake that
it behoves every tourist to visit. The shore of the lake presents an unbroken array of establishments of this order, of every category, from the
"grand hotel" of the newest fashion, with a chalk-white front, a hundred
balconies, and a dozen flags flying from its roof, to the small Swiss pen-
sion of an elder day, with its name inscribed in German-looking lettering
upon a pink or yellow wall and an awkward summer-house in the angle
of the garden. One of the hotels at Vevey, however, is famous, even
classical, being distinguished from many of its upstart neighbours by an
air both of luxury and of maturity. In this region, through the month of
June, American travellers are extremely numerous; it may be said indeed
that Vevey assumes at that time some of the characteristics of an American watering-place. There are sights and sounds that evoke a vision, an
echo, of Newport and Saratoga. There is a flitting hither and thither of
"stylish" young girls, a rustling of muslin flounces, a rattle of dance-
music in the morning hours, a sound of high-pitched voices at all times.
You receive an impression of these things at the excellent inn of the
"Trois Couronnes," and are transported in fancy to the Ocean House or
to Congress Hall. But at the "Trois Couronnes," it must be added, there
are other features much at variance with these suggestions: neat German waiters who look like secretaries of legation; Russian princesses
sitting in the garden; little Polish boys walking about, held by the hand,
with their governors; a view of the snowy crest of the Dent du Midi
and the picturesque towers of the Castle of Chillon.

I hardly know whether it was the analogies or the differences that
were uppermost in the mind of a young American, who, two or three
years ago, sat in the garden of the "Trois Couronnes," looking about him
rather idly at some of the graceful objects I have mentioned. It was a
beautiful summer morning, and in whatever fashion the young American
looked at things they must have seemed to him charming. He had come
from Geneva the day before, by the little steamer, to see his aunt, who
was staying at the hotel—Geneva having been for a long time his place of
residence. But his aunt had a headache—his aunt had almost always a
headache—and she was now shut up in her room smelling camphor, so
that he was at liberty to wander about. He was some seven-and-twenty
years of age; when his friends spoke of him they usually said that he was
at Geneva "studying." When his enemies spoke of him they said—but
after all he had no enemies: he was extremely amiable and generally
liked. What I should say is simply that when certain persons spoke of
him they conveyed that the reason of his spending so much time at Geneva was that he was extremely devoted to a lady who lived there—a foreign lady, a person older than himself. Very few Americans—truly I
think none—had ever seen this lady, about whom there were some singular stories. But Winterbourne had an old attachment for the little capital
of Calvinism; he had been put to school there as a boy and had after-

wards even gone, on trial—trial of the grey old "Academy" on the steep and stony hillside—to college there; circumstances which had led to his forming a great many youthful friendships. Many of these he had kept, and they were a source of great satisfaction to him.

After knocking at his aunt's door and learning that she was indisposed he had taken a walk about the town and then he had come in to his breakfast. He had now finished that repast, but was enjoying a small cup of coffee which had been served him on a little table in the garden by one of the waiters who looked like *attachés*. At last he finished his coffee and lit a cigarette. Presently a small boy came walking along the path —an urchin of nine or ten. The child, who was diminutive for his years, had an aged expression of countenance, a pale complexion and sharp little features. He was dressed in knickerbockers and had red stockings that displayed his poor little spindle-shanks; he also wore a brilliant red cravat. He carried in his hand a long alpenstock, the sharp point of which he thrust into everything he approached—the flower-beds, the garden-benches, the trains of the ladies' dresses. In front of Winterbourne he paused, looking at him with a pair of bright and penetrating little eyes.

"Will you give me a lump of sugar?" he asked in a small sharp hard voice—a voice immature and yet somehow not young.

Winterbourne glanced at the light table near him, on which his coffee-service rested, and saw that several morsels of sugar remained. "Yes, you may take one," he answered; "but I don't think too much sugar good for little boys."

This little boy stepped forward and carefully selected three of the coveted fragments, two of which he buried in the pocket of his knicker-bockers, depositing the other as promptly in another place. He poked his alpenstock, lance-fashion, into Winterbourne's bench and tried to crack the lump of sugar with his teeth.

"Oh blazes: it's har-r-d!" he exclaimed, divesting vowel and consonants, pertinently enough, of any taint of softness.

Winterbourne had immediately gathered that he might have the honour of claiming him as a countryman. "Take care you don't hurt your teeth," he said paternally.

"I haven't got any teeth to hurt. They've all come out. I've only got seven teeth. Mother counted them last night, and one came out right afterwards. She said she'd slap me if any more came out. I can't help it. It's this old Europe. It's the climate that makes them come out. In America they didn't come out. It's these hotels."

Winterbourne was much amused. "If you eat three lumps of sugar your mother will certainly slap you," he ventured.

"She's got to give me some candy then," rejoined his young interlocutor. "I can't get any candy here—any American candy. American candy's the best candy."

"And are American little boys the best little boys?" Winterbourne asked.

"I don't know. *I'm* an American boy," said the child.

"I see you're one of the best!" the young man laughed.

"Are you an American man?" pursued this vivacious infant. And then on his friend's affirmative reply, "American men are the best," he declared with assurance.

His companion thanked him for the compliment, and the child, who had now got astride of his alpenstock, stood looking about him while he attacked another lump of sugar. Winterbourne wondered if he himself had been like this in his infancy, for he had been brought to Europe at about the same age.

"Here comes my sister!" cried his young compatriot. "She's an American girl, you bet!"

Winterbourne looked along the path and saw a beautiful young lady advancing. "American girls are the best girls," he thereupon cheerfully remarked to his visitor.

"My sister ain't the best!" the child promptly returned. "She's always blowing at me."

"I imagine that's your fault, not hers," said Winterbourne. The young lady meanwhile had drawn near. She was dressed in white muslin, with a hundred frills and flounces and knots of pale-coloured ribbon. Bareheaded, she balanced in her hand a large parasol with a deep border of embroidery; and she was strikingly, admirably pretty. "How pretty they are!" thought our friend, who straightened himself in his seat as if he were ready to rise.

The young lady paused in front of his bench, near the parapet of the garden, which overlooked the lake. The small boy had now converted his alpenstock into a vaulting-pole, by the aid of which he was springing about in the gravel and kicking it up not a little. "Why, Randolph," she freely began, "what *are* you doing?"

"I'm going up the Alps!" cried Randolph. "This is the way!" And he gave another extravagant jump, scattering the pebbles about Winterbourne's ears.

"That's the way they come down," said Winterbourne.

"He's an American man!" proclaimed Randolph in his harsh little voice.

The young lady gave no heed to this circumstance, but looked straight at her brother. "Well, I guess you'd better be quiet," she simply observed.

It seemed to Winterbourne that he had been in a manner presented. He got up and stepped slowly toward the charming creature, throwing away his cigarette. "This little boy and I have made acquaintance," he said with great civility. In Geneva, as he had been perfectly aware, a young man wasn't at liberty to speak to a young unmarried lady save under certain rarely-occurring conditions; but here at Vevey what conditions could be better than these?—a pretty American girl coming to stand in front of you in a garden with all the confidence in life. This

pretty American girl, whatever that might prove, on hearing Winterbourne's observation simply glanced at him; she then turned her head
and looked over the parapet, at the lake and the opposite mountains. He
wondered whether he had gone too far, but decided that he must gallantly advance rather than retreat. While he was thinking of something
else to say the young lady turned again to the little boy, whom she addressed quite as if they were alone together. "I should like to know
where you got that pole."

"I bought it!" Randolph shouted.

"You don't mean to say you're going to take it to Italy!"

"Yes, I'm going to take it t' Italy!" the child rang out.

She glanced over the front of her dress and smoothed out a knot or
two of ribbon. Then she gave her sweet eyes to the prospect again.
"Well, I guess you'd better leave it somewhere," she dropped after a
moment.

"Are you going to Italy?" Winterbourne now decided very respectfully to enquire.

She glanced at him with lovely remoteness. "Yes, sir," she then replied.
And she said nothing more.

"And are you—a—thinking of the Simplon?" he pursued with a slight
drop of assurance.

"I don't know," she said. "I suppose it's some mountain. Randolph,
what mountain are we thinking of?"

"Thinking of?"—the boy stared.

"Why going right over."

"Going to where?" he demanded.

"Why right down to Italy"—Winterbourne felt vague emulations.

"I don't know," said Randolph. "I don't want to go t' Italy. I want to go
to America."

"Oh Italy's a beautiful place!" the young man laughed.

"Can you get candy there?" Randolph asked of all the echoes.

"I hope not," said his sister. "I guess you've had enough candy, and
mother thinks so too."

"I haven't had any for ever so long—for a hundred weeks!" cried the
boy, still jumping about.

The young lady inspected her flounces and smoothed her ribbons
again; and Winterbourne presently risked an observation on the beauty
of the view. He was ceasing to be in doubt, for he had begun to perceive
that she was really not in the least embarrassed. She might be cold, she
might be austere, she might even be prim; for that was apparently—he
had already so generalised—what the most "distant" American girls did:
they came and planted themselves straight in front of you to show how
rigidly unapproachable they were. There hadn't been the slightest flush
in her fresh fairness however; so that she was clearly neither offended
nor fluttered. Only she was composed—he had seen that before too—of
charming little parts that didn't match and that made no *ensemble;* and

if she looked another way when he spoke to her, and seemed not particularly to hear him, this was simply her habit, her manner, the result of her having no idea whatever of "form" (with such a tell-tale appendage as Randolph where in the world would she have got it?) in any such connexion. As he talked a little more and pointed out some of the objects of interest in the view, with which she appeared wholly unacquainted, she gradually, none the less, gave him more of the benefit of her attention; and then he saw that act unqualified by the faintest shadow of reserve. It wasn't however what would have been called a "bold" front that she presented, for her expression was as decently limpid as the very cleanest water. Her eyes were the very prettiest conceivable, and indeed Winterbourne hadn't for a long time seen anything prettier than his fair countrywoman's various features—her complexion, her nose, her ears, her teeth. He took a great interest generally in that range of effects and was addicted to noting and, as it were, recording them; so that in regard to this young lady's face he made several observations. It wasn't at all insipid, yet at the same time wasn't pointedly—what point, on earth, could she ever make?—expressive; and though it offered such a collection of small finenesses and neatnesses he mentally accused it—very forgivingly —of a want of finish. He thought nothing more likely than that its wearer would have had her own experience of the action of her charms, as she would certainly have acquired a resulting confidence; but even should she depend on this for her main amusement her bright sweet superficial little visage gave out neither mockery nor irony. Before long it became clear that, however these things might be, she was much disposed to conversation. She remarked to Winterbourne that they were going to Rome for the winter—she and her mother and Randolph. She asked him if he was a "real American"; she wouldn't have taken him for one; he seemed more like a German—this flower was gathered as from a large field of comparison—especially when he spoke. Winterbourne, laughing, answered that he had met Germans who spoke like Americans, but not, so far as he remembered, any American with the resemblance she noted. Then he asked her if she mightn't be more at ease should she occupy the bench he had just quitted. She answered that she liked hanging round, but she none the less resignedly, after a little, dropped to the bench. She told him she was from New York State—"if you know where that is"; but our friend really quickened this current by catching hold of her small slippery brother and making him stand a few minutes by his side.

"Tell me your honest name, my boy." So he artfully proceeded.

In response to which the child was indeed unvarnished truth. "Randolph C. Miller. And I'll tell you hers." With which he levelled his alpenstock at his sister.

"You had better wait till you're asked!" said this young lady quite at her leisure.

"I should like very much to know *your* name," Winterbourne made free to reply.

"Her name's Daisy Miller!" cried the urchin. "But that ain't her real name; that ain't her name on her cards."

"It's a pity you haven't got one of my cards!" Miss Miller quite as naturally remarked.

"Her real name's Annie P. Miller," the boy went on.

It seemed, all amazingly, to do her good. "Ask him *his* now"—and she indicated their friend.

But to this point Randolph seemed perfectly indifferent; he continued to supply information with regard to his own family. "My father's name is Ezra B. Miller. My father ain't in Europe—he's in a better place than Europe." Winterbourne for a moment supposed this the manner in which the child had been taught to intimate that Mr. Miller had been removed to the sphere of celestial rewards. But Randolph immediately added: "My father's in Schenectady. He's got a big business. My father's rich, you bet."

"Well!" ejaculated Miss Miller, lowering her parasol and looking at the embroidered border. Winterbourne presently released the child, who departed, dragging his alpenstock along the path. "He don't like Europe," said the girl as with an artless instinct for historic truth. "He wants to go back."

"To Schenectady, you mean?"

"Yes, he wants to go right home. He hasn't got any boys here. There's one boy here, but he always goes round with a teacher. They won't let him play."

"And your brother hasn't any teacher?" Winterbourne enquired.

It tapped, at a touch, the spring of confidence. "Mother thought of getting him one—to travel round with us. There was a lady told her of a very good teacher; an American lady—perhaps you know her—Mrs. Sanders. I think she came from Boston. She told her of this teacher, and we thought of getting him to travel round with us. But Randolph said he didn't want a teacher travelling round with us. He said he wouldn't have lessons when he was in the cars. And we *are* in the cars about half the time. There was an English lady we met in the cars—I think her name was Miss Featherstone; perhaps you know her. She wanted to know why I didn't give Randolph lessons—give him 'instruction,' she called it. I guess he could give me more instruction than I could give him. He's very smart."

"Yes," said Winterbourne; "he seems very smart."

"Mother's going to get a teacher for him as soon as we get t' Italy. Can you get good teachers in Italy?"

"Very good, I should think," Winterbourne hastened to reply.

"Or else she's going to find some school. He ought to learn some more. He's only nine. He's going to college." And in this way Miss Miller continued to converse upon the affairs of her family and upon other topics. She sat there with her extremely pretty hands, ornamented with very brilliant rings, folded in her lap, and with her pretty eyes now resting upon those of Winterbourne, now wandering over the garden, the people who passed before her and the beautiful view. She addressed her new acquaintance as if she had known him a long time. He found it very pleasant. It was many years since he had heard a young girl talk so much. It might have been said of this wandering maiden who had come and sat down beside him upon a bench that she chattered. She was very quiet, she sat in a charming tranquil attitude; but her lips and her eyes were constantly moving. She had a soft slender agreeable voice, and her tone was distinctly sociable. She gave Winterbourne a report of her movements and intentions, and those of her mother and brother, in Europe, and enumerated in particular the various hotels at which they had stopped. "That English lady in the cars," she said—"Miss Featherstone—asked me if we didn't live in hotels in America. I told her I had never been in so many hotels in my life as since I came to Europe. I've never seen so many—it's nothing but hotels." But Miss Miller made this remark with no querulous accent; she appeared to be in the best humour with everything. She declared that the hotels were very good when once you got used to their ways and that Europe was perfectly entrancing. She wasn't disappointed—not a bit. Perhaps it was because she had heard so much about it before. She had ever so many intimate friends who had been there ever so many times, and that way she had got thoroughly posted. And then she had had ever so many dresses and things from Paris. Whenever she put on a Paris dress she felt as if she were in Europe.

"It was a kind of a wishing-cap," Winterbourne smiled.

"Yes," said Miss Miller at once and without examining this analogy; "it always made me wish I was here. But I needn't have done that for dresses. I'm sure they send all the pretty ones to America; you see the most frightful things here. The only thing I don't like," she proceeded, "is the society. There ain't any society—or if there is I don't know where it keeps itself. Do you? I suppose there's some society somewhere, but I haven't seen anything of it. I'm very fond of society and I've always had plenty of it. I don't mean only in Schenectady, but in New York. I used to go to New York every winter. In New York I had lots of society. Last winter I had seventeen dinners given me, and three of them were by gentlemen," added Daisy Miller. "I've more friends in New York than in Schenectady—more gentlemen friends; and more young lady friends too," she resumed in a moment. She paused again for an instant; she was looking at Winterbourne with all her prettiness in her frank gay eyes and in her clear rather uniform smile. "I've always had," she said, "a great deal of gentlemen's society."

Poor Winterbourne was amused and perplexed—above all he was charmed. He had never yet heard a young girl express herself in just this fashion; never at least save in cases where to say such things was to have at the same time some rather complicated consciousness about them. And yet was he to accuse Miss Daisy Miller of an actual or a potential *arrière-pensée*, as they said at Geneva? He felt he had lived at Geneva so long as to have got morally muddled; he had lost the right sense for the young American tone. Never indeed since he had grown old enough to appreciate things had he encountered a young compatriot of so "strong" a type as this. Certainly she was very charming, but how extraordinarily communicative and how tremendously easy! Was she simply a pretty girl from New York State—were they all like that, the pretty girls who had had a good deal of gentlemen's society? Or was she also a designing, an audacious, in short an expert young person? Yes, his instinct for such a question had ceased to serve him, and his reason could but mislead. Miss Daisy Miller looked extremely innocent. Some people had told him that after all American girls *were* exceedingly innocent, and others had told him that after all they weren't. He must on the whole take Miss Daisy Miller for a flirt—a pretty American flirt. He had never as yet had relations with representatives of that class. He had known here in Europe two or three women—persons older than Miss Daisy Miller and provided, for respectability's sake, with husbands—who were great co-quettes; dangerous terrible women with whom one's light commerce might indeed take a serious turn. But this charming apparition wasn't a coquette in that sense; she was very unsophisticated; she was only a pretty American flirt. Winterbourne was almost grateful for having found the formula that applied to Miss Daisy Miller. He leaned back in his seat; he remarked to himself that she had the finest little nose he had ever seen; he wondered what were the regular conditions and limitations of one's intercourse with a pretty American flirt. It presently became apparent that he was on the way to learn.

"Have you been to that old castle?" the girl soon asked, pointing with her parasol to the far-shining walls of the Château de Chillon.

"Yes, formerly, more than once," said Winterbourne. "You too, I suppose, have seen it?"

"No, we haven't been there. I want to go there dreadfully. Of course I mean to go there. I wouldn't go away from here without having seen that old castle."

"It's a very pretty excursion," the young man returned, "and very easy to make. You can drive, you know, or you can go by the little steamer."

"You can go in the cars," said Miss Miller.

"Yes, you can go in the cars," Winterbourne assented.

"Our courier says they take you right up to the castle," she continued. "We were going last week, but mother gave out. She suffers dreadfully from dyspepsia. She said she couldn't any more go—!" But this sketch of Mrs. Miller's plea remained unfinished. "Randolph wouldn't go either; he says he don't think much of old castles. But I guess we'll go this week if we can get Randolph."

"Your brother isn't interested in ancient monuments?" Winterbourne indulgently asked.

He now drew her, as he guessed she would herself have said, every time. "Why no, he says he don't care much about old castles. He's only nine. He wants to stay at the hotel. Mother's afraid to leave him alone, and the courier won't stay with him; so we haven't been to many places. But it will be too bad if we don't go up there." And Miss Miller pointed again at the Château de Chillon.

"I should think it might be arranged," Winterbourne was thus emboldened to reply. "Couldn't you get some one to stay—for the afternoon—with Randolph?"

Miss Miller looked at him a moment, and then with all serenity, "I wish *you'd* stay with him!" she said.

He pretended to consider it. "I'd much rather go to Chillon with you."

"With me?" she asked without a shadow of emotion.

She didn't rise blushing, as a young person at Geneva would have done; and yet, conscious that he had gone very far, he thought it possible she had drawn back. "And with your mother," he answered very respectfully.

But it seemed that both his audacity and his respect were lost on Miss Daisy Miller. "I guess mother wouldn't go—for *you*," she smiled. "And she ain't much *bent* on going, anyway. She don't like to ride round in the afternoon." After which she familiarly proceeded: "But did you really mean what you said just now—that you'd like to go up there?"

"Most earnestly I meant it," Winterbourne declared.

"Then we may arrange it. If mother will stay with Randolph I guess Eugenio will."

"Eugenio?" the young man echoed.

"Eugenio's our courier. He doesn't like to stay with Randolph—he's the most fastidious man I ever saw. But he's a splendid courier. I guess he'll stay at home with Randolph if mother does, and then we can go to the castle."

Winterbourne reflected for an instant as lucidly as possible: "we" could only mean Miss Miller and himself. This prospect seemed almost too good to believe; he felt as if he ought to kiss the young lady's hand. Possibly he would have done so,—and quite spoiled his chance; but at this moment another person—presumably Eugenio—appeared. A tall handsome man, with superb whiskers and wearing a velvet morning-coat and a voluminous watch-guard, approached the young lady, looking sharply at her companion. "Oh Eugenio!" she said with the friendliest accent.

Eugenio had eyed Winterbourne from head to foot; he now bowed gravely to Miss Miller. "I have the honour to inform Mademoiselle that luncheon's on table."

Mademoiselle slowly rose. "See here, Eugenio, I'm going to that old castle anyway."

"To the Château de Chillon, Mademoiselle?" the courier enquired. "Mademoiselle has made arrangements?" he added in a tone that struck Winterbourne as impertinent.

Eugenio's tone apparently threw, even to Miss Miller's own apprehen-

sion, a slightly ironical light on her position. She turned to Winterbourne with the slightest blush. "You won't back out?"

"I shall not be happy till we go!" he protested.

"And you're staying in this hotel?" she went on. "And you're really
American?"

The courier still stood there with an effect of offence for the young
man so far as the latter saw in it a tacit reflexion on Miss Miller's behaviour and an insinuation that she "picked up" acquaintances. "I shall have
the honour of presenting to you a person who'll tell you all about me,"
he said, smiling, and referring to his aunt.

"Oh well, we'll go some day," she beautifully answered; with which
she gave him a smile and turned away. She put up her parasol and walked
back to the inn beside Eugenio. Winterbourne stood watching her, and
as she moved away, drawing her muslin furbelows over the walk, he
spoke to himself of her natural elegance.

II

He had, however, engaged to do more than proved feasible in promising to present his aunt, Mrs. Costello, to Miss Daisy Miller. As soon as
that lady had got better of her headache he waited on her in her apartment and, after a show of the proper solicitude about her health, asked
if she had noticed in the hotel an American family—a mamma, a daughter and an obstreperous little boy.

"An obstreperous little boy and a preposterous big courier?" said
Mrs. Costello. "Oh yes, I've noticed them. Seen them, heard them and
kept out of their way." Mrs. Costello was a widow of fortune, a person
of much distinction and who frequently intimated that if she hadn't been
so dreadfully liable to sick-headaches she would probably have left a
deeper impress on her time. She had a long pale face, a high nose and a
great deal of very striking white hair, which she wore in large puffs and
over the top of her head. She had two sons married in New York and
another who was now in Europe. This young man was amusing himself
at Homburg and, though guided by his taste, was rarely observed to visit
any particular city at the moment selected by his mother for her appearance there. Her nephew, who had come to Vevey expressly to see her,
was therefore more attentive than, as she said, her very own. He had imbibed at Geneva the idea that one must be irreproachable in all such
forms. Mrs. Costello hadn't seen him for many years and was now greatly
pleased with him, manifesting her approbation by initiating him into
many of the secrets of that social sway which, as he could see she would
like him to think, she exerted from her stronghold in Forty-Second
Street. She admitted that she was very exclusive, but if he had been better
acquainted with New York he would see that one had to be. And her
picture of the minutely hierarchical constitution of the society of that
city, which she presented to him in many different lights, was, to Winterbourne's imagination, almost oppressively striking.

He at once recognised from her tone that Miss Daisy Miller's place in the social scale was low. "I'm afraid you don't approve of them," he pursued in reference to his new friends.

"They're horribly common"—it was perfectly simple. "They're the sort of Americans that one does one's duty by just ignoring."

"Ah you just ignore them?"—the young man took it in.

"I can't *not,* my dear Frederick. I wouldn't if I hadn't to, but I have to."

"The little girl's very pretty," he went on in a moment.

"Of course she's very pretty. But she's of the last crudity."

"I see what you mean of course," he allowed after another pause.

"She has that charming look they all have," his aunt resumed. "I can't think where they pick it up; and she dresses in perfection—no, you don't know how well she dresses. I can't think where they get their taste."

"But, my dear aunt, she's not, after all, a Comanche savage."

"She is a young lady," said Mrs. Costello, "who has an intimacy with her mamma's courier!"

"An 'intimacy' with him?" Ah there it was!

"There's no other name for such a relation. But the skinny little mother's just as bad! They treat the courier as a familiar friend—as a gentleman and a scholar. I shouldn't wonder if he dines with them. Very likely they've never seen a man with such good manners, such fine clothes, so *like* a gentleman—or a scholar. He probably corresponds to the young lady's idea of a count. He sits with them in the garden of an evening. I think he smokes in their faces."

Winterbourne listened with interest to these disclosures; they helped him to make up his mind about Miss Daisy. Evidently she was rather wild. "Well," he said, "I'm not a courier and I didn't smoke in her face, and yet she was very charming to me."

"You had better have mentioned at first," Mrs. Costello returned with dignity, "that you had made her valuable acquaintance."

"We simply met in the garden and talked a bit."

"By appointment—no? Ah that's still to come! Pray what did you say?"

"I said I should take the liberty of introducing her to my admirable aunt."

"Your admirable aunt's a thousand times obliged to you."

"It was to guarantee my respectability."

"And pray who's to guarantee hers?"

"Ah you're cruel!" said the young man. "She's a very innocent girl."

"You don't say that as if you believed it," Mrs. Costello returned.

"She's completely uneducated," Winterbourne acknowledged, "but she's wonderfully pretty, and in short she's very nice. To prove I believe it I'm going to take her to the Château de Chillon."

Mrs. Costello made a wondrous face. "You two are going off there together? I should say it proved just the contrary. How long had you known her, may I ask, when this interesting project was formed? You haven't been twenty-four hours in the house."

"I had known her half an hour!" Winterbourne smiled.

"Then she's just what I supposed."

"And what do you suppose?"

"Why that she's a horror."

Our youth was silent for some moments. "You really think then," he presently began, and with a desire for trustworthy information, "you really think that—" But he paused again while his aunt waited.

"Think what, sir?"

"That she's the sort of young lady who expects a man sooner or later to—well, we'll call it carry her off?"

"I haven't the least idea what such young ladies expect a man to do. But I really consider you had better not meddle with little American girls who are uneducated, as you mildly put it. You've lived too long out of the country. You'll be sure to make some great mistake. You're too innocent."

"My dear aunt, not so much as that comes to!" he protested with a laugh and a curl of his moustache.

"You're too guilty then!"

He continued all thoughtfully to finger the ornament in question. "You won't let the poor girl know you then?" he asked at last.

"Is it literally true that she's going to the Château de Chillon with you?"

"I've no doubt she fully intends it."

"Then, my dear Frederick," said Mrs. Costello, "I must decline the honour of her acquaintance. I'm an old woman, but I'm not too old—thank heaven—to be honestly shocked!"

"But don't they all do these things—the little American girls at home?" Winterbourne enquired.

Mrs. Costello stared a moment. "I should like to see my granddaughters do them!" she then grimly returned.

This seemed to throw some light on the matter, for Winterbourne remembered to have heard his pretty cousins in New York, the daughters of this lady's two daughters, called "tremendous flirts." If therefore Miss Daisy Miller exceeded the liberal licence allowed to these young women it was probable she did go even by the American allowance rather far. Winterbourne was impatient to see her again, and it vexed, it even a little humiliated him, that he shouldn't by instinct appreciate her justly.

Though so impatient to see her again he hardly knew what ground he should give for his aunt's refusal to become acquainted with her; but he discovered promptly enough that with Miss Daisy Miller there was no great need of walking on tiptoe. He found her that evening in the garden, wandering about in the warm starlight after the manner of an indolent sylph and swinging to and fro the largest fan he had ever beheld. It was ten o'clock. He had dined with his aunt, had been sitting with her since dinner, and had just taken leave of her till the morrow. His young friend frankly rejoiced to renew their intercourse; she pronounced it the stupidest evening she had ever passed.

"Have you been all alone?" he asked with no intention of an epigram and no effect of her perceiving one.

"I've been walking round with mother. But mother gets tired walking round," Miss Miller explained.

"Has she gone to bed?"

"No, she doesn't like to go to bed. She doesn't sleep scarcely any—not three hours. She says she doesn't know how she lives. She's dreadfully nervous. I guess she sleeps more than she thinks. She's gone somewhere after Randolph; she wants to try to get him to go to bed. He doesn't like to go to bed."

The soft impartiality of her *constatations,* as Winterbourne would have termed them, was a thing by itself—exquisite little fatalist as they seemed to make her. "Let us hope she'll persuade him," he encouragingly said.

"Well, she'll talk to him all she can—but he doesn't like her to talk to him": with which Miss Daisy opened and closed her fan. "She's going to try to get Eugenio to talk to him. But Randolph ain't afraid of Eugenio. Eugenio's a splendid courier, but he can't make much impression on Randolph! I don't believe he'll go to bed before eleven." Her detachment from any invidious judgement of this was, to her companion's sense, inimitable; and it appeared that Randolph's vigil was in fact triumphantly prolonged, for Winterbourne attended her in her stroll for some time without meeting her mother. "I've been looking round for that lady you want to introduce me to," she resumed—"I guess she's your aunt." Then on his admitting the fact and expressing some curiosity as to how she had learned it, she said she had heard all about Mrs. Costello from the chambermaid. She was very quiet and very *comme il faut;* she wore white puffs; she spoke to no one and she never dined at the common table. Every two days she had a headache. "I think that's a lovely description, headache and all!" said Miss Daisy, chattering along in her thin gay voice. "I want to know her ever so much. I know just what *your* aunt would be; I know I'd like her. She'd be very exclusive. I like a lady to be exclusive; I'm dying to be exclusive myself. Well, I guess we *are* exclusive, mother and I. We don't speak to any one—or they don't speak to us. I suppose it's about the same thing. Anyway, I shall be ever so glad to meet your aunt."

Winterbourne was embarrassed—he could but trump up some evasion. "She'd be most happy, but I'm afraid those tiresome headaches are always to be reckoned with."

The girl looked at him through the fine dusk.

"Well, I suppose she doesn't have a headache every day."

He had to make the best of it. "She tells me she wonderfully does." He didn't know what else to say.

Miss Miller stopped and stood looking at him. Her prettiness was still visible in the darkness; she kept flapping to and fro her enormous fan. "She doesn't want to know me!" she then lightly broke out. "Why don't you say so? You needn't be afraid. *I'm* not afraid!" And she quite crowed for the fun of it.

Winterbourne distinguished however a wee false note in this: he was touched, shocked, mortified by it. "My dear young lady, she knows no one. She goes through life immured. It's her wretched health."

The young girl walked on a few steps in the glee of the thing. "You needn't be afraid," she repeated. "Why should she want to know me?" Then she paused again; she was close to the parapet of the garden, and in front of her was the starlit lake. There was a vague sheen on its surface, and in the distance were dimly-seen mountain forms. Daisy Miller looked out at these great lights and shades and again proclaimed a gay indifference—"Gracious! she *is* exclusive!" Winterbourne wondered if she were seriously wounded and for a moment almost wished her sense of injury might be such as to make it becoming in him to reassure and comfort her. He had a pleasant sense that she would be all accessible to a respectful tenderness at that moment. He felt quite ready to sacrifice his aunt—conversationally; to acknowledge she was a proud rude woman and to make the point that they needn't mind her. But before he had time to commit himself to this questionable mixture of gallantry and impiety, the young lady, resuming her walk, gave an exclamation in quite another tone. "Well, here's mother! I guess she *hasn't* got Randolph to go to bed." The figure of a lady appeared, at a distance, very indistinct in the darkness; it advanced with a slow and wavering step and then suddenly seemed to pause.

"Are you sure it's your mother? Can you make her out in this thick dusk?" Winterbourne asked.

"Well," the girl laughed, "I guess I know my own mother! And when she has got on my shawl too. She's always wearing my things."

The lady in question, ceasing now to approach, hovered vaguely about the spot at which she had checked her steps.

"I'm afraid your mother doesn't see you," said Winterbourne. "Or perhaps," he added—thinking, with Miss Miller, the joke permissible— "perhaps she feels guilty about your shawl."

"Oh it's a fearful old thing!" his companion placidly answered. "I told her she could wear it if she didn't mind looking like a fright. She won't come here because she sees you."

"Ah then," said Winterbourne, "I had better leave you."

"Oh no—come on!" the girl insisted.

"I'm afraid your mother doesn't approve of my walking with you."

She gave him, he thought, the oddest glance. "It isn't for me; it's for you—that is it's for *her*. Well, I don't know who it's for! But mother doesn't like any of my gentlemen friends. She's right down timid. She always makes a fuss if I introduce a gentleman. But I *do* introduce them— almost always. If I didn't introduce my gentlemen friends to mother,"

Miss Miller added, in her small flat monotone, "I shouldn't think I was natural."

"Well, to introduce me," Winterbourne remarked, "you must know my name." And he proceeded to pronounce it.

"Oh my—I can't say all that!" cried his companion, much amused. But by this time they had come up to Mrs. Miller, who, as they drew near, walked to the parapet of the garden and leaned on it, looking intently at the lake and presenting her back to them. "Mother!" said the girl in a tone of decision—upon which the elder lady turned round. "Mr. Frederick Forsyth Winterbourne," said the latter's young friend, repeating his lesson of a moment before and introducing him very frankly and prettily. "Common" she might be, as Mrs. Costello had pronounced her; yet what provision was made by that epithet for her queer little native grace?

Her mother was a small spare light person, with a wandering eye, a scarce perceptible nose, and, as to make up for it, an unmistakeable forehead, decorated—but too far back, as Winterbourne mentally described it—with thin much-frizzled hair. Like her daughter Mrs. Miller was dressed with extreme elegance; she had enormous diamonds in her ears. So far as the young man could observe, she gave him no greeting—she certainly wasn't looking at him. Daisy was near her, pulling her shawl straight. "What are you doing, poking round here?" this young lady enquired—yet by no means with the harshness of accent her choice of words might have implied.

"Well, I don't know"—and the new-comer turned to the lake again.

"I shouldn't think you'd want that shawl!" Daisy familiarly proceeded.

"Well—I do!" her mother answered with a sound that partook for Winterbourne of an odd strain between mirth and woe.

"Did you get Randolph to go to bed?" Daisy asked.

"No, I couldn't induce him"—and Mrs. Miller seemed to confess to the same mild fatalism as her daughter. "He wants to talk to the waiter. He *likes* to talk to that waiter."

"I was just telling Mr. Winterbourne," the girl went on; and to the young man's ear her tone might have indicated that she had been uttering his name all her life.

"Oh yes!" he concurred—"I've the pleasure of knowing your son."

Randolph's mamma was silent; she kept her attention on the lake. But at last a sigh broke from her. "Well, I don't see how he lives!"

"Anyhow, it isn't so bad as it was at Dover," Daisy at least opined.

"And what occurred at Dover?" Winterbourne desired to know.

"He wouldn't go to bed at all. I guess he sat up all night—in the public parlour. He wasn't in bed at twelve o'clock: it seemed as if he couldn't budge."

"It was half-past twelve when I gave up," Mrs. Miller recorded with passionless accuracy.

It was of great interest to Winterbourne. "Does he sleep much during the day?"

"I guess he doesn't sleep *very* much," Daisy rejoined.

"I wish he just *would!*" said her mother. "It seems as if he *must* make it up somehow."

"Well, I guess it's we that make it up. I think he's real tiresome," Daisy pursued.

After which, for some moments, there was silence. "Well, Daisy Miller," the elder lady then unexpectedly broke out, "I shouldn't think you'd want to talk against your own brother!"

"Well, he *is* tiresome, mother," said the girl, but with no sharpness of insistence.

"Well, he's only nine," Mrs. Miller lucidly urged.

"Well, he wouldn't go up to that castle, anyway," her daughter replied as for accommodation. "I'm going up there with Mr. Winterbourne."

To this announcement, very placidly made, Daisy's parent offered no response. Winterbourne took for granted on this that she opposed such a course; but he said to himself at the same time that she was a simple easily-managed person and that a few deferential protestations would modify her attitude. "Yes," he therefore interposed, "your daughter has kindly allowed me the honour of being her guide."

Mrs. Miller's wandering eyes attached themselves with an appealing air to her other companion, who, however, strolled a few steps further, gently humming to herself. "I presume you'll go in the cars," she then quite colourlessly remarked.

"Yes, or in the boat," said Winterbourne.

"Well, of course I don't know," Mrs. Miller returned. "I've never been up to that castle."

"It is a pity you shouldn't go," he observed, beginning to feel reassured as to her opposition. And yet he was quite prepared to find that as a matter of course she meant to accompany her daughter.

It was on this view accordingly that light was projected for him. "We've been thinking ever so much about going, but it seems as if we couldn't. Of course Daisy—she wants to go round everywhere. But there's a lady here—I don't know her name—she says she shouldn't think we'd want to go to see castles *here;* she should think we'd want to wait till we got t' Italy. It seems as if there would be so many there," continued Mrs. Miller with an air of increasing confidence. "Of course we only want to see the principal ones. We visited several in England," she presently added.

"Ah yes, in England there are beautiful castles," said Winterbourne. "But Chillon here is very well worth seeing."

"Well, if Daisy feels up to it—" said Mrs. Miller in a tone that seemed to break under the burden of such conceptions. "It seems as if there's nothing she won't undertake."

"Oh I'm pretty sure she'll enjoy it!" Winterbourne declared. And he desired more and more to make it a certainty that he was to have the privilege of a *tête-à-tête* with the young lady who was still strolling along in front of them and softly vocalising. "You're not disposed, madam," he enquired, "to make the so interesting excursion yourself?"

So addressed Daisy's mother looked at him an instant with a certain scared obliquity and then walked forward in silence. Then, "I guess she had better go alone," she said simply.

It gave him occasion to note that this was a very different type of maternity from that of the vigilant matrons who massed themselves in the forefront of social intercourse in the dark old city at the other end of the lake. But his meditations were interrupted by hearing his name very distinctly pronounced by Mrs. Miller's unprotected daughter. "Mr. Winterbourne!" she piped from a considerable distance.

"Mademoiselle!" said the young man.

"Don't you want to take me out in a boat?"

"At present?" he asked.

"Why of course!" she gaily returned.

"Well, Annie Miller!" exclaimed her mother.

"I beg you, madam, to let her go," he hereupon eagerly pleaded; so instantly had he been struck with the romantic side of this chance to guide through the summer starlight a skiff freighted with a fresh and beautiful young girl.

"I shouldn't think she'd want to," said her mother. "I should think she'd rather go indoors."

"I'm sure Mr. Winterbourne wants to *take* me," Daisy declared. "He's so awfully devoted!"

"I'll row you over to Chillon under the stars."

"I don't believe it!" Daisy laughed.

"Well!" the elder lady again gasped, as in rebuke of this freedom.

"You haven't spoken to me for half an hour," her daughter went on.

"I've been having some very pleasant conversation with your mother," Winterbourne replied.

"Oh pshaw! I want you to take me out in a boat!" Daisy went on as if nothing else had been said. They had all stopped and she had turned round and was looking at her friend. Her face wore a charming smile, her pretty eyes gleamed in the darkness, she swung her great fan about. No, he felt, it was impossible to be prettier than that.

"There are half a dozen boats moored at that landing-place," and he pointed to a range of steps that descended from the garden to the lake. "If you'll do me the honour to accept my arm we'll go and select one of them."

She stood there smiling; she threw back her head; she laughed as for the drollery of this. "I like a gentleman to be formal!"

"I assure you it's a formal offer."

"I was bound I'd make you say something," Daisy agreeably mocked.

"You see it's not very difficult," said Winterbourne. "But I'm afraid you're chaffing me."

"I think not, sir," Mrs. Miller shyly pleaded.

"Do then let me give you a row," he persisted to Daisy.

"It's quite lovely, the way you say that!" she cried in reward.

"It will be still more lovely to do it."

"Yes, it would be lovely!" But she made no movement to accompany him; she only remained an elegant image of free light irony.

"I guess you'd better find out what time it is," her mother impartially contributed.

"It's eleven o'clock, Madam," said a voice with a foreign accent out of the neighbouring darkness; and Winterbourne, turning, recognised the florid personage he had already seen in attendance. He had apparently just approached.

"Oh Eugenio," said Daisy, "I'm going out with Mr. Winterbourne in a boat!"

Eugenio bowed. "At this hour of the night, Mademoiselle?"

"I'm going with Mr. Winterbourne," she repeated with her shining smile. "I'm going this very minute."

"Do tell her she can't, Eugenio," Mrs. Miller said to the courier.

"I think you had better not go out in a boat, Mademoiselle," the man declared.

Winterbourne wished to goodness this pretty girl were not on such familiar terms with her courier; but he said nothing, and she meanwhile added to his ground. "I suppose you don't think it's proper! My!" she wailed; "Eugenio doesn't think anything's proper."

"I'm nevertheless quite at your service," Winterbourne hastened to remark.

"Does Mademoiselle propose to go alone?" Eugenio asked of Mrs. Miller.

"Oh no, with this gentleman!" cried Daisy's mamma for reassurance.

"I *meant* alone with the gentleman." The courier looked for a moment at Winterbourne—the latter seemed to make out in his face a vague presumptuous intelligence as at the expense of their companions—and then solemnly and with a bow, "As Mademoiselle pleases!" he said.

But Daisy broke off at this. "Oh I hoped you'd make a fuss! I don't care to go now."

"Ah but I myself shall make a fuss if you don't go," Winterbourne declared with spirit.

"That's all I want—a little fuss!" With which she began to laugh again.

"Mr. Randolph has retired for the night!" the courier hereupon importantly announced.

"Oh Daisy, now we can go then!" cried Mrs. Miller.

Her daughter turned away from their friend, all lighted with her odd perversity. "Good-night—I hope you're disappointed or disgusted or something!"

He looked at her gravely, taking her by the hand she offered. "I'm puzzled, if you want to know!" he answered.

"Well, I hope it won't keep you awake!" she said very smartly; and, under the escort of the privileged Eugenio, the two ladies passed toward the house.

Winterbourne's eyes followed them; he was indeed quite mystified. He lingered beside the lake a quarter of an hour, baffled by the question of the girl's sudden familiarities and caprices. But the only very definite conclusion he came to was that he should enjoy deucedly "going off" with her somewhere.

Two days later he went off with her to the Castle of Chillon. He waited for her in the large hall of the hotel, where the couriers, the servants, the foreign tourists were lounging about and staring. It wasn't the place he would have chosen for a tryst, but she had placidly appointed it. She came tripping downstairs, buttoning her long gloves, squeezing her folded parasol against her pretty figure, dressed exactly in the way that consorted best, to his fancy, with their adventure. He was a man of imagination and, as our ancestors used to say, of sensibility; as he took in her charming air and caught from the great staircase her impatient confiding step the note of some small sweet strain of romance, not intense but clear and sweet, seemed to sound for their start. He could have believed he was *really* going "off" with her. He led her out through all the idle people assembled—they all looked at her straight and hard: she had begun to chatter as soon as she joined him. His preference had been that they should be conveyed to Chillon in a carriage, but she expressed a lively wish to go in the little steamer—there would be such a lovely breeze upon the water and they should see such lots of people. The sail wasn't long, but Winterbourne's companion found time for many characteristic remarks and other demonstrations, not a few of which were, from the extremity of their candour, slightly disconcerting. To the young man himself their small excursion showed so for delightfully irregular and incongruously intimate that, even allowing for her habitual sense of freedom, he had some expectation of seeing her appear to find in it the same savour. But it must be confessed that he was in this particular rather disappointed. Miss Miller was highly animated, she was in the brightest spirits; but she was clearly not at all in a nervous flutter— as she should have been to match *his* tension; she avoided neither his eyes nor those of any one else; she neither coloured from an awkward consciousness when she looked at him nor when she saw that people were looking at herself. People continued to look at her a great deal, and Winterbourne could at least take pleasure in his pretty companion's distinguished air. He had been privately afraid she would talk loud, laugh overmuch, and even perhaps desire to move extravagantly about the boat. But he quite forgot his fears; he sat smiling with his eyes on her face while, without stirring from her place, she delivered herself of a great number of original reflexions. It was the most charming innocent prattle he had ever heard, for, by his own experience hitherto, when young persons were so ingenuous they were less articulate and when they were so confident were more sophisticated. If he had assented to the idea that she was "common," at any rate, *was* she proving so, after all, or was he simply getting used to her commonness? Her discourse was for the most part of what immediately and superficially surrounded them, but there were moments when it threw out a longer look or took a sudden straight plunge.

"What on *earth* are you so solemn about?" she suddenly demanded, fixing her agreeable eyes on her friend's.

"*Am* I solemn?" he asked. "I had an idea I was grinning from ear to ear."

"You look as if you were taking me to a prayer-meeting or a funeral. If that's a grin your ears are very near together."

"Should you like me to dance a hornpipe on the deck?"

"Pray do, and I'll carry round your hat. It will pay the expenses of our journey."

"I never was better pleased in my life," Winterbourne returned.

She looked at him a moment, then let it renew her amusement. "I like to make you say those things. You're a queer mixture!"

In the castle, after they had landed, nothing could exceed the light independence of her humour. She tripped about the vaulted chambers, rustled her skirts in the corkscrew staircases, flirted back with a pretty little cry and a shudder from the edge of the oubliettes and turned a singularly well-shaped ear to everything Winterbourne told her about the place. But he saw she cared little for mediæval history and that the grim ghosts of Chillon loomed but faintly before her. They had the good fortune to have been able to wander without other society than that of their guide; and Winterbourne arranged with this companion that they shouldn't be hurried—that they should linger and pause wherever they chose. He interpreted the bargain generously—Winterbourne on his side had been generous—and ended by leaving them quite to themselves. Miss Miller's observations were marked by no logical consistency; for anything she wanted to say she was sure to find a pretext. She found a great many, in the tortuous passages and rugged embrasures of the place, for asking her young man sudden questions about himself, his family, his previous history, his tastes, his habits, his designs, and for supplying information on corresponding points in her own situation. Of her own tastes, habits and designs the charming creature was prepared to give the most definite and indeed the most favourable account.

"Well, I hope you know enough!" she exclaimed after Winterbourne had sketched for her something of the story of the unhappy Bonnivard. "I never saw a man that knew so much!" The history of Bonnivard had evidently, as they say, gone into one ear and out of the other. But this easy erudition struck her none the less as wonderful, and she was soon quite sure she wished Winterbourne would travel with them and "go round" with them: they too in that case might learn something about something. "Don't you want to come and teach Randolph?" she asked; "I guess he'd improve with a gentleman teacher." Winterbourne was certain that nothing could possibly please him so much, but that he had unfortunately other occupations. "Other occupations? I don't believe a speck of it!" she protested. "What do you mean now? You're not in business." The young man allowed that he was not in business, but he had engagements which even within a day or two would necessitate his return to Geneva. "Oh bother!" she panted, "I don't believe it!" and she began to talk about something else. But a few moments later, when he was pointing out to her the interesting design of an antique fireplace, she broke out irrelevantly: "You don't mean to say you're going back to Geneva?"

"It is a melancholy fact that I shall have to report myself there tomorrow."

She met it with a vivacity that could only flatter him. "Well, Mr. Winterbourne, I think you're horrid!"

"Oh don't say such dreadful things!" he quite sincerely pleaded—"just at the last."

"The last?" the girl cried; "I call it the very first! I've half a mind to leave you here and go straight back to the hotel alone." And for the next ten minutes she did nothing but call him horrid. Poor Winterbourne was fairly bewildered; no young lady had as yet done him the honour to be so agitated by the mention of his personal plans. His companion, after this, ceased to pay any attention to the curiosities of Chillon or the beauties of the lake; she opened fire on the special charmer in Geneva whom she appeared to have instantly taken it for granted that he was hurrying back to see. How did Miss Daisy Miller know of that agent of his fate in Geneva? Winterbourne, who denied the existence of such a person, was quite unable to discover; and he was divided between amazement at the rapidity of her induction and amusement at the directness of her criticism. She struck him afresh, in all this, as an extraordinary mixture of innocence and crudity. "Does she never allow you more than three days at a time?" Miss Miller wished ironically to know. "Doesn't she give you a vacation in summer? there's no one so hard-worked but they can get leave to go off somewhere at this season. I suppose if you stay another day she'll come right after you in the boat. Do wait over till Friday and I'll go down to the landing to see her arrive!" He began at last even to feel he had been wrong to be disappointed in the temper in which his young lady had embarked. If he had missed the personal accent, the personal accent was now making its appearance. It sounded very distinctly, toward the end, in her telling him she'd stop "teasing" him if he'd promise her solemnly to come down to Rome that winter.

"That's not a difficult promise to make," he hastened to acknowledge. "My aunt has taken an apartment in Rome from January and has already asked me to come and see her."

"I don't want you to come for your aunt," said Daisy; "I want you just to come for me." And this was the only allusion he was ever to hear her make again to his invidious kinswoman. He promised her that at any rate he would certainly come, and after this she forbore from teasing. Winterbourne took a carriage and they drove back to Vevey in the dusk; the girl at his side, her animation a little spent, was now quite distractingly passive.

In the evening he mentioned to Mrs. Costello that he had spent the afternoon at Chillon with Miss Daisy Miller.

"The Americans—of the courier?" asked this lady.

"Ah happily the courier stayed at home."

"She went with you all alone?"

"All alone."

Mrs. Costello sniffed a little at her smelling-bottle. "And that," she exclaimed, "is the little abomination you wanted me to know!"

III

Winterbourne, who had returned to Geneva the day after his excursion to Chillon, went to Rome toward the end of January. His aunt had been established there a considerable time and he had received from her a couple of characteristic letters. "Those people you were so devoted to last summer at Vevey have turned up here, courier and all," she wrote. "They seem to have made several acquaintances, but the courier continues to be the most *intime*. The young lady, however, is also very intimate with various third-rate Italians, with whom she rackets about in a way that makes much talk. Bring me that pretty novel of Cherbuliez's— 'Paule Méré'—and don't come later than the 23d."

Our friend would in the natural course of events, on arriving in Rome, have presently ascertained Mrs. Miller's address at the American banker's and gone to pay his compliments to Miss Daisy. "After what happened at Vevey I certainly think I may call upon them," he said to Mrs. Costello.

"If after what happens—at Vevey and everywhere—you desire to keep up the acquaintance, you're very welcome. Of course you're not squeamish—a man may know every one. Men are welcome to the privilege!"

"Pray what is it then that 'happens'—here for instance?" Winterbourne asked.

"Well, the girl tears about alone with her unmistakeably low foreigners. As to what happens further you must apply elsewhere for information. She has picked up half a dozen of the regular Roman fortune-hunters of the inferior sort and she takes them about to such houses as she may put *her* nose into. When she comes to a party—such a party as she can come to—she brings with her a gentleman with a good deal of manner and a wonderful moustache."

"And where's the mother?"

"I haven't the least idea. They're very dreadful people."

Winterbourne thought them over in these new lights. "They're very ignorant—very innocent only, and utterly uncivilised. Depend on it they're not 'bad.' "

"They're hopelessly vulgar," said Mrs. Costello. "Whether or no being hopelessly vulgar is being 'bad' is a question for the metaphysicians. They're bad enough to blush for, at any rate; and for this short life that's quite enough."

The news that his little friend the child of nature of the Swiss lakeside was now surrounded by half a dozen wonderful moustaches checked Winterbourne's impulse to go straightway to see her. He had perhaps not definitely flattered himself that he had made an ineffaceable impression upon her heart, but he was annoyed at hearing of a state of affairs so little in harmony with an image that had lately flitted in and out of his own meditations; the image of a very pretty girl looking out of an old Roman window and asking herself urgently when Mr. Winterbourne would arrive. If, however, he determined to wait a little before reminding this young lady of his claim to her faithful remembrance, he called with more promtitude on two or three other friends. One of these friends was an American lady who had spent several winters at Geneva, where she had placed her children at school. She was a very accomplished woman and she lived in Via Gregoriana. Winterbourne found her in a little crimson drawing-room on a third floor; the room was filled with southern sunshine. He hadn't been there ten minutes when the servant, appearing in the doorway, announced complacently "Madame Mila!" This announcement was presently followed by the entrance of little Randolph Miller, who stopped in the middle of the room and stood staring at Winterbourne. An instant later his pretty sister crossed the threshold; and then, after a considerable interval, the parent of the pair slowly advanced.

"I guess I know you!" Randolph broke ground without delay.

"I'm sure you know a great many things"—and his old friend clutched him all interestedly by the arm. "How's your education coming on?"

Daisy was engaged in some pretty babble with her hostess, but when she heard Winterbourne's voice she quickly turned her head with a "Well, I declare!" which he met smiling. "I told you I should come, you know."

"Well, I didn't believe it," she answered.

"I'm much obliged to you for that," laughed the young man.

"You might have come to see me then," Daisy went on as if they had parted the week before.

"I arrived only yesterday."

"I don't believe any such thing!" the girl declared afresh.

Winterbourne turned with a protesting smile to her mother, but this lady evaded his glance and, seating herself, fixed her eyes on her son. "We've got a bigger place than this," Randolph hereupon broke out. "It's all gold on the walls."

Mrs. Miller, more of a fatalist apparently than ever, turned uneasily in her chair. "I told you if I was to bring you you'd say something!" she stated as for the benefit of such of the company as might hear it.

"I told *you!*" Randolph retorted. "I tell *you*, sir!" he added jocosely, giving Winterbourne a thump on the knee. "It *is* bigger too!"

As Daisy's conversation with her hostess still occupied her Winterbourne judged it becoming to address a few words to her mother—such as "I hope you've been well since we parted at Vevey."

Mrs. Miller now certainly looked at him—at his chin. "Not very well, sir," she answered.

"She's got the dyspepsia," said Randolph. "I've got it too. Father's got it bad. But I've got it worst!"

This proclamation, instead of embarrassing Mrs. Miller, seemed to soothe her by reconstituting the environment to which she was most accustomed. "I suffer from the liver," she amiably whined to Winterbourne. "I think it's this climate; it's less bracing than Schenectady, especially in the winter season. I don't know whether you know we reside at Schenectady. I was saying to Daisy that I certainly hadn't found any one like Dr. Davis and I didn't believe I *would*. Oh up in Schenectady, he stands first; they think everything of Dr. Davis. He has so much to do, and yet there was nothing he wouldn't do for *me*. He said he never saw anything like my dyspepsia, but he was bound to get at it. I'm sure there was nothing he wouldn't try, and I didn't care what he did to me if he only brought me relief. He was just going to try something new, and I just longed for it, when we came right off. Mr. Miller felt as if he wanted Daisy to see Europe for herself. But I couldn't help writing the other day that I supposed it was all right for Daisy, but that I didn't know as I *could* get on much longer without Dr. Davis. At Schenectady he stands at the very top; and there's a great deal of sickness there too. It affects my sleep."

Winterbourne had a good deal of pathological gossip with Dr. Davis's patient, during which Daisy chattered unremittingly to her own companion. The young man asked Mrs. Miller how she was pleased with Rome. "Well, I must say I'm disappointed," she confessed. "We had heard so much about it—I suppose we had heard too much. But we couldn't help that. We had been led to expect something different."

Winterbourne, however, abounded in reassurance. "Ah wait a little, and you'll grow very fond of it."

"I hate it worse and worse every day!" cried Randolph.

"You're like the infant Hannibal," his friend laughed.

"No I ain't—like any infant!" Randolph declared at a venture.

"Well, that's so—and you never *were!*" his mother concurred. "But we've seen places," she resumed, "that I'd put a long way ahead of Rome." And in reply to Winterbourne's interrogation, "There's Zürich —up there in the mountains," she instanced; "I think Zürich's real lovely, and we hadn't heard half so much about it."

"The best place we've seen's the *City of Richmond!*" said Randolph.

"He means the ship," Mrs. Miller explained. "We crossed in that ship. Randolph had a good time on the *City of Richmond*."

"It's the best place *I've* struck," the child repeated. "Only it was turned the wrong way."

"Well, we've got to turn the right way sometime," said Mrs. Miller with strained but weak optimism. Winterbourne expressed the hope that her daughter at least appreciated the so various interest of Rome, and she declared with some spirit that Daisy was quite carried away. "It's on account of the society—the society's splendid. She goes round everywhere; she has made a great number of acquaintances. Of course she goes round more than I do. I must say they've all been very sweet—they've taken her right in. And then she knows a great many gentlemen. Oh she thinks there's nothing like Rome. Of course it's a great deal pleasanter for a young lady if she knows plenty of gentlemen."

By this time Daisy had turned her attention again to Winterbourne, but in quite the same free form. "I've been telling Mrs. Walker how mean you were!"

"And what's the evidence you've offered?" he asked, a trifle disconcerted, for all his superior gallantry, by her inadequate measure of the zeal of an admirer who on his way down to Rome had stopped neither at Bologna nor at Florence, simply because of a certain sweet appeal to his fond fancy, not to say to his finest curiosity. He remembered how a cynical compatriot had once told him that American women—the pretty ones, and this gave a largeness to the axiom—were at once the most exacting in the world and the least endowed with a sense of indebtedness.

"Why you were awfully mean up at Vevey," Daisy said. "You wouldn't do most anything. You wouldn't stay there when I asked you."

"Dearest young lady," cried Winterbourne, with generous passion, "have I come all the way to Rome only to be riddled by your silver shafts?"

"Just hear him say that!"—and she gave an affectionate twist to a bow on her hostess's dress. "Did you ever hear anything so quaint?"

"So 'quaint,' my dear?" echoed Mrs. Walker more critically—quite in the tone of a partisan of Winterbourne.

"Well, I don't know"—and the girl continued to finger her ribbons. "Mrs. Walker, I want to tell you something."

"Say, mother-r," broke in Randolph with his rough ends to his words, "I tell you you've got to go. Eugenio'll raise something!"

"I'm not afraid of Eugenio," said Daisy with a toss of her head. "Look here, Mrs. Walker," she went on, "you know I'm coming to your party."

"I'm delighted to hear it."

"I've got a lovely dress."

"I'm very sure of that."

"But I want to ask a favour—permission to bring a friend."

"I shall be happy to see any of your friends," said Mrs. Walker, who turned with a smile to Mrs. Miller.

"Oh they're not my friends," cried that lady, squirming in shy repudiation. "It seems as if they didn't take to *me*—I never spoke to one of them!"

"It's an intimate friend of mine, Mr. Giovanelli," Daisy pursued without a tremor in her young clearness or a shadow on her shining bloom.

Mrs. Walker had a pause and gave a rapid glance at Winterbourne. "I shall be glad to see Mr. Giovanelli," she then returned.

"He's just the finest kind of Italian," Daisy pursued with the prettiest serenity. "He's a great friend of mine and the handsomest man in the world—except Mr. Winterbourne! He knows plenty of Italians, but he wants to know some Americans. It seems as if he was crazy about Americans. He's tremendously bright. He's perfectly lovely!"

It was settled that this paragon should be brought to Mrs. Walker's party, and then Mrs. Miller prepared to take her leave. "I guess we'll go right back to the hotel," she remarked with a confessed failure of the larger imagination.

"You may go back to the hotel, mother," Daisy replied, "but I'm just going to walk round."

"She's going to go it with Mr. Giovanelli," Randolph unscrupulously commented.

"I'm going to go it on the Pincio," Daisy peaceably smiled, while the way that she "condoned" these things almost melted Winterbourne's heart.

"Alone, my dear—at this hour?" Mrs. Walker asked. The afternoon was drawing to a close—it was the hour for the throng of carriages and of contemplative pedestrians. "I don't consider it's safe, Daisy," her hostess firmly asserted.

"Neither do I then," Mrs. Miller thus borrowed confidence to add. "You'll catch the fever as sure as you live. Remember what Dr. Davis told you!"

"Give her some of that medicine before she starts in," Randolph suggested.

The company had risen to its feet; Daisy, still showing her pretty teeth, bent over and kissed her hostess. "Mrs. Walker, you're too perfect," she simply said. "I'm not going alone; I'm going to meet a friend."

"Your friend won't keep you from catching the fever even if it *is* his own second nature," Mrs. Miller observed.

"Is it Mr. Giovanelli that's the dangerous attraction?" Mrs. Walker asked without mercy.

Winterbourne was watching the challenged girl; at this question his attention quickened. She stood there smiling and smoothing her bonnet-ribbons; she glanced at Winterbourne. Then, while she glanced and smiled, she brought out all affirmatively and without a shade of hesitation: "Mr. Giovanelli—the beautiful Giovanelli."

"My dear young friend"—and, taking her hand, Mrs. Walker turned to pleading—"don't prowl off to the Pincio at this hour to meet a beautiful Italian."

"Well, he speaks first-rate English," Mrs. Miller incoherently mentioned.

"Gracious me," Daisy piped up, "I don't want to do anything that's going to affect my health—or my character either! There's an easy way to settle it." Her eyes continued to play over Winterbourne. "The Pincio's only a hundred yards off, and if Mr. Winterbourne were as polite as he pretends he'd offer to walk right in with me!"

Winterbourne's politeness hastened to proclaim itself, and the girl gave him gracious leave to accompany her. They passed downstairs before her mother, and at the door he saw Mrs. Miller's carriage drawn up, with the ornamental courier whose acquaintance he had made at Vevey seated within. "Good-bye, Eugenio," cried Daisy; "I'm going to take a walk!" The distance from Via Gregoriana to the beautiful garden at the other end of the Pincian Hill is in fact rapidly traversed. As the day was splendid, however, and the concourse of vehicles, walkers and loungers numerous, the young Americans found their progress much delayed. This fact was highly agreeable to Winterbourne, in spite of his consciousness of his singular situation. The slow-moving, idly-gazing Roman crowd bestowed much attention on the extremely pretty young woman of English race who passed through it, with some difficulty, on his arm; and he wondered what on earth had been in Daisy's mind when she proposed to exhibit herself unattended to its appreciation. His own mission, to her sense, was apparently to consign her to the hands of Mr. Giovanelli; but, at once annoyed and gratified, he resolved that he would do no such thing.

"Why haven't you been to see me?" she meanwhile asked. "You can't get out of that."

"I've had the honour of telling you that I've only just stepped out of the train."

"You must have stayed in the train a good while after it stopped!" she derisively cried. "I suppose you were asleep. You've had time to go to see Mrs. Walker."

"I knew Mrs. Walker—" Winterbourne began to explain.

"I know where you knew her. You knew her at Geneva. She told me so. Well, you knew me at Vevey. That's just as good. So you ought to have come." She asked him no other question than this; she began to prattle about her own affairs. "We've got splendid rooms at the hotel; Eugenio says they're the best rooms in Rome. We're going to stay all winter—if we don't die of the fever; and I guess we'll stay then! It's a great deal nicer than I thought; I thought it would be fearfully quiet—in fact I was sure it would be deadly pokey. I foresaw we should be going round all the time with one of those dreadful old men who explain about the pictures and things. But we only had about a week of that, and now I'm enjoying myself. I know ever so many people, and they're all so charming. The society's extremely select. There are all kinds—English and Germans and Italians. I think I like the English best. I like their style of conversation. But there are some lovely Americans. I never saw anything so hospitable. There's something or other every day. There's not much dancing—but I must say I never thought dancing was everything. I was always fond of conversation. I guess I'll have plenty at Mrs. Walker's—her rooms are so small." When they had passed the gate of the Pincian Gardens Miss Miller began to wonder where Mr. Giovanelli might be. "We had better go straight to that place in front, where you look at the view."

Winterbourne at this took a stand. "I certainly shan't help you to find him."

"Then I shall find him without you," Daisy said with spirit.

"You certainly won't leave me!" he protested.

She burst into her familiar little laugh. "Are you afraid you'll get lost—or run over? But there's Giovanelli leaning against that tree. He's staring at the women in the carriages: did you ever see anything so cool?"

Winterbourne descried hereupon at some distance a little figure that stood with folded arms and nursing its cane. It had a handsome face, a hat artfully poised, a glass in one eye and a nosegay in its buttonhole. Daisy's friend looked at it a moment and then said: "Do you mean to speak to that thing?"

"Do I mean to speak to him? Why you don't suppose I mean to communicate by signs!"

"Pray understand then," the young man returned, "that I intend to remain with you."

Daisy stopped and looked at him without a sign of troubled consciousness, with nothing in her face but her charming eyes, her charming teeth and her happy dimples. "Well, she's a cool one!" he thought.

"I don't like the way you say that," she declared. "It's too imperious."

"I beg your pardon if I say it wrong. The main point's to give you an idea of my meaning."

The girl looked at him more gravely, but with eyes that were prettier than ever. "I've never allowed a gentleman to dictate to me or to interfere with anything I do."

"I think that's just where your mistake has come in," he retorted. "You should sometimes listen to a gentleman—the right one."

At this she began to laugh again. "I do nothing but listen to gentlemen! Tell me if Mr. Giovanelli is the right one."

The gentleman with the nosegay in his bosom had now made out our two friends and was approaching Miss Miller with obsequious rapidity. He bowed to Winterbourne as well as to the latter's compatriot; he seemed to shine, in his coxcombical way, with the desire to please and the fact of his own intelligent joy, though Winterbourne thought him not a bad-looking fellow. But he nevertheless said to Daisy: "No, he's not the right one."

She had clearly a natural turn for free introductions; she mentioned with the easiest grace the name of each of her companions to the other. She strolled forward with one of them on either hand; Mr. Giovanelli, who spoke English very cleverly—Winterbourne afterwards learned that he had practised the idiom upon a great many American heiresses—addressed her a great deal of very polite nonsense. He had the best possible manners, and the young American, who said nothing, reflected on that depth of Italian subtlety, so strangely opposed to Anglo-Saxon simplicity, which enables people to show a smoother surface in proportion as they're more acutely displeased. Giovanelli of course had counted upon something more intimate—he had not bargained for a party of three; but he kept his temper in a manner that suggested far-stretching intentions. Winterbourne flattered himself he had taken his measure. "He's anything but a gentleman," said the young American; "he isn't even a very plausible imitation of one. He's a music-master or a penny-a-liner or a third-rate artist. He's awfully on his good behaviour, but damn his fine eyes!" Mr. Giovanelli had indeed great advantages; but it was deeply disgusting to Daisy's other friend that something in her shouldn't have instinctively discriminated against such a type. Giovanelli chattered and jested and made himself agreeable according to his honest Roman lights. It was true that if he was an imitation the imitation was studied. "Nevertheless," Winterbourne said to himself, "a nice girl ought to know!" And then he came back to the dreadful question of whether this *was* in fact a nice girl. Would a nice girl—even allowing for her being a little American flirt—make a rendezvous with a presumably low-lived foreigner? The rendezvous in this case indeed had been in broad daylight and in the most crowded corner of Rome; but wasn't it possible to regard the choice of these very circumstances as a proof more of vulgarity than of anything else? Singular though it may seem, Winterbourne was vexed that the girl, in joining her *amoroso*, shouldn't appear more impatient of his own company, and he was vexed precisely because of his inclination. It was impossible to regard her as a wholly unspotted flower—she lacked a certain indispensable fineness; and it would therefore much simplify the situation to be able to treat her as the subject of one of the visitations known to romancers as "lawless passions." That she should seem to wish to get rid of him would have helped him to think more lightly of her, just as to be able to think more lightly of her would have made her less perplexing. Daisy at any rate continued on this occasion to present herself as an inscrutable combination of audacity and innocence.

She had been walking some quarter of an hour, attended by her two cavaliers and responding in a tone of very childish gaiety, as it after all struck one of them, to the pretty speeches of the other, when a carriage that had detached itself from the revolving train drew up beside the path. At the same moment Winterbourne noticed that his friend Mrs. Walker—the lady whose house he had lately left—was seated in the vehicle and was beckoning to him. Leaving Miss Miller's side, he hastened to obey her summons—and all to find her flushed, excited, scandalised. "It's really too dreadful"—she earnestly appealed to him. "That crazy girl mustn't do this sort of thing. She mustn't walk here with you two men. Fifty people have remarked her."

Winterbourne—suddenly and rather oddly rubbed the wrong way by this—raised his grave eyebrows. "I think it's a pity to make too much fuss about it."

"It's a pity to let the girl ruin herself!"

"She's very innocent," he reasoned in his own troubled interest.

"She's very reckless," cried Mrs. Walker, "and goodness knows how far—left to itself—it may go. Did you ever," she proceeded to enquire, "see anything so blatantly imbecile as the mother? After you had all left me just now I couldn't sit still for thinking of it. It seemed too pitiful not even to attempt to save them. I ordered the carriage and put on my bonnet and came here as quickly as possible. Thank heaven I've found you!"

"What do you propose to do with us?" Winterbourne uncomfortably smiled.

"To ask her to get in, to drive her about here for half an hour—so that the world may see she's not running absolutely wild—and then take her safely home."

"I don't think it's a very happy thought," he said after reflexion, "but you're at liberty to try."

Mrs. Walker accordingly tried. The young man went in pursuit of their young lady who had simply nodded and smiled, from her distance, at her recent patroness in the carriage and then had gone her way with her own companion. On learning, in the event, that Mrs. Walker had followed her, she retraced her steps, however, with a perfect good grace and with Mr. Giovanelli at her side. She professed herself "enchanted" to have a chance to present this gentleman to her good friend, and immediately achieved the introduction; declaring with it, and as if it were of as little importance, that she had never in her life seen anything so lovely as that lady's carriage-rug.

"I'm glad you admire it," said her poor pursuer, smiling sweetly. "Will you get in and let me put it over you?"

"Oh no, thank you!"—Daisy knew her mind. "I'll admire it ever so much more as I see you driving round with it."

"Do get in and drive round *with* me," Mrs. Walker pleaded.

"That would be charming, but it's so fascinating just as I am!"—with which the girl radiantly took in the gentlemen on either side of her.

"It may be fascinating, dear child, but it's not the custom here," urged the lady of the victoria, leaning forward in this vehicle with her hands devoutly clasped.

"Well, it ought to be then!" Daisy imperturbably laughed. "If I didn't walk I'd expire."

"You should walk with your mother, dear," cried Mrs. Walker with a loss of patience.

"With my mother dear?" the girl amusedly echoed. Winterbourne saw she scented interference. "My mother never walked ten steps in her life. And then, you know," she blandly added, "I'm more than five years old."

"You're old enough to be more reasonable. You're old enough, dear Miss Miller, to be talked about."

Daisy wondered to extravagance. "Talked about? What do you mean?"

"Come into my carriage and I'll tell you."

Daisy turned shining eyes again from one of the gentlemen beside her to the other. Mr. Giovanelli was bowing to and fro, rubbing down his gloves and laughing irresponsibly; Winterbourne thought the scene the most unpleasant possible. "I don't think I want to know what you mean," the girl presently said. "I don't think I should like it."

Winterbourne only wished Mrs. Walker would tuck up her carriage-rug and drive away; but this lady, as she afterwards told him, didn't feel she could "rest there." "Should you prefer being thought a very reckless girl?" she accordingly asked.

"Gracious me!" exclaimed Daisy. She looked again at Mr. Giovanelli, then she turned to her other companion. There was a small pink flush in her cheek; she was tremendously pretty. "Does Mr. Winterbourne think," she put to him with a wonderful bright intensity of appeal, "that—to save my reputation—I ought to get into the carriage?"

It really embarrassed him; for an instant he cast about—so strange was it to hear her speak that way of her "reputation." But he himself in fact had to speak in accordance with gallantry. The finest gallantry here was surely just to tell her the truth; and the truth, for our young man, as the few indications I have been able to give have made him known to the reader, was that his charming friend should listen to the voice of civilised society. He took in again her exquisite prettiness and then said the more distinctly: "I think you should get into the carriage."

Daisy gave the rein to her amusement. "I never heard anything so stiff! If this is improper, Mrs. Walker," she pursued, "then I'm *all* improper, and you had better give me right up. Good-bye; I hope you'll have a lovely ride!"—and with Mr. Giovanelli, who made a triumphantly obsequious salute, she turned away.

Mrs. Walker sat looking after her, and there were tears in Mrs. Walker's eyes. "Get in here, sir," she said to Winterbourne, indicating the place beside her. The young man answered that he felt bound to accompany Miss Miller; whereupon the lady of the victoria declared that if he refused her this favour she would never speak to him again. She was evidently wound up. He accordingly hastened to overtake Daisy and her more faithful ally, and, offering her his hand, told her that Mrs. Walker had made a stringent claim on his presence. He had expected her to answer with something rather free, something still more significant of the perversity from which the voice of society, through the lips of their distressed friend, had so earnestly endeavoured to dissuade her. But she only let her hand slip, as she scarce looked at him, through his slightly awkward grasp; while Mr. Giovanelli, to make it worse, bade him farewell with too emphatic a flourish of the hat.

Winterbourne was not in the best possible humour as he took his seat beside the author of his sacrifice. "That was not clever of you," he said candidly, as the vehicle mingled again with the throng of carriages.

"In such a case," his companion answered, "I don't want to be clever— I only want to be *true!*"

"Well, your truth has only offended the strange little creature—it has only put her off."

"It has happened very well"—Mrs. Walker accepted her work. "If she's so perfectly determined to compromise herself the sooner one knows it the better—one can act accordingly."

"I suspect she meant no great harm, you know," Winterbourne maturely opined.

"So I thought a month ago. But she has been going too far."

"What has she been doing?"

"Everything that's not done here. Flirting with any man she can pick up; sitting in corners with mysterious Italians; dancing all the evening with the same partners; receiving visits at eleven o'clock at night. Her mother melts away when the visitors come."

"But her brother," laughed Winterbourne, "sits up till two in the morning."

"He must be edified by what he sees. I'm told that at their hotel everyone's talking about her and that a smile goes round among the servants when a gentleman comes and asks for Miss Miller."

"Ah we needn't mind the servants!" Winterbourne compassionately signified. "The poor girl's only fault," he presently added, "is her complete lack of education."

"She's naturally indelicate," Mrs. Walker, on her side, reasoned. "Take that example this morning. How long had you known her at Vevey?"

"A couple of days."

"Imagine then the taste of her making it a personal matter that you should have left the place!"

He agreed that taste wasn't the strong point of the Millers—after which he was silent for some moments; but only at last to add: "I suspect, Mrs. Walker, that you and I have lived too long at Geneva!" And he further noted that he should be glad to learn with what particular design she had made him enter her carriage.

"I wanted to enjoin on you the importance of your ceasing your relations with Miss Miller; that of your not appearing to flirt with her; that of your giving her no further opportunity to expose herself; that of your in short letting her alone."

"I'm afraid I can't do anything quite so enlightened as *that*," he returned. "I like her awfully, you know."

"All the more reason you shouldn't help her to make a scandal."

"Well, there shall be nothing scandalous in my attentions to her," he was willing to promise.

"There certainly will be in the way she takes them. But I've said what I had on my conscience," Mrs. Walker pursued. "If you wish to rejoin the young lady I'll put you down. Here, by the way, you have a chance."

The carriage was engaged in that part of the Pincian drive which overhangs the wall of Rome and overlooks the beautiful Villa Borghese. It is bordered by a large parapet, near which are several seats. One of these, at a distance, was occupied by a gentleman and a lady, toward whom Mrs. Walker gave a toss of her head. At the same moment these persons rose and walked to the parapet. Winterbourne had asked the coachman to stop; he now descended from the carriage. His companion looked at him a moment in silence and then, while he raised his hat, drove majestically away. He stood where he had alighted; he had turned his eyes toward Daisy and her cavalier. They evidently saw no one; they were too deeply occupied with each other. When they reached the low garden-wall they remained a little looking off at the great flat-topped pine-clusters of Villa Borghese; then the girl's attendant admirer seated himself familiarly on the broad ledge of the wall. The western sun in the opposite sky sent out a brilliant shaft through a couple of cloud-bars; whereupon the gallant Giovanelli took her parasol out of her hands and opened it. She came a little nearer and he held the parasol over her; then, still holding it, he let it so rest on her shoulder that both of their heads were hidden from Winterbourne. This young man stayed but a moment longer; then he began to walk. But he walked—not toward the couple united beneath the parasol, rather toward the residence of his aunt Mrs. Costello.

IV

He flattered himself on the following day that there was no smiling among the servants when he at least asked for Mrs. Miller at her hotel. This lady and her daughter, however, were not at home; and on the next day after, repeating his visit, Winterbourne again was met by a denial. Mrs. Walker's party took place on the evening of the third day, and in spite of the final reserves that had marked his last interview with that social critic our young man was among the guests. Mrs. Walker was one of those pilgrims from the younger world who, while in contact with the elder, make a point, in their own phrase, of studying European society; and she had on this occasion collected several specimens of diversely-born humanity to serve, as might be, for textbooks. When Winterbourne arrived the little person he desired most to find wasn't there; but in a few moments he saw Mrs. Miller come in alone, very shyly and ruefully. This lady's hair, above the dead waste of her temples, was more frizzled than ever. As she approached their hostess Winterbourne also drew near.

"You see I've come all alone," said Daisy's unsupported parent. "I'm so frightened I don't know what to do; it's the first time I've ever been to a party alone—especially in this country. I wanted to bring Randolph or Eugenio or some one, but Daisy just pushed me off by myself. I ain't used to going round alone."

"And doesn't your daughter intend to favour us with her society?" Mrs. Walker impressively enquired.

"Well, Daisy's all dressed," Mrs. Miller testified with that accent of the dispassionate, if not of the philosophic, historian with which she always recorded the current incidents of her daughter's career. "She got dressed on purpose before dinner. But she has a friend of hers there; that gentleman—the handsomest of the Italians—that she wanted to bring. They've got going at the piano—it seems as if they couldn't leave off. Mr. Giovanelli does sing splendidly. But I guess they'll come before very long," Mrs. Miller hopefully concluded.

"I'm sorry she should come—in that particular way," Mrs. Walker permitted herself to observe.

"Well, I told her there was no use in her getting dressed before dinner if she was going to wait three hours," returned Daisy's mamma. "I didn't see the use of her putting on such a dress as that to sit round with Mr. Giovanelli."

"This is most horrible!" said Mrs. Walker, turning away and addressing herself to Winterbourne. "*Elle s'affiche, la malheureuse.* It's her revenge for my having ventured to remonstrate with her. When she comes I shan't speak to her."

Daisy came after eleven o'clock, but she wasn't, on such an occasion, a young lady to wait to be spoken to. She rustled forward in radiant loveliness, smiling and chattering, carrying a large bouquet and attended by Mr. Giovanelli. Every one stopped talking and turned and looked at her while she floated up to Mrs. Walker. "I'm afraid you thought I never was coming, so I sent mother off to tell you. I wanted to make Mr. Giovanelli practise some things before he came; you know he sings beautifully, and I want you to ask him to sing. This is Mr. Giovanelli; you know I introduced him to you; he's got the most lovely voice and he knows the most charming set of songs. I made him go over them this evening on purpose; we had the greatest time at the hotel." Of all this Daisy delivered herself with the sweetest brightest loudest confidence, looking now at her hostess and now at all the room, while she gave a series of little pats, round her very white shoulders, to the edges of her dress. "Is there anyone I know?" she as undiscourageably asked.

"I think every one knows you!" said Mrs. Walker as with a grand intention; and she gave a very cursory greeting to Mr. Giovanelli. This gentleman bore himself gallantly; he smiled and bowed and showed his white teeth, he curled his moustaches and rolled his eyes and performed all the proper functions of a handsome Italian at an evening party. He sang, very prettily, half a dozen songs, though Mrs. Walker afterwards declared that she had been quite unable to find out who asked him. It was apparently not Daisy who had set him in motion—this young lady being seated a distance from the piano and though she had publicly, as it were, professed herself his musical patroness or guarantor, giving herself to gay and audible discourse while he warbled.

"It's a pity these rooms are so small; we can't dance," she remarked to Winterbourne as if she had seen him five minutes before.

"I'm not sorry we can't dance," he candidly returned. "I'm incapable of a step."

"Of course you're incapable of a step," the girl assented. "I should think your legs *would* be stiff cooped in there so much of the time in that victoria."

"Well, they were very restless there three days ago," he amicably laughed; "all they really wanted was to dance attendance on you."

"Oh my other friend—my friend in need—stuck to me; he seems more at one with his limbs than you are—I'll say that for him. But did you ever hear anything so cool," Daisy demanded, "as Mrs. Walker's wanting me to get into her carriage and drop poor Mr. Giovanelli, and under the pretext that it was proper? People have different ideas! It would have been most unkind; he had been talking about that walk for ten days."

"He shouldn't have talked about it at all," Winterbourne decided to make answer on this: "he would never have proposed to a young lady of this country to walk about the streets of Rome with him."

"About the streets?" she cried with her pretty stare. "Where then would he have proposed to her to walk? The Pincio ain't the streets either, I guess; and I besides, thank goodness, am not a young lady of this country. The young ladies of this country have a dreadfully pokey time of it, by what I can discover; I don't see why I should change my habits for *such* stupids."

"I'm afraid your habits are those of a ruthless flirt," said Winterbourne with studied severity.

"Of course they are!"—and she hoped, evidently, by the manner of it, to take his breath away. "I'm a fearful frightful flirt! Did you ever hear of a nice girl that wasn't? But I suppose you'll tell me now I'm not a nice girl."

He remained grave indeed under the shock of her cynical profession. "You're a very nice girl, but I wish you'd flirt with me, and me only."

"Ah thank you, thank you very much: you're the last man I should think of flirting with. As I've had the pleasure of informing you, you're too stiff."

"You say that too often," he resentfully remarked.

Daisy gave a delighted laugh. "If I could have the sweet hope of making you angry I'd say it again."

"Don't do that—when I'm angry I'm stiffer than ever. But if you won't flirt with me do cease at least to flirt with your friend at the piano. They don't," he declared as in full sympathy with "them," "understand that sort of thing here."

"I thought they understood nothing else!" Daisy cried with startling world-knowledge.

"Not in young unmarried women."

"It seems to me much more proper in young unmarried than in old married ones," she retorted.

"Well," said Winterbourne, "when you deal with natives you must go by the custom of the country. American flirting is a purely American silliness; it has—in its ineptitude of innocence—no place in *this* system. So when you show yourself in public with Mr. Giovanelli and without your mother—"

"Gracious, poor mother!"—and she made it beautifully unspeakable.

Winterbourne had a touched sense for this, but it didn't alter his attitude. "Though *you* may be flirting Mr. Giovanelli isn't—he means something else."

"He isn't preaching at any rate," she returned. "And if you want very much to know, we're neither of us flirting—not a little speck. We're too good friends for that. We're real intimate friends."

He was to continue to find her thus at moments inimitable. "Ah," he then judged, "if you're in love with each other it's another affair altogether!"

She had allowed him up to this point to speak so frankly that he had no thought of shocking her by the force of his logic; yet she now none the less immediately rose, blushing visibly and leaving him mentally to exclaim that the name of little American flirts was incoherence. "Mr. Giovanelli at least," she answered, sparing but a single small queer glance for it, a queerer small glance, he felt, than he had ever yet had from her—"Mr. Giovanelli never says to me such very disagreeable things."

It had an effect on him—he stood staring. The subject of their contention had finished singing; he left the piano, and his recognition of what—a little awkwardly—didn't take place in celebration of this might nevertheless have been an acclaimed operatic tenor's series of repeated ducks before the curtain. So he bowed himself over to Daisy. "Won't you come to the other room and have some tea?" he asked—offering Mrs. Walker's slightly thin refreshment as he might have done all the kingdoms of the earth.

Daisy at last turned on Winterbourne a more natural and calculable light. He was but the more muddled by it, however, since so inconsequent a smile made nothing clear—it seemed at the most to prove in her a sweetness and softness that reverted instinctively to the pardon of offenses. "It has never occurred to Mr. Winterbourne to offer me any tea," she said with her finest little intention of torment and triumph.

"I've offered you excellent advice," the young man permitted himself to growl.

"I prefer weak tea!" cried Daisy, and she went off with the brilliant Giovanelli. She sat with him in the adjoining room, in the embrasure of the window, for the rest of the evening. There was an interesting performance at the piano, but neither of these conversers gave heed to it. When Daisy came to take leave of Mrs. Walker this lady conscientiously repaired the weakness of which she had been guilty at the moment of the girl's arrival—she turned her back straight on Miss Miller and left her to depart with what grace she might. Winterbourne happened to be near the door; he saw it all. Daisy turned very pale and looked at her mother, but Mrs. Miller was humbly unconscious of any rupture of any law or of any deviation from any custom. She appeared indeed to have felt an incongruous impulse to draw attention to her own striking conformity. "Good-night, Mrs. Walker," she said; "we've had a beautiful evening. You see if I let Daisy come to parties without me; I don't want her to go away without me." Daisy turned away, looking with a small white prettiness, a blighted grace, at the circle near the door: Winterbourne saw that for the first moment she was too much shocked and puzzled even for indignation. He on his side was greatly touched.

"That was very cruel," he promptly remarked to Mrs. Walker.

But this lady's face was also as a stone. "She never enters my drawing-room again."

Since Winterbourne then, hereupon, was not to meet her in Mrs. Walker's drawing-room he went as often as possible to Mrs. Miller's hotel. The ladies were rarely at home, but when he found them the devoted Giovanelli was always present. Very often the glossy little Roman, serene in success, but not unduly presumptuous, occupied with Daisy alone the florid salon enjoyed by Eugenio's care, Mrs. Miller being apparently ever of the opinion that discretion is the better part of solicitude. Winterbourne noted, at first with surprise, that Daisy on these occasions was neither embarrassed nor annoyed by his own entrance; but he presently began to feel that she had no more surprises for him and that he really liked, after all, not making out what she was "up to." She showed no displeasure for the interruption of her *tête-à-tête* with Giovanelli; she could chatter as freshly and freely with two gentlemen as with one, and this easy flow had ever the same anomaly for her earlier friend that it was so free without availing itself of its freedom. Winterbourne reflected that if she was seriously interested in the Italian it was odd she shouldn't take more trouble to preserve the sanctity of their interviews, and he liked her the better for her innocent-looking indifference and her inexhaustible gaiety. He could hardly have said why, but she struck him as a young person not formed for a troublesome jealousy. Smile at such a betrayal though the reader may, it was a fact with regard to the women who had hitherto interested him that, given certain contingencies, Winterbourne could see himself afraid—literally afraid—of these ladies. It pleased him to believe that even were twenty other things different and Daisy should love him and he should know it and like it, he would still never be afraid of Daisy. It must be added that this conviction was not altogether flattering to her: it represented that she was nothing every way if not light.

But she was evidently very much interested in Giovanelli. She looked at him whenever he spoke; she was perpetually telling him to do this and to do that; she was constantly chaffing and abusing him. She appeared completely to have forgotten that her other friend had said anything to displease her at Mrs. Walker's entertainment. One Sunday afternoon, having gone to Saint Peter's with his aunt, Winterbourne became aware that the young woman held in horror by that lady was strolling about the great church under escort of her coxcomb of the Corso. It amused him, after a debate, to point out the exemplary pair—even at the cost, as it proved, of Mrs. Costello's saying when she had taken them in through her eye-glass: "That's what makes you so pensive in these days, eh?"

"I hadn't the least idea I was pensive," he pleaded.

"You're very much preoccupied; you're always thinking of something."

"And what is it," he asked, "that you accuse me of thinking of? "

"Of that young lady's, Miss Baker's, Miss Chandler's—what's her name? —Miss Miller's intrigue with that little barber's block."

"Do you call it an intrigue," he asked—"an affair that goes on with such peculiar publicity?"

"That's their folly," said Mrs. Costello, "it's not their merit."

"No," he insisted with a hint perhaps of the preoccupation to which his aunt had alluded—"I don't believe there's anything to be called an intrigue."

"Well"—and Mrs. Costello dropped her glass—"I've heard a dozen people speak of it: they say she's quite carried away by him."

"They're certainly as thick as thieves," our embarrassed young man allowed.

Mrs. Costello came back to them, however, after a little; and Winterbourne recognised in this a further illustration—than that supplied by his own condition—of the spell projected by the case. "He's certainly very handsome. One easily sees how it is. She thinks him the most elegant man in the world, the finest gentleman possible. She has never seen anything like him—he's better even than the courier. It was the courier probably who introduced him, and if he succeeds in marrying the young lady the courier will come in for a magnificent commission."

"I don't believe she thinks of marrying him," Winterbourne reasoned, "and I don't believe he hopes to marry her."

"You may be very sure she thinks of nothing at all. She romps on from day to day, from hour to hour, as they did in the Golden Age. I can imagine nothing more vulgar," said Mrs. Costello, whose figure of speech scarcely went on all fours. "And at the same time," she added, "depend upon it she may tell you any moment that she is 'engaged.' "

"I think that's more than Giovanelli really expects," said Winterbourne.

"And who is Giovanelli?"

"The shiny—but, to do him justice, not greasy—little Roman. I've asked questions about him and learned something. He's apparently a perfectly

respectable little man. I believe he's in a small way a *cavaliere avvocato*.
But he doesn't move in what are called the first circles. I think it really
not absolutely impossible the courier introduced him. He's evidently immensely charmed with Miss Miller. If she thinks him the finest gentleman in the world, he, on his side, has never found himself in personal
contact with such splendour, such opulence, such personal daintiness, as
this young lady's. And then she must seem to him wonderfully pretty
and interesting. Yes, he can't really hope to pull it off. That must appear
to him too impossible a piece of luck. He has nothing but his handsome
face to offer, and there's a substantial, a possibly explosive Mr. Miller in
that mysterious land of dollars and six-shooters. Giovanelli's but too conscious that he hasn't a title to offer. If he were only a count or a *marchese!*
What on earth can he make of the way they've taken him up?"

"He accounts for it by his handsome face and thinks Miss Miller a
young lady *qui se passe ses fantaisies!*"

"It's very true," Winterbourne pursued, "that Daisy and her mamma
haven't yet risen to that stage of—what shall I call it?—of culture, at
which the idea of catching a count or a *marchese* begins. I believe them
intellectually incapable of that conception."

"Ah but the *cavaliere avvocato* doesn't believe them!" cried Mrs. Costello.

Of the observation excited by Daisy's "intrigue" Winterbourne gathered that day at Saint Peter's sufficient evidence. A dozen of the American colonists in Rome came to talk with his relative, who sat on a small
portable stool at the base of one of the great pilasters. The vesper-service
was going forward in splendid chants and organ-tones in the adjacent
choir, and meanwhile, between Mrs. Costello and her friends, much was
said about poor little Miss Miller's going really "too far." Winterbourne
was not pleased with what he heard; but when, coming out upon the
great steps of the church, he saw Daisy, who had emerged before him,
get into an open cab with her accomplice and roll away through the cynical streets of Rome, the measure of her course struck him as simply there
to take. He felt very sorry for her—not exactly that he believed she had
completely lost her wits, but because it was painful to see so much that
was pretty and undefended and natural sink so low in human estimation.
He made an attempt after this to give a hint to Mrs. Miller. He met one
day in the Corso a friend—a tourist like himself—who had just come out
of the Doria Palace, where he had been walking through the beautiful
gallery. His friend "went on" for some moments about the great portrait
of Innocent X, by Velasquez, suspended in one of the cabinets of the
palace, and then said: "And in the same cabinet, by the way, I enjoyed
sight of an image of a different kind; that little American who's so much
more a work of nature than of art and whom you pointed out to me last
week." In answer to Winterbourne's enquiries his friend narrated that
the little American—prettier now than ever—was seated with a companion in the secluded nook in which the papal presence is enshrined.

"All alone?" the young man heard himself disingenuously ask.

"Alone with a little Italian who sports in his button-hole a stack of flowers. The girl's a charming beauty, but I thought I understood from you the other day that she's a young lady *du meilleur monde.*"

"So she is!" said Winterbourne; and having assured himself that his informant had seen the interesting pair but ten minutes before, he jumped into a cab and went to call on Mrs. Miller. She was at home, but she apologised for receiving him in Daisy's absence.

"She's gone out somewhere with Mr. Giovanelli. She's always going round with Mr. Giovanelli."

"I've noticed they're intimate indeed," Winterbourne concurred.

"Oh it seems as if they couldn't live without each other!" said Mrs. Miller. "Well, he's a real gentleman anyhow. I guess I have the joke on Daisy—that she *must* be engaged!"

"And how does your daughter *take* the joke?"

"Oh she just says she ain't. But she might as *well* be!" this philosophic parent resumed. "She goes on as if she was. But I've made Mr. Giovanelli promise to tell me if Daisy don't. I'd want to write to Mr. Miller about it—wouldn't you?"

Winterbourne replied that he certainly should; and the state of mind of Daisy's mamma struck him as so unprecedented in the annals of parental vigilance that he recoiled before the attempt to educate at a single interview either her conscience or her wit.

After this Daisy was never at home and he ceased to meet her at the houses of their common acquaintance, because, as he perceived, these shrewd people had quite made up their minds as to the length she must have gone. They ceased to invite her, intimating that they wished to make, and make strongly, for the benefit of observant Europeans, the point that though Miss Daisy Miller was a pretty American girl all right, her behaviour wasn't pretty at all—was in fact regarded by her compatriots as quite monstrous. Winterbourne wondered how she felt about all the cold shoulders that were turned upon her, and sometimes found himself suspecting with impatience that she simply didn't feel and didn't know. He set her down as hopelessly childish and shallow, as such mere giddiness and ignorance incarnate as was powerless either to heed or to suffer. Then at other moments he couldn't doubt that she carried about in her elegant and irresponsible little organism a defiant, passionate, perfectly observant consciousness of the impression she produced. He asked himself whether the defiance would come from the consciousness of innocence or from her being essentially a young person of the reckless class. Then it had to be admitted, he felt, that holding fast to a belief in her "innocence" was more and more but a matter of gallantry too finespun for use. As I have already had occasion to relate, he was reduced without pleasure to this chopping of logic and vexed at his poor fallibility, his want of instinctive certitude as to how far her extravagance was generic and national and how far it was crudely personal. Whatever it was he had helplessly missed her, and now it was too late. She was "carried away" by Mr. Giovanelli.

A few days after his brief interview with her mother he came across her at that supreme seat of flowering desolation known as the Palace of the Caesars. The early Roman spring had filled the air with bloom and perfume, and the rugged surface of the Palatine was muffled with tender verdure. Daisy moved at her ease over the great mounds of ruin that are embanked with mossy marble and paved with monumental inscriptions. It seemed to him he had never known Rome so lovely as just then. He looked off at the enchanting harmony of line and colour that remotely encircles the city—he inhaled the softly humid odours and felt the freshness of the year and the antiquity of the place reaffirm themselves in deep interfusion. It struck him also that Daisy had never showed to the eye for so utterly charming; but this had been his conviction on every occasion of their meeting. Giovanelli was of course at her side, and Giovanelli too glowed as never before with something of the glory of his race.

"Well," she broke out upon the friend it would have been such mockery to designate as the latter's rival, "I should think you'd be quite lonesome!"

"Lonesome?" Winterbourne resignedly echoed.

"You're always going round by yourself. Can't you get any one to walk with you?"

"I'm not so fortunate," he answered, "as your gallant companion."

Giovanelli had from the first treated him with distinguished politeness; he listened with a deferential air to his remarks; he laughed punctiliously at his pleasantries; he attached such importance as he could find terms for to Miss Miller's cold compatriot. He carried himself in no degree like a jealous wooer; he had obviously a great deal of tact; he had no objection to any one's expecting a little humility of him. It even struck Winterbourne that he almost yearned at times for some private communication in the interest of his character for common sense; a chance to remark to him as another intelligent man that, bless him, *he* knew how extraordinary was their young lady and didn't flatter himself with confident—at least *too* confident and too delusive—hopes of matrimony and dollars. On this occasion he strolled away from his charming charge to pluck a sprig of almond-blossom which he carefully arranged in his button-hole.

"I know why you say that," Daisy meanwhile observed. "Because you think I go round too much with *him!*" And she nodded at her discreet attendant.

"Every one thinks so—if you care to know," was all Winterbourne found to reply.

"Of course I care to know!"—she made this point with much expression. "But I don't believe a word of it. They're only pretending to be shocked. They don't really care a straw what I do. Besides, I don't go round so much."

"I think you'll find they do care. They'll show it—disagreeably," he took on himself to state.

Daisy weighed the importance of that idea. "How—disagreeably?"

"Haven't you noticed anything?" he compassionately asked.

"I've noticed *you*. But I noticed you've no more 'give' than a ramrod the first time ever I saw you."

"You'll find at least that I've more 'give' than several others," he patiently smiled.

"How shall I find it?"

"By going to see the others."

"What will they do to me?"

"They'll show you the cold shoulder. Do you know what that means?"

Daisy was looking at him intently; she began to colour. "Do you mean as Mrs. Walker did the other night?"

"Exactly as Mrs. Walker did the other night."

She looked away at Giovanelli, still titivating with his almond-blossom. Then with her attention again on the important subject: "I shouldn't think you'd let people be so unkind!"

"How can I help it?"

"I should think you'd want to say something."

"I do want to say something"—and Winterbourne paused a moment. "I want to say that your mother tells me she believes you engaged."

"Well, I guess she does," said Daisy very simply.

The young man began to laugh. "And does Randolph believe it?"

"I guess Randolph doesn't believe anything." This testimony to Randolph's scepticism excited Winterbourne to further mirth, and he noticed that Giovanelli was coming back to them. Daisy, observing it as well, addressed herself again to her countryman. "Since you've mentioned it," she said, "I *am* engaged." He looked at her hard—he had stopped laughing. "You don't believe it!" she added.

He asked himself, and it was for a moment like testing a heart-beat; after which, "Yes, I believe it!" he said.

"Oh no, you don't," she answered. "But *if* you possibly do," she still more perversely pursued—"well, I ain't!"

Miss Miller and her constant guide were on their way to the gate of the enclosure, so that Winterbourne, who had but lately entered, presently took leave of them. A week later on he went to dine at a beautiful villa on the Cælian Hill, and, on arriving, dismissed his hired vehicle. The evening was perfect and he promised himself the satisfaction of walking home beneath the Arch of Constantine and past the vaguely-lighted monuments of the Forum. Above was a moon half-developed, whose radiance was not brilliant but veiled in a thin cloud-curtain that seemed to diffuse and equalise it. When on his return from the villa at eleven o'clock he approached the dusky circle of the Colosseum the sense of the romantic in him easily suggested that the interior, in such an atmosphere, would well repay a glance. He turned aside and walked to one of the empty arches, near which, as he observed, an open carriage—one of the little Roman street-cabs—was stationed. Then he passed in among the cavernous shadows of the great structure and emerged upon the clear and silent arena. The place had never seemed to him more impressive. One half of the gigantic circus was in deep shade while the other slept in the luminous dusk. As he stood there he began to murmur Byron's famous lines out of "Manfred"; but before he had finished his quotation he remembered that if nocturnal meditation thereabouts was the fruit of a rich literary culture it was none the less deprecated by medical science. The air of other ages surrounded one; but the air of other ages, coldly analysed, was no better than a villainous miasma. Winterbourne sought, however, toward the middle of the arena, a further reach of vision, intending the next moment a hasty retreat. The great cross in the centre was almost obscured; only as he drew near did he make it out distinctly. He thus also distinguished two persons stationed on the low steps that formed its base. One of these was a woman seated; her companion hovered before her.

Presently the sound of the woman's voice came to him distinctly in the warm night-air. "Well, he looks at us as one of the old lions or tigers may have looked at the Christian martyrs!" These words were winged with their accent, so that they fluttered and settled about him in the darkness like vague white doves. It was Miss Daisy Miller who had released them for flight.

"Let us hope he's not very hungry"—the bland Giovanelli fell in with her humour. "He'll have to take *me* first; you'll serve for dessert."

Winterbourne felt himself pulled up with final horror now—and, it must be added, with final relief. It was as if a sudden clearance had taken place in the ambiguity of the poor girl's appearances and the whole riddle of her contradictions had grown easy to read. She was a young lady about the *shades* of whose perversity a foolish puzzled gentleman need no longer trouble his head or his heart. That once questionable quantity *had* no shades—it was a mere black little blot. He stood there looking at her, looking at her companion too, and not reflecting that though he saw them vaguely he himself must have been more brightly presented. He felt angry at all his shiftings of view—he felt ashamed of all his tender little scruples and all his witless little mercies. He was about to advance again, and then again checked himself; not from the fear of doing her injustice, but from a sense of the danger of showing undue exhilaration for this disburdenment of cautious criticism. He turned away toward the entrance of the place; but as he did so he heard Daisy speak again.

"Why it was Mr. Winterbourne! He saw me and he cuts me dead!"

What a clever little reprobate she was, he was amply able to reflect at this, and how smartly she feigned, how promptly she sought to play off on him, a surprised and injured innocence! But nothing would induce him to cut her either "dead" or to within any measurable distance even of the famous "inch" of her life. He came forward again and went toward the great cross. Daisy had got up and Giovanelli lifted his hat. Winterbourne had now begun to think simply of the madness, on the ground of exposure and infection, of a frail young creature's lounging away such hours in a nest of malaria. What if she *were* the most plausible of little reprobates? That was no reason for her dying of the *perniciosa*. "How long have you been 'fooling round' here?" he asked with conscious roughness.

Daisy, lovely in the sinister silver radiance, appraised him a moment, roughness and all. "Well, I guess all the evening." She answered with spirit and, he could see even then, with exaggeration. "I never saw anything so quaint."

"I'm afraid," he returned, "you'll not think a bad attack of Roman fever very quaint. This is the way people catch it. I wonder," he added to Giovanelli, "that you, a native Roman, should countenance such extraordinary rashness."

"Ah," said this seasoned subject, "for myself I have no fear."

"Neither have I—for you!" Winterbourne retorted in French. "I'm speaking for this young lady."

Giovanelli raised his well-shaped eyebrows and showed his shining teeth, but took his critic's rebuke with docility. "I assured Mademoiselle it was a grave indiscretion, but when was Mademoiselle ever prudent?"

"I never was sick, and I don't mean to be!" Mademoiselle declared. "I don't look like much, but I'm healthy! I was bound to see the Colosseum by moonlight—I wouldn't have wanted to go home without *that*; and we've had the most beautiful time, haven't we, Mr. Giovanelli? If there has been any danger Eugenio can give me some pills. Eugenio has got some splendid pills."

"*I* should advise you then," said Winterbourne, "to drive home as fast as possible and take one!"

Giovanelli smiled as for the striking happy thought. "What you say is very wise. I'll go and make sure the carriage is at hand." And he went forward rapidly.

Daisy followed with Winterbourne. He tried to deny himself the small fine anguish of looking at her, but his eyes themselves refused to spare him, and she seemed moreover not in the least embarrassed. He spoke no word; Daisy chattered over the beauty of the place: "Well, I *have* seen the Colosseum by moonlight—that's one thing I can rave about!" Then noticing her companion's silence she asked him why he was so stiff—it had always been her great word. He made no answer, but he felt his laugh an immense negation of stiffness. They passed under one of the dark archways; Giovanelli was in front with the carriage. Here Daisy stopped a moment, looking at her compatriot. "*Did* you believe I was engaged the other day?"

"It doesn't matter now what I believed the other day!" he replied with infinite point.

It was a wonder how she didn't wince for it. "Well, what do you believe now?"

"I believe it makes very little difference whether you're engaged or not!"

He felt her lighted eyes fairly penetrate the thick gloom of the vaulted passage—as if to seek some access to him she hadn't yet compassed. But Giovanelli, with a graceful inconsequence, was at present all for retreat. "Quick, quick; if we get in by midnight we're quite safe!"

Daisy took her seat in the carriage and the fortunate Italian placed himself beside her. "Don't forget Eugenio's pills!" said Winterbourne as he lifted his hat.

"I don't care," she unexpectedly cried out for this, "whether I have Roman fever or not!" On which the cab-driver cracked his whip and they rolled across the desultory patches of antique pavement.

Winterbourne—to do him justice, as it were—mentioned to no one that he had encountered Miss Miller at midnight in the Colosseum with a gentleman; in spite of which deep discretion, however, the fact of the scandalous adventure was known a couple of days later, with a dozen vivid details, to every member of the little American circle, and was commented accordingly. Winterbourne judged thus that the people about the hotel had been thoroughly empowered to testify, and that after Daisy's return there would have been an exchange of jokes between the porter and the cab-driver. But the young man became aware at the same moment of how thoroughly it had ceased to ruffle him that the little American flirt should be "talked about" by low-minded menials. These sources of current criticism a day or two later abounded still further: the little American flirt was alarmingly ill and the doctors now in possession of the scene. Winterbourne, when the rumour came to him, immediately went to the hotel for more news. He found that two or three charitable friends had preceded him and that they were being entertained in Mrs. Miller's salon by the all-efficient Randolph.

"It's going round at night that way, you bet—that's what has made her so sick. She's always going round at night. I shouldn't think she'd want to—it's so plaguey dark over here. You can't see anything over here without the moon's right up. In America they don't go round by the moon!" Mrs. Miller meanwhile wholly surrendered to her genius for unapparent uses; her salon knew her less than ever, and she was presumably now at least giving her daughter the advantage of her society. It was clear that Daisy was dangerously ill.

Winterbourne constantly attended for news from the sick-room, which reached him, however, but with worrying indirectness, though he once had speech, for a moment, of the poor girl's physician and once saw Mrs. Miller, who, sharply alarmed, struck him as thereby more happily inspired than he could have conceived and indeed as the most noiseless and light-handed of nurses. She invoked a good deal the remote shade of Dr. Davis, but Winterbourne paid her the compliment of taking her after all for less monstrous a goose. To this indulgence indeed something she further said perhaps even more insidiously disposed him. "Daisy spoke of you the other day quite pleasantly. Half the time she doesn't

know what she's saying, but that time I think she did. She gave me a message—she told me to tell you. She wanted you to know she never was engaged to that handsome Italian who was always round. I'm sure I'm very
glad; Mr. Giovanelli hasn't been near us since she was taken ill. I thought
he was so much of a gentleman, but I don't call that very polite! A lady
told me he was afraid I hadn't approved of his being round with her so
much evenings. Of course it ain't as if their evenings were as pleasant as
ours—since *we* don't seem to feel that way about the poison. I guess I
don't see the point now; but I suppose he knows I'm a lady and I'd scorn
to raise a fuss. Anyway, she wants you to realise she ain't engaged. I
don't know why she makes so much of it, but she said to me three times
'Mind you tell Mr. Winterbourne.' And then she told me to ask if you
remembered the time you went up to that castle in Switzerland. But I said
I wouldn't give any such messages as *that*. Only if she ain't engaged I
guess I'm glad to realise it too."

But, as Winterbourne had originally judged, the truth on this question
had small actual relevance. A week after this the poor girl died; it had
been indeed a terrible case of the *perniciosa*. A grave was found for her
in the little Protestant cemetery, by an angle of the wall of imperial
Rome, beneath the cypresses and the thick spring-flowers. Winterbourne
stood there beside it with a number of other mourners; a number larger
than the scandal excited by the young lady's career might have made
probable. Near him stood Giovanelli, who came nearer still before
Winterbourne turned away. Giovanelli, in decorous mourning, showed
but a whiter face; his button-hole lacked its nosegay and he had visibly
something urgent—and even to distress—to say, which he scarce knew
how to "place." He decided at last to confide it with a pale convulsion to
Winterbourne. "She was the most beautiful young lady I ever saw, and
the most amiable." To which he added in a moment: "Also—naturally!—
the most innocent."

Winterbourne sounded him with hard dry eyes, but presently repeated
his words, "The most innocent?"

"The most innocent!"

It came somehow so much too late that our friend could only glare at
its having come at all. "Why the devil," he asked, "did you take her to
that fatal place?"

Giovanelli raised his neat shoulders and eyebrows to within suspicion
of a shrug. "For myself I had no fear; and *she*—she did what she liked."

Winterbourne's eyes attached themselves to the ground. "She did what
she liked!"

It determined on the part of poor Giovanelli a further pious, a further
candid, confidence. "If she had lived I should have got nothing. She
never would have married me."

It had been spoken as if to attest, in all sincerity, his disinterestedness,
but Winterbourne scarce knew what welcome to give it. He said, however, with a grace inferior to his friend's: "I dare say not."

The latter was even by this not discouraged. "For a moment I hoped so. But no. I'm convinced."

Winterbourne took it in; he stood staring at the raw protuberance among the April daisies. When he turned round again his fellow mourner had stepped back.

He almost immediately left Rome, but the following summer he again met his aunt Mrs. Costello at Vevey. Mrs. Costello extracted from the charming old hotel there a value that the Miller family hadn't mastered the secret of. In the interval Winterbourne had often thought of the most interesting member of the trio—of her mystifying manners and her queer adventure. One day he spoke of her to his aunt—said it was on his conscience he had done her injustice.

"I'm sure I don't know"—that lady showed caution. "How did your injustice affect her?"

"She sent me a message before her death which I didn't understand at the time. But I've understood it since. She would have appreciated one's esteem."

"She took an odd way to gain it! But do you mean by what you say," Mrs. Costello asked, "that she would have reciprocated one's affection?"

As he made no answer to this she after a little looked round at him—he hadn't been directly within sight; but the effect of that wasn't to make her repeat her question. He spoke, however, after a while. "You were right in that remark that you made last summer. I was booked to make a mistake. I've lived too long in foreign parts." And this time she herself said nothing.

Nevertheless he soon went back to live at Geneva, whence there continue to come the most contradictory accounts of his motives of sojourn: a report that he's "studying" hard—an intimation that he's much interested in a very clever foreign lady.

❧

THE ASPERN PAPERS

The long tale of *The Aspern Papers*—it is almost a short novel—was written by Henry James very rapidly during the summer of 1887 in Italy and sent off to Thomas Bailey Aldrich, then editor of the *Atlantic Monthly*, where it appeared in the March–May issues of 1888. James felt from the first that he had written a minor masterpiece and critics since that time have tended to agree. As story-telling it moves with the subtle pace of a well-timed thriller; its story, of an unprincipled "publishing scoundrel," who worms his way into the home of a famous poet's mistress and then tries to steal her love letters, is one of great beauty, both in structure and style, though built of light materials. But its lightness of theme does not conceal a deeper plea for the preservation of an artist's life from prying hands, a belief that any artist must be seen in his work alone. At the same time James himself is fascinated by the human elements behind an artist's work, the pulse of life which creates the pulse-beat of a poem. And so James's story is to be read not as a piece of realism—though the Venice of the story is real enough—but as a delicate and beautifully-wrought example of story-telling, and not least in the way the man who tells the story gives us so candid a picture of his own personality.

The "germ" for *The Aspern Papers*, recorded in James's notebooks, stems from an old bit of literary history. A Bostonian Shelley enthusiast named Captain Silsbee discovered that Byron's one-time mistress, Claire Clairmont, had been living in Florence at an advanced age with her niece, a younger Miss Clairmont, of about 50. Convinced that she had in her possession letters of Shelley and Byron, he succeeded in obtaining lodgings in her home to keep a watchful eye on the documents and perhaps gain possession of them. The old lady finally died and Silsbee approached the younger woman, who agreed to give him the letters on the one condition which James includes in his story. James wrote: "Certainly there is a little subject there: the picture of the two faded, queer, poor and discredited old English women—living on into a strange generation, in their musty corner of a foreign town—with these illustrious letters their most precious possession. Then the plot of the Shelley fanatic . . ."

Out of his own vision of Italy, and particularly of Venice, James built this tale which belongs to the golden age of story-telling: a mixture of the pathetic and the comic, centering on the image of an imaginary American Shelley or Byron, whom he named Geoffrey Aspern.

I

I had taken Mrs. Prest into my confidence; without her in truth I should have made but little advance, for the fruitful idea in the whole business dropped from her friendly lips. It was she who found the short cut and loosed the Gordian knot. It is not supposed easy for women to rise to the large free view of anything, anything to be done; but they sometimes throw off a bold conception—such as a man wouldn't have risen to—with singular serenity. "Simply make them take you in on the footing of a lodger"—I don't think that unaided I should have risen to that. I was beating about the bush, trying to be ingenious, wondering by what combination of arts I might become an acquaintance, when she offered this happy suggestion that the way to become an acquaintance was first to become an intimate. Her actual knowledge of the Misses Bordereau was scarcely larger than mine, and indeed I had brought with me from England some definite facts that were new to her. Their name had been mixed up ages before with one of the greatest names of the century, and they now lived obscurely in Venice, lived on very small means, unvisited, unapproachable, in a sequestered and dilapidated old palace: this was the substance of my friend's impression of them. She herself had been established in Venice some fifteen years and had done a great deal of good there; but the circle of her benevolence had never embraced the two shy, mysterious and, as was somehow supposed, scarcely respectable Americans—they were believed to have lost in their long exile all national quality, besides being as their name implied of some remoter French affiliation—who asked no favours and desired no attention. In the early years of her residence she had made an attempt to see them, but this had been successful only as regards the little one, as Mrs. Prest called the niece; though in fact I afterwards found her the bigger of the two in inches. She had heard Miss Bordereau was ill and had a suspicion she was in want, and had gone to the house to offer aid, so that if there were suffering, American suffering in particular, she shouldn't have it on her conscience. The "little one" had received her in the great cold tarnished Venetian *sala*, the central hall of the house, paved with marble and roofed with dim cross-beams, and hadn't even asked her to sit down. This was not encouraging for me, who wished to sit so fast, and I remarked as much to Mrs. Prest. She replied, however, with profundity "Ah, but there's all the difference: I went to confer a favour and you'll go to ask one. If they're proud you'll be on the right side." And she offered to show me their house to begin with—to row me thither in her gondola. I let her know I had already been to look at it half a dozen times; but I accepted her invitation, for it charmed me to hover about the place. I had made my way to it the day after my arrival in Venice—it had been described to me in advance by the friend in England to whom I owed definite information as to their possession of the papers— laying siege to it with my eyes while I considered my plan of campaign. Jeffrey Aspern had never been in it that I knew of, but some note of his voice seemed to abide there by a roundabout implication and in a "dying fall."

Mrs. Prest knew nothing about the papers, but was interested in my curiosity, as always in the joys and sorrows of her friends. As we went, however, in her gondola, gliding there under the sociable hood with the bright Venetian picture framed on either side by the moveable window, I saw how my eagerness amused her and that she found my interest in my possible spoil a fine case of monomania. "One would think you expected from it the answer to the riddle of the universe," she said; and I denied the impeachment only by replying that if I had to choose between that precious solution and a bundle of Jeffrey Aspern's letters I knew indeed which would appear to me the greater boon. She pretended to make light of his genius and I took no pains to defend him. One doesn't defend one's god: one's god is in himself a defence. Besides, today, after his long comparative obscuration, he hangs high in the heaven of our literature for all the world to see; he's a part of the light by which we walk. The most I said was that he was no doubt not a woman's poet: to which she rejoined aptly enough that he had been at least Miss Bordereau's. The strange thing had been for me to discover in England that she was still alive: it was as if I had been told Mrs. Siddons was, or Queen Caroline, or the famous Lady Hamilton, for it seemed to me that she belonged to a generation as extinct. "Why she must be tremendously old—at least a hundred," I had said; but on coming to consider dates I saw it not strictly involved that she should have far exceeded the common span. None the less she was of venerable age and her relations with Jeffrey Aspern had occurred in her early womanhood. "That's her excuse," said Mrs. Prest half sententiously and yet also somewhat as if she were ashamed of making a speech so little in the real tone of Venice. As if a woman needed an excuse for having loved the divine poet! He had been not only one of the most brilliant minds of his day—and in those years, when the century was young, there were, as every one knows, many—but one of the most genial men and one of the handsomest.

The niece, according to Mrs. Prest, was of minor antiquity, and the conjecture was risked that she was only a grand-niece. This was possible; I had nothing but my share in the very limited knowledge of my English fellow worshipper John Cumnor, who had never seen the couple. The world, as I say, had recognised Jeffrey Aspern, but Cumnor and I had recognised him most. The multitude to-day flocked to his temple, but of that temple he and I regarded ourselves as the appointed ministers. We held, justly, as I think, that we had done more for his memory than any one else, and had done it simply by opening lights into his life. He had nothing to fear from us because he had nothing to fear from the truth, which alone at such a distance of time we could be interested in establishing. His early death had been the only dark spot, as it were, on his fame, unless the papers in Miss Bordereau's hands should perversely bring out others. There had been an impression about 1825 that he had "treated her badly," just as there had been an impression that he had "served," as the London populace says, several other ladies in the same masterful way. Each of these cases Cumnor and I had been able to investigate, and we had never failed to acquit him conscientiously of any grossness. I judged him perhaps more indulgently than my friend; certainly, at any rate, it appeared to me that no man could have walked straighter in the given circumstances. These had been almost always difficult and dangerous. Half the women of his time, to speak liberally, had flung themselves at his head, and while the fury raged—the more that it was very catching—accidents, some of them grave, had not failed to occur. He was not a woman's poet, as I had said to Mrs. Prest, in the modern phase of his reputation; but the situation had been different when the man's own voice was mingled with his song. That voice, by every testimony, was one of the most charming ever heard. "Orpheus and the Mænads!" had been of course my foreseen judgement when first I turned over his correspondence. Almost all the Mænads were unreasonable and many of them unbearable; it struck me that he had been kinder and more considerate than in his place—if I could imagine myself in any such box—I should have found the trick of.

It was certainly strange beyond all strangeness, and I shall not take up space with attempting to explain it, that whereas among all these other relations and in these other directions of research we had to deal with phantoms and dust, the mere echoes of echoes, the one living source of information that had lingered on into our time had been unheeded by us. Every one of Aspern's contemporaries had, according to our belief, passed away; we had not been able to look into a single pair of eyes into which his had looked or to feel a transmitted contact in any aged hand that his had touched. Most dead of all did poor Miss Bordereau appear, and yet she alone had survived. We exhausted in the course of months our wonder that we had not found her out sooner, and the substance of our explanation was that she had kept so quiet. The poor lady on the whole had had reason for doing so. But it was a revelation to us that self-effacement on such a scale had been possible in the latter half of the nineteenth century—the age of newspapers and telegrams and photographs and interviewers. She had taken no great trouble for it either—hadn't hidden herself away in an undiscoverable hole, had boldly settled down in a city of exhibition. The one apparent secret of her safety had been that Venice contained so many much greater curiosities. And then accident had somehow favoured her, as was shown for example in the fact that Mrs. Prest had never happened to name her to me, though I had spent three weeks in Venice—under her nose, as it were—five years before. My friend indeed had not named her much to any one; she appeared almost to have forgotten the fact of her continuance. Of course Mrs. Prest hadn't the nerves of an editor. It was meanwhile no explanation of the old woman's having eluded us to say that she lived abroad, for our researches had again and again taken us—not only by correspondence but by personal enquiry—to France, to Germany, to Italy, in which countries, not counting his important stay in England, so many of the too few years of Aspern's career had been spent. We were glad to think at least that in all our promulgations—some people now consider I believe that we have overdone them—we had only touched in passing and in the most discreet manner on Miss Bordereau's connexion. Oddly enough, even if we had had the material—and we had often wondered what could have become of it—this would have been the most difficult episode to handle.

The gondola stopped, the old palace was there; it was a house of the class which in Venice carries even in extreme dilapidation the dignified name. "How charming! It's gray and pink!" my companion exclaimed; and that is the most comprehensive description of it. It was not particularly old, only two or three centuries; and it had an air not so much of decay as of quiet discouragement, as if it had rather missed its career. But its wide front, with a stone balcony from end to end of the *piano nobile* or most important floor, was architectural enough, with the aid of various pilasters and arches; and the stucco with which in the intervals it had long ago been endued was rosy in the April afternoon. It overlooked a clean melancholy rather lonely canal, which had a narrow *riva* or convenient footway on either side. "I don't know why—there are no brick gables," said Mrs. Prest, "but this corner has seemed to me before more Dutch than Italian, more like Amsterdam than like Venice. It's eccentrically neat, for reasons of its own; and though you may pass on foot scarcely any one ever thinks of doing so. It's as negative—considering *where* it is—as a Protestant Sunday. Perhaps the people are afraid of the Misses Bordereau. I dare say they have the reputation of witches."

I forget what answer I made to this—I was given up to two other reflexions. The first of these was that if the old lady lived in such a big and imposing house she couldn't be in any sort of misery and therefore wouldn't be tempted by a chance to let a couple of rooms. I expressed this fear to Mrs. Prest, who gave me a very straight answer. "If she didn't live in a big house how could it be a question of her having rooms to spare? If she were not amply lodged you'd lack ground to approach her. Besides, a big house here, and especially in this *quartier perdu*, proves nothing at all: it's perfectly consistent with a state of penury. Dilapidated old palazzi, if you'll go out of the way for them, are to be had for five shillings a year. And as for the people who live in them—no, until you've explored Venice socially as much as I have, you can form no idea of their domestic desolation. They live on nothing, for they've nothing to live on." The other idea that had come into my head was connected with a high blank wall which appeared to confine an expanse of ground on one side of the house. Blank I call it, but it was figured over with the patches that please a painter, repaired breaches, crumblings of plaster, extrusions of brick that had turned pink with time; while a few thin trees, with the poles of certain rickety trellises, were visible over the top. The place was a garden and apparently attached to the house. I suddenly felt that so attached it gave me my pretext.

I sat looking out on all this with Mrs. Prest (it was covered with the golden glow of Venice) from the shade of our *felze*, and she asked me if I would go in then, while she waited for me, or come back another time. At first I couldn't decide—it was doubtless very weak of me. I wanted still to think I *might* get a footing, and was afraid to meet failure, for it would leave me, as I remarked to my companion, without another arrow for my bow. "Why not another?" she enquired as I sat there hesitating and thinking it over; and she wished to know why even now and before taking the trouble of becoming an inmate—which might be wretchedly uncomfortable after all, even if it succeeded—I hadn't the resource of simply offering them a sum of money down. In that way I might get what I wanted without bad nights.

"Dearest lady," I exclaimed, "excuse the impatience of my tone when I suggest that you must have forgotten the very fact—surely I communicated it to you—which threw me on your ingenuity. The old woman won't have her relics and tokens so much as spoken of; they're personal, delicate, intimate, and she hasn't the feelings of the day, God bless her! If I should sound that note first I should certainly spoil the game. I can arrive at my spoils only by putting her off her guard, and I can put her off her guard only by ingratiating diplomatic arts. Hypocrisy, duplicity are my only chance. I'm sorry for it, but there's no baseness I wouldn't commit for Jeffrey Aspern's sake. First I must take tea with her—then tackle the main job." And I told over what had happened to John Cumnor on his respectfully writing to her. No notice whatever had been taken of his first letter, and the second had been answered very sharply, in six lines, by the niece. "Miss Bordereau requested her to say that she couldn't imagine what he meant by troubling them. They had none of Mr. Aspern's 'literary remains,' and if they *had* had wouldn't have dreamed of showing them to any one on any account whatever. She couldn't imagine what he was talking about and begged he would let her alone." I certainly didn't want to be met that way.

"Well," said Mrs. Prest after a moment and all provokingly, "perhaps they really haven't anything. If they deny it flat how are you sure?"

"John Cumnor's sure, and it would take me long to tell you how his conviction, or his very strong presumption—strong enough to stand against the old lady's not unnatural fib—has built itself up. Besides, he makes much of the internal evidence of the niece's letter."

"The internal evidence?"

"Her calling him 'Mr. Aspern.'"

"I don't see what that proves."

"It proves familiarity, and familiarity implies the possession of mementoes, of tangible objects. I can't tell you how that 'Mr.' affects me—how it bridges over the gulf of time and brings our hero near to me—nor what an edge it gives to my desire to see Juliana. You don't say 'Mr.' Shakespeare."

"Would I, any more, if I had a box full of his letters?"

"Yes, if he had been your lover and some one wanted them!" And I added that John Cumnor was so convinced, and so all the more convinced by Miss Bordereau's tone, that he would have come himself to Venice on the undertaking were it not for the obstacle of his having, for any confidence, to disprove his identity with the person who had written to them, which the old ladies would be sure to suspect in spite of dissimulation and a change of name. If they were to ask him point-blank if he were not their snubbed correspondent it would be too awkward for him to lie; whereas I was fortunately not tied in that way. I was a fresh hand —I could protest without lying.

"But you'll have to take a false name," said Mrs. Prest. "Juliana lives out of the world as much as it is possible to live, but she has none the less probably heard of Mr. Aspern's editors. She perhaps possesses what you've published."

"I've thought of that," I returned; and I drew out of my pocketbook a visiting card neatly engraved with a well-chosen *nom de guerre.*

"You're very extravagant—it adds to your immorality. You might have done it in pencil or ink," said my companion.

" This looks more genuine."

"Certainly you've the courage of your curiosity. But it will be awkward about your letters; they won't come to you in that mask."

"My banker will take them in and I shall go every day to get them. It will give me a little walk."

"Shall you depend all on that?" asked Mrs. Prest. "Aren't you coming to see me?"

"Oh you'll have left Venice for the hot months long before there are any results. I'm prepared to roast all summer—as well as through the long hereafter perhaps you'll say! Meanwhile John Cumnor will bombard me with letters addressed, in my feigned name, to the care of the padrona."

"She'll recognise his hand," my companion suggested.

"On the envelope he can disguise it."

"Well, you're a precious pair! Doesn't it occur to you that even if you're able to say you're not Mr. Cumnor in person they may still suspect you of being his emissary?"

"Certainly, and I see only one way to parry that."

"And what may that be?"

I hesitated a moment. "To make love to the niece."

"Ah," cried my friend, "wait till you see her!"

II

"I must work the garden—I must work the garden," I said to myself five minutes later and while I waited, upstairs, in the long, dusky sala, where the bare scagliola floor gleamed vaguely in a chink of the closed shutters. The place was impressive, yet looked somehow cold and cautious. Mrs. Prest had floated away, giving me a rendezvous at the end of half an hour by some neighbouring water-steps; and I had been let into the house, after pulling the rusty bell-wire, by a small red-headed and white-faced maid-servant, who was very young and not ugly and wore clicking pattens and a shawl in the fashion of a hood. She had not contented herself with opening the door from above by the usual arrangement of a creaking pulley, though she had looked down at me first from an upper window, dropping the cautious challenge which in Italy precedes the act of admission. I was irritated as a general thing by this survival of mediæval manners, though as so fond, if yet so special, an antiquarian I suppose I ought to have liked it; but, with my resolve to be genial from the threshold at any price, I took my false card out of my pocket and held it up to her, smiling as if it were a magic token. It had the effect of one indeed, for it brought her, as I say, all the way down. I begged her to hand it to her mistress, having first written on it in Italian the words: "Could you very kindly see a gentleman, a travelling

American, for a moment?" The little maid wasn't hostile—even that was
perhaps something gained. She coloured, she smiled and looked both
frightened and pleased. I could see that my arrival was a great affair, that
visits in such a house were rare and that she was a person who would
have liked a bustling place. When she pushed forward the heavy door
behind me I felt my foot in the citadel and promised myself ever so
firmly to keep it there. She pattered across the damp stony lower hall
and I followed her up the high staircase—stonier still, as it seemed—without an invitation. I think she had meant I should wait for her below, but
such was not my idea, and I took up my station in the sala. She flitted,
at the far end of it, into impenetrable regions, and I looked at the place
with my heart beating as I had known it to do in dentists' parlours. It
had a gloomy grandeur, but owed its character almost all to its noble
shape and to the fine architectural doors, as high as those of grand front-
ages, which, leading into the various rooms, repeated themselves on either side at intervals. They were surmounted with old faded painted
escutcheons, and here and there in the spaces between them hung brown
pictures, which I noted as speciously bad, in battered and tarnished
frames that were yet more desirable than the canvases themselves. With
the exception of several straw-bottomed chairs that kept their backs to
the wall the grand obscure vista contained little else to minister to effect.
It was evidently never used save as a passage, and scantly even as that. I
may add that by the time the door through which the maid-servant had
escaped opened again my eyes had grown used to the want of light.

I hadn't meanwhile meant by my private ejaculation that I must myself cultivate the soil of the tangled enclosure which lay beneath the windows, but the lady who came toward me from the distance over the hard
shining floor might have supposed as much from the way in which, as I
went rapidly to meet her, I exclaimed, taking care to speak Italian: "The
garden, the garden—do me the pleasure to tell me if it's yours!"

She stopped short, looking at me with wonder; and then, "Nothing
here is mine," she answered in English, coldly and sadly.

"Oh you're English; how delightful!" I ingenuously cried. "But surely
the garden belongs to the house?"

"Yes, but the house doesn't belong to me." She was a long lean pale
person, habited apparently in a dull-coloured dressing-gown, and she
spoke very simply and mildly. She didn't ask me to sit down, any more
than years before—if she were the niece—she had asked Mrs. Prest, and
we stood face to face in the empty pompous hall.

"Well then, would you kindly tell me to whom I must address myself? I'm afraid you will think me horribly intrusive, but you know I
must have a garden—upon my honour I must!"

Her face was not young, but it was candid; it was not fresh, but it
was clear. She had large eyes which were not bright, and a great deal
of hair which was not "dressed," and long fine hands which were—possibly—not clean. She clasped these members almost convulsively as, with

a confused alarmed look, she broke out: "Oh don't take it away from us; we like it ourselves!"

"You have the use of it then?"

"Oh yes. If it wasn't for that—!" And she gave a wan vague smile.

"Isn't it a luxury, precisely? That's why, intending to be in Venice some weeks, possibly all summer, and having some literary work, some reading and writing to do, so that I must be quiet and yet if possible a great deal in the open air—that's why I've felt a garden to be really indispensable. I appeal to your own experience," I went on with as sociable a smile as I could risk. "Now can't I look at yours?"

"I don't know, I don't understand," the poor woman murmured, planted there and letting her weak wonder deal—helplessly enough, as I felt—with my strangeness.

"I mean only from one of those windows—such grand ones as you have here—if you'll let me open the shutters." And I walked toward the back of the house. When I had advanced halfway I stopped and waited as in the belief she would accompany me. I had been of necessity quite abrupt, but I strove at the same time to give her the impression of extreme courtesy. "I've looked at furnished rooms all over the place, and it seems impossible to find any with a garden attached. Naturally in a place like Venice gardens are rare. It's absurd if you like, for a man, but I can't live without flowers."

"There are none to speak of down there." She came nearer, as if, though she mistrusted me, I had drawn her by an invisible thread. I went on again, and she continued as she followed me: "We've a few, but they're very common. It costs too much to cultivate them; one has to have a man."

"Why shouldn't I be the man?" I asked. "I'll work without wages; or rather I'll put in a gardener. You shall have the sweetest flowers in Venice."

She protested against this with a small quaver of sound that might have been at the same time a gush of rapture for my free sketch. Then she gasped: "We don't know you—we don't know you."

"You know me as much as I know you, or rather much more, because you know my name. And if you're English I'm almost a countryman."

"We're not English," said my companion, watching me in practical submission while I threw open the shutters of one of the divisions of the wide high window.

"You speak the language so beautifully: might I ask what you are?" Seen from above the garden was in truth shabby, yet I felt at a glance that it had great capabilities. She made no rejoinder, she was so lost in her blankness and gentleness, and I exclaimed, "You don't mean to say you're also by chance American?"

"I don't know. We used to be."

"Used to be? Surely you haven't changed?"

"It's so many years ago. We don't seem to be anything now."

"So many years that you've been living here? Well, I don't wonder at that; it's a grand old house. I suppose you all use the garden," I went on, "but I assure you I shouldn't be in your way. I'd be very quiet and stay quite in one corner."

"We all use it?" she repeated after me vaguely, not coming close to the window but looking at my shoes. She appeared to think me capable of throwing her out.

"I mean all your family—as many as you are."

"There's only one other than me. She's very old. She never goes down."

I feel again my thrill at this close identification of Juliana; in spite of which, however, I kept my head. "Only one other in all this great house!" I feigned to be not only amazed but almost scandalized. "Dear lady, you must have space then to spare!"

"To spare?" she repeated—almost as for the rich unwonted joy to her of spoken words.

"Why you surely don't live (two quiet women—I see *you* are quiet, at any rate) in fifty rooms!" Then with a burst of hope and cheer I put the question straight: "Couldn't you for a good rent *let* me two or three? That would set me up!"

I had now struck the note that translated my purpose, and I needn't reproduce the whole of the tune I played. I ended by making my entertainer believe me an undesigning person, though of course I didn't even attempt to persuade her I was not an eccentric one. I repeated that I had studies to pursue; that I wanted quiet; that I delighted in a garden and had vainly sought one up and down the city; that I would undertake that before another month was over the dear old house should be smothered in flowers. I think it was the flowers that won my suit, for I afterwards found that Miss Tina—for such the name of this high tremulous spinster proved somewhat incongruously to be—had an insatiable appetite for them. When I speak of my suit as won I mean that before I left her she had promised me she would refer the question to her aunt. I invited information as to who her aunt might be and she answered "Why Miss Bordereau!" with an air of surprise, as if I might have been expected to know. There were contradictions like this in Miss Tina which, as I observed later, contributed to make her rather pleasingly incalculable and interesting. It was the study of the two ladies to live so that the world shouldn't talk of them or touch them, and yet they had never altogether accepted the idea that it didn't hear of them. In Miss Tina at any rate a grateful susceptibility to human contact had not died out, and contact of a limited order there would be if I should come to live in the house.

"We've never done anything of the sort; we've never had a lodger or any kind of inmate." So much as this she made a point of saying to me. "We're very poor, we live very badly—almost on nothing. The rooms are very bare—those you might take; they've nothing at all in them. I don't know how you'd sleep, how you'd eat."

"With your permission I could easily put in a bed and a few tables and chairs. *C'est la moindre des choses* and the affair of an hour or two. I know a little man from whom I can hire for a trifle what I should so briefly want, what I should use; my gondolier can bring the things round in his boat. Of course in this great house you must have a second kitchen, and my servant who's a wonderfully handy fellow"—this personage was an evocation of the moment—"can easily cook me a chop there. My tastes and habits are of the simplest; I live on flowers!" And then I ventured to add that if they were very poor it was all the more reason they should let their rooms. They were bad economists—I had never heard of such a waste of material.

I saw in a moment my good lady had never before been spoken to in any such fashion—with a humorous firmness that didn't exclude sympathy, that was quite founded on it. She might easily have told me that my sympathy was impertinent, but this by good fortune didn't occur to her. I left her with the understanding that she would submit the question to her aunt and that I might come back the next day for their decision.

"The aunt will refuse; she'll think the whole proceeding very *louche!*" Mrs. Prest declared shortly after this, when I had resumed my place in her gondola. She had put the idea into my head and now—so little are women to be counted on—she appeared to take a despondent view of it. Her pessimism provoked me and I pretended to have the best hopes; I went so far as to boast of a distinct prevision of success. Upon this Mrs. Prest broke out,"Oh I see what's in your head! You fancy you've made such an impression in five minutes that she's dying for you to come and can be depended on to bring the old one round. If you do get in you'll count it as a triumph."

I did count it as a triumph, but only for the commentator—in the last analysis—not for the man, who had not the tradition of personal conquest. When I went back on the morrow the little maid-servant conducted me straight through the long sala—it opened there as before in large perspective and was lighter now, which I thought a good omen—into the apartment from which the recipient of my former visit had emerged on that occasion. It was a spacious shabby parlour with a fine old painted ceiling under which a strange figure sat alone at one of the windows. They come back to me now almost with the palpitation they caused, the successive states marking my consciousness that as the door of the room closed behind me I was really face to face with the Juliana of some of Aspern's most exquisite and most renowned lyrics. I grew used to her afterwards, though never completely; but as she sat there before me my heart beat as fast as if the miracle of resurrection had taken place for my benefit. Her presence seemed somehow to contain and express his own, and I felt nearer to him at that first moment of seeing her than I ever had been before or ever have been since. Yes, I remember my emotions in their order, even including a curious little tremor that took me when I saw the niece not to be there. With her, the day before, I had become sufficiently familiar, but it almost exceeded my courage—

much as I had longed for the event—to be left alone with so terrible a
relic as the aunt. She was too strange, too literally resurgent. Then came
a check from the perception that we weren't really face to face, inasmuch
as she had over her eyes a horrible green shade which served for her almost as a mask. I believed for the instant that she had put it on expressly, so that from underneath it she might take me all in without my
getting at herself. At the same time it created a presumption of some
ghastly death's head lurking behind it. The divine Juliana as a grinning
skull—the vision hung there until it passed. Then it came to me that she
was tremendously old—so old that death might take her at any moment,
before I should have time to compass my end. The next thought was a
correction to that; it lighted up the situation. She would die next week,
she would die to-morrow—then I could pounce on her possessions and
ransack her drawers. Meanwhile she sat there neither moving nor speaking She was very small and shrunken, bent forward with her hands in
her lap She was dressed in black and her head was wrapped in a piece
of old black lace which showed no hair.

My emotion keeping me silent she spoke first, and the remark she
made was exactly the most unexpected.

III

"Our house is very far from the centre, but the little canal is very
comme il faut."

"It's the sweetest corner of Venice and I can imagine nothing more
charming," I hastened to reply. The old lady's voice was very thin and
weak, but it had an agreeable, cultivated murmur and there was wonder
in the thought that that individual note had been in Jeffrey Aspern's ear.

"Please to sit down there. I hear very well," she said quietly, as if perhaps I had been shouting; and the chair she pointed to was at a certain
distance. I took possession of it, assuring her I was perfectly aware of my
intrusion and of my not having been properly introduced, and that I
could but throw myself on her indulgence. Perhaps the other lady, the
one I had had the honour of seeing the day before, would have explained
to her about the garden. That was literally what had given me courage to
take a step so unconventional. I had fallen in love at sight with the
whole place—she herself was probably so used to it that she didn't know
the impression it was capable of making on a stranger—and I had felt it
really a case to risk something. Was her own kindness in receiving me a
sign that I was not wholly out in my calculation? It would make me
extremely happy to think so. I could give her my word of honour that
I was a most respectable inoffensive person and that as a co-tenant of the
palace, so to speak, they would be barely conscious of my existence. I
would conform to any regulations, any restrictions, if they would only
let me enjoy the garden. Moreover I should be delighted to give her references, guarantees; they would be of the very best, both in Venice and
in England, as well as in America.

She listened to me in perfect stillness and I felt her look at me with great penetration, though I could see only the lower part of her bleached and shrivelled face. Independently of the refining process of old age it had a delicacy which once must have been great. She had been very fair, she had had a wonderful complexion. She was silent a little after I had ceased speaking; then she began: "If you're so fond of a garden why don't you go to *terra firma*, where there are so many far better than this?"

"Oh it's the combination!" I answered, smiling; and then with rather a flight of fancy; "It's the idea of a garden in the middle of the sea."

"This isn't the middle of the sea; you can't so much as see the water."

I stared a moment, wondering if she wished to convict me of fraud. "Can't see the water? Why, dear madam, I can come up to the very gate in my boat."

She appeared inconsequent, for she said vaguely in reply to this: "Yes, if you've got a boat. I haven't any; it's many years since I have been in one of the *gondole*." She uttered these words as if they designed a curious far-away craft known to her only by hearsay.

"Let me assure you of the pleasure with which I would put mine at your service!" I returned. I had scarcely said this however before I became aware that the speech was in questionable taste and might also do me the injury of making me appear too eager, too possessed of a hidden motive. But the old woman remained impenetrable and her attitude worried me by suggesting that she had a fuller vision of me than I had of her. She gave me no thanks for my somewhat extravagant offer, but remarked that the lady I had seen the day before was her niece; she would presently come in. She had asked her to stay away a little on purpose—had had her reasons for seeing me first alone. She relapsed into silence and I turned over the fact of these unmentioned reasons and the question of what might come yet; also that of whether I might venture on some judicious remark in praise of her companion. I went so far as to say I should be delighted to see our absent friend again: she had been so very patient with me, considering how odd she must have thought me—a declaration which drew from Miss Bordereau another of her whimsical speeches.

"She has very good manners; I bred her up myself!" I was on the point of saying that that accounted for the easy grace of the niece, but I arrested myself in time, and the next moment the old woman went on: "I don't care who you may be—I don't want to know: it signifies very little to-day." This had all the air of being a formula of dismissal, as if her next words would be that I might take myself off now that she had had the amusement of looking on the face of such a monster of indiscretion. Therefore I was all the more surprised when she added in her soft venerable quaver: "You may have as many rooms as you like—if you'll pay me a good deal of money."

I hesitated but an instant, long enough to measure what she meant in particular by this condition. First it struck me that she must have really a large sum in her mind; then I reasoned quickly that her idea of a large sum would probably not correspond to my own. My deliberation, I think, was not so visible as to diminish the promptitude with which I replied: "I will pay with pleasure and of course in advance whatever you may think it proper to ask me."

"Well then, a thousand francs a month," she said instantly, while her baffling green shade continued to cover her attitude.

The figure, as they say, was startling and my logic had been at fault. The sum she had mentioned was, by the Venetian measure of such matters, exceedingly large; there was many an old palace in an out-of-the-way corner that I might on such terms have enjoyed the whole of by the year. But so far as my resources allowed I was prepared to spend money, and my decision was quickly taken. I would pay her with a smiling face what she asked, but in that case I would make it up by getting hold of my "spoils" for nothing. Moreover if she had asked five times as much I should have risen to the occasion, so odious would it have seemed to me to stand chaffering with Aspern's Juliana. It was queer enough to have a question of money with her at all. I assured her that her views perfectly met my own and that on the morrow I should have the pleasure of putting three months' rent into her hand. She received this announcement with apparent complacency and with no discoverable sense that after all it would become her to say that I ought to see the rooms first. This didn't occur to her, and indeed her serenity was mainly what I wanted. Our little agreement was just concluded when the door opened and the younger lady appeared on the threshold. As soon as Miss Bordereau saw her niece she cried out almost gaily: "He'll give three thousand —three thousand to-morrow!"

Miss Tina stood still, her patient eyes turning from one of us to the other; then she brought out, scarcely above her breath: "Do you mean francs?"

"Did you mean francs or dollars?" the old woman asked of me at this.

"I think francs were what you said," I sturdily smiled.

"That's very good," said Miss Tina, as if she had felt how over-reaching her own question might have looked.

"What do *you* know? You're ignorant," Miss Bordereau remarked; not with acerbity but with a strange soft coldness.

"Yes, of money—certainly of money!" Miss Tina hastened to concede.

"I'm sure you've your own fine branches of knowledge," I took the liberty of saying genially. There was something painful to me, somehow, in the turn the conversation had taken, in the discussion of dollars and francs.

"She had a very good education when she was young. I looked into that myself," said Miss Bordereau. Then she added: "But she has learned nothing since."

"I have always been with *you*," Miss Tina rejoined very mildly, and of a certainty with no intention of an epigram.

"Yes, but for that—!" her aunt declared with more satirical force. She evidently meant that but for this her niece would never have got on at all; the point of the observation however being lost on Miss Tina, though she blushed at hearing her history revealed to a stranger. Miss Bordereau went on, addressing herself to me: "And what time will you come to-morrow with the money?"

"The sooner the better. If it suits you I'll come at noon."

"I am always here, but I have my hours," said the old woman as if her convenience were not to be taken for granted.

"You mean the times when you receive?"

"I never receive. But I'll see you at noon when you come with the money."

"Very good, I shall be punctual." To which I added: "May I shake hands with you on our contract?" I thought there ought to be some little form; it would make me really feel easier, for I was sure there would be no other. Besides, though Miss Bordereau couldn't to-day be called personally attractive and there was something even in her wasted antiquity that bade one stand at one's distance, I felt an irresistible desire to hold in my own for a moment the hand Jeffrey Aspern had pressed.

For a minute she made no answer, and I saw that my proposal failed to meet with her approbation. She indulged in no movement of withdrawal which I half expected; she only said coldly: "I belong to a time when that was not the custom."

I felt rather snubbed but I exclaimed good-humouredly to Miss Tina, "Oh you'll do as well!" I shook hands with her while she assented with a small flutter. "Yes, yes, to show it's all arranged!"

"Shall you bring the money in gold?" Miss Bordereau demanded as I was turning to the door.

I looked at her a moment. "Aren't you a little afraid, after all, of keeping such a sum as that in the house?" It was not that I was annoyed at her avidity, but was truly struck with the disparity between such a treasure and such scanty means of guarding it.

"Whom should I be afraid of if I'm not afraid of you?" she asked with her shrunken grimness.

"Ah, well," I laughed, "I shall be in point of fact a protector and I'll bring gold if you prefer."

"Thank you," the old woman returned with dignity and with an inclination of her head which evidently signified my dismissal. I passed out of the room, thinking how hard it would be to circumvent her. As I stood in the sala again I saw that Miss Tina had followed me, and I supposed that as her aunt had neglected to suggest I should take a look at my quarters it was her purpose to repair the omission. But she made no such overture; she only stood there with a dim, though not a languid smile, and with an effect of irresponsible incompetent youth almost comically at variance with the faded facts of her person. She was not infirm, like her aunt, but she struck me as more deeply futile, because her inefficiency was inward, which was not the case with Miss Bordereau's. I waited to see if she would offer to show me the rest of the house but I didn't precipitate the question, inasmuch as my plan was from this moment to spend as much of my time as possible in her society. A minute indeed elapsed before I committed myself.

"I've had better fortune than I hoped. It was very kind of her to see me. Perhaps you said a good word for me."

"It was the idea of the money," said Miss Tina.

"And did you suggest that?"

"I told her you'd perhaps pay largely."

"What made you think that?"

"I told her I thought you were rich."

"And what put that into your head?"

"I don't know; the way you talked."

"Dear me, I must talk differently now," I returned. "I'm sorry to say it's not the case."

"Well," said Miss Tina, "I think that in Venice the *forestieri* in general often give a great deal for something that after all isn't much." She appeared to make this remark with a comforting intention, to wish to remind me that if I had been extravagant I wasn't foolishly singular. We walked together along the sala, and as I took its magnificent measure I said that I was afraid it wouldn't form a part of my *quartiere*. Were my rooms by chance to be among those that opened into it? "Not if you go above—to the second floor," she answered as if she had rather taken for granted I would know my proper place.

"And I infer that that's where your aunt would like me to be."

"She said your apartments ought to be very distinct."

"That certainly would be best." And I listened with respect while she told me that above I should be free to take whatever I might like; that there was another staircase, but only from the floor on which we stood, and that to pass from it to the garden-level or to come up to my lodging I should have in effect to cross the great hall. This was an immense point gained; I foresaw that it would constitute my whole leverage in my relations with the two ladies. When I asked Miss Tina how I was to manage at present to find my way up she replied with an access of that sociable shyness which constantly marked her manner:

"Perhaps you can't. I don't see—unless I should go with you." She evidently hadn't thought of this before.

We ascended to the upper floor and visited a long succession of empty rooms. The best of them looked over the garden; some of the others had above the opposite rough-tiled house-tops a view of the blue lagoon. They were all dusty and even a little disfigured with long neglect, but I saw that by spending a few hundred francs I should be able to make three or four of them habitable enough. My experiment was turning out costly, yet now that I had all but taken possession I ceased to allow this to trouble me. I mentioned to my companion a few of the things I should put in, but she replied rather more precipitately than usual that I might do exactly what I liked: she seemed to wish to notify me that the Misses Bordereau would take none but the most veiled interest in my proceedings. I guessed that her aunt had instructed her to adopt this tone, and I may as well say now that I came afterwards to distinguish perfectly (as I believed) between the speeches she made on her own responsibility and those the old woman imposed upon her. She took no notice of the unswept condition of the rooms and indulged neither in explanations nor in apologies. I said to myself that this was a sign Juliana and her niece—disenchanting idea!—were untidy persons with a low Italian standard; but I afterwards recognised that a lodger who had forced an entrance had no *locus standi* as a critic. We looked out of a good many windows, for there was nothing within the rooms to look at, and still I wanted to linger. I asked her what several different objects in the prospect might be, but in no case did she appear to know. She was evidently not familiar with the view—it was as if she had not looked at it for years—and I presently saw that she was too preoccupied with something else to pretend to care for it. Suddenly she said—the remark was not suggested:

"I don't know whether it will make any difference to you, but the money is for me."

"The money—?"

"The money you're going to bring."

"Why you'll make me wish to stay here two or three years!" I spoke as benevolently as possible, though it had begun to act on my nerves that these women so associated with Aspern should so constantly bring the pecuniary question back.

"That would be very good for me," she answered almost gaily.

"You put me on my honour!"

She looked as if she failed to understand this, but went on: "She wants me to have more. She thinks she's going to die."

"Ah not soon I hope!" I cried with genuine feeling. I had perfectly considered the possibility of her destroying her documents on the day she should feel her end at hand. I believed that she would cling to them till then, and I was as convinced of her reading Aspern's letters over every night or at least pressing them to her withered lips. I would have given a good deal for some view of those solemnities. I asked Miss Tina if her venerable relative were seriously ill, and she replied that she was only very tired—she had lived so extraordinarily long. That was what she said herself—she wanted to die for a change. Besides, all her friends had been dead for ages; either they ought to have remained or she ought to have gone. That was another thing her aunt often said: she was not at all resigned—resigned, that is, to life.

"But people don't die when they like, do they?" Miss Tina inquired. I took the liberty of asking why, if there was actually enough money to maintain both of them, there would not be more than enough in case of her being left alone. She considered this difficult problem a moment and then said: "Oh well, you know, she takes care of me. She thinks that when I'm alone I shall be a great fool and shan't know how to manage."

"I should have supposed rather that you took care of *her*. I'm afraid she's very proud."

"Why, have you discovered that already?" Miss Tina cried with a dimness of glad surprise.

"I was shut up with her there for a considerable time and she struck me, she interested me extremely. It didn't take me long to make my discovery. She won't have much to say to me while I'm here."

"No, I don't think she will," my companion averred.

"Do you suppose she has some suspicion of me?"

Miss Tina's honest eyes gave me no sign I had touched a mark. "I shouldn't think so—letting you in after all so easily."

"You call it easily? She has covered her risk," I said. "But where is it one could take an advantage of her?"

"I oughtn't to tell you if I knew, ought I?" And Miss Tina added, before I had time to reply to this, smiling dolefully: "Do you think we've any weak points?"

"That's exactly what I'm asking. You'd only have to mention them for me to respect them religiously."

She looked at me hereupon with that air of timid but candid and even gratified curiosity with which she had confronted me from the first; after which she said: "There's nothing to tell. We're terribly quiet. I don't know how the days pass. We've no life."

"I wish I might think I should bring you a little."

"Oh we know what we want," she went on. "It's all right."

There were twenty things I desired to ask her: how in the world they did live; whether they had any friends or visitors, any relations in America or in other countries. But I judged such probings premature; I must leave it to a later chance. "Well, don't *you* be proud," I contented myself with saying. "Don't hide from me altogether."

"Oh I must stay with my aunt," she returned without looking at me. And at the same moment, abruptly, without any ceremony of parting, she quitted me and disappeared, leaving me to make my own way downstairs. I stayed a while longer, wandering about the bright desert—the sun was pouring in—of the old house, thinking the situation over on the spot. Not even the pattering little *serva* came to look after me, and I reflected that after all this treatment showed confidence.

IV

Perhaps it did, but all the same, six weeks later, towards the middle of June, the moment when Mrs. Prest undertook her annual migration, I had made no measurable advance. I was obliged to confess to her that I had no results to speak of. My first step had been unexpectedly rapid, but there was no appearance it would be followed by a second. I was a thousand miles from taking tea with my hostess—that privilege of which, as I reminded my good friend, we both had had a vision. She reproached me with lacking boldness and I answered that even to be bold you must have an opportunity: you may push on through a breach, but you can't batter down a dead wall. She returned that the breach I had already made was big enough to admit an army and accused me of wasting precious hours in whimpering in her salon when I ought to have been carrying on the struggle in the field. It is true that I went to see her very often—all on the theory that it would console me (I freely expressed my discouragement) for my want of success on my own premises. But I began to feel that it didn't console me to be perpetually chaffed for my scruples, especially since I was really so vigilant; and I was rather glad when my ironic friend closed her house for the summer. She had expected to gather amusement from the drama of my intercourse with the Misses Bordereau, and was disappointed that the intercourse, and consequently the drama, had not come off. "They'll lead you on to your ruin," she said before she left Venice. "They'll get all your money without showing you a scrap." I think I settled down to my business with more concentration after her departure.

It was a fact that up to that time I had not, save on a single brief occasion, had even a moment's contact with my queer hostesses. The exception had occurred when I carried them according to my promise the terrible three thousand francs. Then I found Miss Tina awaiting me in the hall, and she took the money from my hand with a promptitude that prevented my seeing her aunt. The old lady had promised to receive me, yet apparently thought nothing of breaking that vow. The money was contained in a bag of chamois leather, of respectable dimensions, which my banker had given me, and Miss Tina had to make a big fist to receive it. This she did with extreme solemnity though I tried to treat the affair a little as a joke. It was in no jocular strain, yet it was with a clearness akin to a brightness that she enquired, weighing the money in her two palms: "Don't you think it's too much?" To which I replied that this would depend on the amount of pleasure I should get for it. Hereupon she turned away from me quickly, as she had done the day before, murmuring in a tone different from any she had used hitherto: "Oh pleasure, pleasure—there's no pleasure in this house!"

After that, for a long time, I never saw her, and I wondered the common chances of the day shouldn't have helped us to meet. It could only be evident that she was immensely on her guard against them; and in addition to this the house was so big that for each other we were lost in it. I used to look out for her hopefully as I crossed the sala in my comings and goings, but I was not rewarded with a glimpse of the tail of her dress. It was as if she never peeped out of her aunt's apartment. I used to wonder what she did there week after week and year after year. I had never met so stiff a policy of seclusion; it was more than keeping quiet—it was like hunted creatures feigning death. The two ladies appeared to have no visitors whatever and no sort of contact with the world. I judged at least that people couldn't have come to the house and that Miss Tina couldn't have gone out without my catching some view of it. I did what I disliked myself for doing—considering it but as once in a way: I questioned my servant about their habits and let him infer that I should be interested in any information he might glean. But he gleaned amazingly little for a knowing Venetian: it must be added that where there is a perpetual fast there are very few crumbs on the floor. His ability in other ways was sufficient, if not quite all I had attributed to him on the occasion of my first interview with Miss Tina. He had helped my gondolier to bring me round a boatload of furniture; and when these articles had been carried to the top of the palace and distributed according to our associated wisdom he organized my household with such dignity as answered to its being composed exclusively of himself. He made me in short as comfortable as I could be with my indifferent prospects. I should have been glad if he had fallen in love with Miss Bordereau's maid or, failing this, had taken her in aversion; either event might have brought about some catastrophe, and a catastrophe might have led to some parley. It was my idea that she would have been sociable, and I myself on various occasions saw her flit to and fro· on domestic errands, so that I was sure she was accessible. But I tasted of no gossip from that fountain, and I afterwards learned that Pasquale's affections were fixed upon an object that made him heedless of other women. This was a young lady with a powdered face, a yellow cotton gown and much leisure, who used often to come to see him. She practised, at her convenience, the art of a stringer of beads —these ornaments are made in Venice to profusion; she had her pocket full of them and I used to find them on the floor of my apartment—and kept an eye on the possible rival in the house. It was not for me of course to make the domestics tattle, and I never said a word to Miss Bordereau's cook.

It struck me as a proof of the old woman's resolve to have nothing to do with me that she should never have sent me a receipt for my three months' rent. For some days I looked out for it and then, when I had given it up, wasted a good deal of time in wondering what her reason had been for neglecting so indispensable and familiar a form. At first I was tempted to send her a reminder; after which I put by the idea—against my judgement as to what was right in the particular case—on the general ground of wishing to keep quiet. If Miss Bordereau suspected me of ulterior aims she would suspect me less if I should be businesslike, and yet I consented not to be. It was possible she intended her omission as an impertinence, a visible irony, to show how she could overreach people who attempted to overreach her. On that hypothesis it was well to let her see that one didn't notice her little tricks. The real reading of the matter, I afterwards gathered, was simply the poor lady's desire to emphasise the fact that I was in the enjoyment of a favour as rigidly limited as it had been liberally bestowed. She had given me part of her house, but she wouldn't add to that so much as a morsel of paper with her name on it. Let me say that even at first this didn't make me too miserable, for the whole situation had the charm of its oddity. I foresaw that I should have a summer after my own literary heart, and the sense of playing with my opportunity was much greater after all than any sense of being played with. There could be no Venetian business without patience, and since I adored the place I was much more in the spirit of it for having laid in a large provision. That spirit kept me perpetual company and seemed to look out at me from the revived immortal face—in which all his genius shone—of the great poet who was my prompter. I had invoked him and he had come; he hovered before me half the time; it was as if his bright ghost had returned to earth to assure me he regarded the affair as his own no less than as mine and that we should see it fraternally and fondly to a conclusion. It was as if he had said: "Poor dear, be easy with her; she has some natural prejudices; only give her time. Strange as it may appear to you she was very attractive in 1820. Meanwhile aren't we in Venice together, and what better place is there for the meeting of dear friends? See how it glows with the advancing summer; how the sky and the sea and the rosy air and the marble of the palaces all shimmer and melt together." My eccentric private errand became a part of the general romance and the general glory—I felt even a mystic companionship, a moral fraternity with all those who in the past had been in the service of art. They had worked for beauty, for a devotion; and what else was I doing? That element was in everything that Jeffrey Aspern had written, and I was only bringing it to light.

I lingered in the sala when I went to and fro; I used to watch—as long as I thought decent—the door that led to Miss Bordereau's part of the house. A person observing me might have supposed I was trying to cast a spell on it or attempting some odd experiment in hypnotism. But I was only praying it might open or thinking what treasure probably lurked behind it. I hold it singular, as I look back, that I should never have doubted for a moment that the sacred relics were there; never have failed to know the joy of being beneath the same roof with them. After all they were under my hand—they had not escaped me yet; and they made my life continuous, in a fashion, with the illustrious life they had touched at the other end. I lost myself in this satisfaction to the point of assuming—in my quiet extravagance—that poor Miss Tina also went back, and still went back, as I used to phrase it. She did indeed, the gentle spinster, but not quite so far as Jeffrey Aspern, who was simple hearsay to her quite as he was to me. Only she had lived for years with Juliana, she had seen and handled all mementoes and—even though she was stupid—some esoteric knowledge had rubbed off on her. That was what the old woman represented—esoteric knowledge; and this was the idea with which my critical heart used to thrill. It literally beat faster often, of an evening when I had been out, as I stopped with my candle in the re-echoing hall on my way up to bed. It was as if at such a moment as that, in the stillness and after the long contradiction of the day, Miss Bordereau's secrets were in the air, the wonder of her survival more vivid. These were the acute impressions. I had them in another form, with more of a certain shade of reciprocity, during the hours I sat in the garden looking up over the top of my book at the closed windows of my hostess. In these windows no sign of life ever appeared; it was as if, for fear of my catching a glimpse of them, the two ladies passed their days in the dark. But this only emphasised their having matters to conceal; which was what I had wished to prove. Their motionless shutters became as expressive as eyes consciously closed, and I took comfort in the probability that, though invisible themselves, they kept me in view between the lashes.

I made a point of spending as much time as possible in the garden, to justify the picture I had originally given of my horticultural passion. And I not only spent time, but (hang it! as I said) spent precious money. As soon as I had got my rooms arranged and could give the question proper thought I surveyed the place with a clever expert and made terms for having it put in order. I was sorry to do this, for personally I liked it better as it was, with its weeds and its wild rich tangle, its sweet characteristic Venetian shabbiness. I had to be consistent, to keep my promise that I would smother the house in flowers. Moreover I clung to the fond fancy that by flowers I should make my way—I should succeed by big nosegays. I would batter the old women with lilies—I would bombard their citadel with roses. Their door would have to yield to the pressure when a mound of fragrance should be heaped against it. The place in truth had been brutally neglected. The Venetian capacity for dawdling is of the largest, and for a good many days unlimited litter was all my gardener had to show for his ministrations. There was a great digging of holes and carting about of earth, and after a while I grew so impatient that I had thoughts of sending for my "results" to the nearest stand. But I felt sure my friends would see through the chinks of their shutters where such tribute *couldn't* have been gathered, and might so make up their minds against my veracity. I possessed my soul and finally, though the delay was long, perceived some appearances of bloom. This encouraged me and I waited serenely enough till they multiplied. Meanwhile the real summer days arrived and began to pass, and as I look back upon them they seem to me almost the happiest of my life. I took more and more care to be in the garden whenever it was not too hot. I had an arbour arranged and a low table and an armchair put into it; and I carried out books and portfolios—I had always some business of writing in hand —and worked and waited and mused and hoped, while the golden hours elapsed and the plants drank in the light and the inscrutable old palace turned pale and then, as the day waned, began to recover and flush and my papers rustled in the wandering breeze of the Adriatic.

Considering how little satisfaction I got from it at first it is wonderful I shouldn't have grown more tired of trying to guess what mystic rites of ennui the Misses Bordereau celebrated in their darkened rooms; whether this had always been the tenor of their life and how in previous years they had escaped elbowing their neighbours. It was supposable they had then had other habits, forms and resources; that they must once have been young or at least middle-aged. There was no end to the questions it was possible to ask about them and no end to the answers it was not possible to frame. I had known many of my country-people in Europe and was familiar with the strange ways they were liable to take up there; but the Misses Bordereau formed altogether a new type of the American absentee. Indeed it was clear the American name had ceased to have any application to them—I had seen this in the ten minutes I spent in the old woman's room. You could never have said whence they came from the appearance of either of them; wherever it was they had long ago shed and unlearned all native marks and notes. There was nothing in them one recognised or fitted, and, putting the question of speech aside, they might have been Norwegians or Spaniards. Miss Bordereau, after all, had been in Europe nearly three-quarters of a century; it appeared by some verses addressed to her by Aspern on the occasion of his own second absence from America—verses of which Cumnor and I had after infinite conjecture established solidly enough the date—that she was even then, as a girl of twenty, on the foreign side of the sea. There was a profession in the poem—I hope not just for the phrase—that he had come back for her sake. We had no real light on her circumstances at that moment, any more than we had upon her origin, which we believed to be of the sort usually spoken of as modest. Cumnor had a theory that she had been a governess in some family in which the poet visited and that, in consequence of her position, there was from the first something unavowed, or rather something quite clandestine, in their relations. I on the other hand had hatched a little romance according to which she was the daughter of an artist, a painter or a sculptor, who had left the Western world, when the century was fresh, to study in the ancient schools. It was essential to my hypothesis that this amiable man should have lost his wife, should have been poor and unsuccessful and should have had a second daughter of a disposition quite different from Juliana's. It was also indispensable that he should have been accompanied to Europe by these young ladies and should have established himself there for the remainder of a struggling saddened life. There was a further implication that Miss Bordereau had had in her youth a perverse and reckless, albeit a generous and fascinating character, and that she had braved some wondrous chances. By what passions had she been ravaged, by what adventures and sufferings had she been blanched, what store of memories had she laid away for the monotonous future?

I asked myself these things as I sat spinning theories about her in my arbour and the bees droned in the flowers. It was incontestable that, whether for right or for wrong, most readers of certain of Aspern's poems (poems not as ambiguous as the sonnets—scarcely more divine, I think—of Shakespeare) had taken for granted that Juliana had not always adhered to the steep footway of renunciation. There hovered about her name a perfume of impenitent passion, an intimation that she had not been exactly as the respectable young person in general. Was this a sign that her singer had betrayed her, had given her away, as we say now-adays, to posterity? Certain it is that it would have been difficult to put one's finger on the passage in which her fair fame suffered injury. More-over was not any fame fair enough that was so sure of duration and was associated with works immortal through their beauty? It was a part of my idea that the young lady had had a foreign lover—and say an unedi-fying tragical rupture—before her meeting with Jeffrey Aspern. She had lived with her father and sister in a queer old-fashioned expatriated ar-tistic Bohemia of the days when the æsthetic was only the academic and the painters who knew the best models for *contadina* and *pifferaro* wore peaked hats and long hair. It was a society less awake than the coteries of to-day—in its ignorance of the wonderful chances, the opportunities of the early bird, with which its path was strewn—to tatters of old stuff and fragments of old crockery; so that Miss Bordereau appeared not to have picked up or have inherited many objects of importance. There was no enviable *bric-à-brac*, with its provoking legend of cheapness, in the room in which I had seen her. Such a fact as that suggested bareness, but none the less it worked happily into the sentimental interest I had always taken in the early movements of my countrymen as visitors to Europe. When Americans went abroad in 1820 there was something romantic, almost heroic in it, as compared with the perpetual ferryings of the pres-ent hour, the hour at which photography and other conveniences have annihilated surprise. Miss Bordereau had sailed with her family on a toss-ing brig in the days of long voyages and sharp differences; she had had her emotions on the top of yellow diligences, passed the night at inns where she dreamed of travellers' tales, and was most struck, on reaching the Eternal City, with the elegance of Roman pearls and scarfs and mo-saic brooches. There was something touching to me in all that, and my imagination frequently went back to the period. If Miss Bordereau car-ried it there of course Jeffrey Aspern had at other times done so with greater force. It was a much more important fact, if one was looking at his genius critically, that he had lived in the days before the general transfusion. It had happened to me to regret that he had known Europe at all; I should have liked to see what he could have written without that experience, by which he had incontestably been enriched. But as his fate had ruled otherwise I went with him—I tried to judge how the general old order would have struck him. It was not only there, however, I watched him; the relations he had entertained with the special new had even a livelier interest. His own country after all had had most of his life, and his muse, as they said at that time, was essentially American. That was originally what I had prized him for; that at a period when our native land was nude and crude and provincial, when the famous "atmosphere" it is supposed to lack was not even missed, when literature was lonely there and art and form almost impossible, he had found means to live and write like one of the first; to be free and general and not at all afraid; to feel, understand and express everything.

V

I was seldom at home in the evening, for when I attempted to occupy myself in my apartments the lamplight brought in a swarm of noxious insects, and it was too hot for closed windows. Accordingly I spent the late hours either on the water—the moonlights of Venice are famous—or in the splendid square which serves as a vast forecourt to the strange old church of Saint Mark. I sat in front of Florian's café eating ices, listening to music, talking with acquaintances: the traveller will remember how the immense cluster of tables and little chairs stretches like a promontory into the smooth lake of the Piazza. The whole place, of a summer's evening, under the stars and with all the lamps, all the voices and light footsteps on marble—the only sounds of the immense arcade that encloses it—is an open-air saloon dedicated to cooling drinks and to a still finer degustation, that of the splendid impressions received during the day. When I didn't prefer to keep mine to myself there was always a stray tourist, disencumbered of his Bädeker, to discuss them with, or some domesticated painter rejoicing in the return of the season of strong effects. The great basilica, with its low domes and bristling embroideries, the mystery of its mosaic and sculpture, looked ghostly in the tempered gloom, and the sea-breeze passed between the twin columns of the Piazzetta, the lintels of a door no longer guarded, as gently as if a rich curtain swayed there. I used sometimes on these occasions to think of the Misses Bordereau and of the pity of their being shut up in apartments which in the Venetian July even Venetian vastness couldn't relieve of some stuffiness. Their life seemed miles away from the life of the Piazza, and no doubt it was really too late to make the austere Juliana change her habits. But poor Miss Tina would have enjoyed one of Florian's ices, I was sure; sometimes I even had thoughts of carrying one home to her. Fortunately my patience bore fruit and I was not obliged to do anything so ridiculous.

One evening about the middle of July I came in earlier than usual—I forgot what chance had led to this—and instead of going up to my quarters made my way into the garden. The temperature was very high; it was such a night as one would gladly have spent in the open air, and I was in no hurry to go to bed. I had floated home in my gondola, listening to the slow splash of the oar in the dark narrow canals, and now the only thought that occupied me was that it would be good to recline at one's length in the fragrant darkness on a garden bench. The odour of the canal was doubtless at the bottom of that aspiration, and the breath of the garden, as I entered it, gave consistency to my purpose. It was delicious—just such an air as must have trembled with Romeo's vows when he stood among the thick flowers and raised his arms to his mistress's balcony. I looked at the windows of the palace to see if by chance the example of Verona—Verona being not far off—had been followed; but everything was dim, as usual, and everything was still. Juliana might on the summer nights of her youth have murmured down from open windows at Jeffrey Aspern, but Miss Tina was not a poet's mistress any more than I was a poet. This however didn't prevent my gratification from being great as I became aware on reaching the end of the garden that my younger padrona was seated in one of the bowers. At first I made out but an indistinct figure, not in the least counting on such an overture from one of my hostesses; it even occurred to me that some enamoured maidservant had stolen in to keep a tryst with her sweetheart. I was going to turn away, not to frighten her, when the figure rose to its height and I recognised Miss Bordereau's niece. I must do myself the justice that I didn't wish to frighten her either, and much as I had longed for some such accident I should have been capable of retreating. It was as if I had laid a trap for her by coming home earlier than usual and by adding to that oddity my invasion of the garden. As she rose she spoke to me, and then I guessed that perhaps, secure in my almost inveterate absence, it was her nightly practice to take a lonely airing. There was no trap in truth, because I had had no suspicion. At first I took the words she uttered for an impatience of my arrival; but as she repeated them—I hadn't caught them clearly—I had the surprise of hearing her say: "Oh dear, I'm so glad you've come!" She and her aunt had in common the property of unexpected speeches. She came out of the arbour almost as if to throw herself in my arms.

I hasten to add that I escaped this ordeal and that she didn't even then shake hands with me. It was an ease to her to see me and presently she told me why—because she was nervous when out-of-doors at night alone. The plants and shrubs looked so strange in the dark, and there were all sorts of queer sounds—she couldn't tell what they were—like the noises of animals. She stood close to me, looking about her with an air of greater security but without any demonstration of interest in me as an individual. Then I felt how little nocturnal prowlings could have been her habit, and I was also reminded—I had been afflicted by the same in talking with her before I took possession—that it was impossible to allow too much for her simplicity.

"You speak as if you were lost in the backwoods," I cheeringly laughed. "How you manage to keep out of this charming place when you've only three steps to take to get into it is more than I've yet been able to discover. You hide away amazingly so long as I'm on the premises, I know; but I had a hope you peeped out a little at other times. You and your poor aunt are worse off than Carmelite nuns in their cells. Should you mind telling me how you exist without air, without exercise, without any sort of human contact? I don't see how you carry on the common business of life."

She looked at me as if I had spoken a strange tongue, and her answer was so little of one that I felt it make for irritation. "We go to bed very early—earlier than you'd believe." I was on the point of saying that this only deepened the mystery, but she gave me some relief by adding: "Before you came we weren't so private. But I've never been out at night."

"Never in these fragrant alleys, blooming here under your nose?"

"Ah," said Miss Tina, "they were never nice till now!" There was a finer sense in this and a flattering comparison, so that it seemed to me I had gained some advantage. As I might follow that further by establishing a good grievance I asked her why, since she thought my garden nice, she had never thanked me in any way for the flowers I had been sending up in such quantities for the previous three weeks. I had not been discouraged—there had been, as she would have observed, a daily armful; but I had been brought up in the common forms and a word of recognition now and then would have touched me in the right place.

"Why I didn't know they were for me!"

"They were for both of you. Why should I make a difference?"

Miss Tina reflected as if she might be thinking of a reason for that, but she failed to produce one. Instead of this she asked abruptly: "Why in the world do you want so much to know us?"

"I ought after all to make a difference," I replied. "That question's your aunt's; it isn't yours. You wouldn't ask it if you hadn't been put up to it."

"She didn't tell me to ask you," Miss Tina replied without confusion. She was indeed the oddest mixture of shyness and straightness.

"Well, she has often wondered about it herself and expressed her wonder to you. She has insisted on it, so that she has put the idea into your head that I'm insufferably pushing. Upon my word I think I've been very discreet. And how completely your aunt must have lost every tradition of sociability, to see anything out of the way in the idea that respectable intelligent people, living as we do under the same roof, should occasionally exchange a remark! What could be more natural? We are of the same country and have at least some of the same tastes, since, like you, I'm intensely fond of Venice."

My friend seemed incapable of grasping more than one clause in any proposition, and she now spoke quickly, eagerly, as if she were answering my whole speech: "I'm not in the least fond of Venice. I should like to go far away!"

"Has she always kept you back so?" I went on, to show her I could be as irrelevant as herself.

"She told me to come out to-night; she has told me very often," said Miss Tina. "It is I who wouldn't come. I don't like to leave her."

"Is she too weak, is she really failing?" I demanded, with more emotion, I think, than I meant to betray. I measured this by the way her eyes rested on me in the darkness. It embarrassed me a little, and to turn the matter off I continued genially: "Do let us sit down together comfortably somewhere—while you tell me all about her."

Miss Tina made no resistance to this. We found a bench less secluded, less confidential, as it were, than the one in the arbour; and we were still sitting there when I heard midnight ring out from those clear bells of Venice which vibrate with a solemnity of their own over the lagoon and hold the air so much more than the chimes of other places. We were together more than an hour and our interview gave, as it struck me, a great lift to my undertaking. Miss Tina accepted the situation without a protest, she had avoided me for three months, yet now she treated me almost as if these three months had made me an old friend. If I had chosen I might have gathered from this that though she had avoided me she had given a good deal of consideration to doing so. She paid no attention to the flight of time—never worried at my keeping her so long away from her aunt. She talked freely, answering questions and asking them and not even taking advantage of certain longish pauses by which they were naturally broken to say she thought she had better go in. It was almost as if she were waiting for something—something I might say to her—and intended to give me my opportunity. I was the more struck by this as she told me how much less well her aunt had been for a good many days, and in a way that was rather new. She was markedly weaker; at moments she showed no strength at all; yet more than ever before she wished to be left alone. That was why she had told her to come out—not even to remain in her own room, which was alongside; she pronounced poor Miss Tina "a worry, a bore and a source of aggravation." She sat still for hours together, as if for long sleep; she had always done that, musing and dozing; but at such times formerly she gave, in breaks, some small sign of life, of interest, liking her companion to be near her with her work. This sad personage confided to me that at present her aunt was so motionless as to create the fear she was dead; moreover she scarce ate or drank—one couldn't see what she lived on. The great thing was that she still on most days got up; the serious job was to dress her, to wheel her out of her bedroom. She clung to as many of her old habits as possible and had always, little company as they had received for years, made a point of sitting in the great parlour.

I scarce knew what to think of all this—of Miss Tina's sudden conversion to sociability and of the strange fact that the more the old woman appeared to decline to her end the less she should desire to be looked after. The story hung indifferently together, and I even asked myself if it mightn't be a trap laid for me, the result of a design to make me show my hand. I couldn't have told why my companions (as they could only by courtesy be called) should have this purpoese—why they should try to trip up so lucrative a lodger. But at any hazard I kept on my guard, so that Miss Tina shouldn't have occasion again to ask me what I might really be "up to." Poor woman, before we parted for the night my mind was at rest as to what *she* might be. She was up to nothing at all.

She told me more about their affairs than I had hoped; there was no need to be prying, for it evidently drew her out simply to feel me listen and care. She ceased wondering why I *should*, and at last while describing the brilliant life they had led years before, she almost chattered. It was Miss Tina who judged it brilliant; she said that when they first came to live in Venice, years and years back—I found her essentially vague about dates and the order in which events had occurred—there was never a week they hadn't some visitor or didn't make some pleasant *passeggio* in the town. They had seen all the curiosities; they had even been to the Lido in a boat—she spoke as if I might think there was a way on foot; they had had a collation there, brought in three baskets and spread out on the grass. I asked her what people they had known and she said Oh very nice ones—the Cavaliere Bombicci and the Contessa Altemura, with whom they had had a great friendship! Also English people—the Churtons and the Goldies and Mrs. Stock-Stock, whom they had loved dearly; she was dead and gone, poor dear. That was the case with most of their kind circle—this expression was Miss Tina's own; though a few were left, which was a wonder considering how they had neglected them. She mentioned the names of two or three Venetian old women; of a certain doctor, very clever, who was so attentive—he came as a friend, he had really given up practice; of the *avvocato* Pochintesta, who wrote beautiful poems and had addressed one to her aunt. These people came to see them without fail every year, usually at the *capo d'anno*, and of old her aunt used to make them some little present—her aunt and she together: small things that she, Miss Tina, turned out with her own hand, paper lampshades, or mats for the decanters of wine at dinner, or those woollen things that in cold weather are worn on the wrists. The last few years there hadn't been many presents; she couldn't think what to make and her aunt had lost interest and never suggested. But the people came all the same; if the good Venetians liked you once they liked you for ever.

There was affecting matter enough in the good faith of this sketch of former social glories; the picnic at the Lido had remained vivid through the ages and poor Miss Tina evidently was of the impression that she had had a dashing youth. She had in fact had a glimpse of the Venetian world in its gossiping home-keeping parsimonious professional walks; for I noted for the first time how nearly she had acquired by contact the trick of the familiar soft-sounding almost infantile prattle of the place. I judged her to have imbibed this invertebrate dialect from the natural way the names of things and people—mostly purely local—rose to her lips. If she knew little of what they represented she knew still less of anything else. Her aunt had drawn in—the failure of interest in the tablemats and lamp-shades was a sign of that—and she hadn't been able to mingle in society or to entertain it alone; so that her range of reminiscence struck one as an old world altogether. Her tone, hadn't it been so decent, would have seemed to carry one back to the queer rococo Venice of Goldoni and Casanova. I found myself mistakenly think of her too as one of Jeffrey Aspern's contemporaries; this came from her having so little in common with my own. It was possible, I indeed reasoned, that she hadn't even heard of him; it might very well be that Juliana had forborne to lift for innocent eyes the veil that covered the temple of her glory. In this case she perhaps wouldn't know of the existence of the papers, and I welcomed that presumption—it made me feel more safe with her—till I remembered we had believed the letter of disavowal received by Cumnor to be in the handwriting of the niece. If it had been dictated to her she had of course to know what it was about; though the effect of it withal was to repudiate the idea of any connexion with the poet. I held it probable at all events that Miss Tina hadn't read a word of his poetry. Moreover if, with her companion, she had always escaped invasion and research, there was little occasion for her having got it into her head that people were "after" the letters. People had not been after them, for people hadn't heard of them. Cumnor's fruitless feeler would have been a solitary accident.

When midnight sounded Miss Tina got up; but she stopped at the door of the house only after she had wandered two or three times with me round the garden. "When shall I see you again?" I asked before she went in; to which she replied with promptness that she should like to come out the next night. She added, however, that she shouldn't come— she was so far from doing everything she liked.

"You might do a few things *I* like," I quite sincerely sighed.

"Oh you—I don't believe you!" she murmured at this, facing me with her simple solemnity.

"Why don't you believe me?"

"Because I don't understand you."

"That's just the sort of occasion to have faith." I couldn't say more, though I should have liked to, as I saw I only mystified her; for I had no wish to have it on my conscience that I might pass for having made love to her. Nothing less should I have seemed to do had I continued to beg a lady to "believe in me" in an Italian garden on a midsummer night. There was some merit in my scruples, for Miss Tina lingered and lingered: I made out in her conviction that she shouldn't really soon come down again and the wish therefore to protract the present. She insisted too on making the talk between us personal to ourselves; and altogether her behaviour was such as would have been possible only to a perfectly artless and a considerably witless woman.

"I shall like the flowers better now that I know them also meant for me."

"How could you have doubted it? If you'll tell me the kind you like best I'll send a double lot."

"Oh I like them all best!" Then she went on familiarly: "Shall you study—shall you read and write—when you go up to your rooms?"

"I don't do that at night—at this season. The lamplight brings in the animals."

"You might have known that when you came."

"I did know it!"

"And in winter do you work at night?"

"I read a good deal, but I don't often write." She listened as if these details had a rare interest, and suddenly a temptation quite at odds with all the prudence I had been teaching myself glimmered at me in her plain mild face. Ah yes, she was safe and I could make her safer! It seemed to me from one moment to another that I couldn't wait longer—that I really must take a sounding. So I went on: "In general before I go to sleep (very often in bed; it's a bad habit, but I confess to it) I read some great poet. In nine cases out of ten it's a volume of Jeffrey Aspern."

I watched her well as I pronounced that name, but I saw nothing wonderful. Why should I indeed? Wasn't Jeffrey Aspern the property of the human race?

"Oh *we* read him—we *have* read him," she quietly replied.

"He's my poet of poets—I know him almost by heart."

For an instant Miss Tina hesitated; then her sociability was too much for her. "Oh by heart—that's nothing;" and, though dimly, she quite lighted. "My aunt used to know him, to know him"—she paused an instant and I wondered what she was going to say—"to know him as a visitor."

"As a visitor?" I guarded my tone.

"He used to call on her and take her out."

I continued to stare. "My dear lady, he died a hundred years ago!"

"Well," she said amusingly, "my aunt's a hundred and fifty."

"Mercy on us!" I cried; "why didn't you tell me before? I should like so to ask her about him."

"She wouldn't care for that—she wouldn't tell you," Miss Tina returned.

"I don't care what she cares for! She *must* tell me—it's not a chance to be lost."

"Oh you should have come twenty years ago. Then she still talked about him."

"And what did she say?" I eagerly asked.

" I don't know—that he liked her immensely."

"And she—didn't she like *him?*"

"She said he was a god." Miss Tina gave me this information flatly, without expression; her tone might have made it a piece of trivial gossip. But it stirred me deeply as she dropped the words into the summer night; their sound might have been the light rustle of an old unfolded love-letter.

"Fancy, fancy!" I murmured. And then, "Tell me this, please—has she got a portrait of him? They're distressingly rare."

"A portrait? I don't know," said Miss Tina; and now there was discomfiture in her face. "Well, good-night!" she added; and she turned into the house.

I accompanied her into the wide dusky stone-paved passage that corresponded on the ground floor with our grand sala. It opened at one end into the garden, at the other upon the canal, and was lighted now only by the small lamp always left for me to take up as I went to bed. An extinguished candle which Miss Tina apparently had brought down with her stood on the same table with it. "Good-night, good-night!" I replied, keeping beside her as she went to get her light. "Surely you'd know, shouldn't you, if she had one?"

"If she had what?" the poor lady asked, looking at me queerly over the flame of her candle.

"A portrait of the god. I don't know what I wouldn't give to see it."

"I don't know what she has got. She keeps her things locked up." And Miss Tina went away toward the staircase with the sense evidently of having said too much.

I let her go—I wished not to frighten her—and I contented myself with remarking that Miss Bordereau wouldn't have locked up such a glorious possession as that: a thing a person would be proud of and hang up in a prominent place on the parlour-wall. Therefore of course she hadn't any portrait. Miss Tina made no direct answer to this and, candle in hand, with her back to me, mounted two or three degrees. Then she stopped short and turned round, looking at me across the dusky space.

"Do you write—do you write?" There was a shake in her voice—she could scarcely bring it out.

"Do I write? Oh don't speak of my writing on the same day with Aspern's!"

"Do you write about *him*—do you pry into his life?"

"Ah that's your aunt's question; it can't be yours!" I said in a tone of slightly wounded sensibility.

"All the more reason then that you should answer it. Do you, please?"

I thought I had allowed for the falsehoods I should have to tell, but I found that in fact when it came to the point I hadn't. Besides, now that I had an opening there was a kind of relief in being frank. Lastly—it was perhaps fanciful, even fatuous—I guessed that Miss Tina personally wouldn't in the last resort be less my friend. So after a moment's hesitation I answered: "Yes, I've written about him and I'm looking for more material. In heaven's name have you got any?"

"*Santo Dio!*" she exclaimed without heeding my question; and she hurried upstairs and out of sight. I might count upon her in the last resort, but for the present she was visibly alarmed. The proof of it was that she began to hide again, so that for a fortnight I kept missing her. I found my patience ebbing and after four or five days of this I told the gardener to stop the "floral tributes."

VI

One afternoon, at last, however, as I came down from my quarters to go out, I found her in the sala: it was our first encounter on that ground since I had come to the house. She put on no air of being there by accident; there was an ignorance of such arts in her honest angular diffidence. That I might be quite sure she was waiting for me she mentioned it at once, but telling me with it that Miss Bordereau wished to see me: she would take me into the room at that moment if I had time. If I had been late for a love-tryst I would have stayed for this, and I quickly signified that I should be delighted to wait on my benefactress. "She wants to talk with you—to know you," Miss Tina said, smiling as if she herself appreciated that idea; and she led me to the door of her aunt's apartment. I stopped her a moment before she had opened it, looking at her with some curiosity. I told her that this was a great satisfaction to me and a great honour; but all the same I should like to ask what had made Miss Bordereau so markedly and suddenly change. It had been only the other day that she wouldn't suffer me near her. Miss Tina was not embarrassed by my question; she had as many little unexpected serenities, plausibilities almost, as if she told fibs, but the odd part of them was that they had on the contrary their source in her truthfulness. "Oh my aunt varies," she answered; "it's so terribly dull—I suppose she's tired."

"But you told me she wanted more and more to be alone."

Poor Miss Tina coloured as if she found me too pushing. "Well, if you don't believe she wants to see you, I haven't invented it! I think people often are capricious when they're very old."

"That's perfectly true. I only wanted to be clear as to whether you've repeated to her what I told you the other night."

"What you told me?"

"About Jeffrey Aspern—that I'm looking for materials."

"If I had told her do you think she'd have sent for you?"

"That's exactly what I want to know. If she wants to keep him to herself she might have sent for me to tell me so."

"She won't speak of him," said Miss Tina. Then as she opened the door she added in a lower tone: "I told her nothing."

The old woman was sitting in the same place in which I had seen her last, in the same position, with the same mystifying bandage over her eyes. Her welcome was to turn her almost invisible face to me and show me that while she sat silent she saw me clearly. I made no motion to shake hands with her; I now felt too well that this was out of place for ever. It had been sufficiently enjoined on me that she was too sacred for trivial modernisms—too venerable to touch. There was something so grim in her aspect—it was partly the accident of her green shade—as I stood there to be measured, that I ceased on the spot to doubt her suspecting me, though I didn't in the least myself suspect that Miss Tina hadn't just spoken the truth. She hadn't betrayed me, but the old woman's brooding instinct had served her; she had turned me over and over in the long still hours and had guessed. The worst of it was that she looked terribly like an old woman who at a pinch would, even like Sardanapalus, burn her treasure. Miss Tina pushed a chair forward, saying to me: "This will be a good place for you to sit." As I took possession of it I asked after Miss Bordereau's health; expressed the hope that in spite of the very hot

weather it was satisfactory. She answered that it was good enough—good
enough; that it was a great thing to be alive.

"Oh as to that, it depends upon what you compare it with!" I returned
with a laugh.

"I don't compare—I don't compare. If I did that I should have given
everything up long ago."

I liked to take this for a subtle allusion to the rapture she had known
in the society of Jeffrey Aspern—though it was true that such an allusion
would have accorded ill with the wish I imputed to her to keep him
buried in her soul. What it accorded with was my constant conviction
that no human being had ever had a happier social gift than his, and what
it seemed to convey was that nothing in the world was worth speaking of
if one pretended to speak of that. But one didn't pretend! Miss Tina sat
down beside her aunt, looking as if she had reason to believe some wonderful talk would come off between us.

"It's about the beautiful flowers," said the old lady; "you sent us so
many—I ought to have thanked you for them before. But I don't write
letters and I receive company but at long intervals."

She hadn't thanked me while the flowers continued to come, but she
departed from her custom so far as to send for me as soon as she began
to fear they wouldn't come any more. I noted this; I remembered what
an acquisitive propensity she had shown when it was a question of ex-
tracting gold from me, and I privately rejoiced at the happy thought I
had had in suspending my tribute. She had missed it and was willing to
make a concession to bring it back. At the first sign of this concession I
could only go to meet her. "I'm afraid you haven't had many, of late, but
they shall begin again immediately—to-morrow, to-night."

"Oh do send us some to-night!" Miss Tina cried as if it were a great
affair.

"What else should you do with them? It isn't a manly taste to make a
bower of your room," the old woman remarked.

"I don't make a bower of my room, but I'm exceedingly fond of growing flowers, of watching their ways. There's nothing unmanly in that: it
has been the amusement of philosophers, of statesmen in retirement;
even I think of great captains."

"I suppose you know you can sell them—those you don't use," Miss
Bordereau went on. "I dare say they wouldn't give you much for them;
still, you could make a bargain."

"Oh I've never in my life made a bargain, as you ought pretty well to
have gathered. My gardener disposes of them and I ask no questions."

"I'd ask a few, I can promise you!" said Miss Bordereau; and it was so
I first heard the strange sound of her laugh, which was as if the faint
"walking" ghost of her old-time tone had suddenly cut a caper. I couldn't
get used to the idea that this vision of pecuniary profit was most what
drew out the divine Juliana.

"Come into the garden yourself and pick them; come as often as you
like; come every day. The flowers are all for you," I pursued, addressing
Miss Tina and carrying off this veracious statement by treating it as an
innocent joke. "I can't imagine why she doesn't come down," I added for
Miss Bordereau's benefit.

"You must make her come; you must come up and fetch her," the old
woman said to my stupefaction. "That odd thing you've made in the corner will do very well for her to sit in."

The allusion to the most elaborate of my shady coverts, a sketchy
"summer-house," was irreverent; it confirmed the impression I had already received that there was a flicker of impertinence in Miss Bordereau's talk, a vague echo of the boldness or the archness of her adventurous youth and which had somehow automatically outlived passions and
faculties. None the less I asked: "Wouldn't it be possible for you to come
down there yourself? Wouldn't it do you good to sit there in the shade
and the sweet air?"

"Oh sir, when I move out of this it won't be to sit in the air, and I'm
afraid that any that may be stirring around me won't be particularly
sweet! It will be a very dark shade indeed. But that won't be just yet,"
Miss Bordereau continued cannily, as if to correct any hopes this free
glance at the last receptable of her mortality might lead me to entertain.
"I've sat here many a day and have had enough of arbours in my time.
But I'm not afraid to wait till I'm called."

Miss Tina had expected, as I felt, rare conversation, but perhaps she
found it less gracious on her aunt's side—considering I had been sent for
with a civil intention—that she had hoped. As to give the position a turn
that would put our companion in a light more favourable she said to me:
"Didn't I tell you the other night that she had sent me out? You see I
can do what I like!"

"Do you pity her—do you teach her to pity herself?" Miss Bordereau
demanded, before I had time to answer this appeal. "She has a much
easier life than I had at her age."

"You must remember it has been quite open to me," I said, "to
think you rather inhuman."

"Inhuman? That's what the poets used to call the women a hundred
years ago. Don't try that; you won't do as well as they!" Juliana went on.
"There's no more poetry in the world—that I know of at least. But I
won't bandy words with you," she said, and I well remember the old-
fashioned artificial sound she gave the speech. "You make me talk, talk,
talk! It isn't good for me at all." I got up at this and told her I would take
no more of her time; but she detained me to put a question, "Do you remember, the day I saw you about the rooms, that you offered us the use
of your gondola?" And when I assented promptly, struck again with her
disposition to make a "good thing" of my being there and wondering
what she now had in her eye, she produced: "Why don't you take that
girl out in it and show her the place?"

"Oh dear aunt, what do you want to do with me?" cried the "girl" with a piteous quaver. "I know all about the place!"

"Well then go with him and explain!" said Miss Bordereau, who gave an effect of cruelty to her implacable power of retort. This showed her as a sarcastic profane cynical old woman. "Haven't we heard that there have been all sorts of changes in all these years? You ought to see them, and at your age—I don't mean because you're so young—you ought to take the chances that come. You're old enough, my dear, and this gentleman won't hurt you. He'll show you the famous sunsets, if they still go on—do they go on? The sun set for me so long ago. But that's not a reason. Besides, I shall never miss you; you think you're too important. Take her to the Piazza; it used to be very pretty," Miss Bordereau continued, addressing herself to me. "What have they done with the funny old church? I hope it hasn't tumbled down. Let her look at the shops; she may take some money, she may buy what she likes."

Poor Miss Tina had got up, discountenanced and helpless, and as we stood there before her aunt it would certainly have struck a spectator of the scene that our venerable friend was making rare sport of us. Miss Tina protested in a confusion of exclamations and murmurs; but I lost no time in saying that if she would do me the honour to accept the hospitality of my boat I would engage she really shouldn't be bored. Or if she didn't want so much of my company, the boat itself, with the gondolier, was at her service; he was a capital oar and she might have every confidence. Miss Tina, without definitely answering this speech, looked away from me and out of the window, quite as if about to weep, and I remarked that once we had Miss Bordereau's approval we could easily come to an understanding. We would take an hour, whichever she liked, one of the very next days. As I made my obeisance to the old lady I asked her if she would kindly permit me to see her again.

For a moment she kept me; then she said: "Is it very necessary to your happiness?"

"It diverts me more than I can say."

"You're wonderfully civil. Don't you know it almost kills me?"

"How can I believe that when I see you more animated, more brilliant than when I came in?"

"That's very true, aunt," said Miss Tina. "I think it does you good."

"Isn't it touching, the solicitude we each have that the other shall enjoy herself?" sneered Miss Bordereau. "If you think me brilliant to-day you don't know what you are talking about; you've never seen an agreeable woman. What do you people know about good society?" she cried; but before I could tell her, "Don't try to pay me a compliment; I've been spoiled," she went on. "My door's shut, but you may sometimes knock."

With this she dismissed me and I left the room. The latch closed behind me, but Miss Tina, contrary to my hope, had remained within. I passed slowly across the hall and before taking my way downstairs waited a little. My hope was answered; after a minute my conductress followed me. "That's a delightful idea about the Piazza," I said." When will you go—to-night, to-morrow?"

She had been disconcerted, as I have mentioned, but I had already perceived, and I was to observe again, that when Miss Tina was embarrassed she didn't—as most women would have in like case—turn away, floundering and hedging, but came closer, as it were, with a deprecating, a clinging appeal to be spared, to be protected. Her attitude was a constant prayer for aid and explanation, and yet no woman in the world could have been less of a comedian. From the moment you were kind to her she depended on you absolutely; her self-consciousness dropped and she took the greatest intimacy, the innocent intimacy that was all she could conceive, for granted. She didn't know, she now declared, what possessed her aunt, who had changed so quickly, who had got some idea. I replied that she must catch the idea and let me have it: we would go and take an ice together at Florian's and she should report while we listened to the band.

"Oh it will take me a long time to be able to 'report'!" she said rather ruefully; and she could promise me this satisfaction neither for that night nor for the next. I was patient now, however, for I felt I had only to wait; and in fact at the end of the week, one lovely evening after dinner, she stepped into my gondola, to which in honour of the occasion I had attached a second oar.

We swept in the course of five minutes into the Grand Canal; whereupon she uttered a murmur of ecstasy as fresh as if she had been a tourist just arrived. She had forgotten the splendor of the great water-way on a clear summer evening, and how the sense of floating between marble palaces and reflected lights disposed the mind to freedom and ease. We floated long and far, and though my friend gave no high-pitched voice to her glee I was sure of her full surrender. She was more than pleased, she was transported; the whole thing was an immense liberation. The gondola moved with slow strokes, to give her time to enjoy it, and she listened to the plash of the oars, which grew louder and more musically liquid as we passed into narrow canals, as if it were a revelation of Venice. When I asked her how long it was since she had thus floated, she answered: "Oh I don't know; a long time—not since my aunt began to be ill." This was not the only show of her extreme vagueness about the previous years and the line marking off the period of Miss Bordereau's eminence. I was not at liberty to keep her out long, but we took a considerable *giro* before going to the Piazza. I asked her no questions, holding off by design from her life at home and the things I wanted to know; I poured, rather, treasures of information about the objects before and around us into her ears, describing also Florence and Rome, discoursing on the charms and advantages of travel. She reclined, receptive, on the deep leather cushions, turned her eyes conscientiously to everything I noted and never mentioned to me till some time afterwards that she might be supposed to know Florence better than I, as she had lived there for years with her kinswoman. At last she said with the shy impatience of a child: "Are we not really going to the Piazza? That's what I want to see!" I immediately gave the order that we should go straight, after which we sat silent with the expectation of arrival. As some time still passed, however, she broke out of her own movement: "I've found out what's the matter with my aunt: she's afraid you'll go!"

I quite gasped. "What has put that into her head?"

"She has had an idea you've not been happy. That's why she is different now."

"You mean she wants to make me happier?"

"Well, she wants you not to go. She wants you to stay."

"I suppose you mean on account of the rent," I remarked candidly.

Miss Tina's candour but profited. "Yes, you know; so that I shall have more."

"How much does she want you to have?" I asked with all the gaiety I now felt. "She ought to fix the sum, so that I may stay till it's made up."

"Oh that wouldn't please me," said Miss Tina. "It would be unheard of, your taking that trouble."

"But suppose I should have my own reasons for staying in Venice?"

"Then it would be better for you to stay in some other house."

"And what would your aunt say to that?"

"She wouldn't like it at all. But I should think you'd do well to give up your reasons and go away altogether."

"Dear Miss Tina," I said, "it's not so easy to give up my reasons!"

She made no immediate answer to this, but after a moment broke out afresh: "I think I know what your reasons are!"

"I dare say, because the other night I almost told you how I wished you'd help me to make them good."

"I can't do that without being false to my aunt."

"What do you mean by being false to her?"

"Why she would never consent to what you want. She has been asked, she has been written to. It makes her fearfully angry."

"Then she *has* papers of value?" I precipitately cried.

"Oh, she has everything!" sighed Miss Tina, with a curious weariness, a sudden lapse into gloom.

These words caused all my pulses to throb, for I regarded them as precious evidence. I felt them too deeply to speak, and in the interval the gondola approached the Piazzetta. After we had disembarked I asked my companion if she would rather walk round the square or go and sit before the great café; to which she replied that she would do whichever I liked best—I must only remember again how little time she had. I assured her there was plenty to do both, and we made the circuit of the long arcades. Her spirits revived at the sight of the bright shop-windows, and she lingered and stopped, admiring or disapproving of their contents, asking me what I thought of things, theorizing about prices.

My attention wandered from her; her words of a while before "Oh she has everything!" echoed so in my consciousness. We sat down at last in the crowded circle at Florian's, finding an unoccupied table among those that were ranged in the square. It was a splendid night and all the world out-of-doors; Miss Tina couldn't have wished the elements more auspicious for her return to society. I saw she felt it all even more than she told, but her impressions were well-nigh too many for her. She had forgotten the attraction of the world and was learning that she had for the best years of her life been rather mercilessly cheated of it. This didn't make her angry; but as she took in the charming scene her face had, in spite of its smile of appreciation, the flush of a wounded surprise. She didn't speak, sunk in the sense of opportunities, for ever lost, that ought to have been easy; and this gave me a chance to say to her: "Did you mean a while ago that your aunt has a plan of keeping me on by admitting me occasionally to her presence?"

"She thinks it will make a difference with you if you sometimes see her. She wants you so much to stay that she's willing to make that concession."

"And what good does she consider I think it will do me to see her?"

"I don't know; it must be interesting," said Miss Tina simply. "You told her you found it so."

"So I did; but every one doesn't think that."

"No, of course not, or more people would try."

"Well, if she's capable of making that reflexion she's capable also of making this further one," I went on: "that I must have a particular reason for not doing as others do, in spite of the interest she offers—for not leaving her alone." Miss Tina looked as if she failed to grasp this rather complicated proposition; so I continued: "If you've not told her what I said to you the other night may she not at least have guessed it?"

"I don't know—she's very suspicious."

"But she hasn't been made so by indiscreet curiosity, by persecution?"

"No, no; it isn't that," said Miss Tina, turning on me a troubled face. "I don't know how to say it; it's on account of something—ages ago, before I was born—in her life."

"Something? What sort of thing?"—and I asked it as if I could have no idea.

"Oh she has never told me." And I was sure my friend spoke the truth.

Her extreme limpidity was almost provoking, and I felt for the moment that she would have been more satisfactory if she had been less ingenuous. "Do you suppose it's something to which Jeffrey Aspern's letters and papers—I mean the things in her possession—have reference?"

"I dare say it is!" my companion exclaimed as if this were a very happy suggestion. "I've never looked at any of those things."

"None of them? Then how do you know what they are?"

"I don't," said Miss Tina placidly. "I've never had them in my hands. But I've seen them when she has had them out."

"Does she have them out often?"

"Not now, but she used to. She's very fond of them."

"In spite of their being compromising?"

"Compromising?" Miss Tina repeated as if vague as to what that meant. I felt almost as one who corrupts the innocence of youth.

"I allude to their containing painful memories."

"Oh I don't think anything's painful."

"You mean there's nothing to affect her reputation?"

An odder look even than usual came at this into the face of Miss Bordereau's niece—a confession, it seemed, of helplessness, an appeal to me to deal fairly, generously with her. I had brought her to the Piazza, placed her among charming influences, paid her an attention she appreciated, and now I appeared to show it all as a bribe—a bribe to make her turn in some way against her aunt. She was of a yielding nature and capable of doing almost anything to please a person markedly kind to her; but the greatest kindness of all would be not to presume too much on this. It was strange enough, as I afterwards thought, that she had not the least air of resenting my want of consideration for her aunt's character, which would have been in the worst possible taste if anything less vital—from my point of view—had been at stake. I don't think she really measured it. "Do you mean she ever did something bad?" she asked in a moment.

"Heaven forbid I should say so, and it's none of my business. Besides, if she did," I agreeably put it, "that was in other ages, in another world. But why shouldn't she destroy her papers?"

"Oh she loves them too much."

"Even now, when she may be near her end?"

"Perhaps when she's sure of that she will."

"Well, Miss Tina," I said, "that's just what I should like you to prevent."

"How can I prevent it?"

"Couldn't you get them away from her?"

"And give them to you?"

This put the case, superficially, with sharp irony, but I was sure of her not intending that. "Oh I mean that you might let me see them and look them over. It isn't for myself, or that I should want them at any cost to any one else. It's simply that they would be of such immense interest to the public, such immeasurable importance as a contribution to Jeffrey Aspern's history."

She listened to me in her usual way, as if I abounded in matters she had never heard of, and I felt almost as base as the reporter of a newspaper who forces his way into a house of mourning. This was marked when she presently said: "There was a gentleman who some time ago wrote to her in very much those words. He also wanted her papers."

"And did she answer him?" I asked, rather ashamed of not having my friend's rectitude.

"Only when he had written two or three times. He made her very angry."

"And what did she say?"

"She said he was a devil," Miss Tina replied categorically.

"She used that expression in her letter?"

"Oh no; she said it to me. She made me write to him."

"And what did you say?"

"I told him there were no papers at all."

"Ah poor gentleman!" I groaned.

"I knew there were, but I wrote what she bade me."

"Of course you had to do that. But I hope I shan't pass for a devil."

"It will depend upon what you ask me to do for you," my companion smiled.

"Oh if there's a chance of *your* thinking so my affair's in a bad way! I shan't ask you to steal for me, nor even to fib—for you *can't* fib, unless on paper. But the principal thing is this—to prevent her destroying the papers."

"Why I've no control of her," said Miss Tina. "It's she who controls me."

"But she doesn't control her own arms and legs, does she? The way she would naturally destroy her letters would be to burn them. Now she can't burn them without fire, and she can't get fire unless you give it to her."

"I've always done everything she has asked," my poor friend pleaded. "Besides, there's Olimpia."

I was on the point of saying that Olimpia was probably corruptible, but I thought it best not to sound that note. So I simply put it that this frail creature might perhaps be managed.

"Every one can be managed by my aunt," said Miss Tina. And then she remembered that her holiday was over; she must go home.

I laid my hand on her arm, across the table, to stay her a moment. "What I want of you is a general promise to help me."

"Oh how *can* I, how *can* I?" she asked, wondering and troubled. She was half-surprised, half-frightened at my attaching that importance to her, at my calling on her for action.

"This is the main thing: to watch our friend carefully and warn me in time, before she commits that dreadful sacrilege."

"I can't watch her when she makes me go out."

"That's very true."

"And when you do too."

"Mercy on us—do you think she'll have done anything to-night?"

"I don't know. She's very cunning."

"Are you trying to frighten me?" I asked.

I felt this question sufficiently answered when my companion murmured in a musing, almost envious way: "Oh but she loves them—she loves them!"

This reflexion, repeated with such emphasis, gave me great comfort; but to obtain more of that balm I said: "If she shouldn't intend to destroy the objects we speak of before her death she'll probably have made some disposition by will."

"By will?"

"Hasn't she made a will for your benefit?"

"Ah she has so little to leave. That's why she likes money," said Miss Tina.

"Might I ask, since we're really talking things over, what you and she live on?"

"On some money that comes from America, from a gentleman—I think a lawyer—in New York. He sends it every quarter. It isn't much!"

"And won't she have disposed of that?"

My companion hesitated—I saw she was blushing. "I believe it's mine," she said; and the look and tone which accompanied these words betrayed so the absence of the habit of thinking of herself that I almost thought her charming. The next instant she added: "But she had in an *avvocato* here once, ever so long ago. And some people came and signed something."

"They were probably witnesses. And you weren't asked to sign? Well then," I argued, rapidly and hopefully, "it's because you're the legatee. She must have left all her documents to you!"

"If she has it's with very strict conditions," Miss Tina responded, rising quickly, while the movement gave the words a small character of decision. They seemed to imply that the bequest would be accompanied with a proviso that the articles bequeathed should remain concealed from every inquisitive eye, and that I was very much mistaken if I thought her the person to depart from an injunction so absolute.

"Oh of course you'll have to abide by the terms," I said; and she uttered nothing to mitigate the rigour of this conclusion. None the less, later on, just before we disembarked at her own door after a return which had taken place almost in silence, she said to me abruptly: "I'll do what I can to help you." I was grateful for this—it was very well so far as it went; but it didn't keep me from remembering that night in a worried waking hour that I now had her word for it to re-enforce my own impression that the old woman was full of craft.

VII

The fear of what this side of her character might have led her to do made me nervous for days afterwards. I waited for an intimation from Miss Tina; I almost read it as her duty to keep me informed, to let me know definitely whether or no Miss Bordereau has sacrificed her treasures. But as she gave no sign I lost patience and determined to put the case to the very touch of my own senses. I sent late one afternoon to ask if I might pay the ladies a visit, and my servant came back with surprising news. Miss Bordereau could be approached without the least difficulty; she had been moved out into the sala and was sitting by the window that overlooked the garden. I descended and found this picture correct; the old lady had been wheeled forth into the world and had a certain air, which came mainly perhaps from some brighter element in her dress, of being prepared again to have converse with it. It had not yet, however, begun to flock about her; she was perfectly alone and, though the door leading to her own quarters stood open, I had at first no glimpse of Miss Tina. The window at which she sat had the afternoon shade and, one of the shutters having been pushed back, she could see the pleasant garden, where the summer sun had by this time dried up too many of the plants—she could see the yellow light and the long shadows.

"Have you come to tell me you'll take the rooms for six months more?" she asked as I approached her, startling me by something coarse in her cupidity almost as much as if she hadn't already given me a specimen of it. Juliana's desire to make our acquaintance lucrative had been, as I have sufficiently indicated, a false note in my image of the woman who had inspired a great poet with immortal lines; but I may say here definitely that I after all recognised large allowance to be made for her. It was I who had kindled the unholy flame; it was I who had put into her head that she had the means of making money. She appeared never to have thought of that; she had been living wastefully for years, in a house five times too big for her, on a footing that I could explain only by the presumption that, excessive as it was, the space she enjoyed cost her next to nothing and that, small as were her revenues, they left her, for Venice, an appreciable margin. I had descended on her one day and taught her to calculate, and my almost extravagant comedy on the subject of the garden had presented me irresistibly in the light of a victim. Like all persons who achieve the miracle of changing their point of view late in life, she had been intensely converted; she had seized my hint with a desperate tremulous clutch.

I invited myself to go and get one of the chairs that stood, at a distance, against the wall—she had given herself no concern as to whether I should sit or stand; and while I placed it near her I began gaily: "Oh dear madam, what an imagination you have, what an intellectual sweep! I'm a poor devil of a man of letters who lives from day to day. How can I take palaces by the year? My existence is precarious. I don't know whether six months hence I shall have bread to put in my mouth. I've treated myself for once; it has been an immense luxury. But when it comes to going on——!"

"Are your rooms too dear? If they are you can have more for the same money," Juliana responded. "We can arrange, we can *combinare*, as they say here."

"Well yes, since you ask me, they're too dear, much too dear," I said. "Evidently you suppose me richer than I am."

She looked at me as from the mouth of her cave. "If you write books don't you sell them?"

"Do you mean don't people buy them? A little, a very little—not so much as I could wish. Writing books, unless one be a great genius—and even then!—is the last road to fortune. I think there's no more money to be made by good letters."

"Perhaps you don't choose nice subjects. What do you write about?" Miss Bordereau implacably pursued.

"About the books of other people. I'm a critic, a commentator, an historian, in a small way." I wondered what she was coming to.

"And what other people now?"

"Oh better ones than myself: the great writers mainly—the great philosophers and poets of the past; those who are dead and gone and can't, poor darlings, speak for themselves."

"And what do you say about them?"

"I say they sometimes attached themselves to very clever women!" I replied as for pleasantness. I had measured, as I thought, my risk, but as my words fell upon the air they were to strike me as imprudent. However, I had launched them and I wasn't sorry, for perhaps after all the old woman would be willing to treat. It seemed tolerably obvious that she knew my secret; why therefore drag the process out? But she didn't take what I had said as a confession; she only asked:

"Do you think it's right to rake up the past?"

"I don't feel that I know what you mean by raking it up. How can we get at it unless we dig a little? The present has such a rough way of treading it down."

"Oh I like the past, but I don't like critics," my hostess declared with her hard complacency.

"Neither do I, but I like their discoveries."

"Aren't they mostly lies?"

"The lies are what they sometimes discover," I said, smiling at the quiet impertinence of this. "They often lay bare the truth."

"The truth is God's, it isn't man's; we had better leave it alone. Who can judge of it?—who can say?"

"We're terribly in the dark, I know," I admitted; "but if we give up trying what becomes of all the fine things? What becomes of the work I just mentioned, that of the great philosophers and poets? It's all vain words if there's nothing to measure it by."

"You talk as if you were a tailor," said Miss Bordereau whimsically; and then she added quickly and in a different manner: "This house is very fine; the proportions are magnificent. To-day I wanted to look at this part again. I made them bring me out here. When your man came just now to learn if I would see you I was on the point of sending for you to ask if you didn't mean to go on. I wanted to judge what I'm letting you have. This sala is very grand," she pursued like an auctioneer, moving a little, as I guessed, her invisible eyes. "I don't believe you often have lived in such a house, eh"

"I can't often afford to!" I said.

"Well then how much will you give me for six months?"

I was on the point of exclaiming—and the air of excruciation in my face would have denoted a moral fact—"Don't, Juliana; for *his* sake, don't!" But I controlled myself and asked less passionately: "Why should I remain so long as that?"

"I thought you liked it," said Miss Bordereau with her shrivelled dignity.

"So I thought I should."

For a moment she said nothing more, and I left my own words to suggest to her what they might. I half-expected her to say, coldly enough, that if I had been disappointed we needn't continue the discussion, and this in spite of the fact that I believed her now to have in her mind—however it had come there—what would have told her that my disappointment was natural. But to my extreme surprise she ended by observing: "If you don't think we've treated you well enough perhaps we can discover some way of treating you better." This speech was somehow so incongruous that it made me laugh again, and I excused myself by saying that she talked as if I were a sulky boy pouting in the corner and having to be "brought round." I hadn't a grain of complaint to make; and could anything have exceeded Miss Tina's graciousness in accompanying me a few night before to the Piazza? At this the old woman went on: "Well, you brought it on yourself!" And then in a different tone: "She's a very fine girl." I assented cordially to this proposition, and she expressed the hope that I did so not merely to be obliging, but that I really liked her. Meanwhile I wondered still more what Miss Bordereau was coming to. "Except for me, to-day," she said, "she hasn't a relation in the world." Did she by describing her niece as amiable and unencumbered wish to represent her as a *parti?*

It was perfectly true that I couldn't afford to go on with my rooms at a fancy price and that I had already devoted to my undertaking almost all the hard cash I had set apart for it. My patience and my time were by no means exhausted, but I should be able to draw upon them only on a more usual Venetian basis. I was willing to pay the precious personage with whom my pecuniary dealings were such a discord twice as much as any other *padrona di casa* would have asked, but I wasn't willing to pay her twenty times as much. I told her so plainly, and my plainness appeared to have some success, for she exclaimed: "Very good; you've done what I asked—you've made an offer!"

"Yes, but not for half a year. Only by the month."

"Oh I must think of that then." She seemed disappointed that I wouldn't tie myself to a period, and I guessed that she wished both to secure me and to discourage me; to say severely: "Do you dream that you can get off with less than six months? Do you dream that even by the end of that time you'll be appreciably nearer your victory?" What was most in my mind was that she had a fancy to play me the trick of making me engage myself when in fact she had sacrificed her treasure. There was a moment when my suspense on this point was so acute that I all but broke out with the question, and what kept it back was but an instinctive recoil—lest it should be a mistake—from the last violence of self-exposure. She was such a subtle old witch that one could never tell where one stood with her. You may imagine whether it cleared up the puzzle when, just after she had said she would think of my proposal and without any formal transition, she drew out of her pocket with an embarrassed hand a small object wrapped in crumpled white paper. She held it there a moment and then resumed: "Do you know much about curiosities?"

"About curiosities?"

"About antiquities, the old gimcracks that people pay so much for to-day. Do you know the kind of price they bring?"

I thought I saw what was coming, but I said ingenuously: "Do you want to buy something?"

"No, I want to sell. What would an amateur give me for that?" She unfolded the white paper and made a motion for me to take from her a small oval portrait. I possessed myself of it with fingers of which I could only hope that they didn't betray the intensity of their clutch, and she added: "I would part with it only for a good price."

At the first glance I recognized Jeffrey Aspern, and was well aware that I flushed with the act. As she was watching me however I had the consistency to exclaim: "What a striking face! Do tell me who it is."

"He's an old friend of mine, a very distinguished man in his day. He gave it me himself, but I'm afraid to mention his name, lest you never should have heard of him, critic and historian as you are. I know the world goes fast and one generation forgets another. He was all the fashion when I was young."

She was perhaps amazed at my assurance, but I was surprised at hers; at her having the energy, in her state of health and at her time of life, to wish to sport with me to that tune simply for her private entertainment—the humour to test me and practise on me and befool me. This at least was the interpretation that I put upon her production of the relic, for I couldn't believe she really desired to sell it or cared for any information I might give her. What she wished was to dangle it before my eyes and put a prohibitive price on it. "The face comes back to me, it torments me," I said, turning the object this way and that and looking at it very critically. It was a careful but not a supreme work of art, larger than the ordinary miniature and representing a young man with a remarkbly handsome face, in a high-collared green coat and a buff waistcoat. I felt in the little work a virtue of likeness and judged it to have been painted when the model was about twenty-five. There are, as all the world knows, three other portraits of the poet in existence, but none of so early a date as this elegant image. "I've never seen the original, clearly a man of a past age, but I've seen other reproductions of this face," I went on. "You expressed doubt of this generation's having heard of the gentleman, but he strikes me for all the world as a celebrity. Now who is he? I can't put my finger on him—I can't give him a label. Wasn't he a writer? Surely he's a poet." I was determined that it should be she, not I, who should first pronounce Jeffrey Aspern's name.

My resolution was taken in ignorance of Miss Bordereau's extremely resolute character, and her lips never formed in my hearing the syllables that meant so much for her. She neglected to answer my question, but raised her hand to take back the picture, using a gesture which though impotent was in a high degree peremptory. "It's only a person who should know for himself that would give me my price," she said with a certain dryness.

"Oh then you have a price?" I didn't restore the charming thing; not from any vindictive purpose, but because I instinctively clung to it. We looked at each other hard while I retained it.

"I know the least I would take. What it occurred to me to ask you about is the most I shall be able to get."

She made a movement, drawing herself together as if, in a spasm of dread at having lost her prize she had been impelled to the immense effort of rising to snatch it from me. I instantly placed it in her hand again, saying as I did so: "I should like to have it myself, but with your ideas it would be quite beyond my mark."

She turned the small oval plate over in her lap, with its face down, and I heard her catch her breath as after a strain or an escape. This however did not prevent her saying in a moment: "You'd buy a likeness of a person you don't know by an artist who had no reputation?"

"The artist may have no reputation, but that thing's wonderfully well painted," I replied, to give myself a reason.

"It's lucky you thought of saying that, because the painter was my father."

"That makes the picture indeed precious!" I returned with gaiety; and I may add that a part of my cheer came from this proof I had been right in my theory of Miss Bordereau's origin. Aspern had of course met the young lady on his going to her father's studio as a sitter. I observed to Miss Bordereau that if she would entrust me with her property for twenty-four hours I should be happy to take advice on it; but she made no other reply than to slip it in silence into her pocket. This convinced me still more that she had no sincere intention of selling it during her lifetime, though she may have desired to satisfy herself as to the sum her niece, should she leave it to her, might expect eventually to obtain for it. "Well, at any rate, I hope you won't offer it without giving me notice," I said as she remained irresponsive. "Remember me as a possible purchaser."

"I should want your money first!" she returned with unexpected rudeness; and then, as if she bethought herself that I might well complain of such a tone and wished to turn the matter off, asked abruptly what I talked about with her niece when I went out with her that way of an evening.

"You speak as if we had set up the habit," I replied. "Certainly I should be very glad if it were to become our pleasant custom. But in that case I should feel a still greater scruple at betraying a lady's confidence."

"Her confidence? Has my niece confidence?"

"Here she is—she can tell you herself," I said; for Miss Tina now appeared on the threshold of the old woman's parlour. "Have you confidence, Miss Tina? Your aunt wants very much to know."

"Not in her, not in her!" the younger lady declared, shaking her head with a dolefulness that was neither jocular not affected. "I don't know what to do with her; she has fits of horrid imprudence. She's so easily tired—and yet she has begun to roam, to drag herself about the house." And she looked down at her yoke-fellow of long years with a vacancy of wonder, as if all their contact and custom hadn't made her perversities, on occasion, any more easy to follow.

"I know what I'm about. I'm not losing my mind. I dare say you'd like to think so," said Miss Bordereau with a crudity of cynicism.

"I don't suppose you came out her yourself. Miss Tina must have had to lend you a hand," I interposed for conciliation.

"Oh she insisted we should push her; and when she insists!" said Miss Tina, in the same tone of apprehension; as if there were no knowing what service she disapproved of her aunt might force her next to render.

"I've always got most things done I wanted, thank God! The people I've lived with have humoured me," the old woman continued, speaking out of the white ashes of her vanity.

It took it pleasantly up. "I suppose you mean they've obeyed you."

"Well, whatever it is—when they like one."

"It's just because I like you that I want to resist," said Miss Tina with a nervous laugh."

"Oh I suspect you'll bring Miss Bordereau upstairs next to pay me a visit," I went on; to which the old lady replied:

"Oh no; I can keep an eye on you from here!"

"You're very tired; you'll certainly be ill to-night!" cried Miss Tina.

"Nonsense, dear; I feel better at this moment than I've done for a month. To-morrow I shall come out again. I want to be where I can see this clever gentleman."

"Shouldn't you perhaps see me better in your sitting-room?" I asked.

"Don't you mean shouldn't you have a better chance at *me?*" she returned, fixing me a moment with her green shade.

"Ah I haven't that anywhere! I look at you but don't see you."

"You agitate her dreadfully—and that's not good," said Miss Tina, giving me a reproachful deterrent headshake.

"I want to watch you—I want to watch you!" Miss Bordereau went on. "Well then let us spend as much of our time together as possible—I don't care where. That will give you every facility."

"Oh I've seen you enough for to-day. I'm satisfied. Now I'll go home," Juliana said. Miss Tina laid her hands on the back of the wheeled chair and began to push, but I begged her to let me take her place. "Oh yes, you may move me this way—you shan't in any other!" the old woman cried as she felt herself propelled firmly and easily over the smooth hard floor. Before we reached the door of her own apartment she bade me stop, and she took a long last look up and down the noble *sala*. "Oh it's a prodigious house!" she murmured; after which I pushed her forward. When we had entered the parlour Miss Tina let me know she should now be able to manage, and at the same moment the little red-haired *donna* came to meet her mistress. Miss Tina's idea was evidently to get her aunt immediately back to bed. I confess that in spite of this urgency I was guilty of the indiscretion of lingering; it held me there to feel myself so close to the objects I coveted—which would be probably put away somewhere in the faded unsociable room. The place had indeed a bareness that suggested no hidden values; there were neither dusky nooks nor curtained corners, neither massive cabinets nor chests with iron bands. Moreover it was possible, it was perhaps even likely, that the old lady had consigned her relics to her bedroom, to some battered box that was shoved under the bed, to the drawer of some lame dressing-table, where they would be in the range of vision by the dim night-lamp. None the less I turned an eye on every article of furniture, on every conceivable cover for a hoard, and noticed that there were half a dozen things with drawers, and in particular a tall old secretary with brass ornaments of the style of the Empire—a receptacle somewhat infirm but still capable of keeping rare secrets. I don't know why this article so engaged me, small purpose as I had of breaking into it; but I stared at it so hard that Miss Tina noticed me and changed colour. Her doing this made me think I was right and that, wherever they might have been before, the Aspern papers at that moment languished behind the peevish little lock of the secretary. It was hard to turn my attention from the dull mahogany front when I reflected that a plain panel divided me from the goal of my hopes; but I gathered up my slightly scattered prudence and with an effort took leave of my hostess. To make the effort graceful I said to her that I should certainly bring her an opinion about the little picture.

"The little picture?" Miss Tina asked in surprise.

"What do *you* know about it, my dear?" the old woman demanded. "You needn't mind. I've fixed my price."

"And what may that be?"

"A thousand pounds."

"Oh Lord!" cried poor Miss Tina irrepressibly.

"Is that what she talks to you about?" said Miss Bordereau.

"Imagine your aunt's wanting to know!" I had to separate from my younger friend with only those words, though I should have liked immensely to add: "For heaven's sake meet me to-night in the garden!"

VIII

As it turned out the precaution had not been needed, for three hours later, just as I had finished my dinner, Miss Tina appeared, unannounced, in the open doorway of the room in which my simple repasts were served. I remember well that I felt no surprise at seeing her; which is not a proof of my not believing in her timidity. It was immense, but in a case in which there was a particular reason for boldness it never would have prevented her from running up to my floor. I saw that she was now quite full of a particular reason; it threw her forward—made her seize me, as I rose to meet her, by the arm.

"My aunt's very ill; I think she's dying!"

"Never in the world," I answered bitterly. "Don't you be afraid!

"Do go for a doctor—do, do! Olimpia's gone for the one we always have, but she doesn't come back; I don't know what has happened to her. I told her that if he wasn't at home she was to follow him where he had gone; but apparently she following him all over Venice. I don't know what to do—she looks so as if she were sinking."

"May I see her, may I judge?" I asked. "Of course I shall be delighted to bring some one; but hadn't we better send my man instead, so that I may stay with you?"

Miss Tina assented to this and I dispatched my servant for the best doctor in the neighbourhood. I hurried downstairs with her, and on the way she told me that an hour after I quitted them in the afternoon Miss Bordereau had had an attack of "oppression," a terrible difficulty in breathing. This had subsided, but had left her so exhausted that she didn't come up: she seemed all spent and gone. I repeated that she wasn't gone, that she wouldn't go yet; whereupon Miss Tina gave me a sharper sidelong glance than she had ever favoured me withal and said: "Really, what do you mean? I suppose you don't accuse her of making-believe!" I forget what reply I made to this, but I fear that in my heart I thought the old woman capable of any weird manœuvre. Miss Tina wanted to know what I had done to her; her aunt had told her I had made her so angry. I declared I had done nothing whatever—I had been exceedingly careful; to which my companion rejoined that our friend had assured her she had a scene with me—a scene that had upset her. I answered with some resentment that the scene had been of *her* making—that I couldn't think what she was angry with me for unless for not seeing my way to give a thousand pounds for the portrait of Jeffrey Aspern. "And did she show you that? Oh gracious—oh deary me!" groaned Miss Tina, who seemed to feel the situation pass out of her control and the elements of her fate thickened round her. I answered her I'd give anything to possess it, yet that I had no thousand pounds; but I stopped when we came to the door of Miss Bordereau's room. I had an immense curiosity to pass it, but I thought it my duty to represent to Miss Tina that if I made the invalid angry she ought perhaps to be spared the sight of me. "The sight of you? Do you think she can *see?*" my companion demanded, almost with indignation. I did think so but forbore to say it, and I softly followed my conductress.

I remember that what I said to her as I stood for a moment beside the old woman's bed was: "Does she never show you her eyes then? Have you never seen them?" Miss Bordereau had been divested of her green shade, but—it was not my fortune to behold Juliana in her nightcap—the upper half of her face was covered by the fall of a piece of dingy lacelike muslin, a sort of extemporised hood which, wound round her head, descended to the end of her nose, leaving nothing visible but her white withered cheeks and puckered mouth, closed tightly and, as it were, consciously. Miss Tina gave me a glance of surprise, evidently not seeing a reason for my impatience. "You mean she always wears some-thing? She does it to preserve them."

"Because they're so fine?"

"Oh to-day, to-day!" And Miss Tina shook her head speaking very low. "But they used to be magnificent!"

"Yes indeed—we've Aspern's word for that." And as I looked again at the old woman's wrappings I could imagine her not having wished to al-low any supposition that the great poet had overdone it. But I didn't waste my time in considering Juliana, in whom the appearance of respira-tion was so slight as to suggest that no human attention could ever help her more. I turned my eyes once more all over the room, rummaging with them the closets, the chests of drawers, the tables. Miss Tina at once noted their direction and read, I think, what was in them; but she didn't answer it, turning away restlessly, anxiously, so that I felt rebuked, with reason, for an appetite well-nigh indecent in the presence of our dying companion. All the same I took another view, endeavouring to pick out mentally the receptacle to try first, for a person who should wish to put his hand in Miss Bordereau's papers directly after her death. The place was a dire confusion; it looked like the dressing-room of an old actress. There were clothes hanging over chairs, odd-looking shabby bundles here and there, and various pasteboard boxes piled together, battered, bulging and discoloured, which might have been fifty years old. Miss Tina after a moment noticed the direction of my eyes again, and, as if she guessed how I judged such appearances—forgetting I had no business to judge them at all—said, perhaps to defend herself from the imputation of complicity in the disorder:

"She likes it this way; we can't move things. There are old bandboxes she has had most of her life." Then she added, half-taking pity on my real thought: "Those things were *there*." And she pointed to a small low trunk which stood under a sofa that just allowed room for it. It struck me as a queer superannuated coffer, of painted wood, with elaborate handles and shrivelled straps and with the colour—it had last been endued with a coat of light green—much rubbed off. It evidently had travelled with Juliana in the olden time—in the days of her adventures, which it had shared. It would have made a strange figure arriving at a modern hotel.

"*Were* there—they aren't now?" I asked, startled by Miss Tina's implication.

She was going to answer, but at that moment the doctor came in—the doctor whom the little maid had been sent to fetch and whom she had at last overtaken. My servant, going on his own errand, had met her with her companion in tow, and in the sociable Venetian spirit, retracing his steps with them, had also come up to the threshold of the padrona's room, where I saw him peep over the doctor's shoulder. I motioned him away the more instantly that the sight of his prying face reminded me how little I myself had to do there—an admonition confirmed by the sharp way the little doctor eyed me, his air of taking me for a rival who had the field before him. He was a short fat brisk gentleman who wore the tall hat of his profession and seemed to look at everything but his patient. He kept me still in range, as if it struck him I too should be better for a dose, so that I bowed to him and left him with the women, going down to smoke a cigar in the garden. I was nervous; I couldn't go further; I couldn't leave the place. I don't know exactly what I thought might happen, but I felt it important to be there. I wandered about the alleys—the warm night had come on—smoking cigar after cigar and studying the light in Miss Bordereau's windows. They were open now, I could see; the situation was different. Sometimes the light moved, but not quickly; it didn't suggest the hurry of a crisis. Was the old woman dying or was she already dead? Had the doctor said that there was nothing to be done at her tremendous age but to let her quietly pass away? or had he simply announced with a look a little more conventional that the end of the end had come? Were the other two women just going and coming over the offices that follow in such a case? It made me uneasy not to be nearer, as if I thought the doctor himself might carry away the papers with him. I bit my cigar hard while it assailed me again that perhaps there were now no papers to carry!

I wandered about an hour and more. I looked out for Miss Tina at one of the windows, having a vague idea that she might come there to give me some sign. Wouldn't she see the red tip of my cigar in the dark and feel sure I was hanging on to know what the doctor had said? I'm afraid it's a proof of the grossness of my anxieties that I should have taken in some degree for granted at such an hour, in the midst of the greatest change that could fall on her, poor Miss Tina's having also a free mind for them. My servant came down and spoke to me; he knew nothing save that the doctor had gone after a visit of half an hour. If he had stayed half an hour then Miss Bordereau was still alive: it couldn't have taken so long to attest her decease. I sent the man out of the house; there were moments when the sense of his curiosity annoyed me, and this was one of them. *He* had been watching my cigar-tip from an upper window, if Miss Tina hadn't; he couldn't know what I was after and I couldn't tell him, though I suspected in him fantastic private theories about me which he thought fine and which, had I more exactly known them, I should have thought offensive.

I went upstairs at last, but I mounted no higher than the sala. The door of Miss Bordereau's apartment was open, showing from the parlour the dimness of a poor candle. I went toward it with a light tread, and at the same moment Miss Tina appeared and stood looking at me as I approached. "She's better, she's better," she said even before I had asked. "The doctor has given her something; she woke up, came back to life while he was there. He says there's no immediate danger."

"No immediate danger? Surely he thinks her condition serious!"

"Yes, because she had been excited. That affects her dreadfully."

"It will do so again then, because she works herself up. She did so this afternoon."

"Yes, she mustn't come out any more," said Miss Tina with one of her lapses into a deeper detachment.

"What's the use of making such a remark as that," I permitted myself to ask, "if you begin to rattle her about again the first time she bids you?"

"I won't—I won't do it any more."

"You must learn to resist her," I went on.

"Oh yes, I shall; I shall do so better if you tell me it's right."

"You mustn't do it for me—you must do it for yourself. It all comes back to you, if you're scared and upset."

"Well, I'm not upset now," said Miss Tina placidly enough. "She's very quiet."

"Is she conscious again—does she speak?"

"No, she doesn't speak, but she takes my hand. She holds it fast."

"Yes," I returned, "I can see what force she still has by the way she grabbed that picture this afternoon. But if she holds you fast how comes it that you're here?"

Miss Tina waited a little; though her face was in deep shadow—she had her back to the light in the parlour and I had put down my own candle far off, near the door of the sala—I thought I saw her smile ingenuously. "I came on purpose—I had heard your step."

"Why I came on tiptoe, as soundlessly as possible."

"Well, I had heard you," said Miss Tina.

"And is your aunt alone now?"

"Oh no—Olimpia sits there."

On my side I debated. "Shall we then pass in there?" And I nodded at the parlour; I wanted more and more to be on the spot.

"We can't talk there—she'll hear us."

I was on the point of replying that in that case we'd sit silent, but I felt too much this wouldn't do, there was something I desired so immensely to ask her. Thus I hinted we might walk a little in the sala, keeping more at the other end, where we shouldn't disturb our friend. Miss Tina assented unconditionally; the doctor was coming again, she said, and she would be there to meet him at the door. We strolled through the fine superfluous hall, where on the marble floor—particularly as at first we said nothing—our footsteps were more audible than I had expected. When we reached the other end—the wide window, inveterately closed, connecting with the balcony that overhung the canal—I submitted that we had best remain there, as she would see the doctor arrive the sooner. I opened the window and we passed out on the balcony. The air of the canal seemed even heavier, hotter than that of the sala. The place was hushed and void; the quiet neighborhood had gone to sleep. A lamp, here and there, over the narrow black water, glimmered in double; the voice of a man going homeward singing, his jacket on his shoulder and his hat on his ear, came to us from a distance. This didn't prevent the scene from being very *comme il faut*, as Miss Bordereau had called it the first time I saw her. Presently a gondola passed along the canal with its slow rhythmical plash, and as we listened we watched it in silence. It didn't stop, it didn't carry the doctor; and after it had gone on I said to Miss Tina:

"And where are they now—the things that were in the trunk?"

"In the trunk?"

"That green box you pointed out to me in her room. You said her papers had been there; you seemed to mean she had transferred them."

"Oh yes; they're not in the trunk," said Miss Tina.

"May I ask if you've looked?"

"Yes, I've looked—for you."

"How for me, dear Miss Tina? Do you mean you'd have given them to me if you had found them?"—and I fairly trembled with the question. She delayed to reply and I waited. Suddenly she broke out: "I don't know what I'd do—what I wouldn't!"

"Would you look again—somewhere else?"

She had spoken with a strange unexpected emotion, and she went on in the same tone: "I can't—I can't—while she lies there. It isn't decent."

"No, it isn't decent," I replied gravely. "Let the poor lady rest in peace." And the words, on my lips, were not hypocritical, for I felt reprimanded and shamed.

Miss Tina added in a moment, as if she had guessed this and were sorry for me, but at the same time wished to explain that I did push her, or at least harp on the chord, too much: "I can't deceive her that way. I can't deceive her—perhaps on her deathbed."

"Heaven forbid I should ask you, though I've been guilty myself!"

"You've been guilty?"

"I've sailed under false colours." I felt now I must make a clean breast of it, must tell her I had given her an invented name on account of my fear her aunt would have heard of me and so refuse to take me in. I explained this as well as that I had really been a party to the letter addressed them by John Cumnor months before.

She listened with great attention, almost in fact gaping for wonder, and when I had made my confession she said: "Then your real name—what is it?" She repeated it over twice when I had told her, accompanying it with the exclamation "Gracious, gracious!" Then she added: "I like your own best."

"So do I,"—and I felt my laugh rueful. "Ouf! it's a relief to get rid of the other."

"So it was a regular plot—a kind of conspiracy?"

"Oh a conspiracy—we were only two," I replied, leaving out of course Mrs. Prest.

She considered; I thought she was perhaps going to pronounce us very base. But this was not her way, and she remarked after a moment, as in candid impartial contemplation: "How much you must want them!"

"Oh I do, passionately!" I grinned, I fear to admit. And this chance made me go on, forgetting my compunction of a moment before. "How can she possibly have changed their place herself? How can she walk? How can she arrive at that sort of muscular exertion? How can she lift and carry things?"

"Oh when one wants and when one has so much will!" said Miss Tina as if she had thought over my question already herself and had simply had no choice but that answer—the idea that in the dead of night, or at some moment when the coast was clear, the old woman had been capable of a miraculous effort.

"Have you questioned Olimpia? Hasn't she helped her—hasn't she done it for her?" I asked; to which my friend replied promptly and positively that their servant had had nothing to do with the matter, though without admitting definitely that she had spoken to her. It was as if she were a little shy, a little ashamed now, of letting me see how much she had entered into my uneasiness and had me on her mind. Suddenly she said to me without any immediate relevance:

"I rather feel you a new person, you know, now that you've a new name."

"It isn't a new one; it's a very good old one, thank fortune!"

She looked at me a moment. "Well, I do like it better."

"Oh if you didn't I would almost go on with the other!"

"Would you really?"

I laughed again, but I returned for all answer: "Of course if she can rummage about that way she can perfectly have burnt them."

"You must wait—you must wait," Miss Tina mournfully moralised; and her tone ministered little to my patience, for it seemed after all to accept that wretched possibility. I would teach myself to wait, I declared nevertheless; because in the first place I couldn't do otherwise and in the second I had her promise, given me the other night, that she would help me.

"Of course if the papers are gone that's no use," she said; not as if she wished to recede, but only to be conscientious.

"Naturally. But if you could only find out!" I groaned, quivering again.

"I thought you promised you'd wait."

"Oh you mean wait even for that?"

"For what then?"

"Ah, nothing," I answered rather foolishly, being ashamed to tell her what had been implied in my acceptance of delay—the idea that she would perhaps do more for me than merely find out.

I know not if she guessed this; at all events she seemed to bethink herself of some propriety of showing me more rigour. "I didn't promise to deceive, did I? I don't think I did."

"It doesn't much matter whether you did or not, for you couldn't!"

Nothing is more possible than that she wouldn't have contested this even hadn't she been diverted by our seeing the doctor's gondola shoot into the little canal and approach the house. I noted that he came as fast as if he believed our proprietress still in danger. We looked down at him while he disembarked and then went back into the sala to meet him. When he came up, however, I naturally left Miss Tina to go off with him alone, only asking her leave to come back later for news.

I went out of the house and walked far, as far as the Piazza, where my restlessness declined to quit me. I was unable to sit down; it was very late now though there were people still at the little tables in front of the cafés: I could but uneasily revolve, and I did so half a dozen times. The only comfort, none the less, was in my having told Miss Tina who I really was. At last I took my way home again, getting gradually and all but inextricably lost, as I did whenever I went out in Venice: so that it was considerably past midnight when I reached my door. The sala, upstairs, was as dark as usual and my lamp as I crossed it found nothing satisfactory to show me. I was disappointed, for I had notified Miss Tina that I would come back for a report, and I thought she might have left a light there as a sign. The door of the ladies' apartment was closed; which seemed a hint that my faltering friend had gone to bed in impatience of waiting for me. I stood in the middle of the place, considering, hoping she would hear me and perhaps peep out, saying to myself too that she would never go to bed with her aunt in a state so critical; she would sit up and watch—she would be in a chair, in her dressing-gown. I went nearer the door; I stopped there and listened. I heard nothing at all and at last I tapped gently. No answer came and after another minute I turned the handle. There was no light in the room; this ought to have prevented my entrance, but it had no such effect. If I have frankly stated the importunities, the indelicacies, of which my desire to possess myself of Jeffrey Aspern's papers had made me capable I needn't shrink, it seems to me, from confessing this last indiscretion. I regard it as the worst thing I did, yet there were extenuating circumstances. I was deeply though doubtless not disinterestedly anxious for more news of

Juliana, and Miss Tina had accepted from me, as it were, a rendezvous which it might have been a point of honour with me to keep. It may be objected that her leaving the place dark was a positive sign that she released me, and to this I can only reply that I wished not to be released.

The door to Miss Bordereau's room was open and I could see beyond it the faintness of a taper. There was no sound—my footstep caused no one to stir. I came further into the room; I lingered there lamp in hand. I wanted to give Miss Tina a chance to come to me if, as I couldn't doubt, she were still with her aunt. I made no noise to call her; I only waited to see if she wouldn't notice my light. She didn't, and I explained this—I found afterwards I was right—by the idea that she had fallen asleep. If she had fallen asleep her aunt was not on her mind, and my explanation ought to have led me to go out as I had come. I must repeat again that it didn't, for I found myself at the same moment given up to something else. I had no definite purpose, no bad intention, but felt myself held to the spot by an acute, though absurd, sense of opportunity. Opportunity for what I couldn't have said, inasmuch as it wasn't in my mind that I might proceed to thievery. Even had this tempted me I was confronted with the evident fact that Miss Bordereau didn't leave her secretary, her cupboard and the drawers of her tables gaping. I had no keys, no tools and no ambition to smash her furniture. None the less it came to me that I was now, perhaps alone, unmolested, at the hour of freedom and safety, nearer to the source of my hopes than I had ever been. I held up my lamp, let the light play on the different objects as if it could tell me something. Still there came no movement from the other room. If Miss Tina was sleeping she was sleeping sound. Was she doing so—generous creature—on purpose to leave me the field? Did she know I was there and was just keeping quiet to see what I would do—what I *could* do? Yet might I, when it came to that? She herself knew even better than I how little.

I stopped in front of the secretary, gaping at it vainly and no doubt grotesquely; for what had it to say to me after all? In the first place it was locked, and in the second it almost surely contained nothing in which I was interested. Ten to one the papers had been destroyed, and even if they hadn't the keen old woman wouldn't have put them in such a place as that after removing them from the green trunk—wouldn't have transferred them, with the idea of their safety on her brain, from the better hiding-place to the worse. The secretary was more conspicuous, more exposed in a room in which she could no longer mount guard. It opened with a key, but there was a small brass handle, like a button as well; I saw this as I played my lamp over it. I did something more, for the climax of my crisis; I caught a glimpse of the possibility that Miss Tina wished me really to understand. If she didn't so wish me, if she wished me to keep away, why hadn't she locked the door of communication between the sitting-room and the sala? That would have been a definite sign that I was to leave them alone. If I didn't leave them alone she meant me to come for a purpose—a purpose now represented by the super-subtle inference that to oblige me she had unlocked the secretary. She hadn't left the key, but the lid would probably move if I touched the button. This possibility pressed me hard and I bent very close to judge. I didn't propose to do anything, not even—not in the least—to let down the lid; I only wanted to test my theory, to see if the cover *would* move. I touched the button with my hand—a mere touch would tell me; and as I did so— it is embarrassing for me to relate it—I looked over my shoulder. It was a chance, an instinct, for I had really heard nothing. I almost let my luminary drop and certainly I stepped back, straightening myself up at what I saw. Juliana stood there in her nightdress, by the doorway of her room, watching me; her hands were raised, she had lifted the everlasting curtain that covered half her face, and for the first, the last, the only time I beheld her extraordinary eyes. They glared at me; they were like the sudden drench, for a caught burglar, of a flood of gaslight; they made me horribly ashamed. I never shall forget her strange little bent white tottering figure, with its lifted head, her attitude, her expression; neither shall I forget the tone in which as I turned, looking at her, she hissed out passionately, furiously:

"Ah you publishing scoundrel!"

I can't now say what I stammered to excuse myself, to explain; but I went toward her to tell her I meant no harm. She waved me off with her old hands, retreating before me in horror; and the next thing I knew she had fallen back with a quick spasm, as if death had descended on her, into Miss Tina's arms.

IX

I left Venice the next morning, directly on learning that my hostess had not succumbed, as I feared at the moment, to the shock I had given her—the shock I may also say she had given me. How in the world could I have supposed her capable of getting out of bed by herself? I failed to see Miss Tina before going; I only saw the *donna*, whom I entrusted with a note for her younger mistress. In this note I mentioned that I should be absent but a few days. I went to Treviso, to Bassano, to Castelfranco; I took walks and drives and looked at musty old churches with ill-lighted pictures; I spent hours seated smoking at the doors of cafés, where there were flies and yellow curtains, on the shady side of sleepy little squares. In spite of these pastimes, which were mechanical and perfunctory, I scantly enjoyed my travels: I had had to gulp down a bitter draught and couldn't get rid of the taste. It had been devilish awkward, as the young men say, to be found by Juliana in the dead of night examining the attachment of her bureau; and it had not been less so to have to believe for a good many hours after that it was highly probable I had killed her. My humiliation galled me, but I had to make the best of it, had, in writing to Miss Tina to minimise it, as well as account for the posture in which I had been discovered. As she gave me no word of answer I couldn't know what impression I made on her. It rankled for me that I had been called a publishing scoundrel, since certainly I did publish and no less certainly hadn't been very delicate. There was a moment when I stood convinced that the only way to purge my dishonour was to take myself straight away on the instant; to sacrifice my hopes and relieve the two poor women for ever of the oppression of my intercourse. Then I reflected that I had better try a short absence first, for I must already have had a sense (unexpressed and dim) that in disappearing completely it wouldn't be merely my own hopes I should condemn to extinction. It would perhaps answer if I kept dark long enough to give the elder lady time to believe herself rid of me. That she would wish to be rid of me after this—if I wasn't rid of her—was now not to be doubted: that midnight monstrosity would have cured her of the disposition to put up with my company for the sake of my dollars. I said to myself that after all I couldn't abandon Miss Tina, and I continued to say this even while I noted that she quite ignored my earnest request—I had given her two or three addresses, at little towns, *poste restante*—for some sign of her actual state. I would have made my servant write me news but that he was unable to manage a pen. Couldn't I measure the scorn of Miss Tina's silence—little disdainful as she had ever been? Really the soreness pressed; yet if I had scruples about going back I had others about not doing so, and I wanted to put myself on a better footing. The end of it was that I did return to Venice on the twelfth day; and as my gondola gently bumped against our palace steps a fine palpitation of suspense showed me the violence my absence had done me.

I had faced about so abruptly that I hadn't even telegraphed to my servant. He was therefore not at the station to meet me, but he poked out his head from an upper window when I reached the house. "They have put her into earth, *quella vecchia*," he said to me in the lower hall while he shouldered my valise; and he grinned and almost winked as if he knew I should be pleased with his news.

"She's dead!" I cried, giving him a very different look.

"So it appears, since they've buried her."

"It's all over then? When was the funeral?"

"The other yesterday. But a funeral you could scarcely call it, signore: *roba da niente—un piccolo passeggio brutto* of two gondolas. Poveretta!" the man continued, referring apparently to Miss Tina. His conception of funerals was that they were mainly to amuse the living.

I wanted to know about Miss Tina, how she might be and generally where; but I asked him no more questions till we had got upstairs. Now that the fact had met me I took a bad view of it, especially of the idea that poor Miss Tina had had to manage by herself after the end. What did she know about arrangements, about the steps to take in such a case? Poveretta indeed! I could only hope the doctor had given her support and that she hadn't been neglected by the old friends of whom she had told me, the little band of the faithful whose fidelity consisted in coming

to the house once a year. I elicited from my servant that two old ladies
and an old gentleman had in fact rallied round Miss Tina and had supported her—they had come for her in a gondola of their own—during the
journey to the cemetery, the little red-walled island of tombs which lies
to the north of the town and on the way to Murano. It appeared from
these signs that the Misses Bordereau were Catholics, a discovery I had
never made, as the old woman couldn't go to church and her niece, so
far as I perceived, either didn't, or went only to early mass in the parish
before I was stirring. Certainly even the priests respected their seclusion;
I had never caught the whisk of the curato's skirt. That evening, an hour
later, I sent my servant down with five words on a card to ask if Miss
Tina would see me for a few moments. She was not in the house, where
he had sought her, he told me when he came back, but in the garden
walking about to refresh herself and picking the flowers quite as if they
belonged to her. He had found her there and she would be happy to
see me.

I went down and passed half an hour with poor Miss Tina. She had
always had a look of musty mourning, as if she were wearing out old
robes of sorrow that wouldn't come to an end; and in this particular she
made no different show. But she clearly had been crying, crying a great
deal—simply, satisfyingly, refreshingly, with a primitive retarded sense of
solitude and violence. But she had none of the airs or graces of grief,
and I was almost surprised to see her stand there in the first dusk with her
hands full of admirable roses and smile at me with reddened eyes. Her
white face, in the frame of her mantilla, looked longer, leaner than usual.
I hadn't doubted her being irreconcilably disgusted with me, her considering I ought to have been on the spot to advise her, to help her; and,
though I believed there was no rancour in her composition and no great
conviction of the importance of her affairs, I had prepared myself for a
change in her manner, for some air of injury and estrangement, which
should say to my conscience: "Well, you're a nice person to have professed things!" But historic truth compels me to declare that this poor
lady's dull face ceased to be dull, almost ceased to be plain, as she turned
it gladly to her late aunt's lodger. That touched him extremely and he
thought it simplified his situation until he found it didn't. I was as kind
to her that evening as I knew how to be, and I walked about the garden
with her as long as seemed good. There was no explanation of any sort
between us; I didn't ask her why she hadn't answered my letter. Still less
did I repeat what I had said to her in that communication; if she chose
to let me suppose she had forgotten the position in which Miss Bordereau
had surprised me and the effect of the discovery on the old woman, I
was quite willing to take it that way: I was grateful to her for not treating me as if I had killed her aunt.

We strolled and strolled, though really not much passed between us
save the recognition of her bereavement, conveyed in my manner and in
the expression she had of depending on me now, since I let her see I still

took an interest in her. Miss Tina's was no breast for the pride or the pretense of independence; she didn't in the least suggest that she knew at present what would become of her. I forbore to press on that question, however, for I certainly was not prepared to say that I would take charge of her. I was cautious; not ignobly, I think, for I felt her knowledge of life to be so small that in her unsophisticated vision there would be no reason why—since I seemed to pity her—I shouldn't somehow look after her. She told me how her aunt had died, very peacefully at the last, and how everything had been done afterwards by the care of her good friends—fortunately, thanks to me, she said, smiling, there was money in the house. She repeated that when once the "nice" Italians like you they are your friends for life, and when we had gone into this she asked me about my *giro*, my impressions, my adventures, the places I had seen. I told her what I could, making it up partly, I'm afraid, as in my disconcerted state I had taken little in; and after she had heard me she exclaimed, quite as if she had forgotten her aunt and her sorrow, "Dear, dear, how much I should like to do such things—to take an amusing little journey!" It came over me for the moment that I ought to propose some enterprise, say I would accompany her anywhere she liked; and I remarked at any rate that a pleasant excursion—to give her a change— might be managed; we would think of it, talk it over. I spoke never a word of the Aspern documents, asked no question as to what she had ascertained or what had otherwise happened with regard to them before Juliana's death. It wasn't that I wasn't on pins and needles to know, but that I thought it more decent not to show greed again so soon after the catastrophe. I hoped she herself would say something, but she never glanced that way, and I thought this natural at the time. Later on, however, that night, it occurred to me that her silence was matter for suspicion; since if she had talked of my movements, of anything so detached as the Giorgione at Castelfranco, she might have alluded to what she could easily remember was in my mind. It was not to be supposed that the emotion produced by her aunt's death had blotted out the recollection that I was interested in that lady's relics, and I fidgeted afterwards as it came to me that her reticence might very possibly just mean that no relics survived. We separated in the garden—it was she who said she must go in; now that she was alone on the *piano nobile* I felt that (judged at any rate by Venetian ideas) I was on rather a different footing in regard to the invasion of it. As I shook hands with her for good-night I asked her if she had some general plan, had thought over what she had best do. "Oh yes, oh yes, but I haven't settled anything yet," she replied quite cheerfully. Was her cheerfulness explained by the impression that I would settle for her?

I was glad the next morning that we had neglected practical questions, as this gave me a pretext for seeing her again immediately. There was a practical enough question now to be touched on. I owed it to her to let her know formally that of course I didn't expect her to keep me on as a lodger, as also to show some interest in her own tenure, what she might have on her hands in the way of a lease. But I was not destined, as befell, to converse with her for more than an instant on either of these points. I sent her no message; I simply went down to the sala and walked to and fro there. I knew she would come out; she would promptly see me accessible. Somehow I preferred not to be shut up with her; gardens and big halls seemed better places to talk. It was a splendid morning, with something in the air that told of the waning of the long Venetian summer; a freshness from the sea that stirred the flowers in the garden and made a pleasant draught in the house, less shuttered and darkened now than when the old woman was alive. It was the beginning of autumn, of the end of the golden months. With this it was the end of my experiment—or would be in the course of half an hour, when I should really have learned that my dream had been reduced to ashes. After that there would be nothing left for me but to go to the station; for seriously—and as it struck me in the morning light—I couldn't linger there to act as guardian to a piece of middle-aged female helplessness. If she hadn't saved the papers wherein should I be indebted to her? I think I winced a little as I asked myself how much, if she *had* saved them, I should have to recognise and, as it were, reward such a courtesy. Mightn't that service after all saddle me with a guardianship? If this idea didn't make me more uncomfortable as I walked up and down it was because I was convinced I had nothing to look to. If the old woman hadn't destroyed everything before she pounced on me in the parlour she had done so the next day.

It took Miss Tina rather longer than I had expected to act on my calculation; but when at last she came out she looked at me without surprise. I mentioned I had been waiting for her and she asked why I hadn't let her know. I was glad a few hours later on that I had checked myself before remarking that a friendly intuition might have told her: it turned to comfort for me that I hadn't played even to that mild extent on her sensibility. What I did say was virtually the truth—that I was too nervous, since I expected her now to settle my fate.

"Your fate?" said Miss Tina, giving me a queer look; and as she spoke I noticed a rare change in her. Yes, she was other than she had been the evening before—less natural and less easy. She had been crying the day before and was not crying now, yet she struck me as less confident. It was as if something had happened to her during the night, or at least as if she had thought of something that troubled her—something in particular that affected her relations with me, made them more embarrassing and more complicated. Had she simply begun to feel that her aunt's not being there now altered my position?

"I mean about our papers. *Are* there any? You must know now."

"Yes, there are a great many; more than I supposed." I was struck with the way her voice trembled as she told me this.

"Do you mean you've got them in there—and that I may see them?"

"I don't think you can see them," said Miss Tina, with an extraordinary expression of entreaty in her eyes, as if the dearest hope she had in the world now was that I wouldn't take them from her. But how could she expect me to make such a sacrifice as that after all that had passed between us? What had I come back to Venice for but to see them, to take them? My joy at learning they were still in existence was such that if the poor woman had gone down on her knees to beseech me never to mention them again I would have treated the proceeding as a bad joke. "I've got them but I can't show them," she lamentably added.

"Not even to me? Ah Miss Tina!" I broke into a tone of infinite remonstrance and reproach.

She coloured and the tears came back to her eyes; I measured the anguish it cost her to take such a stand which a dreadful sense of duty had imposed on her. It made me quite sick to find myself confronted with that particular obstacle; all the more that it seemed to me I had been distinctly encouraged to leave it out of account. I quite held Miss Tina to have assured me that if she had no greater hindrance than that——! "You don't mean to say you made her a death-bed promise? It was precisely against your doing anything of that sort that I thought I was safe. Oh I would rather she had burnt the papers outright than have to reckon with such a treachery as that."

"No, it isn't a promise," said Miss Tina.

"Pray what is it then?"

She hung fire, but finally said: "She tried to burn them, but I prevented it. She had hid them in her bed."

"In her bed—?"

"Between the mattresses. That's where she put them when she took them out of the trunk. I can't understand how she did it, because Olimpia didn't help her. She tells me so and I believe her. My aunt only told her afterwards, so that she shouldn't undo the bed—anything but the sheets. So it was very badly made," added Miss Tina simply.

"I should think so! And how did she try to burn them?"

"She didn't try much; she was too weak those last days. But she told me—she charged me. Oh it was terrible! She couldn't speak after that night. She could only make signs."

"And what did you do?"

"I took them away. I locked them up."

"In the secretary?"

"Yes, in the secretary," said Miss Tina, reddening again.

"Did you tell her you'd burn them?"

"No, I didn't—on purpose."

"On purpose to gratify me?"

"Yes, only for that."

"And what good will you have done me if after all you won't show them?"

"Oh none. I know that—I know that," she dismally sounded.

"And did she believe you had destroyed them?"

"I don't know what she believed at the last. I couldn't tell—she was too far gone."

"Then if there was no promise and no assurance I can't see what ties you."

"Oh she hated it so—she hated it so! She was so jealous. But here's the portrait—you may have that," the poor woman announced, taking the little picture, wrapped up in the same manner in which her aunt had wrapped it, out of her pocket.

"I may have it—do you mean you give it to me?" I gasped as it passed into my hand.

"Oh yes."

"But it's worth money—a large sum."

"Well!" said Miss Tina, still with her strange look.

I didn't know what to make of it, for it could scarcely mean that she wanted to bargain like her aunt. She spoke as for making me a present. "I can't take it from you as a gift," I said, "and yet I can't afford to pay you for it according to the idea Miss Bordereau had of its value. She rated it at a thousand pounds."

"Couldn't we sell it?" my friend threw off.

"God forbid! I prefer the picture to the money."

"Well then keep it."

"You're very generous."

"So are you."

"I don't know why you should think so," I returned; and this was true enough, for the good creature appeared to have in her mind some rich reference that I didn't in the least seize.

"Well, you've made a great difference for me," she said.

I looked at Jeffrey Aspern's face in the little picture, partly in order not to look at that of my companion, which had begun to trouble me, even to frighten me a little—it had taken so very odd, so strained and unnatural a cast. I made no answer to this last declaration; I but privately consulted Jeffrey Aspern's delightful eyes with my own—they were so young and brilliant yet so wise and so deep; I asked him what on earth was the matter with Miss Tina. He seemed to smile at me with mild mockery; he might have been amused at my case. I had got into a pickle for him—as if he needed it! He was unsatisfactory for the only moment since I had known him. Nevertheless, now that I held the little picture in my hand I felt it would be a precious possession. "Is this a bribe to make me give up the papers?" I presently and all perversely asked. "Much as I value this, you know, if I were to be obliged to choose the papers are what I should prefer. Ah but ever so much!"

"How can you choose—how can you choose?" Miss Tina returned slowly and woefully.

"I see! Of course there's nothing to be said if you regard the interdiction that rules on you as quite insurmountable. In this case it must seem

to you that to part with them would be an impiety of the worst kind, a
simple sacrilege!"

She shook her head, only lost in the queerness of her case. "You'd understand if you had known her. I'm afraid," she quavered suddenly—
"I'm afraid! She was terrible when she was angry."

"Yes, I saw something of that, that night. She was terrible. Then I saw
her eyes. Lord, they were fine!"

"I see them—they stare at me in the dark!" said Miss Tina.

"You've grown nervous with all you've been through."

"Oh yes, very—very!"

"You mustn't mind; that will pass away," I said kindly. Then I added
resignedly, for it really seemed to me that I must accept the situation:
"Well, so it is, and it can't be helped. I must renounce." My friend, at this,
with her eyes on me, gave a low soft moan, and I went on: "I only wish
to goodness she had destroyed them; then there would be nothing more
to say. And I can't understand why, with her ideas, she didn't."

"Oh she lived on them!" said Miss Tina.

"You can imagine whether that makes me want less to see them," I returned not quite so desperately. "But don't let me stand here as if I had
it in my soul to tempt you to anything base. Naturally, you understand,
I give up my rooms. I leave Venice immediately." And I took up my hat,
which I had placed on a chair. We were still rather awkwardly on our
feet in the middle of the sala. She had left the door of the apartments
open behind her, but had not led me that way.

A strange spasm came into her face as she saw me take my hat. "Immediately—do you mean to-day?" The tone of the words was tragic—
they were a cry of desolation.

"Oh no; not so long as I can be of the least service to you."

"Well, just a day or two more—just two or three days," she panted.
Then controlling herself she added in another manner: "She wanted to
say something to me—the last day—something very particular. But she
couldn't."

"Something very particular?"

"Something more about the papers."

"And did you guess—have you any idea?"

"No, I've tried to think—but I don't know. I've thought all kinds of
things."

"As for instance?"

"Well, that if you were a relation it would be different."

I wondered. "If I were a relation—?"

"If you weren't a stranger. Then it would be the same for you as for
me. Anything that's mine would be yours, and you could do what you
like. I shouldn't be able to prevent you—and you'd have no responsibility."

She brought out this droll explanation with a nervous rush and as if
speaking words got by heart. They gave me an impression of a subtlety

which at first I failed to follow. But after a moment her face helped me to see further, and then the queerest of light came to me. It was embarrassing, and I bent my head over Jeffrey Aspern's portrait. What an odd expression was in his face! "Get out of it as you can, my dear fellow!" I put the picture into the pocket of my coat and said to Miss Tina: "Yes, I'll sell it for you. I shan't get a thousand pounds by any means, but I shall get something good."

She looked at me through pitiful tears, but seemed to try to smile as she returned: "We can divide the money."

"No, no, it shall be all yours." Then I went on: "I think I know what your poor aunt wanted to say. She wanted to give directions that the papers should be buried with her."

Miss Tina appeared to weigh this suggestion; after which she answered with striking decision, "Oh no, she wouldn't have thought that safe!"

"It seems to me nothing could be safer."

"She had an idea that when people want to publish they're capable—!" And she paused, very red.

"Of violating a tomb? Mercy on us, what must she have thought of me!"

"She wasn't just, she wasn't generous!" my companion cried with sudden passion.

The light that had come into my mind a moment before spread further. "Ah don't say that, for we *are* a dreadful race." Then I pursued: "If she left a will that may give you some idea."

"I've found nothing of the sort—she destroyed it. She was very fond of me," Miss Tina added with an effect of extreme inconsequence. "She wanted me to be happy. And if any person should be kind to me—she wanted to speak of that."

I was almost awestricken by the astuteness with which the good lady found herself inspired, transparent astuteness as it was and stitching, as the phrase is, with white thread. "Depend upon it she didn't want to make any provision that would be agreeable to *me*."

"No, not to you, but quite to me. She knew I should like it if you could carry out your idea. Not because she cared for you, but because she did think of me," Miss Tina went on with her unexpected persuasive volubility. "You could see the things—you could use them." She stopped, seeing I grasped the sense of her conditional—stopped long enough for me to give some sign that I didn't give. She must have been conscious, however, that though my face showed the greatest embarrassment ever painted on a human countenance it was not set as a stone, it was also full of compassion. It was a comfort to me a long time afterwards to consider that she couldn't have seen in me the smallest symptom of disrespect. "I don't know what to do; I'm too tormented, I'm too ashamed!" she continued with vehemence. Then turning away from me and burying her face in her hands she burst into a flood of tears. If she didn't know what to do it may be imagined whether I knew better. I stood there dumb, watching her while her sobs resounded in the great empty hall. In a moment she was up at me again with her streaming eyes. "I'd give you everything, and she'd understand, where she is—she'd forgive me!"

"Ah Miss Tina—ah Miss Tina," I stammered for all reply. I didn't know what to do, as I say, but at a venture I made a wild vague movement in consequence of which I found myself at the door. I remember standing there and saying, "It wouldn't do, it wouldn't do!"—saying it pensively, awkwardly, grotesquely, while I looked away to the opposite end of the sala as at something very interesting. The next thing I remembered is that I was downstairs and out of the house. My gondola was there and my gondolier, reclining on the cushions, sprang up as soon as he saw me. I jumped in and to his usual "*Dove commanda?*" replied, in a tone that made him stare: "Anywhere, anywhere; out into the lagoon!"

He rowed me away and I sat there prostrate, groaning softly to myself, my hat pulled over my brow. What in the name of the preposterous did she mean if she didn't mean to offer me her hand? That was the price—that was the price! And did she think I wanted it, poor deluded infatuated extravagant lady? My gondolier, behind me, must have seen my ears red as I wondered, motionless there under the fluttering *tenda* with my hidden face, noticing nothing as we passed—wondered whether her delusion, her infatuation had been my own reckless work. Did she think I had made love to her even to get the papers? I hadn't, I hadn't; I repeated that over to myself for an hour, for two hours, till I was wearied if not convinced. I don't know where, on the lagoon, my gondolier took me; we floated aimlessly and with slow rare strokes. At last I became conscious that we were near the Lido, far up, on the right hand, as you turn your back to Venice, and I made him put me ashore. I wanted to walk, to move, to shed some of my bewilderment. I crossed the narrow strip and got to the sea-beach—I took my way toward Malamocco. But presently I flung myself down again on the warm sand, in the breeze, on the coarse dry grass. It took it out of me to think I had been so much at fault, that I had unwittingly but nonetheless deplorably trifled. But I hadn't given her cause—distinctly I hadn't. I had said to Mrs. Prest that I would make love to her; but it had been a joke without consequences and I had never said it to my victim. I had been as kind as possible because I really liked her; but since when had that become a crime where a woman of such an age and such an appearance was concerned? I am far from remembering clearly the succession of events and feelings during this long day of confusion, which I spent entirely in wandering about, without going home, until late at night; it only comes back to me that there were moments when I pacified my conscience and others when I lashed it into pain. I didn't laugh all day—that I do recollect; the case, however it might have struck others, seemed to me so little amusing. I should have been better employed perhaps in taking in the comic side of it. At any rate, whether I had given cause or not, there was no doubt whatever that I couldn't pay the price. I couldn't accept the proposal. I couldn't, for a bundle of tattered papers, marry a ridiculous pathetic provincial old woman. It was a proof of how little she supposed the idea would come to me that she should have decided to suggest it herself in that practical argumentative heroic way—with the timidity, however, so much more striking than the boldness, that her reasons appeared to come first and her feelings afterward.

As the day went on I grew to wish I had never heard of Aspern's relics, and I cursed the extravagant curiosity that had put John Cumnor on the scent of them. We had more than enough material without them, and my predicament was the just punishment of that most fatal of human follies, our not having known when to stop. It was very well to say it was no predicament, that the way out was simple, that I had only to leave Venice by the first train in the morning, after addressing Miss Tina a note which should be placed in her hand as soon as I got clear of the house; for it was strong proof of my quandary that when I tried to make up the note to my taste in advance—I would put it on paper as soon as I got home, before going to bed—I couldn't think of anything but "How can I thank you for the rare confidence you've placed in me?" That would never do; it sounded exactly as if an acceptance were to follow. Of course I might get off without writing at all, but that would be brutal, and my idea was still to exclude brutal solutions. As my confusion cooled I lost myself in wonder at the importance I had attached to Juliana's crumpled scraps; the thought of them became odious to me and I was as vexed with the old witch for the superstition that had prevented her from destroying them as I was with myself for having already spent more money than I could afford in attempting to control their fate. I forget what I did, where I went after leaving the Lido, and at what hour or with what recovery of composure I made my way back to my boat. I only know that in the afternoon, when the air was aglow with the sunset, I was standing before the church of Saints John and Paul and looking up at the small square-jawed face of Bartolommeo Colleoni, the terrible *condottiere* who sits so sturdily astride of his huge bronze horse on the high pedestal on which Venetian gratitude maintains him. The statue is incomparable, the finest of all mounted figures, unless that of Marcus Aurelius, who rides benignant before the Roman Capitol, be finer: but I was not thinking of that; I only found myself staring at the triumphant captain as if he had had an oracle on his lips. The western light shines into all his grimness at that hour and makes it wonderfully personal. But he continued to look far over my head, at the red immersion of another day—he had seen so many go down into the lagoon through the centuries—and if he were thinking of battles and stratagems they were of a different quality from any I had to tell him of. He couldn't direct me what to do, gaze up at him as I might. Was it before this or after that I wandered about for an hour in the small canals, to the continued stupefaction of my gondolier, who had never seen me so restless and yet so void of a purpose and could extract from me no order but "Go anywhere—everywhere—all over the place?" He reminded me that I had not lunched and expressed therefore respectfully the hope that I would dine earlier. He had had long periods of leisure during the day, when I had left the boat and rambled, so that I was not obliged to consider him, and I told him that till the morrow, for reasons, I should touch no meat. It was an effect of poor Miss Tina's proposal, not altogether auspicious, that I had quite lost my appetite. I don't know why it happened that on this occasion I was more than ever struck with that queer air of sociability, of cousinship and family life, which makes up half the expression of Venice. Without streets and vehicles, the uproar of wheels, the brutality of horses, and with its little winding ways where people crowd together, where voices sound as in the corridors of a house, where the human step circulates as if it skirted the angles of furniture and shoes never wear out, the place has the character of an immense collective apartment, in which Piazza San Marco is the most ornamented corner and palaces and churches, for the rest, play the part of great divans of repose, tables of entertainment, expanses of decoration. And somehow the splendid common domicile, familiar domestic and resonant, also resembles a theatre with its actors clicking over bridges and, in straggling processions, tripping along fondamentas. As you sit in your gondola the footways that in certain parts edge the canals assume to the eye the importance of a stage, meeting it at the same angle, and the Venetian figures, moving to and fro against the battered scenery of their little houses of comedy, strike you as members of an endless dramatic troupe.

I went to bed that night very tired and without being able to compose an address to Miss Tina. Was this failure the reason why I became conscious the next morning as soon as I awoke of a determination to see the poor lady again the first moment she would receive me? That had something to do with it, but what had still more was the fact that during my sleep the oddest revulsion had taken place in my spirit. I found myself aware of this almost as soon as I opened my eyes: it made me jump out of my bed with the movement of a man who remembers that he has left the house-door ajar or a candle burning under a shelf. Was I still in time to save my goods? That question was in my heart; for what had now come to pass was that in the unconscious cerebration of sleep I had swung back to a passionate appreciation of Juliana's treasure. The pieces composing it were now more precious than ever and a positive ferocity had come into my need to acquire them. The condition Miss Tina had attached to that act no longer appeared an obstacle worth thinking of, and for an hour this morning my repentant imagination brushed it aside. It was absurd I should be able to invent nothing; absurd to renounce so easily and turn away helpless from the idea that the only way to become possessed was to unite myself to her for life. I mightn't unite myself, yet I might still have what she had. I must add that by the time I sent down to ask if she would see me I had invented no alternative, though in fact I drew out my dressing in the interest of my wit. This failure was humiliating, yet what

could the alternative be? Miss Tina sent back word I might come; and as
I descended the stairs and crossed the sala to her door—this time she received me in her aunt's forlorn parlour—I hoped she wouldn't think my
announcement was to be "favourable." She certainly would have understood my recoil of the day before.

As soon as I came into the room I saw that she had done so, but I also
saw something which had not been in my forecast. Poor Miss Tina's sense
of her failure had produced a rare alteration in her, but I had been too
full of stratagms and spoils to think of that. Now I took it in; I can
scarcely tell how it startled me. She stood in the middle of the room with
a face of mildness bent upon me, and her look of forgiveness, of absolution, made her angelic. It beautified her; she was younger; she was not a
ridiculous old woman. This trick of her expression, this magic of her
spirit, transfigured her, and while I still noted it I heard a whisper somewhere in the depths of my conscience: "Why not, after all—why not?" It
seemed to me I *could* pay the price. Still more distinctly however than
the whisper I heard Miss Tina's own voice. I was so struck with the different effect she made on me that at first I wasn't clearly aware of what
she was saying; then I recognised she had bade me good-bye—she said
something about hoping I should be very happy.

"Good-bye—good-bye?" I repeated with an inflection interrogative
and probably foolish.

I saw she didn't feel the interrogation, she only heard the words; she
had strung herself up to accepting our separation and they fell upon her
ear as a proof. "Are you going to-day?" she asked. "But it doesn't matter, for whenever you go I shall not see you again. I don't want to." And
she smiled strangely, with an infinite gentleness. She had never doubted
my having left her the day before in horror. How *could* she, since I
hadn't come back before night to contradict, even as a simple form, even
as an act of common humanity, such an idea? And now she had the force
of soul—Miss Tina with force of soul was a new conception—to smile at
me in her abjection.

"What shall you do—where shall you go?" I asked.

"Oh I don't know. I've done the great thing. I've destroyed the papers."

"Destroyed them?" I wailed.

"Yes; what was I to keep them for? I burnt them last night, one by one,
in the kitchen."

"One by one?" I coldly echoed it.

"It took a long time—there were so many." The room seemed to go
round me as she said this and a real darkness for a moment descended on
my eyes. When it passed, Miss Tina was there still, but the transfigura-
tion was over and she had changed back to a plain dingy elderly person.
It was in this character she spoke as she said "I can't stay with you longer,
I can't"; and it was in this character she turned her back upon me, as I
had turned mine upon her twenty-four hours before, and moved to the
door of her room. Here she did what I hadn't done when I quitted her—

she paused long enough to give me one look. I have never forgotten it and I sometimes still suffer from it, though it was not resentful. No, there was no resentment, nothing hard or vindictive in poor Miss Tina; for when, later, I sent her, as the price of the portrait of Jeffrey Aspern, a larger sum of money than I had hoped to be able to gather for her, writing to her that I had sold the picture, she kept it with thanks; she never sent it back. I wrote her that I had sold the picture, but I admitted to Mrs. Prest at the time—I met this other friend in London that autumn— that it hangs above my writing-table. When I look at it I can scarcely bear my loss—I mean of the precious papers.

⚜

THE PUPIL

"The Pupil" belongs to the period of Henry James's career when he was writing a brilliant series of stories about children. He wrote the tale in 1890 and offered it to the *Atlantic Monthly* but the journal rejected it. James placed it in an English magazine, *Longman's*, where it appeared in the March and April issues, 1891. The *Atlantic* editor, Horace Scudder, probably allowed his editorial scruples to prevail over whatever artistic judgment he may have possessed; we may surmise that he feared the *Atlantic* readers would not like the picture of a down-at-the-heels American family wandering about Europe. Posterity has not been worried about this; but it has agreed that the story itself is a delicate psychological study of the relations between a young tutor and his pupil. The tutor is called upon to supply the affection the youth would normally have expected to get from his parents.

The life of the Moreen family as described by James constitutes still another picture in the series the novelist drew of the life of Americans in Europe. Their false standards and values, their facade of pride, their ineffectuality, their sublime belief that the world would provide for their petty luxuries and basic necessities, their strange passivity—all these are shown in their effect on the keen-minded but helpless pupil. He is thoroughly ashamed of his family; but more cutting still is his awareness of their supreme selfishness. Little Morgan dies as much of rejection by those closest to him, as of his heart condition.

I

The poor young man hesitated and procrastinated: it cost him such an effort to broach the subject of terms, to speak of money to a person who spoke only of feelings and, as it were, of the aristocracy. Yet he was unwilling to take leave, treating his engagement as settled, without some

more conventional glance in that direction than he could find an opening
for in the manner of the large, affable lady who sat there drawing a pair
of soiled *gants de Suède* through a fat, jewelled hand and, at once pressing
and gliding, repeated over and over everything but the thing he would
have liked to hear. He would have liked to hear the figure of his salary;
but just as he was nervously about to sound that note the little boy came
back—the little boy Mrs. Moreen had sent out of the room to fetch her
fan. He came back without the fan, only with the casual observation that
he couldn't find it. As he dropped this cynical confession he looked
straight and hard at the candidate for the honour of taking his education
in hand. This personage reflected, somewhat grimly, that the first thing
he should have to teach his little charge would be to appear to address
himself to his mother when he spoke to her—especially not to make her
such an improper answer as that.

When Mrs. Moreen bethought herself of this pretext for getting rid of
their companion, Pemberton supposed it was precisely to approach the
delicate subject of his remuneration. But it had been only to say some
things about her son which it was better that a boy of eleven shouldn't
catch. They were extravagantly to his advantage, save when she lowered
her voice to sigh, tapping her left side familiarly: "And all overclouded
by *this*, you know—all at the mercy of a weakness——!" Pemberton gathered that the weakness was in the region of the heart. He had known the
poor child was not robust: this was the basis on which he had been invited to treat, through an English lady, an Oxford acquaintance, then at
Nice, who happened to know both his needs and those of the amiable
American family looking out for something really superior in the way of
a resident tutor.

The young man's impression of his prospective pupil, who had first
come into the room, as if to see for himself, as soon as Pemberton was admitted, was not quite the soft solicitation the visitor had taken for
granted. Morgan Moreen was, somehow, sickly without being delicate,
and that he looked intelligent (it is true Pemberton wouldn't have enjoyed his being stupid) only added to the suggestion that, as with his big
mouth and big ears he really couldn't be called pretty, he might be unpleasant. Pemberton was modest—he was even timid; and the chance that
his small scholar might prove cleverer than himself had quite figured, to
his nervousness, among the dangers of an untried experiment. He reflected, however, that these were risks one had to run when one accepted
a position, as it was called, in a private family; when as yet one's University honours had, pecuniarily speaking, remained barren. At any rate,
when Mrs. Moreen got up as if to intimate that, since it was understood
he would enter upon his duties within the week she would let him off
now, he succeeded, in spite of the presence of the child, in squeezing out
a phrase about the rate of payment. It was not the fault of the conscious
smile which seemed a reference to the lady's expensive identity, if the allusion did not sound rather vulgar. This was exactly because she became

still more gracious to reply: "Oh! I can assure you that all that will be quite regular."

Pemberton only wondered, while he took up his hat, what "all that" was to amount to—people had such different ideas. Mrs. Moreen's words, however, seemed to commit the family to a pledge definite enough to elicit from the child a strange little comment, in the shape of the mocking foreign ejaculation "Oh, là-là!"

Pemberton, in some confusion, glanced at him as he walked slowly to the window with his back turned, his hands in his pockets and the air in his elderly shoulders of a boy who didn't play. The young man wondered if he could teach him to play, though his mother had said it would never do and that this was why school was impossible. Mrs. Moreen exhibited no discomfiture; she only continued blandly: "Mr. Moreen will be delighted to meet your wishes. As I told you, he has been called to London for a week. As soon as he comes back you shall have it out with him."

This was so frank and friendly that the young man could only reply, laughing as his hostess laughed: "Oh! I don't imagine we shall have much of a battle."

"They'll give you anything you like," the boy remarked unexpectedly, returning from the window. "We don't mind what anything costs—we live awfully well."

"My darling, you're too quaint!" his mother exclaimed, putting out to caress him a practised but ineffectual hand. He slipped out of it, but looked with intelligent, innocent eyes at Pemberton, who had already had time to notice that from one moment to the other his small satiric face seemed to change its time of life. At this moment it was infantine; yet it appeared also to be under the influence of curious intuitions and knowledges. Pemberton rather disliked precocity, and he was disappointed to find gleams of it in a disciple not yet in his teens. Nevertheless he divined on the spot that Morgan wouldn't prove a bore. He would prove on the contrary a kind of excitement. This idea held the young man, in spite of a certain repulsion.

"You pompous little person! We're not extravagant!" Mrs. Moreen gaily protested, making another unsuccessful attempt to draw the boy to her side. "You must know what to expect," she went on to Pemberton.

"The less you expect the better!" her companion interposed. "But we *are* people of fashion."

"Only so far as *you* make us so!" Mrs. Moreen mocked, tenderly. "Well, then, on Friday—don't tell me you're superstitious—and mind you don't fail us. Then you'll see us all. I'm so sorry the girls are out. I guess you'll like the girls. And, you know, I've another son, quite different from this one."

"He tries to imitate me," said Morgan to Pemberton.

"He tries? Why, he's twenty years old!" cried Mrs. Moreen.

"You're very witty," Pemberton remarked to the child—a proposition that his mother echoed with enthusiasm, declaring that Morgan's sallies were the delight of the house. The boy paid no heed to this; he only inquired abruptly of the visitor, who was surprised afterwards that he hadn't struck him as offensively forward: "Do you *want* very much to come?"

"Can you doubt it, after such a description of what I shall hear?" Pemberton replied. Yet he didn't want to come at all; he was coming because he had to go somewhere, thanks to the collapse of his fortune at the end of a year abroad, spent on the system of putting his tiny patrimony into a single full wave of experience. He had had his full wave, but he couldn't pay his hotel bill. Moreover, he had caught in the boy's eyes the glimpse of a far-off appeal.

"Well, I'll do the best I can for you," said Morgan; with which he turned away again. He passed out of one of the long windows; Pemberton saw him go and lean on the parapet of the terrace. He remained there while the young man took leave of his mother, who, on Pemberton's looking as if he expected a farewell from him, interposed with: "Leave him, leave him; he's so strange!" Pemberton suspected she was afraid of something he might say. "He's a genius—you'll love him," she added. "He's much the most interesting person in the family." And before he could invent some civility to oppose to this, she wound up with: "But we're all good, you know!"

"He's a genius—you'll love him!" were words that recurred to Pemberton before the Friday, suggesting, among other things, that geniuses were not invariably lovable. However, it was all the better if there was an element that would make tutorship absorbing: he had perhaps taken too much for granted that it would be dreary. As he left the villa after his interview, he looked up at the balcony and saw the child leaning over it. "We shall have great larks!" he called up.

Morgan hesitated a moment; then he answered, laughing: "By the time you come back I shall have thought of something witty!"

This made Pemberton say to himself: "After all he's rather nice."

II

On the Friday he saw them all, as Mrs. Moreen had promised, for her husband had come back and the girls and the other son were at home. Mr. Moreen had a white moustache, a confiding manner and, in his buttonhole, the ribbon of a foreign order—bestowed, as Pemberton eventually learned, for services. For what services he never clearly ascertained: this was a point—one of a large number—that Mr. Moreen's manner never confided. What it emphatically did confide was that he was a man of the world. Ulick, the firstborn, was in visible training for the same profession—under the disadvantage as yet, however, of a buttonhole only feebly floral and a moustache with no pretensions to type. The girls had hair and figures and manners and small fat feet, but had never been out alone. As for Mrs. Moreen, Pemberton saw on a nearer view that her elegance was intermittent and her parts didn't always match. Her husband, as she had promised, met with enthusiasm Pemberton's ideas in regard to a salary. The young man had endeavoured to make them modest, and Mr. Moreen confided to him that *he* found them positively meagre. He further assured him that he aspired to be intimate with his children, to be their best friend, and that he was always looking out for them. That was what he went off for, to London and other places—to look out; and this vigilance was the theory of life, as well as the real occupation, of the whole family. They all looked out, for they were very frank on the subject of its being necessary. They desired it to be understood that they were earnest people, and also that their fortune, though quite adequate for earnest people, required the most careful administration. Mr. Moreen, as the parent bird, sought sustenance for the nest. Ulick found sustenance mainly at the club, where Pemberton guessed that it was usually served on green cloth. The girls used to do up their hair and their frocks themselves, and our young man felt appealed to to be glad, in regard to Morgan's education, that, though it must naturally be of the best, it didn't cost too much. After a little he *was* glad, forgetting at times his own needs in the interest inspired by the child's nature and education and the pleasure of making easy terms for him.

During the first weeks of their acquaintance Morgan had been as puzzling as a page in an unknown language—altogether different from the obvious little Anglo-Saxons who had misrepresented childhood to Pemberton. Indeed the whole mystic volume in which the boy had been bound demanded some practice in translation. To-day, after a considerable interval, there is something phantasmagoric, like a prismatic reflection or a serial novel, in Pemberton's memory of the queerness of the Moreens. If it were not for a few tangible tokens—a lock of Morgan's hair, cut by his own hand, and the half-dozen letters he got from him when they were separated—the whole episode and the figures peopling it would seem too inconsequent for anything but dreamland. The queerest thing about them was their success (as it appeared to him for a while at the time), for he had never seen a family so brilliantly equipped for failure. Wasn't it success to have kept him so hatefully long? Wasn't it success to have drawn him in that first morning at *déjeuner,* the Friday he came—it was enough to *make* one superstitious—so that he utterly committed himself, and this not by calculation or a *mot d'ordre,* but by a happy instinct which made them, like a band of gipsies, work so neatly together? They amused him as much as if they had really been a band of gipsies. He was still young and had not seen much of the world—his English years had been intensely usual; therefore the reversed conventions of the Moreens (for they had their standards) struck him as topsy-turvy. He had encountered nothing like them at Oxford; still less had any such note been struck to his younger American ear during the four years at Yale in which he had richly supposed himself to be reacting against Puritanism. The reaction of the Moreens, at any rate, went ever so much further. He had thought himself very clever that first day in hitting them all off in his mind with the term "cosmopolite."

Later, it seemed feeble and colourless enough—confessedly, helplessly provisional.

However, when he first applied it to them he had a degree of joy—for an instructor he was still empirical—as if from the apprehension that to live with them would really be to see life. Their sociable strangeness was an intimation of that—their chatter of tongues, their gaiety and good humour, their infinite dawdling (they were always getting themselves up, but it took forever, and Pemberton had once found Mr. Moreen shaving in the drawing-room), their French, their Italian and, in the spiced fluency, their cold, tough slices of American. They lived on macaroni and coffee (they had these articles prepared in perfection), but they knew recipes for a hundred other dishes. They overflowed with music and song, were always humming and catching each other up, and had a kind of professional acquaintance with continental cities. They talked of "good places" as if they had been strolling players. They had at Nice a villa, a carriage, a piano and a banjo, and they went to official parties. They were a perfect calendar of the "days" of their friends, which Pemberton knew them, when they were indisposed, to get out of bed to go to, and which made the week larger than life when Mrs. Moreen talked of them with Paula and Amy. Their romantic initiations gave their new inmate at first an almost dazzling sense of culture. Mrs. Moreen had translated something, at some former period—an author whom it made Pemberton feel *borné* never to have heard of. They could imitate Venetian and sing Neapolitan, and when they wanted to say something very particular they communicated with each other in an ingenious dialect of their own—a sort of spoken cipher, which Pemberton at first took for Volapuk, but which he learned to understand as he would not have understood Volapuk.

"It's the family language—Ultramoreen," Morgan explained to him drolly enough; but the boy rarely condescended to use it himself, though he attempted colloquial Latin as if he had been a little prelate.

Among all the "days" with which Mrs. Moreen's memory was taxed she managed to squeeze in one of her own, which her friends sometimes forgot. But the house derived a frequented air from the number of fine people who were freely named there and from several mysterious men with foreign titles and English clothes whom Morgan called the princes and who, on sofas with the girls, talked French very loud, as if to show they were saying nothing improper. Pemberton wondered how the princes could ever propose in that tone and so publicly: he took for granted cynically that this was what was desired of them. Then he acknowledged that even for the chance of such an advantage Mrs. Moreen would never allow Paula and Amy to receive alone. These young ladies were not at all timid, but it was just the safeguards that made them so graceful. It was a houseful of Bohemians who wanted tremendously to be Philistines.

In one respect, however, certainly, they achieved no rigour—they were wonderfully amiable and ecstatic about Morgan. It was a genuine tenderness, an artless admiration, equally strong in each. They even praised his beauty, which was small, and were rather afraid of him, as if they recognised that he was of a finer clay. They called him a little angel and a little prodigy and pitied his want of health effusively. Pemberton feared at first that their extravagance would make him hate the boy, but before this happened he had become extravagant himself. Later, when he had grown rather to hate the others, it was a bribe to patience for him that they were at any rate nice about Morgan, going on tiptoe if they fancied he was showing symptoms, and even giving up somebody's "day" to procure him a pleasure. But mixed with this was the oddest wish to make him independent, as if they felt they were not good enough for him. They passed him over to Pemberton very much as if they wished to force a constructive adoption on the obliging bachelor and shirk altogether a responsibility. They were delighted when they perceived that Morgan liked his preceptor, and could think of no higher praise for the young man. It was strange how they contrived to reconcile the appearance, and indeed the essential fact, of adoring the child with their eagerness to wash their hands of him. Did they want to get rid of him before he should find them out? Pemberton was finding them out month by month. At any rate, the boy's relations turned their back with exaggerated delicacy, as if to escape the charge of interfering. Seeing in time how little he had in common with them (it was by *them* he first observed it—they proclaimed it with complete humility), his preceptor was moved to speculate on the mysteries of transmission, the far jumps of heredity. Where his detachment from most of the things they represented had come from was more than an observer could say—it certainly had burrowed under two or three generations.

As for Pemberton's own estimate of his pupil, it was a good while before he got the point of view, so little had he been prepared for it by the smug young barbarians to whom the tradition of tutorship, as hitherto revealed to him, had been adjusted. Morgan was scrappy and surprising, deficient in many properties supposed common to the *genus* and abounding in others that were the portion only of supernaturally clever. One day Pemberton made a great stride: it cleared up the question to perceive that Morgan *was* supernaturally clever and that, though the formula was temporarily meagre, this would be the only assumption on which one could successfully deal with him. He had the general quality of a child for whom life had not been simplified by school, a kind of homebred sensibility which might have been bad for himself but was charming for others, and a whole range of refinement and perception—little musical vibrations as taking as picked-up airs—begotten by wandering about Europe at the tail of his migratory tribe. This might not have been an education to recommend in advance, but its results with Morgan were as palpable as a fine texture. At the same time he had in his composition a sharp spice of stoicism, doubtless the fruit of having had to begin early to bear pain, which produced the impression of pluck and made it of less consequence that he might have been thought at school rather a polyglot little beast. Pemberton indeed quickly found himself rejoicing that school was out of the question: in any million of boys it was probably good for all but one, and Morgan was that millionth. It would have made him comparative and superior—it might have made him priggish. Pemberton would try to be school himself—a bigger seminary than five hundred grazing donkeys; so that, winning no prizes, the boy would remain unconscious and irresponsible and amusing—amusing, because, though life was already intense in his childish nature, freshness still made there a strong draught for jokes. It turned out that even in the still air of Morgan's various disabilities jokes flourished greatly. He was a pale, lean, acute, undeveloped little cosmopolite, who liked intellectual gymnastics and who, also, as regards the behavior of mankind, had noticed more things than you might suppose, but who nevertheless had his proper playroom of superstitions, where he smashed a dozen toys a day.

III

At Nice once, towards evening, as the pair sat resting in the open air after a walk, looking over the sea at the pink western lights, Morgan said suddenly to his companion: "Do you like it—you know, being with us all in this intimate way?"

"My dear fellow, why should I stay if I didn't?"

"How do I know you will stay? I'm almost sure you won't, very long."

"I hope you don't mean to dismiss me," said Pemberton.

Morgan considered a moment, looking at the sunset. "I think if I did right I ought to."

"Well, I know I'm supposed to instruct you in virtue; but in that case don't do right."

"You're very young—fortunately," Morgan went on, turning to him again.

"Oh yes, compared with you!"

"Therefore, it won't matter so much if you do lose a lot of time."

"That's the way to look at it," said Pemberton accommodatingly.

They were silent a minute; after which the boy asked: "Do you like my father and mother very much?"

"Dear me, yes. They're charming people."

Morgan received this with another silence; then, unexpectedly, familiarly, but at the same time affectionately, he remarked: "You're a jolly old humbug!"

For a particular reason the words made Pemberton change colour. The boy noticed in an instant that he had turned red, whereupon he turned red himself and the pupil and the master exchanged a longish glance in which there was a consciousness of many more things than are usually touched upon, even tacitly, in such a relation. It produced for Pemberton an embarrassment; it raised, in a shadowy form, a question (this was the first glimpse of it), which was destined to play as singular and, as he imagined, owing to the altogether peculiar conditions, an unprecedented part in his intercourse with his little companion. Later, when he found himself talking with this small boy in a way in which few small boys could ever have been talked with, he thought of that clumsy moment on the bench at Nice as the dawn of an understanding that had broadened. What had added to the clumsiness then was that he thought it his duty to declare to Morgan that he might abuse him (Pemberton) as much as he liked, but must never abuse his parents. To this Morgan had the easy reply that he hadn't dreamed of abusing them; which appeared to be true: it put Pemberton in the wrong.

"Then why am I a humbug for saying *I* think them charming?" the young man asked, conscious of a certain rashness.

"Well—they're not *your* parents."

"They love you better than anything in the world—never forget that," said Pemberton.

"Is that why you like them so much?"

"They're very kind to me," Pemberton replied, evasively.

"You *are* a humbug!" laughed Morgan, passing an arm into his tutor's. He leaned against him, looking off at the sea again and swinging his long, thin legs.

"Don't kick my shins," said Pemberton, while he reflected: "Hang it, I can't complain of them to the child!"

"There's another reason, too," Morgan went on, keeping his legs still.

"Another reason for what?"

"Besides their not being your parents."

"I dont understand you," said Pemberton.

"Well, you will before long. All right!"

Pemberton did understand, fully, before long; but he made a fight even with himself before he confessed it. He thought it the oddest thing to have a struggle with the child about. He wondered he didn't detest the child for launching him in such a struggle. But by the time it began the resource of detesting the child was closed to him. Morgan was a special case, but to know him was to accept him on his own odd terms. Pemberton had spent his aversion to special cases before arriving at knowledge. When at last he did arrive he felt that he was in an extreme predicament. Against every interest he had attached himself. They would have to meet things together. Before they went home that evening, at Nice, the boy had said, clinging to his arm:

"Well, at any rate you'll hang on to the last."

"To the last?"

"Till you're fairly beaten."

"*You* ought to be fairly beaten!" cried the young man, drawing him closer.

IV

A year after Pemberton had come to live with them Mr. and Mrs. Moreen suddenly gave up the villa at Nice. Pemberton had got used to suddenness, having seen it practised on a considerable scale during two jerky little tours—one in Switzerland the first summer, and the other late in the winter, when they all ran down to Florence and then, at the end of ten days, liking it much less than they had intended, straggled back in mysterious depression. They had returned to Nice "for ever," as they said; but this didn't prevent them from squeezing, one rainy, muggy May night, into a second-class railway-carriage—you could never tell by which class they would travel—where Pemberton helped them to stow away a wonderful collection of bundles and bags. The explanation of this manœuvre was that they had determined to spend the summer "in some bracing place"; but in Paris they dropped into a small furnished apartment—a fourth floor in a third-rate avenue, where there was a smell on the staircase and the *portier* was hateful—and passed the next four months in blank indigence.

The better part of this baffled sojourn was for the preceptor and his pupil, who, visiting the Invalides and Notre Dame, the Conciergerie and all the museums, took a hundred remunerative rambles. They learned to know their Paris, which was useful, for they came back another year for a longer stay, the general character of which in Pemberton's memory to-day mixes pitiably and confusedly with that of the first. He sees Morgan's shabby knickerbockers—the everlasting pair that didn't match his blouse and that as he grew longer could only grow faded. He remembers the particular holes in his three or four pairs of coloured stockings.

Morgan was dear to his mother, but he never was better dressed than was absolutely necessary—partly, no doubt, by his own fault, for he was as indifferent to his appearance as a German philosopher. "My dear fellow, you *are* coming to pieces," Pemberton would say to him in sceptical remonstrance; to which the child would reply, looking at him serenely up and down: "My dear fellow, so are you! I don't want to cast you in the shade." Pemberton could have no rejoinder for this—the assertion so closely represented the fact. If however the deficiencies of his own wardrobe were a chapter by themselves he didn't like his little charge to look too poor. Later he used to say: "Well, if we are poor, why, after all, shouldn't we look it?" and he consoled himself with thinking there was something rather elderly and gentlemanly in Morgan's seediness—it differed from the untidiness of the urchin who plays and spoils his things. He could trace perfectly the degrees by which, in proportion as her little son confined himself to his tutor for society, Mrs. Moreen shrewdly forbore to renew his garments. She did nothing that didn't show, neglected him because he escaped notice, and then, as he illustrated this clever policy, discouraged at home his public appearances. Her position was logical enough—those members of her family who did show had to be showy.

During this period and several others Pemberton was quite aware of how he and his comrade might strike people; wandering languidly through the Jardin des Plantes as if they had nowhere to go, sitting, on the winter days, in the galleries of the Louvre, so splendidly ironical to the homeless, as if for the advantage of the *calorifère*. They joked about it sometimes: it was the sort of joke that was perfectly within the boy's compass. They figured themselves as part of the vast, vague, hand-to-mouth multitude of the enormous city and pretended they were proud of their position in it—it showed them such a lot of life and made them conscious of a sort of democratic brotherhood. If Pemberton could not feel a sympathy in destitution with his small companion (for after all Morgan's fond parents would never have let him really suffer), the boy would at least feel it with him, so it came to the same thing. He used sometimes to wonder what people would think they were—fancy they were looked askance at, as if it might be a suspected case of kidnapping. Morgan wouldn't be taken for a young patrician with a preceptor—he wasn't smart enough; though he might pass for his companion's sickly little brother. Now and then he had a five-franc piece, and except once, when they bought a couple of lovely neckties, one of which he made Pemberton accept, they laid it out scientifically in old books. It was a great day, always spent on the quays, rummaging among the dusty boxes that garnish the parapets. These were occasions that helped them to live, for their books ran low very soon after the beginning of their acquaintance. Pemberton had a good many in England, but he was obliged to write to a friend and ask him kindly to get some fellow to give him something for them.

If the bracing climate was untasted that summer the young man had an idea that at the moment they were about to make a push the cup had been dashed from their lips by a movement of his own. It had been his first blow-out, as he called it, with his patrons; his first successful attempt (though there was little other success about it), to bring them to a consideration of his impossible position. As the ostensible eve of a costly journey the moment struck him as a good one to put in a signal protest—to present an ultimatum. Ridiculous as it sounded he had never yet been able to compass an uninterrupted private interview with the elder pair or with either of them singly. They were always flanked by their elder children, and poor Pemberton usually had his own little charge at his side. He was conscious of its being a house in which the surface of one's delicacy got rather smudged; nevertheless he had kept the bloom of his scruple against announcing to Mr. and Mrs. Moreen with publicity that he couldn't go on longer without a little money. He was still simple enough to suppose Ulick and Paula and Amy might not know that since his arrival he had only had a hundred and forty francs; and he was magnanimous enough to wish not to compromise their parents in their eyes. Mr. Moreen now listened to him, as he listened to every one and to everything, like a man of the world, and seemed to appeal to him—though not of course too grossly—to try and be a little more of one himself. Pemberton recognised the importance of the character from the advantage it gave Mr. Moreen. He was not even confused, whereas poor Pemberton was more so than there was any reason for. Neither was he surprised—at least any more than a gentleman had to be who freely confessed himself a little shocked, though not, strictly, at Pemberton.

"We must go into this, mustn't we, dear?" he said to his wife. He assured his young friend that the matter should have his very best attention; and he melted into space as elusively as if, at the door, he were taking an inevitable but deprecatory precedence. When, the next moment, Pemberton found himself alone with Mrs. Moreen it was to hear her say: "I see, I see," stroking the roundness of her chin and looking as if she were only hesitating between a dozen easy remedies. If they didn't make their push Mr. Moreen could at least disappear for several days. During his absence his wife took up the subject again spontaneously, but her contribution to it was merely that she had thought all the while they were getting on so beautifully. Pemberton's reply to this revelation was that unless they immediately handed him a substantial sum he would leave them for ever. He knew she would wonder how he would get away, and for a moment expected her to inquire. She didn't, for which he was almost grateful to her, so little was he in a position to tell.

"You won't, you know you won't—you're too interested," she said. "You *are* interested, you know you are, you dear, kind man!" She laughed, with almost condemnatory archness, as if it were a reproach (but she wouldn't insist), while she flirted a soiled pocket-handerkerchief at him.

Pemberton's mind was fully made up to quit the house the following week. This would give him time to get an answer to a letter he had despatched to England. If he did nothing of the sort—that is, if he stayed another year and then went away only for three months—it was not merely because before the answer to his letter came (most unsatisfactory when it did arrive), Mr. Moreen generously presented him—again with all the precautions of a man of the world—three hundred francs. He was exasperated to find that Mrs. Moreen was right, that he couldn't bear to leave the child. This stood out clearer for the very reason that, the night of his desperate appeal to his patrons, he had seen fully for the first time where he was. Wasn't it another proof of the success with which those patrons practised their arts that they had managed to avert for so long the illuminating flash? It descended upon Pemberton with a luridness which perhaps would have struck a spectator as comically excessive, after he had returned to his little servile room, which looked into a close court where a bare, dirty opposite wall took, with the sound of shrill clatter, the reflection of lighted back-windows. He had simply given himself away to a band of adventurers. The idea, the word itself, had a sort of romantic horror for him—he had always lived on such safe lines. Later it assumed a more interesting, almost a soothing, sense: it pointed a moral, and Pemberton could enjoy a moral. The Moreens were adventurers not merely because they didn't pay their debts, because they lived on society, but because their whole view of life, dim and confused and instinctive, like that of clever colour-blind animals, was speculative and rapacious and mean. Oh! they were "respectable," and that only made them more *immondes*. The young man's analysis of them put it at last very simply—they were adventurers because they were abject snobs. That was the completest account of them—it was the law of their being. Even when this truth became vivid to their ingenious inmate he remained unconscious of how much his mind had been prepared for it by the extraordinary little boy who had now become such a complication in his life. Much less could he then calculate on the information he was still to owe to the extraordinary little boy.

V

But it was during the ensuing time that the real problem came up— the problem of how far it was excusable to discuss the turpitude of parents with a child of twelve, of thirteen, of fourteen. Absolutely inexcusable and quite impossible it of course at first appeared; and indeed the question didn't press for a while after Pemberton had received his three hundred francs. They produced a sort of lull, a relief from the sharpest pressure. Pemberton frugally amended his wardrobe and even had a few francs in his pocket. He thought the Moreens looked at him as if he were almost too smart, as if they ought to take care not to spoil him. If Mr. Moreen hadn't been such a man of the world he would perhaps have said something to him about his neckties. But Mr. Moreen was always enough a man of the world to let things pass—he had certainly shown that. It was singular how Pemberton guessed that Morgan, though saying nothing about it, knew something had happened. But three hundred francs, especially when one owed money, couldn't last for ever; and when they were gone—the boy knew when they were gone—Morgan did say something. The party had returned to Nice at the beginning of the winter, but not to the charming villa. They went to an hotel, where they stayed three months, and then they went to another hotel, explaining that they had left the first because they had waited and waited and couldn't get the rooms they wanted. These apartments, the rooms they wanted, were generally very splendid; but fortunately they never *could* get them—fortunately, I mean, for Pemberton, who reflected always that if they had got them there would have been still less for educational expenses. What Morgan said at last was said suddenly, irrelevantly, when the moment came, in the middle of a lesson, and consisted of the apparently unfeeling words: "You ought to *filer*, you know—you really ought."

Pemberton stared. He had learnt enough French slang from Morgan to know that to *filer* meant to go away. "Ah, my dear fellow, don't turn me off!"

Morgan pulled a Greek lexicon toward him (he used a Greek-German), to look out a word, instead of asking it of Pemberton. "You can't go on like this, you know."

"Like what, my boy?"

"You know they don't pay you up," said Morgan, blushing and turning his leaves.

"Don't pay me?" Pemberton stared again and then feigned amazement. "What on earth put that into your head?"

"It has been there a long time," the boy replied, continuing his search.

Pemberton was silent, then he went on: "I say, what are you hunting for? They pay me beautifully."

"I'm hunting for the Greek for transparent fiction," Morgan dropped.

"Find that rather for gross impertinence, and disabuse your mind. What do I want of money?"

"Oh, that's another question!"

Pemberton hesitated—he was drawn in different ways. The severely correct thing would have been to tell the boy that such a matter was none of his business and bid him go on with his lines. But they were really too intimate for that; it was not the way he was in the habit of treating him; there had been no reason it should be. On the other hand Morgan had quite lighted on the truth—he really shouldn't be able to keep it up much longer; therefore why not let him know one's real motive for forsaking him? At the same time it wasn't decent to abuse to one's pupil the family of one's pupil; it was better to misrepresent than to do that. So in reply to Morgan's last exclamation he just declared, to dismiss the subject, that he had received several payments.

"I say—I say!" the boy ejaculated, laughing.

"That's all right," Pemberton insisted. "Give me your written rendering."

Morgan pushed a copybook across the table, and his companion began to read the page, but with something running in his head that made it no sense. Looking up after a minute or two he found the child's eyes fixed on him, and he saw something strange in them. Then Morgan said: "I'm not afraid of the reality."

"I haven't yet seen the thing that you *are* afraid of—I'll do you that justice!"

This came out with a jump (it was perfectly true), and evidently gave Morgan pleasure. "I've thought of it a long time," he presently resumed.

"Well, don't think of it any more."

The child appeared to comply, and they had a comfortable and even an amusing hour. They had a theory that they were very thorough, and yet they seemed always to be in the amusing part of lessons, the intervals between the tunnels, where there were waysides and views. Yet the morning was brought to a violent end by Morgan's suddenly leaning his arms on the table, burying his head in them and bursting into tears. Pemberton would have been startled at any rate; but he was doubly startled because, as it then occurred to him, it was the first time he had ever seen the boy cry. It was rather awful.

The next day, after much thought, he took a decision and, believing it to be just, immediately acted upon it. He cornered Mr. and Mrs.

Moreen again and informed them that if, on the spot, they didn't pay
him all they owed him, he would not only leave their house, but would
tell Morgan exactly what had brought him to it.

"Oh, you *haven't* told him?" cried Mrs. Moreen, with a pacifying hand
on her well-dressed bosom.

"Without warning you? For what do you take me?"

Mr. and Mrs. Moreen looked at each other, and Pemberton could see
both that they were relieved and that there was a certain alarm in their
relief. "My dear fellow," Mr. Moreen demanded, "what use *can* you have,
leading the quiet life we all do, for such a lot of money?"—an inquiry to
which Pemberton made no answer, occupied as he was in perceiving that
what passed in the mind of his patrons was something like: "Oh, then, if
we've felt that the child, dear little angel, has judged us and how he regards us, and we haven't been betrayed, he must have guessed—and, in
short, it's *general!*" an idea that rather stirred up Mr. and Mrs. Moreen,
as Pemberton had desired that it should. At the same time, if he had
thought that his threat would do something towards bringing them
round, he was disappointed to find they had taken for granted (how little
they appreciated his delicacy!) that he had already given them away to
his pupil. There was a mystic uneasiness in their parental breasts, and that
was the way they had accounted for it. None the less his threat did touch
them; for if they had escaped it was only to meet a new danger. Mr.
Moreen appealed to Pemberton, as usual, as a man of the world; but his
wife had recourse, for the first time since the arrival of their inmate, to
a fine *hauteur*, reminding him that a devoted mother, with her child, had
arts that protected her against gross misrepresentation.

"I should misrepresent you grossly if I accused you of common honesty!" the young man replied; but as he closed the door behind him
sharply, thinking he had not done himself much good, while Mr. Moreen
lighted another cigarette, he heard Mrs. Moreen shout after him, more
touchingly:

"Oh, you do, you *do*, put the knife to one's throat!"

The next morning, very early, she came to his room. He recognised
her knock, but he had no hope that she brought him money; as to which
he was wrong, for she had fifty francs in her hand. She squeezed forward
in her dressing-gown, and he received her in his own, between his bath-
tub and his bed. He had been tolerably schooled by this time to the "foreign ways" of his hosts. Mrs. Moreen was zealous, and when she was
zealous she didn't care what she did; so she now sat down on his bed,
his clothes being on the chairs, and, in her preoccupation, forgot, as she
glanced round, to be ashamed of giving him such a nasty room. What
Mrs. Moreen was zealous about on this occasion was to persuade him that
in the first place she was very good-natured to bring him fifty francs,
and, in the second, if he would only see it, he was really too absurd to
expect to be *paid*. Wasn't he paid enough, without perpetual money—
wasn't he paid by the comfortable, luxurious home that he enjoyed with

them all, without a care, and anxiety, a solitary want? Wasn't he sure of his position, and wasn't that everything to a young man like him, quite unknown, with singularly little to show, the ground of whose exorbitant pretensions it was not easy to discover? Wasn't he paid, above all, by the delightful relation he had established with Morgan—quite ideal, as from master to pupil—and by the simple privilege of knowing and living with so amazingly gifted a child, than whom really—she meant literally what she said—there was no better company in Europe? Mrs. Moreen herself took to appealing to him as a man of the world; she said "Voyons, mon cher," and "My dear sir, look here now"; and urged him to be reasonable, putting it before him that it was really a chance for him. She spoke as if, according as he *should* be reasonable, he would prove himself worthy to be her son's tutor and of the extraordinary confidence they had placed in him.

After all, Pemberton reflected, it was only a difference of theory, and the theory didn't matter much. They had hitherto gone on that of remunerated, as now they would go on that of gratuitous, service; but why should they have so many words about it? Mrs. Moreen, however, continued to be convincing; sitting there with her fifty francs she talked and repeated, as women repeat, and bored and irritated him, while he leaned against the wall with his hands in the pockets of his wrapper, drawing it together round his legs and looking over the head of his visitor at the grey negations of his window. She wound up with saying: "You see I bring you a definite proposal."

"A definite proposal?"

"To make our relations regular, as it were—to put them on a comfortable footing."

"I see—it's a system," said Pemberton. "A kind of blackmail."

Mrs. Moreen bounded up, which was what the young man wanted.

"What do you mean by that?"

"You practise on one's fears—one's fears about the child if one should go away."

"And, pray, what would happen to him in that event?" demanded Mrs. Moreen, with majesty.

"Why, he'd be alone with *you*."

"And pray, with whom *should* a child be but with those whom he loves most?"

"If you think that, why don't you dismiss me?"

"Do you pretend that he loves you more than he loves *us?*" cried Mrs. Moreen.

"I think he ought to. I make sacrifices for him. Though I've heard of those *you* make, I don't see them."

Mrs. Moreen stared a moment; then, with emotion, she grasped Pemberton's hand. "*Will* you make it—the sacrifice?"

Pemberton burst out laughing. "I'll see—I'll do what I can—I'll stay a little longer. Your calculation is just—I *do* hate intensely to give him up;

I'm fond of him and he interests me deeply, in spite of the inconvenience I suffer. You know my situation perfectly; I haven't a penny in the world, and, occupied as I am with Morgan, I'm unable to earn money."

Mrs. Moreen tapped her undressed arm with her folded bank-note. "Can't you write articles? Can't you translate, as *I* do?"

"I don't know about translating; it's wretchedly paid."

"I am glad to earn what I can," said Mrs. Moreen virtuously, with her head high.

"You ought to tell me who you do it for." Pemberton paused a moment, and she said nothing; so he added: "I've tried to turn off some little sketches, but the magazines won't have them—they're declined with thanks."

"You see then you're not such a phœnix—to have such pretensions," smiled his interlocutress.

"I haven't time to do things properly," Pemberton went on. Then as it came over him that he was almost abjectly good-natured to give these explanations he added: "If I stay on longer it must be on one condition—that Morgan shall know distinctly on what footing I am."

Mrs. Moreen hesitated. "Surely you don't want to show off to a child?"

"To show *you* off, do you mean?"

Again Mrs. Moreen hesitated, but this time it was to produce a still finer flower. "And *you* talk of blackmail!"

"You can easily prevent it," said Pemberton.

"And *you* talk of practising on fears," Mrs. Moreen continued.

"Yes, there's no doubt I'm a great scoundrel."

His visitor looked at him a moment—it was evident that she was sorely bothered. Then she thrust out her money at him. "Mr. Moreen desired me to give you this on account."

"I'm much obliged to Mr. Moreen; but we have no account."

"You won't take it?"

"That leaves me more free," said Pemberton.

"To poison my darling's mind?" groaned Mrs. Moreen.

"Oh, your darling's mind!" laughed the young man.

She fixed him a moment, and he thought she was going to break out tormentedly, pleadingly: "For God's sake, tell me what *is* in it!" But she checked this impulse—another was stronger. She pocketed the money—the crudity of the alternative was comical—and swept out of the room with the desperate concession: "You may tell him any horror you like!"

VI

A couple of days after this, during which Pemberton had delayed to profit by Mrs. Moreen's permission to tell her son any horror, the two had been for a quarter of an hour walking together in silence when the boy became sociable again with the remark: "I'll tell you how I know it; I know it through Zénobie."

"Zénobie? Who in the world is *she?*"

" A nurse I used to have—ever so many years ago. A charming woman. I liked her awfully, and she liked me."

"There's no accounting for tastes. What is it you know through her?"

"Why, what their idea is. She went away because they didn't pay her. She did like me awfully, and she stayed two years. She told me all about it—that at last she could never get her wages. As soon as they saw how much she liked me they stopped giving her anything. They thought she'd stay for nothing, out of devotion. And she did stay ever so long—as long as she could. She was only a poor girl. She used to send money to her mother. At last she couldn't afford it any longer, and she went away in a fearful rage one night—I mean of course in a rage against *them*. She cried over me tremendously, she hugged me nearly to death. She told me all about it," Morgan repeated. "She told me it was their idea. So I guessed, ever so long ago, that they have had the same idea with you."

"Zénobie was very shrewd," said Pemberton. "And she made you so."

"Oh, that wasn't Zénobie; that was nature. And experience!" Morgan laughed.

"Well, Zénobie was a part of your experience."

"Certainly I was a part of hers, poor dear!" the boy exclaimed. "And I'm a part of yours."

"A very important part. But I don't see how you know that I've been treated like Zénobie."

"Do you take me for an idiot?" Morgan asked. "Haven't I been conscious of what we've been through together?"

"What we've been through?"

"Our privations—our dark days."

"Oh, our days have been bright enough."

Morgan went on in silence for a moment. Then he said: "My dear fellow, you're a hero!"

"Well, you're another!" Pemberton retorted.

"No, I'm not; but I'm not a baby. I won't stand it any longer. You must get some occupation that pays. I'm ashamed, I'm ashamed!" quavered the boy in a little passionate voice that was very touching to Pemberton.

"We ought to go off and live somewhere together," said the young man.

"I'll go like a shot if you'll take me."

"I'd get some work that would keep us both afloat," Pemberton continued.

"So would I. Why shouldn't *I* work? I ain't such a *crétin!*"

"The difficulty is that your parents wouldn't hear of it," said Pemberton. "They would never part with you; they worship the ground you tread on. Don't you see the proof of it? They don't dislike me; they wish me no harm; they're very amiable people; but they're perfectly ready to treat me badly for your sake."

The silence in which Morgan received this graceful sophistry struck

Pemberton somehow as expressive. After a moment Morgan repeated: "You *are* a hero!" Then he added: "They leave me with you altogether. You've all the responsibility. They put me off on you from morning till night. Why, then, should they object to my taking up with you completely? I'd help you."

"They're not particularly keen about my being helped, and they delight in thinking of you as *theirs*. They're tremendously proud of you."

"I'm not proud of them. But you know *that*," Morgan returned.

"Except for the little matter we speak of they're charming people," said Pemberton, not taking up the imputation of lucidity, but wondering greatly at the child's own, and especially at this fresh reminder of something he had been conscious of from the first—the strangest thing in the boy's large little composition, a temper, a sensibility, even a sort of ideal, which made him privately resent the general quality of his kinsfolk. Morgan had in secret a small loftiness which begot an element of reflection, a domestic scorn not imperceptible to his companion (though they never had any talk about it), and absolutely anomalous in a juvenile nature, especially when one noted that it had not made this nature "old-fashioned," as the word is of children—quaint or wizened or offensive. It was as if he had been a little gentleman and had paid the penalty by discovering that he was the only such person in the family. This comparison didn't make him vain; but it could make him melancholy and a trifle austere. When Pemberton guessed at these young dimnesses he saw him serious and gallant, and was partly drawn on and partly checked, as if with a scruple, by the charm of attempting to sound the little cool shallows which were quickly growing deeper. When he tried to figure to himself the morning twilight of childhood, so as to deal with it safely, he perceived that it was never fixed, never arrested, that ignorance, at the instant one touched it, was already flushing faintly into knowledge, that there was nothing that at a given moment you could say a clever child didn't know. It seemed to him that *he* both knew too much to imagine Morgan's simplicity and too little to disembroil his tangle.

The boy paid no heed to his last remark; he only went on: "I should have spoken to them about their idea, as I call it, long ago, if I hadn't been sure what they would say."

"And what would they say?"

"Just what they said about what poor Zénobie told me—that it was a horrid, dreadful story, that they had paid her every penny they owed her."

"Well, perhaps they had," said Pemberton.

"Perhaps they've paid you!"

"Let us pretend they have, and *n'en parlons plus*."

"They accused her of lying and cheating," Morgan insisted perversely. "That's why I don't want to speak to them."

"Lest they should accuse me, too?"

To this Morgan made no answer, and his companion, looking down at him (the boy turned his eyes, which had filled, away), saw that he couldn't have trusted himself to utter.

"You're right. Don't squeeze them," Pemberton pursued. "Except for that, they *are* charming people."

"Except for *their* lying and *their* cheating?"

"I say—I say!" cried Pemberton, imitating a little tone of the lad's which was itself an imitation.

"We must be frank, at the last; we *must* come to an understanding," said Morgan, with the importance of the small boy who lets himself think he is arranging great affairs—almost playing at shipwreck or at Indians. "I know all about everything," he added.

"I daresay your father has his reasons," Pemberton observed, too vaguely, as he was aware.

"For lying and cheating?"

"For saving and managing and turning his means to the best account. He has plenty to do with his money. You're an expensive family."

"Yes, I'm very expensive," Morgan rejoined, in a manner which made his preceptor burst out laughing.

"He's saving for *you*," said Pemberton. "They think of you in everything they do."

"He might save a little——" The boy paused. Pemberton waited to hear what. Then Morgan brought out oddly: "A little reputation."

"Oh, there's plenty of that. That's all right!"

"Enough of it for the people they know, no doubt. The people they know are awful."

"Do you mean the princes? We mustn't abuse the princes."

"Why not? They haven't married Paula—they haven't married Amy. They only clean out Ulick."

"You *do* know everything!" Pemberton exclaimed.

"No, I don't, after all. I don't know what they live on, or how they live, or *why* they live! What have they got and how did they get it? Are they rich, are they poor, or have they a *modeste aisance?* Why are they always chiveying about—living one year like ambassadors and the next like paupers? Who are they, anyway, and what are they? I've thought of all that—I've thought of a lot of things. They're so beastly worldly. That's what I hate most—oh, I've *seen* it! All they care about is to make an appearance and to pass for something or other. What do they want to pass for? What *do* they, Mr. Pemberton?"

"You pause for a reply," said Pemberton, treating the inquiry as a joke, yet wondering too, and greatly struck with the boy's intense, if imperfect, vision. "I haven't the least idea."

"And what good does it do? Haven't I seen the way people treat them —the 'nice' people, the ones they want to know? They'll take anything from them—they'll lie down and be trampled on. The nice ones hate that—they just sicken them. You're the only really nice person we know."

"Are you sure? They don't lie down for me!"

"Well, you shan't lie down for them. You've got to go—that's what you've got to do," said Morgan.

"And what will become of you?"

"Oh, I'm growing up. I shall get off before long. I'll see you later."

"You had better let me finish you," Pemberton urged, lending himself to the child's extraordinarily competent attitude.

Morgan stopped in their walk, looking up at him. He had to look up much less than a couple of years before—he had grown, in his loose leanness, so long and high. "Finish me?" he echoed.

"There are such a lot of jolly things we can do together yet. I want to turn you out—I want you to do me credit."

Morgan continued to look at him. "To give you credit—do you mean?"

"My dear fellow, you're too clever to live."

"That's just what I'm afraid you think. No, no; it isn't fair—I can't endure it. We'll part next week. The sooner it's over the sooner to sleep."

"If I hear of anything—any other chance, I promise to go," said Pemberton.

Morgan consented to consider this. "But you'll be honest," he demanded; "you won't pretend you haven't heard?"

"I'm much more likely to pretend I have."

"But what can you hear of, this way, stuck in a hole with us? You ought to be on the spot, to go to England—you ought to go to America."

"One would think you were *my* tutor!" said Pemberton.

Morgan walked on, and after a moment he began again: "Well, now that you know that I know and that we look at the facts and keep nothing back—it's much more comfortable, isn't it?"

"My dear boy, it's so amusing, so interesting, that it surely will be quite impossible for me to forgo such hours as these."

This made Morgan stop once more. "You *do* keep something back. Oh, you're not straight—*I* am!"

"Why am I not straight?"

"Oh, you've got your idea!"

"My idea?"

"Why, that I probably shan't live, and that you can stick it out till I'm removed."

"You *are* too clever to live!" Pemberton repeated.

"I call it a mean idea," Morgan pursued. "But I shall punish you by the way I hang on."

"Look out or I'll poison you!" Pemberton laughed.

"I'm stronger and better every year. Haven't you noticed that there hasn't been a doctor near me since you came?"

"*I'm* your doctor," said the young man, taking his arm and drawing him on again.

Morgan proceeded, and after a few steps he gave a sigh of mingled weariness and relief. "Ah, now that we look at the facts, it's all right!"

VII

They looked at the facts a good deal after this; and one of the first consequences of their doing so was that Pemberton stuck it out, as it were, for the purpose. Morgan made the facts so vivid and so droll, and at the same time so bald and so ugly, that there was fascination in talking them over with him, just as there would have been heartlessness in leaving him alone with them. Now that they had such a number of perceptions in common it was useless for the pair to pretend that they didn't judge such people; but the very judgment, and the exchange of perceptions, created another tie. Morgan had never been so interesting as now that he himself was made plainer by the sidelight of these confidences. What came out in it most was the soreness of his characteristic pride. He had plenty of that, Pemberton felt—so much that it was perhaps well it should have had to take some early bruises. He would have liked his people to be gallant, and he had waked up too soon to the sense that they were perpetually swallowing humble-pie. His mother would consume any amount, and his father would consume even more than his mother. He had a theory that Ulick had wriggled out of an "affair" at Nice: there had once been a flurry at home, a regular panic, after which they all went to bed and took medicine, not to be accounted for on any other supposition. Morgan had a romantic imagination, fed by poetry and history, and he would have liked those who "bore his name" (as he used to say to Pemberton with the humour that made his sensitiveness manly) to have a proper spirit. But their one idea was to get in with people who didn't want them and to take snubs as if they were honourable scars. Why people didn't want them more he didn't know—that was people's own affair; after all they were not superficially repulsive—they were a hundred times cleverer than most of the dreary grandees, the "poor swells" they rushed about Europe to catch up with. "After all, they *are* amusing—they are!" Morgan used to say, with the wisdom of the ages. To which Pemberton always replied: "Amusing—the great Moreen troupe? Why, they're altogether delightful; and if it were not for the hitch that you and I (feeble performers!) make in the *ensemble*, they would carry everything before them."

What the boy couldn't get over was that this particular blight seemed, in a tradition of self-respect, so undeserved and so arbitrary. No doubt people had a right to take the line they liked; but why should *his* people have liked the line of pushing and toadying and lying and cheating? What had their forefathers—all decent folk, so far as he knew—done to them, or what had *he* done to them? Who had poisoned their blood with the fifth-rate social ideal, the fixed idea of making smart acquaintances and getting into the *monde chic*, especially when it was foredoomed to failure and exposure? They showed so what they were after; that was what made the people they wanted not want *them*. And never a movement of dignity, never a throb of shame at looking each other in the face, never any independence or resentment or disgust. If his father or his brother would only knock some one down once or twice a year! Clever as they were they never guessed how they appeared. They were good-natured, yes—as good-natured as Jews at the doors of clothing-shops! But was that the model one wanted one's family to follow? Morgan had dim memories of an old grandfather, the maternal, in New York, whom he had been taken across the ocean to see, at the age of five: a gentleman with a high neckcloth and a good deal of pronunciation, who wore a dress-coat in the morning, which made one wonder what he wore in the evening, and had, or was supposed to have, "property" and some-thing to do with the Bible Society. It couldn't have been but that *he* was a good type. Pemberton himself remembered Mrs. Clancy, a widowed sister of Mr. Moreen's, who was as irritating as a moral tale and had paid a fortnight's visit to the family at Nice shortly after he came to live with them. She was "pure and refined," as Amy said, over the banjo, and had the air of not knowing what they meant and of keeping something back. Pemberton judged that what she kept back was an approval of many of their ways; therefore it was to be supposed that she too was of a good type, and that Mr. and Mrs. Moreen and Ulick and Paula and Amy might easily have been better if they would.

But that they wouldn't was more and more perceptible from day to day. They continued to "chivey," as Morgan called it, and in due time became aware of a variety of reasons for proceeding to Venice. They mentioned a great many of them—they were always strikingly frank, and had the brightest friendly chatter, at the late foreign breakfast in espe-cial, before the ladies had made up their faces, when they leaned their arms on the table, had something to follow the *demi-tasse,* and, in the heat of familiar discussion as to what they "really ought" to do, fell in-evitably into the languages in which they could *tutoyer.* Even Pember-ton liked them, then; he could endure even Ulick when he heard him give his little flat voice for the "sweet sea-city." That was what made him have a sneaking kindness for them—that they were so out of the worka-day world and kept him so out of it. The summer had waned when, with cries of ecstasy, they all passed out on the balcony that overhung the Grand Canal; the sunsets were splendid—the Dorringtons had arrived. The Dorringtons were the only reason they had not talked of at break-fast; but the reasons that they didn't talk of at breakfast always came out in the end. The Dorringtons, on the other hand, came out very little; or else, when they did, they stayed—as was natural—for hours, during which periods Mrs. Moreen and the girls sometimes called at their hotel (to see if they had returned) as many as three times running. The gondola was for the ladies; for in Venice too there were "days," which Mrs. Mo-reen knew in their order an hour after she arrived. She immediately took one herself, to which the Dorringtons never came, though on a certain occasion when Pemberton and his pupil were together at St. Mark's— where, taking the best walks they had ever had and haunting a hundred churches, they spent a great deal of time—they saw the old lord turn up with Mr. Moreen and Ulick, who showed him the dim basilica as if it belonged to them. Pemberton noted how much less, among its curiosities, Lord Dorrington carried himself as a man of the world; wondering too whether, for such services, his companions took a fee from him. The autumn, at any rate, waned, the Dorringtons departed, and Lord Verschoyle, the eldest son, had proposed neither for Amy nor for Paula.

One sad November day, while the wind roared round the old palace and the rain lashed the lagoon, Pemberton, for exercise and even somewhat for warmth (the Moreens were horribly frugal about fires—it was a cause of suffering to their inmate), walked up and down the big bare *sala* with his pupil. The scagliola floor was cold, the high battered casements shook in the storm, and the stately decay of the place was unrelieved by a particle of furniture. Pemberton's spirits were low, and it came over him that the fortune of the Moreens was now even lower. A blast of desolation, a prophecy of disaster and disgrace, seemed to draw through the comfortless hall. Mr. Moreen and Ulick were in the Piazza, looking out for something, strolling drearily, in mackintoshes, under the arcades; but still, in spite of mackintoshes, unmistakable men of the world. Paula and Amy were in bed—it might have been thought they were staying there to keep warm. Pemberton looked askance at the boy at his side, to see to what extent he was conscious of these portents. But Morgan, luckily for him, was now mainly conscious of growing taller and stronger and indeed of being in his fifteenth year. This fact was intensely interesting to him—it was the basis of a private theory (which, however, he had imparted to his tutor) that in a little while he should stand on his own feet. He considered that the situation would change— that, in short, he should be "finished," grown up, producible in the world of affairs and ready to prove himself of sterling ability. Sharply as he was capable, at times, of questioning his circumstances, there were happy hours when he was as superficial as a child; the proof of which was his fundamental assumption that he should presently go to Oxford, to Pemberton's college, and, aided and abetted by Pemberton, do the most wonderful things. It vexed Pemberton to see how little, in such a project, he took account of ways and means: on other matters he was so sceptical about them. Pemberton tried to imagine the Moreens at Oxford, and fortunately failed; yet unless they were to remove there as a family there would be no *modus vivendi* for Morgan. How could he live without an allowance, and where was the allowance to come from? He (Pemberton) might live on Morgan; but how could Morgan live on him? What was to become of him anyhow? Somehow, the fact that he was a big boy now, with better prospects of health, made the question of his future more difficult. So long as he was frail the consideration that he inspired seemed enough of an answer to it. But at the bottom of Pemberton's heart was the recognition of his probably being strong enough to live and not strong enough to thrive. He himself, at any rate, was in a period of natural, boyish rosiness about all this, so that the beating of the tempest seemed to him only the voice of life and the challenge of fate. He had on his shabby little overcoat, with the collar up, but he was enjoying his walk.

It was interrupted at last by the appearance of his mother at the end of the *sala*. She beckoned to Morgan to come to her, and while Pemberton saw him, complacent, pass down the long vista, over the damp false marble, he wondered what was in the air. Mrs. Moreen said a word to the boy and made him go into the room she had quitted. Then, having closed the door after him, she directed her steps swiftly to Pemberton. There *was* something in the air, but his wildest flight of fancy wouldn't have suggested what it proved to be. She signified that she had made a pretext to get Morgan out of the way, and then she inquired—without hesitation—if the young man could lend her sixty francs. While, before bursting into a laugh, he stared at her with surprise, she declared that she was awfully pressed for the money; she was desperate for it—it would save her life.

"Dear lady, *c'est trop fort!*" Pemberton laughed. "Where in the world do you suppose I should get sixty francs, *du train dont vous allez?*"

"I thought you worked—wrote things; don't they pay you?"

"Not a penny."

"Are you such a fool as to work for nothing?"

"You ought surely to know that."

Mrs. Moreen stared an instant, then she coloured a little. Pemberton saw she had quite forgotten the terms—if "terms" they could be called—that he had ended by accepting from herself; they had burdened her memory as little as her conscience. "Oh, yes, I see what you mean—you have been very nice about that; but why go back to it so often?" She had been perfectly urbane with him ever since the rough scene of explanation in his room, the morning he made her accept *his* "terms"—the necessity of his making his case known to Morgan. She had felt no resentment, after seeing that there was no danger of Morgan's taking the matter up with her. Indeed, attributing this immunity to the good taste of his influence with the boy, she had once said to Pemberton: "My dear fellow; it's an immense comfort you're a gentleman." She repeated this, in substance, now. "Of course you're a gentleman—that's a bother the less!" Pemberton reminded her that he had not "gone back" to anything; and she also repeated her prayer that, somewhere and somehow, he would find her sixty francs. He took the liberty of declaring that if he could find them it wouldn't be to lend them to *her*—as to which he consciously did himself injustice, knowing that if he had them he would certainly place them in her hand. He accused himself, at bottom and with some truth, of a fantastic, demoralised sympathy with her. If misery made strange bed-fellows it also made strange sentiments. It was moreover a part of the demoralisation and of the general bad effect of living with

such people that one had to make rough retorts, quite out of the tradition of good manners. "Morgan, Morgan, to what pass have I come for
you?" he privately exclaimed, while Mrs. Moreen floated voluminously
down the *sala* again, to liberate the boy; groaning, as she went, that everything was too odious.

Before the boy was liberated there came a thump at the door com-
municating with the staircase, followed by the apparition of a dripping
youth who poked in his head. Pemberton recognised him as the bearer of
a telegram and recognised the telegram as addressed to himself. Morgan
came back as, after glancing at the signature (that of a friend in London),
he was reading the words: "Found jolly job for you—engagement to
coach opulent youth on own terms. Come immediately." The answer,
happily, was paid, and the messenger waited. Morgan, who had drawn
near, waited too, and looked hard at Pemberton; and Pemberton, after a
moment, having met his look, handed him the telegram. It was really by
wise looks (they knew each other so well) that, while the telegraph-boy,
in his waterproof cape, made a great puddle on the floor, the thing was
settled between them. Pemberton wrote the answer with a pencil against
the frescoed wall, and the messenger departed. When he had gone Pemberton said to Morgan:

"I'll make a tremendous charge; I'll earn a lot of money in a short time,
and we'll live on it."

"Well, I hope the opulent youth will be stupid—he probably will—"
Morgan parenthesised, "and keep you a long time."

"Of course, the longer he keeps me the more we shall have for our
old age."

"But suppose *they* don't pay you!" Morgan awfully suggested.

"Oh, there are not two such——!" Pemberton paused, he was on the
point of using an invidious term. Instead of this he said "two such
chances."

Morgan flushed—the tears came to his eyes. "*Dites toujours*, two such
rascally crews!" Then, in a different tone, he added: "Happy opulent
youth!"

"Not if he's stupid!"

"Oh, they're happier then. But you can't have everything, can you?"
the boy smiled.

Pemberton held him, his hands on his shoulders. "What will become of
you, what will you do?" He thought of Mrs. Moreen, desperate for sixty
francs.

"I shall turn into a man." And then, as if he recognised all the bearings
of Pemberton's allusion: "I shall get on with them better when you're
not here."

"Ah, don't say that—it sounds as if I set you against them!"

"You do—the sight of you. It's all right; you know what I mean. I shall
be beautiful. I'll take their affairs in hand; I'll marry my sisters."

"You'll marry yourself!" joked Pemberton; as high, rather tense pleasantry would evidently be the right, or the safest, tone for their separation.

It was, however, not purely in this strain that Morgan suddenly asked: "But I say—how will you get to your jolly job? You'll have to telegraph to the opulent youth for money to come on."

Pemberton bethought himself. "They won't like that, will they?"

"Oh, look out for them!"

Then Pemberton brought out his remedy. "I'll go to the American Consul; I'll borrow some money of him—just for the few days, on the strength of the telegram."

Morgan was hilarious. "Show him the telegram—then stay and keep the money!"

Pemberton entered into the joke enough to reply that, for Morgan, he was really capable of that; but the boy, growing more serious, and to prove that he hadn't meant what he said, not only hurried off to the Consulate (since he was to start that evening, as he had wired to his friend), but insisted on going with him. They splashed through the tortuous perforations and over the humpbacked bridges, and they passed through the Piazza, where they saw Mr. Moreen and Ulick go into a jeweller's shop. The Consul proved accommodating (Pemberton said it wasn't the letter, but Morgan's grand air), and on their way back they went into St. Mark's for a hushed ten minutes. Later they took up and kept up the fun of it to the very end; and it seemed to Pemberton a part of that fun that Mrs. Moreen, who was very angry when he had announced to her his intention, should charge him, grotesquely and vulgarly, and in reference to the loan she had vainly endeavoured to effect, with bolting lest they should "get something out" of him. On the other hand he had to do Mr. Moreen and Ulick the justice to recognise that when, on coming in, *they* heard the cruel news, they took it like perfect men of the world.

VIII

When Pemberton got at work with the opulent youth, who was to be taken in hand for Balliol, he found himself unable to say whether he was really an idiot or it was only, on his own part, the long association with an intensely living little mind that made him seem so. From Morgan he heard half-a-dozen times: the boy wrote charming young letters, a patchwork of tongues, with indulgent postscripts in the family Volapuk and, in little squares and rounds and crannies of the text, the drollest illustrations—letters that he was divided between the impulse to show his present disciple, as a kind of wasted incentive, and the sense of something in them that was profanable by publicity. The opulent youth went up, in due course, and failed to pass; but it seemed to add to the presumption that brilliancy was not expected of him all at once that his parents, condoning the lapse, which they good-naturedly treated as little as possible as if it were Pemberton's, should have sounded the rally again, begged the young coach to keep his pupil in hand another year.

The young coach was now in a position to lend Mrs. Moreen sixty francs, and he sent her a post-office order for the amount. In return for this favour he received a frantic, scribbled line from her: "Implore you to come back instantly—Morgan dreadfully ill." They were on the rebound, once more in Paris—often as Pemberton had seen them depressed he had never seen them crushed—and communication was therefore rapid. He wrote to the boy to ascertain the state of his health, but he received no answer to his letter. Accordingly he took an abrupt leave of the opulent youth and, crossing the Channel, alighted at the small hotel, in the quarter of the Champs Elysées, of which Mrs. Moreen had given him the address. A deep if dumb dissatisfaction with this lady and her companions bore him company: they couldn't be vulgarly honest, but they could live at hotels, in velvety *entresols*, amid a smell of burnt pastilles, in the most expensive city in Europe. When he had left them, in Venice, it was with an irrepressible suspicion that something was going to happen; but the only thing that had happened was that they succeeded in getting away. "How is he? where is he?" he asked of Mrs. Moreen; but before she could speak, these questions were answered by the pressure round his neck of a pair of arms, in shrunken sleeves, which were perfectly capable of an effusive young foreign squeeze.

"Dreadfully ill—I don't see it!" the young man cried. And then, to Morgan: "Why on earth didn't you relieve me? Why didn't you answer my letter?"

Mrs. Moreen declared that when she wrote he was very bad, and Pemberton learned at the same time from the boy that he had answered every letter he had received. This led to the demonstration that Pemberton's note had been intercepted. Mrs. Moreen was prepared to see the fact exposed, as Pemberton perceived, the moment he faced her, that she was prepared for a good many other things. She was prepared above all to maintain that she had acted from a sense of duty, that she was enchanted she had got him over, whatever they might say; and that it was useless of him to pretend that he didn't *know*, in all his bones, that his place at such a time was with Morgan. He had taken the boy away from them, and now he had no right to abandon him. He had created for himself the gravest responsibilities; he must at least abide by what he had done.

"Taken him away from you?" Pemberton exclaimed indignantly.

"Do it—do it, for pity's sake; that's just what I want. I can't stand *this* —and such scenes. They're treacherous!" These words broke from Morgan, who had intermitted his embrace, in a key which made Pemberton turn quickly to him, to see that he had suddenly seated himself, was breathing with evident difficulty and was very pale.

"*Now* do you say he's not ill—my precious pet?" shouted his mother, dropping on her knees before him with clasped hands, but touching him no more than if he had been a gilded idol. "It will pass—it's only for an instant; but don't say such dreadful things!"

"I'm all right—all right," Morgan panted to Pemberton, whom he sat looking up at with a strange smile, his hands resting on either side on the sofa.

"Now do you pretend I've been treacherous—that I've deceived?" Mrs. Moreen flashed at Pemberton as she got up.

"It isn't *he* says it, it's I!" the boy returned, apparently easier, but sinking back against the wall; while Pemberton, who had sat down beside him, taking his hand, bent over him.

"Darling child, one does what one can; there are so many things to consider," urged Mrs. Moreen. "It's his *place*—his only place. You see *you* think it is now."

"Take me away—take me away," Morgan went on, smiling to Pemberton from his white face.

"Where shall I take you, and how—oh, *how*, my boy?" the young man stammered, thinking of the rude way in which his friends in London held that, for his convenience, and without a pledge of instantaneous return, he had thrown them over; of the just resentment with which they would already have called in a successor, and of the little help as regarded finding fresh employment that resided for him in the flatness of his having failed to pass his pupil.

"Oh, we'll settle that. You used to talk about it," said Morgan. "If we can only go, all the rest's a detail."

"Talk about it as much as you like, but don't think you can attempt it. Mr. Moreen would never consent—it would be so precarious," Pemberton's hostess explained to him. Then to Morgan she explained: "It would destroy our peace, it would break our hearts. Now that he's back it will be all the same again. You'll have your life, your work and your freedom, and we'll all be happy as we used to be. You'll bloom and grow perfectly well, and we won't have any more silly experiments, will we? They're too absurd. It's Mr. Pemberton's place—every one in his place. You in yours, your papa in his, me in mine—*n'est-ce pas, chéri?* We'll all forget how foolish we've been, and we'll have lovely times."

She continued to talk and to surge vaguely about the little draped, stuffy *salon*, while Pemberton sat with the boy, whose colour gradually came back; and she mixed up her reasons, dropping that there were going to be changes, that the other children might scatter (who knew?—Paula had her ideas), and that then it might be fancied how much the poor old parent-birds would want the little nestling. Morgan looked at Pemberton, who wouldn't let him move; and Pemberton knew exactly how he felt at hearing himself called a little nestling. He admitted that he had had one or two bad days, but he protested afresh against the iniquity of his mother's having made them the ground of an appeal to poor Pemberton. Poor Pemberton could laugh now, apart from the comicality of Mrs. Moreen's producing so much philosophy for her defence (she seemed to shake it out of her agitated petticoats, which knocked over the light gilt chairs), so little did the sick boy strike him as qualified to repudiate any advantage.

He himself was in for it, at any rate. He should have Morgan on his hands again indefinitely; though indeed he saw the lad had a private theory to produce which would be intended to smooth this down. He was obliged to him for it in advance; but the suggested amendment didn't keep his heart from sinking a little, any more than it prevented him from accepting the prospect on the spot, with some confidence moreover that he would do so even better if he could have a little supper. Mrs. Moreen threw out more hints about the changes that were to be looked for, but she was such a mixture of smiles and shudders (she confessed she was very nervous), that he couldn't tell whether she were in high feather or only in hysterics. If the family were really at last going to pieces why shouldn't she recognise the necessity of pitching Morgan into some sort of lifeboat? This presumption was fostered by the fact that they were established in luxurious quarters in the capital of pleasure; that was exactly where they naturally *would* be established in view of going to pieces. Moreover didn't she mention that Mr. Moreen and the others were enjoying themselves at the opera with Mr. Granger, and wasn't *that* also precisely where one would look for them on the eve of a smash? Pemberton gathered that Mr. Granger was a rich, vacant American—a big bill with a flourishy heading and no items; so that one of Paula's "ideas" was probably that this time she had really done it, which was indeed an unprecedented blow to the general cohesion. And if the cohesion was to terminate what was to become of poor Pemberton? He felt quite enough bound up with them to figure, to his alarm, as a floating spar in case of a wreck.

It was Morgan who eventually asked if no supper had been ordered for him; sitting with him below, later, at the dim, delayed meal, in the presence of a great deal of corded green plush, a plate of ornamental biscuit and a languor marked on the part of the waiter. Mrs. Moreen had explained that they had been obliged to secure a room for the visitor out of the house; and Morgan's consolation (he offered it while Pemberton reflected on the nastiness of lukewarm sauces) proved to be, largely, that this circumstance would facilitate their escape. He talked of their escape (recurring to it often afterwards), as if they were making up a "boy's book" together. But he likewise expressed his sense that there was something in the air, that the Moreens couldn't keep it up much longer. In point of fact, as Pemberton was to see, they kept it up for five or six months. All the while, however, Morgan's contention was designed to cheer him. Mr. Moreen and Ulick, whom he had met the day after his return, accepted that return like perfect men of the world. If Paula and Amy treated it even with less formality an allowance was to be made for them, inasmuch as Mr. Granger had not come to the opera after all. He had only placed his box at their service, with a bouquet for each of the party; there was even one apiece, embittering the thought of his profusion, for Mr. Moreen and Ulick. "They're all like that," was Morgan's comment; "at the very last, just when we think we've got them fast, we're chucked!"

Morgan's comments, in these days, were more and more free; they even included a large recognition of the extraordinary tenderness with which he had been treated while Pemberton was away. Oh, yes, they couldn't do enough to be nice to him, to show him they had him on their mind and make up for his loss. That was just what made the whole thing so sad, and him so glad, after all, of Pemberton's return—he had to keep thinking of their affection less, had less sense of obligation. Pemberton laughed out at this last reason, and Morgan blushed and said: "You know what I mean." Pemberton knew perfectly what he meant; but there were a good many things it didn't make any clearer. This episode of his second sojourn in Paris stretched itself out wearily, with their resumed readings and wanderings and maunderings, their potterings on the quays, their hauntings of the museums, their occasional lingerings in the Palais Royal, when the first sharp weather came on and there was a comfort in warm emanations, before Chevet's wonderful succulent window. Morgan wanted to hear a great deal about the opulent youth—he took an immense interest in him. Some of the details of his opulence—Pemberton could spare him none of them—evidently intensified the boy's appreciation of all his friend had given up to come back to him; but in addition to the greater reciprocity established by such a renunciation he had always his little brooding theory, in which there was a frivolous gaiety too, that their long probation was drawing to a close. Morgan's conviction that the Moreens couldn't go on much longer kept pace with the unexpended impetus with which, from month to month, they did go on. Three weeks after Pemberton had rejoined them they went on to another hotel, a dingier one than the first; but Morgan rejoiced that his tutor had at least still not sacrificed the advantage of a room outside. He clung to the romantic utility of this when the day, or rather the night, should arrive for their escape.

For the first time, in this complicated connection, Pemberton felt sore and exasperated. It was, as he had said to Mrs. Moreen in Venice, *trop fort*—everything was *trop fort*. He could neither really throw off his blighting burden nor find in it the benefit of a pacified conscience or of a rewarded affection. He had spent all the money that he had earned in England, and he felt that his youth was going and that he was getting nothing back for it. It was all very well for Morgan to seem to consider that he would make up to him for all inconveniences by settling himself upon him permanently—there was an irritating flaw in such a view. He saw what the boy had in his mind; the conception that as his friend had had the generosity to come back to him he must show his gratitude by giving him his life. But the poor friend didn't desire the gift—what could he do with Morgan's life? Of course at the same time that Pemberton was irritated he remembered the reason, which was very honourable to Morgan and which consisted simply of the fact that he was perpetually making one forget that he was after all only a child. If one dealt with him on a different basis one's misadventures were one's own fault. So Pemberton waited in a queer confusion of yearning and alarm for the catastrophe which was held to hang over the house of Moreen, of which he certainly at moments felt the symptoms brush his cheek and as to which he wondered much in what form it would come.

Perhaps it would take the form of dispersal—a frightened *sauve qui peut*, a scuttling into selfish corners. Certainly they were less elastic than of yore; they were evidently looking for something they didn't find. The Dorringtons hadn't reappeared, the princes had scattered; wasn't that the beginning of the end? Mrs. Moreen had lost her reckoning of the famous "days"; her social calendar was blurred—it had turned its face to the wall. Pemberton suspected that the great, the cruel, discomfiture had been the extraordinary behaviour of Mr. Granger, who seemed not to know what he wanted, or, what was much worse, what *they* wanted. He kept sending flowers, as if to bestrew the path of his retreat, which was never the path of return. Flowers were all very well, but—Pemberton could complete the proposition. It was now positively conspicuous that in the long run the Moreens were a failure; so that the young man was almost grateful the run had not been short. Mr. Moreen, indeed, was still occasionally able to get away on business, and, what was more surprising, he was also able to get back. Ulick had no club, but you could not have discovered it from his appearance, which was as much as ever that of a person looking at life from the window of such an institution; therefore Pemberton was doubly astonished at an answer he once heard him make to his mother, in the desperate tone of a man familiar with the worst privations. Her question Pemberton had not quite caught; it appeared to be an appeal for a suggestion as to whom they could get to take Amy. "Let the devil take her!" Ulick snapped; so that Pemberton could see that not only they had lost their amiability, but had ceased to believe in themselves. He could also see that if Mrs. Moreen was trying to get people to take her children she might be regarded as closing the hatches for the storm. But Morgan would be the last she would part with.

One winter afternoon—it was a Sunday—he and the boy walked far together in the Bois de Boulogne. The evening was so splendid, the cold lemon-coloured sunset so clear, the stream of carriages and pedestrians so amusing and the fascination of Paris so great, that they stayed out later than usual and became aware that they would have to hurry home to arrive in time for dinner. They hurried accordingly, arm-in-arm, good-humoured and hungry, agreeing that there was nothing like Paris after all and that after all, too, that had come and gone they were not yet sated with innocent pleasures. When they reached the hotel they found that, though scandalously late, they were in time for all the dinner they were likely to sit down to. Confusion reigned in the apartments of the Moreens (very shabby ones this time, but the best in the house), and before the interrupted service of the table (with objects displaced almost as if there had been a scuffle, and a great wine stain from an overturned bottle), Pemberton could not blink the fact that there had been a scene of proprietary mutiny. The storm had come—they were all seeking refuge. The hatches were down—Paula and Amy were invisible (they had never tried the most casual art upon Pemberton, but he felt that they had enough of an eye to him not to wish to meet him as young ladies whose frocks had been confiscated), and Ulick appeared to have jumped overboard. In a word, the host and his staff had ceased to "go on" at the pace of their guests, and the air of embarrassed detention, thanks to a pile of gaping trunks in the passage, was strangely commingled with the air of indignant withdrawal.

When Morgan took in all this—and he took it in very quickly—he blushed to the roots of his hair. He had walked, from his infancy, among difficulties and dangers, but he had never seen a public exposure. Pemberton noticed, in a second glance at him, that the tears had rushed into his eyes and that they were tears of bitter shame. He wondered for an instant, for the boy's sake, whether he might successfully pretend not to understand. Not successfully, he felt, as Mr. and Mrs. Moreen, dinnerless by their extinguished hearth, rose before him in their little dishonoured *salon*, considering apparently with much intensity what lively capital would be next on their list. They were not prostrate, but they were very pale, and Mrs. Moreen had evidently been crying. Pemberton quickly learned however that her grief was not for the loss of her dinner, much as she usually enjoyed it, but on account of a necessity much more tragic. She lost no time in laying this necessity bare, in telling him how the change had come, the bolt had fallen, and how they would all have to turn themselves about. Therefore cruel as it was to them to part with their darling she must look to him to carry a little further the influence he had so fortunately acquired with the boy—to induce his young charge to follow him into some modest retreat. They depended upon him, in a word, to take their delightful child temporarily under his protection—it would leave Mr. Moreen and herself so much more free to give the proper attention (too little, alas! had been given) to the readjustment of their affairs.

"We trust you—we feel that we can," said Mrs. Moreen, slowly rubbing her plump white hands and looking, with compunction, hard at Morgan, whose chin, not to take liberties, her husband stroked with a tentative paternal forefinger.

"Oh, yes; we feel that we can. We trust Mr. Pemberton fully, Morgan," Mr. Moreen conceded.

Pemberton wondered again if he might pretend not to understand; but the idea was painfully complicated by the immediate perception that Morgan had understood.

"Do you mean that he may take me to live with him—for ever and ever?" cried the boy. "Away, away, anywhere he likes?"

"For ever and ever? *Comme vous-y-allez!*" Mr. Moreen laughed indulgently. "For as long as Mr. Pemberton may be so good."

"We've struggled, we've suffered," his wife went on; "but you've made him so your own that we've already been through the worst of the sacrifice."

Morgan had turned away from his father—he stood looking at Pemberton with a light in his face. His blush had died out, but something had come that was brighter and more vivid. He had a moment of boyish joy, scarcely mitigated by the reflection that, with his unexpected consecration of his hope—too sudden and too violent; the thing was a good deal less like a boy's book—the "escape" was left on their hands. The boyish joy was there for an instant, and Pemberton was almost frightened at the revelation of gratitude and affection that shone through his humiliation. When Morgan stammered "My dear fellow, what do you say to *that?*" he felt that he should say something enthusiastic. But he was still more frightened at something else that immediately followed and that made the lad sit down quickly on the nearest chair. He had turned very white and had raised his hand to his left side. They were all three looking at him, but Mrs. Moreen was the first to bound forward. "Ah, his darling little heart!" she broke out; and this time, on her knees before him and without respect for the idol, she caught him ardently in her arms. "You walked him too far, you hurried him too fast!" she tossed over her shoulder at Pemberton. The boy made no protest, and the next instant his mother, still holding him, sprang up with her face convulsed and with the terrified cry "Help, help! he's going, he's gone!" Pemberton saw, with equal horror, by Morgan's own stricken face, that he *was* gone. He pulled him half out of his mother's hands, and for a moment, while they held him together, they looked all their dismay into each other's eyes. "He couldn't stand it with his weak organ," said Pemberton—"the shock, the whole scene, the violent emotion."

"But I thought he *wanted* to go to you!" wailed Mrs. Moreen.

"I *told* you he didn't, my dear," her husband made answer. Mr. Moreen was trembling all over and was in his way as deeply affected as his wife. But after the very first he took his bereavement as a man of the world.

⚜

THE REAL THING

"The Real Thing" was published a year after "The Pupil" and is a tale in another series James was then writing, concerned with the life of painters and writers. The story was suggested to him by his friend the cartoonist and writer George du Maurier, who was visited in his studio by just such a couple as James describes. The stories James wrote about his own craft and the craft of painting often carry within them the elements of a fable. He tells his stories "straight" enough, but they possess always an inner core of meaning. The meaning of "The Real Thing" lies at the heart of all artistic endeavor, and offers a distinction not sufficiently made in our time: the difference between the actual and the imagined, the photographic and the painted, the real and the illusion of reality. The real can be only as real as it is made to be for the reader; and usually it is achieved through the illuminating force of the artist's imagination. In "The Real Thing" James says this with delightful, good-natured humor; and his portrayal of the solid unimaginative pathetic couple and of the bohemian Italian and the little Cockney girl, shows the acuteness of his own observations of London life and his happy faculty for entering into situations; above all his ability to spin the light and the airy in a story and yet say something profound.

I

When the porter's wife (she used to answer the house-bell) announced "A gentleman—with a lady, sir," I had as I often had in those days, for the wish was father to the thought, an immediate vision of sitters. Sitters my visitors in this case proved to be; but not in the sense I should have preferred. However, there was nothing at first to indicate that they might not have come for a portrait. The gentleman, a man of fifty, very high and very straight, with a moustache slightly grizzled and a dark grey walking-coat admirably fitted, both of which I noted professionally—I don't mean as a barber or yet as a tailor—would have struck me as a celebrity if celebrities often were striking. It was a truth of which I had for some time been conscious that a figure with a good deal of frontage was, as one might say, almost never a public institution. A glance at the lady helped to remind me of this paradoxical law: she also looked too distinguished to be a "personality." Moreover one would scarcely come across two variations together.

Neither of the pair spoke immediately—they only prolonged the preliminary gaze which suggested that each wished to give the other a chance. They were visibly shy; they stood there letting me take them in —which, as I afterwards perceived, was the most practical thing they could have done. In this way their embarrassment served their cause. I had seen people painfully reluctant to mention that they desired anything so gross as to be represented on canvas; but the scruples of my new friends appeared almost insurmountable. Yet the gentleman might have said "I should like a portrait of my wife," and the lady might have said "I should like a portrait of my husband." Perhaps they were not husband and wife—this naturally would make the matter more delicate. Perhaps they wished to be done together—in which case they ought to have brought a third person to break the news.

"We come from Mr. Rivet," the lady said at last, with a dim smile which had the effect of a moist sponge passed over a "sunk" piece of painting, as well as of a vague allusion to vanished beauty. She was as tall and straight, in her degree, as her companion, and with ten years less to carry. She looked as sad as a woman could look whose face was not charged with expression; that is her tinted oval mask showed friction as an exposed surface shows it. The hand of time had played over her freely, but only to simplify. She was slim and stiff, and so well-dressed, in dark blue cloth, with lappets and pockets and buttons, that it was clear she employed the same tailor as her husband. The couple had an indefinable air of prosperous thrift—they evidently got a good deal of luxury for their money. If I was to be one of their luxuries it would behove me to consider my terms.

"Ah, Claude Rivet recommended me?" I inquired; and I added that it was very kind of him, though I could reflect that, as he only painted landscape, this was not a sacrifice.

The lady looked very hard at the gentleman, and the gentleman looked round the room. Then staring at the floor a moment and stroking his moustache, he rested his pleasant eyes on me with the remark: "He said you were the right one."

"I try to be, when people want to sit."

"Yes, we should like to," said the lady anxiously.

"Do you mean together?"

My visitors exchanged a glance. "If you could do anything with *me*, I suppose it would be double," the gentleman stammered.

"Oh yes, there's naturally a higher charge for two figures than for one."

"We should like to make it pay," the husband confessed.

"That's very good of you," I returned, appreciating so unwonted a sympathy—for I supposed he meant pay the artist.

A sense of strangeness seemed to dawn on the lady. "We mean for the illustrations—Mr. Rivet said you might put one in."

"Put one in—an illustration?" I was equally confused.

"Sketch her off, you know," said the gentleman, colouring.

It was only then that I understood the service Claude Rivet had rendered me; he had told them that I worked in black and white, for magazines, for story-books, for sketches of contemporary life, and consequently had frequent employment for models. These things were true, but it was not less true (I may confess it now—whether because the aspiration was to lead to everything or to nothing I leave the reader to guess), that I couldn't get the honours, to say nothing of the emoluments, of a great painter of portraits out of my head. My "illustrations" were my pot-boilers; I looked to a different branch of art (far and away the most interesting it had always seemed to me) to perpetuate my fame. There was no shame in looking to it also to make my fortune; but that fortune was by so much further from being made from the moment my visitors wished to be "done" for nothing. I was disappointed; for in the pictorial sense I had immediately *seen* them. I had seized their type—I had already settled what I would do with it. Something that wouldn't absolutely have pleased them, I afterwards reflected.

"Ah, you're—you're—a——?" I began, as soon as I had mastered my surprise. I couldn't bring out the dingy word "models"; it seemed to fit the case so little.

"We haven't had much practice," said the lady.

"We've got to *do* something, and we've thought that an artist in your line might perhaps make something of us," her husband threw off. He further mentioned that they didn't know many artists and that they had gone first, on the off-chance (he painted views of course, but sometimes put in figures—perhaps I remembered), to Mr. Rivet, whom they had met a few years before at a place in Norfolk where he was sketching.

"We used to sketch a little ourselves," the lady hinted.

"It's very awkward, but we absolutely *must* do something," her husband went on.

"Of course, we're not so *very* young," she admitted, with a wan smile.

With the remark that I might as well know something more about them, the husband had handed me a card extracted from a neat new pocket-book (their appurtenances were all of the freshest) and inscribed with the words "Major Monarch." Impressive as these words were they didn't carry my knowledge much further; but my visitor presently added: "I've left the army, and we've had the misfortune to lose our money. In fact our means are dreadfully small."

"It's an awful bore," said Mrs. Monarch.

They evidently wished to be discreet—to take care not to swagger because they were gentlefolks. I perceived they would have been willing to recognise this as something of a drawback, at the same time that I guessed at an underlying sense—their consolation in adversity—that they *had* their points. They certainly had; but these advantages struck me as preponderantly social; such for instance as would help to make a drawing-room look well. However, a drawing-room was always, or ought to be, a picture.

In consequence of his wife's allusion to their age Major Monarch observed: "Naturally, it's more for the figure that we thought of going in. We can still hold ourselves up." On the instant I saw that the figure was indeed their strong point. His "naturally" didn't sound vain, but it lighted up the question. "*She* has got the best," he continued, nodding at his wife, with a pleasant after-dinner absence of circumlocution. I could only reply, as if we were in fact sitting over our wine, that this didn't prevent his own from being very good; which led him in turn to rejoin: "We thought that if you ever have to do people like us, we might be something like it. *She*, particularly—for a lady in a book, you know."

I was so amused by them that, to get more of it, I did my best to take their point of view; and though it was an embarrassment to find myself appraising physically, as if they were animals on hire or useful blacks, a pair whom I should have expected to meet only in one of the relations in which criticism is tacit, I looked at Mrs. Monarch judicially enough to be able to exclaim, after a moment, with conviction: "Oh yes, a lady in a book!" She was singularly like a bad illustration.

"We'll stand up, if you like," said the Major; and he raised himself before me with a really grand air.

I could take his measure at a glance—he was six feet two and a perfect gentleman. It would have paid any club in process of formation and in want of a stamp to engage him at a salary to stand in the principal window. What struck me immediately was that in coming to me they had rather missed their vocation; they could surely have been turned to better account for advertising purposes. I couldn't of course see the thing in detail, but I could see them make someone's fortune—I don't mean their own. There was something in them for a waistcoat-maker, an hotel-keeper or a soap-vendor. I could imagine "We always use it" pinned on their bosoms with the greatest effect; I had a vision of the promptitude with which they would launch a table d'hôte.

Mrs. Monarch sat still, not from pride but from shyness, and presently her husband said to her: "Get up, my dear, and show how smart you are." She obeyed, but she had no need to get up to show it. She walked to the end of the studio, and then she came back blushing, with her fluttered eyes on her husband. I was reminded of an incident I had accidentally had a glimpse of in Paris—being with a friend there, a dramatist about to produce a play—when an actress came to him to ask to be intrusted with a part. She went through her paces before him, walked up and down as Mrs. Monarch was doing. Mrs. Monarch did it quite as well, but I abstained from applauding. It was very odd to see such people apply for such poor pay. She looked as if she had ten thousand a year. Her husband had used the word that described her: she was, in the London current jargon, essentially and typically "smart." Her figure was, in the same order of ideas, conspicuously and irreproachably "good." For a woman of her age her waist was surprisingly small; her elbow moreover had the orthodox crook. She held her head at the conventional angle; but why did she come to *me?* She ought to have tried on jackets at a big shop. I feared my visitors were not only destitute, but "artistic"—which would be a great complication. When she sat down again I thanked her, observing that what a draughtsman most valued in his model was the faculty of keeping quiet.

"Oh, *she* can keep quiet," said Major Monarch. Then he added, jocosely: "I've always kept her quiet."

"I'm not a nasty fidget, am I?" Mrs. Monarch appealed to her husband.

He addressed his answer to me. "Perhaps it isn't out of place to mention—because we ought to be quite business-like, oughtn't we?—that when I married her she was known as the Beautiful Statue."

"Oh dear!" said Mrs. Monarch, ruefully.

"Of course I should want a certain amount of expression," I rejoined.

"Of *course!*" they both exclaimed.

"And then I suppose you know that you'll get awfully tired."

"Oh, we *never* get tired!" they eagerly cried.

"Have you had any kind of practice?"

They hesitated—they looked at each other. "We've been photographed, *immensely*," said Mrs. Monarch.

"She means the fellows have asked us," added the Major.

"I see—because you're so good-looking."

"I don't know what they thought, but they were always after us."

"We always got our photographs for nothing," smiled Mrs. Monarch.

"We might have brought some, my dear," her husband remarked.

"I'm not sure we have any left. We've given quantities away," she explained to me.

"With our autographs and that sort of thing," said the Major.

"Are they to be got in the shops?" I inquired, as a harmless pleasantry.

"Oh, yes; *hers*—they used to be."

"Not now," said Mrs. Monarch, with her eyes on the floor.

II

I could fancy the "sort of thing" they put on the presentation-copies of their photographs, and I was sure they wrote a beautiful hand. It was odd how quickly I was sure of everything that concerned them. If they were now so poor as to have to earn shillings and pence, they never had had much of a margin. Their good looks had been their capital, and they had good-humouredly made the most of the career that this resource marked out for them. It was in their faces, the blankness, the deep intellectual repose of the twenty years of country-house visiting which had given them pleasant intonations. I could see the sunny drawing-rooms, sprinkled with periodicals she didn't read, in which Mrs. Monarch had continuously sat; I could see the wet shrubberies in which she had walked, equipped to admiration for either exercise. I could see the rich covers the Major had helped to shoot and the wonderful garments in which, late at night, he repaired to the smoking-room to talk about them. I could imagine their leggings and waterproofs, their knowing tweeds and rugs, their rolls of sticks and cases of tackle and neat umbrellas; and I could evoke the exact appearance of their servants and the compact variety of their luggage on the platforms of country stations.

They gave small tips, but they were liked; they didn't do anything themselves, but they were welcome. They looked so well everywhere; they gratified the general relish for stature, complexion and "form." They knew it without fatuity or vulgarity, and they respected themselves in consequence. They were not superficial; they were thorough and kept themselves up—it had been their line. People with such a taste for activity had to have some line. I could feel how, even in a dull house, they could have been counted upon for cheerfulness. At present something had happened—it didn't matter what, their little income had grown less, it had grown least—and they had to do something for pocket-money.

Their friends liked them, but didn't like to support them. There was something about them that represented credit—their clothes, their manners, their type; but if credit is a large empty pocket in which an occasional chink reverberates, the chink at least must be audible. What they wanted of me was to help to make it so. Fortunately they had no children—I soon divined that. They would also perhaps wish our relations to be kept secret: this was why it was "for the figure"—the reproduction of the face would betray them.

I liked them—they were so simple; and I had no objection to them if they would suit. But, somehow, with all their perfections I didn't easily believe in them. After all they were amateurs, and the ruling passion of my life was the detestation of the amateur. Combined with this was another perversity—an innate preference for the represented subject over the real one: the defect of the real one was so apt to be a lack of representation. I liked things that appeared; then one was sure. Whether they *were* or not was a subordinate and almost always a profitless question. There were other considerations, the first of which was that I already had two or three people in use, notably a young person with big feet, in alpaca, from Kilburn, who for a couple of years had come to me regularly for my illustrations and with whom I was still—perhaps ignobly—satisfied. I frankly explained to my visitors how the case stood; but they had taken more precautions than I supposed. They had reasoned out their opportunity, for Claude Rivet had told them of the projected *édition de luxe* of one of the writers of our day—the rarest of the novelists—who, long neglected by the multitudinous vulgar and dearly prized by the attentive (need I mention Philip Vincent?) had had the happy fortune of seeing, late in life, the dawn and then the full light of a higher criticism—an estimate in which, on the part of the public, there was something really of expiation. The edition in question, planned by a publisher of taste, was practically an act of high reparation; the woodcuts with which it was to be enriched were the homage of English art to one of the most independent representatives of English letters. Major and Mrs. Monarch confessed to me that they had hoped I might be able to work *them* into my share of the enterprise. They knew I was to do the first of the books, "Rutland Ramsay," but I had to make clear to them that my participation in the rest of the affair—this first book was to be a test—was to depend on the satisfaction I should give. If this should be limited my employers would drop me without a scruple. It was therefore a crisis for me, and naturally I was making special preparations, looking about for new people, if they should be necessary, and securing the best types. I admitted however that I should like to settle down to two or three good models who would do for everything.

"Should we have often to—a—put on special clothes?" Mrs. Monarch timidly demanded.

"Dear, yes—that's half the business."

"And should we be expected to supply our own costumes?"

"Oh, no; I've got a lot of things. A painter's models put on—or put off —anything he likes."

"And do you mean—a—the same?"

"The same?"

Mrs. Monarch looked at her husband again.

"Oh, she was just wondering," he explained, "if the costumes are in *general* use." I had to confess that they were, and I mentioned further that some of them (I had a lot of genuine, greasy last-century things) had served their time, a hundred years ago, on living, world-stained men and women. "We'll put on anything that *fits*," said the Major.

"Oh, I arrange that—they fit in the pictures."

"I'm afraid I should do better for the modern books. I would come as you like," said Mrs. Monarch.

"She has got a lot of clothes at home: they might do for contemporary life," her husband continued.

"Oh, I can fancy scenes in which you'd be quite natural." And indeed I could see the slipshod rearrangements of stale properties—the stories I tried to produce pictures for without the exasperation of reading them— whose sandy tracts the good lady might help to people. But I had to return to the fact that for this sort of work—the daily mechanical grind—I was already equipped; the people I was working with were fully adequate.

"We only thought we might be more like *some* characters," said Mrs. Monarch mildly, getting up.

Her husband also rose; he stood looking at me with a dim wistfulness that was touching in so fine a man. "Wouldn't it be rather a pull sometimes to have—a—to have——?" He hung fire; he wanted me to help him by phrasing what he meant. But I couldn't—I didn't know. So he brought it out, awkwardly: "The *real* thing; a gentleman, you know, or a lady." I was quite ready to give a general assent—I admitted that there was a great deal in that. This encouraged Major Monarch to say, following up his appeal with an unacted gulp: "It's awfully hard—we've tried everything." The gulp was communicative; it proved too much for his wife. Before I knew it Mrs. Monarch had dropped again upon a divan and burst into tears. Her husband sat down beside her, holding one of her hands; whereupon she quickly dried her eyes with the other, while I felt embarrassed as she looked up at me. "There isn't a confounded job I haven't applied for—waited for—prayed for. You can fancy we'd be pretty bad first. Secretaryships and that sort of thing? You might as well ask for a peerage. I'd be *anything*—I'm strong; a messenger or a coal-heaver. I'd put on a gold-laced cap and open carriage-doors in front of the haberdasher's; I'd hang about a station, to carry portmanteaus; I'd be a postman. But they won't *look* at you; there are thousands, as good as yourself, already on the ground. *Gentlemen*, poor beggars, who have drunk their wine, who have kept their hunters!"

I was as reassuring as I knew how to be, and my visitors were presently on their feet again while, for the experiment, we agreed on an hour. We were discussing it when the door opened and Miss Churm came in with a wet umbrella. Miss Churm had to take the omnibus to Maida Vale and then walk half-a-mile. She looked a trifle blowsy and slightly splashed. I scarcely ever saw her come in without thinking afresh how odd it was that, being so little in herself, she should yet be so much in others. She was a meagre little Miss Churm, but she was an ample heroine of romance. She was only a freckled cockney, but she could represent everything, from a fine lady to a shepherdess; she had the faculty, as she might have had a fine voice or long hair. She couldn't spell, and she loved beer, but she had two or three "points," and practice, and a knack, and mother-wit, and a kind of whimsical sensibility, and a love of the theatre, and seven sisters, and not an ounce of respect, especially for the *h*. The first thing my visitors saw was that her umbrella was wet, and in their spotless perfection they visibly winced at it. The rain had come on since their arrival.

"I'm all in a soak; there *was* a mess of people in the 'bus. I wish you lived near a stytion," said Miss Churm. I requested her to get ready as quickly as possible, and she passed into the room in which she always changed her dress. But before going out she asked me what she was to get into this time.

"It's the Russian princess, don't you know?" I answered; "the one with the 'golden eyes,' in black velvet, for the long thing in the *Cheapside.*"

"Golden eyes? I *say!*" cried Miss Churm, while my companions watched her with intensity as she withdrew. She always arranged herself, when she was late, before I could turn round; and I kept my visitors a little, on purpose, so that they might get an idea, from seeing her, what would be expected of themselves. I mentioned that she was quite my notion of an excellent model—she was really very clever.

"Do you think she looks like a Russian princess?" Major Monarch asked, with lurking alarm.

"When I make her, yes."

"Oh, if you have to *make* her——!" he reasoned acutely.

"That's the most you can ask. There are so many that are not makeable."

"Well now, *here's* a lady"—and with a persuasive smile he passed his arm into his wife's—"who's already made!"

"Oh, I'm not a Russian princess," Mrs. Monarch protested, a little coldly. I could see that she had known some and didn't like them. There, immediately, was a complication of a kind that I never had to fear with Miss Churm.

This young lady came back in black velvet—the gown was rather rusty and very low on her lean shoulders—and with a Japanese fan in her red hands. I reminded her that in the scene I was doing she had to look over someone's head. "I forget whose it is; but it doesn't matter. Just look over a head."

"I'd rather look over a stove," said Miss Churm; and she took her station near the fire. She fell into position, settled herself into a tall attitude, gave a certain backward inclination to her head and a certain forward droop to her fan, and looked, at least to my prejudiced sense, distinguished and charming, foreign and dangerous. We left her looking so, while I went downstairs with Major and Mrs. Monarch.

"I think I could come about as near it as that," said Mrs. Monarch.

"Oh, you think she's shabby, but you must allow for the alchemy of art."

However, they went off with an evident increase of comfort, founded on their demonstrable advantage in being the real thing. I could fancy them shuddering over Miss Churm. She was very droll about them when I went back, for I told her what they wanted.

"Well, if *she* can sit I'll tyke to bookkeeping," said my model.

"She's very lady-like," I replied, as an innocent form of aggravation.

"So much the worse for *you*. That means she can't turn round."

"She'll do for the fashionable novels."

"Oh yes, she'll *do* for them!" my model humorously declared. "Ain't they bad enough without her?" I had often sociably denounced them to Miss Churm.

III

It was for the elucidation of a mystery in one of these works that I first tried Mrs. Monarch. Her husband came with her, to be useful if necessary—it was sufficiently clear that as a general thing he would prefer to come with her. At first I wondered if this were for "propriety's" sake—if he were going to be jealous and meddling. The idea was too tiresome, and if it had been confirmed it would speedily have brought our acquaintance to a close. But I soon saw there was nothing in it and that if he accompanied Mrs. Monarch it was (in addition to the chance of being wanted) simply because he had nothing else to do. When she was away from him his occupation was gone—she never *had* been away from him. I judged, rightly, that in their awkward situation their close union was their main comfort and that this union had no weak spot. It was a real marriage, an encouragement to the hesitating, a nut for pessimists to crack. Their address was humble (I remember afterwards thinking it had been the only thing about them that was really professional), and I could fancy the lamentable lodgings in which the Major would have been left alone. He could bear them with his wife—he couldn't bear them without her.

He had too much tact to try and make himself agreeable when he couldn't be useful; so he simply sat and waited, when I was too absorbed in my work to talk. But I liked to make him talk—it made my work, when it didn't interrupt it, less sordid, less special. To listen to him was to combine the excitement of going out with the economy of staying at home. There was only one hindrance: that I seemed not to know any of the people he and his wife had known. I think he wondered extremely, during the term of our intercourse, whom the deuce I *did* know. He hadn't a stray sixpence of an idea to fumble for; so we didn't spin it very fine—we confined ourselves to questions of leather and even of liquor (saddlers and breeches-makers and how to get good claret cheap), and matters like "good trains" and the habits of small game. His lore on these last subjects was astonishing, he managed to interweave the stationmaster with the ornithologist. When he couldn't talk about greater things he could talk cheerfully about smaller, and since I couldn't accompany him into reminiscences of the fashionable world he could lower the conversation without a visible effort to my level.

So earnest a desire to please was touching in a man who could so easily have knocked one down. He looked after the fire and had an opinion on the draught of the stove, without my asking him, and I could see that he thought many of my arrangements not half clever enough. I remember telling him that if I were only rich I would offer him a salary to come and teach me how to live. Sometimes he gave a random sigh, of which the essence was: "Give me even such a bare old barrack as *this*, and I'd do something with it!" When I wanted to use him he came alone; which was an illustration of the superior courage of women. His wife could bear her solitary second floor, and she was in general more discreet; showing by various small reserves that she was alive to the propriety of keeping our relations markedly professional—not letting them slide into sociability. She wished it to remain clear that she and the Major were employed, not cultivated, and if she approved of me as a superior, who could be kept in his place, she never thought me quite good enough for an equal.

She sat with great intensity, giving the whole of her mind to it, and was capable of remaining for an hour almost as motionless as if she were before a photographer's lens. I could see she had been photographed often, but somehow the very habit that made her good for that purpose unfitted her for mine. At first I was extremely pleased with her lady-like air, and it was a satisfaction, on coming to follow her lines, to see how good they were and how far they could lead the pencil. But after a few times I began to find her too insurmountably stiff; do what I would with it my drawing looked like a photograph or a copy of a photograph. Her figure had no variety of expression—she herself had no sense of variety. You may say that this was my business, was only a question of placing her. I placed her in every conceivable position, but she managed to obliterate their differences. She was always a lady certainly, and into the bargain was always the same lady. She was the real thing, but always the same thing. There were moments when I was oppressed by the serenity of her confidence that she *was* the real thing. All her dealings with me and all her husband's were an implication that this was lucky for *me*. Meanwhile I found myself trying to invent types that approached her own, instead of making her own transform itself—in the clever way that was not impossible, for instance, to poor Miss Churm. Arrange as I would and take the precautions

I would, she always, in my pictures, came out too tall—landing me in the dilemma of having represented a fascinating woman as seven feet high, which, out of respect perhaps to my own very much scantier inches, was far from my idea of such a personage.

The case was worse with the Major—nothing I could do would keep *him* down, so that he became useful only for the representation of brawny giants. I adored variety and range, I cherished human accidents, the illustrative note; I wanted to characterise closely, and the thing in the world I most hated was the danger of being ridden by a type. I had quarrelled with some of my friends about it—I had parted company with them for maintaining that one *had* to be, and that if the type was beautiful (witness Raphael and Leonardo), the servitude was only a gain. I was neither Leonardo nor Raphael; I might only be a presumptuous young modern searcher, but I held that everything was to be sacrificed sooner than character. When they averred that the haunting type in question could easily *be* character, I retorted, perhaps superficially: "Whose?" It couldn't be everybody's—it might end in being nobody's.

After I had drawn Mrs. Monarch a dozen times I perceived more clearly than before that the value of such a model as Miss Churm resided precisely in the fact that she had no positive stamp, combined of course with the other fact that what she did have was a curious and inexplicable talent for imitation. Her usual appearance was like a curtain which she could draw up at request for a capital performance. This performance was simply suggestive; but it was a word to the wise—it was vivid and pretty. Sometimes, even, I thought it, though she was plain herself, too insipidly pretty; I made it a reproach to her that the figures drawn from her were monotonously (*bêtement*, as we used to say) graceful. Nothing made her more angry: it was so much her pride to feel that she could sit for characters that had nothing in common with each other. She would accuse me at such moments of taking away her "reputytion."

It suffered a certain shrinkage, this queer quantity, from the repeated visits of my new friends. Miss Churm was greatly in demand, never in want of employment, so I had no scruple in putting her off occasionally, to try them more at my ease. It was certainly amusing at first to do the real thing—it was amusing to do Major Monarch's trousers. They *were* the real thing, even if he did come out colossal. It was amusing to do his wife's back hair (it was so mathematically neat), and the particular "smart" tension of her tight stays. She lent herself especially to positions in which the face was somewhat averted or blurred; she abounded in ladylike back views and *profils perdus*. When she stood erect she took naturally one of the attitudes in which court-painters represent queens and princesses; so that I found myself wondering whether, to draw out this accomplishment, I couldn't get the editor of the *Cheapside* to publish a really royal romance, "A Tale of Buckingham Palace." Sometimes, however, the real thing and the make-believe came into contact; by which I mean that Miss Churm, keeping an appointment or coming to make one on days when I had much work in hand, encountered her invidious rivals. The encounter was not on their part, for they noticed her no more than if she had been the housemaid; not from intentional loftiness, but simply because, as yet, professionally, they didn't know how to fraternise, as I could guess that they would have liked—or at least that the Major would. They couldn't talk about the omnibus—they always walked; and they didn't know what else to try—she wasn't interested in good trains or cheap claret. Besides, they must have felt—in the air—that she was amused at them, secretly derisive of their ever knowing how. She was not a person to conceal her scepticism if she had had a chance to show it. On the other hand Mrs. Monarch didn't think her tidy; for why else did she take pains to say to me (it was going out of the way, for Mrs. Monarch) that she didn't like dirty women?

One day when my young lady happened to be present with my other sitters (she even dropped in, when it was convenient, for a chat), I asked her to be so good as to lend a hand in getting tea—a service with which she was famailiar and which was one of a class that, living as I did in a small way, with slender domestic resources, I often appealed to my models to render. They liked to lay hands on my property, to break the sitting, and sometimes the china—I made them feel Bohemian. The next time I saw Miss Churm after this incident she surprised me greatly by making a scene about it—she accused me of having wished to humiliate her. She had not resented the outrage at the time, but had seemed obliging and amused, enjoying the comedy of asking Mrs. Monarch, who sat vague and silent, whether she would have cream and sugar, and putting an exaggerated simper into the question. She had tried intonations—as if she too wished to pass for the real thing; till I was afraid my other visitors would take offence.

Oh, *they* were determined not to do this; and their touching patience was the measure of their great need. They would sit by the hour, uncomplaining, till I was ready to use them; they would come back on the chance of being wanted, and would walk away cheerfully if they were not. I used to go to the door with them to see in what magnificent order they retreated. I tried to find other employment for them—I introduced them to several artists. But they didn't "take," for reasons I could appreciate, and I became conscious, rather anxiously, that after such disappointments they fell back upon me with a heavier weight. They did me the honour to think that it was I who was most *their* form. They were not picturesque enough for the painters, and in those days there were not so many serious workers in black and white. Besides, they had an eye to the great job I had mentioned to them—they had secretly set their hearts on supplying the right essence for my pictorial vindication of our fine novelist. They knew that for this undertaking I should want no costume-effects, none of the frippery of past ages—that it was a case in which everything would be contemporary and satirical and, presumably, genteel. If I could work them into it their future would be assured, for the labour would of course be long and the occupation steady.

One day Mrs. Monarch came without her husband—she explained his absence by his having had to go to the City. While she sat there in her usual anxious stiffness there came, at the door, a knock which I immediately recognised as the subdued appeal of a model out of work. It was followed by the entrance of a young man whom I easily perceived to be a foreigner and who proved in fact an Italian acquainted with no English word but my name, which he uttered in a way that made it seem to include all others. I had not then visited his country, nor was I proficient in his tongue; but as he was not so meanly constituted—what Italian is?—as to depend only on that member for expression he conveyed to me, in familiar but graceful mimicry, that he was in search of exactly the employment in which the lady before me was engaged. I was not struck with him at first, and while I continued to draw I emitted rough sounds of discouragement and dismissal. He stood his ground, however, not importunately, but with a dumb, dog-like fidelity in his eyes which amounted to innocent impudence—the manner of a devoted servant (he might have been in the house for years), unjustly suspected. Suddenly I saw that this very attitude and expression made a picture, whereupon I told him to sit down and wait till I should be free. There was another picture in the way he obeyed me, and I observed as I worked that there were others still in the way he looked wonderingly, with his head thrown back, about the high studio. He might have been crossing himself in St. Peter's. Before I finished I said to myself: "The fellow's a bankrupt orange-monger, but he's a treasure."

When Mrs. Monarch withdrew he passed across the room like a flash to open the door for her, standing there with the rapt, pure gaze of the young Dante spellbound by the young Beatrice. As I never insisted, in such situations, on the blankness of the British domestic, I reflected that he had the making of a servant (and I needed one, but couldn't pay him to be only that), as well as of a model; in short I made up my mind to adopt my bright adventurer if he would agree to officiate in the double capacity. He jumped at my offer, and in the event my rashness (for I had known nothing about him) was not brought home to me. He proved a sympathetic though a desultory ministrant, and had in a wonderful degree the *sentiment de la pose*. It was uncultivated, instinctive; a part of the happy instinct which had guided him to my door and helped him to spell out my name on the card nailed to it. He had had no other introduction to me than a guess, from the shape of my high north window, seen outside, that my place was a studio and that as a studio it would contain an artist. He had wandered to England in search of fortune, like other itinerants, and had embarked, with a partner and a small green hand-cart, on the sale of penny ices. The ices had melted away and the partner had dissolved in their train. My young man wore tight yellow trousers with

reddish stripes and his name was Oronte. He was sallow but fair, and
when I put him into some old clothes of my own he looked like an Englishman. He was as good as Miss Churm, who could look, when required,
like an Italian.

IV

I thought Mrs. Monarch's face slightly convulsed when, on her coming
back with her husband, she found Oronte installed. It was strange to have
to recognise in a scrap of a lazzarone a competitor to her magnificent Major. It was she who scented danger first, for the Major was anecdotically
unconscious. But Oronte gave us tea, with a hundred eager confusions (he
had never seen such a queer process), and I think she thought better of
me for having at last an "establishment." They saw a couple of drawings
that I had made of the establishment, and Mrs. Monarch hinted that it
never would have struck her that he had sat for them. "Now the drawings you make from *us*, they look exactly like us," she reminded me, smiling in triumph; and I recognised that this was indeed just their defect.
When I drew the Monarchs I couldn't, somehow, get away from them—
get into the character I wanted to represent; and I had not the least desire my model should be discoverable in my picture. Miss Churm never
was, and Mrs. Monarch thought I hid her, very properly, because she was
vulgar; whereas if she was lost it was only as the dead who go to heaven
are lost—in the gain of an angel the more.

By this time I had got a certain start with "Rutland Ramsay," the first
novel in the great projected series; that is I had produced a dozen drawings, several with the help of the Major and his wife, and I had sent them
in for approval. My understanding with the publishers, as I have already
hinted, had been that I was to be left to do my work, in this particular
case, as I liked, with the whole book committed to me; but my connection
with the rest of the series was only contingent. There were moments
when, frankly, it *was* a comfort to have the real thing under one's hand;
for there were characters in "Rutland Ramsay" that were very much like
it. There were people presumably as straight as the Major and women of
as good a fashion as Mrs. Monarch. There was a great deal of country-
house life—treated, it is true, in a fine, fanciful, ironical, generalised way
—and there was a considerable implication of knickerbockers and kilts.
There were certain things I had to settle at the outset; such things for instance as the exact appearance of the hero, the particular bloom of the
heroine. The author of course gave me a lead, but there was a margin for
interpretation. I took the Monarchs into my confidence, I told them
frankly what I was about, I mentioned my embarrassments and alterna-
tives. "Oh, take *him!*" Mrs. Monarch murmured sweetly, looking at her
husband; and "What could you want better than my wife?" the Major
inquired, with the comfortable candour that now prevailed between us.

I was not obliged to answer these remarks—I was only obliged to place
my sitters. I was not easy in mind, and I postponed, a little timidly per-

haps, the solution of the question. The book was a large canvas, the other figures were numerous, and I worked off at first some of the episodes in which the hero and the heroine were not concerned. When once I had set *them* up I should have to stick to them—I couldn't make my young man seven feet high in one place and five feet nine in another. I inclined on the whole to the latter measurement, though the Major more than once reminded me that *he* looked about as young as anyone. It was indeed quite possible to arrange him, for the figure, so that it would have been difficult to detect his age. After the spontaneous Oronte had been with me a month, and after I had given him to understand several different times that his native exuberance would presently constitute an insurmountable barrier to our further intercourse, I waked to a sense of his heroic capacity. He was only five feet seven, but the remaining inches were latent. I tried him almost secretly at first, for I was really rather afraid of the judgment my other models would pass on such a choice. If they regarded Miss Churm as little better than a snare, what would they think of the representation by a person so little the real thing as an Italian street-vendor of a protagonist formed by a public school?

If I went a little in fear of them it was not because they bullied me, because they had got an oppressive foothold, but because in their really pathetic decorum and mysteriously permanent newness they counted on me so intensely. I was therefore very glad when Jack Hawley came home: he was always of such good counsel. He painted badly himself, but there was no one like him for putting his finger on the place. He had been absent from England for a year; he had been somewhere—I don't remember where—to get a fresh eye. I was in a good deal of dread of any such organ, but we were old friends; he had been away for months and a sense of emptiness was creeping into my life. I hadn't dodged a missile for a year.

He came back with a fresh eye, but with the same old black velvet blouse, and the first evening he spent in my studio we smoked cigarettes till the small hours. He had done no work himself, he had only got the eye; so the field was clear for the production of my little things. He wanted to see what I had done for the *Cheapside*, but he was disappointed in the exhibition. That at least seemed the meaning of two or three comprehensive groans which, as he lounged on my big divan, on a folded leg, looking at my latest drawings, issued from his lips with the smoke of the cigarette.

"What's the matter with you?" I asked.

"What's the matter with *you?*"

"Nothing save that I'm mystified."

"You are indeed. You're quite off the hinge. What's the meaning of this new fad?" And he tossed me, with visible irreverence, a drawing in which I happened to have depicted both my majestic models. I asked if he didn't think it good, and he replied that it struck him as execrable, given the sort of thing I had always represented myself to him as wishing to arrive at; but I let that pass, I was so anxious to see exactly what he meant. The two figures in the picture looked colossal, but I supposed this was *not* what he meant, inasmuch as, for aught he knew to the contrary, I might have been trying for that. I maintained that I was working exactly in the same way as when he last had done me the honour to commend me. "Well, there's a big hole somewhere," he answered; "wait a bit and I'll discover it." I depended upon him to do so: where else was the fresh eye? But he produced at last nothing more luminous than "I don't know—I don't like your types." This was lame, for a critic who had never consented to discuss with me anything but the question of execution, the direction of strokes and the mystery of values.

"In the drawings you've been looking at I think my types are very handsome."

"Oh, they won't do!"

"I've had a couple of new models."

"I see you have. *They* won't do."

"Are you sure of that?"

"Absolutely—they're stupid."

"You mean *I* am—for I ought to get round that."

"You *can't*—with such people. Who are they?"

I told him, as far as was necessary, and he declared, heartlessly: "*Ce sont des gens qu'il faut mettre à la porte.*"

"You've never seen them; they're awfully good," I compassionately objected.

"Not seen them? Why, all this recent work of yours drops to pieces with them. It's all I want to see of them."

"No one else has said anything against it—the *Cheapside* people are pleased."

"Everyone else is an ass, and the *Cheapside* people the biggest asses of all. Come, don't pretend, at this time of day, to have pretty illusions about the public, especially about publishers and editors. It's not for *such* animals you work—it's for those who know, *coloro che sanno;* so keep straight for *me* if you can't keep straight for yourself. There's a certain sort of thing you tried for from the first—and a very good thing it is. But this twaddle isn't *in* it." When I talked with Hawley later about "Rutland Ramsay" and its possible successors he declared that I must get back into my boat again or I would go to the bottom. His voice in short was the voice of warning.

I noted the warning, but I didn't turn my friends out of doors. They bored me a good deal; but the very fact that they bored me admonished me not to sacrifice them—if there was anything to be done with them— simply to irritation. As I look back at this phase they seem to me to have pervaded my life not a little. I have a vision of them as most of the time in my studio, seated, against the wall, on an old velvet bench to be out of the way, and looking like a pair of patient courtiers in a royal ante-chamber. I am convinced that during the coldest weeks of the winter they held their ground because it saved them fire. Their newness was losing its gloss, and it was impossible not to feel that they were objects of charity. Whenever Miss Churm arrived they went away, and after I was fairly launched in "Rutland Ramsay" Miss Churm arrived pretty often. They managed to express to me tacitly that they supposed I wanted her for the low life of the book, and I let them suppose it, since they had attempted to study the work—it was lying about the studio—without discovering that it dealt only with the highest circles. They had dipped into the most brilliant of our novelists without deciphering many passages. I still took an hour from them, now and again, in spite of Jack Hawley's warning: it would be time enough to dismiss them, if dismissal should be necessary, when the rigour of the season was over. Hawley had made their acquaintance—he had met them at my fireside—and thought them a ridiculous pair. Learning that he was a painter they tried to approach him, to show him too that they were the real thing; but he looked at them, across the big room, as if they were miles away: they were a compendium of everything that he most objected to in the social system of his country. Such people as that, all convention and patent-leather, with ejaculations that stopped conversation, had no business in a studio. A studio was a place to learn to see, and how could you see through a pair of feather beds?

The main inconvenience I suffered at their hands was that, at first, I was shy of letting them discover how my artful little servant had begun to sit for me for "Rutland Ramsay." They knew that I had been odd enough (they were prepared by this time to allow oddity to artists) to pick a foreign vagabond out of the streets, when I might have had a person with whiskers and credentials; but it was some time before they learned how high I rated his accomplishments. They found him in an attitude more than once, but they never doubted I was doing him as an organ-grinder. There were several things they never guessed, and one of them was that for a striking scene in the novel, in which a footman briefly figured, it occurred to me to make use of Major Monarchs as the menial. I kept putting this off, I didn't like to ask him to don the livery—besides the difficulty of finding a livery to fit him. At last, one day late in the winter, when I was at work on the despised Oronte (he caught one's idea in an instant), and was in the glow of feeling that I was going very straight, they came in, the Major and his wife, with their society laugh about nothing (there was less and less to laugh at), like country-callers—they always reminded me of that—who have walked across the park after church and are presently persuaded to stay to luncheon. Luncheon was over, but they could stay to tea—I knew they wanted it. The fit was on me, however, and I couldn't let my ardour cool and my work wait, with the fading daylight, while my model prepared it. So I asked Mrs. Monarch if she would mind laying it out—a request which, for an instant, brought all the blood to her face. Her eyes were on her husband's for a second, and some mute telegraphy passed between them. Their folly was over the next instant; his cheerful shrewdness put an end to it. So far from pitying their wounded pride, I must add, I was moved to give it as complete a lesson as I could. They bustled about together and got out the cups and saucers and made the kettle boil. I know they felt as if they were waiting on my servant, and when the tea was prepared I said: "He'll have a cup, please—he's tired." Mrs. Monarch brought him one where he stood, and he took it from her as if he had been a gentleman at a party, squeezing a crush-hat with an elbow.

Then it came over me that she had made a great effort for me—made it with a kind of nobleness—and that I owed her a compensation. Each time I saw her after this I wondered what the compensation could be. I couldn't go on doing the wrong thing to oblige them. Oh, it *was* the wrong thing, the stamp of the work for which they sat—Hawley was not the only person to say it now. I sent in a large number of the drawings I had made for "Rutland Ramsay," and I received a warning that was more to the point than Hawley's. The artistic adviser of the house for which I was working was of opinion that many of my illustrations were not what had been looked for. Most of these illustrations were the subjects in which the Monarchs had figured. Without going into the question of what *had* been looked for, I saw at this rate I shouldn't get the other books to do. I hurled myself in despair upon Miss Churm, I put her through all her paces. I not only adopted Oronte publicly as my hero, but one morning when the Major looked in to see if I didn't require him to finish a figure for the *Cheapside,* for which he had begun to sit the week before, I told him that I had changed my mind—I would do the drawing from my man. At this my visitor turned pale and stood looking at me. "Is *he* your idea of an English gentleman?" he asked.

I was disappointed, I was nervous, I wanted to get on with my work; so I replied with irritation: "Oh, my dear Major—I can't be ruined for *you!*"

He stood another moment; then, without a word, he quitted the studio. I drew a long breath when he was gone, for I said to myself that I shouldn't see him again. I had not told him definitely that I was in danger of having my work rejected, but I was vexed at his not having felt the catastrophe in the air, read with me the moral of our fruitless collaboration, the lesson that, in the deceptive atmosphere of art, even the highest respectability may fail of being plastic.

I didn't owe my friends money, but I did see them again. They reappeared together, three days later, and under the circumstances there was something tragic in the fact. It was a proof to me that they could find nothing else in life to do. They had threshed the matter out in a dismal conference—they had digested the bad news that they were not in for the series. If they were not useful to me even for the *Cheapside* their function seemed difficult to determine, and I could only judge at first that they had come, forgivingly, decorously, to take a last leave. This made me rejoice in secret that I had little leisure for a scene; for I had placed both my other models in position together and I was pegging away at a drawing from which I hoped to derive glory. It had been suggested by the passage in which Rutland Ramsay, drawing up a chair to Artemisia's piano-stool, says extraordinary things to her while she ostensibly fingers out a difficult piece of music. I had done Miss Churm at the piano before—it was an attitude in which she knew how to take on an absolutely poetic grace. I wished the two figures to "compose" together, intensely, and my little Italian had entered perfectly into my conception. The pair were vividly before me, the piano had been pulled out; it was a charming picture of blended youth and murmured love, which I had only to catch and keep. My visitors stood and looked at it, and I was friendly to them over my shoulder.

They made no response, but I was used to silent company and went on with my work, only a little disconcerted (even though exhilarated by the sense that *this* was at least the ideal thing) at not having got rid of them after all. Presently I heard Mrs. Monarch's sweet voice beside, or rather above me: "I wish her hair was a little better done." I looked up and she was staring with a strange fixedness at Miss Churm, whose back was turned to her. "Do you mind my just touching it?" she went on—a question which made me spring up for an instant, as with the instinctive fear that she might do the young lady a harm. But she quieted me with a glance I shall never forget—I confess I should like to have been able to paint *that*—and went for a moment to my model. She spoke to her softly, laying a hand upon her shoulder and bending over her; and as the girl, understanding, gratefully assented, she disposed her rough curls, with a few quick passes, in such a way as to make Miss Churm's head twice as charming. It was one of the most heroic personal services I have ever seen rendered. Then Mrs. Monarch turned away with a low sigh and, looking about her as if for something to do, stooped to the floor with a noble humility and picked up a dirty rag that had dropped out of my paint-box.

The Major meanwhile had also been looking for something to do and, wandering to the other end of the studio, saw before him my breakfast things, neglected, unremoved. "I say, can't I be useful *here?*" he called out to me with an irrepressible quaver. I assented with a laugh that I fear was awkward and for the next ten minutes, while I worked, I heard the light clatter of china and the tinkle of spoons and glass. Mrs. Monarch assisted her husband—they washed up my crockery, they put it away. They wandered off into my little scullery, and I afterwards found that they had cleaned my knives and that my slender stock of plate had an unprecedented surface. When it came over me, the latent eloquence of what they were doing, I confess that my drawing was blurred for a moment—the picture swam. They had accepted their failure, but they couldn't accept their fate. They had bowed their heads in bewilderment to the perverse and cruel law in virtue of which the real thing could be so much less precious than the unreal; but they didn't want to starve. If my servants were my models, my models might be my servants. They would reverse the parts—the others would sit for the ladies and gentle-

men, and *they* would do the work. They would still be in the studio—it
was an intense dumb appeal to me not to turn them out. "Take us on,"
they wanted to say—"we'll do *anything*."

When all this hung before me the *afflatus* vanished—my pencil dropped
from my hand. My sitting was spoiled and I got rid of my sitters, who
were also evidently rather mystified and awestruck. Then, alone with
the Major and his wife, I had a most uncomfortable moment. He put
their prayer into a single sentence: "I say, you know—just let *us* do for
you, can't you?" I couldn't—it was dreadful to see them emptying my
slops; but I pretended I could, to oblige them, for about a week. Then
I gave them a sum of money to go away; and I never saw them again. I
obtained the remaining books, but my friend Hawley repeats that Major
and Mrs. Monarch did me a permanent harm, got me into a second-rate
trick. If it be true I am content to have paid the price—for the memory.

THE ART OF FICTION

Henry James's essay "The Art of Fiction" is one of those key pronouncements on a given art which a creator throws off, in a moment
of intense feeling, and which, because it is a spontaneous utterance,
and stems directly from the artist's workshop, attains in after years
the importance of a manifesto, the condensed vitality of a poem.
Many things have been written about the art of the novel in the two
centuries in which that modern form has flourished; but little has
been said that can add to the great generalizations Henry James here
put forth. He was prompted by a lecture delivered by Walter Besant, a minor Victorian novelist and historian, before the Royal Institution in London. Besant spoke on "Fiction as a Fine Art" and
tried to enunciate a series of laws for novel-writing. James found
these much too rigid and didactic, and in his reply, published in
Longman's Magazine in September 1884, asserted the need for the
novelist to have a sense of absolute freedom, a capacity for experiencing life in a manner that enables him to deduce the unknown from
the known, and an awareness of the novel's elasticity. The discussion
was pursued, after James's essay appeared, by Robert Louis Stevenson, who took issue with the realistic school and argued that fiction
must create an illusion of reality, that it cannot pretend to be life
nor genuinely to imitate it. In effect, Stevenson was saying what
James was to say again in his short story, "The Real Thing."

I should not have affixed so comprehensive a title to these few remarks,
necessarily wanting in any completeness upon a subject the full consideration of which would carry us far, did I not seem to discover a pretext
for my temerity in the interesting pamphlet lately published under this

name by Mr. Walter Besant. Mr. Besant's lecture at the Royal Institution [1]—the original form of his pamphlet—appears to indicate that many
persons are interested in the art of fiction, and are not indifferent to such
remarks, as those who practice it may attempt to make it. I am therefore anxious not to lose the benefit of this favorable association, and to
edge in a few words under cover of the attention which Mr. Besant is
sure to have excited. There is something very encouraging in his having
put into form certain of his ideas on the mystery of story-telling.

It is a proof of life and curiosity—curiosity on the part of the brotherhood of novelists as well as on the part of their readers. Only a short
time ago it might have been supposed that the English novel was not
what the French call *discutable*. It had no air of having a theory, a conviction, a consciousness of itself behind it—of being the expression of an
artistic faith, the result of choice and comparison. I do not say it was
necessarily the worse for that: it would take much more courage than I
possess to intimate that the form of the novel as Dickens and Thackeray
(for instance) saw it had any taint of incompleteness. It was, however,
naïf (if I may help myself out with another French word); and evidently
if it be destined to suffer in any way for having lost its *naïveté* it has now
an idea of making sure of the corresponding advantages. During the period I have alluded to there was a comfortable, good-humoured feeling
abroad that a novel is a novel, as a pudding is a pudding, and that our
only business with it could be to swallow it. But within a year or two, for
some reason or other, there have been signs of returning animation—the
era of discussion would appear to have been to a certain extent opened.
Art lives upon discussion, upon experiment, upon curiosity, upon variety
of attempt, upon the exchange of views and the comparison of standpoints; and there is a presumption that those times when no one has anything particular to say about it, and has no reason to give for practice or
preference, though they may be times of honor, are not times of development—are times, possibly even, a little of dullness. The successful application of any art is a delightful spectacle, but the theory too is interesting; and though there is a great deal of the latter without the former I
suspect there has never been a genuine success that has not had a latent
core of conviction. Discussion, suggestion, formulation, these things are
fertilizing when they are frank and sincere. Mr. Besant has set an excellent example in saying what he thinks, for his part, about the way in
which fiction should be written, as well as about the way in which it
should be published; for his view of the "art," carried on into an appen-
dix, covers that too. Other laborers in the same field will doubtless take
up the argument, they will give it the light of their experience, and the
effect will surely be to make our interest in the novel a little more what
it had for some time threatened to fail to be—a serious, active, inquiring

---

[1] Walter Besant (1836–1901), Victorian novelist and historian, delivered the
lecture at the Royal Institution, April 25,
1884.

interest, under protection of which this delightful study may, in moments of confidence, venture to say a little more what it thinks of itself.

It must take itself seriously for the public to take it so. The old superstition about fiction being "wicked" has doubtless died out in England; but the spirit of it lingers in a certain oblique regard directed toward any story which does not more or less admit that it is only a joke. Even the most jocular novel feels in some degree the weight of the proscription that was formerly directed against literary levity: the jocularity does not always succeed in passing for orthodoxy. It is still expected, though perhaps people are ashamed to say it, that a production which is after all only a "make-believe" (for what else is a "story"?) shall be in some degree apologetic—shall renounce the pretension of attempting really to represent life. This, of course, any sensible, wide-awake story declines to do, for it quickly perceives that the tolerance granted to it on such a condition is only an attempt to stifle it disguised in the form of generosity. The old evangelical hostility to the novel, which was as explicit as it was narrow, and which regarded it as little less favorable to our immortal part than a stage play, was in reality far less insulting. The only reason for the existence of a novel is that it does attempt to represent life. When it relinquishes this attempt, the same attempt that we see on the canvas of the painter, it will have arrived at a very strange pass. It is not expected of the picture that it will make itself humble in order to be forgiven; and the analogy between the art of the painter and the art of the novelist is, so far as I am able to see, complete. Their inspiration is the same, their process (allowing for the different quality of the vehicle) is the same, their success is the same. They may learn from each other, they may explain and sustain each other. Their cause is the same, and the honor of one is the honor of another. The Mahometans think a picture an unholy thing, but it is a long time since any Christian did, and it is therefore the more odd that in the Christian mind the traces (dissimulated though they may be) of a suspicion of the sister art should linger to this day. The only effectual way to lay it to rest is to emphasize the analogy to which I just alluded—to insist on the fact that as the picture is reality, so the novel is history. That is the only general description (which does it justice) that we may give of the novel. But history also is allowed to represent life; it is not, any more than painting, expected to apologize. The subject-matter of fiction is stored up likewise in documents and records, and if it will not give itself away, as they say in California, it must speak with assurance, with the tone of the historian. Certain accomplished novelists have a habit of giving themselves away which must often bring tears to the eyes of people who take their fiction seriously. I was lately struck, in reading over many pages of Anthony Trollope, with his want of discretion in this particular. In a digression, a parenthesis or an aside, he concedes to the reader that he and this trusting friend are only "making believe." He admits that the events he narrates have not really happened, and that he can give his narrative any turn the reader may like best. Such a betrayal of a sacred office seems to me, I confess, a terrible crime; it is what I mean by the attitude of apology, and it shocks me every whit as much in Trollope as it would have shocked me in Gibbon or Macaulay. It implies that the novelist is less occupied in looking for the truth (the truth, of course I mean, that he assumes, the premises that we grant him, whatever they may be) than the historian, and in doing so it deprives him at a stroke of all his standing room. To represent and illustrate the past, the actions of men, is the task of either writer, and the only difference that I can see is, in proportion as he succeeds, to the honour of the novelist, consisting as it does in his having more difficulty in collecting his evidence, which is so far from being purely literary. It seems to me to give him a great character, the fact that he has at once so much in common with the philosopher and the painter; this double analogy is a magnificent heritage.

It is of all this evidently that Mr. Besant is full when he insists upon the fact that fiction is one of the *fine* arts, deserving in its turn of all the honours and emoluments that have hitherto been reserved for the successful profession of music, poetry, painting, architecture. It is impossible to insist too much on so important a truth, and the place that Mr. Besant demands for the work of the novelist may be represented, a trifle less abstractly, by saying that he demands not only that it shall be reputed artistic, but that it shall be reputed very artistic indeed. It is excellent that he should have struck this note, for his doing so indicates that there was need of it, that his proposition may be to many people a novelty. One rubs one's eyes at the thought; but the rest of Mr. Besant's essay confirms the revelation. I suspect in truth that it would be possible to confirm it still further, and that one would not be far wrong in saying that in addition to the people to whom it has never occurred that a novel ought to be artistic, there are a great many others who, if this principle were urged upon them, would be filled with an indefinable mistrust. They would find it difficult to explain their repugnance, but it would operate strongly to put them on their guard. "Art," in our Protestant communities, where so many things have got so strangely twisted about, is supposed in certain circles to have some vaguely injurious effect upon those who make it an important consideration, who let it weigh in the balance. It is assumed to be opposed in some mysterious manner to morality, to amusement, to instruction. When it is embodied in the work of the painter (the sculptor is another affair!) you know what it is: it stands there before you, in the honesty of pink and green and a gilt frame; you can see the worst of it at a glance, and you can be on your guard. But when it is introduced into literature it becomes more insidious—there is danger of its hurting you before you know it. Literature should be either instructive or amusing, and there is in many minds an impression that these artistic preoccupations, the search for form, contribute to neither end, interfere indeed with both. They are too frivolous to be edifying, and too serious to be diverting; and they are moreover priggish and paradoxical and superfluous. That, I think, represents the manner in which the latent thought of many people who read novels as an exercise in skipping would explain itself if it were to become articulate. They would argue, of course, that a novel ought to be "good," but they would interpret this term in a fashion of their own, which indeed would vary considerably from one critic to another. One would say that being good means representing virtuous and aspiring characters, placed in prominent positions; another would say that it depends on a "happy ending," on a distribution at the last of prizes, pensions, husbands, wives, babies, millions, appended paragraphs, and cheerful remarks. Another still would say that it means being full of incident and movement, so that we shall wish to jump ahead, to see who was the mysterious stranger, and if the stolen will was ever found, and shall not be distracted from this pleasure by any tiresome analysis or "description." But they would all agree that the "artistic" idea would spoil some of their fun. One would hold it accountable for all the description, another would see it revealed in the absence of sympathy. Its hostility to a happy ending would be evident, and it might even in some cases render any ending at all impossible. The "ending" of a novel is, for many persons, like that of a good dinner, a course of dessert and ices, and the artist in fiction is regarded as a sort of meddlesome doctor who forbids agreeable aftertastes. It is therefore true that this conception of Mr. Besant's of the novel as a superior form encounters not only a negative but a positive indifference. It matters little that as a work of art it should really be as little or as much of its essence to supply happy endings, sympathetic characters, and an objective tone, as if it were a work of mechanics: the association of ideas, however incongruous, might easily be too much for it if an eloquent voice were not sometimes raised to call attention to the fact that it is at once as free and as serious a branch of literature as any other.

Certainly this might sometimes be doubted in presence of the enormous number of works of fiction that appeal to the credulity of our generation, for it might easily seem that there could be no great character in a commodity so quickly and easily produced. It must be admitted that good novels are much compromised by bad ones, and that the field at large suffers discredit from overcrowding. I think, however, that this injury is only superficial, and that the superabundance of written fiction proves nothing against the principle itself. It has been vulgarized, like all other kinds of literature, like everything else today, and it has proved more than some kinds accessible to vulgarization. But there is as much difference as there ever was between a good novel and a bad one: the bad is swept with all the daubed canvases and spoiled marble into some unvisited limbo, or infinite rubbish-yard beneath the back-windows of the world, and the good subsists and emits its light and stimulates our desire for perfection. As I shall take the liberty of making but a single criticism of Mr. Besant, whose tone is so full of the love of his art, I may as well have done with it at once. He seems to me to mistake in attempting to say so definitely beforehand what sort of an affair the good novel will be. To indicate the danger of such an error as that has been the purpose of these few pages; to suggest that certain traditions on the subject, applied *a priori*, have already had much to answer for, and that the good health of an art which undertakes so immediately to reproduce life must demand that it be perfectly free. It lives upon exercise, and the very meaning of exercise is freedom. The only obligation to which in advance we may hold a novel, without incurring the accusation of being arbitrary, is that it be interesting. That general responsibility rests upon it, but it is the only one I can think of. The ways in which it is at liberty to accomplish this result (of interesting us) strike me as innumerable, and such as can only suffer from being marked out or fenced in by prescription. They are as various as the temperament of man, and they are successful in proportion as they reveal a particular mind, different from others. A novel is in its broadest definition a personal, a direct impression of life: that, to begin with, constitutes its value, which is greater or less according to the intensity of the impression. But there will be no intensity at all, and therefore no value, unless there is freedom to feel and say. The tracing of a line to be followed, of a tone to be taken, of a form to be filled out, is a limitation of that freedom and a suppression of the very thing that we are most curious about. The form, it seems to me, is to be appreciated after the fact: then the author's choice has been made, his standard has been indicated; then we can follow lines and directions and compare tones and resemblances. Then in a word we can enjoy one of the most charming of pleasures, we can estimate quality, we can apply the test of execution. The execution belongs to the author alone; it is what is most personal to him, and we measure him by that. The advantage, the luxury, as well as the torment and responsibility of the novelist, is that there is no limit to what he may attempt as an executant—no limit to his possible experiments, efforts, discoveries, successes. Here it is especially that he works, step by step, like his brother of the brush, of whom we may always say that he has painted his picture in a manner best known to himself. His manner is his secret, not necessarily a jealous one. He cannot disclose it as a general thing if he would; he would be at a loss to teach it to others. I say this with a due recollection of having insisted on the community method of the artist who paints a picture and the artist who writes a novel. The painter *is* able to teach the rudiments of his practice, and it is possible, from the study of good work (granted the aptitude), both to learn how to paint and to learn how to write. Yet it remains true, without injury to the *rapprochement*, that the literary artist would be obliged to say to his pupil much more than the other, "Ah, well, you must do it as you can!" It is a question of degree, a matter of delicacy. If there are exact sciences, there are also exact arts, and the grammar of painting is so much more definite that it makes the difference.

I ought to add, however, that if Mr. Besant says at the beginning of his essay that the "laws of fiction may be laid down and taught with as much precision and exactness as the laws of harmony, perspective, and proportion," he mitigates what might appear to be an extravagance by applying his remark to "general" laws, and by expressing most of these rules in a manner with which it would certainly be unaccommodating to disagree. That the novelist must write from his experience, that his "characters must be real and such as might be met with in actual life"; that "a young lady brought up in a quiet country village should avoid descriptions of garrison life," and "a writer whose friends and personal experiences belong to the lower middle-class should carefully avoid introducing his characters into society"; that one should enter one's notes in a common-place book; that one's figures should be clear in outline; that making them clear by some trick of speech or of carriage is a bad method, and "describing them at length" is a worse one; that English Fiction should have a "conscious moral purpose"; that "it is almost impossible to estimate too highly the value of careful workmanship—that is, of style"; that "the most important point of all is the story," that "the story is everything": these are principles with most of which it is surely impossible not to sympathize. That remark about the lower middle-class writer and his knowing his place is perhaps rather chilling; but for the rest I should find it difficult to dissent from any one of these recommendations. At the same time, I should find it difficult positively to assent to them, with the exception, perhaps, of the injunction as to entering one's notes in a common-place book. They scarcely seem to me to have the quality that Mr. Besant attributes to the rules of the novelist—the "precision and exactness" of "the laws of harmony, perspective, and proportion." They are suggestive, they are even inspiring, but they are not exact, though they are doubtless as much so as the case admits of: which is a proof of that liberty of interpretation for which I just contended. For the value of these different injunctions—so beautiful and so vague—is wholly in the meaning one attaches to them. The characters, the situation, which strike one as real will be those that touch and interest one most, but the measure of reality is very difficult to fix. The reality of Don Quixote or of Mr. Micawber is a very delicate shade; it is a reality so colored by the author's vision that, vivid as it may be, one would hesitate to propose it as a model: one would expose one's self to some very embarrassing questions on the part of a pupil. It goes without saying that you will not write a good novel unless you possess the sense of reality; but it will be difficult to give you a recipe for calling that sense into being. Humanity is immense, and reality has a myriad forms; the most one can affirm is that some of the flowers of fiction have the odor of it, and others have not; as for telling you in advance how your nosegay should be composed, that is another affair. It is equally excellent and inconclusive to say that one must write from experience; to our supposititious aspirant such a declaration might savor of mockery. What kind of experience is intended, and where does it begin and end? Experience is never limited, and it is never complete; it is an immense sensibility, a kind of huge spider-web of the finest silken threads suspended in the chamber of consciousness, and catching every air-borne particle in its tissue. It is the very atmophere of the mind; and when the mind is imaginative—much more when it happens to be that of a man of genius—it takes to itself the faintest hints of life, it converts the very pulses of the air into revelations. The young lady living in a village has only to be a damsel upon whom nothing is lost to make it quite unfair (as it seems to me) to declare to her that she shall have nothing to say about the military. Greater miracles have been seen than that, imagination assisting, she should speak the truth about some of these gentlemen. I remember an English novelist, a woman of genius,[2] telling me that she was much commended for the impression she had managed to give in one of her tales of the nature and way of life of the French Protestant youth. She had been asked where she learned so much about his recondite being, she had been congratulated on her peculiar opportunities. These opportunities consisted in her having once, in Paris, as she ascended a staircase, passed an open door where, in the household of a *pasteur,* some of the young Protestants were seated at table round a finished meal. The glimpse made a picture; it lasted only a moment, but that moment was experience. She had got her direct personal impression, and she turned out her type. She knew what youth was, and what Protestantism; she also had the advantage of having seen what it was to be French, so that she converted these ideas into a concrete image and produced a reality. Above all, however, she was blessed with the faculty which when you give it an inch takes an ell, and which for the artist is a much greater source of strength than any accident of residence or of place in the social scale. The power to guess the unseen from the seen, to trace the implication of things, to judge the whole piece by the pattern, the condition of feeling life in general so completely that you are well on your way to knowing any particular corner of it—this cluster of gifts may almost be said to constitute experience, and they occur in country and in town, and in the most differing stages of education. If experience consists of impressions, it may be said that impressions *are* experience, just as (have we not seen it?) they are the very air we breathe. Therefore, if I should certainly say to a novice, "Write from experience and experience only," I should feel that this was rather a tantalizing monition if I were not careful immediately to add, "Try to be one of the people on whom nothing is lost!"

I am far from intending by this to minimize the importance of exactness—of truth of detail. One can speak best from one's own taste, and I may therefore venture to say that the air of reality (solidity of specification) seems to me to be the supreme virtue of a novel—the merit on which all its other merits (including that conscious moral purpose of which Mr. Besant speaks) helplessly and submissively depend. If it be

---

[2] Probably Anne Thackeray, Lady Ritchie, daughter of Thackeray, whose first novel *The Story of Elizabeth* corresponds to James's description.

not there they are all as nothing, and if these be there, they owe their effect to the success with which the author has produced the illusion of life. The cultivation of this success, the study of this exquisite process, form, to my taste, the beginning and the end of the art of the novelist. They are his inspiration, his despair, his reward, his torment, his delight. It is here in very truth that he competes with life; it is here that he competes with his brother the painter in *his* attempt to render the look of things, the look that conveys their meaning, to catch the color, the relief, the expression, the surface, the substance of the human spectacle. It is in regard to this that Mr. Besant is well inspired when he bids him take notes. He cannot possibly take too many, he cannot possibly take enough. All life solicits him, and to "render" the simplest surface, to produce the most momentary illusion, is a very complicated business. His case would be easier, and the rule would be more exact, if Mr. Besant had been able to tell him what notes to take. But this, I fear, he can never learn in any manual; it is the business of his life. He has to take a great many in order to select a few, he has to work them up as he can, and even the guides and philosophers who might have most to say to him must leave him alone when it comes to the application of precepts, as we leave the painter in communion with his palette. That his characters "must be clear in outline," as Mr. Besant says—he feels that down to his boots; but how he shall make them so is a secret between his good angel and himself. It would be absurdly simply if he could be taught that a great deal of "description" would make them so, or that on the contrary the absence of description and the cultivation of dialogue, or the absence of dialogue and the multiplication of "incident," would rescue him from his difficulties. Nothing, for instance, is more possible than that he be of a turn of mind for which this odd, literal opposition of description and dialogue, incident and description, has little meaning and light. People often talk of these things as if they had a kind of internecine distinctness, instead of melting into each other at every breath, and being intimately associated parts of one general effort of expression. I cannot imagine composition existing in a series of blocks, nor conceive, in any novel worth discussing at all, of a passage of description that is not in its intention narrative, a passage of dialogue that is not in its intention descriptive, a touch of truth of any sort that does not partake of the nature of incident, or an incident that derives its interest from any other source than the general and only source of the success of a work of art—that of being illustrative. A novel is a living thing, all one and continuous, like any other organism, and in proportion as it lives will it be found, I think, that in each of the parts there is something of each of the other parts. The critic who over the close texture of a finished work shall pretend to trace a geography of items will mark some frontiers as artificial, I fear, as any that have been known to history. There is an old-fashioned distinction between the novel of character and the novel of incident which must have cost many a smile to the intending fabulist who was keen about his work. It appears to me as little to the point as the equally celebrated distinction between the novel and the romance—to answer as little to any reality. There are bad novels and good novels, as there are bad pictures and good pictures; but that is the only distinction in which I see any meaning, and I can as little imagine speaking of a novel of character as I can imagine speaking of a picture of character. When one says picture one says of character, when one says novel one says of incident, and the terms may be transposed at will. What is character but the determination of incident? What is incident but the illustration of character? What is either a picture or a novel that is *not* of character? What else do we seek in it and find in it? It is an incident for a woman to stand up with her hand resting on a table and look out at you in a certain way; or if it be not an incident I think it will be hard to say what it is. At the same time it is an expression of character. If you say you don't see it (character in *that—allons donc!*), this is exactly what the artist who has reasons of his own for thinking he *does* see it undertakes to show you. When a young man makes up his mind that he has not faith enough after all to enter the church as he intended, that is an incident, though you may not hurry to the end of the chapter to see whether perhaps he doesn't change once more. I do not say that these are extraordinary or startling incidents. I do not pretend to estimate the degree of interest proceeding from them, for this will depend upon the skill of the painter. It sounds almost puerile to say that some incidents are intrinsically much more important than others, and I need not take this precaution after having professed my sympathy for the major ones in remarking that the only classification of the novel that I can understand is into that which has life and that which has it not.

The novel and the romance, the novel of incident and that of character—these clumsy separations appear to me to have been made by critics and readers for their own convenience, and to help them out of some of their occasional queer predicaments, but to have little reality or interest for the producer, from whose point of view it is of course that we are attempting to consider the art fiction. The case is the same with another shadowy category which Mr. Besant apparently is disposed to set up—that of the "modern English novel"; unless indeed it be that in this matter he has fallen into an accidental confusion of standpoints. It is not quite clear whether he intends the remarks in which he alludes to it to be didactic or historical. It is as difficult to suppose a person intending to write a modern English as to suppose him writing an ancient English novel: that is a label which begs the question. One writes the novel, one paints the picture, of one's language and of one's time, and calling it modern English will not, alas! make the difficult task any easier. No more, unfortunately, will calling this or that work of one's fellow-artist a romance—unless it be, of course, simply for the pleasantness of the thing, as for instance when Hawthorne gave this heading to his story of *Blithedale*. The French, who have brought the theory of fiction to remarkable completeness, have but one name for the novel, and have not attempted smaller things in it, that I can see, for that. I can think of no obligation to which the "romancer" would not be held equally with the novelist; the standard of execution is equally high for each. Of course it is of execution that we are talking—that being the only point of a novel that is open to contention. This is perhaps too often lost sight of, only to produce interminable confusions and cross-purposes. We must grant the artist his subject, his idea, his *donnée:* our criticism is applied only to what he makes of it. Naturally I do not mean that we are bound to like it or find it interesting: in case we do not our course is perfectly simple —to let it alone. We may believe that of a certain idea even the most sincere novelist can make nothing at all, and the event may perfectly justify our belief; but the failure will have been a failure to execute, and it is in the execution that the fatal weakness is recorded. If we pretend to respect the artist at all, we must allow him his freedom of choice, in the face, in particular cases, of innumerable presumptions that the choice will not fructify. Art derives a considerable part of its beneficial exercise from flying in the face of presumptions, and some of the most interesting experiments of which it is capable are hidden in the bosom of common things. Gustave Flaubert has written a story [3] about the devotion of a servant-girl to a parrot, and the production, highly finished as it is, cannot on the whole be called a success. We are perfectly free to find it flat, but I think it might have been interesting; and I, for my part, am extremely glad he should have written it; it is a contribution to our knowledge of what can be done—or what cannot. Ivan Turgenev has written a tale about a deaf and dumb serf and a lap-dog,[4] and the thing is touching, loving, a little masterpiece. He struck the note of life where Gustave Flaubert missed it—he flew in the face of a presumption and achieved a victory.

Nothing, of course, will ever take the place of the good old fashion of "liking" a work of art or not liking it: the most improved criticism will not abolish that primitive, that ultimate test. I mention this to guard myself from the accusation of intimating that the idea, the subject, of a novel or a picture, does not matter. It matters, to my sense, in the highest degree, and if I might put up a prayer it would be that artists should select none but the richest. Some, as I have already hastened to admit, are much more remunerative than others, and it would be a world happily arranged in which persons intending to treat them should be exempt from confusions and mistakes. This fortunate condition will arrive only, I fear, on the same day that critics become purged from error. Meanwhile, I repeat, we do not judge the artist with fairness unless we say to him,

"Oh, I grant you your starting-point, because if I did not I should seem to prescribe to you, and heaven forbid I should take that responsibility.

[3] *Un coeur simple.*   [4] *Mumu.*

If I pretend to tell you what you must not take, you will call upon me to tell you then what you must take; in which case I shall be prettily caught. Moreover, it isn't till I have accepted your data that I can begin to measure you. I have the standard, the pitch; I have no right to tamper with your flute and then criticize your music. Of course I may not care for your idea at all; I may think it silly, or stale, or unclean; in which case I wash my hands of you altogether. I may content myself with believing that you will not have succeeded in being interesting, but I shall, of course, not attempt to demonstrate it, and you will be as indifferent to me as I am to you. I needn't remind you that there are all sorts of tastes: who can know it better? Some people, for excellent reasons, don't like to read about carpenters; others, for reasons even better, don't like to read about courtesans. Many object to Americans. Others (I believe they are mainly editors and publishers) won't look at Italians. Some readers don't like quiet subjects; others don't like bustling ones. Some enjoy a complete illusion, others the consciousness of large concessions. They choose their novels accordingly, and if they don't care about your idea they won't, *a fortiori*, care about your treatment."

So that it comes back very quickly, as I have said, to the liking: in spite of M. Zola, who reasons less powerfully than he represents, and who will not reconcile himself to this absoluteness of taste, thinking that there are certain things that people ought to like, and that they can be made to like. I am quite at a loss to imagine anything (at any rate in this matter of fiction) that people *ought* to like or to dislike. Selection will be sure to take care of itself, for it has a constant motive behind it. That motive is simply experience. As people feel life, so they will feel the art that is most closely related to it. This closeness of relation is what we should never forget in talking of the effort of the novel. Many people speak of it as a factitious, artificial form, a product of ingenuity, the business of which is to alter and arrange the things that surround us, to translate them into conventional, traditional moulds. This, however, is a view of the matter which carries us but a very short way, condemns the art to an eternal repetition of a few familiar *clichés*, cuts short its development, and leads us straight up to a dead wall. Catching the very note and trick, the strange irregular rhythm of life, that is the attempt whose strenuous force keeps Fiction upon her feet. In proportion as in what she offers us we see life *without* rearrangement do we feel that we are touching the truth; in proportion as we see it *with* rearrangement do we feel that we are being put off with a substitute, a compromise and convention. It is not uncommon to hear an extraordinary assurance of remark in regard to this matter of rearranging, which is often spoken of as if it were the last word of art. Mr. Besant seems to me in danger of falling into the great error with his rather unguarded talk about "selection." Art is essentially selection, but it is a selection whose main care is to be typical, to be inclusive. For many people art means rose-colored window-panes, and selection means picking a bouquet for Mrs. Grundy. They will tell you glibly that artistic considerations have nothing to do with the disagreeable, with the ugly; they will rattle off shallow commonplaces about the province of art and the limits of art till you are moved to some wonder in return as to the province and the limits of ignorance. It appears to me that no one can ever have made a seriously artistic attempt without becoming conscious of an immense increase—a kind of revelation—of freedom. One perceives in that case—by the light of a heavenly ray—that the province of art is all life, all feeling, all observation, all vision. As Mr. Besant so justly intimates, it is all experience. That is a sufficient answer to those who maintain that it must not touch the sad things of life, who stick into its divine unconscious bosom little prohibitory inscriptions on the end of sticks, such as we see in public gardens—"It is forbidden to walk on the grass; it is forbidden to touch the flowers; it is not allowed to introduce dogs or to remain after dark; it is requested to keep to the right." The young aspirant in the line of fiction whom we continue to imagine will do nothing without taste, for in that case his freedom would be of little use to him; but the first advantage of his taste will be to reveal to him the absurdity of the little sticks and tickets. If he have taste, I must add, of course he will have ingenuity, and my disrespectful reference to that quality just now was not meant to imply that it is useless in fiction. But it is only a secondary aid; the first is a capacity for receiving straight impressions.

Mr. Besant has some remarks on the question of "the story" which I shall not attempt to criticize, though they seem to me to contain a singular ambiguity, because I do not think I understand them. I cannot see what is meant by talking as if there were a part of a novel which is the story and part of it which for mystical reasons is not—unless indeed the distinction be made in a sense in which it is difficult to suppose that any one should attempt to convey anything. "The story," if it represents anything, represents the subject, the idea, the *donnée* of the novel; and there is surely no "school"—Mr. Besant speaks of a school—which urges that a novel should be all treatment and no subject. There must assuredly be something to treat; every school is intimately conscious of that. This sense of the story being the idea, the starting-point, of the novel, is the only one that I see in which it can be spoken of as something different from its organic whole; and since in proportion as the work is successful the idea permeates and penetrates it, informs and animates it, so that every word and every punctuation-point contribute directly to the expression, in that proportion do we lose our sense of the story being a blade which may be drawn more or less out of its sheath. The story and the novel, the idea and the form, are the needle and thread, and I never heard of a guild of tailors who recommended the use of the thread without the needle, or the needle without the thread. Mr. Besant is not the only critic who may be observed to have spoken as if there were certain things in life which constitute stories, and certain others which do not. I find the same odd implication in an entertaining article in the *Pall Mall Gazette,* devoted, as it happens, to Mr. Besant's lecture. "The story is the thing!" says this graceful writer, as if with a tone of opposition to some other idea. I should think it was, as every painter who, as the time for "sending in" his picture looms in the distance, finds himself still in quest of a subject—as every belated artist not fixed about his theme will heartily agree. There are some subjects which speak to us and others which do not, but he would be a clever man who should undertake to give a rule— an *index expurgatorius*—by which the story and the no-story should be known apart. It is impossible (to me at least) to imagine any such rule which shall not be altogether arbitrary. The writer in the *Pall Mall* opposes the delightful (as I suppose) novel of *Margot la Balafrée* [5] to certain tales in which "Bostonian nymphs" appear to have "rejected English dukes for psychological reasons." I am not acquainted with the romance just designated, and can scarcely forgive the *Pall Mall* critic for not mentioning the name of the author, but the title appears to refer to a lady who may have received a scar in some heroic adventure. I am inconsolable at not being acquainted with this episode, but am utterly at a loss to see why it is a story when the rejection (or acceptance) of a duke is not, and why a reason, psychological or other, is not a subject when a cicatrix is. They are all particles of the multitudinous life with which the novel deals, and surely no dogma which pretends to make it lawful to touch the one and unlawful to touch the other will stand for a moment on its feet. It is the special picture that must stand or fall, according as it seem to possess truth or to lack it. Mr. Besant does not, to my sense, light up the subject by intimating that a story must, under penalty of not being a story, consist of "adventures." Why of adventures more than of green spectacles? He mentions a category of impossible things, and among them he places "fiction without adventure." Why without adventure, more than without matrimony, or celibacy, or parturition, or cholera, or hydropathy, or Jansenism? This seems to me to bring the novel back to the hapless little *rôle* of being an artificial, ingenious thing—bring it down from its large, free character of an immense and exquisite correspondence with life. And what *is* adventure, when it comes to that, and by what sign is the listening pupil to recognize it? It is an adventure—an immense one—for me to write this little article; and for a Bostonian nymph to reject an English duke is an adventure only less stirring, I should say, than for an English duke to be rejected by a Bostonian nymph. I see dramas within dramas in that, and innumerable points of view. A psychological reason is, to my imagination, an object adorably pictorial; to catch the tint of its complexion—I feel as that idea might inspire one to Titianesque efforts. There are few things more exciting to me, in short, than a psychological reason, and yet, I protest, the novel seems to me the

---

[5] The author of the "certain tales," fairly obviously, is James himself, and the story alluded to probably *An International* *Episode* (1879). *Margot la Balafrée* is a novel by Fortuné du Boisgobey, published in Paris in 1884.

most magnificent form of art. I have just been reading, at the same time, the delightful story of *Treasure Island*, by Mr. Robert Louis Stevenson and, in a manner less consecutive, the last tale from M. Edmond de Goncourt, which is entitled *Chérie*. One of these works treats of murders, mysteries, islands of dreadful renown, hairbreadth escapes, miraculous coincidences and buried doubloons. The other treats of a little French girl who lived in a fine house in Paris, and died of wounded sensibility because no one would marry her. I call *Treasure Island* delightful, because it appears to me to have succeeded wonderfully in what it attempts; and I venture to bestow no epithet upon *Chérie*, which strikes me as having failed deplorably in what it attempts—that is in tracing the development of the moral consciousness of a child. But one of these productions strikes me as exactly as much of a novel as the other, and as having a "story" quite as much. The moral consciousness of a child is as much a part of life as the islands of the Spanish Main, and the one sort of geography seems to me to have those "surprises" of which Mr. Besant speaks quite as much as the other. For myself (since it comes back in the last resort, as I say, to the preference of the individual), the picture of the child's experience has the advantage that I can at successive steps (an immense luxury, near to the "sensual pleasure" of which Mr. Besant's critic in the *Pall Mall* speaks) say Yes or No, as it may be, to what the artist puts before me. I have been a child in fact, but I have been on a quest for a buried treasure only in supposition, and it is a simple accident that with M. de Goncourt I should have for the most part to say No. With George Eliot, when she painted that country with a far other intelligence, I always said Yes.

The most interesting part of Mr. Besant's lecture is unfortunately the briefest passage—his very cursory allusion to the "conscious moral purpose" of the novel. Here again it is not very clear whether he be recording a fact or laying down a principle; it is a great pity that in the latter case he should not have developed his idea. This branch of the subject is of immense importance, and Mr. Besant's few words point to considerations of the widest reach, not to be lightly disposed of. He will have treated the art of fiction but superficially who is not prepared to go every inch of the way that these considerations will carry him. It is for this reason that at the beginning of these remarks I was careful to notify the reader that my reflections on so large a theme have no pretension to be exhaustive. Like Mr. Besant, I have left the question of the morality of the novel till the last, and at the last I find I have used up my space. It is a question surrounded with difficulties, as witness the very first that meets us, in the form of a definite question, on the threshold. Vagueness, in such a discussion, is fatal, and what is the meaning of your morality and your conscious moral purpose? Will you not define your terms and explain how (a novel being a picture) a picture can be either moral or immoral? You wish to paint a moral picture or carve a moral statue: will you not tell us how you would set about it? We are discussing the Art of Fiction; questions of art are questions (in the widest sense) of execution; questions of morality are quite another affair, and will you not let us see how it is that you find it so easy to mix them up? These things are so clear to Mr. Besant that he has deduced from them a law which he sees embodied in English Fiction, and which is "a truly admirable thing and a great cause for congratulation." It is a great cause for congratulation indeed when such thorny problems become as smooth as silk. I may add that in so far as Mr. Besant perceives that in point of fact English Fiction has addressed itself preponderantly to these delicate questions he will appear to many people to have made a vain discovery. They will have been positively struck, on the contrary, with the moral timidity of the usual English novelist; with his (or with her) aversion to face the difficulties with which on every side the treatment and reality bristles. He is apt to be extremely shy (whereas the picture that Mr. Besant draws is a picture of boldness), and the sign of his work, for the most part, is a cautious silence on certain subjects. In the English novel (by which of course I mean the American as well), more than in any other, there is a traditional difference between that which people know and that which they agree to admit that they know, that which they see and that which they speak of, that which they feel to be a part of life and that which they allow to enter into literature. There is the great difference, in short, between what they talk of in conversation and what they talk of in print. The essence of moral energy is to survey the whole field, and I should directly reverse Mr. Besant's remark and say not that the English novel has a purpose, but that it has a diffidence. To what degree a purpose in a work of art is a source of corruption I shall not attempt to inquire; the one that seems to me least dangerous is the purpose of making a perfect work. As for our novel, I may say lastly on this score that as we find it in England today it strikes me as addressed in a large degree to "young people," and that this in itself constitutes a presumption that it will be rather shy. There are certain things which it is generally agreed not to discuss, not even to mention, before young people. That is very well, but the absence of discussion is not a symptom of the moral passion. The purpose of the English novel—"a truly admirable thing, and a great cause for congratulation"—strikes me therefore as rather negative.

There is one point at which the moral sense and the artistic sense lie very near together; that is in the light of the very obvious truth that the deepest quality of a work of art will always be the quality of the mind of the producer. In proportion as that intelligence is fine will the novel, the picture, the statue partake of the substance of beauty and truth. To be constituted of such elements is, to my vision, to have purpose enough. No good novel will ever proceed from a superficial mind; that seems to me an axiom which, for the artist in fiction, will cover all needful moral ground: If the youthful aspirant take it to heart it will illuminate for him many of the mysteries of "purpose." There are many other useful things that might be said to him, but I have come to the end of my article, and can only touch them as I pass. The critic in the *Pall Mall Gazette,* whom I have already quoted, draws attention to the danger, in speaking of the art of fiction, of generalizing. The danger that he has in mind is rather, I imagine, that of particularizing, for there are some comprehensive remarks which, in addition to those embodied in Mr. Besant's suggestive lecture, might without fear of misleading him be addressed to the ingenuous student. I should remind him first of the magnificence of the form that is open to him, which offers to sight so few restrictions and such innumerable opportunities. The other arts, in comparison, appear confined and hampered; the various conditions under which they are exercised are so rigid and definite. But the only condition that I can think of attaching to the composition of the novel is, as I have already said, that it be sincere. This freedom is a splendid privilege, and the first lesson of the young novelist is to learn to be worthy of it.

"Enjoy it as it deserves [I should say to him]; take possession of it, explore it to its utmost extent, publish it, rejoice in it. All life belongs to you, and do not listen either to those who would shut you up into corners of it and tell you that it is only here and there that art inhabits, or to those who would persuade you that this heavenly messenger wings her way outside of life altogether, breathing a superfine air, and turning away her head from the truth of things. There is no impression of life, no manner of seeing it and feeling it, to which the plan of the novelist may not offer a place; you have only to remember that talents so dissimilar as those of Alexandre Dumas and Jane Austen, Charles Dickens and Gustave Flaubert have worked in this field with equal glory. Do not think too much about optimism and pessimism; try and catch the color of life itself. In France today we see a prodigious effort (that of Émile Zola, to whose solid and serious work no explorer of the capacity of the novel can allude without respect), we see an extraordinary effort vitiated by a spirit of pessimism on a narrow basis. M. Zola is magnificent, but he strikes an English reader as ignorant; he has an air of working in the dark; if he had as much light as energy, his results would be of the highest value. As for the aberrations of a shallow optimism, the ground (of English fiction especially) is strewn with their brittle particles as with broken glass. If you must indulge in conclusions, let them have the taste of a wide knowledge. Remember that your first duty is to be as complete as possible—to make as perfect a work. Be generous and delicate and pursue the prize."

Notes for THE AMBASSADORS

The notebooks of Henry James are among the great documents of American literature. They constitute the record of a private fiction laboratory, preserved by accident, giving us a rare glimpse into the creative process of a remarkable artist. James used to buy cheap scribblers in stationers' shops and carry these about with him during his travels, or keep them at hand in his apartment, to jot down themes which occurred to him and work these out in what amounted to a quiet conversation with himself. He destroyed his notebooks once they had outlived their usefulness; but some half dozen survived, perhaps because they contained jottings for stories he had not yet written. Placed in an old trunk after his death with the remainder of his private papers, they finally came into possession of Harvard University and were published in 1947.

The excerpt given here is the first notation of the idea which later became a novel James considered his most "rounded" work. *The Ambassadors* was written in 1901, six years after the first idea was set down and published in 1903. It differs in a number of ways from the outline James first drafted, as nearly all his stories did; but the central character and the central thread of the story is substantially the same. The W.D.H. mentioned in the opening sentences was William Dean Howells, novelist and editor, for years an intimate friend of James. Jonathan Sturges, who told James the anecdote, was a young New Yorker, a graduate of Princeton, who wrote criticism and short stories and who had made many friends in the artistic worlds of London and Paris.

Torquay, October 31st, 1895.

I was struck last evening with something that Jonathan Sturges, who has been staying here 10 days, mentioned to me: it was only 10 words but I seemed, as usual, to catch a glimpse of a *sujet de nouvelle* in it. We were talking of W.D.H. and of his having seen him during a short and interrupted stay H. had made 18 months ago in Paris—called away—back to America, when he had just come—at the end of 10 days by the news of the death—or illness—of his father. He had scarcely been in Paris, ever, in former days, and he had come there to see his domiciled and initiated son, who was at the Beaux Arts. Virtually in the evening, as it were, of life, it was all new to him: all, all, all. Sturges said he seemed sad —rather brooding; and I asked him what gave him (Sturges) that impression. 'Oh—somewhere—I forget, when I was with him—he laid his hand on my shoulder and said *à propos* of some remark of mine: "Oh, you are young, you are young—be glad of it: be glad of it and *live*. Live all you can: it's a mistake not to. It doesn't so much matter what you do —but live. This place makes it all come over me. I see it now. I haven't done so—and now I'm old. It's too late. It has gone past me—I've lost it. You have time. You are young. Live!"' I amplify and improve a little— but that was the tone. It touches me—I can see him—I can hear him. Immediately, of course—as everything, thank God, does—it suggests a little situation. I seem to see something, of a tiny kind, springing out of it, that would take its place in the little group I should like to do of

Les Vieux—The Old. (What should I call it in English—*Old Fellows?* No, that's trivial and common.) At any rate, it gives me the little idea of the figure of an elderly man who hasn't 'lived,' hasn't at all, in the sense of sensations, passions, impulses, pleasures—and to whom, in the presence of some great human spectacle, some great organization for the Immediate, the Agreeable, for curiosity, and experiment and perception, for Enjoyment, in a word, becomes, *sur la fin,* or toward it, sorrowfully aware. He has never really enjoyed—he has lived only for Duty and conscience—his conception of them; for pure appearances and daily tasks—lived for effort, for surrender, abstention, sacrifice. I seem to see his history, his temperament, his circumstances, his figure, his life. I don't see him as having battled with his passions—I don't see him as harassed by his temperament or as having, in the past, suspected, very much, what he was losing, what he was not doing. The alternative wasn't present to him. He may be an American—he might be an Englishman. I don't altogether like the *banal* side of the revelation of Paris—it's so obvious, so usual to make Paris the vision that opens his eyes, makes him feel his mistake. It might be London—it might be Italy—it might be the general impression of a summer in Europe—abroad. Also, it *may* be Paris. He has been a great worker, a local worker. But of what kind? I can't make him a novelist—too like W.D.H., and too generally *invraisemblable*. But I want him 'intellectual,' I want him *fine,* clever, literary almost: it deepens the irony, the tragedy. A clergyman is too obvious and *usé* and otherwise impossible. A journalist, a lawyer—those men WOULD in a manner have 'lived,' through their contact with life, with the complications and turpitudes and general vitality of mankind. A doctor—an artist too. A mere man of business—he's possible; but not of the intellectual grain that I mean. The Editor of a Magazine—that would come nearest: not at all of a newspaper. A Professor in a college would imply some knowledge of the lives of the young—though there might be a tragic effect in his seeing at the last that he hasn't even suspected what those lives might contain. (They had passed by him—he had passed them by.) He has married very young, and austerely. Happily enough, but charmlessly, and oh, so conscientiously: a wife replete with the New England conscience. But all this must be—oh, so light, so delicately summarized, so merely touched. What I seem to see is the possibility of some little illustrative action. The idea of the tale being the revolution that takes place in the poor man, the impression made on him by the particular experience, the incident in which this revolution and this impression embody themselves, is the point *à trouver*. They are determined by certain circumstances, and they produce a situation, his issue from which is the little drama. I am supposing him, I think, to have 'illustrated,' as I say, in the past, by his issue from some *other* situation, the opposite conditions, those that have determined him in the sense of the sort of life and feeling I have sketched and the memory, the consciousness of which roll over him now with force. He has sacrificed

some one, some friend, some son, some younger brother, to his failure
to feel, to understand, all that his new experience causes to come home
to him in a wave of reaction, of compunction. He has not allowed for
these things, the new things, new sources of emotion, new influences
and appeals—didn't realize them at all. It was in communication with
them that the spirit, the sense, the nature, the temperament of this victim (as now seems to him) of his old ignorance, struggled and suffered.
He was wild—he was free—he was passionate; but there would have
been a way of taking him. Our friend never saw it—never, never: he
perceives that—ever so sadly, so bitterly, now. The young man is dead:
it's all over. Was he a son, was he a ward, a younger brother—or an
elder one? Points to settle: though I'm not quite sure I like the *son.*
Well, my vague little fancy is that he 'comes out,' as it were (to London, to Paris—I'm afraid it *must* be Paris; if he's an American), to take
some step, decide some question with regard to some one, in the sense
of his old feelings and habits, and that the new influences, to state it
roughly, make him act just in the opposite spirit—make him accept on
the spot, with a *volte-face*, a wholly different inspiration. It is a case of
some other person or persons, it is some other young life in regard to
which it's a question of his interfering, rescuing, bringing home. Say
he 'goes out' (partly) to look after, to bring home, some young man
whom his family are anxious about, who won't *come* home, etc.—and
under the operation of the change *se range du côté du jeune homme,*
says to him: 'No; STAY:—*don't* come home.' Say our friend is a widower,
and that the *jeune homme* is the son of a widow to whom he is engaged to be married. *She* is of the strenuous pattern—she is the reflection
of his old self. She has money—she admires and approves him: 5 years
have elapsed since his 1st wife's death, 10 since his own son's. He is 55.
He married at 20! Displeasing the strenuous widow is a sacrifice—an
injury to him. To marry her means rest and security *pour ses vieux
jours.* The 'revolution' endangers immensely his situation with her. But
of course my denouement is that it takes place—that he makes the sacrifice, does the thing I have, vaguely, represented him *supra,* as doing, and
loses the woman he was to marry and all the advantages attaching to
her. It is too late, too late *now,* for HIM to live—but what stirs in him
with a dumb passion of desire, of I don't know what, is the sense that
he may have a little super-sensual hour in the vicarious freedom of another. His little drama is the administration of the touch that contributes
to—that prolongs—that freedom.

STEPHEN CRANE

1871–1900

"I UNDERSTAND," WROTE CRANE, "THAT A MAN IS BORN INTO THIS WORLD with his own pair of eyes, and that he is not at all responsible for his vision—he is merely responsible for his quality of personal honesty." This statement is important in focusing our attention upon two of Crane's major concerns: that he must put his trust in his own experience, rather than building on the received past; and that he must not compromise with truth as he has come to know it. Such an artistic creed is not unique, but Crane's commitment helps to explain the apparent lack of direction in his restless life and the rejections which were necessary before he could become himself. Ultimately, rejections and frenetic activity were constructive: they led him to a few fundamental propositions about man in relation to himself, his God, and the universe, and to the incorporation of these ideas in an important body of work. In his productive years of less than a decade he wrote more than a dozen books, which, though uneven, include two volumes of distinctive verse, some superb short stories, and a classic war novel, *The Red Badge of Courage*.

Crane's career is shot through with paradox. He is historically important as a pioneer in American literary naturalism and as an innovator in poetry, yet he seems to have been almost unconscious of European developments which might have influenced him. He wrote *The Red Badge* without having smelled powder, but his later reports of actual warfare in Greece and Cuba are shallow by comparison. The rather irregular life of a journalist did not justify the gaudy rumors that he was addicted to dope and drink; on the other hand, his union with Mrs. Cora Crane was untouched by scandal, although she had been manager of the Hotel de Dream, a Jacksonville brothel, and it is not known whether they were legally married. As unlikely as anything else in his career was Crane's warm friendship with Joseph Conrad and the fastidious Henry James.

The truths about Crane are often elusive because the documentary evidence of letters and manuscripts is incomplete. Thomas Beer's biography (1923) drew on the recollections of many people who knew Crane, but, despite a flavorsome anecdotal quality and a careful attempt to separate the man from the legend, Beer is often inaccurate. In recent years the picture has been gradually coming into focus, notably through John Berryman's *Stephen Crane* (1950), an acute and informed study for all its dependence on Freudian insights to interpret Crane's personal drives and the latent content of his work. In *Stephen Crane: An Omnibus* (1952) R. W. Stallman has packed much fresh information and a generous selection of his writings, including a new text of *The Red Badge* and pieces not in Wilson Follett's edition of *The Work of Stephen Crane* (1925–26). Daniel Hoffman's study, *The Poetry of Stephen Crane* (1957), draws upon newly available manuscripts to refine the record further. But we still know less than we should like to know about his reading, the influence of literary and artistic acquaintances upon him, and the motivations underlying some of his personal beliefs. This is not mere curiosity, but a valid interest in understanding the creative imagination of an exceptionally talented author who drew almost all his ideas and images from experience and from a private vision of art as truth.

Crane was born in Newark, New Jersey, in November, 1871. His father was a rather benign Methodist minister, while his mother came from a long line of "brimstone" clergymen; this latter inheritance is an important clue to the nihilism of his poetry, for Crane's defiance of the God of vengeance was not only a typical *fin de siècle* gesture but was also a rejection of the joyless views of his mother's forebears. Crane's father, on the other hand, was not so narrowly orthodox and held a kindlier view of man's relation to his God, although he knew little of the world his youngest son was to scrutinize so sensitively. After a childhood spent in various New Jersey towns Crane was sent to the Hudson River Institute in Claverack, New York, a military academy where he distinguished himself in poker and baseball. In the fall of 1890 he enrolled at Lafayette College in Easton, Pennsylvania, transferring the following January to Syracuse University for his final try at schooling. He made an A in English and evidently read a good deal, but we hear more about his abilities as catcher and shortstop. By the end of the spring term he knew he wanted to be a writer and journalism seemed the one immediate outlet for such talents as he had discovered.

Crane had earlier helped his brother Townley with summer newsgathering in Asbury Park and he had written stories for school papers. Now in New York he found work with the *Herald* and later with the *Tribune*, but being more interested in recording impressions than facts he could not satisfy editors. He lost both jobs and never held another regular post: most of his subsequent newspaper writing was done on free-lance assignments. His *Sullivan County Sketches* (1949) was a product of 1892 and five of the ten pieces were printed in the *Tribune* that summer; as stories they are not successful, but they show Crane's style developing into an effective medium for conveying the swift, striking impression in precise, if often self-conscious language ("A scrawny stone dam, clinging in apparent desperation to its foundation, wandered across a wild valley").

In New York he had discovered the Bowery and become acquainted with human degradation and the powerful forces of environment conditioning life in tenements and flophouses. A brief episode in his experience he was later to record in "An Experiment in Misery." Meantime he was at work on a story of a girl who "blossomed in a mud-puddle," was seduced and abandoned by a bartender, and drifted into prostitution and eventual suicide. In 1892 he showed a draft of *Maggie: A Girl of the Streets* to R. W. Gilder, editor of *Century Magazine*, who as Beer tells it objected to a lack of tenderness in the people of Rum Alley and to the objective way in which the narrative unfolded without sentiment or moralizing. "You mean that the story's too honest?" was Crane's response to the editor's criticism of his style. And so *Maggie* found no publisher; in 1893 Crane had it printed at his own expense under the pseudonym "Johnston Smith" but it attracted few readers even after Hamlin Garland praised it in *The Arena*. Not until 1896, following the success of *The Red Badge of Courage*, did it receive conventional publication under Crane's name.

This novella is a landmark in American naturalistic fiction, though Crane's spare, thin manner is at almost polar remove from the massive documentary quality of Dreiser or Zola. But like them he examines ungenteel aspects of society without any sense of obligation to sentimentalize his findings. With cool detachment he sketches the Johnson family whose lives are the product of their wretched surroundings: a father without understanding beyond a few stereotyped precepts, a mother driven to drink and general abuse of children and furniture, a son Jimmie who "menace[s] mankind at the intersections of streets" and becomes a Bowery tough. Maggie, a pretty girl, appears to be untouched by the physical squalor around her, but she is intellectually unformed and is so passive toward the actions and motives of humanity that she mistakes the bartender Pete for a man of character. The rest follows relentlessly, without much emotional stirring in Maggie even when she tries to keep Pete from leaving her. In no sense a plea for reform, the story is simply a report of conditions; Crane stands at a distance and observes, but leaves it to the reader to decide whether this minor tragedy is inevitable or is due to circumstances which society could change. Crane is not quite completely in control of his prose style, for some of his ironies seem contrived and occasionally his avoidance of sentimentality is artificial. But he reproduces the narrow range of language and the psychological motivations of his people with a fidelity worthy of Zola.

Though it has not been established that Crane knew Zola's *L'Assomoir*, which contains some rather general parallels with *Maggie*, he is said to have looked into *La Débâcle* and to have thought that he could improve on Zola's novel of the Franco-Prussian War. He had studied the *Century's* extensive series *Battles and Leaders of the Civil War* and may have given special attention to the battle of Chancellorsville, but what finally appeared late in 1895 as *The Red Badge of Courage* depended very little on books. The generals did not tell him what he needed to know; he had to depend on his own acquaintance with panic and fear to supply the emotional center of this concentrated, intense story of a green soldier in his first battle. We are never really concerned with what a historian would have said happened; reality for Henry Fleming is a compound of anxieties, fear, cowardly actions and bravery which he experiences without understanding. The power of the book lies in its psychological truth (which fiction of more recent wars has verified); its freshness lies in what Crane was prepared to discard of plot machinery, character development, and fully realized scene in order to focus on the succession of impressions, now sharp, now blurred, which constitute Fleming's insignificant world. Central in Crane's method is irony, for he is rejecting the world's romanticized view of battle. The wound which gives Fleming standing among his companions is not a badge of courage, nor is it from an enemy; bravery when it seizes him is as hysterical as was his cowardice; expectations are everywhere turned inside out as Crane allows the elemental responses of the human animal to displace fanciful splendors of glory.

In the spring of 1895 Crane spent several months in the West and in Mexico writing dispatches for a newspaper syndicate. Two of his best stories grew from impressions crowding upon him in Nebraska and Texas, but the writing of "The Blue Hotel" and "The Bride Comes to Yellow Sky" came later. In the same year he published *The Black Riders and Other Lines,* which with *War Is Kind* (1899) constituted almost all the poetry he wrote. *The Red Badge* brought him fame, but characteristically he was "much fonder" of *The Black Riders,* considering it the more ambitious work because his aim "was to comprehend in it the thoughts I have had about life in general, while *The Red Badge* is a mere episode in life, an amplification." The poems found a limited and only partially perceptive public. His "lines," as he always referred to his verse, were terse, iconoclastic allegories in which love did not lead to fulfillment, and the "Blustering God" of his ancestors made sport of man. Yet Crane did not write after the manner of the British decadents, nor did he exhibit any direct indebtedness to the French Symbolists, whom he had probably not read. Howells had introduced him to the intense lyricism of Emily Dickinson, but his rhythms are Biblical where hers are derived from hymnody. His corrosive irony reminds one of Ambrose Bierce, but it had been a staple of his earliest writing. In short, Crane's verse was novel, it was disturbing in its defiance, and its flat, prosy diction broke sharply away from the familiar poetical language of his day. In its compression Crane's free verse is nothing like Whitman's, but rather anticipates the manner—though not the attitudes—of the Imagists almost twenty years later.

In 1896 appeared another short novel of New York, *George's Mother,* along with a collection of Civil War stories, *The Little Regiment.* That November Crane started for Cuba to report on filibustering activities, but his ship sank and he never reached the island. His thirty-six hours in a dinghy after the disaster did, however, lead him to write "The Open Boat," one of his most brilliant and sustained efforts. By March 1897 he was once more on his way to a theater of war, as if impelled to test the correctness of his insights in *The Red Badge.* Greece and Turkey held him briefly; the next year he finally got to Cuba, but his six months in the field did more to undermine his health than his dispatches did to enhance his reputation. Before long tuberculosis seized him and he died in Germany in June 1900. His last three years, spent mostly in England, were unusually productive. In addition to a slight novel, *Active Service* (1899), he published two collections of tales, *The Open Boat* (1898) and *The Monster* (1899). Two other collections, *Whilomville Stories* and *Wounds in the Rain,* appeared in 1900 after his death, and he left material for three further posthumous volumes.

The impressionism of Crane's style is directly related to his belief that he must report, with fidelity, only what his imaginative vision has verified. Thus he seldom indulges in full descriptions or complete dramatizations of scenes. Instead, like the Impressionist painters, he tries to capture the essence of an instant. Just as the Impressionist is interested not in the separate leaves of a tree but in what has registered upon the painter's optical system, so Crane usually conveys not detailed objective truth but a series of "flash" sensory impressions. Thus we have "The sun was pasted in the sky like a red wafer," a vivid image which reduces celestial phenomena to a highly simplified two-dimensional childlike construction. If this is the way it appeared, and if one trusts the senses, this kind of impressionism has a validity, especially if one's fictional world is peopled by observers incapable of abstraction and skeptical of universal truths. It is significant that Crane, who lived with art students for a time, called himself an Impressionist and specifically linked impressionism with truth. A study of Crane's adjectives and verbs ("red years," "pompous and philanthropic whiskers," "The saloon gorged itself with plump men," "The guns squatted in a row like savage chiefs") will reveal the technique he used to distill observable truth. The key words here are meaningless if read literally; their real significance is figurative, suggestive of a complex of image, action, or attitude. As these segments of meaning open out to the imagination they reveal to us not objective facts, but a totality of impact which the context can generate within the mind. The effect is concentrated, and the reader who does not linger a moment to let it work on him may think the texture thin; closer examination, however, will often reveal some of the freshest and most powerful uses of language in Crane's fiction.

"The good writers are Henry James, Stephen Crane, and Mark Twain," said Hemingway, without specifying why these three make up his limited pantheon. One compelling reason is that each of this disparate trio, like Hemingway himself, had to discover a language, a tone, and a form for his individual narrative purposes. Beyond this, there is a special affinity between Hemingway and Crane in their commonly held code of uncompromising honesty, arrived at only after a rejection of the world's slogans and validated by the test of experience. It is this integrity of vision, central in Crane's theory and practice of art, that accounts for the vitality and strength of his best work.

A note on texts: The selections from Crane, most of which appeared originally in periodicals, are taken from first book publication. An exception is "The Blue Battalions," which is reprinted from its original magazine appearance since Crane did not include it in his last collection of poems.

AN EXPERIMENT IN MISERY

This sketch first appeared in the New York *Press* for April 22, 1894, and was reprinted in the English edition of *The Open Boat and Other Stories* (1898), from which the present text is derived. The newspaper version contains an opening and closing framework which makes more explicit—and perhaps more self-conscious—the contrived aspect of the adventure: a youth looks at a tramp and wonders if he might understand the derelict's psychology more clearly if he "went forth to try to eat as the tramp may eat, and sleep as the wanderers sleep." Borrowing clothes from "the studio of an artist friend," he goes "shuffling off down Park Row" and into Chatham Square. At the end he confesses that he may not understand the tramp's point of view any better, but that his own "has undergone a considerable alteration." The reader will find these discarded passages reproduced in *Stephen Crane: An Omnibus,* ed. R. W. Stallman (1952).

It was late at night, and a fine rain was swirling softly down, causing the pavements to glisten with hue of steel and blue and yellow in the rays of the innumerable lights. A youth was trudging slowly, without enthusiasm, with his hands buried deep in his trousers pockets, towards the down-town places where beds can be hired for coppers. He was clothed in an aged and tattered suit, and his derby was a marvel of dust-covered crown and torn rim. He was going forth to eat as the wanderer may eat, and sleep as the homeless sleep. By the time he had reached City Hall Park he was so completely plastered with yells of "bum" and "hobo," and with various unholy epithets that small boys had applied to him at intervals, that he was in a state of the most profound dejection. The sifting rain saturated the old velvet collar of his overcoat, and as the wet cloth pressed against his neck, he felt that there no longer could be pleasure in life. He looked about him searching for an outcast of highest degree that the two might share miseries, but the lights threw a quivering glare over rows and circles of deserted benches that glistened damply, showing patches of wet sod behind them. It seemed that their usual freights had fled on this night to better things. There were only squads of well-dressed Brooklyn people who swarmed towards the bridge.

The young man loitered about for a time and then went shuffling off down Park Row. In the sudden descent in style of the dress of the crowd he felt relief, and as if he were at last in his own country. He began to see tatters that matched his tatters. In Chatham Square there were aimless men strewn in front of saloons and lodging-houses, standing sadly, patiently, reminding one vaguely of the attitudes of chickens in a storm. He aligned himself with these men, and turned slowly to occupy himself with the flowing life of the great street.

Through the mists of the cold and storming night, the cable cars went in silent procession, great affairs shining with red and brass, moving with formidable power, calm and irresistible, dangerful and gloomy, breaking silence only by the loud fierce cry of the gong. Two rivers of people swarmed along the side-walks, spattered with black mud, which made each shoe leave a scar-like impression. Overhead elevated trains with a shrill grinding of the wheels stopped at the station, which upon its leg-like pillars seemed to resemble some monstrous kind of crab squatting over the street. The quick fat puffings of the engines could be heard. Down an alley there were somber curtains of purple and black, on which street lamps dully glittered like embroidered flowers.

A saloon stood with a voracious air on a corner. A sign leaning against the front of the door-post announced "Free hot soup to-night!" The swing doors, snapping to and fro like ravenous lips, made gratified smacks as the saloon gorged itself with plump men, eating with astounding and endless appetite, smiling in some indescribable manner as the men came from all directions like sacrifices to a heathenish superstition.

Caught by the delectable sign the young man allowed himself to be swallowed. A bar-tender placed a schooner of dark and portentous beer on the bar. Its monumental form up-reared until the froth a-top was above the crown of the young man's brown derby.

"Soup over there, gents," said the bar-tender affably. A little yellow man in rags and the youth grasped their schooners and went with speed toward a lunch counter, where a man with oily but imposing whiskers ladled genially from a kettle until he had furnished his two mendicants with a soup that was steaming hot, and in which there were little floating suggestions of chicken. The young man, sipping his broth, felt the cordiality expressed by the warmth of the mixture, and he beamed at the man with oily but imposing whiskers, who was presiding like a priest behind an altar. "Have some more, gents?" he inquired of the two sorry figures before him. The little yellow man accepted with a swift gesture, but the youth shook his head and went out, following a man whose wondrous seediness promised that he would have a knowledge of cheap lodging-houses.

On the side-walk he accosted the seedy man. "Say, do you know a cheap place to sleep?"

The other hesitated for a time gazing sideways. Finally he nodded in the direction of the street, "I sleep up there," he said, "when I've got the price."

"How much?"

"Ten cents."

The young man shook his head dolefully. "That's too rich for me."

At that moment there approached the two a reeling man in strange garments. His head was a fuddle of bushy hair and whiskers, from which his eyes peered with a guilty slant. In a close scrutiny it was possible to distinguish the cruel lines of a mouth which looked as if its lips had just closed with satisfaction over some tender and piteous morsel. He appeared like an assassin steeped in crimes performed awkwardly.

But at this time his voice was tuned to the coaxing key of an affectionate puppy. He looked at the men with wheedling eyes, and began to sing a little melody for charity.

"Say, gents, can't yeh give a poor feller a couple of cents t' git a bed. I got five, and I gits anudder two I gits me a bed. Now, on th' square, gents, can't yeh jest gimme two cents t' git a bed? Now, yeh know how a respecter'ble gentlem'n feels when he's down on his luck, an' I—"

The seedy man, staring with imperturbable countenance at a train which clattered overhead, interrupted in an expressionless voice—"Ah, go t' h—!"

But the youth spoke to the prayerful assassin in tones of astonishment and inquiry. "Say, you must be crazy! Why don't yeh strike somebody that looks as if they had money?"

The assassin, tottering about on his uncertain legs, and at intervals brushing imaginary obstacles from before his nose, entered into a long explanation of the psychology of the situation. It was so profound that it was unintelligible.

When he had exhausted the subject, the young man said to him—

"Let's see th' five cents."

The assassin wore an expression of drunken woe at this sentence, filled with suspicion of him. With a deeply pained air he began to fumble in his clothing, his red hands trembling. Presently he announced in a voice of bitter grief, as if he had been betrayed—"There's on'y four."

"Four," said the young man thoughtfully. "Well, look-a-here, I'm a stranger here, an' if ye'll steer me to your cheap joint I'll find the other three."

The assassin's countenance became instantly radiant with joy. His whiskers quivered with the wealth of his alleged emotions. He seized the young man's hand in a transport of delight and friendliness.

"B' Gawd," he cried, "if ye'll do that, b' Gawd, I'd say yeh was a damned good fellow, I would, an' I'd remember yeh all m' life, I would, b' Gawd, an' if I ever got a chance I'd return the compliment"—he spoke with drunken dignity,—"b' Gawd, I'd treat yeh white, I would, an' I'd allus remember yeh."

The young man drew back, looking at the assassin coldly. "Oh, that's all right," he said. "You show me th' joint—that's all you've got t' do."

The assassin, gesticulating gratitude, led the young man along a dark street. Finally he stopped before a little dusty door. He raised his hand impressively. "Look-a-here," he said, and there was a thrill of deep and ancient wisdom upon his face, "I've brought yeh here, an' that's my part, ain't it? If th' place don't suit yeh, yeh needn't git mad at me, need yeh? There won't be no bad feelin', will there?"

"No," said the young man.

The assassin waved his arm tragically, and led the march up the steep stairway. On the way the young man furnished the assassin with three pennies. At the top a man with benevolent spectacles looked at them through a hole in a board. He collected their money, wrote some names on a register, and speedily was leading the two men along a gloom-shrouded corridor.

Shortly after the beginning of this journey the young man felt his liver turn white, for from the dark and secret places of the building there suddenly came to his nostrils strange and unspeakable odors, that assailed him like malignant diseases with wings. They seemed to be from human bodies closely packed in dens; the exhalations from a hundred pairs of reeking lips; the fumes from a thousand bygone debauches; the expression of a thousand present miseries.

A man, naked save for a little snuff-colored undershirt, was parading sleepily along the corridor. He rubbed his eyes, and, giving vent to a prodigious yawn, demanded to be told the time.

"Half-past one."

The man yawned again. He opened a door, and for a moment his form was outlined against a black, opaque interior. To this door came the three men, and as it was again opened the unholy odors rushed out like fiends, so that the young man was obliged to struggle as against an overpowering wind.

It was some time before the youth's eyes were good in the intense gloom within, but the man with benevolent spectacles led him skilfully, pausing but a moment to deposit the limp assassin upon a cot. He took the youth to a cot that lay tranquilly by the window, and showing him a tall locker for clothes that stood near the head with the ominous air of a tombstone, left him.

The youth sat on his cot and peered about him. There was a gas-jet in a distant part of the room, that burned a small flickering orange-hued flame. It caused vast masses of tumbled shadows in all parts of the place, save where, immediately about it, there was a little gray haze. As the young man's eyes became used to the darkness, he could see upon the cots that thickly littered the floor the forms of men sprawled out, lying in death-like silence, or heaving and snoring with tremendous effort, like stabbed fish.

The youth locked his derby and his shoes in the mummy case near him, and then lay down with an old and familiar coat around his shoulders. A blanket he handled gingerly, drawing it over part of the coat. The cot was covered with leather, and as cold as melting snow. The youth was obliged to shiver for some time on this affair, which was like a slab. Presently, however, his chill gave him peace, and during this period of leisure from it he turned his head to stare at his friend the assassin, whom he could dimly discern where he lay sprawled on a cot in the abandon of a man filled with drink. He was snoring with incredible vigor. His wet hair and beard dimly glistened, and his inflamed nose shone with subdued luster like a red light in a fog.

Within reach of the youth's hand was one who lay with yellow breast and shoulders bare to the cold drafts. One arm hung over the side of the cot, and the fingers lay full length upon the wet cement floor of the room. Beneath the inky brows could be seen the eyes of the man exposed by the partly opened lids. To the youth it seemed that he and this corpse-like being were exchanging a prolonged stare, and that the other threatened with his eyes. He drew back, watching his neighbor from the shadows of his blanket edge. The man did not move once through the night, but lay in this stillness as of death like a body stretched out expectant of the surgeon's knife.

And all through the room could be seen the tawny hues of naked flesh, limbs thrust into the darkness, projecting beyond the cots; up-reared knees, arms hanging long and thin over the cot edges. For the most part they were statuesque, carven, dead. With the curious lockers standing all about like tombstones, there was a strange effect of a graveyard where bodies were merely flung.

Yet occasionally could be seen limbs wildly tossing in fantastic night-mare gestures, accompanied by guttural cries, grunts, oaths. And there was one fellow off in a gloomy corner, who in his dreams was oppressed by some frightful calamity, for of a sudden he began to utter long wails that went almost like yells from a hound, echoing wailfully and weird through this chill place of tombstones where men lay like the dead.

The sound in its high piercing beginnings, that dwindled to final melancholy moans, expressed a red and grim tragedy of the unfathomable possibilities of the man's dreams. But to the youth these were not merely the shrieks of a vision-pierced man: they were an utterance of the meaning of the room and its occupants. It was to him the protest of the wretch who feels the touch of the imperturbable granite wheels, and who then cries with an impersonal eloquence, with a strength not from him, giving voice to the wail of a whole section, a class, a people. This, weaving into the young man's brain, and mingling with his views of the vast and somber shadows that, like mighty black fingers, curled around the naked bodies, made the young man so that he did not sleep, but lay carving the biographies for these men from his meager experience. At times the fellow in the corner howled in a writhing agony of his imaginations.

Finally a long lance-point of gray light shot through the dusty panes of the window. Without, the young man could see roofs drearily white in the dawning. The point of light yellowed and grew brighter, until the golden rays of the morning sun came in bravely and strong. They touched with radiant color the form of a small fat man, who snored in stuttering fashion. His round and shiny bald head glowed suddenly with the valor of a decoration. He sat up, blinked at the sun, swore fretfully, and pulled his blanket over the ornamental splendors of his head.

The youth contentedly watched this rout of the shadows before the bright spears of the sun, and presently he slumbered. When he awoke he heard the voice of the assassin raised in valiant curses. Putting up his head, he perceived his comrade seated on the side of the cot engaged in scratching his neck with long finger-nails that rasped like files.

"Hully Jee, dis is a new breed. They've got can-openers on their feet." He continued in a violent tirade.

The young man hastily unlocked his closet and took out his shoes and hat. As he sat on the side of the cot lacing his shoes, he glanced about and saw that daylight had made the room comparatively commonplace and uninteresting. The men, whose faces seemed stolid, serene or absent, were engaged in dressing, while a great crackle of bantering conversation arose.

A few were parading in unconcerned nakedness. Here and there were men of brawn, whose skins shone clear and ruddy. They took splendid poses, standing massively like chiefs. When they had dressed in their ungainly garments there was an extraordinary change. They then showed bumps and deficiencies of all kinds.

There were others who exhibited many deformities. Shoulders were slanting, humped, pulled this way and pulled that way. And notable among these latter men was the little fat man, who had refused to allow his head to be glorified. His pudgy form, builded like a pear, bustled to and fro, while he swore in fishwife fashion. It appeared that some article of his apparel had vanished.

The young man attired speedily, and went to his friend the assassin. At first the latter looked dazed at the sight of the youth. This face seemed to be appealing to him through the cloud wastes of his memory. He scratched his neck and reflected. At last he grinned, a broad smile gradually spreading until his countenance was a round illumination. "Hello, Willie," he cried cheerily.

"Hello," said the young man. "Are yeh ready t' fly?"

"Sure." The assassin tied his shoe carefully with some twine and came ambling.

When he reached the street the young man experienced no sudden relief from unholy atmospheres. He had forgotten all about them, and had been breathing naturally, and with no sensation of discomfort or distress.

He was thinking of these things as he walked along the street, when he was suddenly startled by feeling the assassin's hand, trembling with excitement, clutching his arm, and when the assassin spoke, his voice went into quavers from a supreme agitation.

"I'll be hully, bloomin' blowed if there wasn't a feller with a night-shirt on up there in that joint."

The youth was bewildered for a moment, but presently he turned to smile indulgently at the assassin's humor.

"Oh, you're a d——d liar," he merely said.

Whereupon the assassin began to gesture extravagantly, and take oath by strange gods. He frantically placed himself at the mercy of remark-able fates if his tale were not true.

"Yes, he did! I cross m'heart thousan' times!" he protested, and at the moment his eyes were large with amazement, his mouth wrinkled in unnatural glee.

"Yessir! A nightshirt! A hully white nightshirt!"

"You lie!"

"No, sir! I hope ter die b'fore I kin git anudder ball [1] if there wasn't a jay wid a hully, bloomin' white nightshirt!"

His face was filled with the infinite wonder of it. "A hully white nightshirt," he continually repeated.

The young man saw the dark entrance to a basement restaurant. There was a sign which read "No mystery about our hash!" and there were other age-stained and world-battered legends which told him that the place was within his means. He stopped before it and spoke to the assassin. "I guess I'll git somethin' t' eat."

At this the assassin, for some reason, appeared to be quite embarrassed. He gazed at the seductive front of the eating place for a moment. Then he started slowly up the street. "Well, good-bye, Willie," he said bravely.

For an instant the youth studied the departing figure. Then he called out, "Hol' on a minnet." As they came together he spoke in a certain fierce way, as if he feared that the other would think him to be charita-ble. "Look-a-here, if yeh wanta git some breakfas' I'll lend yeh three cents t' do it with. But say, look-a-here, you've gota git out an' hustle. I

---

[1] Drink of liquor.

ain't goin' t' support yeh, or I'll go broke b'fore night. I ain't no millionaire."

"I take me oath, Willie," said the assassin earnestly, "th' on'y thing
I really needs is a ball. Me t'roat feels like a fryin'-pan. But as I can't get
a ball, why, th' next bes' thing is breakfast, an' if yeh do that for me,
b' Gawd, I say yeh was th' whitest lad I ever see."

They spent a few moments in dexterous exchanges of phrases, in
which they each protested that the other was, as the assassin had originally said, "a respecter'ble gentlem'n." And they concluded with
mutual assurances that they were the souls of intelligence and virtue.
Then they went into the restaurant.

There was a long counter, dimly lighted from hidden sources. Two
or three men in soiled white aprons rushed here and there.

The youth bought a bowl of coffee for two cents and a roll for one
cent. The assassin purchased the same. The bowls were webbed with
brown seams, and the tin spoons wore an air of having emerged from the
first pyramid. Upon them were black moss-like encrustations of age,
and they were bent and scarred from the attacks of long-forgotten teeth.
But over their repast the wanderers waxed warm and mellow. The
assassin grew affable as the hot mixture went soothingly down his
parched throat, and the young man felt courage flow in his veins.

Memories began to throng in on the assassin, and he brought forth
long tales, intricate, incoherent, delivered with a chattering swiftness as
from an old woman. "—— great job out'n Orange. Boss keep yeh hustlin'
though all time. I was there three days, and then I went an' ask 'im t'
lend me a dollar. 'G-g-go ter the devil,' he ses, an' I lose me job."

"South no good. Damn niggers work for twenty-five an' thirty cents
a day. Run white man out. Good grub though. Easy livin'."

"Yas; useter work little in Toledo, raftin' logs. Make two or three
dollars er day in the spring. Lived high. Cold as ice though in the
winter."

"I was raised in northern N'York. O-o-oh, yeh jest oughto live there.
No beer ner whisky though, way off in the woods. But all th' good hot
grub yeh can eat. B' Gawd, I hung around there long as I could till
th' ol' man fired me. 'Git t' hell outa here, yeh wuthless skunk, git t'
hell outa here, an' go die,' he ses. 'You're a hell of a father,' I ses, 'you
are,' an' I quit 'im."

As they were passing from the dim eating place, they encountered an
old man who was trying to steal forth with a tiny package of food, but
a tall man with an indomitable moustache stood dragon fashion, barring
the way of escape. They heard the old man raise a plaintive protest.
"Ah, you always want to know what I take out, and you never see that
I usually bring a package in here from my place of business."

As the wanderers trudged slowly along Park Row, the assassin began
to expand and grow blithe. "B' Gawd, we've been livin' like kings," he
said, smacking appreciative lips.

"Look out, or we'll have t' pay fer it t'night," said the youth with gloomy warning.

But the assassin refused to turn his gaze toward the future. He went with a limping step, into which he injected a suggestion of lamblike gambols. His mouth was wreathed in a red grin.

In the City Hall Park the two wanderers sat down in the little circle of benches sanctified by traditions of their class. They huddled in their old garments, slumbrously conscious of the march of the hours which for them had no meaning.

The people of the street hurrying hither and thither made a blend of black figures changing yet frieze-like. They walked in their good clothes as upon important missions, giving no gaze to the two wanderers seated upon the benches. They expressed to the young man his infinite distance from all that he valued. Social position, comfort, the pleasures of living, were unconquerable kingdoms. He felt a sudden awe.

And in the background a multitude of buildings, of pitiless hues and sternly high, were to him emblematic of a nation forcing its regal head into the clouds, throwing no downward glances; in the sublimity of its aspirations ignoring the wretches who may flounder at its feet. The roar of the city in his ear was to him the confusion of strange tongues, babbling heedlessly; it was the clink of coin, the voice of the city's hopes which were to him no hopes.

He confessed himself an outcast, and his eyes from under the lowered rim of his hat began to glance guiltily, wearing the criminal expression that comes with certain convictions.

1894, 1898

⚜

A MYSTERY OF HEROISM

This Civil War episode was first printed in the Philadelphia *Press* for August 1–2, 1895, and was republished in *The Little Regiment* (1896), source of the present text. Written after *The Red Badge of Courage* (which the Philadelphia newspaper had serialized in December 1894), it explores the psychological problems of cowardice and courage, fear and bravado which dominate the novel. The irony of the closing paragraphs is consistent with the larger ironies which Crane sees investing heroism itself.

The dark uniforms of the men were so coated with dust from the incessant wrestling of the two armies that the regiment almost seemed a part of the clay bank which shielded them from the shells. On the top of the hill a battery was arguing in tremendous roars with some other guns, and to the eye of the infantry the artillerymen, the guns, the caissons, the horses, were distinctly outlined upon the blue sky. When a piece was fired, a red streak as round as a log flashed low in the heavens, like a monstrous bolt of lightning. The men of the battery wore white duck trousers, which somehow emphasized their legs; and when they ran and crowded in little groups at the bidding of the shouting officers, it was more impressive than usual to the infantry.

Fred Collins, of A Company, was saying: "Thunder! I wisht I had a drink. Ain't there any water round here?" Then somebody yelled, "There goes th' bugler!"

As the eyes of half the regiment swept in one machinelike movement there was an instant's picture of a horse in a great convulsive leap of a deathwound and a rider leaning back with a crooked arm and spread fingers before his face. On the ground was the crimson terror of an exploding shell, with fibres of flame that seemed like lances. A glittering bugle swung clear of the rider's back as fell headlong the horse and the man. In the air was an odor as from a conflagration.

Sometimes they of the infantry looked down at a fair little meadow which spread at their feet. Its long, green grass was rippling gently in a breeze. Beyond it was the gray form of a house half torn to pieces by shells and by the busy axes of soldiers who had pursued firewood. The line of an old fence was now dimly marked by long weeds and by an occasional post. A shell had blown the well-house to fragments. Little lines of gray smoke ribboning upward from some embers indicated the place where had stood the barn.

From beyond a curtain of green woods there came the sound of some stupendous scuffle, as if two animals of the size of islands were fighting. At a distance there were occasional appearances of swift-moving men, horses, batteries, flags, and, with the crashing of infantry volleys were heard, often, wild and frenzied cheers. In the midst of it all Smith and Ferguson, two privates of A Company, were engaged in a heated discussion, which involved the greatest questions of the national existence.

The battery on the hill presently engaged in a frightful duel. The white legs of the gunners scampered this way and that way, and the officers redoubled their shouts. The guns, with their demeanors of stolidity and courage, were typical of something infinitely self-possessed in this clamor of death that swirled around the hill.

One of a "swing" team was suddenly smitten quivering to the ground, and his maddened brethren dragged his torn body in their struggle to escape from this turmoil and danger. A young soldier astride one of the leaders swore and fumed in his saddle, and furiously jerked at the bridle. An officer screamed out an order so violently that his voice broke and ended the sentence in a falsetto shriek.

The leading company of the infantry regiment was somewhat exposed, and the colonel ordered it moved more fully under the shelter of the hill. There was the clank of steel against steel.

A lieutenant of the battery rode down and passed them, holding his right arm carefully in his left hand. And it was as if this arm was not at all a part of him, but belonged to another man. His sober and reflective charger went slowly. The officer's face was grimy and perspiring, and his uniform was tousled as if he had been in direct grapple with an enemy. He smiled grimly when the men stared at him. He turned his horse toward the meadow.

Collins, of A Company, said: "I wisht I had a drink. I bet there's water in that there ol' well yonder!"

"Yes; but how you goin' to git it?"

For the little meadow which intervened was now suffering a terrible onslaught of shells. Its green and beautiful calm had vanished utterly. Brown earth was being flung in monstrous handfuls. And there was a massacre of the young blades of grass. They were being torn, burned, obliterated. Some curious fortune of the battle had made this gentle little meadow the object of the red hate of the shells, and each one as it exploded seemed like an imprecation in the face of a maiden.

The wounded officer who was riding across this expanse said to himself, "Why, they couldn't shoot any harder if the whole army was massed here!"

A shell struck the gray ruins of the house, and as, after the roar, the shattered wall fell in fragments, there was a noise which resembled the flapping of shutters during a wild gale of winter. Indeed, the infantry paused in the shelter of the bank appeared as men standing upon a shore contemplating a madness of the sea. The angel of calamity had under its glance the battery upon the hill. Fewer white-legged men labored about the guns. A shell had smitten one of the pieces, and after the flare, the smoke, the dust, the wrath of this blow were gone, it was possible to see white legs stretched horizontally upon the ground. And at that interval to the rear, where it is the business of battery horses to stand with their noses to the fight awaiting the command to drag their guns out of the destruction or into it or wheresoever these incomprehensible humans demanded with whip and spur—in this line of passive and dumb spectators, whose fluttering hearts yet would not let them forget the iron laws of man's control of them—in this rank of brute-soldiers there had been relentless and hideous carnage. From the ruck of bleeding and prostrate horses, the men of the infantry could see one animal raising its stricken body with its fore legs, and turning its nose with mystic and profound eloquence toward the sky.

Some comrades joked Collins about his thirst. "Well, if yeh want a drink so bad, why don't yeh go git it!"

"Well, I will in a minnet, if yeh don't shut up!"

A lieutenant of artillery floundered his horse straight down the hill with as great concern as if it were level ground. As he galloped past the colonel of the infantry, he threw up his hand in swift salute. "We've got to get out of that," he roared angrily. He was a black-bearded officer, and his eyes, which resembled beads, sparkled like those of an insane man. His jumping horse sped along the column of infantry.

The fat major, standing carelessly with his sword held horizontally behind him and with his legs far apart, looked after the receding horseman and laughed. "He wants to get back with orders pretty quick, or there'll be no batt'ry left," he observed.

The wise young captain of the second company hazarded to the lieutenant colonel that the enemy's infantry would probably soon attack the hill, and the lieutenant colonel snubbed him.

A private in one of the rear companies looked out over the meadow, and then turned to a companion and said, "Look there, Jim!" It was the wounded officer from the battery, who some time before had started to ride across the meadow, supporting his right arm carefully with his left hand. This man had encountered a shell apparently at a time when no one perceived him, and he could now be seen lying face downward with a stirruped foot stretched across the body of his dead horse. A leg of the charger extended slantingly upward precisely as stiff as a stake. Around this motionless pair the shells still howled.

There was a quarrel in A Company. Collins was shaking his fist in the faces of some laughing comrades. "Dern yeh! I ain't afraid t' go. If yeh say much, I will go!"

"Of course, yeh will! You'll run through that there medder, won't yeh?"

Collins said, in a terrible voice, "You see now!" At this ominous threat his comrades broke into renewed jeers.

Collins gave them a dark scowl and went to find his captain. The latter was conversing with the colonel of the regiment.

"Captain," said Collins, saluting and standing at attention—in those days all trousers bagged at the knees—"Captain, I want t' get permission to go git some water from that there well over yonder!"

The colonel and the captain swung about simultaneously and stared across the meadow. The captain laughed. "You must be pretty thirsty, Collins?"

"Yes, sir, I am."

"Well—ah," said the captain. After a moment, he asked, "Can't you wait?"

"No, sir."

The colonel was watching Collins's face. "Look here, my lad," he said, in a pious sort of a voice—"Look here, my lad"—Collins was not a lad—"don't you think that's taking pretty big risks for a little drink of water?"

"I dunno," said Collins uncomfortably. Some of the resentment toward his companions, which perhaps had forced him into this affair, was beginning to fade. "I dunno wether 'tis."

The colonel and the captain contemplated him for a time.

"Well," said the captain finally.

"Well," said the colonel, "if you want to go, why, go."

Collins saluted. "Much obliged t' yeh."

As he moved away the colonel called after him. "Take some of the other boys' canteens with you an' hurry back now."

"Yes, sir, I will."

The colonel and the captain looked at each other then, for it had suddenly occurred that they could not for the life of them tell whether Collins wanted to go or whether he did not.

They turned to regard Collins, and as they perceived him surrounded by gesticulating comrades, the colonel said: "Well, by thunder! I guess he's going."

Collins appeared as a man dreaming. In the midst of the questions, the advice, the warnings, all the excited talk of his company mates, he maintained a curious silence.

They were very busy in preparing him for his ordeal. When they inspected him carefully it was somewhat like the examination that grooms give a horse before a race; and they were amazed, staggered by the whole affair. Their astonishment found vent in strange repetitions.

"Are yeh sure a-goin'?" they demanded again and again.

"Certainly I am," cried Collins, at last furiously.

He strode sullenly away from them. He was swinging five or six canteens by their cords. It seemed that his cap would not remain firmly on his head, and often he reached and pulled it down over his brow.

There was a general movement in the compact column. The long animal-like thing moved slightly. Its four hundred eyes were turned upon the figure of Collins.

"Well, sir, if that ain't th' derndest thing! I never thought Fred Collins had the blood in him for that kind of business."

"What's he goin' to do, anyhow?"

"He's goin' to that well there after water."

"We ain't dyin' of thirst, are we? That's foolishness."

"Well, somebody put him up to it, an' he's doin' it."

"Say, he must be a desperate cuss."

When Collins faced the meadow and walked away from the regiment, he was vaguely conscious that a chasm, the deep valley of all prides, was suddenly between him and his comrades. It was provisional, but the provision was that he return as a victor. He had blindly been led by quaint emotions, and laid himself under an obligation to walk squarely up to the face of death.

But he was not sure that he wished to make a retraction, even if he could do so without shame. As a matter of truth, he was sure of very little. He was mainly surprised.

It seemed to him supernaturally strange that he had allowed his mind to manœuvre his body into such a situation. He understood that it might be called dramatically great.

However, he had no full appreciation of anything, excepting that he was actually conscious of being dazed. He could feel his dulled mind groping after the form and color of this incident. He wondered why he did not feel some keen agony of fear cutting his sense like a knife. He wondered at this, because human expression had said loudly for centuries that men should feel afraid of certain things, and that all men who did not feel this fear were phenomena—heroes.

He was, then, a hero. He suffered that disappointment which we would all have if we discovered that we were ourselves capable of those deeds which we most admire in history and legend. This, then, was a hero. After all, heroes were not much.

No, it could not be true. He was not a hero. Heroes had no shames in their lives, and, as for him, he remembered borrowing fifteen dollars from a friend and promising to pay it back the next day, and then avoiding that friend for ten months. When at home his mother had aroused him for the early labor of his life on the farm, it had often been his fashion to be irritable, childish, diabolical; and his mother had died since he had come to the war.

He saw that, in this matter of the well, the canteens, the shells, he was an intruder in the land of fine deeds.

He was now about thirty paces from his comrades. The regiment had just turned its many faces toward him.

From the forest of terrific noises there suddenly emerged a little uneven line of men. They fired fiercely and rapidly at distant foliage on which appeared little puffs of white smoke. The spatter of skirmish firing was added to the thunder of the guns on the hill. The little line of men ran forward. A color sergeant fell flat with his flag as if he had slipped on ice. There was hoarse cheering from this distant field.

Collins suddenly felt that two demon fingers were pressed into his ears. He could see nothing but flying arrows, flaming red. He lurched from the shock of this explosion, but he made a mad rush for the house, which he viewed as a man submerged to the neck in a boiling surf might view the shore. In the air, little pieces of shell howled and the earthquake explosions drove him insane with the menace of their roar. As he ran the canteens knocked together with a rhythmical tinkling.

As he neared the house, each detail of the scene became vivid to him. He was aware of some bricks of the vanished chimney lying on the sod. There was a door which hung by one hinge.

Rifle bullets called forth by the insistent skirmishers came from the far-off bank of foliage. They mingled with the shells and the pieces of shells until the air was torn in all directions by hootings, yells, howls. The sky was full of fiends who directed all their wild rage at his head.

When he came to the well, he flung himself face downward and peered into its darkness. There were furtive silver glintings some feet from the surface. He grabbed one of the canteens and, unfastening its cap, swung it down by the cord. The water flowed slowly in with an indolent gurgle.

And now as he lay with his face turned away he was suddenly smitten with the terror. It came upon his heart like the grasp of claws. All the power faded from his muscles. For an instant he was no more than a dead man.

The canteen filled with a maddening slowness, in the manner of all bottles. Presently he recovered his strength and addressed a screaming oath to it. He leaned over until it seemed as if he intended to try to push water into it with his hands. His eyes as he gazed down into the well shone like two pieces of metal and in their expression was a great appeal and a great curse. The stupid water derided him.

There was the blaring thunder of a shell. Crimson light shone through the swift-boiling smoke and made a pink reflection on part of the wall of the well. Collins jerked out his arm and canteen with the same motion that a man would use in withdrawing his head from a furnace.

He scrambled erect and glared and hesitated. On the ground near him lay the old well bucket, with a length of rusty chain. He lowered it swiftly into the well. The bucket struck the water and then, turning lazily over, sank. When, with hand reaching tremblingly over hand, he hauled it out, it knocked often against the walls of the well and spilled some of its contents.

In running with a filled bucket, a man can adopt but one kind of gait. So through this terrible field over which screamed practical angels of death Collins ran in the manner of a farmer chased out of a dairy by a bull.

His face went staring white with anticipation—anticipation of a blow that would whirl him around and down. He would fall as he had seen other men fall, the life knocked out of them so suddenly that their knees were no more quick to touch the ground than their heads. He saw the long blue line of the regiment, but his comrades were standing looking at him from the edge of an impossible star. He was aware of some deep wheel ruts and hoofprints in the sod beneath his feet.

The artillery officer who had fallen in this meadow had been making groans in the teeth of the tempest of sound. These futile cries, wrenched from him by his agony, were heard only by shells, bullets. When wild-eyed Collins came running, this officer raised himself. His face contorted and blanched from pain, he was about to utter some great beseeching cry. But suddenly his face straightened and he called: "Say, young man, give me a drink of water, will you?"

Collins had no room amid his emotions for surprise. He was mad from the threats of destruction.

"I can't!" he screamed, and in his reply was a full description of his quaking apprehension. His cap was gone and his hair was riotous. His clothes made it appear that he had been dragged over the ground by the heels. He ran on.

The officer's head sank down and one elbow crooked. His foot in its brass-bound stirrup still stretched over the body of his horse and the other leg was under the steed.

But Collins turned. He came dashing back. His face had now turned gray and in his eyes was all terror. "Here it is! here it is!"

The officer was as a man gone in drink. His arm bent like a twig. His head drooped as if his neck were of willow. He was sinking to the ground, to lie face downward.

Collins grabbed him by the shoulder. "Here it is. Here's your drink. Turn over. Turn over, man, for God's sake!"

With Collins hauling at his shoulder, the officer twisted his body and fell with his face turned toward that region where lived the unspeakable noises of the swirling missiles. There was the faintest shadow of a smile on his lips as he looked at Collins. He gave a sigh, a little primitive breath like that from a child.

Collins tried to hold the bucket steadily, but his shaking hands caused the water to splash all over the face of the dying man. Then he jerked it away and ran on.

The regiment gave him a welcoming roar. The grimed faces were wrinkled in laughter.

His captain waved the bucket away. "Give it to the men!"

The two genial, skylarking young lieutenants were the first to gain possession of it. They played over it in their fashion.

When one tried to drink, the other teasingly knocked his elbow. "Don't, Billie! You'll make me spill it," said the one. The other laughed.

Suddenly there was an oath, the thud of wood on the ground, and a swift murmur of astonishment among the ranks. The two lieutenants glared at each other. The bucket lay on the ground empty.

1895

THE OPEN BOAT

This story first appeared in *Scribner's Magazine* for June 1897 and was reprinted in *The Open Boat and Other Tales of Adventure* (1898), from which the present text comes. As Crane indicated in the epigraph, he drew upon his own experience following the sinking of the *Commodore*. The ship had just left Jacksonville, Florida with a load of munitions for Cuba when it sprang a leak and sank eighteen miles off New Smyrna, January 2, 1897. Crane, who was on his way to report the fighting for the New York *Press*, came away in a ten-foot dinghy with Captain Murphy and two crew members. They battled the sea for thirty hours before they came ashore near Daytona Beach; the oiler, William Higgins, died in the surf much as Crane has described. Press reports of the misadventure have been conveniently gathered in R. W. Stallman's *Stephen Crane: An Omnibus*, pp. 448 ff.

"The Open Boat" focuses on what happened during the thirty hours but even more on the correspondent's attempts to understand his plight. The sea is menacing, the shore treacherous, men's energies are limited, and the wish to survive prompts no pity from the elements or active sympathy from humanity. Thus his own logic leads him to a naturalistic view of the universe, in which men's concerns are of small moment. The correspondent, articulate as Henry Fleming is not, formulates his ideas much more explicitly, but *The Red Badge of Courage* is grounded on similar premises.

A Tale Intended to be after the Fact:
Being the Experience of Four Men
From the Sunk Steamer Commodore

I

None of them knew the color of the sky. Their eyes glanced level, and were fastened upon the waves that swept toward them. These waves were of the hue of slate, save for the tops, which were of foaming white, and all of the men knew the colors of the sea. The horizon narrowed and widened, and dipped and rose, and at all times its edge was jagged with waves that seemed thrust up in points like rocks.

Many a man ought to have a bath-tub larger than the boat which here rode upon the sea. These waves were most wrongfully and barbarously abrupt and tall, and each froth-top was a problem in small-boat navigation.

The cook squatted in the bottom, and looked with both eyes at the six inches of gunwale which separated him from the ocean. His sleeves were rolled over his fat forearms, and the two flaps of his unbuttoned vest dangled as he bent to bail out the boat. Often he said, "Gawd! that was a narrow clip." As he remarked it he invariably gazed eastward over the broken sea.

The oiler, steering with one of the two oars in the boat, sometimes raised himself suddenly to keep clear of water that swirled in over the stern. It was a thin little oar, and it seemed often ready to snap.

The correspondent, pulling at the other oar, watched the waves and wondered why he was there.

The injured captain, lying in the bow, was at this time buried in that profound dejection and indifference which comes, temporarily at least, to even the bravest and most enduring when, willy-nilly, the firm fails, the army loses, the ship goes down. The mind of the master of a vessel is rooted deep in the timbers of her, though he command for a day or a decade; and this captain had on him the stern impression of a scene in the grays of dawn of seven turned faces, and later a stump of a topmast with a white ball on it, that slashed to and fro at the waves, went low and lower, and down. Thereafter there was something strange in his voice.

Although steady, it was deep with mourning, and of a quality beyond oration or tears.

"Keep 'er a little more south, Billie," said he.

"A little more south, sir," said the oiler in the stern.

A seat in this boat was not unlike a seat upon a bucking broncho, and, by the same token, a broncho is not much smaller. The craft pranced and reared and plunged like an animal. As each wave came, and she rose for it, she seemed like a horse making at a fence outrageously high. The manner of her scramble over these walls of water is a mystic thing, and, moreover, at the top of them were ordinarily these problems in white water, the foam racing down from the summit of each wave, requiring a new leap, and a leap from the air. Then, after scornfully bumping a crest, she would slide and race and splash down a long incline, and arrive bobbing and nodding in front of the next menace.

A singular disadvantage of the sea lies in the fact that, after successfully surmounting one wave, you discover that there is another behind it, just as important and just as nervously anxious to do something effective in the way of swamping boats. In a ten-foot dinghy one can get an idea of the resources of the sea in the line of waves that is not probable to the average experience, which is never at sea in a dinghy. As each slaty wall of water approached, it shut all else from the view of the men in the boat, and it was not difficult to imagine that this particular wave was the final outburst of the ocean, the last effort of the grim water. There was a terrible grace in the move of the waves, and they came in silence, save for the snarling of the crests.

In the wan light the faces of the men must have been gray. Their eyes must have glinted in strange ways as they gazed steadily astern. Viewed from a balcony, the whole thing would, doubtless, have been weirdly picturesque. But the men in the boat had no time to see it, and if they had had leisure, there were other things to occupy their minds. The sun swung steadily up the sky, and they knew it was broad day because the color of the sea changed from slate to emerald-green streaked with amber lights, and the foam was like tumbling snow. The process of the breaking day was unknown to them. They were aware only of this effect upon the color of the waves that rolled toward them.

In disjointed sentences the cook and the correspondent argued as to the difference between a life-saving station and a house of refuge. The cook had said: "There's a house of refuge just north of the Mosquito Inlet Light, and as soon as they see us they'll come off in their boat and pick us up."

"As soon as who see us?" said the correspondent.

"The crew," said the cook.

"Houses of refuge don't have crews," said the correspondent. "As I understand them, they are only places where clothes and grub are stored for the benefit of shipwrecked people. They don't carry crews."

"Oh, yes, they do," said the cook.

"No, they don't," said the correspondent.

"Well, we're not there yet, anyhow," said the oiler in the stern.

"Well," said the cook, "perhaps it's not a house of refuge that I'm thinking of as being near Mosquito Inlet Light; perhaps it's a life-saving station."

"We're not there yet," said the oiler in the stern.

II

As the boat bounced from the top of each wave the wind tore through the hair of the hatless men, and as the craft plopped her stern down again the spray slashed past them. The crest of each of these waves was a hill, from the top of which the men surveyed for a moment a broad, tumultuous expanse, shining and wind-riven. It was probably splendid, it was probably glorious, this play of the free sea, wild with lights of emerald and white and amber.

"Bully good thing it's an on-shore wind," said the cook. "If not, where would we be? Wouldn't have a show."

"That's right," said the correspondent.

The busy oiler nodded his assent.

Then the captain, in the bow, chuckled in a way that expressed humor, contempt, tragedy, all in one. "Do you think we've got much of a show now, boys?" said he.

Whereupon the three were silent, save for a trifle of hemming and hawing. To express any particular optimism at this time they felt to be childish and stupid, but they all doubtless possessed this sense of the situation in their minds. A young man thinks doggedly at such times. On the other hand, the ethics of their condition was decidedly against any open suggestion of hopelessness. So they were silent.

"Oh, well," said the captain, soothing his children, "we'll get ashore all right."

But there was that in his tone which made them think; so the oiler quoth, "Yes! if this wind holds."

The cook was bailing. "Yes! if we don't catch hell in the surf."

Canton-flannel gulls flew near and far. Sometimes they sat down on the sea, near patches of brown seaweed that rolled over the waves with a movement like carpets on a line in a gale. The birds sat comfortably in groups, and they were envied by some in the dinghy, for the wrath of the sea was no more to them than it was to a covey of prairie-chickens a thousand miles inland. Often they came very close and stared at the men with black, bead-like eyes. At these times they were uncanny and sinister in their unblinking scrutiny, and the men hooted angrily at them, telling them to be gone. One came, and evidently decided to alight on the top of the captain's head. The bird flew parallel to the boat, and did not circle, but made short sidelong jumps in the air in chicken fashion. His black eyes were wistfully fixed upon the captain's head. "Ugly brute," said the oiler to the bird. "You look as if you were made with a jack-knife." The cook and the correspondent swore darkly at the creature. The captain naturally wished to knock it away with the end of the heavy painter, but he did not dare do it, because anything resembling an emphatic gesture would have capsized this freighted boat; and so, with his open hand, the captain gently and carefully waved the gull away. After it had been discouraged from the pursuit the captain breathed easier on account of his hair, and others breathed easier because the bird struck their minds at this time as being somehow gruesome and ominous.

In the meantime the oiler and the correspondent rowed; and also they rowed. They sat together in the same seat, and each rowed an oar. Then the oiler took both oars; then the correspondent took both oars; then the oiler; then the correspondent. They rowed and they rowed. The very ticklish part of the business was when the time came for the reclining one in the stern to take his turn at the oars. By the very last star of truth, it is easier to steal eggs from under a hen than it was to change seats in the dinghy. First the man in the stern slid his hand along the thwart and moved with care, as if he were of Sèvres. Then the man in the rowing-seat slid his hand along the other thwart. It was all done with the most extraordinary care. As the two sidled past each other, the whole party kept watchful eyes on the coming wave, and the captain cried: "Look out, now! Steady, there!"

The brown mats of seaweed that appeared from time to time were like islands, bits of earth. They were traveling, apparently, neither one way nor the other. They were, to all intents, stationary. They informed the men in the boat that it was making progress slowly toward the land.

The captain, rearing cautiously in the bow after the dinghy soared on a great swell, said that he had seen the lighthouse at Mosquito Inlet. Presently the cook remarked that he had seen it. The correspondent was at the oars then, and for some reason he too wished to look at the lighthouse; but his back was toward the far shore, and the waves were important, and for some time he could not seize an opportunity to turn his head. But at last there came a wave more gentle than the others, and when at the crest of it he swiftly scoured the western horizon.

"See it?" said the captain.

"No," said the correspondent, slowly; "I didn't see anything."

"Look again," said the captain. He pointed. "It's exactly in that direction."

At the top of another wave the correspondent did as he was bid, and this time his eyes chanced on a small, still thing on the edge of the swaying horizon. It was precisely like the point of a pin. It took an anxious eye to find a lighthouse so tiny.

"Think we'll make it, Captain?"

"If this wind holds and the boat don't swamp, we can't do much else," said the captain.

The little boat, lifted by each towering sea and splashed viciously by the crests, made progress that in the absence of seaweed was not apparent to those in her. She seemed just a wee thing wallowing miraculously, top up, at the mercy of five oceans. Occasionally a great spread of water, like white flames, swarmed into her.

"Bail her, cook," said the captain, serenely.

"All right, Captain," said the cheerful cook.

III

It would be difficult to describe the subtle brotherhood of men that was here established on the seas. No one said that it was so. No one mentioned it. But it dwelt in the boat, and each man felt it warm him. They were a captain, an oiler, a cook, and a correspondent, and they were friends—friends in a more curiously iron-bound degree than may be common. The hurt captain, lying against the water-jar in the bow, spoke always in a low voice and calmly; but he could never command a more ready and swiftly obedient crew than the motley three of the dinghy. It was more than a mere recognition of what was best for the common safety. There was surely in it a quality that was personal and heartfelt. And after this devotion to the commander of the boat, there was this comradeship, that the correspondent, for instance, who had been taught to be cynical of men, knew even at the time was the best experience of his life. But no one said that it was so. No one mentioned it.

"I wish we had a sail," remarked the captain. "We might try my overcoat on the end of an oar, and give you two boys a chance to rest." So the cook and the correspondent held the mast and spread wide the overcoat; the oiler steered; and the little boat made good way with her new rig. Sometimes the oiler had to scull sharply to keep a sea from breaking into the boat, but otherwise sailing was a success.

Meanwhile the lighthouse had been growing slowly larger. It had now almost assumed color, and appeared like a little gray shadow on the sky. The man at the oars could not be prevented from turning his head rather often to try for a glimpse of this little gray shadow.

At last, from the top of each wave, the men in the tossing boat could see land. Even as the lighthouse was an upright shadow on the sky, this land seemed but a long black shadow on the sea. It certainly was thinner than paper. "We must be about opposite New Smyrna," said the cook, who had coasted this shore often in schooners. "Captain, by the way, I believe they abandoned that life-saving station there about a year ago."

"Did they?" said the captain.

The wind slowly died away. The cook and the correspondent were not now obliged to slave in order to hold high the oar; but the waves continued their old impetuous swooping at the dinghy, and the little craft, no longer under way, struggled woundily over them. The oiler or the correspondent took the oars again.

Shipwrecks are apropos of nothing. If men could only train for them and have them occur when the men had reached pink condition, there would be less drowning at sea. Of the four in the dinghy none had slept any time worth mentioning for two days and two nights previous to embarking in the dinghy, and in the excitement of clambering about the deck of a foundering ship they had also forgotten to eat heartily.

For these reasons, and for others, neither the oiler nor the correspondent was fond of rowing at this time. The correspondent wondered ingenuously how in the name of all that was sane could there be people who thought it amusing to row a boat. It was not an amusement; it was a diabolical punishment, and even a genius of mental aberrations could never conclude that it was anything but a horror to the muscles and a crime against the back. He mentioned to the boat in general how the amusement of rowing struck him, and the weary-faced oiler smiled in full sympathy. Previously to the foundering, by the way, the oiler had worked double watch in the engine-room of the ship.

"Take her easy now, boys," said the captain. "Don't spend yourselves. If we have to run a surf you'll need all your strength, because we'll sure have to swim for it. Take your time."

Slowly the land arose from the sea. From a black line it became a line of black and a line of white—trees and sand. Finally the captain said that he could make out a house on the shore. "That's the house of refuge, sure," said the cook. "They'll see us before long, and come out after us."

The distant lighthouse reared high. "The keeper ought to be able to make us out now, if he's looking through a glass," said the captain. "He'll notify the life-saving people."

"None of those other boats could have got ashore to give word of the wreck," said the oiler, in a low voice, "else the life-boat would be out hunting us."

Slowly and beautifully the land loomed out of the sea. The wind came again. It had veered from the northeast to the southeast. Finally a new sound struck the ears of the men in the boat. It was the low thunder of the surf on the shore. "We'll never be able to make the lighthouse now," said the captain. "Swing her head a little more north, Billie."

"A little more north, sir," said the oiler.

Whereupon the little boat turned her nose once more down the wind, and all but the oarsman watched the shore grow. Under the influence of this expansion doubt and direful apprehension were leaving the minds of the men. The management of the boat was still most absorbing, but it could not prevent a quiet cheerfulness. In an hour, perhaps, they would be ashore.

Their backbones had become thoroughly used to balancing in the boat, and they now rode this wild colt of a dinghy like circus men. The correspondent thought that he had been drenched to the skin, but happening to feel in the top pocket of his coat, he found therein eight cigars. Four of them were soaked with sea-water; four were perfectly scatheless. After a search, somebody produced three dry matches; and thereupon the four waifs rode in their little boat and, with an assurance of an impending rescue shining in their eyes, puffed at the big cigars, and judged well and ill of all men. Everybody took a drink of water.

IV

"Cook," remarked the captain, "there don't seem to be any signs of life about your house of refuge."

"No," replied the cook. "Funny they don't see us!"

A broad stretch of lowly coast lay before the eyes of the men. It was of low dunes topped with dark vegetation. The roar of the surf was plain, and sometimes they could see the white lip of a wave as it spun up the beach. A tiny house was blocked out black upon the sky. Southward, the slim lighthouse lifted its little gray length.

Tide, wind, and waves were swinging the dinghy northward. "Funny they don't see us," said the men.

The surf's roar was here dulled, but its tone was nevertheless thunderous and mighty. As the boat swam over the great rollers the men sat listening to this roar. "We'll swamp sure," said everybody.

It is fair to say here that there was not a life-saving station within twenty miles in either direction; but the men did not know this fact, and in consequence they made dark and opprobrious remarks concerning the eyesight of the nation's life-savers. Four scowling men sat in the dinghy, and surpassed records in the invention of epithets.

"Funny they don't see us."

The light-heartedness of a former time had completely faded. To their sharpened minds it was easy to conjure pictures of all kinds of incompetency and blindness and, indeed, cowardice. There was the shore of the populous land, and it was bitter and bitter to them that from it came no sign.

"Well," said the captain, ultimately, "I suppose we'll have to make a try for ourselves. If we stay out here too long, we'll none of us have strength left to swim after the boat swamps."

And so the oiler, who was at the oars, turned the boat straight for the shore. There was a sudden tightening of muscles. There was some thinking.

"If we don't all get ashore," said the captain—"if we don't all get ashore, I suppose you fellows know where to send news of my finish?"

They then briefly exchanged some addresses and admonitions. As for the reflections of the men, there was a great deal of rage in them. Perchance they might be formulated thus: "If I am going to be drowned—if I am going to be drowned—if I am going to be drowned, why, in the name of the seven mad gods who rule the sea, was I allowed to come thus far and contemplate sand and trees? Was I brought here merely to have my nose dragged away as I was about to nibble the sacred cheese of life? It is preposterous! If this old ninny-woman, Fate, cannot do better than this, she should be deprived of the management of men's fortunes. She is an old hen who knows not her intention. If she has decided to drown me, why did she not do it in the beginning, and save me all this trouble? The whole affair is absurd. . . . But no; she cannot mean to drown me. She dare not drown me. She cannot drown me. Not after all this work!" Afterward the man might have had an impulse to shake his fist at the clouds. "Just you drown me, now, and then hear what I call you!"

The billows that came at this time were more formidable. They seemed always just about to break and roll over the little boat in a turmoil of foam. There was a preparatory and long growl in the speech of them. No mind unused to the sea would have concluded that the dinghy could ascend these sheer heights in time. The shore was still afar. The oiler was a wily surfman. "Boys," he said swiftly, "she won't live three minutes more, and we're too far out to swim. Shall I take her to sea again, Captain?"

"Yes; go ahead!" said the captain.

This oiler, by a series of quick miracles and fast and steady oarsmanship, turned the boat in the middle of the surf and took her safely to sea again.

There was a considerable silence as the boat bumped over the furrowed sea to deeper water. Then somebody in gloom spoke: "Well, anyhow, they must have seen us from the shore by now."

The gulls went in slanting flight up the wind toward the gray, desolate east. A squall, marked by dingy clouds, and clouds brick-red, like smoke from a burning building, appeared from the southeast.

"What do you think of those life-saving people? Ain't they peaches?"

"Funny they haven't seen us."

"Maybe they think we're out here for sport! Maybe they think we're fishin'. Maybe they think we're damned fools."

It was a long afternoon. A changed tide tried to force them southward, but wind and wave said northward. Far ahead, where coast-line, sea, and sky formed their mighty angle, there were little dots which seemed to indicate a city on the shore.

"St. Augustine?"

The captain shook his head. "Too near Mosquito Inlet."

And the oiler rowed, and then the correspondent rowed; then the oiler rowed. It was a weary business. The human back can become the seat of more aches and pains than are registered in books for the composite anatomy of a regiment. It is a limited area, but it can become the theater of innumerable muscular conflicts, tangles, wrenches, knots, and other comforts.

"Did you ever like to row, Billie?" asked the correspondent.

"No," said the oiler; "hang it!"

When one exchanged the rowing-seat for a place in the bottom of the boat, he suffered a bodily depression that caused him to be careless of everything save an obligation to wiggle one finger. There was cold seawater swashing to and fro in the boat, and he lay in it. His head, pillowed

on a thwart, was within an inch of the swirl of a wave-crest, and sometimes a particularly obstreperous sea came inboard and drenched him
once more. But these matters did not annoy him. It is almost certain that
if the boat had capsized he would have tumbled comfortably out upon
the ocean as if he felt sure that it was a great, soft mattress.

"Look! There's a man on the shore!"

"Where?"

"There! See 'im? See 'im?"

"Yes, sure! He's walking along."

"Now he's stopped. Look! He's facing us!"

"He's waving at us!"

"So he is! By thunder!"

"Ah, now we're all right! Now we're all right! There'll be a boat out
here for us in half an hour."

"He's going on. He's running. He's going up to that house there."

The remote beach seemed lower than the sea, and it required a searching glance to discern the little black figure. The captain saw a floating
stick, and they rowed to it. A bath towel was by some weird chance in
the boat, and, tying this on the stick, the captain waved it. The oarsman
did not dare turn his head, so he was obliged to ask questions.

"What's he doing now?"

"He's standing still again. He's looking, I think. . . . There he goes
again—toward the house. . . . Now he's stopped again."

"Is he waving at us?"

"No, not now; he was, though."

"Look! There comes another man!"

"He's running."

"Look at him go, would you!"

"Why, he's on a bicycle. Now he's met the other man. They're both
waving at us. Look!"

"There comes something up the beach."

"What the devil is that thing?"

"Why, it looks like a boat."

"Why, certainly, it's a boat."

"No; it's on wheels."

"Yes, so it is. Well, that must be the life-boat. They drag them along
shore on a wagon."

"That's the life-boat, sure."

"No, by ——, it's—it's an omnibus."

"I tell you it's a life-boat."

"It is not! It's an omnibus. I can see it plain. See? One of these big
hotel omnibuses."

"By thunder, you're right. It's an omnibus, sure as fate. What do you
suppose they are doing with an omnibus? Maybe they are going around
collecting the life-crew, hey?"

"That's it, likely. Look! There's a fellow waving a little black flag.

He's standing on the steps of the omnibus. There come those other two fellows. Now they're all talking together. Look at the fellow with the flag. Maybe he ain't waving it!"

"That ain't a flag, is it? That's his coat. Why, certainly, that's his coat."

"So it is; it's his coat. He's taken it off and is waving it around his head. But would you look at him swing it!"

"Oh, say, there isn't any life-saving station there. That's just a winter-resort hotel omnibus that has brought over some of the boarders to see us drown."

"What's that idiot with the coat mean? What's he signaling, anyhow?"

"It looks as if he were trying to tell us to go north. There must be a life-saving station up there."

"No; he thinks we're fishing. Just giving us a merry hand. See? Ah, there, Willie!"

"Well, I wish I could make something out of those signals. What do you suppose he means?"

"He don't mean anything; he's just playing."

"Well, if he'd just signal us to try the surf again, or to go to sea and wait, or go north, or go south, or go to hell, there would be some reason in it. But look at him! He just stands there and keeps his coat revolving like a wheel. The ass!"

"There come more people."

"Now there's quite a mob. Look! Isn't that a boat?"

"Where? Oh, I see where you mean. No, that's no boat."

"That fellow is still waving his coat."

"He must think we like to see him do that. Why don't he quit it? It don't mean anything."

"I don't know. I think he is trying to make us go north. It must be that there's a life-saving station there somewhere."

"Say, he ain't tired yet. Look at 'im wave!"

"Wonder how long he can keep that up. He's been revolving his coat ever since he caught sight of us. He's an idiot. Why aren't they getting men to bring a boat out? A fishing-boat—one of those big yawls—could come out here all right. Why don't he do something?"

"Oh, it's all right now."

"They'll have a boat out here for us in less than no time, now that they've seen us."

A faint yellow tone came into the sky over the low land. The shadows on the sea slowly deepened. The wind bore coldness with it, and the men began to shiver.

"Holy smoke!" said one, allowing his voice to express his impious mood, "if we keep on monkeying out here! If we've got to flounder out here all night!"

"Oh, we'll never have to stay here all night! Don't you worry. They've seen us now, and it won't be long before they'll come chasing out after us."

The shore grew dusky. The man waving a coat blended gradually into this gloom, and it swallowed in the same manner the omnibus and the group of people. The spray, when it dashed uproariously over the side, made the voyagers shrink and swear like men who were being branded.

"I'd like to catch the chump who waved the coat. I feel like soaking him one, just for luck."

"Why? What did he do?"

"Oh, nothing, but then he seemed so damned cheerful."

In the meantime the oiler rowed, and then the correspondent rowed, and then the oiler rowed. Gray-faced and bowed forward, they mechanically, turn by turn, plied the leaden oars. The form of the lighthouse had vanished from the southern horizon, but finally a pale star appeared, just lifting from the sea. The streaked saffron in the west passed before the all-merging darkness, and the sea to the east was black. The land had vanished, and was expressed only by the low and drear thunder of the surf.

"If I am going to be drowned—if I am going to be drowned—if I am going to be drowned, why, in the name of the seven mad gods who rule the sea, was I allowed to come thus far and contemplate sand and trees? Was I brought here merely to have my nose dragged away as I was about to nibble the sacred cheese of life?"

The patient captain, drooped over the water-jar, was sometimes obliged to speak to the oarsman.

"Keep her head up! Keep her head up!"

"Keep her head up, sir." The voices were weary and low.

This was surely a quiet evening. All save the oarsman lay heavily and listlessly in the boat's bottom. As for him, his eyes were just capable of noting the tall black waves that swept forward in a most sinister silence, save for an occasional subdued growl of a crest.

The cook's head was on a thwart, and he looked without interest at the water under his nose. He was deep in other scenes. Finally he spoke. "Billie," he murmured dreamfully, "what kind of pie do you like best?"

V

"Pie!" said the oiler and the correspondent, agitatedly. "Don't talk about those things, blast you!"

"Well," said the cook, "I was just thinking about ham sandwiches, and—"

A night on the sea in an open boat is a long night. As darkness settled finally, the shine of the light, lifting from the sea in the south, changed to full gold. On the northern horizon a new light appeared, a small bluish gleam on the edge of the waters. These two lights were the furniture of the world. Otherwise there was nothing but waves.

Two men huddled in the stern, and distances were so magnificent in the dinghy that the rower was enabled to keep his feet partly warm by thrusting them under his companions. Their legs indeed extended far under the rowing-seat until they touched the feet of the captain forward.

Sometimes, despite the efforts of the tired oarsman, a wave came piling into the boat, an icy wave of the night, and the chilling water soaked them anew. They would twist their bodies for a moment and groan, and sleep the dead sleep once more, while the water in the boat gurgled about them as the craft rocked.

The plan of the oiler and the correspondent was for one to row until he lost the ability, and then arouse the other from his sea-water couch in the bottom of the boat.

The oiler plied the oars until his head drooped forward and the over-powering sleep blinded him; and he rowed yet afterward. Then he touched a man in the bottom of the boat, and called his name. "Will you spell me for a little while?" he said meekly.

"Sure, Billie," said the correspondent, awaking and dragging himself to a sitting position. They exchanged places carefully, and the oiler, cuddling down in the sea-water at the cook's side, seemed to go to sleep instantly.

The particular violence of the sea had ceased. The waves came without snarling. The obligation of the man at the oars was to keep the boat headed so that the tilt of the rollers would not capsize her, and to preserve her from filling when the crests rushed past. The black waves were silent and hard to be seen in the darkness. Often one was almost upon the boat before the oarsman was aware.

In a low voice the correspondent addressed the captain. He was not sure that the captain was awake, although this iron man seemed to be always awake. "Captain, shall I keep her making for that light north, sir?"

The same steady voice answered him. "Yes. Keep it about two points off the port bow."

The cook had tied a life-belt around himself in order to get even the warmth which this clumsy cork contrivance could donate, and he seemed almost stove-like when a rower, whose teeth invariably chattered wildly as soon as he ceased his labor, dropped down to sleep.

The correspondent, as he rowed, looked down at the two men sleeping under foot. The cook's arm was around the oiler's shoulders, and, with their fragmentary clothing and haggard faces, they were the babes of the sea—a grotesque rendering of the old babes in the wood.

Later he must have grown stupid at his work, for suddenly there was a growling of water, and a crest came with a roar and a swash into the boat, and it was a wonder that it did not set the cook afloat in his life-belt. The cook continued to sleep, but the oiler sat up, blinking his eyes and shaking with the new cold.

"Oh, I'm awful sorry, Billie," said the correspondent, contritely.

"That's all right, old boy," said the oiler, and lay down again and was asleep.

Presently it seemed that even the captain dozed, and the correspondent thought that he was the one man afloat on all the oceans. The wind had a voice as it came over the waves, and it was sadder than the end.

There was a long, loud swishing astern of the boat, and a gleaming trail of phosphorescence, like blue flame, was furrowed on the black waters. It might have been made by a monstrous knife.

Then there came a stillness, while the correspondent breathed with the open mouth and looked at the sea.

Suddenly there was another swish and another long flash of bluish light, and this time it was alongside the boat, and might almost have been reached with an oar. The correspondent saw an enormous fin speed like a shadow through the water, hurling the crystalline spray and leaving the long glowing trail.

The correspondent looked over his shoulder at the captain. His face was hidden, and he seemed to be asleep. He looked at the babes of the sea. They certainly were asleep. So, being bereft of sympathy, he leaned a little way to one side and swore softly into the sea.

But the thing did not then leave the vicinity of the boat. Ahead or astern, on one side or the other, at intervals long or short, fled the long sparkling streak, and there was to be heard the whiroo of the dark fin. The speed and power of the thing was greatly to be admired. It cut the water like a gigantic and keen projectile.

The presence of this biding thing did not affect the man with the same horror that it would if he had been a picnicker. He simply looked at the sea dully and swore in an undertone.

Nevertheless, it is true that he did not wish to be alone with the thing. He wished one of his companions to awake by chance and keep him company with it. But the captain hung motionless over the water-jar, and the oiler and the cook in the bottom of the boat were plunged in slumber.

VI

"If I am going to be drowned—if I am going to be drowned—if I am going to be drowned, why, in the name of the seven mad gods who rule the sea, was I allowed to come thus far and contemplate sand and trees?"

During this dismal night, it may be remarked that a man would conclude that it was really the intention of the seven mad gods to drown him, despite the abominable injustice of it. For it was certainly an abominable injustice to drown a man who had worked so hard, so hard. The man felt it would be a crime most unnatural. Other people had drowned at sea since galleys swarmed with painted sails, but still—

When it occurs to a man that nature does not regard him as important, and that she feels she would not maim the universe by disposing of him, he at first wishes to throw bricks at the temple, and he hates deeply the fact that there are no bricks and no temples. Any visible expression of nature would surely be pelleted with his jeers.

Then, if there be no tangible thing to hoot, he feels, perhaps, the desire to confront a personification and indulge in pleas, bowed to one knee, and with hands supplicant, saying, "Yes, but I love myself."

A high cold star on a winter's night is the word he feels that she says to him. Thereafter he knows the pathos of his situation.

The men in the dinghy had not discussed these matters, but each had, no doubt, reflected upon them in silence and according to his mind. There was seldom any expression upon their faces save the general one of complete weariness. Speech was devoted to the business of the boat.

To chime the notes of his emotion, a verse mysteriously entered the correspondent's head. He had even forgotten that he had forgotten this verse, but it suddenly was in his mind.

A soldier of the Legion lay dying in Algiers;
There was lack of woman's nursing, there was dearth of woman's
    tears;
But a comrade stood beside him, and he took that comrade's hand,
And he said, "I never more shall see my own, my native land."

In his childhood the correspondent had been made acquainted with the fact that a soldier of the Legion lay dying in Algiers, but he had never regarded it as important. Myriads of his school-fellows had informed him of the soldier's plight, but the dinning had naturally ended by making him perfectly indifferent. He had never considered it his affair that a soldier of the Legion lay dying in Algiers, nor had it appeared to him as a matter for sorrow. It was less to him than the breaking of a pencil's point.

Now, however, it quaintly came to him as a human, living thing. It was no longer merely a picture of a few throes in the breast of a poet, meanwhile drinking tea and warming his feet at the grate; it was an actuality—stern, mournful, and fine.

The correspondent plainly saw the soldier. He lay on the sand with his feet out straight and still. While his pale left hand was upon his chest in an attempt to thwart the going of his life, the blood came between his fingers. In the far Algerian distance, a city of low square forms was set against a sky that was faint with the last sunset hues. The correspondent, plying the oars and dreaming of the slow and slower movements of the lips of the soldier, was moved by a profound and perfectly impersonal comprehension. He was sorry for the soldier of the Legion who lay dying in Algiers.

The thing which had followed the boat and waited had evidently grown bored at the delay. There was no longer to be heard the slash of the cutwater, and there was no longer the flame of the long trail. The light in the north still glimmered, but it was apparently no nearer to the boat. Sometimes the boom of the surf rang in the correspondent's ears, and he turned the craft seaward then and rowed harder. Southward, some one had evidently built a watch-fire on the beach. It was too low and too far to be seen, but it made a shimmering, roseate reflection upon the bluff back of it, and this could be discerned from the boat. The wind came stronger, and sometimes a wave suddenly raged out like a mountain-cat, and there was to be seen the sheen and sparkle of a broken crest.

The captain, in the bow, moved on his water-jar and sat erect. "Pretty long night," he observed to the correspondent. He looked at the shore. "Those life-saving people take their time."

"Did you see that shark playing around?"

"Yes, I saw him. He was a big fellow, all right."

"Wish I had known you were awake."

Later the correspondent spoke into the bottom of the boat.

"Billie!" There was a slow and gradual disentanglement. "Billie, will you spell me?"

"Sure," said the oiler.

As soon as the correspondent touched the cold, comfortable sea-water in the bottom of the boat and had huddled close to the cook's life-belt he was deep in sleep, despite the fact that his teeth played all the popular airs. This sleep was so good to him that it was but a moment before he heard a voice call his name in a tone that demonstrated the last stages of exhaustion. "Will you spell me?"

"Sure, Billie."

The light in the north had mysteriously vanished, but the correspondent took his course from the wide-awake captain.

Later in the night they took the boat farther out to sea, and the captain directed the cook to take one oar at the stern and keep the boat facing the seas. He was to call out if he should hear the thunder of the surf. This plan enabled the oiler and the correspondent to get respite together. "We'll give those boys a chance to get into shape again," said the captain. They curled down and, after a few preliminary chatterings and trembles, slept once more the dead sleep. Neither knew they had bequeathed to the cook the company of another shark, or perhaps the same shark.

As the boat caroused on the waves, spray occasionally bumped over the side and gave them a fresh soaking, but this had no power to break their repose. The ominous slash of the wind and the water affected them as it would have affected mummies.

"Boys," said the cook, with the notes of every reluctance in his voice, "she's drifted in pretty close. I guess one of you had better take her to sea again." The correspondent, aroused, heard the crash of the toppled crests.

As he was rowing, the captain gave him some whisky and water, and this steadied the chills out of him. "If I ever get ashore and anybody shows me even a photograph of an oar—"

At last there was a short conversation.

"Billie! . . . Billie, will you spell me?"

"Sure," said the oiler.

VII

When the correspondent again opened his eyes, the sea and the sky were each of the gray hue of the dawning. Later, carmine and gold was painted upon the waters. The morning appeared finally, in its splendor, with a sky of pure blue, and the sunlight flamed on the tips of the waves.

On the distant dunes were set many little black cottages, and a tall white windmill reared above them. No man, nor dog, nor bicycle appeared on the beach. The cottages might have formed a deserted village.

The voyagers scanned the shore. A conference was held in the boat. "Well," said the captain, "if no help is coming, we might better try a run through the surf right away. If we stay out here much longer we will be too weak to do anything for ourselves at all." The others silently acquiesced in this reasoning. The boat was headed for the beach. The correspondent wondered if none ever ascended the tall wind-tower, and if then they never looked seaward. This tower was a giant, standing with its back to the plight of the ants. It represented in a degree, to the correspondent, the serenity of nature amid the struggles of the individual—nature in the wind, and nature in the vision of men. She did not seem cruel to him then, nor beneficent, nor treacherous, nor wise. But she was indifferent, flatly indifferent. It is, perhaps, plausible that a man in this situation, impressed with the unconcern of the universe, should see the innumerable flaws of his life and have them taste wickedly in his mind and wish for another chance. A distinction between right and wrong seems absurdly clear to him, then, in this new ignorance of the grave-edge, and he understands that if he were given another opportunity he would mend his conduct and his words, and be better and brighter during an introduction or at a tea.

"Now, boys," said the captain, "she is going to swamp sure. All we can do is to work her in as far as possible, and then when she swamps, pile out and scramble for the beach. Keep cool now, and don't jump until she swamps sure."

The oiler took the oars. Over his shoulders he scanned the surf. "Captain," he said, "I think I'd better bring her about, and keep her head-on to the seas, and back her in."

"All right, Billie," said the captain. "Back her in." The oiler swung the boat then, and, seated in the stern, the cook and the correspondent were obliged to look over their shoulders to contemplate the lonely and indifferent shore.

The monstrous inshore rollers heaved the boat high until the men were again enabled to see the white sheets of water scudding up the slanted beach. "We won't get in very close," said the captain. Each time a man could wrest his attention from the rollers, he turned his glance toward the shore, and in the expression of the eyes during this contemplation there was a singular quality. The correspondent, observing the others, knew that they were not afraid, but the full meaning of their glances was shrouded.

As for himself, he was too tired to grapple fundamentally with the fact. He tried to coerce his mind into thinking of it, but the mind was dominated at this time by the muscles, and the muscles said they did not care. It merely occurred to him that if he should drown it would be a shame.

There were no hurried words, no pallor, no plain agitation. The men simply looked at the shore. "Now, remember to get well clear of the boat when you jump," said the captain.

Seaward the crest of a roller suddenly fell with a thunderous crash, and the long white comber came roaring down upon the boat.

"Steady now," said the captain. The men were silent. They turned their eyes from the shore to the comber and waited. The boat slid up the incline, leaped at the furious top, bounced over it, and swung down the long back of the wave. Some water had been shipped, and the cook bailed it out.

But the next crest crashed also. The tumbling, boiling flood of white water caught the boat and whirled it almost perpendicular. Water swarmed in from all sides. The correspondent had his hands on the gunwale at this time, and when the water entered at that place he swiftly withdrew his fingers, as if he objected to wetting them.

The little boat, drunken with this weight of water, reeled and snuggled deeper into the sea.

"Bail her out, cook! Bail her out!" said the captain.

"All right, Captain," said the cook.

"Now, boys, the next one will do for us sure," said the oiler. "Mind to jump clear of the boat."

The third wave moved forward, huge, furious, implacable. It fairly swallowed the dinghy, and almost simultaneously the men tumbled into the sea. A piece of life-belt had lain in the bottom of the boat, and as the correspondent went overboard he held this to his chest with his left hand.

The January water was icy, and he reflected immediately that it was colder than he had expected to find it off the coast of Florida. This appeared to his dazed mind as a fact important enough to be noted at the time. The coldness of the water was sad; it was tragic. This fact was somehow mixed and confused with his opinion of his own situation so that it seemed almost a proper reason for tears. The water was cold.

When he came to the surface he was conscious of little but the noisy water. Afterward he saw his companions in the sea. The oiler was ahead in the race. He was swimming strongly and rapidly. Off to the correspondent's left, the cook's great white and corked back bulged out of the water; and in the rear the captain was hanging with his one good hand to the keel of the overturned dinghy.

There is a certain immovable quality to a shore, and the correspondent wondered at it amid the confusion of the sea.

It seemed also very attractive; but the correspondent knew that it was a long journey, and he paddled leisurely. The piece of life-preserver lay under him, and sometimes he whirled down the incline of a wave as if he were on a hand-sled.

But finally he arrived at a place in the sea where travel was beset with difficulty. He did not pause swimming to inquire what manner of current had caught him, but there his progress ceased. The shore was set before him like a bit of scenery on a stage, and he looked at it, and understood with his eyes each detail of it.

As the cook passed, much farther to the left, the captain was calling to him, "Turn over on your back, cook! Turn over on your back and use the oar."

"All right, sir." The cook turned on his back, and, paddling with an oar, went ahead as if he were a canoe.

Presently the boat also passed to the left of the correspondent, with the captain clinging with one hand to the keel. He would have appeared like a man raising himself to look over a board fence if it were not for the extraordinary gymnastics of the boat. The correspondent marveled that the captain could still hold to it.

They passed on nearer to shore—the oiler, the cook, the captain—and following them went the water-jar, bouncing gaily over the seas.

The correspondent remained in the grip of this strange new enemy, a current. The shore, with its white slope of sand and its green bluff, topped with little silent cottages, was spread like a picture before him. It was very near to him then, but he was impressed as one who, in a gallery, looks at a scene from Brittany or Algiers.

He thought: "I am going to drown? Can it be possible? Can it be possible? Can it be possible?" Perhaps an individual must consider his own death to be the final phenomenon of nature.

But later a wave perhaps whirled him out of this small deadly current, for he found suddenly that he could again make progress toward the shore. Later still he was aware that the captain, clinging with one hand to the keel of the dinghy, had his face turned away from the shore and toward him, and was calling his name. "Come to the boat! Come to the boat!"

In his struggle to reach the captain and the boat, he reflected that when one gets properly wearied drowning must really be a comfortable arrangement—a cessation of hostilities accompanied by a large degree of relief; and he was glad of it, for the main thing in his mind for some moments had been horror of the temporary agony; he did not wish to be hurt.

Presently he saw a man running along the shore. He was undressing with most remarkable speed. Coat, trousers, shirt, everything flew magically off him.

"Come to the boat!" called the captain.

"All right, Captain." As the correspondent paddled, he saw the captain let himself down to bottom and leave the boat. Then the correspondent performed his one little marvel of the voyage. A large wave caught him and flung him with ease and supreme speed completely over the boat and far beyond it. It struck him even then as an event in gymnastics and a true miracle of the sea. An overturned boat in the surf is not a plaything to a swimming man.

The correspondent arrived in water that reached only to his waist, but his condition did not enable him to stand for more than a moment. Each wave knocked him into a heap, and the undertow pulled at him.

Then he saw the man who had been running and undressing, and undressing and running, come bounding into the water. He dragged ashore the cook, and then waded toward the captain; but the captain waved him away and sent him to the correspondent. He was naked—naked as a tree in winter; but a halo was about his head, and he shone like a saint. He gave a strong pull, and a long drag, and a bully heave at the correspondent's hand. The correspondent, schooled in the minor formulæ, said, "Thanks, old man." But suddenly the man cried, "What's that?" He pointed a swift finger. The correspondent said, "Go."

In the shallows, face downward, lay the oiler. His forehead touched sand that was periodically, between each wave, clear of the sea.

The correspondent did not know all that transpired afterward. When he achieved safe ground he fell, striking the sand with each particular part of his body. It was as if he had dropped from a roof, but the thud was grateful to him.

It seemed that instantly the beach was populated with men with blankets, clothes, and flasks, and women with coffee-pots and all the remedies sacred to their minds. The welcome of the land to the men from the sea was warm and generous; but a still and dripping shape was carried slowly up the beach, and the land's welcome for it could only be the different and sinister hospitality of the grave.

When it came night, the white waves paced to and fro in the moonlight, and the wind brought the sound of the great sea's voice to the men on shore, and they felt that they could then be interpreters.

1897

THE BRIDE COMES TO
YELLOW SKY

This southwestern local-color story appeared in *McClure's Magazine* for February 1898; in the same year it was reprinted in *The Open Boat and Other Tales of Adventure*, from which the present text is drawn. One of Crane's best humored stories, it gives an authentic, low-keyed picture of Jack Potter and his unnamed bride who is neither young nor pretty; what suspense there is comes from Potter's expectation of a "shivaree" when they reach Yellow Sky. But excitement of a different kind is furnished by Scratchy Wilson, whose marksmanship makes him dangerous when drunk. Crane successfully establishes the atmosphere of the arid west, though its ingredients are commonplace today and derive in part from Bret Harte. The conclusion is treated romantically when Potter's one word

"Married" reduces Wilson to helplessness and dissolves the potential danger of the situation as if by magic. Crane's theory of human nature is here almost the converse of that motivating "The Blue Hotel," though he avoids revealing it until the closing paragraphs.

I

The great Pullman was whirling onward with such dignity of motion that a glance from the window seemed simply to prove that the plains of Texas were pouring eastward. Vast flats of green grass, dull-hued spaces of mesquit and cactus, little groups of frame houses, woods of light and tender trees, all were sweeping into the east, sweeping over the horizon, a precipice.

A newly married pair had boarded this coach at San Antonio. The man's face was reddened from many days in the wind and sun, and a direct result of his new black clothes was that his brick-colored hands were constantly performing in a most conscious fashion. From time to time he looked down respectfully at his attire. He sat with a hand on each knee, like a man waiting in a barber's shop. The glances he devoted to other passengers were furtive and shy.

The bride was not pretty, nor was she very young. She wore a dress of blue cashmere, with small reservations of velvet here and there, and with steel buttons abounding. She continually twisted her head to regard her puff sleeves, very stiff, straight, and high. They embarrassed her. It was quite apparent that she had cooked, and that she expected to cook, dutifully. The blushes caused by the careless scrutiny of some passengers as she had entered the car were strange to see upon this plain, under-class countenance, which was drawn in placid, almost emotionless lines.

They were evidently very happy. "Ever been in a parlor-car before?" he asked, smiling with delight.

"No," she answered; "I never was. It's fine, ain't it?"

"Great! And then after a while we'll go forward to the diner, and get a big lay-out. Finest meal in the world. Charge a dollar."

"Oh, do they?" cried the bride. "Charge a dollar? Why, that's too much—for us—ain't it, Jack?"

"Not this trip, anyhow," he answered bravely. "We're going to go the whole thing."

Later he explained to her about the trains. "You see, it's a thousand miles from one end of Texas to the other; and this train runs right across it, and never stops but four times." He had the pride of an owner. He pointed out to her the dazzling fittings of the coach; and in truth her eyes opened wider as she contemplated the sea-green figured velvet, the shining brass, silver, and glass, the wood that gleamed as darkly brilliant as the surface of a pool of oil. At one end a bronze figure sturdily held a support for a separated chamber, and at convenient places on the ceiling were frescos in olive and silver.

To the minds of the pair, their surroundings reflected the glory of their marriage that morning in San Antonio; this was the environment of their new estate; and the man's face in particular beamed with an elation that made him appear ridiculous to the negro porter. This individual at times surveyed them from afar with an amused and superior grin. On other occasions he bullied them with skill in ways that did not make it exactly plain to them that they were being bullied. He subtly used all the manners of the most unconquerable kind of snobbery. He oppressed them; but of this oppression they had small knowledge, and they speedily forgot that infrequently a number of travelers covered them with stares of derisive enjoyment. Historically there was supposed to be something infinitely humorous in their situation.

"We are due in Yellow Sky at 3:42," he said, looking tenderly into her eyes.

"Oh, are we?" she said, as if she had not been aware of it. To evince surprise at her husband's statement was part of her wifely amiability. She took from a pocket a little silver watch; and as she held it before her, and stared at it with a frown of attention, the new husband's face shone.

"I bought it in San Anton' from a friend of mine," he told her gleefully.

"It's seventeen minutes past twelve," she said, looking up at him with a kind of shy and clumsy coquetry. A passenger, noting this play, grew excessively sardonic, and winked at himself in one of the numerous mirrors.

At last they went to the dining-car. Two rows of negro waiters, in glowing white suits, surveyed their entrance with the interest, and also the equanimity, of men who had been forewarned. The pair fell to the lot of a waiter who happened to feel pleasure in steering them through their meal. He viewed them with the manner of a fatherly pilot, his countenance radiant with benevolence. The patronage, entwined with the ordinary deference, was not plain to them. And yet, as they returned to their coach, they showed in their faces a sense of escape.

To the left, miles down a long purple slope, was a little ribbon of mist where moved the keening Rio Grande. The train was approaching it at an angle, and the apex was Yellow Sky. Presently it was apparent that, as the distance from Yellow Sky grew shorter, the husband became commensurately restless. His brick-red hands were more insistent in their prominence. Occasionally he was even rather absent-minded and faraway when the bride leaned forward and addressed him.

As a matter of truth, Jack Potter was beginning to find the shadow of a deed weigh upon him like a leaden slab. He, the town marshal of Yellow Sky, a man known, liked, and feared in his corner, a prominent person, had gone to San Antonio to meet a girl he believed he loved, and there, after the usual prayers, had actually induced her to marry him, without consulting Yellow Sky for any part of the transaction. He was now bringing his bride before an innocent and unsuspecting community.

Of course people in Yellow Sky married as it pleased them, in accordance with a general custom; but such was Potter's thought of his duty to his friends, or of their idea of his duty, or of an unspoken form which does not control men in these matters, that he felt he was heinous. He had committed an extraordinary crime. Face to face with this girl in San Antonio, and spurred by his sharp impulse, he had gone headlong over all the social hedges. At San Antonio he was like a man hidden in the dark. A knife to sever any friendly duty, any form, was easy to his hand in that remote city. But the hour of Yellow Sky—the hour of daylight—was approaching.

He knew full well that his marriage was an important thing to his town. It could only be exceeded by the burning of the new hotel. His friends could not forgive him. Frequently he had reflected on the advisability of telling them by telegraph, but a new cowardice had been upon him. He feared to do it. And now the train was hurrying him toward a scene of amazement, glee, and reproach. He glanced out of the window at the line of haze swinging slowly in toward the train.

Yellow Sky had a kind of brass band, which played painfully, to the delight of the populace. He laughed without heart as he thought of it. If the citizens could dream of his prospective arrival with his bride, they would parade the band at the station and escort them, amid cheers and laughing congratulations, to his adobe home.

He resolved that he would use all the devices of speed and plains-craft in making the journey from the station to his house. Once within that safe citadel, he could issue some sort of a vocal bulletin, and then not go among the citizens until they had time to wear off a little of their enthusiasm.

The bride looked anxiously at him. "What's worrying you, Jack?"

He laughed again. "I'm not worrying, girl; I'm only thinking of Yellow Sky."

She flushed in comprehension.

A sense of mutual guilt invaded their minds and developed a finer tenderness. They looked at each other with eyes softly aglow. But Potter often laughed the same nervous laugh; the flush upon the bride's face seemed quite permanent.

The traitor to the feelings of Yellow Sky narrowly watched the speeding landscape. "We're nearly there," he said.

Presently the porter came and announced the proximity of Potter's home. He held a brush in his hand, and, with all his airy superiority gone, he brushed Potter's new clothes as the latter slowly turned this way and that way. Potter fumbled out a coin and gave it to the porter, as he had seen others do. It was a heavy and muscle-bound business, as that of a man shoeing his first horse.

The porter took their bag, and as the train began to slow they moved forward to the hooded platform of the car. Presently the two engines and their long string of coaches rushed into the station of Yellow Sky.

"They have to take water here," said Potter, from a constricted throat and in mournful cadence, as one announcing death. Before the train stopped his eye had swept the length of the platform, and he was glad and astonished to see there was none upon it but the station-agent, who, with a slightly hurried and anxious air, was walking toward the water-tanks. When the train had halted, the porter alighted first, and placed in position a little temporary step.

"Come on, girl," said Potter, hoarsely. As he helped her down they each laughed on a false note. He took the bag from the negro, and bade his wife cling to his arm. As they slunk rapidly away, his hang-dog glance perceived that they were unloading the two trunks, and also that the station-agent, far ahead near the baggage-car, had turned and was running toward him, making gestures. He laughed, and groaned as he laughed, when he noted the first effect of his marital bliss upon Yellow Sky. He gripped his wife's arm firmly to his side, and they fled. Behind them the porter stood, chuckling fatuously.

II

The California express on the Southern Railway was due at Yellow Sky in twenty-one minutes. There were six men at the bar of the Weary Gentleman Saloon. One was a drummer, who talked a great deal and rapidly; three were Texans, who did not care to talk at that time; and two were Mexican sheep-herders, who did not talk as a general practice in the Weary Gentleman Saloon. The barkeeper's dog lay on the board walk that crossed in front of the door. His head was on his paws, and he glanced drowsily here and there with the constant vigilance of a dog that is kicked on occasion. Across the sandy street were some vivid green grass-plots, so wonderful in appearance, amid the sands that burned near them in a blazing sun, that they caused a doubt in the mind. They exactly resembled the grass mats used to represent lawns on the stage. At the cooler end of the railway station, a man without a coat sat in a tilted chair and smoked his pipe. The fresh-cut bank of the Rio Grande circled near the town, and there could be seen beyond it a great plum-colored plain of mesquit.

Save for the busy drummer and his companions in the saloon, Yellow Sky was dozing. The new-comer leaned gracefully upon the bar, and recited many tales with the confidence of a bard who has come upon a new field.

"—and at the moment that the old man fell down-stairs with the bureau in his arms, the old woman was coming up with two scuttles of coal, and of course—"

The drummer's tale was interrupted by a young man who suddenly appeared in the open door. He cried: "Scratchy Wilson's drunk, and has turned loose with both hands." The two Mexicans at once set down their glasses and faded out of the rear entrance of the saloon.

The drummer, innocent and jocular, answered: "All right, old man. S'pose he has? Come in and have a drink, anyhow."

But the information had made such an obvious cleft in every skull in the room that the drummer was obliged to see its importance. All had become instantly solemn. "Say," said he, mystified, "what is this?" His three companions made the introductory gesture of eloquent speech; but the young man at the door forestalled them.

"It means, my friend," he answered, as he came into the saloon, "that for the next two hours this town won't be a health resort."

The barkeeper went to the door, and locked and barred it; reaching out of the window, he pulled in heavy wooden shutters, and barred them. Immediately a solemn, chapel-like gloom was upon the place. The drummer was looking from one to another.

"But say," he cried, "what is this, anyhow? You don't mean there is going to be a gun-fight?"

"Don't know whether there'll be a fight or not," answered one man, grimly; "but there'll be some shootin'—some good shootin'."

The young man who had warned them waved his hand. "Oh, there'll be a fight fast enough, if any one wants it. Anybody can get a fight out there in the street. There's a fight just waiting."

The drummer seemed to be swayed between the interest of a foreigner and a perception of personal danger.

"What did you say his name was?" he asked.

"Scratchy Wilson," they answered in chorus.

"And will he kill anybody? What are you going to do? Does this happen often? Does he rampage around like this once a week or so? Can he break in that door?"

"No; he can't break down that door," replied the barkeeper. "He's tried it three times. But when he comes you'd better lay down on the floor, stranger. He's dead sure to shoot at it, and a bullet may come through."

Thereafter the drummer kept a strict eye upon the door. The time had not yet been called for him to hug the floor, but, as a minor precaution, he sidled near to the wall. "Will he kill anybody?" he said again.

The men laughed low and scornfully at the question.

"He's out to shoot, and he's out for trouble. Don't see any good in experimentin' with him."

"But what do you do in a case like this? What do you do?"

A man responded: "Why, he and Jack Potter—"

"But," in chorus the other men interrupted, "Jack Potter's in San Anton'."

"Well, who is he? What's he got to do with it?"

"Oh, he's the town marshal. He goes out and fights Scratchy when he gets on one of these tears."

"Wow!" said the drummer, mopping his brow. "Nice job he's got."

The voices had toned away to mere whisperings. The drummer

wished to ask further questions, which were born of an increasing anxiety and bewilderment; but when he attempted them, the men merely looked at him in irritation and motioned him to remain silent. A tense waiting hush was upon them. In the deep shadows of the room their eyes shone as they listened for sounds from the street. One man made three gestures at the barkeeper; and the latter, moving like a ghost, handed him a glass and a bottle. The man poured a full glass of whisky, and set down the bottle noiselessly. He gulped the whisky in a swallow, and turned again toward the door in immovable silence. The drummer saw that the barkeeper, without a sound, had taken a Winchester from beneath the bar. Later he saw this individual beckoning to him, so he tiptoed across the room.

"You better come with me back of the bar."

"No, thanks," said the drummer, perspiring; "I'd rather be where I can make a break for the back door."

Whereupon the man of bottles made a kindly but peremptory gesture. The drummer obeyed it, and, finding himself seated on a box with his head below the level of the bar, balm was laid upon his soul at sight of various zinc and copper fittings that bore a resemblance to armor-plate. The barkeeper took a seat comfortably upon an adjacent box.

"You see," he whispered, "this here Scratchy Wilson is a wonder with a gun—a perfect wonder; and when he goes on the war-trail, we hunt our holes—naturally. He's about the last one of the old gang that used to hang out along the river here. He's a terror when he's drunk. When he's sober he's all right—kind of simple—wouldn't hurt a fly—nicest fellow in town. But when he's drunk—whoo!"

There were periods of stillness. "I wish Jack Potter was back from San Anton'," said the barkeeper. "He shot Wilson up once—in the leg—and he would sail in and pull out the kinks in this thing."

Presently they heard from a distance the sound of a shot, followed by three wild yowls. It instantly removed a bond from the men in the darkened saloon. There was a shuffling of feet. They looked at each other. "Here he comes," they said.

III

A man in a maroon-colored flannel shirt, which had been purchased for purposes of decoration, and made principally by some Jewish women on the East Side of New York, rounded a corner and walked into the middle of the main street of Yellow Sky. In either hand the man held a long, heavy, blue-black revolver. Often he yelled, and these cries rang through a semblance of a deserted village, shrilly flying over the roofs in a volume that seemed to have no relation to the ordinary vocal strength of a man. It was as if the surrounding stillness formed the arch of a tomb over him. These cries of ferocious challenge rang against walls of silence. And his boots had red tops with gilded imprints, of the kind beloved in winter by little sledding boys on the hillsides of New England.

The man's face flamed in a rage begot of whisky. His eyes, rolling, , and yet keen for ambush, hunted the still doorways and windows. He walked with the creeping movement of the midnight cat. As it occurred to him, he roared menacing information. The long revolvers in his hands were as easy as straws; they were moved with an electric swiftness. The little fingers of each hand played sometimes in a musician's way. Plain from the low collar of the shirt, the cords of his neck straightened and sank, straightened and sank, as passion moved him. The only sounds were his terrible invitations. The calm adobes preserved their demeanor at the passing of this small thing in the middle of the street.

There was no offer of fight—no offer of fight. The man called to the sky. There were no attractions. He bellowed and fumed and swayed his revolvers here and everywhere.

The dog of the barkeeper of the Weary Gentleman Saloon had not appreciated the advance of events. He yet lay dozing in front of his master's door. At sight of the dog, the man paused and raised his revolver humorously. At sight of the man, the dog sprang up and walked diagonally away, with a sullen head, and growling. The man yelled, and the dog broke into a gallop. As it was about to enter an alley, there was a loud noise, a whistling, and something spat the ground directly before it. The dog screamed, and, wheeling in terror, galloped headlong in a new direction. Again there was a noise, a whistling, and sand was kicked viciously before it. Fear-stricken, the dog turned and flurried like an animal in a pen. The man stood laughing, his weapons at his hips.

Ultimately the man was attracted by the closed door of the Weary Gentleman Saloon. He went to it, and, hammering with a revolver, demanded drink.

The door remaining imperturbable, he picked a bit of paper from the walk, and nailed it to the framework with a knife. He then turned his back contemptuously upon this popular resort, and, walking to the opposite side of the street and spinning there on his heel quickly and lithely, fired at the bit of paper. He missed it by a half-inch. He swore at himself, and went away. Later he comfortably fusilladed the windows of his most intimate friend. The man was playing with this town; it was a toy for him.

But still there was no offer of fight. The name of Jack Potter, his ancient antagonist, entered his mind, and he concluded that it would be a glad thing if he should go to Potter's house, and by bombardment induce him to come out and fight. He moved in the direction of his desire, chanting Apache scalp-music.

When he arrived at it, Potter's house presented the same still front as had the other adobes. Taking up a strategic position, the man howled a challenge. But this house regarded him as might a great stone god. It gave no sign. After a decent wait, the man howled further challenges, mingling with them wonderful epithets.

Presently there came the spectacle of a man churning himself into deepest rage over the immobility of a house. He fumed at it as the winter wind attacks a prairie cabin in the North. To the distance there should have gone the sound of a tumult like the fighting of two hundred Mexicans. As necessity bade him, he paused for breath or to reload his revolvers.

IV

Potter and his bride walked sheepishly and with speed. Sometimes they laughed together shamefacedly and low.

"Next corner, dear," he said finally.

They put forth the efforts of a pair walking bowed against a strong wind. Potter was about to raise a finger to point the first appearance of the new home when, as they circled the corner, they came face to face with a man in a maroon-colored shirt, who was feverishly pushing cartridges into a large revolver. Upon the instant the man dropped his revolver to the ground, and, like lightning, whipped another from its holster. The second weapon was aimed at the bridegroom's chest.

There was a silence. Potter's mouth seemed to be merely a grave for his tongue. He exhibited an instinct to at once loosen his arm from the woman's grip, and he dropped the bag to the sand. As for the bride, her face had gone as yellow as old cloth. She was a slave to hideous rites, gazing at the apparitional snake.

The two men faced each other at a distance of three paces. He of the revolver smiled with a new and quiet ferocity.

"Tried to sneak up on me," he said. "Tried to sneak up on me!" His eyes grew more baleful. As Potter made a slight movement, the man thrust his revolver venomously forward. "No; don't you do it, Jack Potter. Don't you move a finger toward a gun just yet. Don't you move an eyelash. The time has come for me to settle with you, and I'm goin' to do it my own way, and loaf along with no interferin'. So if you don't want a gun bent on you, just mind what I tell you."

Potter looked at his enemy. "I ain't got a gun on me, Scratchy," he said. "Honest, I ain't." He was stiffening and steadying, but yet somewhere at the back of his mind a vision of the Pullman floated: the sea-green figured velvet, the shining brass, silver, and glass, the wood that gleamed as darkly brilliant as the surface of a pool of oil—all the glory of the marriage, the environment of the new estate. "You know I fight when it comes to fighting, Scratchy Wilson; but I ain't got a gun on me. You'll have to do all the shootin' yourself."

His enemy's face went livid. He stepped forward, and lashed his weapon to and fro before Potter's chest. "Don't you tell me you ain't got no gun on you, you whelp. Don't tell me no lie like that. There ain't a man in Texas ever seen you without no gun. Don't take me for no kid."

His eyes blazed with light, and his throat worked like a pump.

"I ain't takin' you for no kid," answered Potter. His heels had not moved an inch backward. "I'm takin' you for a —— fool. I tell you I ain't got a gun, and I ain't. If you're goin' to shoot me up, you better begin now; you'll never get a chance like this again."

So much enforced reasoning had told on Wilson's rage; he was calmer. "If you ain't got a gun, why ain't you got a gun?" he sneered. "Been to Sunday-school?"

"I ain't got a gun because I've just come from San Anton' with my wife. I'm married," said Potter. "And if I'd thought there was going to be any galoots like you prowling around when I brought my wife home, I'd had a gun, and don't you forget it."

"Married!" said Scratchy, not at all comprehending.

"Yes, married. I'm married," said Potter, distinctly.

"Married?" said Scratchy. Seemingly for the first time, he saw the drooping, drowning woman at the other man's side. "No!" he said. He was like a creature allowed a glimpse of another world. He moved a pace backward, and his arm, with the revolver, dropped to his side. "Is this the lady?" he asked.

"Yes; this is the lady," answered Potter.

There was another period of silence.

"Well," said Wilson at last, slowly, "I s'pose it's all off now."

"It's all off if you say so, Scratchy. You know I didn't make the trouble." Potter lifted his valise.

"Well, I 'low it's off, Jack," said Wilson. He was looking at the ground. "Married!" He was not a student of chivalry; it was merely that in the presence of this foreign condition he was a simple child of the earlier plains. He picked up his starboard revolver, and, placing both weapons in their holsters, he went away. His feet made funnel-shaped tracks in the heavy sand.

1898

THE BLUE HOTEL

The setting of "The Blue Hotel" was suggested by a garish piece of light blue architecture Crane saw on a trip through Nebraska in 1895. Although the story is one of his best, it was declined by *Scribner's* and *The Atlantic Monthly*. It appeared in *Collier's Weekly* for November 26 and December 3, 1898, and was collected in *The Monster and Other Stories* (1899), from which the present text is taken. R. W. Stallman, in *Stephen Crane: An Omnibus*, pp. 482–83, summarizes divergent critical opinions of the story and holds that the closing section with its moral preachment is a blemish. True, the attitudes implicit in the body of the story do not require further emphasis at the end. But the last scene contains one piece of information which affects our interpretation of the entire chain of events. Would the story be weakened if we did not learn whether Johnnie cheated the Swede? Or if the truth were revealed earlier?

I

The Palace Hotel at Fort Romper was painted a light blue, a shade that is on the legs of a kind of heron, causing the bird to declare its position against any background. The Palace Hotel, then, was always screaming and howling in a way that made the dazzling winter landscape of Nebraska seem only a gray swampish hush. It stood alone on the prairie, and when the snow was falling the town two hundred yards away was not visible. But when the traveler alighted at the railway station he was obliged to pass the Palace Hotel before he could come upon the company of low clapboard houses which composed Fort Romper, and it was not to be thought that any traveler could pass the Palace Hotel without looking at it. Pat Scully, the proprietor, had proved himself a master of strategy when he chose his paints. It is true that on clear days, when the great trans-continental expresses, long lines of swaying Pullmans, swept through Fort Romper, passengers were overcome at the sight, and the cult that knows the brown-reds and the subdivisions of the dark greens of the East expressed shame, pity, horror, in a laugh. But to the citizens of this prairie town and to the people who would naturally stop there, Pat Scully had performed a feat. With this opulence and splendor, these creeds, classes, egotisms, that streamed through Romper on the rails day after day, they had no color in common.

As if the displayed delights of such a blue hotel were not sufficiently enticing, it was Scully's habit to go every morning and evening to meet the leisurely trains that stopped at Romper and work his seductions upon any man that he might see wavering, gripsack in hand.

One morning, when a snow-crusted engine dragged its long string of freight cars and its one passenger coach to the station, Scully performed the marvel of catching three men. One was a shaky and quick-eyed Swede, with a great shining cheap valise; one was a tall bronzed cowboy, who was on his way to a ranch near the Dakota line; one was a little silent man from the East, who didn't look it, and didn't announce it. Scully practically made them prisoners. He was so nimble and merry and kindly that each probably felt it would be the height of brutality to try to escape. They trudged off over the creaking board sidewalks in the wake of the eager little Irishman. He wore a heavy fur cap squeezed tightly down on his head. It caused his two red ears to stick out stiffly, as if they were made of tin.

At last, Scully, elaborately, with boisterous hospitality, conducted them through the portals of the blue hotel. The room which they entered was small. It seemed to be merely a proper temple for an enormous stove, which, in the center, was humming with godlike violence. At various points on its surface the iron had become luminous and glowed yellow from the heat. Beside the stove Scully's son Johnnie was playing High-Five with an old farmer who had whiskers both gray and sandy. They were quarrelling. Frequently the old farmer turned his face towards a box of sawdust—colored brown from tobacco juice—that was behind the stove, and spat with an air of great impatience and irritation. With a loud flourish of words Scully destroyed the game of cards, and bustled his son up-stairs with part of the baggage of the new guests. He himself conducted them to three basins of the coldest water in the world. The cowboy and the Easterner burnished themselves fiery-red with this water, until it seemed to be some kind of a metal polish. The Swede, however, merely dipped his fingers gingerly and with trepidation. It was notable that throughout this series of small ceremonies the three travelers were made to feel that Scully was very benevolent. He was conferring great favors upon them. He handed the towel from one to the other with an air of philanthropic impulse.

Afterwards they went to the first room, and, sitting about the stove, listened to Scully's officious clamor at his daughters, who were preparing the mid-day meal. They reflected in the silence of experienced men who tread carefully amid new people. Nevertheless, the old farmer, stationary, invincible in his chair near the warmest part of the stove, turned his face from the sawdust box frequently and addressed a glowing commonplace to the strangers. Usually he was answered in short but adequate sentences by either the cowboy or the Easterner. The Swede said nothing. He seemed to be occupied in making furtive estimates of each man in the room. One might have thought that he had the sense of silly suspicion which comes to guilt. He resembled a badly frightened man.

Later, at dinner, he spoke a little, addressing his conversation entirely to Scully. He volunteered that he had come from New York, where for ten years he had worked as a tailor. These facts seemed to strike Scully as fascinating, and afterwards he volunteered that he had lived at Romper for fourteen years. The Swede asked about the crops and the price of labor. He seemed barely to listen to Scully's extended replies. His eyes continued to rove from man to man.

Finally, with a laugh and a wink, he said that some of these Western communities were very dangerous; and after his statement he straightened his legs under the table, tilted his head, and laughed again, loudly. It was plain that the demonstration had no meaning to the others. They looked at him wondering and in silence.

II

As the men trooped heavily back into the front-room, the two little windows presented views of a turmoiling sea of snow. The huge arms of the wind were making attempts—mighty, circular, futile—to embrace the flakes as they sped. A gate-post like a still man with a blanched face stood aghast amid this profligate fury. In a hearty voice Scully announced the presence of a blizzard. The guests of the blue hotel, lighting their pipes, assented with grunts of lazy masculine contentment. No island of the sea could be exempt in the degree of this little room with its humming stove. Johnnie, son of Scully, in a tone which defined his opinion of his ability as a card-player, challenged the old farmer of both gray and sandy whiskers to a game of High-Five. The farmer agreed with a contemptuous and bitter scoff. They sat close to the stove, and squared their knees under a wide board. The cowboy and the Easterner watched the game with interest. The Swede remained near the window, aloof, but with a countenance that showed signs of an inexplicable excitement.

The play of Johnnie and the gray-beard was suddenly ended by another quarrel. The old man arose while casting a look of heated scorn at his adversary. He slowly buttoned his coat, and then stalked with fabulous dignity from the room. In the discreet silence of all [the] other men the Swede laughed. His laughter rang somehow childish. Men by this time had begun to look at him askance, as if they wished to inquire what ailed him.

A new game was formed jocosely. The cowboy volunteered to become the partner of Johnnie, and they all then turned to ask the Swede to throw in his lot with the little Easterner. He asked some questions about the game, and, learning that it wore many names, and that he had played it when it was under an alias, he accepted the invitation. He strode towards the men nervously, as if he expected to be assaulted. Finally, seated, he gazed from face to face and laughed shrilly. This laugh was so strange that the Easterner looked up quickly, the cowboy sat intent and with his mouth open, and Johnnie paused, holding the cards with still fingers.

Afterwards there was a short silence. Then Johnnie said, "Well, let's get at it. Come on now!" They pulled their chairs forward until their knees were bunched under the board. They began to play, and their interest in the game caused the others to forget the manner of the Swede.

The cowboy was a board-whacker. Each time that he held superior cards he whanged them, one by one, with exceeding force, down upon the improvised table, and took the tricks with a glowing air of prowess and pride that sent thrills of indignation into the hearts of his opponents. A game with a board-whacker in it is sure to become intense. The countenances of the Easterner and the Swede were miserable whenever the cowboy thundered down his aces and kings, while Johnnie, his eyes gleaming with joy, chuckled and chuckled.

Because of the absorbing play none considered the strange ways of the Swede. They paid strict heed to the game. Finally, during a lull caused by a new deal, the Swede suddenly addressed Johnnie: "I suppose there have been a good many men killed in this room." The jaws of the others dropped and they looked at him.

"What in hell are you talking about?" said Johnnie.

The Swede laughed again his blatant laugh, full of a kind of false courage and defiance. "Oh, you know what I mean all right," he answered.

"I'm a liar if I do!" Johnnie protested. The card was halted, and the men stared at the Swede. Johnnie evidently felt that as the son of the proprietor he should make a direct inquiry. "Now, what might you be drivin' at, mister?" he asked. The Swede winked at him. It was a wink full of cunning. His fingers shook on the edge of the board. "Oh, maybe you think I have been to nowheres. Maybe you think I'm a tender-foot?"

"I don't know nothin' about you," answered Johnnie, "and I don't give a damn where you've been. All I got to say is that I don't know what you're driving at. There hain't never been nobody killed in this room."

The cowboy, who had been steadily gazing at the Swede, then spoke: "What's wrong with you, mister?"

Apparently it seemed to the Swede that he was formidably menaced. He shivered and turned white near the corners of his mouth. He sent an appealing glace in the direction of the little Easterner. During these moments he did not forget to wear his air of advanced pot-valor. "They say they don't know what I mean," he remarked mockingly to the Easterner.

The latter answered after prolonged and cautious reflection. "I don't understand you," he said, impassively.

The Swede made a movement then which announced that he thought he had encountered treachery from the only quarter where he had expected sympathy, if not help. "Oh, I see you are all against me. I see—"

The cowboy was in a state of deep stupefaction. "Say," he cried, as he tumbled the deck violently down upon the board, "—say, what are you gittin' at, hey?"

The Swede sprang up with the celerity of a man escaping from a snake on the floor. "I don't want to fight!" he shouted. "I don't want to fight!"

The cowboy stretched his long legs indolently and deliberately. His hands were in his pockets. He spat into the sawdust box. "Well, who the hell thought you did?" he inquired.

The Swede backed rapidly towards a corner of the room. His hands were out protectingly in front of his chest, but he was making an obvious struggle to control his fright. "Gentlemen," he quavered, "I suppose I am going to be killed before I can leave this house! I suppose I am going to be killed before I can leave this house!" In his eyes was the dying-swan look. Through the windows could be seen the snow turning blue in the shadow of dusk. The wind tore at the house and some loose thing beat regularly against the clapboards like a spirit tapping.

A door opened, and Scully himself entered. He paused in surprise as he noted the tragic attitude of the Swede. Then he said, "What's the matter here?"

The Swede answered him swiftly and eagerly: "These men are going to kill me."

"Kill you!" ejaculated Scully. "Kill you! What are you talkin'?"

The Swede made the gesture of a martyr.

Scully wheeled sternly upon his son. "What is this, Johnnie?"

The lad had grown sullen. "Damned if I know," he answered. "I can't make no sense to it." He began to shuffle the cards, fluttering them together with an angry snap. "He says a good many men have been killed in this room, or something like that. And he says he's goin' to be killed here too. I don't know what ails him. He's crazy, I shouldn't wonder."

Scully then looked for explanation to the cowboy, but the cowboy simply shrugged his shoulders.

"Kill you?" said Scully again to the Swede. "Kill you? Man, you're off your nut."

"Oh, I know," burst out the Swede. "I know what will happen. Yes, I'm crazy—yes. Yes, of course, I'm crazy—yes. But I know one thing—" There was a sort of sweat of misery and terror upon his face. "I know I won't get out of here alive."

The cowboy drew a deep breath, as if his mind was passing into the last stages of dissolution. "Well, I'm dog-goned," he whispered to himself.

Scully wheeled suddenly and faced his son. "You've been troublin' this man!"

Johnnie's voice was loud with its burden of grievance. "Why, good Gawd, I ain't done nothin' to 'im."

The Swede broke in. "Gentlemen, do not disturb yourselves. I will leave this house. I will go away, because"—he accused them dramatically with his glance—"because I do not want to be killed."

Scully was furious with his son. "Will you tell me what is the matter, you young divil? What's the matter, anyhow? Speak out!"

"Blame it!" cried Johnnie in despair, "don't I tell you I don't know. He —he says we want to kill him, and that's all I know. I can't tell what ails him."

The Swede continued to repeat: "Never mind, Mr. Scully; never mind. I will leave this house. I will go away, because I do not wish to be killed. Yes, of course, I am crazy—yes. But I know one thing! I will go away. I will leave this house. Never mind, Mr. Scully; never mind. I will go away."

"You will not go 'way," said Scully. "You will not go 'way until I hear the reason of this business. If anybody has troubled you I will take care of him. This is my house. You are under my roof, and I will not allow any peaceable man to be troubled here." He cast a terrible eye upon Johnnie, the cowboy, and the Easterner.

"Never mind, Mr. Scully; never mind. I will go away. I do not wish to be killed." The Swede moved towards the door, which opened upon the stairs. It was evidently his intention to go at once for his baggage.

"No, no," shouted Scully peremptorily; but the white-faced man slid by him and disappeared. "Now," said Scully severely, "what does this mane?"

Johnnie and the cowboy cried together: "Why, we didn't do nothin' to 'im!"

Scully's eyes were cold. "No," he said, "you didn't?"

Johnnie swore a deep oath. "Why, this is the wildest loon I ever see. We didn't do nothin' at all. We were jest sittin' here playin' cards, and he—"

The father suddenly spoke to the Easterner. "Mr. Blanc," he asked, "what has these boys been doin'?"

The Easterner reflected again. "I didn't see anything wrong at all," he said at last, slowly.

Scully began to howl. "But what does it mane?" He stared ferociously at his son. "I have a mind to lather you for this, me boy."

Johnnie was frantic. "Well, what have I done?" he bawled at his father.

III

"I think you are tongue-tied," said Scully finally to his son, the cow-boy, and the Easterner; and at the end of this scornful sentence he left the room.

Up-stairs the Swede was swiftly fastening the straps of his great valise. Once his back happened to be half turned towards the door, and, hearing a noise there, he wheeled and sprang up, uttering a loud cry. Scully's wrinkled visage showed grimly in the light of the small lamp he carried. This yellow effulgence, streaming upward, colored only his prominent features, and left his eyes, for instance, in mysterious shadow. He resembled a murderer.

"Man! man!" he exclaimed, "have you gone daffy?"

"Oh, no! Oh, no!" rejoined the other. "There are people in this world who know pretty nearly as much as you do—understand?"

For a moment they stood gazing at each other. Upon the Swede's deathly pale cheeks were two spots brightly crimson and sharply edged, as if they had been carefully painted. Scully placed the light on the table and sat himself on the edge of the bed. He spoke ruminatively. "By cracky, I never heard of such a thing in my life. It's a complete muddle. I can't, for the soul of me, think how you ever got this idea into your head." Presently he lifted his eyes and asked: "And did you sure think they were going to kill you?"

The Swede scanned the old man as if he wished to see into his mind. "I did," he said at last. He obviously suspected that this answer might precipitate an outbreak. As he pulled on a strap his whole arm shook, the elbow wavering like a bit of paper.

Scully banged his hand impressively on the foot-board of the bed. "Why, man, we're goin' to have a line of ilictric street-cars in this town next spring."

"'A line of electric street-cars,'" repeated the Swede, stupidly.

"And," said Scully, "there's a new railroad goin' to be built down from Broken Arm to here. Not to mintion the four churches and the smashin' big brick school-house. Then there's the big factory, too. Why, in two years Romper'll be a met-tro-*pol*-is."

Having finished the preparation of his baggage, the Swede straightened himself. "Mr. Scully," he said, with sudden hardihood, "how much do I owe you?"

"You don't owe me anythin'," said the old man, angrily.

"Yes, I do," retorted the Swede. He took seventy-five cents from his pocket and tendered it to Scully; but the latter snapped his fingers in disdainful refusal. However, it happened that they both stood gazing in a strange fashion at three silver pieces on the Swede's open palm.

"I'll not take your money," said Scully at last. "Not after what's been goin' on here." Then a plan seemed to strike him. "Here," he cried, picking up his lamp and moving towards the door. "Here! Come with me a minute."

"No," said the Swede, in overwhelming alarm.

"Yes," urged the old man. "Come on! I want you to come and see a picter—just across the hall—in my room."

The Swede must have concluded that his hour was come. His jaw dropped and his teeth showed like a dead man's. He ultimately followed Scully across the corridor, but he had the step of one hung in chains.

Scully flashed the light high on the wall of his own chamber. There was revealed a ridiculous photograph of a little girl. She was leaning against a balustrade of gorgeous decoration, and the formidable bang to her hair was prominent. The figure was as graceful as an upright sled-stake, and, withal, it was of the hue of lead. "There," said Scully, tenderly, "that's the picter of my little girl that died. Her name was Carrie. She had the purtiest hair you ever saw! I was that fond of her, she—"

Turning then, he saw that the Swede was not contemplating the picture at all, but, instead, was keeping keen watch on the gloom in the rear.

"Look, man!" cried Scully, heartily. "That's the picter of my little gal that died. Her name was Carrie. And then here's the picter of my oldest boy, Michael. He's a lawyer in Lincoln, an' doin' well. I gave that boy a grand eddycation, and I'm glad for it now. He's a fine boy. Look at 'im now. Ain't he bold as blazes, him there in Lincoln, an honored an' respicted gintleman. An honored and respicted gintleman," concluded Scully with a flourish. And, so saying, he smote the Swede jovially on the back.

The Swede faintly smiled.

"Now," said the old man, "there's only one more thing." He dropped suddenly to the floor and thrust his head beneath the bed. The Swede could hear his muffled voice. "I'd keep it under me piller if it wasn't for that boy Johnnie. Then there's the old woman— Where is it now? I never put it twice in the same place. Ah, now come out with you!"

Presently he backed clumsily from under the bed, dragging with him an old coat rolled into a bundle. "I've fetched him," he muttered. Kneeling on the floor, he unrolled the coat and extracted from its heart a large yellow-brown whisky bottle.

His first manœuvre was to hold the bottle up to the light. Reassured, apparently, that nobody had been tampering with it, he thrust it with a generous movement towards the Swede.

The weak-kneed Swede was about to eagerly clutch this element of strength, but he suddenly jerked his hand away and cast a look of horror upon Scully.

"Drink," said the old man affectionately. He had risen to his feet, and now stood facing the Swede.

There was a silence. Then again Scully said: "Drink!"

The Swede laughed wildly. He grabbed the bottle, put it to his mouth, and as his lips curled absurdly around the opening and his throat worked, he kept his glance, burning with hatred, upon the old man's face.

IV

After the departure of Scully the three men, with the card-board still upon their knees, preserved for a long time an astounded silence. Then Johnnie said: "That's the dod-dangedest Swede I ever see."

"He ain't no Swede," said the cowboy, scornfully.

"Well, what is he then?" cried Johnnie. "What is he then?"

"It's my opinion," replied the cowboy deliberately, "he's some kind of a Dutchman." It was a venerable custom of the country to entitle as Swedes all light-haired men who spoke with a heavy tongue. In consequence the idea of the cowboy was not without its daring. "Yes, sir," he repeated. "It's my opinion this feller is some kind of a Dutchman."

"Well, he says he's a Swede, anyhow," muttered Johnnie, sulkily. He turned to the Easterner: "What do you think, Mr. Blanc?"

"Oh, I don't know," replied the Easterner.

"Well, what do you think makes him act that way?" asked the cowboy.

"Why, he's frightened." The Easterner knocked his pipe against a rim of the stove. "He's clear frightened out of his boots."

"What at?" cried Johnnie and the cowboy together.

The Easterner reflected over his answer.

"What at?" cried the others again.

"Oh, I don't know, but it seems to me this man has been reading dime-novels, and he thinks he's right out in the middle of it—the shootin' and stabbin' and all."

"But," said the cowboy, deeply scandalized, "this ain't Wyoming, ner none of them places. This is Nebrasker."

"Yes," added Johnnie, "an' why don't he wait till he gits *out West?*"

The traveled Easterner laughed. "It isn't different there even—not in these days. But he thinks he's right in the middle of hell."

Johnnie and the cowboy mused long.

"It's awful funny," remarked Johnnie at last.

"Yes," said the cowboy. "This is a queer game. I hope we don't git snowed in, because then we'd have to stand this here man bein' around with us all the time. That wouldn't be no good."

"I wish pop would throw him out," said Johnnie.

Presently they heard a loud stamping on the stairs, accompanied by ringing jokes in the voice of old Scully, and laughter, evidently from the

Swede. The men around the stove stared vacantly at each other. "Gosh!" said the cowboy. The door flew open, and old Scully, flushed and anecdotal, came into the room. He was jabbering at the Swede, who followed him, laughing bravely. It was the entry of two roisterers from a banquet-hall.

"Come now," said Scully sharply to the three seated men, "move up and give us a chance at the stove." The cowboy and the Easterner obediently sidled their chairs to make room for the new-comers. Johnnie, however, simply arranged himself in a more indolent attitude, and then remained motionless.

"Come! Git over, there," said Scully.

"Plenty of room on the other side of the stove," said Johnnie.

"Do you think we want to sit in the draught?" roared the father.

But the Swede here interposed with a grandeur of confidence. "No, no. Let the boy sit where he likes," he cried in a bullying voice to the father.

"All right! All right!" said Scully, deferentially. The cowboy and the Easterner exchanged glances of wonder.

The five chairs were formed in a crescent about one side of the stove. The Swede began to talk; he talked arrogantly, profanely, angrily. Johnnie, the cowboy, and the Easterner maintained a morose silence, while old Scully appeared to be receptive and eager, breaking in constantly with sympathetic ejaculations.

Finally the Swede announced that he was thirsty. He moved in his chair, and said that he would go for a drink of water.

"I'll git it for you," cried Scully at once.

"No," said the Swede, contemptuously. "I'll get it for myself." He arose and stalked with the air of an owner off into the executive parts of the hotel.

As soon as the Swede was out of hearing Scully sprang to his feet and whispered intensely to the others: "Up-stairs he thought I was tryin' to poison 'im."

"Say," said Johnnie, "this makes me sick. Why don't you throw 'im out in the snow?"

"Why, he's all right now," declared Scully. "It was only that he was from the East, and he thought this was a tough place. That's all. He's all right now."

The cowboy looked with admiration upon the Easterner. "You were straight," he said. "You were on to that there Dutchman."

"Well," said Johnnie to his father, "he may be all right now, but I don't see it. Other time he was scared, but now he's too fresh."

Scully's speech was always a combination of Irish brogue and idiom, Western twang and idiom, and scraps of curiously formal diction taken from the story-books and newspapers. He now hurled a strange mass of language at the head of his son. "What do I keep? What do I keep? What do I keep?" he demanded, in a voice of thunder. He slapped his knee impressively, to indicate that he himself was going to make reply, and that all should heed. "I keep a hotel," he shouted. "A hotel, do you mind? A guest under my roof has sacred privileges. He is to be intimidated by none. Not one word shall he hear that would prijudice him in favor of goin' away. I'll not have it. There's no place in this here town where they can say they iver took in a guest of mine because he was afraid to stay here." He wheeled suddenly upon the cowboy and the Easterner. "Am I right?"

"Yes, Mr. Scully," said the cowboy, "I think you're right."

"Yes, Mr. Scully," said the Easterner, "I think you're right."

V

At six-o'clock supper, the Swede fizzed like a fire-wheel. He sometimes seemed on the point of bursting into riotous song, and in all his madness he was encouraged by old Scully. The Easterner was incased in reserve; the cowboy sat in wide-mouthed amazement, forgetting to eat, while Johnnie wrathily demolished great plates of food. The daughters of the house, when they were obliged to replenish the biscuits, approached as warily as Indians, and, having succeeded in their purpose, fled with ill-concealed trepidation. The Swede domineered the whole feast, and he gave it the appearance of a cruel bacchanal. He seemed to have grown suddenly taller; he gazed, brutally disdainful, into every face. His voice rang through the room. Once when he jabbed out harpoon-fashion with his fork to pinion a biscuit, the weapon nearly impaled the hand of the Easterner which had been stretched quietly out for the same biscuit.

After supper, as the men filed towards the other room, the Swede smote Scully ruthlessly on the shoulder. "Well, old boy, that was a good, square meal." Johnnie looked hopefully at his father; he knew that shoulder was tender from an old fall; and, indeed, it appeared for a moment as if Scully was going to flame out over the matter, but in the end he smiled a sickly smile and remained silent. The others understood from his manner that he was admitting his responsibility for the Swede's new view-point.

Johnnie, however, addressed his parent in an aside. "Why don't you license somebody to kick you down-stairs?" Scully scowled darkly by way of reply.

When they were gathered about the stove, the Swede insisted on another game of High-Five. Scully gently deprecated the plan at first, but the Swede turned a wolfish glare upon him. The old man subsided, and the Swede canvassed the others. In his tone there was always a great threat. The cowboy and the Easterner both remarked indifferently that they would play. Scully said that he would presently have to go to meet the 6:58 train, and so the Swede turned menacingly upon Johnnie. For a moment their glances crossed like blades, and then Johnnie smiled and said, "Yes, I'll play."

They formed a square, with the little board on their knees. The Easterner and the Swede were again partners. As the play went on, it was noticeable that the cowboy was not board-whacking as usual. Meanwhile,

Scully, near the lamp, had put on his spectacles and, with an appearance curiously like an old priest, was reading a newspaper. In time he went out to meet the 6:58 train, and, despite his precautions, a gust of polar wind whirled into the room as he opened the door. Besides scattering the cards, it chilled the players to the marrow. The Swede cursed frightfully. When Scully returned, his entrance disturbed a cozy and friendly scene. The Swede again cursed. But presently they were once more intent, their heads bent forward and their hands moving swiftly. The Swede had adopted the fashion of board-whacking.

Scully took up his paper and for a long time remained immersed in matters which were extraordinarily remote from him. The lamp burned badly, and once he stopped to adjust the wick. The newspaper, as he turned from page to page, rustled with a slow and comfortable sound. Then suddenly he heard three terrible words: "You are cheatin'!"

Such scenes often prove that there can be little of dramatic import in environment. Any room can present a tragic front; any room can be comic. This little den was now hideous as a torture-chamber. The new faces of the men themselves had changed it upon the instant. The Swede held a huge fist in front of Johnnie's face, while the latter looked steadily over it into the blazing orbs of his accuser. The Easterner had grown pallid; the cowboy's jaw had dropped in that expression of bovine amazement which was one of his important mannerisms. After the three words, the first sound in the room was made by Scully's paper as it floated forgotten to his feet. His spectacles had also fallen from his nose, but by a clutch he had saved them in air. His hand, grasping the spectacles, now remained poised awkwardly and near his shoulder. He stared at the card-players.

Probably the silence was while a second elapsed. Then, if the floor had been suddenly twitched out from under the men they could not have moved quicker. The five had projected themselves headlong towards a common point. It happened that Johnnie, in rising to hurl himself upon the Swede, had stumbled slightly because of his curiously instinctive care for the cards and the board. The loss of the moment allowed time for the arrival of Scully, and also allowed the cowboy time to give the Swede a great push which sent him staggering back. The men found tongue together, and hoarse shouts of rage, appeal, or fear burst from every throat. The cowboy pushed and jostled feverishly at the Swede, and the Easterner and Scully clung wildly to Johnnie; but, through the smoky air, above the swaying bodies of the peace-compellers, the eyes of the two warriors ever sought each other in glances of challenge that were at once hot and steely.

Of course the board had been overturned, and now the whole company of cards was scattered over the floor, where the boots of the men trampled the fat and painted kings and queens as they gazed with their silly eyes at the war that was waging above them.

Scully's voice was dominating the yells. "Stop now! Stop, I say! Stop, now—"

Johnnie, as he struggled to burst through the rank formed by Scully and the Easterner, was crying, "Well, he says I cheated! He says I cheated! I won't allow no man to say I cheated! If he says I cheated, he's a —— ——!"

The cowboy was telling the Swede, "Quit, now! Quit, d'ye hear—"

The screams of the Swede never ceased: "He did cheat! I saw him! I saw him—"

As for the Easterner, he was importuning in a voice that was not heeded: "Wait a moment, can't you? Oh, wait a moment. What's the good of a fight over a game of cards? Wait a moment—"

In this tumult no complete sentences were clear. "Cheat"—"Quit"—"He says"—these fragments pierced the uproar and rang out sharply. It was remarkable that, whereas Scully undoubtedly made the most noise, he was the least heard of any of the riotous band.

Then suddenly there was a great cessation. It was as if each man had paused for breath; and although the room was still lighted with the anger of men, it could be seen that there was no danger of immediate conflict, and at once Johnnie, shouldering his way forward, almost succeeded in confronting the Swede. "What did you say I cheated for? What did you say I cheated for? I don't cheat, and I won't let no man say I do!"

The Swede said, "I saw you! I saw you!"

"Well," cried Johnnie, "I'll fight any man what says I cheat!"

"No, you won't," said the cowboy. "Not here."

"Ah, be still, can't you?" said Scully, coming between them.

The quiet was sufficient to allow the Easterner's voice to be heard. He was repeating, "Oh, wait a moment, can't you? What's the good of a fight over a game of cards? Wait a moment!"

Johnnie, his red face appearing above his father's shoulder, hailed the Swede again. "Did you say I cheated?"

The Swede showed his teeth. "Yes."

"Then," said Johnnie, "we must fight."

"Yes, fight," roared the Swede. He was like a demoniac. "Yes, fight! I'll show you what kind of a man I am! I'll show you who you want to fight! Maybe you think I can't fight! Maybe you think I can't! I'll show you, you skin, you card-sharp! Yes, you cheated! You cheated! You cheated!"

"Well, let's go at it, then, mister," said Johnnie, coolly.

The cowboy's brow was beaded with sweat from his efforts in intercepting all sorts of raids. He turned in despair to Scully. "What are you goin' to do now?"

A change had come over the Celtic visage of the old man. He now seemed all eagerness; his eyes glowed.

"We'll let them fight," he answered, stalwartly. "I can't put up with it any longer. I've stood this damned Swede till I'm sick. We'll let them fight."

VI

The men prepared to go out-of-doors. The Easterner was so nervous that he had great difficulty in getting his arms into the sleeves of his new leather coat. As the cowboy drew his fur cap down over his ears his hands trembled. In fact, Johnnie and old Scully were the only ones who displayed no agitation. These preliminaries were conducted without words.

Scully threw open the door. "Well, come on," he said. Instantly a terrific wind caused the flame of the lamp to struggle at its wick, while a puff of black smoke sprang from the chimney-top. The stove was in mid-current of the blast, and its voice swelled to equal the roar of the storm. Some of the scarred and bedabbled cards were caught up from the floor and dashed helplessly against the farther wall. The men lowered their heads and plunged into the tempest as into a sea.

No snow was falling, but great whirls and clouds of flakes, swept up from the ground by the frantic winds, were streaming southward with the speed of bullets. The covered land was blue with the sheen of an unearthly satin, and there was no other hue save where, at the low, black railway station—which seemed incredibly distant—one light gleamed like a tiny jewel. As the men floundered into a thigh-deep drift, it was known that the Swede was bawling out something. Scully went to him, put a hand on his shoulder and projected an ear. "What's that you say?" he shouted.

"I say," bawled the Swede again, "I won't stand much show against this gang. I know you'll all pitch on me."

Scully smote him reproachfully on the arm. "Tut, man!" he yelled. The wind tore the words from Scully's lips and scattered them far alee.

"You are all a gang of—" boomed the Swede, but the storm also seized the remainder of this sentence.

Immediately turning their backs upon the wind, the men had swung around a corner to the sheltered side of the hotel. It was the function of the little house to preserve here, amid this great devastation of snow, an irregular V-shape of heavily incrusted grass, which crackled beneath the feet. One could imagine the great drifts piled against the windward side. When the party reached the comparative peace of this spot it was found that the Swede was still bellowing.

"Oh, I know what kind of a thing this is! I know you'll all pitch on me. I can't lick you all!"

Scully turned upon him panther-fashion. "You'll not have to whip all of us. You'll have to whip my son Johnnie. An' the man what troubles you durin' that time will have me to dale with."

The arrangements were swiftly made. The two men faced each other, obedient to the harsh commands of Scully, whose face, in the subtly luminous gloom, could be seen set in the austere impersonal lines that are pictured on the countenances of the Roman veterans. The Easterner's teeth were chattering, and he was hopping up and down like a mechanical toy. The cowboy stood rock-like.

The contestants had not stripped off any clothing. Each was in his ordinary attire. Their fists were up, and they eyed each other in a calm that had the elements of leonine cruelty in it.

During this pause, the Easterner's mind, like a film, took lasting impressions of three men—the iron-nerved master of the ceremony; the Swede, pale, motionless, terrible; and Johnnie, serene yet ferocious, brutish yet heroic. The entire prelude had in it a tragedy greater than the tragedy of action, and this aspect was accentuated by the long, mellow cry of the blizzard, as it sped the tumbling and wailing flakes into the black abyss of the south.

"Now!" said Scully.

The two combatants leaped forward and crashed together like bullocks. There was heard the cushioned sound of blows, and of a curse squeezing out from between the tight teeth of one.

As for the spectators, the Easterner's pent-up breath exploded from him with a pop of relief, absolute relief from the tension of the preliminaries. The cowboy bounded into the air with a yowl. Scully was immovable as from supreme amazement and fear at the fury of the fight which he himself had permitted and arranged.

For a time the encounter in the darkness was such a perplexity of flying arms that it presented no more detail than would a swiftly revolving wheel. Occasionally a face, as if illumined by a flash of light, would shine out, ghastly and marked with pink spots. A moment later, the men might have been known as shadows, if it were not for the involuntary utterance of oaths that came from them in whispers.

Suddenly a holocaust of warlike desire caught the cowboy, and he bolted forward with the speed of a broncho. "Go it, Johnnie! go it! Kill him! Kill him!"

Scully confronted him. "Kape back," he said; and by his glance the cowboy could tell that this man was Johnnie's father.

To the Easterner there was a monotony of unchangeable fighting that was an abomination. This confused mingling was eternal to his sense, which was concentrated in a longing for the end, the priceless end. Once the fighters lurched near him, and as he scrambled hastily backward he heard them breathe like men on the rack.

"Kill him, Johnnie! Kill him! Kill him! Kill him!" The cowboy's face was contorted like one of those agony masks in museums.

"Keep still," said Scully, icily.

Then there was a sudden loud grunt, incomplete, cut short, and Johnnie's body swung away from the Swede and fell with sickening heaviness to the grass. The cowboy was barely in time to prevent the mad Swede from flinging himself upon his prone adversary. "No, you don't," said the cowboy, interposing an arm. "Wait a second."

Scully was at his son's side. "Johnnie! Johnnie, me boy!" His voice had a quality of melancholy tenderness. "Johnnie! Can you go on with it?" He looked anxiously down into the bloody, pulpy face of his son.

There was a moment of silence, and then Johnnie answered in his ordinary voice, "Yes, I—it—yes."

Assisted by his father he struggled to his feet. "Wait a bit now till you git your wind," said the old man.

A few paces away the cowboy was lecturing the Swede. "No, you don't! Wait a second!"

The Easterner was plucking at Scully's sleeve. "Oh, this is enough," he pleaded. "This is enough! Let it go as it stands. This is enough!"

"Bill," said Scully, "git out of the road." The cowboy stepped aside. "Now." The combatants were actuated by a new caution as they advanced toward collision. They glared at each other, and then the Swede aimed a lightning blow that carried with it his entire weight. Johnnie was evidently half stupid from weakness, but he miraculously dodged, and his fist sent the over-balanced Swede sprawling.

The cowboy, Scully, and the Easterner burst into a cheer that was like a chorus of triumphant soldiery, but before its conclusion the Swede had scuffled agilely to his feet and come in berserk abandon at his foe. There was another perplexity of flying arms, and Johnnie's body again swung away and fell, even as a bundle might fall from a roof. The Swede instantly staggered to a little wind-waved tree and leaned upon it, breathing like an engine, while his savage and flame-lit eyes roamed from face to face as the men bent over Johnnie. There was a splendor of isolation in his situation at this time which the Easterner felt once when, lifting his eyes from the man on the ground, he beheld that mysterious and lonely figure, waiting.

"Are you any good yet, Johnnie?" asked Scully in a broken voice.

The son gasped and opened his eyes languidly. After a moment he answered, "No—I ain't—any good—any—more." Then, from shame and bodily ill, he began to weep, the tears furrowing down through the bloodstains on his face. "He was too—too—too heavy for me."

Scully straightened and addressed the waiting figure. "Stranger," he said, evenly, "it's all up with our side." Then his voice changed into that vibrant huskiness which is commonly the tone of the most simple and deadly announcements. "Johnnie is whipped."

Without replying, the victor moved off on the route to the front door of the hotel.

The cowboy was formulating new and unspellable blasphemies. The Easterner was startled to find that they were out in a wind that seemed to come direct from the shadowed arctic floes. He heard again the wail of the snow as it was flung to its grave in the south. He knew now that all this time the cold had been sinking into him deeper and deeper, and he wondered that he had not perished. He felt indifferent to the condition of the vanquished man.

"Johnnie, can you walk?" asked Scully.

"Did I hurt—hurt him any?" asked the son.

"Can you walk, boy? Can you walk?"

Johnnie's voice was suddenly strong. There was a robust impatience in it. "I asked you whether I hurt him any!"

"Yes, yes, Johnnie," answered the cowboy, consolingly; "he's hurt a good deal."

They raised him from the ground, and as soon as he was on his feet he went tottering off, rebuffing all attempts at assistance. When the party rounded the corner they were fairly blinded by the pelting of the snow. It burned their faces like fire. The cowboy carried Johnnie through the drift to the door. As they entered, some cards again rose from the floor and beat against the wall.

The Easterner rushed to the stove. He was so profoundly chilled that he almost dared to embrace the glowing iron. The Swede was not in the room. Johnnie sank into a chair, and, folding his arms on his knees, buried his face in them. Scully, warming one foot and then the other at a rim of the stove, muttered to himself with Celtic mournfulness. The cowboy had removed his fur cap, and with a dazed and rueful air he was running one hand through his tousled locks. From overhead they could hear the creaking of boards, as the Swede tramped here and there in his room.

The sad quiet was broken by the sudden flinging open of a door that led towards the kitchen. It was instantly followed by an inrush of women. They precipitated themselves upon Johnnie amid a chorus of lamentation. Before they carried their prey off to the kitchen, there to be bathed and harangued with that mixture of sympathy and abuse which is a feat of their sex, the mother straightened herself and fixed old Scully with an eye of stern reproach. "Shame be upon you, Patrick Scully!" she cried. "Your own son, too. Shame be upon you!"

"There, now! Be quiet, now!" said the old man, weakly.

"Shame be upon you, Patrick Scully!" The girls, rallying to this slogan, sniffed disdainfully in the direction of those trembling accomplices, the cowboy and the Easterner. Presently they bore Johnnie away, and left the three men to dismal reflection.

VII

"I'd like to fight this here Dutchman myself," said the cowboy, breaking a long silence.

Scully wagged his head sadly. "No, that wouldn't do. It wouldn't be right. It wouldn't be right."

"Well, why wouldn't it?" argued the cowboy. "I don't see no harm in it."

"No," answered Scully, with mournful heroism. "It wouldn't be right. It was Johnnie's fight, and now we mustn't whip the man just because he whipped Johnnie."

"Yes, that's true enough," said the cowboy; "but—he better not get fresh with me, because I couldn't stand no more of it."

"You'll not say a word to him," commanded Scully, and even then they heard the tread of the Swede on the stairs. His entrance was made theatric. He swept the door back with a bang and swaggered to the middle of the room. No one looked at him. "Well," he cried, insolently, at Scully, "I s'pose you'll tell me now how much I owe you?"

The old man remained stolid. "You don't owe me nothin'."

"Huh!" said the Swede, "huh! Don't owe 'im nothin'."

The cowboy addressed the Swede. "Stranger, I don't see how you come to be so gay around here."

Old Scully was instantly alert. "Stop!" he shouted, holding his hand forth, fingers upward. "Bill, you shut up!"

The cowboy spat carelessly into the sawdust box. "I didn't say a word, did I?" he asked.

"Mr. Scully," called the Swede, "how much do I owe you?" It was seen that he was attired for departure, and that he had his valise in his hand.

"You don't owe me nothin'," repeated Scully in his same imperturbable way.

"Huh!" said the Swede. "I guess you're right. I guess if it was any way at all, you'd owe me somethin'. That's what I guess." He turned to the cowboy. "'Kill him! Kill him! Kill him!'" he mimicked, and then guffawed victoriously. "'Kill him!'" He was convulsed with ironical humor.

But he might have been jeering the dead. The three men were immovable and silent, staring with glassy eyes at the stove.

The Swede opened the door and passed into the storm, giving one derisive glance backward at the still group.

As soon as the door was closed, Scully and the cowboy leaped to their feet and began to curse. They trampled to and fro, waving their arms and smashing into the air with their fists. "Oh, but that was a hard minute!" wailed Scully. "That was a hard minute! Him there leerin' and scoffin'! One bang at his nose was worth forty dollars to me that minute! How did you stand it, Bill?"

"How did I stand it?" cried the cowboy in a quivering voice. "How did I stand it? Oh!"

The old man burst into sudden brogue. "I'd loike to take that Swade," he wailed, "and hould 'im down on a shtone flure and bate 'im to a jelly wid a shtick!"

The cowboy groaned in sympathy. "I'd like to git him by the neck and ha-ammer him"—he brought his hand down on a chair with a noise like a pistol-shot—"hammer that there Dutchman until he couldn't tell himself from a dead coyote!"

"I'd bate 'im until he—"

"I'd show *him* some things—"

And then together they raised a yearning, fanatic cry—"Oh-o-oh! if we only could—"

"Yes!"

"Yes!"

"And then I'd—"

"O-o-oh!"

VIII

The Swede, tightly gripping his valise, tacked across the face of the storm as if he carried sails. He was following a line of little naked, gasping trees, which he knew must mark the way of the road. His face, fresh from the pounding of Johnnie's fists, felt more pleasure than pain in the wind and the driving snow. A number of square shapes loomed upon him finally, and he knew them as the houses of the main body of the town. He found a street and made travel along it, leaning heavily upon the wind whenever, at a corner, a terrific blast caught him.

He might have been in a deserted village. We picture the world as thick with conquering and elate humanity, but here, with the bugles of the tempest pealing, it was hard to imagine a peopled earth. One viewed the existence of man then as a marvel, and conceded a glamour of wonder to these lice which were caused to cling to a whirling, fire-smitten,[1] ice-locked, disease-stricken, space-lost bulb. The conceit of man was explained by this storm to be the very engine of life. One was a coxcomb not to die in it. However, the Swede found a saloon.

In front of it an indomitable red light was burning, and the snowflakes were made blood-color as they flew through the circumscribed territory of the lamp's shining. The Swede pushed open the door of the saloon and entered. A sanded expanse was before him, and at the end of it four men sat about a table drinking. Down one side of the room extended a radiant bar, and its guardian was leaning upon his elbows listening to the talk of the men at the table. The Swede dropped his valise upon the floor, and, smiling fraternally upon the barkeeper, said, "Gimme some whisky, will you?" The man placed a bottle, a whisky-glass, and a glass of ice-thick water upon the bar. The Swede poured himself an abnormal portion of whisky and drank it in three gulps. "Pretty bad night," remarked the bartender, indifferently. He was making the pretension of blindness which is usually a distinction of his class; but it could have been seen that he was furtively studying the half-erased blood-stains on the face of the Swede. "Bad night," he said again.

"Oh, it's good enough for me," replied the Swede, hardily, as he poured himself some more whisky. The barkeeper took his coin and manœuvred it through its reception by the highly nickelled cash-machine. A bell rang; a card labelled "20 cts." had appeared.

"No," continued the Swede, "this isn't too bad weather. It's good enough for me."

---

[1] Crane wrote "fire-smote."

"So?" murmured the barkeeper, languidly.

The copious drams made the Swede's eyes swim, and he breathed a trifle heavier. "Yes, I like this weather. I like it. It suits me." It was apparently his design to impart a deep significance to these words.

"So?" murmured the bartender again. He turned to gaze dreamily at the scroll-like birds and bird-like scrolls which had been drawn with soap upon the mirrors back of the bar.

"Well, I guess I'll take another drink," said the Swede, presently. "Have something?"

"No, thanks; I'm not drinkin'," answered the bartender. Afterwards he asked, "How did you hurt your face?"

The Swede immediately began to boast loudly. "Why, in a fight. I thumped the soul out of a man down here at Scully's hotel."

The interest of the four men at the table was at last aroused.

"Who was it?" said one.

"Johnnie Scully," blustered the Swede. "Son of the man what runs it. He will be pretty near dead for some weeks, I can tell you. I made a nice thing of him, I did. He couldn't get up. They carried him in the house. Have a drink?"

Instantly the men in some subtle way incased themselves in reserve. "No, thanks," said one. The group was of curious formation. Two were prominent local business men; one was the district-attorney; and one was a professional gambler of the kind known as "square." But a scrutiny of the group would not have enabled an observer to pick the gambler from the men of more reputable pursuits. He was, in fact, a man so delicate in manner, when among people of fair class, and so judicious in his choice of victims, that in the strictly masculine part of the town's life he had come to be explicitly trusted and admired. People called him a thoroughbred. The fear and contempt with which his craft was regarded was undoubtedly the reason that his quiet dignity shone conspicuous above the quiet dignity of men who might be merely hatters, billiard-markers, or grocery-clerks. Beyond an occasional unwary traveler who came by rail, this gambler was supposed to prey solely upon reckless and senile farmers, who, when flush with good crops, drove into town in all the pride and confidence of an absolutely invulnerable stupidity. Hearing at times in circuitous fashion of the despoilment of such a farmer, the important men of Romper invariably laughed in contempt of the victim, and, if they thought of the wolf at all, it was with a kind of pride at the knowledge that he would never dare think of attacking their wisdom and courage. Besides, it was popular that this gambler had a real wife and two real children in a neat cottage in a suburb, where he led an exemplary home life; and when any one even suggested a discrepancy in his character, the crowd immediately vociferated descriptions of this virtuous family circle. Then men who led exemplary home lives, and men who did not lead exemplary home lives, all subsided in a bunch, remarking that there was nothing more to be said.

However, when a restriction was placed upon him—as, for instance, when a strong clique of members of the new Pollywog Club refused to permit him, even as a spectator, to appear in the rooms of the organization—the candor and gentleness with which he accepted the judgment disarmed many of his foes and made his friends more desperately partisan. He invariably distinguished between himself and a respectable Romper man so quickly and frankly that his manner actually appeared to be a continual broadcast compliment.

And one must not forget to declare the fundamental fact of his entire position in Romper. It is irrefutable that in all affairs outside of his business, in all matters that occur eternally and commonly between man and man, this thieving card-player was so generous, so just, so moral, that, in a contest, he could have put to flight the consciences of nine-tenths of the citizens of Romper.

And so it happened that he was seated in this saloon with the two prominent local merchants and the district-attorney.

The Swede continued to drink raw whisky, meanwhile babbling at the barkeeper and trying to induce him to indulge in potations. "Come on. Have a drink. Come on. What—no? Well, have a little one, then. By gawd, I've whipped a man to-night, and I want to celebrate. I whipped him good, too. Gentlemen," the Swede cried to the men at the table, "have a drink?"

"Ssh!" said the barkeeper.

The group at the table, although furtively attentive, had been pretending to be deep in talk, but now a man lifted his eyes towards the Swede and said, shortly, "Thanks. We don't want any more."

At this reply the Swede ruffled out his chest like a rooster. "Well," he exploded, "it seems I can't get anybody to drink with me in this town. Seems so, don't it? Well!"

"Ssh!" said the barkeeper.

"Say," snarled the Swede, "don't you try to shut me up. I won't have it. I'm a gentleman, and I want people to drink with me. And I want 'em to drink with me now. *Now*—do you understand?" He rapped the bar with his knuckles.

Years of experience had calloused the bartender. He merely grew sulky. "I hear you," he answered.

"Well," cried the Swede, "listen hard then. See those men over there? Well, they're going to drink with me, and don't you forget it. Now you watch."

"Hi!" yelled the barkeeper, "this won't do!"

"Why won't it?" demanded the Swede. He stalked over to the table, and by chance laid his hand upon the shoulder of the gambler. "How about this?" he asked, wrathfully. "I asked you to drink with me."

The gambler simply twisted his head and spoke over his shoulder. "My friend, I don't know you."

"Oh, hell!" answered the Swede, "come and have a drink."

"Now, my boy," advised the gambler, kindly, "take your hand off my shoulder and go 'way and mind your own business." He was a little, slim man, and it seemed strange to hear him use this tone of heroic patronage to the burly Swede. The other men at the table said nothing.

"What! You won't drink with me, you little dude? I'll make you then! I'll make you!" The Swede had grasped the gambler frenziedly at the throat, and was dragging him from his chair. The other men sprang up. The barkeeper dashed around the corner of his bar. There was a great tumult, and then was seen a long blade in the hand of the gambler. It shot forward, and a human body, this citadel of virtue, wisdom, power, was pierced as easily as if it had been a melon. The Swede fell with a cry of supreme astonishment.

The prominent merchants and the district-attorney must have at once tumbled out of the place backward. The bartender found himself hanging limply to the arm of a chair and gazing into the eyes of a murderer.

"Henry," said the latter, as he wiped his knife on one of the towels that hung beneath the bar-rail, "you tell 'em where to find me. I'll be home, waiting for 'em." Then he vanished. A moment afterwards the barkeeper was in the street dinning through the storm for help, and, moreover, companionship.

The corpse of the Swede, alone in the saloon, had its eyes fixed upon a dreadful legend that dwelt atop of the cash-machine: "This registers the amount of your purchase."

IX

Months later, the cowboy was frying pork over the stove of a little ranch near the Dakota line, when there was a quick thud of hoofs outside, and presently the Easterner entered with the letters and the papers.

"Well," said the Easterner at once, "the chap that killed the Swede has got three years. Wasn't much, was it?"

"He has? Three years?" The cowboy poised his pan of pork, while he ruminated upon the news. "Three years. That ain't much."

"No. It was a light sentence," replied the Easterner as he unbuckled his spurs. "Seems there was a good deal of sympathy for him in Romper."

"If the bartender had been any good," observed the cowboy, thoughtfully, "he would have gone in and cracked that there Dutchman on the head with a bottle in the beginnin' of it and stopped all this here murderin'."

"Yes, a thousand things might have happened," said the Easterner, tartly.

The cowboy returned his pan of pork to the fire, but his philosophy continued. "It's funny, ain't it? If he hadn't said Johnnie was cheatin' he'd be alive this minute. He was an awful fool. Game played for fun, too. Not for money. I believe he was crazy."

"I feel sorry for that gambler," said the Easterner.

"Oh, so do I," said the cowboy. "He don't deserve none of it for killin' who he did."

"The Swede might not have been killed if everything had been square."

"Might not have been killed?" exclaimed the cowboy. "Everythin' square? Why, when he said that Johnnie was cheatin' and acted like such a jackass? And then in the saloon he fairly walked up to git hurt?" With these arguments the cowboy browbeat the Easterner and reduced him to rage.

"You're a fool!" cried the Easterner, viciously. "You're a bigger jackass than the Swede by a million majority. Now let me tell you one thing. Let me tell you something. Listen! Johnnie *was* cheating!"

" 'Johnnie,' " said the cowboy, blankly. There was a minute of silence, and then he said, robustly, "Why, no. The game was only for fun."

"Fun or not," said the Easterner, "Johnnie was cheating. I saw him. I know it. I saw him. And I refused to stand up and be a man. I let the Swede fight it out alone. And you—you were simply puffing around the place and wanting to fight. And then old Scully himself! We are all in it! This poor gambler isn't even a noun. He is kind of an adverb. Every sin is the result of a collaboration. We, five of us, have collaborated in the murder of this Swede. Usually there are from a dozen to forty women really involved in every murder, but in this case it seems to be only five men—you, I, Johnnie, old Scully; and that fool of an unfortunate gambler came merely as a culmination, the apex of a human movement, and gets all the punishment."

The cowboy, injured and rebellious, cried out blindly into this fog of mysterious theory: "Well, I didn't do anythin', did I?"

1898

FROM THE BLACK RIDERS AND
OTHER LINES

3

In the desert
I saw a creature, naked, bestial,
Who, squatting upon the ground,
Held his heart in his hands,
And ate of it.   5
I said, "Is it good, friend?"
"It is bitter—bitter," he answered;
"But I like it
Because it is bitter,
And because it is my heart."   10

6

God fashioned the ship of the world carefully.
With the infinite skill of an All-Master
Made He the hull and the sails,
Held He the rudder
Ready for adjustment.   5
Erect stood He, scanning His work proudly.
Then—at fateful time—a wrong called,
And God turned, heeding.
Lo, the ship, at this opportunity, slipped slyly,
Making cunning noiseless travel down the ways.   10
So that, forever rudderless, it went upon the seas
Going ridiculous voyages,
Making quaint progress,
Turning as with serious purpose
Before stupid winds.   15
And there were many in the sky
Who laughed at this thing.

10

Should the wide world roll away,
Leaving black terror,
Limitless night,
Nor God, nor man, nor place to stand
Would be to me essential,   5
If thou and thy white arms were there,
And the fall to doom a long way.

13

If there is a witness to my little life,
To my tiny throes and struggles,
He sees a fool;
And it is not fine for gods to menace fools.

18

In heaven,
Some little blades of grass
Stood before God.
"What did you do?"
Then all save one of the little blades   5
Began eagerly to relate
The merits of their lives.
This one stayed a small way behind,
Ashamed.
Presently, God said,   10
"And what did you do?"
The little blade answered, "Oh, my Lord,

Memory is bitter to me,
For, if I did good deeds,
I know not of them."
Then God, in all His splendor,
Arose from His throne.
"Oh, best little blade of grass!" He said.

21

There was, before me,
Mile upon mile
Of snow, ice, burning sand.
And yet I could look beyond all this,
To a place of infinite beauty;
And I could see the loveliness of her
Who walked in the shade of the trees.
When I gazed,
All was lost
But this place of beauty and her.
When I gazed,
And in my gazing, desired,
Then came again
Mile upon mile,
Of snow, ice, burning sand.

36

I met a seer.
He held in his hands
The book of wisdom.
"Sir," I addressed him,
"Let me read."
"Child—" he began.
"Sir," I said,
"Think not that I am a child,
For already I know much
Of that which you hold.
Aye, much."

He smiled.
Then he opened the book
And held it before me.—
Strange that I should have grown so suddenly blind.

68

A spirit sped
Through spaces of night;
And as he sped, he called,
"God! God!"
He went through valleys

Of black death-slime,
Ever calling,
"God! God!"
Their echoes
From crevice and cavern   10
Mocked him:
"God! God! God!"
Fleetly into the plains of space
He went, ever calling,
"God! God!"   15
Eventually, then, he screamed,
Mad in denial,
"Ah, there is no God!"
A swift hand,
A sword from the sky,   20
Smote him,
And he was dead.

                              1895

THE BLUE BATTALIONS

Aside from its compressed metaphoric language, the most striking aspect of this poem is its image of an understanding God who does not scorn mankind. Suggesting a kind of militant judgment day, "The Blue Battalions" is free from the irony and outrage usually characteristic of Crane's verse. It is here reprinted from Elbert Hubbard's magazine *Philistine*, June 1898, where it first appeared. In the same year it was anthologized in a volume of *Spanish-American War Songs*, but it was not inspired by that conflict, having been written no later than 1896. Crane did not include it in *War Is Kind*, although Follett mistakenly added it to that volume in *Work* and *Collected Poems*. Hoffman, who considers it the author's "most significant poem," gives a detailed and appreciative analysis in *The Poetry of Stephen Crane*, pp. 163-74.

When a people reach the top of a hill
Then does God lean toward them,
Shortens tongues and lengthens arms.
A vision of their dead comes to the weak.
    The moon shall not be too old   5
    Before the new battalions rise,
        Blue battalions.
    The moon shall not be too old
    When the children of change shall fall
    Before the new battalions,   10
        The blue battalions.

Mistakes and virtues will be trampled deep.
A church and a thief shall fall together.
A sword will come at the bidding of the eyeless.
The God-led, turning only to beckon,   15
  Swinging a creed like a censer
  At the head of the new battalions,
    Blue battalions.
March the tools of nature's impulse,
Men born of wrong, men born of right,   20
Men of the new battalions,
  The blue battalions.

The clang of swords is thy wisdom,
The wounded make gestures like thy Son's,
The feet of mad horses is one part—   25
Aye, another is the hand of a mother on the brow of a youth.
  Then, swift as they charge thro a shadow,
  The men of the new battalions,
    Blue battalions.
God lead them high, God lead them far,   30
God lead them far, God lead them high,
These new battalions,
  The blue battalions.

                                              1898

From WAR IS KIND AND OTHER LINES

I

Do not weep, maiden, for war is kind.
Because your lover threw wild hands toward the sky
And the affrighted steed ran on alone,
Do not weep.
War is kind.   5

  Hoarse, booming drums of the regiment,
  Little souls who thirst for fight,
  These men were born to drill and die.
  The unexplained glory flies above them,
  Great is the battle-god, great, and his kingdom—   10
  A field where a thousand corpses lie.

Do not weep, babe, for war is kind.
Because your father tumbled in the yellow trenches,
Raged at his breast, gulped and died,
Do not weep.
War is kind.   15

Swift blazing flag of the regiment,
Eagle with crest of red and gold,
These men were born to drill and die.
Point for them the virtue of slaughter,   20
Make plain to them the excellence of killing
And a field where a thousand corpses lie.

Mother whose heart hung humble as a button
On the bright splendid shroud of your son,
Do not weep.   25
War is kind.

5

"Have you ever made a just man?"
"Oh, I have made three," answered God,
"But two of them are dead,
And the third—
Listen! Listen!   5
And you will hear the thud of his defeat."

6

I explain the silvered passing of a ship at night,
The sweep of each sad lost wave,
The dwindling boom of the steel thing's striving,
The little cry of a man to a man,
A shadow falling across the greyer night,   5
And the sinking of the small star;

Then the waste, the far waste of waters,
And the soft lashing of black waves
For long and in loneliness.

Remember, thou, O ship of love,   10
Thou leavest a far waste of waters,
And the soft lashing of black waves
For long and in loneliness.

12

A newspaper is a collection of half-injustices
Which, bawled by boys from mile to mile,
Spreads its curious opinion
To a million merciful and sneering men,
While families cuddle the joys of the fireside   5
When spurred by tale of dire lone agony.
A newspaper is a court
Where every one is kindly and unfairly tried
By a squalor of honest men.
A newspaper is a market   10

Where wisdom sells its freedom
And melons are crowned by the crowd.
A newspaper is a game
Where his error scores the player victory
While another's skill wins death.   15
A newspaper is a symbol;
A collection of loud tales
It is fetless [1] life's chronicle,
Concentrating eternal stupidities,
That in remote ages lived unhaltered,   20
Roaming through a fenceless world.

13

The wayfarer,
Perceiving the pathway to truth,
Was struck with astonishment.
It was thickly grown with weeds.
"Ha," he said,   5
"I see that none has passed here
In a long time."
Later he saw that each weed
Was a singular knife.
"Well," he mumbled at last,   10
"Doubtless there are other roads."

21

A man said to the universe:
"Sir, I exist!"
"However," replied the universe,
"The fact has not created in me
A sense of obligation."   5

25

Each small gleam was a voice,
A lantern voice—
In little songs of carmine, violet, green, gold.
A chorus of colors came over the water;
The wondrous leaf-shadows no longer wavered,   5
No pines crooned on the hills,
The blue night was elsewhere a silence,
When the chorus of colors came over the water,
Little songs of carmine, violet, green, gold.

Small glowing pebbles   10
Thrown on the dark plane of evening
Sing good ballads of God

[1] Crane probably meant "feckless," a reading adopted by Follett in *Work* and *Collected Poems*.

And eternity, with soul's rest.
Little priests, little holy fathers,
None can doubt the truth of your hymning,   15
When the marvellous chorus comes over the water,
Songs of carmine, violet, green, gold.

                                        1899

EUGENE O'NEILL

1888–1953

E UGENE GLADSTONE O'NEILL WROTE HALF A HUNDRED PLAYS DURING THREE
decades of lonely work—lonely save for the few early years when he was
associated with the Provincetown players on Cape Cod and in Greenwich
Village. He was by nature solitary and rather sombre; and he was driven
by great tension and nervous energy. During the 1920's he wrote more
successful plays than most dramatists produce in a lifetime and they won
him recognition upon the stages of the world. Other Americans had written significant drama before him but none gained the international recognition given O'Neill. He was awarded the Nobel prize at a moment
when the Swedish Academy was still chary in recognizing American literary achievement; and in his own country he received the Pulitzer prize
three times.

O'Neill tended to hold aloof from the professional literary world. He
was a man of the theatre rather than a man of letters; his plays live on the
stage rather than in the library. This, no doubt, is where plays are supposed to live; but it must be recognized that the dramatist, by the very
fact that he uses words, is involved in a literary process. The best "theatre" of the ages has been a part of literature. And although O'Neill possessed a distinctly poetic imagination he could not find language noble
enough to give expression to it. He could create extraordinary tension
behind the proscenium; yet more often than not it was conveyed by an
impoverished and stale speech. Only when his characters express themselves in their own idiom do the plays acquire poetic as well as theatric
force. Other of his characters speak in the clichés of romantic drama.

The dramatic imagination of Eugene O'Neill was dark and fatalistic.
The genius of comedy usually fled the theatre when O'Neill approached.
Ah Wilderness! was his isolated venture into comedy and it derives its
humor from its wistfulness rather than from genuine comic situations and

comic dialogue. He wrote, to be sure, a play called *Lazarus Laughed*, but the laughter is the laughter of despair. For Eugene O'Neill saw life as savage and without hope: an endless struggle by man against forces which mould him—and doom him. In this sense O'Neill can be said to be a naturalist. His plays are deterministic and his characters are the helpless pawns of heredity and environment. They curse the land; but they remain on it. They curse the sea, but they always return to their ships. Whiskey is their general anaesthetic and prostitutes their sole anodyne. The sense of fate is large and oppressive in the dramas of Eugene O'Neill.

As a dramatist O'Neill marked the end of a period in the American theatre as well as a beginning. He ended the naturalistic phase which had come to us from Zola and had been reflected in the fiction of Crane, Norris, and Dreiser. But he opened up the era of expressive symbolism on the stage, seeking a still greater realism in the theatre by discovering symbolic ways of rendering life. His early masters were Ibsen and Strindberg and the Russian novelists; later he learned from certain of the avant-garde Germans and notably the "expressionists." To suggest rather than to reproduce, to create an atmosphere and a mood on the stage which serves to convey reality rather than to represent it, this was the method of the symbolists in the theatre as on the printed page. The task of the dramatist in these circumstances was to find the setting and action for projecting the given emotion.

From the first O'Neill showed himself to be a restless explorer of stage effect. The use of recurrent sound (the beating of tom-toms, or the vibrant monotone of fog-horns); the introduction of masks, as in the classic Greek plays, adapted to modern use; the attempt to bring "stream of consciousness" into the theatre by reviving monologue, soliloquy and aside; the use of simultaneous action, as first attempted by the Europeans (by removing, for instance, the façade of a house and showing what is going on in several rooms at the same time); the "stylization" of certain scenes (as in the Fifth Avenue episode in *The Hairy Ape* in which passersby are represented as automatons)—O'Neill, with great boldness, used whatever technique or device could serve him best to render his subject. At a time when theatrical producers stressed old-time rigidities and brevity, in order to squeeze a play between supper and suburban train, O'Neill wrote longer and longer plays. He asked his audiences to squeeze *their* suppers between the opening action of his play and its later portion. To the surprise of commercial producers, O'Neill's audiences willingly accepted these changes and flocked to see him. As for the time-worn speech taboos, O'Neill utterly defied them. What he lacked in poetry he made up in profanity. He never hesitated to use uncouth language if that was the way a character was supposed to speak; and the anomaly is, as we have noted, that when he achieved realistic utterance, he was at his most poetic.

These theatrical innovations may now seem commonplace; but in O'Neill's time they made for an experimental theatre and created a sense of excitement in the audience. One remarkable experiment of another kind which O'Neill made late in life did not belong to the realm of technique. This was his writing for production after his death of certain autobiographical plays, of which *Long Day's Journal into Night* is the best known. Criticism does not seem to have done sufficient justice to the high originality of O'Neill's concept: that of writing autobiography in his own medium. Whenever playwrights have written their memoirs they have usually done so in the form of a book, not of a play. O'Neill was the first playwright to write a play which, while being a valid, and indeed remarkable, vehicle in the theatre, was at the same time a biographical document. *Long Day's Journey* seems to assert the dramatist's right to use the stage for telling his personal story, without disguising it in fictional dress.

To arrive at this final experiment, Eugene O'Neill passed through a long apprenticeship. He was born into the theatre. His father was a popular romantic actor who had cherished great dreams of becoming a supreme tragedian; instead he trouped through the cities and towns of America playing a hackneyed version of *The Count of Monte Cristo*. His tours were financial successes; but he undertook them with a feeling that he was sacrificing his art for money. O'Neill's mother, who had once planned to enter a convent, travelled with her husband and spent many lonely hours in small-town hotels. Through poor medical treatment she became a drug addict. Eugene on his side was a precocious alcoholic and frequenter of brothels. By his mid-twenties the future dramatist had sailed the seas as a common sailor, tramped in many harbors, been a beachcomber, prospected for gold, and tried his hand at journalism. There came a moment, in 1912, when he discovered that he had tuberculosis. This he later regarded (as his autobiographical plays show) as the climactic moment in his life.

O'Neill's experience in the sanatorium for consumptives was not unlike that of Thomas Mann's hero in *The Magic Mountain*. He was not seriously ill and his recovery was rapid. Nevertheless, weeks of enforced idleness gave him an opportunity to reflect upon his life. It had been a life largely of thoughtless action and of derelict wandering. He had been an "outsider," a tramp, a young man in revolt and in flight alike from family and from self. Now he began to channel his youthful rebellion into plays; what he had acted out in life he could project successfully as action in the theatre—his bitter feeling of not "belonging," the sustained sense that he was caught in old forces and in a sordid world from which his only escape thus far had been through illness. The plays of Eugene O'Neill mirrored his own tragic tension; they also contained a vivid projection of the social conditions and the seamy life he had come to know at first hand.

His first plays were melodramas; certain of these he published in a volume called *Thirst*. Others he destroyed, but only after depositing scripts in Washington for copyright purposes. Years later these were exhumed by other hands and published without O'Neill's consent as his "lost" plays. They serve, however, as a record of his early fumblings for dramatic statement. On leaving the sanatorium O'Neill briefly went to Harvard to take a course in play-writing, and then had the good fortune to fall in with a group of writers and artists in Provincetown. Here his plays received a trying-out in the wharf theatre. Later in Greenwich Village, in a converted stable in Macdougal Street, the Provincetown experimental theatre was established as an off-Broadway "Playwrights Theater." It made its mark on the contemporary stage, largely by launching O'Neill. What the group gave the dramatist was a chance to see his plays come to life—and an audience. By the time this workshop phase was over he was an established playwright.

This was the first phase of O'Neill's career and it lasted from 1913 to 1918. Out of it emerged the one-act plays of the sea, among them *The Moon of the Caribbees, Bound East for Cardiff,* and *The Long Voyage Home.* In these plays O'Neill was not only learning how to construct his plays, but also searching to find the language of dramatic statement. His protagonists are nearly all helpless individuals, caught up in life and yielding to it in bewilderment. In one a sailor dies in a brawl on deck as the ship is lying in a Caribbean harbor; in another a seaman is dying, after an accident, with a sense of his life unlived; in another a sailor is shanghaied. O'Neill's subjects here are pathetic rather than tragic; there is no struggle—only defeat.

On a deeper level the plays of this first phase seem to be saying to us that however much one may journey upon the face of the earth, life is but a round of ports and bars and prostitutes, a series of illusions carried out to sea and brought back to shore. The "old devil" sea, like an all-embracing mother, reclaims her sons, whether they live or die; and in their wanderings they seem to be completely in a fog—that recurrent symbol of O'Neill's plays—lost and without direction.

The second phase of O'Neill's career marked a sharp change. It lasted from 1918 to 1925, and during this time he wrote some sixteen plays (several had been sketched earlier), of which nearly all reached the stage. To this period belongs his universal success, *The Emperor Jones,* a stark drama of a Negro porter's rise to be "emperor" among a group of savages on a remote island by convincing them that he has a charmed life; and his regression to the savage state in a few hours of jungle nightmare. Also in this period came *The Hairy Ape,* with its vivid scenes of life in a ship's stokehole; *Beyond the Horizon,* dealing with a frustrated dreamer on a farm; and *Anna Christie,* one of O'Neill's best-liked plays, the story of a prostitute who seeks to marry and lead a normal life. There was also a forthright play about race relations, *All God's Chillun Got Wings;* and the period ended with one of O'Neill's most powerful dramas, *Desire Under the Elms,* in which he described a struggle for power between a farmer and his sons on a granite New England farm.

Viewed in the light of biography, this second period was O'Neill's large effort to escape from the fog in which he had been groping in the early plays. Some of his characters seek grandeur, they think themselves "different"; they try to change themselves into something finer than they are, but they fail. The Negro porter has made himself into an "Emperor" and almost convinced himself that he is unconquerable; the stoker in *The Hairy Ape* fancies himself the very pivot of the world, the keeper of its Promethean flame. And the drama resides in his discovery that he does not "belong," that he is the obscurest of the obscure, hidden in his grimy stokehole. Anna Christie also cannot escape her past. She may swear an oath of fidelity to her husband in spite of her sordid earlier life, but the doubt in her husband-lover's mind is not erased. Similarly in *Desire Under the Elms* the characters are possessed by old circumstances and primitive passions; sons are turned against the father, a son possesses his step-mother, the ill-gotten child is strangled in the cradle. Blind passion, pre-determined by earlier passions, rules. In the characteristic plays of this period the struggle against fate has been on a much larger scale than in the earlier ones; but the defeat in the end is the same.

The third phase of O'Neill's career extended from 1925 to 1934 and again marked a significant change. The attempt to resist fate now becomes secondary to the idea of appearance and reality. Primitive passion is abandoned; the plays are contemplative, pseudo-philosophical, often romantic, and pseudo-poetical. The period was inaugurated by an experimental adaptation of *The Ancient Mariner* in which O'Neill used masks. He followed this with *The Great God Brown*, in which characters put on and removed masks at various times, thus expressing their dual personalities; the masked faces they turn upon the world conceal their real faces, the aspect they cannot hide from themselves. *Strange Interlude*, which followed, was on the surface O'Neill's attempt to show the thoughts of his characters as Joyce had done; but in reality it also was a kind of mask play, only here the masks are verbal. What the characters say to one another conceals what they think; and their thoughts are often at variance with their actions. There were excursions into such fantasies as *The Fountain*, a play about the search for eternal youth, and *Marco Millions*, in which the wandering philistine Marco might be seen as the actor-wanderer that O'Neill's father had been. But O'Neill returned from such fantasies to inner conflict, and out of the darker side of his experience he now fashioned *Mourning Becomes Electra*, which some regard as his finest play. Produced in the autumn of 1931, it was an ambitious trilogy. Acted, like *Strange Interlude*, from late afternoon into late evening with an interval for supper, it attempted to recreate, in modern conditions, the *Oresteia* of Aeschylus. Treating the American Civil War as if it had been the Trojan War, O'Neill traced the destructive forces within a family in which adultery and murder engender more murder until in the end the modern Electra is left alone to shut herself up in the family house with her ghostly past. O'Neill spoke of this play as "a grim, savage, gloomy country of my own making," and we might add that it was a country out of his own childhood, the country of early family hate and love and guilt.

In O'Neill not only is there no escape from such a past; it can, in the end, only smother its participants.

Even as O'Neill's Electra shuts herself away with her family ghosts, so the dramatist now shut himself away from the world. His fourth period has been called the period of "non-communication." He seemed to be writing for himself; manuscripts piled up on his desk, but they were not brought into the theatre. The withdrawal may have marked his oncoming illness; it may have been partly involuntary, due to the erection of too many protective barriers which encouraged him to batten on his past rather than to move forward with his present. There had been a fore-shadowing, however, of this phase in *Dynamo* in 1928 and *Days Without End* in 1932, two of O'Neill's unsuccessful plays. In *Dynamo* the hero embraces the machine as if it were a mother, and dies: "I don't want any miracle, Mother! I don't want to know the truth! I only want you to hide me, Mother! Never let me go from you again! Please, Mother!" In *Days Without End* the protagonist embraces with similar passion and longing the Mother Church, and in Electra the withdrawal is into the very womb of the family. *Mourning Becomes Electra*, it might be noted, is dedicated to his wife, and he addresses her as "mother and wife and mistress and friend." And in writing *The Iceman Cometh*, the only new play produced at the end of this period, he said: "I felt I had locked my-self in with my memories."

In this retreat he finally removed his mask and was reliving his life. He was ready now to face the data of his own early experience. In giving us *Long Day's Journey into Night* and *A Moon for the Misbegotten* he seemed to be saying in the end: "I have for too long taken bits and pieces of my life and fashioned them into art; now, for once, let me take art—the art of the theatre—and use it to illuminate my life." In writing *Long Day's Journey*, the story of that long-ago day in the family house in New London, Connecticut, when he discovered that he had tuberculosis, O'Neill made of himself an historic literary case: he linked his own per-son more closely to his dramas than any playwright had ever done before. The implication in this for criticism is clear enough; however much an artist may want his works to be regarded by his audience as impersonal and divorced from his own life—and therefore possessing a life of their own—the reality is that they contain inevitably some emanation of the writer's temperament, some overflow of his personal experience. This was the reality which O'Neill now recognized.

With the passage of time his plays had grown longer and longer. He projected elaborate cycles: an eleven-play series about a family, its his-tory in America from the eighteenth century to the present, titled *A Tale of Possessors, Self-Dispossessed*. It was in the midst of this work that he wrote his autobiographies; having done this he had difficulty returning to the cycle and he never completed it. He projected a second cycle, *By Way of Obit*, but only a one-act play survives, titled *Hughie*.

The four periods of O'Neill's creative life thus show that however much he may have shifted from subject to subject, from ships to farms, from jungles to brothels, or taken his long leaps into the romantic distance—Ponce de Leon, Marco Polo, Lazarus—he had one major theme upon which these were bold variations. That theme is stated for us in its primal simplicity in *Long Day's Journey:* the imprisonment of the individual within a past and in a state of disharmony with those closest to him. From this condition O'Neill could find no escape and neither do the characters which his mind projected upon the stage. However much they might reach out for the new, the old re-asserted itself. Whatever mask they put on had sooner or later to be laid off. His autobiographies show us the face behind the mask: that of a youth caught in the love-hate of a father, with a dependency and attachment—and idealization—of the mother.

The entire work of O'Neill is that of a dramatist seeking to cast off this past, yet aware that he cannot do so. And the haunted heroes of O'Neill bring about their own downfall when they announce that they have transcended their past. In this O'Neill was duplicating, in modern terms, the primitive basis of Greek tragedy: in the Greek plays the Oracle has spoken, man's fate is determined; he struggles knowing nothing can be altered. The flaw within him contributes to his downfall; and this inner weakness is usually the sense in the O'Neill protagonist of having conquered, when in reality he has only listened to the voice of his own pride.

O'Neill held up his life to illuminate his work; and by this illumination we read its essential pattern. His power and his creativity derived from the intensity of his early emotional experience and his life-long need—and failure—to fathom it. This experience had in it the simple dynamism which impressed Greek tragedy upon the western world. It enabled O'Neill to bring a high seriousness into the American theatre and by the good fortune of a childhood spent in the wings of theatres he was able to endow his plays with a stagecraft which helped revolutionize the New World theatre. Had he been a poet, rather than merely possessing a "touch of the poet," he might very well have become a modern Shakespeare. The stuff of great drama was in him. But he could not match the tragic tone to his tragic vision. Nevertheless that vision was so powerful that within the theatre it was able to transcend his poetic limitations. O'Neill had what Joseph Wood Krutch described as "an instinctive perception" of what a modern tragedy would have to be. He came as close to writing it as any dramatist in our time.

THE LONG VOYAGE HOME

A Play in One Act

This play was first produced in the Playwrights' Theater in Mac-dougal Street in Greenwich Village on November 2, 1917, and was also among the O'Neill plays published during that year in the magazine *Smart Set* edited by H. L. Mencken and George Jean Nathan. It had been written in 1916, at a time when O'Neill was still working largely in the one-act form. In 1919 the play was published in the volume *The Moon of the Caribbees and Six Other Plays of the Sea*.

The principal characters of *The Long Voyage Home* are the same as those in *The Moon of the Caribbees, In the Zone*, and *Bound East for Cardiff*. All are crew-members of the S.S. Glencairn, a British tramp steamer. In later years the one-act Glencairn plays were given as a group. "The individual plays are complete in themselves," O'Neill said in an interview, "yet the identity of the crew goes through the series and welds the four one-acts into a long play." The group might be seen as the earliest "cycle" of plays conceived by O'Neill.

The title *The Long Voyage Home* brings to mind the title of one of the last plays of O'Neill written many years later, *Long Day's Journey into Night*. Indeed both plays, written at the beginning and at the end of Eugene O'Neill's career, use the symbolic concept of the "long journey," the end of which can only be death. In both plays the central character meets defeat; Ollie wants to put an end to his voyaging but is shanghaied: Edmund, the actor's son, has aspirations which are cut short by his discovering that he has tuberculosis.

CHARACTERS

FAT JOE, *proprietor of a dive.*
NICK, *a crimp.*
MAG, *a barmaid.*

OLSON
COCKY
DRISCOLL } *Seamen of the British tramp steamer Glencairn.*
IVAN
KATE
FREDA
TWO ROUGHS

SCENE—*The bar of a low dive on the London water front—a squalid, dingy room dimly lighted by kerosene lamps placed in brackets on the walls. On the left, the bar. In front of it, a door leading to a side room. On the right, tables with chairs around them. In the rear, a door leading to the street.*

A slovenly barmaid with a stupid face sodden with drink is mopping off the bar. Her arm moves back and forth mechanically and her eyes are half shut as if she were dozing on her feet. At the far end of the bar stands FAT JOE, *the proprietor, a gross bulk of a man with an enormous stomach. His face is red and bloated, his little piggish eyes being almost concealed by rolls of fat. The thick fingers of his big hands are loaded with cheap rings and a gold watch chain of cable-like proportions stretches across his checked waistcoat.*

At one of the tables, front, a round-shouldered young fellow is sitting, smoking a cigarette. His face is pasty, his mouth weak, his eyes shifting and cruel. He is dressed in a shabby suit, which must have once been cheaply flashy, and wears a muffler and cap.

It is about nine o'clock in the evening.

JOE (*yawning*). Blimey if bizness ain't 'arf slow to-night. I donnow wot's 'appened. The place is like a bleedin' tomb. Where's all the sailor men, I'd like to know? (*Raising his voice.*) Ho, you Nick! (NICK *turns around listlessly.*) Wot's the name o' that wessel put in at the dock below jest arter noon?

NICK (*laconically*). Glencairn—from Bewnezerry. (Buenos Aires.)

JOE. Ain't the crew been paid orf yet?

NICK. Paid orf this arternoon, they tole me. I 'opped on board of 'er an' seen 'em. 'Anded 'em some o' yer cards, I did. They promised faithful they'd 'appen in to-night—them as whose time was done.

JOE. Any two-year men to be paid orf?

NICK. Four—three Britishers an' a square-'ead.

JOE (*indignantly*). An' yer popped orf an' left 'em? An' me a-payin' yer to 'elp an' bring 'em in 'ere!

NICK (*grumblingly*). Much you pays me! An' I ain't slingin' me 'ook abaht the 'ole bleedin' town fur now man. See?

JOE. I ain't speakin' on'y fur meself. Down't I always give yer yer share, fair an' square, as man to man?

NICK (*with a sneer*). Yus—b'cause you 'as to.

JOE. 'As to? Listen to 'im! There's many'd be 'appy to 'ave your berth, me man!

NICK. Yus? Wot wiv the peelers li'ble to put me away in the bloody jail fur crimpin', an' all?

JOE (*indignantly*). We down't do no crimpin'.

NICK (*sarcastically*). Ho, now! Not arf!

JOE (*a bit embarrassed*). Well, on'y a bit now an' agen when there ain't no reg'lar trade. (*To hide his confusion he turns to the barmaid angrily. She is still mopping off the bar, her chin on her breast, half-asleep.*) 'Ere, me gel, we've 'ad enough o' that. You been a-moppin', an' a-moppin', an' a-moppin' the blarsted bar fur a 'ole 'our. 'Op it aht o' this! You'd fair guv a bloke the shakes a-watchin' yer.

MAG (*beginning to sniffle*). Ow, you do frighten me when you 'oller at me, Joe. I ain't a bad gel, I ain't. Gawd knows I tries to do me best fur you. (*She bursts into a tempest of sobs.*)

JOE (*roughly*). Stop yer grizzlin'! An' 'op it aht of 'ere!

NICK (*chuckling*). She's drunk, Joe. Been 'ittin' the gin, eh, Mag?

MAG (*ceases crying at once and turns on him furiously*). You little crab, you! Orter wear a muzzle, you ort! A-openin' of your ugly mouth to a 'onest woman what ain't never done you no 'arm. (*Commencing to sob again.*) H'abusin' me like a dawg cos I'm sick an' orf me oats, an' all.

JOE. Orf yer go, me gel! Go hupstairs and 'ave a sleep. I'll wake yer if I wants yer. An' wake the two gels when yer goes hup. It's 'arpas' nine an' time as some one was a-comin' in, tell 'em. D'yer 'ear me?

MAG (*stumbling around the bar to the door on left—sobbing*). Yus, yus, I 'ears you. Gawd knows wot's goin' to 'appen to me, I'm that sick. Much you cares if I dies, down't you? (*She goes out.*)

JOE (*still brooding over* NICK's *lack of diligence—after a pause*). Four two-year men paid orf wiv their bloody pockets full o' sovereigns—an' yer lorst 'em. (*He shakes his head sorrowfully.*)

NICK (*impatiently*). Stow it! They promised faithful they'd come, I tells yer. They'll be walkin' in in 'arf a mo'. There's lots o' time yet. (*In a low voice.*) 'Ave yer got the drops? We might wanter use 'em.

JOE (*taking a small bottle from behind the bar*). Yus; 'ere it is.

NICK (*with satisfaction*). Righto! (*His shifty eyes peer about the room searchingly. Then he beckons to* JOE, *who comes over to the table and sits down.*) Reason I arst yer about the drops was 'cause I seen the capt'n of the Amindra this arternoon.

JOE. The Amindra? Wot ship is that?

NICK. Bloody windjammer—skys'l yarder—full rigged—painted white—been layin' at the dock above 'ere fur a month. You knows 'er.

JOE. Ho, yus. I knows now.

NICK. The capt'n says as 'e wants a man special bad—ter-night. They sails at daybreak termorrer.

JOE. There's plenty o' 'ands lyin' abaht waitin' fur ships, I should fink.

NICK. Not fur this ship, ole buck. The capt'n an' mate are bloody slave-drivers, an' they're bound down round the 'Orn. They 'arf starved the 'ands on the larst trip 'ere, an' no one'll dare ship on 'er. (*After a pause.*) I promised the capt'n faithful I'd get 'im one, and ter-night.

JOE (*doubtfully*). An' 'ow are yer goin' to git 'im?

NICK (*with a wink*). I was thinkin' as one of 'em from the Glencairn'd do—them as was paid orf an' is comin' 'ere.

JOE (*with a grin*). It'd be a good 'aul, that's the troof. (*Frowning.*) If they comes 'ere.

NICK. They'll come, an' they'll all be rotten drunk, wait an' see. (*There is the noise of loud, boisterous singing from the street.*) Sounds like 'em, now. (*He opens the street door and looks out.*) Gawd blimey if it ain't the four of 'em! (*Turning to* JOE *in triumph.*) Naw, what d'yer say? They're lookin' for the place. I'll go aht an' tell 'em. (*He goes out.*)

JOE *gets into position behind the bar, assuming his most oily smile. A moment later the door is opened, admitting* DRISCOLL, COCKY, IVAN *and* OLSON. DRISCOLL *is a tall, powerful Irishman;* COCKY, *a wizened runt of a man with a straggling gray mustache;* IVAN, *a hulking oaf of a peasant;* OLSON, *a stocky, middle-aged Swede with round, childish blue eyes. The first three are all very drunk, especially* IVAN *who is managing his legs with difficulty.* OLSON *is perfectly sober. All are dressed in their ill-fitting shore clothes and look very uncomfortable.* DRISCOLL *has unbuttoned his stiff collar and its ends stick out sideways. He has lost his tie.* NICK *slinks into the room after them and sits down at a table in rear. The seamen come to the table, front.*)

JOE (*with affected heartiness*). Ship ahoy, mates! 'Appy to see yer 'ome safe an' sound.

DRISCOLL (*turns round, swaying a bit, and peers at him across the bar*). So ut's you, is ut? (*He looks about the place with an air of recognition.*) 'An the same damn rat's-hole, sure enough. I remimber foive or six years back 'twas here I was sthripped av me last shillin' whin I was aslape. (*With sudden fury.*) God stiffen ye, come none av your dog's thricks on me this trip or I'll—— (*He shakes his fist at* JOE.)

JOE (*hastily interrupting*). Yer must be mistaiken. This is a 'onest place, this is.

COCKY (*derisively*). Ho, yus! An' you're a bleedin' angel, I s'pose?

IVAN (*vaguely taking off his derby hat and putting it on again—plaintively*). I don' li-ike dis place.

DRISCOLL (*going over to the bar—as genial as he was furious a moment before*). Well, no matther, 'tis all past an' gone an' forgot. I'm not the man to be holdin' harrd feelin's on me first night ashore, an' me dhrunk as a lord. (*He holds out his hand, which* JOE *takes very gingerly.*) We'll all be havin' a dhrink, I'm thinkin'. Whiskey for the three av us—*Irish* whiskey!

COCKY (*mockingly*). An' a glarse o' ginger beer fur our blarsted lovechild 'ere. (*He jerks his thumb at* OLSON.)

OLSON (*with a good-natured grin*). I bane a good boy dis night, for one time.

DRISCOLL (*bellowing, and pointing to* NICK *as* JOE *brings the drinks to the table*). An' see what that crimpin' son av a crimp'll be wantin'—an' have your own pleasure. (*He pulls a sovereign out of his pocket and slams it on the bar.*)

NICK. Guv me a pint o' beer, Joe. (JOE *draws the beer and takes it down to the far end of the bar.* NICK *comes over to get it and* JOE *gives him a significant wink and nods toward the door on the left.* NICK *signals back that he understands.*)

COCKY (*drink in hand—impatiently*). I'm that bloody dry! (*Lifting his glass to* DRISCOLL.) Cheero, ole dear, cheero!

DRISCOLL (*pocketing his change without looking at it*). A toast for ye: Hell roast that divil av a bo'sun! (*He drinks.*)

Cocky. Righto! Gawd strike 'im blind! (*He drains his glass.*)

Ivan (*half-asleep*). Dot's gude. (*He tosses down his drink in one gulp.*
Olson *sips his ginger ale.* Nick *takes a swallow of his beer and then
comes round the bar and goes out the door on left.*)

Cocky (*producing a sovereign*). Ho there, you Fatty! Guv us another!

Joe. The saime, mates?

Cocky. Yus.

Driscoll. No, ye scut! I'll be havin' a pint av beer. I'm dhry as a loime
kiln.

Ivan (*suddenly getting to his feet in a befuddled manner and nearly
upsetting the table*). I don' li-ike dis place! I wan' see girls—plenty girls.
(*Pathetically.*) I don't li-ike dis place. I wan' dance with girl.

Driscoll (*pushing him back on his chair with a thud*). Shut up, ye
Rooshan baboon! A foine Romeo you'd make in your condishun. (Ivan
blubbers some incoherent protest—then suddenly falls asleep.)

Joe (*bringing the drinks—looks at* Olson). An' you, matey?

Olson (*shaking his head*). Noting dis time, thank you.

Cocky (*mockingly*). A-saivin' of 'is money, 'e is! Goin' back to 'ome
an' mother. Goin' to buy a bloomin' farm an' punch the blarsted dirt,
that's wot 'e is! (*Spitting disgustedly.*) There's a funny bird of a sailor
man for yer, Gawd blimey!

Olson (*wearing the same good-natured grin*). Yust what I like, Cocky.
I wus on farm long time when I wus kid.

Driscoll. Lave him alone, ye bloody insect! 'Tis a foine sight to see a
man wid some sense in his head instead av a damn fool the loike av us. I
only wisht I'd a mother alive to call me own. I'd not be dhrunk in this
divil's hole this minute, maybe.

Cocky (*commencing to weep dolorously*). Ow, down't talk, Drisc! I
can't bear to 'ear you. I ain't never 'ad no mother, I ain't——

Driscoll. Shut up, ye ape, an' don't be makin' that squealin'. If ye cud
see your ugly face, wid the big red nose av ye all screwed up in a knot,
ye'd never shed a tear the rist av your loife. (*Roaring into song.*) We
ar-re the byes av We-e-exford who fought wid hearrt an' hand! (*Speaking.*) To hell wid Ulster! (*He drinks and the others follow his example.*)
An' I'll strip to any man in the city av London won't dhrink to that toast.
(*He glares truculently at* Joe, *who immediately downs his beer.* Nick *enters again from the door on the left and comes up to* Joe *and whispers in
his ear. The latter nods with satisfaction.*)

Driscoll (*glowering at them*). What divil's thrick are ye up to now,
the two av ye? (*He flourishes a brawny fist.*) Play fair wid us or ye deal
wid me!

Joe (*hastily*). No trick, shipmate! May Gawd kill me if that ain't troof!

Nick (*indicating* Ivan, *who is snoring*). On'y your mate there was
arskin' fur gels an' I thorght as 'ow yer'd like 'em to come dawhn and 'ave
a wet wiv yer.

JOE (*with a smirking wink*). Pretty, 'olesome gels they be, ain't they, Nick?

NICK. Yus.

COCKY. Aar! I knows the gels you 'as, not 'arf! They'd fair blind yer, they're that 'omely. None of yer bloomin' gels fur me, ole Fatty. Me an' Drisc knows a place, down't we, Drisc?

DRISCOLL. Divil a lie, we do. An' we'll be afther goin' there in a minute. There's music there an' a bit av a dance to liven a man.

JOE. Nick, 'ere, can play yer a tune, can't yer, Nick?

NICK. Yus.

JOE. An' yer can 'ave a dance in the side room 'ere.

DRISCOLL. Hurroo! Now you're talkin'. (*The two women, FREDA and KATE, enter from the left. FREDA is a little, sallow-faced blonde. KATE is stout and dark.*)

COCKY (*in a loud aside to DRISCOLL*). Gawd blimey, look at 'em! Ain't they 'orrible? (*The women come forward to the table, wearing their best set smiles.*)

FREDA (*in a raspy voice*). 'Ullo, mates.

KATE. 'Ad a good voyage?

DRISCOLL. Rotten; but no matther. Welcome, as the sayin' is, an' sit down, an' what'll ye be takin' for your thirst? (*To KATE.*) You'll be sittin' by me, darlin'—what's your name?

KATE (*with a stupid grin*). Kate. (*She stands by his chair.*)

DRISCOLL (*putting his arm around her*). A good Irish name, but you're English by the trim av ye, an' be damned to you. But no matther. Ut's fat ye are, Katy dear, an' I never cud endure skinny wimin. (*FREDA favors him with a viperish glance and sits down by OLSON.*) What'll ye have?

OLSON. No, Drisc. Dis one bane on me. (*He takes out a roll of notes from his inside pocket and lays one on the table. JOE, NICK, and the women look at the money with greedy eyes. IVAN gives a particularly violent snore.*)

FREDA. Waike up your fren'. Gawd, 'ow I 'ates to 'ear snorin'.

DRISCOLL (*springing to action, smashes IVAN's derby over his ears*). D'you hear the lady talkin' to ye, ye Rooshan swab? (*The only reply to this is a snore. DRISCOLL pulls the battered remains of the derby off IVAN's head and smashes it back again.*) Arise an' shine, ye dhrunken swine! (*Another snore. The women giggle. DRISCOLL throws the beer left in his glass into IVAN's face. The Russian comes to in a flash, spluttering. There is a roar of laughter.*)

IVAN (*indignantly*). I tell you—dot's someting I don' li-ike!

COCKY. Down't waste good beer, Drisc.

IVAN (*grumblingly*). I tell you—dot is not ri-ight.

DRISCOLL. Ut's your own doin', Ivan. Ye was moanin' for girrls an' whin they come you sit gruntin' loike a pig in a sty. Have ye no manners? (*IVAN seems to see the women for the first time and grins foolishly.*)

KATE (*laughing at him*). Cheero, ole chum, 'ows Russha?

IVAN (*greatly pleased—putting his hand in his pocket*). I buy a drink.

OLSON. No; dis one bane on me. (*To* JOE.) Hey, you faller!

JOE. Wot'll it be, Kate?

KATE. Gin.

FREDA. Brandy.

DRISCOLL. An' Irish whiskey for the rist av us—wid the excipshun av our timperance friend, God pity him!

FREDA (*to* OLSON). You ain't drinkin'?

OLSON (*half-ashamed*). No.

FREDA (*with a seductive smile*). I down't blame yer. You got sense, you 'ave. I on'y tike a nip o' brandy now an' agen fur my 'ealth. (JOE *brings the drinks and* OLSON's *change.* COCKY *gets unsteadily to his feet and raises his glass in the air.*)

COCKY. 'Ere's a toff toast for yer: The ladies, Gawd—(*He hesitates—then adds in a grudging tone.*)—bless 'em.

KATE (*with a silly giggle*). Oo-er! That wasn't what you was goin' to say, you bad Cocky, you! (*They all drink.*)

DRISCOLL (*to* NICK). Where's the tune ye was promisin' to give us?

NICK. Come ahn in the side 'ere an' you'll 'ear it.

DRISCOLL (*getting up*). Come on, all av ye. We'll have a tune an' a dance if I'm not too dhrunk to dance, God help me. (COCKY *and* IVAN *stagger to their feet.* IVAN *can hardly stand. He is leering at* KATE *and snickering to himself in a maudlin fashion. The three, led by* NICK, *go out the door on the left.* KATE *follows them.* OLSON *and* FREDA *remain seated.*)

COCKY (*calling over his shoulder*). Come on an' dance, Ollie.

OLSON. Yes, I come. (*He starts to get up. From the side room comes the sound of an accordion and a boisterous whoop from* DRISCOLL, *followed by a heavy stamping of feet.*)

FREDA. Ow, down't go in there. Stay 'ere an' 'ave a talk wiv me. They're all drunk an' you ain't drinkin'. (*With a smile up into his face.*) I'll think yer don't like me if yer goes in there.

OLSON (*confused*). You wus wrong, Miss Freda. I don't—I mean I do like you.

FREDA (*smiling—puts her hand over his on the table*). An' I likes you. Yer a genelman. You don't get drunk an' hinsult poor gels wot 'as a 'ard an' uneppy life.

OLSON (*pleased but still more confused—wriggling his feet*). I bane drunk many time, Miss Freda.

FREDA. Then why ain't yer drinkin' now? (*She exchanges a quick, questioning glance with* JOE, *who nods back at her—then she continues persuasively.*) Tell me somethin' abaht yeself.

OLSON (*with a grin*). There ain't noting to say, Miss Freda. I bane poor devil sailor man, dat's all.

FREDA. Where was you born—Norway? (OLSON *shakes his head*.) Denmark?

OLSON. No. You guess once more.

FREDA. Then it must be Sweden.

OLSON. Yes. I wus born in Stockholm.

FREDA (*pretending great delight*). Ow, ain't that funny! I was born there, too—in Stockholm.

OLSON (*astonished*). You wus born in Sweden?

FREDA. Yes; you wouldn't think it, but it's Gawd's troof. (*She claps her hands delightedly*.)

OLSON (*beaming all over*). You speak Swedish?

FREDA (*trying to smile sadly*). Now. Y'see my ole man an' woman come 'ere to England when I was on'y a baby an' they was speakin' English b'fore I was old enough to learn. Sow I never knew Swedish. (*Sadly*.) Wisht I 'ad! (*With a smile*.) We'd 'ave a bloomin' lark of it if I 'ad, wouldn't we?

OLSON. It sound nice to hear the old talk yust once in a time.

FREDA. Righto! No place like yer 'ome, I says. Are yer goin' up to—to Stockholm b'fore yer ships away agen?

OLSON. Yes. I go home from here to Stockholm. (*Proudly*.) As passenger!

FREDA. An' you'll git another ship up there arter you've 'ad a vacation?

OLSON. No. I don't never ship on sea no more. I got all sea I want for my life—too much hard work for little money. Yust work, work, work on ship. I don't want more.

FREDA. Ow, I see. That's why you give up drinkin'.

OLSON. Yes. (*With a grin*.) If I drink I yust get drunk and spend all money.

FREDA. But if you ain't gointer be a sailor no more, what'll yer do? You been a sailor all yer life, ain't yer?

OLSON. No. I work on farm till I am eighteen. I like it, too—it's nice—work on farm.

FREDA. But ain't Stockholm a city same's London? Ain't no farms there, is there?

OLSON. We live—my brother and mother live—my father iss dead—on farm yust a little way from Stockholm. I have plenty money, now. I go back with two years' pay and buy more land yet; work on farm. (*Grinning*.) No more sea, no more bum grub, no more storms—yust nice work.

FREDA. Ow, ain't that luv'ly! I s'pose you'll be gittin' married, too?

OLSON (*very much confused*). I don't know. I like to, if I find nice girl, maybe.

FREDA. Ain't yer got some gel back in Stockholm? I bet yer 'as.

OLSON. No. I got nice girl once before I go on sea. But I go on ship, and I don't come back, and she marry other faller. (*He grins sheepishly*).

FREDA. Well, it's nice for yer to be goin' 'ome, anyway.

OLSON. Yes. I tank so. (*There is a crash from the room on left and the music abruptly stops. A moment later* COCKY *and* DRISCOLL *appear, supporting the inert form of* IVAN *between them. He is in the last stage of intoxication, unable to move a muscle.* NICK *follows them and sits down at the table in rear.*)

DRISCOLL (*as they zigzag up to the bar*). Ut's dead he is, I'm thinkin', for he's as limp as a blarsted corpse.

CORKY (*puffing*). Gawd, 'e ain't 'arf 'eavy!

DRISCOLL (*slapping* IVAN'S *face with his free hand*). Wake up, ye divil, ye. Ut's no use. Gabriel's trumpet itself cudn't rouse him. (*To* JOE.) Give us a dhrink for I'm perishing wid the thirst. 'Tis harrd worrk, this.

JOE. Whiskey?

DRISCOLL. *Irish* whiskey, ye swab. (*He puts down a coin on the bar.* JOE *serves* COCKY *and* DRISCOLL. *They drink and then swerve over to* OLSON'S *table.*)

OLSON. Sit down and rest for time, Drisc.

DRISCOLL. No, Ollie, we'll be takin' this lad home to his bed. Ut's late for wan so young to be out in the night. An' I'd not trust him in this hole as dhrunk as he is, an' him wid a full pay day on him. (*Shaking his fist at* JOE). Oho, I know your games, me sonny bye!

JOE (*with an air of grievance*). There yer goes again—hinsultin' a 'onest man!

COCKY. Ho, listen to 'im! Guv 'im a shove in the marf, Drisc.

OLSON (*anxious to avoid a fight—getting up*). I help you take Ivan to boarding house.

FREDA (*protestingly*). Ow, you ain't gointer leave me, are yer? An' we 'avin' sech a nice talk, an' all.

DRISCOLL (*with a wink*). Ye hear what the lady says, Ollie. Ye'd best stay here, me timperance lady's man. An' we need no help. 'Tis only a bit av a way and we're two strong men if we are dhrunk. Ut's no hard shift to take the remains home. But ye can open the door for us, Ollie. (OLSON *goes to the door and opens it.*) Come on, Cocky, an' don't be fallin' aslape yourself. (*They lurch toward the door. As they go out* DRISCOLL *shouts back over his shoulder.*) We'll be comin' back in a short time, surely. So wait here for us, Ollie.

OLSON. All right. I wait here, Drisc. (*He stands in the doorway uncertainly.* JOE *makes violent signs to* FREDA *to bring him back. She goes over and puts her arm around* OLSON'S *shoulder.* JOE *motions to* NICK *to come to the bar. They whisper together excitedly.*)

FREDA (*coaxingly*). You ain't gointer leave me, are yer, dearie? (*Then irritably.*) Fur Gawd's sake, shet that door! I'm fair freezin' to death wiv the fog. (OLSON *comes to himself with a start and shuts the door.*)

OLSON (*humbly*). Excuse me, Miss Freda.

FREDA (*leading him back to the table—coughing*). Buy me a drink o' brandy, will yer? I'm sow cold.

OLSON. All you want, Miss Freda, all you want. (*To* JOE, *who is still whispering instructions to* NICK.) Hey, Yoe! Brandy for Miss Freda. (*He lays a coin on the table.*)

JOE. Righto! (*He pours out her drink and brings it to the table.*) 'Avin' somethink yeself, shipmate?

OLSON. No. I don't tank so. (*He points to his glass with a grin.*) Dis iss only belly-wash, no? (*He laughs.*)

JOE (*hopefully*). 'Ave a man's drink.

OLSON. I would like to—but no. If I drink one I want drink one tousand. (*He laughs again.*)

FREDA (*responding to a vicious nudge from* JOE's *elbow*). Ow, tike somethin'. I ain't gointer drink all be meself.

OLSON. Den give me a little yinger beer—small one. (JOE *goes back of the bar, making a sign to* NICK *to go to their table.* NICK *does so and stands so that the sailor cannot see what* JOE *is doing.*)

NICK (*to make talk*). Where's yer mates popped orf ter? (JOE *pours the contents of the little bottle into* OLSON's *glass of ginger beer.*)

OLSON. Dey take Ivan, dat drunk faller, to bed. They come back. (JOE *brings* OLSON's *drink to the table and sets it before him.*)

JOE (*to* NICK—*angrily*). 'Op it, will yer? There ain't no time to be dawdlin'. See? 'Urry!

NICK. Down't worry, ole bird, I'm orf. (*He hurries out the door.* JOE *returns to his place behind the bar.*)

OLSON (*after a pause—worriedly*). I tank I should go after dem. Cocky iss very drunk, too, and Drisc——

FREDA. Aar! The big Irish is all right. Don't yer 'ear 'im say as 'ow they'd surely come back 'ere, an' fur you to wait fur 'em?

OLSON. Yes; but if dey don't come soon I tank I go see if dey are in boarding house all right.

FREDA. Where is the boardin' 'ouse?

OLSON. Yust little way back from street here.

FREDA. You stayin' there, too?

OLSON. Yes—until steamer sail for Stockholm—in two day.

FREDA (*she is alternately looking at* JOE *and feverishly trying to keep* OLSON *talking so he will forget about going away after the others*). Yer mother won't be arf glad to see yer agen, will she? (OLSON *smiles.*) Does she know yer comin'?

OLSON. No. I tought I would yust give her surprise. I write to her from Bonos Eres but I don't tell her I come home.

FREDA. Must be old, ain't she, yer ole lady?

OLSON. She iss eighty-two. (*He smiles reminiscently.*) You know, Miss Freda, I don't see my mother or my brother in—let me tank—(*he counts laboriously on his fingers*) must be more than ten year. I write once in while and she write many time; and my brother he write me, too. My mother say in all letter I should come home right away. My brother he write same ting, too. He want me to help him on farm. I write back always I come soon; and I mean all time to go back home at end of voyage.

But I come ashore, I take one drink, I take many drinks, I get drunk, I spend all money, I have to ship away for other voyage. So dis time I say to myself: Don't drink one drink, Ollie, or, sure, you don't get home. And I want go home dis time. I feel homesick for farm and to see my people again. (*He smiles.*) Yust like little boy, I feel homesick. Dat's why I don't drink noting to-night but dis—belly-wash! (*He roars with childish laughter, then suddenly becomes serious.*) You know, Miss Freda, my mother get very old, and I want to see her. She might die and I would never——

FREDA (*moved a lot in spite of herself*). Ow, don't talk like that! I jest 'ates to 'ear any one speakin' abaht dyin'. (*The door to the street is opened and* NICK *enters, followed by two rough-looking, shabbily-dressed men, wearing mufflers, with caps pulled down over their eyes. They sit at the table nearest to the door.* JOE *brings them three beers, and there is a whispered consultation, with many glances in the direction of* OLSON.)

OLSON (*starting to get up—worriedly*). I tank I go round to boarding house. I tank someting go wrong with Drisc and Cocky.

FREDA. Ow, down't go. They kin take care of theyselves. They ain't babies. Wait 'arf a mo'. You ain't 'ad yer drink yet.

JOE (*coming hastily over to the table, indicates the men in the rear with a jerk of his thumb*). One of them blokes wants yer to 'ave a wet wiv 'im.

FREDA. Righto! (*To* OLSON.) Let's drink this. (*She raises her glass. He does the same.*) 'Ere's a toast fur yer: Success to yer bloomin' farm an' may yer live long an' 'appy on it. Skoal! (*She tosses down her brandy. He swallows half his glass of ginger beer and makes a wry face.*)

OLSON. Skoal! (*He puts down his glass.*)

FREDA (*with feigned indignation*). Down't yer like my toast?

OLSON (*grinning*). Yes. It iss very kind, Miss Freda.

FREDA. Then drink it all like I done.

OLSON. Well—— (*He gulps down the rest.*) Dere! (*He laughs.*)

FREDA. Done like a sport!

ONE OF THE ROUGHS (*with a laugh*). Amindra, ahoy!

NICK (*warningly*). Sssshh!

OLSON (*turns around in his chair*). Amindra? Iss she in port? I sail on her once long time ago—three mast, full rig, skys'l yarder? Iss dat ship you mean?

THE ROUGH (*grinning*). Yus; right you are.

OLSON (*angrily*). I know dat damn ship—worst ship dat sail to sea. Rotten grub and dey make you work all time—and the Captain and Mate wus Bluenose devils. No sailor who know anyting ever ship on her. Where iss she bound from here?

THE ROUGH. Round Cape 'Orn—sails at daybreak.

OLSON. Py yingo, I pity poor fallers make dat trip round Cape Stiff dis time year. I bet you some of dem never see port once again. (*He passes his hand over his eyes in a dazed way. His voice grows weaker.*) Py golly, I feel dizzy. All the room go round and round like I wus drunk. (*He gets weakly to his feet.*) Good night, Miss Freda. I bane feeling sick. Tell Drisc—I go home. (*He takes a step forward and suddenly collapses over a chair, rolls to the floor, and lies there unconscious.*)

JOE (*from behind the bar*). Quick, nawh! (NICK *darts forward with* JOE *following.* FREDA *is already beside the unconscious man and has taken the roll of money from his inside pocket. She strips off a note furtively and shoves it into her bosom, trying to conceal her action, but* JOE *sees her. She hands the roll to* JOE, *who pockets it.* NICK *goes through all the other pockets and lays a handful of change on the table.*)

JOE (*impatiently*). 'Urry, 'urry, can't yer? The other blokes'll be 'ere in 'arf a mo'. (*The two* ROUGHS *come forward.*) 'Ere, you two, tike 'im in under the arms like 'e was drunk. (*They do so.*) Tike 'im to the Amindra —yer knows that, don't yer?—two docks above. Nick'll show yer. An' you, Nick, down't yer leave the bleedin' ship till the capt'n guvs yer this bloke's advance—full month's pay—five quid, d'yer 'ear?

NICK. I knows me bizness, ole bird. (*They support* OLSON *to the door.*)

THE ROUGH (*as they are going out*). This silly bloke'll 'ave the s'prise of 'is life when 'e wakes up on board of 'er. (*They laugh. The door closes behind them.* FREDA *moves quickly for the door on the left but* JOE *gets in her way and stops her.*)

JOE (*threateningly*). Guv us what yer took!

FREDA. Took? I guv yer all 'e 'ad.

JOE. Yer a liar! I seen yer a-playin' yer sneakin' tricks, but yer can't fool Joe. I'm too old a 'and. (*Furiously.*) Guv it to me, yer bloody cow! (*He grabs her by the arm.*)

FREDA. Lemme alone! I ain't got no——

JOE (*hits her viciously on the side of the jaw. She crumples up on the floor.*) That'll learn yer! (*He stoops down and fumbles in her bosom and pulls out the banknote, which he stuffs into his pocket with a grunt of satisfaction.* KATE *opens the door on the left and looks in—then rushes to* FREDA *and lifts her head up in her arms.*)

KATE (*gently*). Pore dearie! (*Looking at* JOE *angrily.*) Been 'ittin' 'er agen, 'ave yer, yer cowardly swine!

JOE. Yus; an' I'll 'it you, too, if yer don't keep yer marf shut. Tike 'er aht of 'ere! (KATE *carries* FREDA *into the next room.* JOE *goes behind the bar. A moment later the outer door is opened and* DRISCOLL *and* COCKY *come in.*)

DRISCOLL. Come on, Ollie. (*He suddenly sees that* OLSON *is not there, and turns to* JOE.) Where is ut he's gone to?

JOE (*with a meaning wink*). 'E an' Freda went aht t'gether 'bout five minutes past. 'E's fair gone on 'er, 'e is.

DRISCOLL (*with a grin*). Oho, so that's ut, is ut? Who'd think Ollie'd be sich a divil wid the wimin? 'Tis lucky he's sober or she'd have him stripped to his last ha'penny. (*Turning to* COCKY, *who is blinking sleepily.*) What'll ye have, ye little scut? (*To* JOE.) Give me whiskey, *Irish* whiskey!

(*The Curtain Falls*)

DESIRE UNDER THE ELMS

Desire Under the Elms was produced in the Greenwich Village Theater in New York on November 11, 1924. Written during the winter and spring of that year, it ran for twelve months and was widely played by two road companies. Some efforts were made by officials to censor the play because of its theme and its overt sexuality, but these failed. The play came to be acknowledged in later years as one of O'Neill's strongest and most characteristic works in the tragic mode.

The portrait of the family—that is of the farmer and his sons—suggests the portrait of the O'Neill family in *Long Day's Journey.* In both plays sons are in conflict with their father; and in the autobiographical play there is a distinct bond of empathy between Edmund [Eugene] and his mother, as in *Desire* there is the overt passion between Eben and his step-mother. In psychological terms it can be seen that what is implied in the autobiography—the deep attachment of the son for the mother—is openly expressed in the "unconscious autobiography" of *Desire.*

It is equally interesting to note that in *Long Day's Journey* O'Neill left out one autobiographical fact of importance. As his second wife remarks in her memoirs: "Who, having seen *Long Day's Journey into Night* would ever realize that Edmund, the younger son [who is Eugene] had been married and divorced, and was the father of a child nearly three years old on that August evening in 1912," when the play takes place. In *Desire,* Eben becomes a father in an adulterous and quasi-incestuous union with his step-mother. And the child is murdered. In real life Eugene O'Neill did not see the child of his first marriage until the boy was ten.

There is thus a very real connection between the autobiographical data of *Desire Under the Elms,* which O'Neill reshaped into a work of art, and *Long Day's Journey* in which much of the data is given to us without the re-shaping process. An illuminating psychoanalytical study of these two plays was published in the *Journal of the American Psychoanalytical Association* in July 1957, (Vol. V, No. 3) by Philip Weissman, M.D., titled "Conscious and Unconscious Autobiographical Dramas of Eugene O'Neill."

CHARACTERS

EPHRAIM CABOT

SIMEON ⎫
PETER   ⎬ *His sons*
EBEN   ⎭

ABBIE PUTNAM

Young Girl, Two Farmers, The Fiddler, A Sheriff,
and other folk from the neighboring farms.

The action of the entire play takes place in, and immediately outside of,
the Cabot farmhouse in New England, in the year 1850. The south end
of the house faces front to a stone wall with a wooden gate at center
opening on a country road. The house is in good condition but in need of
paint. Its walls are a sickly grayish, the green of the shutters faded. Two
enormous elms are on each side of the house. They bend their trailing
branches down over the roof. They appear to protect and at the same
time subdue. There is a sinister maternity in their aspect, a crushing, jealous absorption. They have developed from their intimate contact with
the life of man in the house an appalling humaneness. They brood oppressively over the house. They are like exhausted women resting their
sagging breasts and hands and hair on its roof, and when it rains their tears
trickle down monotonously and rot on the shingles.

There is a path running from the gate around the right corner of the
house to the front door. A narrow porch is on this side. The end wall facing us has two windows in its upper story, two larger ones on the floor
below. The two upper are those of the father's bedroom and that of the
brothers. On the left, ground floor, is the kitchen—on the right, the parlor,
the shades of which are always drawn down.

PART ONE—SCENE ONE

*Exterior of the Farmhouse. It is sunset of a day at the beginning of sum-
mer in the year 1850. There is no wind and everything is still. The sky
above the roof is suffused with deep colors, the green of the elms glows,
but the house is in shadow, seeming pale and washed out by contrast.*

A door opens and EBEN CABOT *comes to the end of the porch and stands
looking down the road to the right. He has a large bell in his hand and
this he swings mechanically, awakening a deafening clangor. Then he
puts his hands on his hips and stares up at the sky. He sighs with a puzzled awe and blurts out with halting appreciation.*

EBEN. God! Purty! (*His eyes fall and he stares about him frowningly.
He is twenty-five, tall and sinewy. His face is well-formed, good-looking,
but its expression is resentful and defensive. His defiant, dark eyes remind
one of a wild animal's in captivity. Each day is a cage in which he finds*

himself trapped but inwardly unsubdued. There is a fierce repressed vitality about him. He has black hair, mustache, a thin curly trace of beard. He is dressed in rough farm clothes.

He spits on the ground with intense disgust, turns and goes back into the house.

SIMEON *and* PETER *come in from their work in the fields. They are tall men, much older than their half-brother* [SIMEON *is thirty-nine and* PETER *thirty-seven*], *built on a squarer, simpler model, fleshier in body, more bovine and homelier in face, shrewder and more practical. Their shoulders stoop a bit from years of farm work. They clump heavily along in their clumsy thick-soled boots caked with earth. Their clothes, their faces, hands, bare arms and throats are earth-stained. They smell of earth. They stand together for a moment in front of the house and, as if with the one impulse, stare dumbly up at the sky, leaning on their hoes. Their faces have a compressed, unresigned expression. As they look upward, this softens.*)

SIMEON (*grudgingly*). Purty.

PETER. Ay-eh.

SIMEON (*suddenly*). Eighteen year ago.

PETER. What?

SIMEON. Jenn. My woman. She died.

PETER. I'd fergot.

SIMEON. I rec'lect—now an' agin. Makes it lonesome. She'd hair long's a hoss' tail—an' yaller like gold!

PETER. Waal—she's gone. (*This with indifferent finality—then after a pause*) They's gold in the West, Sim.

SIMEON (*still under the influence of sunset-vaguely*). In the sky?

PETER. Waal—in a manner o' speakin'—thar's the promise. (*Growing excited*) Gold in the sky—in the West—Golden Gate—Californi-a!—Goldest West!—fields o' gold!

SIMEON (*excited in his turn*). Fortunes layin' just atop o' the ground waitin' t' be picked! Solomon's mines, they says! (*For a moment they continue looking up at the sky—then their eyes drop.*)

PETER (*with sardonic bitterness*). Here—it's stones atop o' the ground—stones atop o' stones—makin' stone walls—year atop o' year—him 'n' yew 'n' me 'n' then Eben—makin' stone walls fur him to fence us in!

SIMEON. We've wuked. Give our strength. Give our years. Plowed 'em under in the ground,—(*he stamps rebelliously*)—rottin'—makin' soil for his crops! (*A pause*) Waal—the farm pays good for hereabouts.

PETER. If we plowed in Californi-a, they'd be lumps o' gold in the furrow!

SIMEON. Californi-a's t'other side o' earth, a'most. We got t' calc'late—

PETER (*after a pause*). 'Twould be hard fur me, too, to give up what we've 'arned here by our sweat. (*A pause.* EBEN *sticks his head out of the dining-room window, listening.*)

SIMEON. Ay-eh. (*A pause*) Mebbe—he'll die soon.

PETER (*doubtfully*). Mebbe.

SIMEON. Mebbe—fur all we knows—he's dead now.

PETER. Ye'd need proof.

SIMEON. He's been gone two months—with no word.

PETER. Left us in the fields an evenin' like this. Hitched up an' druv off into the West. That's plum onnateral. He hain't never been off this farm 'ceptin' t' the village in thirty year or more, not since he married Eben's maw. (*A pause. Shrewdly*) I calc'late we might git him declared crazy by the court.

SIMEON. He skinned 'em too slick. He got the best o' all on 'em. They'd never b'lieve him crazy. (*A pause*) We got t' wait—till he's under ground.

EBEN (*with a sardonic chuckle*). Honor thy father! (*They turn, startled, and stare at him. He grins, then scowls*) I pray he's died. (*They stare at him. He continues matter-of-factly*) Supper's ready.

SIMEON and PETER (*together*). Ay-eh.

EBEN (*gazing up at the sky*). Sun's downin' purty.

SIMEON and PETER (*together*). Ay-eh. They's gold in the West.

EBEN. Ay-eh. (*Pointing*) Yonder atop o' the hill pasture, ye mean?

SIMEON and PETER (*together*). In Californi-a!

EBEN. Hunh? (*Stares at them indifferently for a second, then drawls*) Waal—supper's gittin' cold. (*He turns back into kitchen.*)

SIMEON (*startled—smacks his lips*). I air hungry!

PETER (*sniffing*). I smells bacon!

SIMEON (*with hungry appreciation*). Bacon's good!

PETER (*in same tone*). Bacon's bacon! (*They turn, shouldering each other, their bodies bumping and rubbing together as they hurry clumsily to their food, like two friendly oxen toward their evening meal. They disappear around the right corner of house and can be heard entering the door.*)

CURTAIN

Scene Two

The color fades from the sky. Twilight begins. The interior of the kitchen is now visible. A pine table is at center, a cookstove in the right rear corner, four rough wooden chairs, a tallow candle on the table. In the middle of the rear wall is fastened a big advertizing poster with a ship in full sail and the word "California" in big letters. Kitchen utensils hang from nails. Everything is neat and in order but the atmosphere is of a men's camp kitchen rather than that of a home.

Places for three are laid. EBEN takes boiled potatoes and bacon from the stove and puts them on the table, also a loaf of bread and a crock of water. SIMEON and PETER shoulder in, slump down in their chairs without a word. EBEN joins them. The three eat in silence for a moment, the two elder as naturally unrestrained as beasts of the field, EBEN picking at his food without appetite, glancing at them with a tolerant dislike.

SIMEON (*suddenly turns to* EBEN). Looky here! Ye'd oughtn't t' said that, Eben.

PETER. 'Twa'n't righteous.

EBEN. What?

SIMEON. Ye prayed he'd died.

EBEN. Waal—don't yew pray it? (*A pause.*)

PETER. He's our Paw.

EBEN (*violently*). Not mine!

SIMEON (*dryly*). Ye'd not let no one else say that about yer Maw! Ha! (*He gives one abrupt sardonic guffaw.* PETER *grins.*)

EBEN (*very pale*). I meant—I hain't his'n—I hain't like him—he hain't me!

PETER (*dryly*). Wait till ye've growed his age!

EBEN (*intensely*). I'm Maw—every drop o' blood! (*A pause. They stare at him with indifferent curiosity.*)

PETER (*reminiscently*). She was good t' Sim 'n' me. A good Stepmaw's scurse.

SIMEON. She was good t' everyone.

EBEN (*greatly moved, gets to his feet and makes an awkward bow to each of them—stammering*). I be thankful t' ye. I'm her—her heir. (*He sits down in confusion.*)

PETER (*after a pause—judicially*). She was good even t' him.

EBEN (*fiercely*). An' fur thanks he killed her!

SIMEON (*after a pause*). No one never kills nobody. It's allus somethin'. That's the murderer.

EBEN. Didn't he slave Maw t' death?

PETER. He's slaved himself t' death. He's slaved Sim 'n' me 'n' yew t' death—on'y none o' us hain't died—yit.

SIMEON. It's somethin'—drivin' him—t' drive us!

EBEN (*vengefully*). Waal—I hold him t' jedgment! (*Then scornfully*) Somethin'! What's somethin'?

SIMEON. Dunno.

EBEN (*sardonically*). What's drivin' yew to Californi-a, mebbe? (*They look at him in surprise*) Oh, I've heerd ye! (*Then, after a pause*) But ye'll never go t' the gold fields!

PETER (*assertively*). Mebbe!

EBEN. Whar'll ye git the money?

PETER. We kin walk. It's an a'mighty ways—Californi-a—but if yew was t' put all the steps we've walked on this farm end t' end we'd be in the moon!

EBEN. The Injuns'll skulp ye on the plains.

SIMEON (*with grim humor*). We'll mebbe make 'em pay a hair fur a hair!

EBEN (*decisively*). But t'aint that. Ye won't never go because ye'll wait here fur yer share o' the farm, thinkin' allus he'll die soon.

SIMEON (*after a pause*). We've a right.

PETER. Two-thirds belongs t'us.

EBEN (*jumping to his feet*). Ye've no right! She wa'n't yewr Maw! It was her farm! Didn't he steal it from her? She's dead. It's my farm.

SIMEON (*sardonically*). Tell that t' Paw—when he comes! I'll bet ye a dollar he'll laugh—fur once in his life. Ha! (*He laughs himself in one single mirthless bark.*)

PETER (*amused in turn, echoes his brother*). Ha!

SIMEON (*after a pause*). What've ye got held agin us, Eben? Year arter year it's skulked in yer eye—somethin'.

PETER. Ay-eh.

EBEN. Ay-eh. They's somethin'. (*Suddenly exploding*) Why didn't ye never stand between him 'n' my Maw when he was slavin' her to her grave—t' pay her back fur the kindness she done t' yew? (*There is a long pause. They stare at him in surprise.*)

SIMEON. Waal—the stock'd got t' be watered.

PETER. 'R they was woodin' t' do.

SIMEON. 'R plowin'.

PETER. 'R hayin'.

SIMEON. 'R spreadin' manure.

PETER. 'R weedin'.

SIMEON. 'R prunin'.

PETER. 'R milkin'.

EBEN (*breaking in harshly*). An' makin' walls—stone atop o' stone— makin' walls till yer heart's a stone ye heft up out o' the way o' growth onto a stone wall t' wall in yer heart!

SIMEON (*matter-of-factly*). We never had no time t' meddle.

PETER (*to* EBEN). Yew was fifteen afore yer Maw died—an' big fur yer age. Why didn't ye never do nothin'?

EBEN (*harshly*). They was chores t' do, wa'n't they? (*A pause—then slowly*) It was on'y arter she died I come to think o' it. Me cookin'—doin' her work—that made me know her, suffer her sufferin'—she'd come back t' help—come back t' bile potatoes—come back t' fry bacon—come back t' bake biscuits—come back all cramped up t' shake the fire, an' carry ashes, her eyes weepin' an' bloody with smoke an' cinders same's they used t' be. She still comes back—stands by the stove thar in the evenin'—she can't find it nateral sleepin' an' restin' in peace. She can't git used t' bein' free— even in her grave.

SIMEON. She never complained none.

EBEN. She'd got too tired. She'd got too used t' bein' too tired. That was what he done. (*With vengeful passion*) An' sooner'r later, I'll meddle. I'll say the thin's I didn't say then t' him! I'll yell 'em at the top o' my lungs. I'll see t' it my Maw gits some rest an' sleep in her grave! (*He sits down again, relapsing into a brooding silence. They look at him with a queer indifferent curiosity.*)

PETER (*after a pause*). Whar in tarnation d'ye s'pose he went, Sim?

SIMEON. Dunno. He druv off in the buggy, all spick an' span, with the mare all breshed an' shiny, druv off clackin' his tongue an' wavin' his whip. I remember it right well. I was finishin' plowin', it was spring an' May an' sunset, an' gold in the West, an' he druv off into it. I yells "Whar ye goin', Paw?" an' he hauls up by the stone wall a jiffy. His old snake's eyes was glitterin' in the sun like he'd been drinkin' a jugful an' he says with a mule's grin: "Don't ye run away till I come back!"

PETER. Wonder if he knowed we was wantin' fur Californi-a?

SIMEON. Mebbe. I didn't say nothin' and he says, lookin' kinder queer an' sick: "I been hearin' the hens cluckin' an' the roosters crowin' all the durn day. I been listenin' t' the cows lowin' an' everythin' else kickin' up till I can't stand it no more. It's spring an' I'm feelin' damned," he says. "Damned like an old bare hickory tree fit on'y fur burnin'," he says. An' then I calc'late I must've looked a mite hopeful, fur he adds real spry and vicious: "But don't git no fool idee I'm dead. I've sworn t' live a hundred an' I'll do it, if on'y t' spite yer sinful greed! An' now I'm ridin' out t' learn God's message t' me in the spring, like the prophets done. An' yew git back t' yer plowin'," he says. An' he druv off singin' a hymn. I thought he was drunk—'r I'd stopped him goin'.

EBEN (scornfully). No, ye wouldn't! Ye're scared o' him. He's stronger —inside—than both o' ye put together!

PETER (sardonically). An' yew—be yew Samson?

EBEN. I'm gittin' stronger. I kin feel it growin' in me—growin' an' growin'—till it'll bust out—! (He gets up and puts on his coat and a hat. They watch him, gradually breaking into grins. EBEN avoids their eyes sheepishly) I'm goin' out fur a spell—up the road.

PETER. T' the village?

SIMEON. T' see Minnie?

EBEN (defiantly). Ay-eh!

PETER (jeeringly). The Scarlet Woman!

SIMEON. Lust—that's what's growin' in ye!

EBEN. Waal—she's purty!

PETER. She's been purty fur twenty year!

SIMEON. A new coat o' paint'l make a heifer out of forty.

EBEN. She hain't forty!

PETER. If she hain't, she's teeterin' on the edge.

EBEN (desperately). What d'yew know—

PETER. All they is . . . Sim knew her—an' then me arter—

SIMEON. An' Paw kin tell yew somethin' too! He was fust!

EBEN. D'ye mean t' say he . . . ?

SIMEON (with a grin). Ay-eh! We air his heirs in everythin'!

EBEN (intensely). That's more to it! That grows on it! It'll bust soon! (Then violently) I'll go smash my fist in her face! (He pulls open the door in rear violently.)

SIMEON (with a wink at PETER—drawlingly). Mebbe—but the night's wa'm—purty—by the time ye git thar mebbe ye'll kiss her instead!

PETER. Sart'n he will! (They both roar with coarse laughter. EBEN

rushes out and slams the door—then the outside front door—comes around the corner of the house and stands still by the gate, staring up at the sky.)
SIMEON (*looking after him*). Like his Paw.
PETER. Dead spit an' image!
SIMEON. Dog'll eat dog!
PETER. Ay-eh. (*Pause. With yearning*) Mebbe a year from now we'll be in Californi-a.
SIMEON. Ay-eh. (*A pause. Both yawn*) Let's git t'bed. (*He blows out the candle. They go out door in rear.* EBEN *stretches his arms up to the sky—rebelliously.*)
EBEN. Waal—thar's a star, an' somewhar's they's him, an' here's me, an' thar's Min up the road—in the same night. What if I does kiss her? She's like t'night, she's soft 'n' wa'm, her eyes kin wink like a star, her mouth's wa'm, her arms're wa'm, she smells like a wa'm plowed field, she's purty . . . Ay-eh! By God A'mighty she's purty, an' I don't give a damn how many sins she's sinned afore mine or who she's sinned 'em with, my sin's as purty as any one on 'em! (*He strides off down the road to the left.*)

SCENE THREE

It is the pitch darkness just before dawn. EBEN *comes in from the left and goes around to the porch, feeling his way, chuckling bitterly and cursing half-aloud to himself.*
EBEN. The cussed old miser! (*He can be heard going in the front door. There is a pause as he goes upstairs, then a loud knock on the bedroom door of the brothers*) Wake up!
SIMEON (*startedly*). Who's thar?
EBEN (*pushing open the door and coming in, a lighted candle in his hand. The bedroom of the brothers is revealed. Its ceiling is the sloping roof. They can stand upright only close to the center dividing wall of the upstairs.* SIMEON *and* PETER *are in a double bed, front.* EBEN'S *cot is to the rear.* EBEN *has a mixture of silly grin and vicious scowl on his face*). I be!
PETER (*angrily*). What in hell's-fire . . . ?
EBEN. I got news fur ye! Ha! (*He gives one abrupt sardonic guffaw.*)
SIMEON (*angrily*). Couldn't ye hold it 'til we'd got our sleep?
EBEN. It's nigh sunup. (*Then explosively*) He's gone an' married agen!
SIMEON *and* PETER (*explosively*). Paw?
EBEN. Got himself hitched to a female 'bout thirty-five—an' purty, they says . . .
SIMEON (*aghast*). It's a durn lie!
PETER. Who says?
SIMEON. They been stringin' ye!
EBEN. Think I'm a dunce, do ye? The hull village says. The preacher from New Dover, he brung the news—told it t'our preacher—New Dover,

that's whar the old loon got himself hitched—that's whar the woman lived—

PETER (*no longer doubting—stunned*). Waal . . . !

SIMEON (*the same*). Waal . . . !

EBEN (*sitting down on a bed—with vicious hatred*). Ain't he a devil out o' hell? It's jest t' spite us—the damned old mule!

PETER (*after a pause*). Everythin'll go t' her now.

SIMEON. Ay-eh. (*A pause—dully*) Waal—if it's done—

PETER. It's done us. (*Pause—then persuasively*) They's gold in the fields o' Californi-a, Sim. No good a-stayin' here now.

SIMEON. Jest what I was a-thinkin'. (*Then with decision*) S'well fust's last! Let's light out and git this mornin'.

PETER. Suits me.

EBEN. Ye must like walkin'.

SIMEON (*sardonically*). If ye'd grow wings on us we'd fly thar!

EBEN. Ye'd like ridin' better—on a boat, wouldn't ye? (*Fumbles in his pocket and takes out a crumpled sheet of foolscap*) Waal, if ye sign this ye kin ride on a boat. I've had it writ out an' ready in case ye'd ever go. It says fur three hundred dollars t' each ye agree yewr shares o' the farm is sold t' me. (*They look suspiciously at the paper. A pause.*)

SIMEON (*wonderingly*). But if he's hitched agen—

PETER. An' whar'd yew git that sum o' money, anyways?

EBEN (*cunningly*). I know whar it's hid. I been waitin'—Maw told me. She knew whar it lay fur years, but she was waitin' . . . It's her'n—the money he hoarded from her farm an' hid from Maw. It's my money by rights now.

PETER. Whar's it hid?

EBEN (*cunningly*). Whar yew won't never find it without me. Maw spied on him—'r she'd never knowed. (*A pause. They look at him suspiciously, and he at them*) Waal, is it fa'r trade?

SIMEON. Dunno.

PETER. Dunno.

SIMEON (*looking at window*). Sky's grayin'.

PETER. Ye better start the fire, Eben.

SIMEON. An' fix some vittles.

EBEN. Ay-eh. (*Then with a forced jocular heartiness*) I'll git ye a good one. If ye're startin' t' hoof it t' Californi-a ye'll need somethin' that'll stick t' yer ribs. (*He turns to the door, adding meaningly*) But ye kin ride on a boat if ye'll swap. (*He stops at the door and pauses. They stare at him.*)

SIMEON (*suspiciously*). Whar was ye all night?

EBEN (*defiantly*). Up t' Min's. (*Then slowly*) Walkin' thar, fust I felt 's if I'd kiss her; then I got a-thinkin' o' what ye'd said o' him an' her an' I says, I'll bust her nose fur that! Then I got t' the village an' heerd the news an' I got madder'n hell an' run all the way t' Min's not knowin' what I'd do— (*He pauses—then sheepishly but more defiantly*) Waal—

when I seen her, I didn't hit her—nor I didn't kiss her nuther—I begun t' beller like a calf an' cuss at the same time, I was so durn mad—an' she got scared—an' I jest grabbed holt an' tuk her! (*Proudly*) Yes, sirree! I tuk her. She may've been his'n—an' your'n, too—but she's mine now!

SIMEON (*dryly*). In love, air yew?

EBEN (*with lofty scorn*). Love! I don't take no stock in sech slop!

PETER (*winking at* SIMEON). Mebbe Eben's aimin' t' marry, too.

SIMEON. Min'd make a true faithful he'pmeet! (*They snicker.*)

EBEN. What do I care fur her—'ceptin' she's round an' wa'm? The p'int is she was his'n—an' now she b'longs t' me! (*He goes to the door—then turns—rebelliously*) An' Min hain't sech a bad un. They's worse'n Min in the world, I'll bet ye! Wait'll we see this cow the Old Man's hitched t'! She'll beat Min, I got a notion! (*He starts to go out.*)

SIMEON (*suddenly*). Mebbe ye'll try t' make her your'n, too?

PETER. Ha! (*He gives a sardonic laugh of relish at this idea.*)

EBEN (*spitting with disgust*). Her—here—sleepin' with him—stealin' my Maw's farm! I'd as soon pet a skunk 'r kiss a snake! (*He goes out. The two stare after him suspiciously. A pause. They listen to his steps receding.*)

PETER. He's startin' the fire.

SIMEON. I'd like t' ride t' Californi-a—but—

PETER. Min might o' put some scheme in his head.

SIMEON. Mebbe it's all a lie 'bout Paw maryin'. We'd best wait an' see the bride.

PETER. An' don't sign nothin' till we does!

SIMEON. Nor till we've tested it's good money! (*Then with a grin*) But if Paw's hitched we'd be sellin' Eben somethin' we'd never git no-how!

PETER. We'll wait an' see. (*Then with sudden vindictive anger*) An' till he comes, let's yew 'n' me not wuk a lick, let Eben tend to thin's if he's a mind t', let's us jest sleep an' eat an' drink likker, an' let the hull damned farm go t' blazes!

SIMEON (*excitedly*). By God, we've 'arned a rest! We'll play rich fur a change. I hain't a-going to stir outa bed till breakfast's ready.

PETER. An' on the table!

SIMEON (*after a pause—thoughtfully*). What d'ye calc'late she'll be like—our new Maw? Like Eben thinks?

PETER. More'n' likely.

SIMEON (*vindictively*). Waal—I hope she's a she-devil that'll make him wish he was dead an' livin' in the pit o' hell fur comfort!

PETER (*fervently*). Amen!

SIMEON (*imitating his father's voice*). "I'm ridin' out t' learn God's message t' me in the spring like the prophets done," he says. I'll bet right then an' thar he knew plumb well he was goin' whorin', the stinkin' old hypocrite!

Scene Four

Same as Scene Two—shows the interior of the kitchen with a lighted candle on table. It is gray dawn outside. SIMEON *and* PETER *are just finishing their breakfast.* EBEN *sits before his plate of untouched food, brooding frowningly.*

PETER (*glancing at him rather irritably*). Lookin' glum don't help none.

SIMEON (*sarcastically*). Sorrowin' over his lust o' the flesh!

PETER (*with a grin*). Was she yer fust?

EBEN (*angrily*). None o' yer business. (*A pause*) I was thinkin' o' him. I got a notion he's gittin' near—I kin feel him comin' on like yew kin feel malaria chill afore it takes ye.

PETER. It's too early yet.

SIMEON. Dunno. He'd like t' catch us nappin'—jest t' have somethin' t' hoss us 'round over.

PETER (*mechanically gets to his feet.* SIMEON *does the same*). Waal—let's git t' wuk. (*They both plod mechanically toward the door before they realize. Then they stop short.*)

SIMEON (*grinning*). Ye're a cussed fool, Pete—and I be wuss! Let him see we hain't wukin'! We don't give a durn!

PETER (*as they go back to the table*). Not a damned durn! It'll serve t' show him we're done with him. (*They sit down again.* EBEN *stares from one to the other with surprise.*)

SIMEON (*grins at him*). We're aimin' t' start bein' lilies o' the field.

PETER. Nary a toil 'r spin 'r lick o' wuk do we put in!

SIMEON. Ye're sole owner—till he comes—that's what ye wanted. Waal, ye got t' be sole hand, too.

PETER. The cows air bellerin'. Ye better hustle at the milkin'.

EBEN (*with excited joy*). Ye mean ye'll sign the paper?

SIMEON (*dryly*). Mebbe.

PETER. Mebbe.

SIMEON. We're considerin'. (*Peremptorily*) Ye better git t' wuk.

EBEN (*with queer excitement*). It's Maw's farm agen! It's my farm! Them's my cows! I'll milk my durn fingers off fur cows o' mine! (*He goes out door in rear, they stare after him indifferently.*)

SIMEON. Like his Paw.

PETER. Dead spit 'n' image!

SIMEON. Waal—let dog eat dog! (EBEN *comes out of front door and around the corner of the house. The sky is beginning to grow flushed with sunrise.* EBEN *stops by the gate and stares around him with glowing, possessive eyes. He takes in the whole farm with his embracing glance of desire.*)

EBEN. It's purty! It's damned purty! It's mine! (*He suddenly throws his head back boldly and glares with hard, defiant eyes at the sky*) Mine, d'ye hear? Mine! (*He turns and walks quickly off left, rear, toward the barn. The two brothers light their pipes.*)

SIMEON (*putting his muddy boots up on the table, tilting back his chair, and puffing defiantly*). Waal—this air solid comfort—fur once.

PETER. Ay-eh. (*He follows suit. A pause. Unconsciously they both sigh.*)

SIMEON (*suddenly*). He never was much o' a hand at milkin', Eben wa'n't.

PETER (*with a snort*). His hands air like hoofs! (*A pause.*)

SIMEON. Reach down the jug thar! Let's take a swaller. I'm feelin' kind o' low.

PETER. Good idee! (*He does so—gets two glasses—they pour out drinks of whiskey*) Here's t' the gold in Californi-a!

SIMEON. An' luck t' find it! (*They drink—puff resolutely—sigh—take their feet down from the table.*)

PETER. Likker don't pear t' sot right.

SIMEON. We hain't used t' it this early. (*A pause. They become very restless.*)

PETER. Gittin' close in this kitchen.

SIMEON (*with immense relief*). Let's git a breath o' air. (*They arise briskly and go out rear—appear around house and stop by the gate. They stare up at the sky with a numbed appreciation.*)

PETER. Purty!

SIMEON. Ay-eh. Gold's t' the East now.

PETER. Sun's startin' with us fur the Golden West.

SIMEON (*staring around the farm, his compressed face tightened, unable to conceal his emotion*). Waal—it's our last mornin'—mebbe.

PETER (*the same*). Ay-eh.

SIMEON (*stamps his foot on the earth and addresses it desperately*). Waal—ye've thirty year o' me buried in ye—spread out over ye—blood an' bone an' sweat—rotted away—fertilizin' ye—richin' yer soul—prime manure, by God, that's what I been t' ye!

PETER. Ay-eh! An' me!

SIMEON. An' yew, Peter. (*He sighs—then spits*) Waal—no use'n cryin' over spilt milk.

PETER. They's gold in the West—an' freedom, mebbe. We been slaves t' stone walls here.

SIMEON (*defiantly*). We hain't nobody's slaves from this out—nor no thin's slaves nuther. (*A pause—restlessly*) Speakin' o' milk, wonder how Eben's managin'?

PETER. I s'pose he's managin'.

SIMEON. Mebbe we'd ought t' help—this once.

PETER. Mebbe. The cows knows us.

SIMEON. An' likes us. They don't know him much.

PETER. An' the hosses, an' pigs, an' chickens. They don't know him much.

SIMEON. They knows us like brothers—an' likes us! (*Proudly*) Hain't we raised 'em t' be fust-rate, number one prize stock?

PETER. We hain't—not no more.

SIMEON (*dully*). I was fergittin'. (*Then resignedly*) Waal, let's go help Eben a spell an' git waked up.

PETER. Suits me. (*They are starting off down left, rear, for the barn when* EBEN *appears from there hurrying toward them, his face excited.*)

EBEN (*breathlessly*). Waal—har they be! The old mule an' the bride! I seen 'em from the barn down below at the turnin'.

PETER. How could ye tell that far?

EBEN. Hain't I as far-sight as he's near-sight? Don't I know the mare 'n' buggy, an' two people settin' in it? Who else . . . ? An' I tell ye I kin feel 'em a-comin', too! (*He squirms as if he had the itch.*)

PETER (*beginning to be angry*). Waal—let him do his own unhitchin'!

SIMEON (*angry in his turn*). Let's hustle in an' git our bundles an' be a-goin' as he's a-comin'. I don't want never t' step inside the door agen arter he's back. (*They both start back around the corner of the house.* EBEN *follows them.*)

EBEN (*anxiously*). Will ye sign it afore ye go?

PETER. Let's see the color o' the old skinflint's money an' we'll sign. (*They disappear left. The two brothers clump upstairs to get their bundles.* EBEN *appears in the kitchen, runs to window, peers out, comes back and pulls up a strip of flooring in under stove, takes out a canvas bag and puts it on table, then he sets the floorboard back in place. The two brothers appear a moment after. They carry old carpet bags.*)

EBEN (*puts his hand on bag guardingly*). Have ye signed?

SIMEON (*shows paper in his hand*). Ay-eh. (*Greedily*) Be that the money?

EBEN (*opens bag and pours out pile of twenty-dollar gold pieces*). Twenty-dollar pieces—thirty on 'em. Count 'em. (*Peter does so, arranging them in stacks of five, biting one or two to test them.*)

PETER. Six hundred. (*He puts them in bag and puts it inside his shirt carefully.*)

SIMEON (*handing paper to* EBEN). Har ye be.

EBEN (*after a glance, folds it carefully and hides it under his shirt—gratefully*). Thank yew.

PETER. Thank yew fur the ride.

SIMEON. We'll send ye a lump o' gold fur Christmas. (*A pause.* EBEN *stares at them and they at him.*)

PETER (*awkwardly*). Waal—we're a-goin'.

SIMEON. Comin' out t' the yard?

EBEN. No. I'm waitin' in here a spell. (*Another silence. The brothers edge awkwardly to door in rear—then turn and stand.*)

SIMEON. Waal—good-by.

PETER. Good-by.

EBEN. Good-by. (*They go out. He sits down at the table, faces the stove and pulls out the paper. He looks from it to the stove. His face, lighted up by the shaft of sunlight from the window, has an expression of trance. His lips move. The two brothers come out to the gate.)*

PETER (*looking off toward barn*). Thar he be—unhitchin'.

SIMEON (*with a chuckle*). I'll bet ye he's riled!

PETER. An' thar she be.

SIMEON. Let's wait 'n' see what our new Maw looks like.

PETER (*with a grin*). An' give him our partin' cuss!

SIMEON (*grinning*). I feel like raisin' fun. I feel light in my head an' feet.

PETER. Me, too. I feel like laffin' till I'd split up the middle.

SIMEON. Reckon it's the likker?

PETER. No. My feet feel itchin' t' walk an' walk—an' jump high over thin's—an'. . . .

SIMEON. Dance? (*A pause.*)

PETER (*puzzled*). It's plumb onnateral.

SIMEON (*a light coming over his face*). I calc'late it's 'cause school's out. It's holiday. Fur once we're free!

PETER (*dazedly*). Free?

SIMEON. The halter's broke—the harness is busted—the fence bars is down—the stone walls air crumblin' an' tumblin'! We'll be kickin' up an' tearin' away down the road!

PETER (*drawing a deep breath—oratorically*). Anybody that wants this stinkin' old rock-pile of a farm kin hev it. T'ain't our'n, no sirree!

SIMEON (*takes the gate off its hinges and puts it under his arm*). We harby 'bolishes shet gates, an' open gates, an' all gates, by thunder!

PETER. We'll take it with us fur luck an' let 'er sail free down some river.

SIMEON (*as a sound of voices comes from left, rear*). Har they comes! (*The two brothers congeal into two stiff, grim-visaged statues.* EPHRAIM CABOT *and* ABBIE PUTNAM *come in.* CABOT *is seventy-five, tall and gaunt, with great, wiry, concentrated power, but stoop-shouldered from toil. His face is as hard as if it were hewn out of a boulder, yet there is a weakness in it, a petty pride in its own narrow strength. His eyes are small, close together, and extremely near-sighted, blinking continually in the effort to focus on objects, their stare having a straining, ingrowing quality. He is dressed in his dismal black Sunday suit.* ABBIE *is thirty-five, buxom, full of vitality. Her round face is pretty but marred by its rather gross sensuality. There is strength and obstinacy in her jaw, a hard determination in her eyes, and about her whole personality the same unsettled, untamed, desperate quality which is so apparent in* EBEN.)

CABOT (*as they enter—a queer strangled emotion in his dry cracking voice*). Har we be t' hum, Abbie.

ABBIE (*with lust for the word*). Hum! (*Her eyes gloating on the house without seeming to see the two stiff figures at the gate*) It's purty—purty! I can't b'lieve it's r'ally mine.

CABOT (*sharply*). Yewr'n? Mine! (*He stares at her penetratingly. She stares back. He adds relentingly*) Our'n—mebbe! It was lonesome too long. I was growin' old in the spring. A hum's got t' hev a woman.

ABBIE (*her voice taking possession*). A woman's got t' hev a hum!

CABOT (*nodding uncertainly*). Ay-eh. (*Then irritably*) Whar be they? Ain't thar nobody about—'r wukin'—'r nothin'?

ABBIE (*sees the brothers. She returns their stare of cold appraising contempt with interest—slowly*). Thar's two men loafin' at the gate an' starin' at me like a couple o' strayed hogs.

CABOT (*straining his eyes*). I kin see 'em—but I can't make out. . . .

SIMEON. It's Simeon.

PETER. It's Peter.

CABOT (*exploding*). Why hain't ye wukin'?

SIMEON (*dryly*). We're waitin' t' welcome ye hum—yew an' the bride!

CABOT (*confusedly*). Huh? Waal—this be yer new Maw, boys. (*She stares at them and they at her.*)

SIMEON (*turns away and spits contemptuously*). I see her!

PETER (*spits also*). An' I see her!

ABBIE (*with the conqueror's conscious superiority*). I'll go in an' look at *my* house. (*She goes slowly around to porch.*)

SIMEON (*with a snort*). Her house!

PETER (*calls after her*). Ye'll find Eben inside. Ye better not tell him it's *yewr* house.

ABBIE (*mouthing the name*). Eben. (*Then quietly*) I'll tell Eben.

CABOT (*with a contemptuous sneer*). Ye needn't heed Eben. Eben's a dumb fool—like his Maw—soft an' simple!

SIMEON (*with his sardonic burst of laughter*). Ha! Eben's a chip o' yew —spit 'n' image—hard 'n' bitter's a hickory tree! Dog'll eat dog. He'll eat ye yet, old man!

CABOT (*commandingly*). Ye git t' wuk!

SIMEON (*as ABBIE disappears in house—winks at PETER and says tauntingly*). So that thar's our new Maw, be it? Whar in hell did ye dig her up? (*He and PETER laugh.*)

PETER. Ha! Ye'd better turn her in the pen with the other sows. (*They laugh uproariously, slapping their thighs.*)

CABOT (*so amazed at their effrontery that he stutters in confusion*). Simeon! Peter! What's come over ye? Air ye drunk?

SIMEON. We're free, old man—free o' yew an' the hull damned farm! (*They grow more and more hilarious and excited.*)

PETER. An' we're startin' out fur the gold fields o' Californi-a!

SIMEON. Ye kin take this place an' burn it!

PETER. An' bury it—fur all we cares!

SIMEON. We're free, old man! (*He cuts a caper.*)

PETER. Free! (*He gives a kick in the air.*)

SIMEON (*in a frenzy*). Whoop!

PETER. Whoop! (*They do an absurd Indian war dance about the old man who is petrified between rage and the fear that they are insane.*)

SIMEON. We're free as Injuns! Lucky we don't skulp ye!

PETER. An' burn yer barn an' kill the stock!

SIMEON. An' rape yer new woman! Whoop! (*He and* PETER *stop their dance, holding their sides, rocking with wild laughter.*)

CABOT (*edging away*). Lust fur gold—fur the sinful, easy gold o' Californi-a! It's made ye mad!

SIMEON (*tauntingly*). Wouldn't ye like us to send ye back some sinful gold, ye old sinner?

PETER. They's gold besides what's in Californi-a! (*He retreats back beyond the vision of the old man and takes the bag of money and flaunts it in the air above his head, laughing.*)

SIMEON. And sinfuller, too!

PETER. We'll be voyagin' on the sea! Whoop! (*He leaps up and down.*)

SIMEON. Livin' free! Whoop! (*He leaps in turn.*)

CABOT (*suddenly roaring with rage*). My cuss on ye!

SIMEON. Take our'n in trade fur it! Whoop!

CABOT. I'll hev ye both chained up in the asylum!

PETER. Ye old skinflint! Good-by!

SIMEON. Ye old blood sucker! Good-by!

CABOT. Go afore I . . . !

PETER. Whoop! (*He picks a stone from the road.* SIMEON *does the same.*)

SIMEON. Maw'll be in the parlor.

PETER. Ay-eh! One! Two!

CABOT (*frightened*). What air ye . . . ?

PETER. Three! (*They both throw, the stones hitting the parlor window with a crash of glass, tearing the shade.*)

SIMEON. Whoop!

PETER. Whoop!

CABOT (*in a fury now, rushing toward them*). If I kin lay hands on ye— I'll break yer bones fur ye! (*But they beat a capering retreat before him,* SIMEON *with the gate still under his arm.* CABOT *comes back, panting with impotent rage. Their voices as they go off take up the song of the gold-seekers to the old tune of "Oh, Susannah!"*)

> "I jumped aboard the Liza ship,
> And traveled on the sea,
> And every time I thought of home
> I wished it wasn't me!
> Oh! Californi-a,
> That's the land fur me!
> I'm off to Californi-a!
> With my wash bowl on my knee."

(*In the meantime, the window of the upper bedroom on right is raised and* ABBIE *sticks her head out. She looks down at* CABOT—*with a sigh of relief.*)

ABBIE. Waal—that's the last o' them two, hain't it? (*He doesn't answer. Then in possessive tones*) This here's a nice bedroom, Ephraim. It's a r'al nice bed. Is it my room, Ephraim?

CABOT (*grimly—without looking up*). Our'n! (*She cannot control a grimace of aversion and pulls back her head slowly and shuts the window. A sudden horrible thought seems to enter* CABOT'S *head*) They been up to somethin'! Mebbe—mebbe they've pizened the stock—'r somethin'! (*He almost runs off down toward the barn. A moment later the kitchen door is slowly pushed open and* ABBIE *enters. For a moment she stands looking at* EBEN. *He does not notice her at first. Her eyes take him in penetratingly with a calculating appraisal of his strength as against hers. But under this her desire is dimly awakened by his youth and good looks. Suddenly he becomes conscious of her presence and looks up. Their eyes meet. He leaps to his feet, glowering at her speechlessly.*)

ABBIE (*in her most seductive tones which she uses all through this scene*). Be you—Eben? I'm Abbie—(*She laughs*) I mean, I'm yer new Maw.

EBEN (*viciously*). No, damn ye!

ABBIE (*as if she hadn't heard—with a queer smile*). Yer Paw's spoke a lot o' yew. . . .

EBEN. Ha!

ABBIE. Ye mustn't mind him. He's an old man. (*A long pause. They stare at each other*) I don't want t' pretend playin' Maw t' ye, Eben. (*Admiringly*) Ye're too big an' too strong fur that. I want t' be frens with ye. Mebbe with me fur a fren ye'd find ye'd like livin' here better. I kin make it easy fur ye with him, mebbe. (*With a scornful sense of power*) I calc'late I kin git him t' do most anythin' fur me.

EBEN (*with bitter scorn*). Ha! (*They stare again,* EBEN *obscurely moved, physically attracted to her—in forced stilted tones*) Yew kin go t' the devil!

ABBIE (*calmly*). If cussin' me does ye good, cuss all ye've a mind t'. I'm all prepared t' have ye agin me—at fust. I don't blame ye nuther. I'd feel the same at any stranger comin' t' take my Maw's place. (*He shudders. She is watching him carefully*) Yew must've cared a lot fur yewr Maw, didn't ye? My Maw died afore I'd growed. I don't remember her none. (*A pause*) But yew won't hate me long, Eben. I'm not the wust in the world—an' yew an' me've got a lot in common. I kin tell that by lookin' at ye. Waal—I've had a hard life, too—oceans o' trouble an' nuthin' but wuk fur reward. I was a orphan early an' had t' wuk fur others in other folks' hums. Then I married an' he turned out a drunken spreer an' so he had to wuk fur others an' me too agen in other folks' hums, an' the baby died, an' my husband got sick an' died too, an' I was glad sayin' now I'm free fur once, on'y I diskivered right away all I was free fur was t' wuk agen in other folks' hums, doin' other folks' wuk till I'd most give up hope o' ever doin' my own wuk in my own hum, an' then your Paw come. . . . (CABOT *appears returning from the barn. He comes to the gate and looks down the road the brothers have gone. A faint strain of their retreating voices is head: "Oh, Californi-a! That's the place for me." He stands glowering, his fist clenched, his face grim with rage.*)

EBEN (*fighting against his growing attraction and sympathy—harshly*). An' bought yew—like a harlot! (*She is stung and flushes angrily. She has been sincerely moved by the recital of her troubles. He adds furiously*) An' the price he's payin' ye—this farm—was my Maw's, damn ye!—an' mine now!

ABBIE (*with a cool laugh of confidence*). Yewr'n? We'll see 'bout that! (*Then strongly*) Waal—what if I did need a hum? What else'd I marry an old man like him fur?

EBEN (*maliciously*). I'll tell him ye said that!

ABBIE (*smiling*). I'll say ye're lyin' a-purpose—an' he'll drive ye off the place!

EBEN. Ye devil!

ABBIE (*defying him*). This be my farm—this be my hum—this be my kitchen—!

EBEN (*furiously, as if he were going to attack her*). Shut up, damn ye!

ABBIE (*walks up to him—a queer coarse expression of desire in her face and body—slowly*). An' upstairs—that be my bedroom—an' my bed! (*He stares into her eyes, terribly confused and torn. She adds softly*) I hain't bad nor mean—'ceptin' fur an enemy—but I got t' fight fur what's due me out o' life, if I ever 'spect t' git it. (*Then putting her hand on his arm—seductively*) Let's yew 'n' me be frens, Eben.

EBEN (*stupidly—as if hypnotized*). Ay-eh. (*Then furiously flinging off her arm*) No, ye durned old witch! I hate ye! (*He rushes out the door.*)

ABBIE (*looks after him smiling satisfiedly—then half to herself, mouthing the word*). Eben's nice. (*She looks at the table, proudly*) I'll wash up my dishes now. (EBEN *appears outside, slamming the door behind him. He comes around corner, stops on seeing his father, and stands staring at him with hate.*)

CABOT (*raising his arms to heaven in the fury he can no longer control*). Lord God o' Hosts, smite the undutiful sons with Thy wust cuss!

EBEN (*breaking in violently*). Yew 'n' yewr God! Allus cussin' folks —allus naggin' 'em!

CABOT (*oblivious to him—summoningly*). God o' the old! God o' the lonesome!

EBEN (*mockingly*). Naggin' His sheep t' sin! T' hell with yewr God! (CABOT *turns. He and* EBEN *glower at each other.*)

CABOT (*harshly*). So it's yew. I might've knowed it. (*Shaking his finger threateningly at him*) Blasphemin' fool! (*Then quickly*) Why hain't ye t' wuk?

EBEN. Why hain't yew? They've went. I can't wuk it all alone.

CABOT (*contemptuously*). Nor noways! I'm wuth ten o' ye yit, old's I be! Ye'll never be more'n half a man! (*Then, matter-of-factly*) Waal—let's git t' the barn. (*They go. A last faint note of the "Californi-a" song is heard from the distance.* ABBIE *is washing her dishes.*)

CURTAIN

PART TWO—SCENE ONE

The exterior of the farmhouse, as in Part One—a hot Sunday afternoon two months later. ABBIE, *dressed in her best, is discovered sitting in a rocker at the end of the porch. She rocks listlessly, enervated by the heat, staring in front of her with bored, half-closed eyes.*

EBEN *sticks his head out of his bedroom window. He looks around furtively and tries to see—or hear—if anyone is on the porch, but although he has been careful to make no noise,* ABBIE *has sensed his movement. She stops rocking, her face grows animated and eager, she waits attentively.* EBEN *seems to feel her presence, he scowls back his thoughts of her and spits with exaggerated disdain—then withdraws back into the room.* ABBIE *waits, holding her breath as she listens with passionate eagerness for every sound within the house.*

EBEN *comes out. Their eyes meet. His falter, he is confused, he turns away and slams the door resentfully. At this gesture,* ABBIE *laughs tantalizingly, amused but at the same time piqued and irritated. He scowls, strides off the porch to the path and starts to walk past her to the road with a grand swagger of ignoring her existence. He is dressed in his store suit, spruced up, his face shines from soap and water.* ABBIE *leans forward on her chair, her eyes hard and angry now, and, as he passes her, gives a sneering, taunting chuckle.*

EBEN (*stung—turns on her furiously*). What air yew cacklin' 'bout?

ABBIE (*triumphant*). Yew!

EBEN. What about me?

ABBIE. Ye look all slicked up like a prize bull.

EBEN (*with a sneer*). Waal—ye hain't so durned purty yerself, be ye? (*They stare into each other's eyes, his held by hers in spite of himself, hers glowingly possessive. Their physical attraction becomes a palpable force quivering in the hot air.*)

ABBIE (*softly*). Ye don't mean that, Eben. Ye may think ye mean it, mebbe, but ye don't. Ye can't. It's agin nature, Eben. Ye been fightin' yer nature ever since the day I come—tryin' t' tell yerself I hain't purty t'ye. (*She laughs a low humid laugh without taking her eyes from his. A pause —her body squirms desirously—she murmurs languorously*) Hain't the sun strong an' hot? Ye kin feel it burnin' into the earth—Nature—makin' thin's grow—bigger 'n' bigger—burnin' inside ye—makin' ye want t' grow —into somethin' else—till ye're jined with it—an' it's your'n—but it owns ye, too—an' makes ye grow bigger—like a tree—like them elums— (*She laughs again softly, holding his eyes. He takes a step toward her, compelled against his will)* Nature'll beat ye, Eben. Ye might's well own up t' it fust 's last.

EBEN *(trying to break from her spell—confusedly)*. If Paw'd hear ye goin' on. . . . *(Resentfully)* But ye've made such a damned idjit out o' the old devil . . . ! *(ABBIE laughs.)*

ABBIE. Waal—hain't it easier fur yew with him changed softer?

EBEN *(defiantly)*. No. I'm fightin' him—fightin' yew—fightin' fur Maw's rights t' her hum! *(This breaks her spell for him. He glowers at her)* An' I'm onto ye. Ye hain't foolin' me a mite. Ye're aimin' t' swaller up everythin' an' make it your'n. Waal, you'll find I'm a heap sight bigger hunk nor yew kin chew! *(He turns from her with a sneer.)*

ABBIE *(trying to regain her ascendancy—seductively)*. Eben!

EBEN. Leave me be! *(He starts to walk away.)*

ABBIE *(more commandingly)*. Eben!

EBEN *(stops—resentfully)*. What d'ye want?

ABBIE *(trying to conceal a growing excitement)*. Whar air ye goin'?

EBEN *(with malicious nonchalance)*. Oh—up the road a spell.

ABBIE. T' the village?

EBEN *(airily)*. Mebbe.

ABBIE *(excitedly)*. T' see that Min, I s'pose?

EBEN. Mebbe.

ABBIE *(weakly)*. What d'ye want t' waste time on her fur?

EBEN *(revenging himself now—grinning at her)*. Ye can't beat Nature, didn't ye say? *(He laughs and again starts to walk away.)*

ABBIE *(bursting out)*. An ugly old hake!

EBEN *(with a tantalizing sneer)*. She's purtier'n yew be!

ABBIE. That every wuthless drunk in the country has. . . .

EBEN *(tauntingly)*. Mebbe—but she's better'n yew. She owns up fa'r 'n' squar' t' her doin's.

ABBIE *(furiously)*. Don't ye dare compare. . . .

EBEN. She don't go sneakin' an' stealin'—what's mine.

ABBIE *(savagely seizing on his weak point)*. Your'n? Yew mean—my farm?

EBEN. I mean the farm yew sold yerself fur like any other old whore—my farm!

ABBIE *(stung—fiercely)*. Ye'll never live t' see the day when even a stinkin' weed on it 'll belong t' ye! *(Then in a scream)* Git out o' my sight! Go on t' yer slut—disgracin' yer Paw 'n' me! I'll git yer Paw t' horsewhip ye off the place if I want t'! Ye're only livin' here 'cause I tolerate ye! Git along! I hate the sight o' ye! *(She stops, panting and glaring at him.)*

EBEN *(returning her glance in kind)*. An' I hate the sight o' yew! *(He turns and strides off up the road. She follows his retreating figure with concentrated hate. Old CABOT appears coming up from the barn. The hard, grim expression of his face has changed. He seems in some queer way softened, mellowed. His eyes have taken on a strange, incongruous dreamy quality. Yet there is no hint of physical weakness about him— rather he looks more robust and younger. ABBIE sees him and turns away quickly with unconcealed aversion. He comes slowly up to her.*)

CABOT (*mildly*). War yew an' Eben quarrelin' agen?

ABBIE (*shortly*). No.

CABOT. Ye was talkin' a'mighty loud. (*He sits down on the edge of porch.*)

ABBIE (*snappishly*). If ye heerd us they hain't no need askin' questions.

CABOT. I didn't hear what ye said.

ABBIE (*relieved*). Waal—it wa'n't nothin' t' speak on.

CABOT (*after a pause*). Eben's queer.

ABBIE (*bitterly*). He's the dead spit 'n' image o' yew!

CABOT (*queerly interested*). D'ye think so, Abbie? (*After a pause, ruminatingly*) Me 'n' Eben's allus fit 'n' fit. I never could b'ar him noways. He's so thunderin' soft—like his Maw.

ABBIE (*scornfully*). Ay-eh! 'Bout as soft as yew be!

CABOT (*as if he hadn't heard*). Mebbe I been too hard on him.

ABBIE (*jeeringly*). Waal—ye're gittin' soft now—soft as slop! That's what Eben was sayin'.

CABOT (*his face instantly grim and ominous*). Eben was sayin'? Waal, he'd best not do nothin' t' try me 'r he'll soon diskiver. . . . (*A pause. She keeps her face turned away. His gradually softens. He stares up at the sky*) Purty, hain't it?

ABBIE (*crossly*). I don't see nothin' purty.

CABOT. The sky. Feels like a wa'm field up thar.

ABBIE (*sarcastically*). Air yew aimin' t' buy up over the farm too? (*She snickers contemptuously.*)

CABOT (*strangely*). I'd like t' own my place up thar. (*A pause*) I'm gittin' old, Abbie. I'm gittin' ripe on the bough. (*A pause. She stares at him mystified. He goes on*) It's allus lonesome cold in the house—even when it's bilin' hot outside. Hain't yew noticed?

ABBIE. No.

CABOT. It's wa'm down t' the barn—nice smellin' an' warm—with the cows. (*A pause*) Cows is queer.

ABBIE. Like yew?

CABOT. Like Eben. (*A pause*) I'm gittin' t' feel resigned t' Eben—jest as I got t' feel 'bout his Maw. I'm gittin' t' learn to b'ar his softness—jest like her'n. I calc'late I c'd a'most take t' him—if he wa'n't sech a dumb fool! (*A pause*) I s'pose it's old age a-creepin' in my bones.

ABBIE (*indifferently*). Waal—ye hain't dead yet.

CABOT (*roused*). No, I hain't, yew bet—not by a hell of a sight—I'm sound 'n' tough as hickory! (*Then moodily*) But arter three score and ten the Lord warns ye t' prepare. (*A pause*) That's why Eben's come in my head. Now that his cussed sinful brothers is gone their path t' hell, they's no one left but Eben.

ABBIE (*resentfully*). They's me, hain't they? (*Agitatedly*) What's all this sudden likin' ye've tuk to Eben? Why don't ye say nothin' 'bout me? Hain't I yer lawful wife?

CABOT (*simply*). Ay-eh. Ye be. (*A pause—he stares at her desirously—his eyes grow avid—then with a sudden movement he seizes her hands and squeezes them, declaiming in a queer camp meeting preacher's tempo*) Yew air my Rose o' Sharon! Behold, yew air fair; yer eyes air doves; yer lips air like scarlet; yer two breasts air like two fawns; yer navel be like a round goblet; yer belly be like a heap o' wheat. . . . (*He covers her hand with kisses. She does not seem to notice. She stares before her with hard angry eyes.*)

ABBIE (*jerking her hands away—harshly*). So ye're plannin' t' leave the farm t' Eben, air ye?

CABOT (*dazedly*). Leave. . . ? (*Then with resentful obstinacy*) I hain't a-givin' it t' no one!

ABBIE (*remorselessly*). Ye can't take it with ye.

CABOT (*thinks a moment—then reluctantly*). No, I calc'late not. (*After a pause—with a strange passion*) But if I could, I would, by the Etarnal! 'R if I could, in my dyin' hour, I'd set it afire an' watch it burn—this house an' every ear o' corn an' every tree down t' the last blade o' hay! I'd sit an' know it was all a-dying with me an' no one else'd ever own what was mine, what I'd made out o' nothin' with my own sweat 'n' blood! (*A pause—then he adds with a queer affection*) 'Ceptin' the cows. Them I'd turn free.

ABBIE (*harshly*). An' me?

CABOT (*with a queer smile*). Ye'd be turned free, too.

ABBIE (*furiously*). So that's the thanks I git fur marryin' ye—t' have ye change kind to Eben who hates ye, an' talk o' turnin' me out in the road.

CABOT (*hastily*). Abbie! Ye know I wa'n't. . . .

ABBIE (*vengefully*). Just let me tell ye a thing or two 'bout Eben! Whar's he gone? T' see that harlot, Min! I tried fur t' stop him. Disgracin' yew an' me—on the Sabbath, too!

CABOT (*rather guiltily*). He's a sinner—nateral-born. It's lust eatin' his heart.

ABBIE (*enraged beyond endurance—wildly vindictive*). An' his lust fur me! Kin ye find excuses fur that?

CABOT (*stares at her—after a dead pause*). Lust—fur yew?

ABBIE (*defiantly*). He was tryin' t' make love t' me—when ye heerd us quarrelin'.

CABOT (*stares at her—then a terrible expression of rage comes over his face—he springs to his feet shaking all over*). By the A'mighty God—I'll end him!

ABBIE (*frightened now for* EBEN). No! Don't ye!

CABOT (*violently*). I'll git the shotgun an' blow his soft brains t' the top o' them elums!

ABBIE (*throwing her arms around him*). No, Ephraim!

CABOT (*pushing her away violently*). I will, by God!

ABBIE (*in a quieting tone*). Listen, Ephraim. 'Twa'n't nothin' bad—on'y a boy's foolin'—'twa'n't meant serious—jest jokin' an' teasin'. . . .

CABOT. Then why did ye say—lust?

ABBIE. It must hev sounded wusser'n I meant. An' I was mad at thinkin' —ye'd leave him the farm.

CABOT (*quieter but still grim and cruel*). Waal then, I'll horsewhip him off the place if that much'll content ye.

ABBIE (*reaching out and taking his hand*). No. Don't think o' me! Ye mustn't drive him off. 'Tain't sensible. Who'll ye get to help ye on the farm? They's no one hereabouts.

CABOT (*considers this—then nodding his appreciation*). Ye got a head on ye. (*Then irritably*) Waal, let him stay. (*He sits down on the edge of the porch. She sits beside him. He murmurs contemptuously*) I oughtn't t' git riled so—at that 'ere fool calf. (*A pause*) But har's the p'int. What son o' mine'll keep on here t' the farm—when the Lord does call me? Simeon an' Peter air gone t' hell—an' Eben's follerin' 'em.

ABBIE. They's me.

CABOT. Ye're on'y a woman.

ABBIE. I'm yewr wife.

CABOT. That hain't me. A son is me—my blood—mine. Mine ought t' git mine. An' then it's still mine—even though I be six foot under. D'ye see?

ABBIE (*giving him a look of hatred*). Ay-eh. I see. (*She becomes very thoughtful, her face growing shrewd, her eyes studying* CABOT *craftily.*)

CABOT. I'm gittin' old—ripe on the bough. (*Then with a sudden forced reassurance*) Not but what I hain't a hard nut t' crack even yet—an' fur many a year t' come! By the Eternal, I kin break most o' the young fellers' backs at any kind o' work any day o' the year!

ABBIE (*suddenly*). Mebbe the Lord'll give *us* a son.

CABOT (*turns and stares at her eagerly*). Ye mean—a son—t' me 'n' yew?

ABBIE (*with a cajoling smile*). Ye're a strong man yet, hain't ye? 'Tain't noways impossible, be it? We know that. Why d'ye stare so? Hain't ye never thought o' that afore? I been thinkin' o' it all along. Ay-eh—an' I been prayin' it'd happen, too.

CABOT (*his face growing full of joyous pride and a sort of religious ecstasy*). Ye been prayin', Abbie?—fur a son?—t' us?

ABBIE. Ay-eh. (*With a grim resolution*) I want a son now.

CABOT (*excitedly clutching both of her hands in his*). It'd be the blessin' o' God, Abbie—the blessin' o' God A'mighty on me—in my old age—in my lonesomeness! They hain't nothin' I wouldn't do fur ye then, Abbie. Ye'd hev on'y t' ask it—anythin' ye'd a mind t'!

ABBIE (*interrupting*). Would ye will the farm t' me then—t' me an' it . . . ?

CABOT (*vehemently*). I'd do anythin' ye axed, I tell ye! I swar it! May I be everlastin' damned t' hell if I wouldn't! (*He sinks to his knees pulling her down with him. He trembles all over with the fervor of his hopes*) Pray t' the Lord agen, Abbie. It's the Sabbath! I'll jine ye! Two prayers air better nor one. "An' God hearkened unto Rachel"! An' God hearkened unto Abbie! Pray, Abbie! Pray fur him to hearken! (*He bows his head, mumbling. She pretends to do likewise but gives him a side glance of scorn and triumph.*)

SCENE TWO

About eight in the evening. The interior of the two bedrooms on the top floor is shown. EBEN *is sitting on the side of his bed in the room on the left. On account of the heat he has taken off everything but his undershirt and pants. His feet are bare. He faces front, brooding moodily, his chin propped on his hands, a desperate expression on his face.*

In the other room CABOT *and* ABBIE *are sitting side by side on the edge of their bed, an old four-poster with feather mattress. He is in his night shirt, she in her nightdress. He is still in the queer, excited mood into which the notion of a son has thrown him. Both rooms are lighted dimly and flickeringly by tallow candles.*

CABOT. The farm needs a son.

ABBIE. I need a son.

CABOT. Ay-eh. Sometimes ye air the farm an' sometimes the farm be yew. That's why I clove t' ye in my lonesomeness. (*A pause. He pounds his knee with his fist*) Me an' the farm has got t' beget a son!

ABBIE. Ye'd best go t' sleep. Ye're gittin' thin's all mixed.

CABOT (*with an impatient gesture*). No, I hain't. My mind's clear's a well. Ye don't know me, that's it. (*He stares hopelessly at the floor.*)

ABBIE (*indifferently*). Mebbe. (*In the next room* EBEN *gets up and paces up and down distractedly.* ABBIE *hears him. Her eyes fasten on the intervening wall with concentrated attention.* EBEN *stops and stares. Their hot glances seem to meet through the wall. Unconsciously he stretches out his arms for her and she half rises. Then aware, he mutters a curse at himself and flings himself face downward on the bed, his clenched fists above his head, his face buried in the pillow.* ABBIE *relaxes with a faint sigh but her eyes remain fixed on the wall; she listens with all her attention for some movement from* EBEN.)

CABOT (*suddenly raises his head and looks at her—scornfully*). Will ye ever know me—'r will any man 'r woman? (*Shaking his head*) No. I calc'late 't wa'n't t' be. (*He turns away.* ABBIE *looks at the wall. Then, evidently unable to keep silent about his thoughts, without looking at his wife, he puts out his hand and clutches her knee. She starts violently, looks at him, sees he is not watching her, concentrates again on the wall and pays no attention to what he says*) Listen, Abbie. When I come here fifty odd year ago—I was jest twenty an' the strongest an' hardest ye ever seen—ten times as strong an' fifty times as hard as Eben. Waal—this place was nothin' but fields o' stones. Folks laughed when I tuk it. They couldn't know what I knowed. When ye kin make corn sprout out o' stones,

God's livin' in yew! They wa'n't strong enuf fur that! They reckoned God was easy. They laughed. They don't laugh no more. Some died hereabouts. Some went West an' died. They're all under ground—fur follerin' arter an easy God. God hain't easy. (*He shakes his head slowly*) An' I growed hard. Folks kept allus sayin' he's a hard man like 'twas sinful t' be hard, so's at last I said back at 'em: Waal then, by thunder, ye'll git me hard an' see how ye like it! (*Then suddenly*) But I give in t' weakness once. 'Twas arter I'd been here two year. I got weak—despairful—they was so many stones. They was a party leavin', givin' up, goin' West. I jined 'em. We tracked on 'n' on. We come t' broad medders, plains, whar the soil was black an' rich as gold. Nary a stone. Easy. Ye'd on'y to plow an' sow an' then set an' smoke yer pipe an' watch thin's grow. I could o' been a rich man—but somethin' in me fit me an fit me—the voice o' God sayin': "This hain't wuth nothin' t' Me. Git ye back t' hum!" I got afeerd o' that voice an' I lit out back t' hum here, leavin' my claim an' crops t' whoever'd a mind t' take 'em. Ay-eh. I actoolly give up what was rightful mine! God's hard, not easy! God's in the stones! Build my church on a rock—out o' stones an' I'll be in them! That's what He meant t' Peter! (*He sighs heavily—a pause*) Stones. I picked 'em up an' piled 'em into walls. Ye kin read the years o' my life in them walls, every day a hefted stone, climbin' over the hills up and down, fencin' in the fields that was mine, whar I'd made thin's grow out o' nothin'—like the will o' God, like the servant o' His hand. It wa'n't easy. It was hard an' He made me hard fur it. (*He pauses*) All the time I kept gittin' lonesomer. I tuk a wife. She bore Simeon an' Peter. She was a good woman. She wuked hard. We was married twenty year. She never knowed me. She helped but she never knowed what she was helpin'. I was allus lonesome. She died. After that it wa'n't so lonesome fur a spell. (*A pause*) I lost count o' the years. I had no time t' fool away countin' 'em. Sim an' Peter helped. The farm growed. It was all mine! When I thought o' that I didn't feel lonesome. (*A pause*) But ye can't hitch yer mind t' one thin' day an' night. I tuk another wife—Eben's Maw. Her folks was contestin' me at law over my deeds t' the farm—my farm! That's why Eben keeps a-talkin' his fool talk o' this bein' his Maw's farm. She bore Eben. She was purty—but soft. She tried t' be hard. She couldn't. She never knowed me nor nothin'. It was lonesomer 'n hell with her. After a matter o' sixteen odd years. she died. (*A pause*) I lived with the boys. They hated me 'cause I was hard. I hated them 'cause they was soft. They coveted the farm without knowin' what it meant. It made me bitter 'n wormwood. It aged me—them coveting what I'd made fur mine. Then this spring the call come—the voice o' God cryin' in my wilderness, in my lonesomeness—t' go out an' seek an' find! (*Turning to her with strange passion*) I sought ye an' I found ye! Yew air my Rose o' Sharon! Yer eyes air like. . . . (*She has turned a blank face, resentful eyes to his. He stares at her for a moment—then harshly*) Air ye any the wiser fur all I've told ye?

ABBIE (*confusedly*). Mebbe.

CABOT (*pushing her away from him—angrily*). Ye don't know nothin'—nor never will. If ye don't hev a son t' redeem ye. . . . (*This in a tone of cold threat.*)

ABBIE (*resentfully*). I've prayed, hain't I?

CABOT (*bitterly*). Pray agen—fur understandin'!

ABBIE (*a veiled threat in her tone*). Ye'll have a son out o' me, I promise ye.

CABOT. How kin ye promise?

ABBIE. I got second-sight mebbe. I kin foretell. (*She gives a queer smile.*)

CABOT. I believe ye have. Ye give me the chills sometimes. (*He shivers*) It's cold in this house. It's oneasy. They's thin's pokin' about in the dark—in the corners. (*He pulls on his trousers, tucking in his night shirt, and pulls on his boots.*)

ABBIE (*surprised*). Whar air ye goin'?

CABOT (*queerly*). Down whar it's restful—whar it's warm—down t' the barn. (*Bitterly*) I kin talk t' the cows. They know. They know the farm an' me. They'll give me peace. (*He turns to go out the door.*)

ABBIE (*a bit frightenedly*). Air ye ailin' tonight, Ephraim?

CABOT. Growin'. Growin' ripe on the bough. (*He turns and goes, his boots clumping down the stairs. EBEN sits up with a start, listening. ABBIE is conscious of his movement and stares at the wall. CABOT comes out of the house around the corner and stands by the gate, blinking at the sky. He stretches up his hands in a tortured gesture*) God A'mighty, call from the dark! (*He listens as if expecting an answer. Then his arms drop, he shakes his head and plods off toward the barn. EBEN and ABBIE stare at each other through the wall. EBEN sighs heavily and ABBIE echoes it. Both become terribly nervous, uneasy. Finally ABBIE gets up and listens, her ear to the wall. He acts as if he saw every move she was making, he becomes resolutely still. She seems driven into a decision—goes out the door in rear determinedly. His eyes follow her. Then as the door of his room is opened softly, he turns away, waits in an attitude of strained fixity. ABBIE stands for a second staring at him, her eyes burning with desire. Then with a little cry she runs over and throws her arms about his neck, she pulls his head back and covers his mouth with kisses. At first, he submits dumbly; then he puts his arms about her neck and returns her kisses, but finally, suddenly aware of his hatred, he hurls her away from him, springing to his feet. They stand speechless and breathless, panting like two animals.*)

ABBIE (*at last—painfully*). Ye shouldn't, Eben—ye shouldn't—I'd make ye happy!

EBEN (*harshly*). I don't want t' be happy—from yew!

ABBIE (*helplessly*). Ye do, Eben! Ye do! Why d'ye lie?

EBEN (*viciously*). I don't take t'ye, I tell ye! I hate the sight o' ye!

ABBIE (*with an uncertain troubled laugh*). Waal, I kissed ye anyways—an' ye kissed back—yer lips was burnin'—ye can't lie 'bout that! (*In-*

tensely) If ye don't care, why did ye kiss me back—why was yer lips burnin'?

EBEN (*wiping his mouth*). It was like pizen on 'em. (*Then tauntingly*) When I kissed ye back, mebbe I thought 'twas someone else.

ABBIE (*wildly*). Min?

EBEN. Mebbe.

ABBIE (*torturedly*). Did ye go t' see her? Did ye r'ally go? I thought ye mightn't. Is that why ye throwed me off jest now?

EBEN (*sneeringly*). What if it be?

ABBIE (*raging*). Then ye're a dog, Eben Cabot!

EBEN (*threateningly*). Ye can't talk that way t' me!

ABBIE (*with a shrill laugh*). Can't I? Did ye think I was in love with ye —a weak thin' like yew? Not much! I on'y wanted ye fur a purpose o' my own—an' I'll hev ye fur it yet 'cause I'm stronger'n yew be!

EBEN (*resentfully*). I knowed well it was on'y part o' yer plan t' swaller everythin'!

ABBIE (*tauntingly*). Mebbe!

EBEN (*furious*). Git out o' my room!

ABBIE. This air my room an' ye're on'y hired help!

EBEN (*threateningly*). Git out afore I murder ye!

ABBIE (*quite confident now*). I hain't a mite afeerd. Ye want me, don't ye? Yes, ye do! An' yer Paw's son'll never kill what he wants! Look at yer eyes! They's lust fur me in 'em, burnin' 'em up! Look at yer lips now! They're tremblin' an' longin' t' kiss me, an' yer teeth t' bite! (*He is watching her now with a horrible fascination. She laughs a crazy triumphant laugh*) I'm a-goin' t' make all o' this hum my hum! They's one room hain't mine yet, but it's a-goin' t' be tonight. I'm a-goin' down now an' light up! (*She makes him a mocking bow*) Won't ye come courtin' me in the best parlor, Mister Cabot?

EBEN (*staring at her—horribly confused—dully*). Don't ye dare! It hain't been opened since Maw died an' was laid out thar! Don't ye . . . ! (*But her eyes are fixed on his so burningly that his will seems to wither before hers. He stands swaying toward her helplessly.*)

ABBIE (*holding his eyes and putting all her will into her words as she backs out the door*). I'll expect ye afore long, Eben.

EBEN (*stares after her for a while, walking toward the door. A light appears in the parlor window. He murmurs*). In the parlor? (*This seems to arouse connotations for he comes back and puts on his white shirt, collar, half ties the tie mechanically, puts on coat, takes his hat, stands barefooted looking about him in bewilderment, mutters wonderingly*) Maw! Whar air yew? (*Then goes slowly toward the door in rear.*)

SCENE THREE

A few minutes later. The interior of the parlor is shown. A grim, repressed room like a tomb in which the family has been interred alive.

ABBIE *sits on the edge of the horsehair sofa. She has lighted all the candles and the room is revealed in all its preserved ugliness. A change has come over the woman. She looks awed and frightened now, ready to run away.*

The door is opened, and EBEN *appears. His face wears an expression of obsessed confusion. He stands staring at her, his arms hanging disjointedly from his shoulders, his feet bare, his hat in his hand.*

ABBIE (*after a pause—with a nervous, formal politeness*). Won't ye set?

EBEN (*dully*). Ay-eh. (*Mechanically he places his hat carefully on the floor near the door and sits stiffly beside her on the edge of the sofa. A pause. They both remain rigid, looking straight ahead with eyes full of fear.*)

ABBIE. When I fust come in—in the dark—they seemed somethin' here.

EBEN (*simply*). Maw.

ABBIE. I kin still feel—somethin'. . . .

EBEN. It's Maw.

ABBIE. At fust I was feered o' it. I wanted t' yell an' run. Now—since yew come—seems like it's growin' soft an' kind t' me. (*Addressing the air—queerly*) Thank yew.

EBEN. Maw allus loved me.

ABBIE. Mebbe it knows I love yew, too. Mebbe that makes it kind t' me.

EBEN (*dully*). I dunno. I should think she'd hate ye.

ABBIE (*with certainty*). No. I kin feel it don't—not no more.

EBEN. Hate ye fur stealin' her place—here in her hum—settin' in her parlor whar she was laid— (*He suddenly stops, staring stupidly before him.*)

ABBIE. What is it, Eben?

EBEN (*in a whisper*). Seems like Maw didn't want me t' remind ye.

ABBIE (*excitedly*). I knowed, Eben! It's kind t' me! It don't b'ar me no grudges fur what I never knowed an' couldn't help!

EBEN. Maw b'ars him a grudge.

ABBIE. Waal, so does all o' us.

EBEN. Ay-eh. (*With passion*) I does, by God!

ABBIE (*taking one of his hands in hers and patting it*). Thar! Don't git riled thinkin' o' him. Think o' yer Maw who's kind t' us. Tell me about yer Maw, Eben.

EBEN. They hain't nothin' much. She was kind. She was good.

ABBIE (*putting one arm over his shoulder. He does not seem to notice—passionately*). I'll be kind an' good t' ye!

EBEN. Sometimes she used t' sing fur me.

ABBIE. I'll sing fur ye!

EBEN. This was her hum. This was her farm.

ABBIE. This is my hum! This is my farm!

EBEN. He married her t' steal 'em. She was soft an 'easy. He couldn't 'preciate her.

ABBIE. He can't 'preciate me!

EBEN. He murdered her with his hardness.

ABBIE. He's murderin' me!

EBEN. She died. (*A pause*) Sometimes she used to sing fur me. (*He bursts into a fit of sobbing.*)

ABBIE (*both her arms around him—with wild passion*). I'll sing fur ye! I'll die fur ye! (*In spite of her overwhelming desire for him, there is a sincere maternal love in her manner and voice—a horribly frank mixture of lust and mother love*) Don't cry, Eben! I'll take yer Maw's place! I'll be everythin' she was t' ye! Let me kiss ye, Eben! (*She pulls his head around. He makes a bewildered pretense of resistance. She is tender*) Don't be afeered! I'll kiss ye pure, Eben—same 's if I was a Maw t' ye—an' ye kin kiss me back 's if yew was my son—my boy—sayin' good-night t' me! Kiss me, Eben. (*They kiss in restrained fashion. Then suddenly wild passion overcomes her. She kisses him lustfully again and again and he flings his arms about her and returns her kisses. Suddenly, as in the bedroom, he frees himself from her violently and springs to his feet. He is trembling all over, in a strange state of terror.* ABBIE *strains her arms toward him with fierce pleading*) Don't ye leave me, Eben! Can't ye see it hain't enuf—lovin' ye like a Maw—can't ye see it's got t' be that an' more—much more—a hundred times more—fur me t' be happy—fur yew t' be happy?

EBEN (*to the presence he feels in the room*). Maw! Maw! What d'ye want? What air ye tellin' me?

ABBIE. She's tellin' ye t' love me. She knows I love ye an' I'll be good t' ye. Can't ye feel it? Don't ye know? She's tellin' ye t' love me, Eben!

EBEN. Ay-eh. I feel—mebbe she—but—I can't figger out—why—when ye've stole her place—here in her hum—in the parlor whar she was—

ABBIE (*fiercely*). She knows I love ye!

EBEN (*his face suddenly lighting up with a fierce, triumphant grin*). I see it! I sees why. It's her vengeance on him—so's she kin rest quiet in her grave!

ABBIE (*wildly*). Vengeance o' God on the hull o' us! What d'we give a durn? I love ye, Eben! God knows I love ye! (*She stretches out her arms for him.*)

EBEN (*throws himself on his knees beside the sofa and grabs her in his arms—releasing all his pent-up passion*). An' I love yew, Abbie!—now I kin say it! I been dyin' fur want o' ye—every hour since ye come! I love ye! (*Their lips meet in a fierce, bruising kiss.*)

SCENE FOUR

Exterior of the farmhouse. It is just dawn. The front door at right is opened and EBEN *comes out and walks around to the gate. He is dressed in his working clothes. He seems changed. His face wears a bold and confident expression, he is grinning to himself with evident satisfaction. As he gets near the gate, the window of the parlor is heard opening and the shutters are flung back and* ABBIE *sticks her head out. Her hair tumbles over her shoulders in disarray, her face is flushed, she looks at* EBEN *with tender, languorous eyes and calls softly.*)

ABBIE. Eben. (*As he turns—playfully*) Jest one more kiss afore ye go. I'm goin' to miss ye fearful all day.

EBEN. An' me yew, ye kin bet! (*He goes to her. They kiss several times. He draws away, laughingly*) Thar. That's enuf, hain't it? Ye won't hev none left fur next time.

ABBIE. I got a million o' 'em left fur yew! (*Then a bit anxiously*) D'ye r'ally love me, Eben?

EBEN (*emphatically*). I like ye better'n any gal I ever knowed! That's gospel!

ABBIE. Likin' hain't lovin'.

EBEN. Waal then—I love ye. Now air yew satisfied?

ABBIE. Ay-eh, I be. (*She smiles at him adoringly.*)

EBEN. I better git t' the barn. The old critter's liable t' suspicion an' come sneakin' up.

ABBIE (*with a confident laugh*). Let him! I kin allus pull the wool over his eyes. I'm goin' t' leave the shutters open and let in the sun 'n' air. This room's been dead long enuf. Now it's goin' t' be my room!

EBEN (*frowning*). Ay-eh.

ABBIE (*hastily*). I meant—our room.

EBEN. Ay-eh.

ABBIE. We made it our'n last night, didn't we? We give it life—our lovin' did. (*A pause.*)

EBEN (*with a strange look*). Maw's gone back t' her grave. She kin sleep now.

ABBIE. May she rest in peace! (*Then tenderly rebuking*) Ye oughtn't t' talk o' sad thin's—this mornin'.

EBEN. It jest come up in my mind o' itself.

ABBIE. Don't let it. (*He doesn't answer. She yawns*) Waal, I'm a-goin' t' steal a wink o' sleep. I'll tell the Old Man I hain't feelin' pert. Let him git his own vittles.

EBEN. I see him comin' from the barn. Ye better look smart an' git upstairs.

ABBIE. Ay-eh. Good-by. Don't ferget me. (*She throws him a kiss. He grins—then squares his shoulders and awaits his father confidently.* CABOT *walks slowly up from the left, staring up at the sky with a vague face.*)

EBEN (*jovially*). Mornin', Paw. Star-gazin' in daylight?

CABOT. Purty, hain't it?

EBEN (*looking around him possessively*). It's a durned purty farm.

CABOT. I mean the sky.

EBEN (*grinning*). How d'ye know? Them eyes o' your'n can't see that fur. (*This tickles his humor and he slaps his thigh and laughs*) Ho-ho! That's a good un!

CABOT (*grimly sarcastic*). Ye're feelin' right chipper, hain't ye? Whar'd ye steal the likker?

EBEN (*good-naturedly*). 'Tain't likker. Jest life. (*Suddenly holding out his hand—soberly*) Yew 'n' me is quits. Let's shake hands.

CABOT (*suspiciously*). What's come over ye?

EBEN. Then don't. Mebbe it's jest as well. (*A moment's pause*) What's come over me? (*Queerly*) Didn't ye feel her passin'—goin' back t' her grave?

CABOT (*dully*). Who?

EBEN. Maw. She kin rest now an' sleep content. She's quits with ye.

CABOT (*confusedly*). I rested. I slept good—down with the cows. They know how t' sleep. They're teachin' me.

EBEN (*suddenly jovial again*). Good fur the cows! Waal—ye better git t' work.

CABOT (*grimly amused*). Air yew bossin' me, ye calf?

EBEN (*beginning to laugh*). Ay-eh! I'm bossin' yew! Ha-ha-ha! See how ye like it! Ha-ha-ha! I'm the prize rooster o' this roost. Ha-ha-ha! (*He goes off toward the barn laughing.*)

CABOT (*looks after him with scornful pity*). Soft-headed. Like his Maw. Dead spit 'n' image. No hope in him! (*He spits with contemptuous disgust*) A born fool! (*Then matter-of-factly*) Waal—I'm gittin' peckish. (*He goes toward door.*)

CURTAIN

PART THREE—SCENE ONE

A night in late spring the following year. The kitchen and the two bedrooms upstairs are shown. The two bedrooms are dimly lighted by a tallow candle in each. EBEN is sitting on the side of the bed in his room, his chin propped on his fists, his face a study of the struggle he is making to understand his conflicting emotions. The noisy laughter and music from below where a kitchen dance is in progress annoy and distract him. He scowls at the floor.

In the next room a cradle stands beside the double bed.

In the kitchen all is festivity. The stove has been taken down to give more room to the dancers. The chairs, with wooden benches added, have been pushed back against the walls. On these are seated, squeezed in tight against one another, farmers and their wives and their young folks of both sexes from the neighboring farms. They are all chattering and laughing loudly. They evidently have some secret joke in common. There is no end of winking, of nudging, of meaning nods of the head toward CABOT who, in a state of extreme hilarious excitement increased by the amount he has drunk, is standing near the rear door where there is a small keg of whisky and serving drinks to all the men. In the left corner, front, dividing the attention with her husband, ABBIE *is sitting in a rocking chair, a shawl wrapped about her shoulders. She is very pale, her face is thin and drawn, her eyes are fixed anxiously on the open door in rear as if waiting for someone.*

The musician is tuning up his fiddle, seated in the far right corner. He is a lanky young fellow with a long, weak face. His pale eyes blink incessantly and he grins about him slyly with a greedy malice.

ABBIE (*suddenly turning to a young girl on her right*). Whar's Eben?

YOUNG GIRL (*eying her scornfully*). I dunno, Mrs. Cabot. I hain't seen Eben in ages. (*Meaningly*) Seems like he's spent most o' his time t' hum since yew come.

ABBIE (*vaguely*). I tuk his Maw's place.

YOUNG GIRL. Ay-eh. So I've heerd. (*She turns away to retail this bit of gossip to her mother sitting next to her.* ABBIE *turns to her left to a big stoutish middle-aged man whose flushed face and starting eyes show the amount of "likker" he has consumed.*)

ABBIE. Ye hain't seen Eben, hev ye?

MAN. No, I hain't. (*Then he adds with a wink*) If yew hain't, who would?

ABBIE. He's the best dancer in the county. He'd ought t' come an' dance.

MAN (*with a wink*). Mebbe he's doin' the dutiful an' walkin' the kid t' sleep. It's a boy, hain't it?

ABBIE (*nodding vaguely*). Ay-eh—born two weeks back—purty's a picter.

MAN. They all is—t' their Maws. (*Then in a whisper, with a nudge and a leer*) Listen, Abbie—if ye ever git tired o' Eben, remember me! Don't fergit now! (*He looks at her uncomprehending face for a second—then grunts disgustedly*) Waal—guess I'll likker agin. (*He goes over and joins* CABOT *who is arguing noisily with an old farmer over cows. They all drink.*)

ABBIE (*this time appealing to nobody in particular*). Wonder what Eben's a-doin'? (*Her remark is repeated down the line with many a guffaw and titter until it reaches the fiddler. He fastens his blinking eyes on* ABBIE.)

FIDDLER (*raising his voice*). Bet I kin tell ye, Abbie, what Eben's doin'! He's down t' the church offerin' up prayers o' thanksgivin'. (*They all titter expectantly.*)

A MAN. What fur? (*Another titter.*)

FIDDLER. 'Cause unto him a—(*He hesitates just long enough*) brother is born! (*A roar of laughter. They all look from* ABBIE *to* CABOT. *She is oblivious, staring at the door.* CABOT, *although he hasn't heard the words, is irritated by the laughter and steps forward, glaring about him. There is an immediate silence.*)

CABOT. What're ye all bleatin' about—like a flock o' goats? Why don't ye dance, damn ye? I axed ye here t' dance—t' eat, drink an' be merry— an' thar ye set cacklin' like a lot o' wet hens with the pip! Ye've swilled my likker an' guzzled my vittles like hogs, hain't ye? Then dance fur me, can't ye? That's fa'r an' squar', hain't it? (*A grumble of resentment goes around but they are all evidently in too much awe of him to express it openly.*)

FIDDLER (*slyly*). We're waitin' fur Eben. (*A suppressed laugh.*)

CABOT (*with a fierce exultation*). T'hell with Eben! Eben's done fur now! I got a new son! (*His mood switching with drunken suddenness*) But ye needn't t' laugh at Eben, none o' ye! He's my blood, if he be a dumb fool. He's better nor any o' yew! He kin do a day's work a'most up t' what I kin—an' that'd put any o' yew pore critters t' shame!

FIDDLER. An' he kin do a good night's work, too! (*A roar of laughter.*)

CABOT. Laugh, ye damn fools! Ye're right jist the same, Fiddler. He kin work day an' night too, like I kin, if need be!

OLD FARMER (*from behind the keg where he is weaving drunkenly back and forth—with great simplicity*). They hain't many t' touch ye, Ephraim—a son at seventy-six. That's a hard man fur ye! I be on'y sixty-eight an' I couldn't do it. (*A roar of laughter in which* CABOT *joins uproariously.*)

CABOT (*slapping him on the back*) I'm sorry fur ye, Hi. I'd never suspicion sech weakness from a boy like yew!

OLD FARMER. An' I never reckoned yew had it in ye nuther, Ephraim. (*There is another laugh.*)

CABOT (*suddenly grim*). I got a lot in me—a hell of a lot—folks don't know on. (*Turning to the fiddler*) Fiddle 'er up, durn ye! Give 'em somethin' t' dance t'! What air ye, an ornament? Hain't this a celebration? Then grease yer elbow an' go it!

FIDDLER (*seizes a drink which the* OLD FARMER *holds out to him and downs it*). Here goes! (*He starts to fiddle "Lady of the Lake." Four young fellows and four girls form in two lines and dance a square dance. The* FIDDLER *shouts directions for the different movements, keeping his words in the rhythm of the music and interspersing them with jocular personal remarks to the dancers themselves. The people seated along the walls stamp their feet and clap their hands in unison.* CABOT *is especially active in this respect. Only* ABBIE *remains apathetic, staring at the door as if she were alone in a silent room.*)

FIDDLER. Swing your partner t' the right! That's it, Jim! Give her a b'ar hug! Her Maw hain't lookin'. (*Laughter*) Change partners! That suits ye, don't it, Essie, now ye got Reub afore ye? Look at her redden up, will ye? Waal, life is short an' so's love, as the feller says. (*Laughter.*)

CABOT (*excitedly, stamping his foot*). Go it, boys! Go it, gals!

FIDDLER (*with a wink at the others*). Ye're the spryest seventy-six ever I sees, Ephraim! Now if ye'd on'y good eye-sight . . . ! (*Suppressed laughter. He gives* CABOT *no chance to retort but roars*) Promenade!

Ye're walkin' like a bride down the aisle, Sarah! Waal, while they's life they's allus hope, I've heerd tell. Swing your partner to the left! Gosh A'mighty, look at Johnny Cook high-steppin'! They hain't goin' t'be much strength left fur howin' in the corn lot t'morrow. (*Laughter.*)

CABOT. Go it! Go it! (*Then suddenly, unable to restrain himself any longer, he prances into the midst of the dancers, scattering them, waving his arms about wildly*) Ye're all hoofs! Git out o' my road! Give me room! I'll show ye dancin'. Ye're all too soft! (*He pushes them roughly away. They crowd back toward the walls, muttering, looking at him resentfully.*)

FIDDLER (*jeeringly*). Go it, Ephraim! Go it! (*He starts "Pop, Goes the Weasel," increasing the tempo with every verse until at the end he is fiddling crazily as fast as he can go.*)

CABOT (*starts to dance, which he does very well and with tremendous vigor. Then he begins to improvise, cuts incredibly grotesque capers, leaping up and cracking his heels together, prancing around in a circle with body bent in an Indian war dance, then suddenly straightening up and kicking as high as he can with both legs. He is like a monkey on a string. And all the while he intersperses his antics with shouts and derisive comments.*) Whoop! Here's dancin' fur ye! Whoop! See that! Seventy-six, if I'm a day! Hard as iron yet! Beatin' the young 'uns like I allus done! Look at me! I'd invite ye t' dance on my hundredth birthday on'y ye'll all be dead by then. Ye're a sickly generation! Yer hearts air pink, not red! Yer veins is full o' mud an' water! I be the on'y man in the county! Whoop! See that! I'm a Injun! I've killed Injuns in the West afore ye was born—an' skulped 'em too! They's a arrer wound on my backside I c'd show ye! The hull tribe chased me. I outrun 'em all—with the arrer stuck in me! An' I tuk vengeance on 'em. Ten eyes fur an eye, that was my motter! Whoop! Look at me! I kin kick the ceilin' off the room! Whoop!

FIDDLER (*stops playing—exhaustedly*). God A'mighty, I got enuf. Ye got the devil's strength in ye.

CABOT (*delightedly*). Did I beat yew, too? Wa'al, ye played smart. Hev a swig. (*He pours whisky for himself and FIDDLER. They drink. The others watch CABOT silently with cold, hostile eyes. There is a dead pause. The FIDDLER rests. CABOT leans against the keg, panting, glaring around him confusedly. In the room above, EBEN gets to his feet and tiptoes out the door in rear, appearing a moment later in the other bedroom. He moves silently, even frightenedly, toward the cradle and stands there looking down at the baby. His face is as vague as his reactions are confused, but there is a trace of tenderness, of interested discovery. At the same moment that he reaches the cradle, ABBIE seems to sense something. She gets up weakly and goes to CABOT.*)

ABBIE. I'm goin' up t' the baby.

CABOT (*with real solicitation*). Air ye able fur the stairs? D'ye want me t' help ye, Abbie?

ABBIE. No. I'm able. I'll be down agen soon.

CABOT. Don't ye git wore out! He needs ye, remember—our son does! (*He grins affectionately, patting her on the back. She shrinks from his touch.*)

ABBIE (*dully*). Don't—tech me. I'm goin'—up. (*She goes.* CABOT *looks after her. A whisper goes around the room.* CABOT *turns. It ceases. He wipes his forehead streaming with sweat. He is breathing pantingly.*)

CABOT. I'm a-goin' out t' git fresh air. I'm feelin' a mite dizzy. Fiddle up thar! Dance, all o' ye! Here's likker fur them as wants it. Enjoy yerselves. I'll be back. (*He goes, closing the door behind him.*)

FIDDLER (*sarcastically*). Don't hurry none on our account! (*A suppressed laugh. He imitates* ABBIE) Whar's Eben? (*More laughter.*)

A WOMAN (*loudly*). What's happened in this house is plain as the nose on yer face! (ABBIE *appears in the doorway upstairs and stands looking in surprise and adoration at* EBEN *who does not see her.*)

A MAN. Ssshh! He's li'ble t' be listenin' at the door. That'd be like him. (*Their voices die to an intensive whispering. Their faces are concentrated on this gossip. A noise as of dead leaves in the wind comes from the room.* CABOT *has come out from the porch and stands by the gate, leaning on it, staring at the sky blinkingly.* ABBIE *comes across the room silently.* EBEN *does not notice her until quite near.*)

EBEN (*starting*). Abbie!

ABBIE. Ssshh! (*She throws her arms around him. They kiss—then bend over the cradle together*) Ain't he purty?—dead spit 'n' image o' yew!

EBEN (*pleased*). Air he? I can't tell none.

ABBIE. E-zactly like!

EBEN (*frowningly*). I don't like this. I don't like lettin' on what's mine's his'n. I been doin' that all my life. I'm gittin' t' the end o' b'arin' it!

ABBIE (*putting her finger on his lips*). We're doin' the best we kin. We got t' wait. Somethin's bound t' happen. (*She puts her arms around him*) I got t' go back.

EBEN. I'm goin' out. I can't b'ar it with the fiddle playin' an' the laughin'.

ABBIE. Don't git feelin' low. I love ye, Eben. Kiss me. (*He kisses her. They remain in each other's arms.*)

CABOT (*at the gate, confusedly*). Even the music can't drive it out—somethin'. Ye kin feel it droppin' off the elums, climbin' up the roof, sneakin' down the chimney, pokin' in the corners! They's no peace in houses, they's no rest livin' with folks. Somethin's always livin' with ye. (*With a deep sigh*) I'll go t' the barn an' rest a spell. (*He goes wearily toward the barn.*)

FIDDLER (*tuning up*). Let's celebrate the old skunk gittin' fooled! We kin have some fun now he's went. (*He starts to fiddle "Turkey in the Straw." There is real merriment now. The young folks get up to dance.*)

Scene Two

*A half hour later—Exterior—*Eben *is standing by the gate looking up at the sky, an expression of dumb pain bewildered by itself on his face.* Cabot *appears, returning from the barn, walking wearily, his eyes on the ground. He sees* Eben *and his whole mood immediately changes. He becomes excited, a cruel, triumphant grin comes to his lips, he strides up and slaps* Eben *on the back. From within comes the whining of the fiddle and the noise of stamping feet and laughing voices.*

Cabot. So har ye be!

Eben (*startled, stares at him with hatred for a moment—then dully*). Ay-eh.

Cabot (*surveying him jeeringly*). Why hain't ye been in t' dance? They was all axin' fur ye.

Eben. Let 'em ax!

Cabot. They's a hull passel o' purty gals.

Eben. T' hell with 'em!

Cabot. Ye'd ought t' be marryin' one o' 'em soon.

Eben. I hain't marryin' no one.

Cabot. Ye might 'arn a share o' a farm that way.

Eben (*with a sneer*). Like yew did, ye mean? I hain't that kind.

Cabot (*stung*). Ye lie! 'Twas yer Maw's folks aimed t' steal my farm from me.

Eben. Other folks don't say so. (*After a pause—defiantly*) An' I got a farm, anyways!

Cabot (*derisively*). Whar?

Eben (*stamps a foot on the ground*). Har!

Cabot (*throws his head back and laughs coarsely*). Ho-ho! Ye hev, hev ye? Waal, that's a good un!

Eben (*controlling himself—grimly*). Ye'll see!

Cabot (*stares at him suspiciously, trying to make him out—a pause—then with scornful confidence*). Ay-eh. I'll see. So'll ye. It's ye that's blind —blind as a mole underground. (Eben *suddenly laughs, one short sardonic bark:* "Ha." *A pause.* Cabot *peers at him with renewed suspicion*) Whar air ye hawin' 'bout? (Eben *turns away without answering.* Cabot *grows angry*) God A'mighty, yew air a dumb dunce! They's nothin' in that thick skull o' your'n but noise—like a empty keg it be! (Eben *doesn't seem to hear.* Cabot's *rage grows*) Yewr farm! God A'mighty! If ye wa'n't a born donkey ye'd know ye'll never own stick nor stone on it, specially now arter him bein' born. It's his'n, I tell ye—his'n arter I die— but I'll live a hundred jest t' fool ye all—an' he'll be growed then—yewr age a'most! (Eben *laughs again his sardonic* "Ha." *This drives* Cabot *into a fury*) Ha? Ye think ye kin git 'round that someways, do ye? Waal, it'll be her'n, too—Abbie's—ye won't git 'round her—she knows yer tricks— she'll be too much fur ye—she wants the farm her'n—she was afeerd o' ye

—she told me ye was sneakin' 'round tryin' t' make love t' her t' git her on yer side . . . ye . . . ye mad fool, ye! (*He raises his clenched fists threateningly.*)

EBEN (*is confronting him, choking with rage*). Ye lie, ye old skunk! Abbie never said no sech thing!

CABOT (*suddenly triumphant when he sees how shaken* EBEN *is*). She did. An' I says, I'll blow his brains t' the top o' them elums—an' she says no, that hain't sense, who'll ye git t'help ye on the farm in his place—an' then she says yew'n me ought t' have a son—I know we kin, she says—an' I says, if we do, ye kin have anythin' I've got ye've a mind t'. An' she says, I wants Eben cut off so's this farm'll be mine when ye die! (*With terrible gloating*) An' that's what's happened, hain't it? An' the farm's her'n! An' the dust o' the road—that's you'rn! Ha! Now who's hawin'?

EBEN (*has been listening, petrified with grief and rage—suddenly laughs wildly and brokenly*). Ha-ha-ha! So that's her sneakin' game—all along! —like I suspicioned at fust—t' swaller it all—an' me, too . . . ! (*Madly*) I'll murder her! (*He springs toward the porch but* CABOT *is quicker and gets in between.*)

CABOT. No, ye don't!

EBEN. Git out o' my road! (*He tries to throw* CABOT *aside. They grapple in what becomes immediately a murderous struggle. The old man's concentrated strength is too much for* EBEN. CABOT *gets one hand on his throat and presses him back across the stone wall. At the same moment,* ABBIE *comes out on the porch. With a stifled cry she runs toward them.*)

ABBIE. Eben! Ephraim! (*She tugs at the hand on* EBEN's *throat*) Let go, Ephraim! Ye're chokin' him!

CABOT (*removes his hand and flings* EBEN *sideways full length on the grass, gasping and choking. With a cry,* ABBIE *kneels beside him, trying to take his head on her lap, but he pushes her away.* CABOT *stands looking down with fierce triumph.*) Ye needn't t've fret, Abbie, I wa'n't aimin' t' kill him. He hain't wuth hangin' fur—not by a hell of a sight! (*More and more triumphantly*) Seventy-six an' him not thirty yit—an' look whar he be fur thinkin' his Paw was easy! No, by God, I hain't easy! An' him upstairs, I'll raise him t' be like me! (*He turns to leave them*) I'm goin' in an' dance!—sing an' celebrate! (*He walks to the porch—then turns with a great grin*) I don't calc'late it's left in him, but if he gits pesky, Abbie, ye jest sing out. I'll come a-runnin' an' by the Etarnal, I'll put him across my knee an' birch him! Ha-ha-ha! (*He goes into the house laughing. A moment later his loud "whoop" is heard.*)

ABBIE (*tenderly*). Eben. Air ye hurt? (*She tries to kiss him but he pushes her violently away and struggles to a sitting position.*)

EBEN (*gaspingly*). T' hell—with ye!

ABBIE (*not believing her ears*). It's me, Eben—Abbie—don't ye know me?

EBEN (*glowering at her with hatred*). Ay-eh—I know ye—now! (*He suddenly breaks down, sobbing weakly.*)

ABBIE (*fearfully*). Eben—what's happened t' ye—why did ye look at me 's if ye hated me?

EBEN (*violently, between sobs and gasps*). I do hate ye! Ye're a whore —a damn trickin' whore!

ABBIE (*shrinking back horrified*). Eben! Ye don't know what ye're sayin'!

EBEN (*scrambling to his feet and following her—accusingly*). Ye're nothin' but a stinkin' passel o' lies! Ye've been lyin' t' me every word ye spoke, day an' night, since we fust—done it. Ye've kept sayin' ye loved me. . . .

ABBIE (*frantically*). I do love ye! (*She takes his hands but he flings hers away.*)

EBEN (*unheeding*). Ye've made a fool o' me—a sick, dumb fool— a-purpose! Ye've been on'y playin' yer sneakin', stealin' game all along— gittin' me t' lie with ye so's ye'd hev a son he'd think was his'n, an' makin' him promise he'd give ye the farm and let me eat dust, if ye did git him a son! (*Staring at her with anguished, bewildered eyes*) They must be a devil livin' in ye! T'ain't human t' be as bad as that be!

ABBIE (*stunned—dully*). He told yew . . . ?

EBEN. Hain't it true? It hain't no good in yew lyin'.

ABBIE (*pleadingly*). Eben, listen—ye must listen—it was long ago—afore we done nothin'—yew was scornin' me—goin' t' see Min—when I was lovin' ye—an' I said it t' him t' git vengeance on ye!

EBEN (*unheedingly. With tortured passion*). I wish ye was dead! I wish I was dead along with ye afore this come! (*Ragingly*) But I'll git my vengeance too! I'll pray Maw t' come back t' help me—t' put her cuss on yew an' him!

ABBIE (*brokenly*). Don't ye, Eben! Don't ye! (*She throws herself on her knees before him, weeping*) I didn't mean t' do bad t' ye! Fergive me, won't ye?

EBEN (*not seeming to hear her—fiercely*). I'll git squar' with the old skunk—an' yew! I'll tell him the truth 'bout the son he's so proud o'! Then I'll leave ye here t' pizen each other—with Maw comin' out o' her grave at nights—an' I'll go t' the gold fields o' Californi-a whar Sim an' Peter be!

ABBIE (*terrified*). Ye won't—leave me? Ye can't!

EBEN (*with fierce determination*). I'm a-goin', I tell ye! I'll git rich thar an' come back an' fight him fur the farm he stole—an' I'll kick ye both out in the road—t' beg an' sleep in the woods—an' yer son along with ye—t' starve an' die! (*He is hysterical at the end.*)

ABBIE (*with a shudder—humbly*). He's yewr son, too, Eben.

EBEN (*torturedly*). I wish he never was born! I wish he'd die this minit! I wish I'd never sot eyes on him! It's him—yew havin' him—a-purpose t' steal—that's changed everythin'!

ABBIE (*gently*). Did ye believe I loved ye—afore he come?

EBEN. Ay-eh—like a dumb ox!

ABBIE. An' ye don't believe no more?

EBEN. B'lieve a lyin' thief! Ha!

ABBIE (*shudders—then humbly*). An' did ye r'ally love me afore?

EBEN (*brokenly*). Ay-eh—an' ye was trickin' me!

ABBIE. An' ye don't love me now!

EBEN (*violently*). I hate ye, I tell ye!

ABBIE. An' ye're truly goin' West—goin' t' leave me—all account o' him being born?

EBEN. I'm a-goin' in the mornin'—or may God strike me t' hell!

ABBIE (*after a pause—with a dreadful cold intensity—slowly*). If that's what his comin's done t' me—killin' yewr love—takin' yew away—my on'y joy—the on'y joy I ever knowed—like heaven t' me—purtier'n heaven— then I hate him, too, even if I be his Maw!

EBEN (*bitterly*). Lies! Ye love him! He'll steal the farm fur ye! (*Brokenly*) But t'ain't the farm so much—not no more—it's yew foolin' me— gittin' me t' love ye—lyin' yew loved me—jest t' git a son t' steal!

ABBIE (*distractedly*). He won't steal! I'd kill him fust! I do love ye! I'll prove t' ye . . . !

EBEN (*harshly*). T'ain't no use lyin' no more. I'm deaf t' ye! (*He turns away*) I hain't seein' ye agen. Good-by!

ABBIE (*pale with anguish*). Hain't ye even goin' t' kiss me—not once— arter all we loved?

EBEN (*in a hard voice*). I hain't wantin' t' kiss ye never agen! I'm wantin' t' forgit I ever sot eyes on ye!

ABBIE. Eben!—ye mustn't—wait a spell—I want t' tell ye. . . .

EBEN. I'm a-goin' in t' git drunk. I'm a-goin' t' dance.

ABBIE (*clinging to his arm—with passionate earnestness*). If I could make it—'s if he'd never come up between us—if I could prove t' ye I wa'n't schemin' t' steal from ye—so's everythin' could be jest the same with us, lovin' each other jest the same, kissin' an' happy the same's we've been happy afore he come—if I could do it—ye'd love me agen, wouldn't ye? Ye'd kiss me agen? Ye wouldn't never leave me, would ye?

EBEN (*moved*). I calc'late not. (*Then shaking her hand off his arm— with a bitter smile*) But ye hain't God, be ye?

ABBIE (*exultantly*). Remember ye've promised! (*Then with strange intensity*) Mebbe I kin take back one thin' God does!

EBEN (*peering at her*). Ye're gittin' cracked, hain't ye? (*Then going towards door*) I'm a-goin' t' dance.

ABBIE (*calls after him intensely*). I'll prove t' ye! I'll prove I love ye better'n. . . . (*He goes in the door, not seeming to hear. She remains standing where she is, looking after him—then she finishes desperately*) Better'n everythin' else in the world!

SCENE THREE

Just before dawn in the morning—shows the kitchen and CABOT'S *bedroom. In the kitchen, by the light of a tallow candle on the table,* EBEN *is sitting, his chin propped on his hands, his drawn face blank and expressionless. His carpetbag is on the floor beside him. In the bedroom, dimly lighted by a small whale-oil lamp,* CABOT *lies asleep.* ABBIE *is bending over the cradle, listening, her face full of terror yet with an undercurrent of desperate triumph. Suddenly, she breaks down and sobs, appears about to throw herself on her knees beside the cradle; but the old man turns restlessly, groaning in his sleep, and she controls herself, and, shrinking away from the cradle with a gesture of horror, backs swiftly toward the door in rear and goes out. A moment later she comes into the kitchen and, running to* EBEN, *flings her arms about his neck and kisses him wildly. He hardens himself, he remains unmoved and cold, he keeps his eyes straight ahead.*

ABBIE (*hysterically*). I done it, Eben! I told ye I'd do it! I've proved I love ye—better'n everythin'—so's ye can't never doubt me no more!

EBEN (*dully*). Whatever ye done, it hain't no good now.

ABBIE (*wildly*). Don't ye say that! Kiss me, Eben, won't ye? I need ye t' kiss me arter what I done! I need ye t' say ye love me!

EBEN (*kisses her without emotion—dully*). That's fur good-by. I'm a-goin' soon.

ABBIE. No! No! Ye won't go—not now!

EBEN (*going on with his own thoughts*). I been a-thinkin'—an' I hain't goin' t' tell Paw nothin'. I'll leave Maw t' take vengeance on ye. If I told him, the old skunk'd jest be stinkin' mean enuf to take it out on that baby. (*His voice showing emotion in spite of him*) An' I don't want nothin' bad t' happen t' him. He hain't t' blame fur yew. (*He adds with a certain queer pride*) An' he looks like me! An' by God, he's mine! An' some day I'll be a-comin' back an' . . . !

ABBIE (*too absorbed in her own thoughts to listen to him—pleadingly*) They's no cause fur ye t' go now—they's no sense—it's all the same's it was—they's nothin' come b'tween us now—arter what I done!

EBEN (*something in her voice arouses him. He stares at her a bit frightenedly*). Ye look mad, Abbie. What did ye do?

ABBIE. I—I killed him, Eben.

EBEN (*amazed*). Ye killed him?

ABBIE (*dully*). Ay-eh.

EBEN (*recovering from his astonishment—savagely*). An' serves him right! But we got t' do somethin' quick t' make it look s'if the old skunk'd killed himself when he was drunk. We kin prove by 'em all how drunk he got.

ABBIE (*wildly*). No! No! Not him! (*Laughing distractedly*) But that's what I ought t' done, hain't it? I oughter killed him instead! Why didn't ye tell me?

EBEN (*appalled*). Instead? What d'ye mean?

ABBIE. Not him.

EBEN (*his face grown ghastly*). Not—not that baby!

ABBIE (*dully*). Ay-eh!

EBEN (*falls to his knees as if he'd been struck—his voice trembling with horror*). Oh, God A'mighty! A'mighty God! Maw, whar was ye, why didn't ye stop her?

ABBIE (*simply*). She went back t' her grave that night we fust done it, remember? I hain't felt her about since. (*A pause.* EBEN *hides his head in his hands, trembling all over as if he had the ague. She goes on dully*) I left the piller over his little face. Then he killed himself. He stopped breathin'. (*She begins to weep softly.*)

EBEN (*rage beginning to mingle with grief*). He looked like me. He was mine, damn ye!

ABBIE (*slowly and brokenly*). I didn't want t' do it. I hated myself fur doin' it. I loved him. He was so purty—dead spit 'n' image o' yew. But I loved yew more—an' yew was goin' away—far off whar I'd never see ye agen, never kiss ye, never feel ye pressed agin me agen—an' ye said ye hated me fur havin' him—ye said ye hated him an' wished he was dead— ye said if it hadn't been fur him comin' it'd be the same's afore between us.

EBEN (*unable to endure this, springs to his feet in a fury, threatening her, his twitching fingers seeming to reach out for her throat*). Ye lie! I never said—I never dreamed ye'd— I'd cut off my head afore I'd hurt his finger!

ABBIE (*piteously, sinking on her knees*). Eben, don't ye look at me like that—hatin' me—not after what I done fur ye—fur us—so's we could be happy agen—

EBEN (*furiously now*). Shut up, or I'll kill ye! I see yer game now—the same old sneakin' trick—ye're aimin' t' blame me fur the murder ye done!

ABBIE (*moaning—putting her hands over her ears*). Don't ye, Eben! Don't ye! (*She grasps his legs.*)

EBEN (*his mood suddenly changing to horror, shrinks away from her*). Don't ye tech me! Ye're pizen! How could ye—t' murder a pore little critter— Ye must've swapped yer soul t' hell! (*Suddenly raging*) Ha! I kin see why ye done it! Not the lies ye jest told—but 'cause ye wanted t' steal agen—steal the last thin' ye'd left me—my part o' him—no, the hull o' him—ye saw he looked like me—ye knowed he was all mine—an' ye couldn't b'ar it—I know ye! Ye killed him fur bein' mine! (*All this has driven him almost insane. He makes a rush past her for the door—then turns—shaking both fists at her, violently*) But I'll take vengeance now! I'll git the Sheriff! I'll tell him everythin'! Then I'll sing "I'm off to Californi-a!" an' go—gold—Golden Gate—gold sun—fields o' gold in the West! (*This last he half shouts, half croons incoherently, suddenly breaking off passionately*) I'm a-goin' fur the Sheriff t' come an' git ye! I want ye tuk away, locked up from me! I can't stand t' luk at ye! Murderer an' thief 'r not, ye still tempt me! I'll give ye up t' the Sheriff! (*He turns and runs out, around the corner of house, panting and sobbing, and breaks into a swerving sprint down the road.*)

ABBIE (*struggling to her feet, runs to the door, calling after him*). I love ye, Eben! I love ye! (*She stops at the door weakly, swaying, about to fall*) I don't care what ye do—if ye'll on'y love me agen— (*She falls limply to the floor in a faint.*)

SCENE FOUR

About an hour later. Same as Scene Three. Shows the kitchen and CABOT's *bedroom. It is after dawn. The sky is brilliant with the sunrise. In the kitchen,* ABBIE *sits at the table, her body limp and exhausted, her head bowed down over her arms, her face hidden. Upstairs,* CABOT *is still asleep but awakes with a start. He looks toward the window and gives a snort of surprise and irritation—throws back the covers and begins hurriedly pulling on his clothes. Without looking behind him, he begins talking to* ABBIE *whom he supposes beside him.*

CABOT. Thunder 'n' lightnin', Abbie! I hain't slept this late in fifty year! Looks 's if the sun was full riz a'most. Must've been the dancin' an' likker. Must be gittin' old. I hope Eben's t' wuk. Ye might've tuk the trouble t' rouse me, Abbie. (*He turns—sees no one there—surprised*) Waal—whar air she? Gittin' vittles, I calc'late. (*He tiptoes to the cradle and peers down—proudly*) Mornin', sonny. Purty's a picter! Sleepin' sound. He don't beller all night like most o' 'em. (*He goes quietly out the door in rear—a few moments later enters kitchen—sees* ABBIE—*with satisfaction*) So thar ye be. Ye got any vittles cooked?

ABBIE (*without moving*). No.

CABOT (*coming to her, almost sympathetically*). Ye feelin' sick?

ABBIE. No.

CABOT (*pats her on shoulder. She shudders*). Ye'd best lie down a spell. (*Half jocularly*) Yer son'll be needin' ye soon. He'd ought t' wake up with a gnashin' appetite, the sound way he's sleepin'.

ABBIE (*shudders—then in a dead voice*). He hain't never goin' t' wake up.

CABOT (*jokingly*). Takes after me this mornin'. I hain't slept so late in . . .

ABBIE. He's dead.

CABOT (*stares at her—bewilderedly*). What. . . .

ABBIE. I killed him.

CABOT (*stepping back from her—aghast*). Air ye drunk—'r crazy—'r . . . !

ABBIE (*suddenly lifts her head and turns on him—wildly*). I killed him, I tell ye! I smothered him. Go up an' see if ye don't b'lieve me! (*CABOT stares at her a second, then bolts out the rear door, can be heard bounding up the stairs, and rushes into the bedroom and over to the cradle. ABBIE has sunk back lifelessly into her former position. CABOT puts his hand down on the body in the crib. An expression of fear and horror comes over his face.*)

CABOT (*shrinking away—tremblingly*). God A'mighty! God A'mighty. (*He stumbles out the door—in a short while returns to the kitchen—comes to* ABBIE, *the stunned expression still on his face—hoarsely*) Why did ye do it? Why? (*As she doesn't answer, he grabs her violently by the shoulder and shakes her*) I ax ye why ye done it! Ye'd better tell me 'r . . . !

ABBIE (*gives him a furious push which sends him staggering back and springs to her feet—with wild rage and hatred*). Don't ye dare tech me! What right hev ye t' question me 'bout him? He wa'n't yewr son! Think I'd have a son by yew? I'd die fust! I hate the sight o' ye an' allus did! It's yew I should've murdered, if I'd had good sense! I hate ye! I love Eben. I did from the fust. An' he was Eben's son—mine an' Eben's—not your'n!

CABOT (*stands looking at her dazedly—a pause—finding his words with an effort—dully*). That was it—what I felt—pokin' round the corners—while ye lied—holdin' yerself from me—sayin' ye'd a'ready conceived—(*He lapses into crushed silence—then with a strange emotion*) He's dead, sart'n. I felt his heart. Pore little critter! (*He blinks back one tear, wiping his sleeve across his nose.*)

ABBIE (*hysterically*). Don't ye! Don't ye! (*She sobs unrestrainedly.*)

CABOT (*with a concentrated effort that stiffens his body into a rigid line and hardens his face into a stony mask—through his teeth to himself*) I got t' be—like a stone—a rock o' jedgment! (*A pause. He gets complete control over himself—harshly*) If he was Eben's, I be glad he air gone! An' mebbe I suspicioned it all along. I felt they was somethin' onnateral—somewhars—the house got so lonesome—an' cold—drivin' me down t' the barn—t' the beasts o' the field. . . . Ay-eh. I must've suspicioned—somethin'. Ye didn't fool me—not altogether, leastways—I'm too old a bird—growin' ripe on the bough. . . . (*He becomes aware he is wandering, straightens again, looks at* ABBIE *with a cruel grin*) So ye'd liked t' hev murdered me 'stead o' him, would ye? Waal, I'll live to a hundred! I'll live t' see ye hung! I'll deliver ye up t' the jedgment o' God an' the law! I'll git the Sheriff now. (*Starts for the door.*)

ABBIE (*dully*). Ye needn't. Eben's gone fur him.

CABOT (*amazed*). Eben—gone fur the Sheriff?

ABBIE. Ay-eh.

CABOT. T' inform agen ye?

ABBIE. Ay-eh.

CABOT (*considers this—a pause—then in a hard voice*). Waal, I'm thankful fur him savin' me the trouble. I'll git t' wuk. (*He goes to the door—then turns—in a voice full of strange emotion*) He'd ought t' been my son, Abbie. Ye'd ought t' loved me. I'm a man. If ye'd loved me, I'd never told no Sheriff on ye no matter what ye did, if they was t' brile me alive!

ABBIE (*defensively*). They's more to it nor yew know, makes him tell.

CABOT (*dryly*). Fur yewr sake, I hope they be. (*He goes out—comes around to the gate—stares up at the sky. His control relaxes. For a moment he is old and weary. He murmurs despairingly*) God A'mighty, I be lonesomer'n ever! (*He hears running footsteps from the left, immedi-*

ately is himself again. EBEN *runs in, panting exhaustedly, wild-eyed and mad looking. He lurches through the gate.* CABOT *grabs him by the shoulder.* EBEN *stares at him dumbly*) Did ye tell the Sheriff?

EBEN (*nodding stupidly*). Ay-eh.

CABOT (*gives him a push away that sends him sprawling—laughing with withering contempt*). Good fur ye! A prime chip o' yer Maw ye be! (*He goes toward the barn, laughing harshly.* EBEN *scrambles to his feet. Suddenly* CABOT *turns—grimly threatening*) Git off this farm when the Sheriff takes her—or, by God, he'll have t' come back an' git me fur murder, too! (*He stalks off.* EBEN *does not appear to have heard him. He runs to the door and comes into the kitchen.* ABBIE *looks up with a cry of anguished joy.* EBEN *stumbles over and throws himself on his knees beside her—sobbing brokenly.*)

EBEN. Fergive me!

ABBIE (*happily*). Eben! (*She kisses him and pulls his head over against her breast.*)

EBEN. I love ye! Fergive me!

ABBIE (*ecstatically*). I'd fergive ye all the sins in hell fur sayin' that! (*She kisses his head, pressing it to her with a fierce passion of possession.*)

EBEN (*brokenly*). But I told the Sheriff. He's comin' fur ye!

ABBIE. I kin b'ar what happens t' me—now!

EBEN. I woke him up. I told him. He says, wait 'til I git dressed. I was waiting. I got to thinkin' o' yew. I got to thinkin' how I'd loved ye. It hurt like somethin' was bustin' in my chest an' head. I got t' cryin'. I knowed sudden I loved ye yet, an' allus would love ye!

ABBIE (*caressing his hair—tenderly*). My boy, hain't ye?

EBEN. I begun t' run back. I cut across the fields an' through the woods. I thought ye might have time t' run away—with me—an' . . . .

ABBIE (*shaking her head*). I got t' take my punishment—t' pay fur my sin.

EBEN. Then I want t' share it with ye.

ABBIE. Ye didn't do nothin'.

EBEN. I put it in yer head. I wisht he was dead! I as much as urged ye t' do it!

ABBIE. No. It was me alone!

EBEN. I'm as guilty as yew be! He was the child o' our sin.

ABBIE (*lifting her head as if defying God*). I don't repent that sin! I hain't askin' God t' fergive that!

EBEN. Nor me—but it led up t' the other—an' the murder ye did, ye did 'count o' me—an' it's my murder, too, I'll tell the Sheriff—an' if ye deny it, I'll say we planned it t'gether—an' they'll all b'lieve me, fur they suspicion everythin' we've done, an' it'll seem likely an' true to 'em. An' it is true—way down. I did help ye—somehow.

ABBIE (*laying her head on his—sobbing*). No! I don't want yew t' suffer!

EBEN. I got t' pay fur my part o' the sin! An' I'd suffer wuss leavin' ye, goin' West, thinkin' o' ye day an' night, bein' out when yew was in— (*Lowering his voice*) 'r bein' alive when yew was dead. (*A pause*) I want t' share with ye, Abbie—prison 'r death 'r hell 'r anythin'! (*He looks into her eyes and forces a trembling smile*) If I'm sharin' with ye, I won't feel lonesome, leastways.

ABBIE (*weakly*). Eben! I won't let ye! I can't let ye!

EBEN (*kissing her—tenderly*). Ye can't he'p yerself. I got ye beat fur once!

ABBIE (*forcing a smile—adoringly*). I hain't beat—s'long's I got ye!

EBEN (*hears the sound of feet outside*). Ssshh! Listen! They've come t' take us!

ABBIE. No, it's him. Don't give him no chance to fight ye, Eben. Don't say nothin'—no matter what he says. An' I won't neither. (*It is* CABOT. *He comes up from the barn in a great state of excitement and strides into the house and then into the kitchen.* EBEN *is kneeling beside* ABBIE, *his arm around her, hers around him. They stare straight ahead.*)

CABOT (*stares at them, his face hard. A long pause—vindictively*). Ye make a slick pair o' murderin' turtle doves! Ye'd ought t' be both hung on the same limb an' left thar t' swing in the breeze an' rot—a warnin' t' old fools like me t' b'ar their lonesomeness alone—an' fur young fools like ye t' hobble their lust. (*A pause. The excitement returns to his face, his eyes snap, he looks a bit crazy*) I couldn't work today. I couldn't take no interest. T' hell with the farm! I'm leavin' it! I've turned the cows an' other stock loose! I've druv 'em into the woods whar they kin be free! By freein' 'em, I'm freein' myself! I'm quittin' here today! I'll set fire t' house an' barn an' watch 'em burn, an' I'll leave yer Maw t' haunt the ashes, an' I'll will the fields back t' God, so that nothin' human kin never touch 'em! I'll be a-goin' to Californi-a—t' jine Simeon an' Peter—true sons o' mine if they be dumb fools—an' the Cabots'll find Solomon's Mines t'gether! (*He suddenly cuts a mad caper*) Whoop! What was the song they sung? "Oh, Californi-a! That's the land fur me." (*He sings this— then gets on his knees by the floor-board under which the money was hid*) An' I'll sail thar on one o' the finest clippers I kin find! I've got the money! Pity ye didn't know whar this was hidden so's ye could steal. . . . (*He has pulled up the board. He stares—feels—stares again. A pause of dead silence. He slowly turns, slumping into a sitting position on the floor, his eyes like those of a dead fish, his face the sickly green of an attack of nausea. He swallows painfully several times—forces a weak smile at last*) So—ye did steal it!

EBEN (*emotionlessly*). I swapped it t' Sim an' Peter fur their share o' the farm—t' pay their passage t' Californi-a.

CABOT (*with one sardonic*). Ha! (*He begins to recover. Gets slowly to his feet—strangely*) I calc'late God give it to 'em—not yew! God's hard, not easy! Mebbe they's easy gold in the West but it hain't God's gold. It hain't fur me. I kin hear His voice warnin' me agen t' be hard an' stay on my farm. I kin see his hand usin' Eben t' steal t' keep me from weakness. I kin feel I be in the palm o' His hand, His fingers guidin' me. (*A pause— then he mutters sadly*) It's a-goin' t' be lonesomer now than ever it war afore—an' I'm gittin' old, Lord—ripe on the bough. . . . (*Then stiffen- ing*) Waal—what d'ye want? God's lonesome, hain't He? God's hard an' lonesome! (*A pause. The* SHERIFF *with two men comes up the road from the left. They move cautiously to the door. The* SHERIFF *knocks on it with the butt of his pistol.*)

SHERIFF. Open in the name o' the law! (*They start.*)

CABOT. They've come fur ye. (*He goes to the rear door*) Come in, Jim! (*The three men enter.* CABOT *meets them in doorway*) Jest a minit, Jim. I got 'em safe here. (*The* SHERIFF *nods. He and his companions re- main in the doorway.*)

EBEN (*suddenly calls*). I lied this mornin', Jim. I helped her to do it. Ye kin take me, too.

ABBIE (*brokenly*). No!

CABOT. Take 'em both. (*He comes forward—stares at* EBEN *with a trace of grudging admiration*) Purty good—fur yew! Waal, I got t' round up the stock. Good-by.

EBEN. Good-by.

ABBIE. Good-by. (CABOT *turns and strides past the men—comes out and around the corner of the house, his shoulders squared, his face stony, and stalks grimly toward the barn. In the meantime the* SHERIFF *and men have come into the room.*)

SHERIFF (*embarrassedly*). Wall—we'd best start.

ABBIE. Wait. (*Turns to* EBEN) I love ye, Eben.

EBEN. I love ye, Abbie. (*They kiss. The three men grin and shuffle em- barrassedly.* EBEN *takes* ABBIE's *hand. They go out the door in rear, the men following, and come from the house, walking hand in hand to the gate.* EBEN *stops there and points to the sunrise sky*) Sun's a-rizin'. Purty, hain't it?

ABBIE. Ay-eh. (*They both stand for a moment looking up raptly in at- titudes strangely aloof and devout.*)

SHERIFF (*looking around at the farm enviously—to his companion*). It's a jim-dandy farm, no denyin'. Wished I owned it!

CURTAIN

ROBERT FROST

1874–

THE POPULARITY OF ROBERT FROST CAN BE EXPLAINED AS A NATURAL RESULT of his clarity and directness, his easily communicated wit, his vivid translation of local experience into universal terms. Today it may be difficult to realize that he was almost forty years old before his poetry began to reach the public, despite his steady besieging of editors with poems that are now widely familiar. Since Frost is usually considered a traditionalist, we perhaps overlook the fact that in his use of colloquial language and the rhythms of speech he challenged Victorian poetic diction drawn largely from a formal literary vocabulary. Though his metrical forms were familiar, his "voice" was fresh, for he very early purged the outworn conventionalities from his work. Some of his poems, grounded in the New Hampshire and Vermont rural scene, may seem to be simple and transparent genre pieces, but they can seldom be dismissed so lightly. They are not merely a local colorist's insights into the oddities and whimsicalities of an isolated group; the atmosphere of authenticity is unmistakable, but Frost is moved by human concerns that transcend the New England countryside. In "An Old Man's Winter Night" he is acutely sensitive to some of the universal qualities of old age; in " 'Out, Out—' " the tragic woodlot scene ends with an unglossed view of stoically endured grief; the familiar "Birches" is almost an allegory of human growth through trial and error. The widening circles of meaning which expand from the local to the universal are indications not that the poet finds "lessons" in the humble scene about him, but that his response to experience is more complex than may be apparent at first glance. The deceptive simplicity of the surface is in reality perhaps a high form of sophistication. His wisdom is a product of life that has touched the world at many points, has seen all kinds and conditions of men, and is neither despairing nor shallowly optimistic toward man as an individual, though he may be healthily skeptical of what Steinbeck calls "group man."

As we might expect, there is more than New England in Frost's background. His mother was born in Edinburgh and came to live with relatives in Columbus, Ohio, where she taught in the local schools. In 1872 she moved to a teaching position in Lewiston, Pennsylvania, and there met William Prescott Frost, who had just taken his degree with honors at Harvard. They married and moved to San Francisco where the poet was born in 1874. Although the elder Frost was a New Englander, he had been a Confederate sympathizer to the extent of trying to join Southern troops during the Civil War, and not unnaturally named his son Robert Lee Frost. The California years left their impress in memories of Democratic political activity in which the son accompanied his father, and memories of a different sort registered years later in a few poems such as "A Peck of Gold." Upon her husband's untimely death in 1885 Mrs. Frost took her two children to live with grandfather Frost in Lawrence, Massachusetts. She resumed school teaching while young Frost, who had been "turned out of doors" in San Francisco, began belatedly to get a formal education. He stood at the top of his class when he graduated from Lawrence high school in 1892. That fall he entered Dartmouth but left after three months, and for five years held a succession of jobs as teacher, millhand, reporter, salesman, and farmer. In 1895 he married a Lawrence classmate, Elinor White, and spent 1897–99 at Harvard, continuing his acquaintance with the classics and studying philosophy with Santayana without becoming a disciple. At the age of twenty-five he was evidently impatient with undergraduate routines and left Harvard without taking a degree. For the next dozen years his principal occupation was farming near Derry, New Hampshire, but he also did part-time teaching at Pinkerton Academy in Derry; in 1911–12 he taught psychology in the State Normal School in nearby Plymouth, N.H.

Frost's first poem was written in 1890, when he was fifteen, and was immediately published in the Lawrence school magazine. "La Noche Triste," inspired by his reading of Prescott's *Conquest of Mexico*, is a ballad on Cortez, a promising piece of juvenilia without hint of the distinctive idiom he would soon develop.[1] In the succeeding two decades Frost placed a handful of poems in *The Independent*, for a total return of about $100, but most other magazines were indifferent to his work. From 1912 to early 1915 he and his family lived in England, where he continued to farm and write, but in an atmosphere more congenial to the growth of poetry. His friendship with the Georgian poets Lascelles Abercrombie, Edward Thomas, and Wilfrid Gibson is commemorated in a poem of Gibson's which describes Frost "Holding us with shrewd turns and racy quips" as they talked in the lamplight. In London he met Ezra Pound, who wanted Frost to join his circle that gathered weekly to

---

[1] The poem, which Frost has never reprinted, may be found in Louis Untermeyer's *The Road Not Taken* (1951), pp. 231–35.

prune the adjectives from each other's verse. Frost wisely declined to be drawn into the Imagist movement which Pound was promoting, though when one of his poems fell under Pound's gaze it proved tightly enough knit to resist the Pound blue pencil. In 1913, *A Boy's Will* was published in London, to be followed by *North of Boston* the next year. The two volumes were warmly reviewed on both sides of the ocean and were soon issued in America. Frost returned to this country in 1915 to find himself acclaimed and his position as a poet assured. Amy Lowell devoted part of a critical volume to his work; in 1916 he became poet in residence at Amherst, and later at Michigan and at Dartmouth; in 1924 the first of four Pulitzer prizes was awarded him.

Frost has never written as voluminously as Tennyson or Browning, for his is a gift of concise, spare statement. By the same token, the quality of almost every poem is high: Frost has done his own winnowing and has not allowed himself to be hurried into print. But as the years have passed, new volumes have steadily continued to appear: *Mountain Interval* (1916), *New Hampshire* (1923), *West-Running Brook* (1928), *A Further Range* (1936), *A Witness Tree* (1942), *A Masque of Reason* (1945), *A Masque of Mercy* and *Steeple Bush* (1947), *And All We Call American* (1959).

Many of Frost's most characteristic poems show him to be a pastoral poet, comfortably at home in the outdoors and with country people. But his range is much wider. A long poem "Build Soil" owes something to the Virgilian eclogue, but he calls it "a political pastoral" and notes that it was publicly spoken at Columbia University prior to the national party conventions of 1932. Many poems in more recent years reveal him as a citizen of the world, conscious of the dilemma we face when science with its "complacent ministry of fear" is no longer the simple liberator of other days. "Fire and Ice" and "Desert Places" express the human predicament of man on an inferior planet. They are different views of the cosmic order, humanized by the polarities of love and hate in the one poem and by the perils of personal loneliness in the other.

For all his lyric gift, Frost often captures the essence of an experience in dramatic form. "Home Burial" is a penetrating little psychological drama which reveals a bereft wife's inability to reconcile herself to the loss of her child or to accept her husband's quite different mode of living with grief. In more muted tones "The Death of the Hired Man" depicts a couple's concern for a wornout farm worker who considers their place home and has returned to die. Both poems, like many others of their sort, are dialogues which skillfully characterize the speakers through their own words and actions, without the intrusion of the author. The two masques are, of course, formal one-act dramas. Other poems, like "Brown's Descent" and "One More Brevity," although not dramatic, narrate an episode whose significance is contained in the action itself and may not require any comment from the poet-spokesman.

Frost has been content to use traditional verse forms, but under his hand they seem anything but outworn. The blank verse of " 'Out, Out—' " and "Two Look at Two" has attained uncommon flexibility, for the speech rhythms are an overlay upon the five-beat line and demand to be read with the syncopations and emphases of spoken language. Sometimes the same effect prevails in stanzaic patterns, as in "Brown's Descent" with its numerous "run-on" lines. The classic regularity of "Stopping by Woods on a Snowy Evening" is a triumph of another sort, for in the simplest diction he invests a commonplace verse pattern with strength and dignity which are the mark of a master. Frost finds an inviting challenge in formal metrics, a restraining element within which the craftsman can exercise freedom in proportion to the perfectness of his control. If the poet must pad or squeeze, or if his rhymes are not inevitable, he betrays his lack of mastery, for within a formal structure his obligations cannot be concealed. Frost has thus found his freedom without resorting to free verse, but his attitude is a measure of his zest and not a mark of narrow conservatism.

Wise, tolerant, skeptical, shrewd, humorous—these describe the Frost who has given us the essence of himself, his New England, his age. The essence of his art cannot be so easily summed up, for first-rate poetry possesses an elusive magic, whether of image or idea. Frost's poems flash with that special quality of perfected craftsmanship which, even if inexplicable, is unmistakable.

A note on texts: The texts here used are taken from *Complete Poems of Robert Frost* (1949), except for "One More Brevity," which was privately issued in 1953. The dates appended to each selection are those of first publication.

THE FIGURE A POEM MAKES [1]

Abstraction is an old story with the philosophers, but it has been like a new toy in the hands of the artists of our day. Why can't we have any one quality of poetry we choose by itself? We can have in thought. Then it will go hard if we can't in practice. Our lives for it.

Granted no one but a humanist much cares how sound a poem is if it is only *a* sound. The sound is the gold in the ore. Then we will have the sound out alone and dispense with the inessential. We do till we make the discovery that the object in writing poetry is to make all poems sound as different as possible from each other, and the resources for that of vowels, consonants, punctuation, syntax, words, sentences, meter are not enough. We need the help of context—meaning—subject matter. That is the greatest help towards variety. All that can be done with words is

---

[1] Preface to the 1939 edition of *Collected Poems*.

soon told. So also with meters—particularly in our language where there are virtually but two, strict iambic and loose iambic. The ancients with many were still poor if they depended on meters for all tune. It is painful to watch our sprung-rhythmists straining at the point of omitting one short from a foot for relief from monotony. The possibilities for tune from the dramatic tones of meaning struck across the rigidity of a limited meter are endless. And we are back in poetry as merely one more art of having something to say, sound or unsound. Probably better if sound, because deeper and from wider experience.

Then there is this wildness whereof it is spoken. Granted again that it has an equal claim with sound to being a poem's better half. If it is a wild tune, it is a poem. Our problem then is, as modern abstractionists, to have the wildness pure; to be wild with nothing to be wild about. We bring up as aberrationists, giving way to undirected associations and kicking ourselves from one chance suggestion to another in all directions as of a hot afternoon in the life of a grasshopper. Theme alone can steady us down. Just as the first mystery was how a poem could have a tune in such a straightness as meter, so the second mystery is how a poem can have wildness and at the same time a subject that shall be fulfilled.

It should be of the pleasure of a poem itself to tell how it can. The figure a poem makes. It begins in delight and ends in wisdom. The figure is the same as for love. No one can really hold that the ecstasy should be static and stand still in one place. It begins in delight, it inclines to the impulse, it assumes direction with the first line laid down, it runs a course of lucky events, and ends in a clarification of life—not necessarily a great clarification, such as sects and cults are founded on, but in a momentary stay against confusion. It has denouement. It has an outcome that though unforeseen was predestined from the first image of the original mood— and indeed from the very mood. It is but a trick poem and no poem at all if the best of it was thought of first and saved for the last. It finds its own name as it goes and discovers the best waiting for it in some final phrase at once wise and sad—the happy-sad blend of the drinking song.

No tears in the writer, no tears in the reader. No surprise for the writer, no surprise for the reader. For me the initial delight is in the surprise of remembering something I didn't know I knew. I am in a place, in a situation, as if I had materialized from cloud or risen out of the ground. There is a glad recognition of the long lost and the rest follows. Step by step the wonder of unexpected supply keeps growing. The impressions most useful to my purpose seem always those I was unaware of and so made no note of at the time when taken, and the conclusion is come to that like giants we are always hurling experience ahead of us to pave the future with against the day when we may want to strike a line of purpose across it for somewhere. The line will have the more charm for not being mechanically straight. We enjoy the straight crookedness of a good walking stick. Modern instruments of precision are being used to make things crooked as if by eye and hand in the old days.

I tell how there may be a better wildness of logic than of inconsequence. But the logic is backward, in retrospect, after the act. It must be more felt than seen ahead like prophecy. It must be a revelation, or a series of revelations, as much for the poet as for the reader. For it to be that there must have been the greatest freedom of the material to move about in it and to establish relations in it regardless of time and space, previous relation, and everything but affinity. We prate of freedom. We call our schools free because we are not free to stay away from them till we are sixteen years of age. I have given up my democratic prejudices and now willingly set the lower classes free to be completely taken care of by the upper classes. Political freedom is nothing to me. I bestow it right and left. All I would keep for myself is the freedom of my material —the condition of body and mind now and then to summons aptly from the vast chaos of all I have lived through.

Scholars and artists thrown together are often annoyed at the puzzle of where they differ. Both work from knowledge; but I suspect they differ most importantly in the way their knowledge is come by. Scholars get theirs with conscientious thoroughness along projected lines of logic; poets theirs cavalierly and as it happens in and out of books. They stick to nothing deliberately, but let what will stick to them like burrs where they walk in the fields. No acquirement is on assignment, or even self-assignment. Knowledge of the second kind is much more available in the wild free ways of wit and art. A schoolboy may be defined as one who can tell you what he knows in the order in which he learned it. The artist must value himself as he snatches a thing from some previous order in time and space into a new order with not so much as a ligature clinging to it of the old place where it was organic.

More than once I should have lost my soul to radicalism if it had been the originality it was mistaken for by its young converts. Originality and initiative are what I ask for my country. For myself the originality need be no more than the freshness of a poem run in the way I have described: from delight to wisdom. The figure is the same as for love. Like a piece of ice on a hot stove the poem must ride on its own melting. A poem may be worked over once it is in being, but may not be worried into being. Its most precious quality will remain its having run itself and carried away the poet with it. Read it a hundred times: it will forever keep its freshness as a metal keeps its fragrance. It can never lose its sense of a meaning that once unfolded by surprise as it went.

1942

RELUCTANCE

Out through the fields and the woods
And over the walls I have wended;
I have climbed the hills of view
And looked at the world, and descended;

I have come by the highway home, 5
And lo, it is ended.

The leaves are all dead on the ground,
Save those that the oak is keeping
To ravel them one by one
And let them go scraping and creeping 10
Out over the crusted snow,
When others are sleeping.

And the dead leaves lie huddled and still,
No longer blown hither and thither;
The last lone aster is gone; 15
The flowers of the witch-hazel wither;
The heart is still aching to seek,
But the feet question "Whither?"

Ah, when to the heart of man
Was it ever less than a treason 20
To go with the drift of things,
To yield with a grace to reason,
And bow and accept the end
Of a love or a season?

1912

THE TUFT OF FLOWERS

I went to turn the grass once after one
Who mowed it in the dew before the sun.

The dew was gone that made his blade so keen
Before I came to view the leveled scene.

I looked for him behind an isle of trees; 5
I listened for his whetstone on the breeze.

But he had gone his way, the grass all mown,
And I must be, as he had been,—alone,

"As all must be," I said within my heart,
"Whether they work together or apart." 10

But as I said it, swift there passed me by
On noiseless wing a bewildered butterfly,

Seeking with memories grown dim o'er night
Some resting flower of yesterday's delight.

And once I marked his flight go round and round, 15
As where some flower lay withering on the ground.

And then he flew as far as eye could see,
And then on tremulous wing came back to me.

I thought of questions that have no reply,
And would have turned to toss the grass to dry; 20

But he turned first, and led my eye to look
At a tall tuft of flowers beside a brook,

A leaping tongue of bloom the scythe had spared
Beside a reedy brook the scythe had bared.

The mower in the dew had loved them thus, 25
By leaving them to flourish, not for us,

Nor yet to draw one thought of ours to him,
But from sheer morning gladness at the brim.

The butterfly and I had lit upon,
Nevertheless, a message from the dawn, 30

That made me hear the wakening birds around,
And hear his long scythe whispering to the ground,

And feel a spirit kindred to my own;
So that henceforth I worked no more alone;

But glad with him, I worked as with his aid, 35
And weary, sought at noon with him the shade;

And dreaming, as it were, held brotherly speech
With one whose thought I had not hoped to reach.

"Men work together," I told him from the heart,
"Whether they work together or apart." 40

1913

HOME BURIAL

He saw her from the bottom of the stairs
Before she saw him. She was starting down,
Looking back over her shoulder at some fear.
She took a doubtful step and then undid it
To raise herself and look again. He spoke 5
Advancing toward her: "What is it you see

From up there always—for I want to know."
She turned and sank upon her skirts at that,
And her face changed from terrified to dull.
He said to gain time: "What is it you see," 10
Mounting until she cowered under him.
"I will find out now—you must tell me, dear."
She, in her place, refused him any help
With the least stiffening of her neck and silence.
She let him look, sure that he wouldn't see, 15
Blind creature; and awhile he didn't see.
But at last he murmured, "Oh," and again, "Oh."

"What is it—what?" she said.

                        "Just that I see."

"You don't," she challenged. "Tell me what it is." 20

"The wonder is I didn't see at once.
I never noticed it from here before.
I must be wonted to it—that's the reason.
The little graveyard where my people are!
So small the window frames the whole of it. 25
Not so much larger than a bedroom, is it?
There are three stones of slate and one of marble,
Broad-shouldered little slabs there in the sunlight
On the sidehill. We haven't to mind *those*.
But I understand: it is not the stones, 30
But the child's mound—"

                "Don't, don't, don't, don't," she cried.

She withdrew shrinking from beneath his arm
That rested on the bannister, and slid downstairs;
And turned on him with such a daunting look, 35
He said twice over before he knew himself:
"Can't a man speak of his own child he's lost?"

"Not you! Oh, where's my hat? Oh, I don't need it!
I must get out of here. I must get air.
I don't know rightly whether any man can." 40

"Amy! Don't go to someone else this time.
Listen to me. I won't come down the stairs."
He sat and fixed his chin between his fists.
"There's something I should like to ask you, dear."

"You don't know how to ask it." 45

"Help me, then."

Her fingers moved the latch for all reply.

"My words are nearly always an offense.
I don't know how to speak of anything
So as to please you. But I might be taught
I should suppose. I can't say I see how.   50
A man must partly give up being a man
With women-folk. We could have some arrangement
By which I'd bind myself to keep hands off
Anything special you're a-mind to name.   55
Though I don't like such things 'twixt those that love.
Two that don't love can't live together without them.
But two that do can't live together with them."
She moved the latch a little. "Don't—don't go.
Don't carry it to someone else this time.
Tell me about it if it's something human.   60
Let me into your grief. I'm not so much
Unlike other folks as your standing there
Apart would make me out. Give me my chance.
I do think, though, you overdo it a little.
What was it brought you up to think it the thing   65
To take your mother-loss of a first child
So inconsolably—in the face of love.
You'd think his memory might be satisfied—"

"There you go sneering now!"   70

                         "I'm not, I'm not!
You make me angry. I'll come down to you.
God, what a woman! And it's come to this,
A man can't speak of his own child that's dead."

"You can't because you don't know how to speak.   75
If you had any feelings, you that dug
With your own hand—how could you?—his little grave;
I saw you from that very window there,
Making the gravel leap and leap in air,
Leap up, like that, like that, and land so lightly   80
And roll back down the mound beside the hole.
I thought, Who is that man? I didn't know you.
And I crept down the stairs and up the stairs
To look again, and still your spade kept lifting.
Then you came in. I heard your rumbling voice   85
Out in the kitchen, and I don't know why,
But I went near to see with my own eyes.
You could sit there with the stains on your shoes

Of the fresh earth from your own baby's grave
And talk about your everyday concerns.   90
You had stood the spade up against the wall
Outside there in the entry, for I saw it."

"I shall laugh the worst laugh I ever laughed.
I'm cursed. God, if I don't believe I'm cursed."

"I can repeat the very words you were saying.   95
'Three foggy mornings and one rainy day
Will rot the best birch fence a man can build.'
Think of it, talk like that at such a time!
What had how long it takes a birch to rot
To do with what was in the darkened parlor.   100
You *couldn't* care! The nearest friends can go
With anyone to death, comes so far short
They might as well not try to go at all.
No, from the time when one is sick to death,
One is alone, and he dies more alone.   105
Friends make pretense of following to the grave,
But before one is in it, their minds are turned
And making the best of their way back to life
And living people, and things they understand.
But the world's evil. I won't have grief so   110
If I can change it. Oh, I won't, I won't!"

"There, you have said it all and you feel better.
You won't go now. You're crying. Close the door.
The heart's gone out of it: why keep it up.
Amy! There's someone coming down the road!"   115

"*You*—oh, you think the talk is all. I must go—
Somewhere out of this house. How can I make you—"

"If—you—do!" She was opening the door wider.
"Where do you mean to go? First tell me that.
I'll follow and bring you back by force. I *will!*—"   120

1914

After Apple-Picking

My long two-pointed ladder's sticking through a tree
Toward heaven still,
And there's a barrel that I didn't fill
Beside it, and there may be two or three
Apples I didn't pick upon some bough.   5
But I am done with apple-picking now.
Essence of winter sleep is on the night,

The scent of apples: I am drowsing off.
I cannot rub the strangeness from my sight
I got from looking through a pane of glass   10
I skimmed this morning from the drinking trough
And held against the world of hoary grass.
It melted, and I let it fall and break.
But I was well
Upon my way to sleep before it fell,   15
And I could tell
What form my dreaming was about to take.
Magnified apples appear and disappear,
Stem end and blossom end,
And every fleck of russet showing clear.   20
My instep arch not only keeps the ache,
It keeps the pressure of a ladder-round.
I feel the ladder sway as the boughs bend.
And I keep hearing from the cellar bin
The rumbling sound   25
Of load on load of apples coming in.
For I have had too much
Of apple-picking: I am overtired
Of the great harvest I myself desired.
There were ten thousand thousand fruit to touch,   30
Cherish in hand, lift down, and not let fall.
For all
That struck the earth,
No matter if not bruised or spiked with stubble,
Went surely to the cider-apple heap   35
As of no worth.
One can see what will trouble
This sleep of mine, whatever sleep it is.
Were he not gone,
The woodchuck could say whether it's like his   40
Long sleep, as I describe its coming on,
Or just some human sleep.

1914

THE WOOD-PILE

Out walking in the frozen swamp one gray day,
I paused and said, "I will turn back from here.
No, I will go on farther—and we shall see."
The hard snow held me, save where now and then
One foot went through. The view was all in lines   5
Straight up and down of tall slim trees
Too much alike to mark or name a place by
So as to say for certain I was here
Or somewhere else: I was just far from home.

A small bird flew before me. He was careful　　　　10
To put a tree between us when he lighted,
And say no word to tell me who he was
Who was so foolish as to think what *he* thought.
He thought that I was after him for a feather—
The white one in his tail; like one who takes　　　15
Everything said as personal to himself.
One flight out sideways would have undeceived him.
And then there was a pile of wood for which
I forgot him and let his little fear
Carry him off the way I might have gone,　　　　20
Without so much as wishing him good-night.
He went behind it to make his last stand.
It was a cord of maple, cut and split
And piled—and measured, four by four by eight.
And not another like it could I see.　　　　　25
No runner tracks in this year's snow looped near it.
And it was older sure than this year's cutting,
Or even last year's or the year's before.
The wood was gray and the bark warping off it
And the pile somewhat sunken. Clematis　　　30
Had wound strings round and round it like a bundle.
What held it though on one side was a tree
Still growing, and on one a stake and prop,
These latter about to fall. I thought that only
Someone who lived in turning to fresh tasks　　　35
Could so forget his handiwork on which
He spent himself, the labor of his ax,
And leave it there far from a useful fireplace
To warm the frozen swamp as best it could
With the slow smokeless burning of decay.　　　40

An Old Man's Winter Night

All out-of-doors looked darkly in at him
Through the thin frost, almost in separate stars,
That gathers on the pane in empty rooms.
What kept his eyes from giving back the gaze
Was the lamp tilted near them in his hand.　　　5
What kept him from remembering what it was
That brought him to that creaking room was age.
He stood with barrels round him—at a loss.
And having scared the cellar under him
In clomping here, he scared it once again　　　10
In clomping off;—and scared the outer night,
Which has its sounds, familiar, like the roar
Of trees and crack of branches, common things,

But nothing so like beating on a box.
A light he was to no one but himself   15
Where now he sat, concerned with he knew what,
A quiet light, and then not even that.
He consigned to the moon, such as she was,
So late-arising, to the broken moon
As better than the sun in any case   20
For such a charge, his snow upon the roof,
His icicles along the wall to keep;
And slept. The log that shifted with a jolt
Once in the stove, disturbed him and he shifted,
And eased his heavy breathing, but still slept.   25
One aged man—one man—can't keep a house,
A farm, a countryside, or if he can,
It's thus he does it of a winter night.

1916

"OUT, OUT—"

The buzz saw snarled and rattled in the yard
And made dust and dropped stove-length sticks of wood,
Sweet-scented stuff when the breeze drew across it.
And from there those that lifted eyes could count
Five mountain ranges one behind the other   5
Under the sunset far into Vermont.
And the saw snarled and rattled, snarled and rattled,
As it ran light, or had to bear a load.
And nothing happened: day was all but done.
Call it a day, I wish they might have said   10
To please the boy by giving him the half hour
That a boy counts so much when saved from work.
His sister stood beside them in her apron
To tell them "Supper." At the word, the saw,
As if to prove saws knew what supper meant,   15
Leaped out at the boy's hand, or seemed to leap—
He must have given the hand. However it was,
Neither refused the meeting. But the hand!
The boy's first outcry was a rueful laugh,
As he swung toward them holding up the hand   20
Half in appeal, but half as if to keep
The life from spilling. Then the boy saw all—
Since he was old enough to know, big boy
Doing a man's work, though a child at heart—
He saw all spoiled. "Don't let him cut my hand off—   25
The doctor, when he comes. Don't let him, sister!"
So. But the hand was gone already.
The doctor put him in the dark of ether.
He lay and puffed his lips out with his breath.
And then—the watcher at his pulse took fright.   30

No one believed. They listened at his heart.
Little—less—nothing!—and that ended it.
No more to build on there. And they, since they
Were not the one dead, turned to their affairs.

1916

Brown's Descent

or

The Willy-Nilly Slide

Brown lived at such a lofty farm
    That everyone for miles could see
His lantern when he did his chores
    In winter after half-past three.

And many must have seen him make   5
    His wild descent from there one night,
'Cross lots, 'cross walls, 'cross everything,
    Describing rings of lantern light.

Between the house and barn the gale
    Got him by something he had on   10
And blew him out on the icy crust
    That cased the world, and he was gone!

Walls were all buried, trees were few:
    He saw no stay unless he stove
A hole in somewhere with his heel.   15
    But though repeatedly he strove

And stamped and said things to himself,
    And sometimes something seemed to yield,
He gained no foothold, but pursued
    His journey down from field to field.   20

Sometimes he came with arms outspread
    Like wings, revolving in the scene
Upon his longer axis, and
    With no small dignity of mien.

Faster or slower as he chanced,   25
    Sitting or standing as he chose,
According as he feared to risk
    His neck, or thought to spare his clothes.

He never let the lantern drop.
    And some exclaimed who saw afar   30
The figures he described with it,
    "I wonder what those signals are

"Brown makes at such an hour of night!
  He's celebrating something strange.
I wonder if he's sold his farm,   35
  Or been made Master of the Grange."

He reeled, he lurched, he bobbed, he checked;
  He fell and made the lantern rattle
(But saved the light from going out.)
  So halfway down he fought the battle,   40

Incredulous of his own bad luck.
  And then becoming reconciled
To everything, he gave it up
  And came down like a coasting child.

"Well—I—be—" that was all he said,   45
  As standing in the river road,
He looked back up the slippery slope
  (Two miles it was) to his abode.

Sometimes as an authority
  On motor-cars, I'm asked if I   50
Should say our stock was petered out,
  And this is my sincere reply:

Yankees are what they always were.
  Don't think Brown ever gave up hope
Of getting home again because   55
  He couldn't climb that slippery slope;

Or even thought of standing there
  Until the January thaw
Should take the polish off the crust.
  He bowed with grace to natural law,   60

And then went round it on his feet,
  After the manner of our stock;
Not much concerned for those to whom,
  At that particular time o'clock,

It must have looked as if the course   65
  He steered was really straight away
From that which he was headed for—
  Not much concerned for them, I say;

No more so than became a man—
  And politician at odd seasons.   70
I've kept Brown standing in the cold
  While I invested him with reasons;

But now he snapped his eyes three times;
Then shook his lantern, saying, "Ile's
'Bout out!" and took the long way home   75
By road, a matter of several miles.

1916

Fire and Ice

Some say the world will end in fire,
Some say in ice.
From what I've tasted of desire
I hold with those who favor fire.
But if it had to perish twice,   5
I think I know enough of hate
To say that for destruction ice
Is also great
And would suffice.

1920

Stopping by Woods on a Snowy Evening

Whose woods these are I think I know.
His house is in the village though;
He will not see me stopping here
To watch his woods fill up with snow.

My little horse must think it queer   5
To stop without a farmhouse near
Between the woods and frozen lake
The darkest evening of the year.

He gives his harness bells a shake
To ask if there is some mistake.   10
The only other sound's the sweep
Of easy wind and downy flake.

The woods are lovely, dark and deep,
But I have promises to keep,
And miles to go before I sleep,   15
And miles to go before I sleep.

1923

To Earthward

Love at the lips was touch
As sweet as I could bear;
And once that seemed too much;
I lived on air

That crossed me from sweet things   5
The flow of—was it musk
From hidden grapevine springs
Down hill at dusk?

I had the swirl and ache
From sprays of honeysuckle   10
That when they're gathered shake
Dew on the knuckle.

I craved strong sweets, but those
Seemed strong when I was young;
The petal of the rose   15
It was that stung.

Now no joy but lacks salt
That is not dashed with pain
And weariness and fault;
I crave the stain   20

Of tears, the aftermark
Of almost too much love,
The sweet of bitter bark
And burning clove.

When stiff and sore and scarred   25
I take away my hand
From leaning on it hard
In grass and sand,

The hurt is not enough:
I long for weight and strength   30
To feel the earth as rough
To all my length.

1923

Two Look at Two

Love and forgetting might have carried them
A little further up the mountainside
With night so near, but not much further up.
They must have halted soon in any case
With thoughts of the path back, how rough it was   5
With rock and washout, and unsafe in darkness;
When they were halted by a tumbled wall
With barbed-wire binding. They stood facing this,
Spending what onward impulse they still had
In one last look the way they must not go,   10

On up the failing path, where, if a stone
Or earthslide moved at night, it moved itself;
No footstep moved it. "This is all," they sighed,
"Good-night to woods." But not so; there was more.
A doe from round a spruce stood looking at them   15
Across the wall, as near the wall as they.
She saw them in their field, they her in hers.
The difficulty of seeing what stood still,
Like some up-ended boulder split in two,
Was in her clouded eyes: they saw no fear there.   20
She seemed to think that two thus they were safe.
Then, as if they were something that, though strange,
She could not trouble her mind with too long,
She sighed and passed unscared along the wall.
"*This*, then, is all. What more is there to ask?"   25
But no, not yet. A snort to bid them wait.
A buck from round the spruce stood looking at them
Across the wall as near the wall as they.
This was an antlered buck of lusty nostril,
Not the same doe come back into her place.   30
He viewed them quizzically with jerks of head,
As if to ask, "Why don't you make some motion?
Or give some sign of life? Because you can't.
I doubt if you're as living as you look."
Thus till he had them almost feeling dared   35
To stretch a proffering hand—and a spell-breaking.
Then he too passed unscared along the wall.
Two had seen two, whichever side you spoke from.
"This *must* be all." It was all. Still they stood,
A great wave from it going over them,   40
As if the earth in one unlooked-for favor
Had made them certain earth returned their love.

1923

ONCE BY THE PACIFIC

The shattered water made a misty din.
Great waves looked over others coming in,
And thought of doing something to the shore
That water never did to land before.
The clouds were low and hairy in the skies,   5
Like locks blown forward in the gleam of eyes.
You could not tell, and yet it looked as if
The shore was lucky in being backed by cliff,
The cliff in being backed by continent;
It looked as if a night of dark intent   10
Was coming, and not only a night, an age.
Someone had better be prepared for rage.

There would be more than ocean-water broken
Before God's last *Put out the Light* was spoken.

1926

TREE AT MY WINDOW

Tree at my window, window tree,
My sash is lowered when night comes on;
But let there never be curtain drawn
Between you and me.

Vague dream-head lifted out of the ground,   5
And thing next most diffuse to cloud,
Not all your light tongues talking aloud
Could be profound.

But, tree, I have seen you taken and tossed,
And if you have seen me when I slept,   10
You have seen me when I was taken and swept
And all but lost.

That day she put our heads together,
Fate had her imagination about her,
Your head so much concerned with outer,   15
Mine with inner, weather.

1927

A PECK OF GOLD

Dust always blowing about the town,
Except when sea-fog laid it down,
And I was one of the children told
Some of the blowing dust was gold.

All the dust the wind blew high   5
Appeared like gold in the sunset sky,
But I was one of the children told
Some of the dust was really gold.

Such was life in the Golden Gate:
Gold dusted all we drank and ate,   10
And I was one of the children told,
"We all must eat our peck of gold."

1928

DESERT PLACES

Snow falling and night falling fast, oh, fast
In a field I looked into going past,

And the ground almost covered smooth in snow,
But a few weeds and stubble showing last.

The woods around it have it—it is theirs.   5
All animals are smothered in their lairs.
I am too absent-spirited to count;
The loneliness includes me unawares.

And lonely as it is that loneliness
Will be more lonely ere it will be less—   10
A blanker whiteness of benighted snow
With no expression, nothing to express.

They cannot scare me with their empty spaces
Between stars—on stars where no human race is.
I have it in me so much nearer home   15
To scare myself with my own desert places.

                                        1934

DEPARTMENTAL

An ant on the tablecloth
Ran into a dormant moth
Of many times his size.
He showed not the least surprise.
His business wasn't with such.   5
He gave it scarcely a touch,
And was off on his duty run.
Yet if he encountered one
Of the hive's enquiry squad   9
Whose work is to find out God
And the nature of time and space,
He would put him onto the case.
Ants are a curious race;
One crossing with hurried tread
The body of one of their dead   15
Isn't given a moment's arrest—
Seems not even impressed.
But he no doubt reports to any
With whom he crosses antennae,
And they no doubt report   20
To the higher up at court.
Then word goes forth in Formic:
"Death's come to Jerry McCor-
      mic,

Our selfless forager Jerry.
Will the special Janizary   25
Whose office it is to bury
The dead of the commissary
Go bring him home to his people.
Lay him in state on a sepal.
Wrap him for shroud in a
      petal.   30
Embalm him with ichor of nettle.
This is the word of your Queen."
And presently on the scene
Appears a solemn mortician;
And taking formal position   35
With feelers calmly atwiddle,
Seizes the dead by the middle,
And heaving him high in air,
Carries him out of there.
No one stands round to stare.   40
It is nobody else's affair.

It couldn't be called ungentle.
But how thoroughly departmen-
      tal.

                                        1935

A Drumlin Woodchuck

One thing has a shelving bank,
Another a rotting plank,
To give it cozier skies
And make up for its lack of size.

My own strategic retreat   5
Is where two rocks almost meet,
And still more secure and snug,
A two-door burrow I dug.

With those in mind at my back
I can sit forth exposed to attack
As one who shrewdly pretends   11
That he and the world are friends.

All we who prefer to live
Have a little whistle we give,
And flash, at the least alarm   15
We dive down under the farm.

We allow some time for guile
And don't come out for a while
Either to eat or drink.
We take occasion to think.   20

And if after the hunt goes past
And the double-barreled blast
(Like war and pestilence
And the loss of common sense),

If I can with confidence say   25
That still for another day,
Or even another year,
I will be there for you, my dear,

It will be because, though small
As measured against the All,   30
I have been so instinctively thorough
About my crevice and burrow.

1936

A Considerable Speck

A speck that would have been beneath my sight
On any but a paper sheet so white
Set off across what I had written there.
And I had idly poised my pen in air
To stop it with a period of ink   5
When something strange about it made me think.
This was no dust speck by my breathing blown,
But unmistakably a living mite
With inclinations it could call its own.
It paused as with suspicion of my pen,   10
And then came racing wildly on again
To where my manuscript was not yet dry;
Then paused again and either drank or smelt—
With loathing, for again it turned to fly.
Plainly with an intelligence I dealt.   15
It seemed too tiny to have room for feet,
Yet must have had a set of them complete
To express how much it didn't want to die.
It ran with terror and with cunning crept.
It faltered: I could see it hesitate;   20
Then in the middle of the open sheet
Cower down in desperation to accept

Whatever I accorded it of fate.
I have none of the tenderer-than-thou
Collectivistic regimenting love   25
With which the modern world is being swept.
But this poor microscopic item now!
Since it was nothing I knew evil of
I let it lie there till I hope it slept.

I have a mind myself and recognize   30
Mind when I meet with it in any guise.
No one can know how glad I am to find
On any sheet the least display of mind.

                                        1939

TRIPLE BRONZE

The Infinite's being so wide
Is the reason the Powers provide
For inner defense my hide.
For next defense outside

I make myself this time   5
Of wood or granite or lime
A wall too hard for crime
Either to breach or climb.

Then a number of us agree
On a national boundary.   10
And that defense makes three
Between too much and me.

                                        1939

COME IN

As I came to the edge of the woods,
Thrush music—hark!
Now if it was dusk outside,
Inside it was dark.

Too dark in the woods for a bird   5
By sleight of wing
To better its perch for the night,
Though it still could sing.

The last of the light of the sun
That had died in the west   10
Still lived for one song more
In a thrush's breast.

Far in the pillared dark
Thrush music went—
Almost like a call to come in   15
To the dark and lament.

But no, I was out for stars:
I would not come in.
I meant not even if asked,
And I hadn't been.   20

1941

THE GIFT OUTRIGHT

The land was ours before we were the land's.
She was our land more than a hundred years
Before we were her people. She was ours
In Massachusetts, in Virginia,
But we were England's, still colonials,   5
Possessing what we still were unpossessed by,
Possessed by what we now no more possessed.
Something we were withholding made us weak
Until we found out that it was ourselves
We were withholding from our land of living,   10
And forthwith found salvation in surrender.
Such as we were we gave ourselves outright
(The deed of gift was many deeds of war)
To the land vaguely realizing westward,
But still unstoried, artless, unenhanced,   15
Such as she was, such as she would become.

1942

A YOUNG BIRCH

The birch begins to crack its outer sheath
Of baby green and show the white beneath,
As whosoever likes the young and slight
May well have noticed. Soon entirely white
To double day and cut in half the dark   5
It will stand forth, entirely white in bark,
And nothing but the top a leafy green—
The only native tree that dares to lean,
Relying on its beauty, to the air.
(Less brave perhaps than trusting are the fair.) 10
And someone reminiscent will recall
How once in cutting brush along the wall
He spared it from the number of the slain,
At first to be no bigger than a cane,
And then no bigger than a fishing pole,   15

But now at last so obvious a bole
The most efficient help you ever hired
Would know that it was there to be admired,
And zeal would not be thanked that cut it down
When you were reading books or out of town.   20
It was a thing of beauty and was sent
To live its life out as an ornament.

1946

One Step Backward Taken

Not only sands and gravels
Were once more on their travels,
But gulping muddy gallons
Great boulders off their balance
Bumped heads together dully   5
And started down the gully.
Whole capes caked off in slices.
I felt my standpoint shaken
In the universal crisis.
But with one step backward taken   10
I saved myself from going.
A world torn loose went by me.
Then the rain stopped and the blowing
And the sun came out to dry me.

1947

Why Wait for Science

Sarcastic Science she would like to know,
In her complacent ministry of fear,
How we propose to get away from here
When she has made things so we have to go
Or be wiped out. Will she be asked to show   5
Us how by rocket we may hope to steer
To some star off there say a half light-year
Through temperature of absolute zero?
Why wait for Science to supply the how
When any amateur can tell it now?   10
The way to go away should be the same
As fifty million years ago we came—
If anyone remembers how that was.
I have a theory, but it hardly does.

1947

One More Brevity

I opened the door so my last look
Should be taken outside a house and book.

Before I gave up seeing and slept
I said I would see how Sirius kept
His watch dog eye on what remained   5
To be gone into if not explained.
But scarcely was my door ajar
When past the leg I thrust for bar
Slipped in to be my problem guest
Not a heavenly dog made manifest,   10
But an earthly dog of the carriage breed,
Who having failed of the modern speed,
Now asked asylum—and I was stirred
To be the one so dog-preferred.
He dumped himself like a bag of bones,   15
He sighed himself a couple of groans,
And head to tail then firmly curled
Like swearing off on the traffic world.
I set him water, I set him food.
He rolled an eye with gratitude   20
(Or merely manners it may have been),
But never so much as lifted chin.
His hard tail loudly smacked the floor
As if beseeching me, "Please, no more
I can't explain—tonight at least."   25
His brow was perceptibly trouble-creased.
So I spoke in tones of adoption thus:
"Gustie, old boy, Dalmatian Gus
You're right, there's nothing to discuss.
Don't try to tell me what's on your mind,   30
The sorrow of having been left behind,
Or the sorrow of having run away.
All that can wait for the light of day.
Meanwhile feel obligation-free.
Nobody has to confide in me."   35
'Twas too one sided a dialogue,
And I wasn't sure I was talking dog.
I broke off puzzled. But all the same
In fancy I ratified his name,
Gustie, Dalmatian Gus, that is,   40
And started shaping my life to his,
Finding him his right supplies
And sharing his miles of exercise.

Next morning the minute I was about
He went to the door to be let out   45
As much as to say, "I have paid my call.
You mustn't be hurt if now I'm all
For getting back somewhere or further on."
I opened the door and he was gone.
I was to taste in little the grief   50

That comes of dogs' lives being so brief,
Only a fraction of ours at most.
He might have been the dream of a ghost
In spite of the way his tail had smacked
My floor so hard and matter-of-fact.   55
And things have been going so strangely since
I wouldn't be too hard to convince,
I might even claim, he was Sirius
(Think of presuming to call him Gus),
The star itself, Heaven's greatest star,   60
Not a meteorite, but an avatar,
Who had made an overnight descent
To show by deeds he didn't resent
My profiting by his virtue so long,
Yet doing so little about it in song.   65
A symbol was all he could hope to convey,
An intimation, a shot of ray,
A meaning I was supposed to seek,
And finding, was indisposed to speak.

1953

T. S. ELIOT

1888–

*A*LTHOUGH T. S. ELIOT CONSIDERS HIMSELF A "CLASSICIST IN LITERATURE" and a conservative in politics and religion, he has been anything but classical and conservative in his creativity. He has tended, to be sure, to frame his imaginative life within austere and even rigid borders; and he has spoken of himself in one of his poems as possessing a grim brow, a prim mouth, and features of clerical cut. A careful reader discovers, however, that Mr. Eliot is giving us a cat's-eye view of himself. Our own view, when we read his poems, is quite likely to show a different face, or a series of faces, and we might remember the line in *Prufrock* about preparing a face "to meet the faces that you meet." For, if the frame around the Eliot canvas is rigid and dark, the canvas itself—the canvas, that is, of his work—often looks like a Picasso painting; or it might even be described as resembling one of the strange polished creations of Salvador Dali, in which battered and bent clock visages are scattered amid dry bones and rocks on endless sand in a timeless and arrested world. The "grim" Eliot brow, it may be ventured, is also often relaxed; the prim mouth knows how to soften into a smile. And we may even assume that a symbolical beret, slightly askew, might be allowed to replace, on occasion, a clerical hat.

The real face of T. S. Eliot is that of a highly original poet, not that of the staunch and sometimes platitudinous defender of orthodoxy. If the New England puritan in Eliot speaks for rigidity, he paradoxically defends the very things the Puritans fled. He is royalist in politics, Anglo-Catholic in religion. The other side of Eliot defends the rebels in art, the twentieth-century experimenters of the *avant-garde:* Joyce, whose genius he recognized and admired to the end; his old friend Ezra Pound; or such gifted and idiosyncratic figures as the painter-prosateur Wyndham Lewis. Eliot may be the author of a series of meditations on the Lambeth

Conference of the Church of England, but this has not kept him from writing a preface to a novel about Parisian prostitutes and pimps called *Bubu of Montparnasse*.

The major figures in any advance guard are not those who seek mere novelty for the sake of novelty. They are the men who, having incorporated a tradition into their experience of life, are sufficiently at home with it to use it and even bold enough to modify it. Eliot's career, in this respect, and in many others, has distinct parallels with that of Henry James. On the surface we might speak of their long residence in England, their transfer of loyalty to the British Crown while guarding a strong spiritual allegiance to the United States, their receiving the coveted Order of Merit from the hands of the British sovereign, their ready acceptance of Old World traditions and standards and even their prolonged tenancy of flats in the same apartment house in Kensington—as if Eliot sought to be a posthumous neighbor to an illustrious predecessor. These, nevertheless, are surface parallels. A deeper resemblance is to be found in their cast of mind, and above all in their ability to mold tradition into new forms. Like James, Eliot is both creator and critic. This is not as common as might be supposed. Many writers attempt criticism but few significant writers, in all the history of literature, have also become significant critics. In Eliot, however, the two faculties mingle to such a degree that it is difficult to say sometimes whether Eliot is a poet writing criticism, or a critic writing poetry. As James was the great theorist of fiction of his time and ours, so Eliot has been the great—and certainly the most widely influential—theorist of poetry. His works themselves have an internal resemblance to James's. A finished poem by Eliot, like a Jamesian novel, is at several meditated removes from the original emotional stirrings that prompted it. The poetic passion, the intense moment of creation, is filtered through a complex verbal wall and dressed in metaphors which flow from the intellect. Neither the novelist nor the poet is capable of taking the reader on a journey into the blackness of the night; if they brilliantly examine what the darkness has meant they do so in broad daylight. We do not always experience their passion: but we look upon it through the illumination of their intellect and their civilization—and by this process are led to new experience.

In their experiments with form they stand on common ground, both as artists and as Americans. Their strong sense of "craft" may be discerned as a national trait, as artist-products of a civilization concerned with the highest skills and the greatest efficiencies. As James was the exponent of "point of view" in the novel, so Eliot has espoused it consistently in poetry. It is a method essentially dramatic and it stems, originally, from the monologues of Browning which influenced both the American novelist and the American poet. What Eliot has done has been simply to move the thoughts of his speaker more deeply into the consciousness; the monologue—understandably in the era of Joyce—is more "inner" than it was in the time of James and Browning. Eliot has explained in an illuminating lecture on *The Three Voices of Poetry* that when we read a poem we hear the voice of the poet talking to himself; or again, the voice may be addressing an audience; or (and this would be the third voice), the poet may speak through a character of his own creation, or in the guise of some figure out of the past. This very formulation reveals to us Eliot's acute sense of poetry as drama, and as embodying within it the dynamism of the audible as well as the visual. The voice we hear in the theatre is always the third voice, that of characters imagined by the dramatist, acting themselves out in words before our eyes. They live for us in what they say and what they reveal of themselves.

The poet speaking to himself, the poet addressing an audience in his own voice, or in an assumed one—what are these if not the voices of soliloquy and the chorus of the ancient and modern stage? In our century, however, precisely through the understanding of *point of view* or *field of vision*, we have penetrated more deeply into the inner modes and the inner life of these voices, so that sometimes we are brought closer to the actual flow of thought in the speaker. His "stream of consciousness," or "inner monologue," translated into verbal images or symbols, places us, the readers or listeners, close to the actual emotional experience of the character. The words and the images, the symbols they place before us, are (in Eliot's complex statement of this complex creative process) the *objective correlative* of the emotional state of the creator, as a shadow is a projection of an image of the body. Helen Gardner, in her study of Eliot's art, gives us an admirable example of the process by quoting a passage from the poet's prose and showing us the manner in which the same data was used by him in his poetry. The prose passage is to be found in Eliot's essay on *The Uses of Poetry*. He is speaking of the poet's imagery and he says:

> It comes from the whole of his sensitive life since early childhood. Why, for all of us, out of all that we have heard, seen, felt, in a lifetime, do certain images recur, charged with emotion, rather than others? The song of one bird, the leap of one fish, at a particular place and time, the scent of one flower, an old woman on a German mountain path, six ruffians seen through an open window playing cards at night at a small French railway junction where there was a watermill; such memories may have symbolic value, but of what we cannot tell, for they come to represent depths of feeling into which we cannot peer.

That we can sometimes peer into these depths Proust has shown. But what is significant for us is that this "felt life," as James called it, without necessarily being analyzed, makes its way into artistic utterance. Let us see how the third voice of poetry—the voice of an old man in the *Journey of the Magi*—takes these items of Eliot's experience into the realm of general symbolic experience:

Then at dawn we came down to a temperate valley,
Wet, below the snow line, smelling of vegetation;
With a running stream and a water-mill beating the darkness,
And three trees on the low sky,
And an old white horse galloped away in the meadow.
Then we came to a tavern with vine-leaves over the lintel,
Six hands at an open door dicing for pieces of silver,
And feet kicking the empty wine-skins.

Here the old personal memories of Eliot have melted together with older memories of the history of man and of Calvary, the three trees, the six hands dicing for silver, the blood-wine.

Eliot places us usually within the dramatized thoughts and reflections of himself as poet, or those he has imparted to his created character whether it be Prufrock, the aged narrator in the *Magi*, or the lady of his *Portrait of a Lady*. And this becomes one of the difficulties we experience in reading him, for we must recognize for ourselves the peculiar voice that addresses us, and then try to capture from the sequence of images the quality and the emotion of the utterance. A further difficulty is created by Eliot's cautious borrowing of lines and phrases from literature, past and present. Such depth of allusion is an endless source of fascination for explicators and footnote writers (whom Eliot seems to have partly emulated and partly mocked in his notes to *The Waste Land*) but it tends to confuse the reader accustomed to the old lucidities and simplicities of lyric and dramatic poetry. He may experience a slight irritation when he discovers that a certain line he has admired is not in reality Eliot, but Spenser or Shakespeare, or is taken from some obscure long-ago sermon. Such irritation may be overcome—and is certainly groundless—if we recognize how often in our daily speech we ourselves use phrases out of the past, from the Bible or the Declaration of Independence or books or poems read and reread, without it ever occurring to us that we must acknowledge these borrowings; often, indeed, we have forgotten that we are quoting someone else. We have only to recall how many of Churchill's and Roosevelt's phrases coined during the Second World War became a part of daily speech to recognize that we are always drawing upon the past of our language and our literature; that even Churchill and Roosevelt themselves salted their sentences with homely phrases out of their reading or their private oral tradition. Verbal experience, like all experience, is a constant composite of old and new, and when Eliot records memories of things he has read, which become a part of *his* experience of the moment, he is concerned not with the source of this or that quotation he may be using, but with the emotion which the line or lines may contain for him. These lines are so many possessions of his own consciousness, or of the character he has adumbrated and made to speak to us in the poem.

We must see Eliot's poetry, therefore, as part of a complex projection into words of states of consciousness, some seemingly inchoate, some as organized and meditative as the old-fashioned soliloquies. And this "life-time burning in every moment" involves the poet and his readers in problems of time—not the mechanical time of the clock but the human or psychological time which can make a second seem an hour and an hour a second. "Time present and time past," Eliot says in the first of his *Quartets,* are "both perhaps present in time future," as time future is contained in time past. Time is irreversible; the past stretches behind us; the present fleets by; we are always advancing into a future. But we are constantly using our past in this evanescent, flowing present, and when we do, we make it a part of the *new present*—before it flows once more into the past. Thus when Eliot evokes the Thames in *The Waste Land,* it is certainly the river that runs through London now; it is also, how-ever, the river on which the royalty of England rode in their barges cen-turies ago; and the very word *Thames* has a history, is charged with his-toric memory as well as personal memory, not only for the Londoners of our time but for persons in far-off places who have never been in Lon-don. When Eliot, in writing of London and its river, uses Spenser's "Sweet Themmes! runne softly, till I end my Song," he is resorting to a famous line which occurs to him while he is also speaking of a Thames in which we discern not sweetness but the flotsam and jetsam of the great London present—as well as the shadowy accretions of the past. "In some minds," Eliot once said, "certain memories, both from reading and from life, become charged with emotional significance. All these are used, so that intensity is gained at the expense of clarity."

In his willingness to sacrifice clarity to intensity, Eliot is ranged with the symbolists in literature, those experimenters who sought to widen the dimensions of a literary work by placing upon words the burden not only of expressing coherent and logical ideas, but also of conveying the experience of the senses. The romantic poets stressed emotion as well; but the important difference between them and a writer like Eliot is that the old poets spoke of emotion as they experienced it—clouds and daffo-dils or the pain or joy of love—whereas Eliot is concerned, like Proust, with capturing the deeper associational experience and creating or evok-ing an analogous experience for the reader. He is not interested in tell-ing the reader about a flowery perfume, or the odor of certain streets; he tries to capture in words the essence of these perfumes or odors, so that the reader will experience them out of his own sensory memories. There is a presumption in everything Eliot has written that the reader will be attentive and collaborative.

The work of T. S. Eliot has been a progress from an early cynicism and self-deflation through the depths of depression and despair to a grad-ual reconciliation with the anomalies of existence arrived at by intro-spection, meditation, and religious emotion. In this we may see a kind of development which takes its identification and inspiration from the journey of Dante in his trilogy, and we know that Dante is the poet with whom Eliot has most intimately been concerned. The early Eliot poems mock polite society and the tea-hound or "cookie-pusher," the man who has measured out his life with coffee spoons, while at the same time being aware of his feeling of impotence and his frustrated strivings. The petty conformities of the drawing-room, symbol of an ordered and vacuous world, are invoked; already the poet is smiling at his hostesses while he murders them with a phrase or a thought; and Prufrock, wandering on the beach, finds his buried feelings and deeper intensities expressed in the surging waves, the breaking foam. He is hardly a Hamlet; but he possesses Hamlet's inner melancholy, and his indecision. The voice of the poet, speaking to us in the guise of Prufrock, or of the elderly lady who gives us her self-portrait, is that of an individual who has depths of feeling which have been tamed and cultivated and disciplined, and therefore have never been fully expressed. Reticence, gentility, petty conformity, have smothered emotion; the poet buries his youth and assumes the guise of the disillusioned middle-aged, who have found little meaning in life and wonder whether "it has been worth while after all." This mood of boredom and futility—and sterility—reaches climactic utterance in *The Waste Land*, which Eliot published in 1922 (the year of Joyce's *Ulysses*). In this poem, life and history are seen as drained of all fertility; there has been a monstrous dehydration of the land and of the soul; the world is drab, uniform, mechanized. Questions are asked for which there are no answers:

> Do
> You know nothing? Do you see nothing? Do you remember
> Nothing?

Or if there is an answer, it is death:

> I remember
> Those are pearls that were his eyes.

The universal symbol in *The Waste Land* is that of water; the drama derives from its absence. As water is fertility and life, so the absence of water is sterility, death, decay. Water itself can bring death as well as life, and the drowned Phoenician sailor or the water-sense of *The Tempest* are evoked to suggest this. The tension in *The Waste Land* resides in a series of visions and moods, the brooding of Tiresias, the blind seer of tragedy and the central consciousness of the poem, filled with the insight of the sightless. The images of drought and disintegration, dryness and decay, multiply—dusty trees, desert rocks, dry bones, empty cisterns —while Eliot plays his game of juxtaposing the beautiful and the ugly. Sometimes the effect is to make us doubly aware of the beauty; sometimes the ugliness prevails. So past and present are juxtaposed, the drab and the exquisite, in a London in which people have through the centuries worked and made love in a kind of sleep-walking routine. It is an "unreal city," phantom-crowded, yet having the reality of history and the palpability of its people. And *The Waste Land* ends with an evocation of thunder and rain, the implication that fertility may return.

If we read Eliot's work in sequence, we find at its center, immediately following *The Waste Land*, a poem to which he gave the title *The Hollow Men*. It is of 1925 and, with its quotation from Conrad as epigraph, and its evocation of "death's other kingdom," it suggests that at this point the poet reached the heart of his darkness:

> shape without form, shade without colour,
> Paralysed force, gesture without motion.

The Waste Land still has the awareness of its sterility; and its images of dryness, and the fear embodied in dust, still partake of life. But the "waste land" of *The Hollow Men* is waste indeed. It is the soul's emptiness, when life has lost all meaning; the hollow men, stuffed with straw, are scarecrows in vague human shape; the dehumanization is complete. The poem can end only with the babble of fragments of the Lord's Prayer mingled with nursery rhyme and

> the world ends
> Not with a bang but a whimper.

Ash-Wednesday, which came five years after *The Hollow Men,* marks the ascent from the nether regions, the long climb, as it were, through Purgatory. The poet, now speaking in his first or second voice, to himself and to an audience, seems to be looking for some center of peace, and seeking to find his salvation; he has set foot outside the dryness of waste-land, away from the miasma of the heart of darkness. As its title suggests, *Ash-Wednesday* is a deeply religious poem. The voice speaking to us has embraced Christianity and has come to terms with past and present, "for what is done . . . May the judgement not be too heavy upon us." The poet rejoices, "having to construct something/ Upon which to rejoice." The symbolism of this poem is intricate and derives from religious ritual and religious meditation. There are ambiguities of feeling and uncertainties, doubts, and indecisions; the poem may well be explored by some future biographer for its testimony of some personal crisis which Eliot seeks to resolve by purification and holiness. The lines themselves are as of the chants and responses, the incantations and reiterations, of the religious service. Only by writing such a poem can the poet be ready for peace, as Dante was for the *Paradiso*. He could move forward in his work toward that repose of the heart which comes from the knowledge of agitation surmounted, tranquillity experienced.

He had always been a dramatic poet and he was prepared now to write his plays and to reformulate his feelings in a series of "quartets" as Beethoven, in his late phase, resorted to the subtleties of chamber music for the expression, in a highly organized form, of the felt intensities and accumulated visions of his life. In *Four Quartets* (1940–1942),

Eliot wrote a poetic summing up of the twenty years of his middle life, between the two world wars which, since it belonged also to the continuum of his experience was, in reality, a summing up of his entire life. In these poems he only occasionally seems to be addressing an audience; for the most part he meditates—on time, on history, on feeling, on the poet's craft. History is "a pattern of timeless moments." The poet's craft makes him spokesman for the moment,

> last year's words belong to last year's language
> And next year's words await another voice.

For most men there is "only the unattended/Moment, the moment in and out of time." For the rest, there is "prayer, observance, discipline, thought and action." The quartets are compounded of the visual and the dramatic; by a series of subtle devices Eliot expresses, in the loftiest and also the most delicately shaded phrasings, his deep sense of man's inner tumult and the calm that awaits him through sentience, expression of feeling, as in prayer, self-acceptance, and acceptance of Christian love—

> Love is most nearly itself
> When here and now cease to matter.

But to sum up, in this fashion, certain of the ideas in the quartets does not suggest their intricacy of pattern and nuance of thought. The critics have seen that each quartet deals with one of the four elements: *East Coker* with earth, *Burnt Norton* with air, *The Dry Salvages* with water and *Little Gidding* with fire. The air raids on London brought fire and water together; but water is also baptism, and fire purges—and water (as in *The Waste Land*) betokens fertility while fire is a destroyer as well as a renewer of life. Thus Eliot sounds the universal symbols and the eternal ambiguities. The quartets are of a piece with *The Waste Land*, but in them the search and the questioning are over. The poet has discovered his answers and now knows repose and the large dimensions of serenity.

In his plays Eliot re-invigorated poetic drama as Yeats had done before him. *Murder in the Cathedral* (1935) dramatized the death and martyrdom centuries ago of Thomas à Becket. *The Family Reunion* (1939) and *The Cocktail Party* (1950) dealt with crises in the emotional life of certain individuals and their search for self-understanding. Eliot chooses nearly always a minor domestic episode—a family reunion, a cocktail party—as situation for the self-exploration of the characters. The result is that his plays seem strangely to combine the trivial with the significant. Eliot's theory of dramatic poetry is that the play must establish a "musical pattern" which intensifies the action and the resulting emotion. And he warns against allowing "bursts of poetry" to substitute for action. His most recent plays are *The Confidential Clerk* (1955) and *The Elder Statesman* (1958).

In criticism Eliot has provided for the present generation a reassessment of certain writers of the past as well as an active discussion of the problems in his own poetic workshop. He has confined himself almost wholly to the criticism of poetry and drama, and in his focus upon a given work or works and the "purity" of the critical act, has had a remarkable influence upon certain critics who have used his ideas as touchstones for wider criticism. Unlike them, however, Eliot has always been concerned with the experience of reading and the sharpening of critical insight by this experience. His is the criticism of a poet seeking always the deeper awarenesses of his craft.

Thomas Stearns Eliot was born in St. Louis in 1888. His family came from Massachusetts, guarding its New England traditions and its sense of a more distant English past—its descent from Andrew Eliot who left East Coker in the seventeenth century for the colonies. The future poet studied at Harvard, the University of Paris, and at Oxford; he settled in England in 1914, when he was twenty-six, taught for a while, worked in a bank, and later became a member of the publishing house now known as Faber & Faber, as well as editor of the critical journal, the *Criterion*, which he founded. *The Love Song of J. Alfred Prufrock* was published in 1915 and *Poems* in 1920, a volume enlarged during his later years to contain his complete poetical writings. His first collection of essays, *The Sacred Wood*, was of 1920 and was followed by other collections, the most recent of which is *On Poetry and Poets*. In 1948 he received the Nobel Prize. He has been a British citizen since the mid-twenties, but he returns occasionally to his homeland to lecture and to read his poetry.

Thus in the circumstances of his life he has been, like Henry James, a trans-Atlantic figure, a writer with strong American roots who has recovered older roots in England. We may speculate that the admixture of Old and New World elements, the sense of trans-Atlantic cultural differences, the reforging of an old civilization on a new continent, compounded in Eliot (as in James) a degree of complexity and technical virtuosity which few writers of England have possessed, since they are part of a more homogeneous civilization and attached to a narrower part of the earth's surface. Eliot is fundamentally a visionary and a psychological writer tugging at the sources of feeling, a philosopher of man's journey into the abyss and his struggle to escape from it. As such he is linked inevitably in the critical mind, as indeed in his own, with Dante rather than with Milton, and with metaphysical poetry rather than with the romantics. Whatever his ties, he is the one poet of our time who has infused an extraordinary vitality into the language of poetry and been at the same time a very real scholar in his art. His influence has been extensive wherever English is spoken and read; and his is the dominant voice in poetry and the poetic drama in the middle of our century.

THE LOVE SONG OF
J. ALFRED PRUFROCK

This poem was first published in the June 1915 number of *Poetry* and gave its name to T. S. Eliot's first volume of verse, *Prufrock and Other Observations*, 1917. It remains one of his best-known poems; certain lines in it have a currency beyond any other poetry written in our time. Critics have seen this work as reflecting the manner and idiom of the French poet Jules Laforgue; but whatever the sources, it is clear that Eliot converted them to his own use and to the creation of a dramatic monologue expressive of the disillusion and frustration of a middle-aged man, or one who thinks of himself as prematurely old.

As with most of Eliot's poems, we must pay close attention to the quotation affixed at the head of the poem, for it carries in it an overtone of the work, some association in the poet's mind linked to the center of his feeling in the poem. In this case he has chosen certain lines from Dante, a passage from Canto XXVII of the *Inferno*. The speaker is Guido da Montefeltro, reduced in hell to a hovering flame because he gave false counsel. He tells Dante in these lines that if he believed he were answering the questions of someone returning to earth (as Dante was supposed to return) he would be at rest. But since he is sure that there is no turning back from hell for anyone, he can speak without fear of infamy. In the rest of the canto he tells Dante about his life as a deceiver, how his needs were those of the sly fox rather than of a bold lion. If we search the inner meaning of the passage in Dante and the substance of "Prufrock," we see that Eliot too has written a poem about false counsel. A man who is a deceiver is not true to himself. And J. Alfred Prufrock has bowed, and smirked, measured out his life with coffee spoons, put on a face other than his own, done what he was socially supposed to do, instead of yielding to his own natural feelings. Moreover he dares not depart from this role. He is afraid: and has been afraid to do what he really wanted, afraid even to speak his love to women. He longs to be daring; to walk along the beach in carefree fashion and in informal attire; to talk boldly to mermaids; but if he did, he is sure they would not reply. He has become a middle-aged Little Lord Fauntleroy; his hesitations are hardly those of a Hamlet. The fear of self-assertion is combined with the fear that he might meet rebuff. All this makes him see himself as rather a fool, a jester in life.

Like Guido, who deceived and tried to conform to other people's values, he has ended by playing a rather frightful trick on himself. For in being untrue to oneself one ends by being untrue to others. The "love song" of Mr. Prufrock is ironic; being incapable of any love but self-love, and facing the world with a mask of deceit, he must sing his love song, so to speak, to himself.

*S'io credesse che mia risposta fosse
A persona che mai tornasse al mondo,
Questa fiamma staria senza piu scosse.
Ma perciocche giammai di questo fondo
Non torno vivo alcun, s'i'odo il vero,
Senza tema d'infamia ti rispondo.*

Let us go then, you and I,
When the evening is spread out against the sky
Like a patient etherised upon a table;
Let us go, through certain half-deserted streets,
The muttering retreats   5
Of restless nights in one-night cheap hotels
And sawdust restaurants with oyster-shells:
Streets that follow like a tedious argument
Of insidious intent
To lead you to an overwhelming question.   10
Oh, do not ask, 'What is it?'
Let us go and make our visit.

In the room the women come and go
Talking of Michelangelo.

The yellow fog that rubs its back upon the window-panes,   15
The yellow smoke that rubs its muzzle on the window-panes
Licked its tongue into the corners of the evening,
Lingered upon the pools that stand in drains,
Let fall upon its back the soot that falls from chimneys,
Slipped by the terrace, made a sudden leap,   20
And seeing that it was a soft October night,
Curled once about the house, and fell asleep.

And indeed there will be time
For the yellow smoke that slides along the street
Rubbing its back upon the window-panes;
There will be time, there will be time   25
To prepare a face to meet the faces that you meet;
There will be time to murder and create,
And time for all the works and days of hands
That lift and drop a question on your plate;   30
Time for you and time for me,
And time yet for a hundred indecisions,
And for a hundred visions and revisions,
Before the taking of a toast and tea.

In the room the women come and go   35
Talking of Michelangelo.

And indeed there will be time
To wonder, 'Do I dare?' and, 'Do I dare?'
Time to turn back and descend the stair,
With a bald spot in the middle of my hair—   40
[They will say: 'How his hair is growing thin!']
My morning coat, my collar mounting firmly to the chin,
My necktie rich and modest, but asserted by a simple pin—
[They will say: 'But how his arms and legs are thin!']
Do I dare   45
Disturb the universe?
In a minute there is time
For decisions and revisions which a minute will reverse.

For I have known them all already, known them all—
Have known the evenings, mornings, afternoons,   50
I have measured out my life with coffee spoons;
I know the voices dying with a dying fall
Beneath the music from a farther room.
    So how should I presume?

And I have known the eyes already, known them all—   55
The eyes that fix you in a formulated phrase,
And when I am formulated, sprawling on a pin,
When I am pinned and wriggling on the wall,
Then how should I begin
To spit out all the butt-ends of my days and ways?   60
    And how should I presume?

And I have known the arms already, known them all—
Arms that are braceleted and white and bare
[But in the lamplight, downed with light brown hair!]
Is it perfume from a dress   65
That makes me so digress?
Arms that lie along a table, or wrap about a shawl.
    And should I then presume?
    And how should I begin?

          .   .   .   .   .

Shall I say, I have gone at dusk through narrow streets   70
And watched the smoke that rises from the pipes
Of lonely men in shirt-sleeves, leaning out of windows? . . .

I should have been a pair of ragged claws
Scuttling across the floors of silent seas.

          .   .   .   .   .

And the afternoon, the evening, sleeps so peacefully!   75
Smoothed by long fingers,
Asleep . . . tired . . . or it malingers,
Stretched on the floor, here beside you and me.
Should I, after tea and cakes and ices,
Have the strength to force the moment to its crisis?   80
But though I have wept and fasted, wept and prayed,
Though I have seen my head [grown slightly bald] brought in upon a
    platter,
I am no prophet—and here's no great matter;
I have seen the moment of my greatness flicker,
And I have seen the eternal Footman hold my coat, and snicker,   85
And in short, I was afraid.
And would it have been worth it, after all,
After the cups, the marmalade, the tea,
Among the porcelain, among some talk of you and me,
Would it have been worth while,   90
To have bitten off the matter with a smile,
To have squeezed the universe into a ball
To roll it toward some overwhelming question,
To say: 'I am Lazarus, come from the dead,
Come back to tell you all, I shall tell you all'—   95
If one, settling a pillow by her head,
  Should say: 'That is not what I meant at all.
  That is not it, at all.'

And would it have been worth it, after all,
Would it have been worth while,   100
After the sunsets and the dooryards and the sprinkled streets,
After the novels, after the teacups, after the skirts that trail along the
    floor—
And this, and so much more?—
It is impossible to say just what I mean!
But as if a magic lantern threw the nerves in patterns on a screen: 105
Would it have been worth while
If one, settling a pillow or throwing off a shawl,
And turning toward the window, should say:
  'That is not it at all,
  That is not what I meant, at all.'   110

No! I am not Prince Hamlet, nor was meant to be;
Am an attendant lord, one that will do
To swell a progress, start a scene or two,
Advise the prince; no doubt, an easy tool,
Deferential, glad to be of use,   115
Politic, cautious, and meticulous;

Full of high sentence, but a bit obtuse;
At times, indeed, almost ridiculous—
Almost, at times, the Fool.

I grow old . . . I grow old . . .   120
I shall wear the bottoms of my trousers rolled.

Shall I part my hair behind? Do I dare to eat a peach?
I shall wear white flannel trousers, and walk upon the beach.
I have heard the mermaids singing, each to each.

I do not think that they will sing to me.   125

I have seen them riding seaward on the waves
Combing the white hair of the waves blown back
When the wind blows the water white and black.

We have lingered in the chambers of the sea
By sea-girls wreathed with seaweed red and brown   130
Till human voices wake us, and we drown.

1915

PRELUDES

The "Preludes," published in 1915, carry over the poet's sense of boredom and sadness—the emotional stasis—characteristic of "Prufrock." As with Chopin's preludes, isolated introductory fragments, these announce themes but go no farther than announcement. They express the single mood: despondency at the end of the day; the jaded awakening to a depressed world; a night of fantasy and nightmare; the general sense of the City as a prison with its dark streets and slum waste, its impassive people "assured of certain certainties." But amid this monotone world of the daily round, the poet experiences flights of fancy which remove him from the hard images of a hard world. They fill life with a sense of gentleness and of suffering.

I

The winter evening settles down
With smell of steaks in passageways.
Six o'clock.
The burnt-out ends of smoky days.
And now a gusty shower wraps   5
The grimy scraps
Of withered leaves about your feet
And newspapers from vacant lots;

The showers beat
On broken blinds and chimney-pots,   10
And at the corner of the street
A lonely cab-horse steams and stamps.
And then the lighting of the lamps.

II

The morning comes to consciousness
Of faint stale smells of beer   15
From the sawdust-trampled street
With all its muddy feet that press
To early coffee-stands.
With the other masquerades
That time resumes,   20
One thinks of all the hands
That are raising dingy shades
In a thousand furnished rooms.

III

You tossed a blanket from the bed,
You lay upon your back, and waited;   25
You dozed, and watched the night revealing
The thousand sordid images
Of which your soul was constituted;
They flickered against the ceiling.
And when all the world came back   30
And the light crept up between the shutters
And you heard the sparrows in the gutters,
You had such a vision of the street
As the street hardly understands;
Sitting along the bed's edge, where   35
You curled the papers from your hair,
Or clasped the yellow soles of feet
In the palms of both soiled hands.

IV

His soul stretched tight across the skies
That fade behind a city block,   40
Or trampled by insistent feet
At four and five and six o'clock;
And short square fingers stuffing pipes,
And evening newspapers, and eyes
Assured of certain certainties,   45
The conscience of a blackened street
Impatient to assume the world.
I am moved by fancies that are curled
Around these images, and cling:

The notion of some infinitely gentle   50
Infinitely suffering thing.
Wipe your hand across your mouth, and laugh;
The worlds revolve like ancient women
Gathering fuel in vacant lots.

1915

SWEENEY AMONG THE NIGHTINGALES

The Greek epigraph for this poem can be translated "Alas, I am struck a mortal blow within"—the climactic cry of the betrayed Agamemnon in the tragedy by Aeschylus. The effect is ironic: a memory of high tragedy is invoked for a tale of a thick-necked individual named Sweeney, threatened by death in some gangster dive. To the nightingales—as to the worms in Hamlet—this is a matter of complete indifference. The nightingales will sing alike for King or gangster; as a consequence of the industry of worms, a King may make a progress through the guts of a beggar. The exquisite music of the nightingales sounded when the mortal blow was struck in Ancient Greece; and they sing while Sweeney is under the eye of the man in mocha brown and has his little adventure with the intoxicated nighttown lady in the Spanish cape. Eliot has been quoted as saying that he is aware only of having tried to create in his poem a "sense of foreboding." But the effect, up to the last two stanzas, is rather that of movie-melodrama and comedy. Then the mood changes: the poet is suddenly solemn, meditative, philosophical. He muses on the fact that the deaths of a king and of a man named Sweeney are of equal importance, even if one is a tragic hero and the other is ape-like and commonplace. Beauty and ugliness are juxtaposed; the tragic emotion and the pathetic; and the nightingales offer a requiem of indifference for one or the other, much as the droppings of the birds are indifferent to the shroud that decks the remains of a king.

ὤμοι, πέπληγμαι καιρίαν πληγὴν ἔσω

Apeneck Sweeney spreads his knees
Letting his arms hang down to laugh,
The zebra stripes along his jaw
Swelling to maculate giraffe.

The circles of the stormy moon   5
Slide westward toward the River Plate,
Death and the Raven drift above
And Sweeney guards the hornèd gate.

Gloomy Orion and the Dog
Are veiled; and hushed the shrunken seas; 10
The person in the Spanish cape
Tries to sit on Sweeney's knees

Slips and pulls the table cloth
Overturns a coffee-cup,
Reorganized upon the floor 15
She yawns and draws a stocking up:

The silent man in mocha brown
Sprawls at the window-sill and gapes;
The waiter brings in oranges
Bananas figs and hothouse grapes; 20

The silent vertebrate in brown
Contracts and concentrates, withdraws;
Rachel *née* Rabinovitch
Tears at the grapes with murderous paws;

She and the lady in the cape 25
Are suspect, thought to be in league;
Therefore the man with heavy eyes
Declines the gambit, shows fatigue,

Leaves the room and reappears
Outside the window, leaning in, 30
Branches of wistaria
Circumscribe a golden grin;

The host with someone indistinct
Converses at the door apart,
The nightingales are singing near 35
The convent of the Sacred Heart,

And sang within the bloody wood
When Agamemnon cried aloud,
And let their liquid siftings fall
To stain the stiff dishonoured shroud. 40

1918

THE WASTE LAND

T. S. Eliot's *The Waste Land* and James Joyce's *Ulysses* both appeared in 1922 and both have since that time exercised a profound influence upon English—and indeed world—literature. In these two works the spirit of the age, perhaps of the whole twentieth century, has found full reflection. Joyce, with extraordinary vitality and imaginative power, sought to assert himself and the power of language by plucking—in words—a single day out of all eternity. Eliot's vision was a gloomy, introspective, and quasi-philosophical meditation upon the decay of civilization, reflecting a deep malaise and sense of depression, but also revealing a fount of vitality and a consummate sense of language. Joyce's work, although containing a highly original exploration of subjectivity, was in itself extrovert. Eliot's was introvert. Or we might borrow an analogy from the Russian novelist Turgenev, and speak of *Ulysses* as embodying the tradition of *Don Quixote* and *The Waste Land* as belonging to the tradition of *Hamlet*.

As always it is necessary to look closely at the epigraph. In this case Eliot is quoting Petronius, and the Greek words, set into the Latin, are question and response: "With my own eyes I saw the Sybil suspended in a glass bottle at Cumae, and when the boys said to her: *Sybil what is the matter?* she would always respond: *I yearn to die.*"

Thus, if we consider Eliot's poetry in sequence, the frustration and impotence and the boredom of the earlier poems, and the foreboding of Sweeney, has become utter despair and a yearning for death. The waste land is that inner drying up of the will to live, because life has lost its meaning and the pain of existence craves the anaesthesia of death. But if the yearning for death is self-destructive and a negation of life, the desire to escape from the waste land can carry in it an affirmation of life as well: it is that affirmation which Hamlet voices when, in his great soliloquy, he fears eternal sleep in case it may be disrupted by dream. So the poet in the waste land, his senses numbed by the drying-up of life, finds that they are still capable of responding to all that is fertile and beautiful and waste-defeating. There is not yet that deadly apathy and emptiness of despair which could turn the wish for death into an act of self-annihilation. The eyes that look upon the desert-land know also that what has been lost may be recovered.

If we allow some such emotions as constituting the deepest sources of this poem—and we take our cue for them from the epigraph—we can then reread the work, keeping in mind Eliot's formulation of the "objective correlative," and see in the images and symbols projected by the poet the concretions into which the emotions have been translated. To search out the meaning of the poem by annotating it even beyond the annotations of Mr. Eliot is perhaps a pleasant intellectual exercise, and on occasion a scholarly necessity, but the way to the heart of *The Waste Land* lies elsewhere. For the reader concerned with the poem's essence it is more profitable to see how the image of a waste land, the central image, is translated into its multiple forms and into its antithesis. If, on the one hand, we are in a desert world of heat and dryness, shadowless life, empty cisterns and decayed cities, we are also led to reflect on opposites: the return of the seasons, the freshness of the water, the age-old vegetation and fertility myths, the rituals surrounding birth and growth, life and death, and the relation of the cycles of life to a Divine order.

The reader who is willing to accept Eliot's sacrifice of lucidity for intensity, and to treat the poem not as a test of memory or an elaborate literary puzzle, may not grasp all that he will read and yet be capable of capturing the force and beauty of the language and the poetic pictures—and emotions—evoked. The poem is a series of visions, narrative moments expressed in lyric and dramatic terms. We begin with the round of the seasons, old memories, the fortuneteller, we move into a Prufrockian London, ("unreal city,") we listen to a conversation in a pub, we meditate Hamlet-like with the poet, or see with the aid of the blind seer Tiresias such episodes as that of the tired typist and her carbuncular young man and their love-making, as automatic as their gramophone. The Thames flows sweetly through the poem, with its unsweet burden and its historic memories; and the poet, standing in London, possesses the historic memory of Carthage, burning and leveled to waste land. (Years later this will seem almost prophetic when the poet will actually see London ablaze during the war.) If fire consumes, so can water. Phlebas the Phoenician has been drowned and Eliot's lyric recounts this in a kind of water-music. And then the voice of Thunder, the emanation of the unknown and the final images of dessication and death, the deserts of the world and the soul, but the hope also for rain and for eternal calm.

That *The Waste Land* possessed much meaning for its readers is clear, for it was read by many—and for years—without benefit of explication. And if we listen to Eliot's "three voices of poetry" in it we can figure the poem as a discovery of the dark wood into which the poet has wandered, in the middle of the journey. The poet is descending into the abyss.

'Nam Sibyllam quidem Cumis ego ipse oculis meis
vidi in ampulla pendere, et cum illi pueri dicerent:
ἰΣβυλλα τί θέλεις; respondebat illa: ἀποθανεῖν θέλω.'
For Ezra Pound
il miglior fabbro.

I. THE BURIAL OF THE DEAD

April is the cruellest month, breeding
Lilacs out of the dead land, mixing
Memory and desire, stirring
Dull roots with spring rain.
Winter kept us warm, covering   5
Earth in forgetful snow, feeding
A little life with dried tubers.
Summer surprised us, coming over the Starnbergersee
With a shower of rain; we stopped in the colonnade,
And went on in sunlight, into the Hofgarten,   10

And drank coffee, and talked for an hour.
Bin gar keine Russin, stamm' aus Litauen, echt deutsch.
And when we were children, staying at the arch-duke's,
My cousin's, he took me out on a sled,
And I was frightened. He said, Marie,   15
Marie, hold on tight. And down we went.
In the mountains, there you feel free.
I read, much of the night, and go south in the winter.

What are the roots that clutch, what branches grow
Out of this stony rubbish? Son of man,   20
You cannot say, or guess, for you know only
A heap of broken images, where the sun beats,
And the dead tree gives no shelter, the cricket no relief,
And the dry stone no sound of water. Only
There is shadow under this red rock   25
(Come in under the shadow of this red rock),
And I will show you something different from either
Your shadow at morning striding behind you
Or your shadow at evening rising to meet you;
I will show you fear in a handful of dust.   30
   Frisch weht der Wind
   Der Heimat zu
   Mein Irisch Kind,
   Wo weilest du?
'You gave me hyacinths first a year ago;   35
'They called me the hyacinth girl.'
—Yet when we came back, late, from the Hyacinth garden
Your arms full, and your hair wet, I could not
Speak, and my eyes failed, I was neither
Living nor dead, and I knew nothing,   40
Looking into the heart of light, the silence.
Oe'd und leer das Meer.

Madame Sosostris, famous clairvoyante,
Had a bad cold, nevertheless
Is known to be the wisest woman in Europe,
With a wicked pack of cards. Here, said she,   45
Is your card, the drowned Phoenician Sailor,
(Those are pearls that were his eyes. Look!)
Here is Belladonna, the Lady of the Rocks,
The lady of situations.   50
Here is the man with three staves, and here the Wheel
And here is the one-eyed merchant, and this card,
Which is blank, is something he carries on his back,
Which I am forbidden to see. I do not find
The Hanged Man. Fear death by water.   55
I see crowds of people, walking round in a ring.
Thank you. If you see dear Mrs. Equitone,

Tell her I bring the horoscope myself:
One must be so careful these days.

Unreal City, 60
Under the brown fog of a winter dawn,
A crowd flowed over London Bridge, so many,
I had not thought death had undone so many.
Sighs, short and infrequent, were exhaled,
And each man fixed his eyes before his feet. 65
Flowed up the hill and down King William Street,
To where Saint Mary Woolnoth kept the hours
With a dead sound on the final stroke of nine.
There I saw one I knew, and stopped him, crying: 'Stetson!
'You who were with me in the ships at Mylae! 70
'That corpse you planted last year in your garden,
'Has it begun to sprout? Will it bloom this year?
'Or has the sudden frost disturbed its bed?
'Oh keep the Dog far hence, that's friend to men,
'Or with his nails he'll dig it up again! 75
'You! hypocrite lecteur!—mon semblable,—mon frère!'

II. A GAME OF CHESS

The Chair she sat in, like a burnished throne,
Glowed on the marble, where the glass
Held up by standards wrought with fruited vines
From which a golden Cupidon peeped out 80
(Another hid his eyes behind his wing)
Doubled the flames of sevenbranched candelabra
Reflecting light upon the table as
The glitter of her jewels rose to meet it,
From satin cases poured in rich profusion; 85
In vials of ivory and coloured glass
Unstoppered, lurked her strange synthetic perfumes,
Unguent, powdered, or liquid—troubled, confused
And drowned the sense in odours; stirred by the air
That freshened from the window, these ascended 90
In fattening the prolonged candle-flames,
Flung their smoke into the laquearia,
Stirring the pattern on the coffered ceiling.
Huge sea-wood fed with copper
Burned green and orange, framed by the coloured stone, 95
In which sad light a carvèd dolphin swam.
Above the antique mantel was displayed
As though a window gave upon the sylvan scene
The change of Philomel, by the barbarous king
So rudely forced; yet there the nightingale 100
Filled all the desert with inviolable voice
And still she cried, and still the world pursues,

'Jug Jug' to dirty ears.
And other withered stumps of time
Were told upon the walls; staring forms   105
Leaned out, leaning, hushing the room enclosed.
Footsteps shuffled on the stair.
Under the firelight, under the brush, her hair
Spread out in fiery points
Glowed into words, then would be savagely still.   110

   'My nerves are bad to-night. Yes, bad. Stay with me.
'Speak to me. Why do you never speak. Speak.
   'What are you thinking of? What thinking? What?
'I never know what you are thinking. Think.'

   I think we are in rats' alley   115
Where the dead men lost their bones.

   'What is that noise?'
              The wind under the door.
'What is that noise now? What is the wind doing?'
              Nothing again nothing.   120
                       'Do
'You know nothing? Do you see nothing? Do you remember
'Nothing?'

     I remember
Those are pearls that were his eyes.   125
'Are you alive, or not? Is there nothing in your head?'
                           But
O O O O that Shakespeherian Rag—
It's so elegant
So intelligent   130
'What shall I do now? What shall I do?'
'I shall rush out as I am, and walk the street
'With my hair down, so. What shall we do to-morrow?
'What shall we ever do?
              The hot water at ten.   135
And if it rains, a closed car at four.
And we shall play a game of chess,
Pressing lidless eyes and waiting for a knock upon the door.

    When Lil's husband got demobbed, I said—
I didn't mince my words, I said to her myself,   140
HURRY UP PLEASE ITS TIME
Now Albert's coming back, make yourself a bit smart.
He'll want to know what you done with that money he gave you
To get yourself some teeth. He did, I was there.
You have them all out, Lil, and get a nice set,   145

He said, I swear, I can't bear to look at you.
And no more can't I, I said, and think of poor Albert,
He's been in the army four years, he wants a good time,
And if you don't give it him, there's others will, I said.
Oh is there, she said. Something o' that, I said.   150
Then I'll know who to thank, she said, and give me a straight look.
HURRY UP PLEASE ITS TIME
If you don't like it you can get on with it, I said.
Others can pick and choose if you can't.
But if Albert makes off, it won't be for lack of telling.   155
You ought to be ashamed, I said, to look so antique.
(And her only thirty-one.)
I can't help it, she said, pulling a long face,
It's them pills I took, to bring it off, she said.
(She's had five already, and nearly died of young George.)   160
The chemist said it would be all right, but I've never been the same.
You *are* a proper fool, I said.
Well, if Albert won't leave you alone, there it is, I said,
What you get married for if you don't want children?
HURRY UP PLEASE ITS TIME   165

Well, that Sunday Albert was home, they had a hot gammon,
And they asked me in to dinner, to get the beauty of it hot—
HURRY UP PLEASE ITS TIME
HURRY UP PLEASE ITS TIME
Goonight Bill. Goonight Lou. Goonight May. Goonight.   170
Ta ta. Goonight. Goonight.
Good night, ladies, good night, sweet ladies, good night, good night.

III. THE FIRE SERMON

The river's tent is broken: the last fingers of leaf
Clutch and sink into the wet bank. The wind
Crosses the brown land, unheard. The nymphs are departed.   175
Sweet Thames, run softly, till I end my song.
The river bears no empty bottles, sandwich papers,
Silk handkerchiefs, cardboard boxes, cigarette ends
Or other testimony of summer nights. The nymphs are departed.
And their friends, the loitering heirs of city directors—   180
Departed, have left no addresses.
By the waters of Leman I sat down and wept . . .
Sweet Thames, run softly till I end my song,
Sweet Thames, run softly, for I speak not loud or long.
But at my back in a cold blast I hear   185
The rattle of the bones, and chuckle spread from ear to ear.
A rat crept softly through the vegetation
Dragging its slimy belly on the bank
While I was fishing in the dull canal
On a winter evening round behind the gashouse   190

Musing upon the king my brother's wreck
And on the king my father's death before him.
White bodies naked on the low damp ground
And bones cast in a little low dry garret,
Rattled by the rat's foot only, year to year.   195
But at my back from time to time I hear
The sound of horns and motors, which shall bring
Sweeney to Mrs. Porter in the spring.
O the moon shone bright on Mrs. Porter
And on her daughter   200
They wash their feet in soda water
Et O ces voix d'enfants, chantant dans la coupole!
   Twit twit twit
Jug jug jug jug jug jug
So rudely forc'd.   205
Tereu

   Unreal City
Under the brown fog of a winter noon
Mr. Eugenides, the Smyrna merchant
Unshaven, with a pocket full of currants   210
C.i.f. London: documents at sight,
Asked me in demotic French
To luncheon at the Cannon Street Hotel
Followed by a weekend at the Metropole.

   At the violet hour, when the eyes and back   215
Turn upward from the desk, when the human engine waits
Like a taxi throbbing waiting,
I Tiresias, though blind, throbbing between two lives,
Old man with wrinkled female breasts, can see
At the violet hour, the evening hour that strives   220
Homeward, and brings the sailor home from sea,
The typist home at teatime, clears her breakfast, lights
Her stove, and lays out food in tins.
Out of the window perilously spread
Her drying combinations touched by the sun's last rays,   225
On the divan are piled (at night her bed)
Stockings, slippers, camisoles, and stays.
I Tiresias, old man with wrinkled dugs
Perceived the scene, and foretold the rest—
I too awaited the expected guest.   230
He, the young man carbuncular, arrives,
A small house agent's clerk, with one bold stare,
One of the low on whom assurance sits
As a silk hat on a Bradford millionaire.
The time is now propitious, as he guesses,   235
The meal is ended, she is bored and tired,

Endeavours to engage her in caresses
Which still are unreproved, if undesired.
Flushed and decided, he assaults at once;
Exploring hands encounter no defence;   240
His vanity requires no response,
And makes a welcome of indifference.
(And I Tiresias have foresuffered all
Enacted on this same divan or bed;
I who have sat by Thebes below the wall   245
And walked among the lowest of the dead.)
Bestows one final patronising kiss,
And gropes his way, finding the stairs unlit . . .

She turns and looks a moment in the glass,
Hardly aware of her departed lover;   250
Her brain allows one half-formed thought to pass:
'Well now that's done: and I'm glad it's over.'
When lovely woman stoops to folly and
Paces about her room again, alone,
She smoothes her hair with automatic hand,   255
And puts a record on the gramophone.

'This music crept by me upon the waters'
And along the Strand, up Queen Victoria Street.
O City city, I can sometimes hear
Beside a public bar in Lower Thames Street,   260
The pleasant whining of a mandoline
And a clatter and a chatter from within
Where fishmen lounge at noon: where the walls
Of Magnus Martyr hold
Inexplicable splendour of Ionian white and gold.   265

    The river sweats
    Oil and tar
    The barges drift
    With the turning tide
    Red sails   270
    Wide
    To leeward, swing on the heavy spar.
    The barges wash
    Drifting logs
    Down Greenwich reach   275
    Past the Isle of Dogs.
        Weialala leia
        Wallala leialala

    Elizabeth and Leicester
    Beating oars   280
    The stern was formed

A gilded shell
Red and gold
the brisk swell
Rippled both shores   285
Southwest wind
Carried down stream
The peal of bells
White towers
 Weialala leia   290
 Wallala leialala

 'Trams and dusty trees.
Highbury bore me. Richmond and Kew
Undid me. By Richmond I raised my knees
Supine on the floor of a narrow canoe.'   295

 'My feet are at Moorgate, and my heart
Under my feet. After the event
He wept. He promised "a new start."
I made no comment. What should I resent?'

 'On Margate Sands.   300
I can connect
Nothing with nothing.
The broken fingernails of dirty hands.
My people humble people who expect
Nothing.'   305
 la la

To Carthage then I came

Burning burning burning burning
O Lord Thou pluckest me out
O Lord Thou pluckest   310

burning

IV. DEATH BY WATER

Phlebas the Phoenician, a fortnight dead,
Forgot the cry of gulls, and the deep sea swell
And the profit and loss.
    A current under sea   315
Picked his bones in whispers. As he rose and fell
He passed the stages of his age and youth
Entering the whirlpool.
    Gentile or Jew
O you who turn the wheel and look to windward,   320
Consider Phlebas, who was once handsome and tall as you.

V. WHAT THE THUNDER SAID

After the torchlight red on sweaty faces
After the frosty silence in the gardens
After the agony in stony places
The shouting and the crying   325
Prison and palace and reverberation
Of thunder of spring over distant mountains
He who was living is now dead
We who were living are now dying
With a little patience   330

  Here is no water but only rock
Rock and no water and the sandy road
The road winding above among the mountains
Which are mountains of rock without water
If there were water we should stop and drink   335
Amongst the rock one cannot stop or think
Sweat is dry and feet are in the sand
If there were only water amongst the rock
Dead mountain mouth of carious teeth that cannot spit
Here one can neither stand nor lie nor sit   340
There is not even silence in the mountains
But dry sterile thunder without rain
There is not even solitude in the mountains
But red sullen faces sneer and snarl
From doors of mudcracked houses   345
                             If there were water

    And no rock
    If there were rock
    And also water
    And water   350
    A spring
    A pool among the rock
    If there were the sound of water only
    Not the cicada
    And dry grass singing   355
    But sound of water over a rock
    Where the hermit-thrush sings in the pine trees
    Drip drop drip drop drop drop drop
    But there is no water

    Who is the third who walks always beside you?   360
When I count, there are only you and I together
But when I look ahead up the white road
There is always another one walking beside you
Gliding wrapt in a brown mantle, hooded
I do not know whether a man or a woman   365
—But who is that on the other side of you?

What is that sound high in the air
Murmur of maternal lamentation
Who are those hooded hordes swarming
Over endless plains, stumbling in cracked earth   370
Ringed by the flat horizon only
What is the city over the mountains
Cracks and reforms and bursts in the violet air
Falling towers
Jerusalem Athens Alexandria   375
Vienna London
Unreal

    A woman drew her long black hair out tight
And fiddled whisper music on those strings
And bats with baby faces in the violet light   380
Whistled, and beat their wings
And crawled head downward down a blackened wall
And upside down in air were towers
Tolling reminiscent bells, that kept the hours
And voices singing out of empty cisterns and exhausted wells.   385

    In this decayed hole among the mountains
In the faint moonlight, the grass is singing
Over the tumbled graves, about the chapel
There is the empty chapel, only the wind's home.
It has no windows, and the door swings,   390
Dry bones can harm no one.
Only a cock stood on the rooftree
Co co rico co co rico
In a flash of lightning. Then a damp gust
Bringing rain   395

    Ganga was sunken, and the limp leaves
Waited for rain, while the black clouds
Gathered far distant, over Himavant.
The jungle crouched, humped in silence.
Then spoke the thunder   400
DA
Datta: what have we given?
My friend, blood shaking my heart
The awful daring of a moment's surrender
Which an age of prudence can never retract   405
By this, and this only, we have existed
Which is not to be found in our obituaries
Or in memories draped by the beneficent spider
Or under seals broken by the lean solicitor
In our empty rooms   410
DA

Dayadhvan: I have heard the key
Turn in the door once and turn once only
We think of the key, each in his prison
Thinking of the key, each confirms a prison   415
Only at nightfall, aethereal rumours
Revive for a moment a broken Coriolanus
D*A*
Damyata: The boat responded
Gaily, to the hand expert with sail and oar   420
The sea was calm, your heart would have responded
Gaily, when invited, beating obedient
To controlling hands

                I sat upon the shore
Fishing, with the arid plain behind me   425
Shall I at least set my lands in order?
London Bridge is falling down falling down falling down
Poi s'ascose nel foco che gli affina
Quando fiam uti chelidon—O swallow swallow
Le Prince d'Aquitaine à la tour abolie   430
These fragments I have shored against my ruins
Why then Ile fit you. Hieronymo's mad againe.
Datta. Dayadhvam. Damyata.
          Shantih   shantih   shantih

Notes on "The Waste Land"

In a lecture entitled "The Frontiers of Criticism" delivered at the University of Minnesota in 1956, T. S. Eliot described how he came to write the notes to *The Waste Land*. His original intention had been to source all his quotations, so as to spike "the guns of critics of my earlier poems who had accused me of plagiarism." When *The Waste Land* was to be printed as a book it was found, however, that the poem was "inconveniently short." Eliot accordingly expanded his notes "in order to provide a few more pages of printed matter." And he added: "I have sometimes thought of getting rid of these notes; but now they can never be unstuck. They have had almost greater popularity than the poem itself—anyone who bought my book of poems, and found that the notes to *The Waste Land* were not in it, would demand his money back." Eliot described his notes as being "bogus scholarship" and added that what he regretted was that they had stimulated "the wrong kind of interest among the seekers of sources."

Not only the title, but the plan and a good deal of the incidental symbolism of the poem were suggested by Miss Jessie L. Weston's book on the Grail legend: *From Ritual to Romance* (Cambridge). Indeed, so deeply am I indebted, Miss Weston's book will elucidate the difficulties of the poem much better than my notes can do; and I recommend it (apart from the great interest of the book itself) to any who think such elucidation of the poem worth the trouble. To another work of anthropology I am indebted in general, one which has influenced our generation profoundly; I mean *The Golden Bough;* I have used especially the two volumes *Adonis, Attis, Osiris.* Anyone who is acquainted with these works will immediately recognize in the poem certain references to vegetation ceremonies.

I. THE BURIAL OF THE DEAD

Line 20. Cf. *Ezekiel* II, i.

23. Cf. *Ecclesiastes* XII, v.

31. V. *Tristan und Isolde,* I, verses 5–8.

42. Id. III, verse 24.

46. I am not familiar with the exact constitution of the Tarot pack of cards, from which I have obviously departed to suit my own convenience. The Hanged Man, a member of the traditional pack, fits my purpose in two ways: because he is associated in my mind with the Hanged God of Frazer, and because I associate him with the hooded figure in the passage of the disciples to Emmaus in Part V. The Phoenician Sailor and the Merchant appear later; also the "crowds of people," and Death by Water is executed in Part IV. The Man with Three Staves (an authentic member of the Tarot pack) I associate, quite arbitrarily, with the Fisher King himself.

60. Cf. Baudelaire:
"Fourmillante cité, cité, pleine de rêves,
"Où le spectre en plein jour raccroche le paessant."

63. Cf. *Inferno,* III, 55–7:
"si lunga tratta
di gente, ch'io non avrei mai creduto
che morte tanta n'avesse disfatta."

64. Cf. *Inferno,* IV, 25–7:
"Quivi, secondo che per ascoltare,
"non avea pianto, ma' che di sospiri,
"che l'aura eterna facevan tremare."

68. A phenomenon which I have often noticed.

74. Cf. the Dirge in Webster's *White Devil.*

76. V. Baudelaire, Preface to *Fleurs du Mal.*

II. A GAME OF CHESS

77. Cf. *Antony and Cleopatra,* II, ii, l. 190.

92. Laquearia. V. *Aeneid,* I, 726:
dependent lychni laquearibus aureis
incensi, et noctem flammis funalia vincunt.

98. Sylvan scene. V. Milton, *Paradise Lost*, IV, 140.
99. V. Ovid, *Metamorphoses*, VI, Philomela.
100. Cf. Part III, l. 204.
115. Cf. Part III, l. 195.
118. Cf. Webster: "Is the wind in that door still?"
126. Cf. Part I, l. 37, 48.
138. Cf. the game of chess in Middleton's *Women beware Women*.

III. THE FIRE SERMON

176. V. Spenser, *Prothalamion*.
192. Cf. *The Tempest*, I, ii.
196. Cf. Marvell, *To His Coy Mistress*.
197. Cf. Day, *Parliament of Bees:*

> "When of the sudden, listening, you shall hear,
> "A noise of horns and hunting, which shall bring
> "Actaeon to Diana in the spring,
> "Where all shall see her naked skin . . ."

199. I do not know the origin of the ballad from which these lines are taken: it was reported to me from Sydney, Australia.
202. V. Verlaine, *Parsifal*.
210. The currants were quoted at a price "carriage and insurance free to London"; and the Bill of Lading, etc., were to be handed to the buyer upon payment of the sight draft.
218. Tiresias, although a mere spectator and not indeed a "character," is yet the most important personage in the poem, uniting all the rest. Just as the one-eyed merchant, seller of currants, melts into the Phoenician Sailor, and the latter is not wholly distinct from Ferdinand Prince of Naples, so all the women are one woman, and the two sexes meet in Tiresias. What Tiresias *sees*, in fact, is the substance of the poem. The whole passage from Ovid is of great anthropological interest:

> ". . . Cum Iunone iocos et maior vestra profecto est
> Quam, quae contingit maribus," dixisse, "voluptas."
> Illa negat; placuit quae sit sententia docti
> Quaerere Tiresiae: venus huic erat utraque nota.
> Nam duo magnorum viridi coeuntia silva
> Corpora serpentum baculi violaverat ictu
> Deque viro factus, mirabile, femina septem
> Egerat autumnos; octavo rursus eosdem
> Vidit et "est vestrae si tanta potentia plagae,"
> Dixit "ut auctoris sortem in contraria mutet,
> Nunc quoque vos feriam!" percussis anguibus isdem
> Forma prior rediit genetivaque venit imago.
> Arbiter hic igitur sumptus de lite iocosa
> Dicta Iovis firmat; gravius Saturnia iusto
> Nec pro materia fertur doluisse suique

Iudicis aeterna damnavit lumina nocte,
At pater omnipotens (neque enim licet inrita cuiquam
Facta dei fecisse deo) pro lumine adempto
Scire futura dedit poenamque levavit honore.

221. This may not appear as exact as Sappho's lines, but I had in mind the "longshore" or "dory" fisherman, who returns at nightfall.

253. V. Goldsmith, the song in *The Vicar of Wakefield*.

257. V. *The Tempest*, as above.

264. The interior of St. Magnus Martyr is to my mind one of the finest among Wren's interiors. See *The Proposed Demolition of Nineteen City Churches* (P. S. King & Son, Ltd.).

266. The Song of the (three) Thames-daughters begins here. From line 292 to 306 inclusive they speak in turn. V. *Götterdämmerung*, III, i: the Rhine-daughters.

279. V. Froude, *Elizabeth*, Vol. I, ch. iv, letter of De Quadra to Philip of Spain:

"In the afternoon we were in a barge, watching the games on the river. (The queen) was alone with Lord Robert and myself on the poop, when they began to talk nonsense, and went so far that Lord Robert at last said, as I was on the spot there was no reason why they should not be married if the queen pleased."

293. Cf. *Purgatorio*, V, 133:

"Ricorditi di me, che son la Pia;
"Siena mi fe', disfecemi Maremma."

307. V. St. Augustine's *Confessions:* "to Carthage then I came, where a cauldron of unholy loves sang all about mine ears."

308. The complete text of the Buddha's Fire Sermon (which corresponds in importance to the Sermon on the Mount) from which these words are taken, will be found translated in the late Henry Clarke Warren's *Buddhism in Translation* (Harvard Oriental Series). Mr. Warren was one of the great pioneers of Buddhist studies in the Occident.

309. From St. Augustine's *Confessions* again. The collocation of these two representatives of eastern and western asceticism, as the culmination of this part of the poem, is not an accident.

V. WHAT THE THUNDER SAID

In the first part of Part V three themes are employed: the journey to Emmaus, the approach to the Chapel Perilous (see Miss Weston's book) and the present decay of eastern Europe.

357. This is *Turdus aonalaschkae pallasii*, the hermit-thrush which I have heard in Quebec County. Chapman says (*Handbook of Birds of Eastern North America*) "it is most at home in secluded woodland and thickety retreats. . . . Its notes are not remarkable for variety or volume, but in purity and sweetness of tone and exquisite modulation they are unequalled." Its "water-dripping song" is justly celebrated.

360. The following lines were stimulated by the account of one of the Antarctic expeditions (I forget which, but I think one of Shackleton's): it was related that the party of explorers, at the extremity of their strength, had the constant delusion that there was *one more member* than could actually be counted.

367–77. Cf. Hermann Hesse, *Blick ins Chaos:* "Schon ist halb Europa, schon ist zumindest der halbe Osten Europas auf dem Wege zum Chaos, fährt betrunken im heiligen Wahn am Abgrund entlang und singt dazu, singt betrunken und hymnisch wie Dmitri Karamasoff sang. Ueber diese Lieder lacht der Bürger beleidigt, der Heilige und Seher hört sie mit Tränen."

402. "Datta, dayadhvam, damyata" (Give, sympathize, control). The fable of the meaning of the Thunder is found in the *Brihadaranyaka—Upanishad*, 5, 1. A translation is found in Deussen's *Sechzig Upanishads des Veda*, p. 489.

408. Cf. Webster, *The White Devil*, V, vi:

> "... they'll remarry
> Ere the worm pierce your winding-sheet, ere the spider
> Make a thin curtain for your epithaphs."

412. Cf. *Inferno*, XXXIII, 46:

> "ed io sentii chiavar l'uscio di sotto all'orribile torre."

Also F. H. Bradley, *Appearance and Reality*, p. 346. "My external sensations are no less private to myself than are my thoughts or my feelings. In either case my experience falls within my own circle, a circle closed on the outside; and, with all its elements alike, every sphere is opaque to the others which surround it. ... In brief, regarded as an existence which appears in a soul, the whole world for each is peculiar and private to that soul."

425. V. Weston: *From Ritual to Romance;* chapter on the Fisher King.

428. V. *Purgatorio*, XXVI, 148:

> " 'Ara vos prec, per equella valor
> 'que vos guida al som de l'escalina,
> 'sovegna vos a temps de ma dolor.'
> Poi s'ascose nel foco che gli affina."

429. V. *Pervigilium Veneris*. Cf. Philomela in Parts II and III.

430. V. Gerard de Nerval, Sonnet *El Desdichado*.

432. V. Kyd's *Spanish Tragedy*.

434. Shantih. Repeated as here, a formal ending to an Upanishad. "The Peace which passeth understanding" is our equivalent to this word.

1922

THE HOLLOW MEN

Again it is the epigraph which offers us the key. "Mistah Kurtz—
he dead" is the ominous climax of Joseph Conrad's *Heart of Darkness*, the tale of the dark journey of an individual into the primitive
depths of the self, those depths of the unconscious which Kurtz
reached when he espoused the savagery of the jungle. The second
epigraph, "A penny for the Old Guy" alludes to another figure of
violence, the Guy Fawkes of English history, whose gunpowder plot
was foiled and who to this day is burned in effigy. In the poem itself
there are allusions to Dante—to death's other kingdom, death's dream
kingdom, and to the multifoliate rose. The heart of darkness is also
the bottom of hell; and it is the bottom of one's own despair. *The
Waste Land* is now a dead land; there is no longer an awareness of
the multiplicity of life, the richness of history, the recuperative power
of man. Men are made of straw; the Lord's Prayer breaks into fragments and is jumbled in the consciousness with a nursery rhyme; and
the Guy Fawkes explosion, which would have ended the world with
a bang, ends in a whimper. "The Hollow Men," with its image of the
swinging tree, the broken column, the stone images, the broken jaw
of some animal which becomes the metaphor for a lost kingdom, "this
last of meeting places" by the river where the shades wait to be
ferried into the regions from which there is no return, possesses the
indifference of death. There is no longer a yearning to die; there is
only emptiness and death.

Mistah Kurtz—he dead.

A penny for the Old Guy

I

We are the hollow men
We are the stuffed men
Leaning together
Headpiece filled with straw. Alas!
Our dried voices, when   5
We whisper together
Are quiet and meaningless
As wind in dry grass
Or rats' feet over broken glass
In our dry cellar   10

Shape without form, shade without colour,
Paralysed force, gesture without motion;

Those who have crossed
With direct eyes, to death's other Kingdom
Remember us—if at all—not as lost   15
Violent souls, but only
As the hollow men
The stuffed men.

II

Eyes I dare not meet in dreams
In death's dream kingdom   20
These do not appear:
There, the eyes are
Sunlight on a broken column
There, is a tree swinging
And voices are   25
In the wind's singing
More distant and more solemn
Than a fading star.

Let me be no nearer
In death's dream kingdom   30
Let me also wear
Such deliberate disguises
Rat's coat, crowskin, crossed staves
In a field
Behaving as the wind behaves   35
No nearer—

Not that final meeting
In the twilight kingdom

III

This is the dead land
This is cactus land   40
Here the stone images
Are raised, here they receive
The supplication of a dead man's hand
Under the twinkle of a fading star.

Is it like this   45
In death's other kingdom
Walking alone
At the hour when we are
Trembling with tenderness
Lips that would kiss   50
Form prayers to broken stone.

IV

The eyes are not here
There are no eyes here
In this valley of dying stars
In this hollow valley   55
This broken jaw of our lost kingdoms

In this last of meeting places
We grope together
And avoid speech
Gathered on this beach of the tumid river   60

Sightless, unless
The eyes reappear
As the perpetual star
Multifoliate rose
Of death's twilight kingdom   65
The hope only
Of empty men.

V

Here we go round the prickly pear
Prickly pear prickly pear
Here we go round the prickly pear   70
At five o'clock in the morning.

Between the idea
And the reality
Between the motion
And the act   75
Falls the Shadow
                    For Thine is the Kingdom

Between the conception
And the creation
Between the emotion   80
And the response
Falls the Shadow
                    Life is very long

Between the desire
And the spasm   85
Between the potency
And the existence
Between the essence
And the descent
Falls the Shadow   90
                    For Thine is the Kingdom

For Thine is
Life is
For Thine is the

This is the way the world ends   95
This is the way the world ends
This is the way the world ends
Not with a bang but a whimper.

1925

JOURNEY OF THE MAGI

Between the publication of "The Hollow Men" in 1925 and *Ash-Wednesday* in 1930, T. S. Eliot published little poetry, although his critical pen was active. A few fragments show him already experimenting with drama. But three poems, known (with others later written) as the Ariel Poems (because they were part of a publisher's series of that name), came out in the three years betwen 1927 and 1930. They seem to be steppingstones on the way to Eliot's full acceptance of Christianity. In his work up to and including "The Hollow Men," Christianity has no particular place. But with the *Journey of the Magi* (1927) Eliot seems to be thinking of birth and rebirth; of the birth of Christ as representing for the world a rebirth and a new way of life. *The Waste Land* had in it a yearning for death; "The Hollow Men" represented inner death. Now rebirth is visioned. And the two other poems of this time are consonant with the "Journey of the Magi." In "A Song for Simeon" (1928) there is a prayer for peace; "Animula" (1929) ends with the line "Pray for us now and at the hour of our birth." The "Journey of the Magi" is told by one of the wise men, long afterwards; the hardships of the journey, the vision of the Crucifixion, the knowledge that death will come also to him, but that he also had been a witness of resurrection and rebirth.

'A cold coming we had of it,
Just the worst time of the year
For a journey, and such a long journey:
The ways deep and the weather sharp,
The very dead of winter.'   5
And the camels galled, sore-footed, refractory,
Lying down in the melting snow.
There were times we regretted
The summer palaces on slopes, the terraces,
And the silken girls bringing sherbert.   10
Then the camel men cursing and grumbling
And running away, and wanting their liquor and women,

And the night-fires going out, and the lack of shelters,
And the cities hostile and the towns unfriendly
And the villages dirty and charging high prices: 15
A hard time we had of it.
At the end we preferred to travel all night,
Sleeping in snatches,
With the voices singing in our ears, saying
That this was all folly.   20

Then at dawn we came down to a temperate valley,
Wet, below the snow line, smelling of vegetation;
With a running stream and a water-mill beating the darkness,
And three trees on the low sky,
And an old white horse galloped away in the meadow.   25
Then we came to a tavern with vine-leaves over the lintel,
Six hands at an open door dicing for pieces of silver,
And feet kicking the empty wine-skins.
But there was no information, and so we continued
And arrived at evening, not a moment too soon   30
Finding the place; it was (you may say) satisfactory.

All this was a long time ago, I remember,
And I would do it again, but set down
This set down
This: were we led all that way for   35
Birth or Death? There was a Birth, certainly,
We had evidence and no doubt. I had seen birth and death,
But had thought they were different: this Birth was
Hard and bitter agony for us, like Death, our death.
We returned to our places, these Kingdoms,   40
But no longer at ease here, in the old dispensation,
With an alien people clutching their gods.
I should be glad of another death.

                                                                1927

ASH–WEDNESDAY

In the year after "Journey of the Magi" T. S. Eliot became a British subject—that is he took an oath of allegiance to the King of England. At the same time he accepted the dogma of the Church of England, thereby pledging loyalty to an historic Church as well as an historic Crown. His statement announcing himself royalist in politics, Anglo-Catholic in religion, followed. For an American who had come from St. Louis, on the Mississippi River, this was a re-birth indeed. The six-part poem, *Ash-Wednesday*, which began to appear between 1927 and 1930, and was published as a separate book in 1930, is a poetic record of the poet's passage through a sort of Purgatory, of rebirth and purification, by which he might enter into the fullest awareness of Christian belief. The poet's turning to God, his acceptance, his humility, his travail through the "time of tension between dying and birth," these are some of the elements in the poem. *Ash-Wednesday* is, in reality, a group of poems strung together, concerned with a single theme, that of penitence. Since the poems appeared in various journals and not in their final order, they may be regarded as having an individual rather than total genesis. The sixth and final poem here given contains the poet's expression of sensual delight in the world's beauties, while the second half reveals his unwavering determination to achieve "Our peace in His will."

VI

Although I do not hope to turn again
Although I do not hope
Although I do not hope to turn

Wavering between the profit and the loss
In this brief transit where the dreams cross   5
The dreamcrossed twilight between birth and dying
(Bless me father) though I do not wish to wish these things
From the wide window towards the granite shore
The white sails still fly seaward, seaward flying
Unbroken wings   10

And the lost heart stiffens and rejoices
In the lost lilac and the lost sea voices
And the weak spirit quickens to rebel
For the bent golden-rod and the lost sea smell
Quickens to recover   15
The cry of quail and the whirling plover
And the blind eye creates
The empty forms between the ivory gates
And smell renews the salt savour of the sandy earth

This is the time of tension between dying and birth   20
The place of solitude where three dreams cross
Between blue rocks
But when the voices shaken from the yew-tree drift away
Let the other yew be shaken and reply.
Blessèd sister, holy mother, spirit of the fountain, spirit of the garden,
Suffer us not to mock ourselves with falsehood   26
Teach us to care and not to care
Teach us to sit still
Even among these rocks,
Our peace in His will

And even among these rocks
Sister, mother
And spirit of the river, spirit of the sea,
Suffer me not to be separated

And let my cry come unto Thee.   35

1930

LANDSCAPES

The brief series of five "Landscapes" which Eliot wrote in 1934–
1935, of which three are here given, suggest not only the familiar scenery of the painter's art, but the *paysages* of a composer like Debussy.
They combine American memory with a kind of French impressionism, plastic and tonal: the orchard in New Hampshire which sym-
bolizes the swift passage of the years; the river, the heat, the mockingbird of Virginia, which inspire "iron thoughts"; the palaver of
birds at Cape Ann dominated by the cry of the gulls. These verses
are both audible and visual, and in their quiet brevity contain also
overtones of autobiography. The titles—names of places—already fore-
shadow the sense of place that will give the titles and much of the
substance to the *Four Quartets,* and there is a relationship between
the voices of the birds filling the air at Cape Ann, and the rocks
known as "The Dry Salvages," which supply the title to the third
Quartet. These are also located at Cape Ann on the New England
coast.

New Hampshire

Children's voices in the orchard
Between the blossom- and the fruit-time:
Golden head, crimson head,
Between the green tip and the root.
Black wing, brown wing, hover over;   5
Twenty years and the spring is over;
To-day grieves, to-morrow grieves,
Cover me over, light-in-leaves;
Golden head, black wing
Cling, swing   10
Spring, sing,
Swing up into the apple-tree.

Virginia

Red river, red river,
Slow flow heat is silence
No will is still as a river   15

Still. Will heat move
Only through the mocking-bird
Heard once? Still hills
Wait. Gates wait. Purple trees,
White trees, wait, wait.   20
Delay, decay. Living, living,
Never moving. Ever moving
Iron thoughts came with me
And go with me:
Red river, river, river.   25

CAPE ANN

O quick quick quick, quick hear the song-sparrow,
Swamp-sparrow, fox-sparrow, vesper-sparrow
At dawn and dusk. Follow the dance
Of the goldfinch at noon. Leave to chance
The Blackburnian warbler, the shy one. Hail   30
With shrill whistle the note of the quail, the bob-white
Dodging by bay-bush. Follow the feet
Of the walker, the water-thrush. Follow the flight
Of the dancing arrow, the purple martin. Greet
In silence the bullbat. All are delectable. Sweet sweet sweet   35
But resign this land at the end, resign it
To its true owner, the tough one, the sea-gull.
The palaver is finished.

LITTLE GIDDING

In the *Four Quartets,* published between 1940 and 1942, that is, during the bleak first years of the Second World War, T. S. Eliot summed up the middle years of his life and all that his experience had meant to him. The *Quartets* are at once personal and impersonal; they are meditative, as Wordsworth meditated in his *Prelude,* gathering memories out of the past the better to see the world of the present. So Eliot, in these mature poems of late middle life, sees again how a certain kind of inner death can be a rebirth and a beginning. And now he has attained understanding and Christian love, the solace of prayer, the relationship between the poet's sensual awareness of the world and his spiritual awareness. His total view is endowed, in the *Quartets,* with his sense of history: and history for him is not unlike the Viconian view which James Joyce incorporated in *Finnegans Wake,* the long experimental book he published just before Joyce's first *Quartet* appeared. Vico saw history as cyclical: and believed that once the full cycle has run its course, we return to the beginning. Thus *Finnegans Wake* opens in the middle of a sentence, the beginning of which is at the end of the book. (One could, by this system, go from the end of the book to the beginning to complete the sentence, and if one reads on, the cycle is repeated—which is the idea Vico and Joyce sought to convey). The first words of the second *Quartet,* "East Coker," are: "In my beginning is my end." And this can be reversed, as Eliot does in the last *Quartet:* "to make an end is to make a beginning." For Eliot too life can come full cycle; or it may be a backward and forward flow. This is the sense of the epigraph from Heraclitus at the head of the *Quartets:* "The way upward and downward are one and the same."

The *Quartets*—"Burnt Norton," "East Coker," "The Dry Salvages," and "Little Gidding"—are written in many styles, dry rhythmic statement, colloquial passages, passages of high lyricism, imitations of various poets: all the elements of the earlier poems are here but refined and developed. The *Quartets,* however, are not dramatic as the earlier poems are. Only now and again does the poet invoke the dramatic or third voice, as in the Dantesque passage here given, from "Little Gidding." This *Quartet* derives its name from a place of religious memory, in Huntingdonshire, dedicated to prayer. Eliot departs in "Little Gidding" from his meditation at this moment to record a conversation. The moment chosen by him has a touch of actuality, it is the "uncertain hour" when the "dark dove with the flickering tongue" has dropped below the horizon and the poet patrols the street as a fire warden amid acrid smoke and a wasted London. At this hour he meets a stranger whom he seems to recognize, a dead master, "known, forgotten, half recalled" who seems to embody the qualities of his various masters, the poets of the past, a "compound ghost." One feels in the lines, written in a modified *terza rima,* not only Dante but Milton; Virgil and Mallarmé are quoted. The concept put forth by this "ghost" in the early morning amid the ruins is that of the dynamism of poetry; its capacity for renewing itself; its need to be of the present as well as of the past. The poet is the purifier of "the dialect of the tribe," as fire is a purifier as well as a destroyer. This moving sequence, with its overtones of a still recent and horrible war, and its glimpse of oncoming old age, ends with the blowing of the "All clear." The ghost vanishes; his words remain.

> In the uncertain hour before the morning
> Near the ending of interminable night
> At the recurrent end of the unending
> After the dark dove with the flickering tongue
> Had passed below the horizon of his homing   5
> While the dead leaves still rattled on like tin
> Over the asphalt where no other sound was
> Between three districts whence the smoke arose
> I met one walking, loitering and hurried
> As if blown towards me like the metal leaves   10
> Before the urban dawn wind unresisting.
> And as I fixed upon the down-turned face

That pointed scrutiny with which we challenge
  The first-met stranger in the waning dusk
  I caught the sudden look of some dead master   15
Whom I had known, forgotten, half recalled
  Both one and many; in the brown baked features
  The eyes of a familiar compound ghost
Both intimate and unidentifiable.
  So I assumed a double part, and cried   20
  And heard another's voice cry: 'What are *you* here?'
Although we were not. I was still the same,
  Knowing myself yet being someone other—
  And he a face still forming; yet the words sufficed
To compel the recognition they preceded.   25
  And so, compliant to the common wind,
  Too strange to each other for misunderstanding,
In concord at this intersection time
  Of meeting nowhere, no before and after,
  We trod the pavement in a dead patrol.   30
I said: 'The wonder that I feel is easy,
  Yet ease is cause of wonder. Therefore speak:
  I may not comprehend, may not remember.'
And he: 'I am not eager to rehearse
  My thought and theory which you have forgotten.   35
  These things have served their purpose: let them be.
So with your own, and pray they be forgiven
  By others, as I pray you to forgive
  Both bad and good. Last season's fruit is eaten
And the fullfed beast shall kick the empty pail.   40
  For last year's words belong to last year's language
  And next year's words await another voice.
But, as the passage now presents no hindrance
  To the spirit unappeased and peregrine
  Between two worlds become much like each other,   45
So I find words I never thought to speak
  In streets I never thought I should revisit
  When I left my body on a distant shore.
Since our concern was speech, and speech impelled us
  To purify the dialect of the tribe   50
  And urge the mind to aftersight and foresight,
Let me disclose the gifts reserved for age
  To set a crown upon your lifetime's effort.
  First, the cold friction of expiring sense
Without enchantment, offering no promise   55
  But bitter tastelessness of shadow fruit
  As body and soul begin to fall asunder.
Second, the conscious impotence of rage
  At human folly, and the laceration
  Of laughter at what ceases to amuse.   60

And last, the rending pain of re-enactment
  Of all that you have done, and been; the shame
  Of motives late revealed, and the awareness
Of things ill done and done to others' harm
  Which once you took for exercise of virtue.   65
  Then fools' approval stings, and honour stains.
From wrong to wrong the exasperated spirit
  Proceeds, unless restored by that refining fire
  Where you must move in measure, like a dancer.'
The day was breaking. In the disfigured street   70
  He left me, with a kind of valediction,
  And faded on the blowing of the horn.

MACAVITY: THE MYSTERY CAT

In 1939, T. S. Eliot published his *Old Possum's Book of Practical Cats*, a volume of lively verses describing the habits and characteristics of various cats, presumably certain observed pets of his own. The verses showed a genuine warmth and affection for the domestic animal which embodies so much of the grace and beauty of jungle creatures, but may be possessed in tame softness within the household. A large literature exists about cats ever since the days when the animal was regarded by the Egyptians as sacred, and in our time it figures prominently in the delicate and subtle novels of the French writer Colette; or may be seen in the studies of Foujita, the Japanese artist who has devoted his life to making drawings of cats. To this cat-art, T. S. Eliot added a book of great charm. The poem selected from this volume treats of Macavity, the elusive cat, endowed, as are the other Eliot cats, with human qualities. This one is, among other things, a master spy, a stealer of state documents. The verses show the suppleness of Eliot's verse, the direct, hard use of language, and of ingenious rhyme. That Eliot was early aware of the body-movement of cats and their softness may be seen by examining the image in the opening lines of "Prufrock" in which the smoke and fog of the city are described in a metaphor, as of a cat curling about a house.

Macavity's a Mystery Cat: he's called the Hidden Paw—
For he's the master criminal who can defy the Law.
He's the bafflement of Scotland Yard, the Flying Squad's despair:
For when they reach the scene of crime—*Macavity's not there!*

Macavity, Macavity, there's no one like Macavity,   5
He's broken every human law, he breaks the law of gravity.
His powers of levitation would make a fakir stare,
And when you reach the scene of crime—*Macavity's not there!*
You may seek him in the basement, you may look up in the air—
But I tell you once and once again, *Macavity's not there!*   10

Macavity's a ginger cat, he's very tall and thin;
You would know him if you saw him, for his eyes are sunken in.
His brow is deeply lined with thought, his head is highly domed;
His coat is dusty from neglect, his whiskers are uncombed.
He sways his head from side to side, with movements like a snake;   15
And when you think he's half asleep, he's always wide awake.

Macavity, Macavity, there's no one like Macavity,
For he's a fiend in feline shape, a monster of depravity.
You may meet him in a by-street, you may see him in the square—
But when a crime's discovered, then *Macavity's not there!*   20

He's outwardly respectable. (They say he cheats at cards.)
And his footprints are not found in any file of Scotland Yard's.
And when the larder's looted, or the jewel-case is rifled,
Or when the milk is missing, or another Peke's been stifled,
Or the greenhouse glass is broken, and the trellis past repair—   25
Ay, there's the wonder of the thing! *Macavity's not there!*

And when the Foreign Office find a Treaty's gone astray,
Or the Admiralty lose some plans and drawings by the way,
There may be a scrap of paper in the hall or on the stair—
But it's useless to investigate—*Macavity's not there!*   30
And when the loss has been disclosed, the Secret Service say:
"It *must* have been Macavity!"—but he's a mile away.
You'll be sure to find him resting, or a-licking of his thumbs,
Or engaged in doing complicated long division sums.

Macavity, Macavity, there's no one like Macavity,   35
There never was a Cat of such deceitfulness and suavity.
He always has an alibi, and one or two to spare:
At whatever time the deed took place—MACAVITY WASN'T THERE!
And they say that all the Cats whose wicked deeds are widely known
(I might mention Mungojerrie, I might mention Griddlebone)   40
Are nothing more than agents for the Cat who all the time
Just controls their operations: the Napoleon of Crime!

⚜

TWO LECTURES

In 1950 T. S. Eliot delivered the Theodore Spencer Memorial Lecture at Harvard on "Poetry and Drama," drawing upon his experiences in the theatre to describe the manner in which he believes verse should be used on the stage. In 1953 he delivered a lecture on "The Three Voices of Poetry" before the National Book League of England. Both discourses were reprinted in his recent volume *Of Poetry and Poets* for which Eliot made certain revisions in his original text so as to convert the lectures into essays. They illustrate Eliot's skill and lucidity as a writer of prose; they demonstrate no less the subtle critical mind of the poet while showing at the same time how he functions as a dramatist.

POETRY AND DRAMA

Reviewing my critical output for the last thirty-odd years, I am surprised to find how constantly I have returned to the drama, whether by examining the work of the contemporaries of Shakespeare, or by reflecting on the possibilities of the future. It may even be that people are weary of hearing me on this subject. But, while I find that I have been composing variations on this theme all my life, my views have been continually modified and renewed by increasing experience; so that I am impelled to take stock of the situation afresh at every stage of my own experimentation.

As I have gradually learned more about the problems of poetic drama, and the conditions which it must fulfil if it is to justify itself, I have made a little clearer to myself, not only my own reasons for wanting to write in this form, but the more general reasons for wanting to see it restored to its place. And I think that if I say something about these problems and conditions, it should make clearer to other people whether and if so why poetic drama has anything potentially to offer the playgoer that prose drama cannot. For I start with the assumption that if poetry is merely a decoration, an added embellishment, if it merely gives people of literary tastes the pleasure of listening to poetry at the same time that they are witnessing a play, then it is superfluous. It must justify itself dramatically, and not merely be fine poetry shaped into a dramatic form. From this it follows that no play should be written in verse for which prose is *dramatically* adequate. And from this it follows, again, that the audience, its attention held by the dramatic action, its emotions stirred by the situation between the characters, should be too intent upon the play to be wholly conscious of the medium.

Whether we use prose or verse on the stage, they are both but means to an end. The difference, from one point of view, is not so great as we might think. In those prose plays which survive, which are read and produced on the stage by later generations, the prose in which the characters speak is as remote, for the best part, from the vocabulary, syntax, and rhythm of our ordinary speech—with its fumbling for words, its constant recourse to approximation, its disorder and its unfinished sentences—as verse is. Like verse, it has been written, and rewritten. Our two greatest prose stylists in the drama—apart from Shakespeare and the other Elizabethans who mixed prose and verse in the same play—are, I believe, Congreve and Bernard Shaw. A speech by a character of Congreve or of Shaw has—however clearly the characters may be differentiated—that unmistakable personal rhythm which is the mark of a prose style, and of which only the most accomplished conversationalists—who are for that matter usually monologuists—show any trace in their talk. We have all heard (too often!) of Molière's character who expressed surprise when told that he spoke prose. But it was M. Jourdain who was right, and not his mentor or his creator: he did not speak prose—he only talked. For I mean to draw a triple distinction: between prose, and verse, and our ordinary speech which is mostly below the level of either verse or prose. So if you look at it in this way, it will appear that prose, on the stage, is as artificial as verse: or alternatively, that verse can be as natural as prose. But while the sensitive member of the audience will appreciate, when he hears fine prose spoken in a play, that this is something better than ordinary conversation, he does not regard it as a wholly different language from that which he himself speaks, for that would interpose a barrier between himself and the imaginary characters on the stage. Too many people, on the other hand, approach a play which they know to be in verse, with the consciousness of the difference. It is unfortunate when they are repelled by verse, but can also be deplorable when they are attracted by it—if that means that they are prepared to enjoy the play and the language of the play as two separate things. The chief effect and style and rhythm in dramatic speech, whether it be in prose or verse, should be unconscious.

From this it follows that a mixture of prose and verse in the same play is generally to be avoided: each transition makes the auditor aware, with a jolt, of the medium. It is, we may say, justifiable when the author wishes to produce this jolt: when, that is, he wishes to transport the audience violently from one plane of reality to another. I suspect that this kind of transition was easily acceptable to an Elizabethan audience, to whose ears both prose and verse came natually; who liked highfalutin and low comedy in the same play; and to whom it seemed perhaps proper that the more humble and rustic characters should speak in a homely language, and that those of more exalted rank should rant in verse. But even in the plays of Shakespeare some of the prose passages seem to be designed for an effect of contrast which, when achieved, is something that can never become old-fashioned. The knocking at the gate in *Macbeth* is an example that comes to everyone's mind; but it has long seemed to me that the alternation of scenes in prose with scenes in verse in *Henry IV* points an ironic contrast between the world of high politics and the world of common life. The audience probably thought they were getting their accustomed chronicle play garnished with amusing scenes of low life; yet the prose scenes of both Part I and Part II provide a sardonic comment upon the bustling ambitions of the chiefs of the parties in the insurrection of the Percys.

Today, however, because of the handicap under which verse drama suffers, I believe that in verse drama prose should be used very sparingly indeed; that we should aim at a form of verse in which everything can be said that has to be said; and that when we find some situation which is intractable in verse, it is merely that our form of verse is inelastic. And if there prove to be scenes which we cannot put in verse, we must either develop our verse, or avoid having to introduce such scenes. For we have to accustom our audiences to verse to the point at which they will cease to be conscious of it; and to introduce prose dialogue would only be to distract their attention from the play itself to the medium of its expression. But if our verse is to have so wide a range that it can say anything that has to be said, it follows that it will not be "poetry" all the time. It will only be "poetry" when the dramatic situation has reached such a point of intensity that poetry becomes the natural utterance, because then it is the only language in which the emotions can be expressed at all.

It is indeed necessary for any long poem, if it is to escape monotony, to be able to say homely things without bathos, as well as to take the highest flights without sounding exaggerated. And it is still more important in a play, especially if it is concerned with contemporary life. The reason for writing even the more pedestrian parts of a verse play in verse instead of prose is, however, not only to avoid calling the audience's attention to the fact that it is at other moments listening to poetry. It is also that the verse rhythm should have its effect upon the hearers, without their being conscious of it. A brief analysis of one scene of Shakespeare's may illustrate this point. The opening scene of *Hamlet*—as well constructed an opening scene as that of any play ever written—has the advantage of being one that everybody knows.

What we do not notice, when we witness this scene in the theatre, is the great variation of style. Nothing is superfluous, and there is no line of poetry which is not justified by its dramatic value. The first twenty-two lines are built of the simplest words in the most homely idiom. Shakespeare had worked for a long time in the theatre, and written a good many plays, before reaching the point at which he could write those twenty-two lines. There is nothing quite so simplified and sure in his previous work. He first developed conversational, colloquial verse in the monologue of the character part—Faulconbridge in *King John*, and later the Nurse in *Romeo and Juliet*. It was a much further step to carry it unobtrusively into the dialogue of brief replies. No poet has begun to master dramatic verse until he can write lines which, like these in *Hamlet*, are *transparent*. You are consciously attending, not to the poetry, but to the meaning of the poetry. If you were hearing *Hamlet* for the first time, without knowing anything about the play, I do not think that it would occur to you to ask whether the speakers were speaking in verse or prose. The verse is having a different effect upon us from prose; but, at the moment, what we are aware of is the frosty night, the officers keeping watch on the battlements, and the foreboding of a tragic action. I do not say that there is no place for the situation in which part of one's pleasure will be the enjoyment of hearing beautiful poetry—

providing that the author gives it, in that place, dramatic inevitability. And of course, when we have both seen a play several times and read it between performances, we begin to analyse the means by which the author has produced his effects. But in the immediate impact of this scene we are unconscious of the medium of its expression.

From the short, brusque ejaculations at the beginning, suitable to the situation and to the character of the guards—but not expressing more character than is required for their function in the play—the verse glides into a slower movement with the appearance of the courtiers Horatio and Marcellus.

> *Horatio says 'tis but our fantasy . . .*

and the movement changes again on the appearance of Royalty, the ghost of the King, into the solemn and sonorous

> *What art thou, that usurp'st this time of night . . .*

(and note, by the way, this anticipation of the plot conveyed by the use of the verb *usurp*); and majesty is suggested in a reference reminding us whose ghost this is:

> *So frown'd he once, when, in an angry parle,*
> *He smote the sledded Polacks on the ice.*

There is an abrupt change to staccato in Horatio's words to the Ghost on its second appearance; this rhythm changes again with the words

> *We do it wrong, being so majestical,*
> *To offer it the show of violence;*
> *For it is, as the air, invulnerable,*
> *And our vain blows malicious mockery.*

The scene reaches a resolution with the words of Marcellus:

> *It faded on the crowing of the cock.*
> *Some say that ever 'gainst that season comes*
> *Wherein our Saviour's birth is celebrated,*
> *The bird of dawning singeth all night long . . .*

and Horatio's answer:

> *So have I heard and do in part believe it.*
> *But, look, the morn, in russet mantle clad,*
> *Walks o'er the dew of yon high eastern hill.*
> *Break we our watch up . . .*

This is great poetry, and it is dramatic; but besides being poetic and dramatic, it is something more. There emerges, when we analyse it, a kind of musical design also which reinforces and is one with the dramatic movement. It has checked and accelerated the pulse of our emotion without our knowing it. Note that in these last words of Marcellus

there is a deliberate brief emergence of the poetic into consciousness.
When we hear the lines

> *But, look, the morn, in russet mantle clad,*
> *Walks o'er the dew of yon high eastern hill*

we are lifted for a moment beyond character, but with no sense of un-
fitness in the words coming, and at this moment, from the lips of
Horatio. The transitions in the scene obey laws of the music of dramatic poetry. Note that the two lines of Horatio which I have quoted
twice are preceded by a line of the simplest speech which might be
either verse or prose:

> *So have I heard and do in part believe it*

and that he follows them abruptly with a half line which is hardly more
than a stage direction:

> *Break we our watch up.*

It would be interesting to pursue, by a similar analysis, this problem of
the double pattern in great poetic drama—the pattern which may be
examined from the point of view of stagecraft or from that of the music.
But I think that the examination of this one scene is enough to show us
that verse is not merely a formalization, or an added decoration, but
that it intensifies the drama. It should indicate also the importance of
the unconscious effect of the verse upon us. And lastly, I do not think
that this effect is felt only by those members of an audience who "like
poetry" but also by those who go for the play alone. By the people who
do not like poetry, I mean those who cannot sit down with a book of
poetry and enjoy reading it: these people also, when they go to a play
in verse, should be affected by the poetry. And these are the audiences
whom the writer of such a play ought to keep in mind.

At this point I might say a word about those plays which we call
poetic, though they are written in prose. The plays of John Millington
Synge form rather a special case, because they are based upon the idiom
of a rural people whose speech is naturally poetic, both in imagery and
in rhythm. I believe that he even incorporated phrases which he had
heard from these country people of Ireland. The language of Synge is
not available except for plays set among that same people. We can draw
more general conclusions from the plays in prose, (so much admired in
my youth and now hardly even read) by Maeterlinck. These plays are
in a different way restricted in their subject matter; and to say that the
characterization in them is dim is an understatement. I do not deny that
they have some poetic quality. But in order to be poetic in prose, a
dramatist has to be so consistently poetic that his scope is very limited.
Synge wrote plays about characters whose originals in life talked poeti-
cally, so he could make them talk poetry and remain real people. The

poetic prose dramatist who has not this advantage has to be too poetic. The poetic drama in prose is more limited by poetic convention, or by our conventions as to what subject matter is poetic, than is the poetic drama in verse. A really dramatic verse can be employed, as Shakespeare was able to employ it, to say the most matter-of-fact things.

Yeats is a very different case from Maeterlinck or Synge. A study of his development as a dramatist would show, I think, the great distance he went, and the triumph of his last plays. In his first period, he wrote plays in verse about subjects conventionally accepted as suitable for verse, in a metric which—though even at that early stage having the personal Yeats rhythm—is not really a form of speech quite suitable for anybody except mythical kings and queens. His middle-period *Plays for Dancers* are very beautiful, but they do not solve any problem for the dramatist in verse: they are poetic prose plays with important interludes in verse. It was only in his last play *Purgatory* that he solved his problem of speech in verse, and laid all his successors under obligation to him.

II

Now, I am going to venture to make some observations based on my own experience, which all lead me to comment on my intentions, failures, and partial successes, in my own plays. I do this in the belief that any explorer or experimenter in new territory may, by putting on record a kind of journal of his explorations, say something of use to those who follow him into the same regions and who will perhaps go further.

The first thing of any importance that I discovered was that a writer who has worked for years, and achieved some success, in writing other kinds of verse, has to approach the writing of a verse play in a different frame of mind from that to which he has been accustomed in his previous work. In writing other verse, I think that one is writing, so to speak, in terms of one's own voice: the way it sounds when you read it to yourself is the test. For it is yourself speaking. The question of communication, of what the reader will get from it, is not paramount: if your poem is right to you, you can only hope that the readers will eventually come to accept it. The poem can wait a little while; the approval of a few sympathetic and judicious critics is enough to begin with; and it is for future readers to meet the poet more than half way. But in the theatre, the problem of communication presents itself immediately. You are deliberately writing verse for other voices, not for your own, and you do not know whose voices they will be. You are aiming to write lines which will have an immediate effect upon an unknown and unprepared audience, to be interpreted to that audience by unknown actors rehearsed by an unknown producer. And the unknown audience cannot be expected to show any indulgence towards the poet. The poet cannot afford to write his play merely for his admirers, those who know his nondramatic work and are prepared to receive favourably anything he puts his name to. He must write with an audience in view which knows nothing and cares nothing about any previous success he may have had before he ventured into the theatre. Hence one finds out that many of the things one likes to do, and knows how to do, are out of place; and that every line must be judged by a new law, that of dramatic relevance.

When I wrote *Murder in the Cathedral* I had the advantage for a beginner of an occasion which called for a subject generally admitted to be suitable for verse. Verse plays, it has been generally held, should either take their subject matter from some mythology, or else should be about some remote historical period, far enough away from the present for the characters not to need to be recognizable as human beings, and therefore for them to be licensed to talk in verse. Picturesque period costume renders verse much more acceptable. Furthermore, my play was to be produced for a rather special kind of audience—an audience of those serious people who go to "festivals" and expect to have to put up with poetry—though perhaps on this occasion some of them were not quite prepared for what they got. And finally it was a religious play, and people who go deliberately to a religious play at a religious festival expect to be patiently bored and to satisfy themselves with the feeling that they have done something meritorious. So the path was made easy.

It was only when I put my mind to thinking what sort of play I wanted to do next, that I realized that in *Murder in the Cathedral* I had not solved any general problem; but that from my point of view the play was a dead end. For one thing, the problem of language which that play had presented to me was a special problem. Fortunately, I did not have to write in the idiom of the twelfth century, because that idiom, even if I knew Norman French and Anglo-Saxon, would have been unintelligible. But the vocabulary and style could not be exactly those of modern conversation—as in some modern French plays using the plot and personages of Greek drama—because I had to take my audience back to an historical event; and they could not afford to be archaic, first because archaism would only have suggested the wrong period, and second because I wanted to bring home to the audience the contemporary relevance of the situation. The style therefore had to be *neutral*, committed neither to the present nor to the past. As for the versification, I was only aware at this stage that the essential was to avoid any echo of Shakespeare, for I was persuaded that the primary failure of nineteenth-century poets when they wrote for the theatre (and most of the greatest English poets had tried their hand at drama) was not in their theatrical technique, but in their dramatic language; and that this was due largely to their limitation to a strict blank verse which, after extensive use for non-dramatic poetry, had lost the flexibility which blank verse must have if it is to give the effect of conversation. The rhythm of regular blank verse had become too remote from the movement of modern speech. Therefore what I kept in mind was the versification of *Everyman*, hoping that anything unusual in the sound of it would be on the whole, advantageous. An avoidance of too much iambic, some use of alliteration, and occasional unexpected rhyme, helped to distinguish the versification from that of the nineteenth century.

The versification of the dialogue in *Murder in the Cathedral* has therefore, in my opinion, only a *negative* merit: it succeeded in avoiding what had to be avoided, but it arrived at no positive novelty; in short, in so far as it solved the problem of speech in verse for writing today, it solved it for this play only, and provided me with no clue to the verse I should use in another kind of play. Here, then, were two problems left unsolved: that of the idiom and that of the metric (it is really one and the same problem), for general use in any play I might want to write in future. I next became aware of my reasons for depending, in that play, so heavily upon the assistance of the chorus. There were two reasons for this, which in the circumstances justified it. The first was that the essential action of the play—both the historical facts and the matter which I invented—was somewhat limited. A man comes home, foreseeing that he will be killed, and he is killed. I did not want to increase the number of characters, I did not want to write a chronicle of twelfth-century politics, nor did I want to tamper unscrupulously with the meagre records as Tennyson did (in introducing Fair Rosamund, and in suggesting that Becket had been crossed in love in early youth). I wanted to concentrate on death and martyrdom. The introduction of a chorus of excited and sometimes hysterical women, reflecting in their emotion the significance of the action, helped wonderfully. The second reason was this: that a poet writing for the first time for the stage is much more at home in choral verse than in dramatic dialogue. This, I felt sure, was something I could do, and perhaps the dramatic weaknesses would be somewhat covered up by the cries of the women. The use of a chorus strengthened the power and concealed the defects of my theatrical technique. For this reason I decided that next time I would try to integrate the chorus more closely into the play.

I wanted to find out also, whether I could learn to dispense altogether with the use of prose. The two prose passages in *Murder in the Cathedral* could not have been written in verse. Certainly, with the kind of dialogue verse which I used in that play, the audience would have been uncomfortably aware that it was verse they were hearing. A sermon cast in verse is too unusual an experience for even the most regular churchgoers: nobody could have responded to it as a sermon at all. And in the speeches of the knights, who are quite aware that they are addressing an audience of people living eight hundred years after they themselves are dead, the use of platform prose is intended of course to have a special effect: to shock the audience out of their complacency. But this is a kind of trick: that is, a device tolerable only in one play and of no use for any other. I may, for aught I know, have been slightly under the influence of *St. Joan*.

I do not wish to give you the impression that I would rule out of dramatic poetry these three things: historical or mythological subject mat-

ter, the chorus, and traditional blank verse. I do not wish to lay down
any law that the only suitable characters and situations are those of modern life, or that a verse play should consist of dialogue only, or that a
wholly new versification is necessary. I am only tracing out the route
of exploration of one writer, and that one myself. If the poetic drama
is to reconquer its place, it must, in my opinion, enter into overt competition with prose drama. As I have said, people are prepared to put up
with verse from the lips of personages dressed in the fashion of some distant age; therefore they should be made to hear it from people dressed
like ourselves, living in houses and apartment like ours, and using tele-
phones and motor cars and radio sets. Audiences are prepared to accept
poetry recited by a chorus, for that is a kind of poetry recital, which it
does them credit to enjoy. And audiences (those who go to a verse play
because it is in verse) expect poetry to be in rhythms which have lost
touch with colloquial speech. What we have to do is to bring poetry into
the world in which the audience lives and to which it returns when it
leaves the theatre; not to transport the audience into some imaginary
world totally unlike their own, an unreal world in which poetry can be
spoken. What I should hope might be achieved, by a generation of dramatists having the benefit of our experience, is that the audience should
find, at the moment of awareness that it is hearing poetry, that it is saying to itself: "*I* could talk in poetry too!" Then we should not be transported into an artificial world; on the contrary, our own sordid, dreary,
daily world would be suddenly illuminated and transfigured.

I was determined, therefore, in my next play to take a theme of contemporary life, with characters of our own time living in our own world.
The Family Reunion was the result. Here my first concern was the problem of the versification, to find a rhythm close to contemporary speech,
in which the stresses could be made to come wherever we should naturally put them, in uttering the particular phrase on the particular occasion. What I worked out is substantially what I have continued to
employ: a line of varying length and varying number of syllables, with
a caesura and three stresses. The caesura and the stresses may come at
different places, almost anywhere in the line; the stresses may be close
together or well separated by light syllables, the only rule being that there
must be one stress on one side of the caesura and two on the other. In
retrospect, I soon saw that I had given my attention to versification, at
the expense of plot and character. I had, indeed, made some progress in
dispensing with the chorus; but the device of using four of the minor
personages, representing the Family, sometimes as individual character
parts and sometimes collectively as chorus, does not seem to me very satisfactory. For one thing, the immediate transition from individual, characterized part to membership of a chorus is asking too much of the actors:
it is a very difficult transition to accomplish. For another thing, it seemed
to me another trick, one which, even if successful, could not have been
applicable in another play. Furthermore, I had in two passages used the

device of a lyrical duet further isolated from the rest of the dialogue by being written in shorter lines with only two stresses. These passages are in a sense "beyond character," the speakers have to be presented as falling into a kind of trance-like state in order to speak them. But they are so remote from the necessity of the action that they are hardly more than passages of poetry which might be spoken by anybody; they are too much like operatic arias. The member of the audience, if he enjoys this sort of thing, is putting up with a suspension of the action in order to enjoy a poetic fantasia: these passages are really less related to the action than are the choruses in *Murder in the Cathedral*. I observed that when Shakespeare, in one of his mature plays, introduces what might seem a purely poetic line or passage, it never interrupts the action, or is out of character, but on the contrary, in some mysterious way supports both action and character. When Macbeth speaks his so often quoted words beginning

Tomorrow and tomorrow and tomorrow

or when Othello, confronted at night with his angry father-in-law and friends, utters the beautiful line

Keep up your bright swords, for the dew will rust them

we do not feel that Shakespeare has thought of lines which are beautiful poetry and wishes to fit them in somehow, or that he has for the moment come to the end of his dramatic inspiration and has turned to poetry to fill up with. The lines are surprising, and yet they fit in with the character; or else we are compelled to adjust our conception of the character in such a way that the lines will be appropriate to it. The lines spoken by Macbeth reveal the weariness of the weak man who had been forced by his wife to realize his own halfhearted desires and her ambitions, and who, with her death, is left without the motive to continue. The line of Othello expresses irony, dignity, and fearlessness; and incidentally reminds us of the time of night in which the scene takes place. Only poetry could do this; but it is *dramatic* poetry: that is, it does not interrupt but intensifies the dramatic situation.

It was not only because of the introduction of passages which called too much attention to themselves as poetry, and could not be dramatically justified, that I found *The Family Reunion* defective: there were two weaknesses which came to strike me as more serious still. The first was that I had employed far too much of the strictly limited time allowed to a dramatist in presenting a situation, and not left myself enough time, or provided myself with enough material, for developing it in action. I had written what was, on the whole, a good first act; except that for a first act it was much too long. When the curtain rises again, the audience is expecting, as it has a right to expect, that something is going to happen. Instead, it finds itself treated to a further exploration of the background: in other words, to what ought to have been given much earlier if at all.

The beginning of the second act presents much the most difficult problem to producer and cast: for the audience's attention is beginning to wander. And then, after what must seem to the audience an interminable time of preparation, the conclusion comes so abruptly that we are, after all, unready for it. This was an elementary fault in mechanics.

But the deepest flaw of all was in a failure of adjustment between the Greek story and the modern situation. I should either have stuck closer to Aeschylus or else taken a great deal more liberty with his myth. One evidence of this is the appearance of those ill-fated figures, the Furies. They must, in future, be omitted from the cast, and be understood to be visible only to certain of my characters, and not to the audience. We tried every possible manner of presenting them. We put them on the stage, and they looked like uninvited guests who had strayed in from a fancy-dress ball. We concealed them behind gauze, and they suggested a still out of a Walt Disney film. We made them dimmer, and they looked like shrubbery just outside the window. I have seen other expedients tried: I have seen them signalling from across the garden, or swarming onto the stage like a football team, and they are never right. They never succeed in being either Greek goddesses or modern spooks. But their failure is merely a symptom of the failure to adjust the ancient with the modern.

A more serious evidence is that we are left in a divided frame of mind, not knowing whether to consider the play the tragedy of the mother or the salvation of the son. The two situations are not reconciled. I find a confirmation of this in the fact that my sympathies now have come to be all with the mother, who seems to me, except perhaps for the chauffeur, the only complete human being in the play; and my hero now strikes me as an insufferable prig.

Well, I had made some progress in learning how to write the first act of a play, and I had—the one thing of which I felt sure—made a good deal of progress in finding a form of versification and an idiom which would serve all my purposes, without recourse to prose, and be capable of unbroken transition between the most intense speech and the most relaxed dialogue. You will understand, after my making these criticisms of *The Family Reunion,* some of the errors that I endeavoured to avoid in designing *The Cocktail Party.* To begin with, no chorus, and no ghosts. I was still inclined to go to a Greek dramatist for my theme, but I was determined to take this merely as a point of departure, and to conceal the origins so well that nobody would identify them until I pointed them out myself. In this at least I have been successful; for no one of my acquaintance (and no dramatic critics) recognised the source of my story in the *Alcestis* of Euripides. In fact, I have had to go into detailed explanation to convince them—I mean, of course, those who were familiar with the plot of that play—of the genuineness of the inspiration. But those who were at first disturbed by the eccentric behaviour of my unknown guest, and his apparently intemperate habits and tendency to burst into song, have found some consolation after I have called their attention to the behaviour of Heracles in Euripides' play.

In the second place, I laid down for myself the ascetic rule to avoid poetry which could not stand the test of strict dramatic utility: with such success, indeed, that it is perhaps an open question whether there is any poetry in the play at all. And finally, I tried to keep in mind that in a play, from time to time, something should happen; that the audience should be kept in the constant expectation that something is going to happen; and that, when it does happen, it should be different, but not too different, from what the audience has been led to expect.

I have not yet got to the end of my investigation of the weaknesses of this play, but I hope and expect to find more than those of which I am yet aware. I say "hope" because while one can never repeat a success, and therefore must always try to find something different, even if less popular, to do, the desire to write something which will be free of the defects of one's last work is a very powerful and useful incentive. I am aware that the last act of my play only just escapes, if indeed it does escape, the accusation of being not a last act but an epilogue; and I am determined to do something different, if I can, in this respect. I also believe that while the self-education of a poet trying to write for the theatre seems to require a long period of disciplining his poetry, and putting it, so to speak, on a very thin diet in order to adapt it to the needs of the stage, he may find that later, when (and if) the understanding of theatrical technique has become second nature, at which he can dare to make more liberal use of poetry and take greater liberties with ordinary coloquial speech. I base that belief on the evolution of Shakespeare, and on some study of the language in his late plays.

In devoting so much time to an examination of my own plays, I have, I believe, been animated by a better motive than egotism. It seems to me that if we are to have a poetic drama, it is more likely to come from poets learning how to write plays, than from skilful prose dramatists learning to write poetry. That some poets can learn how to write plays, and write good ones, may be only a hope, but I believe a not unreasonable hope; but that a man who has started by writing successful prose plays should then learn how to write good poetry, seems to me extremely unlikely. And, under present-day conditions, and until the verse play is recognised by the larger public as a possible source of entertainment, the poet is likely to get his first opportunity to work for the stage only after making some sort of reputation for himself as the author of other kinds of verse. I have therefore wished to put on record, for what it may be worth to others, some account of the difficulties I have encountered, and the mistakes into which I have fallen, and the weaknesses I have had to try to overcome.

I should not like to close without attempting to set before you, though only a dim outline, the ideal towards which it seems to me that poetic drama should strive. It is an unattainable ideal: and that is why it interests me, for it provides an incentive towards further experiment and exploration, beyond any goal which there is prospect of attaining. It is a function of all art to give us some perception of an order in life, by imposing an order upon it. The painter works by selection, combination, and emphasis among the elements of the visible world; the musician, in the world of sound. It seems to me that beyond the nameable, classifiable emotions and motives of our conscious life when directed towards action —the part of life which prose drama is wholly adequate to express—there is a fringe of indefinite extent, of feeling which we can only detect, so to speak, out of the corner of the eye and can never completely focus; of feeling which we are only aware in a kind of temporary detachment from action. There are great prose dramatists—such as Ibsen and Chekhov —who have at times done things of which I would not otherwise have supposed prose to be capable, but who seem to me, in spite of their success, to have been hampered in expression by writing in prose. This peculiar range of sensibility can be expressed by dramatic poetry, at its moments of great intensity. As such moments, we touch the border of those feelings which only music can express. We can never emulate music, because to arrive at the condition of music would be the annihilation of poetry, and especially of dramatic poetry. Nevertheless, I have before my eyes a kind of mirage of the perfection of verse drama, which would be a design of human action and of words, such as to present at once the two aspects of dramatic and of musical order. It seems to me that Shakespeare achieved this at least in certain scenes—even rather early, for there is the balcony scene of *Romeo and Juliet*—and that this was what he was striving towards in his late plays. To go as far in this direction as it is possible to go, without losing that contact with the ordinary everyday world with which drama must come to terms, seems to me the proper aim of dramatic poetry. For it is ultimately the function of art, in imposing a credible order upon ordinary reality, and thereby eliciting some perception of an order *in* reality, to bring us to a condition of serenity, stillness, and reconciliation; and then leave us, as Virgil left Dante, to proceed toward a region where that guide can avail us no further.

The Three Voices of Poetry

The first voice is the voice of the poet talking to himself—or to nobody. The second is the voice of the poet addressing an audience, whether large or small. The third is the voice of the poet when he attempts to create a dramatic character speaking in verse; when he is saying, not what he would say in his own person, but only what he can say within the limits of one imaginary character addressing another imaginary character. The distinction between the first and the second voice, between the poet speaking to himself and the poet speaking to other people, points to the problem of poetic communication; the distinction between the poet addressing other people in either his own voice or an assumed voice, and the poet inventing speech in which imaginary characters address each other, points to the problem of the difference between dramatic, quasi-dramatic, and non-dramatic verse.

I wish to anticipate a question that some of you may well raise. Cannot a poem be written for the ear, or for the eye, of one person alone? You may say simply, "Isn't love poetry at times a form of communication between one person and one other, with no thought of a further audience?"

There are at least two people who might have disagreed with me on this point: Mr and Mrs Robert Browning. In the poem "One Word More," written as an epilogue to *Men and Women*, and addressed to Mrs Browning, the huband makes a striking value judgment:

> Rafael made a century of sonnets,
> Made and wrote them in a certain volume,
> Dinted with the silver-pointed pencil
> Else he only used to draw Madonnas:
> These, the world might view—but one, the volume.
> Who that one, you ask? Your heart instructs you . . .
>
> You and I would rather read that volume . . .
> Would we not? than wonder at Madonnas . . .
>
> Dante once prepared to paint an angel:
> Whom to please? You whisper "Beatrice" . . .
> You and I would rather see that angel,
> Painted by the tenderness of Dante,
> Would we not?—than read a fresh Inferno.

I agree that one *Inferno*, even by Dante, is enough; and perhaps we need not too much regret the fact that Rafael did not live to multiply his Madonnas: but I can only say that I feel no curiosity whatever about Dante's sonnets or Rafael's angel. If Dante wrote, or Rafael painted, for the eyes of one person alone, let their privacy be respected. We know that Mr and Mrs Browning liked to write poems to each other, because they published them, and some of them are good poems. We know that Rossetti thought that he was writing his "House of Life" sonnets for one person, and that he was only persuaded by his friends to disinter them. Now, I do not deny that a poem may be addressed to one person: there is a well-known form, not always amatory in content, called The Epistle. We shall never have conclusive evidence: for the testimony of poets as to what they thought they were doing when they wrote a poem, cannot be taken altogether at its face value. But my opinion is, that a good love poem, though it may be addressed to one person, is always meant to be overheard by other people. Surely, the proper language of love—that is, of communication to the beloved and to no one else—is prose.

Having dismissed as an illusion the voice of the poet talking to one person only, I think that the best way for me to try to make my three voices audible to you, is to trace the genesis of the distinction in my own mind. The writer to whose mind the distinction is most likely to occur is probably the writer like myself, who has spent a good many years in writing poetry, before attempting to write for the stage at all. It may be, as I have read, that there is a dramatic element in much of my early work. It may be that from the beginning I aspired unconsciously to the theatre —or, unfriendly critics might say, to Shaftesbury Avenue and Broadway. I have, however, gradually come to the conclusion that in writing verse for the stage both the process and the outcome are very different from what they are in writing verse to be read or recited. Twenty years ago I was commissioned to write a pageant play to be called *The Rock*. The invitation to write the words for this spectacle—the occasion of which was an appeal for funds for church-building in new housing areas—came at a moment when I seemed to myself to have exhausted my meagre poetic gifts, and to have nothing more to say. To be, at such a moment, commissioned to write something which, good or bad, must be delivered by a certain date, may have the effect that vigorous cranking sometimes has upon a motor-car when the battery is run down. The task was clearly laid out: I had only to write the words of prose dialogue for scenes of the usual historical pageant pattern, for which I had been given a scenario. I had also to provide a number of choral passages in verse, the content of which was left to my own devices: except for the reasonable stipulation that all the choruses were expected to have some relevance to the purpose of the pageant, and that each chorus was to occupy a precise number of minutes of stage time. But in carrying out this second part of my task, there was nothing to call my attention to the third, or dramatic voice: it was the second voice, that of myself addressing—indeed harangu-ing—an audience, that was most distinctly audible. Apart from the obvi-ous fact that writing to order is not the same thing as writing to please oneself, I learnt only that verse to be spoken by a choir should be differ-ent from verse to be spoken by one person; and that the more voices you have in your choir, the simpler and more direct the vocabulary, the syn-tax, and the content of your lies must be. This chorus of *The Rock* was not a dramatic voice; though many lines were distributed, the personages were unindividuated. Its members were speaking *for me*, not uttering words that really represented any supposed character of their own.

The chorus in *Murder in the Cathedral*, does, I think, represent some advance in dramatic development: that is to say, I set myself the task of writing lines, not for an anonymous chorus, but for a chorus of women of Canterbury—one might almost say, charwomen of Canterbury. I had to make some effort to identify myself with these women, instead of merely identifying them with myself. But as for the dialogue of the play, the plot had the drawback (from the point of view of my own dramatic education) of presenting only one dominant character; and what dramatic conflict there is takes place within the mind of that character. The third, or dramatic voice, did not make itself audible to me until I first attacked the problem of presenting two (or more) characters, in some sort of conflict, misunderstanding, or attempting to understand each other, characters with each of whom I had to try to identify myself while writing the words for him or her to speak. You may remember that Mrs Cluppins, in the trial of the case of Bardell *v.* Pickwick, testified that "the voices was very loud, sir, and forced themselves upon my ear." "Well, Mrs Cluppins," said Sergeant Buzfuz, "you were not listening, but you heard the voices." It was in 1938, then, that the third voice began to force itself upon my ear.

At this point I can fancy the reader murmuring: "I'm sure he has said all this before." I will assist memory by supplying the reference. In a lecture on "Poetry and Drama," delivered exactly three years ago and subsequently published, I said:

> In writing other verse (i.e. non-dramatic verse) I think that one is writing, so to speak, in terms of one's own voice: the way it sounds when you read it to yourself is the test. For it is yourself speaking. The question of communication, of what the reader will get from it, is not paramount . . .

There is some confusion of pronouns in this passage, but I think that the meaning is clear; so clear, as to be a glimpse of the obvious. At that stage, I noted only the difference between speaking for oneself, and speaking for an imaginary character; and I passed on to other considerations about the nature of poetic drama. I was beginning to be aware of the difference between the first and the third voice, but gave no attention to the second voice, of which I shall say more presently. I am now trying to penetrate a little further into the problem. So, before going on to consider the other voices, I want to pursue for a few moments the complexities of the third voice.

In a verse play, you will probably have to find words for several characters differing widely from each other in background, temperament, education, and intelligence. You cannot afford to identify one of these characters with yourself, and give him (or her) all the "poetry" to speak. The poetry (I mean, the language at those dramatic moments when it reaches intensity) must be as widely distributed as characterization permits; and each of your characters, when he has words to speak which are poetry and not merely verse, must be given lines appropriate to himself. When the poetry comes, the personage on the stage must not give the impression of being merely a mouthpiece for the author. Hence the author is limited by the kind of poetry, and the degree of intensity in its kind, which can be plausibly attributed to each character in his play. And these lines of poetry must also justify themselves by their development of the situation in which they are spoken. Even if a burst of magnificent poetry is suitable enough for the character to which it is assigned, it must also convince us that it is necessary to the action; that it is helping to extract the utmost emotional intensity out of the situation. The poet writing for the theatre may, as I have found, make two mistakes: that of assigning to a personage lines of poetry not suitable to be spoken by that personage, and that of assigning lines which, however suitable to the personage, yet fail to forward the action of the play. There are, in some of the minor Elizabethan dramatists, passages of magnificent poetry which are in both respects out of place—fine enough to preserve the play for ever as literature, but yet so inappropriate as to prevent the play from being a dramatic masterpiece. The best-known instances occur in Marlowe's *Tamburlaine.*

How have the very great dramatic poets—Sophocles, or Shakespeare, or Racine—dealt with this difficulty? This is, of course, a problem which concerns all imaginative fiction—novels and prose plays—in which the characters may be said to live. I can't see, myself, any way to make a character live except to have a profound sympathy with that character. Ideally, a dramatist, who has usually far fewer characters to manipulate than a novelist, and who has only two hours or so of life to allow them, should sympathise profoundly with all of his characters: but that is a counsel of perfection, because the plot of a play with even a very small cast may require the presence of one or more characters in whose reality, apart from their contribution to the action, we are uninterested. I wonder, however, whether it is possible to make completely real a wholly villainous character—one toward whom neither the author nor anyone else can feel anything but antipathy. We need an admixture of *weakness* with either heroic virtue or satanic villainy, to make character plausible. Iago frightens me more than Richard III; I am not sure that Parolles, in *All's Well That Ends Well,* does not disturb me more than Iago. (And I am quite sure that Rosamund Vincy, in *Middlemarch,* frightens me far more than Goneril or Regan.) It seems to me that what happens, when an author creates a vital character, is a sort of give-and-take. The author may put into that character, besides its other attributes, some trait of his own, some strength or weakness, some tendency to violence or to indecision, some eccentricity even, that he has found in himself. Something perhaps never realized in his own life, something of which those who know him best may be unaware, something not restricted in transmission to characters of the same temperament, the same age, and, least of all, of the same sex. Some bit of himself that the author gives to a character may be the germ from which the life of that character starts. On the other hand, a character which succeeds in interesting its author may elicit from the author latent potentialities of his own being. I believe that the author imparts something of himself to his characters, but I also believe that he is influenced by the characters he creates. It would be only too easy to lose oneself in a maze of speculation about the process by which an imaginary character can become as real for us as people we have known. I have penetrated into this maze so far only to indicate the difficulties, the limitations, the fascination, for a poet who is used to writing poetry in his own person, of the problem of making imaginary personages talk poetry. And the difference, the abyss, between writing for the first and for the third voice.

The peculiarity of my third voice, the voice of poetic drama, is brought out in another way by comparing it with the voice of the poet in non-dramatic poetry which has a dramatic element in it—and conspicuously in the dramatic monologue. Browning, in an uncritical moment, addressed himself as "Robert Browning, you writer of plays." How many of us have read a play by Browning more than once; and, if we have read it more than once, was our motive the expectation of enjoyment? What personage, in a play by Browning, remains living in our mind? On the other hand, who can forget Fra Lippo Lippi, or Andrea del Sarto, or Bishop Blougram, or the other bishop who ordered his tomb? It would seem without further examination, from Browning's mastery of the dramatic monologue, and his very moderate achievement in the drama, that the two forms must be essentially different. Is there, perhaps, another voice which I have failed to hear, the voice of the dramatic poet whose dramatic gifts are best exercised outside of the theatre? And certainly, if any poetry, not of the stage, deserves to be characterized as "dramatic," it is Browning's.

In a play, as I have said, an author must have divided loyalties; he must sympathize with characters who may be in no way sympathetic to each other. And he must allocate the "poetry" as widely as the limitations of each imaginary character permit. This necessity to divide the poetry implies some variation of the style of the poetry according to the character to whom it is given. The fact that a number of characters in a play have claims upon the author, for their allotment of poetic speech, compels him to try to extract the poetry from the character, rather than impose his poetry upon it. Now, in the dramatic monologue we have no such check. The author is just as likely to identify the character with himself, as himself with the character: for the check is missing that will prevent him from doing so—and that check is the necessity for identifying himself with some other character replying to the first. What we normally hear, in fact, in the dramatic monologue, is the voice of the poet, who has put on the costume and make-up either of some historical character, or of one out of fiction. His personage must be identified to us—as an individual, or at least as a type—before he begins to speak. If, as frequently with Browning, the poet is speaking in the role of an historical personage, like Lippo Lippi, or in the role of a known character of fiction, like Caliban, he has taken possession of that character. And the difference is most evident in his "Caliban upon Setebos." In *The Tempest*, it is Caliban who speaks; in "Caliban upon Setebos," it is Browning's voice that we hear, Browning talking aloud through Caliban. It was Browning's greatest disciple, Mr Ezra Pound, who adopted the term "persona" to indicate the several historical characters through whom he spoke: and the term is just.

I risk the generalization also, which may indeed be far too sweeping, that dramatic monologue cannot create a character. For character is created and made real only in an action, a communication between imaginary people. It is not irrelevant that when the dramatic monologue is not put into the mouth of some character already known to the reader—from history or from fiction—we are likely to ask the question "Who was the original?" About Bishop Blougram people have always been impelled to ask, how far was this intended to be a portrait of Cardinal Manning, or of some other ecclesiastic? The poet, speaking, as Browning does, in his own voice, cannot bring a character to life: he can only mimic a character otherwise known to us. And does not the point of mimicry lie in the recognition of the person mimicked, and in the incompleteness of the illusion? We have to be aware that the mimic and the person mimicked are different people: if we are actually deceived, mimicry becomes impersonation. When we listen to a play by Shakespeare, we listen not to Shakespeare but to his characters; when we read a dramatic monologue by Browning, we cannot suppose that we are listening to any other voice than that of Browning himself.

In the dramatic monologue, then, it is surely the second voice, the voice of the poet talking to other people, that is dominant. The mere fact that he is assuming a role, that he is speaking through a mask, implies the presence of an audience: why should a man put on fancy dress and a mask only to talk to himself? The second voice is, in fact, the voice most often and most clearly heard in poetry that is not of the theatre: in all poetry, certainly, that has a conscious social purpose—poetry intended to amuse or to instruct, poetry that tells a story, poetry that preaches or points a moral, or satire which is a form of preaching. For what is the point of a story without an audience, or of a sermon without a congregation? The voice of the poet addressing other people is the dominant voice of epic, though not the only voice. In Homer, for instance, there is heard also, from time to time, the dramatic voice: there are moments when we hear, not Homer telling us what a hero said, but the voice of the hero himself. *The Divine Comedy* is not in the exact sense an epic, but here also we hear men and women speaking to us. And we have no reason to suppose that Milton's sympathy with Satan was so exclusive as to seal him from the Devil's Party. But the epic is essentially a tale told to an audience, while drama is essentially an action exhibited to an audience.

Now, what about the poetry of the first voice—that which is not primarily an attempt to communicate with anyone at all?

I must make the point that this poetry is not necessarily what we call loosely "lyric poetry." The term "lyric" itself is unsatisfactory. We think first of verse intended to be sung—from the songs of Campion and Shakespeare and Burns, to the arias of W. S. Gilbert, or the words of the latest "musical number." But we apply it also to poetry that was never intended for a musical setting, or which we dissociate from its music: we speak of the "lyric verse" of the metaphysical poets, of Vaughan and Marvell as well as Donne and Herbert. The very definition of "lyric," in the Oxford Dictionary, indicates that the word cannot be satisfactorily defined:

> *Lyric:* Now the name for short poems, usually divided into stanzas or strophes, and directly expressing the poet's own thoughts and sentiments.

How short does a poem have to be, to be called a "lyric"? The emphasis on brevity, and the suggestion of division into stanzas, seem residual from the association of the voice with music. But there is no necessary relation between brevity and the expression of the poet's own thoughts and feelings. "Come unto these yellow sands" or "Hark! hark! the lark" are lyrics —are they not?—but what sense is there in saying that they express directly the poet's own thoughts and sentiments? *London, The Vanity of Human Wishes*, and *The Deserted Village* are all poems which appear to express the poet's own thoughts and sentiments, but do we ever think of such poems as "lyrical"? They are certainly not short. Between them, all the poems I have mentioned seem to fail to qualify as lyrics, just as Mr Daddy Longlegs and Mr Floppy Fly failed to qualify as courtiers:

> One never more can go to court,
> Because his legs have grown too short;
> The other cannot sing a song,
> Because his legs have grown too long!

It is obviously the lyric in the sense of a poem "directly expressing the poet's own thoughts and sentiments," not in the quite unrelated sense of a short poem intended to be set to music, that is relevant to my first voice— the voice of the poet talking to himself—or to nobody. It is in this sense that the German poet Gottfried Benn, in a very interesting lecture entitled *Probleme der Lyrik*, thinks of lyric as the poetry of the first voice: he includes, I feel sure, such poems as Rilke's Duinese Elegies and Valéry's *La Jeune Parque*. Where he speaks of "lyric poetry," then, I should prefer to say "meditative verse."

What, asks Herr Benn in this lecture, does the writer of such a poem, "addressed to no one," start with? There is first, he says, an inert embryo or "creative germ" (*ein dumpfer schöpferischer Keim*) and, on the other hand, the Language, the resources of the words at the poet's command. He has something germinating in him for which he must find words; but he cannot know what words he wants until he has found the words; he cannot identify this embryo until it has been transformed into an arrangement of the right words in the right order. When you have the words for it, the "thing" for which the words had to be found has disappeared, replaced by a poem. What you start from is nothing so definite as an emotion, in any ordinary sense; it is still more certainly not an idea; it is—to adapt two lines of Beddoes to a different meaning—a

> bodiless childful of life in the gloom
> Crying with frog voice, "what shall I be?"

I agree with Gottfried Benn, and I would go a little further. In a poem which is neither didactic nor narrative, and not animated by any other social purpose, the poet may be concerned solely with expressing in verse —using all his resources of words, with their history, their connotations, their music—this obscure impulse. He does not know what he has to say until he has said it, and in the effort to say it he is not concerned with making other people understand anything. He is not concerned, at this stage, with other people at all: only with finding the right words or, anyhow, the least wrong words. He is not concerned whether anybody else will ever listen to them or not, or whether anybody else will ever understand them if he does. He is oppressed by a burden which he must bring to birth in order to obtain relief. Or, to change the figure of speech, he is haunted by a demon, a demon against which he feels powerless, because in its first manifestation it has no face, no name, nothing; and the words, the poem he makes, are a kind of form of exorcism of this demon. In other words again, he is going to all that trouble, not in order to communicate with anyone, but to gain relief from acute discomfort; and when the words are finally arranged in the right way—or in what he comes to accept as the best arrangement he can find—he may experience a moment of exhaustion, of appeasement, of absolution, and of something very near annihilation, which is in itself indescribable. And then he can say to the poem: "Go away! Find a place for yourself in a book—and don't expect *me* to take any further interest in you."

I don't believe that the relation of a poem to its origins is capable of being more clearly traced. You can read the essays of Paul Valéry, who studied the workings of his own mind in the composition of a poem more perseveringly than any other poet has done. But if, either on the basis of what poets try to tell you, or by biographical research, with or without the tools of the psychologist, you attempt to explain a poem, you will probably be getting further and further away from the poem without arriving at any other destination. The attempt to explain the poem by tracing it back to its origins will distract attention from the poem, to direct it on to something else which, in the form in which it can be apprehended by the critic and his readers, has no relation to the poem and throws no light upon it. I should not like you to think that I am trying to make the writing of a poem more of a mystery than it is. What I am maintaining is, that the first effort of the poet should be to achieve clarity for himself, to assure himself that the poem is the right outcome of the process that has taken place. The most bungling form of obscurity is that of the poet who has not been able to express himself *to* himself; the shoddiest form is found when the poet is trying to persuade himself that he has something to say when he hasn't.

So far I have been speaking, for the sake of simplicity, of the three voices as if they were mutually exclusive: as if the poet, in any particular poem, was speaking *either* to himself or to others, and as if neither of the first two voices was audible in good dramatic verse. And this indeed is the conclusion to which Herr Benn's argument appears to lead him: he speaks as if the poetry of the first voice—which he considers, moreover, to be on the whole a development of our own age—was a totally different kind of poetry from that of the poet addressing an audience. But for me the voices are most often found together—the first and second, I mean, in non-dramatic poetry; and together with the third in dramatic poetry too. Even though, as I have maintained, the author of a poem may have written it primarily without thought of an audience, he will also want to know what the poem which has satisfied *him* will have to say to other people. There are, first of all, those few friends to whose criticism he may wish to submit it before considering it completed. They can be very helpful, in suggesting a word or a phrase which the author has not been able to find for himself; though their greatest service perhaps is to say simply "this passage won't do"—thus confirming a suspicion which the author had been suppressing from his own consciousness. But I am not thinking primarily of the few judicious friends whose opinion the author prizes, but of the larger and unknown audience—people to whom the author's name means only his poem which they have read. The final handing over, so to speak, of the poem to an unknown audience, for what that audience will make of it, seems to me the consummation of the process begun in solitude and without thought of the audience, the long process of gestation of the poem, because it marks the final separation of the poem from the author. Let the author, at this point, rest in peace.

So much for the poem which is primarily a poem of the first voice. I think that in every poem, from the private meditation to the epic or the drama, there is more than one voice to be heard. If the author never spoke to himself, the result would not be poetry, though it might be magnificent rhetoric; and part of our enjoyment of great poetry is the enjoyment of *overhearing* words which are not addressed to us. But if the poem were exclusively for the author, it would be a poem in a private and unknown language; and a poem which was a poem only for the author would not be a poem at all. And in poetic drama, I am inclined to believe that all three voices are audible. First, the voice of each character —an individual voice different from that of any other character: so that of each utterance we can say, that it could only have come from that character. There may be from time to time, and perhaps when we least notice it, the voices of the author and the character in unison, saying something appropriate to the character, but something which the author could say for himself also, though the words may not have quite the same meaning for both. That may be a very different thing from the ventriloquism which makes the character only a mouthpiece for the author's ideas or sentiments.

Tomorrow and tomorrow and tomorrow . . .

Is not the perpetual shock and surprise of these hackneyed lines evidence
that Shakespeare and Macbeth are uttering the words in unison, though
perhaps with somewhat different meaning? And finally there are the
lines, in a play by one of the supreme poetic dramatists, in which we
hear a more impersonal voice still than that of either the character or the
author.

Ripeness is all

or

Simply the thing I am
Shall make me live.

And now I should like to return for a moment to Gottfried Benn and
his unknown, dark *psychic material*—we might say, the octopus or angel
with which the poet struggles. I suggest that between the three kinds of
poetry to which my three voices correspond there is a certain difference
of process. In the poem in which the first voice, that of the poet talking
to himself, dominates, the *psychic material* tends to create its own form
—the eventual form will be to a greater or less degree the form for that
one poem and for no other. It is misleading, of course, to speak of the
material as creating or imposing its own form: what happens is a simultaneous development of form and material; for the form affects the material at every stage; and perhaps all the material does is to repeat "not
that! not that!" in the face of each unsuccessful attempt at formal organization; and finally the material is identified with its form. But in poetry
of the second and in that of the third voice, the form is already to some
extent given. However much it may be *trans*formed before the poem is
finished, it can be represented from the start by an outline or scenario. If
I choose to tell a story, I must have some notion of the plot of the story
I propose to tell; if I undertake satire, moralizing, or invective, there is
already something given which I can recognize and which exists for
others as well as myself. And if I set out to write a play, I start by an act
of choice: I settle upon a particular emotional situation, out of which
characters and a plot will emerge, and I can make a plain prose outline
of the play in advance—however much that outline may be altered before the play is finished, by the way in which the characters develop. It
is likely, of course, that it is in the beginning the pressure of some rude
unknown *psychic material* that directs the poet to tell that particular
story, to develop that particular situation. And on the other hand, the
frame, once chosen, within which the author has elected to work, may
itself evoke other psychic material; and then, lines of poetry may come
into being, not from the original impulse, but from a secondary stimulation of the unconscious mind. All that matters is, that in the end the
voices should be heard in harmony; and, as I have said, I doubt whether
in any real poem only one voice is audible.

The reader may well, by now, have been asking himself what I have been up to in all these speculations. Have I been toiling to weave a laboured web of useless ingenuity? Well, I have been trying to talk, not to myself—as you may have been tempted to think—but to the reader of poetry. I should like to think that it might interest the reader of poetry to test my assertions in his own reading. Can you distinguish these voices in the poetry you read, or hear recited, or hear in the theatre? If you complain that a poet is obscure, and apparently ignoring you, the reader, or that he is speaking only to a limited circle of initiates from which you are excluded—remember that what he may have been trying to do, was to put something into words which could not be said in any other way, and therefore in a language which may be worth the trouble of learning. If you complain that a poet is too rhetorical, and that he addresses you as if you were a public meeting, try to listen for the moments when he is not speaking to you, but merely allowing himself to be overheard: he may be a Dryden, a Pope, or a Byron. And if you have to listen to a verse play, take it first at its face value, as entertainment, for each character speaking for himself with whatever degree of reality his author has been able to endow him. Perhaps, if it is a great play, and you do not try too hard to hear them, you may discern the other voices too. For the work of a great poetic dramatist, like Shakespeare, constitutes a world. Each character speaks for himself, but no other poet could have found those words for him to speak. If you seek for Shakespeare, you will find him only in the characters he created; for the one thing in common between the characters is that no one but Shakespeare could have created any of them. The world of a great poetic dramatist is a world in which the creator is everywhere present, and everywhere hidden.

WILLIAM FAULKNER

1897–

AT VARIOUS TIMES DURING THE LAST CENTURY AND A HALF, CERTAIN areas of the world, visited by defeat and persecution, long silent and voiceless, have suddenly found themselves creating a great literature. One thinks of feudal Russia, which at the moment of its freeing of the serfs produced Turgenev, Tolstoy, Dostoevsky; of Ireland, in our time, creating, after wars and poverty and long-nursed hatreds, the poetry of Yeats, the tradition-shattering prose of Joyce. When we contemplate this relation between disaster and literature, we can understand why the American South was silent for so long and how, within the last twenty-five years, it has become brilliantly articulate. For decades after the Civil War there was impoverishment and stasis, an emotional collapse, self-laceration, the cultivation of a nostalgia for a perished order to cushion aching wounds. And with this, the ever-present racial tension and a feeling of impotence beside the strength and the expansion of the North.

These are broad generalizations, but they contain a great fund of truth. Much more might be said about the way in which peoples who are forced through defeat, distress and moral despair to suppress heroic emotions, sooner or later produce the writers who give these emotions form and utterance. In our time the South has found such a voice in the novelist William Faulkner. Indeed it might be said that he is writing the authentic history of the South. It is not, to be sure, the history of its plantation days, its era of slavery and of prosperity, the great battles and the collapse and ruin of the fratricidal war. That central drama in American life belongs in the regular history books. Faulkner's record has been rather the emotions of this drama, his vision, in depth, of the South's great moral tragedy from the days of the Indians, through the ironic moments when both Indians and whites were slave-owners and beyond into the era of defeat and degeneration.

The growth of Faulkner's art and the development of his large fictional canvas was rapid; the growth of his reputation, slow. In 1945 all seventeen of his books were out of print. Since then the award of the Nobel Prize has brought him universal fame and the United States has become aware that the world esteems Faulkner as one of America's most fertile masters of fiction in this century.

Faulkner's novels, in their sprawling picture of an entire Southern landscape, give the impression at times of a legendary world, as in the Old Testament, of people driven by passion and pride to acts of violence under the eyes of an unforgiving God of punishment. His themes—he spoke of them in his Nobel Prize speech—partake of the "old verities." And he named them, "love and honor and pity and pride and compassion and sacrifice." We might observer, however, that in the Faulknerian world, pride is often founded upon a false code of honor; love is often lust; compassion and pity and sacrifice are functions of an obsessive guilt. Faulkner's tales are touched with wildness and nightmare, they depict man's driven state in an uncompromising world in which instinct determines his needs and history his environment. The best Faulkner can offer is a belief in man's endurance in spite of a past which continually engulfs and destroys his present. Life would be different, Faulkner seems to say, if there had not been certain events long ago: if our ancestors had not sinned, if the Indians had not been despoiled, if the Negro had not been enslaved, if there had not been a Civil War. He seems, in a word, to be saying anew that the sins of the fathers are visited upon the children.

All this suggests a highly moralistic view of life; it suggests also a writer concerned not so much with ideas as with ambiguities of feeling, anomalies of experience. Faulkner writes not out of reason but out of passion; the wild, the grotesque, the macabre and the violent, these are the ingredients of Faulkner's fiction, heightened by a bold and brilliant, if sometimes windy, rhetoric. But the strange thing is that no matter how grotesque and how wild, Faulkner has the capacity to endow his material with high plausibility. And this results from the intensity of his vision. The wildest of his tales becomes real because it is "real" to him and because he possesses a prose which conveys his own tension and a technique which imposes order upon the chaos of his Southern world. Yet for all his vividness and his technical resources, he is regarded by many of his readers as "difficult," and most critics agree that he is uneven of performance.

The "difficult" in Faulkner stems from his endless and imaginative delight in experiments with language and with form. He narrates his stories from many angles of vision, as if he were using a moving picture camera; he resorts to flashbacks and to movement forward and backward in time; he places us within the consciousness of his personages and asks us to know them only through their thoughts and perceptions. The reader is assigned the task (and few readers want a task in the midst of reading!) of putting together the fragments of scrambled experience Faulkner prepares for them. Faulkner's experiments in letting a story tell itself instead of explaining every step of his narrative, place him with Henry James and James Joyce in the history of modern fiction. At his best he is a formidable craftsman and a vigorous and original stylist, possessing the courage to alter language as necessary and even to invent words in his constant effort to evoke mental atmospheres and the sensory world. At his worst he can write interminable sentences and inflate his prose with strange and elaborate pomposities. More often than not he is mastered by his art rather than being the master of it. This is the source of much of his power; it also explains his unevenness, his lack of what might be called the sense of the "professional."

To grasp Faulkner's vision of the South, it is useful to compare it with the vision of another writer we might deem to have been "unprofessional"—Hawthorne and his New England. The two writers, for all the years that divide them, have much in common. There is, in the first place, a distinct similarity of temperament—both shy and aloof, dreaming their dreams at their writing desk, writing, it would seem, not so much to tell stories to their fellow men as to unburden themselves of a weight of inner emotion. Faulkner long ago expressed his affinity for Hawthorne by naming his first book of verse *The Marble Fawn*, and perhaps in another way as well, by altering his family name from Falkner, as Hawthorne changed his from Hathorne. In this way both seem to have dissociated themselves from an ancestral past and given themselves a name and identity of their own. And as Hawthorne wrote of religious bigotry in New England and the manner in which American pitted himself against American over differences in faith and doctrine, so in the South Faulkner's work carries within it the constant memory of the Civil War and a gnawing sense of the chasm it created in American life. Hawthorne mingled the fanciful and the real, and Faulkner endows his people and their acts with lurid melodrama—so that both derive from the old Gothic novels of exaggerated terror. A more fundamental parallel however lies in their love for their particular land, their awareness of what it means to be attached to the soil of a given region, its haunted memories, the passion of its people. Hawthorne, in his life-long reverie, brooded over his ancestors who hanged witches in Salem; Faulkner on his side broods over his hot-blooded progenitors who instituted slavery and who lynched Negroes.

These are the deeper resemblances of the two, but we need not push our parallels further. Hawthorne, after all, was writing of a small seaboard society and of the early days of New England's history; the novel itself as a form, was, moreover, then still in its youth. Faulkner has almost a century of additional American history to draw upon including the cataclysmic Civil War and the vast changes it wrought in the South. And he works with a literary form which has evolved markedly since the simple story-telling days of Hawthorne. The novel, in modern times, has developed into a complex and subtle vehicle capable of evoking whole areas of human experience Hawthorne believed unreachable to the writer. We might even venture to argue that Faulkner's emergence as a writer dates from the moment Joyce placed in his hands, so to speak, those instruments which gave form to the Southern myth he carried within him and sought to express. By opening avenues into the exploration of subjective experience, the Irish writer made it possible for the American to render the tormented clock-beat of a region where time is out of joint and where day-dreams of past glories have annihilated immediate realities.

Faulkner's most important novels deal with Yoknapatawpha County in Mississippi, which is the fictional name for his own Lafayette County where he lives in the town of Oxford, the "Jefferson" of his novels. The Yoknapatawpha County series has been compared often with the *Comédie Humaine* of Balzac in which the French novelist focused on various areas of life, Parisian and regional, and carried over his personages from volume to volume. But if there is a resemblance in this respect, it is useful to remember that Balzac himself had been inspired by Sir Walter Scott's Waverley novels and that Scott was widely read in the old South. Indeed Faulkner's great-grandfather, Col. William Falkner (the original of John Sartoris) built a railway from Oxford to Memphis and named the way-stations after characters in the Waverley series. Like Scott, Faulkner is the historian of a region—historian of its emotions as much as of its events—and certain of his books are historical novels, in that particular sense. The fictional country of Faulkner has been carefully mapped by him: it lies between the Tallahatchie and the Yoknapatawpha rivers, in Mississippi, and involves an area of 2400 square miles. Its Faulknerian population consists of 6,298 whites and 9,313 Negroes. To the map Faulkner appended these words: "William Faulkner, Sole Owner & Proprietor."

The ownership is unchallengeable, and the owner moves about freely in his territory, picking up this story or that, weaving his genealogies and chronicles of certain families whose sagas have made up the history of the County from the days of the Chicasaw Indians to the present. If we unscramble the tales and sort out their chronology we arrive at a picture of the Sartorises, the Compsons, the black and white descendants of Carothers McCaslin and tales of the Snopeses and the Bundrens. We move, as it were, through the history of a feudal society, for there are the landed aristocrats and their slaves; then comes the break-up of the estates and the decline of the power of the old families; we see the middlemen in the towns, the landless who live by their labor, or their cunning, and the way in which their mendacity waters down old codes and old moralities. Faulkner treats his people and their acts, their incest and murder, their jumbled sense of past and present, with compassion, ironic humor and sometimes simply (as with the Snopeses), exaggerated caricature. And like Cervantes, a writer he reads constantly, he shrugs his shoulders over inconsistencies and contradictions in his saga. He seems unconcerned that a house may be of brick in one passage and later be described as of wood; or he will sometimes alter a character carried over from a previous novel. His principal structure, however, is consistent and he is concerned with essence as much as with detail.

The novels were not written in the chronological order of Yoknapatawpha history and so we have been given the various stories piece-meal, and the novels themselves tell their stories in bits and fragments. The aristocracy is first mapped for us in *Sartoris* (1929) in the days after the Civil War; but *The Unvanquished* (1938) harks back to their war period; *The Sound and the Fury* (1929), considered by many to be Faulkner's finest work, traces the decay of the Compson family and the society of which it is the symbol; *As I Lay Dying* (1930) is the history of still another family, the poor-white Bundrens. *Sanctuary,* the lurid gangster novel Faulkner published in 1931 as an avowed pot-boiler, records the advent of the Snopes clan and the sinister city riff-raff represented by Popeye. In *Absalom, Absalom!* (1936) a member of the Compson family describes the rise and fall of the Sutpen plantation dynasty in a brilliant narrative which dramatizes one of the most poignant themes in Faulkner, the Southern fear of mixed blood. The same theme is at the heart of one of Faulkner's least subjective novels, a work in the naturalist mode narrated with great power, *Light in August* (1932). This contains one of the novelist's most remarkable studies of a driven and conflicted individual who believes himself to be part Negro (whether he is or is not is never told). In *The Hamlet* (1940) we are again with the Snopeses and Faulkner may well have coined a name which will add the word *snope-ism* to the English language. The Snopeses are the crawling worms among Yoknapatawpha's humans, predatory, cunning, tough, shrewd, ludicrous, devoid of morals and standards, yet capable by sheer tenacity of worming their way into high places.

Faulkner's Negroes may be said to be among the first, in the long line of Negroes in Southern literature, who are treated in a realistic fashion. He neither idealizes them nor caricatures them, as other writers have tended to do. They are shown to us as creatures of their hard environment, the haunted and the hunted, the insulted and the injured of history, and Faulkner sees them in their human dignity as well as in their weaknesses as group and as individuals. For the maternal Negro woman, the loyal family servant, Faulkner shows a particular warmth and deep emotion, as may be seen in his creation of Dilsey, in *The Sound and the Fury*. Indeed he seems to possess more warmth for this type of character than for any of his white women. Faulkner admires above all in his Negroes their capacity to "endure," their rock-like quality which has enabled them to surmount the wear and tear and the destructive forces of the white man's world. He has by no means treated the Negro problem in all of its sociological aspects; but he has remained within his novelist's province of trying to see the Negroes as they are within the Southern society. In an indirect way he has dramatized the Negro-White problems in his stories of the Indians in their earlier slave-owning days in Yoknapa-tawpha County. The irony of this is driven home in a masterpiece of short story telling such as "Red Leaves," when one of the Indians, speaking of the two races which are upon his soil, remarks of the Negroes "they are worse than the white people." If this, on the one hand, coincides with certain Southern white feelings, it no less surely puts these whites in their place.

No bald account of Faulkner's world can quite convey the peculiar vividness he evokes. Told in sequence his Yoknapatawpha saga becomes merely a long tale of crime and horror. But a glance at *The Sound and the Fury* may suggest to some degree the qualities of his work and his "scrambled" methods of storytelling. In this novel Faulkner conveys to us the decay of the Compson family and by the same token the decay of the South. He achieves this by placing us first inside the consciousness of Benjy, the idiot son of the Compsons who is thirty-three when the novel starts, but who has the awareness of a three-year-old. Possessing no language, merely capable of animal sound, for he never learned to speak, having no sense of time, his inner being is a timeless world, an incoherence of conditioned sensations. Life is winter at one moment for him, and summer the next; he remembers only through sensation, and Faulkner conveys the idiot experience not so much by stream-of-consciousness —since Benjy has no awareness—but rather stream-of-sensation. The dark is a series of noises to him; things come to him rather than he to things. The spoon "came up and I ate," and "the bowl steamed up to my face." The lawn approaches him and goes away. Now, neither Faulkner nor anyone else has ever been inside the head of an idiot; and the daring achievement of the novelist has been to observe idiots so closely as to deduce the unknown from the known: observation, empathy, compassion, have enabled him to extrapolate the idiot condition. It is, moreover, a non-verbal condition and Faulkner has found the language for this purpose. The poet, the novelist, in such instances, becomes the voice for those who are silent.

In the second part of the novel, Faulkner places us in the consciousness of Benjy's brother Quentin, at Harvard in 1910 on the day on which he commits suicide because he is unable to tolerate any longer the burden of his fantasies of incest with his sister, Caddy. Quentin is the poetic, the verbal consciousness of the Compsons. He has a great awareness of the world around him, but is unable to bring it into proper focus so that he may understand it. The third part deals with Jason, the third brother, who is low-minded, self-frustrating, cunning, but not cunning enough, a Snopes among the gentry. Thus through the angle of vision of three different temperaments we are enabled to recover the past of the Compson family and its decay. The family's history resides in the memories and perceptions of the brothers even though we see them at different times. The Benjy section is dated April 7, 1928; we are with Quentin on June 2, 1910; we see Jason's world on April 6, 1928, the day before we were feeling our way among Benjy's perceptions. Having observed this family "from the inside" we are taken, in the final section, into the objective world and move about with Dilsey, the faithful Negro servant, on April 8, 1928. Thus we finally see the Compsons "from the outside." Time has been thoroughly scrambled; and by this method Faulkner has shown us how confused the Southern sense of time is, and how by living in a vanished past, confusion and distortion is generated in the immediate present. *The Sound and the Fury* is the post-bellum South: Benjy is its timelessness and inarticulateness; Quentin is its voice and its sensibility in brooding conflict over itself; and Jason is its poor-white decadence. Dilsey is its enduring Negro.

As might be expected in a writer so distinctively regional and historical, Faulkner has lived most of his life in his native Mississippi. He was born in 1897 at New Albany in that state, and shortly thereafter his family moved to Oxford where the novelist continues to make his home. He did not finish high school. He was, however, an inveterate reader and an attentive listener. From his earliest days he listened to stories of the old South and of his legendary great-grandfather whose name he bears: how he built the railway, fought as a guerrilla in the Civil War and even wrote a best-selling novel. In 1918, in the last days of the First World War, Faulkner enlisted in the Canadian air force but did not go overseas. We may speculate that to an historically conscious young man, sensitive to the merging of past and present, the old war he had refought in his imagination—the war of the States—blended with the new war which he also had to fight in his mind. There is a story that he did get to Europe and was stationed near Oxford, England. Faulkner himself might have created such a legend. To be in Oxford, England, when one comes from Oxford, Mississippi, is to be aware of historical contrasts and how the same name can represent two different environments and cultures. It is not uncommon in Faulkner's novels to find him using similar names to heighten profound differences.

At the end of the war Faulkner returned to Oxford in Mississippi and took some courses at the university. He continued to read, but studied little. In 1924 he went to New Orleans, where he became the friend of Sherwood Anderson, and began to write. In that year he issued his volume of verses and completed his first two novels. In 1929 he began to publish, after travel abroad and a stay in New York, what has since been recognized as his major work. In less than ten years he brought out *The Sound and the Fury, Light in August* and *Absalom, Absalom! Sanctuary*, written as a "shocker," succeeded in its effect. It brought Faulkner his first measure of recognition at the end of the 1920's. Since that time he has published more than twenty volumes of novels and tales. His most recent works in the Yoknapatawpha series have been *Intruder in the Dust* (1948), and *The Town* (1957) which carries on the stories of the Snopeses. Outside the series, perhaps his most striking work, though much criticized, was *The Fable* (1955) which was awarded the Pulitzer

Prize. In it Faulkner rewrote the story of the Crucifixion in terms of the First World War and enunciated those sentiments which animated his Nobel Prize speech.

Faulkner's success outside the United States has been phenomenal. He was recognized in France long before his full stature had been measured in his own country. Perhaps a Europe that felt itself disintegrating after two world wars could identify itself more strongly with the South than the powerful America of the twentieth century. Whatever the reasons, Faulkner now dominates American fiction. Less professional than Henry James, having no sense of himself as a "man of letters," (as T. S. Eliot has), he is nevertheless that unique and mystical being, a literary genius whose own life and that of his region are so intertwined that every word he sets down speaks not only for himself as a teller of fables, but for his land.

RED LEAVES

The principal stories of William Faulkner treat of the frontier, the growth of the settlements, the Civil War and modern times in Yoknapatawpha County. Some of the tales read as if they were episodes written for the novels and later set aside; the same characters reappear and new light is thrown on details merely sketched in the earlier and longer fiction. Each tale, in effect, has been cut from the same cloth as the novels—the continuing history of Yoknapatawpha County; but while it is a part of a whole, it also stands independently.

"Red Leaves" takes us back to the frontier days in Mississippi. The Chickasaw Indians still own land, but they were hardly cut out to be plantation owners or gentlemen farmers. Limited in movement, where they once could roam freely, they have lapsed into a kind of inertia and lost little time in picking up the worst habits of the white man. And if they had their own kind of slavery in early days, they now buy Negro slaves, like the whites, but do not have the same ability to exploit them. The story is woven out of the two primitive forces prevailing on the frontier in Yoknapatawpha, that of the Indian and the Negro, as well as of the corrupting force of the white man.

The Indians, patient and implacable, will carry out their age-old ritual; the Negro in this case will be their victim; and what they do will be a prophetic enactment of the later history of the South—the white posse seeking its quarry for the modern but even more primitive ritual of lynching. Out of such deeply historical elements, and with intimate realistic detail, Faulkner wrote this tale, among the most powerful he has set down. "Red Leaves" is an early story, published in Faulkner's first collection, *These Thirteen,* in 1931. Later he included it in his *Collected Stories,* in the group dealing with "The Wilderness."

_____

I

The two Indians crossed the plantation toward the slave quarters. Neat with whitewash, of baked soft brick, the two rows of houses in which lived the slaves belonging to the clan, faced one another across the mild shade of the lane marked and scored with naked feet and with a few homemade toys mute in the dust. There was no sign of life.

"I know what we will find," the first Indian said.

"What we will not find," the second said. Although it was noon, the lane was vacant, the doors of the cabins empty and quiet; no cooking smoke rose from any of the chinked and plastered chimneys.

"Yes. It happened like this when the father of him who is now the Man, died."

"You mean, of him who was the Man."

"Yao."

The first Indian's name was Three Basket. He was perhaps sixty. They were both squat men, a little solid, burgher-like; paunchy, with big heads, big, broad, dust-colored faces of a certain blurred serenity like carved heads on a ruined wall in Siam or Sumatra, looming out of a mist. The sun had done it, the violent sun, the violent shade. Their hair looked like sedge grass on burnt-over land. Clamped through one ear Three Basket wore an enameled snuffbox.

"I have said all the time that this is not the good way. In the old days there were on quarters, no Negroes. A man's time was his own then. He had time. Now he must spend most of it finding work for them who prefer sweating to do."

"They are like horses and dogs."

"They are like nothing in this sensible world. Nothing contents them save sweat. They are worse than the white people."

"It is not as though the Man himself had to find work for them to do."

"You said it. I do not like slavery. It is not the good way. In the old days, there was the good way. But not now."

"You do not remember the old way either."

"I have listened to them who do. And I have tried this way. Man was not made to sweat."

"That's so. See what it has done to their flesh."

"Yes. Black. It has a bitter taste, too."

"You have eaten of it?"

"Once. I was young then, and more hardy in the appetite than now. Now it is different with me."

"Yes. They are too valuable to eat now."

"There is a bitter taste to the flesh which I do not like."

"They are too valuable to eat, anyway, when the white men will give horses for them."

They entered the lane. The mute, meager toys—the fetish-shaped objects made of wood and rags and feathers—lay in the dust about the patinaed doorsteps, among bones and broken gourd dishes. But there was no sound from any cabin, no face in any door; had not been since yesterday, when Issetibbeha died. But they already knew what they would find.

It was in the central cabin, a house a little larger than the others, where at certain phases of the moon the Negroes would gather to begin their ceremonies before removing after nightfall to the creek bottom, where they kept the drums. In this room they kept the minor accessories, the cryptic ornaments, the ceremonial records which consisted of sticks daubed with red clay in symbols. It had a hearth in the center of the floor, beneath a hole in the roof, with a few cold wood ashes and a suspended iron pot. The window shutters were closed; when the two Indians entered, after the abashless sunlight they could distinguish nothing with the eyes save a movement, shadow, out of which eyeballs rolled, so that the place appeared to be full of Negroes. The two Indians stood in the doorway.

"Yao," Basket said. "I said this is not the good way."

"I don't think I want to be here," the second said.

"That is black man's fear which you smell. It does not smell as ours does."

"I don't think I want to be here."

"Your fear has an odor too."

"Maybe it is Issetibbeha which we smell."

"Yao. He knows. He knows what we will find here. He knew when he died what we should find here today." Out of the rank twilight of the room the eyes, the smell, of Negroes rolled about them. "I am Three Basket, whom you know," Basket said into the room. "We are come from the Man. He whom we seek is gone?" The Negroes said nothing. The smell of them, of their bodies, seemed to ebb and flux in the still hot air. They seemed to be musing as one upon something remote, inscrutable. They were like a single octopus. They were like the roots of a huge tree uncovered, the earth broken momentarily upon the writhen, thick, fetid tangle of its lightless and outraged life. "Come," Basket said. "You know our errand. Is he whom we seek gone?"

"They are thinking something," the second said. "I do not want to be here."

"They are knowing something," Basket said.

"They are hiding him, you think?"

"No. He is gone. He has been gone since last night. It happened like this before, when the grandfather of him who is now the Man died. It took us three days to catch him. For three days Doom lay above the ground, saying 'I see my horse and my dog. But I do not see my slave. What have you done with him that you will not permit me to lie quiet?' "

"They do not like to die."

"Yao. They cling. It makes trouble for us, always. A people without honor and without decorum. Always a trouble."

"I do not like it here."

"Nor do I. But then, they are savages; they cannot be expected to regard usage. That is why I say that this way is a bad way."

"Yao. They cling. They would even rather work in the sun than to enter the earth with a chief. But he is gone."

The Negroes had said nothing, made no sound. The white eyeballs rolled, wild, subdued; the smell was rank, violent. "Yes, they fear," the second said. "What shall we do now?"

"Let us go and talk with the Man."

"Will Moketubbe listen?"

"What can he do? He will not like to. But he is the Man now."

"Yao. He is the Man. He can wear the shoes with the red heels all the time now." They turned and went out. There was no door in the door frame. There were no doors in any of the cabins.

"He did that anyway," Basket said.

"Behind Issetibbeha's back. But now they are his shoes, since he is the Man."

"Yao. Issetibbeha did not like it. I have heard. I know that he said to Moketubbe: 'When you are the Man, the shoes will be yours. But until then, they are my shoes.' But now Moketubbe is the Man; he can wear them."

"Yao," the second said. "He is the Man now. He used to wear the shoes behind Issetibbeha's back, and it was not known if Issetibbeha knew this or not. And then Issetibbeha became dead, who was not old, and the shoes are Moketubbe's, since he is the Man now. What do you think of that?"

"I don't think about it," Basket said. "Do you?"

"No," the second said.

"Good," Basket said. "You are wise."

II

The house sat on a knoll, surrounded by oak trees. The front of it was one story in height, composed of the deck house of a steamboat which had gone ashore and which Doom, Issetibbeha's father, had dismantled with his slaves and hauled on cypress rollers twelve miles home overland. It took them five months. His house consisted at the time of one brick wall. He set the steamboat broadside on to the wall, where now the chipped and flaked gilding of the rococo cornices arched in faint splendor above the gilt lettering of the stateroom names above the jalousied doors.

Doom had been born merely a subchief, a Mingo, one of three children on the mother's side of the family. He made a journey—he was a young man then and New Orleans was a European city—from north Mississippi to New Orleans by keel boat, where he met the Chevalier Sœur Blonde de Vitry, a man whose social position, on its face, was as equivocal as Doom's own. In New Orleans, among the gamblers and cutthroats of the river front, Doom, under the tutelage of his patron, passed as the chief, the Man, the hereditary owner of that land which belonged to the male side of the family; it was the Chevalier de Vitry who called him *du homme*, and hence Doom.

They were seen everywhere together—the Indian, the squat man with a bold, inscrutable, underbred face, and the Parisian, the expatriate, the friend, it was said, of Carondelet and the intimate of General Wilkinson. Then they disappeared, the two of them, vanishing from their old equivocal haunts and leaving behind them the legend of the sums which Doom was believed to have won, and some tale about a young woman, daughter of a fairly well-to-do West Indian family, the son and brother of whom sought Doom with a pistol about his old haunts for some time after his disappearance.

Six months later the young woman herself disappeared, boarding the St. Louis packet, which put in one night at a wood landing on the north Mississippi side, where the woman, accompanied by a Negro maid, got off. Four Indians met her with a horse and wagon, and they traveled for three days, slowly, since she was already big with child, to the plantation, where she found that Doom was now chief. He never told her how he accomplished it, save that his uncle and his cousin had died suddenly. At that time the house consisted of a brick wall built by shiftless slaves, against which was propped a thatched lean-to divided into rooms and littered with bones and refuse, set in the center of ten thousand acres of matchless parklike forest where deer grazed like domestic cattle. Doom and the woman were married there a short time before Issetibbeha was born, by a combination itinerant minister and slave trader who arrived on a mule, to the saddle of which was lashed a cotton umbrella and a three-gallon demijohn of whisky. After that, Doom began to acquire more slaves and to cultivate some of his land, as the white people did. But he never had enough for them to do. In utter idleness the majority of them led lives transplanted whole out of African jungles, save on the occasions when, entertaining guests, Doom coursed them with dogs.

When Doom died, Issetibbeha, his son, was nineteen. He became proprietor of the land and of the quintupled herd of blacks for which he had no use at all. Though the title of Man rested with him, there was a hierarchy of cousins and uncles who ruled the clan and who finally gathered in squatting conclave over the Negro question, squatting profoundly beneath the golden names above the doors of the steamboat.

"We cannot eat them," one said.

"Why not?"

"There are too many of them."

"That's true," a third said. "Once we started, we should have to eat them all. And that much flesh diet is not good for man."

"Perhaps they will be like deer flesh. That cannot hurt you."

"We might kill a few of them and not eat them," Issetibbeha said.

They looked at him for a while. "What for?" one said.

"That is true," a second said. "We cannot do that. They are too valuable; remember all the bother they have caused us, finding things for them to do. We must do as the white men do."

"How is that?" Issetibbeha said.

"Raise more Negroes by clearing more land to make corn to feed them, then sell them. We will clear the land and plant it with food and raise Negroes and sell them to the white men for money."

"But what will we do with this money?" a third said.

They thought for a while.

"We will see," the first said. They squatted, profound, grave.

"It means work," the third said.

"Let the Negroes do it," the first said.

"Yao. Let them. To sweat is bad. It is damp. It opens the pores."

"And then the night air enters."

"Yao. Let the Negroes do it. They appear to like sweating."

So they cleared the land with the Negroes and planted it in grain. Up to that time the slaves had lived in a huge pen with a lean-to roof over one corner, like a pen for pigs. But now they began to build quarters, cabins, putting the young Negroes in the cabins in pairs to mate; five years later Issetibbeha sold forty head to a Memphis trader, and he took the money and went abroad upon it, his maternal uncle from New Orleans conducting the trip. At that time the Chevalier Sœur Blonde de Vitry was an old man in Paris, in a toupee and a corset, with a careful toothless old face fixed in a grimace quizzical and profoundly tragic. He borrowed three hundred dollars from Issetibbeha and in return he introduced him into certain circles; a year later Issetibbeha returned home with a gilt bed, a pair of girandoles by whose light it was said that Pompadour arranged her hair while Louis smirked at his mirrored face across her powdered shoulder, and a pair of slippers with red heels. They were too small for him, since he had not worn shoes at all until he reached New Orleans on his way abroad.

He brought the slippers home in tissue paper and kept them in the remaining pocket of a pair of saddlebags filled with cedar shavings, save when he took them out on occasion for his son, Moketubbe, to play with. At three years of age Moketubbe had a broad, flat, Mongolian face that appeared to exist in a complete and unfathomable lethargy, until confronted by the slippers.

Moketubbe's mother was a comely girl whom Issetibbeha had seen one day working in her shift in a melon patch. He stopped and watched her for a while—the broad, solid thighs, the sound back, the serene face. He was on his way to the creek to fish that day, but he didn't go any farther; perhaps while he stood there watching the unaware girl he may have remembered his own mother, the city woman, the fugitive with her fans and laces and her Negro blood, and all the tawdry shabbiness of that sorry affair. Within the year Moketubbe was born; even at three he could not get his feet into the slippers. Watching him in the still, hot afternoons as he struggled with the slippers with a certain monstrous repudiation of fact, Issetibbeha laughed quietly to himself. He laughed at Moketubbe and the shoes for several years, because Moketubbe did not give up trying to put them on until he was sixteen. Then he quit. Or Issetibbeha thought he had. But he had merely quit trying in Issetibbeha's presence. Issetibbeha's newest wife told him that Moketubbe had stolen and hidden the shoes. Issetibbeha quit laughing then, and he sent the woman away, so that he was alone. "Yao," he said. "I too like being alive, it seems." He sent for Moketubbe. "I give them to you," he said.

Moketubbe was twenty-five then, unmarried. Issetibbeha was not tall, but he was taller by six inches than his son and almost a hundred pounds lighter. Moketubbe was already diseased with flesh, with a pale, broad, inert face and dropsical hands and feet. "They are yours now," Issetibbeha said, watching him. Moketubbe had looked at him once when he entered, a glance brief, discreet, veiled.

"Thanks," he said.

Issetibbeha looked at him. He could never tell if Moketubbe saw anything, looked at anything. "Why will it not be the same if I give the slippers to you?"

"Thanks," Moketubbe said. Issetibbeha was using snuff at the time; a white man had shown him how to put the powder into his lip and scour it against his teeth with a twig of gum or of alphea.

"Well," he said, " a man cannot live forever." He looked at his son, then his gaze went blank in turn, unseeing, and he mused for an instant. You could not tell what he was thinking, save that he said half aloud: "Yao. But Doom's uncle had no shoes with red heels." He looked at his son again, fat, inert. "Beneath all that, a man might think of doing anything and it not be known until too late." He sat in a splint chair hammocked with deer thongs. "He cannot even get them on; he and I are both frustrated by the same gross meat which he wears. He cannot even get them on. But is that my fault?"

He lived for five years longer, then he died. He was sick one night, and though the doctor came in a skunk-skin vest and burned sticks, he died before noon.

That was yesterday; the grave was dug, and for twelve hours now the People had been coming in wagons and carriages and on horseback and afoot, to eat the baked dog and the succotash and the yams cooked in ashes and to attend the funeral.

III

"It will be three days," Basket said, as he and the other Indian returned to the house. "It will be three days and the food will not be enough; I have seen it before."

The second Indian's name was Louis Berry. "He will smell too, in this weather."

"Yao. They are nothing but a trouble and a care."

"Maybe it will not take three days."

"They run far. Yao. We will smell this Man before he enters the earth. You watch and see if I am not right."

They approached the house.

"He can wear the shoes now," Berry said. "He can wear them now in man's sight."

"He cannot wear them for a while yet," Basket said. Berry looked at him. "He will lead the hunt."

"Moketubbe?" Berry said. "Do you think he will? A man to whom even talking is travail?"

"What else can he do? It is his own father who will soon begin to smell."

"That is true," Berry said. "There is even yet a price he must pay for the shoes. Yao. He has truly bought them. What do you think?"

"What do you think?"

"What do you think?"

"I think nothing."

"Nor do I. Issetibbeha will not need the shoes now. Let Moketubbe have them; Issetibbeha will not care."

"Yao. Man must die."

"Yao. Let him; there is still the Man."

The bark roof of the porch was supported by peeled cypress poles, high above the texas of the steamboat, shading an unfloored banquette where on the trodden earth mules and horses were tethered in bad weather. On the forward end of the steamboat's deck sat an old man and two women. One of the women was dressing a fowl, the other was shelling corn. The old man was talking. He was barefoot, in a long linen frock coat and a beaver hat.

"This world is going to the dogs," he said. "It is being ruined by white men. We got along fine for years and years, before the white men foisted their Negroes upon us. In the old days the old men sat in the shade and ate stewed deer's flesh and corn and smoked tobacco and talked of honor and grave affairs; now what do we do? Even the old wear themselves into the grave taking care of them that like sweating." When Basket and Berry crossed the deck he ceased and looked up at them. His eyes were querulous, bleared; his face was myriad with tiny wrinkles. "He is fled also," he said.

"Yes," Berry said, "he is gone."

"I knew it. I told them so. It will take three weeks, like when Doom died. You watch and see."

"It was three days, not three weeks," Berry said.

"Were you there?"

"No," Berry said. "But I have heard."

"Well, I was there," the old man said. "For three whole weeks, through the swamps and the briers—" They went on and left him talking.

What had been the saloon of the steamboat was now a shell, rotting slowly; the polished mahogany, the carving glinting momentarily and fading through the mold in figures cabalistic and profound; the gutted windows were like cataracted eyes. It contained a few sacks of seed or grain, and the fore part of the running gear of a barouche, to the axle of which two C-springs rusted in graceful curves, supporting nothing. In one corner a fox cub ran steadily and soundlessly up and down a willow cage; three scrawny gamecocks moved in the dust, and the place was pocked and marked with their dried droppings.

They passed through the brick wall and entered a big room of chinked logs. It contained the hinder part of the barouche, and the dismantled body lying on its side, the window slatted over with willow withes, through which protruded the heads, the still, beady, outraged eyes and frayed combs of still more game chickens. It was floored with packed clay; in one corner leaned a crude plow and two hand-hewn boat paddles. From the ceiling, suspended by four deer thongs, hung the gilt bed which Issetibbeha had fetched from Paris. It had neither mattress nor springs, the frame crisscrossed now by a neat hammocking of thongs.

Issetibbeha had tried to have his newest wife, the young one, sleep in the bed. He was congenitally short of breath himself, and he passed the nights half reclining in his splint chair. He would see her to bed and, later, wakeful, sleeping as he did but three or four hours a night, he would sit in the darkness and simulate slumber and listen to her sneak infinitesimally from the gilt and ribboned bed, to lie on a quilt pallet on the floor until just before daylight. Then she would enter the bed quietly again and in turn simulate slumber, while in the darkness beside her Issetibbeha quietly laughed and laughed.

The girandoles were lashed by thongs to two sticks propped in a corner where a ten-gallon whisky keg lay also. There was a clay hearth; facing it, in the splint chair, Moketubbe sat. He was maybe an inch better than five feet tall, and he weighed two hundred and fifty pounds. He wore a broadcloth coat and no shirt, his round, smooth copper balloon of belly swelling above the bottom piece of a suit of linen underwear. On his feet were the slippers with the red heels. Behind his chair stood a stripling with a punkah-like fan made of fringed paper. Moketubbe sat motionless, with his broad, yellow face with its closed eyes and flat nostrils, his flipperlike arms extended. On his face was an expression profound, tragic, and inert. He did not open his eyes when Basket and Berry came in.

"He has worn them since daylight?" Basket said.

"Since daylight," the stripling said. The fan did not cease. "You can see."

"Yao," Basket said. "We can see." Moketubbe did not move. He looked like an effigy, like a Malay god in frock coat, drawers, naked chest, the trivial scarlet-heeled shoes.

"I wouldn't disturb him, if I were you," the stripling said.

"Not if I were you," Basket said. He and Berry squatted. The stripling moved the fan steadily. "O Man," Basket said, "listen." Moketubbe did not move. "He is gone," Basket said.

"I told you so," the stripling said. "I knew he would flee. I told you."

"Yao," Basket said. "You are not the first to tell us afterward what we should have known before. Why is it that some of you wise men took no steps yesterday to prevent this?"

"He does not wish to die," Berry said.

"Why should he not wish it?" Basket said.

"Because he must die some day is no reason," the stripling said. "That would not convince me either, old man."

"Hold your tongue," Berry said.

"For twenty years," Basket said, "while others of his race sweat in the fields, he served the Man in the shade. Why should he not wish to die, since he did not wish to sweat?"

"And it will be quick," Berry said. "It will not take long."

"Catch him and tell him that," the stripling said.

"Hush," Berry said. They squatted, watching Moketubbe's face. He might have been dead himself. It was as though he were cased so in flesh that even breathing took place too deep within him to show.

"Listen, O Man," Basket said. "Issetibbeha is dead. He waits. His dog and his horse we have. But his slave has fled. The one who held the pot for him, who ate of his food, from his dish, is fled. Issetibbeha waits."

"Yao," Berry said.

"This is not the first time," Basket said. "This happened when Doom, thy grandfather, lay waiting at the door of the earth. He lay waiting three days, saying, 'Where is my Negro?' And Issetibbeha, thy father, answered, 'I will find him. Rest; I will bring him to you so that you may begin the journey.'"

"Yao," Berry said.

Moketubbe had not moved, had not opened his eyes.

"For three days Issetibbeha hunted in the bottom," Basket said. "He did not even return home for food, until the Negro was with him; then he said to Doom, his father, 'Here is thy dog, thy horse, thy Negro; rest.' Issetibbeha, who is dead since yesterday, said it. And now Issetibbeha's Negro is fled. His horse and his dog wait with him, but his Negro is fled."

"Yao," Berry said.

Moketubbe had not moved. His eyes were closed; upon his supine monstrous shape there was a colossal inertia, something profoundly immobile, beyond and impervious to flesh. They watched his face, squatting.

"When thy father was newly the Man, this happened," Basket said.

"And it was Issetibbeha who brought back the slave to where his father waited to enter the earth." Moketubbe's face had not moved, his eyes had not moved. After a while Basket said, "Remove the shoes."

The stripling removed the shoes. Moketubbe began to pant, his bare chest moving deep, as though he were rising from beyond his unfathomed flesh back into life, like up from the water, the sea. But his eyes had not opened yet.

Berry said, "He will lead the hunt."

"Yao," Basket said. "He is the Man. He will lead the hunt."

IV

All that day the Negro, Issetibbeha's body servant, hidden in the barn, watched Issetibbeha's dying. He was forty, a Guinea man. He had a flat nose, a close, small head; the inside corners of his eyes showed red a little, and his prominent gums were a pale bluish red above his square, broad teeth. He had been taken at fourteen by a trader off Kamerun, before his teeth had been filed. He had been Issetibbeha's body servant for twenty-three years.

On the day before, the day on which Issetibbeha lay sick, he returned to the quarters at dusk. In that unhurried hour the smoke of the cooking fires blew slowly across the street from door to door, carrying into the opposite one the smell of the identical meat and bread. The women tended them; the men were gathered at the head of the lane, watching him as he came down the slope from the house, putting his naked feet down carefully in a strange dusk. To the waiting men his eyeballs were a little luminous.

"Issetibbeha is not dead yet," the headman said.

"Not dead," the body servant said. "Who not dead?"

In the dusk they had faces like his, the different ages, the thoughts sealed inscrutable behind faces like the death masks of apes. The smell of the fires, the cooking, blew sharp and slow across the strange dusk, as from another world, above the lane and the pickaninnies naked in the dust.

"If he lives past sundown, he will live until daybreak," one said.

"Who says?"

"Talk says."

"Yao. Talk says. We know but one thing." They looked at the body servant as he stood among them, his eyeballs a little luminous. He was breathing slow and deep. His chest was bare; he was sweating a little. "He knows. He knows it."

"Let us let the drums talk."

"Yao. Let the drums tell it."

The drums began after dark. They kept them hidden in the creek bottom. They were made of hollowed cypress knees, and the Negroes kept them hidden; why, none knew. They were buried in the mud on the bank of a slough; a lad of fourteen guarded them. He was undersized, and a mute; he squatted in the mud there all day, clouded over with mosquitoes, naked save for the mud with which he coated himself against the mosquitoes, and about his neck a fiber bag containing a pig's rib to which black shreds of flesh still adhered, and two scaly barks on a wire. He slobbered onto his clutched knees, drooling; now and then Indians came noiselessly out of the bushes behind him and stood there and contemplated him for a while and went away, and he never knew it.

From the loft of the stable where he lay hidden until dark and after, the Negro could hear the drums. They were three miles away, but he could hear them as though they were in the barn itself below him, thudding and thudding. It was as though he could see the fire too, and the black limbs turning into and out of the flames in copper gleams. Only there would be no fire. There would be no more light there than where he lay in the dusty loft, with the whispering arpeggios of rat feet along the warm and immemorial ax-squared rafters. The only fire there would be the smudge against mosquitoes where the women with nursing children crouched, their heavy sluggish breasts nippled full and smooth into the mouths of men children; contemplative, oblivious of the drumming, since a fire would signify life.

There was a fire in the steamboat, where Issetibbeha lay dying among his wives, beneath the lashed girandoles and the suspended bed. He could see the smoke, and just before sunset he saw the doctor come out, in a waistcoat made of skunk skins, and set fire to two clay-daubed sticks at the bows of the boat deck. "So he is not dead yet," the Negro said into the whispering gloom of the loft, answering himself; he could hear the two voices, himself and himself:

"Who not dead?"

"You are dead."

"Yao, I am dead," he said quietly. He wished to be where the drums were. He imagined himself springing out of the bushes, leaping among the drums on his bare, lean, greasy, invisible limbs. But he could not do that, because man leaped past life, into where death was; he dashed into death and did not die, because when death took a man, it took him just this side of the end of living. It was when death overran him from behind, still in life. The thin whisper of rat feet died in fainting gusts along the rafters. Once he had eaten rat. He was a boy then, but just come to America. They had lived ninety days in a three-foot-high 'tween-deck in tropic latitudes, hearing from topside the drunken New England captain intoning aloud from a book which he did not recognize for ten years afterward to be the Bible. Squatting in the stable so, he had watched the rat, civilized, by association with man reft of its inherent cunning of limb and eye; he had caught it without difficulty, with scarce a movement of his hand, and he ate it slowly, wondering how any of the rats had escaped so long. At that time he was still wearing the single white garment which the trader, a deacon in the Unitarian church, had given him, and he spoke then only his native tongue.

He was naked now, save for a pair of dungaree pants bought by Indians from white men, and an amulet slung on a thong about his hips. The amulet consisted of one half of a mother-of-pearl lorgnon which Issetibbeha had brought back from Paris, and the skull of a cottonmouth moccasin. He had killed the snake himself and eaten it, save the poison head. He lay in the loft, watching the house, the steamboat, listening to the drums, thinking of himself among the drums.

He lay there all night. The next morning he saw the doctor come out, in his skunk vest, and get on his mule and ride away, and he became quite still and watched the final dust from beneath the mule's delicate feet die away, and then he found that he was still breathing and it seemed strange to him that he still breathed air, still needed air. Then he lay and watched quietly, waiting to move, his eyeballs a little luminous, but with a quiet light, and his breathing light and regular, and saw Louis Berry come out and look at the sky. It was good light then, and already five Indians squatted in their Sunday clothes along the steamboat deck; by noon there were twenty-five there. That afternoon they dug the trench in which the meat would be baked, and the yams; by that time there were almost a hundred guests—decorous, quiet, patient in their stiff European finery—and he watched Berry lead Issetibbeha's mare from the stable and tie her to a tree, and then he watched Berry emerge from the house with the old hound which lay beside Issetibbeha's chair. He tied the hound to the tree too, and it sat there, looking gravely about at the faces. Then it began to howl. It was still howling at sundown, when the Negro climbed down the back wall of the barn and entered the spring branch, where it was already dusk. He began to run then. He could hear the hound howling behind him, and near the spring, already running, he passed another Negro. The two men, the one motionless and the other running, looked for an instant at each other as though across an actual boundary between two different worlds. He ran on into full darkness, mouth closed, fists doubled, his broad nostrils bellowing steadily.

He ran on in the darkness. He knew the country well, because he had hunted it often with Issetibbeha, following on his mule the course of the fox or the cat beside Issetibbeha's mare; he knew it as well as did the men who would pursue him. He saw them for the first time shortly before sunset of the second day. He had run thirty miles then, up the creek bottom, before doubling back; lying in a pawpaw thicket he saw the pursuit for the first time. There were two of them, in shirts and straw hats, carrying their neatly rolled trousers under their arms, and they had no weapons. They were middle-aged, paunchy, and they could not have moved very fast anyway; it would be twelve hours before they could return to where he lay watching them. "So I will have until midnight to rest," he said. He was near enough to the plantation to smell the cooking fires, and he thought how he ought to be hungry, since he had not eaten in thirty hours. "But it is more important to rest," he told himself. He continued to tell himself that, lying in the pawpaw thicket, because the effort of resting, the need and the haste to rest, made his heart thud the same as the running had done. It was as though he had forgot how to rest, as though the six hours were not long enough to do it in, to remember again how to do it.

As soon as dark came he moved again. He had thought to keep going steadily and quietly through the night, since there was nowhere for him to go, but as soon as he moved he began to run at top speed, breasting his panting chest, his broad-flaring nostrils through the choked and whipping darkness. He ran for an hour, lost by then, without direction, when suddenly he stopped, and after a time his thudding heart unraveled from the sound of the drums. By the sound they were not two miles away; he followed the sound until he could smell the smudge fire and taste the acrid smoke. When he stood among them the drums did not cease; only the headman came to him where he stood in the drifting smudge, panting, his nostrils flaring and pulsing, the hushed glare of his ceaseless eyeballs in his mud-daubed face as though they were worked from lungs.

"We have expected thee," the headman said. "Go, now."

"Go?"

"Eat, and go. The dead may not consort with the living; thou knowest that."

"Yao. I know that." They did not look at one another. The drums had not ceased.

"Wilt thou eat?" the headman said.

"I am not hungry. I caught a rabbit this afternoon, and ate while I lay hidden."

"Take some cooked meat with thee, then."

He accepted the cooked meat, wrapped in leaves, and entered the creek bottom again; after a while the sound of the drums ceased. He walked steadily until daybreak. "I have twelve hours," he said. "Maybe more, since the trail was followed by night." He squatted and ate the meat and wiped his hands on his thighs. Then he rose and removed the dungaree pants and squatted again beside a slough and coated himself with mud—face, arms, body and legs—and squatted again, clasping his knees, his head bowed. When it was light enough to see, he moved back into the swamp and squatted again and went to sleep so. He did not dream at all. It was well that he moved, for, waking suddenly in broad daylight and the high sun, he saw the two Indians. They still carried their neatly rolled trousers; they stood opposite the place where he lay hidden, paunchy, thick, soft-looking, a little ludicrous in their straw hats and shirt tails.

"This is wearying work," one said.

"I'd rather be at home in the shade myself," the other said. "But there is the Man waiting at the door to the earth."

"Yao." They looked quietly about; stooping, one of them removed from his shirt tail a clot of cockleburs. "Damn that Negro," he said.

"Yao. When have they ever been anything but a trial and a care to us?"

In the early afternoon, from the top of a tree, the Negro looked down into the plantation. He could see Issetibbeha's body in a hammock between the two trees where the horse and the dog were tethered, and the concourse about the steamboat was filled with wagons and horses and mules, with carts and saddle-horses, while in bright clumps the women and the smaller children and the old men squatted about the long trench where the smoke from the barbecuing meat blew slow and thick. The men and the big boys would all be down there in the creek bottom behind him, on the trail, their Sunday clothes rolled carefully up and wedged into tree crotches. There was a clump of men near the door to the house, to the saloon of the steamboat, though, and he watched them, and after a while he saw them bring Moketubbe out in a litter made of buckskin and persimmon poles; high hidden in his leafed nook the Negro, the quarry, looked quietly down upon his irrevocable doom with an expression as profound as Moketubbe's own. "Yao," he said quietly. "He will go then. That man whose body has been dead for fifteen years, he will go also."

In the middle of the afternoon he came face to face with an Indian. They were both on a footlog across a slough—the Negro gaunt, lean, hard, tireless and desperate; the Indian thick, soft-looking, the apparent embodiment of the ultimate and the supreme reluctance and inertia. The Indian made no move, no sound; he stood on the log and watched the Negro plunge into the slough and swim ashore and crash away into the undergrowth.

Just before sunset he lay behind a down log. Up the log in slow procession moved a line of ants. He caught them and ate them slowly, with a kind of detachment, like that of a dinner guest eating salted nuts from a dish. They too had a salt taste, engendering a salivary reaction out of all proportion. He ate them slowly, watching the unbroken line move up the log and into oblivious doom with a steady and terrific undeviation. He had eaten nothing else all day; in his caked mud mask his eyes rolled in reddened rims. At sunset, creeping along the creek bank toward where he had spotted a frog, a cottonmouth moccasin slashed him suddenly across the forearm with a thick, sluggish blow. It struck clumsily, leaving two long slashes across his arm like two razor slashes, and half sprawled with its own momentum and rage, it appeared for the moment utterly helpless with its own awkwardness and choleric anger. "Olé, grandfather," the Negro said. He touched its head and watched it slash him again across his arm, and again, with thick, raking, awkward blows. "It's that I do not wish to die," he said. Then he said it again—"It's that I do not wish to die"—in a quiet tone, of slow and low amaze, as though it were something that, until the words had said themselves, he found that he had not known, or had not known the depth and extent of his desire.

V

Moketubbe took the slippers with him. He could not wear them very long while in motion, not even in the litter where he was slung reclining, so they rested upon a square of fawnskin upon his lap—the cracked, frail slippers a little shapeless now, with their scaled patent-leather surfaces and buckleless tongues and scarlet heels, lying upon the supine obese shape just barely alive, carried through swamp and brier by swinging relays of men who bore steadily all day long the crime and its object, on the business of the slain. To Moketubbe it must have been as though, himself immortal, he were being carried rapidly through hell by doomed spirits which, alive, had contemplated his disaster, and, dead, were oblivious partners to his damnation.

After resting for a while, the litter propped in the center of the squatting circle and Moketubbe motionless in it, with closed eyes and his face at once peaceful for the instant and filled with inescapable foreknowledge, he could wear the slippers for a while. The stripling put them on him, forcing his big, tender, dropsical feet into them; whereupon into his face came again that expression tragic, passive and profoundly attentive, which dyspeptics wear. Then they went on. He made no move, no sound, inert in the rhythmic litter out of some reserve of inertia, or maybe of some kingly virtue such as courage or fortitude. After a time they set the litter down and looked at him, at the yellow face like that of an idol, beaded over with sweat. Then Three Basket or Had-Two-Fathers would say: "Take them off. Honor has been served." They would remove the shoes. Moketubbe's face would not alter, but only then would his breathing become perceptible, going in and out of his pale lips with a faint ah-ah-ah sound, and they would squat again while the couriers and the runners came up.

"Not yet?"

"Not yet. He is going east. By sunset he will reach Mouth of Tippah. Then he will turn back. We may take him tomorrow."

"Let us hope so. It will not be too soon."

"Yao. It has been three days now."

"When Doom died, it took only three days."

"But that was a old man. This one is young."

"Yao. A good race. If he is taken tomorrow, I will win a horse."

"May you win it."

"Yao. This work is not pleasant."

That was the day on which the food gave out at the plantation. The guests returned home and came back the next day with more food, enough for a week longer. On that day Issetibbeha began to smell; they could smell him for a long way up and down the bottom when it got hot toward noon and the wind blew. But they didn't capture the Negro on that day, nor on the next. It was about dusk on the sixth day when the couriers came up to the litter; they had found blood. "He has injured himself."

"Not bad, I hope," Basket said. "We cannot send with Issetibbeha one who will be of no service to him."

"Nor whom Issetibbeha himself will have to nurse and care for," Berry said.

"We do not know," the courier said. "He has hidden himself. He has crept back into the swamp. We have left pickets."

They trotted with the litter now. The place where the Negro had crept into the swamp was an hour away. In the hurry and excitement they had forgotten that Moketubbe still wore the slippers; when they reached the place Moketubbe had fainted. They removed the slippers and brought him to.

With dark, they formed a circle about the swamp. They squatted, clouded over with gnats and mosquitoes; the evening star burned low and close down the west, and the constellations began to wheel overhead. "We will give him time," they said. "Tomorrow is just another name for today."

"Yao. Let him have time." Then they ceased, and gazed as one into the darkness where the swamp lay. After a while the noise ceased, and soon the courier came out of the darkness.

"He tried to break out."

"But you turned him back?"

"He turned back. We feared for a moment, the three of us. We could smell him creeping in the darkness, and we could smell something else, which we did not know. That was why we feared, until he told us. He said to slay him there, since it would be dark and he would not have to see the face when it came. But it was not that which we smelled; he told us what it was. A snake had struck him. That was two days ago. The arm swelled, and it smelled bad. But it was not that which we smelled then, because the swelling had gone down and his arm was no larger than that of a child. He showed us. We felt the arm, all of us did; it was no larger than that of a child. He said to give him a hatchet so he could chop the arm off. But tomorrow is today also."

"Yao. Tomorrow is today."

"We feared for a while. Then he went back into the swamp."

"That is good."

"Yao. We feared. Shall I tell the Man?"

"I will see," Basket said. He went away. The courier squatted, telling again about the Negro. Basket returned. "The Man says that it is good. Return to your post."

The courier crept away. They squatted about the litter; now and then they slept. Sometime after midnight the Negro waked them. He began to shout and talk to himself, his voice coming sharp and sudden out of the darkness, then he fell silent. Dawn came; a white crane flapped slowly across the jonquil sky. Basket was awake. "Let us go now," he said. "It is today."

Two Indians entered the swamp, their movements noisy. Before they reached the Negro they stopped, because he began to sing. They could see him, naked and mud-caked, sitting on a log, singing. They squatted silently a short distance away, until he finished. He was chanting something in his own language, his face lifted to the rising sun. His voice was clear, full, with a quality wild and sad. "Let him have time," the Indians said, squatting, patient, waiting. He ceased and they approached. He looked back and up at them through the cracked mud mask. His eyes were bloodshot, his lips cracked upon his square short teeth. The mask of mud appeared to be loose on his face, as if he might have lost flesh since he put it there; he held his left arm close to his breast. From the elbow down it was caked and shapeless with black mud. They could smell him, a rank smell. He watched them quietly until one touched him on the arm. "Come," the Indian said. "You ran well. Do not be ashamed."

VI

As they neared the plantation in the tainted bright morning, the Negro's eyes began to roll a little, like those of a horse. The smoke from the cooking pit blew low along the earth and upon the squatting and waiting guests about the yard and upon the steamboat deck, in their bright, stiff, harsh finery; the women, the children, the old men. They had sent couriers along the bottom, and another on ahead, and Issetibbeha's body had already been removed to where the grave waited, along with the horse and the dog, though they could still smell him in death about the house where he had lived in life. The guests were beginning to move toward the grave when the bearers of Moketubbe's litter mounted the slope.

The Negro was the tallest there, his high, close, mud-caked head looming above them all. He was breathing hard, as though the desperate effort of the six suspended and desperate days had catapulted upon him at once; although they walked slowly, his naked scarred chest rose and fell above the close-clutched left arm. He looked this way and that continuously, as if he were not seeing, as though sight never quite caught up with the looking. His mouth was open a little upon his big white teeth; he began to pant. The already moving guests halted, pausing, looking back, some with pieces of meat in their hands, as the Negro looked about at their faces with his wild, restrained, unceasing eyes.

"Will you eat first?" Basket said. He had to say it twice.

"Yes," the Negro said. "That's it. I want to eat."

The throng had begun to press back toward the center; the word passed to the outermost: "He will eat first."

They reached the steamboat. "Sit down," Basket said. The Negro sat on the edge of the deck. He was still panting, his chest rising and falling, his head ceaseless with its white eyeballs, turning from side to side. It was as if the inability to see came from within, from hopelessness, not from absence of vision. They brought food and watched quietly as he tried to eat it. He put the food into his mouth and chewed it, but chewing, the half-masticated matter began to emerge from the corners of his mouth and to drool down his chin, onto his chest, and after a while he stopped chewing and sat there, naked, covered with dried mud, the plate on his knees, and his mouth filled with a mass of chewed food, open, his eyes wide and unceasing, panting and panting. They watched him, patient, implacable, waiting.

"Come," Basket said at last.

"It's water I want," the Negro said. "I want water."

The well was a little way down the slope toward the quarters. The slope lay dappled with the shadows of noon, of that peaceful hour when, Issetibbeha napping in his chair and waiting for the noon meal and the long afternoon to sleep in, the Negro, the body servant, would be free. He would sit in the kitchen door then, talking with the women who prepared the food. Beyond the kitchen the lane between the quarters would be quiet, peaceful, with the women talking to one another across the lane and the smoke of the dinner fires blowing upon the pickaninnies like ebony toys in the dust.

"Come," Basket said.

The Negro walked among them, taller than any. The guests were moving on toward where Issetibbeha and the horse and the dog waited. The Negro walked with his high ceaseless head, his panting chest. "Come," Basket said. "You wanted water."

"Yes," the Negro said. "Yes." He looked back at the house, then down to the quarters, where today no fire burned, no face showed in any door, no pickaninny in the dust, panting. "It struck me here, raking me across this arm; once, twice, three times. I said, 'Olé, Grandfather.'"

"Come now," Basket said. The Negro was still going through the motion of walking, his knee action high, his head high, as though he were on a treadmill. His eyeballs had a wild, restrained glare, like those of a horse. "You wanted water," Basket said. "Here it is."

There was a gourd in the well. They dipped it full and gave it to the Negro, and they watched him try to drink. His eyes had not ceased as he tilted the gourd slowly against his caked face. They could watch his throat working and the bright water cascading from either side of the gourd, down his chin and breast. Then the water stopped. "Come," Basket said.

"Wait," the Negro said. He dipped the gourd again and tilted it against his face, beneath his ceaseless eyes. Again they watched his throat working and the unswallowed water sheathing broken and myriad down his chin, channeling his caked chest. They waited, patient, grave, decorous, implacable; clansman and guest and kin. Then the water ceased, though still the empty gourd tilted higher and higher, and still his black throat aped the vain motion of his frustrated swallowing. A piece of water-loosened mud carried away from his chest and broke at his muddy feet, and in the empty gourd they could hear his breath: ah-ah-ah.

"Come," Basket said, taking the gourd from the Negro and hanging it back in the well.

MY GRANDMOTHER MILLARD[1]

Faulkner calls the Civil War period in Yoknapatawpha County "the middle ground" of its history. Memories of the war haunt the modern story of the County; and these bitter memories have been carried over into a later time, where they are no longer relevant. Yet they linger as if the war were still on, or had just been fought. And it is with these memories that Faulkner has been concerned. He has written, however, a series of tales dealing explicitly with "the middle ground," seeking to recapture the actual moment of the Southern tragedy. Certain of these stories, loosely strung together, constitute *The Unvanquished*, published in 1938. Each episode is a story in itself, and in nearly all the episodes is to be found the indomitable Grandmother Millard. She is decidedly one of the unvanquished. She maintains her dignity and her authority in a world crumbling about her; she tries to carry on the old order in the midst of chaos. Whatever may happen to the South, the personal world of Grandmother Millard cannot disintegrate.

The comic episode here recounted by Faulkner, in spite of its loose and digressive storytelling, reveals the strong vein of fancy and of humor he is capable of injecting into narrative. The digressions tend to add charm to the tale: they remind one of the way in which Cervantes, in *Don Quixote*, rambles and philosophizes, but comes back always to his main story amid an embroidery of anecdote. We meet here certain figures whose descendants will be subjects of later novels and stories, not least Ab Snopes, the self-styled "horse-captain" concerned however not with fighting but with horse-thievery. In this tale Faulkner shows how much of the detail of daily life, and the gentle ironies of habit and custom, can exist on the margin of the large tragedy of war and national disaster.

I

It would be right after supper, before we had left the table. At first, beginning with the day the news came that the Yankees had taken Memphis, we did it three nights in succession. But after that, as we got better and better and faster and faster, once a week suited Granny. Then after Cousin Melisandre finally got out of Memphis and came to live with us, it would be just once a month, and when the regiment in Virginia voted Father out of the colonelcy and he came home and stayed three months while he made a crop and got over his mad and organized his cavalry troop for General Forrest's command, we quit doing it at all.

[1] The full title of this story is "My Grandmother Millard and General Bedford Forrest and The Battle of Harrykin Creek."

That is, we did it one time with Father there too, watching, and that night Ringo and I heard him laughing in the library, the first time he had laughed since he came home, until in about a half a minute Granny came out already holding her skirts up and went sailing up the stairs. So we didn't do it any more until Father had organized his troop and was gone again.

Granny would fold her napkin beside her plate. She would speak to Ringo standing behind her chair without even turning her head: "Go call Joby and Lucius."

And Ringo would go back through the kitchen without stopping. He would just say, "All right. Look out," at Louvinia's back and go to the cabin and come back with not only Joby and Lucius and the lighted lantern but Philadelphia too, even though Philadelphia wasn't going to do anything but stand and watch and then follow to the orchard and back to the house until Granny said we were done for that time and she and Lucius could go back home to bed. And we would bring down from the attic the big trunk (we had done it so many times by now that we didn't even need the lantern any more to go to the attic and get the trunk) whose lock it was my job to oil every Monday morning with a feather dipped in chicken fat, and Louvinia would come in from the kitchen with the unwashed silver from supper in a dishpan under one arm and the kitchen clock under the other and set the clock and the dishpan on the table and take from her apron pocket a pair of Granny's rolled-up stockings and hand them to Granny and Granny would unroll the stockings and take from the toe of one of them a wadded rag and open the rag and take out the key to the trunk and unpin her watch from her bosom and fold it into the rag and put the rag back into the stocking and roll the stockings back into a ball and put the ball into the trunk. Then with Cousin Melisandre and Philadelphia watching, and Father too on that one time when he was there, Granny would stand facing the clock, her hands raised and about eight inches apart and her neck bowed so she could watch the clock-face over her spectacles, until the big hand reached the nearest hour-mark.

The rest of us watched her hands. She wouldn't speak again. She didn't need to. There would be just the single light loud pop of her palms when the hand came to the nearest hour-mark; sometimes we would be already moving, even before her hands came together, all of us that is except Philadelphia. Granny wouldn't let her help at all, because of Lucius, even though Lucius had done nearly all the digging of the pit and did most of the carrying of the trunk each time. But Philadelphia had to be there. Granny didn't have to tell her but once. "I want the wives of all the free men here too," Granny said. "I want all of you free folks to watch what the rest of us that aint free have to do to keep that way."

That began about eight months ago. One day even I realized that something had happened to Lucius. Then I knew that Ringo had already seen it and that he knew what it was, so that when at last Louvinia came and told Granny, it was not as if Lucius had dared his mother to tell her but as if he had actually forced somebody, he didn't care who, to tell her. He had said it more than once, in the cabin one night probably for the first time, then after that in other places and to other people, to Negroes from other plantations even. Memphis was already gone then, and New Orleans, and all we had left of the River was Vicksburg and although we didn't believe it then, we wouldn't have that long. Then one morning Louvinia came in where Granny was cutting down the worn-out uniform pants Father had worn home from Virginia so they would fit me, and told Granny how Lucius was saying that soon the Yankees would have all of Mississippi and Yoknapatawpha County too and all the niggers would be free and that when that happened, he was going to be long gone. Lucius was working in the garden that morning. Granny went out to the back gallery, still carrying the pants and the needle. She didn't even push her spectacles up. She said, "You, Lucius," just once, and Lucius came out of the garden with the hoe and Granny stood looking down at him over the spectacles as she looked over them at everything she did, from reading or sewing to watching the clock-face until the instant came to start burying the silver.

"You can go now," she said. "You needn't wait on the Yankees."

"Go?" Lucius said. "I aint free."

"You've been free for almost three minutes," Granny said. "Go on."

Lucius blinked his eyes while you could have counted about ten. "Go where?" he said.

"I can't tell you," Granny said. "I aint free. I would imagine you will have all Yankeedom to move around in."

Lucius blinked his eyes. He didn't look at Granny now. "Was that all you wanted?" he said.

"Yes," Granny said. So he went back to the garden. And that was the last we heard about being free from him. That is, it quit showing in the way he acted, and if he talked any more of it, even Louvinia never thought it was worth bothering Granny with. It was Granny who would do the reminding of it, especially to Philadelphia, especially on the nights when we would stand like race-horses at the barrier, watching Granny's hands until they clapped together.

Each one of us knew exactly what he was to do. I would go upstairs for Granny's gold hatpin and her silver-headed umbrella and her plumed Sunday hat because she had already sent her ear-rings and brooch to Richmond a long time ago, and to Father's room for his silver-backed brushes and to Cousin Melisandre's room after she came to live with us for her things because the one time Granny let Cousin Melisandre try to help too, Cousin Melisandre brought all her dresses down. Ringo would go to the parlor for the candlesticks and Granny's dulcimer and the medallion of Father's mother back in Carolina. And we would run back to the dining-room where Louvinia and Lucius would have the sideboard almost cleared, and Granny still standing there and watching the clock-face and the trunk both now with her hands ready to pop again and they would pop and Ringo and I would stop at the cellar door just long enough to snatch up the shovels and run on to the orchard and snatch the brush and grass and the criss-crossed sticks away and have the pit open and ready by the time we saw them coming: first Louvinia with the lantern, then Joby and Lucius with the trunk and Granny walking beside it and Cousin Melisandre and Philadelphia (and on that one time Father, walking along and laughing) following behind. And on that first night, the kitchen clock wasn't in the trunk. Granny was carrying it, while Louvinia held the lantern so that Granny could watch the hand, Granny made us put the trunk into the pit and shovel the dirt back and smooth it off and lay the brush and grass back over it again and then dig up the trunk and carry it back to the house. And one night, it seemed like we had been bringing the trunk down from the attic and putting the silver into it and carrying it out to the pit and uncovering the pit and then covering the pit again and turning around and carrying the trunk back to the house and taking the silver out and putting it back where we got it from all winter and all summer too;—that night, and I don't know who thought of it first, maybe it was all of us at once. But anyway the clock-hand had passed four hour-marks before Granny's hands even popped for Ringo and me to run and open the pit. And they came with the trunk and Ringo and I hadn't even put down the last armful of brush and sticks, to save having to stoop to pick it up again, and Lucius hadn't even put down his end of the trunk for the same reason and I reckon Louvinia was the only one that knew what was coming next because Ringo and I didn't know that the kitchen clock was still sitting on the dining-room table. Then Granny spoke. It was the first time we had ever heard her speak between when she would tell Ringo, "Go call Joby and Lucius," and then tell us both about thirty minutes later: "Wash your feet and go to bed." It was not loud and not long, just two words: "Bury it." And we lowered the trunk into the pit and Joby and Lucius threw the dirt back in and even then Ringo and I didn't move with the brush until Granny spoke again, not loud this time either: "Go on. Hide the pit." And we put the brush back and Granny said, "Dig it up." And we dug up the trunk and carried it back into the house and put the things back where we got them from and that was when I saw the kitchen clock still sitting on the dining-room table. And we all stood there watching Granny's hands until they popped together and that time we filled the trunk and carried it out to the orchard and lowered it into the pit quicker than we had ever done before.

II

And then when the time came to really bury the silver, it was too late. After it was all over and Cousin Melisandre and Cousin Philip were finally married and Father had got done laughing, Father said that always happened when a heterogeneous collection of people who were cohered simply by an uncomplex will for freedom engaged with a tyrannous machine. He said they would always lose the first battles, and if they were outnumbered and outweighed enough, it would seem to an outsider that they were going to lose them all. But they would not. They could not be defeated; if they just willed that freedom strongly and completely enough to sacrifice all else for it—ease and comfort and fatness of spirit and all, until whatever it was they had left would be enough, no matter how little it was—that very freedom itself would finally conquer the machine as a negative force like drouth or flood could strangle it. And later still, after two more years and we knew we were going to lose the war, he was still saying that. He said, "I won't see it but you will. You will see it in the next war, and in all the wars Americans will have to fight from then on. There will be men from the South in the forefront of all the battles, even leading some of them, helping those who conquered us defend that same freedom which they believed they had taken from us." And that happened: thirty years later, and General Wheeler, whom Father would have called apostate, commanding in Cuba, and whom old General Early did call apostate and matricide too in the office of the Richmond editor when he said: "I would like to have lived so that when my time comes, I will see Robert Lee again. But since I haven't, I'm certainly going to enjoy watching the devil burn that blue coat off Joe Wheeler."

We didn't have time. We didn't even know there were any Yankees in Jefferson, let alone within a mile of Sartoris. There never had been many. There was no railroad then and no river big enough for big boats and nothing in Jefferson they would have wanted even if they had come, since this was before Father had had time to worry them enough for General Grant to issue a general order with a reward for his capture. So we had got used to the war. We thought of it as being definitely fixed and established as a railroad or a river is, moving east along the railroad from Memphis and south along the River toward Vicksburg. We had heard tales of Yankee pillage and most of the people around Jefferson stayed ready to bury their silver fast too, though I don't reckon any of them practiced doing it like we did. But nobody we knew was even kin to anyone who had been pillaged, and so I don't think that even Lucius really expected any Yankees until that morning.

It was about eleven o'clock. The table was already set for dinner and everybody was beginning to kind of ease up so we would be sure to hear when Louvinia went out to the back gallery and rang the bell, when Ab Snopes came in at a dead run, on a strange horse as usual. He was a member of Father's troop. Not a fighting member; he called himself father's horse-captain, whatever he meant by it, though we had a pretty good idea, and none of us at least knew what he was doing in Jefferson when the troop was supposed to be up in Tennessee with General Bragg, and probably nobody anywhere knew the actual truth about how he got the horse, galloping across the yard and right through one of Granny's flower beds because I reckon he figured that carrying a message he could risk it, and on around to the back because he knew that, message or no message, he better not come to Granny's front door hollering that way, sitting that strange blown horse with a U.S. army brand on it you could read three hundred yards and yelling up at Granny that General Forrest was in Jefferson but there was a whole regiment of Yankee cavalry not a half a mile down the road.

So we never had time. Afterward Father admitted that Granny's error was not in strategy nor tactics either, even though she had copied from someone else. Because he said it had been a long time now since originality had been a component of military success. It just happened too fast. I went for Joby and Lucius and Philadelphia because Granny had already sent Ringo down to the road with a cup towel to wave when they came in sight. Then she sent me to the front window where I could watch Ringo. When Ab Snopes came back from hiding his new Yankee horse, he offered to go upstairs to get the things there. Granny had told us a long time ago never to let Ab Snopes go anywhere about the house unless somebody was with him. She said she would rather have Yankees in the house any day because at least Yankees would have more delicacy, even if it wasn't anything but good sense, than to steal a spoon or candlestick and then try to sell it to one of her own neighbors, as Ab Snopes would probably do. She didn't even answer him. She just said, "Stand over there by that door and be quiet." So Cousin Melisandre went upstairs after all and Granny and Philadelphia went to the parlor for the candlesticks and the medallion and the dulcimer, Philadelphia not only helping this time, free or not, but Granny wasn't even using the clock.

It just all happened at once. One second Ringo was sitting on the gatepost, looking up the road. The next second he was standing on it and waving the cup towel and then I was running and hollering, back to the dining-room, and I remember the whites of Joby's and Lucius's and Philadelphia's eyes and I remembered Cousin Melisandre's eyes where she leaned against the sideboard with the back of her hand against her mouth, and Granny and Louvinia and Ab Snopes glaring at one another across the trunk and I could hear Louvinia's voice even louder than mine:

"Miz Cawmpson! Miz Cawmpson!"

"What?" Granny cried. "What? Mrs. Compson?" Then we all remembered. It was when the first Yankee scouting patrol entered Jefferson over a year ago. The war was new then and I suppose General Compson was the only Jefferson soldier they had heard of yet. Anyway, the officer asked someone in the Square where General Compson lived and old Doctor Holston sent his Negro boy by back alleys and across lots to warn Mrs. Compson in time, and the story was how the Yankee officer sent some of his men through the empty house and himself rode around to the back where old Aunt Roxanne was standing in front of the outhouse behind the closed door of which Mrs. Compson was sitting, fully dressed even to her hat and parasol, on the wicker hamper containing her plate and silver. "Miss in dar," Roxanne said. "Stop where you is." And the story told how the Yankee officer said, "Excuse me," and raised his hat and even backed the horse a few steps before he turned and called his men and rode away. "The privy!" Granny cried.

"Hell fire, Miz Millard!" Ab Snopes said. And Granny never said anything. It wasn't like she didn't hear, because she was looking right at him. It was like she didn't care; that she might have even said it herself. And that shows how things were then: we just never had time for anything. "Hell fire," Ab Snopes said, "all north Missippi has done heard about that! There aint a white lady between here and Memphis that aint setting in the back house on a grip full of silver right this minute."

"Then we're already late," Granny said. "Hurry."

"Wait!" Ab Snopes said. "Wait! Even them Yankees have done caught onto that by now!"

"Then let's hope these are different Yankees," Granny said. "Hurry."

"But Miz Millard!" Ab Snopes cried. "Wait! Wait!"

But then we could hear Ringo yelling down at the gate and I remember Joby and Lucius and Philadelphia and Louvinia and the balloon-like swaying of Cousin Melisandre's skirts as they ran across the back yard, the trunk somewhere among them; I remember how Joby and Lucius tumbled the trunk into the little tall narrow flimsy sentry-box and Louvinia thrust Cousin Melisandre in and slammed the door and we could hear Ringo yelling good now, almost to the house, and then I was back at the front window and I saw them just as they swept around the house in a kind of straggling-clump—six men in blue, riding fast yet with something curious in the action of the horses, as if they were not only yoked together in spans but were hitched to a single wagon-tongue, then Ringo on foot running and not yelling now, and last of all the seventh rider, bareheaded and standing in his stirrups and with a sabre over his head. Then I was on the back gallery again, standing beside Granny above that moil of horses and men in the yard, and she was wrong. It was as if these were not only the same ones who had been at Mrs. Compson's last year, but somebody had even told them exactly where our outhouse was. The horses were yoked in pairs, but it was not a wagon-tongue, it was a pole, almost a log, twenty feet long, slung from saddle to saddle between the three span; and I remember the faces, unshaven and wan and not so much peering as frantically gleeful, glaring up at us for an instant before the men leaped down and unslung the pole and jerked the horses aside and picked up the pole, three to a side, and began to run across the yard with it as the last rider came around the house, in gray (an officer: it was Cousin Philip, though of course we didn't know that then, and there was going to be a considerable more uproar and confusion before he finally became Cousin Philip and of course we didn't know that either), the sabre still lifted and not only standing in the stirrups but almost lying down along the horse's neck. The six Yankees never saw him. And we used to watch Father drilling his troop in the pasture, changing them from column to troop front at full gallop, and you could hear his voice even above the sound of the galloping hooves but it wasn't a bit louder than Granny's. "There's a lady in there!" she said. But the Yankees never heard her any more than they had seen Cousin Philip yet, the whole mass of them, the six men running with the pole and Cousin Philip on the horse, leaning out above them with a lifted sabre, rushing on across the yard until the end of the pole struck the outhouse door. It didn't just overturn, it exploded. One second it stood there, tall and narrow and flimsy; the next second it was gone and there was a boil of yelling men in blue coats darting and dodging around under Cousin Philip's horse and the flashing sabre until they could find a chance to turn and run. Then there was a scatter of planks and shingles and Cousin Melisandre sitting beside the trunk in the middle of it, in the spread of her hoops, her eyes shut and her mouth open, still screaming, and after a while a feeble popping of pistol-shots from down along the creek that didn't sound any more like war than a boy with firecrackers.

"I tried to tell you to wait!" Ab Snopes said behind us, "I tried to tell you them Yankees had done caught on!"

After Joby and Lucius and Ringo and I finished burying the trunk in the pit and hiding the shovel-marks, I found Cousin Philip in the summer house. His sabre and belt were propped against the wall but I don't reckon even he knew what had become of his hat. He had his coat off too and was wiping it with his handkerchief and watching the house with one eye around the edge of the door. When I came in he straightened up and I thought at first he was looking at me. Then I don't know what he was looking at. "That beautiful girl," he said. "Fetch me a comb."

"They're waiting for you in the house," I said. "Granny wants to know what's the matter." Cousin Melisandre was all right now. It took Louvinia and Philadelphia both and finally Granny to get her into the house but Louvinia brought the elder-flower wine before Granny had time to send her after it and now Cousin Melisandre and Granny were waiting in the parlor.

"Your sister," Cousin Philip said. "And a hand-mirror."

"No, Sir," I said. "She's just our cousin. From Memphis. Granny says—" Because he didn't know Granny. It was pretty good for her to wait any time for anybody. But he didn't even let me finish.

"That beautiful, tender girl," he said. "And send a nigger with a basin of water and a towel." I went back toward the house. This time when I looked back I couldn't see his eye around the door-edge. "And a clothes brush," he said.

Granny wasn't waiting very much. She was at the front door. "Now what?" she said. I told her. "Does the man think we are giving a ball here in the middle of the day? Tell him I said to come on in and wash on the back gallery like we do. Louvinia's putting dinner on, and we're already late." But Granny didn't know Cousin Philip either. I told her again. She looked at me. "What did he say?" she said.

"He didn't say anything," I said. "Just that beautiful girl."

"That's all he said to me too," Ringo said. I hadn't heard him come in. " 'Sides the soap and water. Just that beautiful girl."

"Was he looking at you either when he said it?" I said.

"No," Ringo said. "I just thought for a minute he was."

Now Granny looked at Ringo and me both. "Hah," she said, and afterward when I was older I found out that Granny already knew Cousin Philip too, that she could look at one of them and know all the other Cousin Melisandres and Cousin Philips both without having to see them. "I sometimes think that bullets are just about the least fatal things that fly, especially in war.—All right," she said. "Take him his soap and water. But hurry."

We did. This time he didn't say "that beautiful girl." He said it twice. He took off his coat and handed it to Ringo. "Brush it good," he said. "Your sister, I heard you say."

"No, you didn't," I said.

"No matter," he said. "I want a nosegay. To carry in my hand."

"Those flowers are Granny's," I said.

"No matter," he said. He rolled up his sleeves and began to wash. "A small one. About a dozen blooms. Get something pink."

I went and got the flowers. I don't know whether Granny was still at the front door or not. Maybe she wasn't. At least she never said anything. So I picked the ones Ab Snopes' new Yankee horse had already trampled down and wiped the dirt off of them and straightened them out and went back to the summer house where Ringo was holding the hand-glass while Cousin Philip combed his hair. Then he put on his coat and buckled on his sabre again and held his feet out one at a time for Ringo to wipe his boots off with the towel, and Ringo saw it. I wouldn't have spoken at all because we were already later for dinner than ever now, even if there hadn't never been a Yankee on the place. "You tore your britches on them Yankees," Ringo said.

So I went back to the house. Granny was standing in the hall. This time she just said, "Yes?" It was almost quiet.

"He tore his britches," I said. And she knew more about Cousin Philip than even Ringo could find out by looking at him. She had the needle already threaded in the bosom of her dress. And I went back to the summer house and then we came back to the house and up to the front door and I waited for him to go into the hall but he didn't, he just stood there holding the nosegay in one hand and his hat in the other, not very old, looking at that moment anyway not very much older than Ringo and me for all his braid and sash and sabre and boots and spurs, and even after just two years looking like all our soldiers and most of the other people too did: as if it had been so long now since he had had all he wanted to eat at one time that even his memory and palate had forgotten and only his body remembered, standing there with his nosegay and that beautiful-girl look in his face like he couldn't have seen anything even if he had been looking at it.

"No," he said. "Announce me. It should be your nigger. But no matter." He said his full name, all three of them, twice, as if he thought I might forget them before I could reach the parlor.

"Go on in," I said. "They're waiting for you. They had already been waiting for you even before you found your pants were torn."

"Announce me," he said. He said his name again. "Of Tennessee. Lieutenant, Savage's Battalion, Forrest's Command, Provisional Army, Department of the West."

So I did. We crossed the hall to the parlor, where Granny stood between Cousin Melisandre's chair and the table where the decanter of elder-flower wine and three fresh glasses and even a plate of the tea cakes Louvinia had learned to make from cornmeal and molasses were sitting, and he stopped again at that door too and I know he couldn't even see Cousin Melisandre for a minute, even though he never had looked at anything else but her. "Lieutenant Philip St-Just Backhouse," I said. I said it loud, because he had repeated it to me three times so I would be sure to get it right and I wanted to say it to suit him too since even if he had made us a good hour late for dinner, at least he had saved the silver. "Of Tennessee," I said. "Savage's Battalion, Forrest's Command, Provisional Army, Department of the West."

While you could count maybe five, there wasn't anything at all. Then Cousin Melisandre screamed. She sat bolt upright on the chair like she had sat beside the trunk in the litter of planks and shingles in the back yard this morning, with her eyes shut and her mouth open again, screaming.

III

So we were still another half an hour late for dinner. Though this time it never needed anybody but Cousin Philip to get Cousin Melisandre upstairs. All he needed to do was to try to speak to her again. Then Granny came back down and said, "Well, if we don't want to just quit and start calling it supper, we'd better walk in and eat it within the next hour and a half at least." So we walked in. Ab Snopes was already waiting in the dining-room. I reckon he had been waiting longer than anybody, because after all Cousin Melisandre wasn't any kin to him. Ringo drew Granny's chair and we sat down. Some of it was cold. The rest of it had been on the stove so long now that when you ate it it didn't matter whether it was cold or not. But Cousin Philip didn't seem to mind. And maybe it didn't take his memory very long to remember again what it was like to have all he wanted to eat, but I don't think his palate ever tasted any of it. He would sit there eating like he hadn't seen any food of any kind in at least a week, and like he was expecting what was even already on his fork to vanish before he could get it into his mouth. Then he would stop with the fork halfway to his mouth and sit there looking at Cousin Melisandre's empty place, laughing. That is, I don't know what else to call it but laughing. Until at last I said,

"Why don't you change your name?"

Then Granny quit eating too. She looked at me over her spectacles. Then she took both hands and lifted the spectacles up her nose until she could look at me through them. Then she even pushed the spectacles up into her front hair and looked at me. "That's the first sensible thing I've heard said on this place since eleven o'clock this morning," she said. "It's so sensible and simple that I reckon only a child could have thought of it." She looked at him. "Why don't you?"

He laughed some more. That is, his face did the same way and he made the same sound again. "My grandfather was at King's Mountain, with Marion all through Carolina. My uncle was defeated for Governor of Tennessee by a corrupt and traitorous cabal of tavern-keepers and Republican Abolitionists, and my father died at Chapultepec. After that, the name they bore is not mine to change. Even my life is not mine so long as my country lies bleeding and ravished beneath an invader's iron heel." Then he stopped laughing, or whatever it was. Then his face looked surprised. Then it quit looking surprised, the surprise fading out of it steady at first and gradually faster but not very much faster like the heat fades out of a piece of iron on a blacksmith's anvil until his face just looked amazed and quiet and almost peaceful. "Unless I lose it in battle," he said.

"You can't very well do that sitting here," Granny said.

"No," he said. But I don't think he even heard her except with his ears. He stood up. Even Ab Snopes was watching him now, his knife stopped halfway to his mouth with a wad of greens on the end of the blade. "Yes," Cousin Philip said. His face even had the beautiful-girl look on it again. "Yes," he said. He thanked Granny for his dinner. That is, I reckon that's what he had told his mouth to say. It didn't make much sense to us, but I don't think he was paying any attention to it at all. He bowed. He wasn't looking at Granny nor at anything else. He said "Yes" again. Then he went out. Ringo and I followed to the front door and watched him mount his horse and sit there for a minute, bareheaded, looking up at the upstairs windows. It was Granny's room he was looking at, with mine and Ringo's room next to it. But Cousin Melisandre couldn't have seen him even if she had been in either one of them, since she was in bed on the other side of the house with Philadelphia probably still wringing the cloths out in cold water to lay on her head. He sat the horse well. He rode it well too: light and easy and back in the saddle and toes in and perpendicular from ankle to knee as Father had taught me. It was a good horse too.

"It's a damn good horse," I said.

"Git the soap," Ringo said.

But even then I looked quick back down the hall, even if I could hear

Granny talking to Ab Snopes in the dining-room. "She's still in there," I said.

"Hah," Ringo said. "I done tasted soap in my mouth for a cuss I thought was a heap further off than that."

Then Cousin Philip spurred the horse and was gone. Or so Ringo and I thought. Two hours ago none of us had ever even heard of him; Cousin Melisandre had seen him twice and sat with her eyes shut screaming both times. But after we were older, Ringo and I realized that Cousin Philip was probably the only one in the whole lot of us that really believed even for one moment that he had said goodbye forever, that not only Granny and Louvinia knew better but Cousin Melisandre did too, no matter what his last name had the bad luck to be.

We went back to the dining-room. Then I realized that Ab Snopes had been waiting for us to come back. Then we both knew he was going to ask Granny something because nobody wanted to be alone when they had to ask Granny something even when they didn't know they were going to have trouble with it. We had known Ab for over a year now. I should have known what it was like Granny already did. He stood up. "Well, Miz Millard," he said. "I figger you'll be safe all right from now on, with Bed Forrest and his boys right there in Jefferson. But until things quiet down a mite more, I'll just leave the horses in your lot for a day or two."

"What horses?" Granny said. She and Ab didn't just look at one another. They watched one another.

"Them fresh-captured horses from this morning," Ab said.

"What horses?" Granny said. Then Ab said it.

"My horses." Ab watched her.

"Why?" Granny said. But Ab knew what she meant.

"I'm the only grown man here," he said. Then he said, "I see them first. They were chasing me before——" Then he said, talking fast now; his eyes had gone kind of glazed for a second but now they were bright again, looking in the stubbly dirt-colored fuzz on his face like two chips of broken plate in a worn-out door-mat: "Spoils of war! I brought them here! I tolled them in here: a military and-bush! And as the only and ranking Confedrit military soldier present——"

"You ain't a soldier," Granny said. "You stipulated that to Colonel Sartoris yourself while I was listening. You told him yourself you would be his independent horse-captain but nothing more."

"Ain't that just exactly what I am trying to be?" he said. "Didn't I bring all six of them horses in here in my own possession, the same as if I was leading them on a rope?"

"Hah," Granny said. "A spoil of war or any other kind of spoil don't belong to a man or a woman either until they can take it home and put it down and turn their back on it. You never had time to get home with even the one you were riding. You ran in the first open gate you came to, no matter whose gate it was."

"Except it was the wrong one," he said. His eyes quit looking like china. They didn't look like anything. But I reckon his face would still look like an old door-mat even after he had turned all the way white. "So I reckon I got to even walk back to town," he said. "The woman that would . . ." His voice stopped. He and Granny looked at one another.

"Don't you say it," Granny said.

"Nome," he said. He didn't say it. ". . . a man of seven horses ain't likely to lend him a mule."

"No," Granny said. "But you won't have to walk."

We all went out to the lot. I don't reckon that even Ab knew until then that Granny had already found where he thought he had hidden the first horse and had it brought up to the lot with the other six. But at least he already had his saddle and bridle with him. But it was too late. Six of the horses moved about loose in the lot. The seventh one was tied just inside the gate with a piece of plow-line. It wasn't the horse Ab had come on because that horse had a blaze. Ab had known Granny long enough too. He should have known. Maybe he did. But at least he tried. He opened the gate.

"Well," he said, "it ain't getting no earlier. I reckon I better——"

"Wait," Granny said. Then we looked at the horse which was tied to the fence. At first glance it looked the best one of the seven. You had to see it just right to tell its near leg was sprung a little, maybe from being worked too hard too young under too much weight. "Take that one," Granny said.

"That ain't mine," Ab said. "That's one of yourn. I'll just——"

"Take that one," Granny said. Ab looked at her. You could have counted at least ten.

"Hell fire, Miz Millard," he said.

"I've told you before about cursing on this place," Granny said.

"Yessum," Ab said. Then he said it again: "Hell fire." He went into the lot and rammed the bit into the tied horse's mouth and clapped the saddle on and snatched the piece of plow-line off and threw it over the fence and got up and Granny stood there until he had ridden out of the lot and Ringo closed the gate and that was the first time I noticed the chain and padlock from the smokehouse door and Ringo locked it and handed Granny the key and Ab sat for a minute, looking down at her. "Well, good-day," he said. "I just hope for the sake of the Confedricy that Bed Forrest don't never tangle with you with all the horses he's got." Then he said it again, maybe worse this time because now he was already on a horse pointed toward the gate: "Or you'll damn shore leave him just one more passel of infantry before he can spit twice."

Then he was gone too. Except for hearing Cousin Melisandre now and then, and those six horses with U.S. branded on their hips standing in the lot, it might never have happened. At least Ringo and I thought that was all of it. Every now and then Philadelphia would come downstairs with the pitcher and draw some more cold water for Cousin Melisandre's cloths but we thought that after a while even that would just wear out and quit. Then Philadelphia came down again and came in to where Granny was cutting down a pair of Yankee pants that Father had worn home last time so they would fit Ringo. She didn't say anything. She just stood in the door until Granny said, "All right. What now?"

"She want the banjo," Philadelphia said.

"What?" Granny said. "My dulcimer? She can't play it. Go back upstairs."

But Philadelphia didn't move. "Could I ax Mammy to come help me?"

"No," Granny said. "Louvinia's resting. She's had about as much of this as I want her to stand. Go back upstairs. Give her some more wine if you can't think of anything else." And she told Ringo and me to go somewhere else, anywhere else, but even in the yard you could still hear Cousin Melisandre talking to Philadelphia. And once we even heard Granny though it was still mostly Cousin Melisandre telling Granny that she had already forgiven her, that nothing whatever had happened and that all she wanted now was peace. And after a while Louvinia came up from the cabin without even being sent for and went upstairs and then it began to look like we were going to be late for supper too. But Philadelphia finally came down and cooked it and carried Cousin Melisandre's tray up and then we quit eating; we could hear Louvinia overhead, in Granny's room now, and she came down and set the untasted tray on the table and stood beside Granny's chair with the key to the trunk in her hand.

"All right," Granny said. "Go call Joby and Lucius." We got the lantern and the shovels. We went to the orchard and removed the brush and dug up the trunk and got the dulcimer and buried the trunk and put the brush back and brought the key in to Granny. And Ringo and I could hear her from our room and Granny was right. We heard her for a long time and Granny was surely right; she just never said but half of it. The moon came up after a while and we could look down from our window into the garden, at Cousin Melisandre sitting on the bench with the moonlight glinting on the pearl inlay of the dulcimer, and Philadelphia squatting on the sill of the gate with her apron over her head. Maybe she was asleep. It was already late. But I don't see how.

So we didn't hear Granny until she was already in the room, her shawl over her nightgown and carrying a candle. "In a minute I'm going to have about all of this I aim to stand too," she said. "Go wake Lucius and tell him to saddle the mule," she told Ringo. "Bring me the pen and ink and a sheet of paper." I fetched them. She didn't sit down. She stood at the bureau while I held the candle, writing even and steady and not very much, and signed her name and let the paper lie open to dry until Lucius came in. "Ab Snopes said that Mr. Forrest is in Jefferson," she told Lucius. "Find him. Tell him I will expect him here for breakfast in the morning and to bring that boy." She used to know General Forrest in Memphis before he got to be a general. He used to trade with Grandfather Millard's supply house and sometimes he would come out to sit with Grandfather on the front gallery and sometimes he would eat with them. "You can tell him I have six captured horses for him," she said. "And never mind patter-rollers or soldiers either. Haven't you got my signature on that paper?"

"I ain't worrying about them," Lucius said. "But suppose them Yan-kees——"

"I see," Granny said. "Hah. I forgot. You've been waiting for Yankees, haven't you? But those this morning seemed to be too busy trying to stay free to have much time to talk about it, didn't they?—Get along," she said. "Do you think any Yankee is going to dare ignore what a Southern soldier or even a patter-roller wouldn't?—And you go to bed," she said.

We lay down, both of us on Ringo's pallet. We heard the mule when Lucius left. Then we heard the mule and at first we didn't know we had been asleep, the mule coming back now and the moon had started down the west and Cousin Melisandre and Philadelphia were gone from the garden, to where Philadelphia at least could sleep better than sitting on a square sill with an apron over her head, or at least where it was quieter. And we heard Lucius fumbling up the stairs but we never heard Granny at all because she was already at the top of the stairs, talking down at the noise Lucius was trying not to make. "Speak up," she said. "I ain't asleep but I ain't a lip-reader either. Not in the dark."

"Genl Fawhrest say he respectful compliments," Lucius said, "and he can't come to breakfast this morning because he gonter to be whuppin Genl Smith at Tallahatchie Crossing about that time. But providin he ain't too fur away in the wrong direction when him and Genl Smith git done, he be proud to accept your invitation next time he in the neigh-borhood. And he say 'whut boy'."

While you could count about five, Granny didn't say anything. Then she said, "What?"

"He say 'whut boy'," Lucius said.

Then you could have counted ten. All we could hear was Lucius breathing. Then Granny said: "Did you wipe the mule down?"

"Yessum," Lucius said.

"Did you turn her back into the pasture?"

"Yessum," Lucius said.

"Then go to bed," Granny said. "And you too," she said.

General Forrest found out what boy. This time we didn't know we had been asleep either, and it was no one mule now. The sun was just rising. When we heard Granny and scrambled to the window, yesterday wasn't a patch on it. There were at least fifty of them now, in gray; the whole outdoors was full of men on horses, with Cousin Philip out in front of them, sitting his horse in almost exactly the same spot where he had been yesterday, looking up at Granny's window and not seeing it or anything else this time either. He had a hat now. He was holding it clamped over his heart and he hadn't shaved and yesterday he had looked younger than Ringo because Ringo always had looked about ten years older than me. But now, with the first sun-ray making a little soft fuzz in the gold-colored stubble on his face, he looked even younger than I did, and gaunt and worn in the face like he hadn't slept any last night and something else in his face too: like he not only hadn't slept last night but by godfrey he wasn't going to sleep tonight either as long as he had anything to do with it. "Goodbye," he said. "Goodbye," and whirled his horse, spurring, and raised the new hat over his head like he had carried the sabre yesterday and the whole mass of them went piling back across flower beds and lawns and all and back down the drive toward the gate while Granny still stood at her window in her nightgown, her voice louder than any man's anywhere, I don't care who he is or what he would be doing: "Backhouse! Backhouse! You, Backhouse!"

So we ate breakfast early. Granny sent Ringo in his nightshirt to wake Louvinia and Lucius both. So Lucius had the mule saddled before Louvinia even got the fire lit. This time Granny didn't write a note. "Go to Tallahatchie Crossing," she told Lucius. "Sit there and wait for him if necessary."

"Suppose they done already started the battle?" Lucius said.

"Suppose they have?" Granny said. "What business is that of yours or mine either? You find Bedford Forrest. Tell him this is important; it won't take long. But don't you show your face here again without him."

Lucius rode away. He was gone four days. He didn't even get back in time for the wedding, coming back up the drive about sundown on the fourth day with two soldiers in one of General Forrest's forage wagons with the mule tied to the tailgate. He didn't know where he had been and he never did catch up with the battle. "I never even heard it," he told Joby and Lucius and Louvinia and Philadelphia and Ringo and me. "If wars always moves that far and that fast, I don't see how they ever have time to fight."

But it was all over then. It was the second day, the day after Lucius left. It was just after dinner this time and by now we were used to soldiers. But these were different, just five of them, and we never had seen just that few of them before and we had come to think of soldiers as either jumping on and off horses in the yard or going back and forth through Granny's flower beds at full gallop. These were all officers and I reckon maybe I hadn't seen so many soldiers after all because I never saw this much braid before. They came up the drive at a trot, like people just taking a ride, and stopped without trompling even one flower bed and General Forrest got down and came up the walk toward where Granny waited on the front gallery—a big, dusty man with a big beard so black it looked almost blue and eyes like a sleepy owl, already taking off his hat. "Well, Miss Rosie," he said.

"Don't call me Rosie," Granny said. "Come in. Ask your gentlemen to alight and come in."

"They'll wait there," General Forrest said. "We are a little rushed. My plans have. . . ." Then we were in the library. He wouldn't sit down. He looked tired all right, but there was something else a good deal livelier than just tired. "Well, Miss Rosie," he said. "I——"

"Don't call me Rosie," Granny said. "Can't you even say Rosa?"

"Yessum," he said. But he couldn't. At least, he never did. "I reckon we both have had about enough of this. That boy——"

"Hah," Granny said. "Night before last you were saying what boy. Where is he? I sent you word to bring him with you."

"Under arrest," General Forrest said. It was a considerable more than just tired. "I spent four days getting Smith just where I wanted him. After that, this boy here could have fought the battle." He said 'fit' for fought just as he said 'druv' for drove and 'drug' for dragged. But maybe when you fought battles like he did, even Granny didn't mind how you talked. "I won't bother you with details. He didn't know them either. All he had to do was exactly what I told him. I did everything but draw a diagram on his coat-tail of exactly what he was to do, no more and no less, from the time he left me until he saw me again: which was to make contact and then fall back. I gave him just exactly the right number of men so that he couldn't do anything else but that. I told him exactly how fast to fall back and how much racket to make doing it and even how to make the racket. But what do you think he did?"

"I can tell you," Granny said. "He sat on his horse at five o'clock yesterday morning, with my whole yard full of men behind him, yelling goodbye at my window."

"He divided his men and sent half of them into the bushes to make a noise and took the other half who were the nearest to complete fools and led a sabre charge on that outpost. He didn't fire a shot. He drove it clean back with sabres onto Smith's main body and scared Smith so that he threw out all his cavalry and pulled out behind it and now I don't know whether I'm about to catch him or he's about to catch me. My provost finally caught the boy last night. He had come back and got the other thirty men of his company and was twenty miles ahead again, trying to find something to lead another charge against. 'Do you want to be killed?' I said. 'Not especially,' he said. 'That is, I don't especially care one way or the other.' 'Then neither do I,' I said. 'But you risked a whole company of my men.' 'Ain't that what they enlisted for?' he said. 'They enlisted into a military establishment the purpose of which is to expend each man only at a profit. Or maybe you don't consider me a shrewd enough trader in human meat?' 'I can't say,' he said. 'Since day before yesterday I ain't thought very much about how you or anybody else runs this war.' 'And just what were you doing day before yesterday that changed your ideas and habits?' I said. 'Fighting some of it,' he said. 'Dispersing the enemy.' 'Where?' I said. 'At a lady's house a few miles from Jefferson,' he said. 'One of the niggers called her Granny like the white boy did. The others called her Miss Rosie.'" This time Granny didn't say anything. She just waited.

"Go on," she said.

" 'I'm still trying to win battles, even if since day before yesterday you ain't,' I said. 'I'll send you down to Johnston at Jackson,' I said. 'He'll put you inside Vicksburg, where you can lead private charges day and night too if you want.' 'Like hell you will,' he said. And I said—excuse me— 'Like hell I won't.' " And Granny didn't say anything. It was like day before yesterday with Ab Snopes: not like she hadn't heard but as if right now it didn't matter, that this was no time either to bother with such.

"And did you?" she said.

"I can't. He knows it. You can't punish a man for routing an enemy four times his weight. What would I say back there in Tennessee, where we both live, let alone that uncle of his, the one they licked for Governor six years ago, on Bragg's personal staff now, with his face over Bragg's shoulder every time Bragg opens a dispatch or picks up a pen. And I'm still trying to win battles. But I can't. Because of a girl, one single lone young female girl that ain't got anything under the sun against him except that, since it was his misfortune to save her from a passel of raiding enemy in a situation that everybody but her is trying to forget, she can't seem to bear to hear his last name. Yet because of that, every battle I plan from now on will be at the mercy of a twenty-two-year-old shavetail— excuse me again—who might decide to lead a private charge any time he can holler at least two men in gray coats into moving in the same direction." He stopped. He looked at Granny. "Well?" he said.

"So now you've got to it," Granny said. "Well what, Mr. Forrest?"

"Why, just have done with this foolishness. I told you I've got that boy, in close arrest, with a guard with a bayonet. But there won't be any trouble there. I figured even yesterday morning that he had already lost his mind. But I reckon he's recovered enough of it since the Provost took him last night to comprehend that I still consider myself his commander even if he don't. So all necessary now is for you to put your foot down. Put it down hard. Now. You're her grandma. She lives in your home. And it looks like she is going to live in it a good while yet before she gets back to Memphis to that uncle or whoever it is that calls himself her guardian. So just put your foot down. Make her. Mr. Millard would have already done that if he had been here. And I know when. It would have been two days ago by now."

Granny waited until he got done. She stood with her arms crossed, holding each elbow in the other. "Is that all I'm to do?" she said.

"Yes," General Forrest said. "If she don't want to listen to you right at first, maybe as his commander——"

Granny didn't even say "Hah." She didn't even send me. She didn't even stop in the hall and call. She went upstairs herself and stood there and I thought maybe she was going to bring the dulcimer too and I thought how if I was General Forrest I would go back and get Cousin Philip and make him sit in the library until about supper-time while Cousin Melisandre played the dulcimer and sang. Then he could take

Cousin Philip on back and then he could finish the war without worrying.

She didn't have the dulcimer. She just had Cousin Melisandre. They came in and Granny stood to one side again with her arms crossed, holding her elbows. "Here she is," she said. "Say it—This is Mr. Bedford Forrest," she told Cousin Melisandre. "Say it," she told General Forrest.

He didn't have time. When Cousin Melisandre first came, she tried to read aloud to Ringo and me. It wasn't much. That is, what she insisted on reading to us wasn't so bad, even if it was mostly about ladies looking out windows and playing on something (maybe they were dulcimers too) while somebody else was off somewhere fighting. It was the way she read it. When Granny said this is Mister Forrest, Cousin Melisandre's face looked exactly like her voice would sound when she read to us. She took two steps into the library and curtsied, spreading her hoops back, and stood up. "General Forrest," she said. "I am acquainted with an associate of his. Will the General please give him the sincerest wishes for triumph in war and success in love, from one who will never see him again?" Then she curtsied again and spread her hoops backward and stood up and took two steps backward and turned and went out.

After a while Granny said, "Well, Mr. Forrest?"

General Forrest began to cough. He lifted his coattail with one hand and reached the other into his hip pocket like he was going to pull at least a musket out of it and got his handkerchief and coughed into it a while. It wasn't very clean. It looked about like the one Cousin Philip was trying to wipe his coat off with in the summer house day before yesterday. Then he put the handkerchief back. He didn't say "Hah" either. "Can I reach the Holly Branch road without having to go through Jefferson?" he said.

Then Granny moved. "Open the desk," she said. "Lay out a sheet of note-paper." I did. And I remember how I stood at one side of the desk and General Forrest at the other, and watched Granny's hand move the pen steady and not very slow and not very long across the paper because it never did take her very long to say anything, no matter what it was, whether she was talking it or writing it. Though I didn't see it then, but only later, when it hung framed under glass above Cousin Melisandre's and Cousin Philip's mantel: the fine steady slant of Granny's hand and General Forrest's sprawling signatures below it that looked itself a good deal like a charge of massed cavalry:

Lieutenant P. S. Backhouse, Company D, Tennessee Cavalry, was this day raised to the honorary rank of Brevet Major General & killed while engaging the enemy. Vice whom Philip St-Just Backus is hereby appointed Lieutenant, Company D, Tennessee Cavalry.

N. B. Forrest Genl

I didn't see it then. General Forrest picked it up. "Now I've got to have a battle," he said. "Another sheet, son." I laid that one out on the desk.

"A battle?" Granny said.

"To give Johnston," he said. "Confound it, Miss Rosie, can't you understand either that I'm just a fallible mortal man trying to run a military command according to certain fixed and inviolable rules, no matter how foolish the business looks to superior outside folks?"

"All right," Granny said. "You had one. I was looking at it."

"So I did," General Forrest said. "Hah," he said. "The battle of Sartoris."

"No," Granny said. "Not at my house."

"They did all the shooting down at the creek," I said.

"What creek?" he said.

So I told him. It ran through the pasture. Its name was Hurricane Creek but not even the white people called it hurricane except Granny. General Forrest didn't either when he sat down at the desk and wrote the report to General Johnston at Jackson:

A unit of my command on detached duty engaged a body of the enemy & drove him from the field & dispersed him this day 28th ult. April 1862 at Harrykin Creek. With loss of one man.

N. B. Forrest Genl

I saw that. I watched him write it. Then he got up and folded the sheets into his pocket and was already going toward the table where his hat was.

"Wait," Granny said. "Lay out another sheet," she said. "Come back here."

General Forrest stopped and turned. "Another one?"

"Yes!" Granny said. "A furlough, pass—whatever you busy military establishments call them! So John Sartoris can come home long enough to——" and she said it herself, she looked straight at me and even backed up and said some of it over as though to make sure there couldn't be any mistake: "——can come back home and give away that damn bride!"

IV

And that was all. The day came and Granny waked Ringo and me before sunup and we ate what breakfast we had from two plates on the back steps. And we dug up the trunk and brought it into the house and polished the silver and Ringo and I brought dogwood and redbud branches from the pasture and Granny cut the flowers, all of them, cutting them herself with Cousin Melisandre and Philadelphia just carrying the baskets; so many of them until the house was so full that Ringo and I would believe we smelled them even across the pasture each time we came up. Though of course we could, it was just the food—the last ham from the smokehouse and the chickens and the flour which Granny had been saving and the last of the sugar which she had been saving along with the bottle of champagne for the day when the North surrendered—which Louvinia had been cooking for two days now, to remind us each time we approached the house of what was going on and that the flowers were there. As if we could have forgotten about the food. And they dressed Cousin Melisandre and, Ringo in his new blue pants and I in my gray ones which were not so new, we stood in the late afternoon on the gallery—Granny and Cousin Melisandre and Louvinia and Philadelphia and Ringo and I—and watched them enter the gate. General Forrest was not one. Ringo and I had thought maybe he might be, if only to bring Cousin Philip. Then we thought that maybe, since Father was coming anyway, General Forrest would let Father bring him, with Cousin Philip maybe handcuffed to Father and the soldier with the bayonet following, or maybe still just handcuffed to the soldier until he and Cousin Melisandre were married and Father unlocked him.

But General Forrest wasn't one, and Cousin Philip wasn't handcuffed to anybody and there was no bayonet and not even a soldier because these were all officers too. And we stood in the parlor while the homemade candles burnt in the last of sunset in the bright candlesticks which Philadelphia and Ringo and I had polished with the rest of the silver because Granny and Louvinia were both busy cooking and even Cousin Melisandre polished a little of it although Louvinia could pick out the ones she polished without hardly looking and hand them to Philadelphia to polish again:—Cousin Melisandre in the dress which hadn't needed to be altered for her at all because Mother wasn't much older than Cousin Melisandre even when she died, and which would still button on Granny too just like it did the day she married in it, and the chaplain and Father and Cousin Philip and the four others in their gray and braid and sabres and Cousin Melisandre's face was all right now and Cousin Philip's was too because it just had the beautiful-girl look on it and none of us had ever seen him look any other way. Then we ate, and Ringo and I anyway had been waiting on that for three days and then we did it and then it was over too, fading just a little each day until the palate no longer remembered and only our mouths would run a little water as we would name the dishes aloud to one another, until even the water would run less and less and less and it would take something we just hoped to eat some day if they ever got done fighting, to make it run at all.

And that was all. The last sound of wheel and hoof died away, Philadelphia came in from the parlor carrying the candlesticks and blowing out the candles as she came, and Louvinia set the kitchen clock on the table and gathered the last of soiled silver from supper into the dishpan and it might never have even been. "Well," Granny said. She didn't move, leaning her forearms on the table a little and we had never seen that before. She spoke to Ringo without turning her head: "Go call Joby and Lucius." And even when we brought the trunk in and set it against the wall and opened back the lid, she didn't move. She didn't even look at Louvinia either. "Put the clock in too," she said. "I don't think we'll bother to time ourselves tonight."

THAT EVENING SUN

The history of the Compson family, symbol of Southern decay, is told in its greatest detail in *The Sound and the Fury* (see pp. 855–856), but one episode in the lives of the Compson children is to be found in Faulkner's short story, "That Evening Sun." The narrator is Quentin Compson, the most sensitive member of the family, doomed to die young by his own hand, who is also the narrator of the events in the novel *Absalom, Absalom!* He is recalling the time when one of the Compson family's Negro servants, Nancy, feared that she would be killed by her husband. We do not learn, in the story, what happened. It is in the novel that we discover, in an incidental allusion, that she was indeed murdered and her body left in a ditch.

The story offers us much more than a further glimpse of the Compson family—the alert Candace (Caddy), the cowardly Jason, the whining mother, the harassed father and also the steadfast and maternal Negro housekeeper, Dilsey. What the art of Faulkner conveys above all, in his narrative, is the angle of vision of the children: they are dimly aware of grave and violent things in the air about them, but can grasp Nancy's anguish only in their own childlike ways. They do not know that Nancy is with child by a white man; nor do they know why she is threatened by her husband. Their very innocence gives the tale its great tension and poignancy.

In this story can be seen also Faulkner's feeling that the Negro represents an element of stability and endurance in the South. We catch only a glimpse of Dilsey in her patience and her dignity; but we experience something of the terror of Nancy and the force of the would-be murderer, into whose mouth Faulkner places one of the most effective statements in the story: "I can't hang around white man's kitchen. But white man can hang around mine. White man can come in my house, but I can't stop him. When white man want to come in my house, I ain't got no house." It is this sense of the spiritual dispossession of the Negro which Faulkner records—this and the emotions of the children, poised and innocent, on the perimeter of sordid domestic tragedy.

I

Monday is no different from any other weekday in Jefferson now. The streets are paved now, and the telephone and electric companies are cutting down more and more of the shade trees—the water oaks, the maples and locusts and elms—to make room for iron poles bearing clusters of bloated and ghostly and bloodless grapes, and we have a city laundry which makes the rounds on Monday morning, gathering the bundles of clothes into bright-colored, specially-made motor cars: the soiled wearing of a whole week now flees apparitionlike behind alert and irritable electric horns, with a long diminishing noise of rubber and asphalt like tearing silk, and even the Negro women who still take in white people's washing after the old custom, fetch and deliver it in automobiles.

But fifteen years ago, on Monday morning the quiet, dusty, shady streets would be full of Negro women with, balanced on their steady, turbaned heads, bundles of clothes tied up in sheets, almost as large as cotton bales, carried so without touch of hand between the kitchen door of the white house and the blackened washpot beside a cabin door in Negro Hollow.

Nancy would set her bundle on the top of her head, then upon the bundle in turn she would set the black straw sailor hat which she wore winter and summer. She was tall, with a high, sad face sunken a little where her teeth were missing. Sometimes we would go a part of the way down the lane and across the pasture with her, to watch the balanced bundle and the hat that never bobbed nor wavered, even when she walked down into the ditch and up the other side and stooped through the fence. She would go down on her hands and knees and crawl through the gap, her head rigid, uptilted, the bundle steady as a rock or a balloon, and rise to her feet again and go on.

Sometimes the husbands of the washing women would fetch and deliver the clothes, but Jesus never did that for Nancy, even before father told him to stay away from our house, even when Dilsey was sick and Nancy would come to cook for us.

And then about half the time we'd have to go down the lane to Nancy's cabin and tell her to come on and cook breakfast. We would stop at the ditch, because father told us to not have anything to do with Jesus —he was a short black man, with a razor scar down his face—and we would throw rocks at Nancy's house until she came to the door, leaning her head around it without any clothes on.

"What yawl mean, chunking my house?" Nancy said. "What you little devils mean?"

"Father says for you to come on and get breakfast," Caddy said. "Father says it's over a half an hour now, and you've got to come this minute."

"I aint studying no breakfast," Nancy said. "I going to get my sleep out."

"I bet you're drunk," Jason said. "Father says you're drunk. Are you drunk, Nancy?"

"Who says I is?" Nancy said. "I got to get my sleep out. I aint studying no breakfast."

So after a while we quit chunking the cabin and went back home. When she finally came, it was too late for me to go to school. So we thought it was whisky until that day they arrested her again and they were taking her to jail and they passed Mr Stovall. He was the cashier in the bank and a deacon in the Baptist church, and Nancy began to say:

"When you going to pay me, white man? When you going to pay me, white man? It's been three times now since you paid me a cent—" Mr Stovall knocked her down, but she kept on saying, "When you going to pay me, white man? It's been three times now since—" until Mr Stovall kicked her in the mouth with his heel and the marshal caught Mr Stovall back, and Nancy lying in the street, laughing. She turned her head and spat out some blood and teeth and said, "It's been three times now since he paid me a cent."

That was how she lost her teeth, and all that day they told about Nancy and Mr Stovall, and all that night the ones that passed the jail could hear Nancy singing and yelling. They could see her hands holding to the window bars, and a lot of them stopped along the fence, listening to her and to the jailer trying to make her stop. She didn't shut up until almost daylight, when the jailer began to hear a bumping and scraping upstairs and he went up there and found Nancy hanging from the window bar. He said that it was cocaine and not whisky, because no nigger would try to commit suicide unless he was full of cocaine, because a nigger full of cocaine wasn't a nigger any longer.

The jailer cut her down and revived her; then he beat her, whipped her. She had hung herself with her dress. She had fixed it all right, but when they arrested her she didn't have on anything except a dress and so she didn't have anything to tie her hands with and she couldn't make her hands let go of the window ledge. So the jailer heard the noise and ran up there and found Nancy hanging from the window, stark naked, her belly already swelling out a little, like a little balloon.

When Dilsey was sick in her cabin and Nancy was cooking for us, we could see her apron swelling out; that was before father told Jesus to stay away from the house. Jesus was in the kitchen, sitting behind the stove, with his razor scar on his black face like a piece of dirty string. He said it was a watermelon that Nancy had under her dress.

"It never come off of your vine, though," Nancy said.

"Off of what vine?" Caddy said.

"I can cut down the vine it did come off of," Jesus said.

"What makes you want to talk like that before these chillen?" Nancy said. "Whyn't you go on to work? You done et. You want Mr Jason to catch you hanging around his kitchen, talking that way before these chillen?"

"Talking what way?" Caddy said. "What vine?"

"I cant hang around white man's kitchen," Jesus said. "But white man can hang around mine. White man can come in my house, but I cant stop him. When white man want to come in my house, I aint got no house. I cant stop him, but he cant kick me outen it. He cant do that."

Dilsey was still sick in her cabin. Father told Jesus to stay off our place. Dilsey was still sick. It was a long time. We were in the library after supper.

"Isn't Nancy through in the kitchen yet?" mother said. "It seems to me that she has had plenty of time to have finished the dishes."

"Let Quentin go and see," father said. "Go and see if Nancy is through, Quentin. Tell her she can go on home."

I went to the kitchen. Nancy was through. The dishes were put away and the fire was out. Nancy was sitting in a chair, close to the cold stove. She looked at me.

"Mother wants to know if you are through," I said.

"Yes," Nancy said. She looked at me. "I done finished." She looked at me.

"What is it?" I said. "What is it?"

"I aint nothing but a nigger," Nancy said. "It aint none of my fault."

She looked at me, sitting in the chair before the cold stove, the sailor hat on her head. I went back to the library. It was the cold stove and all, when you think of a kitchen being warm and busy and cheerful. And with a cold stove and the dishes all put away, and nobody wanting to eat at that hour.

"Is she through?" mother said.

"Yessum," I said.

"What is she doing?" mother said.

"She's not doing anything. She's through."

"I'll go and see," father said.

"Maybe she's waiting for Jesus to come and take her home," Caddy said.

"Jesus is gone," I said. Nancy told us how one morning she woke up and Jesus was gone.

"He quit me," Nancy said. "Done gone to Memphis, I reckon. Dodging them city *po*-lice for a while, I reckon."

"And a good riddance," father said. "I hope he stays there."

"Nancy's scaired of the dark," Jason said.

"So are you," Caddy said.

"I'm not," Jason said.

"Scairy cat," Caddy said.

"I'm not," Jason said.

"You, Candace!" mother said. Father came back.

"I am going to walk down the lane with Nancy," he said. "She says that Jesus is back."

"Has she seen him?" mother said.

"No. Some Negro sent her word that he was back in town. I wont be long."

"You'll leave me alone, to take Nancy home?" mother said. "Is her safety more precious to you than mine?"

"I wont be long," father said.

"You'll leave these children unprotected, with that Negro about?"

"I'm going too," Caddy said. "Let me go, Father."

"What would he do with them, if he were unfortunate enough to have them?" father said.

"I want to go, too," Jason said.

"Jason!" mother said. She was speaking to father. You could tell that by the way she said the name. Like she believed that all day father had been trying to think of doing the thing she wouldn't like the most, and that she knew all the time that after a while he would think of it. I stayed quiet, because father and I both knew that mother would want him to make me stay with her if she just thought of it in time. So father didn't look at me. I was the oldest. I was nine and Caddy was seven and Jason was five.

"Nonsense," father said. "We wont be long."

Nancy had her hat on. We came to the lane. "Jesus always been good to me," Nancy said. "Whenever he had two dollars, one of them was mine." We walked in the lane. "If I can just get through the lane," Nancy said, "I be all right then."

The lane was always dark. "This is where Jason got scared on Hallowe'en," Caddy said.

"I didn't," Jason said.

"Cant Aunt Rachel do anything with him?" father said. Aunt Rachel was old. She lived in a cabin beyond Nancy's, by herself. She had white hair and she smoked a pipe in the door, all day long; she didn't work any more. They said she was Jesus' mother. Sometimes she said she was and sometimes she said she wasn't any kin to Jesus.

"Yes, you did," Caddy said. "You were scairder than Frony. You were scairder than T.P even. Scairder than niggers."

"Cant nobody do nothing with him," Nancy said. "He say I done woke up the devil in him and aint but one thing going to lay it down again."

"Well, he's gone now," father said. "There's nothing for you to be afraid of now. And if you'd just let white men alone."

"Let what white men alone?" Caddy said. "How let them alone?"

"He aint gone nowhere," Nancy said. "I can feel him. I can feel him now, in this lane. He hearing us talk, every word, hid somewhere, waiting. I aint seen him, and I aint going to see him again but once more, with that razor in his mouth. That razor on that string down his back, inside his shirt. And then I aint going to be even surprised."

"I wasn't scaired," Jason said.

"If you'd behave yourself, you'd have kept out of this," father said. "But it's all right now. He's probably in St. Louis now. Probably got another wife by now and forgot all about you."

"If he has, I better not find out about it," Nancy said. "I'd stand there right over them, and every time he wropped her, I'd cut that arm off. I'd cut his head off and I'd slit her belly and I'd shove—"

"Hush," father said.

"Slit whose belly, Nancy?" Caddy said.

"I wasn't scaired," Jason said. "I'd walk right down this lane by myself."

"Yah," Caddy said. "You wouldn't dare to put your foot down in it if we were not here too."

II

Dilsey was still sick, so we took Nancy home every night until mother said, "How much longer is this going on? I to be left alone in this big house while you take home a frightened Negro?"

We fixed a pallet in the kitchen for Nancy. One night we waked up, hearing the sound. It was not singing and it was not crying, coming up the dark stairs. There was a light in mother's room and we heard father going down the hall, down the back stairs, and Caddy and I went into the hall. The floor was cold. Our toes curled away from it while we listened to the sound. It was like singing and it wasn't like singing, like the sounds that Negroes make.

Then it stopped and we heard father going down the back stairs, and we went to the head of the stairs. Then the sound began again, in the stairway, not loud, and we could see Nancy's eyes halfway up the stairs, against the wall. They looked like cat's eyes do, like a big cat against the wall, watching us. When we came down the steps to where she was, she quit making the sound again, and we stood there until father came back up from the kitchen, with his pistol in his hand. He went back down with Nancy and they came back with Nancy's pallet.

We spread the pallet in our room. After the light in mother's room went off, we could see Nancy's eyes again. "Nancy," Caddy whispered, "are you asleep, Nancy?"

Nancy whispered something. It was oh or no, I dont know which. Like nobody had made it, like it came from nowhere and went nowhere, until it was like Nancy was not there at all; that I had looked so hard at her eyes on the stairs that they had got printed on my eyeballs, like the sun does when you have closed your eyes and there is no sun. "Jesus," Nancy whispered. "Jesus."

"Was it Jesus?" Caddy said. "Did he try to come into the kitchen?"

"Jesus," Nancy said. Like this: Jeeeeeeeeeeeeeeesus, until the sound went out, like a match or a candle does.

"It's the other Jesus she means," I said.

"Can you see us, Nancy?" Caddy whispered. "Can you see our eyes too?"

"I aint nothing but a nigger," Nancy said. "God knows. God knows."

"What did you see down there in the kitchen?" Caddy whispered. "What tried to get in?"

"God knows," Nancy said. We could see her eyes. "God knows."

Dilsey got well. She cooked dinner. "You'd better stay in bed a day or two longer," father said.

"What for?" Dilsey said. "If I had been a day later, this place would be to rack and ruin. Get on out of here now, and let me get my kitchen straight again."

Dilsey cooked supper too. And that night, just before dark, Nancy came into the kitchen.

"How do you know he's back?" Dilsey said. "You aint seen him."

"Jesus is a nigger," Jason said.

"I can feel him," Nancy said. "I can feel him laying yonder in the ditch."

"Tonight?" Dilsey said. "Is he there tonight?"

"Dilsey's a nigger too," Jason said.

"You try to eat something," Dilsey said.

"I dont want nothing," Nancy said.

"I aint a nigger," Jason said.

"Drink some coffee," Dilsey said. She poured a cup of coffee for Nancy. "Do you know he's out there tonight? How come you know it's tonight?"

"I know," Nancy said. "He's there, waiting. I know. I done lived with him too long. I know what he is fixing to do fore he know it himself."

"Drink some coffee," Dilsey said. Nancy held the cup to her mouth and blew into the cup. Her mouth pursed out like a spreading adder's, like a rubber mouth, like she had blown all the color out of her lips with blowing the coffee.

"I aint a nigger," Jason said. "Are you a nigger, Nancy?"

"I hellborn, child," Nancy said. "I wont be nothing soon. I going back where I come from soon."

III

She began to drink the coffee. While she was drinking, holding the cup in both hands, she began to make the sound again. She made the sound into the cup and the coffee sploshed out onto her hands and her dress. Her eyes looked at us and she sat there, her elbows on her knees, holding the cup in both hands, looking at us across the wet cup, making the sound. "Look at Nancy," Jason said. "Nancy cant cook for us now. Dilsey's got well now."

"You hush up," Dilsey said. Nancy held the cup in both hands, looking at us, making the sound, like there were two of them: one looking at us and the other making the sound. "Whyn't you let Mr Jason telefoam the marshal?" Dilsey said. Nancy stopped then, holding the cup in her long brown hands. She tried to drink some coffee again, but it sploshed out of the cup, onto her hands and her dress, and she put the cup down. Jason watched her.

"I cant swallow it," Nancy said. "I swallows but it wont go down me."

"You go down to the cabin," Dilsey said. "Frony will fix you a pallet and I'll be there soon."

"Wont no nigger stop him," Nancy said.

"I aint a nigger," Jason said. "Am I, Dilsey?"

"I reckon not," Dilsey said. She looked at Nancy. "I dont reckon so. What you going to do, then?"

Nancy looked at us. Her eyes went fast, like she was afraid there wasn't time to look, without hardly moving at all. She looked at us, at all three of us at one time. "You member that night I stayed in yawls' room?" she said. She told about how we waked up early the next morning, and played. We had to play quiet, on her pallet, until father woke up and it was time to get breakfast. "Go and ask your maw to let me stay here tonight," Nancy said. "I wont need no pallet. We can play some more."

Caddy asked mother. Jason went too. "I cant have Negroes sleeping in the bedrooms," mother said. Jason cried. He cried until mother said he couldn't have any dessert for three days if he didn't stop. Then Jason said he would stop if Dilsey would make a chocolate cake. Father was there.

"Why dont you do something about it?" mother said. "What do we have officers for?"

"Why is Nancy afraid of Jesus?" Caddy said. "Are you afraid of father, mother?"

"What could the officers do?" father said. "If Nancy hasn't seen him, how could the officers find him?"

"Then why is she afraid?" mother said.

"She says he is there. She says she knows he is there tonight."

"Yet we pay taxes," mother said. "I must wait here alone in this big house while you take a Negro woman home."

"You know that I am not lying outside with a razor," father said.

"I'll stop if Dilsey will make a chocolate cake," Jason said. Mother told us to go out and father said he didn't know if Jason would get a chocolate cake or not, but he knew what Jason was going to get in about a minute. We went back to the kitchen and told Nancy.

"Father said for you to go home and lock the door, and you'll be all right," Caddy said. "All right from what, Nancy? Is Jesus mad at you?" Nancy was holding the coffee cup in her hands again, her elbows on her knees and her hands holding the cup between her knees. She was looking into the cup. "What have you done that made Jesus mad?" Caddy said. Nancy let the cup go. It didn't break on the floor, but the coffee spilled out, and Nancy sat there with her hands still making the shape of the cup. She began to make the sound again, not loud. Not singing and not unsinging. We watched her.

"Here," Dilsey said. "You quit that, now. You get holt of yourself. You wait here. I going to get Versh to walk home with you." Dilsey went out.

We looked at Nancy. Her shoulders kept shaking, but she quit making the sound. We watched her. "What's Jesus going to do to you?" Caddy said. "He went away."

Nancy looked at us. "We had fun that night I stayed in yawls' room, didn't we?"

"I didn't," Jason said. "I didn't have any fun."

"You were asleep in mother's room," Caddy said. "You were not there."

"Let's go down to my house and have some more fun," Nancy said.

"Mother wont let us," I said. "It's too late now."

"Dont bother her," Nancy said. "We can tell her in the morning. She wont mind."

"She wouldn't let us," I said.

"Dont ask her now," Nancy said. "Dont bother her now."

"She didn't say we couldn't go," Caddy said.

"We didn't ask," I said.

"If you go, I'll tell," Jason said.

"We'll have fun," Nancy said. "They won't mind, just to my house. I been working for yawl a long time. They won't mind."

"I'm not afraid to go," Caddy said. "Jason is the one that's afraid. He'll tell."

"I'm not," Jason said.

"Yes, you are," Caddy said. "You'll tell."

"I won't tell," Jason said. "I'm not afraid."

"Jason ain't afraid to go with me," Nancy said. "Is you, Jason?"

"Jason is going to tell," Caddy said. The lane was dark. We passed the pasture gate. "I bet if something was to jump out from behind that gate, Jason would holler."

"I wouldn't," Jason said. We walked down the lane. Nancy was talking loud.

"What are you talking so loud for, Nancy?" Caddy said.

"Who; me?" Nancy said. "Listen at Quentin and Caddy and Jason saying I'm talking loud."

"You talk like there was five of us here," Caddy said. "You talk like father was here too."

"Who; me talking loud, Mr Jason?" Nancy said.

"Nancy called Jason 'Mister,'" Caddy said.

"Listen how Caddy and Quentin and Jason talk," Nancy said.

"We're not talking loud," Caddy said. "You're the one that's talking like father—"

"Hush," Nancy said; "hush, Mr Jason."

"Nancy called Jason 'Mister' aguh—"

"Hush," Nancy said. She was talking loud when we crossed the ditch and stooped through the fence where she used to stoop through with the clothes on her head. Then we came to her house. We were going fast then. She opened the door. The smell of the house was like the lamp and the smell of Nancy was like the wick, like they were waiting for one another to begin to smell. She lit the lamp and closed the door and put the bar up. Then she quit talking loud, looking at us.

"What're we going to do?" Caddy said.

"What do yawl want to do?" Nancy said.

"You said we would have some fun," Caddy said.

There was something about Nancy's house; something you could smell besides Nancy and the house. Jason smelled it, even. "I don't want to stay here," he said. "I want to go home."

"Go home, then," Caddy said.

"I don't want to go by myself," Jason said.

"We're going to have some fun," Nancy said.

"How?" Caddy said.

Nancy stood by the door. She was looking at us, only it was like she had emptied her eyes, like she had quit using them. "What do you want to do?" she said.

"Tell us a story," Caddy said. "Can you tell a story?"

"Yes," Nancy said.

"Tell it," Caddy said. We looked at Nancy. "You don't know any stories."

"Yes," Nancy said. "Yes, I do."

She came and sat in a chair before the hearth. There was a little fire there. Nancy built it up, when it was already hot inside. She built a good blaze. She told a story. She talked like her eyes looked, like her eyes watching us and her voice talking to us did not belong to her. Like she was living somewhere else, waiting somewhere else. She was outside the cabin. Her voice was inside and the shape of her, the Nancy that could stoop under a barbed wire fence with a bundle of clothes balanced on her head as though without weight, like a balloon, was there. But that was all. "And so this here queen come walking up to the ditch, where that bad man was hiding. She was walking up to the ditch, and she say, 'If I can just get past this here ditch,' was what she say . . ."

"What ditch?" Caddy said. "A ditch like that one out there? Why did a queen want to go into a ditch?"

"To get to her house," Nancy said. She looked at us. "She had to cross the ditch to get into her house quick and bar the door."

"Why did she want to go home and bar the door?" Caddy said.

IV

Nancy looked at us. She quit talking. She looked at us. Jason's legs stuck straight out of his pants where he sat on Nancy's lap. "I don't think that's a good story," he said. "I want to go home."

"Maybe we had better," Caddy said. She got up from the floor. "I bet they are looking for us right now." She went toward the door.

"No," Nancy said. "Don't open it." She got up quick and passed Caddy. She didn't touch the door, the wooden bar.

"Why not?" Caddy said.

"Come back to the lamp," Nancy said. "We'll have fun. You don't have to go."

"We ought to go," Caddy said. "Unless we have a lot of fun." She and Nancy came back to the fire, the lamp.

"I want to go home," Jason said. "I'm going to tell."

"I know another story," Nancy said. She stood close to the lamp. She looked at Caddy, like when your eyes look up at a stick balanced on your nose. She had to look down to see Caddy, but her eyes looked like that, like when you are balancing a stick.

"I won't listen to it," Jason said. "I'll bang on the floor."

"It's a good one," Nancy said. "It's better than the other one."

"What's it about?" Caddy said. Nancy was standing by the lamp. Her hand was on the lamp, against the light, long and brown.

"Your hand is on that hot globe," Caddy said. "Don't it feel hot to your hand?"

Nancy looked at her hand on the lamp chimney. She took her hand away, slow. She stood there, looking at Caddy, wringing her long hand as though it were tied to her wrist with a string.

"Let's do something else," Caddy said.

"I want to go home," Jason said.

"I got some popcorn," Nancy said. She looked at Caddy and then at Jason and then at me and then at Caddy again. "I got some popcorn."

"I don't like popcorn," Jason said. "I'd rather have candy."

Nancy looked at Jason. "You can hold the popper." She was still wringing her hand; it was long and limp and brown.

"All right," Jason said. "I'll stay a while if I can do that. Caddy can't hold it. I'll want to go home again if Caddy holds the popper."

Nancy built up the fire. "Look at Nancy putting her hands in the fire," Caddy said. "What's the matter with you, Nancy?"

"I got popcorn," Nancy said. "I got some." She took the popper from under the bed. It was broken. Jason began to cry.

"Now we can't have any popcorn," he said.

"We ought to go home, anyway," Caddy said. "Come on, Quentin."

"Wait," Nancy said; "wait. I can fix it. Don't you want to help me fix it?"

"I don't think I want any," Caddy said. "It's too late now."

"You help me, Jason," Nancy said. "Don't you want to help me?"

"No," Jason said. "I want to go home."

"Hush," Nancy said; "hush. Watch. Watch me. I can fix it so Jason can hold it and pop the corn." She got a piece of wire and fixed the popper.

"It won't hold good," Caddy said.

"Yes, it will," Nancy said. "Yawl watch. Yawl help me shell some corn."

The popcorn was under the bed too. We shelled it into the popper and Nancy helped Jason hold the popper over the fire.

"It's not popping," Jason said. "I want to go home."

"You wait," Nancy said. "It'll begin to pop. We'll have fun then." She was sitting close to the fire. The lamp was turned up so high it was beginning to smoke.

"Why don't you turn it down some?" I said.

"It's all right," Nancy said. "I'll clean it. Yawl wait. The popcorn will start in a minute."

"I don't believe it's going to start," Caddy said. "We ought to start home, anyway. They'll be worried."

"No," Nancy said. "It's going to pop. Dilsey will tell um yawl with me. I been working for yawl long time. They won't mind if yawl at my house. You wait, now. It'll start popping any minute now."

Then Jason got some smoke in his eyes and he began to cry. He dropped the popper into the fire. Nancy got a wet rag and wiped Jason's face, but he didn't stop crying.

"Hush," she said. "Hush." But he didn't hush. Caddy took the popper out of the fire.

"It's burned up," she said. "You'll have to get some more popcorn, Nancy."

"Did you put all of it in?" Nancy said.

"Yes," Caddy said. Nancy looked at Caddy. Then she took the popper and opened it and poured the cinders into her apron and began to sort the grains, her hands long and brown, and we watching her.

"Haven't you got any more?" Caddy said.

"Yes," Nancy said; "yes. Look. This here ain't burnt. All we need to do is—"

"I want to go home," Jason said. "I'm going to tell."

"Hush," Caddy said. We all listened. Nancy's head was already turned toward the barred door, her eyes filled with red lamplight. "Somebody is coming," Caddy said.

Then Nancy began to make that sound again, not loud, sitting there above the fire, her long hands dangling between her knees; all of a sudden water began to come out on her face in big drops, running down her face, carrying in each one a little turning ball of firelight like a spark until it dropped off her chin. "She's not crying," I said.

"I ain't crying," Nancy said. Her eyes were closed. "I ain't crying. Who is it?"

"I don't know," Caddy said. She went to the door and looked out. "We've got to go now," she said. "Here comes father."

"I'm going to tell," Jason said. "Yawl made me come."

The water still ran down Nancy's face. She turned in her chair. "Listen. Tell him. Tell him we going to have fun. Tell him I take good care of yawl until in the morning. Tell him to let me come home with yawl and sleep on the floor. Tell him I won't need no pallet. We'll have fun. You member last time how we had so much fun?"

"I didn't have fun," Jason said. "You hurt me. You put smoke in my eyes. I'm going to tell."

V

Father came in. He looked at us. Nancy did not get up.

"Tell him," she said.

"Caddy made us come down here," Jason said. "I didn't want to."

Father came to the fire. Nancy looked up at him. "Can't you go to Aunt Rachel's and stay?" he said. Nancy looked up at father, her hands between her knees. "He's not here," father said. "I would have seen him. There's not a soul in sight."

"He in the ditch," Nancy said. "He waiting in the ditch yonder."

"Nonsense," father said. He looked at Nancy. "Do you know he's there?"

"I got the sign," Nancy said.

"What sign?"

"I got it. It was on the table when I come in. It was a hog-bone, with blood meat still on it, laying by the lamp. He's out there. When yawl walk out that door, I gone."

"Gone where, Nancy?" Caddy said.

"I'm not a tattletale," Jason said.

"Nonsense," father said.

"He out there," Nancy said. "He looking through that window this minute, waiting for yawl to go. Then I gone."

"Nonsense," father said. "Lock up your house and we'll take you on to Aunt Rachel's."

"'Twont do no good," Nancy said. She didn't look at father now, but he looked down at her, at her long, limp, moving hands. "Putting it off wont do no good."

"Then what do you want to do?" father said.

"I don't know," Nancy said. "I can't do nothing. Just put it off. And that don't do no good. I reckon it belong to me. I reckon what I going to get ain't no more than mine."

"Get what?" Caddy said. "What's yours?"

"Nothing," father said. "You all must get to bed."

"Caddy made me come," Jason said.

"Go on to Aunt Rachel's," father said.

"It won't do no good," Nancy said. She sat before the fire, her elbows on her knees, her long hands between her knees. "When even your own kitchen wouldn't do no good. When even if I was sleeping on the floor in the room with your chillen, and the next morning there I am, and blood—"

"Hush," father said. "Lock the door and put out the lamp and go to bed."

"I scared of the dark," Nancy said. "I scared for it to happen in the dark."

"You mean you're going to sit right here with the lamp lighted?" father said. Then Nancy began to make the sound again, sitting before the fire, her long hands between her knees. "Ah, damnation," father said. "Come along, chillen. It's past bedtime."

"When yawl go home, I gone," Nancy said. She talked quieter now, and her face looked quiet, like her hands. "Anyway, I got my coffin money saved up with Mr. Lovelady." Mr. Lovelady was a short, dirty man who collected the Negro insurance, coming around to the cabins or the kitchens every Saturday morning, to collect fifteen cents. He and his wife lived at the hotel. One morning his wife committed suicide. They had a child, a little girl. He and the child went away. After a week or two he came back alone. We could see him going along the lanes and the back streets on Saturday mornings.

"Nonsense," father said. "You'll be the first thing I'll see in the kitchen tomorrow morning."

"You'll see what you'll see, I reckon," Nancy said. "But it will take the Lord to say what that will be."

VI

We left her sitting before the fire.

"Come and put the bar up," father said. But she didn't move. She didn't look at us again, sitting quietly there between the lamp and the fire. From some distance down the lane we could look back and see her through the open door.

"What, Father?" Caddy said. "What's going to happen?"

"Nothing," father said. Jason was on father's back, so Jason was the tallest of all of us. We went down into the ditch. I looked at it, quiet. I couldn't see much where the moonlight and the shadows tangled.

"If Jesus is hid here, he can see us, cant he?" Caddy said.

"He's not there," father said. "He went away a long time ago."

"You made me come," Jason said, high; against the sky it looked like father had two heads, a little one and a big one. "I didn't want to."

We went up out of the ditch. We could still see Nancy's house and the open door, but we couldn't see Nancy now, sitting before the fire with the door open, because she was tired. "I just done got tired," she said. "I just a nigger. It ain't no fault of mine."

But we could hear her, because she began just after we came up out of the ditch, the sound that was not singing and not unsinging. "Who will do our washing now, Father?" I said.

"I'm not a nigger," Jason said, high and close above father's head.

"You're worse," Caddy said, "you are a tattletale. If something was to jump out, you'd be scairder than a nigger."

"I wouldn't," Jason said.

"You'd cry," Caddy said.

"Caddy," father said.

"I wouldn't," Jason said.

"Scairy cat," Caddy said.

"Candace!" father said.

AS I LAY DYING

When William Faulkner was invited to record passages from his works, he chose to read several pages from his novel *As I Lay Dying* (1930). These pages are reproduced here. Faulkner has always said he considers this novel his best and certainly it is a vivid and original piece of writing, perhaps the most sustained of all his work. He wrote it, by his own account, during the period in Oxford, Mississippi, when he was employed as a night worker in a power plant. He filled most of the quiet early morning hours with his literary task; his desk was an upturned wheelbarrow.

The novel shows Faulkner's boldness in fictional experiment. It is told entirely through "inner monologue." This is the method of telling a story "from the inside out"—the author attempting to put the reader into the thoughts and feelings of the character. We are, in the book, at every turn in the consciousness of the members of one family, the Bundrens, and for brief moments in that of their neighbors, or one or two persons they encounter during their strange funeral trip from the backwoods area of Yoknapatawpha County to Jefferson. At no point in the story does the author intrude to tell us anything about his people or the scene, or the events. Everything is learned by the reader from what the characters think, feel, or say, about themselves, each other, or the central situation. Faulkner's handling of his series of inner monologues is extremely adroit. He is never at a loss in the double act—the act of letting the persons he has invented reveal their secret inner life (thereby characterizing themselves), and the act of showing their relationship to everything else in the book. And at certain points, with the warmth and compassion he feels for his people, he is the poet, the seer, who supplies the words for those feelings of his personages which would never be verbalized.

The main outline of the novel can be deduced from the excerpts Faulkner selected for his reading. His first passage takes us into the thoughts of Tull, a neighbor of the poor-white Bundrens, and his talk with Anse Bundren who is waiting for his wife Addie to die. He has solemnly promised her that she will be buried in her home town, in Jefferson cemetery. Cash, one of the sons, a carpenter, is busy hammering together the coffin under the window of the room in which Addie Bundren lies dying, and we meet certain of the other children, such as the child Vardaman, carrying the large fish he has caught. The family and the situation is seen through the neighbor's eyes and the words of the father.

In the second excerpt we are in the consciousness of Darl, another of the Bundren sons and the most articulate. Darl experiences life with the heightened reality—and the distortion—of one touched by madness, and he will go stark mad before the book ends. Through Darl's perceptions we have etched for us, in a moving scene of primitive feeling, Addie Bundren's last moments and her death. We get glimpses of some of the other children, of Jewel, another son, Dewey Dell, the daughter, the practical Cash, and the deeply disturbed—because he does not understand—Vardaman. Jewel, we learn in the novel, was born of the mother's secret love affair with the preacher Whitfield, and this kind of echo of Hawthorne (the name Jewel reminds us of the name Pearl, in *The Scarlet Letter,*) as we have seen, runs through Faulkner's work.

The remaining two passages read by Faulkner and given here are remarkable in the effort to create the illusion of the consciousness of the youngest child, Vardaman, who in his fumbling way, and with infantile logic, is trying to understand the nature of death. The fish he has caught has been chopped up to be eaten; the mother is laid in her coffin. Both are dead; death is the common denominator for little Vardaman of mother and fish, and he recognizes this but does not understand it. In handling the childish thoughts, in showing us Vardaman's tears and his rage as well as his fancies, Faulkner displays the same kind of empathy and poetry he used in creating the idiot Benjy in *The Sound and the Fury*, published a year before this novel.

The rest of the novel tells of the journey. During their crawling trip the entire family becomes involved in various adventures; the coffin is almost lost in a flooding river; it is rescued from fire; each member of the family in the end is concerned no longer with death but with his own need to cope with everyday life. At the end, once Addie is buried, the father promptly finds himself another wife and gets himself the false teeth he has long needed: the trip to the city has been not so much the enactment of a promise to a dead mother as the fulfillment of promises to each member of this family. We move among their shifting angles of vision and as we read we take hold of an increasing number of threads making up the story. The book is rich in the flavor of the Bundren idiom and the lyrical qualities with which Faulkner endows his human material. There are touches of farce; there is melodrama and brutality; but we are at every turn close to life, to feeling—and to the poetry of feeling.

Tull

Anse keeps on rubbing his knees. His overalls are faded; on one knee a serge patch cut out of a pair of Sunday pants, wore iron-slick. "No man mislikes it more than me," he says.

"A fellow's got to guess ahead now and then," I say. "But, come long and short, it won't be no harm done neither way."

"She'll want to get started right off," he says. "It's far enough to Jefferson at best."

"But the roads is good now," I say. It's fixing to rain tonight, too. His folks buries at New Hope, too, not three miles away. But it's just like him to marry a woman born a day's hard ride away and have her die on him.

He looks out over the land, rubbing his knees. "No man so mislikes it," he says.

"They'll get back in plenty of time," I say. "I wouldn't worry none."

"It means three dollars," he says.

"Might be it won't be no need for them to rush back, noways," I say. "I hope it."

"She's a-going," he says. "Her mind is set on it." It's a hard life on women, for a fact. Some women. I mind my mammy lived to be seventy and more. Worked every day, rain or shine; never a sick day since her last chap was born until one day she kind of looked around her and then she went and taken that lace-trimmed night-gown she had had forty-five years and never wore out of the chest and put it on and laid down on the bed and pulled the covers up and shut her eyes. "You all will have to look out for pa the best you can," she said. "I'm tired."

Anse rubs his hands on his knees. "The Lord giveth," he says. We can hear Cash a-hammering and sawing beyond the corner.

It's true. Never a truer breath was ever breathed. "The Lord giveth," I say.

That boy comes up the hill. He is carrying a fish nigh long as he is. He slings it to the ground and grunts "Hah" and spits over his shoulder like a man. Durn nigh long as he is.

"What's that?" I say. "A hog? Where'd you get it?"

"Down to the bridge," he says. He turns it over, the under-side caked over with dust where it is wet, the eye coated over, humped under the dirt.

"Are you aiming to leave it laying there?" Anse says.

"I aim to show it to ma," Vardaman says. He looks toward the door. We can hear the talking, coming out on the draught. Cash, too, knocking and hammering at the boards. "There's company in there," he says.

"Just my folks," I say. "They'd enjoy to see it, too."

He says nothing, watching the door. Then he looks down at the fish laying in the dust. He turns it over with his foot and prods at the eye-bump with his toe, gouging at it. Anse is looking out over the land. Vardaman looks at Anse's face, then at the door. He turns, going toward the corner of the house, when Anse calls him without looking around.

"You clean that fish," Anse says.

Vardaman stops. "Why can't Dewey Dell clean it?" he says.

"You clean that fish," Anse says.

"Aw, pa," Vardaman says.

"You clean it," Anse says. He don't look around. Vardaman comes back and picks up the fish. It slides out of his hands, smearing wet dirt on to him, and flops down, dirtying itself again, gap-mouthed, goggle-eyed, hiding into the dust like it was ashamed of being dead, like it was in a hurry to get back hid again. Vardaman cusses it. He cusses it like a grown man, standing a-straddle of it. Anse don't look around. Vardaman picks it up again. He goes on around the house, toting it in both arms like an armful of wood, it overlapping him on both ends, head and tail. Durn nigh big as he is.

Anse's wrists dangle out of his sleeves: I never see him with a shirt on that looked like it was his in all my life. They all looked like Jewel might have give him his old ones. Not Jewel, though. He's long-armed, even if he is spindling. Except for the lack of sweat. You could tell they ain't been nobody else's but Anse's that way without no mistake. His eyes look like pieces of burnt-out cinder fixed in his face, looking out over the land.

When the shadow touches the steps he says "It's five o'clock."

Just as I get up Cora comes to the door and says it's time to get on. Anse reaches for his shoes. "Now, Mr. Bundren," Cora says, "don't you get up now." He puts his shoes on, stomping into them, like he does everything like he is hoping all the time he really can't do it and can quit trying to. When we go up the hall we can hear them clumping on the floor like they was iron shoes. He comes toward the door where she is, blinking his eyes, kind of looking ahead of hisself before he sees, like he is hoping to find her setting up, in a chair maybe or maybe sweeping, and looks into the door in that surprised way like he looks in and finds her still in bed every time and Dewey Dell still a-fanning her with the fan. He stands there, like he don't aim to move again nor nothing else.

"Well, I reckon we better get on," Cora says. "I got to feed the chickens." It's fixing to rain, too. Clouds like that don't lie, and the cotton making every day the Lord sends. That'll be something else for him. Cash is still trimming at the boards. "If there's ere a thing we can do," Cora says.

"Anse'll let us know," I say.

Anse don't look at us. He looks around, blinking, in that surprised way, like he had wore hisself down being surprised and was even surprised at that. If Cash just works that careful on my barn.

"I told Anse it likely won't be no need," I say. "I so hope it."

"Her mind is set on it," he says. "I reckon she's bound to go."

"It comes to all of us," Cora says. "Let the Lord comfort you."

"About that corn," I say. I tell him again I will help him out if he gets into a tight, with her sick and all. Like most folks around here, I done help him so much already I can't quit now.

"I aimed to get to it today," he says. "Seems like I can't get my mind on nothing."

"Maybe she'll hold out till you are laid by," I say.

"If God wills it," he says.

"Let Him comfort you," Cora says.

If Cash just works that careful on my barn. He looks up when we pass. "Don't reckon I'll get to you this week," he says.

" 'Tain't no rush," I say. "Whenever you get around to it."

We get into the wagon. Cora sets the cake-box on her lap. It's fixing to rain, sho.

"I don't know what he'll do," Cora says. "I just don't know."

"Poor Anse," I say. "She kept him at work for thirty-odd years. I reckon she is tired."

"And I reckon she'll be behind him for thirty years more," Kate says. "Or if it ain't her, he'll get another one before cotton-picking."

"I reckon Cash and Darl can get married now," Eula says.

"That poor boy," Cora says. "The poor little tyke."

"What about Jewel?" Kate says.

"He can, too," Eula says.

"Humph," Kate says. "I reckon he will. I reckon so. I reckon there's more gals than one around here that don't want to see Jewel tied down. Well, they needn't to worry."

"Why, Kate!" Cora says. The wagon begins to rattle. "The poor little tyke," Cora says.

It's fixing to rain this night. Yes, sir. A rattling wagon is mighty dry weather, for a Birdsell. But that'll be cured. It will for a fact.

"She ought to taken them cakes after she said she would," Kate says.

DARL

Pa stands beside the bed. From behind his leg Vardaman peers, with his round head and his eyes round and his mouth beginning to open. She looks at pa; all her failing life appears to drain into her eyes, urgent, irremediable. "It's Jewel she wants," Dewey Dell says.

"Why, Addie," pa says, "him and Darl went to make one more load. They thought there was time. That you would wait for them, and that three dollars and all . . . ." He stoops, laying his hand on hers. For a while yet she looks at him, without reproach, without anything at all, as if her eyes alone are listening to the irrevocable cessation of his voice. Then she raises herself, who has not moved in ten days. Dewey Dell leans down, trying to press her back.

"Ma," she says; "ma."

She is looking out the window, at Cash stooping steadily at the board in the failing light, labouring on toward darkness and into it as though the stroking of the saw illumined its own motion, board and saw engendered.

"You, Cash," she shouts, her voice harsh, strong, and unimpaired. "You, Cash!"

He looks up at the gaunt face framed by the window in the twilight. It is a composite picture of all time since he was a child. He drops the saw and lifts the board for her to see, watching the window in which the face has not moved. He drags a second plank into position and slants the two of them into their final juxtaposition, gesturing toward the ones yet on the ground, shaping with his empty hand in pantomime the finished box. For a while still she looks down at him from the composite picture, neither with censure nor approbation. Then the face disappears.

She lies back and turns her head without so much as glancing at pa. She looks at Vardaman; her eyes, the life in them, rushing suddenly upon them; the two flames glare up for a steady instant. Then they go out as though someone had leaned down and blown upon them.

"Ma," Dewey Dell says; "ma!" Leaning above the bed, her hands lifted a little, the fan still moving like it has for ten days, she begins to keen. Her voice is strong, young, tremulous and clear, rapt with its own timbre and volume, the fan still moving steadily up and down, whispering the useless air. Then she flings herself across Addie Bundren's knees, clutching her, shaking her with the furious strength of the young before sprawling suddenly across the handful of rotten bones that Addie Bundren left, jarring the whole bed into a chattering sibilance of mattress shucks, her arms outflung and the fan in one hand still beating with expiring breath into the quilt.

From behind pa's leg Vardaman peers, his mouth full open and all colour draining from his face into his mouth, as though he has by some means fleshed his own teeth in himself, sucking. He begins to move slowly backward from the bed, his eyes round, his pale face fading into the dusk like a piece of paper pasted on a failing wall, and so out of the door.

Pa leans above the bed in the twilight, his humped silhouette partaking of that owl-like quality of awry-feathered, disgruntled outrage within which lurks a wisdom too profound or too inert for even thought.

"Durn them boys," he says.

Jewel, I say. Overhead the day drives level and grey, hiding the sun by a flight of grey spears. In the rain the mules smoke a little, splashed yellow with mud, the off one clinging in sliding lunges to the side of the road above the ditch. The tilted lumber gleams dull yellow, water-soaked and heavy as lead, tilted at a steep angle into the ditch above the broken wheel; about the shattered spokes and about Jewel's ankles a runnel of yellow neither water nor earth swirls, curving with the yellow road neither of earth nor water, down the hill dissolving into a streaming mass of dark green neither of earth nor sky. Jewel, I say.

Cash comes to the door, carrying the saw. Pa stands beside the bed, humped, his arms dangling. He turns his head, his shabby profile, his chin collapsing slowly as he works the snuff against his gums.

"She's gone," Cash says.

"She taken and left us," pa says. Cash does not look at him. "How nigh are you done?" pa says. Cash does not answer. He enters, carrying the saw. "I reckon you better get at it," pa says. "You'll have to do the best you can, with them boys gone off that-a-way." Cash looks down at her face. He is not listening to pa at all. He does not approach the bed. He stops in the middle of the floor, the saw against his leg, his sweating arms powdered lightly with sawdust, his face composed. "If you get in a tight, maybe some of them'll get here tomorrow and help you," pa says. "Vernon could." Cash is not listening. He is looking down at her peaceful, rigid face fading into the dusk as though darkness were a precursor of the ultimate earth, until at last the face seems to float detached upon it, lightly as the reflection of a dead leaf. "There is Christians enough to help you," pa says. Cash is not listening. After a while he turns without looking at pa and leaves the room. Then the saw begins to snore again. "They will help us in our sorrow," pa says.

The sound of the saw is steady, competent, unhurried, stirring the dying light so that at each stroke her face seems to wake a little into an expression of listening and of waiting, as though she were counting the strokes. Pa looks down at the face, at the black sprawl of Dewey Dell's hair, the outflung arms, the clutched fan now motionless on the fading quilt. "I reckon you better get supper on," he says.

Dewey Dell does not move.

"Git up, now, and put supper on," pa says. "We got to keep our strength up. I reckon Doctor Peabody's right hungry, coming all this way. And Cash'll need to eat quick and get back to work so he can finish it in time."

Dewey Dell rises, heaving to her feet. She looks down at the face. It is like a casting of fading bronze upon the pillow, the hands alone still with any semblance of life: a curled, gnarled inertness; a spent yet alert quality from which weariness, exhaustion, travail has not yet departed, as though they doubted even yet the actuality of rest, guarding with horned and penurious alertness the cessation which they know cannot last.

Dewey Dell stoops and slides the quilt from beneath them and draws it up over them to the chin, smoothing it down, drawing it smooth. Then without looking at pa she goes around the bed and leaves the room.

She will go out where Peabody is, where she can stand in the twilight and look at his back with such an expression that, feeling her eyes and turning, he will say; I would not let it grieve me, now. She was old, and sick too. Suffering more than we knew. She couldn't have got well. Vardaman's getting big now, and with you to take good care of them all. I would try not to let it grieve me. I expect you'd better go and get some supper ready. It don't have to be much. But they'll need to eat, and she looking at him, saying You could do so much for me if you just would. If you just knew. I am I and you are you and I know it and you don't know it and you could do so much for me if you just would and if you just would then I could tell you and then nobody would have to know it except you and me and Darl.

Pa stands over the bed, dangle-armed, humped, motionless. He raises his hand to his head, scouring his hair, listening to the saw. He comes nearer and rubs his hand, palm and back, on his thigh and lays it on her face and then on the hump of quilt where her hands are. He touches the quilt as he saw Dewey Dell do, trying to smooth it up to the chin, but disarranging it instead. He tries to smooth it again, clumsily, his hand awkward as a claw, smoothing at the wrinkles which he made and which continue to emerge beneath his hand with perverse ubiquity, so that at last he desists, his hand falling to his side and stroking itself again, palm and back, on his thigh. The sound of the saw snores steadily into the room. Pa breathes with a quiet, rasping sound, mouthing the snuff against his gums. "God's will be done," he says. "Now I can get them teeth."

Jewel's hat droops limp about his neck, channelling water on to the soaked tow-sack tied about his shoulders as, ankle-deep in the running ditch, he pries with a slipping two-by-four, with a piece of rotting log for fulcrum, at the axle. Jewel, I say, she is dead, Jewel. Addie Bundren is dead.

Vardaman

Then I begin to run. I run toward the back and come to the edge of the porch and stop. Then I begin to cry. I can feel where the fish was in the dust. It is cut up into pieces of not-fish now, not-blood on my hands and overalls. Then it wasn't so. It hadn't happened then. And now she is getting so far ahead I cannot catch her.

The trees look like chickens when they ruffle out into the cool dust on the hot days. If I jump off the porch I will be where the fish was, and it all cut up into not-fish now. I can hear the bed and her face and them and I can feel the floor shake when he walks on it that came and did it. That came and did it when she was all right but he came and did it.

"The fat son of a bitch."

I jump from the porch, running. The top of the barn comes swooping up out of the twilight. If I jump I can go through it like the pink lady in the circus, into the warm smelling, without having to wait. My hands grab at the bushes; beneath my feet the rocks and dirt go rubbling down.

Then I can breathe again, in the warm smelling. I enter the stall, trying to touch him, and then I cry then I vomit the crying. As soon as he gets through kicking I can and then I can cry, the crying can.

"He kilt her. He kilt her."

The life in him runs under the skin, under my hand, running through the splotches, smelling up into my nose where the sickness is beginning to cry, vomiting the crying, and then I can breathe, vomiting it. It makes a lot of noise. I can smell the life running up from under my hands, up my arms, and then I can leave the stall.

I cannot find it. In the dark, along the dust, the walls I cannot find it. The crying makes a lot of noise. I wish it wouldn't make so much noise. Then I find it in the wagon-shed, in the dust, and I run across the lot and into the road, the stick jouncing on my shoulder.

They watch me as I run up, beginning to jerk back, their eyes rolling, snorting, jerking back on the hitch rein. I strike. I can hear the stick striking; I can see it hitting their heads, the breast-yoke, missing altogether sometimes as they rear and plunge, but I am glad.

"You kilt my maw!"

The stick breaks, they rearing and snorting, their feet popping loud on the ground; loud because it is going to rain and the air is empty for the rain. But it is still long enough. I run this way and that as they rear and jerk at the hitch-rein, striking.

"You kilt her!"

I strike at them, striking, they wheeling in a long lunge, the buggy wheeling on to two wheels and motionless like it is nailed to the ground and the horses motionless like they are nailed by the hind feet to the centre of a whirling-plate.

I run in the dust. I cannot see, running in the sucking dust where the buggy vanishes tilted on two wheels. I strike, the stick hitting into the ground, bouncing, striking into the dust and then into the air again and the dust sucking on down the road faster than if a car was in it. And then I can cry, looking at the stick. It is broken down to my hand, not longer than stove wood that was a long stick. I throw it away and I can cry. It does not make so much noise now.

The cow is standing in the barn door, chewing. When she sees me come into the lot she lows, her mouth full of flopping green, her tongue flopping.

"I ain't a-goin' to milk you. I ain't a-goin' to do nothing for them."

I hear her turn when I pass. When I turn she is just behind me with her sweet, hot, hard breath.

"Didn't I tell you I wouldn't?"

She nudges me, snuffing. She moans deep inside, her mouth closed. I jerk my hand, cursing her like Jewel does.

"Git, now."

I stoop my hand to the ground and run at her. She jumps back and whirls away and stops, watching me. She moans. She goes on to the path and stands there, looking up the path.

It is dark in the barn, warm, smelling, silent. I can cry quietly, watching the top of the hill.

Cash comes to the hill, limping where he fell off of the church. He looks down at the spring, then up the road and back toward the barn. He comes down the path stiffly and looks at the broken hitch-rein and at the dust in the road and then up the road, where the dust is gone.

"I hope they've got clean past Tull's by now. I so hope hit."

Cash turns and limps up the path.

"Durn him. I showed him. Durn him."

I am not crying now. I am not anything. Dewey Dell comes to the hill and calls me. "Vardaman." I am not anything. I am quiet. "You, Vardaman." I can cry quiet now, feeling and hearing my tears.

"Then hit want. Hit hadn't happened then. Hit was a-layin' right there on the ground. And now she's gittin ready to cook hit."

It is dark. I can hear wood, silence: I know them. But not living sounds, not even him. It is as though the dark were resolving him out of his integrity, into an unrelated scattering of components—snuffings and

stampings; smells of cooling flesh and ammoniac hair; an illusion of a
coordinated whole of splotched hide and strong bones within which, detached and secret and familiar, an *is* different from my *is*. I see him dissolve—legs, a rolling eye, a gaudy splotching like cold flames—and float
upon the dark in fading solution; all one yet neither; all either yet none.
I can see hearing coil toward him, caressing, shaping his hard shape—fet-
lock, hip, shoulder and head; smell and sound. I am not afraid.

"Cooked and et. Cooked and et."

[In the novel, the monologue of Dewey Dell follows at this point, then Vardaman's
monologue is resumed.]

When they get it finished they are going to put her in it and then for
a long time I couldn't say it. I saw the dark stand up and go whirling
away and I said "Are you going to nail her up in it, Cash? Cash? Cash?" I
got shut up in the crib the new door it was too heavy for me it went
shut I couldn't breathe because the rat was breathing up all the air. I
said "Are you going to nail it shut, Cash? Nail it? *Nail* it?"

Pa walks around. His shadow walks around, over Cash going up and
down above the saw, at the bleeding plank.

Dewey Dell said we will get some bananas. The train is behind the
glass, red on the track. When it runs the track shines on and off. Pa said
flour and sugar and coffee costs so much. Because I am a country boy because boys in town. Bicycles. Why do flour and sugar and coffee cost so
much when he is a country boy. "Wouldn't you ruther have some bananas instead?" Bananas are gone, eaten. Gone. When it runs on the track
shines again. "Why ain't I a town boy, pa?" I said God made me. I did
not said to God to made me in the country. If He can make the train,
why can't He make them all in the town because flour and sugar and
coffee. "Wouldn't you ruther have bananas?"

He walks around. His shadow walks around.

It was not her. I was there, looking. I saw. I thought it was her, but it
was not. It was not my mother. She went away when the other one laid
down in her bed and drew the quilt up. She went away. "Did she go as
far as town?" "She went farther than town." "Did all those rabbits and
possums go farther than town?" God made the rabbits and possums. He
made the train. Why must He make a different place for them to go if
she is just like the rabbit.

Pa walks around. His shadow does. The saw sounds like it is asleep.

And so if Cash nails the box up, she is not a rabbit, and so if she is not
a rabbit I couldn't breathe in the crib and Cash is going to nail it up.
And so if she lets him it is not her. I know. I was there. I saw when it did
not be her. I saw. They think it is and Cash is going to nail it up.

It was not her because it was laying right yonder in the dirt. And now
it's all chopped up. I chopped it up. It's laying in the kitchen in the bleeding pan, waiting to be cooked and et. Then it wasn't and she was, and
now it is and she wasn't. And tomorrow it will be cooked and et and she
will be him and pa and Cash and Dewey Dell and there won't be anything

in the box and so she can breathe. It was laying right yonder on the ground. I can get Vernon. He was there and he seen it, and with both of us it will be and then it will not be.

⚜

From THE OLD MAN

The passage given below from William Faulkner's short novel *The Old Man* was also selected by him for his recording. *The Old Man* was originally contained in a novel, *The Wild Palms* (1939) in which it was narrated, in alternation, with another story, both stories having analogous and complementary themes. Most critics felt the alternation to be artificial; certainly *The Old Man* stands by itself as a short novel. It is a vivid narrative of an unnamed Mississippi convict, who is put to work with other convicts to help control a raging flood. He is ordered to rescue a woman isolated by the rushing waters. When he reaches her, he discovers she is in an advanced stage of pregnancy and about to give birth. They drift in the flood waters, thrown together by a disaster, uninterested in each other, both merely seeking survival, yet forced to co-operate. The convict has temporary freedom and does not know how to use it. The episode read by Faulkner is from the chapter in which the rescue is achieved and the baby is born. The story's final irony is that the convict, having carried out his duty, is sentenced to an extra ten years for "attempted escape." By the time he wrote this story, Faulkner had developed his long, rhythmic sentences and his use of them, in spinning his narrative, may be studied in this striking passage.

Even when he tried to tell it, even after the seven weeks and he safe, secure, riveted warranted and doubly guaranteed by the ten years they had added to his sentence for attempted escape, something of the old hysteric incredulous outrage came back into his face, his voice, his speech. He never did even get on the other boat. He told how he clung to a strake (it was a dirty unpainted shanty boat with a drunken rake of tin stove pipe, it had been moving when he struck it and apparently it had not even changed course even though the three people on it must have been watching him all the while—a second man, barefoot and with matted hair and beard also at the steering sweep, and then—he did not know how long—a woman leaning in the door, in a filthy assortment of men's garments, watching him too with the same cold speculation) being dragged violently along, trying to state and explain his simple (and to him at least) reasonable desire and need; telling it, trying to tell it, he could feel again the old unforgettable affronting like an ague fit as he watched the abortive tobacco rain steadily and faintly from between his shaking hands and then the paper itself part with a thin dry snapping report:

"Burn my clothes?" the convict cried. "Burn them?"

"How in hell do you expect to escape in them bill-boards?" the man with the shotgun said. He (the convict) tried to tell it, tried to explain as he had tried to explain not to the three people on the boat alone but to the entire circumambience—desolate water and forlorn trees and sky —not for justification because he needed none and knew that his hearers, the other convicts, required none from him, but rather as, on the point of exhaustion, he might have picked dreamily and incredulously at a suffocation. He told the man with the gun how he and his partner had been given the boat and told to pick up a man and a woman, how he had lost his partner and failed to find the man, and now all in the world he wanted was something flat to leave the woman on until he could find an officer, a sheriff. He thought of home, the place where he had lived almost since childhood, his friends of years whose ways he knew and who knew his ways, the familiar fields where he did work he had learned to do well and to like, the mules with characters he knew and respected as he knew and respected the characters of certain men; he thought of the barracks at night, with screens against the bugs in summer and good stoves in winter and someone to supply the fuel and the food too; the Sunday ball games and the picture shows—things which, with the exception of the ball games, he had never known before. But most of all, his own character (Two years ago they had offered to make a trusty of him. He would not longer need to plow or feed stock, he would only follow those who did with a loaded gun, but he declined. "I reckon I'll stick to plowing," he said, absolutely without humor. "I done already tried to use a gun one time too many.") his good name, his responsibility not only toward those who were responsible toward him but to himself, his own honor in the doing of what was asked of him, his pride in being able to do it, no matter what it was. He thought of this and listened to the man with the gun talking about escape and it seemed to him that, hanging there, being dragged violently along (it was here he said that he first noticed the goats' beards of moss in the trees, though it could have been there for several days so far as he knew. It just happened that he first noticed it here.) that he would simply burst.

"Cant you get it into your head that the last thing I want to do is run away?" he cried. "You can set there with that gun and watch me; I give you fair lief. All I want is to put this woman—"

"And I told you she could come aboard," the man with the gun said in his level voice. "But there aint no room on no boat of mine for nobody hunting a sheriff in no kind of clothes, let alone a penitentiary suit."

"When he steps aboard, knock him in the head with the gun barrel," the man at the sweep said. "He's drunk."

"He aint coming aboard," the man with the gun said. "He's crazy."

Then the woman spoke. She didnt move, leaning in the door, in a pair of faded and patched and filthy overalls like the two men: "Give them some grub and tell them to get out of here." She moved, she crossed the

deck and looked down at the convict's companion with her cold sullen
face. "How much more time have you got?"

"It wasn't due till next month," the woman in the boat said. "But I—"
The woman in overalls turned to the man with the gun.

"Give them some grub," she said. But the man with the gun was still
looking down at the woman in the boat.

"Come on," he said to the convict. "Put her aboard, and beat it."

"And what'll happen to you," the woman in overalls said, "when you
try to turn her over to an officer. When you lay alongside a sheriff and
the sheriff asks you who you are?" Still the man with the gun didn't even
look at her. He hardly even shifted the gun across his arm as he struck
the woman across the face with the back of his other hand, hard. "You
son of a bitch," she said. Still the man with the gun did not even look at
her.

"Well?" he said to the convict.

"Dont you see I cant?" the convict cried. "Cant you see that?"

Now, he said, he gave up. He was doomed. That is, he knew now that
he had been doomed from the very start never to get rid of her, just as
the ones who sent him out with the skiff knew that he never would actually give up; when he recognized one of the objects which the woman
in overalls was hurling into the skiff to be a can of condensed milk, he
believed it to be a presage, gratuitous and irrevocable as a death-notice
over the telegraph, that he was not even to find a flat stationary surface
in time for the child to be born on it. So he told how he held the skiff
alongside the shanty-boat while the first tentative toying of the second
wave made up beneath him, while the woman in overalls passed back and
forth between house and rail, flinging the food—the hunk of salt meat, the
ragged and filthy quilt, the scorched lumps of cold bread which she
poured into the skiff from a heaped dishpan like so much garbage—while
he clung to the strake against the mounting pull of the current, the new
wave which for the moment he had forgotten because he was still trying
to state the incredible simplicity of his desire and need until the man
with the gun (the only one of the three who wore shoes) began to
stamp at his hands, he snatching his hands away one at a time to avoid
the heavy shoes, then grasping the rail again until the man with the gun
kicked at his face, he flinging himself sideways to avoid the shoe and so
breaking his hold on the rail, his weight canting the skiff off at a tangent
on the increasing current so that it began to leave the shanty boat behind and he paddling again now, violently, as a man hurries toward the
precipice for which he knows at last he is doomed, looking back at the
other boat, the three faces sullen derisive and grim and rapidly diminishing across the widening water and at last, apoplectic, suffocating with the
intolerable fact not that he had been refused but that he had been refused so little, had wanted so little, asked for so little, yet there had been
demanded of him in return the one price out of all breath which (they

must have known) if he could have paid it, he would not have been where he was, asking what he asked, raising the paddle and shaking it and screaming curses back at them even after the shotgun flashed and the charge went scuttering past along the water to one side.

So he hung there, he said, shaking the paddle and howling, when suddenly he remembered that other wave, the second wall of water full of houses and dead mules building up behind him back in the swamp. So he quit yelling then and went back to paddling. He was not trying to outrun it. He just knew from experience that when it overtook him, he would have to travel in the same direction it was moving in anyway, whether he wanted to or not, and when it did overtake him, he would begin to move too fast to stop, no matter what places he might come to where he could leave the woman, land her in time. Time: that was his itch now, so his only chance was to stay ahead of it as long as he could and hope to reach something before it struck. So he went on, driving the skiff with muscles which had been too tired so long they had quit feeling it, as when a man has had bad luck for so long that he ceases to believe it is even bad, let alone luck. Even when he ate—the scorched lumps the size of baseballs and the weight and durability of cannel coal even after having lain in the skiff's bilge where the shanty boat woman had thrown them—the iron-like lead-heavy objects which no man would have called bread outside of the crusted and scorched pan in which they had cooked—it was with one hand, begrudging even that from the paddle.

He tried to tell that too—that day while the skiff fled on among the bearded trees while every now and then small quiet tentative exploratory feelers would come up from the wave behind and toy for a moment at the skiff, light and curious, then go on with a faint hissing sighing, almost a chuckling, sound, the skiff going on, driving on with nothing to see but trees and water and solitude: until after a while it no longer seemed to him that he was trying to put space and distance behind him or shorten space and distance ahead but that both he and the wave were now hanging suspended simultaneous and unprogressing in pure time, upon a dreamy desolation in which he paddled on not from any hope even to reach anything at all but merely to keep intact what little of distance the length of the skiff provided between himself and the inert and inescapable mass of female meat before him; then night and the skiff rushing on, fast since any speed over anything unknown and invisible is too fast, with nothing before him and behind him the outrageous idea of a volume of moving water toppling forward, its crest frothed and shredded like fangs, and then dawn again (another of those dreamlike alterations day to dark then back to day again with that quality truncated, anacronic and unreal as the waxing and waning of lights in a theatre scene) and the skiff emerging now with the woman no longer supine beneath the shrunken soaked private's coat but sitting bolt upright, gripping the gunwales with both hands, her eyes closed and her lower lip caught between her teeth and he driving the splintered board furiously now, glaring at her out of his wild swollen sleepless face and crying, croaking, "Hold on! For God's sake hold on!"

"I'm trying to," she said. "But hurry! Hurry!" He told it, the unbelievable: hurry, hasten: the man falling from a cliff being told to catch onto something and save himself; the very telling of it emerging shadowy and burlesque, ludicrous, comic and mad, from the ague of unbearable forgetting with a quality more dreamily furious than any fable behind proscenium lights:

He was in a basin now—"A basin?" the plump convict said. "That's what you wash in."

"All right," the tall one said, harshly, above his hands. "I did." With a supreme effort he stilled them long enough to release the two bits of cigarette paper and watched them waft in light fluttering indecision to the floor between his feet, holding his hands motionless even for a moment longer—a basin, a broad peaceful yellow sea which had an abruptly and curiously ordered air, giving him, even at that moment, the impression that it was accustomed to water even if not total submersion; he even remembered the name of it, told to him two or three weeks later by someone: Atchafalaya—

"Louisiana?" the plump convict said. "You mean you were clean out of Mississippi? Hell fire." He stared at the tall one. "Shucks," he said. "That aint but just across from Vicksburg."

"They never named any Vicksburg across from where I was," the tall one said. "It was Baton Rouge they named." And now he began to talk about a town, a little neat white portrait town nestling among enormous very green trees, appearing suddenly in the telling as it probably appeared in actuality, abrupt and airy and mirage-like and incredibly serene before him behind a scattering of boats moored to a line of freight cars standing flush to the doors in water. And now he tried to tell that too: how he stood waist-deep in water for a moment looking back and down at the skiff in which the woman half lay, her eyes still closed, her knuckles white on the gunwales and a tiny thread of blood creeping down her chin from her chewed lip, and he looking down at her in a kind of furious desperation.

"How far will I have to walk?" she said.

"I don't know, I tell you!" he cried. "But it's land somewhere yonder! It's land, houses."

"If I try to move, it wont even be born inside a boat," she said. "You'll have to get closer."

"Yes," he cried, wild, desperate, incredulous. "Wait, I'll go and surrender, then they will have—" He didn't finish, wait to finish; he told that too: himself splashing, stumbling, trying to run, sobbing and gasping; now he saw it—another loading platform standing above the yellow flood, the khaki figures on it as before, identical, the same; he said how the intervening days since that first innocent morning telescoped, vanished as if they had never been, the two contiguous succeeding instants (succeeding? simultaneous) and he transported across no intervening space but merely turned in his own footsteps, plunging, splashing, his arms raised, croaking harshly. He heard the startled shout, "There's one of them!", the command, the clash of equipment, the alarmed cry: "There he goes! There he goes!"

"Yes!" he cried, running, plunging, "here I am! Here! Here!" running on, into the first scattered volley, stopping among the bullets, waving his arms, shrieking, "I want to surrender! I want to surrender!" watching not in terror but in amazed and absolutely unbearable outrage as a squatting clump of the khaki figures parted and he saw the machine gun, the blunt thick muzzle slant and drop and probe toward him and he still screaming in his hoarse crow's voice, "I want to surrender! Cant you hear me?" continuing to scream even as he whirled and plunged splashing, ducking, went completely under and heard the bullets going thuck-thuck-thuck on the water above him and he scrabbling still on the bottom, still trying to scream even before he regained his feet and still all submerged save his plunging unmistakable buttocks, the outraged screaming bubbling from his mouth and about his face since he merely wanted to surrender. Then he was comparatively screened, out of range, though not for long. That is (he didn't tell how nor where) there was a moment in which he paused, breathed for a second before running again, the course back to the skiff open for the time being though he could still hear the shouts behind him and now and then a shot, and he panting, sobbing, a long savage tear in the flesh of one hand, got when and how he did not know, and he wasting precious breath, speaking to no one now any more than the scream of the dying rabbit is addressed to any mortal ear but rather an indictment of all breath and its folly and suffering, its infinite capacity for folly and pain, which seems to be its only immortality: "All in the world I want is just to surrender."

He returned to the skiff and got in and took up his splintered plank. And now when he told this, despite the fury of element which climaxed it, it (the telling) became quite simple; he now even creased another cigarette paper between fingers which did not tremble at all and filled the paper from the tobacco sack without spilling a flake, as though he had passed from the machine-gun's barrage into a bourne beyond any more amazement: so that the subsequent part of his narrative seemed to reach his listeners as though from beyond a sheet of slightly milky though still transparent glass, as something not heard but seen—a series of shadows, edgeless yet distinct, and smoothly flowing, logical and unfrantic and making no sound: They were in the skiff, in the center of the broad placid trough which had no boundaries and down which the tiny forlorn skiff flew to the irresistible coercion of a current going once more he knew not where, the neat small liveoak-bowered towns unattainable and miragelike and apparently attached to nothing upon the airy and unchanging horizon. He did not believe them, they did not matter, he was doomed; they were less than the figments of smoke or of delirium, and he driving his unceasing paddle without destination or even hope now, looking now and then at the woman sitting with her knees drawn up and locked and her entire body one terrific clench while the threads of bloody saliva crept from her teeth-clenched lower lip. He was going nowhere and fleeing from nothing, he merely continued to paddle because he had paddled so long now that he believed if he stopped his muscles would scream in agony. So when it happened he was not surprised. He heard the sound which he knew well (he had heard it but once before, true enough, but no man needed hear it but once) and he had been expecting it; he looked back, still driving the paddle, and saw it, curled, crested with its strawlike flotsam of trees and debris and dead beasts and he glared over his shoulder at it for a full minute out of that attenuation far beyond the point of outragement where even suffering, the capability of being further affronted, had ceased, from which he now contemplated with savage and invulnerable curiosity the further extent to which his now anesthetised nerves could bear, what next could be invented for them to bear, until the wave actually began to rear above his head into its thunderous climax. Then only did he turn his head. His stroke did not falter, it neither slowed nor increased; still paddling with that spent hypnotic steadiness, he saw the swimming deer. He did not know what it was nor that he had altered the skiff's course to follow it, he just watched the swimming head before him as the wave boiled down and the skiff rose bodily in the old familiar fashion on a welter of tossing trees and houses and bridges and fences, he still paddling even while the paddle found no purchase save air and still paddled even as he and the deer shot forward side by side at arm's length, he watching the deer now, watching the deer begin to rise out of the water bodily until it was actually running along upon the surface, rising still, soaring clear of the water altogether, vanishing upward in a dying crescendo of splashings and snapping branches, its damp scut flashing upward, the entire animal vanishing upward as smoke vanishes. And now the skiff struck and canted and he was out of it too, standing knee-deep, springing out and falling to his knees, scrambling up, glaring after the vanished deer. "Land!" he croaked. "Land! Hold on! Just hold on!" He caught the woman beneath the arms, dragging her out of the boat, plunging and panting after the vanished deer. Now earth actually appeared—an acclivity smooth and swift and steep, bizarre, solid and unbelievable; an Indian mound, and he plunging at the muddy slope, slipping back, the woman struggling in his muddy hands.

"Let me down!" she cried. "Let me down!" But he held her, panting, sobbing, and rushed again at the muddy slope; he had almost reached the flat crest with his now violently unmanageable burden when a stick under his foot gathered itself with thick convulsive speed. *It was a snake,* he thought as his feet fled beneath him and with the indubitable last of his strength he half pushed and half flung the woman up the bank as he shot feet first and face down back into that medium upon which he had lived for more days and nights than he could remember and from which he himself had never completely emerged, as if his own failed and spent flesh were attempting to carry out his furious unflagging will for severance at any price, even that of drowning, from the burden with which, unwitting and without choice, he had been doomed. Later it seemed to him that he had carried back beneath the surface with him the sound of the infant's first mewling cry.

THE NOBEL PRIZE SPEECH
AND A FABLE

In 1950 Faulkner was awarded the Nobel Prize for literature and journeyed to Stockholm to receive what one of his predecessors— William Butler Yeats—called "the bounty of Sweden." Never one to make long speeches, Faulkner read only a few sentences, which he later recorded, in a matter-of-fact, quiet voice. But when his words were cabled around the world, they excited much admiration for their dignity and their passion: in their slightly old-fashioned rhetoric there was the ring of a man sincerely devoted to his craft and to the truth of feeling, "the human heart in conflict with itself."

Four years later *A Fable*, Faulkner's novel about the First World War, was published. Some readers noticed that one section in it—the "Thursday Night" section—contained the ideas and even phrases and sentences from the Nobel Prize speech. In the recorded reading, Faulkner juxtaposed the speech with this section, and the two, placed together, amplify the novelist's views of the endurance of man and his capacity to be aware of his fate. *A Fable* deals with a mutiny during the First World War and the events which lead to an execution. Faulkner, in his characteristic way, built his modern story upon the symbolism of Passion Week.

THE STOCKHOLM ADDRESS

I feel that this award was not made to me as a man but to my work— a life's work in the agony and sweat of the human spirit, not for glory and least of all for profit, but to create out of the materials of the human spirit something which did not exist before. So this award is only mine in trust. It will not be difficult to find a dedication for the money part of it commensurate with the purpose and significance of its origin. But I would like to do the same with the acclaim too, by using this moment as a pinnacle from which I might be listened to by the young men and women already dedicated to the same anguish and travail, among whom is already that one who will some day stand here where I am standing.

Our tragedy today is a general and universal physical fear so long sustained by now that we can even bear it. There are no longer problems of the spirit. There is only the question: When will I be blown up? Because of this, the young man or woman writing today has forgotten the problems of the human heart in conflict with itself which alone can make good writing because only that is worth writing about, worth the agony and the sweat.

He must learn them again. He must teach himself that the basest of all things is to be afraid; and, teaching himself that, forget it forever, leaving no room in his workshop for anything but the old verities and truths of the heart, the old universal truths lacking which any story is ephemeral and doomed—love and honor and pity and pride and compassion and sacrifice. Until he does so, he labors under a curse. He writes not of love but of lust, of defeats in which nobody loses anything of value, of victories without hope and, worst of all, without pity or compassion. His griefs grieve on no universal bones, leaving no scars. He writes not of the heart but of the glands.

Until he relearns these things, he will write as though he stood alone and watched the end of man. I decline to accept the end of man. It is easy enough to say that man is immortal simply because he will endure; that when the last ding-dong of doom has clanged and faded from the last worthless rock hanging tideless in the last red and dying evening, that even then there will still be one more sound: that of his puny inexhaustible voice, still talking. I refuse to accept this. I believe that man will not merely endure: he will prevail. He is immortal, not because he alone among creatures has an inexhaustible voice but because he has a soul, a spirit capable of compassion and sacrifice and endurance. The poet's, the writer's, duty is to write about these things. It is his privilege to help man endure by lifting his heart, by reminding him of the courage and honor and hope and pride and compassion and pity and sacrifice which have been the glory of his past. The poet's voice need not merely be the record of man, it can be one of the props, the pillars to help him endure and prevail.

FROM A FABLE

"Don't be afraid," the corporal said. "There's nothing to be afraid of. Nothing worth it."

For a moment the old general didn't seem to have heard the corporal at all, standing a head below the other's high mountain one, beneath the seemingly insuperable weight of the blue-and-scarlet hat cross-barred and dappled with gold braid and heavy golden leaves. Then he said, "Afraid? No no, it's not I but you who are afraid of man; not I but you who believe that nothing but a death can save him. I know better. I know that he has that in him which will enable him to outlast even his wars; that in him more durable than all his vices, even that last and most fearsome one; to outlast even this next avatar of his servitude which he now faces: his enslavement to the demonic progeny of his own mechanical curiosity, from which he will emancipate himself by that one ancient tried-and-true method by which slaves have always freed themselves: by inculcating their masters with the slaves' own vices—in this case the vice of war and that other one which is no vice at all but instead is the quality-mark and warrant of man's immortality: his deathless folly. He has already begun to put wheels under his patio his terrace and his front veranda; even at my age I may see the day when what was once his house has become a storage-place for his bed and stove and razor and spare clothing; you with your youth could (remember that bird) see the day when he will have invented his own private climate and moved it stove bathroom bed clothing kitchen and all into his automobile and what he once called home will have vanished from human lexicon: so that he won't dismount from his automobile at all because he won't need to: the entire earth one unbroken machined de-mountained dis-rivered expanse of concrete paving protuberanceless by tree or bush or house or anything which might constitute a corner or a threat to visibility, and man in his terrapin myriads enclosed clothesless from birth in his individual wheeled and glove-like envelope, with pipes and hoses leading upward from underground reservoirs to charge him with one composite squirt which at one mutual instant will fuel his mobility, pander his lusts, sate his appetites and fire his dreams; peripatetic, unceasing and long since no longer countable, to die at last at the click of an automatic circuit-breaker on a speedometer dial, and, long since freed of bone and organ and gut, leaving nothing for communal scavenging but a rusting and odourless shell—the shell which he does not get out of because he does not need to, but which presently for a time he will not emerge from because he does not dare because the shell will be his only protection from the hail-like iron refuse from his wars. Because by that time his wars will have dispossessed him by simple out-distance; his simple frail physique will be no longer able to keep up, bear them, attend them, be present. He will try of course and for a little while he will even hold his own; he will build tanks bigger and faster and more impervious and with more firepower than any before, he will build aircraft bigger and faster and capable of more load and more destruction than any yet; for a little while he will accompany, direct, as he thinks control them, even after he has finally realised that it is not another frail and mortal dissident to his politics or his notions of national boundaries that he is contending with, but the very monster itself which he inhabits. It will not be someone firing bullets at him who for the moment doesn't like him. It will be his own frankenstein which roasts him alive with heat, asphyxiates him with speed, wrenches loose his still-living entrails in the ferocity of its prey-seeking stoop. So he will not be able to go along with it at all, though for a little while longer it will permit him the harmless delusion that he controls it from the ground with buttons. Then that will be gone too; years, decades then centuries will have elapsed since it last answered his voice; he will have even forgotten the very location of its breeding-grounds and his last contact with it will be a day when he will crawl shivering out of his cooling burrow to crouch among the delicate stalks of his dead antennae like a fairy geometry, beneath a clangourous rain of dials and meters and switches and bloodless fragments of metal epidermis, to watch the final two of them engaged in the last gigantic wrestling against the final and dying sky robbed even of darkness and filled with the inflectionless uproar of the two mechanical voices bellowing at each other polysyllabic and verbless patriotic nonsense. Oh yes, he will survive it because he has that in him which will endure even beyond the ultimate worthless tideless rock freezing slowly in the last red and heatless sunset, because already the next star in the blue immensity of space will be already clamorous with the uproar of his debarkation, his puny and inexhaustible voice still talking, still planning; and there too after the last ding dong of doom has rung and died there will still be one sound more: his voice, planning still to build something higher and faster and louder; more efficient and louder and faster than ever before, yet it too inherent with the same old primordial fault since it too in the end will fail to eradicate him from the earth. I don't fear man. I do better: I respect and admire him. And pride: I am ten times prouder of that immortality which he does possess than ever he of that heavenly one of his delusion. Because man and his folly—"

"Will endure," the corporal said.

"They will do more," the old general said proudly. "They will prevail."

BIBLIOGRAPHY

GENERAL

For extensive bibliographies on the authors in this text as well as for background material, the student should consult Volume III (*Bibliography*) of *Literary History of the United States*, 1948 (supplement, 1959), edited by Spiller, Thorp, Johnson, and Canby. Also useful is *Eight American Authors: A Review of Research and Criticism*, 1956, edited by Floyd Stovall. The books named below will serve as general guides to the cultural background of American literature; all of them contain bibliographies.

Charles A. and Mary R. Beard, *The Rise of American Civilization*, rev. and enl., 4 vols., 1942, deals chiefly with the economic factors that have shaped American society. Sociological elements are likewise stressed in Harry J. Carman and Harold C. Syrett, *A History of the American People*, 2 vols., 1952. Merle Curti's *The Growth of American Thought*, 2nd ed., 1951, is a social history from colonial times. Similarly useful is Ralph H. Gabriel, *The Course of American Democratic Thought: An Intellectual History since 1815*, 2nd ed., 1956. Oscar Cargill, *Intellectual America: Ideas on the March*, 1941, chiefly concerned with the twentieth century, deals with the European impact. Henry S. Commager, *The American Mind: An Interpretation of American Thought and Character since the 1880's*, 1950; and Max Lerner, *America as a Civilization: Life and Thought in the United States Today*, 1957, are stimulating and informed. Richard D. Mosier, *The American Temper: Patterns of Our Intellectual Heritage*, 1952, treats especially phases of puritanism, enlightenment, romanticism, and modernism.

Authoritative studies of particular cultural aspects are Herbert W. Schneider, *A History of American Philosophy*, 1946, a source book and survey; Morris R. Cohen, *American Thought: A Critical Sketch*, 1954, a study of philosophical points of view; and William W. Sweet, *Religion in the Development of American Culture, 1765–1840*, 1952. The fine and applied arts are treated in Oliver W. Larkin, *Art and Life in America*, 1949; and Marshall B. Davidson, *Life in America*, 2 vols., 1951.

Important for their stimulating ideas are D. H. Lawrence, *Studies in Classic American Literature*, 1923; Lewis Mumford, *The Golden Day*, 1926; Constance Rourke, *American Humor*, 1931; F. O. Mattiessen, *American Renaissance*, 1941; R. W. B. Lewis, *The American Adam*, 1955; and Daniel J. Boorstin, *The Americans: The Colonial Experience*, 1958.

WALT WHITMAN

The standard edition is *The Complete Writings of Walt Whitman,* 10 vols., 1902. This edition was issued by Whitman's literary executors, Horace L. Traubel, Richard M. Bucke, and Thomas B. Harned; Oscar L. Triggs supplied additional bibliographical and critical material. There is no collected edition of Whitman's letters. There are several volumes of Whitman's unpublished work and newspaper articles. Horace Traubel, *With Walt Whitman in Camden,* covering the years 1888–1889 and published in four volumes in 1906, 1908, 1914, and 1958, is a record of daily conversations with Whitman. The best guide to Whitman scholarship is Gay Wilson Allen, *Walt Whitman Handbook,* 1946.

Allen, Gay Wilson, *The Solitary Singer: A Critical Biography of Walt Whitman,* 1955. The definitive biography.
Catel, Jean, *Walt Whitman: La Naissance du Poète,* 1929. A psycho-biographical study.
Chase, Richard, *Walt Whitman Reconsidered,* 1955. A stimulating reappraisal.
Hindus, Milton (ed.), *Leaves of Grass: One Hundred Years After,* 1955. Essays in reappraisal.
Holloway, Emory, *Whitman: An Interpretation in Narrative,* 1926. The fullest account of Whitman the journalist and editor.
Long, Haniel, *Walt Whitman and the Springs of Courage,* 1938. A valuable study of how Whitman strengthened himself by means of phrenology, Emerson's writings, and contact with people and friends.
Matthiessen, F. O., *American Renaissance: Art and Expression in the Age of Emerson and Whitman,* 1941. The best study of Whitman's art.
Miller, James E., Jr., *A Critical Guide to* Leaves of Grass, 1957. A study of Whitman's artistry in selected poems and in the whole of *Leaves of Grass.*
Perry, Bliss, *Walt Whitman, His Life and Work,* 1906. The first thorough, objective account of Whitman.
Schyberg, Frederik, *Walt Whitman,* 1951. This translation by Evie A. Allen of the revised 1933 Danish edition extends Catel's study of the development of the poet.
Shephard, Esther, *Walt Whitman's Pose,* 1938. Discovers Whitman's masks and "poses."

EMILY DICKINSON

The bulk of the Dickinson manuscripts, and it is large, is about evenly divided between the Houghton Library at Harvard and Amherst College Library. Authoritative editions are *The Poems of Emily Dickinson, including variant readings, critically compared with all known manuscripts,* 3 vols., 1955; and *The Letters of Emily Dickinson,* 3 vols., 1958; both edited by T. H. Johnson. The selections herein adopt the numbering and follow the text of the variorum edition.

Bingham, Millicent Todd, *Ancestors' Brocades*, 1945. Useful source material.
Bingham, Millicent Todd, *Emily Dickinson: A Revelation*, 1954. Additional source material.
Bingham, Millicent Todd, *Emily Dickinson's Home*, 1955. Further source material.
Chase, Richard, *Emily Dickinson*, 1951. A critical study.
Johnson, T. H., *Emily Dickinson: An Interpretative Biography*, 1955. Written by the editor of the poems and the letters.
Whicher, George F., *This Was a Poet*, 1938. Sympathetic and informed biography.

MARK TWAIN

The most extensive of the many collected editions is *The Writings of Mark Twain*, 37 vols., 1922–1925, edited by Albert B. Paine. *Mark Twain's Autobiography*, 2 vols., 1924, edited by Albert B. Paine, has been supplemented by *Mark Twain in Eruption*, 1940, edited by Bernard DeVoto. Paine's edition of *Mark Twain's Letters*, 2 vols., 1917, is quite incomplete; important additions include, among others, *The Love Letters of Mark Twain*, 1949, edited by Dixon Wecter, and the correspondence in Clara Clemens' *My Father, Mark Twain*, 1931, and Samuel C. Webster's *Mark Twain, Business Man*, 1946; a definitive edition is badly needed. Merle Johnson's *A Bibliography of the Works of Mark Twain*, 1935, is authoritative for first editions.

Bellamy, Gladys C., *Mark Twain as a Literary Artist*, 1950. A much needed book which not only synthesizes the work of recent scholars but also provides many fresh insights.
DeVoto, Bernard, *Mark Twain at Work*, 1942. Illuminating essays on the making of *Tom Sawyer*, *Huckleberry Finn*, and *The Mysterious Stranger*.
DeVoto, Bernard, *Mark Twain's America*, 1932. Vivid treatment of the frontier and of Twain's indebtedness to Southern and Western traditions of humor.
Ferguson, DeLancey, *Mark Twain: Man and Legend*, 1943. A serviceable biography.
Howells, William Dean, *My Mark Twain*, 1910. Warm personal recollections.
Paine, Albert B., *Mark Twain, A Biography*, 3 vols., 1912. The authorized life, invaluable for its documentary detail but limited by Paine's rather pedestrian imagination.
Wecter, Dixon, *Sam Clemens of Hannibal*, 1952. An excellent study of Twain's formative years.

HENRY ADAMS

The bulk of the manuscripts of the Adams family, now being edited by Lyman H. Butterfield, is in the Massachusetts Historical Library. For details of the publication of Henry Adams's extensive correspondence, for the many reprints of his major works, and for the great number of special studies, many of which have appeared in the last decade, the student should consult the Adams bibliography in *Literary History of the United States*, 1948, and its supplement, 1959.

Levenson, J. C., *The Mind and Art of Henry Adams*, 1957. A critical study.
Samuels, Ernest, *The Young Henry Adams*, 1948; *Henry Adams: The Middle Years*, 1958. Detailed biography, to be completed by a final volume.
Stevenson, Elizabeth, *Henry Adams: A Biography*, 1955. A balanced study.

HENRY JAMES

Henry James's novels and tales were revised and edited by him in a selective edition known as the *New York Edition*, 24 vols., 1907–1909. Two additional volumes were added posthumously. A collective edition of all but his earliest stories and the stories written from his plays, in thirty-five volumes, came out in London in 1921, edited by Percy Lubbock. Recent collections of his other writings have included *The Art of the Novel*, 1934, edited by R. P. Blackmur, which contains the prefaces to the *New York Edition; The Notebooks of Henry James*, 1947, edited by F. O. Matthiessen and Kenneth B. Murdock; *The Complete Plays of Henry James*, 1949, edited by Leon Edel; *The Ghostly Tales of Henry James*, 1949, edited by Leon Edel; *The Scenic Art*, 1948, edited by Allan Wade, which contains James's dramatic criticisms; *The Painter's Eye*, 1956, edited by J. L. Sweeney, a selection of James's art criticism, and *Parisian Sketches*, 1957, his letters to the New York *Tribune*, edited by Leon Edel and Ilse D. Lind; *The Letters of Henry James*, 1920, edited by Percy Lubbock, appeared in two volumes; *The Selected Letters*, 1956, edited by Leon Edel; *Henry James and H. G. Wells*, letters of the two writers, edited by Leon Edel and Gordon N. Ray. See also *A Bibliography of Henry James*, 1957, by Leon Edel and Dan H. Laurence, which lists all of James's writings.

Beach, Joseph Warren, *The Method of Henry James*, 1918. An early and still valuable study of James's fictional techniques.
Brooks, Van Wyck, *The Pilgrimage of Henry James*, 1927. A speculative book arguing James would have been a better writer if he had not lived abroad.
Dupee, F. W., *Henry James*, 1951. A compact sketch of the life and work of the novelist.

Dupee, F. W. (ed.), *The Question of Henry James*, 1945. An anthology of essays on James, early and late.

Edel, Leon, *Henry James: The Untried Years*, 1953. The writer's life from 1843 to 1870, first volume of a three-volume biography.

Grattan, C. H., *The Three Jameses*, 1932. An early study of the senior Henry James and his two sons, William and Henry.

Lubbock, Percy, *The Craft of Fiction*, 1921. The first critic to recognize the significance of James's technique of the "point of view" and the importance of the final novels.

Matthiessen, F. O., *Henry James: The Major Phase*, 1944. Develops Lubbock's discussion of the final novels.

Matthiessen, F. O., *The James Family*, 1947. An anthology of the writings of the two Henrys, William, and Alice James.

Nowell-Smith, Simon (ed.), *The Legend of the Master*, 1948. A witty compilation of Jamesian anecdotes.

Wilson, Edmund, *The Triple Thinkers*, 1938. Contains a highly perceptive discussion of James's writings after 1895.

STEPHEN CRANE

Crane's writings have been collected in *The Work of Stephen Crane*, 12 vols., 1925–1926, edited by Wilson Follett. Additional early fiction is represented by *The Sullivan County Sketches of Stephen Crane*, 1949, edited by Melvin Schoberlin. Follett has also edited *The Collected Poems of Stephen Crane*, 1930. *Stephen Crane: An Omnibus*, 1952, edited by R. W. Stallman, is important for its new text of *The Red Badge of Courage*, based upon the original manuscripts, and for its sizable collection of letters. Ames W. Williams and Vincent Starrett's *Stephen Crane: A Bibliography*, 1948, is an invaluable guide.

Beer, Thomas, *Stephen Crane: A Study in American Letters*, 1923. An important early biography, full of anecdotal material supplied by many persons who knew Crane.

Berryman, John, *Stephen Crane*, 1950. An acute biographical and critical study with psychoanalytical bias.

Hoffman, Daniel G., *The Poetry of Stephen Crane*, 1957. A substantial contribution to Crane criticism; contains fresh biographical information.

EUGENE O'NEILL

Editions of the collected plays of Eugene O'Neill were issued at various times starting in 1924. In 1941 a convenient three-volume edition was issued containing all the plays except for the early one-acters O'Neill himself published in 1914 under the title *Thirst*, the so-called "lost" plays, which O'Neill believed he had destroyed and which were printed without his authorization in 1950, and *The Iceman Cometh*, published in 1946. Since O'Neill's death, the Yale University Press has published his posthumously produced plays, including *Long Day's Journey into Night* and *A Touch of the Poet*.

Boulton, Agnes, *Part of a Long Story*, 1958. O'Neill's second wife tells of O'Neill's Provincetown days.

Clark, Barrett H., *Eugene O'Neill*, rev. ed., 1947. The essential facts of the playwright's life are told in a reportorial fashion.

Engel, Edwin A., *The Haunted Heroes of Eugene O'Neill*, 1953. A detailed study of the plays.

Falk, Doris V., *Eugene O'Neill and the Tragic Tension*, 1958. An attempt to apply psychoanalytical theory to the plays.

Winther, Sophus Keith, *Eugene O'Neill, A Poet's Quest*, 1935. A useful appraisal.

ROBERT FROST

The Frost canon is represented by *Complete Poems of Robert Frost*, 1949, together with a more recent volume, *And All We Call American*, 1959. Two useful bibliographical aids are William B. Clymer and Charles R. Green, *Robert Frost: A Bibliography*, 1937, and Louis and Esther Mertins, *The Intervals of Robert Frost: A Critical Bibliography*, 1947.

Cook, Reginald L., *The Dimensions of Robert Frost*, 1958. An intimate view of Frost's personality and his art.

Cox, Sidney, *A Swinger of Birches*, 1957. A portrait by a lifelong friend.

Jarrell, Randall, *Poetry and the Age*, 1953, pp. 28–69. Two discriminating essays on Frost's work.

Munson, Gorham B., *Robert Frost: A Study in Sensibility and Good Sense*, 1927. A valuable early estimate.

Thompson, Lawrance, *Fire and Ice: The Art and Thought of Robert Frost*, 1942. The most comprehensive study.

T. S. ELIOT

The Complete Poems and Plays of T. S. Eliot, published in 1952, contains the largest part of the poet's imaginative work. Since it appeared, there has been separate publication of the later plays, *The Confidential Clerk*, 1954, and *The Elder Statesman*, 1959. Eliot's prose works are to be found in the *Selected Essays* of 1932 and in the enlarged American edition of 1950. His most recent volume of essays, *On Poetry and Poets*, appeared in 1957. A full listing of Eliot's writings, including a collation of all his editions, can be found in Donald Gallup's *T. S. Eliot: A Bibliography*, 1952.

Blackmur, R. P., *The Double Agent*, 1935. Contains a preceptive discussion of Eliot's poetry.

Braybrooke, Neville (ed.), *T. S. Eliot, A Symposium*, 1958. Essays collected in honor of the poet's seventieth birthday, containing some biographical information.

Drew, Elizabeth, *T. S. Eliot, The Design of His Poetry*, 1950. A close and valuable examination of the work.

Gardner, Helen, *The Art of T. S. Eliot*, 1950. The most lucid and penetrating study of the poet and a valuable critical work.

March, Richard, and Tambimuttu (eds.), *T. S. Eliot, A Symposium*, 1948. Contains much biographical data.

Matthiessen, F. O., *The Achievement of T. S. Eliot*, rev. ed., 1947. A wide exploration of Eliot's meaning and a sensitive reading of his poems.

Wilson, Edmund, *Axel's Castle*, 1931. Contains one of the earliest critical essays on Eliot showing his relationship to the French symbolists.

WILLIAM FAULKNER

Most of Faulkner's novels are now in print in various editions, many in paperback issues. *The Collected Stories of William Faulkner* was published in 1950. *The Portable Faulkner*, edited by Malcolm Cowley, explains the Yoknapatawpha series and contains a map of the county. *Faulkner at Nagano*, published in Tokyo in 1956, contains a transcript of the novelist's seminar in Japan conducted at Nagano during the summer of 1955. See also R. W. Daniel, *A Catalogue of the Writings of William Faulkner*, 1942.

Campbell, Harry Modean, and Foster, Ruel E., *William Faulkner, A Critical Appraisal*, 1951. A discussion of imagery, symbolism and technique in Faulkner.

Hoffman, F. J., and Vickery, O. W. (eds.), *William Faulkner: Two Decades of Criticism*, 1951. An anthology containing certain key essays on Faulkner.

Howe, Irving, *William Faulkner, A Critical Study*, 1952. A limited but perceptive critical study.

Note: When the title and the first line of a poem are the same, only the title is given.